The first historian to make full use of the relevant documentation, Fine has not only created a compelling portrait of an enlightened politician and administrator, he has also considerably increased our understanding of the New Deal years.

SIDNEY FINE is Andrew Dickson White Professor of History at the University of Michigan. His *Frank Murphy: The Detroit Years,* the first volume of the biography, is published by the University of Michigan Press. The third volume, *Frank Murphy: The Washington Years,* will be published by the University of Chicago Press.

D1154219

FRANK MURPHY

Governor Murphy

FRANK MURPHY

MURPHY The New Deal Years

Sidney Fine

Chicago and London   The University of Chicago Press

SIDNEY FINE is Andrew Dickson White Professor
of History at the University of Michigan. His
Frank Murphy: The Detroit Years, the first
volume of the biography, is published by The
University of Michigan Press. The third volume,
Frank Murphy: The Washington Years, will be
published by The University of Chicago Press.

The University of Chicago Press, Chicago 60637
The University of Chicago Press, Ltd., London

© 1979 by The University of Chicago
All rights reserved. Published 1979
Printed in the United States of America
83 82 81 80 79   5 4 3 2 1

Library of Congress Cataloging in Publication Data

Fine, Sidney, 1920–
  Frank Murphy.

  Vols. 2– have imprint: Chicago, University of
Chicago Press.
    Bibliography: v. 1, p.
    Includes index.
    CONTENTS: [1] The Detroit years—[2] The New Deal
years.
    1. Murphy, Frank, 1890–1949.
KF8745.M8F49   347'.73'2634 [B]   74–25945
ISBN 0–472–32949–9 (v. 1)
ISBN 0–226–24934–4 (v. 2)

To the memory of
Verner W. Crane and Dwight Lowell Dumond

Contents

Preface

Frank Murphy, a *Detroit News* reporter observed at the close of Murphy's governorship, could not be ignored because he was "different from the ruck of public officials who rise and fall without any public excitement." It is not primarily Murphy's fascinating personal qualities, however, that have led me to deal in so extended a way with his career but rather the great matters that occupied his attention in the various public positions that he held. "Frank Murphy," Mary Margaret Clarke has correctly noted, "had an amazing facility for holding official positions at times of crisis that thrust him into the public limelight. As a result, his career was enmeshed in the major issues of American society from 1930 to 1950." In devoting three volumes to the life and times of Frank Murphy, I have been as much concerned with these "major issues" as I have been with Murphy himself.

In his long career, Murphy served as a criminal court judge, mayor of a great city, a colonial official in the United States' most important overseas possession, governor of a major state, a federal cabinet officer, and a justice of the United States Supreme Court. In his Detroit years, the subject of Volume 1, he achieved distinction as a member of one of the nation's leading criminal courts, and he was obliged as mayor to deal with the consequences of the Great Depression in the big city hardest hit by that cataclysmic event. In his New Deal years, the focus of the present volume, he was the chief American official in the Philippines at a time when the islands were being transformed from colony to Commonwealth, beginning the transition period that led to independence. As governor of Michigan, he became actively involved as a peacemaker in the great labor upheaval of 1937 and successfully mediated what was probably the most important strike in the nation's history. His administration, at the same time, was also responsible for one of the few successful New Deals at the state level. In the Washington phase of his career, reserved for Volume 3, he served an eventful year as attorney general and then became the foremost civil libertarian on the United States Supreme

Court during one of the most turbulent and interesting periods in its history. Few American public officials have served in so many roles at the various levels of our federal system, and few have been associated in an important way with so many great events.

It is a pleasure to acknowledge the assistance that I received in writing this book. My research and the final typing of the manuscript were facilitated by grants from the Horace H. Rackham School of Graduate Studies of the University of Michigan. A grant from the Earhart Foundation made it possible for me to devote more time to the writing of the manuscript than otherwise would have been possible. As with the first volume, my colleague Bradford Perkins read the entire manuscript with meticulous care and made many suggestions for its improvement. My colleague Norman G. Owen read the Philippine chapters of the manuscript and gave me the benefit of his considerable knowledge of Philippine history. Robert M. Warner, who also gave my Michigan chapters a discriminating reading, Richard M. Doolen, and Mary Jo Pugh of the Michigan Historical Collections provided me with superb service during the course of my research. I am especially indebted to Thomas E. Powers of the Michigan Historical Collections, who responded to my many inquiries with professional competence and unfailing courtesy. Richard M. Maxwell of the National Archives and Records Service guided me through the intricacies of Record Groups 126 and 350 and also provided me with a copy of his study of the office of high commissioner to the Philippines. My manuscript research was also aided by Philip P. Mason and Warner W. Pflug of the Archives of Labor History and Urban Affairs of Wayne State University, Alice Dalligan and the staff of the Burton Historical Collection, David Olson of the State Archives, Michigan History Division, William R. Emerson and the staff of the Franklin Roosevelt Library, John C. Broderick and the staff of the Manuscript Division of the Library of Congress, and Joseph D. Howerton, Donald Mossholder, Judith Koucky, Thomas E. Hohmann, and John Taylor of the National Archives and Records Service. Daniel J. Leab kindly arranged for the photocopying of relevant documents in the Daniel Bell Papers, and Richard Storatz supplied me with copies of some Murphy items in the Herbert H. Lehman Papers. Martin S. Hayden made the Murphy file of the *Detroit News* available to me, and the late Raymond Moley permitted me to examine his Murphy file. Irving Bernstein permitted me to examine his notes on a file of CIO material that I was unable to locate. Edward Magdol kindly sent me a copy of the paper on the Michigan press in the state's 1938 gubernatorial election that he had prepared in collaboration with Robert Perlman.

Thomas W. Hare provided me with excellent translations of documents in the Japanese Ministry of Foreign Affairs Archives. I am grateful to Deborah Lanyi and Jeanette Ranta for their expert typing of a difficult-to-read manuscript. My wife, Jean Fine, was, as always, my indispensable collaborator.

The University of Michigan Press has permitted me to use portions of my *Sit-Down: The General Motors Strike of 1936-1937*, and the New York State School of Industrial and Labor Relations has similarly permitted me to adapt "Frank Murphy, Law and Order, and Labor Relations in Michigan," in David B. Lipsky, ed., *Union Power and Public Policy*. Unless otherwise noted, the photographs reproduced in the text were generously made available to me by the Michigan Historical Collections.

PHILIPPINE ISLANDS

INDEX TO PROVINCES

Laoag

Tuguegarao

Baguio

Tarlac

LUZON

Philippine Sea

Manila

CATANDUANES I.

Legaspi

MINDORO

MASBATE

SAMAR

PANAY

Tacloban

LEYTE

Bacolod

CEBU

NEGROS

Surigao

Dumaguete

Puerto Princesa

PALAWAN

Sulu   Sea

MINDANAO

Cotabato

Davao

Zamboanga

BASILAN I.

0   50   100   150 MILES
0   50   100   150 KILOMETERS

1

"A Perfect Corner . . .
of the Lord's Footstool"

I

" . . . you will think a little of all that you have left behind you, but more of what is ahead, because that is the way you are made," one of Frank Murphy's lady friends wrote him shortly after Franklin D. Roosevelt appointed him governor-general of the Philippines.[1] If Murphy did indeed "think a little" about his past as he sailed for the Philippines on May 19, 1933, he must have been pleased with his ruminations.

Born in 1890 in Sand Beach (now Harbor Beach), Michigan, the third of the four children of John F. and Mary Brennan Murphy, Murphy had enjoyed a happy childhood before departing for Ann Arbor in 1908 to attend the University of Michigan. After receiving a bachelor of laws degree in 1914, he worked briefly for a Detroit law firm and enjoyed a good deal of success. He attended the Reserve Officers Training Camp at Fort Sheridan, Illinois, shortly after the United States entered World War I, was commissioned a first lieutenant in the infantry, and served overseas. He was sworn in as first assistant United States attorney for the Eastern District of Michigan on August 9, 1919, serving with distinction in that capacity until March 1, 1922. After resigning his federal position, Murphy joined his friend Edward G. Kemp in private law practice. He very quickly became one of the most successful attorneys in the city of Detroit.

In February 1923 Murphy filed as a candidate for a judgeship on the Detroit Recorder's Court, a court with a unified criminal jurisdiction that had attracted the favorable attention of students of criminal jurisprudence. Campaigning against the court's ruling bloc of four judges who had become identified with a tough law-and-order approach to crime, Murphy led the field in the final election, taking office on January 1, 1924. During his six and one-half years on the court—he was reelected in 1929—his social views "crystallized," he won the support of Detroit's liberal elements, blacks, and the city's white ethnic groups, and he became widely recognized as one of the few outstanding municipal court judges in the nation.

1

Following the recall of Mayor Charles W. Bowles in July 1930, Murphy decided to run for mayor of Detroit, a nonpartisan post. He defeated four opponents in a campaign in which he stressed unemployment as the major issue confronting the city and the nation and attacked the "conspiracy of silence" surrounding the problem. He served as mayor from September 22, 1930, to May 10, 1933, easily winning reelection in November 1931.

As mayor, Murphy provided Detroit with a socially minded and clean government that was committed to free speech and freedom of assembly, and he maintained close ties with organized labor. Sometimes lacking in decisiveness, he selected excellent men for administrative positions and gave them his full support. He received nationwide attention for his determined efforts to cope with the unemployment crisis in Detroit and to secure federal aid for local relief, but there was, concomitantly, a good deal of uninformed criticism of the alleged "dole spree" in the city.

As the chief executive of a nonpartisan city, Murphy remained largely aloof from Democratic politics until the 1932 campaign, when he supported the presidential candidacy of Franklin D. Roosevelt. The new president rewarded Murphy by nominating him on April 7, 1933, to serve as governor-general of the Philippine Islands.

An immensely self-centered person, Murphy was obsessed with the importance of whatever he was doing. He was sentimental and tenderhearted, but he gloried in the strenuous life and possessed an unmistakable bellicose streak. Although outwardly calm, he was inwardly tense, and his mild manner concealed a fierce resolve. Exceedingly ambitious, he aspired to the presidency itself, eschewing alcohol and tobacco and exercising regularly because he regarded physical fitness as essential to political success. He enjoyed the company of the rich and well-born, but he had a genuine compassion for the afflicted and the unfortunate. He was unusually attractive to women, and he craved their affection, but he loved his own career more. Although always his own man, he was in his fashion a devout Catholic and was influenced by Catholic social thought.[2]

Although he would have preferred to become attorney general of the United States, Murphy—the youngest man, the only bachelor, and the second Catholic to serve as governor-general of the Philippines—was attracted to the insular post because of the opportunity that it provided him both to help create a new nation and to make his mark in national politics. He was aware that one of his predecessors, William Howard Taft, had gone from the Philippines to the presidency and another, Henry L. Stimson, had become secretary of state.[3]

James A. Farley was not mistaken in informing Murphy that the news of his appointment had been "well-received in every section of the country," but the general approbation of the president's choice did not include the nation's foremost academic student of the Philippines, University of Michigan political science professor Joseph R. Hayden. Hayden, who had served as an assistant in an American history course in which Murphy had been enrolled, thought that Murphy was "an extremely likeable and very intelligent Irishman with superb gifts for the great Irish game of politics" but that he was also a politician who had appealed to the "emotions and prejudices" of Detroit's voters and had "recklessly" employed the "dole system" to drive the city into bankruptcy. What most disturbed Hayden was that Murphy knew "absolutely nothing" about the Philippines. Hayden thought it "an outrageous travesty upon every principle of good government and sound judgment" that such a man should have been appointed governor-general.[4]

Before leaving the United States Murphy attempted to fill in at least a portion of the immense gap in his knowledge concerning the Philippines. He conferred with many persons both inside and outside the United States government who had knowledge of the archipelago, as well as with Manuel Quezon, the president of the Philippine Senate, Manuel Roxas, the speaker of the Philippine House, and other members of the Philippine Legislative Mission then in Washington; he read some books on the subject; and he received a considerable amount of documentary material from the Bureau of Insular Affairs, the War Department agency charged with administrative responsibility for the Philippines.[5]

Quite apart from what Murphy may have learned from his brief exposure to Philippine matters before he left the United States, he brought qualities to his new post that augured well for his success and that men like Hayden failed to consider in evaluating Murphy's suitability for the position: a charismatic personality, the experience of having governed a great city in time of crisis, the ability to relate successfully to persons and groups of varying backgrounds and aspirations, a lofty conception of his role as a public servant, and the capacity as an administrator to inspire his aides to give the best that was in them in the performance of their duties.[6]

Murphy left Detroit for California on May 14. He was accompanied by his adoring sister, Marguerite, who was to serve as hostess in the Philippines for the bachelor governor-general; her husband, William Teahan; Sanger Williams, Murphy's black chauffeur; and several former Detroit aides who were to serve on his Philippine staff. On the West Coast, Murphy, having the time of his life, was royally entertained in Hollywood by screen-star and one-time girl friend Ann Harding, visited at San Simeon with William Randolph Hearst, the publisher of the consistently pro-Murphy *Detroit Times*, and talked in San Francisco with California Democratic leaders, the president of the Philippine Sugar Association, and American businessmen with interests in the islands.[7]

Aboard the S.S. *Coolidge*, Murphy continued his cram course on the Philippines by reading some of the documentary material that he had taken along and talking with fellow passengers Quezon, General Creed F. Cox, newly nominated to serve as chief of the Bureau of Insular Affairs, and George A. Malcolm, a Michigan native who had served on the Philippine Supreme Court for twenty-five years. After his physically punishing experience as mayor of Detroit during the darkest days of the Great Depression, Murphy thoroughly enjoyed the restful, four-week ocean voyage to Manila. He had never "felt stronger or more rested," he informed his older brother, Harold. "It is the first time in years," he wrote, "that I feel all the kinks ironed out and am ready to stand up like a soldier and slug it out with anyone." Frank's reading matter included "all those sorrowful love letters" he had received from "*all the girls*" that he had left behind. None of the women aboard ship, however, aroused his interest, Marguerite observing that not one of them was physically attractive.[8]

The *Coolidge* docked in Honolulu, Shanghai, Hongkong, and Yokohama. When the passengers debarked in Honolulu, Malcolm was mistaken for Murphy, was adorned with leis, and made a short speech of thanks. In Shanghai, Quezon left the ship before Murphy and was welcomed by a band and a large delegation of Filipinos, a reception that the American consul general thought had been "prearranged" to impress Murphy. The acting secretary of finance of the Philippine government and the undersecretary of the department boarded the *Coolidge* at Shanghai, at Murphy's request, so that he might examine relevant financial data before presenting his first budget to the Philippine legislature. In Hongkong, the Murphy party was met by Abe Garfinkel, the veteran military aide of Philippine governors-general, whose assignment it was to guide Murphy through the intricacies of the inauguration ceremony. From Yokohama, Murphy was driven to Tokyo, where he called on Premier Hiroshi Saito and Foreign Minister Yasuya Ichida and lunched with Ambassador Joseph Grew. On one occasion before the ship left Japanese waters, Murphy came down from the upper deck in casual attire after a handball game and was mistaken for one of the stewards by an army lieutenant. "Boy," the lieutenant said, "bring me a deck chair," and Murphy did.[9]

From Japan, the *Coolidge* sailed directly for the Philippines. An archipelago of 7,083 islands and approximately 115,000 square miles, with a population in 1933 of more than 13.5 million people,[10] the Philippine Islands had passed from Spanish into American hands as the result of the Spanish-American war of 1898 and the Treaty of Paris of the same year. When the American victory over Spain did not lead to immediate independence for the Philippines, indigenous forces led by Emilio Aguinaldo felt themselves betrayed. Fighting between Filipino and American troops began on February 4, 1899, and the Filipinos were not subdued until 1902.[11]

The objectives of American rule in the Philippines were set forth by President William McKinley in instructions issued to the Second Philippine Commission on April 7, 1900:

the Commission [McKinley stated] should bear in mind that the government is designed not for our satisfaction or for the expression of our theoretical views, but for the happiness, peace, and prosperity of the people of the Philippine Islands, and the measures adopted should be made to conform to their customs, their habits, and even their prejudices, to the fullest extent consistent with the accomplishment of the indispensable requisites of just and effective government. At the same time, the Commission should bear in mind, and the people of the islands should be made plainly to understand, that there are certain great principles of government which have been made the basis of our governmental system, which we deem essential to the rule of law and the maintenance of individual freedom . . . ; that there are also certain practical rules of government which we have found to be essential to the preservation of these great principles of liberty and law, and that these principles and these rules of government must be established and maintained in their islands for the sake of their liberty and happiness, however much they may be in conflict with the customs or laws of procedure with which they are familiar.

Over the years American policy in the Philippines tended to emphasize first one and then the other of the twin objectives of American rule set forth by McKinley, conformity to Philippine traditions on the one hand and the maintenance of American principles and governmental practices on the other. To some extent, the oscillation in policy reflected "a perceptible difference in emphasis and style" between Republican governors-general and a "conservative Republican tradition" and Democratic governors-general and a "liberal Democratic tradition."[12]

Civil government in the Philippines was inaugurated on July 4, 1901, when Taft became the civil governor (the title was changed to governor-general in 1905). Two months later three Filipinos were added to the five Americans who composed the Second Philippine Commission, in which legislative authority was lodged. Beginning in 1907 the Commission shared its legislative power with an elective

Philippine Assembly, consisting entirely of Filipinos. When Wilson became president in 1913, he appointed Francis Burton Harrison to be governor-general, and the president informed the Filipinos through Harrison that " 'every step' " taken by the administration would have as its objective " 'the ultimate independence' " of the Philippines. Consistent with this goal, Harrison reconstituted the Commission to provide for a Filipino majority and hence Filipino control of the legislature, and he pressed for speedy Filipinization of the government service. Congress declared in the preamble to the Jones Act of 1916 that it was the intent of the United States to grant the Philippine Islands their independence "as soon as a stable government can be established therein." The statute provided for an elective Senate to replace the Commission as the upper house of the legislature.

Following the enactment of the Jones Act, Harrison, who now thought of himself, in Peter W. Stanley's words, as "a constitutional monarch presiding over a government of Filipinos," deferred to the elective officials of the government and permitted the legislature to increase its control over the executive departments, make the cabinet "an arm of the majority party," and increase the powers of department heads as compared to the governor-general. In 1918 he established the Council of State, consisting of the governor-general, members of the cabinet, the Speaker of the House, and the president of the Senate, and permitted it not only to play a major role in the preparation of the budget and the formulation of legislative proposals but to dominate the executive in certain respects. He also placed control over the newly established government-owned companies in the hands of a Board of Control composed of the governor-general, the Speaker of the House, and the president of the Senate. Although the Jones Act vested the supreme executive power in the governor-general, Harrison surrendered much of his authority to the Filipino leadership in the legislature.

Leonard Wood, Harrison's Republican successor who served as governor-general from 1921 to 1927, sought to regain some of the authority that he believed Harrison had wrongly surrendered to the Filipino political leadership. He insisted on the right to veto legislation of local significance as well as legislation affecting American sovereignty, refused to appoint members of the legislature to cabinet posts, and made it clear that department heads were responsible to the governor-general, not the legislature. He virtually suspended the Council of State, and he abolished the Board of Control. The Filipino members of the cabinet and Council of State resigned in 1923, ostensibly because of opposition to Wood's policies and procedures, but Michael Paul Onorato has attributed the resignations more to the exigencies of Filipino politics than to constitutional issues. When Wood died in the course of a brain operation in the United States in August 1927, he was replaced by Henry L. Stimson, who restored amicable relations between the governor-general and the legislature. Stimson reconstituted the Council of State, adding the majority floor leaders of the legislature to the body, but he used the Council only as an advisory agency. He appointed cabinet members from the majority party, as Harrison had done, and he gained legislative approval in 1928 for the Belo Act, a measure that provided funding for a staff of experts to advise the governor but who were not to have administrative responsibilities.[13] Like Stimson, his successors, Dwight F. Davis and Theodore Roosevelt, Jr., maintained cordial relations with the Filipinos. Roosevelt permitted Quezon virtually to run the insular government and, according to an American bureau chief in the Philippines, was " 'led about by Quezon to an extent which even . . . Harrison would not have . . . allowed.' " As it turned out, Roosevelt was the last Republican governor-general of the Philippines. When his kinsman Franklin D. Roosevelt won the presidential election in 1932, Theodore Roosevelt remarked, "I am a cousin about to be removed." His successor was Frank Murphy.[14]

If American policy regarding the political institutions of the Philippines pointed in the direction of independence, American tariff policy as it applied to the archipelago appeared to be oriented in precisely the opposite direction. After having reduced the tariff on Philippine products in 1902 to 75 percent of existing rates, Congress in 1909, as part of the Payne-Aldrich tariff, stipulated that American products were to enter the Philippines without duty and provided for the free admission into the United States of all Philippine products except sugar and tobacco exceeding a specified quota and rice. Four years later the Underwood-Simmons tariff removed all restrictions of the free importation of Philippine products. The effect of free trade on Philippine exports to the United States was dramatic: in 1899, 18 percent of Philippine exports by value were exported to the United States; in 1908, 35 percent; and in 1933, 86 percent. Free trade, moreover, encouraged the Philippines to specialize in the production of the few crops for which there was a ready American market and discouraged the development of local manufacturing and a more diversified agriculture, resulting in the growth of "a colonial economy of the classical type." At the same time, the tariff advantage enjoyed by American products gave the United States an increasing share of the Philippine market (9 percent of total imports by value in 1899,

17 percent in 1908, and 58 percent in 1933) and accustomed Filipino consumers to American products. The Philippines consistently enjoyed a favorable commodity balance of trade with the United States, the net sum in 1933, P95,545,240 (two pesos = $1), exceeding the expenses of the insular government. When not only merchandise items but gold and silver shipments, service items, interest and dividends, and capital movements are taken into account, the Philippines in 1933 had a net credit balance with the United States of P95,178,000, a net debit with the remainder of the world of P47,630,000, and a net credit overall of P47,548,000.[15]

Of the Philippine exports to the United States, sugar and coconut products were most important, and both were decisively affected by the advent of free trade. Almost all Philippine sugar was exported to the United States, and sugar alone, as of 1933, accounted for almost 63 percent of the export income of the Philippines and about 70 percent of Philippine exports to the United States by value. Two million Filipinos were directly dependent on the sugar industry, another four million were indirectly dependent on it, and about 30 percent of the national income and more than 40 percent of the government's revenue were derived from this single source. The high cost of production and transportation of Philippine sugar, as compared to this cost for the competition, especially Cuban sugar, would have debarred Philippine sugar from the United States market had it not been for free trade.

Although the culture of sugar cane had been known in the Philippines even before Magellan discovered the islands, the first modern *central* to mill the raw product was not built until 1910, the year after the Philippines had been granted a duty-free quota in the American market. In 1915, two years after the quota restriction had been lifted, the insular legislature established the Sugar Central Board to promote sugar production in the islands, and the Philippine government provided funds through the Philippine National Bank for crop loans to planters and to finance the expansion of centrals. Sugar production rose from 466,912 short tons in 1920 to 1,342,975 short tons in 1933 as the acreage under cultivation increased 36 percent (from 487,775 to 663,365), the average yield per acre more than doubled (from .957 short tons to 2.186) following the use of new varieties of cane, and new centrifugal mills were constructed.

The two principal elements of the Philippine sugar industry as of the middle 1930s were the 23,734 planters, 175,000 tenants, and 100,000 plantation laborers who grew the cane and the 46 centrals and their 25,000 employees that milled it. Milling contracts generally ran for thirty years and usually provided for a fifty-fifty division between planters and centrals. Some planters were small peasant proprietors growing cane on two to five hectares (1 hectare = 2.47 acres), others were large landowners (*hacenderos*) whose land was cultivated by tenant farmers, who paid their landlords 6–22 percent of their crop in rent, or transient laborers. The centrals were the dominant factor in the industry, and their organization, the Philippine Sugar Association, was a powerful force in Philippine politics. Although 80 percent of the land devoted to sugar was owned by Filipinos, the large amount of capital required to build mills that used the centrifugal process limited Filipino investment in the centrals to about 45 percent of the total, the remainder being supplied by Americans (30 percent) or Spaniards (25 percent).[16]

Between 1928 and 1933 coconut products (copra, coconut oil, copra cake and meal, and dessicated coconuts) ranged from 16.2 percent to 34 percent of Philippine exports by value. About 80 percent of these products by value went to the United States. The coconut industry was the second most important export industry of the Philippines, the value of the crop being exceeded only by that of the sugar and rice crops. Taxes on coconut-bearing land yielded 15 percent of all real property taxes in the archipelago, excluding Manila and Baguio, and more than 50 percent of such taxes in eight provinces; and almost four million persons were dependent on the industry. About 90 percent of the investment in the industry was in Philippine hands.

The production and export of copra had been an important activity in the Philippines from the middle of the nineteenth century, but there were no coconut mills in the islands before the advent of free trade, and the bulk of the copra, into which most of the crop was converted, was shipped to Europe. Although six coconut mills were established in the Philippines between 1910 and 1914, the major expansion of the industry came in World War I in response to the demand for coconut oil, whose high glycerine content made it a valuable ingredient in the manufacture of explosives. By the end of the war period there were more than forty crushing mills in the Philippines, but most of them were forced to close soon thereafter as demand slackened. Copra-crushing survived as an export industry only because the two-cent per pound duty on coconut oil imposed by the Fordney-McCumber tariff in 1922 virtually excluded all but Philippine-produced coconut oil from the American market. The same tariff act imposed duties on copra cake and meal (the residue remaining after coconut oil is expressed from the copra) and dessicated coconuts, thus favoring the Philippine export of these products as well. Since copra was on the free list, Philippine copra, which accounted for about 40 percent of United States copra imports, enjoyed no special advantage in the American market.

Most of the coconut crop in the Philippines was grown on plots of less than ten acres. The crop was generally produced on a share-tenantry basis, the tenant commonly receiving one-third of the proceeds from the sale of the copra. About 10–20 percent of the coconut crop was consumed locally; the remainder was exported, principally in the form of copra and coconut oil. The 1,398,000 acres devoted to the coconut crop in 1933 were almost entirely Filipino-owned, but Filipinos owned only one of the eight large mills that produced coconut oil for export; Americans, Englishmen, and Spaniards each owned two, and the Chinese, one.[17]

In addition to sugar and coconut oil, the American market as of 1933 absorbed a substantial proportion of the other principal products exported by the Philippines: 23.8 percent of the abaca; 53.3 percent of the cordage; 92.1 percent of the cigars; 97.4 percent of the scrap tobacco; 20.6 percent of the logs and lumber; 99.7 percent of the cotton embroideries; 70 percent of the hats; and almost all the pearl buttons. Among these exports, cigars, scrap tobacco, embroideries, and pearl buttons, like sugar and coconut oil, appeared to be dependent on privileged access to the United States market.[18]

Rice, which was grown on about half the acreage under cultivation, was the chief food crop of the Philippines. More Filipinos were engaged in its production than in any other economic activity, and more capital was invested in its production, processing, and marketing than in any other industry. Only about 20 percent of the rice produced in the islands, however, entered commercial production, and the Philippines normally imported more rice than it exported. The reason was that Filipinos found it more economical to specialize in crops like sugar and coconuts that yielded a higher net return per acre than rice. Also, partly because of poor methods of cultivation, the cost of producing rice in the Philippines tended to be higher than the cost of production in such places as Indo-China, Siam, and India. Rice was mainly grown by tenants, who divided the crop with their landlords.[19]

The depressed condition of the rice tenant pointed up one of the shortcomings of American rule in the Philippines despite achievements in such areas as education and health. The United States pursued a policy of accommodation and "suasion" in the Philippines that largely defused hostility, but it equated the interests of "wealthy agriculturists'' with the interests of the Philippines as a whole, and it relied on the Filipino elite to effect its program. This limited the ability of American administrators to cope with one of the critical issues in the Philippines, the relationship between the landowning elite, the *caciques*, and the tenants, the rural poor, the "common taos." About 65 percent of the Philippine labor force over ten years of age was engaged in agriculture, and about 35 percent of those so employed were tenants; another 15.6 percent owned only part of their land, and only 49.2 percent of the farmers owned all their land. Some tenants were cash tenants, but many more were share tenants. The tenants were dependent for their subsistence on credit advanced by their landlords, a condition that was aggravated by free trade since the emphasis on cash crops meant that the peasant was unlikely to grow his own food supply. The *caciques* commonly extended credit at usurious rates, leaving the *tao* perpetually indebted and "almost a slave" to his landlord. "Usury," an authority has stated, was "the darkest aspect of the relations between landlord and tenant" in the Philippines. Many tenants worked fewer than two hectares of land and found it impossible to eke out even "a bare living." They were often "mercilessly and illegally" deprived of their share of the crops, were forced to render services to their landlords without just compensation, and were not really free to express their grievances. Conditions were at their worst in central Luzon, where tenancy rates were above 50 percent and the individual plots of land were especially small. Agrarian unrest had been endemic in Philippine history, and central Luzon was a center of disaffection, especially after 1927.[20]

Although the educational system that American rule brought to the Philippines provided an avenue for social mobility and was largely responsible for the development of a small middle class, probably the most advanced in southeast Asia, "the major class difference" in the Philippines was "simply between the wealthy and the poor," between the top 15–20 percent of mixed Malay, Chinese, and Spanish blood and the bottom 80 percent of unmixed Malay blood. The United States did relatively little to bridge the gap between rich and poor, to combat the widespread rural and urban poverty, or to modify a "rigid land tenure system." It did delimit the amount of public agricultural land that could be acquired by individuals (144 hectares) and corporations (1,024 hectares), and it purchased 410,000 acres of friar lands in 1903 for resale to tenants; but the wealthy and the educated prevented the *taos* from deriving much benefit from this, just as the Filipino leadership largely frustrated the efforts of Governors-General W. Cameron Forbes and Stimson to achieve meaningful land reform. In February 1933 Governor-General Roosevelt persuaded the legislature to enact a Rice Share Tenancy Act designed to protect the rice tenant against usurious interest rates and other *cacique* abuses. The law could be implemented in a province, however, only if a majority of its municipal councils petitioned the governor-general to apply the statute; since the councils were controlled by the landlords, no such petitions were presented.[21]

Just as economic power in the Philippines was lodged in the hands of the landowning elite, so political power was the preserve of the few. Since the press, which reflected the views of Filipino political leaders or the American business community in the islands, neither represented nor reached the great mass of the people, "effective public opinion," similarly, was the opinion of the relatively small group that controlled the central and provincial governments.[22]

Despite the American desire for a two-party system in the Philippines, the overwhelming stress in Filipino politics on independence, or at least autonomy, militated against the achievement of that goal. A single party, the Partido Nacionalista, dominated Philippine politics from the time of the party's formation in 1907. The party was plagued by factionalism, however, its two principal leaders, Quezon and Sergio Osmeña, splitting the Nacionalistas into warring groups between 1921 and 1924 and again in 1933, just before Murphy arrived in the Philippines.[23]

The diminutive, vain, and foppish Quezon, who had fought both the Spaniards and the Americans, served as the Philippine resident commissioner to the United States from 1909 to 1916, as president of the Senate from its creation in 1916, and as president of the Nacionalistas beginning in 1924. A charismatic personality, "an impulsive, dynamic man whose actions often . . . [had] a large element of the emotional and dramatic in them," and a brilliant orator in English, Spanish, and Tagalog, Quezon was mercurial in temperament and inconsistent in behavior—" 'There is no place for consistency in government,' " he once declared. Quezon, who actually was not one but many men, was capable of taking on the character that the situation seemed to him to require. "For every man, for every situation," Theodore Friend has written, "Quezon had a special tone and special touch." The urbane and scholarly Osmeña, a Chinese mestizo who dominated Philippine politics from 1907 to 1921 as Speaker of the Assembly and House of Representatives and president of the Nacionalistas and then became president pro tempore of the Senate, was a more reserved and consistent person than Quezon. Of the two, Quezon, the more skillful politician, was more admired by his countrymen, and he bested his rival when they contended for the leadership of the Nacionalistas and of their people. The politics that men like Quezon and Osmeña practiced was the politics of patronage rather than of ideology. Filipino politics was based not on programs but on the personal following a leader was able to develop as the result of his popularity, his wealth, and the political favors he bestowed.[24]

The Philippine legislature served mainly as "a background for the national 'leadership,' " and it developed more as "an instrument for the attainment of independence" than as a "normal law-making body." The *New York Times* correspondent in Manila, who was secretly attached to the office of the assistant chief of staff, G-2, of the United States Army, advised the army in 1934 that the legislature was "not particularly competent" and had "little or no sense of fiscal responsibility, no competent bill drafting division, no correctly organized calendar, no correctly kept record, and no very high sense of public responsibility." For all its faults, however, the Philippine legislature played a larger part in the affairs of government than legislatures normally played in the colonies of other imperial powers.[25]

As of 1913, a corps of 2,623 Americans, 29 percent of the total, directed and gave tone to the Philippine civil service. Harrison's policy of "immediate Filipinization" reduced the number of Americans by 1921 to 614, or 4 percent of the civil service, and the "purging at the top" was "even more drastic." By the time Murphy arrived in the Philippines, there were only 376 Americans among the 21,612 persons in the Philippine civil service.[26] The merit system introduced at the outset of American rule continued in effect, but the Filipinos assumed that the kin of persons in office were entitled to preferential treatment in the making of appointments. The result was that the government service, as one observer put it, was "cluttered up with a vast array of cousins, second cousins, brothers-in-law, nephews-by-marriage and other connections, close and distant," of persons with influence in the government. It is not surprising, therefore, that government offices and bureaus were "over-staffed and under-worked" and that the concept of honest and efficient administration as an end in itself, or as a necessary condition of good government, found little support in theory or in practice.[27]

As was evident in the staffing of the civil service, Filipinos extended the concept of family to include not only paternal and maternal relatives but even nonfamily persons such as godparents, godchildren, and marriage sponsors. It was this extended bilateral family rather than the nation that defined the Filipino "sense of community." As is characteristic in traditional agrarian societies, the Filipinos were deferential to authority and to "big men," a tendency that was strengthened by Spanish and American rule. The Filipino was thus predisposed to support the party in power, and he gave his loyalty to the "top man" in the governmental power structure.[28]

Although consisting of more than forty ethnographic groups and speaking at least eighty languages and dialects, the Filipino people, most of whom were Malay in origin, were predominantly a homogeneous people ethnologically. In addition to the indigenous inhabitants, the population of the Philippines as of 1930 included 80,000–100,000 Chinese, 16,000 Japanese, 8,700 Americans, and 4,600 Spaniards. There had been a good deal of intermarriage between Chinese and Filipinos, and about 750,000 Filipinos, visibly, had Chinese blood. The Chinese, who had begun to settle in the Philippines in the last quarter of the sixteenth century, conducted the bulk of the retail trade in the islands. They and their property were periodically the victims of mob violence, and they also were subjected to discriminatory taxation and legislation. They remained an unpopular minority while Murphy served as governor-general, but the Japanese by that time aroused far greater fears among the Filipino leadership.[29]

About 90 percent of the inhabitants of the Philippines were Christians, 80 percent of them being Roman Catholics and 9–10 percent being Aglipayans, members of the nationalistic but essentially Catholic Philippine Independent Church that had been formed in the early years of the twentieth century, taking its name from Gregorio Aglipay, an excommunicated Catholic priest who had served as chaplain general of Aguinaldo's army. About 4 percent of the Filipinos were Muslims (Moros), and another 4 percent were pagans. There was a vast "cultural chasm" between the Christians and the non-Christians that Filipinos underestimated and that American rule only partially bridged.[30]

From 1905, when the Partido Federal abandoned statehood as its political objective, political independence became the professed and reiterated goal of the Filipino political leadership. When the Partido Nacionalista was formed in 1907, its platform called for " 'the immediate independence of the Philippine Islands . . . under a democratic government without prejudice to the adoption in due time of any form of guarantee.' " Independence, however, was more an "ideal" than a program for action, and some of its prominent advocates really may have preferred some form of binationalism such as dominion status. This, however, was not a view that could be publicly expressed since the leadership had proclaimed independence to be "synonymous with national honor and personal happiness," and it had become both "the cement of unity and the sanction of class rule."[31]

On December 5, 1931, the Ninth Independence Mission left Manila for the United States. Headed by Osmeña and Manuel Roxas, the OsRox mission, as it was dubbed, was given "entire freedom" by the Philippine legislature to seek "the earliest concession of independence" that it could obtain from the United States. By the time the mission was authorized, the impact of the Great Depression and Japanese aggression in Manchuria had made Philippine independence the goal not only of the Filipino leadership but of influential groups within the United States as well.[32]

It was, to be sure, in the economic interests of many Americans for the United States to retain its hold on the Philippines. Americans who had invested funds in the Philippines (American direct and portfolio investments in the Philippines in 1932 totaled more than $257 million, and American capital was "dominant" or an "important factor" in 189 Philippine concerns), importers and processors of duty-free Philippine products, manufacturers and exporters of American products sent to the Philippines (the ninth largest market for United States goods), owners of American ships in the Philippine trade, and American businessmen and other Americans resident in the Philippines all had reason to oppose the grant of independence. These groups made their views known through the Philippine-American Chamber of Commerce in New York and the American Chamber of Commerce in Manila, and the *Manila Daily Bulletin* bespoke their interests.[33]

The advocates of Philippine independence in the United States—economic interests that believed themselves disadvantageously affected by the competition of Philippine imports, opponents of Filipino immigration, isolationists or those who thought the Philippines militarily indefensible, and anti-imperialists—proved to be more powerful politically than the opponents of independence. Although "the cumulative impact of the anti-imperial tradition" is essential to an understanding of the measure, the Hare-Hawes-Cutting Act that the OsRox mission took back to the Philippines in 1933 was designed less to satisfy Filipino aspirations for independence than to respond to the demands of Americans who believed that independence was in their own best interests. As Senator Arthur H. Vandenberg wryly indicated, the intent of the measure was "not to free the Philippines from the United States, but to free the United States from the Philippines."[34]

Farm organizations, bankers, and cordage manufacturers were among the influential lobbyists for Philippine independence. Responding to a slump in the world sugar market that began in 1925 and was aggravated by the general economic collapse of 1929 and the following years of depression, American sugar beet and cane growers thought that they could increase the price for their product if they could limit the import of duty-free Philippine sugar. Philippine sugar exports to the United States increased more than seven-fold from 1921 to 1933, partly because of the increase in the duty on other sugar (from 1.256 cents to 2.206 cents per pound) imposed by the Fordney-McCumber tariff of 1922 and partly because Philippine sugar producers, increasingly concerned that American independence legislation might limit the amount of Philippine sugar that could be exported to the United States, were intent upon establishing as large a claim as possible upon any quota that might be fixed on their product. The reduced import of Philippine sugar, however, would not have aided American sugar producers to any great extent since the price of sugar in the American market was determined by the world price plus the preferential tariff on Cuban sugar. American firms that had invested in Cuban sugar, particularly the National City Bank of New York, which had seen the Cuban share of the American sugar market decline from almost 55 percent in 1927 to 25.34 percent in 1933 while the Philippine share rose from 8.2 to 19.65 percent, did stand to benefit from any limitation that might be imposed on Philippine sugar; and so they lobbied quietly to protect their economic interests. No doubt they reminded legislators that the American investment in Cuban sugar exceeded the total value of American investments in the Philippines.[35]

Although United States dairy and cottonseed oil interests complained that coconut oil imported from the Philippines competed with domestic oils and fats, there was little substance to this allegation. About two-thirds of the imported coconut oil was used in the manufacture of soap, and the Philippine product was not only far better suited for this purpose than animal fat and cottonseed oil but was also so much cheaper than animal fat that the duty of a few cents per pound on imported oil that was being suggested would not have discouraged its use. A little more than 22 percent of Philippine coconut oil went into the production of oleomargarine (most Philippine coconut oil was unsuitable for edible purposes), but since butter was selling for about eighteen cents more per pound than oleo, the contemplated duty would not have led to the increased consumption of butter. The American Cordage Institute, by contrast, was on firmer ground when it complained that processed Philippine cordage imported into the United States competed with Philippine abaca that American cordage manufacturers imported and processed. Since the Philippines enjoyed a virtual monopoly in the growing of abaca, there was no American complaint about the import of the raw product.[36]

Since about 90 percent of the sixty thousand Filipinos resident in the United States as of 1932 were males under thirty years of age, the American Federation of Labor (AFL) alleged that they were a source of job and wage competition for American union members even though most Filipinos worked as agricultural laborers or domestic servants. The AFL at first pressed for Filipino exclusion, but, when this effort failed, it gave its support to independence legislation as the means of curbing Filipino immigration. It was joined in this cause by the patriotic societies, which, ignoring the evidence, charged that Filipinos were unassimilable.[37]

For isolationists and those who doubted the ability of the United States to defend the Philippines against a Japanese attack, Japanese aggression in Manchuria demonstrated the danger of a continued American presence in the Orient. The Joint Board of the Army and Navy, on the other hand, had several times recorded its opposition to independence as "detrimental to the best interests of the United States," and War Plan Orange, the contingency plan for war with Japan, called for American retention of Manila Bay until reinforcements arrived. Some army officers in the Philippines, however, did not regard War Plan Orange as realistic, and key figures in Congress like Senator Harry B. Hawes did not believe that the Philippines were defensible.[38]

The Hare-Hawes-Cutting bill that Congress approved at the end of 1932 was to take effect only when accepted either by a concurrent resolution of the Philippine legislature or by a convention called for that purpose. Were the legislation to be accepted, the Philippine legislature was authorized to arrange for a constitutional convention to draft a constitution that would provide for a republican form of government, include a bill of rights, and assure the continuation of American authority. The constitution was to be submitted to the president of the United States for his approval and was to go into effect if approved by a majority of Filipino voters.

The Hare-Hawes-Cutting bill provided for the independence of the Philippines on July 4 following the expiration of a period of ten years from the date of the inauguration of a new Commonwealth government. The president of the United States, however, might reserve land for "military and other reservations" that the United States could use after independence. He was also to enter into negotiations with other countries to seek the neutralization of the Philippines.

There was to be no change in existing trade relations between the United States and the Philippines during the first five years of the Commonwealth except that the full United States tariff was to apply to annual imports from the Philippines of unrefined sugar in excess of 800,000 long tons (896,000 short), refined sugar in excess of 50,000 long tons (56,000 short), coconut oil in excess of 200,000 long tons (224,000 short), and cordage in excess of 3 million pounds. American products were to enter the Philippines duty-free during the entire Commonwealth period, but beginning with the sixth year of the Commonwealth the Philippine government was to impose a tax equal to 5 percent of the United States tariff on all exports, and these rates were to increase an additional 5 percent each year for the remaining five years of the Commonwealth. The money derived from the export tax was to be placed in a sinking fund and used to pay the bonded debt of the Philippine government. After independence, Philippine imports were to pay the full United States duty. There was, however, to be a joint conference between representatives of the United States and Philippine governments at least one year before the date of independence to formulate recommendations that would govern future trade relations between the two. Such a conference was needed since the imposition of the full American tariff on Philippine goods seemed likely to destroy or at least seriously damage the major Philippine export industries.

Just as the independence bill imposed restrictions on the movement of goods from the Philippines to the United States, so it restricted the movement of people as well. During the Commonwealth period the Philippines were to be allowed a quota of fifty immigrants, but once independence had been attained, American immigration statutes excluding Orientals were to apply to Filipinos other than Philippine Scout veterans of World War I.

Although the Philippine government was to exercise a substantial degree of control over local affairs during the Commonwealth period, the Hare-Hawes-Cutting bill imposed some restraints on its behavior, placed foreign affairs under the control of the United States government, and authorized American intervention in the Philippines under certain circumstances. A high commissioner appointed by the president was to represent the United States in the Philippines during the Commonwealth period.[39]

The OsRox mission does not appear to have been particularly concerned about the strategic implications of the Hare-Hawes-Cutting bill, and it was willing to accept restrictions on Filipino immigration partly because many businessmen in the Philippines and many provincial governors preferred that Filipino laborers remain in the islands. The members of the mission, on the other hand, were painfully aware of what the application of American tariff duties on Philippine exports portended for the Philippine economy and the viability of an independent Philippine state. They nevertheless agreed to accept the bill because they were pleased with its political provisions, which made greater concessions to Philippine interests than they had anticipated, and because they knew that the trade terms were the "best" that they could obtain. As they saw it, if disaster occurred during the ten-year transition period, the United States would have to assume the responsibility for dealing with it; and if both sides wished to continue the status quo after ten years, independence could be delayed. This was not something that members of the mission could say publicly, but after lengthy conversations with the OsRox group, Professor Hayden concluded that this was their view.[40]

Lame-duck President Herbert Hoover was especially troubled about the strategic implications of the independence measure, fearing that the bill's adoption would upset the balance of power in the Far East. This was also Great Britain's view, and Britain might have refused to accept the limitations on naval construction imposed by the London Naval Conference in 1930 had not Hoover pledged that the United States would retain the Philippines. Hawes had apparently inserted the provision in the independence measure regarding military and other reservations "to quiet international discussion" concerning America's withdrawal from the Philippines, but this did not satisfy Hoover, who vetoed the measure on January 13, 1933. Congress, however, overrode the veto.[41]

If Hoover was powerless to block congressional approval of the independence bill, Manuel Quezon, who had remained in Manila "to watch the home front of the independence battle," demonstrated that he had the power to prevent its acceptance by the Philippine legislature. While in the United States in 1931 Quezon, who like so many Filipino leaders was ambivalent about independence, had discussed dominion status for the Philippines and had also considered a "Free State" plan advanced by American businessmen interested in the Philippines. He seems to have favored an arrangement that would have granted the Philippines autonomy for ten years, after which a plebiscite would resolve the independence issue; but there was little support for this idea in the Philippines, and Quezon had found himself outflanked by vocal advocates of immediate independence like Osmeña. Fearing that his position in the Philippines was weakening vis-à-vis Osmeña, Quezon asked the Os-Rox mission to return home after the independence bill had become stalled in the Senate in July 1932. The mission, however, ignored this request. After Roosevelt won the presidential election, Quezon, abandoning any idea of "partnership" with the United States, cabled the mission to work for immediate independence; and after Congress had passed the Hare-Hawes-Cutting bill, he vainly sought to persuade the Philippine legislature to request Hoover to veto the measure.[42]

In March 1933 Quezon left for the United States with a "mixed mission" that was without official standing. In coming to the United States, Quezon hoped to assert his primacy in Philippine politics by securing important amendments to the Philippine Independence (Hare-Hawes-Cutting) Act, which, he alleged, was "a disgraceful piece of legislation," or at least by obtaining a commitment from the new president that he would support such amendments in the future. Senator Key Pittman, the chairman of the Senate Committee on Foreign Relations, informed Murphy that Quezon would "not obtain such commitments." At a meeting in Pittman's office honoring Murphy that was attended by members of the Foreign Relations Committee, Quezon, according to Norman Hill's recollection, referred to the Stars and Stripes as an "alien flag." This angered Senator Joseph Robinson, the majority leader of the Senate, who informed the Filipino leader that he should be grateful for the measure that had been approved and that he could not expect a better bill from the new Senate. When Roosevelt later conferred with Quezon and the OsRox group, he told them that the Filipinos would have to act on the independence measure themselves before the matter could receive any further consideration in Washington. Their differences over the Independence Act unresolved, the Filipino leaders decided to return to Manila.[43]

II

The *Coolidge* arrived at its Manila destination on June 15. About sixty decorated launches met the ship outside the breakwater and escorted her to the pier, while an aerial escort flew overhead, and the bands on the pier blared a greeting. A crowd of about fifteen thousand was on hand to join in the "grand[,] glorious welcome." Those who caught a glimpse of the new governor-general might have noted that he was of medium height (5'11") and had a slight build, a high forehead, receding red hair, a freckled face, keen blue eyes, a longish nose, and a ready smile. His "most distinctive feature" was his bushy eyebrows, which he combed downward for emphasis. After receiving a seventeen-gun salute, Murphy reviewed the military escort drawn up at the pier and then went to the speaker's stand to promise that he would administer his responsibilities "in a spirit of broad understanding, sympathy, and tolerance." He stated that he would not seek to influence the Filipino decision regarding the burning question of independence and would provide the islands with an efficient and economical government that would be concerned with social justice and the attainment of a better-balanced economy. After the speech a rifle troop of the 26th Cavalry and a motorcycle squad escorted the Murphy party to Malacañan Palace, the official residence of the governor-general. A battalion of the Philippine Constabulary tendered the honors there, and the Murphys, "bewildered at it all," entered the palace. They inspected the building and received callers, after which Frank and the Teahans went to the Santo Domingo Church to offer a prayer. Following a dinner for thirty guests in the palace, the Murphys went to the Manila Hotel for a mammoth reception honoring the governor-general that was attended by more than seven thousand persons.[44]

As governor-general, Murphy was vested with the "supreme executive power" in the Philippines. The governor-general appointed not only the members of his cabinet and subordinate officials but also the members of the legislature who represented the Moros and the pagan tribes. His veto power included the right to veto individual items in appropriation bills. Vetoes could be overridden by a two-thirds vote of each house of the legislature, but when this occurred the bills were referred to the president of the United States for a final decision. Tariff bills and bills dealing with public lands, immigration, coinage, and the currency required the approval of both the governor-general and the president.

As governor-general, Murphy received a salary of $18,000 and was entitled to the use of Malacañan Palace in Manila and Mansion House in Baguio. He could spend up to P30,000 in discretionary funds, and a coast guard cutter was available for his use. In addition to an office staff and custodial forces for Malacañan and Mansion House, the governor-general could designate an aide-de-camp and military and naval aides, and the aforementioned Belo Act provided him with a standing appropriation of P250,000 per annum for the salaries and expenses of such technical personnel and civilian assistants as he saw fit to employ.[45]

Murphy's authority as governor-general was enhanced by the fact that President Roosevelt and congressional leaders went "out of their way to make it plain" to the Filipino leadership that the new governor-general would receive "100% backing" from Washington. This, Hayden thought, would make Murphy "a harder man" for the Filipinos to " 'handle' " than his immediate predecessors had been. On the other hand, the fact that independence was imminent served as a constraint on the exercise of executive power by the governor-general. Also, since the heads of the executive departments were Filipinos and the legislature was entirely a Filipino body, the governor-general had to secure the cooperation of the Filipino leadership if he were to accomplish anything. "There is no other road to a successful administration or even to a tolerable existence," Hayden had written in 1931. It was advisable under the circumstances for a governor-general to rule by "indirection," by persuading the Filipino leadership that his program was really theirs. When Theodore Roosevelt, Jr., became governor-general, former governor-general W. Cameron Forbes advised him to take the position with the Filipinos that he had not come to the islands to govern them but rather to assist them to govern themselves. "The velvet glove," Forbes wrote, "is of utmost importance." [46]

Like the governor-general, the vice-governor was a presidential appointee. Since he doubted that Murphy, because of his ignorance of the Philippines, could "manage to swing it," Cameron Forbes advised Roosevelt to compensate for the governor-general's "deficiency" by appointing a knowledgeable vice-governor. This was also Murphy's view, and, after conversing with Hayden at a dinner party in Ann Arbor before leaving for the Philippines, the governor-general decided that Hayden was the right man for the position. Born on September 24, 1887, in Keokuk, Iowa, Hayden received a B.S. degree from Knox College before entering graduate school at the University of Michigan, where he was awarded the Ph.D. in political science in 1915. He joined the Michigan Naval Militia in World War I and apparently fired the "last official shot of the war," a fact commemorated by a bronze plaque in the Smithsonian Institution. He taught at the University of the Philippines in 1922 and 1930 and served as an advisor to the Carmi A. Thompson mission that President Coolidge sent to the Philippines in 1926. A great admirer of the performance of Leonard Wood as governor-general, Hayden, whom Quezon characterized as "one of those 'Nordics' who look down on colored races," believed that the Philippines were economically unprepared for independence and was therefore opposed to the Hare-

Hawes-Cutting Act. Hayden was a Republican, and at least one other candidate for the vice-governorship, George A. Malcolm, enjoyed the support of influential Democrats; but Murphy wanted Hayden, and the president obliged the governor-general.[47]

The vice-governor of the Philippines headed the department of public instruction, which included the bureaus of education, health, and welfare. Hayden's responsibilities under Murphy, however, encompassed a far wider sphere than this. Murphy thought that as the number-two man in the insular government and the resident American expert on the Philippines, Hayden should serve as the governor-general's chief advisor, "cognizant of everything that is going on, and . . . prepared to take over at any time should this become necessary." As it turned out, Hayden's responsibilities became virtually coterminous with Murphy's. The scholarly and rather dour vice-governor and the sentimental and idealistic governor-general quickly developed a "happy" working relationship. "In spite of their obvious contrasts of temperament, character and political persuasion," the two men, an old Philippine hand observed, "pulled together well at Malacañan."[48]

The insular auditor of the Philippines, like the vice-governor, was a presidential appointee. Murphy's choice for the position was G. Hall Roosevelt, the president's brother-in-law, who had been Detroit's controller while Murphy was the city's mayor; but the appointment was given to J. Weldon Jones, a thirty-seven-year-old assistant professor of accounting at Ohio State University. Jones, who was very good at his job, developed a close relationship with the vice-governor.[49]

Murphy's staff of administrative assistants, "the Belo boys," consisted of holdovers from the previous administration as well as some aides whom he had brought with him from Detroit. Among the latter, the most important were Joseph R. Mills, who had been commissioner of public works and general manager of the Detroit Street Railways while Murphy was mayor, and Ed Kemp. Mills, whom Murphy had once described as "the most perfect public servant" he had ever encountered, was the governor-general's economic and financial advisor, his responsibilities encompassing budget-making by both the central and the provincial governments, the operation of government-owned companies, industrial development, and a variety of other economic matters. "Overworked," he died on April 6, 1934. Kemp, Murphy's closest friend and confidant, served the governor-general as legal advisor.[50]

Of the staff members already serving in the Philippines when Murphy arrived, he relied most heavily on Major George C. Dunham and Evett D. Hester. Dunham, whose particular responsibility had been sanitation, played an "indispensable" role in shaping Murphy's health and welfare program. Hester, who had served as both senior trade commissioner in Manila and as "extramural advisor" at Mala-cañan since May 1930, joined Murphy as a full-time advisor in February 1934. "I warned him [Murphy]," Hester wrote Theodore Roosevelt, Jr., "I was a very black Republican, a Philippine reten-tionist, a protectionist, a mason, socially a boor, sociologically a Bourbon, with just a slight touch of liberalism acquired from you," but, Hester observed, his "unregenerate status didn't seem to phase" Murphy. When Mills died, Hester succeeded to most of his responsi-bilities. On the advice of the Bureau of Insular Affairs and because they had become "permanent fixtures," Murphy retained as part of his secretarial staff both Charles W. Franks, who had been in the Philippine service since 1901, and Richard R. Ely, who had entered the Philippine service in 1917. Norman H. Hill, who had been Mayor Murphy's executive secretary, served as the governor-general's prin-cipal secretary; the post of assistant secretary went to Eleanor M. Bumgardner, a former secretary in a Detroit bank who remained with Murphy in a secretarial capacity for the rest of his life.[51]

A *Manila Bulletin* correspondent characterized Murphy's staff as "the strongest and most loyal" ever assembled by a governor-general, and the Manila correspondent of the *New York Times* concluded after Murphy's first year in the Philippines that "no governor in recent times . . . [had] had a better staff."[52] Murphy's success as governor-general, like his success in other positions in the public ser-vice, was in no small measure due to the excellent aides with whom he surrounded himself.

Although a member of Murphy's family thought it strange that President Roosevelt had not provided the govornor-general with in-structions regarding his assignment, the nation's chief executives had customarily left governors-general free to proceed as they thought best. As Murphy conceived his role, one of his objectives was to administer his office in such a manner that the president would not have to trouble himself about the Philippines and could take pride in what the American regime was accomplishing. Murphy hoped to infuse Philippine political life with the same sort of humanitarianism and idealism that had characterized his mayoralty. He also wished to interpret for the Filipinos "the spirit of America's best intentions toward them" and to prepare the islands for independence so that, when American rule came to an end, the Filipinos would take over a government that was "sound, orderly and just." As long as he remained at the head of the Philippine government, finally, he thought it his duty to press Filipino claims in the United States as vigorously as he could. He knew that there were many able men in the United States to present the American position, whereas the advocacy of the Filipino case, he thought, rested primarily on his shoulders. "I was so anxious to do them justice," he wrote toward the end of his tenure, "that, with the eyes of my reason wide open, if an error was to be made I wanted to err on the side of doing justice to the Philippines."[53]

Despite his profound sympathy for the aspirations of the Filipinos and his desire to encourage them to be self-reliant, Murphy was determined to permit no one to encroach upon the powers and prerogatives of the governor-general as outlined in the Jones Act. Making this evident to department heads and bureau chiefs at the outset of his administration, Murphy "re-established the vigorous American leadership" that had characterized the Wood regime and the pre-1913 period of American rule. Although he consulted with the Filipino leadership before making major appointments, in preparing his legislative program, and before vetoing legislation, he left no doubt in their minds that the final decision and the ultimate responsibility regarding these matters were his. Because of his fairness, tact, and diplomatic skill—"He tells you things you don't like in a way that make you like them—and him," an American business-man involved in the Philippine trade noted—Murphy retained the confidence of all factions in the Philippines. After "a brief 'trying out' period," they "tacitly accepted" his interpretation of the scope of his powers.[54]

Because Manuel Quezon was the dominant figure in Philippine political life—"There isn't anything that Quezon can't do politically in the Philippines," Murphy reportedly said—Murphy took special care to establish cordial relations with the Nacionalista leader. Careful always to permit Quezon to save face and anxious to avoid a rupture between the two of them lest it weaken the governor-general in the Philippines and embarrass him politically in the United States, Murphy was accused by some Americans of "continuous kowtowing to Quezon" and of being dominated by the Filipino leader. The reverse, however, seems to have been more nearly true. Murphy, Hayden observed at the close of Murphy's service in the Philippines, was "smart enough politically to make M.L.Q. do more things that this gentleman did not want to do and prevent him from doing more things that he did want to do than has any other Governor-General, and do it in such a way that Quezon could not come into an open break with him. Of course, Quezon got some things out of Murphy too, but there was never any bargaining, and Quezon got little that was not in accord with the public interest.''

Although ''there were times when he [Quezon] nearly wore the G-G out,'' Murphy admired and respected the Filipino leader. In a diary-like note of January 1935 the governor-general wrote of Quezon, ''From the first day in the Islands . . . through every disagreement and every struggle, he has been consistently loyal and helpful . . . he manifests a stability overlooked by those who underestimate him or who may be biased about him.'' It is not easy to know Quezon's true feelings about Murphy since the Filipino leader realized the importance for himself and his people of having Murphy's support and was probably aware of the governor-general's susceptibility to flattery. Although Quezon privately criticized some of Murphy's policies and actions and complained that he was ''so very 'good' it made him [Quezon] uncomfortable,'' the Filipino leader was impressed that Murphy ''always looked at things from a very common-sense point of view and decided questions on the merits of the case without allowing himself to be disturbed too much by political angles.'' Quezon valued Murphy's advice and appreciated all that he did for the Filipino cause and for Quezon himself. ''Nothing I can say,'' Quezon wrote Murphy toward the end of his service in the Philippines, ''will ever fully express my appreciation of what you have done for my country[,] my administration[,] and me personally.''[55]

Whatever Quezon may have thought about Murphy, we can be certain, at the very least, that inside the Quezon household, Aurora Quezon, fascinated by Murphy as women of all ages were apt to be, lobbied with her husband in Murphy's behalf. ''Where could I find another friend like you?'' she wrote Murphy in 1936. ''Never even if I go around the world. I don't intend to have another one. You are my *first* and my *last*.''[56]

In his efforts to secure executive-legislative cooperation, Murphy relied on his good relations with Quezon and the inclusion of important legislators in his cabinet rather than on the Council of State. The Council ''virtually ceased to be a deliberative body'' during the Murphy regime, meeting rarely and then only to grant formal approval to decisions already reached by the governor-general, the cabinet, and legislative leaders. When the Filipino political leadership attempted to add the phrase ''by and with the consent of the Council of State'' to legislative measures, Murphy adopted a ''thumbs down attitude'' lest this hamstring the island's chief executive. This was one way of letting the Filipinos know who was ''boss'' in their country.[57]

Murphy informed cabinet members that although he did not intend "to relax the duty of the Governor-General," he wanted to encourage a sense of self-reliance on the part of high government officials. He advised them to bear in mind that they were "members of the Cabinet of a great government," it was not becoming their "dignity" to spend their time at cabinet meetings on trivial patronage matters, and they should discuss the big questions of government and the "doing [of] things that are worth doing." What he required of cabinet members, he said, was "loyalty to the public trust" rather than to the governor-general.[58]

Murphy's staff, "an informal, extra-official council of advice," met with the governor-general the day before the weekly cabinet meeting. Staff members served as Murphy's "eyes and ears," keeping him informed about matters that were to come to him for decision and about the departments to which they were assigned. Although staff members, for the most part, worked harmoniously with the Filipino executives and legislators to whom their duties related, the Nacionalista press complained at the end of 1934 that Murphy was assigning the Belo boys duties that properly belonged to cabinet members. The latter, however, refused to rise to the bait and expressed their satisfaction with the way the governor-general was conducting his administration.[59]

Committed to the merit system, Murphy ordered officials to follow the merit principle in filling all positions not expressly unclassified. He vetoed a bill stipulating that persons licensed to practice certain professions be eligible for appointment to the government service without meeting normal civil service requirements. Concerned about a decline in the "dignity and competence" of some government agencies and the substitution of "direct political control" for "responsible technical control," Murphy gave first consideration to professional competence rather than politics in appointing persons to positions requiring technical skills, did not hesitate to suspend or dismiss the incompetent and the "unworthy," and instructed department undersecretaries to limit their political activities.[60]

Some officials had expected to find in Murphy "a glad-handed careless politician," but they discovered instead, as Hester put it, "a coldly ascetic celt equipped with that almost peculiar, almost fanatic depth of devotion and tenseness." Stating that a new governor-general had the choice of "being window dressing or getting down to work," Murphy broke precedent and "made a big hit" with both the Filipino and American communities by not making the usual inspection tour at the outset of his administration. As at the start of his mayoralty, he began work in the Philippines at a feverish pace, applying himself "studiously and with the greatest of determination." Hayden reported at the end of the year that Murphy, who was seeking to set an example for government servants, had been at his desk "almost without a break" since his arrival in the Philippines. Although Hayden later concluded that no governor-general had "worked harder" than Murphy, Murphy actually worked in spurts after the initial few months, putting in long hours when this appeared to be necessary but working only a few hours a day on other occasions and finding a good deal of time for athletic activity and afternoon siestas. However many hours per day Murphy labored at his official tasks, however, he had a "devotion to his work" that Hayden accurately characterized as "passionate." ". . . government *per se*," Hayden wrote a faculty colleague about Murphy, "is his devouring interest in life. No political scientist ever thought more constantly upon this subject."[61]

"As in Detroit," Murphy wrote his brother George, "I am making . . . integrity the dominant strain throughout the administration and its every policy. Nothing captures public support so much as honesty in government." Aware that the government service was "honeycombed with inefficiency, corruption, and extravagance," he stressed the importance of punctuality, thoroughness, orderliness, and honesty on the part of government servants, insisted upon the proper care of government property, and called for "a constant effort to improve the worth and usefulness of ourselves to the government and of the government to the public." Since he knew that what went on in Malacañan was "pretty closely watched and reflected on the outside," he instructed staff members to "keep driving at things," not to "let down," and to be at their desks during working hours. Also, as in Detroit, he created a General Committee on Efficiency and Economy and similar committees in the various departments. "Everybody feels that Murphy is constantly on the watch," Osmeña declared. The governor-general, he observed, not only fought graft and dishonesty in the public service but even the appearance of same.[62]

In the Philippines as in Detroit, Murphy was acutely conscious of the value of favorable publicity and the importance of establishing good relations with the press. He generally saw reporters twice a day, at noon for the benefit of afternoon papers and in the afternoon to accommodate morning papers. He told newsmen the truth and developed a relationship of "confidence and friendship" with both the American and Filipino press, admittedly inclined to sing the praises of governors-general, that was "unique" in the American experience in the islands.[63]

Murphy not only wished Filipinos to think of him as a hardworking governor-general but as a man of unostentatious tastes as well. It was for this reason that he ordered the discontinuance of the traditional practice of providing elaborate receptions for Malacañan officials when they visited the provinces. The press applauded this decision, the *Philippines Herald* proclaiming that Murphy was "a simple man absolutely free from pretension." "How," it asked, as Murphy no doubt hoped it would, "can he be expected to like the ways of flattery, the insincerity of adulation?"

Murphy used his tours of the archipelago not only to familiarize himself with the problems of local government and to demonstrate the closeness between government and the people but also to spread "the gospel of good government." Since he attached a good deal of importance to the role of leader as exhorter, a role in which he excelled, it is not surprising that a Murphy tour became "as much . . . an evangelistic crusade as a series of inspection visits." He provided his listeners with "sermons on fiscal integrity," sought to arouse them to the need for "a progressive social program," and lectured them on "civil rights and civil duties." " 'You cannot stay in the Philippines a week,' " the historian A. B. Hart had written in 1909, " 'without realizing that the Insular Government is in reality a big mission, the bishop of which is the governor general.' " No governor-general came closer to fulfilling Hart's ecclesiastical definition of the position than Frank Murphy. The governor-general was " 'more like Billy Sunday than a high dignitary,' " Robert Aura Smith concluded after accompanying Murphy on a tour of the southern islands.[64]

Although Murphy did not always translate his "preachments" into action and could procrastinate when difficult decisions had to be made, he was far from being an inefficient administrator. He was not "brilliant," but the principles on which he acted were "fundamentally sound," and Hayden thought that the governor-general could "see the heart of a political or administrative problem as quickly as anyone" Hayden had ever known. Murphy, Hayden observed, remembered what had gone before, and he could "state . . . a case under consideration with beautiful clarity." As in Detroit, moreover, Murphy's earnestness, his dedication to his job, and the loftiness of his purposes made a strong impression on those who worked under him, and many of them sought to emulate his example. Murphy raised the tone of public service in the Philippines just as he had done in Detroit.[65]

As could have been predicted, Murphy came to view the position he held as "the most attractive" in the government service save the presidency. He thought the Filipino people "the kindliest, gentlest and the most considerate" he had ever met, he was impressed with the "charm" of Manila, and he was overwhelmed with the beauty of Baguio. When he accepted the post, he observed that it was "a rather disappointing commentary on the times" that those with whom he discussed the job dwelt on the perquisites of the office—the palace, the servants, the yachts—rather than on the service he could render. Dissimulating, as was his habit, Murphy protested that the trappings of office interested him not at all, that the last thing he desired was to live like an "oriental potentate." As he confided to his brother George, however, Murphy very much enjoyed "the ease and emoluments" of his position. He thought that the palace and all that went with it were "grand" (" 'Oh boy, it's some palace,' " he told a lady friend), was "extremely fond of the official social life," and liked being treated "like a king." Indeed, he so much enjoyed the perquisites of his office and the accompanying pomp and ceremony that he felt a bit guilty about the matter.[66]

In the final analysis, though, it was less the perquisites of office than what the position enabled him to accomplish and the contrast with the conditions he had faced as mayor that especially appealed to Murphy. Long an advocate of Irish independence, he considered himself "privileged to assist and direct" while a nation was "being born and a people . . . [were] coming into their destiny." As he looked back upon his mayoralty, it seemed to him that the city's "heartbreaking indebtedness" and "the colossal problem of unemployment" had cast a pall over his administration and had overshadowed his accomplishments. He found it satisfying, therefore, to administer a government that was "unhampered" by debt and substantial unemployment. Because of the more favorable circumstances, he thought, "the progress made always shows itself."[67]

No doubt Murphy's enjoyment of his position was enhanced by the knowledge that the Filipinos "virtually worshipped" him. The American associate editor of the *Philippines Free Press* was quite correct in his judgment that Murphy "had a way with Filipinos." He "recognized their rights, sympathized with their aspirations, showed a real understanding and respect for their feelings, and always appealed to the best within them." One of Murphy's predecessors as governor-general, aware of the importance that Filipinos attached to "self-esteem" and "face," thought it important for occupants of the position to understand that Filipinos valued "social recognition" above "political concession[s]" and were upset if they received less consideration in Malacañan than Americans did. "They are very touchy about that kind of thing," Cameron Forbes noted. Murphy understood that this was so and also that Filipinos liked Americans who reposed trust in them and did not "shame" them in conversation or give offense in any way. "They want to be treated with dignity and justice," Murphy wrote his brother George, "and as I see it that is the way to their hearts."[68]

In arranging formal dinners at Malacañan, Murphy was careful to include a substantial number of Filipinos—"They work over the guest lists like they were budgets," the governor-general's sister-in-law remarked. When some Americans in the islands complained that Murphy was more hospitable to Filipinos than his predecessors had been, the governor-general's reply was, "Well, it's their palace and they feed me." It was, however, not only the welcome extended to them in Malacañan and the fact that Murphy socialized more with Filipinos than with the American community that pleased the people of the Philippines; they also reacted appreciatively to Murphy's democratic manner, his oratory, his "dreamy idealism," his sentimentality, his heart-on-the-sleeve patriotism, his commitment to them "to do my best to preserve your traditions, your culture, and everything that is distinctively yours as a people," and, most important of all, his Catholicism. It would "help very much," Quezon thought, for Murphy to "show very openly and plainly" that he was "a practical Catholic, a religious man." In the Catholic Murphy the Filipinos recognized that they had a governor-general of their "own kind."[69]

Murphy acted from the outset on the understanding that his religion was "a great asset" in the performance of his role as governor-general. He had contemplated arranging a public service in the Manila cathedral immediately upon his arrival in the Philippines, but Quezon advised against this lest anticlericals complain that the new governor-general had come to the Philippines not to provide "just government" but to be "unfairly Catholic." As noted, however, Murphy did visit a Manila church on the day of his arrival for the purpose of "meditation and gratitude."

In an interview with a reporter soon after he became governor-general, Murphy stated that he was related to twenty-seven priests on his mother's side, which is hardly credible, was proud to be a Catholic and to carry a rosary, had been a professor in a Jesuit school (the University of Detroit), and followed the *Rerum Novarum* of Pope Leo XIII as "my philosophy of life." Catholic clerics were seen in Malacañan more often than in the past, the governor-general attended weekday mass in a chapel in the palace, and he made it a point to attend a different church every Sunday.[70]

"All of us having the same religious faith, we thank our Lord for having given you to us as the Governor of our country in its most critical period,'' Aurora Quezon wrote Murphy. The Catholic hierarchy was delighted with the ''good example'' that Murphy set for the Catholics of the Philippines, a point made by the apostolic delegate to the Philippines and by the pope himself. The pontiff, Murphy was advised, ''learned with paternal joy that the expression of your loyalty is no mere formula, and that you esteem your catholic faith as your greatest treasure, and its practice your greatest privilege.'' Even some devout Protestants in the Philippines were pleased to have a governor-general who, unlike some of his predecessors, attended church regularly. The Episcopal bishop of the Philippines, ''carried away'' by Murphy's ''earnestness,'' expressed pleasure that Murphy paid heed to the ''religious side'' of life and stressed the importance of practicing one's religion.[71]

Proud of his faith, Murphy respected other religions as well and did not permit his Catholicism to determine his actions as a public official. Despite their praise for Murphy's practice of his religion, Catholic leaders found fault with some of his actions as governor-general. Murphy, for example, ignored the advice of the apostolic delegate that he not attend YMCA functions, just as he did not necessarily heed the wishes of the church in making appointments. He urged the archbishop of Manila, with whom the governor-general's relations were ''quite strained,'' to divest himself of his substantial business holdings in the Philippines and to invest his funds outside the country; he urged a divorce law on the legislature; and he resisted ''all kinds of . . . religious pressure'' for the immediate pardon of a prominent Catholic woman convicted and jailed for accepting bribes to falsify bar examination papers.[72]

Murphy did not have the same rapport with the American community in the Philippines that he did with the native population, but the conclusion of the insular auditor that ''the Filipinos liked Murphy and . . . the American community disliked him'' overstates the matter. Americans, to a large extent, led ''a barricaded . . . life'' in the Philippines, insulating themselves from the life of the country as much as possible and institutionalizing their color prejudice by establishing their own schools, churches, and clubs. '' 'The Americans treat us like niggers,' '' a prominent Filipina complained. Some ''old-timers'' (''a limited few of our old professional knockers,'' Hester called them) were disturbed by Murphy's New Dealism, his support of independence, his occasional flouting of the social conventions, his close association with members of the Spanish community, and, above all, his ignoring of the racial barriers they had erected. They complained that the governor-general was "beginning to play to the native," and some of them even refused to attend affairs at Malacañan. The leaders of the community, however, including the most prominent businessmen, were favorably impressed with Murphy's reassertion of the powers of the governor-general, the way in which he looked after American business interests, his high-mindedness, and the effective manner in which he discharged his duties.[73]

III

The three years that Murphy spent in the Philippines were the happiest of his adult life. "What a perfect corner this is of the Lord's footstool!" he wrote. "I doubt if any place on earth is so enchanting." There was "a peacefulness and happiness" about his work and style of life that contrasted sharply with the rush and turmoil of his Detroit years and that he found enormously satisfying.[74]

The Malacañan community consisted of about seventy persons. Murphy's sister-in-law described it as "truly a royal Court with all the military and diplomatic ceremony that prevails around a Palace." When meals were served, five servants attended the Murphy family in the dining room while a chief cook and two assistants labored in the kitchen. When state dinners were held, Major Garfinkel announced the guests, and a military band entertained them from the patio. On some occasions there were forty diners—Filipinos, Americans, and Spaniards—and another hundred guests would arrive after dinner for the dancing. The abstemious Murphy did not like to have a bar set up for such occasions—"banks of thirsty men were looking for a drink," Francis Burton Harrison observed regarding a reception that the governor-general gave for the secretary of war. In addition to the nonalcoholic punch, however, Murphy sometimes permitted the use of a basement room to dispense hard liquor. On evenings when the Murphys were not entertaining, they were themselves entertained. Since the governor-general discovered that dining out in the Philippines often had an adverse effect on his delicate digestive system, he would eat his meal in the palace before attending a banquet and then pretend to eat when the food was served.[75]

It was characteristic of Frank Murphy to assume that something was due him for the sacrifice he believed he was making to serve the public. When Marguerite, expressing her delight that just about everything in the Philippines was free to the Murphys, wrote to brother George that "we are entitled to all that goes with this [position]," she surely was speaking for Frank as well. The governor-general, indeed, seems to have thought that a good deal "went" with his position. Not only did he expend the entire discretionary fund allotted his office, but one year, in what was apparently an unprecedented action, he asked that a portion of the Belo fund also be used for that purpose. Murphy abused his authority in seeking personal services for himself, members of his family, and his staff. He arranged with the United States Army to provide him with horses, a jump course, and a twenty-four hour guard at Baguio; he improperly allowed his Filipino servants to take advantage of the governor-general's commissary privileges; he permitted two aides to live in Malacañan even though the palace was supposedly reserved for the governor-general and his family; he employed William Teahan on Belo fund money despite the fact that, as a Canadian, he was ineligible for such an appointment; and he sought in vain to have the federal government pay for the transportation of members of his family when they visited the Philippines. A model of rectitude in dealing with large public matters, Murphy was inclined to be indiscreet, to say the least, in his interpretation of the privileges of public office.[76]

Since he believed that "good health" was "the base of every . . . success with any durability to it" and that "commanding physical condition" was an important ingredient of a person's character, Murphy must have been pleased that his new position, less burdensome than his mayoralty, brought with it an improvement in his health and a restoration of physical vigor. Murphy, however, could not escape the ear, nose, and throat ailments that plagued him throughout his adult life: he suffered from the effects of a tonsil infection in the latter part of 1934, underwent a tonsillectomy in May 1935, and had to undergo an operation on his right ear in August 1935.[77]

Believing that regular exercise was essential to the maintenance of good health, Murphy engaged in some type of athletic activity virtually every day that he was in the Philippines. He played tennis and golf, swam in the palace pool, and regularly indulged his passion for horseback riding. Every other Sunday before mass he enjoyed "thrilling rides" with members of the Carabao Wallow Club over an eight-mile course spotted with jumps. They rode in formation and had breakfast under a field tent while the Constabulary band played for their enjoyment. Murphy entered jumping events at horse shows and played "a little poor polo." Although exercise was his chief form of relaxation, Murphy, in his sometimes pretentious way, wished it to be known that he spent some of his time reading the literary masters and pondering "the transcendent problems of life and destiny."

" . . . once in a while," he said, "I wish to escape from the bitterness of mundane realities. That is why I read and study and think.''[78]

On his way to the Philippines, Murphy, who had lost much of his private " 'fortune' " as the result of the decline in common-stock values, sanctimoniously and inaccurately informed the press that, once he had decided on a public career, it had become his goal to divest himself of his wealth, and he had now attained his goal. Since he was able to live on his expense allowance, Murphy did "a regular Cal Coolidge" with his salary, and he was soon seeking profitable investments in the United States. By the time he left the Philippines, he held about 116,000 shares of General Motors, Chrysler, Packard, and United States Steel stock. He earned $13,375 in dividends in 1936 alone, all of which was exempt from United States taxes.[79]

When Murphy told a correspondent in 1935 that his financial resources were limited because he had "substantial family obligations" even though he was a bachelor, he was dissimulating about his resources but not about his family obligations. The Murphys were an unusually close-knit family, and distance did not loosen the bonds of affection and loyalty that had always united them. Frank financed visits to the Philippines by George and by Harold and his family and contributed generously to the support of both his brothers.[80]

Murphy left a bevy of girl friends behind when he departed for the Philippines, and few of them forgot him. A Detroit socialite wrote him that when she tried to solve her "life problem," thoughts of the governor-general intruded, and an actress friend wondered if she must "weep forever" because of him. Not all of Frank's American girl friends expressed their love from afar; as his sister-in-law noted in December 1933, "Frank's girls" were beginning "to come to the Orient by the boat loads." Two were already there, and two more, she noted, were "heaving in" after the holidays. One female visitor returned to the states, spurned and unhappy, and yet, despite referring to "a scar that will never come off," wrote him as she was about to marry, "You will always be the noonday Sun for me. I hope you will always let me be your bedside candle.''[81] Frank Murphy was not the marrying kind, but it was not unusual for his girl friends to retain a strong affection for him after they belatedly discovered that fact and decided to marry someone else.

Murphy's principal girl friend while he was governor-general was Anna May Walker, member of a family with which the Murphy clan had long been friendly. Anna May had been attracted to Frank Murphy while he was mayor. After he assumed his Philippine post, she left college to become Marguerite's social secretary and to be close to the governor-general. When after "six sweet and unforgettable months" in the Philippines, she returned to Detroit because of her father's illness, Frank wrote her passionate, tender letters in which he spoke of his love for her and his great loneliness and conceded, as was obvious from his letters, that he felt like "an adolescent kid unable to find" himself. Craving female affection, he feared without reason that he was "gradually slipping out" of her "heart and mind"; but although, as his sister-in-law observed, he was "heroic devotion itself," he never "got around to mentioning the time and place," the obvious solution for the love that he professed for Miss Walker and the "crushing anguish" he experienced when they were apart.[82]

It was not only American girls who were drawn to Frank Murphy; Filipino girls and daughters of "the Spanish mestizo aristocracy" also responded to the fascination of the bachelor governor-general. When he departed from the Philippines, a Manila newspaper ran a story under the headline, "Manila Maids Mourn Murphy's Leaving." It has been alleged that Murphy's "dallying with young Filipino girls brought sharp criticism from Filipino fathers and [that reports of] his supposed celibacy . . . brought giggles and snide remarks from Filipino women." A Filipino woman sitting on the platform during the ceremonies inaugurating the Philippine Commonwealth referred to Murphy as " 'a virgin' " and then hastily stated that she had used the wrong word. When a reporter relayed the story to Murphy, he commented, "I am glad she qualified it." Murphy, who delighted in stories of this sort, also enjoyed the circulation in the Philippines of the persistent rumor that he had fathered two illegitimate mestizo children while serving in the archipelago. When an American journalist who had lived in the Philippines was asked whether the stories concerning Murphy's romances were true, the journalist replied, "It is hard to believe them; it is equally hard to doubt them."[83]

Although Murphy found time in the Philippines for his girl friends, his family, social affairs, and exercise, his work, as always, was the center of his attention and his greatest joy. "I have work to do and a short time in which to do it," he wrote George, "and I intend to keep it supreme in my life instead of life's heartaches." When a reporter asked the governor-general for a picture of himself at play, he obliged the newsman but noted that he preferred pictures of himself at work since that was his "best fun anyway." He could not "remember the time," he observed, "when work did not come first."[84]

The initial reaction to Murphy in the Philippines was universally favorable, as all elements of the insular community were impressed with the vigorous manner in which he assumed the responsibilities of his office. "No other chief executive of these islands has accomplished more in one month's time," the *Manila Daily Bulletin* commented at the end of Murphy's first month in office. "The New Philippine Deal is with us," a newspaper man wrote to Murphy shortly thereafter.[85]

2

*"I'm Going
to Set These People Free"*

As he left the Michigan Central depot to begin his journey to the
Philippines, Frank Murphy dramatically told his brother George, "I
have one ambition. I'm going to set these people free."[1] Had he
heard these words, Senator Harry B. Hawes would have been delighted, since he believed that the decision of the Filipinos regarding
the offer of independence could be decisively influenced by the
governor-general of the islands. The governor-general, Hawes had
written President-elect Franklin D. Roosevelt, was in a position to put
"very strong, almost compelling pressure" on the insular legislature
to accept or reject the Independence Act.[2]

Murphy's Irish heritage was a major factor inclining him to favor
the independence of the Philippines. In explaining his support of the
Irish cause, Murphy had written a girl friend in 1922 that he was
"consistent" in his "Irish attitude . . . for my views and principles
on self-government, imperialistic and militaristic aggression I would
apply in just the same spirit anywhere as I do in the case of Ireland."
When first informed of his nomination as governor-general, Murphy
remarked, "Any race that has its future to make interests me"; he
pointedly told the OsRox mission that he was of "Irish extraction"
and that his heritage was one of "oppression." The thought that he
might play a large role in the birth of an independent Philippine
nation also appealed to the romantic side of Murphy's nature and to
his longstanding conviction that he was destined to do great things in
the political realm.[3]

Murphy's predisposition to favor Philippine independence did not
mean that he had committed himself to the terms of the Hare-
Hawes-Cutting Act or, indeed, that he had given any real thought
before leaving the United States to the merits of the statute as an
independence measure. The Filipinos themselves, of course, were
divided in their opinion of the Independence Act, the OsRox forces,
the "pros," favoring its adoption and the "antis," led by the
redoubtable Quezon, opposing that course. ". . . the Philippine
political pot is boiling as it never has boiled before," a Manila

38

correspondent noted, and he thought that the new governor-general would have "to exercise a great deal of judgment to prevent himself from being scalded."[4]

In his inaugural address and his first message to the Philippine legislature, Murphy, although urging prompt action, announced that he was leaving it to the Filipinos themselves, "without interference and uncontrolled by any force or influence whatsoever," to determine whether or not they wished to accept the Hare-Hawes-Cutting Act. Publicly, at least, Murphy adhered to this policy, exerting no pressure to influence the decision, abstaining from local politics, and avoiding even the making of appointments lest it appear that he was favoring one side or the other. By tactfully pursuing what he described as "a 'hands off,' strict neutrality, 'self determination' policy" on the explosive independence issue, Murphy was able to retain the support of all "combatants and leaders" in the internecine independence struggle.[5]

Although Murphy has been given a good deal of credit for his policy of neutrality while the Filipinos debated the Independence Act and for avoiding the kind of political blunder regarding this question that would have jeopardized the success of his administration, he was in all probability simply following the advice of the Bureau of Insular Affairs. As F. LeJ. Parker, the acting chief of the bureau and an "active and relentless opponent" of the Independence Act informed the secretary of war on May 11, 1933, and as he must have told Murphy, the Filipino leaders, having "clamored" for independence, were now in the "embarrassing predicament" of either accepting terms that they regarded with "apprehension" or rejecting a measure that promised independence. Under these circumstances, Parker advised, a policy of "impartial detachment" on the part of the governor-general was "most desirable" lest Filipino leaders attempted to evade "unpopular responsibility" by claiming that they had "more or less" been compelled to accept the act by American authorities, an argument that they also might later employ to justify a demand that the statute be amended.[6]

In the struggle between the pros and the antis, the OsRox group had the backing of "leading educators" and such newspapers as the *Manila Tribune*. Quezon, on the other hand, enjoyed the support not only of most "business interests," especially the large sugar planters and the owners of the sugar centrals, but also of those who favored immediate independence and those who opposed independence or at least preferred a longer transition period than the act provided.[7]

Quezon offered a variety of reasons for his opposition to the Hare-Hawes-Cutting Act. He claimed that the proposed American retention of bases in the Philippines after independence gave the United States "sovereignty and control" over important territory in the islands and thus "destroyed the very essence of independent existence for the Philippines." The provisions of the statute regarding trade relations during the transition period, Quezon charged, would close the United States market to the principal Philippine products, destroy the Philippine economy, and bankrupt the insular government. Quezon also complained that the powers reserved to the United States during the transition period were so broad and so poorly defined that the autonomy of the proposed Commonwealth would be "largely, if not completely, neutralized." Patriot though he was, however, Quezon was probably less concerned about the merits of the Hare-Hawes-Cutting Act than he was about the political advantage that he could gain at home by pointing to the shortcomings of an independence statute that had been negotiated by his principal rivals. Issues, Theodore Friend has correctly observed, were "subordinated to a contest of naked power for supremacy in Philippine politics."[8]

The political necessity of defeating the pros without, however, appearing to oppose independence, the supreme goal of Philippine politics, undoubtedly explains Quezon's uncertainty regarding the proper tactics for him to pursue in combating the Independence Act. It is not likely that Quezon's preferred choice of procedure was to submit the issue to the Filipino electorate, but when Osmeña challenged him to follow the plebiscitary route, Quezon found it difficult to disagree. Murphy urged this procedure whenever he was consulted by the Filipino leadership, but although the two factions agreed in principle to a plebiscite, they could not agree on the precise questions to be submitted to the voters; and in the end it was the Filipino legislature, not the Filipino electorate, that made the decision.[9]

The outcome in the legislature was forecast on June 20 when Quezon forced the resignation of Manuel Roxas as Speaker of the House, and the Senate, by a vote of 16–5, refused to accept the resignation of Quezon as president of the body but concurred by a vote of 15–2 in the resignation of Osmeña as president pro tem. The master now of the legislature and of Philippine politics, Quezon waited for ten weeks before asking for a vote on the independence question. He delayed primarily because negotiations were under way in Washington to allocate quotas to the principal sugar producers supplying the American market, and he did not wish to jeopardize Philippine efforts to secure a larger quota than the Hare-Hawes-Cutting Act provided. In part because of Murphy's effective presentation of the Philippine case, the Washington conferees assigned the Philippines a quota of 1.1 million long tons (1.23 million short), as compared to the 850,000-ton figure in the independence statute. The sugar matter apparently disposed of—Secretary of Agriculture Henry A. Wallace later rejected the agreement as unfair to consumers—the Philippine Senate on October 7 "declined to accept" the Independence Act by a vote of 15–4, and the House followed suit four days later by a vote of 55–22. On October 17 the legislature agreed to dispatch still another independence mission to Washington to secure the amendment of the Hare-Hawes-Cutting Act or adoption of an entirely new measure. Headed by Quezon and consisting entirely of members of the majority faction since the pros declined to participate, the delegation left for the United States on November 4.[10]

Asked by the secretary of war for his views concerning the Independence Act, Murphy, who by this time had been made aware by his staff of the "serious" economic consequences for the Philippines should the statute be approved, correctly replied that free trade had "unbalanced" the Philippine economy and that the United States was now trying to respond to the "incompatible policies of economic dependence and political independence by creating economic and political independence simultaneously." He observed that there was "grave doubt" should the act be implemented whether the Filipinos could maintain "an independent government, with adequate revenue to insure domestic stability and security against foreign aggression." He had no doubt about the "ability and capacity" of the Filipinos to govern themselves, but he thought that the realization of America's "traditional political objectives" in the Philippines required "a preliminary and preparatory modification of economic policy that would tend rationally toward economic independence" even though this postponed the "definite determination of the political status." He recommended that President Roosevelt give Quezon "as much time" as was "reasonable and appropriate" before the next session of Congress, that the mission be invited to submit specific proposals to remedy "objectionable provisions" of the Independence Act, and that Congress be requested to amend the statute or to enact a more satisfactory measure.[11]

Murphy offered his advice despite the fact that Senator Key Pittman had informed him that the Filipinos had lost "quite a number of friends" in Congress because of their failure to approve the

Independence Act and that the issue of Philippine independence would not be brought up in Congress in 1934, an election year. Murphy's views also ran counter to the position of the Bureau of Insular Affairs that it was not a "favorable" time for the enactment of new independence legislation because of "abnormal" conditions in the United States. If the president agreed to recommend changes in the independence measure, the bureau advised Secretary of War George Dern, the Filipinos would contend that Congress was obligated to follow his recommendations. The bureau's opinion was echoed in Manila by Evett Hester, who recommended that Murphy advise the president to tell Quezon that the independence statute was "a dead issue" and that the "political status quo" would be maintained for the time being. Murphy's contrary advice to Washington was not followed to the letter, but it may have persuaded the administration to yield something to Quezon rather than to accept the recommendation of the hard-liners.[12]

Quezon obviously deemed it essential to his political future to return to the Philippines with an independence measure that differed in at least some particular from the statute identified with the OsRox faction. Before leaving the Far East, he provided Murphy with three different independence plans that the Filipino leader contended provided "a just resolution of the Philippine Question." The first two plans, submitted on November 3 and 4, were quite similar in nature, calling for an amended Hare-Hawes-Cutting Act. They both provided for a transition period, the elimination of the excise tax, a larger quota than Congress had provided for sugar and perhaps for coconut oil and cordage as well, and the possible retention of American naval bases, but not military bases.

From Hongkong on November 7, Quezon, writing to Murphy, "My hope is placed in you," submitted a third independence plan proposing that the Hare-Hawes-Cutting Act be "discarded altogether." Quezon now suggested that the Philippines be granted independence in two or three years, the United States retain neither military nor naval bases, and the Philippines be granted free access to the United States market for ten to twenty years except that the United States could limit annual sugar imports to 1.2 million long tons (1.34 million short) and annual coconut oil imports to 200,000 long tons (224,000 short). Justifying a period of free trade after independence, Quezon alleged that the United States was obligated to grant the Philippines the time to "undo the economic tie" between the two nations that American policy had forged. The period of free trade, he contended, would also enable the two nations to decide whether a special trade relationship after that time was in their mutual interest. Knowing of the American desire to ease tensions in East Asia, Quezon argued that the decision of the United States not to retain any bases in the Philippines after independence would reassure Japan regarding American intentions in the Far East and, coupled with the special American-Philippine trade relationship, would guarantee the Philippines against a possible Japanese attack. Quezon, who was advancing his third plan for the record, obviously did not expect to be taken seriously in Washington. If Roosevelt rejected his suggestions, Quezon informed Murphy, he was willing to accept the Hare-Hawes-Cutting Act with the amendments he had previously specified.[13]

During the next several weeks Quezon, adjusting his remarks to his audience and to the circumstances of the moment and probably "saying ten things he didn't mean to everyone that he did," pressed his campaign to secure an independence measure that would bear the Quezon imprimatur. In Japan, en route to the United States, he threatened to conclude a commercial pact with that nation if he could not secure a satisfactory independence law from the United States government, and he stated that an independent Philippines would not require the protection of the United States. In the United States, however, he told men like Henry L. Stimson that Japan would seize the Philippines in two or three years unless the United States worked out a special trade relationship with the islands. He assured Philippine retentionists like Stimson and Theodore Roosevelt, Jr., that his preference was dominion status for the Philippines or that he was willing to continue the status quo, but he told others that he favored independence in anywhere from two to six years or, if the United States intended to cut off commerce with the Philippines, immediately. Quezon's most insistent request to whomever he spoke was for free trade between the United States and the Philippines during the transition period, more generous quotas for sugar, coconut oil, and cordage than were stipulated in the Hare-Hawes-Cutting Act, and a "special" trade relationship between the two nations after independence had been attained.[14]

Quezon learned that there was a profound reluctance in Washington to alter the basic terms of the Independence Act. Rejecting the idea of immediate independence, the president told him that it would be extremely difficult to amend the measure in any way. Senator Millard Tydings, chairman of the Senate Committee on Territories and Insular Affairs, stated that the only change Congress would consider would be to allow the Philippines additional time to accept the Independence Act, and he indicated that President Roose-velt would regard final rejection of the measure as evidence that the Filipinos did not desire independence. Quezon also learned that the Bureau of Insular Affairs did not believe that the Filipinos should be permitted to elect their own chief executive during the Common-wealth period, as the independence statute provided, because this would not properly safeguard the interests of the United States as the sovereign power in the islands. Quezon, surprisingly, suggested that the bureau's objection could be met by giving the president of the United States the power to remove the Commonwealth's president; but General Cox, who regarded independence as "a bad thing," thought this "an impossible arrangement," preferring that the American president appoint the Filipino president.[15]

The one Quezon request to which there was a sympathetic reaction in Washington was the Filipino leader's opposition to retention of American military bases in the Philippines. Although willing to defer a decision on American retention of naval bases for later negotiation between the two countries, Quezon repeatedly stated that the Ameri-can retention of military bases in the islands was inconsistent with Philippine independence. It posed no problem for the president and Congress to concede this point since the secretary of war, the acting secretary of war, Chief of Staff Douglas MacArthur, the chief of naval operations, and the chief of the Bureau of Insular Affairs secretly agreed on February 1, 1934, and so advised the president, that when the Philippines achieved full independence American naval and military forces should be "entirely withdrawn" from the islands and American naval and military reservations should be "abandoned." They revealed that neither the War nor Navy Depart-ments had had "anything to do" with the inclusion of the provisions regarding bases in the Hare-Hawes-Cutting Act, and they contended that the statute would be improved if the provision in question were eliminated. In Congress, also, both proponents and opponents of the independence statute were willing to abandon American military bases in the Philippines, but they thought that the United States should leave open the possibility of retaining a naval base to strengthen its hands in "dealing with the Japanese relative to disarmament."[16]

Given the views of the army and navy, the political realities in Washington, and his political needs in Manila, the best solution for the independence problem from Quezon's point of view and the "common meeting ground" for the Quezon mission and the Ameri-can government was the enactment of a new independence measure identical with the Hare-Hawes-Cutting Act but which omitted the provision sanctioning American military bases after independence and left open the question of naval bases for subsequent negotiation. Quezon knew that Congress would not modify the trade provisions of the Hare-Hawes-Cutting Act, but he was prepared to accept these provisions for the time being if the president would commit himself to recommend that Congress should later remedy imperfections in the independence law. President Roosevelt was willing to accept this arrangement since he agreed with his "adviser of last resort" on the question, Frank Murphy, that there had to be "some amelioration" of the trade provisions of the independence statute. As the president told Stimson, the independence law "put the pressure on too quickly."[17]

The bargain between Quezon and congressional leaders had been struck by February 17, 1934, when Quezon cabled Murphy that "everything" was "satisfactory." Roosevelt sent a special message to Congress on March 2 recommending the agreed-upon changes regarding American bases in an independent Philippines but stating that the remainder of the original Hare-Hawes-Cutting Act should not be altered. "Where imperfections or inequalities exist," the president asserted with regard to the statute, "I am confident that they can be corrected after proper hearing and in fairness to both peoples." Although he wished to grant "complete independence" to the Philippines at the earliest practicable moment, he asserted that it would be "a definite injustice" to do so without permitting sufficient time to elapse for "necessary political and economic adjustments."[18]

By the time Roosevelt sent his message to Congress, Senator Tydings had received assurances that not only Quezon but Osmeña, Roxas, Aguinaldo, and others among the Philippine leadership would accept what the president was proposing. The senator, by then, probably had also agreed to the Filipino request that a congressional group visit the Philippines after the independence statute had been approved to hear complaints regarding the measure. There was some further wavering by Quezon, inspired by proposed new restraints on Philippine exports, but the Philippine Independence (Tydings-McDuffie) Act was officially approved by the president on March 4. Quezon and others in the Philippines gave Murphy a good deal of credit for what had occurred since they believed that his influence with the president had led to the reopening of the independence question after Congress had indicated that it would not reconsider the issue unless specifically requested to do so by the White House.[19]

When Murphy heard that the Tydings-McDuffie Act had been approved, his first words were, " 'Blessed be God.' " ". . . you have to choose to be a sincere friend of the Commonwealth and the coming republic or a weak and indifferent one," Murphy wrote the editor of the *Detroit News*. "I am for it with whatever might is mine." Murphy thought the "principle" of independence to be "right and just," and he believed that the Filipinos had "the right to accept disadvantages economically—if it is their will—to secure the political independence which may have greater significance to them." If members of his family are to be believed, however, he had privately become "reluctant" by this time "to see these beautiful and wealthy Islands pass out of our hands," fearing that independence under the terms provided meant revolution and a Japanese takeover. This is what was in his mind when he privately told Quezon before he sailed for America that the Filipinos would "hang themselves" if they accepted an unamended Hare-Hawes-Cutting Act.[20]

The OsRox faction preferred that the Philippine decision on the Tydings-McDuffie Act be made by the legislature that would be chosen in the general election scheduled for June 5. The antis, however, urged that a special session of the existing legislature be called to decide the matter so that there would be enough time, should the act be approved, to permit the election of delegates to the constitutional convention that had to be held no later than October 1 according to the terms of the Tydings-McDuffie Act. Although Murphy thought it "desirable and preferable" to entrust the decision to the new legislature, the time constraints on compliance imposed by the statute made this impracticable, and so he called a special session for April 30.[21]

Murphy was given "a great ovation" when he entered the crowded hall of the House of Representatives on April 30 to deliver his address to the special joint session of the legislature. The governor-general stated that it had been his "undeviating policy" to leave the decision on independence to the Filipinos themselves, but he spoke now as though the decision was no longer in doubt. Although the *Manila Daily Bulletin* thought that it was "not the moment to eulogize American generosity," Murphy, who knew what the proprieties required, used the occasion to characterize the grant of independence as a demonstration of American "altruism." If, he asserted, economic factors had played some part in the framing of the independence law, the decision for independence had been "fundamentally conditioned and sustained and inspired by the political idealism and altruism of the American people." The day following

Murphy's speech Quezon and Osmeña appeared on the Senate floor "arm in arm," and on May 2 the legislature unanimously accepted the Tydings-McDuffie Act by a concurrent resolution stating that certain provisions of the statute required "further consideration" but noting what President Roosevelt had said about this matter in his March 2 message. In the bitterly contested election on June 5 Quezon's faction won a decisive victory over Osmeña's pros, and on July 10 delegates were elected to the constitutional convention that convened on July 30.[22]

Among the delegates participating in the constitutional convention the antis and their allies outnumbered the pros by a margin of better than three-to-one, and Senator Claro Recto, the chairman of the convention, was a Quezon partisan. Delegates who protested that convention proceedings were being directed by Quezon, who was not a delegate, were "steamrollered out of the way." Although many able men were included among the delegates, Hayden reported that "many . . . members . . . evinced more interest in increasing their per diems and securing a flat sum bonus than in any other matters." The constitution was adopted on February 8, 1935, with but a single dissent, and was signed by the delegates, one of whom used his blood as ink, two weeks later.[23]

Although the delegates knew that the constitution they adopted would have no validity unless the president of the United States certified that it conformed to the requirements of the Tydings-McDuffie Act, they made their decisions without any overt assistance or guidance from Washington and with the governor-general remaining discreetly in the background. "Some [Filipino] leaders" had led Hatton W. Sumners, the chairman of the House Committee on the Judiciary, to believe that Quezon wanted him to assist in drafting the constitution, and Sumners sent Quezon some suggestions for the document; but when the congressman inquired if he should come to the Philippines to aid in the drafting, Murphy "strongly" advised that he remain in the United States. On September 3 John Brabner Smith, apparently at Sumner's instigation, appeared in Manila carrying a letter that assigned him to the convention as a special assistant to the attorney general of the United States. Smith registered at a hotel under an assumed name, but when Murphy learned of his presence the governor-general advised him to return home at once. Smith sailed for the United States on September 5. This could not have displeased the Bureau of Insular Affairs since it believed it "inappropriate" in view of the Tydings-McDuffie Act for the United States to do anything that might "hamper or in any way embarrass the actions of the Philippine government in connection with the work of drafting a constitution."[24]

Murphy was so intent on avoiding even the appearance of an American role in the convention that he declined an invitation to attend the opening session, a tactful and symbolic decision that was much praised in the Philippines. Murphy, however, assigned one of his aides "to watch and report on" the convention; he followed its deliberations with "intense interest"; and when a draft of the constitution became available, he asked Hayden, Kemp, and Hester to study it thoroughly and to advise him regarding provisions bearing on "fundamental questions of government," the Tydings-McDuffie Act, and the continuing American interest in the Philippines. In January the president of the convention, anxious not to include anything in the document that might cause Roosevelt to find it deficient, sought Murphy's advice on several key sections of the constitution, but if Murphy responded to his request, which is unlikely, he did not do so in writing.[25] Murphy, however, did intervene behind the scenes to secure the inclusion of a female suffrage article, and we may assume that it was he who persuaded the convention to agree to the creation of a unicameral legislature for the Philippines.

The movement to enact female suffrage in the Philippines was initiated in the early years of the twentieth century. The Philippine Senate, heeding the advice of Governor-General Harrison, passed a female suffrage bill in 1919, but the measure died in the House. In part because he believed that women were "endowed by nature and experience with sympathy and a strong sense of duty," Murphy had called on the country's lawmakers in his first address to the legislature to extend "the full right of suffrage" to the women of the islands. Responding to the pressure exerted by the governor-general, the legislature had enacted a measure in December 1933 that made female suffrage effective as of January 1, 1935. The law, however, was opposed by the Catholic church and was very unpopular among legislators, who feared its effect on "the whole established political machine."[26]

Since a majority of the delegates were unenthusiastic, to say the least, about female suffrage, the president of the constitutional convention was "strongly adverse" to the idea, and Quezon professed concern that the extension of the vote to women imperiled the "sanctity of the home," the convention almost certainly would have limited the suffrage to males had not Murphy interceded. Meeting privately with Quezon and then with Osmeña, Murphy "made it plain" that he regarded the abandonment of female suffrage an "unwise[,] backward step" and "would disapprove the change if made." Quezon thereupon assured Murphy that the effort to kill female suffrage "would not get beyond our control," and it was probably intervention by the president of the Senate that accounted for the compromise clause in the constitution providing for female suffrage if, in a plebiscite held within two years of the adoption of the document, not less than 300,000 women approved the idea. This condition was met in a plebiscite of May 14, 1937, and female suffrage was enacted into law four months later.[27]

An admirer of George W. Norris, Murphy believed that the unicameral legislature contributed to the "cause of good government," and he so advised convention leaders. Quezon preferred a bicameral legislature, but because of Murphy's intercession when it appeared that the convention would not accept the idea, because the delegates could not agree on an electoral basis for an upper house, and because some delegates thought a unicameral legislature would reduce the cost of government, the proposal for a unicameral legislature carried in a close vote. It is likely, also, that the provisions of the constitution regarding "the promotion of social justice" and the "protection" of the laborer reflected not only concerns of the era but the policy commitments of the governor-general.[28]

The constitution approved by the convention was designed to serve as the fundamental law not only for the Commonwealth of the Philippines but also for the Republic of the Philippines that would come into being when American sovereignty was withdrawn. Although the document contained a bill of rights, it subordinated the rights of the individual to those of the state, specifying that all citizens might be required to render "personal military or civil service" in defense of the state, vesting ownership of natural resources in the state, and authorizing the state to "establish and operate industries and means of transportation and communication."

Although Philippine constitutional development during the period of American rule had tended in the direction of a parliamentary or semiparliamentary form of government, the new constitution provided for a presidential system of government, undoubtedly because Quezon thought it prudent to follow the American precedent, at least for the time being, lest Roosevelt decide to reject the document. The president of the Commonwealth, however, was granted powers that exceeded those the United States Constitution bestowed on the American chief executive, including the item veto, authority to recommend appropriations that could not, for the most part, be increased by the legislature, general supervision over local government, and "indefinite dictatorial power" that the National Assembly could grant him in an emergency. The government that was to be established, Hayden advised Murphy, might be "democratic in form," but "it probably would be in effect an irresponsible autocracy." Hayden thought that this kind of autocracy was "in harmony with the instincts, traditions and past practices of the Filipino people" and was "the *natural* system for the people of these islands in their present state of political development." Although the "spirit" of the Filipino constitution was quite different from that of the American constitution, nothing in the document, Hayden informed Murphy, contravened the terms of the Tydings-McDuffie Act. There was, nevertheless, concern among the Filipino leadership that President Roosevelt would find some provisions objectionable.[29]

When a Filipino mission submitted the constitution to Roosevelt, Murphy, who was in the United States at the time, advised the president to say nothing in accepting the document that indicated his approval of its specific terms lest the constitution prove "unworkable" or be seen as having "objectionable features." Murphy believed that it was even more "important" for the president to say that during the Commonwealth period the United States retained "*all* powers commensurate with sovereign responsibilities," which is what Murphy himself had said when the document had been presented to him in the Philippines. After consulting with the State and War Departments, Murphy supplied the president with drafts of statements along these lines that the president used, in the main, when he officially accepted the constitution on March 23 in a ceremony in the White House attended by Murphy, members of the Filipino mission, and high administrative and congressional officials.[30]

In leaving the White House ceremony, Quezon paused in the entrance hall before table that Aguinaldo had given Roosevelt and thanked Murphy in the name of the Filipino people for having paved the way for the president's acceptance of the constitution. The Filipino leadership was aware that it was Murphy, who hyperbolically praised the constitution as "second to none in the world," to whom Roosevelt had turned for assurance that the constitution could be accepted as written. "Your Philippine record," a *Manila Daily Bulletin* correspondent wrote Murphy in the exaggerated language that came so easily to Filipinos, "stands matchless in colonial history."[31]

When Quezon informed an expectant Manila shortly after midnight on March 24 that President Roosevelt had accepted the constitution, church bells pealed, factories sounded their sirens, boats in the harbor blared their horns, fireworks were shot off into the night, and hotels, restaurants, and places of amusement played the national anthem. From one side of the archipelago to the other, Filipinos "gloriously celebrated" the news that independence, that talismanic concept, was one step closer to realization. At Murphy's instruction, Hayden called the legislature into special session to draft legislation providing for the submission of the constitution to the voters. Meeting on April 8, the legislature passed a bill providing for a national referendum on May 14, 1935. When Hayden expressed his intention to declare May 14 a public holiday and to urge a large voter turnout, Murphy cautioned him to adhere to the established Murphy policy of noninterference with the Filipino decision for independence.[32] As Murphy advised, Malacañan did not try to influence the May 14 vote, but the only organized opposition to the Nacionalistas, the Sakdalistas, sought by an abortive revolt to frustrate the election and to block the establishment of the Commonwealth.

Sakdalism was accurately described by Hayden as "a blow against *caciquism* as well as for independence." Sakdalistas identified American domination with the landlords, moneylenders, and local officials whom they viewed as the source of their misery, and they believed that they could more effectively deal with their oppressors if the Americans left the islands. Independence for the unlettered *tao* was a magic word that meant "a remedy for all their ills. They dream of it," a Murphy staff member noted, "as making living easier, days happier, work lighter, debts wiped out, money more plentiful, an end to petty injustices, taxes non-existent or greatly lessened, and . . . a share in the property now possessed by others." Susceptible to radical appeals because of their low standard of living, the peasants of central Luzon, who had staged unsuccessful uprisings on three occasions between 1925 and 1931, were disposed to believe leaders who told them that the proposed constitution would both delay independence and perpetuate a social and economic system that enriched the few and impoverished the many. "Exploiting landlords, blood-sucking money lenders, stupid and callous local officials, the indifference of those in better circumstances around them, what better ground could agitators desire," the editor of the *Philippine Magazine* commented.[33]

The leader of the Sakdalistas was Benigno Ramos, described by one historian as "the most commanding and charismatic figure in prewar Filipino nationalism." Born on February 10, 1893, the son of a minor bureaucrat, Ramos served in a provincial government office in Malolos and taught in a village school before moving to Manila in 1912.

He secured a position as a translator in the Philippine Senate in 1917 and in 1929 became director of its clipping division. His participation in an anti-American high school teachers' strike in 1930 antagonized Quezon, who forced Ramos's resignation from the government service. A few months later Ramos founded the *Sakdal* (the word means "to accuse" or "to strike"), a four-page weekly that sharply attacked the Nacionalistas and called for immediate independence. The divisive struggle between the pros and antis persuaded Ramos to arrange for a convention in Manila on October 29, 1933, that led to the formation of the Sakdal party and the designation of Ramos as its president and campaign manager. He spent two months in California attempting to win support for his cause among the Filipino community and then proceeded to Washington just as the Tydings-McDuffie Act was being approved. In a petition addressed to President Roosevelt, Ramos criticized the statute and called for immediate independence. He then returned to the Philippines, arriving in time to participate in the national elections of June 1934.[34]

The Sakdals entered candidates in two Senate races, three House races, and for local offices in eight provinces, seven of them in densely populated central Luzon. The Sakdal platform called for complete independence by December 31, 1935, division among the poor of the landed estates of the church and the rich, abolition of the cedula (poll) tax, and salary increases for petty government employees, which the middle-class leadership of the party advocated in an effort to attract middle-class support. In "a remarkable showing of political strength," the party won the three House seats that it contested, elected one provincial governor, and garnered more than twenty municipal posts.[35]

Following the election, the Sakdalista leadership intensified its propaganda attack on the Philippine establishment and began to look to Japan for assistance in achieving the party's goals. Pretending that he was on his way to Washington to protest the Tydings-McDuffie Act, Ramos in November 1934 sailed for Japan, where he was "welcomed with open arms by certain ultranationalist Pan-Asian extremists." His chief Japanese sponsor was Matsumoto Kumpei, a former Diet member and the organizer of the Congress of Young Asia; but Ambassador Joseph Grew later reported that Ramos had not been supported by "any of the large and powerful reactionary organizations," and he apparently received no "concrete aid" from the Japanese government itself. Ramos, who was "in constant touch" with Sakdalista leaders inside the Philippines, nevertheless assured his followers that if they could sustain a rebellion, Japanese aid would be forthcoming. Mysteriously and ominously, many prominent Filipinos received a letter purportedly written by a Major Hiroshi Tomura, who claimed to be a Japanese artillery officer in Formosa, attacking Quezon as a traitor to the cause of Philippine independence and assuring the Filipinos of Japanese support in their "hour of need."[36]

Within the Philippines, planning for a revolt was initiated by the more radical wing of the Sakdal party in March 1935. The purpose of the revolt was to prevent the adoption of the new constitution, thwart the establishment of the Commonwealth, and induce the United States to modify its position on independence. The propaganda line of the Sakdals was that the Tydings-McDuffie Act was not really an independence statute, Japan was the only nation interested in Filipino freedom, the Filipino leadership was really opposed to independence but the Sakdals would secure it by the end of the year, and Quezon and other leaders did nothing for the mass of the people.[37]

On April 1, 1935, a publication entitled *Free Filipinos*, largely written by Ramos and containing columns printed in Japanese, English, Spanish, and Tagalog, was smuggled into the Philippines from Japan. It contended that American government was "the Government of Invasion, of Assault, of Foreign Intrusion, of Imperial Domination,—the Enemy of the Filipino people and their Freedom," it attacked Murphy as "a real despot" and a "Frankenstein" who favored the Tydings-McDuffie Act so that he could retain his lucrative position, and it denounced Quezon as the "first and number one slave of the American interests in the Philippines." In an appeal to Philippine nationalism and Pan-Asian sentiments, *Free Filipinos* portrayed the Sakdalistas as favoring the revival of the Filipino "family tradition," Filipino culture, and Filipino industries and commerce, the elimination of "unsound foreign influences," and the fashioning of "a strong and eternal union between all countries of the Far East."[38]

In early March 1935 the insular government began to take notice of the "seditious activities" of the Sakdalistas in the provinces near Manila. "The mood of the poverty stricken elements of our population is such," the secretary of agriculture and commerce warned Hayden, who was acting governor-general while Murphy was in the United States, "that a psychological situation is being created and spread fertile for the sowing of communistic doctrines by the radicals." The insular government attempted to counteract Sakdalista propaganda by launching an educational campaign to acquaint the populace with the terms of the new constitution and with government programs designed to serve the masses, requesting the press "to handle the news about the 'Sakdalistas' in such a way as not to augment their strength falsely," requiring permits for Sakdalista meetings, revoking the second-class mailing privileges of the *Sakdal*, and arresting and prosecuting Sakdalistas allegedly guilty of seditiously conspiring to overthrow the government and to assassinate government leaders.[39]

The oppressed tenants to whom the Sakdalistas appealed were persuaded that, if they rose in revolt, the Constabulary and the municipal police would not fire on their countrymen, the Philippine Scouts would provide the rebels with arms, and Japan would come to their assistance. A revolt was scheduled for May 2, twelve days before the plebiscite the Sakdalistas hoped to block, but Ramos, at the eleventh hour and too late to alter plans, urged a May 14 date for the uprising. The ensuing confusion may explain why some Sakdalistas remained quiescent when the revolt occurred.[40]

Although the Constabulary began to receive information from intelligence agents on April 29 that there would be a Sakdalista uprising that year, possibly before May 14, it was not until the morning of May 2 that an undercover agent who had penetrated the Sakdalista "inner circle" the day before reported that the Sakdalistas were preparing for an "armed uprising" that night. Despite the report, when the revolt occurred on the night of May 2, both the American and Filipino high commands were absent from Manila. Murphy and Quezon were in the United States; Hayden, the secretary of the interior, and the insular auditor, assured by the head of the Constabulary that he did not anticipate any trouble "in the immediate future," had left on April 30 for an eight-day inspection trip in Mountain Province; and the head of the Constabulary inexplicably departed for an inspection trip on the evening of May 2 on an intercoastal steamer that lacked a radio. The ranking official in Malacañan on May 2 was Richard R. Ely, an assistant secretary to the governor-general.[41]

About 8:30 P.M. on May 2 reports reached Manila that the wires had been cut north and south of the city. At about the same time approximately two hundred Sakdalistas stormed the municipal building in Santa Rosa, Laguna, a town forty kilometers from Manila. A small Constabulary detachment arrived while the action was underway and barricaded itself in nearby buildings. When reinforcements arrived, the government force took the offensive and, at a cost to itself of three killed and five wounded, dispersed the mob, killing four Sakdalistas and wounding sixteen. At approximately 2:00 A.M. on

May 3 about 150 Sakdalistas took possession of the *presidencia* in San Ildefonso, Bulacan, sixty-six kilometers north of Manila, but were forced to surrender by a Constabulary force after a brief exchange of fire that resulted in the death of one Constabulary member and two Sakdalistas. Early that same morning several hundred Sakdalistas seized the *presidencia* in Cabuyao, Laguna, forty-six kilometers north of Manila. A Constabulary force of five officers and thirty-two men was quickly dispatched to the municipality and in a brief churchyard battle killed fifty-three Sakdalistas and wounded nineteen more at a cost to itself of four wounded. That night a Sakdalista band seized the acting governor of Cavite and took him to Tanza, twenty-six kilometers north of Manila, but the Sakdalistas fled when they found the Constabulary waiting for them. Sakdalista mobs in several other places in Luzon also scattered when they discovered a Constabulary force prepared to resist.

All in all, Sakdalista mobs totaling from five to seven thousand men and women, armed with pistols, revolvers, shotguns, and lesser weapons, had attempted to capture the municipal buildings or governments in fourteen towns north and southwest of Manila. By 9:00 P.M. on May 3 all was quiet, but central Luzon for a time had "reeled and shuddered" from the impact of the uprising. Prominent families had fled from Manila, expecting an attack on the capital, and Malacañan had alerted United States Army units in the area of the uprising.[42]

The Constabulary had quickly subdued the Sakdalista revolt, but in Cabuyao at least it had "used more force than [was] necessary." Defenders of the Constabulary justified its behavior at Cabuyao on the grounds that quick action was required since the commanding officer had reason to expect an attack by Sakdalista reinforcements on his rear and flank, and they attributed the heavy Sakdalista casualties to the compact massing of the peasant force. Since the Sakdalistas, however, were lightly armed with a few shotguns and a small number of homemade pistols, bolos, daggers, and clubs and were not threatening an attack, the *Philippine Magazine* was correct in charging that the affray was "nothing but a massacre." The Constabulary, unfortunately, had not received any training in "accepted police methods of handling mobs," and it had attacked its bedraggled, poorly armed foe as though it were in action against a military force.[43]

In response to the uprising, the insular government ordered the arrest of 1,121 persons, including nearly all the leaders of the Sakdal party. Since the evidence available to the prosecution was "meager and very often unreliable," 736 of the prisoners were released within two months; nineteen others were acquitted after a trial in which the government's chief witness confessed that the Constabulary had suborned his testimony. Ninety-four of the accused, including two Sakdalista legislative members, had been convicted by early August, receiving jail sentences ranging from two to sixteen years.[44]

The most prominent of the Sakdalistas, Benigno Ramos, escaped arrest because the Japanese government refused to extradite him. In Tokyo interviews Ramos charged that Philippine authorities had "trapped" the Sakdalistas into a premature revolt by tampering with cables he had sent that changed the date of the uprising. He conceded that he had "incited" the revolt, but when he sought a visa the next year to come to the United States, he denied any connection with the uprising, attributing the affair to the evil designs of his "political enemies." He returned to the Philippines from Japan in August 1938 and was tried, convicted, and imprisoned for instigating the revolt. He was freed by the Japanese in April 1942, after which he collaborated with them in organizing the fanatical Makapili, "a volunteer militia of opportunists and Japanophiles." He was killed in 1945 while fighting alongside the Japanese.[45]

Some American congressmen interpreted the Sakdalista revolt to mean the the Filipinos were not ready for independence. The journalist Carlos Romulo bluntly told Quezon that, "stripped of camouflage, the Sakdalista uprising was a protest against" his "leadership," but Quezon defensively contended that the real cause was the trade provisions of the Tydings-McDuffie Act. The Philippine secretary of justice thought that it was the free-speech policy of the Murphy regime that had permitted "the seeds of dangerous propaganda" to take root among the masses, and the secretary of agriculture and commerce not only urged that the Sakdalistas be subjected to "constant vigilance" but also advocated the organization of "all good law-abiding and peace-loving citizens who are possessors of shot-guns for night patrol purposes."[46]

When Murphy learned of the Sakdalista uprising, he publicly sought to dismiss the event as simply "an incident of the local political situation" rather than reflecting "a widespread or general condition" or hostility to the United States. Aware, however, of the social and economic conditions in the Philippines that bred discontent in the barrios and city slums, Murphy instructed Hayden to request the Constabulary and two Malacañan staff members to ascertain the "root causes" of the uprising and to recommend measures that might be helpful in the affected areas.

Because of the excessive bloodshed and the absence of government leaders from their posts, some favored a public inquiry into the Sakdalista uprising. Murphy was prepared to yield to this demand, but Hayden preferred a private investigation by the governor-general's staff, contending that it might be difficult to appoint a representative commission of prominent persons whom the public would consider "disinterested" since the uprising was at least in part directed against the Filipino leadership. Murphy accepted Hayden's recommendation of a staff inquiry, but this angered Quezon, who believed that Hayden's preference for an investigation conducted by the Malacañan staff indicated that he either did not trust Filipino officials or thought that information secured by Americans was "more reliable" than information secured by Filipinos. The Filipino leader unsurprisingly favored an investigation by Filipino civil officials beholden to Quezon himself.[47]

The private report of the Malacañan committee, which was "hurriedly made," was based on the interrogation of 120 individuals involved in the uprising, most of them Sakdalista prisoners. The report concluded that there was "no evidence of any considerable degree of bitterness against the government or the present political leaders because of economic or social distress," but this judgment was contradicted in the body of the report. The staff committee found that the Constabulary had acted with "dispatch and efficiency," although the loss of life at Cabuyao was declared to have been "excessive" and one committee member criticized the Constabulary's tactics in the engagement as "unjustified." Publicly, Murphy stated that the Constabulary had acted with "commendable promptness and courage"; but he conceded after returning to the Philippines that human life had been wantonly sacrificed, and he instructed the secretary of the interior to give highest priority in the Constabulary training program to riot- and mob-control, which was also the recommendation of the Malacañan investigating committee. No one satisfactorily explained why the head of the Constabulary was absent from Manila at the beginning of the Sakdalista uprising, and this remains a mystery.[48]

The day preceding the May 14 plebiscite the insular government, in a precautionary move that probably resulted from a confidential agent's report that the Sakdalistas planned an attack on Manila that night, arrested a number of men believed to be the "directing heads" of a possible uprising. Perhaps because "An Open Letter to All Sakdalistas" of May 23 called for "secret assassination" as the "only scientific way of removing rascals from public life," there was a "tense atmosphere" in Manila when Murphy and Quezon returned to the city from the United States on July 8. Since there was fear that the pier where they were to embark would be "blown up," the public was excluded from the area, the Thirty-first Infantry of the United States Army was on hand as "a guard of honor" for Murphy, and Constabulary soldiers were placed at strategic points between the pier and Quezon's residence. The Constabulary continued to keep the Sakdalistas under surveillance, and they were to be heard from both before and after the Commonwealth was inaugurated, but they were no longer an effective force in Philippine politics following the uprising of May 2 and 3 and the arrests that followed. The leadership among the *taos* passed to Pedro Abad Santos and the socialists, who eventually merged with the Communists in a united front, and class antagonism increased rather than decreased despite the efforts of the Murphy regime and the Commonwealth government to allay discontent by purchasing large estates for resale to tenants and despite a variety of Commonwealth programs designed to improve the lot of the agricultural poor.[49]

About two-thirds of the registered voters participated in the referendum, 1,213,046 of them voting in favor of the constitution, and 44,963 voting against. Included were about 200,000 women, voting for the first time in the history of the Philippines. The stage was now set for the national elections, scheduled for September 17, 1935, to determine the composition of the new Commonwealth government. The pro and anti wings of the Nacionalista party, which had been discussing reunification since the end of 1934, were given an added reason to join forces by the Sakdalista revolt and the consequent fear of "proletarian violence." They agreed on June 16 to coalesce in support of a ticket consisting of Quezon as the presidential candidate and Osmeña as the vice-presidential nominee.[50]

Quezon was opposed for the presidency by Emilio Aguinaldo, the sixty-year-old president of the First Philippine Republic, leader of Los Veteranos de la Revolucion Filipina, and "a sort of permanent first unofficial citizen of the Philippines"; and by Bishop Gregorio Aglipay, head of the Philippine Independent Church. Neither had an effective political organization, but they appealed to the "have nots," those who were dissatisfied with American rule, and those who wanted independence at an earlier date than the Tydings-McDuffie Act promised. Although the Sakdalistas decided not to take part in the election, it was assumed that their votes would go to Aguinaldo.[51]

In February 1935, months before there were any announced candidates, Murphy stated that the Filipinos would choose wisely if they selected Quezon and Osmeña to lead them. When the governor-general returned to Manila in June, he declared that he would maintain strict neutrality in the election, but Aguinaldo's National Socialist party soon complained that Murphy was "partial and unfair," cabinet secretaries were campaigning for Quezon and Osmeña, government servants were being compelled to contribute to the Nacionalistas and were taking an active part in the campaign, the Constabulary was maintaining surveillance of Aguinaldo's headquarters, and government officials were intimidating the general in one way or another. Responding to these charges, Murphy protested his impartiality, stated that cabinet members were campaigning as party leaders not as cabinet members, forbade undersecretaries to engage in political activity, insisted on rigorous compliance with executive orders and legislation forbidding civil servants to engage in political activities, and instructed the Constabulary to eschew harassment tactics. Although Murphy was undoubtedly sincere in his avowals of neutrality and on one occasion even convinced a large delegation of protesting Aguinaldistas that this was so ("They came with fire in their eyes and went away like lambs," Marguerite remarked), it is unlikely that his instructions regarding campaign behavior were scrupulously observed.[52]

In the balloting on September 17 Quezon received 69 percent of the votes (694,104); Aguinaldo 17.5 percent (179,390); and Aglipay 14 percent (147,951). Considering the long Nacionalista dominance in Philippine politics, Hayden was justified in interpreting the large vote for Quezon's opponents as "a violent protest against the *Presidente* and all his works."[53]

Expecting victory, Aguinaldo took his defeat "very hard." A newspaperman who enjoyed the general's confidence but was secretly reporting on his behavior to the insular government thought that the "crushing defeat" was "so shocking to his [Aguinaldo's] sense of pride as to upset his mental balance." Aguinaldo, the informant believed, suffered from "a persecution complex," and his "nagging wife," according to the same source, intensified his "revengeful proclivities" and his "morbid propensity to secure a remedy, legal or illegal."[54]

Declaring, "I still believe we have not yet lost," Aguinaldo charged that he had been deprived of victory in "a dirty election." Beginning on September 19, he held nightly meetings of his supporters on the ample grounds of his Kawit home to keep alive a sense of outrage among them and to devise an appropriate course of action. Constabulary agents were not only present at these meetings, generally attended by several hundred persons and on one occasion by as many as three thousand, but the government was also able to obtain information on the secret meetings of the Aguinaldistas that were held in different homes in Kawit and in the home of Aguinaldo's sister. Constabulary agents who reported on the outdoor meetings characterized Aguinaldo's supporters as "rabid fanatics who would follow him even to hell itself." Although Aguinaldo always counseled patience and moderation at the outdoor meetings, he spoke without restraint at the "sinister" private meetings, where strategy was formulated.[55]

The Aguinaldistas, charging that the election did not reflect the popular will and verbally attacking the Filipino leadership and the governor-general, considered various means of preventing the peaceful inauguration of the Quezon government. There was much talk of assassinating Quezon, which Aguinaldo privately said would be "the greatest blessing" that could come to the Philippines, and some planning, "jokingly" referred to as " 'an elimination contest,' " to rid the country of Quezon, Osmeña, and Roxas. One fanciful scheme called for an assassin to place cyanide acid on a piece of bubble gum on his palm and to kill Quezon by shaking hands with him at the inaugural ball. There was also talk of gathering arms for an eventual revolt, but the tactic most seriously considered was a giant "protest parade" of the discontented, the poor, and radical elements to coincide with the inauguration ceremonies in Manila and to impress visiting American dignitaries and journalists with the extent of opposition to a Quezon administration.[56]

The Constabulary was not content merely to observe and report on Aguinaldo's public meetings; it placed "strong patrols" on the road leading to his residence, and its agents took the names of those attending the meetings and searched them for weapons. One agent, not surprisingly, reported that these tactics were having a "demoralizing effect" on the meetings. "Bitterly" resenting the Constabulary's behavior, Aguinaldo took his protests directly to Murphy in meetings of October 8 and 10. Murphy told the general that, although assemblies advocating assassination would not be tolerated, the right of the Aguinaldistas to assemble peacefully would not be abridged; the governor-general summoned Basilio Valdes, the head of the Constabulary, to one of the meetings to reinforce the point. Aguinaldo understood Murphy to have ordered Valdes to withdraw the Constabulary from the vicinity of the Kawit home, but if Murphy issued such an order it was not observed. Murphy told Aguinaldo that he could expect justice from Quezon, to which the general replied that one could hardly expect justice from a "rascal" who had won the election by fraud. When the governor-general asked if plans were afoot to assassinate Quezon, Aguinaldo replied that he had several times protected Quezon from assassination. Murphy wanted to know if Aguinaldo was planning a protest parade for November 15, to which Aguinaldo responded that he was planning a large one.[57]

Murphy had told Hayden before Aguinaldo's first visit that Quezon was " 'doomed,' " revolution was brewing, and it would be a " 'miracle' " if the Commonwealth were peacefully inaugurated. After his second meeting with Aguinaldo, the governor-general informed the vice-governor that he expected an "armed uprising" before November 15. "Each day now seems tense, there is talk of revolution—trouble," Marguerite recorded in her diary. Since the Sakdalista uprising, Quezon had been "guarded as is no other man in the world," Hayden reported, and the president-elect was living in "hourly, momentary terror of assassination," his home and grounds having become "an armed camp." Quezon's and Murphy's fears of an impending revolution were shared by Murphy's "level headed[,] conservative" aide George C. Dunham, who thought that the radical leaders were determined to " 'get' " the landlords, and, to some extent, by Hayden, who believed that the impoverished tenants of central Luzon had "been ground down until they . . . [were] ready for anything." Although Aguinaldo was the leader of "the forces of discontent," his grievances were "only incidental," Hayden realized, since the movement of protest rested on "a wide and deep foundation of injustice and abuse, economic and political."[58]

After his second visit to Murphy, Aguinaldo wrote the governor-general that he did not intend "to obstruct in any way the ushering in of the new regime" but wished to demonstrate that the election had not been "clean and above-board." He requested Murphy not to certify the results until the "unprecedented frauds" had been investigated by an impartial investigator who would be joined by Aguinaldo or his representatives. Murphy replied that the legislature had certified the election results to him in accordance with the law and that he had then certified the results to President Roosevelt, as the Tydings-McDuffie Act specified. He advised Aguinaldo that he was referring his charges to the legislature as the body legally authorized to determine election results and was directing the secretary of justice to investigate the general's complaints. Retorting that this would not be an independent investigation, Aguinaldo asked that the relevant correspondence be forwarded to Roosevelt, a request with which the governor-general complied.

Aguinaldo refused to supply evidence to the secretary of justice or to honor a subpoena that he issued and also refused to appear before a joint session of the elections committees of the legislature to which the matter had been referred. The committees then declared the matter closed and reported that even if the election results were nullified in all the provinces where fraud allegedly had occurred, Quezon would still have won a decisive victory. Aguinaldo, to be sure, had "ample grounds" for his charges of fraud, but even one of his closest associates conceded the correctness of the committees' finding. As for President Roosevelt, he instructed Murphy to inform Aguinaldo that there was no federal law authorizing the president to inject himself into the matter.[59]

Just before the legislature, on October 22, rendered its report on the election, a "much perturbed" Quezon appeared at Malacañan and told Murphy that the only way to avert trouble was for the governor-general to inform Aguinaldo that the United States Army would deal forcibly with any disturbance he created. Murphy professed to be startled at this proposal, telling Quezon that he would not consider it even for a moment. Since the Filipinos, Murphy said, had assumed certain responsibilities for their own governance, they must do all that was in their power to meet these responsibilities before he would call in the army. For American troops to kill a single Filipino, the governor-general remonstrated, was simply "unthinkable." Quezon did not pursue the matter, deciding apparently to deal with Aguinaldo in his own way.[60]

In explaining Quezon's "methods of disposing of troublesome opponents," Louis J. Van Schaick, a veteran member of the Malacañan staff, told Hayden that the president-elect had been "working on" Aguinaldo's associates, had offered one of them a major position in the Commonwealth government, and reportedly had indicated that, if Aguinaldo called off his meetings and his proposed demonstration in Manila, the government would return land to him that he had lost or was about to lose because of failure to pay his taxes. Hayden's comment on this information was, "Hardly possible!" If Hayden, however, had been present on January 19, 1935, when Quezon told Murphy that "A[guinaldo] would do anything for money," the vice-governor might not have thought the news the staff member gave him all that far-fetched. Toward the end of October several high officials of the insular government, including Osmeña and the head of the Constabulary, met with one of Aguinaldo's principal aides, and the parties agreed that the Constabulary would be withdrawn from the Kawit home and that there would be no more nightly meetings and no more seditious speeches after November 2, the day Secretary of War Dern was to arrive in Manila. If Aguinaldo remained "quiet" from then on, the government officials implied, the Commonwealth government would "condone his unpaid taxes on the Paliparan Estate through special legislation."[61]

When Aguinaldo hinted at a rally, after the agreement had been reached, that the meetings would soon be suspended, his followers suspected that he had been bribed. "We are advising him not to commit another ridiculous act," the Aguinaldo confidant supplying information to the Constabulary reported, "but some of his other advisers are pushing him on to the edge of the precipice," and the informant thought that Aguinaldo was inclined to follow them. "He would as soon doublecross Quezon and Osmeña as he would sell his people," the informant noted. Perhaps, however, the agent speculated, Aguinaldo was just bluffing in order to get an "immediate cash bribe" instead of a "mere promise" about his Paliparan estate.[62]

Aguinaldo suspended his nightly meetings on November 2, telling a secret caucus that he was doing so because the cost of holding the meetings had become excessive. It is unclear whether the secret meetings also came to an end, but it is known that they continued for a time after the bargain of late October had been struck and that, as the Aguinaldo confidant reported, "the same murderous inclinations and obsessions" characterized "these sinister confabs." Since the threat of a protest parade continued to hang over the inauguration, Murphy, thinking back no doubt to what Quezon had proposed as the way to avert trouble, met with Aguinaldo on November 7 to dissuade him from engaging in any kind of demonstration. When Aguinaldo stated that he would bring fifty to sixty thousand persons to Manila on inauguration day to demonstrate his popular support, Murphy said that since a demonstration meant bloodshed, which would be very embarrassing to both the governor-general and the high American officials who would be present, he would resort to force if this were necessary. Murphy, who could "talk a bird out of a tree," was his usual affable self with the Filipino general; but Aguinaldo, understanding that the governor-general's compliments and sweet words were in this instance simply a mask for his resolve, promised that he would call off the demonstration. Aguinaldo did not even appear in Manila for the inauguration ceremonies, and there was no Aguinaldista demonstration to mar the proceedings.[63]

When Secretary of War Dern arrived in the Philippines on November 2, Aguinaldo invited him to Kawit in a letter in which the general noted that his followers were "only waiting for my orders." Subsequently briefed by Murphy on the events of the preceding several weeks, Dern waited until 2:00 P.M. on November 11 to inform Aguinaldo that he would arrive in Kawit three hours later. Despite the short notice, about twenty-five hundred persons lined the streets of the city to welcome the secretary. Murphy, who accompanied Dern, tactfully wrote in the general's guest book, "A moment under the roof of the patriotic Aguinaldo is a happy one." Dern concluded from the visit that, although Aguinaldo still had "a devoted following," his prestige had suffered "a severe decline" as the result of his futile entry into politics.[64]

Although Aguinaldo posed the major threat to the peaceful inauguration of the Commonwealth, the insular government was also concerned about the intentions of the Sakdalistas. Reports from undercover agents indicated that the Sakdalistas were planning an uprising for November 15 in Manila and nearby provinces and planned to entice the Constabulary away from the city by creating a disturbance elsewhere the day before. There was also "alarming news" that Ramos had informed his followers that he would arrive from Japan with arms some time between November 14 and 16 to join forces with the Aguinaldistas and the Communists. An intercepted Ramos letter alerted the Sakdalistas not to be surprised if he returned to the Philippines in a Japanese battleship. When he gave the signal, the letter advised, they were to burn Manila, kill the Constabulary forces stationed there and seize their arms, and kidnap Murphy, the archbishop, all "big Americans," and businessmen and their families. According to Ramos, Murphy would then have to declare a cease-fire, cable the United States to grant the Philippines independence within twenty-four hours, and give all government positions to Sakdalistas.[65]

Murphy's military aide characterized the Ramos letter as the "ravings of a maniac," an understandable conclusion; but that the Sakdalistas had plans for wholesale incendiarism and kidnappings on November 15 was confirmed when the Constabulary later arrested a Ramos follower returning from Japan and seized documents in his possession. When it was discovered preceding inauguration day that two thousand tickets for the proceedings had been stolen, the Constabulary feared that the tickets had fallen into Sakdalista hands or that Aguinaldo's men had somehow acquired them and would pack the stands with bolo-men, another indication of the apprehension that surrounded the inauguration ceremonies. The Constabulary was on the alert on inauguration day, and guards armed with riot guns swarmed around Malacañan. The inflammatory rhetoric of Ramos and his followers, however, was not translated into action; as Murphy informed President Roosevelt, the inauguration ceremonies were conducted "without the slightest incident to mar the happy occasion."[66] The Filipinos were now safely on the road to independence, and Frank Murphy, who had hoped "to set these people free," had reason to be pleased with the role that he had played, both in Washington and Manila, in achieving that result.

3

The Philippine New Deal

As governor-general of the Philippines, Murphy acted on the presumption that his principal responsibility at a time when the Filipinos seemed likely to be granted independence was to strengthen the insular government in preparation for the responsibilities it was soon likely to assume and to inaugurate the kind of program an enlightened state should pursue. For Murphy, this meant providing the Philippines with a government that was fiscally sound and socially progressive.[1]

Murphy told the Filipinos at the outset of his tenure in the islands that his "first and primary concern" was to balance the insular government's budget and not to permit deficits "to creep into our balance sheets." He was determined to bring an end to the deficits of the preceding few years, to replenish the general fund, and "to turn over this government to the Filipinos . . . with every account balanced and securely in the black."[2]

In committing himself to a policy of fiscal conservatism, Murphy was reflecting the conventional American wisdom regarding what was right and what was wrong in the realm of public finance. As he informed Senator Millard Tydings, he was "actuated by the conviction that all good government flows from a sound and stable fiscal policy." Only a government that was "economically stable," he contended, could "fulfill its primary responsibility of helpfulness to its people and make practical its ideals of service." There is no reason to doubt that Murphy believed what he said about balanced budgets, but politics also impelled him to stress the point. As mayor of depression-ridden Detroit he had acquired an undeserved national reputation for having spent the city into bankruptcy, and he undoubtedly wished to refurbish his tarnished public image. Also, as the New Deal came under increasing attack for its budget deficits, Murphy thought that the American electorate would be impressed by the quite different record of the New Dealer in Manila. "I am a new sort of a new dealer," he noted. "I am balancing the budget. . . ."[3]

In the three calendar years 1930–32 the Philippine government had incurred a net deficit of P19.78 million, and it had balanced the budget only by drawing on the surplus that had been accumulated in preceding years of prosperity. Theodore Roosevelt, Jr., had sought toward the end of his term to counteract the deficit by securing a reorganization of the governmental structure and reducing the salaries of government employees, but it was the Murphy administration that converted the deficit into a surplus. The budget surplus in the calendar year 1933 was almost P500,000 despite a decrease in government revenue of about P4.7 million as compared to 1932 (from P74.7 million in 1932 to P70 million in 1933). In 1934 the budget surplus was almost P8 million; and the surplus amounted to slightly less than P2.5 million for the last ten and one-half months of American rule in 1935.[4]

Murphy achieved his budget goals by creating an "institutional interest in economy," submitting budgets to the legislature that called for reduced spending, eliminating the traditional pork-barrel funds from the budget, and instituting new controls over the budgetary process. The General Efficiency and Economy Committee that he had established and similar subcommittees in the various bureaus of the government suggested ways to reduce expenditures, restraints were placed on promotions and salary increases, and economies were effected in the use of equipment and supplies. Enforcing economy "with an iron hand," as Evett Hester observed, Murphy generally withheld expenditures when an appropriation act gave him the discretionary authority to do so or the appropriation was conditional.

In the past, as part of the cherished Philippine pork barrel, the public works appropriation assigned a specific sum for each legislator to expend in his district. Murphy, however, withheld the expenditure of pork-barrel items in the existing 1933 budget; and in an almost unprecedented action that displeased Quezon and others, he entirely eliminated the pork-barrel feature from the 1934 budget, the first that he himself submitted to the legislature. When the lawmakers threatened to unbalance the budget by exceeding his budget requests, Murphy made liberal use of his item veto power. Finally, he instituted the kind of "arduous and detailed" budget controls that he had developed during his mayoralty to restrain spending—the allocation of appropriations on a monthly basis and the requirement that executive departments reserve 5 percent of their appropriation as a protection against possible deficits.[5]

Even more impressive than his management of the insular government's budget was the control that Murphy exercised over local finances. Prior to Murphy's service the central government had not attempted to supervise the financial behavior of provincial and municipal governments, with the result that many had been guilty of slipshod budgetary practices and had regularly incurred deficits. A survey conducted for Murphy just after he assumed his post revealed that eleven of the forty-nine provinces had begun the year 1933 with overdrafts and twenty-seven had spent more than half of their 1933 appropriation by the end of May. Deciding on a system of central control over local finance, Murphy transferred effective supervision of the problem from the Department of the Interior to the Malacañan staff, specifically to Joseph Mills, and he firmly supported Mills's efforts to bring local finances under control.

Working with a committee of provincial treasurers, Mills devised a system of monthly reports by the provinces that revealed the exact state of their finances. When these reports indicated that a provincial treasury was running a deficit, the provincial governor and treasurer might be called to Manila and advised how to correct the imbalance. Murphy sent out general communications to the provinces on the need for economy, and when a province was guilty of improper fiscal behavior, the governor-general was apt to send it a special letter. As J. Weldon Jones recalled, this was "a new and startling activity for the Governor-General's Office," and it "brought results." Murphy also spread the gospel of fiscal responsibility on his tours of the provinces. He told provincial officers "right from the shoulder," Norman Hill wrote, "that fiscal stability and integrity is the backbone of government" and that he expected them to balance their budgets.[6]

Admonishing local officials not to look to Manila for financial aid in balancing their accounts, Murphy insisted on the "prompt and full collection" of taxes by provincial governments. In his first veto he forestalled the enactment of a bill remitting the penalty for the late payment of the real estate tax, the chief source of provincial and municipal revenue. Also, unlike Theodore Roosevelt, Jr., at the outset of his service Murphy resisted efforts to extend the due date for the payment of the cedula, the two-peso tax paid by adult males that was a source of local revenue. Although he believed the cedula an inequitable tax, he later vetoed a bill abolishing this impost since the measure made no provision for an alternative source of revenue. Government, Murphy lectured local officials, "is much like a commodity—the amount of its services are [sic] closely measured by the amount of taxes paid."[7]

The methods introduced by the Murphy regime to control local finances largely achieved their objective: the provinces were in "excellent financial condition'' by the end of 1934, having converted a 1932 aggregate deficit of P1.6 million into a P856,979 surplus. The system of financial control introduced in 1933 was continued after the establishment of the Commonwealth government, a Murphy legacy to the new government.[8]

The Murphy policy of sound fiscal management was also extended to the government companies under the governor-general's supervision—the Philippine National Bank, the Manila Railroad Company, the Manila Hotel, the National Development Company, and the Cebu Portland Cement Company. Murphy insisted that these companies, established to spur Philippine economic development, be operated in an efficient, businesslike, nonpolitical manner. The companies, he advised, should have two objectives: they should be of service to the people, but they should also strive to be self-sustaining and, of lesser importance, to earn a profit. In an effort to improve the performance of government companies, Murphy arranged for the appointment of able men like Mills, who served as president of the Manila Railroad Company and vice-chairman of the Philippine National Bank, to direct their affairs. The results were impressive: all the companies showed a profit in 1933, and only the Manila Railroad Company, which had to pay off some of its bonds in foreign currency and was suffering the effects of reduced internal traffic, failed to remain in the black in 1934.[9]

When the Commonwealth government was inaugurated on November 15, 1935, it had a surplus of P14 million in its general fund, and the central government, the local governments, and the government companies were all in far sounder condition than they had been when Murphy assumed his Philippine post. The *Manila Daily Bulletin* was correct in its judgment that ''no other chief executive'' of the Philippines had been ''so consistently determined upon the fiscal integrity and stability of the Philippine Government'' as the last governor-general of the islands.[10]

If Murphy believed that ''the adoption of a sound financial policy was ... the problem demanding ... [his] first attention,'' the impending change in the status of the Philippine government and prevailing attitudes in the Philippines persuaded him that ''a very strong effort'' had to be made ''to establish a broad and comprehensive social program'' in the islands that would be continued, he hoped, after American control had come to an end. In making this ''effort,'' Murphy provided the Philippines with ''at least the outward symbol of a New Deal.''[11] Although the Philippine New Deal was less sweeping than the Roosevelt New Deal, the Murphy regime initiated the most ambitious program of social reform in the history of American rule in the Philippines.

Because of Spanish neglect, the fatalistic attitude of the Filipino masses toward suffering, the lack of any real sense of community responsibility among the wealthy and educated, the "inertia" of those in authority, and the prevalence of the *pariente* system, which required the members of a family to provide for one another (the bilateral, extended Filipino family has been characterized as "a ready-made social security system"), the Philippines had lagged behind occidental countries in the development of government services for health and welfare. These same circumstances placed a special responsibility on the governor-general if the obstacles to government action in the welfare field were to be overcome. Comfortable in the role, Murphy discharged this responsibility admirably. Not only did he help to educate public opinion on the subject, but under his "aggressive . . . leadership," the insular government, for the first time, "assumed full and complete responsibility for the relief of distress due to any cause." In his speeches and tours of the country, Murphy sought to arouse the social conscience of the Filipinos, to persuade them to assign first place to "human relations" in their thoughts about the future, and to provide them and their leaders with an appreciation of the role of a modern government in the welfare field. "Battling against the dead weight of acquiescent inertia," the *New York Times*'s Manila correspondent reported after the governor-general's first year in the Philippines, Murphy had "succeeded in galvanizing the public into genuine social thinking and some distinct accomplishments."[12]

Although Murphy characterized social justice as "a subject little enthused about" before his arrival in the Philippines, American rule, unlike Spanish rule, had been marked by a concern for the health and welfare of the archipelago's inhabitants. Significant progress was made in the period 1898–1914 and during Leonard Wood's governor-generalship in the eradication of various diseases endemic in the Philippines, such as small pox and cholera, the improvement of medical education, the training of public health nurses, and the improvement of Filipino dietary habits. There was some retrogression in the public health field in the Harrison era, but during these years the Philippine government laid the foundation for a public welfare program and encouraged the efforts of private organizations to deal with tuberculosis and maternal and child health.

In 1932 the uncoordinated health and welfare functions of the government were consolidated in two bureaus (Bureau of Health,

Bureau of Public Welfare) and placed under the Department of Public Instruction, headed by the vice-governor. As of 1933, however, public health nursing and social services had yet to be extended into the homes of the poor; the Bureau of Public Welfare confined its activities largely to Manila; no place in the Philippines had a water supply that was entirely safe; less than one-half of the persons in the provinces had access to toilets; and Filipinos, because of their diet of polished rice and fish, suffered from beri-beri and other nutritional diseases and had a low resistance to infections. In the five years before 1933 the infant death rate, "the best index of health conditions," averaged 150–160 per thousand in the Philippines as compared to 80 per thousand in the United States.[13]

In his inaugural address Murphy affirmed that an "enlightened and progressive" Philippine government would have to be concerned with the social and economic conditions of its people and would have to correct "gross inequalities and social injustices." It would have to "help the underprivileged,... protect the weak and untutored against the strong and unscrupulous; and ... make education, healthful living conditions, fair and impartial justice, steady employment at a fair wage, adequate care of the sick and indigent, and all the other benefits of civilized society, available to every man, woman and child." Murphy told his Filipino audience, as he had informed his Detroit constituents, that "if in administrative and fiscal matters the government succeeds, while social justice in the community fails or remains unsolved, the great task of governmental management is still incomplete."[14]

Murphy outlined a "sociological program" for the Philippines that embraced "almost every field of humanitarian activity"—public health in all its aspects, improved institutional care, child and family welfare, recreation, crime and corrections, assistance to the working-man, relief for the unemployed, improved housing and slum clearance, and rural improvement. Only expenditures in the health and welfare field escaped the economy axe that Murphy wielded in devising his budgets. In the decade before he became governor-general, the largest sum provided by special appropriation for public health and social services was P550,000 in 1928, and the 1933 budget that Murphy inherited provided only P92,791 for this purpose; but in 1934 and 1935 the legislature appropriated almost P1.5 million for Murphy's health and social programs over and above appropriations for routine activities and not including P2 million appropriated for typhoon relief and colonization.[15]

Murphy was assisted in devising and implementing his health and welfare program by the competent Filipino administrators in the Bureau of Health and Bureau of Public Welfare, and he found "the perfect technical collaborator" in the sanitarian and public health administrator Major George C. Dunham. "A big Newfoundland dog type," Dunham, in Hayden's view, exercised "an influence in the Islands . . . never . . . exceeded by . . . any other health officer." Dunham, in turn, viewed Murphy as "the health official's dream come true."[16]

It was Dunham's premise that in the Philippines, to a far greater extent than in the United States and Europe, the rehabilitation of "socially inadequate" families was intimately related to public health activity. " . . . the most important social needs of the Filipino people," he contended, "are based fundamentally on certain conditions of public health." As Dunham saw it, social problems such as unemployment and crime were directly or indirectly related to disease, malnutrition, and poor living conditions and could best be controlled by public health activity. Since both government and private health and welfare agencies tended to slight the health and social problems of the family, devoting their principal efforts to sanitation, immunization, research, and teaching, and since thousands of deaths each year were attributable to unsanitary home conditions, Dunham thought that Murphy's health and welfare program should be designed to carry public health practices and social services into the home and make them "an inherent part of family life."[17]

The principal Philippine institution devoted to family health problems when Murphy became governor-general was the puericulture center. An agency concerned primarily with maternal and child health and generally staffed by a doctor, nurses, and sometimes a midwife, the puericulture center treated its patients in clinics and, less frequently, by home visits. Puericulture centers had been established in various municipalities and provinces beginning in 1921 at the instigation, usually, of women's clubs or interested private individuals. The centers had to be incorporated or, at least, endorsed by the local municipal or provincial government, which sometimes supplemented the voluntary contributions with public funds, and had to conform to standards set by the insular government. The insular government usually contributed one-half of the funds to operate a puericulture center provided that the other half was raised locally, a condition that tended to confine the centers to the most affluent communities in the Philippines rather than to those that most needed their services. When Murphy became governor-general, 174 peuriculture centers were in operation, but 80 percent of the archipelago's municipalities lacked such centers.[18]

Believing that the Philippines required a minimum of five hundred puericulture centers or at least one for every two municipalities, Murphy urged an increase in insular government funding for the program. The legislature responded in 1934 by appropriating an additional P170,000 for this purpose, which made possible the establishment of 146 publicly financed centers in 1935 in addition to the 202 centers functioning at the end of 1934. When the Bureau of Health lagged in implementing the program, Hayden insisted on action. "The needs of the public and the good name of the Department," he informed the commissioner of health and welfare, "demand that this be done."[19]

Although the puericulture center appeared to be an effective institution in meeting the health needs of less densely populated areas and regions where the standard of living was relatively high, the poor in the slums of Manila and other large cities and in the most impoverished barrios required a government agency that would cater not only to their health needs but to their material and social needs as well. In Manila alone, an estimated fifteen thousand families with a family income of less than P15 per month—P30 per month was considered to be the minimum for a "wholesome" standard of living—suffered from malnutrition, tuberculosis, poor housing, and overcrowding. In August 1933, after a survey of a portion of the Tondo slum district of Manila by the Philippine chapter of the American Red Cross revealed deplorable conditions in the area stemming from poverty and poor health, the insular government, on an experimental basis, established a community health-social center in the district to serve its maternal and child health needs, to combat tuberculosis, and to foster the "social and economic rehabilitation" of its people. Dealing with the family as a "health-social unit," as Dunham had prescribed, the center, although operating a clinic, stressed home visits by public health nurses and social workers. "Action in the fields and not words in the office are necessary," Dunham declared.

The excellent results obtained by the Tondo center persuaded the Murphy administration to press for the establishment of additional community health-social centers in Manila and in the provinces. By the end of 1935 ten such centers were in operation, four in Manila, three in the cities of Iloilo, Cebu, and Zamboanga, and three in the larger barrios of Occidental Negros. All the centers were funded by the government, although they had been subsidized initially by the Red Cross and the Philippine Islands Anti-Tuberculosis Society. Each center consisted of a child and maternal health section, a general clinic and dispensary, a dental clinic, a tuberculosis section, and a social rehabilitation section. The social rehabilitation sections not only engaged in social work but also operated kindergartens and conducted sewing classes and classes for illiterate mothers. The community health-social center, Hayden concluded, was "the most effective agency yet devised for reaching the people and helping them to solve their health and social problems."[20]

In addition to the establishment of community health-social centers, the insular government in 1934 appropriated funds for the first time for community public health nurses to provide nursing and social services to the needy in communities of less than ten thousand people. By the fall of 1935 these nurses were visiting the homes of the poor to deal with their health and social problems and holding weekly clinics in 149 communities selected because of their poverty and high infant mortality rates.[21]

The Murphy administration's health program also involved the reorganization of the 628-bed Philippine General Hospital, which catered mainly to charity patients. "Under fire" for years, the hospital was refusing admission to twenty persons daily, and patients were being discharged prematurely to provide space for the incoming sick. The administration of the hospital was also "markedly impersonal and machine like in character." Following the report of a committee of doctors and laymen appointed by Hayden to investigate the hospital's performance, the vice-governor at the beginning of 1935 ordered the hospital to organize a "partially complete visiting service" to follow into their homes patients denied admission because of a shortage of space and convalescent patients discharged before full recovery. The director of the hospital reported at the end of the year that the institution's new extension service was functioning satisfactorily, and the reopening of two wards that had been closed because of lack of funds increased the hospital's bed capacity.[22]

Shortly before Murphy became governor-general, the Bureau of Health set up a Nutrition Section to combat the chronic malnutrition that afflicted the Filipino poor. Murphy supplemented this action in September 1933 by establishing a Committee on Nutrition on which the dozen or so agencies concerned with the subject were represented. The community health-social centers and the puericulture centers provided mothers with instruction in improved nutritional practices, such as the use of fruits and vegetables to supplement the family diet, and conducted tests to ensure compliance with pure food and drug laws.[23]

A campaign initiated on April 1, 1933, to provide one latrine per family resulted in the building of more than 550,000 latrines by June 30, 1935. When the Metropolitan Water District Board tabled the recommendation of a mayor's committee to filter the central water supply of Manila, Murphy secured a reversal of the decision, with the result that a new filtration plant was opened for the city in the summer of 1935.[24]

Murphy visited the Insular Psychopathic Hospital late in July 1934 to focus attention on the "scandalous" treatment of the "helpless victims of melancholy" who were housed there. "I like visiting asylums, prisons and hospitals," Murphy wrote a girl friend, "largely for the reason it affords the opportunity to do so many acts of personal kindness and mercy. That is the most satisfying experience in high public life. . . . Mercy, mercy, mercy. I love it because I expect and depend upon it myself. . . . Balancing the budget, fiscal stability, good government, social justice and all the rest are shibboleths and phrases and of course to a great degree the means of progress in politics[,] but when it's all done there is an empty satisfaction unless there is the record of individual acts of righteousness and kindness and mercy that should mark the human being and not the mere political pontiff."[25]

It would be easy to dismiss the above remarks as another evidence of the sanctimoniousness that was a Murphy characteristic, but they are nevertheless revealing of the very personal way in which he approached his responsibilities regarding the custodial care of the afflicted and the unfortunate. One can thus easily imagine the pleasure Murphy derived from ordering a halt to the shackling of recalcitrant inmates of public institutions, a routine Filipino procedure that had led to the death of eleven inmates of the National Girls Training School. He would rather see inmates escape, Murphy declared, than expose them to death as the result of some disaster.[26]

It is hardly surprising that the deplorable manner in which the Filipinos cared for the insane, "one of the sorest spots in the Philippine social economy," aroused the concern of Murphy and his aides. The Insular Psychopathic Hospital, which dated from Leonard Wood's governor-generalship, was designed for eight hundred patients but housed eleven hundred as of 1933 and failed to provide them with satisfactory treatment. It was, in Hayden's words, "little more than a frightfully overcrowded cage," and Murphy characterized it as a " 'medieval madhouse.' " Conditions were "even worse" in the equally overcrowded City Sanatorium in Manila, which treated its 250 patients in a "disgraceful" and "uncivilized" manner. The less seriously ill in the facility were assigned to overcrowded wards, and the acutely insane were confined in tiny cages and cells in an outbuilding. The main building, a fire trap, constituted "a grave menace'' to the safety of the inmates. Since there were no facilities at all for the mentally ill in places other than Manila, they were consigned to jails or remained at large.[27]

Describing the institutionalized insane as "our guests," Murphy insisted that they receive "humane and adequate treatment." At his behest, the legislature appropriated P280,000 for three buildings designed to increase the capacity of the Insular Psychopathic Hospital to eighteen hundred. When the buildings were completed in 1935, patients were transferred to them from the City Sanatorium, and more satisfactory arrangements were devised for the patients who remained in the city facility.[28]

Until 1935 the insular government made no special provision for the care and treatment of feebleminded children, assigning them to the Insular Psychopathic Hospital or the training schools for delinquent boys and girls if it took heed of them at all. Asserting that there was a "crying need for the better care of mentally defective children," Murphy persuaded the 1934 legislature to appropriate P90,000 for a school for such children at Welfareville, the government institution in Manila for "the socially helpless and handicapped." The new Home for Mentally Defective Children opened on February 1, 1935, as the fifth of the child-care institutions at Welfareville.[29]

One of the most troublesome problems regarding the care of the afflicted that Murphy faced as governor-general was the treatment of leprous patients. As of 1935, more than eighty-seven hundred bacteriologically positive lepers were being subjected to group segregation and treatment, more than seven thousand of them in the leper colony on the island of Culion, the largest leper colony in the world, and sixteen hundred in four regional treatment centers and three small local leprosaria. In addition, eleven hundred bacteriologically negative lepers, regarded as incapable of infecting others, were registered in skin clinics, and perhaps two thousand negative cases were on parole. Since leprosy was normally contracted in childhood, segregation was designed to prevent the transmission of the disease from positive lepers to their children. There was no scientific evidence that the disease could be cured, but treatment could arrest its progress and aid in rendering a leper bacteriologically negative.

If a leper remained bacteriologically negative for a year, regulations permitted his release. In 1935, however, the legislature passed a bill permitting the release of lepers who had been bacteriologically negative for four consecutive weeks even though the record showed that those who became bacteriologically negative for short periods generally relapsed and became bacteriologically positive again. On the advice of health authorities, Murphy, who had visited Culion on his first southern tour and promised "a new deal for leprous patients," vetoed the bill as endangering the public health. Following this action, he appointed a Leprosy Commission headed by Dunham to make appropriate recommendations. The commission concluded in its report that the segregation of lepers in their own homes was "impracticable as a control measure" and that group segregation should be continued. It recommended an increase in the number of regional treatment centers, establishment of regional agricultural colonies to which physically fit lepers could be assigned, provision of proper facilities for the observation of bacteriologically negative lepers both prior to their parole and thereafter, separation of children of leprous patients from their parents at birth, and provision of additional facilities for their care at Welfareville. The report met with "almost unanimous public approval," and the process of implementing its provisions was soon initiated.[30]

The Murphy program of social reform in the Philippines involved a concern not only for the public health and the proper care of the afflicted but also for housing of the poor, relief of the destitute, and the improvement of rural life. In the Tondo district of Manila, the families lived in small, poorly built "nipa shacks standing back to back and face to face on low lots and near swamps"; in the San Nicolas and Intramuros slums of the city they were housed in filthy tenements that lacked toilet facilities and in which fifteen to twenty persons might be crowded into a single room. Believing that the eradication of slum conditions was "one of the most urgent duties of the government," Murphy appointed a Housing Committee in October 1933 to initiate "action" on the problem. As an experiment, the committee decided to reconstruct a small, miserable area in the Tondo district. Frustrated by legal technicalities and the attitude of slum property-owners, it arranged for the demolition of sixty-four dwellings and the building of thirty-one model homes at a cost of about P10,500, the money provided by the city of Manila and the Red Cross. The project was then turned over to the city, and the homes were rented at the small sum of P3 or P3.50 per month.

On the basis of its initial experiment, the housing committee devised a comprehensive plan for a government-sponsored project to house twenty-five hundred families supposedly able to purchase or rent low-cost dwellings, and the legislature then appropriated P250,000 for the purpose. The low-income laborers for whom the dwellings were intended, however, could not afford the rentals set by the measure; and although the legislature subsequently appropriated additional funds, slum clearance and low-income housing, as Murphy had feared, became "a matter of conversation instead of accomplishment."[31]

Murphy enjoyed greater success in urging that public playgrounds be provided, particularly for underprivileged children. There were only two public playgrounds in Manila when Murphy became governor-general, but at his urging the city of Manila provided funds in 1933 to open thirteen school playgrounds for public use, steps were taken to provide eight additional municipal playgrounds, and a large number of playgrounds were also opened in the provinces.[32]

Although the Great Depression did not result in joblessness in the Philippines to anywhere near the extent that it did in industrialized nations, the Bureau of Labor estimated that there were about ninety-eight thousand unemployed persons in the Philippines in 1933. Insofar as the destitute were cared for outside the family, the burden traditionally had been assumed by the Associated Charities, aided by the Bureau of Public Welfare; but relief of the unemployed, as distinguished from those in distress for other reasons, had not been a concern of either the charity organization or the government.

Following the precedent he had established in Detroit and consistent with his desire to have government play the decisive role in the alleviation of distress, Murphy on July 20, 1933, created an Unemployment Committee of representative citizens to study the relief needs of the islands and to make appropriate recommendations. Aided by a legislative appropriation of P30,000 in 1933 and P50,000 in 1934 and a P5,000 contribution from the city of Manila, the committee began to serve as a coordinating agency for the relief efforts of the Associated Charities, the Red Cross, the Bureau of Public Welfare, and the Bureau of Labor. It aided the Associated Charities in meeting the immediate relief needs of the unemployed, which generally took the form of work relief or relief in kind, sought to find jobs for them, encouraged the charity organization to establish small industries like mat-making and clothing repair, and provided free transportation to the provinces for the unemployed who were willing to leave Manila. It provided free medicine to the unemployed certified to it by the Associated Charities, and it arranged with the Bureau of Education to permit children of the jobless to enter city schools without the payment of matriculation fees.[33]

On the recommendation of the Unemployment Committee, Murphy in October 1934 established a National Emergency Relief Board (NERB) made up of representatives from private and public life to deal with distress caused by unemployment. The NERB subsequently established similar committees in each of the provinces and municipalities. Like the Unemployment Committee, the NERB made funds available to the Associated Charities to aid the destitute, and it sought to reduce unemployment by encouraging the development of home industries and securing the assignment of the jobless to public work projects.[34]

Before the Murphy years the Red Cross had been responsible for disaster relief in the Philippines. When typhoons and floods, however, ravaged twenty-eight provinces in the last four months of 1934, affecting the well-being of 1.5 million people, Murphy, who saw the disaster as a test case for his welfare state policies, decided that the insular government should direct the entire relief effort. He appointed a Typhoon Relief Committee to coordinate and expedite a relief program, and the legislature appropriated a total of P1.1 million in 1934 and 1935 for the relief of indigent typhoon victims and the repair of school buildings. The government, Murphy declared in response to those who "raised a hue and cry" about the diminished role of the Red Cross in the disaster effort, "is willing to go as far as it can in granting recognition and authority to the Red Cross short of transferring to it and taking from the government the responsibility for relief which the government must meet."

As it worked out, the Red Cross provided immediate relief, the Bureau of Health provided medical relief and sought to guard against epidemics, and the Department of Public Works and Communications sought to cope with the transportation and communication problems resulting from the disaster. After immediate relief had been provided, fifteen rehabilitation units, each consisting of a doctor, three public health nurses, an agronomist, and aides, were sent to the devastated areas, where they operated clinics, provided welfare services for the indigent, and distributed free seeds. The entire operation was so effectively directed by the government that the epidemics that had often followed natural disasters in the Philippines in the past were this time avoided.[35]

When typhoons, a short crop, and "manipulations and profiteering" by rice dealers caused a rice shortage and a sharp rise in the price of rice in September 1935, Murphy, once again resorting to governmental authority in coping with a crisis, authorized the Bureau of Commerce to import rice free of the usual duty and to sell the commodity at cost. The governor-general, at the same time, invoked existing legislation penalizing the monopolization and hoarding of rice. Although the government action forced down the price of rice and helped somewhat to alleviate the shortage, it did not solve the problem of hunger, and mobs of hungry persons resorted to violence in parts of the Philippines. "The rice problem," as Charles O. Houston, Jr., pointed out, "became one of Quezon's major headaches" as president of the Commonwealth. His government established a National Rice and Corn Corporation in April 1936 to insure a steady supply of rice and corn and to stabilize prices at levels fair to both the producer and the consumer, but this did not solve the problem, which was getting worse when war came to the Philippines.[36]

In his efforts to prepare the Philippine Islands for the responsibilities of independence, Murphy sought to improve the standard of living not only of the urban poor but also of tenants and small farmers in the rural areas. He appointed a Rural Improvement Committee in August 1933 to survey rural conditions and to promote the growing of secondary crops by barrio people. The committee selected the Gapan district in Nueva Ecija and San Miguel in Bulacan, both areas in which rice was the chief crop and "perennial centers of agrarian conflicts," to demonstrate that the farmers could meet part of their food needs and also derive some income by growing fruits and vegetables on the home lots that they owned or that landlords might be willing to provide them. The committee was responsible for the planting of 750 gardens in 1933 and 1934, which demonstrated the feasibility of the idea and led to the extension of the program to additional farmers in central Luzon, but what was done had only a minimal effect on the countryside. The committee, as a matter of fact, concluded after six months of effort that the farmers in the demonstration areas did not lack for food, although their diets were unbalanced, and that it was the low price of agricultural products and the uneconomical size of their landholdings that accounted for their plight.[37]

Although Murphy envisioned tenant relief as the purpose of the Rural Improvement Committee, the committee decided at its first meeting that it would not concern itself with the critical question of farm leases and would not, at least at the outset, seek to alter existing relationships between landlords and tenants. The insular government also failed to make a frontal assault on the problem of usury. The government created an Anti-Usury Board in the Bureau of Labor in 1933, but the board did not accomplish anything of note. The Murphy administration, however, sought to use the Philippine National Bank, in which the insular government owned the controlling interest, to make credit more readily available to small farmers and to combat the usurer. Responding to policy guidelines established by the governor-general, the bank substantially lowered interest rates for agricultural loans, granted loans to small farmers on crops deposited in warehouses, and provided loans to small farmers in remote and in underdeveloped areas by extending its agency arrangement with provincial treasurers (the number of small loans increased from 62 in 1933 to 4,692 in 1934). Insofar as *caciquism* and usury had a "strangle-hold" on the *tao*, however, the Murphy regime, unwilling to challenge the Filipino leadership on the eve of the Commonwealth, failed to weaken that hold.[38]

Although Murphy did not attain all his social objectives in the Philippines, he provided the islands with "a broad and comprehensive program of health and social service" that compared very favorably with the achievements of his predecessors. What had been accomplished, moreover, as the *Manila Daily Bulletin* observed, was not to be measured solely in terms of bills passed and pesos spent; Murphy, the newspaper noted, had "succeeded in bringing social thinking to a more prominent place than it ... [had] ever occupied in Philippine history." When Murphy arrived in the Philippines, a Filipino observer remarked as the Commonwealth began its history, "social justice" was a "little known" concept in the islands; "today, 'social justice' is a household word—it is the framework upon which the entire social structure rests."[39]

Although Murphy was anxious to develop a welfare program that would have an impact on the Philippines of the future, the Filipino approval of the Tydings-McDuffie Act and the approach of the Commonwealth inhibited long-range planning by the American regime. Hayden made this clear to his American correspondents, noting that the circumstances were hardly conducive to the introduction of new programs and that the chief American task had become one of "liquidation, not construction." Murphy thought that his social program was "firmly entrenched," but Hayden, who lamented that the Commonwealth government would "express almost completely Spanish-Malayan and not Anglo-Saxon psychology" and that this would produce "unhappy" results in the health and welfare field, feared that Murphy was "not fully aware of the impermanent foundations" of his program. "If he is to live as a realist and not as a romanticist," Hayden wrote of Murphy, "he must recognize that he is dealing with a national psychology that is very different from our own."[40]

Insofar as the immediate future of health and welfare activity in the Philippines was concerned, it was Hayden's pessimism, rather than Murphy's optimism, that was excessive. When he published his important study of the Philippines in 1942, Hayden noted: "Since being placed upon their own responsibility, the Filipinos have continued the general health and welfare policies and agencies which had been developed during the period when final control lay in American hands. They have adhered to and carried forward the modern, long-time inclusive program initiated during the last years of the American regime." One of Murphy's Filipino correspondents informed him at the end of 1937, "you started social justice. . . . Now everyone talks social justice, and what's more, demands it." Contrary to what Hayden had forecast, the health-welfare program became an "essential part of the broader drive for 'social justice' " that was "the most important policy of the Quezon administration." Although the performance of the Commonwealth government in its efforts to promote social justice did not always match its rhetoric, it nevertheless enacted a substantial amount of social legislation. It was World War II that destroyed what the Murphy regime and the Commonwealth government had wrought.[41]

Shortly after Murphy arrived in the Philippines, the secretary of the Philippine Labor Congress, noting that labor in his country was "more abused, uncared for and exploited" than in the United States, expressed the hope that the new governor-general would demonstrate the same sympathy for the workingman in the Philippines that he had for the workingman in Detroit. It was not long before Murphy provided evidence that his little New Deal in the Philippines would not ignore the islands' laborers.[42]

One of the principal demands of the Philippine Labor Congress was that Murphy investigate Cayetano Ligot, the Philippine resident labor commissioner in Hawaii. Several thousand Filipino laboreres were employed by the Hawaiian Sugar Planters' Association, and there were allegations that the labor commissioner was "over-friendly" with the Association and was more interested in his personal well-being than in the well-being of the laborers whom he was supposed to serve. Murphy's predecessors had ignored these charges, but when the governor-general concluded that there was substance to the allegations, he relieved Ligot and replaced him with an official drawn from labor's own ranks.[43]

The two principal legislative measures relating to labor enacted while Murphy was governor-general—workers described the measures as "their triumphs"—were an eight-hour law applying to laborers doing work requiring great physical effort or working under "difficult, dangerous, or unhealthful conditions" and a statute elevating the Bureau of Labor to departmental rank. Although urged by his legal advisors to veto the eight-hour bill, Murphy signed the measure into law once assured that it enjoyed labor support. The elevation of the Bureau of Labor to departmental rank was hailed in one Filipino newspaper as "the greatest official victory of the Philippine proletariat." The Philippine Labor Congress recommended Ramon Torres, a pro-labor legislator from Occidental Negros, to head the department, and Murphy accepted the suggestion.

The Department of Labor, which began to function on May 1, 1934, was made up of four principal divisions: conciliation, unemployment, women and children, and statistics. Torres reported in March 1936 that the department's conciliation division, performing a function previously ignored in the Philippines, had helped to adjust 117 strikes, seventy-four of them in favor of the strikers and forty-three in favor of the employers. In the period before the Commonwealth was inaugurated, the department found jobs for 3,730 workers and also dispatched 5,259 homesteaders to Mindanao and elsewhere in an effort to remove surplus population from congested areas. Although pleased with the performance of the department's conciliation and unemployment divisions, Murphy was not satisfied with the performance of its division of women and children and with the failure of the department to put an end to the exploitation of workers by private employment exchanges.[44]

"The existence of a strike," Murphy declared at the outset of his governor-generalship, "shows that things are not in their natural order, that something is wrong. The government, therefore[,] should intervene in such conflicts ... to protect ... the interest of the public."[45] Murphy's view of the proper role for government in a labor dispute was put to its most severe test while he was in the Philippines when, in August 1934, about eleven thousand workers in twenty-one cigar factories in Manila and neighboring municipalities struck in an effort to secure higher wages for unskilled laborers. Although government officials, the police, and employers alleged that "radical elements," including Communists, were playing a prominent role in the strike, there is no reason to doubt that the workers struck because of poor working conditions—cigar-making in the Philippines was carried on "practically under sweatshop conditions"—even if Communists sought to capitalize on the event.[46]

There was a violent clash between strikers and police on September 17, 1934, when the former, shouting "Let us kill all policemen and secret service men," forcibly sought to enter the Minerva Cigar Factory in Manila. Before the fighting stopped, four strikers had been killed, and additional strikers, ten policemen, and two passers-by had been injured. In response to a request for information from the American Civil Liberties Union (ACLU), Murphy stated that he had done all that he could to prevent "this regrettable and unnecessary incident," which is almost certainly inaccurate. Expressing some "misgiving" about the police conduct, Roger N. Baldwin, the director of the ACLU and an admirer of the governor-general because of his civil liberties record as mayor of Detroit, chided Murphy, "At such times of excitement you know fully as well as we, it is possible for wise policing to avoid the kind of tragic conflict which here took place." Murphy learned his lesson in the cigar strike, and later, as governor of Michigan, he demonstrated in the General Motors sit-down strike that "wise policing" could avoid the loss of life even in a strike with a considerable potential for violence.[47]

Murphy's advice to the strikers, whom he viewed not as radicals but as " 'poor people' " who wanted " 'more pay to bring up their families,' " was to settle the dispute by arbitration rather than force. Following the procedure that he had adopted as mayor of Detroit in dealing with the Briggs strike,[48] Murphy appointed a Fact-Finding Board on September 14 to investigate the dispute and to determine the pertinent facts. One week later Torres arranged a return to work by the strikers at slightly increased pay, pending the report of the board. In its report, the board concluded that the provisional wage increase was "justified and reasonable" and suggested that management might consider an additional increase to bring wages more in line with the cost of living. Torres informed the cabinet a few weeks later that only one factory had objected to the report's findings.[49]

Although cigarmakers had marched with the Communists in the May Day parade in 1934, they did not repeat that action in 1935. Murphy's policies, the secretary of labor thought, had won over the laborers of Manila, including the cigarmakers; and Torres reported that the labor unions, whose membership appears to have increased substantially while Murphy was governor-general, had never before shown so much confidence in the government. "Our efforts," he wrote Murphy, "are now devoted to extend this policy (that of taking care of the laborers and the poor) to all nooks and corners of the Philippine Islands, and we will not stop until the farm laborers in the most distant barrios and the logging man in the depth of the forest, can feel by their side as if it were their guardian angel, the protecting hand of the Government." Much, to be sure, remained to be done. When Quezon became president of the Commonwealth, the average daily wage (P0.70) of the workingman was below the cost of living for a family of five, and working conditions were "miserable."[50]

A government, Murphy told the Philippine legislature in his first address to that body, revealed its "attitude toward human beings and its real understanding of them" just as much in its "administration of justice" as in its "treatment of socially inadequate persons." Seeking to build the kind of institutional infrastructure in the Philippines that would enable an independent Philippine government to function in an enlightened manner, Murphy was just as intent upon modernizing the judicial system of the islands and impressing upon the leadership and the populace the importance of governmental concern for civil liberties as he was in expanding government services in the health and welfare field. What Murphy sought to achieve reflected his experience as a criminal court judge and as mayor and his long-standing commitment to a reformative brand of justice and to civil liberties.[51]

The entire Philippine judiciary was appointive, Supreme Court justices being appointed by the president of the United States and judges of the courts of first instance and justices of the peace being appointed by the governor-general. In an effort to secure the selection of the most qualified persons to serve on the bench and to remove politics from the appointment process, Murphy established a Judicial Council in August 1934 consisting of the chief justice of the Philippine Supreme Court, the secretary of justice, the senior judge of the court of first instance in Manila, the dean of the law school of the University of the Philippines, and a member of the board of bar examiners to make recommendations for judicial posts when requested to do so by the governor-general. The members of the council, the order specified, were to be "kept entirely free from the molestation and annoyance of outside influence or solicitation."[52]

Long convinced of the need for public defenders, Murphy persuaded the Philippine legislature to enact a bill providing for the appointment of attorneys to serve as defense counsel for the indigent in criminal cases. Especially necessary in a country where the poor and ignorant were commonly exploited, the public defenders not only represented the indigent in criminal cases but also helped abandoned wives and children to obtain support from "heartless" husbands and parents, assisted homesteaders in applying for land and the unemployed in seeking jobs, sought to adjust labor and landlord-tenant disputes, aided workers in compensation cases and in pressing wage claims and claims for benefit payments from sugar planters, and disseminated information on the rights and duties of citizens and on available government services. Although some of the first public defenders failed to meet their responsibilities, the fifty-three officials serving in 1940 were reported by Hayden to be ''performing valuable services both for the individuals whom they aid[ed] and the state.''[53]

''One of the tragedies of government,'' as Murphy saw it, was ''the mismanagement of penal institutions.'' He believed that ''penal institutions should not be considered as places where human derelicts are to be punished, . . . whipped and lashed'' but rather as places where they were ''to be reformed.'' Soon after becoming governor-general he ordered the Department of Justice to conduct a census of prisoners as a basis for overhauling the prison system, and he sent Colonel Paulino Santos, the director of prisons, to visit prisons in the United States so that he might familiarize himself with modern prison practices. Murphy urged the segregation of short-term and long-term prisoners, had one of his aides survey the islands' prisons and interview prisoners to ascertain if they had been imprisoned unjustly or were eligible for parole, sought assurances that remote district jails were being kept in sanitary condition and were ''good morally,'' and took steps to provide prisoners with improved medical and dental care.[54]

Murphy was not able to improve the Philippine prison system to the extent that he desired, but he was successful in persuading the insular legislature to enact legislation providing indeterminate sentences and a system of probation. The indeterminate sentence, Murphy believed, facilitated the absorption of inmates into society and served to correct the errors of trial judges. His experience as a trial judge, he said, had convinced him of the soundness of the principle, and he was certain that the Philippines could safely adopt the scheme. At his urging, the legislature in 1933 passed a bill creating an indeterminate sentence board, composed of a psychiatrist, a clergyman or educator, at least one woman, and the secretary of justice as chairman, that was empowered to order the parole of prisoners who had served their minimum sentence and were deemed fit for release. During the first twenty months that the measure was in effect, only three of 645 parolees violated their parole, and the government was able to save a good deal of money in the process. There seems, however, to have been little local interest in the measure, and many in the American community incorrectly thought that Murphy was simply trying to court popularity by sponsoring the reform.[55]

Probation, for Murphy, was designed to achieve ''the separation of those elements in society who are not criminals, but who, by the force of circumstances, are led to commit crime.'' It was ''a measure of economy and social progress,'' he told his cabinet, and a proven and effective means of achieving ''reformation.'' Murphy submitted his probation bill to the legislature in August 1934, but because of the "great opposition" among legislators, the measure was not approved until a year later. It authorized the probation of adult offenders convicted of minor offenses and the suspension of sentences imposed on minors. In accordance with Murphy's view that a probation system must be conducted in conformity with professional standards and that a psychological clinic was its "indispensable adjunct," the statute provided for the selection of probation officers on the basis of the merit system, and the Probation Office employed three psychiatrists and a psychologist. Although Murphy thought that the probation law, along with the indeterminate sentence statute, had "just about revolutionized the attitude of the people and the spirit of the law toward offenders," the Filipino leadership, less enamored of the probation concept than he was, repealed the measure in 1937.[56]

In practice, the Murphy program of judicial reform included the abolition of capital punishment. Rejecting all advice to the contrary, Murphy, long a foe of capital punishment, commuted every death sentence while he was governor-general. Quezon pledged himself to follow the Murphy precedent as president of the Commonwealth, and he remained true to his word, commuting all death sentences during the six years preceding the Japanese attack on the Philippines. Murphy's judicial reforms did not prove to be his "most lasting monument in the Islands," as the *Philippines Herald* had predicted, but what he had achieved was of some significance both for his own governor-generalship and for the Commonwealth that followed.[57]

Although the substantive law stemming from the Code Napoleon largely remained in effect during the period of American rule in the Philippines, the American Bill of Rights, minus the right of the people to bear arms and the right to trial by jury, was made effective in the islands by the Organic Acts of 1902 and 1916. No governor-general made a more determined effort than Murphy to ensure that the rights granted to Filipino citizens on paper were observed by public officials in practice. The government, he declared in his initial message to the legislature, should encourage a "spirit and zest for liberty" and should provide an example for the citizenry by avoiding illegal searches and seizures and unwarranted interference with free speech, a free press, and freedom of assembly.[58]

Responding to complaints of the pros that their right to assemble and speak freely was being curbed by the Quezon forces, Murphy issued an executive order in February 1934 stating that it was "indefensible for police officials to intervene and attempt ... to prevent or obstruct public assemblies and free associations of the people for political or other lawful purposes.'' The rights of public assembly and free speech, the order declared, ''may not be conditioned, limited, or circumscribed without danger to free institutions. While their exercise may properly be regulated as to time and place in the interest of public convenience and order, such orders must not discriminate against particular individuals or groups, nor diminish or curtail the rights themselves except as clearly defined and permitted by valid general statutes.''[59]

Murphy supplemented his free-speech order with a letter to the secretary of interior and labor—labor was a bureau in the Department of Industry and Labor until May 1934—advising him that when the exercise of free speech and freedom of assembly seemed likely to result in ''serious hostilities'' between groups, the policy of the government should be to provide added police protection rather than to restrict the exercise of constitutional rights. The governor-general further instructed that permits for meetings should be granted ''as a matter of right and without restriction on attendance or freedom of utterance.'' The government, Murphy said, might restrict freedom of speech and assembly ''only in extreme cases of grave public emergency.'' A grateful *Manila Tribune*, an OsRox organ, editorialized that Murphy was helping the Filipinos to ''grow up.'' Later, following the Sakdalista uprising, Murphy told his cabinet that he favored a ''liberal attitude'' in the government's dealings with the Sakdalistas. They should be permitted to hold meetings, he instructed, as long as their purpose was not to disturb the peace or to advance ''doctrines subversive of government.'' On one occasion Murphy specifically ordered that a permit be granted the Sakdalistas to hold a mass meeting in Manila, and he forbade discrimination against them in the distribution of relief.[60]

When Murphy learned that a dentist had been arrested for the illegal possession of firearms and then bound and gagged after he had attempted to prevent an illegal effort by the Constabulary to search his premises, he pardoned the dentist and condemned unlawful searches and seizures as a violation of the Philippine bill of rights. The governor-general had a legal aide investigate all search-and-seizure cases brought to Malacañan's attention. Murphy, the aide stated, ''wanted every poor man . . . to be safeguarded in the free exercise of his constitutional rights.'' In addition to speaking out against illegal searches and seizures, Murphy was the first American governor-general to issue an executive order banning the use of the third degree by the Constabulary and the police. The order was later embodied in statute form.[61]

The most troublesome civil liberties problem for Murphy as governor-general stemmed from the insular government's enforcement of the Sedition Act of 1907, which Baldwin characterized as "the toughest law of its sort in [the] American jurisdiction." The statute was the principal weapon used by the Constabulary to prosecute the leaders of the small Communist party that had been launched in the Philippines in 1930. The party itself was outlawed by the Philippine Supreme Court in a decision of October 1932, but its activities continued both underground and through legal organizations. Baldwin urged Murphy to secure the repeal or at least amendment of the sedition statute because its language was "so vague and all-inclusive," and the ACLU director also requested the governor-general to grant executive clemency to those already convicted of sedition, all of them apparently Communists, if their activities had not involved overt acts of violence.[62]

Murphy believed that a sedition law was required in the Philippines to enable the authorities to cope with groups such as the Moros that used armed force against the government. He nevertheless directed his legal aides to study the statute to ascertain whether its definition of what was seditious could be narrowed. Although Ed Kemp thought that the language was indeed "too broad and susceptible of use for political oppression," another Murphy staff man concluded that there was no evidence that the statute had been improperly used. Murphy, in the end, did not seek the law's modification, perhaps because he did not wish to challenge the political leadership of the Philippines on the issue. "He is not the whole show, as he well knows," Baldwin advised a correspondent regarding Murphy and the sedition issue.[63]

Murphy sought to oblige Baldwin regarding clemency for those convicted of sedition by granting conditional pardons in 1934 to twenty-seven prisoners who had been sentenced under the sedition law and by paroling three others. Most of the prisoners about whom the ACLU had expressed concern were released, but a few remained in jail because they refused to accept pardons obliging them to comply with the law and to refrain from seditious activities. Murphy also extended pardons to the Sakdalistas who had been convicted following the uprising of May 1935, except for those who had incited and led the revolt. In his last act as governor-general he extended conditional pardons to thirty political prisoners, some of them Communists but not including Crisanto Evangelista, the party's dominant figure. Although he claimed that he did not believe in imprisoning persons for their political views, Quezon privately complained that Murphy had "made a mistake" in freeing the Communists.[64]

The ACLU's national secretary and one of the organization's Philippine contacts agreed early in 1934 that it was not necessary to establish a Philippine branch of the civil liberties organization since Murphy was "quite alert" to what was required regarding civil liberties and could be depended upon to protect the Philippine people against encroachment on their rights. Although the ACLU was not completely satisfied with Murphy's civil liberties record as governor-general, it found more to praise than to criticize in his behavior; and Baldwin, as he informed one Filipino, continued to believe that Murphy was "a man of high integrity and . . . rare courage for . . . [one] so long in public life."[65]

II

In seeking to prepare the Philippine Islands for independence, Murphy sought to counter the potential threat posed to the stability of a future Philippine government by the presence in the islands of a large, unassimilated minority, the Moros. Of the 593,507 Moros in the Philippines, more than 236,000 lived in the Sulu archipelago; the remainder lived in six provinces in Mindanao, especially in Lanao and Cotabato. Spain, using Christian Filipinos as the "shock troops" of its armies, had been unable to establish its rule over the Moros or to spread Christianity among them, but the United States Army conquered and disarmed the Moros after a long struggle and gained their acquiescence in American rule. Civilian government replaced military government in Moroland in 1913, with the Department of Mindanao and Sulu serving as the supervisory administrative agency. The insular government abolished the department in 1920, replacing it with the Bureau of Non-Christian Tribes, which was lodged in the Department of the Interior. The official objective of the Philippine government regarding the Moros was their integration in a united Philippines, but the so-called " 'policy of attraction' " the Filipinos pursued in an effort to assimilate the Moros was a dismal failure. Filipino officials, who manned most government positions in Moroland and among whom, according to one local observer, there was "plenty of dead wood, false alarms and dumb bells," often abused their power, could not conceal their poor opinion of the people they governed, and failed altogether to gain their trust.[66]

Hayden, an authority on the subject, described the Moros as a "proud, ignorant, stubborn and highly courageous people." Whereas the Filipinos were Christians, the Moros were Moslems, and religion was for them "the fundamental, all-embracing force of life."

Distinctive in their religion and their cultural traits, the Moros were also distinctive in appearance since they filed their teeth to points and their consumption of betel-nut juice gave their lips a vermilion hue.[67]

The governing body of the individual Moro provinces typically consisted of an appointive governor and treasurer and a "third member," elected by the municipal officials of the province. The governors had always been Americans, the third member was normally a Moro, and the remaining officials were generally Christian Filipinos. The power of the governor in a Moro province was less than complete since the agencies of the insular government in his province were not subject to his control and since his authority was superimposed on a competing Moro system of authority. The 152,922 Moros in Lanao were thus loyal to their *datus* or headmen, about one hundred in number, and the 140,362 Moros in Cotabato gave their allegiance to a smaller number of "relatively powerful chiefs."[68]

The clash of authority systems was most evident and most troublesome in the group of 448 islands making up the Sulu archipelago, "the most highly developed" region in Moroland both politically and culturally. Here, since 1899, Americans and Filipinos had had to contend with Sultan Hadji Mohammed Jamalul Kiram II, scion of a dynasty that boasted a history of more than four hundred years, the head of the Mohammedan religion in Sulu and, theoretically but not actually, throughout Moroland, and a man who "spent much time and money in dissipations." Since the sultan, in Moro eyes, was the fount of political as well as religious authority and since the Moros did not make any sharp distinction between the religious and the secular, the delimitation of the sultan's role by the insular government proved to be a very vexing problem.

By the so-called Carpenter agreement of 1915, the sultan, who was already receiving a subsidy from the United States government, was recognized as the spiritual head of the Mohammedans in Sulu, and he, in turn, recognized United States sovereignty, including the jurisdiction of government courts in all civil and criminal cases "falling within the laws and orders of the Government." The interpretation of the agreement was in dispute from the moment of its adoption, the sultan alleging that, as head of the Mohammedan religion, he was, at the very least, entitled to decide all cases that were religious in nature, particularly disputes arising under the Agama, "the body of Mohammedan law governing marital relations in all their ramifications." Moros were under no obligation to take any cases to the Agama or ecclesiastical courts, but the sultan and his agents induced them to believe that even cases to which the penal code applied should be brought to the Agama courts, which thus became a " 'Government within a Government.' "

The interest in the Agama courts of the sultan and his entourage, "generally a grasping extortionate lot," seems primarily to have been the fines that the courts illegally collected (only duly organized courts of justice could legally collect fines), estimated in 1934 at P3,000 annually. Some of this money went to the sultan, some to his agents. There was nothing resembling due process in the Agama courts, and the *wakils* (religious judges) apparently imposed fines whether the accused party was guilty or not. The Agama courts, moreover, were legally unable to enforce their decisions; and when the guilty party ignored a court decision, the offended party sometimes resorted to violence, creating turmoil in the province.[69]

Sulu was plagued not only by the graft and corruption stemming from the Agama courts but also by cattle stealing, banditry, murder, and clashes between the Constabulary and disaffected Moros. It was into this troubled environment that James R. Fugate was plunged when he was appointed governor of Sulu province in 1928. Described by Hayden as "one of those rare men who are the natural rulers of primitive people," Fugate had served in the Philippines since 1899 as soldier, teacher, and then head of the Episcopalian school for boys in Jolo, the principal island of the Sulu group, and had in the process acquired a knowledge of Moro dialects and Moro customs. Basing his administration of Sulu province on his deep understanding of the inhabitants, he made "trust" in the Moros the "keynote" of his policy.

The most effective administrative technique employed by Fugate was to hold weekly meetings in each municipal district of Jolo at which the governor and other provincial officials virtually put the Agama courts out of business by applying Moro law and custom to the solution of such problems as had arisen in the district. Since crime decreased, the revenue increased, and peace and harmony prevailed while Fugate was Sulu's governor, Hayden described the Fugate regime in superlatives. The governor's policies, however, aroused the ire of powerful opponents who sought his ouster. The sultan and his entourage were antagonized by Fugate's curbing of the Agama courts; Filipino officials complained that he kowtowed to the Moros and convinced them that Christian Filipinos were hostile to them; the provincial Constabulary commander, Captain Leon Angeles, who believed that Moros could be "governed only by bullets and bayonets" and had "a deserved reputation as a killer" on the basis of his previous service in Lanao, was antagonized by Fugate's establishment of a municipal police force to maintain order; and resident Americans, whose vested interests Fugate challenged, thought that he did not understand that Moros were deceitful persons who could not be trusted. The governor had to leave for the United States in August 1931 to receive medical attention—he had suffered from indigestion since his youth and had been eating only one meal per day since 1905. When he was about to return to his post, in November 1932, his enemies persuaded an "uninformed" Theodore Roosevelt, Jr., to dismiss him.[70]

With Fugate out of the way and Arthur G. Spiller, a "weak" replacement serving as acting governor, the sultan and his niece Dayang Dayang Hadji Pindao, the power behind the throne, combined with Captain Angeles to undo what Fugate had achieved. Twenty-seven members of the Constabulary and seventy-five Moros were killed during the Spiller-Angeles regime, cattle stealing became "rampant" once again, the Agama courts flourished, and "chaos and terror reigned in Jolo."[71]

When Hayden first learned of Murphy's appointment as governor-general, he guessed that Murphy would be unwilling to face up to the Moro problem and would simply follow the wishes of the Filipino leadership in the matter. Hayden nevertheless "outlined the whole Moro problem" for Murphy, and when the new governor-general asked what he could do so as to be able to leave the Philippines with "a decent conscience" about the Moros, Hayden responded that Murphy could restore Fugate to his former post as governor of Sulu.[72]

Pending the working out of a suitable policy for the Moros, Murphy believed that law and order must be restored in Moroland so that life could go on "without the dangers of death and wounds and robbery at every turn." Murphy was convinced, however, that brute force was not the solution to the Moro problem. "It is foolish to presume," he declared, "that a mere display of force can reach to the bottom of a complex and vital situation which has in its background racial, social and religious elements."[73]

Realizing how well informed on the Moro question Hayden was, Murphy decided to add non-Christian affairs to the vice-governor's responsibilities. "This was putting a pretty sick baby on my doorstep," Hayden wrote a faculty colleague, "and the situation was made worse by the fact that the Baby's daddy is the Secretary of the Interior," whose department was not within Hayden's jurisdiction. The "Baby's daddy" had by that time forwarded to Murphy a communication from Teopisto Guingona, the head of the Bureau of Non-Christian Tribes, giving the bureau's view of the Moro problem.

"We have to train, educate and develop its [Sulu's] inhabitants," Guingona advised, *"moulding them to the type which we want,* in order to amalgamate them later with the rest of the nation." Although he believed that the insular government should follow the traditional policy of attraction, Guingona urged that the Moros be made to understand that this did not signify governmental approval of "abuses" and tolerance of crime. "Describing it graphically," he stated, "it might be said that in the management of the affairs of Moroland, the government should have sugar in one hand and a whip in the other." The "whip," as Guingona explained it, meant an increase in the size of the Constabulary force, the maintenance of a secret service unit in Moroland, and even the assignment of a bombing plane to the area. The "sugar" was to take the form of an increase in funds for Mindanao and Sulu so that the government could carry out a program of moral, social, political, and economic development in the region.[74]

Murphy was also receiving advice from other quarters as to how to deal with the Moro question,[75] but it was Hayden's advice, transmitted in the form of a memorandum toward the end of January 1934, that counted most with Murphy. There was no "solution" for the Moro problem, Hayden wrote, but improvement was possible. While the Moros would have to respect the authority of the government, the government, in turn, would have to respect the personal and property rights of the Moros and their distinctive religious and cultural institutions. Insofar as conditions permitted, Hayden thought, the Moros should be afforded equal access with Christians to government services in education and health. In the administration of these services, the government should adapt its procedures and personnel to local conditions, and Moros should be employed to the extent possible in communities where they predominated.

To coordinate insular services in Moroland and to concentrate authority in the provincial governors, Hayden recommended that the heads of the various insular services in Sulu, Lanao, and Cotobato be assigned and promoted only with the concurrence of the provincial governor. For Sulu, Hayden recommended the return of Fugate as governor, the transfer of Angeles, the appointment of Frederick W. Roth, a former schoolteacher and a businessman with a considerable experience in Mindanao, as deputy provincial governor-at-large, and additional changes in personnel. Finally, Hayden advised that the secretary of the interior be associated with whatever announcement Murphy made concerning Moro policy.

Since Hayden's advice was consonant with Murphy's desire to

proclaim a "New Deal" for the Moros, his belief in the need to Moroize government employment in Mindanao and Sulu, and his commitment to cultural pluralism, he accepted his vice-governor's recommendations virtually in their entirety. Murphy "sold" the Hayden plan to the secretary of the interior, thus securing Filipino support for "the 'new deal' in Moroland."[76]

About a month after receiving Hayden's memorandum, Murphy officially announced his Moro New Deal. He relieved Spiller as acting governor of Sulu and returned Fugate to the post. The sultan's niece was "not pleased," but for Fugate, who was something of a fanatic— a woman who knew him well described him as " 'half-God and Half-Devil!' "—the return to the Philippines was "the highest thing in life—the only life—all there is to life." Murphy appointed Roth to the new position of deputy provincial governor-at-large, replaced Angeles, and made most of the other personnel changes Hayden had recommended.[77]

An affirmative action program for Moros, to use today's terminology, was an essential part of Murphy's Moro New Deal. It had, indeed, long been government policy to employ non-Christians insofar as consistent with "a reasonable degree of efficiency." Since Murphy, however, became aware that the policy was not really being implemented and that educated Moros had become "discouraged" because they could not find suitable employment, he insisted on "a new and more vigorous representation" of Moros in the government service. As a test of what might be achieved, he asked Fugate to compile a list of local non-Christians in Sulu qualified by education or experience for service with the insular or provincial government and a list of the positions that they could satisfactorily fill. It was Murphy's intention, Hayden wrote Fugate, to compel the appointment of additional Moros to government jobs.

Roth, who took responsibility for the employment survey, went beyond his instructions and made himself, in effect, "a personnel and placement officer." He concluded that there was "much truth" to the allegation that Christians were being given jobs for which Moros were qualified. When a Filipino head of a government office complained that a Christian was more qualified for a particular position than a Moro applicant, Roth reminded him that that was precisely how American bureau chiefs had reacted when the issue was the employment of Filipinos in preference to Americans.

The pressure exerted from Manila—when the division superintendent of schools in Sulu proved reluctant to hire Moro teachers, he was replaced by a new superintendent who implemented the affirmative action policy—and the provincial governor's office had its effect in Sulu: in the first month after Roth completed the employment survey the number of Christian employees in Sulu decreased from 857 to 850, but the number of non-Christians employed rose from 718 to 891; whereas there were 73 Moro teachers in Sulu in 1933 (32 percent of the total), the number had increased to 144 by 1936 (46.4 percent of the total). In Lanao, the number of native employees increased from 194 in 1933 to 242 in 1935.[78]

The Moro New Deal promised the non-Christians "opportunities for development equal to those given the inhabitants of the other provinces through the public schools, the public health service, and all of the other agencies through which the government serves the people." Malacañan did not forget this pledge. Little had been done in Sulu before 1933 to make government services generally available, but the insular government now established a puericulture center in Jolo, and it assigned community public health nurses "to take health and social work into the homes of the people." The Moro provinces also received their fair share of insular funds for the construction of school buildings. The new buildings were required since the increase in the number of Moro teachers and the assignment of American teachers sympathetic to the Moro New Deal led to a substantial increase in Moro school attendance.[79]

If there were to be a New Deal for the Moros, Murphy asserted, "its foundation" had to be Moro "respect for law and order and unquestioned recognition of, and loyalty to," the Philippine government. As Fugate saw it, the task of reducing crime, upholding law and order, and keeping Sulu peaceful and progressive meant restraining the sultan, opposing "the slimy practices" of the Agama courts, and encouraging "progressive" elements among the Moro population. As the principal means of implementing his policies, Fugate held daily meetings in the districts of his province at which the governor and his aides attempted to persuade those present to help themselves "in all that enters into their daily lives . . . be it social, religious, or civic." "Their official lives," Fugate reported of himself and his colleagues, "is [*sic*] one well-nigh of travel, to carry 'government' in its simplest, most enlightened and just form to the people in the most remote parts and to the least intelligent." He sought at these meetings, which he characterized as "adult schools in citizenship and improved living," to "humanize" government for the Moros, relate it to their "controlling customs and practices," and build popular support for education, sanitation, law and order, and civil peace.

The results that the Fugate administration achieved were nothing short of remarkable: cattle stealing virtually ceased in Sulu; armed conflict between the Constabulary and the Moros came to an end, partly because Fugate once again placed reliance on the development of a local police force, while the Constabulary remained in the background; and Jolo was "transformed from a place of terror and chaos to one of relative security and order." Fugate's success demonstrated the correctness of Roth's appraisal that the way to bring law and order to Moroland was to treat the Moros fairly. The Moro, he believed, would not bow to force, which he did not fear, as long as he felt himself treated unjustly.[80]

The curbing of the sultan and his Agama courts proved to be the most troublesome problem of Fugate's governorship. Soon after assuming his post, Fugate instructed the deputy governors and the justices of the peace in Sulu that existing agreements defining and delimiting the sultan's powers must be observed. The sultan and his representatives were told that they could not try criminal cases, could impose fines only in certain religious cases " 'as purely indemnity and intended for and delivered to the parties involved,' " could not impose any " 'correctional punishments,' " could not solicit or receive contributions, and could exercise " 'religious power' " only over persons voluntarily submitting to their jurisdiction. The sultan, however, ignored these guidelines, and the jurisdictional conflict was exacerbated when plaintiffs who lost in the Agama courts took their cases to the government courts.[81]

The sultan, for his part, complained to Murphy that "certain government officials," contrary to existing agreements and the Moro New Deal, had been making "organized efforts to invade the powers and prerogatives of the Sultan as the Supreme Head of the Mohammedan Ecclesiastical Affairs" in Sulu by themselves attempting to dispose of religious cases. In a letter of October 17, 1934, Murphy, who had come to regard the sultan as lacking in "moral and mental qualifications" and had declined to reappoint him as a senator in 1934, reminded the sultan of his obligation not to infringe on the rights of civil authorities but pledged at the same time that "the powers and prerogatives" of the sultan as head of the Mohammedan religion would be respected.

Murphy's letter was enclosed with a letter to Fugate instructing him to confer with the sultan about his complaints. "No government official in Sulu," the letter to Fugate stated, "should take any action that might give the color of truth to charges that the religious powers of the Sultan or the special religion and customs of the Moro inhabitants are being improperly interfered with by the Philippine Government.'' Hayden was the real author of the letters to the sultan and Fugate, and his purpose, obviously, was to place the governor-general in an ''invulnerable position'' regarding his Moro policy. Since Hayden thought that the sultan would not ''submit to the loss of his Agama graft without a struggle'' and that his advisors would ''stop at nothing,'' he believed that the Murphy administration had to watch ''every step with care.'' As he later conceded, he should have asked the sultan to document his charges and should have given Fugate the opportunity to comment on the letter to the sultan before transmitting it.[82]

Hayden personally sealed and posted the letter to Fugate and the enclosed copy of the letter to the sultan, but the envelope was ''abstracted'' from the mails and did not reach Fugate. Not until almost three months later, after the accumulation of evidence that the sultan was ''stepping over the traces'' did Fugate and Roth see the correspondence. In the meantime, the sultan and his agents, misrepresenting Murphy's letter, were alleging that the governor-general had expressed his support for the sultan's rather than Fugate's interpretation of the proper role of the Agama courts. The ''incident,'' as Hayden noted, had ''to be entered upon the debit side of the column.'' Once Murphy's ''clear and unequivocal'' letter became known, however, the issue of the Agama courts was resolved, and the division of authority spelled out in the Carpenter agreement and the Murphy letter was largely observed during the remainder of Murphy's governor-generalship.[83]

Murphy's Moro policy had been oriented primarily toward Sulu, and Hayden concluded that it had been ''100 per cent successful.'' At the time the Commonwealth was established, Sulu, in Hayden's judgment, was ''more peaceful and better governed than it had ... been in its five centuries of tumultuous history.'' What the United States had accomplished there, he thought, was ''a part of our final chapter in the Islands of which we can be proud.''[84]

In Lanao, as in Sulu, the provincial governor at the beginning of the Commonwealth reported the ''growth of a more neighborly feeling between the Christians and non-Christians, a feeling of live and let live.'' If the Moro New Deal, however, was designed to ease Moro concern about their place in an independent Philippines, it had failed to attain its goal since the Moros viewed that prospect with alarm, much preferring the continuation of American rule. The Moro leaders of Lanao, complaining about the American grant of independence, thus wrote President Roosevelt regarding the Moros of

Mindanao and Sulu, "We are like a small cow that is still sucking, that if its mother abandon her, she will be without protector and will later be eaten by a more powerful animal."[85]

The Moros had reason to be concerned. Quezon, who had been in the United States when Murphy proclaimed his Moro New Deal, had later asked Murphy to dismiss Fugate and had said that the only language the Moros understood was the language of force. " 'When I take over this government,' " he declared, " 'the Constabulary will show them [the Moros] who is master.' " When he became president of the Commonwealth, Quezon, who disliked and distrusted the Moros, abolished the Bureau of Non-Christian Tribes, which the Moros saw as their "protector, . . . guide and adviser." Then, in an action that Murphy described as "something of a jar to me," the Filipino president transferred Fugate to Manila to serve as an advisor in the Department of the Interior and replaced him as governor of Sulu with Leon Angeles, who had commanded the Constabulary force in the Cabuyao massacre of the Sakdalistas and was hated by the Moros. The Commonwealth government could have done "nothing more sinister or more darkly portending tragedy," Hayden thought, and so it must have seemed to the Moros also.

Despite Murphy's and Hayden's fears, Fugate reported in 1938 that Quezon was attempting to implement "the entire [Murphy-Hayden Moro] policy," and there was, to be sure, a "high degree of Muslim participation in the political system" during the Common-wealth period. The Commonwealth government, however, seeking to promote the economic development of Mindanao and to encourage migration to the area of landless Christian Filipinos, thought of the Moros "largely in negative terms," ignored their concerns, and met their resistance to government policies with force. Although the Moros cooperated with Christian Filipinos who resisted the Japanese occupation during World War II, events of the postwar era proved that the Moros had been right to worry about their fate in an independent Philippines. As for their friend Fugate, allegedly the only American in Jolo who did not carry a gun, he was murdered in Upi, in Moroland, on December 14, 1938. His death, in a symbolic sense, marked the close of a hopeful interlude in the unhappy history of the Moros in the Philippines.[86]

The Murphy New Deal in the Philippines was extended not only to the Moros but also, to a much lesser extent, to the 213,701 pagan Igorots living in Mountain Province,[87] in northern Luzon. A student of the Igorots, Hayden thought that except for health services, which he characterized as "little more than farcical," conditions in the pagan region were "good, taken by and large." Hayden and Dunham sought to cope with the health problem by assigning four community public health nurses and two traveling clinics to Mountain Province to supplement the three hospitals in the area. This action, coupled with the construction of toilets in most of the cities, helped to improve health conditions among the Igorots. The Murphy administration found it difficult to cope with the conflict over land and water rights between the mining companies and the native people resulting from the gold rush in northern Luzon in 1933 and 1934, but the problem seems to have been largely resolved by the time the Commonwealth was established. As in Mindanao and Sulu, the Murphy administration favored the employment of more natives in the government service in the pagan provinces. The visible symbol of this policy was the selection of a native of Mountain Province to serve as deputy governor, the first time this had occurred.[88]

Although Murphy's policies regarding public finance, health and welfare, education, labor, justice, and the non-Christians had their impact on the Philippine Commonwealth, they were of less concern to the Filipinos as they anxiously contemplated independence than the presence in their midst of an unassimilated and cohesive Japanese minority, their ability to defend themselves against a foreign foe, and, above all else, the probable impact on their economy of the Tydings-McDuffie Act. These three matters occupied a good deal of Murphy's time as the last governor-general of the Philippines.

4

"Fear for the Future"

I

"I fear for the future," Manuel Quezon told Frank Murphy in January 1935. "Japan is the great peril to our Independence." Japan, Quezon warned, would seize the Philippines by military force "at the right time" and would seek economic ascendancy "at once." Quezon often told American officials what they wanted to hear, but he was on this occasion expressing a genuine concern of the Filipino leadership as Commonwealth status loomed.[1]

Slightly more than twenty thousand Japanese resided in the Philippines as of 1934, their number having increased from less than one thousand at the beginning of the century. Unlike the more numerous Chinese who came to the Philippines, the Japanese brought their wives and children with them, and there was little intermarriage between them and Filipinos. Most Japanese in the Philippines were agriculturists, fishermen, or artisans, but an increasing number of them entered retail trade when the Chinese in the Philippines, late in 1931, initiated a boycott of Japanese goods in response to the Japanese attack on Manchuria. By 1933 approximately 25 percent of the retail trade in the Philippines was in Japanese hands. Japanese residents occupied an even more conspicious place in the fishing industry: as of 1933, more than 60 percent of the licensed commercial fishing boats in the Philippines were Japanese-owned, 81 percent of the licensed fishermen were Japanese, and the Japanese were responsible for 79 percent of the fish caught in deep-sea waters.[2]

About two-thirds (13,745) of the Japanese in the Philippines in 1934 resided in the province of Davao in southeastern Mindanao. The first small group of Japanese had arrived in Davao in 1904 following the completion of the zigzag road leading to Baguio in northern Luzon for whose construction they had been brought in from Japan and Okinawa the year before. The growing of hemp (abaca) became the predominant activity of the Japanese in Davao; by the 1930s they were responsible for about 40–45 percent of all the hemp produced in the Philippines. The manner in which they acquired the land for the growing of hemp and for other purposes became a subject of intense controversy in the Philippines while Murphy was governor-general.

The Public Land Act of 1903 permitted an individual to purchase a maximum of 144 hectares (one hectare = 2.471 acres) of public land, and legally organized corporations could buy or lease 1,024 hectares. Japanese corporations acquired some land under this statute and additional land by purchase from private owners or by sublease from American, Spanish, or Filipino lessors. Since the Public Land Act of 1919 prohibited land acquisition by aliens and stipulated that a corporation could purchase or lease land only if 61 percent of its capital stock was owned by Filipinos or Americans, the Japanese acquired land after that date primarily by creating dummy corporations nominally owned by Filipinos, many of them lawyers, or by the so-called *pakiao* system, whereby a Japanese corporation or individual contracted with a nominal Filipino landowner or lessor to develop his land as a laborer and to retain 85–90 percent of the profits therefrom. What was nominally a labor contract was actually an illegal lease. As of February 1935 the Japanese owned or controlled 57,350 hectares of Davao land; they had purchased only 8,119 hectares and were leasing the remainder by one means or another. Although the total land area of the province was almost two million hectares, the Japanese held about two-thirds of the cultivated land and were responsible for 80 percent of the hemp, 50 percent of the copra, and all the lumber produced in the province. In addition to the eighty thousand indigenous non-Christians in the area, there were about 105,000 Christian Filipinos in Davao, about twelve thousand of whom were employed by the Japanese. Unlike the Japanese, the Filipinos lacked capital, organization, and leadership.

The Japanese government supervised the selection of immigrants for Davao and maintained close ties with Japanese organizations and individuals in the province. The self-contained Japanese community, with its "well-nigh perfect organization for the economic penetration and development of a new country," had aroused the concern of both Filipino and American officials even before the passage of the Tydings-McDuffie Act although, in the opinion of historian Grant K. Goodman, "no evidence whatever exists . . . that the Japanese colony was in any way a bridgehead for the ultimate seizure of the Philippines." The secretary of agriculture and natural resources recommended in 1930 that consideration be given to closing Davao as a port of entry into the Philippines, and early in 1932, following the Japanese attack on Manchuria, Acting Governor-General George Butte reserved large tracts of land in Davao for Filipino homesteaders and cancelled one hundred applications by Filipinos for shore leases on the Gulf of Davao because he believed that they were " 'acting for Japanese third parties.' " Japanese businessmen and consular officials and Filipinos who benefited from the status quo in Davao, such as *pakiao* landlords and Filipino attorneys, consistently opposed the demand that " 'something be done' " about the Japanese in Davao.[3]

As the inauguration of the Commonwealth approached, the Japanese began "an extensive campaign of . . . cultural penetration" designed "to bring the Philippines within the Japanese orbit." The American chargé d'affaires ad interim in Japan reported in September 1934 that Japan had displayed an "unusual interest" in the Philippines since the passage of the Independence Act, and he thought that this presaged "an intention to exercise a certain degree of tutelage over the Islands at some time in the future." The chargé made special note of a speech in Manila by the Japanese consul general in the Philippines, Hiroshi Kimura, who reportedly had recently changed from a "retiring, discreet Oriental diplomat" into "an aggressive and bold propagandist," in which he advised the Filipinos to cast their lot with the countries of Asia, not with the United States. A small number of Filipinos decided to do just that, but the Filipino leadership and, it would seem, the majority of informed Filipinos viewed Japan as a potential threat to the Philippines. They were concerned about Japanese political and economic behavior in the Far East, the influx into the Philippines of low-priced Japanese goods, and the "danger" posed by the "miniature Japan" in Davao. When the leaders of the insular legislature met with Murphy on January 21, 1935, they were "unanimous" in their belief that the "future safety and security" of the Philippines were "menaced" by the "martial tendency of Japan."[4]

Murphy shared the concern of the Philippine leadership regarding Japanese intentions. When he stopped in China en route to the United States at the end of January 1935, he listened sympathetically as the Chinese minister of finance, H. H. Kung, told him that Japan's ambition was "to rule the world." Moving on to Japan, Murphy informed the American ambassador, Joseph C. Grew, that the Filipinos were concerned about "the Japanese expansion and ascendancy program" in the Far East. Grew confirmed that "expansion and dreams of empire" were "widespread in Japan." In Washington, Murphy talked of "the menace of Japanese propaganda" in the Philippines, provided "alarming details" about Japanese subsidization of key Filipinos, and warned that Japan had embarked on a program of political and economic expansion in eastern Asia. He thought that the possession of the Philippines, both for economic and strategic reasons, was a Japanese objective, and he advised that the United States must frustrate the Japanese design.[5]

Privately, Murphy did not see the issue of Japan versus the Philippines in simple black-and-white terms. He thought that "fundamental racial ties, Anglo-Saxon and Nordic conceit, and historical exploitation" of the region, along with "the superior prestige, power and progressive leadership" of Japan, were bringing the people of Asia together for "mutual security" despite differences among them. He thought that Americans were extraordinarily naive about the Far East and, "largely ... because of vanity," were disposed "to ignore any current excepting the ones drawing people" to them. He was impressed with "the energy of character, the discipline, capacity to sacrifice, [the] enterprise and above all the simplicity of life among the Japanese," but he nevertheless believed that his own countrymen had "built a better society" that they must "keep ... secure from greed, luxury, pleasure-loving softness and centralization of wealth."[6]

The belligerent behavior of the crew of a Japanese fishing vessel, the *Haiun Maru*, more than any other single event, "aroused Filipino apprehension regarding Japanese activities" while Murphy was governor-general. The *Haiun Maru* was a fifty-foot power fishing boat, with a crew of twenty-three, that had been operating off Balabac, at the southern end of Palawan. Members of the crew came ashore on September 11, 1934, and allegedly stole three hundred coconuts. A patrol unit consisting of three Constabulary officers and a sergeant of the local police boarded the boat to investigate the complaint, but the crew attacked them with hatchets, robbed them, and threw them overboard. They reached shore by clinging to a floating log while the *Haiun Maru* sailed off to Formosa. The court of first instance in Palawan issued a warrant for the arrest of the crew members, and the prosecuting attorney, responding to "intense public concern," requested Murphy to seek their extradition. The secretary of justice, Murphy informed Washington, regarded what had occurred as so "serious" an affront to the Philippines and the United States and as so endangering the territorial integrity of the Philippines that he believed it "imperative" that the case be tried in the Philippines.

In view of the transitional status of the Philippines, the State Department thought that the department, rather than the governor-general, should initiate the request for extradition, but in the end it was Murphy, seeking to avoid delay, who requested Grew to seek the extradition of the captain and the crew. The Japanese government was not required by treaty to comply with this request, and it chose not to do so, a foreign office spokesman professing his government's inability " 'to understand why certain newspapers in the Philippines' " were " 'making a sensation of a small affair.' " The crew members were eventually tried in Formosa, where a Takao court imposed a two-year sentence on the captain, one-year sentences on the chief engineer and the boatswain, and six-month suspended sentences on six crew members. On appeal, the captain's sentence was reduced to one and one-half years, and the one-year sentences were suspended.[7]

Although the *Haiun Maru* affair, as Hayden later wrote, had "a profound effect" on the Philippines,[8] it was the insular government's efforts to resolve the troublesome problem of illegal Japanese landholdings in Davao that posed the greatest threat to Philippine-Japanese relations while Murphy was governor-general. The initiative in dealing with the matter was taken by Eulogio Rodriguez, the secretary of agriculture and commerce, but with Murphy's knowledge and approval. In a memorandum of December 12, 1934, Rodriguez informed Murphy that he was gathering data on violations of Philippine land laws by the Japanese in Davao, that there were "constant agitations" in the press for an investigation, and that he believed "a definite policy" should be established "to guide this Department in this delicate matter." If the Japanese had acquired their lands legally, agitation should cease, but if they had not, Rodriguez asserted, "I would suggest that the full force of the law be brought to bear upon such violations." He believed that action should be taken "immediately," before the Commonwealth government was inaugurated, since the Philippines might not "be able, as a nation, to enforce . . . [its] demands."[9]

On January 7, 1935, Rodriguez sent a six-man committee of investigation to Davao under the chairmanship of Alfredo Fajardo of the Bureau of Lands. When Rodriguez himself decided at the end of the month to go to Davao, he asked Hayden—Murphy was then en route to the United States—whether a member of the governor-general's staff should accompany the secretary. Hayden replied in the negative on the grounds that the governor-general's office did "not want to be mixed up in that question." The governor-general's office, however, was already "mixed up" in the affair since Murphy had "personally approved" the trip, and, as Hayden had observed at a cabinet meeting, the investigation was "for the Executive."[10]

On the basis of Fajardo's report and his own investigation, Rodriguez informed Hayden on February 15 that the Japanese were occupying twenty-nine thousand hectares in Davao that they had illegally sublet from Filipinos or Americans. Hayden told Rodriguez that, quite apart from the issue of legality, it was essential to consider "the international significance of this thing" and that nothing should therefore be done without consulting Washington. Even though the Japanese leases could be cancelled, Hayden advised that consideration be given to the fact that the leases had continued for many years without protest from the insular government and that the Japanese had made improvements on the land with the "acquiescence" of American and Filipino officials.[11]

Before leaving for Davao, Rodriguez had assured Kimura that the purpose of the trip was to remove an obstacle to good relations between Japan and the Philippines. By gathering the facts, Rodriguez said, he hoped to lessen Filipino apprehension regarding Davao, and he asserted that it would do more harm than good to cancel illegal Japanese leases. The report that Rodriguez submitted, however, was hardly what the Japanese had been led to expect. He noted that Japan controlled "the whole situation" in the province and that the illegal leases might endanger the territorial integrity of the Philippines. He recommended the temporary suspension of action on all public land grants in Davao and several other provinces, firmer control over the issuance of pasture permits since Filipinos were allegedly using these permits to acquire large tracts of land that they then turned over to the Japanese, subdivision of public lands in Davao and other provinces into small parcels that would be available only to qualified applicants, cancellation of leases and rejection of applications for land of Filipino government officials who had illegally leased or subleased land to the Japanese, cancellation of all other illegal leases or subleases, nonrenewal of leases illegally held by aliens before these leases expired, and the future checking of all notarized land contracts to which one party was an alien.

Rodriguez stated that he would proceed to implement his recommendations, as he was legally entitled to do, unless Murphy advised him to the contrary. Actually, only the proposal to cancel illegal leases raised issues of importance, and Rodriguez, for the moment anyhow, would have been content to receive authorization to proceed only against leases illegally sublet by Filipino officials. Quezon, who had learned of Rodriguez's trip to Davao only after Murphy had approved it, agreed that this was the way to begin if only for "moral and political effect" in the Philippines. Although he told the Japanese vice-consul in Davao that he was "not . . . pleased" that the trip had been undertaken, he was nevertheless impressed by the "extensive publicity" Rodriguez's action had received and the "editorial demand" for prompt action.[12]

Rodriguez presented an oral summary of his report at a cabinet meeting on February 20. After discussing the report from "all angles," the cabinet decided to cable the substance of the document to Murphy so that he could consult about the matter in Washington. Rodriguez, in the meantime, was to make "a thorough study of the legal questions involved." Continuing to worry about the international implications of any strong Filipino action in Davao, Hayden wrote Murphy that the cancellation of the illegal leases would leave the Philippines with a dispossessed Japanese population, and he wondered what the Filipinos proposed to do about that. If the Japanese used force to resist cancellation, as was being threatened, and were the Constabulary unable to deal with the situation, would the United States send in the army and navy, and would the American people support a war over a few thousand hectares of land in Davao? Even if war did not result from the cancellation, Hayden wondered, would not the action engender a Japanese desire for revenge that might be satisfied after the United States left the Philippines? Did not an independent Philippine government, he asked, need Japanese friendship more than it needed to "punish" Filipino officials and others guilty of illegally subleasing land? "A far simpler solution" than cancellation, Hayden believed, would be to legalize existing subleases and to prohibit such subleases in the future. Hayden did think, however, that the local situation required that Rodriguez's other recommendations, which were "wholly unobjectionable," be approved. After discussing the matter with the chief of the Bureau of Insular Affairs, Murphy concurred.[13]

The approved Rodriguez proposals were put into effect in March and April. In Washington in the meantime, Murphy, ignoring his own role in the matter, was saying that the Davao affair had " 'been made too much a matter of excitement.' " Characterizing cancellation as "a legal problem" rather than "an international question," Murphy urged that the issue be settled in the courts and that it be treated as a matter involving the protection of the "public patrimony" rather than as a "Japanese problem." This was the position agreed upon in Washington before the governor-general returned to Manila.[14]

When Murphy returned to the Philippines, Rodriguez secured his consent to cancel or reject the "leases or other applications" of government officials who had illegally leased or subleased their holdings. Following this, he was authorized to proceed against the illegal leases or subleases of former government officials and wives of government officials and, last of all, against persons who had leased or subleased land to third parties without the consent of the secretary of agriculture and commerce. The government, Rodriguez asserted, was "duty bound to enforce the law no matter whether the violator be a Filipino, an American, or a foreigner"; but for the time being Rodriguez was to proceed only against Filipino officials.[15]

The insular government declared the *pakiao* system illegal on June 24, and it had cancelled ninety-eight leases by the middle of September but without dispossessing the Japanese occupants of the land. The Japanese in Davao became "exceedingly excited" about these developments, and the Japanese government quietly informed Rodriguez that it was "very much concerned" about the situation, warning that the manner in which the problem was disposed of would have "great importance" for future relations between Japan and the Philippines. Both Murphy and Rodriguez let it be known that the cancellations were directed against Filipinos who had broken the law and were not intended to "punish" third parties. It is likely—at least so the Japanese consul general in the Philippines thought—that the cancellations were designed to curry popular favor in advance of the September 17 elections. In any event, Rodriguez assured the consul general just before the elections that the government would cease its "coercive" actions, and he soon issued orders to that effect.

Despite press reports as Commonwealth inauguration day loomed that two-thirds of the illegal Davao leases had been cancelled, nothing had really changed, Rodriguez stating that he could not initiate ejection proceedings until he received a signal from " 'top-side.' " His reference was to Quezon and Murphy, and neither wished to take any action that would disturb Japanese-American or Japanese-Philippine relations. Also, when General Creed F. Cox, the chief of the Bureau of Insular Affairs, was in the Philippines for the inauguration of the Commonwealth, he advised Rodriguez and other government officials that insofar as land was illegally held in Davao, the remedy should be sought in the courts. "Otherwise," Cox warned, "a serious, and even dangerous political situation might be created that might prove very detrimental to Philippine interests."[16]

Weeks before he became president of the Philippines on November 15, Quezon, who thought that his countrymen were more troubled about the Japanese invasion of the Philippine fisheries than about Davao, privately reassured the Japanese government concerning his intentions with regard to the province. Although he told the consul general that he was reluctant to intervene in the situation before he became president, particularly if Rodriguez had been acting on Murphy's orders, he made it evident that once he assumed the presidency, he would "keep ... [Japanese] interests in mind" and would stop the implementation of Rodriguez's orders. Soon after his inauguration, Quezon secretly ordered Rodriguez to take no administrative action regarding Davao, and a member of the legislature known to be close to Quezon introduced a bill legalizing all Davao leases.[17]

In a conversation with Murphy on December 26, 1935, Quezon remarked that prominent Americans had urged him to take "drastic action" regarding Davao as evidence of his pro-Americanism. Murphy advised Quezon to prevent the further leasing of land to the Japanese in Davao—Quezon characterized Filipinos who had illegally sublet land as *"traitors"*—and to proceed against existing leases in the courts but to refrain from evictions or "violent measures" if the matter could be handled by negotiation or other means. Murphy also advised that the Philippine government should "fully recognize" Japanese "equitable rights" in the illegally leased land. At Murphy's behest, Quezon agreed to take no action regarding Davao before first consulting with the high commissioner and Washington.[18]

Having taken personal charge of the Davao problem, Quezon visited the province in April 1936 to make his own appraisal of the situation. Upon his return to Manila, he sought to use the issue as a weapon to extract a promise from the United States to grant the Philippines postindependence trade concessions. In a letter to Murphy, Quezon, who told the Japanese one thing and the Americans another, stated that any recommendation about Davao that he might make to the National Assembly depended on American policy regarding the Philippines. If the United States intended to cut its ties with the Philippines after independence, he would seek an arrangement with Japan whereby landholders in Davao could remain on the land that they had leased but with the understanding that the Japanese would not seek to acquire any additional land. He would also adopt a policy of cooperation with Japan for the economic development of the Philippines. There was, to be sure, some risk in this policy, he said, but it was the only course the Philippines could follow that would not antagonize Japan and provide her with an excuse to convert the Philippines into another Manchuria. This would mean, he warned, "the entire elimination of American participation in the trade and commerce as well as in the development of the natural resources of the Philippine Islands."

Quezon wrote that he preferred a policy of economic cooperation with the United States since he knew that Americans could be granted special economic privileges without endangering Philippine liberties or threatening the Philippine economy. The United States,

however, would have to commit itself to a special economic relationship with the Philippines if it wished to share in Philippine economic
development. In that event, the Davao situation could be settled
strictly in accordance with the law, although Japanese leaseholders
might be permitted to remain on the land they occupied until their
leases expired. "We have to decide now and not leave it to chance,"
Quezon melodramatically stated, "whether we are to find our partnership with America or with Japan—the only two alternatives left to
us in view of our past history and our geographical position. Our
choice is America, but if America is unwilling to be our partner, we
have to go to Japan under the best conditions that Filipino statesmanship can evolve." Quezon asked Murphy to present this alternative to
Roosevelt and the State Department. If Roosevelt were willing to
recommend that Congress approve a trade arrangement between the
United States and the Philippines that would continue after independence and if he agreed that the United States would occupy
certain portions of the Philippines as naval reservations, Quezon
would not make any specific proposals regarding Davao at the next
session of the Commonwealth legislature but would simply provide it
with a confidential report on the province and an outline of his
thoughts.[19]

Quezon, of course, was engaging in diplomatic blackmail, but his
tactic could have been effective only if the United States were determined to secure the cancellation of the illegal Davao leases even at
the cost of jeopardizing Japanese-American relations. Quezon, however, knew that this was not in accord with Murphy's policy, and
Murphy's policy was in this instance United States policy.[20] As long as
the United States remained the sovereign power in the Philippines,
moreover, it was not likely that Quezon could carry out his threat to
marry the Philippines to Japan, and Quezon knew this as well as
Murphy.

A few days after receiving Quezon's letter, Murphy told the
Japanese consul general that the United States wanted to avoid any
dispute over Davao. He asserted that Japanese contractual rights in
the province should be respected and that it might be well to renew
expiring leases if conditions were appropriate. It is likely that Murphy, in essence, said the same thing to Quezon in response to his
letter, telling him, in effect, "to find a way to deal with the Davao
situation that . . . [would] protect . . . [Philippine] interests and
give neither undue advantage nor undue offense to the Japanese."
When Quezon addressed the National Assembly in June, he minimized the significance of the issue, stating " 'There is nothing in the

so-called Davao problem that should cause serious concern.' '' His "solution" for the possible danger posed to the Philippines by the strong and cohesive Japanese colony to whose "full protection" Japan seemed committed was to spur the development of the remainder of Mindanao by the Filipinos and to confine the Japanese to the limited space they then occupied by preventing any further acquisition of public land by foreigners. Quezon and Murphy, even though the latter was telling Washington that the Japanese position in Davao constituted "a potential menace to the security of Philippine authority" after independence, were determined not to provoke Japan over Davao. The policy of nonconfrontation that they adopted continued without change until the Japanese attacked the Philippines. Indeed, shortly before that attack, the Commonwealth government agreed with Japan to accept the status quo in Davao until independence made direct, bilateral negotiations possible, and Japan promised to check any further illegal land acquisitions.[21]

II

The American and Filipino concern about Japanese intentions regarding the Philippines was interrelated with the more general question of planning for the defense of the Philippines both during the Commonwealth period, when the United States would continue to be the sovereign power, and after independence. In an analysis of April 1933 General Stanley D. Embick, the commander of the Harbor Defenses of Manila and Subic Bays, an expert on grand strategy, and "the foremost military advocate" of "a limited [American] defense perimeter," dissented sharply from the thinking behind War Plan Orange, which called for American retention of Manila Bay in the event of war with Japan. Characterizing the Philippines as "a military liability of a constantly increasing gravity," he criticized the possible implementation of War Plan Orange as "literally an act of madness" and called for the neutralization of the Philippines and the withdrawal from the islands of the American military garrison and the naval shore establishment. Major General E. E. Booth, the commanding general of the Philippine Department, as the American army garrison in the islands was known, concurred in this appraisal and so informed Washington, but the War Department rejected the recommendation.[22]

When Murphy became governor-general, the Philippine Department consisted of about eleven thousand officers and men, of whom more than six thousand were enrolled in the Philippine Scouts, a United States Army unit made up primarily of Filipino enlisted men.

The fortifications and military defenses in the Philippines had not been improved for many years and, like the armed forces in the islands, were altogether inadequate to fulfill the role assigned to local defenses by War Plan Orange, as the new Philippine Department commander, General Frank Parker, and the commander of the Asiatic fleet advised Washington in a joint note in March 1934.

In July 1934 the adjutant general of the army asked Parker to submit recommendations concerning the American military position in the Philippines during the approaching Commonwealth period. After consulting with Murphy and his staff, Parker, with Murphy concurring, replied that the Philippines after independence would be "practically indefensible by the Philippine government against the aggression of a strong foreign power." He therefore advised that the Commonwealth armed forces be limited to what was required to maintain "internal order only." Assuming that the responsibility of defending the Commonwealth against a foreign foe would rest with the United States, Parker also recommended an increase of United States forces in the Philippines during the Commonwealth period and their "rapid employment" in the event of an emergency. In November the War Plans Division of the army, then headed by Embick, went beyond Parker and Murphy and the terms of the Tydings-McDuffie Act and urged the withdrawal of United States troops from the Philippines *during* the Commonwealth period. Although it had already indicated that the Philippine base would not be strengthened either in men or materiel, the War Department disapproved this recommendation. The official United States position at the time has been accurately described as one of "no improvements, no reinforcements, no withdrawals."[23]

Although the Filipinos had no army of their own, the Philippine Constabulary, which had been organized as a national police force in 1901, was "semi-military in character" in both its training and organization. It was this force that Parker and Murphy recommended should be augmented to serve as the agency to maintain internal order during the Commonwealth period. When Murphy became governor-general, the strength of the Constabulary was slightly less than 5,500 officers and men, its ranks having been depleted in the preceding years. It lacked "proper leaders," political influence rather than merit often determined assignments and promotions, the stability of its pension and retirement funds was in doubt, its efficiency left a good deal to be desired, and morale, not surprisingly under the circumstances, was "at a low ebb."[24]

In a letter to the secretary of interior and labor in March 1934

Murphy called for the immediate "reformation and rehabilitation" of the Constabulary to make it a body of "high morale and discipline." He stipulated that henceforth promotion in the lower ranks was to be on the basis of seniority; promotions and transfers in the higher grades were to be based solely on merit and the needs of the service and were to be under the exclusive control of the chief of the Constabulary; the effort by any outsider to advance the status of a member of the force would be charged as a "demerit" against that individual; the Constabulary was to be relieved of all nonpolice and nonmilitary duties; quarters and equipment were to be renovated; retirement and pension funds were to be placed on a sound basis; and there was to be a gradual increase in personnel. Rejecting the advice of his military aide not to appoint a Filipino to head the Constabulary since it would mean jumping him over whites, Murphy, soon after announcing his Constabulary reforms, appointed Lieutenant Colonel Basilio J. Valdes as commanding officer of the Constabulary, only the second time a Filipino had headed the force. "You have been a real god-send to the Philippines in general and the local constabulary in particular," a group of admiring Constabulary officers wrote Murphy late in June. "If we could only do so publicly, we will be more than willing to kiss your feet as a token of our profound gratefulness."[25]

By the time the Commonwealth was inaugurated the Constabulary had been enlarged to a force of 549 officers and 8,512 men, and its efficiency had noticeably increased.[26] Quezon, however, had decided that the Commonwealth government should not limit its military capability to a police force adequate only to maintain law and order, as Murphy and Parker had advised, but should rather create an army that could defend the islands against aggression. Only a veto by Murphy had prevented the insular government from taking the first step late in 1934 to create an independent defense force in addition to the Constabulary. The vetoed measure provided for a Bureau of National Defense, the establishment of "the different branches of military service" that might be necessary to defend the Philippines, the creation of a reserve corps, and "military and citizenship training" for all schoolchildren. A select number of Filipinos were to be sent for training to military and naval academies and the schools of aviation in the United States and elsewhere, and the United States government was to be requested to detail army and navy officers and men to serve as instructors in Philippine schools. The statute appropriated slightly more than P2.3 million for its implementation during the next four years.[27]

The Bureau of National Defense bill was a badly thought-out measure that not only aroused the opposition of school authorities but was inconsistent with the Murphy-Parker judgment concerning the defensibility of the Philippines. In a well-reasoned veto message, Murphy pointed out that the measure might be inconsistent with the provisions of the Tydings-McDuffie Act regarding neutralization of the Philippines, might impair the educational system of the islands, confused citizenship training and military training, and imposed too heavy a financial burden on the Commonwealth.[28]

Murphy was concerned about the role of the airplane in the defense of the Philippines throughout his tenure in the islands. Even before he left the United States for Manila, he had indicated to Bureau of Insular Affairs officials that he sympathized with the proposition that franchises to operate aircraft in the Philippines deemed " 'inexpedient' " from the point of view of defense should not be granted pending a review in Washington. Murphy was advised by the War Department that the defense problem in the Philippines would be simplified if airline franchises were granted only to companies owned and operated by Americans or Filipinos.[29]

When Murphy arrived in the Philippines, he discovered that the field of civil aviation had been "practically untouched." Only ten civilian aircraft were operating in the islands, and the Philippines had no trained pilots, few airplane mechanics, and no radio weather broadcasts. Two commercial companies serviced the islands, the Philippine Aerial Taxi Company, which flew mail and passengers between Manila and Baguio, and the Iloilo-Negros Air Express Company, which maintained air service between Manila and Iloilo and between Iloilo and several other points. The latter company had attempted to secure a franchise for the entire Philippines. When it failed to do so, it persuaded the legislature shortly before Murphy became governor-general to pass Act 4033, which provided that no air public carrier could operate within the Philippines without having secured a franchise by December 9, 1933. Since the company enjoyed "very strong political support," the assumption was that the legislature would in the end grant it a monopoly over all Philippine air transportation, except for the Manila-Baguio run, already serviced by the Philippine Aerial Taxi Company.

Believing that Act 4033 would limit the number of aircraft operators in the Philippines, Murphy regarded the measure both as "prejudicial" to United States interests from a defense standpoint and "highly detrimental" to the development of air commerce in the Philippines. The measure also posed a threat to the entry of Pan

American into the Philippines, which both the War Department and the Department of Commerce were anxious to secure. Having urged Pan American in May 1933 to "take whatever steps ... seem to be practicable to operate in and out of as well as within the Philippines," the chief of the Aeronautics Trade Division of the Department of Commerce had informed the company, "We are anxious to help Pan American Airways in any way possible."[30]

Following the advice of his technical advisor for aeronautics, Captain R. L. Maughan, Murphy, in his first message to the legislature, urged that Act 4033 be amended to vest exclusive control over the airplane business in an executive agency. He also recommended that the insular and provincial governments cooperate in the building of airports, landing fields, and other aviation facilities, the law be amended to permit the use of gasoline-fund money for the construction and maintenance of landing fields, and consideration be given to the formation of a governmental unit, perhaps within the Constabulary, to serve as the "nucleus for a national air service."[31] Rebuffing Murphy's efforts to have Act 4033 amended and to have the American Air Commerce Act extended to the Philippines so that United States international lines could operate there, the insular legislature, spurred on by "a powerful lobby," granted twenty-five year franchises in November 1933 to the Iloilo-Negros Air Express Company and the Philippine Aerial Taxi Company, gave them prior rights to operate in territory not covered by their franchises, in effect forbade competition with them as long as they provided satisfactory service, and required that 75 percent of their stock be owned by Filipinos or Americans *resident in the Philippines*. The legislature, at the same time, refused to grant permission to Pan American to fly from Hongkong to Manila and interior points in the Philippines largely because this concession was strongly opposed by the Iloilo company, which feared the competition on local runs. Secretary of War Dern advised Murphy to veto the measure, which was what he proposed to do in any event.[32]

In his veto message, Murphy criticized the monopolistic character of the two franchises, asserting that the success of the American policy of "freedom of the air" made it inadvisable for the Philippines to pursue a contrary policy. He contended that the stock-ownership provisions of the legislation were of "questionable constitutionality" and were, in any event, "impolitic" at a time when the United States absorbed 80 percent of Philippine exports. He also called attention to the War Department's opposition to the granting of long-term franchises that "might give rise to conditions inexpedient from the standpoint of national defense.'' He sought to assure the legislature that there was no truth to the rumor that he was vetoing the bill because of its "failure to grant franchises to other applicants," but it is doubtful that many lawmakers believed him.

Although Murphy continued to press the legislature to alter its air commerce policy, Act 4033 remained in effect, and the lawmakers appeared determined to retain their power to grant franchises and to protect the two favored local companies from the competition of American or foreign air lines. This troubled Murphy and the War Department because of the implications for national defense. It was also of concern to the Commerce and State Departments since they regarded the Philippines as "a strategic air base" for international airline operations and thought that authorization for foreign airlines to operate into and through the Philippines would be "an effective means" to secure privileges for Americans to operate in other parts of Asia and thus to expand American foreign trade.[33]

The defense and commercial interests of the United States in the development of aviation in the Philippines were brought into focus in August 1934 when the Royal Netherlands Aviation Company (KNILM) sought an air connection between the Netherlands East Indies (NEI) and the Philippines. When Washington referred the proposal to Murphy for an opinion, he replied that under existing conditions, with the Iloilo line operating at a loss, the Dutch line would "dominate" Philippine aviation if permitted to operate locally. He noted that this could be prevented "under present arrangements" but that the future Commonwealth government would be able to grant the franchise unless this could be forestalled by "moral pressure" or by amending the Tydings-McDuffie Act to vest control over foreign air lines operating in the Philippines in the United States government, an action regarded as unlikely in Washington. Agreeing with Murphy, the secretary of war advised the State Department to inform the Dutch company that its request could not be granted.[34]

Shortly thereafter Juan T. Trippe of Pan American, which was seeking a Manila-Netherlands East Indies connection, urgently requested the State Department to declare that the United States government would favorably consider a KNILM application to maintain air service between the NEI and Manila via Zamboanga. Trippe's request, initiated because it was "customary" to inaugurate international air service across the territory of other powers on the basis of "strict reciprocity," set off a prolonged controversy between the Departments of State and Commerce on one side and the War and Navy Departments on the other.

Murphy at his desk in Malacañan

Malacañan Palace

Entertaining at
Malacañan. Right to
left: Frank Murphy,
Marguerite Murphy,
Manuel Quezon,
Aurora Quezon

Murphy and Quezon

Left to right: Quezon, Murphy, Sergio Osmeña

Murphy and riding companions. Front row, left to right: Joseph R. Hayden, Murphy,
General Frank Parker

Murphy and his American staff. First row, left to right: Captain W. H. Allen, Edward G. Kemp, Joseph Ralston Hayden, Murphy, Eleanor Bumgardner, Colonel Louis J. Van Schaick, William Teahan. Second row, left to right: Charles W. Franks, Richard E. Ely, Lt. Comdr. J. E. Kiernan, Colonel Frederick W. Manley, Major J. MacDowal, Major Abraham Garfinkel, E. D. Hester. Third row, left to right: Major H. Prosser, Norman H. Hill, J. Weldon Jones, H. C. Anderson, Major George C. Dunham, Elisha Lee.

Roosevelt approves the Philippine constitution, March 23, 1935. Seated, left to right: George Dern, Roosevelt, Quezon. Cordell Hull is to Murphy's left.

Inauguration of the Philippine Commonwealth, November 15, 1935. Dern is at the podium. John Nance Garner, Murphy, and Quezon are seated behind him.

Council of State banquet for Murphy. Murphy is flanked on his left by Quintin Paredes and on his right by Douglas MacArthur and Francis Burton Harrison.

Murphy and Ann Parker. Copyright by Harris and Ewing.

Charlie Chaplin and Murphy aboard the S.S. *Coolidge*, June 4, 1936.

The State and Commerce Departments contended that rejection of the Dutch company's request would limit the extension of American air transport in the international sphere to the detriment of American foreign trade. The War Department, supported by the Navy Department, recognized that approval of the Pan American request would result in "undeniable advantages" for the company and for air transport in general, but it was more concerned about the "deleterious effect" on national defense if the entry of a foreign air line into the Philippines served as a precedent for permitting foreign lines to enter Hawaii and the Canal Zone. ". . . with respect to our outlying possessions, at which we are, under existing limitations, unable to maintain the forces essential to defense, and which would be difficult to reinforce on [the] outbreak of war," Dern wrote Secretary of State Cordell Hull, "it is felt that the interest of commercial companies must yield to those of national defense." The War Department position was that the interests of the United States and the Philippines would be best served if only American lines were allowed to enter the Philippines, if they were permitted to handle local traffic, and if no company was permitted to establish an aviation monopoly in the islands. Murphy and the chief of the Bureau of Insular Affairs had a good deal of sympathy for the State Department position despite their concern for national defense. The hard-liners in the War Department prevailed, however, and the interests of national defense, as they conceived it, triumphed over the interests of foreign commerce as conceived by Pan American, the Department of State, and the Department of Commerce.[35]

After a good deal of deliberation, the Interdepartmental Committee on Civil International Aviation decided in May 1935 to abandon the concept of reciprocity and to have Pan American deal directly with the Philippine legislature to obtain permission to fly to the Philippines. The committee, which believed that "the weight of this Government should be placed behind the Pan American airways," agreed that Murphy should be instructed to use his "good offices in every practicable way" to insure that the franchise was granted. The Department of Commerce representative on the committee remarked that if there had been an appreciation of the importance of aviation at an earlier time, it "would have been a good argument to kill independence."

Murphy, on July 5, requested the insular legislature to grant Pan American a franchise to maintain air service between the Philippines and the United States and any other country. Responding to the governor-general's prodding, the legislature granted Pan American a twenty-five year franchise to operate air transport service to and from the Philippines. The legislature also granted franchises of similar duration to the two local companies. Japan made "a sort of diplomatic complaint" about the Pan American concession, contending that it could be viewed as "military preparations in the guise of civilian enterprise."[36]

It had been assumed both in Washington and Manila that the Commonwealth government would have exclusive control over aviation within and into the Philippines. The Interdepartmental Committee, however, decided otherwise in 1936, and the Department of Justice, to which the issue was referred, agreed that permission to authorize *foreign* airlines to enter the Philippines rested with the United States government under the Tydings-McDuffie Act as an aspect of foreign affairs.[37]

When toward the end of 1935 the Dutch once again sought to establish a Philippine air connection, the War Department initially opposed the concession, as it had in the past, but it reversed itself at the end of May 1936. It did so not only because Pan American's trans-Pacific air service was by then "an established fact" but also because the department had concluded that the Dutch request could be granted without jeopardizing national defense provided Pan American received reciprocal rights to operate in the NEI and provided the concession was not construed as a precedent insofar as other United States territories and possessions were concerned. The Interdepartmental Committee decided that under these circumstances the United States should approve the Dutch application and should also seek the Commonwealth government's approval. The Dutch, however, had still not received the permission they sought when Murphy's service in the Philippines came to a close at the end of 1936.[38]

While the issue of air transportation into the Philippines was receiving so much attention in Washington, Murphy continued to push for the development of air commerce within the Philippines, stressing the urgency of the matter for national defense in a country where land transport was difficult and water transport was slow. He recommended "a comprehensive development program" to the 1934 legislature very much along the lines that he had proposed in 1933, but the legislature approved only a portion of the program: it allocated P200,000 for the development of landing fields, and it enacted legislation creating an aviation unit in the Constabulary.[39]

As Murphy pointed out in his final message as governor-general, the major credit for the acquisition and construction of landing fields at strategic points in the Philippines belonged to General Frank Parker, "the Flying General," and the Army Air Corps. Although the army in 1931 and 1932 had built some landing fields on army property and on land it had leased in Mindanao, it was Parker who mapped a system of air fields and air routes to link the scattered islands of the Philippine archipelago. Some of the funds to construct landing fields came from the United States government, but most of the money was supplied by the insular government.[40]

Murphy thought it essential for the Philippine government to create an aviation unit that could deal with internal disorder and that could be expanded into an organization of sufficient strength to aid in the defense of the archipelago. Although the ten pilots and ten aircraft provided for by the legislature in 1934 when it appropriated P259,000 to establish an aviation unit in the Constabulary were sufficient only for internal police purposes, the insular government requested the War Department to assign an army officer to serve as a technical advisor to the unit and also detailed a Filipino to study military aviation in the United States.[41] The more vigorous exploitation of the airplane as a weapon of national defense awaited the inauguration of the Commonwealth and the implementation of the ambitious defense plan devised for it by General Douglas MacArthur.

III

As Murphy and the Filipino political and economic leadership were well aware, it was the economic provisions of the Tydings-McDuffie Act that posed the greatest threat to the future of an independent Philippines. Since the Philippine economy was dependent on the free entry into the United States of Philippine sugar, coconut oil, and other products, the projected end of free trade necessitated a fundamental readjustment of the economy if an independent Philippines were not to become an economic basket case. The required restructuring of the economy could hardly be accomplished without some degree of government "control and guidance," a fact that Murphy recognized in his initial addresses as governor-general when he called for economic planning and the initiation of "corrective measures" to prevent unbalanced production and the maldistribution of wealth. "In the world of to-day," he observed, "the consequences of inaction and leaderless drifting are fatal."[42] What this seemed to mean was the encouragement of local industries and the diversification of agricultural production, but little was actually accomplished in this regard. The major Philippine effort in the economic sphere was less directed toward restructuring the insular economy than toward the preservation of a special trade relationship with the United States.

Although the Philippine Islands were rich in some raw materials useful in manufacturing, they lacked the power to fuel any significant industrial development, and there was an apparent scarcity of labor adaptable to factory conditions. Most Philippine manufacturing, like hat making, cotton weaving, and embroidery production, was of the household, handicraft variety; of the industries utilizing machine power, only a few such as sugar milling, rice milling, and some branches of tobacco manufacturing involved any substantial number of workers.

When the Manila Trading Center and Exchange was opened on August 17, 1933, Murphy proclaimed the following week "Made-in-the-Philippines Week" and urged the Filipinos to cultivate the "spirit of economic nationalism" and to develop local industries. A year later the cabinet approved the expenditure of the small sum of P83,000 to implement rather modest industrialization plans worked out by the Department of Agriculture and Commerce. Shortly thereafter Murphy ordered the release of P100,000 to construct a building to house a government cotton mill and to support relevant research.[43]

In October 1934 Murphy revived the government's virtually moribund National Development Company, which had been established in 1919 to promote Philippine enterprises. After appointing his wealthy friend Joaquin (Mike) Elizalde to head the company, Murphy laid down a series of policy guidelines for the company that included the preparation of technical studies regarding industries that might be developed in the Philippines. In the year or so that remained until the Commonwealth was established, the National Development Company could do little more regarding industrialization than to study the feasibility of cotton manufacturing and a few other industries.

When the Commonwealth government assumed control of Philippine domestic affairs, it converted the National Development Company into a public corporation, increased its capitalization, and enlarged its powers. The company established a variety of new subsidiaries—the National Food Products Corporation, the National Power Corporation, and the National Footwear Corporation—but the principal result of its efforts insofar as major factory production was concerned was the opening in August 1939 of the textile mill for whose construction the Murphy regime had provided the initial impetus. Although cotton textile manufacturing was "the industry offering the greatest potentiality" for the Philippines, this was the single textile mill in the islands when the Japanese attacked the Philippines, and it was operating at a loss.[44]

Some of the capital required to promote industrial development would have been available to the Philippine government had the United States government agreed to transfer to the Philippines the dollar profit realized on Philippine government deposits in the United States when the American dollar was officially devalued in terms of gold in January 1934. With the approval of the United States government, the Philippine government had been keeping its monetary reserves in United States banks in the form of currency; as of January 31, 1934, the insular government had about $56 million on deposit in forty-one American banks. It had sought in late 1932 and early 1933 to withdraw its deposits in coin, but the War Department had blocked these efforts.

After the Gold Standard Act was passed, Roosevelt and the secretary of war thought that Congress should enact legislation reimbursing the Philippine government for the diminution in the value of its monetary reserves. Lewis Douglas, the director of the budget, argued, however, that such a measure seemingly would acknowledge that the "moral equities" of the people of an American dependency were greater than those of citizens of the United States itself. Secretary of the Treasury Henry Morgenthau thought that the interest earned on the deposits should be deducted from the total sum appropriated for the Philippines. When the Philippine secretary of finance agreed to this, Quezon was "furious" and called him an " 'Ass' " for permitting the United States to " 'gyp' " the Philippine government out of $7.5 million. In June 1934 Congress approved a bill authorizing the president to credit the Philippine government with almost $24 million as the result of the devaluation, an action that the *Philippines Herald* characterized as a victory for the Philippines second only to independence. Congress, however, failed to appropriate the funds the bill had authorized. "They got exactly what they put in," one senator declared. "We have simply changed our bookkeeping arrangements." Murphy vigorously pressed the Filipino claim, but to no avail.[45]

In January 1936 Senator Alva Adams introduced a bill that repealed the law authorizing the payment of the devaluation profit to the Philippine government. Noting that the sum involved was "a mere trifle" for the United States government but of "tremendous importance to us," Quezon regarded the Adams bill as a "great injustice" to the Philippines. J. Weldon Jones, the insular auditor, thought that there was "no legal basis" for the Filipino claim unless the peso could be considered a foreign currency, which it was not; but Murphy, who believed that the United States government should view the question not as a purely legal matter but in terms of its

"moral responsibility," favored the presentation of "every meri-
torious argument" that could be advanced in support of the payment
of the devaluation profit. After the Adams bill had passed the
Senate, President Roosevelt, partly because of Murphy's opposition,
arranged to "slip word" to the Speaker of the House not to permit
the measure to emerge from committee. This killed the bill for the
time being, but the Philippine government did not receive the funds
it had been led to believe would be forthcoming.[46]

Jones was later to argue that, as a gold producer, the Philippine
Islands gained more than they lost because of the devaluation of the
dollar. There was a gold mining boom under way in the Philippines
while Murphy served there, production increasing from P10.2 million
(about 247,000 ounces) in 1932 to about P43.5 million (about
622,000 ounces) in 1936 and employment growing from fifty-six
hundred to twenty thousand in the same years. Murphy described
gold production in 1936 as "the outstanding feature" of the year,
noting that gold by then ranked in value ahead of all Filipino exports
except sugar and coconut products. Americans supplied most of the
capital for the Philippine gold mining industry, and the management
of the mining companies was in American or foreign hands.[47]

Murphy recognized that, in order to prepare for the economic
shock of independence, it was necessary for the Filipinos not only to
develop local industries but also to diversify their agricultural production. Enticed by free trade to concentrate on the production of the
few crops for which there was a large American market, the Filipinos
did not produce enough foodstuffs to feed themselves, agricultural
products constituting almost 19 percent of Filipino imports by value
in 1932. Murphy believed that the Philippine Islands were "perfectly
adapted" to become self-sufficient in food and also to grow food
crops for the foreign market, a view that was largely shared by the
Bureau of Plant Industry and the Philippine Economic Association.
Murphy thought that the government would have to play the directing role if Philippine agriculture were to be diversified, and his rural
improvement program was partly designed with this objective in
view, but the effort to encourage rice farmers to grow secondary crops
was too limited in its geographical scope to have any significant
impact. Like the attempt to spur the industrialization of the Philippines, the campaign to diversify its agriculture and to encourage the
growing of such crops as cotton and onions achieved next to nothing
in the 1930s.[48]

Despite the rhetoric about industrialization and agricultural diversification, sugar, coconut oil, and products of lesser importance like

cordage continued to dominate the Philippine economy. Each was affected by special legislation adopted by the United States Congress following the enactment of the Tydings-McDuffie Act. Seeking to win friends in Washington but looking out at the same time for what they considered their own best interests, Filipino sugar producers persuaded the insular legislature toward the end of 1933 to approve a sugar limitation bill that permitted each planter to produce no more sugar in one year than he had produced in any one of the crop years 1931–32, 1932–33, and 1933–34 and also altered existing contracts between planters and sugar centrals in favor of the former.

Characterizing the measure as "a piece of class legislation of a most shameless type," Murphy vetoed the bill on the grounds that its production formula "practically guarantee[d]" that the 1934–35 sugar crop would be the largest yet produced in the islands, time constraints made it impossible to enforce the measure, and the proposed alteration in existing contracts between planters and millers impaired the obligation of contracts. What had occurred persuaded him that, if sugar production in the Philippines were to be reduced, the authority to impose crop controls must rest with the governor-general, not the legislature. As Murphy informed Washington, the Filipino political leadership, although recognizing the need for limitation, was unable to withstand the pressure of the planters, and a large fraction of the legislators were themselves stockholders of sugar centrals or sugar plantations. The governor-general requested the secretaries of war and agriculture to grant him the necessary authority to limit annual sugar production both for export and domestic consumption.[49]

Failing to receive the authority that he had requested, Murphy in February 1934 asked the centrals and the planters to agree among themselves to limit the 1934–35 sugar crop by 14 percent lest the large surplus that was looming have serious consequences for the Philippine economy. It soon became evident, however, that because of differences among the planters regarding the manner in which the reduction should be achieved and the resistance of what Murphy characterized as "selfish interests" devoid of "all sense of citizenship and responsibility," compulsion would be required if Philippine sugar production were to be effectively limited.[50]

When the Jones-Costigan Sugar Control Act became law on May 9, 1934, seven days after the Philippine legislature had approved the Tydings-McDuffie Act, Secretary of Agriculture Henry A. Wallace assigned the Philippines a quota of 1,015,000 short tons (as compared to the duty-free quota of 952,000 short tons specified in the independence legislation). The quotas recommended for American territories and insular possessions and for Cuba were allocated on the basis of their average annual shipments to the United States in the three most representative years during the period 1925–33 and the anticipated American consumption in 1934. Although in selecting the years 1931–33 as the basis for the Philippine quota, the secretary had picked the three most favorable years from the point of view of Philippine sugar producers, Murphy and the Philippine sugar interests would have preferred an even larger quota for the islands for 1934 (the quota provisions of the Tydings-McDuffie Act did not go into effect until 1936). The State Department and the large New York banks interested in Cuban sugar prevented this, however, doubtlessly pointing out that the Philippine share of the American sugar market had been increasing more rapidly since the early 1920s than the share of any other area supplying the United States.

More troubling to Philippine sugar producers than the size of their quota was the fact that the Jones-Costigan Act made the 1934 quota retroactive to January 1. Since the Philippine crop year began in the middle of the year, since less than forty-five thousand short tons of the 1933–34 crop of about 1.4 million tons had reached the United States before January 1, 1934, and since it appeared too late to keep the 1934–35 crop below the 1933–34 level, the retroactivity feature threatened to leave the Philippines at the end of 1934 with an enormous surplus to carry over into the next quota year. Always "adept at advocating local interests," particularly the interests of Philippine export industries, Murphy had therefore sought to have the Jones-Costigan Act amended so that the quota year coincided with the fiscal year. His efforts, however, proved unavailing since what he proposed would have created a large surplus in the United States in the calendar year 1934 and would have benefited the Philippines at the expense of other sugar producing regions.[51]

Wallace appointed Murphy to serve as sugar administrator for the Philippines, which meant that it was his responsibility to allocate the Philippine quota among Philippine sugar producers. Although the Tydings-McDuffie Act specified that the duty-free quota assigned the Philippines once the Commonwealth had been established should be allocated among the centrals on the basis of their average annual production for the years 1931–33, the Jones-Costigan Act did not include any allocation guidelines for the governor-general. This led to "open war" between the long-established larger centrals and planters favoring an averaging method and the smaller central owners and planters who preferred that the quota be allocated on the basis of the best crop year for any producer during the period 1930-34. Whereas newer units alleged that the averaging method favored the older units, the latter, having little room to expand, objected to the best-year method because they claimed that they had been restricting their production while the newer units were expanding theirs despite industry and government warnings.[52]

Murphy announced toward the end of June 1934 that he would not allocate the 1934 quota because of the lateness of the date but would charge the surplus above the quota figure (estimated at 500,000 short tons) against the allocation assigned producers for 1935. After an audit of all centrals, planters, and firms handling sugar, the 1935 quota was to be allotted among the mills in proportion to their average annual production during the calendar years 1931-33, with each mill's allotment to be suballocated among its associated planters on the same basis and in accordance with the usual arrangements as to crop shares. This method, the governor-general noted, would disadvantage those who had recently increased their production in the face of warnings not to do so. Insofar as the industry as a whole suffered hardship, he asserted, it was because of the 500,000 tons that would have to be subtracted from the 1935 quota rather than because of the allotment formula he had promulgated. Rafael Alunan, the president of the Philippine Sugar Association, characterized the Murphy plan as " 'the best' " that could be devised under the circumstances; and although some of the smaller centrals were displeased, the president of the congress of small centrals also professed to be satisfied.[53]

In December 1934 Murphy signed the Sugar Limitation Act, which empowered the governor-general to fix the amount of sugar that could be produced for export to the United States, determine the amount to be manufactured for local consumption and to be held in an emergency reserve, and allocate each of these quotas among the mill and plantation owners. The act set the quota for domestic consumption for 1935 at 70,000 short tons and the emergency reserve at 100,000 short tons. The effect of the legislation was to give the governor-general "complete control" over the centrifugal and refined sugar produced in the Philippines beginning with the 1934-35 crop.[54]

Murphy placed Jones in charge of the audit of the Philippine sugar industry, but the actual task of allocation and enforcement was performed by the Computation and Records Dvision, headed by the governor-general's economic advisor, Evett D. Hester. The audit led to the suballocation of the Philippine quota to 47 centrals, 21,229 plantations, and 23,734 planters. The planter allowances were allocated to the actual operators of plantations who delivered sugar cane to the mills in their own names, whether or not they actually owned the plantations. The allocation system recognized the planters as the entities with a right to participate in the quotas; the sugar mills were entitled to quotas only because of their contracts with planters. The domestic and emergency reserve quotas were allocated in the same manner as the United States quota except that "amelioration" quantities were allotted to four submarginal and four marginal sugar districts and the quotas were distributed among mills, plantations, and planters on the basis of their production during the crop years 1932-33 or 1933-34, whichever was the greater, a formula that pleased the smaller planters and centrals.[55]

Since no allotments were made for the quota year 1934, Murphy worked out an agreement with the Agricultural Adjustment Administration (AAA), which administered the Jones-Costigan Act, whereby all Philippine sugar shipped to the United States before October 15, 1934, would be admitted into the United States, with the excess above the 1934 quota held in bond until January 1, 1935, and then charged against the 1935 quota. The 1935 quota, as revised, was 981,958 short tons, but when the excess 1934 shipments were deducted from this figure, the effective quota became 505,672 tons. The Confederacion de Associaciones y Plantadores de Caña Dulce, the association of sugar planters, sought to persuade Murphy to permit the milling of one million short tons of the 1934-35 crop and to carry over the surplus for absorption in future years, but Murphy confined the milling of the crop to the marketable quantity so that the Philippines could produce a 1935-36 crop of "relatively normal proportion." Responding to a request by Murphy, however, Wallace permitted Philippine sugar producers to convert excess cane into a maximum of twenty million gallons of molasses.[56]

The 1936 quota was first set at 965,000 short tons but was subsequently raised to 1,067,681 short tons. Since the Philippines, however, had a short crop in 1935-36, reserve stocks were limited, nearly all mills had closed for the season before the increase was announced, and the bulk of the increase would have been subject by then to duty under the Tydings-McDuffie Act and thus would have earned less for the producers than the same sugar sold in the domestic market, the Philippine Sugar Association and the confederation of planters decided to ship only the amount of sugar that was duty free. The result was that 1936 shipments totaled 969,106 short tons.[57]

The AAA established a Philippine branch of its Sugar Section in

July 1934 to assist the governor-general in the implementation of the Jones-Costigan Act. To man the Manila office, the Sugar Section selected Dr. Carl Rosenquist, an economist, and Thurman Arnold, who represented the general counsel of the AAA. The Manila and Washington sugar officials worked together without conspicuous discord, avoiding the difficulties that occurred in Puerto Rico and Hawaii, but Hester, who despised the New Deal and all its works, was contemptuous of the AAA bureaucracy in general and of the Sugar Section's representatives in Manila in particular. Describing his experience in administering the sugar program, Hester wrote about "committee meetings by a cable with a bunch in Washington who hadn't the slightest idea about the Philippines; receiving several consignments of avid ND's [New Dealers], showing them their first stalk of sugarcane; having daily knock-downs with a 'legal mind' sired by Jerome Franks [*sic*] out of Felix Frankfurter [Arnold]; settling quarrels between five separate AAA offices set up in Manila for 'service.' "[58]

Although the Manila branch of the Sugar Section assisted in the enforcement of the allotment program, its primary concerns were the benefit payments available to planters who reduced their sugar acreage and the disposition of the funds created by the payment of the processing tax on sugar sent to the United States for refining. The principles governing the benefit payments were worked out by Murphy's sugar advisors and were then accepted by the AAA. The benefits, which the AAA fixed at P2.40 per picul (133.33 pounds), were to be distributed only to planters. Those receiving benefit payments were required to agree to destroy or ratoon cane in excess of their 1935 allotment and to guarantee not to cultivate cane in excess of 120 percent of their 1936 allotment. They were originally obliged not to plant any basic food crop on the land taken out of production other than for their own consumption, but they were later released from this requirement because of a rice shortage in the Philippines. No planter was to receive a benefit payment unless he had paid all accrued wages to his laborers and settled all share claims of his sharecroppers.

The first benefit checks were issued in January 1935. By the time the payments were discontinued on July 1, 1936, after the AAA had been declared unconstitutional, more than eighteen thousand Philippine planters had received payments totaling P30.7 million. The payments were "a life-giving boon" to the industry, as the *Philippines Free Press* put it, especially in 1935, when the P25 million distributed supplemented the sharply reduced income resulting from the limited sugar shipments of that year.[59]

It had been assumed that the one-half cent per pound processing tax on Philippine sugar sent to the United States would produce funds sufficient to meet not only the cost of benefit payments but also to aid insular agriculture in general, as the applicable legislation and an executive order provided. Murphy requested funds for a variety of programs to relieve agricultural distress, and he was informally advised in the spring of 1935 that $3.1 million would be made available for this purpose. In the end, however, the Philippine government did not receive the money since the sum used for benefit payments to sugar planters depleted the fund from which the relief money was to have come.[60]

"We are getting along quite famously in respect to sugar," Hester informed Murphy in February 1935. Hester's summation accurately describes the implementation and enforcement of the sugar program in the Philippines. The insular sugar administration "enjoyed the full support" of both the centrals and the planters, and in not a single instance while Murphy was governor-general did it have to invoke the sanctions provided in the Jones-Costigan Act or the local sugar limitation law. Hester, who worked fourteen hours a day administering the program, "grew grey, developed a nasty temper, and wrote no letters," but, as he informed Theodore Roosevelt, Jr., "we made it [the sugar control program] work . . . partly by forcing dictatorial unconstitutional . . . legislation locally, and largely by the truly fine backing that Murphy gave me in every step, even when I ran counter to the bedlam theories in Washington."[61]

Although sugar production was reduced from about 1.5 million short tons in 1933–34 to 750,000 in 1934–35 and 1 million in 1935–36, not a single mill had to close, all made "good money," and no plantation had to be sold or foreclosed because its production had been limited. In 1933, the year before the crop control program went into effect, 1,193,244 short tons of sugar valued at P128,665,804 were exported from the Philippines to the United States; in 1934, 1,275,250 short tons valued at P130,907,242; in 1935, 572,724 short tons valued at P65,923,186; and in 1936, 991,466 short tons valued at P123,854,368. The addition of benefit payments in 1935 and 1936 raised the average annual value of the sugar crop sold in the American market to about P110 million in those two years. This was well above the figures for the years before 1932 but somewhat below the average annual income for the peak years 1932–34, when the sugar industry was rapidly expanding its production because of the likelihood that the United States would restrict the import of insular sugar.[62] Given the vital importance of sugar to the Philippine economy, the Murphy administration had every reason to be pleased with the efficient manner in which it had implemented the sugar control program, the high degree of support for its efforts among millers and planters alike, and the success with which the industry had adjusted to the program.

Like the sugar industry, the coconut industry, the second most important in the Philippines, not only faced the threat of extinction as the result of the Tydings-McDuffie Act but had to adjust to special legislation that Congress enacted before the economic provisions of the independence statute went into effect. When it seemed that a marketing agreement being devised as part of the AAA program would require that oleomargarine be made exclusively with ingredients produced in the United States, Murphy, "again at the firing line in defense of the economic interest" of the Philippines, protested that the agreement would be "discriminatory and contrary to the spirit of reciprocal free trade."[63] The restriction to which he objected was not included in the agreement, but he was unable to stave off a tax on Philippine coconut oil included in the Revenue Act of 1934.

Early in 1934 Congress began considering the imposition of a five-cent per pound excise on imported coconut oil and oil crushed from copra in the United States because of concern that the processing tax imposed by the AAA on the butter and animal fat industries would make it more difficult for American dairy, cottonseed, cattle, and hog interests to compete with oil producers in the Philippines and elsewhere. Claiming that the excise, which would have doubled the wholesale price of Philippine coconut oil in the United States, would have a "disastrous" effect on the Philippines, Murphy proposed either that 200,000 long tons of coconut oil and 250,000 long tons of copra, which exceeded the amounts the Philippines were shipping to the United States, be exempted from the excise or that Philippine coconut oil used in nonedible products, the principal American use of Philippine coconut oil, be exempted from the excise. The latter proposal would probably have given the Philippines the entire United States market for coconut oil used for nonedible purposes.[64]

President Roosevelt, Secretary of War Dern, Senator Tydings, and Congressman John McDuffie all criticized the proposed coconut oil excise, and a compilation by the White House of the editorial opinion of four hundred daily newspapers failed to reveal even one that favored the tax. Although Murphy bombarded Washington with messages of protest and warnings of disaster, Congress rejected his proposals as well as the advice of the president, but it did modify the revenue bill to provide a preference for Philippine coconut oil. In the form in which it passed the Congress early in May 1934, the bill included a three-cent per pound excise on oil extracted from copra of Philippine origin but retained the five-cent tax on oil from copra of foreign origin. Congress also stipulated that the tax collected on coconut oil of Philippine origin be returned to the Philippines on the condition that the insular government not pay any subsidy to producers of copra, coconut oil, or allied products.[65]

The Philippine coconut industry dismissed the two-cent per pound differential in its favor as "but an empty gesture." The arguments of the industry and of refiners of Philippine coconut oil in the United States were that a tax exceeding the price of the commodity being taxed (the price of coconut oil was then 2¼ cents per pound FOB Pacific Coast ports) would substantially reduce the consumption of that commodity; that Philippine coconut oil had now lost its advantage over products like palm kernel oil that competed directly with it and were also subject to a duty of only three cents per pound; that there would now be an incentive to gather various excise-free South and Central American nuts like Babassu from which lauric acid could be extracted but whose cost had previously been too high; that the tax rebate would be of no aid to the coconut industry; and that since 70 percent of all coconut oil consumed in the United States went into soap, the excise would substantially increase the price of soap to the American consumer. The Philippine legislature approved a concurrent resolution urging Congress to reconsider the measure or, failing this, requesting the president to veto the bill, a request that Murphy seconded. Lacking the item veto, Roosevelt approved the measure, and it became law on May 10, 1934. Murphy thought that the new tax was "embarrassing and injudicious and a breach of understanding" between the United States and the Philippines.[66]

The immediate effect of the coconut oil excise was a reduction in the price of Philippine copra and coconut oil, a relative decrease in the use of coconut oil in the manufacture of soap and oleomargarine, a substantial increase in the amount of cottonseed oil used in the manufacture of oleomargarine, and a 28 percent reduction in the tonnage (from 402,901 to 319,029 short tons) and a 31 percent reduction in the value (from $14,976,301 to $10,296,587) of copra and coconut oil shipped to the United States from the Philippines in 1934 as compared to 1933. It is not surprising under the circumstances that Quezon sought the repeal of the excise, insisting that this was "much more important than even the sugar question." The fact that Tayabas and Laguna, both important centers of the coconut industry, were the only two provinces from which Sakdalistas were elected to the Philippine legislature in 1934 helped to convince Quezon of the seriousness of the issue.

The Philippine coconut industry prospered in 1935, in contrast to 1934, as drought and the reduced production of cotton and hogs in the United States, coupled with a world shortage of oils and fats, drove the price of copra and coconut oil to record highs and once again increased American demand for Philippine coconut products. The tonnage of Philippine coconut oil and copra sent to the United States in 1935 returned to 1933 levels, and the combined value of the two products (more than $21 million) was double that of 1934 and 42 percent above 1933. The favorable trend continued in 1936, with the result that there was no longer much "popular agitation" in the Philippines for the repeal of the tax. The rebate of the excise tax was in the meantime being held up by a court test of its constitutionality. The Supreme Court upheld the rebate in May 1937, at which time about $48 million, a sum almost equal to the total receipts of the Philippine government in 1936, was transferred from the United States to the Philippine government. From then until the Japanese attack on the Philippines, the coconut oil excise netted the Commonwealth government about $17 million per annum, making up about one-third of its revenue and enabling it to balance its budget.[67]

Just as the provisions of the Tydings-McDuffie Act regarding sugar and coconut oil were modified before they could be implemented, so the statute's limitation of duty-free cordage to three million pounds per annum was altered prior to the date that it was to take effect. Unlike sugar and coconut oil, however, cordage accounted for only about 1 percent of Philippine exports, and the United States was receiving only about half of the cordage that the Philippines exported. The four Philippine cordage factories employed only a little more than one thousand workers, and only about $3 million, slightly more than half of which was American money, was invested in the industry.[68]

Designed to protect the American cordage industry, which claimed it was losing money as the result of Filipino competition and wanted that competition "throttled," the Cordage Act of June 1935 raised the duty-free amount of Filipino cordage that could be admitted annually to the United States to six million pounds for a three-year period beginning in May 1935, subject to a three-year renewal at the discretion of the president, but forbade the import of any Philippine cordage beyond that amount. Since Philippine cordage shipments to the United States had exceeded six million pounds in all but two years since 1929 and had totaled almost nine million pounds in 1934, the statute required a substantial reduction in the volume of Philippine cordage exports to the United States. Murphy was very much opposed to the cordage law, another "piecemeal modification" of the Tydings-McDuffie Act that he regarded as prejudicial to the "larger interests" of both the Philippines and the United States, but the Cordage Institute carried greater weight with Congress on this issue than the governor-general did.[69]

The allocation of the Philippine quota among the Philippine cordage factories was left to the governor-general, who ruled that the average amount shipped to the United States by any company during the calendar years 1931, 1932, and 1933 should determine its share of the quota. This was essentially the proposal of Elizalde and Company, the leading firm in the industry and a conspicuous beneficiary of the formula. In 1936 and 1937 Philippine cordage exports to the United States fell well below the permissible amount, primarily because freight rate differentials favored the shipment of abaca as compared to finished rope—another example, as with coconut oil, of the manner in which unanticipated economic factors modified the predicted results of economic legislation.[70]

IV

Given the normal reluctance of human beings to alter established modes of behavior in any significant way, it is hardly surprising that the Filipino leadership was less inclined to restructure the Philippine economy as the price to pay for independence than it was to maintain existing trading relationships with the United States with as little change as possible. Quezon and his associates were anxious to eliminate the progressive export tax called for by the Tydings-McDuffie Act, to increase the amount of duty-free Philippine imports permitted by the statute, and, most important of all, to arrange for a preferential trade relationship with the United States that would continue after independence. The Filipino leadership as well as Murphy consequently attached very great importance both to President Roosevelt's statement to Congress of March 2, 1934, regarding the correction of "injustices and inequities" resulting from the independence statute and to the language of the act providing for a Filipino-American conference at least one year before independence "for the purpose of formulating recommendations as to future trade relations" between the two.[71]

In the opinion of Roy Veatch, the official in the Office of Economic Adviser of the State Department most concerned with Philippine affairs, most Filipino political leaders, although they could not disclose their "real feelings" to their people, were "more concerned with the economic welfare of the country than . . . with political independence" and would "fight strenuously against being cut off from the United States." Filipino leaders, to be sure, wanted both political independence and economic security, but if they could not "hold" the American market with independence, they were prepared, in Veatch's opinion, to negotiate an arrangement that would permit the Philippines to hold that market without independence. The State Department thought that this was also the view of "practically every business and industrial leader in the Philippines," especially the powerful sugar barons and American businessmen in the Philippines who sold American products to Filipinos "behind the very considerable tariff wall" that had been erected in their favor.[72]

When Quezon came to the United States in the fall of 1934, he emphasized in discussions with the Bureau of Insular Affairs the desire of the Philippines for "a permanent special trade relationship" with the United States "no matter what the political relationship" was. He was "not very much interested," he indicated, in changing the political terms of the independence statute, but he nevertheless stated that he wished to see "a relationship [between the two countries] more or less permanently established." When General Cox asked if that meant the Commonwealth status should be "a permanent relationship," Quezon, who for many years had been privately expressing doubts about the merits of Philippine independence to American officials who he knew were dubious about the idea, replied, in effect, in the affirmative.[73]

Murphy also wondered if the apprehension among the Filipino leadership about the economic consequences of independence meant that they were beginning to have second thoughts about the subject. He asked both Quezon and Osmeña in August 1934 whether "sentiment" among their countrymen was developing in favor of "a new arrangement" with the United States after the Commonwealth period on a "Dominion basis or something similar." Notes that Murphy made of these conversations reveal that Osmeña "firmly and plainly" opposed dominion status and indicated that only the sugar barons favored the idea. Quezon also replied in the negative when Murphy put the same question to him, but Murphy thought that Osmeña's "personal repugnance" at the suggestion seemed "more noticeable" than Quezon's.[74]

Although the Filipinos were understandably concerned about their economic future, men like Veatch were probably incorrect in their judgment that, if worst came to worst, the political leaders of the islands were prepared to jeopardize their political careers in order to retain the American market for Philippine products. Their objective was a continuing economic relationship with the United States, but

Murphy, at least, understood that they were not willing to sacrifice independence to attain their economic goals.[75]

In an effort to win American support for continued free trade or tariff preference for the Philippines, the Filipino leadership decided that it would be expedient for the insular government to revise Philippine tariff schedules so as to increase the import of American products, which, of course, were duty free. They reasoned that if American interests became convinced of the importance of the Filipino market and the economic threat that Philippine independence posed for American exports, perhaps they would abet the Filipinos in their attempt to secure revision of the Tydings-McDuffie Act.[76] It seemed especially important for the Filipino leadership to address itself to this question because of the extent to which Philippine commodity exports to the United States in 1933 exceeded Philippine imports from the United States. The Philippines had consistently enjoyed a favorable commodity balance in its trade with the United States, but while Filipino exports to the United States in 1933 increased by more than 10 percent as compared to 1932 (from $82,648,000 to $91,313,000), American imports, although still constituting about two-thirds of all Philippine imports, decreased by about 15 percent (from $51,298,000 to $43,540,000). As one Murphy aide noted, the trade figures for 1933 were "dangerous from the standpoint of Philippine interests in Washington."[77]

Since American cotton textile exports to the Philippines had constituted about 31 percent of all American cotton textile exports in 1932 (an abnormally high figure because of the Chinese boycott of Japanese goods in the Philippines that year), the decline in Philippine imports of such goods from 88,065,000 square meters in 1932 (71.9 percent of Philippine textile imports) to 67,711,639 square meters in 1933 and 47,875,816 square meters in 1934 (40.5 percent of Philippine textile imports) and the increase in Japanese textile exports to the Philippines during the same period from 20,621,000 square meters to 56,345,000 square meters (53 percent of Philippine textile imports) occupied a central place in the consideration of Philippine-American trade relations in both countries. Whatever the causes for the changed pattern of Philippine textile imports—the lower prices of Japanese cotton goods (anywhere from 10 to 50 percent below American prices on individual items), their greater suitability for many Filipino consumers, and Japanese merchandising methods largely explain what was happening—neither American textile exporters nor the Filipino leadership was disposed to allow market forces to be the sole determinant of the matter. They looked instead to a revision of the Filipino tariff as the means to redirect the flow of Philippine textile imports in America's favor.[78]

The basic Philippine tariff law had been enacted in 1909 and had been subject to "only very limited revision" since that time. The fall in commodity prices due to the Depression, however, increased the effectiveness of the many specific duties in the tariff act; and the Philippine Parity Law of December 1932, requiring that invoices for foreign goods be converted into pesos for tariff purposes at the "parities of exchange" specified in the act rather than at the actual rate (Japanese goods were thus converted into pesos in 1933 at a rate of fifty cents per yen even though the exchange rate was twenty cents) also effectively served to increase the degree of protection. Thus the ad valorem equivalent of the specific rates on dutiable goods, which was calculated at 18.65 percent in 1932, had risen to 32.03 percent in 1933 and 27.04 percent in 1934. There was a close correlation in most instances between the share of the Philippine market supplied by United States products and the degree of protection afforded those products.[79]

When Quezon visited the United States in the winter of 1933–34, he reached an agreement with American textile exporters that called for the Philippines to give added protection to American imports and for American export interests to support the Philippine campaign for a preferential trading relationship with the United States. Representatives of the textile exporters later informed the State Department that the proposed revision of the textile schedules in the Philippine tariff law had been devised in their offices, and proposed changes in the Philippine wheat schedule probably were also worked out in Washington.[80]

The campaign to alter the Philippine tariff to favor American exporters was officially launched on July 16, 1934, when Murphy noted in his message to the insular legislature that the Filipinos had been reducing their purchase of American goods, even though Filipino goods were favored in the American market, and recommended that the legislature reciprocate by increasing tariff rates on those items in which American exporters were "specially interested." About three weeks later Murphy appointed a committee made up of representatives of the legislature, the executive, and the business community to recommend the revision of the insular tariff. The tariff changes proposed by American exporters had already been transmitted to the Philippines by that time, and Murphy had also received suggestions for tariff revision from the American trade commissioner in Manila. The recommendations of the commissioner were actually a composite of the views of local representatives of the American Textile Export Association; the Philippine Shoe Manufacturers Association; the president of the Pacific Commercial Company, which was the "largest American mercantile interest in the Philippines"; and Evett D. Hester, a protectionist.[81]

Murphy's tariff committee not only was anxious to favor American products because it hoped that this would aid the Philippines in securing desired revisions in the Tydings-McDuffie Act, but it also was responding to a fear of Japan and of Japanese economic penetration of the islands by seeking closer economic ties with the United States. The desire for a permanent or long-term preferential trading relationship with the United States was also being expressed by a newly formed Philippine-American Trade Association, "fomented and organized" by Quezon's majority party. Made up of Filipino businessmen and American businessmen in the Philippines, the organization was seeking to mount an educational campaign in the United States to " 'sell' " Americans on the importance of the Philippine market. " 'Trans-Pacific Trade War Begins' " was the way a Japanese financial paper headlined a story on what was taking place in the Philippines, and the Japanese Foreign Office, expressing fear that the proposed changes in the Philippine tariff would "adversely affect the friendly relations" between the United States and Japan, instructed the Japanese chargé d'affaires in Washington to discuss the matter with the State Department. Japanese interests in the Philippines also vociferously opposed any tariff changes that would discriminate against Japanese imports.[82]

Murphy explained to Washington that the tariff bill his committee was forging was designed to protect local industries, increase the American share of Philippine imports to 70 percent,[83] and increase duties on certain luxury items not normally imported from the United States to offset the revenue loss that would result from the planned decrease of non-American imports. Murphy later told Washington officials that he had "carefully worked out the bill with his cabinet" and that it was a "moderate" measure "conditioned on the good of [the] Filipino economy." The bill, actually, was quite different from Murphy's description of it. Most of the increases that it provided were double or triple existing rates, and few were less than 50 percent higher. The cotton textile rates averaged almost 300 percent ad valorem and, according to a State Department economist, vastly exceeded what was required to equalize most Japanese and American prices.[84]

The proposed Philippine tariff revision received a hostile reception in Washington, particularly from the Department of State. The bill, for one thing, was seen as running counter to the American policy of reducing trade barriers and as possibly harmful to the American negotiation of reciprocal trade agreements with other nations. Washington also feared that if Philippine tariff barriers reduced foreign sales to the Philippines, the countries adversely affected might, in turn, buy less from the United States. Japan, for example, the country whose exports would have been most severely affected by the bill, had a large unfavorable balance of trade with the United States and, if it sold less to the Philippines, might be inclined to transfer its American purchases to other markets. The tariff bill, it was also pointed out in Washington, would have adverse effects on the Philippines since it would increase consumer prices, decrease customs receipts, and perhaps delay needed diversification of the economy. It seemed proper, moreover, for the decision on the Philippine tariff to be made by the Commonwealth government rather than by a government that was soon to come to an end. Washington, finally, was concerned that enactment of the bill would be interpreted in the Philippines as obligating the United States to make reciprocal concessions, which was, of course, the major purpose of the measure.[85]

The State Department was especially troubled about the impact of the Philippine tariff bill on the "confused and delicate nature" of the international situation, by which it meant the tension between the United States and Japan stemming from Japanese policy regarding China and Manchuria. The department viewed the matter so seriously that it dispatched Assistant Secretaries R. Walton Moore and Francis B. Sayre to Hyde Park on September 13 to discuss the ramifications of the tariff measure with President Roosevelt. Secretary of State Hull confidentially informed Secretary of War Dern a few days later that " 'the President felt that in view of the delicacy of the present situation with respect to Japan and other nations, and in view of the complex nature of the questions raised by the proposed tariff, it would be wise, if possible, for the Philippine Legislature to take no action regarding this or similar matters during the present session.' " Hull made the same recommendation to Murphy, and Dern bluntly informed him on September 22 that, because of the opposition of the State Department and the United States Tariff Commission, the tariff measure, if enacted, would not be approved in Washington (Philippine tariff measures required the approval of the president). The secretary of war advised that action should be deferred until after the inauguration of the Commonwealth.[86]

Guilty of not having sounded out the War Department before

committing himself on the tariff matter, an embarrassed Murphy replied that he would discourage legislative action on the proposed tariff. He asked, at the same time, whether there was objection to a moderate tariff increase designed only to protect local industries. The Bureau of Insular Affairs replied in a few days that neither it nor the Tariff Commission objected but that the views of the State Department had not yet been ascertained. Since foreign economic policy was primarily the responsibility of the State Department and since the department had been the principal Washington opponent of Philippine tariff revision, Murphy should have bided his time until advised of the department's opinion. Perhaps, however, because he was under "considerable [local] pressure" to act, because Washington's opposition to the original bill had left him "out on a limb," and because he was not feeling well and did not appreciate that Washington had not yet provided him with its final answer, Murphy issued a public statement on October 8 that he had been "informally advised" that, although the United States government believed a tariff measure increasing protection for the benefit of American producers would interfere with existing trade policy, there was "no objection to legislation for the reasonable protection of local Philippine industries."[87]

What Murphy did not know was that on the same day that he issued his statement, the State Department informed the secretary of war that it would be " 'unfortunate for the Philippine legislature to move for increased tariffs, unless there . . . [was] a real emergency and then only during and to the extent of the emergency.' " The Bureau of Insular Affairs now had to advise Murphy that "responsible officials" in Washington preferred that all tariff legislation be delayed for the time being. Inexplicably, the chief of the bureau privately informed Quezon at the same time that there was "no serious objection on the part of anybody" to a "moderate" tariff increase to protect local industries.[88]

The revised Philippine tariff bill, designed allegedly only to protect local industries, was actually a slightly scaled-down version of the original bill to which Washington had objected. Working closely with the Philippine tariff committee, the American exporters, "under the guise of protection for local industries," succeeded in keeping tariff rates in the revised bill at about 90 percent of the very high figures in the original bill. Although they claimed that this eliminated the " 'gravy' " from the original measure, the revised bill would have substantially improved the position of American exporters in the Philippine market, and it could hardly be characterized as a measure solely to protect home industries. Murphy, who had not examined the bill as closely as he should have, seemed unaware of its nature. He conferred with the Filipino leadership after learning of Washington's opposition and then informed the secretary of war that the legislature was "unlikely" to approve any tariff legislation in the session then nearing its end. The reason was perfectly obvious: the Filipino leadership was far less interested in the protection of home industries than it was in securing a tariff bill that would win friends and influence people in the United States, and it had become apparent that the United States government would not approve such a measure.[89]

In a public statement of October 26 that he had cleared with Washington, Murphy, although reiterating that the United States government did not object "to reasonable protection and development of local Philippine industries," asserted that it had been "deemed advisable after consultation with Washington to leave the larger matter of trade relations with the United States to later consideration and disposition." Regarding such trade relations—his real concern in the tariff controversy—he was "authorized to state," he declared, that the United States government intended to give the Philippine government "every possible assistance in preparing for an independent existence."[90]

When it became evident as the result of Murphy's statement that Washington's opposition had prevented the Philippine legislature from revising the insular tariff to increase protection for American products, textile exporters and their political allies angrily protested the Roosevelt administration's behavior. Asserting that the cotton trade was threatened with "the complete loss" of its Philippine market, a textile spokesman informed the White House that the industry could not "meekly acquiesce in this supine surrender of a lucrative market to the merchants of a low wage nation producing goods of an inferior quality under conditions which would not be tolerated within the United States or its territories." The United States Chamber of Commerce asked the president to intervene to protect American interests in the Philippine market, and Representative Hamilton Fish of New York, a congressional spokesman for the textile industry, was "on the warpath against the [State] Department for not doing everything possible to help our cotton textile exporters." When a State Department representative met with Fish and a group of cotton textile exporters, the congressman let it be known that he was prepared to make a political issue of the State Department's policy regarding the Philippine tariff. He told the cotton textile representatives that the issue was "political dynamite" in twenty states.[91]

Aware that the State Department was blocking an action favored by practically all Filipino leaders, by the governor-general, and by the politically powerful textile industry in the United States, department officials decided that it might be prudent to yield a bit by agreeing to temporary legislation that would limit the flow of Japanese textile products into the Philippine market. The problem was discussed with the president, who indicated that he wanted "some steps taken to meet the emergency" lest United States textiles be displaced in the Philippines. Murphy was consequently informed on November 1 that the United States government did not object to emergency legislation limiting the import of non-American cotton and rayon products for one year unless the same result could be achieved by a voluntary agreement among the principal suppliers of the Philippine market.

Dissatisfied with the mildness of the November 1 message, cotton textile interests insisted that the administration pressure the Philippine legislature to act before it adjourned on November 8. The president responded by asserting that he wished a letter sent to the Philippines stating, " 'We [the United States government] feel action should be taken.' " The chief of the Bureau of Insular Affairs, who thought it of " 'doubtful wisdom' " to permit " 'small group interests to force our hands' " and who was also concerned about the effect of a tariff increase on the cost of living in the Philippines, disagreed with the president. He noted, moreover, that it had "not been considered a very wise thing" for Washington to suggest legislation that it wished the Philippine legislature to enact and that, in view of the passage of the Tydings-McDuffie Act, such action was "out of line with the declared intent of Congress." In the end, the president retreated and General Cox prevailed, and the message sent to the Philippines simply asked for information about the textile tariff. By the time the communication reached the Philippines, the leadership had decided to defer action on tariff matters pending a thorough study of United States-Philippine trade relations, and it was unwilling to reconsider its decision.[92]

As the American share of the Philippine textile market continued to dwindle in the next few months, the textile exporters pressed even more vigorously for relief. The Philippine Committee of the Textile Export Association of the United States advised a visiting delegation of congressmen in late December that United States firms were then selling only "distress lots" that mills could not dispose of in the United States. The same group told Murphy that United States textiles would "disappear practically entirely" from the Philippine market within a few months. Responding to the mounting pressure, Cordell Hull, despite his commitment to freer trade and his reluctance to give Japan any cause for complaint in view of an "uncertain and chaotic" international situation that had been aggravated by the Japanese decision to renounce existing restrictions on naval construction, informed Congressman Joseph W. Martin, Jr., of the textile state of Massachusetts that the State Department was not opposed to temporary measures designed to protect American textiles in the Philippine market. When Murphy visited Washington in March 1935, he assured both Martin and Fish that the next Philippine legislature would provide protection for American textiles.[93]

The question in Washington in March and April 1935 was not whether Japanese textile shipments to the Philippines should be limited but only how that result should be achieved. "What steps can be taken to appease the textile people here?" was the way Cox accurately phrased the question in a discussion of the problem by the interested departments. Departmental representatives voiced the familiar arguments against an increase in the Philippine tariff, but political realities by this time had become a more important factor in the decision-making process than economic theories. The economic arguments against additional protection were clearly recognized, Sayre remarked to the Interdepartmental Committee that had been established to deal with Philippine affairs, but "there is a political situation here which must be taken into account." The textile group, he continued, could be "a strong political influence," and President Roosevelt, who had some very important legislation that he wanted passed, could be placed in "a difficult and embarrassing position" because of the textile problem. "In pure theory," Roosevelt had earlier said to the secretary of state, "you and I think alike but every once in a while we have to modify principle to meet a hard and disagreeable fact! Witness the Japanese avalanche of cotton goods into the Philippines during the past six months."[94]

The alternatives considered in Washington were a quota on Japanese exports, adjustment of the Philippine tariff, or a voluntary agreement with Japan to limit textile exports. ". . . the slant of the President's mind is in the direction of quotas," Sayre reported to the Interdepartmental Committee. "'. . . we've got to hold our nose and put a quota on,'" the president had said. Although Sayre thought that they would be "violently attacked" if they opposed a quota, the preponderant opinion among departmental representatives was that a quota on textile imports was "inadvisable." In their view, it was a tactic of economic warfare to which the United States was normally opposed; it was "a dangerous precedent" and might lead to retaliation from abroad.

Murphy, who met with the Interdepartmental Committee on this issue on three occasions and who also discussed the subject at "great length" with Cox, favored the tariff approach to the textile problem. From the start, however, his concern had been less the immediate problems of the American textile industry than the long-range economic relationship between the Philippines and the United States. He complained to the Interdepartmental Committee that "the textile problem" and "the whole Philippine problem" had been looked at "too much in the light of the immediate past and future rather than [from] a long-range view and all the implications of trade and commerce in that part of the world 25 years from now." The textile issue, he thought, should be subordinated to the general tariff question, as it had been in the Philippines in 1934, and he hoped that the possibility of a "moderate tariff increase" could be "explored sympathetically." Although obviously miffed that he had been checkmated by Washington in his attempt to deal with the tariff problem, Murphy asserted that his "major purpose" was to cooperate with the State Department, and he denied rumors that he would resign his post because of differences with the department.[95]

No one, of course, objected to the negotiation of a voluntary agreement with Japan regarding Philippine textile imports. The likelihood that such an agreement could be concluded was substantially enhanced when the United States Senate voted on March 29, 1935, to investigate Japanese textile exports to the United States. Faced now with the possibility, if they appeared unreasonable, of having a limitation imposed on their textile exports to the large American market, the Japanese were prepared to accept some limitation on textile shipments to the much smaller Philippine market. After speaking to the Japanese commercial attaché, a representative of the United States Tariff Commission reported to the Interdepartmental Committee on April 4 that the Japanese were "in an excellent frame of mind" to minimize their competition with American textile exporters in the Philippine market. It was this knowledge that undoubtedly led Murphy and the State Department to agree that same day to recommend to the president that the department attempt to negotiate a voluntary textile agreement with the Japanese government. If additional assistance to American textile interests was considered "advisable," they agreed that the Philippine legislature, as Murphy had urged, should be advised to enact a "moderate" tariff increase on textiles for approximately one year, pending the holding of joint Philippine-American trade discussions. The president concurred in these recommendations.[96]

Negotiations between the United States and Japan were initiated on April 11 when Sayre met with the Japanese ambassador, Hiroshi Saito, and were not concluded until a joint agreement was reached on October 11. The negotiations proceeded against a backdrop of continued calls in Congress for the Philippine government to take "prompt and decisive action" to protect American textile exports by passing an emergency tariff measure. Believing that tariff revision was consistent with the recommendations for dealing with the textile problem that the president had approved, Murphy sent a message to the legislature on July 9 stating that "satisfactory adjustment" of Philippine trade relations with the United States would be "materially aided by an effective adjustment of import duties on textiles and other products that would afford prompt relief to American and Philippine interests." The War Department and the State Department, however, were opposed to this course of action, and the Japanese government advised the State Department that it regarded Murphy's message as "somewhat disturbing" while negotiations for a textile agreement were underway. Although the Philippine legislature withheld action on Murphy's proposal, what had occurred probably gave point to the State Department's warning to Japan at the outset of the textile negotiations that, unless Japan acted voluntarily to reduce textile exports to the Philippines, "the resulting political pressure might become unmanageable." The United States, the Japanese were told, had no desire to exclude Japan from the Philippine market but neither did it wish to see the American share of Philippine imports reduced to "negligible figures."[97]

The agreement reached between the United States and Japan on October 11, 1935, specified that the newly created Association of Japanese Exporters of Cotton Goods to the Philippine Islands would for a two-year period beginning on August 1, 1935, and provided the Philippine government did not increase the tariff on cotton piece goods, limit annual exports to the Philippines to forty-five million square meters (as compared to more than fifty-six million square meters in 1934 and almost sixty million square meters in the twelve months preceding September 1, 1935). It was further provided that imports during the first year of the agreement could be as much as 10 percent more or 10 percent less that the agreed-upon figure, with the necessary adjustment to be made in the second year. Although nothing was said about the matter in the memorandum of conversation setting forth the terms of the agreement, Sayre stated to the Japanese ambassador that the assurances provided by the United States that it would not initiate action to increase the Philippine tariff on cotton goods were in no way binding on the Philippine government. This was consistent with the view of the Bureau of Insular Affairs that Washington should not dictate the legislation that the insular legislature should pass. In this instance, however, what was said was for the record since Murphy, whose advice had been sought by the State Department, had indicated that the agreement was "acceptable as a temporary measure," Quezon had given his approval, and the State Department had promised to "utilize as far as appropriate such influence as it possesses" to discourage Philippine tariff action.

Although Murphy had advised that Japanese textiles arriving in the Philippines from intermediate points should be included in the Japanese quota, the published agreement made no mention of transshipments. "After some show of reluctance," Japan, however, privately agreed to include Japanese cotton piece goods transshipped at Hongkong and other places within the quota and also to "do its best" to prevent the shipment of piece goods produced in Japanese mills in China. The Japanese government wanted "no public reference" made to this understanding lest it create the impression that there was "suspicion" about Japanese intentions. Nothing in the agreement, finally, precluded discussion between the United States and the Philippines regarding their long-term trading relationship, a point on which Murphy had insisted when he was consulted by the State Department.[98]

The implementation of the Japanese-American textile agreement proved to be more difficult than anticipated. The Japanese government and the Association of Japanese Exporters, for one thing, seemed unable to control the transshipment of cotton goods from Hongkong and elsewhere; by July 31, 1936, an estimated 7,527,000 square meters had reached the Philippines in that way. The heavy shipment of Japanese rayon goods (24,327,025 square meters in 1936 as compared to 13,692,338 square meters in 1935), which were not included in the agreement, also constituted "a distinct threat" to the agreement from the point of view of American textile exporters, as did the increased Philippine import of cotton piece goods of Chinese origin. Neither the Japanese government nor the American government, moreover, seemed aware that there was a time lag of several weeks between the arrival of goods in the Philippines and the liquidation of the duty on these goods, the basis for determining the volume of imports under the agreement. The result was that several million square meters of Japanese textile goods that had arrived in the Philippines before August 1, the beginning date of the agreement, were not included in the statistics based on liquidation of duties until after August 1.[99]

Although Japanese shipments for the first year of the textile agreement (52,675,000 square meters) exceeded the quota limit for the year, including the 10 percent tolerance, by more than three million square meters, the State Department thought that there was "no more satisfactory alternative" to the quota agreement. Murphy also favored negotiations to "salvage" the agreement. The agreement was renewed for one year shortly after its expiration date and annually thereafter until Japanese-American trade came to an end in July 1941. Largely because of transshipments, Japanese textile exports again exceeded the quota in the year ending July 31, 1937; but during the remainder of the period in which the quota was in effect Japanese textile exports, primarily because of the disruptive effect on Japanese industry of the Sino-Japanese war, fell well below quota limits, and United States textiles regained their dominant position in the Philippine market. Whereas the United States had supplied only 33 percent of the cotton cloth imported by the Philippines in 1936–37, the American share rose to 62 percent in 1939–40, while the Japanese share of the Philippine textile market fell during the same period from 56 percent to 25 percent.[100]

It will be recalled that the Philippine legislature had adopted a concurrent resolution on May 2, 1934, inviting the president to appoint a committee of representatives of the United States government to visit the Philippines to ascertain whether "imperfections and inequalities" existed in the independence statute that warranted its modification. Senator Tydings was receptive to the idea but thought it undesirable to send a congressional committee to the Philippines during the summer "as there would be a large clamor for places on the committee that would make a junketing trip out of it." Tydings regarded the period after the November elections as the appropriate time for the trip. At his urging, President Roosevelt requested Congress to appoint members from each house to serve as the visiting committee. The vice-president and the Speaker each appointed five members to the committee.[101]

Acting as "an advance scout" for the Tydings committee, Senator Carl Hayden left for the Philippines at the end of June. After a preliminary investigation in the islands, he reported back to Tydings that the application of United States tariff legislation as provided in the Tydings-McDuffie Act would mean the failure of "this experiment in self government." The way to avoid this dolorous result, he thought, was for the United States to negotiate a reciprocal trade agreement with the Commonwealth government that would provide for a special trading relationship between the two. He recommended that the State, War, and Commerce Departments initiate studies of the Philippine-American commercial relationship preparatory to the negotiation of such an agreement. Tydings was ready to follow this advice, but the president, although amenable to the idea, preferred to delay the appointment of an interdepartmental study committee until he had received a similar recommendation from the Tydings committee as a whole.[102]

The Tydings committee arrived in the Philippines on December 9 prepared to consider all matters pertaining to the Philippine economy and Philippine independence. The Filipino business and political leadership predictably informed the congressmen that they favored free trade during the Commonwealth period, the abolition of the export tax, larger quotas for the principal Philippine exports, tariff autonomy for the Commonwealth, and commercial relations with the United States after independence on the basis of reciprocity. Although Alguinaldo's organization of veterans called for independence in three to five years, other Filipinos, fearful about the future, expressed a preference for some kind of enduring relationship with the United States. Tydings concluded that there was "a considerable sentiment" against independence and that with "a little judicious steering" the United States, if it wished, could induce the Filipinos to request a reconsideration of the grant of independence.[103]

Whether or not Tydings accurately judged the sentiment of the Filipinos regarding independence, some members of the mission, notably Senator Ernest W. Gibson of Utah, Senator Kenneth McKellar of Tennessee, and Tydings himself, came away from their visit quite pessimistic about the viability of an independent Philippines. Independence, Gibson feared, meant "economic suicide" for the Philippines and Japanese domination of the islands—"Japan . . . is moving in as we are moving out," he declared. He publicly regretted his vote for the Tydings-McDuffie Act, expressing a preference now for dominion status or a modified form of statehood for the Philippines. McKellar, who had also voted for independence, declared that it would be "a monumental disaster" for the Philippines to become independent and advised the Filipinos to petition Congress to establish the Philippines as "a completely self-governing local political entity" but not as an independent nation. Tydings, the principal author of the independence statute, stated that if the Filipinos themselves took the initiative in asking for a reconsideration of independence, he would be inclined to favor the retention of the islands. The principal recommendation of the committee, which was conveyed to the president on December 31, 1934, was, however, simply the implementation of Hayden's earlier suggestion that an interdepartmental committee be appointed to study United States-Philippine trade relations.[104]

Meeting at the invitation of Secretary of State Hull, representatives of the Tariff Commission and the War, State, Commerce, and Agriculture Departments agreed on January 11, 1935, to establish an Interdepartmental Committee on the Philippines to conduct the trade studies recommended by the Tydings mission. The committee quickly became "a study group for the entire Philippine problem, with special emphasis upon the economic factors involved."[105]

In the meantime, Murphy, who was preparing to visit the United States, sought to ascertain precisely what changes in the Tydings-McDuffie Act the Filipino leadership favored and whether there had been any change in their views concerning independence since his last discussion of the subject with them. When he met with Quezon, Osmeña, Roxas, and Quintin Paredes, the Speaker of the Philippine House, on January 21, Quezon stated that there was "strong sentiment" in the islands for reducing the length of the Commonwealth period, but only Paredes agreed with this judgment. They all favored larger quotas for Philippine sugar and cordage during the transition period and the abolition of the coconut excise as well as a special trade relationship with the United States after independence. They also wanted an understanding with the United States that would make Japan think twice before taking any action against the Philippines or that would "entirely eliminate her efforts at political or economic domination." They made it clear, finally, that they regarded any arrangement with the United States not based on Philippine independence as "impractical and not to be considered." Murphy's estimate of the situation after the conference was that the Filipinos continued to favor independence but that there was "a growing sense of realism" among them both about their "economic structure" and about the threat of Japanese expansionism.[106]

The day after his conference with the Filipino leadership Murphy attended a mammoth banquet in the Manila Hotel that the Philippine government had arranged in his honor preparatory to his trip to the United States. Believing that he must play the role of "an understanding and sympathetic friend and guide" of a people that had taken the first step toward independence, Murphy used the occasion to deliver a forty-minute extemporaneous address designed to "clear the atmosphere" and to give the Filipinos courage as they faced an uncertain future. "Suspicions, ugly rumors, uncertainty and worse still incredible efforts to turn back on our policy and pledges in connection with the establishment of the Commonwealth had to be destroyed with a single blow," Murphy wrote in a note about his speech, "and I resolved to deliver the necessary punch at this banquet." He sought to persuade his audience that the difficulties of the "near and far future" were being "overemphasized" and were "soluble with courage and prudence." "There is not any cause for the Filipino people and others of this community to have fear," he declared. "This country is not going to ruin. This civilization is not going to crumble. There is not any necessity for this nation to step back." Independence, Murphy observed in his note about the speech, is "dearer to me . . . than anything man possesses." If, "as a matter of self-determination," the Filipinos chose a "further relationship" with the United States, that could be arranged, and "it might be wise from our [the American] viewpoint," but he hoped that they would opt for "complete independence as soon as practicable." [107]

The next morning Murphy met with his cabinet and outlined the policies he wanted followed in his absence, including "every step in the procedure to set up the Commonwealth without delay." He lunched with his staff and their families, and then Quezon and the cabinet accompanied him to his ship. Murphy was accorded a seventeen-gun salute when he arrived at the pier, where he inspected the troops of the 31st Infantry and shook hands with some among the large crowd, "the humble and the great" of Manila, that had come to bid him a temporary farewell. Once on the ship, "the excitement swept" the Murphy party. The governor-general went up to the bridge to wave at the cheering crowd, some of whom were in tears. The *Augusta*, the flagship of the Asiatic fleet, boomed another seventeen-gun salute, ships in the harbor blew their whistles, and the band on the *Augusta* played the Star Spangled Banner and Auld Lang Syne. "I watched Manila and the Harbor fade away," the sentimental Murphy wrote of the event, "and then returned to my apartment moved by the sincere, heartfelt farewell from the people among whom I have so happily labored." [108]

En route home and in the United States Murphy, continuing to serve as the Filipino "friend in court," repeatedly sounded the refrain that the Filipinos were "ready for independence" under the terms of the Independence Act and that their economic problems could and should be solved with American aid. "We can't arbitrarily wash our hands of their economic problems after having sustained them" for so many years, he told one interviewer. In his conversations with officials from the president on down, Murphy consistently maintained that there must be no shortening of the transition period but no retreat from the plans to establish the Commonwealth. He thought it "unwise" to consider neutralization of the Philippines or the establishment of an American protectorate over the islands as political arrangements to accompany a changed trading relationship, and he recommended that the United States declare at an early date that, when she withdrew from the Philippines, she would do so "entirely." [109]

Murphy, who had long considered the economic problem as "the most important" problem facing an independent Philippines, discussed this matter on several occasions with the Interdepartmental Committee. At the March 7 meeting of the committee, he recommended the negotiation of a reciprocal trade agreement between the two countries that would provide as "effective" protection for United States manufactured goods in the Philippine market as Philippine raw materials received in the United States but that would alleviate any "undesirable" competition between Philippine and American goods. When Sayre asked how Japan would react to such an arrangement, Murphy replied that it was "undesirable" to consider the Japanese reaction, but he anticipated no difficulty in that area. A representative of the Department of Commerce contended that if Murphy's recommendations were followed, Japan would simply set up factories in the Philippines behind the Philippine tariff wall and would "destroy" the effectiveness of the tariff preference granted the United States. Murphy responded that this was preferable to opening the Philippine market to Japanese goods without restriction and would at least mean the entry of capital into the Philippines and jobs for Filipinos. When asked if the trade agreement he advocated should continue indefinitely, Murphy replied that, unlike the Filipino leadership, which favored a permanent arrangement, he preferred an agreement "conditioned on progressive steps to support and build up an independent economy in the Philippine Islands." It was essential, he remarked, for the United States to aid the Philippines to "adjust" their economy, and he indicated that he could not "speak too strongly against those who say, 'Well, just let them go to the dogs.'"

When Murphy indicated that the Filipinos were realistically aware that they must help to correct the unfavorable American balance of trade with the Philippines, a committee member pointed out that, because of "the triangulation of trade," it did not matter whether the trade between any two countries was in balance. Murphy, who knew relatively little about the economics of international trade and who probably had never given a thought to the "triangulation of trade," naively "expressed interest in this point of view and said that he would like to follow it further." He correctly observed, however, that "from the political angle," to which both the Filipino leadership and he were sensitive, the balance between the two was important and that members of Congress frequently pointed to the unfavorable American balance as a reason for restricting Philippine imports.[110]

As the result of its discussions with Murphy and its own deliberations, the Interdepartmental Committee drafted a "Confidential Memorandum on the Settlement of Philippine-United States Trade Relations after Independence" that Hull forwarded to the president on March 18, 1935. Pointing to the "serious consequences" for both countries that would result from the imposition of full tariff rates when the Philippines became independent, the committee recommended the negotiation of an agreement during the Commonwealth period providing for "a more gradual mutual adjustment of tariff rates" after independence so as "to minimize the shock of transition." Since industries in both the United States and the Philippines would be kept in "a state of indecision" throughout the Commonwealth period if the decision on future trade relations were postponed, the committee recommended an early settlement of the matter and the holding of the joint trade conference provided for in the Tydings-McDuffie Act at "as early a date as practicable" after the establishment of the Commonwealth.[111]

Roosevelt approved the Interdepartmental Committee's recommendations and instructed the committee to continue with its trade studies so that "the necessary basic material" would be available when the joint trade conference was held. The president at the same time told Murphy to initiate similar studies in the Philippines. Murphy hailed the president's decision regarding the early holding of a joint trade conference, for which the governor-general deserved a good deal of the credit, as "the start of our efforts to stabilize [the] Philippine economy."[112]

The Interdepartmental Committee dispatched two Tariff Commission analysts, Drs. Frank M. Waring and Ben B. Dorfman, to study "relevant economic conditions" in the Philippines. By the time the two men arrived in the Philippines on September 9, the economic fact-gathering process was already underway there, Murphy on July 9 having appointed a Technical Trade Committee of nine persons, most of them prominent business figures, and a Philippine Interdepartmental Committee of three cabinet members to prepare the necessary data for the joint conference.[113]

The American experts completed their fieldwork in the Philippines early in January 1936, submitted a brief memorandum to Murphy on their findings, and then returned to the United States. In a preliminary report to the Interdepartmental Committee, they predicted that, because of the effect of the export tax and the full American tariff on the principal Philippine exports, the emergence of the Philippines as an independent state would be accompanied by "grave economic dislocation, acute depression, and social unrest" and the Philippine government would be unable to preserve peace and order. American exports to the Philippines, the survey team thought, would decline with independence and the end of tariff preference for American goods, and the Philippines would become less attractive as a field for investment, but the Philippine market would not be lost to the United States.[114]

In its final report, the Philippine Technical Trade Committee urged the repeal of the coconut oil excise and the Tydings-McDuffie export taxes, a larger duty-free quota for sugar than provided in the independence statute, and a larger duty-free quota for cordage than specified in the Cordage Act. Although the Tydings-McDuffie Act had allegedly been designed to prepare the Philippines for independence, the chairman of the committee concluded that the statute was "not preparatory but liquidatory of our major agricultural industries." In addition to the Technical Trade Committee's proposals, Manuel Roxas submitted his own plan for "Philippine Island Independence without Free Trade" that Quezon told Murphy "practically presents the views of my administration." A rather complex plan, it called in essence for complete free trade during the transition period, an agreement by the United States during that time to purchase its copra and hemp exclusively from the Philippines, upward revision of the Philippine tariff to protect American goods during the transition period, and Philippine action before independence to curtail the production of commodities dependent on free trade and to make them more competitive. After independence, the Roxas plan, which Hester considered the "least realistic and most selfish program" that had been advanced, called for a gradual increase in the tariff rates each country imposed on the other's goods except that lower rates were to be set for goods that could not afford to pay the stipulated rate. Whether Quezon was actually wedded to the details of the Roxas plan is doubtful, but he left no doubt in Murphy's mind that he favored some kind of "economic partnership" with the United States.[115]

Murphy, who took an "active interest" in the preparations for the trade conference, regarded it as of critical significance to the future of the Philippines and to his own place in the history of the islands. When he left the Philippines in May 1936, not to return for another ten years, he was determined that Washington should "know that we want something done and want it done right." The "something" was the joint trade conference, and Murphy was anxious that it be held before the end of the year. He thought that the scheduling of the conference for an early date was essential to counteract pessimism in the Philippines regarding American intentions, because of the growing Japanese influence in the islands, and because American and Philippine business interests were reluctant to make long-term investments in the Philippines as long as they remained uncertain about its economic future. What Murphy did not say was that he wanted to play a role in the trade conference, which, as one Philippine newspaper put it, was his "baby," and 1936 was to be the final year that he could do so.[116]

Although Quezon shared Murphy's desire for an early trade conference, there was a much more relaxed attitude about the matter in Washington than there was in Manila. The Interdepartmental Committee and the War Department thought that the United States would not be "fully prepared" for a conference any time in 1936 and that Congress was not likely to be in the proper frame of mind in an election year to react favorably to recommendations for the amendment of the Tydings-McDuffie Act. Murphy pressed for at least a preliminary meeting in 1936 at which experts from the two countries could exchange views and could prepare the agenda for the final conference. The Interdepartmental Committee did not object to "discussions of an entirely informal nature" that might lessen a tendency in the Philippines to regard the projected conference as "mainly an opportunity for trade bargaining," but the State Department and the other government agencies decided that the United States would not be prepared even to enter into preliminary discussions with the Filipinos until March 1937. Although Murphy, by that time, was serving as Michigan's governor, he hoped to be identified with the conference in some way.[117]

As the principle that should govern the joint preliminary discussions between the United States and the Philippines, the Interdepartmental Committee recommended to the president in February

1937 that the preferential trade relationship that the Philippines enjoyed with the United States should be terminated "at the earliest practicable date consistent with affording the Philippines a reasonable opportunity to adjust their national economy." According to the Interdepartmental Committee, the trade preferences the Philippines then enjoyed brought "substantial losses" to the United States, and the continuation of this relationship after independence might prejudice the chance to secure the neutralization of the Philippines. After the president approved the Interdepartmental Committee's recommendation, the principle that the committee had formulated was incorporated in a joint statement issued by President Quezon and Assistant Secretary of State Sayre. After independence, the joint statement declared, trade between the two countries would be "regulated in accordance with a reciprocal trade agreement on a non-preferential basis."[118]

The Joint Preparatory Committee on Philippine Affairs that was appointed in April 1937 conducted public hearings in Washington and San Francisco in June and July and in Manila in September and then issued its report in May 1938. In what has been characterized as "an essentially somber" document, the committee recommended that the trade preferences scheduled by the Tydings-McDuffie Act to expire on July 4, 1946, should continue until 1961. President Roosevelt had basically approved this principle in advance in order to mollify Quezon, who had become "increasingly upset" about the work of the committee because he thought that the American representatives had been acting as a unit in opposition to Philippine interests. The committee proposed that the export taxes, scheduled to rise to 25 percent of existing American duties by January 1, 1945, and 100 percent by the date of independence, July 4, 1946, should remain at 25 percent but should be converted after independence into a 25 percent duty on United States imports and should be increased by 5 percent annually until January 1, 1961, when the full Philippine duties would go into effect. The United States, in turn, was to impose a duty on Philippine imports on July 4, 1946, equal to 25 percent of existing duties, and the tariff was to be increased by 5 percent annually until January 1, 1961, when the full tariff would be imposed. Annually declining duty-free quotas, exempt from the export tax, were proposed for the years 1940–46 for coconut oil, cigars, scrap tobacco, and pearl buttons, but no change was recommended in the independence statute's provision for sugar. The committee also recommended that abaca and copra be admitted into the United States during the Commonwealth period free of duty and that cordage in excess of six million pounds be subject to duty after the expiration of the Cordage Act on May 1, 1941. The report, Sayre wrote Governor Murphy, was "built upon the ideas that you and I have many times discussed." The report was also influenced by the proposals of Murphy's Technical Trade Committee, the Roxas plan, the deliberations of the Interdepartmental Committee, and the recommendations of the survey team that the committee had sent to the Philippines.[119]

Senator Tydings introduced a bill in January 1939 that incorporated the principal recommendations of the Joint Preparatory Committee, but a congressional majority influenced by lobbyists for the interested American industries and by an "isolationist brand of anti-imperialism" revised the measure so that it made no provision for trade relations between the two countries after independence and offered the Philippines "almost nothing" for the remainder of the Commonwealth period. Congress was in a somewhat more generous mood after World War II; the Bell Trade Act of 1946 provided for eight years of free trade and then for gradual annual tariff increases until 1974, when the full American duty went into effect on Philippine imports.[120] Frank Murphy was a member of the United States Supreme Court when the Bell Act was passed, but his interest in the Philippines remained strong.

5

"A New Federal Relationship"

I

The constitution of the Commonwealth of the Philippine Islands, as Joseph R. Hayden saw it, provided for "a new federal relationship, unique not only in our own [America's] rich experience with federalism, but in the history of federal, colonial, or imperial government anywhere." There were no longer any American officials "within" the Philippine government, which was granted "the maximum measure of autonomy consistent with the responsibility, interests, and dignity of the United States as the sovereign power in the Islands."[1]

The powers reserved to the United States government in the Commonwealth by the Tydings-McDuffie Act seemed clear enough, but the precise role to be played by the United States high commissioner to the Commonwealth government was left uncertain. The Philippine government could not contract foreign loans without the consent of the president of the United States; all acts affecting the currency, coinage, imports, exports, and immigration required his approval; amendments to the Philippine constitution had to be submitted for his approval; and he was authorized to "suspend" any law, contract, or executive order that he thought could result in the failure of the Commonwealth government to fulfill its contracts, meet its bonded debt, provide for its sinking funds, or that could impair its currency reserves or violate the international obligations of the United States. The foreign affairs of the Commonwealth were placed under "the direct supervision and control" of the United States; the Philippine government recognized the right of the United States government to expropriate property for public uses, maintain military and other reservations and armed forces in the Philippines, and call into service such armed forces as the Philippine government might organize; and, by presidential proclamation, the United States government could "intervene" to preserve and maintain the government of the Commonwealth, protect life, property, and individual liberty, and secure the discharge of government obligations. The United States Supreme Court not only retained its power to review

Philippine cases but was also authorized to review cases involving the Commonwealth constitution.

The United States high commissioner to the Philippines, appointed by the president with the advice and consent of the Senate, was to represent the president in the Philippines. He was to have access to the records of the Commonwealth government and its subdivisions and was to be supplied with such information as he requested. If the Commonwealth government failed to pay its bonded debt or to fulfill its contracts, the high commissioner was to report the facts to the president of the United States, who could direct the high commissioner to take over and administer the customs offices of the Commonwealth. The high commissioner was to perform "such additional duties and functions" as the president might delegate to him under the independence statute.[2]

Since there was no other official in the American government precisely like the high commissioner and since the Tydings-McDuffie Act did not define his status with precision, a Philippine newspaper concluded that he would play "the real mystery role" in the Commonwealth. Seeking to characterize the essence of that role, observers at the time variously described the high commissioner as "an observer in behalf of the President . . . vested with diplomatic rather than political authority," "a mere presence that can be conveniently ignored so long as the actual actors follow the rules," "an Ambassador . . . with added statutory functions," "a glorified bill collector," and "the 'watch dog' of the United States government in the Philippines." What was evident was that, unlike the governor-general, the high commissioner did not exercise "the supreme executive power" in the Philippines. He was not authorized to approve or veto legislation, appoint government officials, or intervene in the day-to-day affairs of government.

In vetoing the Hare-Hawes-Cutting bill, President Hoover complained that " 'the powers which the high commissioner can exercise on his own initiative are unimportant, and those which can be delegated to him by the President over legislation are doubtful and indirect.' " The chief of the Bureau of Insular Affairs, however, thought that the "preeminence" of the high commissioner in the Commonwealth was assured since he was the representative of the president, and Quezon complained to President Roosevelt early in 1934 that the "wide" and "not very well defined" powers of the high commissioner authorized by the independence legislation "largely, if not completely neutralized" the autonomy of the proposed Commonwealth.[3]

Frank Murphy was virtually the unanimous choice of the Filipinos to serve as the first high commissioner. Quezon made this recommendation "definite and urgent" in a conversation with the chief of the Bureau of Insular Affairs in November 1934. ". . . a man on the ground who already had the reins of the government in his hand and understood the general set-up throughout the Islands," Quezon stated, "would be an enormous contributing factor to the proper functioning of the Commonwealth government." Murphy was initially disinclined to accept the high commissionership if it was offered to him, describing the position as "a swell job—good pay[,] no work—which I don't want and seems an anti-climax." He could conceive of himself as playing the role, he indicated, "simply to help these good people over the bridge," but he believed that "the firing line" was "the place" for him, and the high commissionership, "a step down" from the governor-generalship in his view, did not satisfy this criterion. " 'I don't think he wants to stay there,' " Senator Millard Tydings concluded after visiting the Philippines late in 1934. When President Roosevelt, however, definitely offered the position to Murphy in March 1935, he agreed to stay on for about three months after the inauguration of the Commonwealth, "long enough to get it going and establish a sort of standard."[4]

Roosevelt nominated Murphy as the high commissioner on June 25, 1935, and the Senate unanimously approved the appointment without even referring it to committee. Although Murphy by this time was saying to those closest to him that he "would like the job," he had no desire to remain in the post for more than a few months. His hope was that the president would summon him to Washington late in 1935 or early in 1936 to serve in an "appropriate post," by which Murphy meant the attorney generalship, for which he thought himself "best equipped," the secretaryship of war, which he was confident he could "handle," or the secretaryship of state, which appealed to him. Failing such an appointment, Murphy intended to return to the United States in May or June 1936 to enter the Michigan gubernatorial race or to "otherwise assist" President Roosevelt in the 1936 campaign.[5]

The president apparently intended to replace Murphy, after the Commonwealth had been safely launched, with the chief of staff of the United States Army, General Douglas MacArthur. Learning in May 1935 that MacArthur was under consideration as a successor to Murphy, Quezon asked the general whether it was more to his interest and that of their two countries for him to serve as high commissioner or as military advisor to the Philippines, the position

MacArthur was then slated to fill. MacArthur, who for several months had been considering the possibility of becoming high commissioner, replied that he had "no inkling" that he was to succeed Murphy, who, the general wrote, "fills the job admirably" and should be persuaded to remain in the position "indefinitely." As between the two positions, MacArthur asserted that nothing could "tempt" him to give up the job of military advisor. Despite these words, when Roosevelt offered MacArthur the high commissionership on September 3, 1935, he was quite receptive. When he discovered that he could not accept a civilian appointment without resigning from the army, the general, professing himself to be "dismayed and nonplussed," wondered whether Congress might resolve the matter in his favor by special legislation. Roosevelt thought that this could be arranged with "little or no trouble on the Hill," but the president in the end let the matter drop.[6]

The appointment of Murphy as high commissioner was hailed in the Philippines as "the best that could have been made." The legislature unanimously approved a joint resolution lauding Murphy's selection as "a fitting recognition of his able, high-minded, and statesmanlike discharge of the duties" of governor-general. In remarks on the Senate floor, Quezon, not one to speak in moderation on such occasions, declared that none of Murphy's predecessors as governor-general excelled him in "his sympathetic understanding of our problems, in his devotion to his duties, in his love of justice, in his courage to fight the wrong and to stand by the right, and in his vision as a statesman."[7]

"It is of the utmost importance," Murphy advised the Bureau of Insular Affairs a few weeks after the approval of the Tydings-McDuffie Act, "that the position, status and authority of the High Commissioner be clearly defined, established, and understood before surrendering control to [the] new government." Unless this were done, Murphy feared that it would be "difficult, if not impossible," for the high commissioner "to support and maintain in practice the position of preeminence, rank and respect necessary for effective discharge of his responsibilities under the law." What Murphy had in mind, he later wrote Roosevelt, was a statement by the president similar to the instructions that President McKinley had issued to William Howard Taft and the Philippine Commission in 1900 and Secretary of War Newton D. Baker had issued to Francis B. Harrison after the passage of the Jones Act. The Bureau of Insular Affairs and the War Department initially supported Murphy's position, and when Senator Carl Hayden visited the Philippines in September 1934, he too became "convinced" that Murphy's estimate of the situation was correct.[8]

Shortly before Murphy arrived in Washington in March 1935, General Cox advised the secretary of war that General MacArthur and the judge advocate general both had reacted unfavorably to drafts of instructions to the high commissioner that had been prepared by the Bureau of Insular Affairs. They contended that the powers the United States surrendered to the Commonwealth should be granted "graciously," without "reservation" and without any implication that the Philippine government would not faithfully observe the mandatory provisions of the independence statute. Because of the opposition to his views regarding instructions that Murphy encountered in Washington, Cox thought that the governor-general might be "inclined to veer away" from the idea of instructions, but Murphy soon set the general straight on the matter, reiterating that the position of the United States vis-à-vis the Commonwealth had to be "made plain" in advance. "Important and paramount national interests," Murphy declared, "should not be left to uncertainty or future negotiation or local Philippine policy."⁹

When Murphy left the United States in May, he thought that his ideas about the high commissionership had been "approved in a general way" by the president, the secretary of state, and the Bureau of Insular Affairs. After "a very careful and prolonged study" and after efforts to draft suitable instructions "seemed to result merely in a repetition of the legal provisions [of the Tydings-McDuffie Act] without adding to their clarity," Cox, however, advised the secretary of war that it was "hardly practicable to lay down definite rules" regarding the relationship of the high commissioner and the Commonwealth. As he saw it, reliance would have to be placed on "the ability, judgment, and tact" of the high commissioner to deal with specific situations as they arose. Secretary Dern, who believed that the high commissioner "should remain in the background so far as possible, and should not appear to have any voice in the conduct of the proper affairs of the Commonwealth government," promptly converted the Cox memorandum into an August 16 letter from the secretary of war to Murphy and gained the president's approval of the document. In Hayden's opinion, and Murphy must have agreed, Dern's letter was "so inadequate as to be puerile."¹⁰

The very same day that the secretary of war advised Murphy that Washington had rejected his request for detailed instructions, Cox sent the governor-general some notes concerning the ceremonies inaugurating the Commonwealth that called for a gun salute for the president of the Commonwealth but not for the high commissioner. Since Murphy believed that the high commissioner must be the ranking official in the Commonwealth, Cox's inaugural suggestions initiated a prolonged and acrimonious controversy between Murphy and the War Department regarding the proper honors and salutes to be accorded the president and the high commissioner that became intertwined with the equally troublesome dispute concerning instructions for the high commissioner.[11]

About the same time that Cox wrote Murphy about the inauguration ceremonies, the Bureau of Insular Affairs recommended that the president of the Commonwealth, like the high commissioner, should receive a nineteen-gun salute rather than the twenty-one gun salute accorded a head of state. MacArthur, however, advised the secretary of war that he "disagree[d] utterly" with this recommendation. The United States, the general declared, could "make no greater mistake . . . than to attempt to belittle and diminish the social prestige of the governing head of this new country." If the bureau's "unnecessary and uncalled for ruling" were implemented, he warned, it would "create a sense of resentment and insult in the breasts of all Filipinos" and would engender "a bitter quarrel" between the two nations. Since the secretary of war agreed with MacArthur, Cox informed Murphy on September 6 that the president would be accorded a twenty-one gun salute and the high commissioner a nineteen-gun salute, thus giving the head of the new government precedence over the chief American official in the islands.[12]

Strongly dissenting from the position taken in Washington and viewing the matter with "the greatest concern," Murphy cabled Cox on September 11 that "without premier rank and commensurate authority for its chief representative," the American position in the Philippines would become "untenable." Since the Commonwealth, he correctly pointed out, would not be a sovereign state, the high commissioner, as the representative of the president and the sovereign authority, should be "superior in rank and dignity to all Commonwealth officials." Any view to the contrary was "inconsistent with [the] plain and express provisions of the [Independence] Act, practical experience, and sound principles of administrative policy." The matter was of such great importance to American interests in the Philippines and in the Orient, Murphy stated, that it should be submitted to the president for decision.[13]

The next day Murphy sent Cox a draft of the instructions that the governor-general thought should be issued to the high commissioner. The document had been prepared by Murphy and Ed Kemp with some help from Hayden, and "every word" had been "weighed and re-weighed." It should be American policy, the draft proposed, to avoid interference with the "broad autonomy" granted the Commonwealth government so long as its authority was exercised in accordance with the Tydings-McDuffie Act and the Constitution. The United States government, however, the document contended, "by virtue of its sovereign position as well as express provisions of the Act, retains a large measure of responsibility for maintenance of orderly, stable, and just government in the Philippines, together with commensurate authority for the performance of its responsibility." As the chief representative of the sovereign government, the high commissioner was "to make such dispositions and actuations" as he thought "necessary for effective exercise and discharge of the authority and responsibility" reserved to the United States government.

Quite apart from the powers entrusted to the president by the independence law, Murphy argued, "there exist undefined obligations and responsibilities that necessarily inhere in a situation and relationship of this sort, rights and duties that are not susceptible of legislative definition or statement, and these also must be assumed and implemented by executive authority in accordance with the recognized purposes of the Act." The actions of the president would necessarily have to be guided largely by information and advice furnished by the high commissioner; the president, in practice, might find it "convenient and even necessary" to entrust the discharge of some of his functions to the high commissioner. There might even be occasions when the high commissioner would have to take "prompt or summary action" without sanction of "special authorization." The high commissioner, in Murphy's view, was not only to perform the duties expressly assigned in the independence statute or delegated by the president but also "to take whatever action shall at any time be required to protect and promote those interests that are the legitimate concern of this government in the administration of the affairs of the Philippine Government." If the Commonwealth government seriously neglected or flagrantly disregarded its obligations or the provisions of its constitution, he might "make appropriate representations" to it "for correction or abatement of such conditions." If necessary to preserve law and order or to protect the interests of the United States government, he could call on the military for assistance. Murphy also insisted that the high commissioner must have "unrestricted access to all government records" and that the president of the Commonwealth should be "enjoined" to furnish the high commissioner with whatever information he requested.[14]

The high commissioner envisioned in Murphy's draft instructions, a powerful figure possessed of inherent executive power, bore little resemblance to the official whom others in Washington and Manila characterized as an "observer," "ambassador," "glorified bill collector," or "watch dog of the United States." Concerned, apparently, that the War Department might not comply with his request to forward his letters regarding instructions and honors and salutes to the president, Murphy sent copies directly to the White House and suggested that the president should review the subject and should also refer the matter to the attorney general for study.[15]

Continuing the flurry of messages to Washington regarding the status and authority of the high commissioner, Murphy cabled the secretary of war on September 23 to protest the department's apparent decision to subordinate the high commissioner to the president of the Commonwealth. Since the "local policy and practice" had always been "to enlarge local control and diminish American authority" to the extent possible, the relegation of the high commissioner to a "secondary position," Murphy contended, would be "fatal" to the "effective maintenance and exercise" of that authority.[16]

As the War Department saw it, Murphy's barrage of cables "[set] forth . . . an absolutely unwarranted assumption of authority for the High Commissioner." The chief influence in the molding of Philippine policy in the department was now Douglas MacArthur, who as third-ranking member in the department ran the agency after Dern left to attend the inauguration ceremonies in Manila. In the view of Murphy and his staff—so Hayden wrote a faculty colleague in Ann Arbor—there was "a deliberate plan afoot to inaugurate the Philippine Commonwealth as a semi-independent state, or protectorate and to give its President the status of the chief executive of such an entity." Quezon and MacArthur were seen as plotting "to set up a situation" contrary to the Tydings-McDuffie Act and to do so through MacArthur's control of the War Department—when Murphy had been in Washington in the spring, MacArthur had told him that Dern, who, to be sure, had "no knowledge of and little interest in the Army" and whose health was failing, was unaware that " 'we have relieved him of most of his work' "—and while President Roosevelt was preoccupied with other matters.

The manifestations of the " 'plot,' " as seen in Manila, were the Dern letter of August 16 rejecting Murphy's plea for detailed instructions; plans for the inauguration of the Commonwealth, including the twenty-one gun salute for Quezon; "covert opposition" to Murphy in the Bureau of Insular Affairs; evidence that MacArthur was furnishing Quezon with bureau documents or their substance; Quezon's arranging to have MacArthur detailed to the Philippines as military advisor to the Commonwealth government; confidential

War Department instructions, to be noted later, that, from Mala-cañan's perspective, made MacArthur the "No. 1 U.S. Army man" in the Philippines and placed the American army in the Philippines at Quezon's disposal; and the consideration being given in Washington to the appointment of MacArthur to succeed Murphy as high commissioner. Hayden was especially concerned about MacArthur's possible succession to the high commissionership since the vice-governor thought that the general was too close to Quezon—they were "compadres"—and would be regarded by many Filipinos as Quezon's man.[17]

After MacArthur read Murphy's draft instructions, he left word that Murphy was to be informed that the views he had expressed were "widely different" from those prevailing in Washington, which was precisely what was at issue. "Hell's a-popping!" commented D. C. McDonald, acting chief of the Bureau of Insular Affairs during Cox's absence from Washington, when Murphy's cable to Roosevelt asking him personally to review the matter was forwarded to the War Department for decoding. Since MacArthur, who was acting secretary of war, was soon to leave for the Philippines, McDonald was "pushing" for the chief of staff to take the matter up with Roosevelt lest the entire War Department be "upset" by what McDonald viewed as a challenge to its authority by Murphy. McDonald and MacArthur discussed the question at some length on September 23, and the general then began dictating a letter on the subject to the president. That night Major Dwight D. Eisenhower came to McDonald's residence, the two men "revamped" MacArthur's letter, and Eisenhower further revised the letter the next morning.

Later that same day McDonald attended a meeting that the State Department had called to discuss the issue of honors and salutes as it pertained to the Philippine Commonwealth. McDonald argued for a twenty-one gun salute for the president of the Commonwealth, but State Department representatives, viewing the matter as Murphy did, contended that the twenty-one gun salute should be reserved for heads of state and that it would be a mistake "even by inference" to convey the impression that the Commonwealth was a sovereign state. They not only favored a nineteen-gun salute for Quezon but maintained that the high commissioner should be "the number one man" in the Philippines. Since Richard Southgate, the chief of the Division of Protocol and Conference of the State Department, had agreed with the War Department's position on gun salutes the previous week, McDonald was astonished at the view expressed by State Department representatives—Southgate "went back on the State Department's approval of your 21 guns,'' McDonald informed MacArthur—and he thought it ''a grave mistake'' for the position of the secretary of war, the chief of staff, and the Bureau of Insular Affairs to be reversed by the State Department. Bureaucratic rivalry now became commingled with issues of principle in the effort to define the position of the high commissioner in the Philippine Commonwealth.[18]

The participants in the State-War Department conference of September 24 agreed that the salute issue was of such great importance that it should be resolved by the president himself. The conferees decided that the State Department should prepare a brief statement on the matter and should then present it to the War Department for concurrence before submitting it to Roosevelt. Fearing, however, that the State Department might take the matter directly to the president without giving the War Department a chance to set forth its views, McDonald urged the prompt dispatch to Roosevelt of the MacArthur letter to the president concerning Murphy's cables. Agreeing, Mac-Arthur signed the letter on September 26, and McDonald, waging the bureaucratic battle with a vengeance, delivered it to the White House in person that same morning. When he returned to Mac-Arthur's office at 10:57 A.M., McDonald learned that William Phillips, the acting secretary of state, was to see Roosevelt at 11:00 A.M. Since MacArthur thought it ''imperative'' that the president see the War Department's letter and the background documents that accompanied it before he talked to Phillips, McDonald called Rudolph Forster, the White House executive clerk, who promised to place the material before the president immediately.[19]

In his letter to the president, MacArthur contended that the Tydings-McDuffie Act did not call for ''an inter-governmental procedure designed to perpetuate a state and feeling of American authority in the Islands'' but rather ''the maximum assumption of independent action on the part of the Island authorities consistent with the interests of the United States and the plain language of the law. In effect,'' he stated, confirming Malacañan's fears, ''independence has been proclaimed.'' It was ''self-evident'' to MacArthur that the president of the Commonwealth should be accorded a ''social status'' equivalent to that of an elected head of state.

Despite the clear intent of the independence law, the general insisted, Murphy was seeking ''even greater authority'' than he exercised as governor-general. His definition of the role of the high commissioner would ''practically ignore the explicit provisions of the Tydings-McDuffie Act ... and would actually limit, rather than extend, the degree of autonomy ... enjoyed by the Filipinos.'' Depicting Murphy's position as a challenge to the authority of the president of the United States, MacArthur extravagantly contended that if Murphy's recommendations were implemented, the high commissioner would become "a super-President of the Commonwealth" and would exercise "many of the powers heretofore exercised only by the President of the United States. . . . The War Department," MacArthur observed, "knows of no appointive official in any government having powers as great as those desired by . . . Murphy."

"The main function" of the high commissioner, as MacArthur saw it, was "to act as a general adviser to the Commonwealth Government and to keep the President of the United States informed as to the significant developments . . . in the Islands." Murphy should therefore be advised, MacArthur recommended, that the Dern letter of August 16 represented "the considered views of the Administration," and the terms of that letter, MacArthur counseled, "should not be materially changed."[20]

Just before seeing the president on September 26, Phillips visited with MacArthur. Although the general thought that he had "sold" the acting secretary of state on the gun-salute issue, when Phillips talked to the president, he simply presented the differing views on the matter of the State Department and the War Department. Acting Attorney General Stanley Reed advised the president that same day that the August 16 letter "tactfully expressed" the proper relationship of the high commissioner to the Philippine government, that the limited role the letter prescribed for the high commissioner could be "construed as a sign of weakness" but that it was "worth while to try" the approach, and that the Commonwealth president should be accorded "priority of rank." After weighing the matter carefully, the president, as Murphy was informed, decided to accept the War Department's advice regarding both instructions to the high commissioner and the salute to be accorded the president of the Commonwealth. Although the victory of MacArthur and the War Department seemed complete, on October 1, while MacArthur was en route to the Philippines, the president relieved him of his position as chief of staff even though Dern had recommended that this not take place until December 15. MacArthur, who was reduced by the president's action from four-star to two-star general, thought that he had been betrayed, but Hayden and, presumably, Murphy, concluding that Roosevelt had discovered that he was being "used" by MacArthur, were delighted.[21]

On October 4 the *Philippines Herald*, Quezon's principal newspaper, published a precedence list for the inauguration ceremonies, prepared in Washington for the benefit of the commanding general of the Philippine Department, that made Quezon the ranking official in the islands. An angry Murphy, who had not been sent a copy of the document, cabled the Bureau of Insular Affairs to ascertain responsibility for the list and its legal justification. The bureau replied that it had prepared the list in collaboration with the Protocol Division of the State Department and the adjutant general's office but that it was merely "suggestive" and "entirely unofficial," which left unexplained how Filipino sources had acquired the document. Murphy protested to the secretary of war that the list had created "surprise and confusion" in the Philippines.[22]

Ill with bleeding ulcers, Manuel Quezon had remained in the background while the conflict between Murphy and the War Department escalated. He joined the argument on November 2, however, with a long twenty-five point memorandum to Murphy that challenged the governor-general's definition of the high commissioner's role as set forth in the draft instructions that he had submitted to Washington. Someone in the War Department had supplied the Filipino leader with this and other pertinent documents, as Hayden correctly suspected. Quezon, who had privately remarked that Murphy would "have nothing to do as High Commissioner," stated that he agreed with Roosevelt that instructions were unnecessary. If they were to be issued, however, they must conform not only to the specific provisions of the Tydings-McDuffie Act but also to its "intent and spirit." Quezon's thesis was that, except for "the specific reservations and limitations" in the independence law, Congress had transferred "the plenary powers of government" to the Filipino nation. The United States government, as a consequence, now possessed only certain enumerated powers as regards the Philippines, and to contend, as Murphy did, that it had "other indeterminate powers" inhering in sovereignty was to assume that no change in government was to occur as the result of the establishment of the Commonwealth. The powers reserved to the United States, moreover, were not to be exercised in the regular and orderly functioning of government. *"They partake,"* Quezon argued, *"of the nature of supervisory powers to be held in reserve and only to be used in the emergencies specifically mentioned in the [Tydings-McDuffie] Act."* Doubts as to how these powers were to be exercised should be resolved in favor of the Commonwealth.

Actions by the United States regarding the Commonwealth, Quezon concluded, were to be determined by the president, not by the high commissioner "accredited" to the Philippines. "Congress,"

Quezon insisted, "took special pains to avoid giving any power of administration or control directly to the High Commissioner, in order that there be no excuse for unauthorized intermeddling on his part in the orderly functioning of the Government." Congress had vested the powers of supervision in the president rather than the high commissioner, Quezon argued, since the former, unlike the latter, would not be influenced by the local political and social atmosphere or by "considerations of a personal nature" and could therefore consider questions "in the light of broad principles and sound administration alone." Although as the representative of the president the high commissioner had "a standing of the highest order," the Tydings-McDuffie Act granted him no "power of government, whether direct or supervisory in nature," and he was not to participate in "the conduct of public affairs in the Commonwealth." Essentially only "an official observer," he could take no action regarding the Commonwealth unless authorized to do so by the president, and the only power that the president could specifically delegate to him was the authority to take over the Philippine customs if the Commonwealth government failed to pay its indebtedness. In short, Quezon summarized, the high commissioner was "not a pro-consul or a colonial administrator of the old type . . . with the strings of power at his finger tips" but rather "the dignified symbol of American sovereignty, detached from the actual work of government but ready to give . . . friendly advice when necessary."

In a handwritten note at the end of his memorandum, Quezon recalled for Murphy that, when Hoover had vetoed the Hare-Hawes-Cutting bill because he thought it denied the United States "effective authority," Congress had overridden the president. Quezon conveniently neglected to mention that he himself had alleged that the statute vested excessive power in the high commissioner.[23]

Quezon's memorandum confirmed Murphy's worst fears concerning the Quezon-MacArthur view of the nature of the Commonwealth and the role of the high commissioner. In a point-by-point rebuttal of the document that echoed constitutional arguments of an earlier era regarding the nature of the American federal system, Murphy attacked what he regarded as Quezon's confusion concerning the sovereignty of the United States and his narrowly circumscribed definition of the authority of the high commissioner. The United States, Murphy contended, possessed "plenary sovereign power," not "enumerated" powers, and although the authority of United States officials was limited by the independence statute, that of the United States government was limited neither by the Tydings-

McDuffie Act nor by the Philippine constitution. As a "creature of Congress," the Commonwealth government, by contrast, was a government of "granted powers," and doubts as to where a particular power was lodged were therefore to be resolved in favor of the sovereign authority.

The president, Murphy argued, could delegate to the high commissioner any of the powers assigned to the chief executive by the Tydings-McDuffie Act. To describe the high commissioner as an official "accredited" to the Philippines, as Quezon had done, was in itself a "fundamental error," Murphy charged. He was neither an "ambassador" nor a mere " 'symbol of American sovereignty' " but an official vested by law with certain duties and prerogatives and "empowered to exercise large local authority under delegation of the President."[24]

When Dern and Cox arrived in the Philippines on November 2, Murphy did not go to the dock to meet them. The details of the secretary's reception, Cox observed, were complete insofar as the army was concerned, but he thought that "there was a certain lack of completeness . . . at Malacanang [sic]." Before Dern was able to get to his room in the palace, Murphy was already pressing him with questions about the Commonwealth and the high commissioner. Murphy discovered that the secretary knew very little either about the Philippines or about the issues regarding the status and prerogatives of the high commissioner that so concerned the governor-general. Dern, Cox, Murphy, Hayden, and J. Weldon Jones continued the discussion the next day, and Murphy, according to Hayden, "went after Cox pretty hard" and "shot the logic and the law of their [Dern and Cox] position pretty much to pieces."[25]

On November 4 Dern gave Hayden a copy of MacArthur's September 26 letter to the president—the copy was unsigned, but typist's marks revealed its authorship—in which the general accused Murphy of wishing to become "a super-President of the Commonwealth." The letter, according to Hayden, "set up a man of straw and proceeded to demolish it," and Murphy and his aides were determined to rebut the general's factually inaccurate statements. At lunch the next day Murphy, Hayden, and Kemp canvassed the situation from every angle. They remained convinced that what was at stake was the position of the United States in the Commonwealth and the likelihood that the United States would have to withdraw from the Philippines before the end of the transition period if the War Department's interpretation of the status and prerogatives of the high commissioner prevailed. In further conversations with Dern on November

6, Murphy contended that to accord Quezon a twenty-one gun salute would give him "an erroneous conception of his importance and latitude of action" and would make it difficult for the United States "to keep a restraining hand" on the new government. Murphy disavowed any personal interest in the matter of rank and precedence and succeeded in convincing Dern that his "motives" were "above question." [26]

Dern and Cox discovered that the War Department's views regarding the status and authority of the high commissioner were opposed not only by Murphy and his staff but by all the army and navy officers with whom they talked. "Very positive" that the high commissioner should be "the No. 1 Man in the Islands," the officers were "considerably perturbed" at the prospects of the demotion of the United States to "second place." Dern's "faith" in the War Department's position had been "somewhat weakened" when he read Murphy's cables to Washington, which did not reach the secretary until after his arrival in the Philippines, and he was "considerably impressed" by the additional arguments advanced in Manila by Murphy, Hayden, and others. Not only did Dern become aware of the exaggerated character of MacArthur's "super-President" letter, but he also learned for the first time of the plans for the inauguration ceremonies. " 'I thought that I was coming out here to inaugurate a Commonwealth, not merely a President,' " a concerned secretary of war commented. [27]

Since the controversy regarding the status of the high commissioner looked quite different to the secretary in Manila than it had in Washington, "at a distance from the scene of action," he agreed on November 7 to send Roosevelt a message that Murphy had drafted. This involved a reversal of the War Department's position, and so Dern decided that he must first discuss the matter with MacArthur, who turned up at Malacañan that night and talked with the secretary until 1:00 A.M. the next morning. The general apparently sought to convince Dern that the " 'Malacañan crowd' " simply wished to "hang on" to their privileges, and the secretary, probably overawed by the manner and presence of the general and unable to "break loose" from his influence, began to have second thoughts about the message to Roosevelt. He now decided simply to advise the president of Murphy's position, but when he supplied Malacañan with the message, undoubtedly the handiwork of Cox, Murphy and his staff found it "unsatisfactory, incorrect, and improper."

A discouraged Hayden feared that MacArthur had "won." The status of the high commissioner, Hayden bitterly noted, was being decided by two generals, "one of whom [Cox]" was "a mush-head, and the other [MacArthur] Quezon's agent!" Hayden was also dismayed that the congressional delegation visiting the Philippines for the inauguration appeared to be under the tutelage of former senator Harry B. Hawes, the lobbyist through whom Quezon, according to the vice-governor, hoped to control Congress. "The whole thing," Hayden concluded, "is shameful and suggests that we are not fit to have colonies, dependencies, protectorates, or any authority beyond our boundaries." Hayden, however, erred in his estimate of the situation. MacArthur had not "won," and "the MacArthur set-up in Washington" was not as formidable as the professor thought.[28]

Cabling the president on November 9, Dern noted that "some discord" had developed regarding the inauguration. He set forth Murphy's views concerning the twenty-one gun salute for Quezon and relayed the governor-general's recommendation that he and Quezon, in that order, should receive nineteen-gun salutes. Dern reported that Murphy's views were shared by his staff and the principal army and navy officers in the Philippines, with the sole exception of MacArthur. The secretary conceded that he was "somewhat impressed" with Murphy's position and that the subject might be more important than the secretary had once thought; but, echoing MacArthur, he expressed fear that a revision of the president's order regarding honors and precedence "would do more harm than good" since it was essential to retain the good will and cooperation of the Philippine government. Dern, consequently, did not recommend any change in the president's order, but he noted that if the president disagreed with this conclusion, it had been suggested that the firing of the same number of guns for both the high commissioner and the president of the Commonwealth would "relieve the situation." It is not clear whom Roosevelt consulted after receiving Dern's cable, but he now decided that Murphy had been right all along about the salute issue. In a reply cable to Dern that same day, the president instructed that Quezon was to receive the same nineteen-gun salute accorded state governors.[29]

When Quezon heard that he was to receive only a nineteen-gun salute, he rushed to Malacañan to complain to Murphy and Dern. He threatened to remain away from the inauguration ceremonies and to have the chief justice of the Philippine Supreme Court come to his home to administer the oath, after which he would proceed to the palace to assume his duties. According to Quezon's account of the conversation, "Murphy turned blue and Dern pink." After Quezon had been given the opportunity "to vent his grievances fully," Dern and Murphy sought to soothe his ruffled feelings; Murphy, according to Quezon, even offered to resign as prospective high commissioner if he had lost the Filipino leader's confidence. Quezon had assumed that Murphy, "under American 'Old Timer' influence in Manila," was responsible for the gun-salute reversal, but he now learned that Roosevelt had made the decision. The discussion appeared to end amicably, Dern informing Roosevelt that Quezon had said that he was "perfectly satisfied" with the new arrangement. Quezon, however, was play-acting, and he never forgave Murphy for his part in the affair. The Filipino leader had been made to lose "face," and if, on the one hand, he referred to the gun-salute controversy as "a small matter" and claimed that he was indifferent to honors, he also said that it meant "a great deal" and that it was the honor due his country that was at issue. As for remaining away from his inauguration, "nothing," as Hayden later observed, "could have kept the *Presidente* from that occasion except his own demise."[30]

The Roosevelt cable of November 9, although settling the issue of the gun salute, made no reference to the equally troublesome matter of the order of precedence as between the high commissioner and the president of the Commonwealth. When the program for the inauguration was submitted to Dern for revision, however, the secretary and Murphy "took pains to outline a procedure which implied the seniority of the High Commissioner." In the meantime, the State Department was counseling the president that the high commissioner could more effectively discharge his duties and the United States could better fulfill its responsibilities as the sovereign power in the Philippines if the high commissioner were the ranking official in the islands. Heeding this advice, Roosevelt informed Dern on November 13 that, although the high commissioner and the president of the Commonwealth were to be regarded as of equal rank and were to receive the same honors, the high commissioner was to take precedence as between the two of them. As soon as this message was received in Manila, Murphy provided Quezon with a copy. Dern, however, preferring that the order be officially released in Washington, decided not to make the message public in Manila "for fear of scratching the wound which had just been healed." Dern thought that "a difficult situation" now had been "happily ended," a view to which Murphy, but not Quezon, subscribed.[31]

When Quezon visited the United States early in 1937, he made it evident in conversations with State Department officials that he was "greatly irked" by the fact that the high commissioner outranked the president of the Commonwealth. He talked about the gun-salute reversal, which Joseph E. Jacobs, the head of the department's new Office of Philippine Affairs, thought had become "almost an obsession" with him, "in a tone of rancor and impatience." Quezon, Stanley K. Hornbeck, chief of the Division of Far Eastern Affairs, observed, "nurses a grievance," and this, Hornbeck thought, made it difficult for him to approach "problems" in Philippine-American relations in an objective manner. Hornbeck quite correctly noted that the issue had been "badly handled," and he was aware that "a high officer of the Army" was ultimately responsible.[32]

Victorious on the issue of honors and precedence, Murphy failed to sway Dern or Roosevelt on the issue of instructions. Undoubtedly influenced by Cox and seeking "to terminate the discussion" before the inauguration, the secretary wrote Murphy on November 13 that he was "particularly impressed with the idea that concrete instructions might tend to unfortunate situations because of their mandatory nature, whereas without too many restrictions in the form of orders," the high commissioner and the Commonwealth president could resolve "most situations . . . through . . . cooperative efforts." Unpersuaded by this line of argument, Murphy on November 14 handed Dern a suggested draft of instructions to consider on his return trip to the United States. There the matter rested until after the inauguration of the Commonwealth on November 15.[33]

II

Vice-President John Nance Garner, Secretary of War Dern, twenty-six members of the House of Representatives, seventeen senators, and ten American newsmen—"the most distinguished group that ever left our [American] shores for one purpose," according to Hawes— were on hand for the inauguration ceremonies. Murphy, who accommodated the vice-president, the secretary of war, and their wives in Malacañan, made a profoundly favorable impression on both John and Mrs. Garner. The vice-president later told Roosevelt that Murphy was "one of the most substantial men this Republic has," and Mrs. Garner, succumbing to Murphy's fabled fascination for women, regardless of age, wrote him shortly after the inauguration, "I have one beloved son . . . if I had two, I would have liked the other one to be just like you. I have never said this about any other boy I have ever known."[34]

Garner and Speaker of the House Joseph T. Byrns addressed a joint session of the insular legislature on November 12. Greeted with "salvos of applause," the governor-general delivered his final address to the legislature the next day. He noted some of the accomplishments of his administration and advised the government that was about to be formed that success in government came from "loyalty to the principles of sound finance and social justice, freedom from measures that are selfish and oppressive, steadfast devotion to the ideals and principles of democracy." Thinking no doubt about the provisions of the new Philippine constitution, he counseled that "the personal aspect of government must be minimized. All officials should be humble before the majesty of the law." In a sardonic commentary on the speech, J. P. McEvoy observed in the *Saturday Evening Post* that "what Murphy said diplomatically in ten thousand well-chosen words could have been sent in the following wire: Boys Keep Your Feet Out of the Trough. Stop. Love. Murphy."[35]

Dern and Murphy drove together to the inaugural ceremonies, preceded by a cavalry escort, and a similar escort preceded Quezon and his family. An enormous assemblage of about 250,000 persons was on hand for the proceedings. After an address by Dern, Murphy read a proclamation announcing the results of the September 17 elections. When Quezon rose to take his oath of office, he received a nineteen-gun salute, followed by ruffles and flourishes and the playing of the Philippine national anthem. Dern then read a proclamation on behalf of President Roosevelt terminating the existing insular government and stating that the Commonwealth government was to "enter upon its rights, privileges, powers, and duties" as provided in its constitution. Quezon, following this, delivered an inaugural address, which brought the morning ceremonies to a close. Cox had specified that in leaving the inaugural ceremonies, Murphy was to withdraw to the Manila Hotel under escort and was to be accorded appropriate honors but was not to receive a gun salute. In "a last minute change" in the arrangements, however, it had been decided that Murphy would be rendered a nineteen-gun salute when he arrived at the hotel, which is the procedure that was followed.

Shortly after the conclusion of Quezon's address a bugle call sounded the beginning of the inaugural parade, which was witnessed by one-half million people, the largest crowd that had ever assembled in Manila. The opening session of the National Assembly took place in the afternoon, there was a fireworks display in the evening in front of the New Luneta on Manila Bay, and an inaugural ball concluded what the *New York Herald Tribune* characterized as "one of the most elaborate Presidential inaugural ceremonies the world has ever witnessed."[36]

Using the bible that his "darling Mama" had given him when he graduated from high school, Murphy took his oath of office as high commissioner on November 14 in a simple ceremony attended by Quezon, Dern, and a few others. In a laudatory self-appraisal of his governor-generalship, Murphy noted in his brief remarks that the new government was fortunate to begin its existence with "a balanced budget, an awakened social consciousness and in an atmosphere of peace and good will." Concerned about the discord generated by the salute controversy, Murphy ignored protocol and sought to appease "hurt feelings" by making an official call on Quezon the morning after the inauguration, shortly before the Commonwealth president made his first official call on the high commissioner. This "planted a time bomb" for J. Weldon Jones, who served as acting high commissioner when Murphy returned to the United States in 1936, and Murphy later conceded that what he had done "was a mistake."[37]

The inauguration of the Commonwealth did not end the controversy between the high commissioner and Quezon regarding rank and precedence, nor did it lessen Murphy's insistence on the need for detailed instructions. On November 22, 1935, Roosevelt directed that his message according senior rank to the high commissioner be "announced" as "the rule governing rank and precedence," which Murphy thought was "perfect." He played down publicity with respect to the rule lest it prove "offensive" to local leaders, but he saw to it that the consular corps and American and Commonwealth officials were advised of Roosevelt's order, and he instructed subordinates to cite the document whenever this was necessary to clarify a particular situation.[38]

When a French war vessel visited Manila shortly after the Commonwealth was inaugurated, the commanding officer made an official call on the high commissioner, a fact noted in the American-owned press but "somewhat smothered" in the Philippine press. A few days later, however, when a Pan American clipper completed the air line's first airmail flight to Manila, the airmen called on Quezon but ignored the high commissioner. Questioned about this, Murphy replied that he was "totally disinterested in the matter of honors, salutes and courtesies for their own sake," but the high commissioner, as Jones noted, felt the snub "very keenly." Murphy wrote Norman Hill some months later that the indifference to the interests of their own country of Pan American officials, whose company he had befriended, was "a little shocking" but that he should have known from past experience that public utilities were "stone cold to obligations of this kind. I haven't seen much proof that they know a flag or a country." Although Murphy noted at the end of February 1936 that the Pan American action had been the "one act of disrespect, [the] one offense," as far as the status of the high commissioner was concerned, his aides soon became aware that another "act of disrespect" was being committed by foreign consuls in the Philippines, who sometimes communicated directly with the Commonwealth government, rather than through the high commissioner, even though the foreign relations of the Commonwealth were supposedly the preserve of the United States government. When Paul V. McNutt succeeded Murphy, he insisted that the practice be halted.[39]

The continued sensitivity in Manila about the matter of honors became evident when J. Weldon Jones began his service as acting high commissioner on September 15, 1936. Quezon proposed an exchange of formal calls, with Jones making the first call, as Murphy had done following the inauguration of the Commonwealth. American civil and military officials advised Jones that this was contrary to Washington orders and that Quezon must make the first call. Jones so advised Quezon, but since he did not wish to offend the Philippine president, he told Osmeña that he was willing to forgo the ceremony of official calls.

Angrily responding to Jones's proposal, Quezon insisted in a letter to Jones that the " 'rules of ordinary courtesy' " required that a new high commissioner call on the head of the government even if one conceded, which Quezon did only for the sake of argument, that the high commissioner outranked the Commonwealth president. " 'I am not going to allow that once more,' " Quezon asserted, " 'the Army and Navy officers of the U.S. with their officiousness place unnecessary and unjustified obstacles in the way of sending this government the honors that are its due.' " He had yielded in the twenty-one gun salute controversy, he said, but " 'this time I am standing pat.' " He would not call on anyone save the American president, and he would not " 'obey any order' " to the contrary. As long as he remained president, Quezon concluded, " 'no High Commissioner will ever receive any official call who does not first call on me.' "

Continuing the argument the next day, Quezon contended that the Commonwealth was " 'a new situation under the American flag,' " which, of course, was why the controversy had developed, that the United States had no applicable precedents bearing on the relationship of the high commissioner to the new government, and that he would not abide by the precedents of other countries respecting the relationship of their high commissioners to " 'puppet native rulers' " since the United States " 'did not set up a puppet' " in the Philippines and he " 'would not be one any way.' " Having made his point, Quezon quickly expressed himself " 'satisfied' " that neither man should make an official call on the other. " 'Let us be practical and realistic,' " he wrote Jones. " 'Our job is too important to be interfered with by . . . such childish affairs as so-called official calls.' "[40]

The issue of precedence remained a troublesome one. When Quezon while en route to the United States early in 1937 visited China, he was received as a head of state, and the Japanese accorded him a twenty-one gun salute. The State Department advised that he should receive no more attention in Washington than a state governor and that it would be "wise" to let him know that he was "in a sense an American official." Hull informed Roosevelt that, since the inauguration of the Commonwealth, Quezon had evidenced "a marked tendency . . . to seize every opportunity to arrogate to himself the rank and honors of a chief of state." The question of ranks and salutes was in itself of minor significance, Hull noted, but it was "an index to the political and international status of the Philippine Commonwealth" and was "particularly important in the Far East[,] where such matters are very seriously regarded." This, of course, was precisely the point that Murphy had made. The advice of the State Department was followed in Washington, but when Quezon resumed his world tour he continued to act and be treated as a head of state, much to the State Department's annoyance. When he returned to Manila, however, Quezon stated publicly that the Commonwealth was " 'not an independent government,' " and the honors issue finally subsided in importance.[41]

It had been Murphy's contention that to avoid any misconception on the part of the Commonwealth government regarding its status, such as Murphy thought Quezon had evidenced in his tiff with Jones over official calls, it was essential for the United States government to issue instructions to the high commissioner defining his powers and prerogatives. The note on the subject that Murphy had handed Dern on November 14 failed, however, to persuade the secretary that anything more than his letter of August 16, 1935, was required; and the War Department did not even respond when the high commissioner later forwarded Quezon's memorandum of November 2, 1935, that so narrowly defined the powers of the high commissioner. Murphy consequently decided that since Washington was unlikely to provide him with "appropriate instructions," he would "set them up" himself. ". . . I can't wait for another several months," he wrote Hayden in December, "while the War Department[,] either in over its head in this matter or unable to act because of designers[,] further delays or confuses the situation. . . . I am here to do justice to the Filipinos but I have a primary duty to protect, pursue and further legitimate U.S. interests in the Philippines so long as the flag flies here."[42]

Murphy accordingly informed the War Department on December 10 that, unless advised to the contrary, he would henceforth act on the assumption that the high commissioner should have "unrestricted access to all government records"; should advise the president of the United States concerning "all important matters" affecting the Commonwealth government; report to the president whenever the Commonwealth government defaulted on its contractual obligations and, at the president's direction, take over its customs offices; take appropriate action in an "emergency," or when there was "serious and flagrant disregard" of the provisions of the Tydings-McDuffie Act or the Constitution, or when this was necessary to protect "the legitimate interests of the United States"; render such official reports as required by the Tydings-McDuffie Act; perform such additional duties as the president of the United States might delegate to him; and advise the president of the Commonwealth on matters involving the interests of the United States. Murphy stated that he would avoid "unnecessary interference" in Commonwealth government affairs.[43]

Murphy's definition of "appropriate instructions," more specific than the draft he had submitted on September 12, failed to persuade the War Department, which concluded that the issuance of further instructions would "raise an immediate controversy with Quezon" and would be "resented and contested" in Manila. Although probably correct, this was hardly a valid reason for the department's decision, which Murphy's staff interpreted as a refusal to grant the high commissioner "any real authority."[44]

Controversy that developed between Jones and the Commonwealth government during the final months of 1936 reinforced Murphy's conviction of the need for a "clear definition" of the high commissioner's authority. In a meeting of December 28 attended by Sayre, the chief of staff of the army, Embick, and Jacobs, Murphy, "with evidence of much feeling," stressed that the indefinite status of the high commissioner made it "impossible for him to function efficiently" and contended that Philippine officials were "assuming" that the islands were already independent.

In contrast to Murphy, Cox obdurately maintained that the history of the first year of the Commonwealth confirmed the soundness of the War Department's argument that it was "impossible to issue any comprehensive instructions in this new situation" and that it was best for the high commissioner to deal pragmatically with issues as they arose. Cox nevertheless conceded that it might be wise for the president to define the functions and status of the high commissioner somewhat more fully than had already been done. Cox prepared a draft of a letter of instructions, but it was couched in very general terms and fell far short of what Murphy had in mind. In a letter to the secretary of war on December 31, 1936, his last day in office as high commissioner, Murphy, buttressing his request with documents relating to events that had occurred since the inauguration of the Commonwealth, made a final plea for a "better definition . . . by responsible Washington authority of the position of the High Commissioner for the guidance of himself and the Commonwealth authorities."[45]

When Paul McNutt was appointed to succeed Murphy early in 1937, President Roosevelt provided him with a letter of instructions that the State Department had prepared and which incorporated suggestions of both Murphy and the War Department. "It is clearly understood," the president wrote, "that the United States will exercise sovereignty over the Islands and that certain authority arising out of the exercise of sovereign rights is still reserved to the Government of the United States." Murphy's influence was evident in this assertion as well as in a paragraph of the letter regarding the inherent authority of the high commissioner as the representative of the sovereign power:

> Aside from the duties and powers entrusted by the Independence Act to the President of the United States and the High Commissioner, there exist undefined obligations and responsibilities naturally inherent in a relationship which exists between the United States and the Philippines, as well as rights and duties that are not susceptible of legislative definition or statement. When situations arise involving such undefined obligations, responsibilities, rights and duties, it will be your duty to make appropriate representations to the Commonwealth Government and to tender in a spirit of sincere cooperation such suggestions or counsel as you may deem prudent or helpful.[46]

The president's letter lacked the specificity that Murphy thought desirable, the War Department having prevailed on this point, but his persistence regarding the matter of appropriate instructions for the high commissioner had not been without effect.

The residence of the high commissioner and the size and nature of his staff were issues that in Murphy's thinking were related to the broader question of the status and authority of the president's representative in the Philippines. Since Malacañan, the residential symbol of the governor-general's authority, was to be transferred to the president of the Commonwealth, Murphy thought that the residence provided for the high commissioner should be "at least equal" to the palace. Echoing the judgment of Cameron Forbes that the residence of the high commissioner went "right to the heart of his influence and prestige," Murphy wrote the War Department in September 1934 that "the practical importance of properly housing the first H.C. with a degree of prestige in the public mind" could "scarcely be over estimated." If the residence of the high commissioner were of an inferior sort, Murphy contended, this would "adversely affect [the] . . . response" to his suggestions and would make his position "difficult and wanting in effectiveness." Senator Carl Hayden agreed with Murphy. "Oriental peoples," he wrote Senator Tydings, "like magnificence and they will not have respect for a high commissioner who lives in a small house in Manila and has an office in some building occupied by others."[47]

After some initial hesitation, Quezon agreed to make Baguio's Mansion House temporarily available to the high commissioner as a residence. The United States government decided to construct a permanent building for a residence and offices for the high commissioner on reclaimed land in Manila Harbor. When Cox arrived in Manila for the inauguration ceremonies, he was dismayed to discover that Murphy had failed to make arrangements for temporary office and living space in Manila. Prodded by the general, Murphy a few days later contracted for office space in the Elks Club and reserved a suite in the Manila Hotel as his living quarters. Work on the permanent residence did not begin until the end of 1935, when a contract was let for the construction of a retaining wall in the harbor. The structure that was finally completed in 1940 became known as " 'Murphy's Mud Flat' " and was architecturally not too well suited to the tropics.[48]

Taking a "first-class" diplomatic mission of the United States in Europe as the "gross model," Murphy initially requested an appropriation of $263,100 for the operation of the high commissioner's office during the first year of the Commonwealth, with $82,000 of this sum budgeted as nonrecurring. Although the Bureau of the Budget regarded this sum as "too liberal," Murphy insisted that he required a staff equal in number to the staff of the governor-general because of "considerations of prestige" and the extensive responsibilities of the office. When Quezon became aware of the substantial staff Murphy contemplated, the Filipino leader "showed some anxiety about it" because, as Cox put it, "he [Quezon] thought we were leaving more of an observation post than he had . . . contemplated," another indication of Quezon's constricted view of the role of the high commissioner. In the end, Congress appropriated $165,000 for the high commissioner's office for the final seven-and-one-half months of the fiscal year 1936, a sum Murphy regarded as insufficient.[49]

Murphy split his staff between Baguio and Manila, and the high commissioner commuted between the two places by army plane at least once a week. Life at Mansion House was now "very quiet"; there were few visitors and "no more large parties." There was more activity in the high commissioner's Manila office, described by the *New York Times* as "the most gigantic place of record" in the Philippines. The author of a satirical article on the Philippines published early in 1936 reported, however, that Murphy now had no one to talk to but himself. The United States had never before had a high commissioner, the author noted, so "we forgot to tell him just what he is supposed to do." Actually, in addition to the general responsibilities vested in the high commissioner by the Tydings-McDuffie Act, the president assigned him a variety of duties and responsibilities: he was authorized to supervise the sugar program in the Philippines insofar as exports to the United States were concerned, issue passports, prescribe the documents required of aliens wishing to enter the Philippines, review Commonwealth proceedings in deportation cases and extradite fugitives, and issue licenses for the export and import of arms.[50]

It would always be his policy as high commissioner, Murphy informed Roosevelt, "to show proper respect for the dignity and authority of the Commonwealth Government." As high commissioner, Murphy consistently evidenced sympathy for the nationalist aspirations of the Philippines, but in dealing with such matters as Quezon's effort to vest control over deportations in the hands of the president of the Commonwealth and to impose duties on goods imported into the Philippines from foreign countries for the United States Army and Navy and in reacting to a legal opinion that the Securities Exchange Commission lacked jurisdiction over the Manila Stock Exchange, the high commissioner revealed his sensitivity to possible Commonwealth encroachment upon United States powers and prerogatives and his conviction that the office he held must be "something more than an observer's outpost."[51]

The effective discharge of his responsibilities, Murphy believed, required that the high commissioner's office be fully informed of the actions of the Commonwealth government. He therefore put his staff to work soon after the new government was established to prepare a list of the types of documents and reports it should be required to furnish the high commissioner. The list Murphy submitted to Quezon ran to four pages; as Weldon Jones remarked, "We asked for a plenty while we were asking." Kemp informed a friend that the high commissioner's office intended "to keep well informed of everything that goes on in the government" so that it could keep Washington apprised of Commonwealth affairs, particularly financial affairs. "It is our theory," Kemp declared, "that preventive action is preferable to major repairs and rehabilitation measures."[52]

The Commonwealth government readily complied with the high commissioner's request for documents except for the minutes of the Philippine National Bank and information concerning the use of the Belo fund, which after November 15, 1935, was disbursed by the president of the Commonwealth. Quezon told Francis Burton Harrison that he had instructed the bank to supply the minutes but had not pressed the matter when it refused to comply. The Commonwealth government justified its refusal to supply the minutes on the grounds of confidentiality and because, it contended, the bank was not a "subdivision" of the government and hence was exempt from the application of the Tydings-McDuffie Act. Rebutting this argument, Jones, the high commissioner's financial expert, contended that the bank was "the heart of governmental finance." Quezon eventually proposed that a representative of the high commissioner examine the minutes at the bank, but Jones, as acting high commissioner, rejected this offer and threatened to take the matter to Washington. It was not until January 1937 that Quezon yielded and transmitted the minutes to the high commissioner's office.[53]

Since the high commissioner, as Quezon put it, knew his "most intimate personal affairs," the Filipino president expressed a willingness to provide Murphy, as an individual, with information concerning appointments paid for with the P250,000 Belo fund money. Quezon, however, argued that it would be a dangerous precedent for him to concede that the high commissioner's office had a right to review the president's expenditure of such funds. The high commissioner's office did not yield to Quezon because, as Jones put it, the details concerning the expenditure of the fund were "more significant in showing the *nature* and *character* of the [Commonwealth] Government ... than the expenditure of any like sum anywhere in the Government." Believing that the fund made it possible for Quezon to reward his friends and to achieve "personal government" and regarding its continuation as "something of a blow at constitutional government" and as subject to abuse by "those affected by the Spanish influence," Murphy advised Quezon to abolish the fund.

Although resentful that Murphy wished him to do without money that Murphy had availed himself of as governor-general, Quezon heeded the high commissioner's advice and recommended in June 1936 that the National Assembly repeal the Belo Act as of January 1, 1938. He remained adamant, however, about supplying information regarding use of the Belo money. Although Murphy thought it "a healthy sign that . . . Quezon manifests a jealous and sensitive interest in these matters," the high commissioner regarded his right of access to Commonwealth records as unrestricted. He was, nevertheless, disinclined to permit the affair to grow into "a serious issue," and so the high commissioner's office did not press the matter during the remainder of Murphy's tenure.[54]

As Murphy's advice to Quezon regarding the Belo fund indicates, the high commissioner believed that he was "entitled . . . to counsel and admonish the local government." Hayden was not surprised that Quezon and his associates turned to Murphy for advice since the political scientist thought that Murphy had "long since established an intellectual and moral ascendancy in that group" and that "dependence upon some patron more able or more powerful than himself is one of the deepest traits of Malayan character." Quezon consulted with Murphy "in a personal and unofficial manner, without solicitation or suggestion," on an almost daily basis and sought the high commissioner's advice on a variety of pending Commonwealth government matters, including even matters that were "strictly none of . . . [the High Commissioner's] business." Quezon committed himself to send his legislative proposals to the high commissioner, and he sought Murphy's "counsel and advice" on most pending legislation and on bills awaiting the Commonwealth president's signature.[55]

Quezon turned to Murphy for advice when Manuel Roxas refused the Commonwealth president's invitation to become secretary of finance in the new government. Murphy, who concluded that Quezon did not really want Roxas in his cabinet, "tried to close the gap" between the two men. "Personal political fortunes," he told Roxas, must be subordinated to the good of the Commonwealth. Murphy thought that Roxas was "splendid" about the matter and correctly predicted, "He will rule some day." Thanks to Murphy's mediation, a role in which he excelled, a "serious break" in the leadership ranks of the Commonwealth was avoided, even though Roxas, in the end, declined the position and went into private law practice.[56]

Since the United States reserved the right to intervene should the Commonwealth government fail to meet its financial obligations, the high commissioner was especially concerned about the government's fiscal behavior. He instructed Jones to use the authority of the high commissioner's office to discourage "premature, half-baked and ill considered plans" of the Commonwealth regarding its currency, informally counseled Commonwealth officials regarding the revenue needed to finance government operations, and was "always after them to balance the budget." Cooperating with the high commissioner, Quezon sought Jones's advice before submitting his budget message to the legislature in June 1936, but the emotional and sensitive Commonwealth president threw a public tantrum when press accounts made it appear that the high commissioner's office was exercising a veto power over the fiscal transactions of the new government.

After Quezon conferred with Jones on July 17 concerning a proposed P7-million bond issue for road construction, Jones submitted a memorandum to the Filipino president setting forth the reasons for and against the bond issue but without advising a course of action. On the basis of information obtained from a member of the Assembly, the *Manila Daily Bulletin* incorrectly reported that the high commissioner's office had "turned thumbs down" on the proposed bond issue. Quezon thereupon issued a public statement labeling the story "false" and "mischievous" and stating that he wished it to be clearly understood that "no American official from the President . . . down to the High Commissioner" had "any authority, powers, prerogatives or privileges in the government of the Commonwealth except those granted in the Independence Law." Neither the president of the United States nor the high commissioner, Quezon asserted, could veto legislation approved by the Assembly, and nothing in the Tydings-McDuffie Act required the prior approval of the high commissioner for acts the Assembly approved. Similarly, he declared, the Assembly was free to issue bonds that did not exceed the indebtedness limits set by Congress. In conclusion, Quezon criticized "elements in the community" who opposed Philippine independence and erroneously believed that the high commissioner was "in fact the government of the Commonwealth."

When Jones discussed the controversy with Quezon, the Filipino president said that he had reacted so strongly both because he had been ill and because he was sensitive to anything reflecting on the legal prerogatives of the Commonwealth government. Since Jones complained that the incident had made him appear to be a meddler, Quezon promised to provide the press with an accurate account of what had occurred. He did so at his next press conference although without abandoning his view, as Jones put it, that the Tydings-McDuffie Act did not permit the United States government or the high commissioner " 'to do anything until they [the Commonwealth government] had done something.' " To Murphy, as might have been expected, the episode graphically revealed the need for the United States government to issue suitable instructions to the high commissioner.[57]

Since the high commissioner operated behind the scenes, performing his duties "quietly and inconspicuously," some observers in the Philippines thought that Murphy displayed a "supine attitude" toward the Commonwealth government and was a "mere figurehead" as high commissioner. The American newspaperman Frederic S. Marquardt commented that the high commissioner was supposed to be a "super-policeman" but that Murphy was a "poor cop" who was insufficiently concerned about American sovereignty and who set precedents embarrassing to his successors. This mistaken conception of Murphy's performance as high commissioner is echoed by Garel A. Grunder and William E. Livezey in their study, *The Philippines and the United States*, in which Murphy, incredibly, is portrayed as "not interested in matters of social precedence." Actually, because he brought to his office the glamor and prestige of the governor-generalship, his intimate knowledge of the local situation, his great skill in dealing with people, and the fact that he enjoyed the confidence of the Philippine leadership and had the support of the president of the United States, Murphy exercised a subtle influence on Philippine affairs as high commissioner. If he was not "a Power behind the curtain," as Jones depicted him, he nevertheless made the position "one of great usefulness and help to the Philippines," as Quezon said, aiding the Filipinos in launching their new government successfully and in securing their "full day in court" in the United States while he zealously protected the interests of the sovereign power.[58]

Murphy did not find the position of high commissioner as satisfying as that of governor-general. Always one to stress the critical importance of the task in which he was engaged, he put the best face on matters, observing how "thrilling" it was "to be on the ground floor in the establishment of historic precedents which will tend to shape the destinies of an emergent government for all times." There was a soupçon of truth in what Murphy said, but whatever modest satisfaction he may have derived from the position was more than offset by the loss of the power, responsibilities, and glamor of the governor-general's office. An energetic man who loved the limelight, he now was shunted to the background and had relatively little to do. He liked to say that this gave him the opportunity to study "the larger international phases" of the Philippine position; it really meant that he gave more and more of his time to the "social whirl," went riding even more frequently than before, and dreamed increasingly about his political future in the United States.[59]

III

The Commonwealth government operated rather "smoothly" while Murphy was high commissioner, and many of its actions were pleasing to him. He thought that Quezon's appointments were "exceptionally good" and that the Filipino president showed "a zest for policies which mean good and incorrupt government." He was delighted that, after a "bad start," Quezon had committed himself to "fiscal stability" and that the Commonwealth government continued and expanded the program of social welfare and social justice that his own regime had inaugurated.[60] He was disturbed, however, at what he thought was the "real Achilles heel" of the Commonwealth governmental structure, "a disconcerting concentration of power" in the hands of one man, "a striking tendency toward personal government" and "dictatorship." While he remained in the Philippines, he "inoffensively" sought to correct this "tendency," but he did not succeed. The Commonwealth government, newspaperman Robert Aura Smith reported toward the end of Murphy's service, was not a democratic government but "a one-man show with a one-goat power assembly yelling 'Yes' till it has tonsilitis."[61]

Of the major programs of the Commonwealth none aroused greater concern in the office of the high commissioner than Quezon's effort to provide his country with a system of national defense. While in Washington in November 1934 Quezon informed Dern that it was "of the most urgent importance" that the Philippines have a defense system in "a state of reasonable efficiency" before independence was attained. Since the Philippines, Quezon wrote, required "the friendly counsel and exclusive use of professionally trained military leaders of wide experience" for at least five or six years, he requested that a 1926 statute permitting the United States government to furnish military missions to certain Latin American countries be amended to include the Philippines as well. Having obtained the agreement of the Navy and State departments, Dern urged the action on Congress, and the appropriate legislation became law on May 14, 1935.[62]

Before requesting amendment of the military-mission statute, Quezon had asked Chief of Staff Douglas MacArthur if he thought an independent Philippines defensible. MacArthur, not one to state his opinions in moderate terms, replied, " 'I don't think so. I know that the Islands can be protected, provided, of course, that you have the money which will be required.' "[63] Since MacArthur had served in the Philippines on several occasions, including a stint as commander of the Philippine Department, Quezon asked the general if he would be willing to become the military advisor to the Commonwealth government. MacArthur, who was fond of Quezon and the Philippine people and whose service as chief of staff, in any event, was coming to an end, agreed, provided that this met with the approval of the president and the secretary of war. After accompanying Dern to the While House late in 1934, MacArthur informed Quezon that both the president and the secretary were " 'not only in complete sympathy but were enthusiastic.' " MacArthur himself drafted the amendment authorizing the military mission to the Philippines, urged its enactment, and wrote the letter in which Quezon requested the general's appointment.[64]

When Quezon, shortly after the military mission had been authorized, learned that MacArthur was being considered for the high commissionership, he asked the general whether he would prefer that office or the post of military advisor. In his customary grandiloquent prose, MacArthur replied, "The great work involved as your Military Adviser seems to me to transcend in ultimate importance anything else that is conceivable. I am prepared to devote the remainder of my life if necessary to securing a proper defense for the Philippine Nation. No question that confronts it in ultimate analysis is of such importance. Some day it will mean the difference between life and death for your people."[65]

After the military-mission bill had been enacted, Quezon and MacArthur agreed that MacArthur would be appointed field marshal by the Commonwealth government, would receive the same salary and emoluments as the governor-general had received, and would be responsible directly to the president of the Commonwealth. An unsigned copy of the agreement in the MacArthur Memorial Library states that, if MacArthur were appointed high commissioner, he would furnish the Commonwealth with the defense plans and recommendations he had prepared, in return for which he would receive compensation equivalent to his salary and allowances for two years. As high commissioner, he would "supervise the operation and further development of plans for Philippine defense." Another version of the agreement provided that, whether or not he became high commissioner or commander of the Philippine Department, MacArthur was to receive a very substantial "commission" over a seven-year period for the defense plan that he had prepared, once it was accepted by the Philippine government, and while he advised the Commonwealth regarding its implementation. Since the plan was being drafted by United States government personnel on government time, both versions of the agreement, insofar as they involved compensation to MacArthur for the preparation of the plan, were in violation of American law.[66]

MacArthur was officially detailed by the United States government on September 18, 1935, to "act as the Military Adviser to the Commonwealth Government in the establishment and development of a system of National Defense." In a confidential letter to the general, the adjutant general, by order of the secretary of war, authorized MacArthur to take to the Philippines such officers and enlisted men as he required, to request the department commander in the Philippines to furnish additional officers and men, and to call on him for "such service from his command" as MacArthur deemed advisable. MacArthur, who was authorized to confer directly with the secretary of war and the chief of staff or deputy chief of staff, was given "the greatest latitude and general authorities" in carrying out his mission: "Your mission must be accomplished," the letter read, "Ways and means are largely left to you." In another letter of the same date the secretary of war confidentially ordered the commanding general of the Philippine Department to furnish MacArthur "every reasonable assistance" and to provide him with "every possible help."[67]

The remarkable War Department orders of September 18 had actually been "prepared and signed" by MacArthur himself after Dern, who knew "very little or nothing" about MacArthur's plans, had left Washington for the Philippines. General Frank Parker, the commanding general of the Philippine Department, told Murphy that he had not seen such orders in his entire career, and Hayden rightly concluded that the orders made MacArthur the "No. 1 U.S. Army man" in the Philippines.[68]

Murphy and his staff were greatly concerned both about the creation of the Military Mission to the Commonwealth and the orders to the Philippine Department regarding its relationship to the mission. Although agreeable to the designation of MacArthur as the mission's head, Murphy had told Roosevelt shortly before the enactment of the mission legislation, which had been cleared neither with the governor-general nor the commanding general of the Philippine Department, that he saw no need for the mission. The War

Department, furthermore, had not supplied Murphy with a copy of the September 18 order to the Philippine Department, which General Parker brought to his attention. Already embroiled in a controversy with MacArthur and the War Department concerning the proper salute to the president of the Commonwealth and the issuance of instructions to the high commissioner, Murphy and his staff were disposed to see the September 18 order as another element in the " 'plot' " concocted by MacArthur and Quezon to establish the Commonwealth as a "semi-independent state." How, Murphy and his staff wondered, could the United States government effectively exercise its right of intervention during the Commonwealth period if the department commander, under certain circumstances, could become subject to the authority of the military advisor to the Commonwealth, whom Quezon allegedly referred to as " 'my aide' "? Murphy became increasingly concerned about this matter when he learned early in 1936 that General Lucius Holbrook, a MacArthur man, was to become the new department commander.

It was essential, Murphy and his aides believed, to clarify the status of the mission and its relationship to the department commander and the high commissioner so that they could "perform their proper duties and responsibilities without control or interference, and with full information of the Mission's activities." If this were not done, Murphy and his staff thought, "divided counsel and confusion of responsibility . . . [might] result, to the prejudice of American policy and interests in the Philippines." The extent to which the Philippine Department cooperated in the implementation of the Commonwealth defense plan, Murphy quite properly advised the War Department, should be determined by the department commander, not the military advisor to the Commonwealth government, and the military advisor, like the Commonwealth government, should communicate with Washington only through the high commissioner.[69]

There was a good deal of sympathy for Murphy's position in the chief of staff's office in Washington. Staff personnel drafted new instructions for the military advisor, but they were not issued. After MacArthur, however, began late in 1936 to draw officers and enlisted men from the Philippine Department for his personal staff, Holbrook protested to the War Department, which responded by requiring MacArthur to gain its approval before he could secure personnel from the Philippine command.[70]

The initial defense plan for the Philippines was prepared in Washington by Major James B. Ord, with the aid of Major Dwight D. Eisenhower and Army War College personnel. MacArthur informed

Murphy that the General Staff of the army had helped to develop the plan, but Chief of Staff Malin Craig informed Murphy that this misrepresented the facts. After first telling Murphy that he had explained the plan to Roosevelt and Dern, MacArthur later conceded that Dern knew nothing about it. Neither Murphy nor the commanding general of the Philippine Department was consulted about the plan or its implementation.[71]

The plan that Ord and Eisenhower initially developed called for an annual expenditure by the Philippine government of P50 million over a ten-year period. After consulting with Quezon, however, MacArthur told the planners that this sum would have to be cut in half. The two majors then discarded their initial scheme and started afresh only to be told that the maximum annual expenditure for Commonwealth defense could not exceed P16 million. "This," Eisenhower recalled, "made for a paper-thin plan." MacArthur, nevertheless, exuded optimism about the ability of the Filipinos to defend themselves, telling Quezon at the end of 1934 that " 'before the close of the ten-year period the Commonwealth, no matter what betides, will be secure from foreign aggression.' " Five months later the general wrote Quezon, "I will forge for you a weapon which will spell the safety of your nation from brutal aggression until the end of time." The potential aggressor was obviously Japan, but Quezon, hedging his bets in customary fashion, told the Japanese consul general in the Philippines just a week before the inauguration of the Commonwealth that the purpose of the defense plan was to create an army that could assure domestic peace lest the inability of the Commonwealth government to deal with internal disorder serve as an excuse for the United States government to postpone Philippine independence.[72]

The day after the inauguration of the Commonwealth Quezon appointed MacArthur Military Adviser to the President of the Philippines—MacArthur received the title of field marshal as of June 18, 1936. The first measure Quezon presented to the Commonwealth legislature was the National Defense bill, and it was enacted into law as Commonwealth Act No. 1 on December 21, 1935. The measure, which MacArthur described as offering "the maximum in national security at the least possible cost," made all Filipinos liable for military service and obligated to undergo "preparatory military training." Schoolchildren were to receive training from age ten until age eighteen, and service in the junior reserve was to extend from age eighteen until age twenty-one. All male citizens were to register during April of the calendar year in which they became twenty-one and, unless selected for the "regular force," were to receive "trainee instruction" during the next two years for a period not to exceed five and one-half months. Trainees then went into the reserve force, where they were to receive training for not more than thirty days each year until age fifty. The number of officers and men in the regular force, which included three-year enlistees and assigned trainees, was not specified but was rather to be prescribed each year by the chief of staff. The Constabulary was henceforth to be a part of the regular force.

The measure appropriated approximately P16 million for defense, and it was anticipated that a like sum would be appropriated annually during the Commonwealth period. MacArthur planned to use these funds to develop a regular force of eleven thousand men, provide annual training for forty thousand reservists, and build and maintain a military academy, " 'lesser service schools,' " and 120 training camps. The plan also envisioned the acquisition by the Commonwealth of 250 airplanes and fifty torpedo boats. Although MacArthur recognized that the development of Philippine battle and air fleets was "outside the realm of practicability," he thought that a small navy and air arm could serve to deny the use of Philippine waters to a hostile fleet and to preserve communications among the islands of the archipelago.[73]

MacArthur did not supply the high commissioner with a copy of the National Defense bill until after its introduction in the legislature. As soon as he received a copy, Murphy ordered a staff study of the measure. As Jones wrote Hayden, the high commissioner and his staff viewed the National Defense Act as "the biggest proposal we may have to face here for the entire ten years. In fact all else we may do may well be *conditioned* on the fact that an army with arms is here." Murphy and the men around him felt themselves "on the spot," as having to demonstrate either that there was no reason for the high commissioner to take any action regarding the measure or that there were grounds for recommending that the president of the United States should suspend the operation of the law.[74]

Whether the Commonwealth government could afford the cost of its new national defense program was a major concern of the high commissioner's office. Largely because of the size of the defense budget, total estimated appropriations for the first year of the plan exceeded estimated revenue by almost P3.5 million. Moreover, the cost of some important items in the defense budget appeared to be underestimated, and a heavy cost would eventually have to be incurred to pay for ships and aircraft. Viewing these facts in conjunction with the narrow tax base in the Philippines and the probable adverse effect on revenues of the limitations imposed on Philippine exports by the Tydings-McDuffie Act, the high commissioner's office had "grave doubts" about the ability of the Commonwealth government to finance the defense plan and meet its other obligations at the same time. On the other hand, the government had a cash surplus in its general fund of more than P8.7 million as of January 1, 1936, and its income was about to be augmented by funds accumulating in the United States as the result of the coconut oil excise, the export tax that would be collected during the last five years of the Common- wealth, and possibly the sum the Filipinos were claiming was due them because of the devaluation of the dollar. Under the circum- stances, Jones could not prove that the plan would result in default despite his fear that the Commonwealth had embarked on a course "disastrous to the stability of Public Finance."[75]

MacArthur's response to complaints about the cost of the defense plan was to contend that it was "a fundamental error in reasoning" to argue that the plan in itself would unbalance the budget and undermine the governmental structure since Philippine independence would be meaningless without adequate security. Defense, therefore, had to be treated as a first charge on the budget, not the last charge. He also noted that the net cost increase of the plan per annum would be P9 million, not P16 million, since P7 million was already being expended on the Constabulary.[76]

Whether or not the Commonwealth government could afford its national defense plan, Murphy had concluded even before MacArthur became the government's military advisor that the Filipinos could not defend themselves against external aggression. He favored the reten- tion of a strong United States presence in the Philippines "up to the very day of independence," but he did not believe that the United States should assume any responsibility for Philippine defense after independence, and he thought that American retention of military and naval bases in the islands would simply "invite trouble." He had agreed with General Parker's judgment that the islands were "prac- tically indefensible," and he was also influenced by General Embick's analysis that the American retention of a naval base in the Philippines or its assumption of "any other commitment" in the Far East would be "the gravest error committed in our entire history."[77]

When Murphy discussed Philippine defense with Roosevelt and State Department officials in April 1935, he discovered that they largely agreed with his views. In a letter to the secretary of the navy on May 3 the president rejected an army-navy proposal that the Manila-

Subic Bay area be retained as "a permanent defense area," stating that he regarded the maintenance of an American naval base in an independent Philippines as "a military-naval liability instead of an asset." Although the navy contended that an American retreat in the western Pacific would lead to " 'usurpation by the yellow race of the rights of the white race in the Far East,' " there was a growing conviction among army and navy planners by the end of 1935 that the Philippines could not be held.[78]

As General Embick, who became head of the War Plans Division in early 1935, saw it, in the event of an attack on an independent Philippines the enemy navy would control the intervening water areas of the archipelago. Since the projected Filipino army could not be concentrated to resist the attack, small enemy forces could capture the various islands. Because the Filipinos lacked the resources to defend themselves, Embick thought that the only value of the proposed Philippine military establishment, should the Philippines be attacked, would be to supplement measures that the United States might take to defend the islands. "This thought, openly expressed by some," he contended, "must be in the back of the minds of all informed proponents of such an establishment." Embick's poor opinion of the MacArthur defense plan was shared, Murphy discovered, by nearly all the high military and naval officers to whom he spoke, and MacArthur himself told Murphy either late in 1935 or early in 1936 that ten years was too brief a time to prepare an army for the defense of the Philippines. Murphy would probably have looked askance at any Philippine defense plan authored by MacArthur, but expert opinion, including that of the chief of staff, supported the high commissioner's conclusion that the particular plan incorporated in the National Defense Act would not protect the Philippines against an attack by a first-class power.[79]

Quite apart from its cost and adequacy, there were implications of the defense plan that troubled Murphy. Beginning with its second year the plan was to provide the Commonwealth government with an army that would be larger than the United States garrison in the Philippines, and this, Murphy feared, would effectively nullify the ability of the United States to intervene under the Tydings-McDuffie Act. He thought that compulsory military training, beginning at age ten, was inconsistent with American traditions. He believed that the powers vested in the Commonwealth president by the plan were "so complete as to make him a dictator in the matter of [its] execution" and, coupled with the authority already granted the president by the Philippine constitution, constituted a threat to democracy in the islands. He was convinced that Japan would see the purpose of the plan as the increase in the size of the American military establishment in the Far East and thus a threat. If the plan failed, the high commissioner and his staff thought, the United States would be blamed since the scheme had originated in the War Department. Finally, Murphy was perturbed about the "unusual character and status" of the Military Mission.[80]

The questions raised by the National Defense Act took on a more "somber aspect" when MacArthur, without the knowledge of the high commissioner, asked the War Department at the end of 1935 whether the Commonwealth government could purchase 400,000 World War I Enfield rifles and 4,500 Browning automatics. Both Embick and Hornbeck thought it "undesirable" for the United States government to comply, and the secretary of state agreed with them. Embick, who contended that the Commonwealth army had immediate need for only a small portion of the arms requested and that arms already in storage in the Philippines could satisfactorily meet that need, urged that Murphy be consulted before any decision was reached regarding the arms request. The matter was carried to the president, and, so that he might be "fully informed," the War Department requested Murphy and MacArthur to confer about what appeared to the department to be "an excessive quantity of arms at this stage."[81]

Murphy was in Sternberg Hospital at the time, but MacArthur and three members of his staff called on the high commissioner to plead their case. MacArthur insisted that the number of weapons requested was "the minimum amount necessary," and he "spoke with feeling," as Murphy put it, "about the views apparently adopted in Washington not encouragingly [sic] to the defense plan." The United States did not need the weapons in question, MacArthur argued, and if it refused to meet the request, "the Oriental countries would be more than pleased to let them [the Filipinos] have the rifles for nothing." If his defense plan was scrapped in Washington, MacArthur said, he would return to the United States and issue a statement "to protect his position as a soldier." When Murphy noted the fears that had been expressed about placing arms in such quantities in the hands of Filipinos and about the possible reaction of Japan, MacArthur dismissed these concerns as "groundless" and speculated that views of this sort had been conveyed to the president by Roger N. Baldwin and, probably, the Japanese as well. "We must never forget," Eisenhower recorded in his diary of the Military Mission, "that every question is settled in Washington today on the basis of getting votes next November. To decide this matter completely in our favor would gain no votes, while to disapprove the request and give the matter some publicity might be considered as a vote getting proposition among the pacifists and the other misguided elements of the American electorate.''[82]

After additional conferences with MacArthur's staff, Murphy advised the secretary of war that the arms request was ''reasonable and proper'' in view of the terms of the National Defense Act. He recommended, however, that only 100,000 rifles be furnished the Commonwealth during the first year of the defense plan, with future transfers to be made only as the need arose. Following Murphy's advice, the president approved the transfer to the Philippines of 100,000 Enfields and 600 Browning automatics. Since Eisenhower and Ord thought that if they were able to obtain 40,000 or 50,000 rifles during the year, there was ''no reason to despair as to ultimate success,'' they were pleased with the president's decision. The rifles cost the Philippine government more than Eisenhower had anticipated, but their price was nevertheless about P47 per rifle less than the Springfield rifles that the Commonwealth would otherwise have been required to purchase. ''The amount involved and the saving obtained in this single transaction,'' a grateful Quezon wrote MacArthur, ''is in itself more than enough to justify the engagement of your services by me.''[83]

Just before he left the Philippines for Washington in May 1936, Murphy sent the War Department a forty-one page analysis of the National Defense Act setting forth the reasons why the high commissioner's office had found the measure so troubling. As ''a sort of trustee'' for the Philippine people, Murphy commented, the United States government had both the right and duty to prevent the Commonwealth government from creating ''a burdensome military establishment'' that an independent Philippines could sustain only by sacrificing much of what had been achieved under American rule. Although he regarded the plan as ''improvident'' in view of the problems likely to attend independence, he was unwilling to make a specific recommendation regarding its suspension, as he should have, stating rather that this was a matter for the president to decide. If American intervention were deemed unwarranted, the Commonwealth government, Murphy advised, should be asked to submit ''a practical and sound financial plan'' specifying how it intended to finance the program. If a plan could be formulated that assured the financing of the defense effort without the impairment of essential services, if suitable action were taken to prevent the weakening of

American authority in the islands during the Commonwealth period, and if arrangements were made that limited American responsibility should the defense program fail, he stated that his objections to the defense plan could be set aside.[84]

While Murphy pressed his concern in Washington, MacArthur early in July urged the transfer to "War Reserve" in the Philippines of substantial quantities of American military equipment classified as nonstandard or substitute-standard, including rifles, machine rifles, and 75-mm guns. Washington also learned about the same time that the Commonwealth government was negotiating with the Remington Arms Company for the construction of a munitions plant in the Philippines (a project that was in the end abandoned), was considering the purchase of eleven million rounds of 30-caliber ammunition from the same company, and had ordered seven hundred automatic machine-gun rifles from the Colt Patent Firearms Manufacturing Company. Urging the State, War, and Navy departments to devise "a thoughtful and co-ordinated policy" regarding Philippine defense and armaments, Murphy advised that further shipment of arms and ammunition to the Philippines be halted until such a policy had been formulated. He made a strong impression in Washington, and it was undoubtedly because of concerns that Murphy, Embick, and the State Department had expressed that Chief of Staff Craig informed MacArthur that there was "much apprehension" in Washington regarding the rapid rate at which the Filipinos were acquiring munitions and arms. Although there was much confidence in Quezon, Craig noted, he might pass from the scene or might be unable to control "a severe disaffection imperiling American sovereignty." As for MacArthur's most recent request, Craig advised that until reserve arms stocks in the Philippine Department increased, the equipment should be retained as American property and should be loaned to the Filipinos only for active training, with nonexpendable items to be returned to the United States. The War Department eventually approved this arrangement as the means of meeting MacArthur's request.[85]

Miffed that the army General Staff had not been consulted about the Philippine defense plan, dubious about its validity, and concerned about the buildup of arms in Philippine hands, Craig regarded the Philippine situation as "critical" and thought that the time was "more than ripe" for a presidential resolution of the matter. Since he was sensitive to the political implications of the issue in an election year, the acting secretary of war, Harry H. Woodring, thought that after Murphy, the State Department, and the War Department had expressed their concerns to Roosevelt, MacArthur should be called home to present his side of the question. Otherwise, Woodring feared, MacArthur might ask to be relieved, and this, the secretary and, perhaps, the president thought, "would be unfortunate from the purely political view, especially at this time." When Craig asked the White House on September 11 whether he should permit the Commonwealth government to acquire machine guns, Roosevelt responded that the general and Woodring should see him about arms for the Philippines *after* the election.[86]

Willing to talk about Philippine defense in a preliminary way before the election, Roosevelt discussed the subject with Craig, Woodring, and Hull on September 14. After the conference, the State Department advised the War Department that the implementation of the Philippine defense plan should be undertaken "only after the fullest study and joint consideration" of the matter by the departments concerned and a final decision by the president on "certain fundamental issues." Further steps regarding the development of "an independent Philippine armament," the State Department urged, should be deferred until the high commissioner and the interested departments had assured themselves that this was "not inconsistent" with the United States government's Far Eastern policies and plans.[87]

The specific concern of the State Department appears to have been the relationship of the defense plan to the neutralization of the Philippines and the possible American retention of a naval base there. When Assistant Secretary of State Francis B. Sayre discussed these matters with Roosevelt shortly after the election, the president said that he had not formulated any plans for neutralization but that he might call an informal conference of the interested powers at which the United States might propose the neutralization not only of the Philippines but of the Japanese mandated islands. The results of such a conference, the president said, might determine whether he would enter into negotiations for the neutralization of the Philippines. If Japan attacked the Philippines, Roosevelt predicted, the United States would have to evacuate the islands temporarily if it still retained forces there. Nothing much would happen for two years after that, but the United States "would gradually move westward in an island-hopping operation."[88] What happened in the Pacific after the Japanese attack on Pearl Harbor could hardly have come as much of a surprise to President Roosevelt.

In his last days as high commissioner, Murphy made a final effort to persuade Washington to follow his advice regarding the MacArthur mission. In a meeting of December 28 with Craig, Embick, Sayre, and Jacobs, Murphy "emphasized more than anything else the growing menace" of the Military Mission to the Philippines. He stated emphatically that the mission should not have been dispatched in the first place and recommended that it "be abandoned as soon as practicable." Describing MacArthur as "a 'lone horse' who was very difficult to deal with," Craig agreed with Murphy and asserted that the mission should be recalled no later than July 1, 1937. Embick supported Craig but noted that the government "would have a difficult situation on its hands in General MacArthur," who would probably "propagandize" for his cause in the United States. Sayre expressed his "perfect" agreement with Murphy and the two generals, although he declared that he could not commit the State Department without first talking to the secretary or acting secretary. "The most satisfactory solution," the conferees agreed, was for the secretaries of state and war, Murphy, Craig, Embick, and Sayre to present the facts to the president so that he might decide the question.[89]

Although the proposed White House conference apparently did not materialize, Craig sent MacArthur a confidential cable on August 6, 1937, instructing him to return to the United States for a new assignment after he had completed two years of service in the Philippines and specifically revoking the remarkable order of September 18, 1935. Unwilling to accept a subordinate command in the United States, MacArthur responded to Craig's letter by applying for retirement from the army, a request that the department granted effective as of the end of the year.[90]

MacArthur's biographer, D. Clayton James, appears to accept the view of friends of the general that Craig was "not responsible" for forcing MacArthur's retirement, and James speculates that Murphy, among others, may have been involved in the effort to recall the general.[91] Murphy, to be sure, had advised that the MacArthur mission be recalled; but Craig had agreed with this position, and his recall letter was entirely consistent with his views concerning the mission.

The Interdepartmental Committee on Philippine Affairs recommended in February 1937 that the president seek the neutralization of the Philippines and, before this, that the United States government decide whether to retain naval bases in the Philippines. The committee, as Murphy had urged, also recommended that consideration be given to the relationship of defense expenditures to the economic adjustments required of the Philippines by the independence law. Although the Joint Preparatory Committee on Philippine

Affairs subsequently made a study of Philippine government finance and included recommendations on the subject in its 1938 report, no action was taken on these recommendations, nor did the United States government seek to achieve the neutralization of the Philippines.[92]

MacArthur and the Commonwealth government proceeded with the implementation of the National Defense Act despite the misgivings of Murphy and the army command in Washington. MacArthur's high hopes for the defense plan were not to be realized, and Quezon himself eventually began to doubt the plan's validity. The year 1936 was devoted to the building of camps, the organization of cadres, and the training of instructors. It did not take long for friction to develop between MacArthur and his staff and the staff of the Filipino army. " 'You are not here a day,' " the Manila representative of the Remington Arms Company reported to his firm, " 'without feeling that there is quite some discontent [among the Filipinos] against the decisions which have been reached in policies which they could not dictate.' " After a discussion with the chief of staff of the Philippine army, the Remington man concluded that the Filipino leadership was " 'not going to sit by quietly and be dictated to by the American advisers.' "

If the Filipinos were dissatisfied with the Americans, the Americans were also dissatisfied with the Filipinos. "We have learned to expect from the Filipinos with whom we deal," Eisenhower wrote in his diary regarding Ord and himself, "a minimum of performance from a maximum of promise." Eisenhower was also disturbed about the lack of communication between the Commonwealth government and the Military Mission. "Things happen and we know nothing of them," he complained in his diary. He thought the problem could be resolved if MacArthur had a weekly meeting with Quezon, but MacArthur, Eisenhower recorded, "apparently thinks it would not be in keeping with his rank and position for him to do so!!!!!"[93]

Eisenhower and Ord had planned on calling twenty thousand Filipinos into service on January 1, 1937. Quezon, however, insisted that the number be raised to about forty thousand, and this caused "considerable changes" in the conduct of the training program, made it difficult to provide an adequate number of qualified instructors, and depleted Commonwealth financial reserves. As it turned out, 36,601 reserves had been trained by the end of 1937, and the contemplated figure of forty thousand trainees per year was never reached. As of July 1941, the regular force consisted of 4,163 officers and men, and the poorly trained and poorly equipped reserve force, which existed largely on paper, numbered 132,000. The quality and morale of the regular force left a good deal to be desired, as did the educational level of both regulars and reserves. The training program had been marred by trainee strikes, terrorism by some units, and poorly executed maneuvers.

The seven-thousand man Philippine Constabulary had originally been consolidated with the regular force, and a separate state police force had been formed. When this proved unsatisfactory, the state force was abolished, and the Constabulary, in May 1938, was detached from the regular force to resume its former role. The air corps as of the end of 1940 consisted of forty planes, one hundred pilots, and three hundred ground personnel; and two torpedo boats obtained from the British constituted the Commonwealth naval force. The budget allotted for defense rose to P25 million in the second year of the plan, but the sum was reduced to about P16 million per annum thereafter, about 14 percent of the Commonwealth budget.[94]

Quezon, in the meantime, became increasingly disillusioned with the defense plan and with its author. He stated in the fall of 1939 that the Philippines could not be defended by the Filipinos, and soon thereafter he told High Commissioner Sayre that the MacArthur plan was " 'idiotic.' " Quezon talked about relieving MacArthur of his position, and the Filipino president began to communicate with the field marshal only through a secretary. The defense budget for 1941 reduced the number of trainees by half and required the closing of sixty-one training camps. There is no reason to believe that MacArthur could have forged an impregnable defense instrument for the Philippines by the scheduled date for independence had not war intervened at the end of 1941 to render that question moot. More than four months before the bombs rained down on Pearl Harbor and Clark Field, the Philippine Army had been called into United States service, and the United States government had selected Douglas MacArthur to head a newly created Far Eastern Command.[95]

By the time MacArthur returned to active duty in the United States Army, his erstwhile antagonist in the Philippines, Frank Murphy, was serving on the United States Supreme Court. He had left the Philippines on May 13, 1936, at President Roosevelt's request, partly to deal with Philippine affairs but also with the expectation that he would enter the 1936 gubernatorial race in Michigan. "Washington must be enlightened on some Philippine matters, the country must be saved, and perhaps the State [of Michigan] too," Kemp observed about the Murphy journey to the United States.[96]

Murphy spent a busy morning in his office on his last day in the

Philippines, and numerous friends called to bid farewell. He held his final press conference shortly before noon, telling the journalists, "The moment calls for soldiery spirit, not for sentimentality. But I can't help being sentimental to the Filipino people." He then attended a luncheon at the Manila Hotel tendered in his honor by his former cabinet. After lunch, the high commissioner, Marguerite, a military aide, and a local belle "made a last grateful visit to Santo Domingo Church," where Murphy had prayed on the day of his arrival in the Philippines. There were no other worshipers in the church, but the Dominicans were chanting in the choir loft. "The hush in the empty church, broken only by the solemn voices of the fathers droning away their hymns of adoration . . . as they had through the ages," Murphy wrote, "moved me during these last few moments on Filipino soil and swept me back into the past for the moment."

From the church, Murphy went to the pier, where a troop escort rendered him final honors. After boarding the S.S. *Coolidge*, he went on deck to say a last good-bye to Commonwealth officials, General Holbrook, representatives of the consular corps, and members of the Filipino, Spanish, and American communities of Manila. There was a large crowd at the pier, including several Murphy girl friends, a fact the high commissioner did not fail to note. It especially "hurt" Murphy to say farewell to Aurora Quezon, and "there were tears" among the Murphy party and those who were there to see them depart.

Quezon, Roxas, and Jose Yulo accompanied Murphy for part of the journey to continue the discussion of Philippine affairs. The first stop was Hongkong, where the American consul general gave a tea in the high commissioner's honor. Murphy attended a dinner dance at a Hongkong hotel that evening, and he was impressed with the "many attractive Filipino and Chinese girls" who were present. The next stop was Shanghai, where Murphy discussed Chinese affairs with H. H. Kung. The *Coolidge* then proceeded to Japan. In Kobe, reporters questioned Murphy about Davao, and he answered "without getting on thin ice." He visited an industrial fair in Osaka but was not permitted to see the military exhibit. In Tokyo he talked with Ambassador Joseph Grew, who took the high commissioner to see the emperor.

Among the passengers on the *Coolidge* when it sailed for Japan, Murphy found Charlie Chaplin and Paulette Goddard to be the "most interesting." He thought Chaplin to be "a profound man" who had an "interest in the underdog" and supported Roosevelt and the New Deal. Impressed with the good looks of Paulette Goddard, Murphy concluded that "she likes the choice and fine things in this life." Chaplin, Goddard, and Murphy continued to think well of one another long after the *Coolidge* had reached its destination.

It was a "thrill" to set foot in the United States again, Murphy wrote Ann Walker after the *Coolidge* arrived in San Francisco. "It will always be thus with the patriot," he noted, but he was "anything but happy at leaving the Philippines and the dear Filipino friends. Maybe," he wrote, "it is in part because in a small measure I have fathered the new nation and assisted in preparation for it; maybe it is in part due to an appreciation that I am not needed here in our strong, well established country and that over there where a people are struggling to their feet a friend, such as I have been, is a need."[97]

After "a short sojourn among the movie queens" in Hollywood and Los Angeles, a "long visit" with William Randolph Hearst, and the receipt of an honorary doctor of laws degree at Loyola University of Los Angeles, Murphy resumed his eastward journey. He visited Roosevelt in Washington and Hyde Park, attended the Democratic national convention in Philadelphia, and devoted time to Philippine affairs both before he became active in the Michigan gubernatorial race and between the election and his inauguration. He gave some thought to flying back to the Philippines before assuming his gubernatorial post, but this proved to be impossible. As he wrote a Philippine friend, however, he was "forever . . . bound to the Islands and their welfare. Nothing can deter this union we have made." For Murphy, his Philippine years had been "happy years among a good people," and he retained an interest in the islands and an affection for their people for the rest of his life.[98]

Murphy had every reason to be pleased with what he had accomplished in the Philippines. Not only had he established the new office of high commissioner on a sound basis, but his record as governor-general compared favorably with that of his predecessors. When Hayden contended that the Murphy administration was "the most satisfactory we have ever had in the Islands," he was manifesting his enthusiasm for an administration of which he had been an important member and for a man who, contrary to the professor's expectations, had dazzled him; he was also rendering a judgment that others, less committed to Murphy, shared in large degree. After visiting the Philippines at the time the Commonwealth was inaugurated, Secretary of War Dern reported to President Roosevelt that Filipino leaders had "complete confidence" in Murphy, the Filipino masses trusted and loved him, and American army and navy officers in the islands praised him as a man who had defended American interests in the Philippines. Murphy, Dern concluded, had been one of the greatest of the eleven governors-general who had served in the Philippines.[99]

As governor-general, Murphy provided the Philippines with an efficient and economical government, balanced the insular budget, and greatly improved the character of fiscal management at the provincial level. He aggressively supported democratic principles and civil liberties, modernized the system of criminal justice, and rehabilitated the Constabulary. He was "the first [Philippine] chief executive to lay special stress on social problems," evidenced greater concern for the "forgotten" men, women, and children of the islands than his predecessors had, and provided a "New Deal" for the Moros. Insofar as the Philippine-American relationship was concerned, he was probably more assiduous than any of his predecessors in pressing the Philippine cause in the United States, and he played a helpful part in the transformation of the Philippines from colony into Commonwealth. Although careful always to uphold the "dignity" of his position, he sympathized with Filipino aspirations and demonstrated "a real understanding and respect" for their feelings. In sum, he presented the Filipinos with a commendable model of rectitude and high purpose and personified some of the best qualities of his nation as a colonial power.

Murphy did relatively little to spur the badly needed restructuring of the Philippine economy, but it is difficult to know what more he could have accomplished given the entrenched power of export agriculture and the relatively brief time available to him as governor-general. His performance in this and other areas did not always match his rhetoric—hardly an unusual failing in a public figure—and he underestimated the weight of tradition in the islands, as subsequent events were to demonstrate. Not everyone was impressed with him, and some considered him a "pious fraud"; but even one of his sometime critics predicted in 1937 that, in accounts of American rule in the Philippines, the name of Frank Murphy would be "high on the list, and written in golden letters."[100]

6

"Me-and-Roosevelt"

Ambitious for higher office, Frank Murphy did not ignore his political base in the United States while he performed his proconsular role in the Philippines. En route to the Philippines, he asked his brother George to send him the names of Democratic officeholders in Michigan and members of the Democratic state and county organizations so that he could "keep in touch with the prominent members of the party." He also indicated a desire to maintain contact with the leaders of organized labor in Detroit and with the Catholic clergy in the city. Always a strong believer in publicity and overly fond of seeing his name in headlines, Murphy had his staff forward to influential persons and makers of opinion in the United States the laudatory references to his performance that regularly appeared in the Philippine press. Delighted as he was by the praise from Philippine sources, Murphy was even more pleased when he read press clippings from the United States, where he received "splendid publicity" throughout his service in the Philippines. Murphy, a Washington, D.C., newspaper editorialized, was "a model of what ALL our domestic officials should be."[1]

From the Philippines, Murphy sought to remain in friendly contact with Father Charles E. Coughlin, the Detroit radio priest with whom Murphy had been closely associated since the late 1920s and whose political influence was at its height when Murphy left the United States for the Philippines. As Coughlin toward the end of 1933 became increasingly disenchanted with Franklin D. Roosevelt, Murphy sought to restrain the priest, and for a time the governor-general appeared to be succeeding. Coughlin, however, was not appeased by the soothing words emanating from Manila. Roosevelt, he complained to Murphy in the middle of 1934, had "not gone to the bottom of our national cesspool. . . . I refer," the priest explained, "to the glaring fact that he has not driven the money changers from the temple in the persons of the Federal Reserve bankers and the international bankers."[2]

The next step after the governor-generalship in Murphy's quest for

the presidency, as he saw it, was to secure a cabinet-level appointment or to become Michigan's governor or a United States senator.
Before he had completed his first year in the Philippines, Murphy was
already sending word to Washington that he was "available" for
another position. "Somehow or other I feel that I ought to be doing
more for the President," he wrote Louis Howe in April 1934. He was
happy in the Philippines, the governor-general truthfully remarked,
but his place was nevertheless "on the firing line." When George
Murphy left for the United States in July 1934 after a visit in the
Philippines, he sailed with instructions from his brother to talk with
Cordell Hull, Raymond Moley, and Coughlin about Frank's availability for a Washington assignment. Whenever he was queried
about leaving the Philippines, Murphy would say something like, "I
belong here." "On the other hand," he reminded George, making
it evident that his preference was to be somewhere else, "I have more
than my quota of the stuff they call ambition and if conditions are
right I'm restless unless forging ahead."[3]

When Murphy returned to the United States in the spring of 1935,
there were rumors that he was about to be nominated for one or
another important federal post. Pearson and Allen claimed the governor-general himself as the source for a story that he would replace
Frances Perkins as secretary of labor, and Perkins, we do know, placed
Murphy's name at the head of a long list of persons whom she called
to the president's attention for positions on the National Labor
Relations Board. It does not appear, however, that the president
offered Murphy a new position in the administration.[4]

If Murphy preferred a cabinet post to a test of Michigan's political
waters, the choice was understandable: Michigan's Democratic party,
which in 1932 had broken the Republican stranglehold on the state
government, was in disarray during almost the entire period of
Murphy's incumbency in the Philippines. Settled originally by mi-
grants from New England and the Middle Atlantic states and then by
immigrants from Great Britain, Germany, and Holland, Michigan
was a one-party Republican state from the founding of the party until
the Great Depression. It was, in this respect, unlike neighboring
Ohio, Indiana, and Illinois, where residents of southern origin had
brought Democratic politics with them to challenge the Republicans
for ascendancy. Between 1854 and 1928 the Democrats failed to carry
Michigan in any presidential election; won the governorship only
four times, taking advantage on these occasions of division in Republican ranks or successfully practicing fusion tactics; elected a
subordinate state official only in 1890; and gained control of the state

legislature on only one occasion. During the years 1919–30 there was not a single Democrat in Michigan's thirty-two member Senate, and the number of Democrats in the one-hundred member House ranged from zero to five. Michigan Democrats did not have a real statewide organization, and the main concern of party leaders and the chief source of friction among them was the distribution of patronage when a Democratic president was in the White House.

A few wealthy men paid the expenses of the state Democratic party and directed its affairs, selecting its candidates and writing its platforms. Following a practice initiated in 1922, the party met in convention before the state primary to endorse candidates for office, hoping that one of the persons whom it might endorse for a particular office would consent to become a candidate. The dominant figure in the party in the 1920s was William A. Comstock, the party's state chairman from 1920 to 1924, a member of the Democratic National Committee from 1924 to 1930, and the party's unsuccessful candidate for governor in 1926, 1928, and 1930. A native of Alpena, Michigan, and the inheritor of lumber wealth, to which he added by a variety of business activities, Comstock was the party's financial angel in the 1920s, loaning it $37,000 in 1924 to pay its debts and financing his own gubernatorial campaigns in 1926 and 1928. Horatio J. Abbott, a Comstock ally and, like him, a major contributor to the party, succeeded Comstock as state chairman. He served in the post until 1930, when he replaced Comstock as Michigan's Democratic national committeeman.

Although the Republicans won the Michigan gubernatorial election in 1930, Comstock received 42 percent of the vote, compared to 37.6 percent in 1928, and he carried Detroit and Wayne County. Two years later the Democrats scored a stunning victory in depression-ridden Michigan. Not only did Franklin D. Roosevelt add the state to the Democratic electoral column, but Comstock, running ahead of Roosevelt in the popular vote, won the governorship, the Democrats captured ten of seventeen congressional races in the state as well as all the elective state offices save that of secretary of state, and they won control of both houses of the Michigan legislature.[5]

"Able to take defeat, but not success," as one Michigan Democrat shrewdly observed, Comstock failed to seize the opportunity that his 1932 victory provided to build a strong Democratic party in Michigan. He did not file a campaign expense report, as the law required, until the press called attention to his dereliction; and when he complied with the law, his report revealed that the entire cost of the campaign, a modest $9,354, had been met by a single individual, Isaiah Leebove.

A Pittsburgh-born attorney, Leebove had represented notorious underworld characters in New York before moving in 1929 to Harrison, Michigan, where he formed a friendship and business relationship with Comstock. There was much speculation concerning Leebove's precise role in the new Comstock administration, some seeing him as its "kingpin" while Comstock attacked this view as a "myth."[6]

Comstock, who had promised to abolish the State Police if elected, failed to do so and further antagonized labor and liberal elements when he dispatched the troopers to Highland Park during a 1933 strike at the Briggs Motor Company plants in the Detroit area. The 3 percent sales tax that the state legislature enacted in 1933 produced needed revenue but nevertheless displeased taxpayers, as did the $2 head tax imposed by the lawmakers to finance the state's old-age pension plan. Comstock foolishly appointed Alfred Debo, chairman of the Democratic State Central Committee, commissioner of pardons and paroles; and the propriety and wisdom of the paroles the commissioner approved, along with the pardons granted by the governor to several "bandits and hardened criminals," reflected adversely on both the state administration and the state's Democratic party. In 1934 a grand jury began looking into allegations of graft in the state administration stemming from a bribery charge that involved a prominent Democratic legislator and a Democratic lobbyist. The probe proved fruitless, but it was nevertheless damaging to the party's image.

The Comstock administration could point to some accomplishments—an old-age pension law, bank reform legislation, a new liquor control system, and effective administration of public relief—but its shortcomings, emphasized by the state's overwhelmingly Republican press, received more attention than its achievements. More could have been accomplished, no doubt, had not the Democratic majority in the legislature been so lacking in experience—only two of the Democrats had served in the legislature before 1933—and had Comstock been possessed of greater skill as a legislative leader. As it was, the relationship of the governor and the legislature degenerated into "one long nightmare of obstructionism" and "mutual recrimination."[7]

Continuing to behave like a minority-party leader, Comstock failed to integrate into the Democratic party the former Republicans and the new voters who had cast their ballots for the Democrats in 1932. The governor was most comfortable with the old-line Democratic leaders who had kept the party alive when state conventions could be held in the "sample rooms of hotels," and he had scant regard for those whom he regarded as Johnny-come-lately Democrats or "political self-starters." The old-line Democrats, a party leader observed, "would sooner sing in [the] choir of the minority party than sit in the church proper of the majority party."

The conflict between the old Democratic party and the new Democratic party that began to emerge in Michigan in 1932 manifested itself most conspicuously in a bitter struggle over patronage, an issue that divided the party throughout the period that Frank Murphy served in the Philippines. The chief protagonists in the fratricidal patronage conflict were Comstock, Abbott, and Debo on the one hand and the ten Democratic congressmen elected in 1932 on the other. At the state Democratic convention in the spring of 1932 Debo had read a letter from James A. Farley, Roosevelt's campaign manager and soon to become chairman of the Democratic National Committee, promising that federal patronage would be channeled through the state organization if Roosevelt were elected. The Democratic congressmen, however, insisted that they play a major role in the distribution of patronage in their districts, as Democratic congressmen had done when Woodrow Wilson was president. Failing this, they contended, the state organization would award jobs to old-line Democrats rather than use patronage to forge a New Deal party in the state.

Insofar as positions were filled in Michigan in 1933 and 1934, they went to "relatives and friends" of the Comstock group since Farley, as he said, "always supported the regular organization in any of these fights." Abbott and Debo secured the most important jobs for themselves, the former becoming collector of internal revenue in Detroit, the latter becoming collector of customs. Abbott was forced to resign his government position in May 1934 when it was discovered that two of his employees had solicited funds for the Democratic party from large taxpayers, but he retained his post as Democratic national committeeman. Debo, similarly, remained in his position despite allegations that he had misappropriated funds contributed to the 1932 Roosevelt-Comstock campaign.

Although some Michigan positions were filled, many important jobs remained unfilled as the internecine conflict in the party and Washington's mounting annoyance at the behavior of Michigan's Democrats led to a patronage "stalemate of growing bitterness." Complaining that they had been left "entirely in the cold" in the award of patronage, the Michigan congressmen demanded the resignation of Abbott and Debo, while the Comstock Democrats berated the congressmen as "newcomers" who were "trying to dictate everything.'' There were also constant complaints from Michigan Democrats that Republicans, so strongly entrenched in the state, were retaining or securing federal jobs even though the Democrats had won the 1932 election. A bitter Congressman John Lesinski, who represented Michigan's Sixteenth Congressional District, asked Farley if he was attempting ''to wreck the Democratic party in Michigan'' by giving jobs to the opposition. The constant squabbling about ''all this job distribution stuff'' lessened the attractiveness of the state Democratic party to the Michigan electorate, but national party leaders appeared to be unable to resolve the conflict.[8]

It was common knowledge in Michigan that Frank Murphy and William Comstock were not the same kind of Democrats and were not particularly fond of one another. Having been elected on non-partisan tickets as criminal court judge and mayor and aware that Michigan's Democratic party was a miniscule, ineffective, and conservative organization, Murphy in the 1920s and early 1930s played down his Democratic affiliations, stressed his independence from the conventional politics of party and organization, and categorized himself as an ''Independent Progressive.'' When Comstock sought to create ''a 'Me and Murphy' impression'' in the 1930 gubernatorial contest by attempting to capitalize on Murphy's popularity in Detroit and other industrial centers, Mayor Murphy let it be known that he would ''greatly regret'' any attempt to involve him in ''party politics,'' a comment that Comstock and his political allies did not forget. They were consequently ''lukewarm,'' to say the least, when a Murphy-for-vice-president boomlet developed the next year. Abbott stated that Michigan Democrats would give their support to party members ''who were ready to stand up at all times and be counted'' rather than to men like Murphy.

Relations between Murphy and Comstock deteriorated further during the early months of the Comstock governorship when the mayor publicly complained about the state government's reluctance to aid Detroit in meeting its staggering relief problem. Like many other Democrats, Murphy was dismayed by the general tone of the Comstock administration and by the ''improprieties'' of which he thought it guilty. He conceded that it had done ''some creditable things,'' but he thought that its record had been marred by an ''endless series of scandals, inefficiency, mismanagement, and a general picture of poor enthusiasm for good government.''[9]

Writing to Farley while en route to the Philippines, Murphy reported that he found the state of party affairs in Michigan ''disquieting and disconcerting.'' He advised Farley to consult about

Michigan Democratic affairs with two men of "unquestioned integrity," Arthur J. Lacy, former judge of the defunct Detroit Domestic Relations Court, and George E. Bushnell, who had just been elected to the Michigan Supreme Court. Murphy, who sent the two men copies of his letter to Farley, advised them to give the Democratic chairman the "sickening" facts about the state party. He wanted them to meet with his brother George, who served as Frank's spokesman while he was in the Philippines, and to surround themselves with other Democrats who understood that there was "no escape from the duty of men in earnest within the party" to purge it of "corrupt and sinister influences." Lacy and Bushnell met with Farley when he visited Detroit toward the end of June, but they did not agree on any plan of action even though Bushnell informed Frank that Farley "fully" concurred in his appraisal of Michigan's Democratic party.[10]

Indicating to Farley that he had no personal "interest in patronage other than to see that the faithful" were "rewarded . . . and the party . . . strengthened in Michigan," Murphy advised that Michigan's Democratic congressmen be accorded "every consideration possible" in the distribution of federal jobs. Aware that the base of the state party would have to be widened, Murphy regarded Washington support for the congressmen as "an indispensable factor in the maintenance of party supremacy in Michigan."[11]

The bitter struggle within Michigan's Democratic party, typical of the conflict in many states between old-line Democrats and new elements attracted to the party by the Depression and the New Deal, reached a climax in 1934 when the anti-Comstock forces sought to defeat the governor in the state primary. Their candidate was Lacy, who had long since become disillusioned with Comstock. Although Lacy did not wish to become a gubernatorial candidate, preferring to run for the Senate, the Democratic congressmen protested that they would be defeated in 1934 if Comstock were on the ticket, and other candidates, notably Bushnell and Frank Murphy, were unavailable. The congressmen invited Lacy to Washington to urge him to run, and after attending a baseball game with the president, he concluded that he had Roosevelt's support should he challenge Comstock.

"Sick about it" and fearing that he would have "a terrific, horrible battle with Comstock," Lacy announced himself a candidate for governor on May 11, 1934. Roosevelt had asked Lacy if the White House could resolve the troubled Michigan political situation by appointing Comstock to a federal post, and Lacy urged this course of action. If a position was offered Comstock, however, he declined it.

In opposing Comstock, Lacy sought to link himself to Roosevelt and the New Deal, but the president, who remained aloof from the 1934 elections, refused to endorse the Lacy candidacy.[12]

Since Frank Murphy had invited Lacy to play a leadership role in rescuing Michigan's Democratic party, it was logical for Lacy to assume that the governor-general would support his candidacy. Although Lacy later claimed that George Murphy specifically urged him to run, this seems unlikely since George, as an attorney on the staff of the state's attorney general, Patrick H. O'Brien, felt obliged to support Comstock. Not only did George's position in the Comstock administration pose a problem for Frank, but he was also aware that Coughlin opposed Lacy, regarding him as "totally smeared" with Michigan's bank failures because of the role that he played in the reorganization of the Detroit Trust Company. For these reasons and perhaps because he thought it best not to take sides in the divisive campaign lest he decide to enter the race for a United States Senate seat or, failing that, lest it adversely affect his political future in the state, Murphy chose to remain aloof from the contest, lamely offering "long absence" from Michigan and his "distance from the scene" as the explanation.[13]

Both sides made last-minute attempts before the September 11 primary to make it appear that the popular Murphy favored their candidate. A Lacy supporter to whom Murphy had written that "the questionable and rackateering [sic] element should be lashed right out of the capitol" advised the press on this basis that Murphy opposed Comstock, which the governor-general regarded as an "improper straining" of the facts. A few days later George Murphy, who had received a message from his brother stating, "Hope all goes well with the administration," made a speech in Detroit in which he stressed that his brother credited Comstock with being "the guiding force behind some of the most progressive legislation in the state's history." When George finished the speech, Lacy, who was present, demanded an explanation. George asserted that he had not intended to imply that his brother was " 'taking sides,' " but he refused to issue a clarifying statement. In speaking as he had, George may have been seeking to correct the impression that his brother favored Lacy lest this further impair Frank's standing with party regulars, or he may have been under pressure from the Comstock administration to make the speech if he wished to retain his state job—Lacy later claimed that George had been "constrained if not intimidated."[14]

In a radio address delivered shortly after George's speech, Frank Picard, a political friend of Frank Murphy, a Comstock supporter, and a candidate for the United States Senate, alleged that the governor-general had informed his brother that he favored Comstock. Regarding this speech as "one of the most disastrous blows" that he "had to take in the entire campaign," Lacy cabled Murphy for an explanation. The governor-general promptly replied that he was maintaining an "attitude of openmindedness and neutrality" regarding the primary.[15]

Lacy defeated Comstock in the September primary by about ten thousand votes. At the Democratic state convention at the end of the month, Lacy sought to reunite the warring factions in the party by accepting Comstock men as candidates for attorney general and treasurer. At the same time Lacy secured the election of Elmer B. O'Hara, the Wayne County clerk, to replace Debo as chairman of the Democratic State Central Committee. Murphy publicly endorsed the Democratic ticket, stating that it was led by men of "exceptional competence and proved fidelity to the cause of good government."[16]

In the November election Republican Frank D. Fitzgerald defeated Lacy by 82,699 votes. The Democrats also sustained a net loss of four congressional seats. Among the many reasons for Lacy's defeat were the entrenched strength of the Republican party in Michigan and the effectiveness of its campaign. Lacy, "a weak candidate" and a poor campaigner, was also handicapped by the unpopularity of the Comstock administration, whose "atmosphere," Lacy wrote, "hung over my election campaign like a cloud." Comstock endorsed Lacy four days before the election, but it seems likely that the Comstock group "worked under cover, quietly yet actively," to defeat their Democratic rival.[17]

Frank Murphy's name did not appear on Michigan's 1934 ballot, but it was only because prolonged, largely behind-the-scenes efforts to persuade him to become a candidate for the United States Senate had proved unavailing. A few days after the 1932 election Picard advised Murphy to begin making preparations to become a candidate for the Senate seat held by Republican Arthur H. Vandenberg. Others in Michigan offered Murphy the same advice after he became governor-general, and the Roosevelt administration was reportedly interested in a Murphy senatorial candidacy as a means of defeating a man then viewed as a possible contender for the Republican presidential nomination in 1936. Murphy, on the other hand, also received advice that he would be "a fool" to seek the Senate post in view of the electorate's negative reaction to the Comstock administration.[18]

While publicly professing that he intended to remain in the Philippines, Murphy gave much more than passing thought to a senatorial candidacy, taking soundings in Michigan about the possibility as early as November 1933. After visiting the Philippines toward the end of 1933, Congressman John Dingell, who represented Michigan's Fifteenth Congressional District, concluded that Murphy would run if his work in the Philippines had been completed or was nearly complete, the welfare of the Democratic party in Michigan demanded it, and the president did not object.

Pressed by Dingell for "a confidential expression" of his intentions, Murphy made his views known to George in a letter of March 28, 1934, so that he could discuss the subject with key people in Michigan. Since Frank thought that the Philippine Commonwealth might be established by the summer of 1935 and since a senator elected in November 1934 would not, in that pre-Lame-Duck-Amendment era, have had to take his seat until December 1935, he explained that he would be able to complete his assignment as governor-general before moving to the Senate if he decided to enter the race and if he were victorious, "both 'ifs,' " as he put it, "being strong ones." "The job [of Senator]," he wrote, "doesn't hold an especial lure but how I would like to get out on the hustings and over the crossroads preaching the gospel of good government and the New Deal." Since Murphy did not wish to appear eager to run for the Senate, preferring to be seen as responding to a call from the Roosevelt administration or the people of Michigan, he almost certainly understated his desire for the senatorship in his letter to George. His true feelings were probably revealed in a letter that his sister-in-law, then in the Philippines, wrote at about the same time Frank wrote to George: Frank, Irene Murphy stated, "wants to go to the Senate next."[19]

Before he left for the Philippines in April 1934, George tested sentiment in Michigan for Frank's senatorial candidacy. Since Michigan's senior senator, James Couzens, was a Detroiter, Frank was especially concerned that his candidacy might be viewed with disfavor by voters in the western part of the state as violating "the unwritten law" that no more than one Michigan senator should come from the eastern part of the state. The prominent Grand Rapids Democrat, Thomas F. McAllister, advised George, however, that the "serious objection" to two senators from Detroit did not apply if one of them was Frank Murphy because of his "state-wide" popularity and because only he would be able to "mark the distinct cleavage in the popular mind between the New Deal and the past."[20]

George, who spoke to Farley before leaving the United States, later claimed that Farley had wanted Frank to become a candidate and that the trip to the Philippines had actually been made at the behest of "authoritative sources" specifically to discuss the matter. When George arrived in the Philippines, he announced that the Democratic National Committee wished to launch a Murphy candidacy, but Farley failed to corroborate this allegation. Although Farley probably favored a Murphy candidacy, he felt that "he could not very well ring in on this matter as much as he would like to" because of Roosevelt's refusal to become involved in the 1934 elections. Farley, however, may have sought to stimulate a Murphy candidacy by assigning Emil Hurja, the vice-chairman of the Democratic National Committee and a Michigan native to plot Vandenberg's defeat. Dingell, we know, discussed a Murphy candidacy with Farley, who promised to take up the question with the "boss"; but he said not a word about the Senate race when he visited Michigan late in May.

The president wired Murphy in late June that although he "personally" would be happy to see Murphy in the Senate, he would have to be "consistent in taking no part in Senatorial or Congressional candidacies." Expressing his approval of Murphy's record as governor-general, Roosevelt concluded, "My feeling is best expressed by the wish that you would be in both places at the same time." Since Murphy had decided that he would remain in the Philippines "unless ordered away," the president's refusal to intervene, despite Murphy's later allegations that Roosevelt had cabled "importuning" him "to run," appeared to doom a Murphy candidacy.[21]

When George left the Philippines early in July, the instructions he carried from his brother related to his interest in a cabinet post, not a senatorship. A few days later, however, Frank received a letter from a trusted Michigan Democrat stating that the chances were "good" that he could be both nominated and elected. "Itching to go" home, Frank now considered permitting his Michigan friends to place his name on the primary ballot while he remained in the Philippines. As he wrote George in a letter that did not reach him until after the filing date for the primary, he did not want to return to the United States, but "my decision in [the] event the people voted for me while here is another matter."[22]

While George was still homeward bound, the old-line Democrats, no doubt thinking that it might aid Comstock in securing the Democratic gubernatorial nomination, quietly decided to circulate Murphy-for-senator petitions so that Murphy would be able to run for the office should he desire to do so. The task of gathering the necessary signatures was assigned to Walter McKenzie, a prominent Comstock ally, but, for reasons that are not self-evident, he failed to carry out his assignment in the short time available to him. Dingell was also tempted to circulate Murphy petitions, and Lacy favored the idea, indicating support for Murphy in both factions of the state party. Dingell, however, decided against the action because, as he wrote Murphy, he did not wish "to compromise your job or embarrass you." Had Dingell known the contents of Frank's letter to George concerning "the Senatorial thing"—the length of the sea voyage between Manila and the United States prevented that—the congressman would certainly have arranged for the circulation of Murphy petitions. As it was, Picard became the Democratic senatorial candidate, and he was defeated by Vandenberg in November by about 52,000 votes. Had Murphy rather than Picard opposed Vandenberg, it is possible that Vandenberg's senatorial career would have come to an end in 1934. Vandenberg understandably breathed a sigh of relief when it became evident that Murphy would not be his Democratic opponent in November.[23]

Insofar as Murphy considered returning to the United States to run for elective office after the 1934 election, his focus was on the Michigan governorship. That office was occupied beginning in January 1935 by Frank D. Fitzgerald. Born in Grand Ledge, Michigan, in 1885, Fitzgerald had served as deputy secretary of state and business manager of the state's Highway Department before being elected secretary of state in 1930. He had been reelected in 1932, the only Republican to win a statewide administrative post in that Democratic year. An able politician but "a weak man," Fitzgerald was inclined to take a stand on a particular issue and then to retreat in the face of "comparatively minor opposition." The "strongest man" behind the governor was Frank D. McKay, characterized by a former *Detroit Free Press* reporter and campaign worker for Fitzgerald as "the sub rosa governor of Michigan." McKay "never comes out far in the open but he pulls the strings and pulls them very shrewdly," Howard O. Hunter, a Federal Emergency Relief Administration field representative, informed Harry Hopkins.

A self-made man who was reputed to have been "a business genius," McKay became a major force in the Republican party in the 1920s when he served three terms as state treasurer, was the chief legislative lobbyist for Governor Fred W. Green, and chaired the highway and finance committees of the state's Administrative Board. A close associate of Fitzgerald since the early 1920s, he "reached the zenith of his influence" when Fitzgerald became governor. It was "widely believed" in Michigan that anyone wishing to sell to the state had to do so through McKay or one of his dummy corporations; and it was an "open secret" that to secure a job in the state's liquor control agency or to obtain a liquor order, one had to see McKay first.

Both the federal and state governments later sought to convict McKay on one charge or another, but two trials ended in acquittals, a third in a hung jury, and other indictments were dropped.[24]

Michigan's Democratic party continued to be wracked with division following Lacy's defeat in 1934. The state chairman of the party, Elmer O'Hara, whom Picard accused of being "out to wreck the party," was indicted in July 1935 for having violated the state's election laws by staging a fraudulent recount of the 1934 contests for the offices of secretary of state and attorney general. Since he refused to resign his party post despite his legal difficulties and the very strong opposition to his leadership, the Democratic State Central Committee stripped him of his powers soon after his indictment and vested party authority in the executive secretary of a newly created executive committee.[25]

"Smarting" from the defeat they had sustained in the 1934 primary, the Comstock-Abbott-Debo forces sought to regain control of the state party following the election. The old-line Democrats, as these men saw it, had sustained the party in its lean years and had led it to victory in 1932 whereas their enemies in the party, the Comstock group alleged, had contributed little to its well-being. "You are much like a woman who knows the joy of being a mother without undergoing the pains of travail," one Comstock supporter wrote Murphy. "You have had all the honors and none of the grief." Lacy was correct, however, in characterizing the Comstock group as "a hollow shell." Representing mostly out-state Michigan, they had discredited themselves with the electorate when they finally gained power in 1932. They were simply "a bunch of no good politicians and four-flushers," a Michigan Democrat advised the White House.[26]

A new third force emerged in the Michigan Democratic party after 1933 led by Highway Commissioner Murray D. Van Wagoner and his close associate, G. Donald Kennedy. A graduate of the University of Michigan, where he had received a civil engineering degree, Van Wagoner had twice been elected drain commissioner of Oakland County before being elected in 1933 to a four-year term as state highway commissioner, the first Democrat to hold the post. Kennedy and Van Wagoner had been roommates at the University of Michigan and had graduated together in 1921. After serving as a consulting engineer for several years, Kennedy became assistant city engineer and then engineer of Jackson, Michigan. While Van Wagoner served as Oakland County's drain commissioner, Kennedy assisted him in building up a "very splendid organization," based in part on University of Michigan and engineering profession contacts.

When Van Wagoner took office as highway commissioner on

July 1, 1933, he appointed Kennedy the department's business manager. The two men took advantage of their positions to fashion a formidable political organization, gaining friends through the astute distribution of highway funds and patronage—the Highway Department employed about 22 percent of the state's fourteen thousand employees—appointing "the most ingratiating group of subordinates to be found anywhere in Lansing," inducing county highway departments to provide amenable convention delegates, and creating a "voluntary" highway campaign fund. "It is intelligently manned, efficiently operated, and they know something about the value of organization work," a prominent Michigan Democrat said of the Highway Department in the summer of 1936. The vice-chairman of the Democratic State Central Committee advised Farley at the same time that Van Wagoner's head was "slightly swelled," claiming that she once had heard him say, " 'The Highway runs Michigan and I am King of the Highway.' " Van Wagoner belonged to the conservative wing of the Democratic party, but he did not identify with the Comstock forces.[27]

The factionalism within the Michigan Democratic party not only made it difficult for the national administration to resolve the patronage conflict that had contributed to the state party's 1934 defeat but also loomed as an obstacle to Democratic victory in the state in 1936. Roosevelt saw Frank Murphy as the Michigan Democrat best able to bring an end to Michigan's "patronage war" and to unite the warring factions in the state, and it was partly for this reason that the president summoned the governor-general to Washington early in 1935. ". . . all Michigan things are waiting for the return of Murphy from the Philippines," Louis Howe noted in February. "This is the President's wish."[28]

While in the United States, Murphy discussed the thorny patronage problem with Michigan Democrats as well as with Roosevelt, Farley, and Howe, to whom the president had assigned responsibility for Michigan since administration stalwarts like Hopkins, Henry Morgenthau, and Harold Ickes were disinclined to follow Farley's lead in Michigan patronage matters. Murphy's suggestion to resolve the patronage conflict was the appointment of a "committee of referees" consisting of three "representative and substantial Democrats" to decide on major appointments in consultation with the national committeeman and the state chairman. This proposal was opposed by the accredited party leaders in Michigan and by Farley, and the likelihood that it would be accepted was further diminished when Howe became ill on the day Murphy was scheduled to make a formal presentation of his plan.

The patronage pact that was finally agreed to by the parties of interest in Michigan at the beginning of April, with Murphy, the "uncrowned king of the [state] party," playing the role of mediator, provided that in districts where there was a Democratic congressman, the congressman and the chairman of the Democratic county committee were to be "supreme"; the county committee was to play the key role in consultation with the state party chairman in districts without a Democratic congressman. What was not revealed was that Murphy, despite his protestations that he had been "released" from further involvement in patronage matters, was henceforth to play an advisory role in the distribution of Michigan jobs (he could recommend appointments but not "cinch anything"), and the names of potential appointees were to be cleared with him. Murphy designated his brother George, Hall Roosevelt, and Thomas Chawke, a prominent Detroit criminal lawyer who had defended Henry Sweet in Judge Murphy's courtroom in 1926, to represent the governor-general in patronage matters.[29]

Murphy recognized that the patronage solution was "far from ideal" and did not harmonize party differences. It did, however, break Michigan's patronage logjam and led to the release after two years of hundreds of federal positions in the state, including, at long last, the positions of collector of internal revenue and collector of customs. The most important federal position filled in the spring of 1935 was that of state administrator of the new Works Progress Administration (WPA), and Murphy was instrumental in the selection of H. Lynn Pierson for the post. Pierson, the president of the Detroit Harvester Company, was a longtime friend of the president, having been associated with him in polio fund-raising efforts. Since the Pierson appointment was nonpartisan in character—"what I know about politics could be written on the back of a postage stamp," Pierson told Murphy—there were rumblings among Michigan Democrats. Murphy explained that it was necessary to appoint someone who was both loyal to the president and acceptable to Michigan's Republican but progressive-minded senator, James Couzens, and Pierson satisfied these criteria. Because of the numerous administrative positions that the WPA would be able to fill, Murphy recognized the agency's considerable potential for the rebuilding of Michigan's Democratic party along New Deal lines. He knew that the "machine gang" would seek to gain control of WPA patronage, and so he arranged for Pierson to seek the guidance of Chawke, Hall Roosevelt, and George.[30]

After consulting with Murphy's Michigan triumvirate and others, Pierson appointed a WPA advisory board of outstanding citizens to combat the view that the new agency would serve as a "political grab-bag." Since Dr. William Haber had run Michigan's emergency relief program in an efficient and nonpartisan manner, Pierson appointed the professor to serve as deputy WPA administrator; and the state WPA absorbed most of the personnel of the state's Emergency Relief Administration's work division despite Democratic allegations that the division was "too decidedly Republican in flavor." Pierson was under a "tremendous amount of pressure" from Democratic influentials to appoint their friends to WPA positions, but he successfully resisted most importunities.

Complaints that Pierson was ignoring the party's faithful poured in to Murphy, his Michigan representatives, Democratic national headquarters, the WPA in Washington, and the White House. The WPA was "the last hope" of Democrats who had worked for Roosevelt's election, a Michigan Democrat protested to the White House, but he contended that the relief administration's efforts to keep politics out of the program and Pierson's appointment of "'sympathetic' Republicans" were likely to lead to "a complete break-down in the morale of the Democratic organization." The executive secretary of the Wayne County Democratic Committee, who had previously stated, "If we muff this opportunity presented by the WPA we are unalloyed 120 Horse-power political asses," protested at the end of August 1935 that 96 percent of the key WPA positions in Wayne County had been awarded to Republicans. "If the WPA is to be non-partisan," he stated in an "Appeal by the Wayne County Democratic Organization for Fair Treatment" addressed to the White House and the Democratic National Committee, "at least dignify the Democratic Party to the extent of putting it on a parity with Republicans instead of as it is at present ignominiously suffering the same consideration as would be accorded the Communists. . . . This faithful horde of Chairmen, Delegates, Captains, group leaders and workers [should] be allowed not only the chance to share in the success of the WPA, but also to have a few nickels in their pockets." "Our recommendees are swarming the streets," John Dingell remonstrated. "Incorrigible Republicans cannot be transformed into Democrats and Democrats cannot live on hope or [the] perpetual idealism of President Roosevelt," the congressman declared. Organized labor in Detroit, which had received assurances from Murphy that the WPA would recognize its "fair demands," also complained that it was being excluded from "every major function" of the relief organization.[31]

"Lynn, these political boys are on my neck about you," WPA head Harry L. Hopkins told Pierson in a phone conversation on July 9.

Pierson responded that he had "forgotten politics" in making "major appointments." His appointees, he thought, were mostly "Roosevelt men but . . . not Democratic wheelhorses," and that was the rub. George Murphy informed his brother that the WPA appointees were mostly independents, some were identified with Republicans, and two or three had ties with the Democratic party organization but all were in sympathy with Roosevelt. ". . . a new color is being given the Democratic Party here in Michigan," George concluded. This is exactly what Frank had hoped to hear, and he endorsed all that Pierson had done. As for the "little boys" who were "crowding in" on Pierson, they were the "same ones," a WPA field observer reported, "who rushed pell mell for the trough in 1933, whose grunts and squeals could be heard from the Straits of Mackinac to Lake St. Clair. They're the boys who got the party in wrong in Michigan."[32]

Murphy's concern about patronage matters and the state of the Democratic party in Michigan was necessarily related to the possibility that he might seek Michigan's governorship in 1936. When the Michigan press reported shortly after the 1934 state election that George Murphy was saying that Frank would run for governor in 1936, Marguerite wrote George, "of course Frank couldn't say that he would [run]—but he said it was perfectly alright for you to say so." Since Murphy, as Congressman Prentiss Brown noted, had been "out of the fight" in 1934, he was "in a mighty good position to lead the [Democratic] party" in the state. Although unwilling to commit himself to a gubernatorial candidacy, Murphy did not discourage efforts to promote that candidacy.[33]

The role that Frank Murphy was to play in domestic politics in 1935 and 1936 was determined less by his own wishes than by the political needs of the Roosevelt administration and by the president's desire to stave off a possible third-party threat to his chances for reelection in 1936. That threat stemmed in part from the behavior of Father Coughlin, who in November 1934 founded the National Union for Social Justice (NUSJ), "the first step toward a complete break" between the priest and the Roosevelt administration. Picard informed Murphy that there was a "grave fear" in both Michigan and Washington that, given the state of the economy, "inflammatory appeals to the masses" of the Coughlin variety might even "lead to bloodshed." The Coughlin movement, the president of the Brotherhood of Teamsters advised Farley, "should not be considered lightly by anyone in political life whose political philosophy Coughlin opposes." Coughlin made his first direct public attack on Roosevelt at the end of January 1935, and one of the purposes for which Murphy visited the United States soon thereafter was to serve as the administration's "unofficial liaison to placate" the radio priest.³⁴

In returning to the United States Murphy was interested not only in running political errands for the national administration but in strengthening his own political base in Michigan. Although feigning to oppose "elaborate" reception arrangements for his Detroit arrival, he was careful to advise George to include "my labor friends" and "my old workers" among those who would greet him. When he reached Chicago on February 19, about one hundred Michigan Democrats, comprising "leaders, would-be leaders, corporals and privates in the Democratic ranks," were on hand, most of them beseeching him to assume the party's leadership.

When the governor-general arrived in Detroit the next day, he was greeted by what the *Detroit Times* described as "the largest and most impressive homecoming ceremonies ever accorded a Detroiter." Large crowds met Murphy at the Michigan Central terminal, lined the streets along his route to City Hall and a meeting with Mayor Frank Couzens, and waited outside the building to catch a glimpse of their former mayor. Eight hundred persons, including Comstock, Lacy, and several Murphy girl friends, attended a Murphy homecoming banquet that night.

Before leaving Detroit for Washington, Murphy received a "tumultuous welcome" at a Detroit and Wayne County Federation of Labor (DWCFL) affair, conferred with Democrats from all over the state, delivered two addresses, and met with Father Coughlin. When questioned by reporters about the Coughlin meeting, Murphy replied that he thought the NUSJ program was "splendid" and that he was "a close friend and ardent admirer of Father Coughlin." Murphy privately believed that he had taken "steps . . . to iron out the bumps" in the path of reconciliation between Roosevelt and Coughlin. While Murphy was in Washington, however, Coughlin scathingly described the first two years of the New Deal as " 'two years of failure, two years of compromise[,] and two years of pitting the puny and puerile brains of idealists against the vicious and virile brains of industrial monopolists and big finance.' "³⁵

Murphy seems to have arranged for a Detroit priest with whom he was friendly to talk to the Reverend Michael J. Gallagher, Coughlin's bishop, about Coughlin's attacks on the president, but the bishop made no apparent effort to restrain Coughlin. Murphy once again turned to that task himself during his final days in Detroit before returning to the Philippines. While in the hospital recovering from an "unusually tough" tonsillectomy, he spoke "at length and favorably," he thought, with Coughlin, telling him, it would seem, that Roosevelt was "a great leader whose heart and soul" were "on the people's side" even if some of his aides were guilty of insensitivity and despite a "trend toward experimentation." Murphy's efforts were abetted by the prominent Catholic Joseph P. Kennedy, who arrived in Detroit on May 12 to confer with Murphy and Coughlin. Murphy thought Kennedy was the logical person to play the role of peacemaker between Coughlin and the administration after Murphy returned to the Philippines.

The governor-general informed the White House after his conversation with Coughlin that he was confident the priest would not align himself with "disaffected elements" and would support the president, particularly if "his [Coughlin's] case is given the intimate and persistent attention it deserves." In a final radio address before leaving Detroit Murphy praised both Roosevelt and Coughlin and pointedly predicted that the people would not abandon the president either for "extremists" or the advocates of laissez-faire. Both Coughlin and Bishop Gallagher were among the crowd of well-wishers who bade Murphy farewell as he began the rail journey from Detroit to San Francisco. At a White House meeting shortly before Murphy's departure, the president, according to Farley, reported that Murphy was "doing a splendid job in handling Coughlin." Roosevelt indicated that, although he intended to appoint Murphy high commissioner, he would bring him home shortly thereafter so that he could "devote his entire time to the Coughlin situation."[36]

It is possible that while in Washington Murphy met with another bitter critic of the Roosevelt administration, Huey Long. Long and Coughlin had joined forces in January 1935 to prevent ratification of a treaty that would have led to United States membership in the World Court. This led to speculation thereafter about a Long-Coughlin alliance that might affect the outcome of the 1936 presidential election. In the summer of 1935 Long dictated the draft of a book, *My First Days in the White House*, which was published in the fall, shortly after Huey's death. The attorney general in President Long's cabinet was none other than Frank Murphy, attaining in this fictional account the position he had coveted since Roosevelt's election in 1932. Long related in the book that, in his first conversation with Murphy, he had felt Murphy's "piercing eyes boring into my soul." The senator described an interview with his attorney general that concluded with Murphy's saying, "Mr. President, we shall restore Justice in America."

Long's presidential dreams came to an end in September 1935, when Huey was felled by an assassin's bullet. By a curious coincidence, the news of the assassination reached Father Coughlin while he was conferring in New York with Joseph Kennedy, who, playing the role of mediator that Murphy had assigned him, was in the process of arranging a meeting between the president and the priest.[37]

That the meeting between Roosevelt and Coughlin on September 11 would not lead to a reconciliation was foretold a few days before Long's death. "More disgusted than ever" with the national administration, Coughlin charged in a letter to Murphy of September 5 that Roosevelt had broken virtually all his promises and had used methods smacking of socialism and communism. After his visit with the president, Coughlin described Roosevelt as "a socialist of the radical type." The president, the priest wrote, "like every other radical, either willingly or unwillingly determined that the nation shall be a country of, by and for the bankers." Conceding that Roosevelt would be reelected barring some "unforeseen miracle," the priest reported that his allies and he were setting out to rid the Congress of members who rubber-stamped the president's proposals, thus making it impossible for Roosevelt "to hold a whip" over the next Congress. The "more progressive Republicans," Coughlin claimed, were willing to help reelect Roosevelt "for the purpose of ruining him entirely together with the hopes of the Tugwells, the Frankfurters and the rest of the Jews who surround him." "The plot," Coughlin reported, was "deeply laid" and enjoyed the almost unanimous support of Republicans, Progressives, Townsendites, the NUSJ, and some smaller organizations. Coughlin had been off the air during the summer, and so there had been a lull in his criticism of the New Deal. He returned to the air early in November, however, and during the next few months he publicly broke with the Roosevelt administration.[38]

Although Long's death eliminated the Louisiana senator as a possible threat to a Roosevelt victory in 1936, it did not end the administration's concern about the election's outcome. The administration had been receiving disturbing reports that the president had "slipped" in Michigan because of its business-controlled Republican press, complaints that the New Deal's relief program was "making bums out of people," and "the mess that the Democratic party" seemed "to have got itself into." Michigan Democrats were warning the administration that, without "diligent and painstaking" effort before the 1936 election, it could "expect to see Michigan once more piling up a majority for the republican presidential candidate." It became increasingly evident that, whether or not Murphy wished to remain in the Philippines, the president would bring him back to the United

States in 1936 to play a part in the campaign, most probably "to pull the Democratic party in the state [Michigan] together and to help carry the state for Roosevelt."[39]

During his 1935 trip to the United States Murphy not only sought to placate Father Coughlin but also to persuade Senator Couzens to run as a Democrat in 1936. Murphy's argument to Couzens, a Republican who supported much of the New Deal and was popular with the voters but not with the Republican leadership in Michigan, was that he could win as a Democrat but not as a Republican. Telling Couzens that he could "manage" the Democratic part of the arrangement, Murphy claimed that the idea of a Couzens party switch had come to him after a group of wealthy Detroiters, to whom Couzens was anathema, had offered him a $500,000 campaign fund if he would run against the senator. Although it is not clear whether Murphy was acting on his own to enhance Democratic chances in Michigan in 1936, including his own, or was running another errand for the national administration, we do know that agents of Farley made the same proposal to Couzens the next year. Couzens had no intention of abandoning the Republican party, unless, as he wrote Governor Fitzgerald, it "again came under the control of the stand-pat and reactionary leaders who . . . heretofore had control of the Party." He did, however, seriously consider entering the primaries of both parties or running on a separate ticket as "an independent Republican." In the end, he contested for the nomination on the Republican ticket, and, as Murphy had predicted, he was defeated.[40]

Murphy's trip to the United States, Tom McAllister informed the governor-general, had aroused the "keenest anticipation" that he would become a gubernatorial candidate. "There is a spontaneous and unanimous demand for you to return and regenerate the Party," McAllister wrote. There was, indeed, a Murphy-for-governor boom in the state, and George Murphy announced that "if there was a proper demand made for his candidacy," Frank "would accept." Frank did not reveal his intentions publicly, but Congressman Prentiss Brown concluded "from somewhat frequent contacts" with Murphy during his mainland visit that he would run for governor unless the president appointed him to "some major place." When he returned to the Philippines in the middle of June, Frank privately informed George that, if he did not receive a cabinet post and became high commissioner, he would return to the United States in May or June 1936 to run for governor or "otherwise assist" Roosevelt in the presidential campaign.[41]

During the next several months Murphy received a number of letters and reports from Michigan designed to encourage his candidacy and predicting his victory. On the other hand, he knew that Michigan's Democratic party was "a rabble of snarling factions," the Comstock forces were committed to a " 'Stop Murphy Campaign,' " Father Coughlin opposed his candidacy on the Democratic ticket, and victory in Republican Michigan was far from a sure thing. In replies to his correspondents, Murphy generally indicated satisfaction with his Philippine post without however foreclosing the possibility that he might, under certain circumstances, seek the governorship. Regardless of his own wishes, he knew that the president might request his return, and so he thought it prudent to prepare for that eventuality. He therefore requested his brother to join with Chawke and Hall Roosevelt in selecting "a competent organizer" to establish Murphy-for-governor clubs in the state that would "feel out sentiment" so that "we would be prepared if things take a turn in that direction."[42]

George informed Frank late in July 1935 that Don Kennedy had been offered the position of executive secretary of the Democratic State Central Committee to run the 1936 state campaign but would not take the post unless he received "some word more or less definite as to your intentions." Although Frank cabled back urging that Kennedy accept the position, the message did not arrive until after he had decided not to take the job. In follow-up letters Frank asked George to explore the possibility of support for a Murphy candidacy from the Hearst-owned and by then anti-Roosevelt *Detroit Times*, which, Frank asserted, had "made possible every campaign victory I have enjoyed." Before the year was out Frank learned from a friendly *Times* reporter that the *Times* and Murphy would "continue to fight together" and Frank was informed later that Hearst himself had given "full approval."[43]

Before George returned to the Philippines at the end of 1935, Kennedy summarized for him what he thought would have to be done if Frank were to be elected governor. The governor-general, for one thing, would have to make a confidential commitment in the near future that he would become a candidate, Kennedy advised, so that those planning his campaign could begin a "long-term build-up." Such a commitment would also prevent the development within the party of "movements of a dangerous character," by which Kennedy probably meant the entry into the race of other Democratic candidates. Frank's reaction to Kennedy's advice was to tell the Highway Department business manager to "continue with your plans," but he thought it premature to make the commitment that Kennedy thought desirable. Although protesting that, "despite belief to the contra,'' he was ''not coy about either love or politics,'' all that he would do about his possible candidacy as 1935 came to a close was to say that he would be pleased if his friends were to '' 'make-way-the-road' '' for him while he awaited developments regarding his duty. He recognized that this might be ''something of a selfish policy,'' but he rationalized that groups organized in his behalf could later be transferred to another candidate if he did not himself enter the race. If he did become a candidate, he informed a close friend, it would be because he decided that he owed it to the president to do so. ''He [Roosevelt] won't have to ask me to do my duty.''[44]

As it turned out, the president did find it necessary to ask Murphy ''to do'' his ''duty.'' In a letter to the high commissioner of January 7, 1936, Roosevelt characterized the forthcoming election as the most important since the Civil War. After careful study, the president stated, the administration had concluded that the only solution for the ''demoralized state'' of the Democratic party in Michigan was for Murphy to ''assemble the discordant elements. No one,'' the president wrote, ''has been able to suggest a candidate for the Governorship who shows the slightest likelihood of a successful outcome with the exception of yourself.'' Farley, the president indicated, had been in touch with Van Wagoner and Kennedy, and they had promised their full support, with Kennedy agreeing to serve as Murphy's campaign manager. He favored the appointment of Picard to the vacant federal judgeship in Michigan, but since Picard, like Murphy, was a Catholic, the president deviously suggested that the position initially go to a Protestant, with the understanding that he would resign on November 15, after the election, so that Picard could then be given the position! The president also thought of Picard as a possible senatorial candidate, especially if Murphy ''did not accord with the nomination of a Protestant because proper material is not available.'' Roosevelt pressed Murphy for an ''immediate answer,'' assuring him that if he lost the election but Roosevelt was reelected, ''your work would obviously be recognized.''[45]

Since the president regarded a Murphy decision about the Michigan governorship to be a matter of some urgency, it is difficult to understand why the January 7 letter was not cabled to Manila but was rather sent by sea, not arriving in the Philippines until the beginning of February. Murphy promptly cabled his political informants in Michigan for their assessment of the political situation in the state. After receiving several encouraging responses, the governor-general, who could hardly have replied otherwise, cabled Roosevelt on February 7, ''Will gladly undertake without conditions errand suggested. . . .

It will be no sacrifice on my part to make any effort that may be helpful to you.'' Murphy, at the same time, rejected the president's opportunistic suggestion regarding the federal judgeship in Michigan as injecting politics into judicial appointments.[46]

Although his friends had begun to circulate petitions in his behalf in late January, Murphy still refused to commit himself publicly. He did send messages to the United States urging that ''a real delegation'' be sent to the state Democratic convention in the spring, advising that the influence of the Young Democrats be made ''vital and effective,'' appealing to Coughlin to support Roosevelt against ''the ruthless pack seeking . . . [his] destruction'' and promising, if victorious, to follow policies that Coughlin and the NUSJ could approve.[47]

Fearing that ''the chances'' if he entered the race were ''much more'' that his ''head would roll into a basket than that it . . . [would] wear a crown,'' Murphy was more guarded when he sent a promised follow-up letter to the president on March 7 than he had been in his cable. He would, of course, become a gubernatorial candidate or undertake any other mission that would aid the president in the fall election, but ''proper consideration,'' he said, also had to be given to ''preserving the present satisfactory state of affairs in the Philippines.'' He noted, furthermore, that reports from Michigan indicated that the outlook for the party in the state, ''if not hopeless,'' was ''at least very doubtful.'' Despite a specific denial in the letter, Murphy was obviously seeking to impress the president with the extent of the ''sacrifice'' he would be making were he to become a candidate for governor. Doubting that ''the realities of the Michigan situation'' had been ''fairly presented'' to the president and also anxious to discuss Philippine matters with him, Murphy sought and apparently received assurances from Roosevelt that the status quo regarding the Philippines and the Murphy candidacy would be maintained until the high commissioner returned to the United States and spoke with the president.[48]

Despite his protestations to the contrary, Murphy did not wish to remain in the Philippines, thinking that there was little more that he could do there either to aid the Filipinos or to advance his career. As Weldon Jones noted, ''barring the fortuitous and more or less accidental which might give the High Commissioner national headlines, this post is a long way from home and gives its occupant little chance to make a national reputation and less chance to keep in touch with alliances behind the curtains.'' Murphy, indeed, was being advised by Michigan Democrats that if he remained in the Philippines much longer, he would be forgotten in his home state and would remove himself from ''the track and trend of affairs.'' Murphy, however, did not have much appetite for a losing race in Michigan. When he received a letter asking "WHO in hell" he thought "could carry this State" if he did not run, he wondered if even he could win. Coughlin, for one, was telling him that he could not win on a Roosevelt ticket, and Murphy grossly exaggerated the political power that Coughlin wielded in Michigan.

Although Murphy knew that in the end he would have to do what Roosevelt asked of him, it is likely that when he left the Philippines in May 1936 he was not particularly eager to become a candidate for governor and preferred instead to aid the president in the 1936 campaign in some other way. Whatever the final decision was to be, he thought it best to return to the United States as high commissioner reporting on Philippine affairs rather than as a politician seeking office at the president's behest. It was politically necessary, as Farley, Hall Roosevelt, and George Murphy all agreed, for Frank to counteract the impression created by Michigan's Republican press that the president was meddling in Michigan's political affairs by compelling Murphy to give up his Philippine post to run for governor.[49]

Murphy's supporters in Michigan had counseled him that the longer he delayed the announcement of his candidacy, the more likely he would face opposition in the Democratic primary. Their fears materialized when George W. Welsh on April 14, 1936, announced his candidacy for the governorship. Welsh, who had served as a member and Speaker of the Michigan House, lieutenant governor of the state, and city manager of Grand Rapids, was a recent convert to the Democratic party who had supported Comstock in the 1932 gubernatorial campaign after having unsuccessfully opposed Wilber M. Brucker in the Republican primary. Since there was speculation that Van Wagoner, State Treasurer Theodore I. Fry, and Picard would emulate Welsh, Farley, in an effort to forestall these "rumored candidacies," secretly persuaded George A. Schroeder, the Democratic Speaker of the Michigan House, to proclaim his candidacy, with the understanding that he would withdraw when Murphy declared himself. At the request of Farley's aide Emil Hurja, Van Wagoner issued "a very strong public statement" to the effect that he would not be a candidate for governor. Another threat to Murphy's candidacy was averted when the Catholic Picard, who would have liked to run for the Senate again, rejected the offer of a "sizable campaign fund" for a senatorial race from foes of Murphy who "wanted to get a catholic at that end of the ticket so that Frank Murphy wouldn't run at the other end. It wasn't so much love for me," Picard observed, "as it was desire to squelch Murphy."[50]

In an address to the delegates at the Michigan Democratic party's pre-primary convention on May 20, Farley sought to refute the view that the Roosevelt administration was insisting on a Murphy candidacy. "The whole thing is up to the Democrats of Michigan," he misleadingly asserted. "We are not interfering from Washington." Deferring a party showdown, the delegates endorsed Murphy, Welsh, Fry (who soon announced that he would not enter the race), and Schroeder as possible candidates deserving party support. Whereas the demonstration for Murphy at the convention was lackluster and looked "very artificial," the Welsh candidacy was enhanced as the result of the "good impression" he made on the delegates, the endorsement that he received from Comstock and Don W. Canfield, the state party's executive secretary, the hostility to Murphy of many old-line and out-state Democrats, and the belief of many delegates, despite Farley's disclaimers, that the Murphy candidacy was being " 'jammed through' " by the national administration.[51]

When he arrived in San Francisco on June 3, Murphy insisted that he had been called home "in the line of duty" and denied that the administration had demanded that he become a candidate. After meeting with the president on June 20, Murphy informed his sister that, although no final decision had been reached, the president was "not too keen about . . . [his] running for governor" and believed that he could do more to aid the Democratic cause in 1936 "campaigning around the country." One may surmise that the president was thinking along these lines not only because opposition had developed to Murphy in Michigan but also because of the president's concern about the Catholic vote in the presidential election. The day before the Roosevelt-Murphy meeting Coughlin announced that he would support William Lemke for president on a new Union party ticket that was also likely to enjoy the backing of Francis Townsend and Gerald L. K. Smith, who was attempting to wear Huey Long's mantle. Although a Gallup poll of late June 1936 revealed that a Coughlin endorsement was far more likely to hurt than to help a candidate, the radio priest's activities were viewed as "the most dangerous indication of Catholic dissatisfaction" with the administration. Alfred E. Smith's opposition to the president and the New Deal, charges that Communists had infiltrated the administration, and Catholic complaints that the administration was insufficiently concerned about anticlericalism in Mexico also aroused fears in Washington concerning Catholic allegiance to the Democrats, fears that Murphy might help to allay.[52]

With the final decision about his gubernatorial candidacy still pending, Murphy journeyed to the Democratic national convention in Philadelphia as chairman of the Philippine delegation and as a delegate-at-large from Michigan. The oratory at the convention was interminable since the arrangements called for a member of each delegation to second the nomination of Franklin D. Roosevelt. Murphy, who had been disappointed in his expectation of making a seconding speech at the 1932 Democratic convention, was given his opportunity this time. When he wisely confined his remarks to a single sentence—"The Philippine Islands gratefully second the nomination of Franklin Delano Roosevelt"—the audience roared its approval. While at the convention, Murphy interceded with the Michigan delegation to help secure the appointment of Edmund C. Shields, a former chairman of the Democratic State Central Committee and a former University of Michigan regent, to serve as Michigan's Democratic national committeeman.[53]

The decision that Murphy should become a candidate for governor was made by Roosevelt, for all practical purposes, in a meeting with Murphy at Roosevelt's Hyde Park home on June 29. The president stated that the advice he had received from Hall Roosevelt and others was that the Democrats would lose Michigan unless Murphy headed the state ticket. The party needed the Detroit vote to win, Roosevelt contended, and Murphy could best attract that vote. The president was also undoubtedly aware, as Murphy was, of polling data gathered in the spring of 1936 by the Highway Department, following "approved scientific methods" used by Emil Hurja, which indicated that a race between Roosevelt and a Republican challenger would be very close in Michigan, the strongest Democratic ticket would be Roosevelt for president, Murphy for governor, and Couzens for senator, and "Murphy alone would add sufficient strength [to the ticket] to carry his office and the Presidency." Hurja predicted that Murphy would defeat Fitzgerald by forty thousand votes, a remarkably accurate forecast.

As might have been expected, Murphy protested that his Philippine experience and his knowledge of the Far East should not be "scrapped without careful consideration" and that, in any event, he might be of greater assistance in the national campaign than by running for governor. "I was firm," Murphy recorded in a memorandum he made of the Hyde Park conference, but "so was he—all the while smiling." Michigan might be the pivotal state in the election, Roosevelt said; if he lost it, he might lose the election. Roosevelt told Murphy to think it over, but it was "obvious," Murphy realized, that the president wanted him to run. "He didn't order me to run," Murphy wrote. "He didn't say that I should but he was thinking it and in an adroit, silent, forceful way he commanded it. He was entirely cordial and friendly.'' Although Murphy did not commit himself to run, as he left the conference he told Marguerite LeHand, the president's secretary, that he felt like a prisoner being sentenced to a two-year term. After the conference he said to reporters that he had come to Hyde Park to discuss "confidential matters" regarding the Philippines and that there had been "just a passing reference" to national politics at the meeting.[54]

In an address in Detroit on July 2, Murphy, drawing a distinction between the politics of ideology and the politics of patronage and setting the stage for his own candidacy, sharply criticized politicians who stressed the distribution of spoils rather than "the great problems of the day.... There should be men and women in public service," he asserted, "with the courage and intelligence to stand for things that are basic and fundamental, rather than mere job hucksters; simple, honest, earnest men who are willing to be evangelical." He cited George Norris and Robert La Follette, Jr., as examples, but he was really seeking to describe Frank Murphy.[55]

Following Shields's advice, Murphy arranged for the state's top Democrats to confer with Roosevelt on July 9. Knowing that Van Wagoner and Fry had indicated that they would be "neutral" in the primary and fearing that the opposition press might extract "embarrassing statements" from them, Murphy, in a meeting with Kennedy, Shields, and the two men just before they all went to the White House, stressed the importance of party unity. They wanted to be "coaxed or bargained with," Murphy wrote in a note that he made of the meeting, and since he was unwilling to do the latter he did the former "enthusiastically." They were "friendly" but "noncommittal." In a characteristic performance, Roosevelt continued the task of persuasion, complimenting Van Wagoner, listening "with approval" to what Shields had to say about patronage, and giving Kennedy the opportunity to discuss highway problems. In a jovial mood, Roosevelt stated he had hoped that he could cut Murphy in half and keep one half in the Philippines and the other in Michigan. Since he could not do this, he said, he would keep Murphy in Michigan, and the Democrats would carry the state. The Roosevelt magic worked, and the party leaders left the conference "happy and charmed."[56]

In advance of the July 9 conference, the White House released a letter from Murphy announcing his resignation as high commissioner and his candidacy for the governorship. In his letter, Murphy stated that he had decided to enter the gubernatorial race because what was of "first importance" was the continuation of Roosevelt's leadership and the success of the Democratic party in the state and the nation. Party leaders in Michigan, Murphy asserted, had assured him that his candidacy would meet with "the general approval" of the state party and would "materially promote" Roosevelt's success. In a letter of reply that the *Detroit News* characterized as "one of the strongest notes of praise that has ever emerged from the presidential office," Roosevelt stressed what Murphy had accomplished as governor-general and high commissioner both for his "country and the cause of humanity." The president attributed to Murphy's efforts "a feeling of cordiality and mutual trust without parallel in the history of relations between a sovereign and a dependent people."

Uncertain about the Michigan outcome, Roosevelt decided to hold Murphy's resignation in abeyance. Murphy was to continue as high commissioner until September 5, a few days before the primary—he said that he would campaign only on weekends—and then, his primary victory being assumed, he was to receive a two-month leave of absence without pay to campaign against his Republican opponent. Murphy stated that the president had arranged matters in this way so that the high commissioner could participate in a Philippine-American trade conference in November. Murphy was, indeed, pressing for such a conference, but it is more likely that the resignation was held in abeyance so that he could return to the Philippines should he be defeated. This was why *Time* characterized the resignation as "riskless."[57]

II

In announcing his gubernatorial candidacy, Murphy declared that, if elected, he would establish in Lansing "those humane and enlightened social conditions envisioned by the New Deal." He would attempt to "modernize and simplify" the business of government by applying "progressive methods employed in private business" insofar as that was possible. A fiscally conservative New Dealer, he promised both a balanced budget, "except in conditions of extreme emergency," and the attainment of "a larger measure of social justice." Above all, he declared, he would free the state government from "the bane of sinister influences and of selfish men seeking their own advantage at the expense of the public interest."[58]

Schroeder, a stalking horse for Murphy, withdrew from the race as soon as Murphy announced his candidacy. Welsh, however, remained a candidate. In an effort to contrast his own candidacy with Murphy's, Welsh stated that he was not in the race at anyone's solicitation, was seeking no help from Washington, and was "not the

favorite candidate, nor the rubber stamp, of any group or clique."
Echoing the same view and giving evidence that Murphy and he had
"come to the parting of the political ways," Coughlin stated that
"people don't want state candidates chosen at Washington." The
reaction in the Philippines to Murphy's decision was one of dismay
not only because of the high commissioner's immense popularity but
also because it seemed evident once again that "political considerations" had ranked above Philippine-American relations in the United
States government's ordering of priorities.

The Republican press of Michigan, while noting that Murphy was
"superlatively good looking" and had "vast personal charm," commented in a disparaging way about his abilities. In a sarcastic editorial
entitled "Sad Case of Mr. Murphy," the *Detroit Free Press* observed
that "anyone who knows Mr. Murphy must realize what it means for
a young man of his social disposition to have to give up even
temporarily a highly paid job in the Orient, where the climate is
seductive, where servants are cheap and there are no dinner checks to
pay, to gamble on getting a $5,000 job in this State." The *Detroit
News* wondered just what votes Murphy could add to the Roosevelt
column that the president could not win on his own.[59] The answer to
that reasonable question had to await the outcome of the November
election in Michigan.

For the Roosevelt administration's Michigan strategy to be put to
the test, Murphy first had to defeat Welsh in the state primary.
Murphy was handicapped because he had to limit his campaigning
until September 5, but it was "the local political situation" that
posed the greatest threat to a Murphy victory. It was predictable, of
course, that old-line Democrats like Comstock, "bitter, hurt, revengeful, anti-Roosevelt and anti-Frank Murphy," would support
Welsh. Introducing Welsh for a campaign address, Comstock, conveniently forgetting Welsh's recent conversion to the Democratic
party, stated that the man who won the primary should be "a good
party man . . . a regular organization man" rather than someone
who thought himself chosen by God.[60]

More troubling to Murphy than the opposition of the Comstock
group, a faction of dwindling importance in Michigan politics, was
the attitude of the powerful Highway Department organization.
Although Murphy had been led to believe that the Highway wing of
the party would support him in the primary, Van Wagoner advanced
the novel thesis that, as an elected state official, he would have to
remain neutral in the campaign. Important Democrats in the state
thought that Van Wagoner was not behaving like a neutral but was

rather "conspiring" to defeat Murphy, and there was evidence to support this belief in at least some parts of the state. The chairman of the Young Democratic Clubs of Michigan thought that Van Wagoner and Kennedy had "cooled" toward Murphy because he had not selected Kennedy to manage his campaign and had refused to promise the Highway Department exclusive control over patronage if he won the election. Evidence is lacking to support these allegations, but they are not, in any event, a sufficient explanation for the Highway Department's less than friendly attitude toward Murphy's candidacy. It is more likely, as some Michigan Democrats believed, that Van Wagoner's ambition was to gain control of the state Democratic party and that he saw a Murphy victory as a major obstacle to that goal. If, however, the Democrats lost the state election—Welsh was a less likely winner than Murphy—and Van Wagoner won re-election in 1937, the Highway Department would be "the head and tail and the 'all' " of the Michigan party.[61]

The Highway Department demonstrated its political muscle when on July 28, 1936, Elmer O'Hara at long last resigned his chairmanship of the Democratic State Central Committee. The Highway Department's candidate to succeed O'Hara was Edward J. Fry, the superintendent of the state capitol and the brother of the state treasurer. Without consulting Murphy and "without previous notice," the Van Wagoner faction "railroaded" Fry's appointment through a meeting of the State Central Committee "jammed with proxies in the hands of Highway representatives." According to the chairman of the Ingham County Democratic Committee, Fry stated after his selection, " 'I think we can beat Murphy.' " A few weeks later Fry allegedly asserted, " 'I am going to kill Murphy, then my brother will be the big democrat.' " Fry not only sought to conciliate Comstock, but he appointed a Welsh supporter as his assistant and field representative. This led the chairman of the Sanilac County Democratic Committee to wonder whether "there was a Nigger somewhere in the activities of the Chairman's office." The *Detroit Free Press* thought that Fry's selection and his efforts to appease Comstock marked the "ascendancy" of Welsh over Murphy in the party. Although this grossly overstated the matter, what had occurred was certainly troubling to Murphy.[62]

Emil Hurja and the vice-chairman of the Democratic State Central Committee urged Farley to "bang down on the Highway Department" and to impress upon Van Wagoner the necessity of "getting behind" Murphy. Farley conferred with two Highway representatives, probably Van Wagoner and Kennedy, in the latter part of July and then informed Murphy, "I am sure that they will come through all right." Van Wagoner and Fry met with Farley early in August following press reports of "thinly veiled hints" that Michigan might encounter difficulties in securing federal highway funds if the department opposed Murphy. Fry and Kennedy denied that pressure was being exerted by the national administration, but there is every reason to think that that is precisely what occurred. "I think the smart thing for me to do right now is take a vacation," Van Wagoner declared after the campaign had been under way for a few weeks.[63]

Murphy was also concerned about the support accorded Welsh by two Detroit area Democratic congressmen, George Sadowski and John Lesinski. Both men represented constituencies with large numbers of voters of Polish descent, an ethnic group that had overwhelmingly supported Murphy in the past. "The Polack [sic] Congressmen in Detroit," except for Dingell, a leading Michigan Democrat wrote Farley, "are, as usual, off on the wrong foot." He thought, however, that Sadowski and Lesinski would be unable to carry their constituencies with them.[64]

The Murphy camp anticipated that the Coughlinites and Townsendites in the Democratic party would vote against Murphy, but the electoral strength of those two groups was uncertain. When Townsend, who normally only endorsed congressional candidates, urged his followers to support Welsh, the *Detroit News* speculated that this might decide the primary. The respected Ann Arbor Democrat, George Burke, disagreed, contending that the Townsend endorsement would do Welsh more harm than good. One Democrat believed that Coughlin's influence in the state had become "negligible" as the result of his attack on the president, but a priest in Macomb County informed Murphy that he was going to lose the county because of Coughlin's strength there. There was additional worry in the Murphy camp that Couzens's presence on the Republican ticket as a senatorial candidate would attract voters to the Republican primary who would otherwise have cast their ballots for Murphy. This partly explains Murphy's vain effort to persuade Couzens to switch to the Democratic party. Couzens endorsed Roosevelt during the course of the Michigan primary, but that did not add votes to the Murphy column.[65]

Murphy's religion also appeared to be an obstacle to his success. Murphy was a Catholic, Michigan's national committeewoman noted, but Michigan, excepting Wayne County, was "not a Catholic state." Although the religious issue, according to a pre-primary analysis of the Michigan political situation, was "way in the background" and might "never be dragged out," Murphy later complained that religion had been used against him "in every conceivable way." Murphy was seen not just as a Catholic but as a wet—as mayor he had been a conspicuous proponent of repeal. The minister editor of the *Michigan Christian Advocate*, a Methodist paper, observed that Murphy's "exceedingly wet policy" did not make him "popular with our crowd."[66]

Murphy was also concerned about newspaper opposition to his candidacy. Not only were Michigan's newspapers overwhelmingly Republican—there were 255 Republican daily and weekly newspapers in the state as compared to a single Democratic daily (in Marshall, with a population of five thousand) and fifteen Democratic weeklies—but they were almost all opposed to Murphy, "many of them violently" so. Because of his relief policies as mayor, Detroit's inability at the end of his mayoralty to meet payments on its bonded indebtedness, and the fact that he had resigned three positions since 1930, the Republican press pictured Murphy as "a reckless demagogue, wasteful of the public money, leaving one office as soon as it is to his advantage to do so, and otherwise unscrupulous and self-seeking." Murphy had been led to believe that the *Detroit Times*, at least, would take up the cudgels in his behalf, but Hearst in the end was willing to place the *Times* behind Murphy only if he denounced Roosevelt, which, of course, he would not do. Complaining to Hearst on August 4 that the *Times* had joined the *Detroit Free Press* in the "vicious campaign" against his candidacy, Murphy appealed to the publisher for support. A few days later, possibly because Hearst had passed the word, possibly because the editorial staff of the *Times* was pro-Murphy, the newspaper announced editorially that, although it would not support Murphy, it would not say a word against him.[67]

Despite some liabilities, Murphy had many assets as a candidate. He had an attractive personality; he was a marvelous campaigner and a superb orator—no other political figure in the state could sway an audience as he could; factory workers were solidly behind Roosevelt and the New Deal; economic conditions in the state had been improving since the beginning of the year; the state's national committeeman and most Democratic county chairmen supported him rather than Welsh; and the national administration, despite Roosevelt's proclaimed refusal to intervene in Democratic primaries, obviously favored Murphy and quietly aided his candidacy. Welsh's support, on the other hand, came mainly from "the old Comstock following" and "some of the same fellows who helped to make a mess of the Comstock administration." It was for these reasons that

George Burke, in an astute analysis of the Michigan political situation, concluded, "If he [Murphy] confines his talks to the Brotherhood of Man and the Fatherhood of God, there will be nothing to it."[68]

To direct his primary campaign, Murphy turned to Harry Mead, an earthy practitioner of the old politics who had managed Murphy's successful mayoralty campaigns in 1930 and 1931. Employed at the time as an attorney in the Public Works Administration (PWA), Mead secured a leave from his position to take charge of the Murphy campaign. Mead, who thought that he had not been amply rewarded for his direction of previous Murphy campaigns, told Josephine Gomon, who had been Mayor Murphy's assistant secretary, that "he had pinned him [Murphy] down and Murphy had definitely promised him something this time." Mead also told Gomon that he was "going to try to shake down the PWA contractors" for campaign contributions.[69]

Advising Mead regarding the nature of the campaign organization he wished to establish, Murphy asserted that he wanted a statewide organization perfected that would include a steering committee and campaign units in every county and congressional district of the state. He instructed that "a very active but . . . tactful woman" be selected to organize and address women's groups and that the publicity man for the campaign be "on the job morning, noon and night sending dope to the local and state press." Knowing that he was especially popular with blacks and white ethnic groups because of his record as judge and mayor, he told Mead to organize "our old minority groups" in Detroit and to set up branch headquarters in Polish, Hungarian, Jewish, Italian, Greek, Slovak, and black areas in Detroit.

Since Sadowski and Lesinski were supporting Welsh, Murphy thought that special attention had to be devoted to Detroit's Polish voters. He wanted the campaign in the First Congressional District, a bastion of Polish electoral strength, to be "extraordinarily effective." He asked Mead to confer with Polish leaders in the district who had been associated with Murphy as mayor, he advised that Murphy meetings be organized in the district to counteract Welsh meetings, he wanted advertisements placed in the *Polish Daily News* to offset Sadowski advertisements for Welsh, and he suggested that the Polish radio hour be utilized to deliver the Murphy message. It quickly became evident that Murphy enjoyed a good deal of support among the leadership of Detroit's Polish community and among other white ethnic groups as well.[70]

Months before Murphy announced his candidacy, Moses Walker, a prominent Detroit black who was active in the National Association for the Advancement of Colored People, organized a Murphy for Governor Club among black WPA workers. After Murphy became a candidate, Walker lined up meetings in his behalf, one of which was addressed by Robert Vann, editor of the *Pittsburgh Courier*. Murphy's friend and ardent admirer Beulah Young, editor of the *Detroit People's News*, a black newspaper, organized a nonpartisan Murphy for Governor Committee and appealed to blacks who were Republicans, the party of most Detroit blacks until 1932, to support Murphy. "He Fed the Hungry and Clothed the Poor," she declared in an editorial; a black Republican who voted for him, she commented, need not conclude that he was becoming "a complete" Democrat but rather that he knew "a worthy man" when he saw one.[71]

Because of his long, friendly association with organized labor in Detroit, it is hardly surprising that both the DWCFL and the United Automobile Workers endorsed Murphy's candidacy. Murphy, DWCFL president Frank Martel wrote a Grand Rapids unionist who had said that Murphy was "an unknown quantity in this part of the state," had "rendered valuable service to the trade union movement. He had been its spirited champion in season and out of season, advocating a policy of dealing with the duly elected representatives of the trade union movement rather than through back door methods."[72]

In an effort to counteract the unfavorable publicity accorded his candidacy in the Republican press, Murphy instructed his campaign staff to keep "a running file of publicity" about the Murphy campaign in the foreign-language press and in church and parish weeklies and to arrange for billboard advertising and campaign signs. It was, however, to "a well organized and well manned radio campaign" that Murphy looked as the principal weapon to bring his message to the public. "Our campaign," he advised, "must be won over the radio." He wanted contact established with the people who ran the "minority and small group radio periods," and he directed that the major Detroit radio stations be provided with daily information about his schedule, a sentence or two on his major speech of the previous night, and effective spot lines. An extremely effective radio speaker—one associate thought him a "radio genius"—Murphy used the medium for several campaign addresses.

Since the management of Detroit station WJR, which had an "enormous following," had offered to help him, Murphy advised his campaign manager to make something available to the station for both its daily news broadcasts. George Trendle, the president of the corporation that owned station WXYZ in Detroit as well as stations in seven other Michigan cities, not only agreed to broadcast Murphy announcements and news items whenever possible but also promised to slip them into the daily news broadcast sponsored by Alka-Seltzer even though the contract for the program forbade the use of political items of this sort. "In my opinion," Murphy counseled, "everything ought to be subordinated to our efforts to get the greatest utility possible out of these two large radio stations [WJR, WXYZ]." Murphy and other Democrats sought to reward Trendle for his support by urging the Federal Communications Commission to grant WXYZ the additional wattage that it was seeking.[73]

Attempting to counteract opposition to Murphy because of his religion, the Murphy campaign staff arranged for letters to be sent to selected individuals in which the sender stated that, although he was not a Catholic, he was voting for Murphy because "*he's on the side of all of us who have to work for a living*. A man's religion," the letter continued, "is his own business, but good government is the business of all of us." The recipient of the letter was requested to write in the same vein to ten others. At the same time, the Murphy forces quietly appealed to Catholics to "get . . . in line" and to support their coreligionist. In one of his speeches Murphy made a plea for religious tolerance and said that to oppose a man for office because of his religion violated the Constitution and the Declaration of Independence. Political veterans in the state asserted that they could not recall another occasion when a gubernatorial candidate "dared to preach religious tolerance," but the *Free Press* accused Murphy of injecting the religious issue into the campaign.[74]

Although Murphy advised Farley that a Roosevelt visit to Michigan on Labor Day would provide a boost to the Murphy candidacy, the president refused to deviate from his public policy of noninterference in Democratic primaries. It appears that persons close to Murphy sought to persuade Welsh to drop out of the race, possibly by offering him a position in a Murphy administration. Remaining a candidate, Welsh challenged Murphy to a debate; Murphy, in the manner of the front-runner, rejected the idea as likely to prove divisive.[75]

Murphy claimed that the total cost of his primary campaign was less than $7,500, but this considerably understated the actual expenditures in his behalf. The detailed but rather confusing statement submitted by the Murphy campaign committee to the clerk of Wayne County listed disbursements of $17,021 for the primary and unpaid debts of $5,300. The debts included a $2,500 loan from the Democratic National Committee, later converted into a gift, making the committee the largest single contributor to the Murphy primary campaign despite the administration's protestations of neutrality. There is every reason to believe that the cost of the Welsh campaign considerably exceeded that of the Murphy campaign.[76]

The essence of Murphy's campaign speeches, which he delivered across the state to large and enthusiastic audiences, was that he was in the campaign to aid Roosevelt and the New Deal and to bring Michigan "a modern, progressive, kindly government, conducted in the interests of the public." The *Detroit Free Press*, which had nothing good to say about Murphy, was not incorrect in charging him with conducting a " 'Me-and-Roosevelt' " campaign. Murphy portrayed Roosevelt as the savior of the nation's political and economic institutions and the friend of "the average man," whereas he characterized the president's opponents as "special pleaders for the rich and privileged." "I am just droning away for the President and progressive government in Michigan," Murphy wrote Hayden near the end of the campaign; and the *Michigan Democratic Forum* stated that a vote against Murphy was a vote against Roosevelt—he [Murphy] is more or less of a symbol."[77]

Murphy claimed that he had decided to enter the race when he became convinced that "some person was needed to pry Michigan loose from a thoroughly incompetent and wasteful administration, in the grip of an invisible government, where the Governor was a puppet in the hands of unseen and predatory influences." Consistently attacking "McKayism," Murphy contended that the way to end this style of government was to place men in high office who did not have "questionable associates" and for whom government service was "a holy mission." He pointed to his own record in Detroit and the Philippines as evidence that he was a public servant of this type. He complained that the incumbent administration had failed to take full advantage of the Social Security Act, criticized the state's old-age pension statute as "entirely inadequate," and chastised the governor for refusing to provide relief to strikers.[78]

Murphy promised if elected to provide Michigan with "the most progressive government of any state in the Union." It was "the common herd" about whom he was most concerned, he said, and he pledged himself to help the poor, the unemployed, and the afflicted and to provide "reasonable security" for all. He proclaimed his support for an unemployment insurance law, adequate assistance for the aged, modernization and centralization of the state's welfare activities, an occupational disease law, a civil service reform law, and a teacher-tenure law.

Murphy told organized labor that he would make the state's Department of Labor and Industry more "active and effective" and would not permit the State Police to interfere with peaceful picketing. ". . . I am heart and soul in the Labor Movement," he declared in a telephone interview with the *Detroit Labor News*. "I have yet to go contrary to the expressed will of Organized Labor in matters that affect it, and as expressed by its official chosen representatives, and you all know that I shall never do so." In farm areas and the thinly populated Upper Peninsula, Murphy stressed his support for rural electrification, and he criticized the Fitzgerald administration for blocking the efforts of the Rural Electrification Administration to bring electricity to Michigan farms. In speaking to Polish-Americans and Irish-Americans, he recounted his efforts to aid the Moros and to gain the Filipinos their freedom ("you and your ancestors know what it means to fight for liberty"), and he reminded blacks what he had done for them as Detroit's mayor. Defending himself against charges that he had been fiscally irresponsible as mayor, he asked if his opponents would have denied food to the hungry; he noted that he had been able under more fortunate circumstances in the Philippines to balance the budget without raising taxes or neglecting social needs.[79]

Throughout the primary campaign Murphy referred to Welsh in respectful terms if he noted his existence at all. No doubt Murphy agreed with Shields that it was in the best interests of the party and of victory in November "to let them [Welsh and his supporters] have their contest, if possible, without any personal antagonism or vituperation." In his final campaign speech, however, Murphy cautioned the Democratic electorate not to vote for a candidate whose party allegiance was suspect and who was "compromised by the support of interests" opposed to Roosevelt's reelection. As the underdog, Welsh directed his attack at Murphy, conducting what a Murphy adherent described as "an aggressive but an abusive and nasty campaign." Among other things, Welsh criticized his opponent for drawing his Philippine salary during part of the campaign and for allegedly returning to the United States with a Filipino valet, which was a distortion. Welsh's criticism of Murphy was abetted by the press—a front-page cartoon in the *Detroit Free Press* pictured Farley, the words "Tammany Hall" emblazoned on his shirt, his arms encircling Murphy and holding money bags labeled "Patronage Dough," saying, "Here's the man I've picked to be your governor. What are you going to do about it?" The Fitzgerald camp sought to abet Welsh's efforts by doing what it could to secure Murphy's defeat.[80]

As it turned out, Murphy won 70 percent of the Democratic vote in the September 15 primary, netting 278,967 votes to Welsh's 130,537. Murphy carried seventy-four of the state's eighty-three counties, defeating his opponent by more than 100,000 votes in populous Wayne County (Detroit) and losing to him only in eight thinly populated agricultural and forest counties and one urbanized county, Kent (Grand Rapids), which was Welsh's home county. The *Detroit News* thought that the "outstanding feature" of the primary in the state's largest city was "the amazing shift" of the black vote to the Democratic party. According to its estimate, the Republicans had received 80 percent of the city's black vote in the 1932 primary but only 40 percent in 1936. Harold E. Bledsoe, the director of Negro Democratic activities in Michigan, attributed this result to both Roosevelt and Murphy. "Mayor Murphy," Bledsoe asserted, "was the best friend the Negro people ever had in City Hall. The Negro people have not forgotten."[81]

Conceding nothing to Murphy, the *Free Press* argued that it was "regimented WPA workers and relief beneficiaries" who had defeated Welsh, and the *Detroit Saturday Night*, in similar fashion, concluded that Murphy had won "the boondoggle vote in Michigan." Sniping by the opposition press did not detract from the impressive character of Murphy's victory. Murphy's success, the *Richmond Times-Dispatch* editorialized, "catapults him into the national political picture, and even makes him a presidential possibility for 1940. . . . The sky should be the limit of his political potentialities." To which Murphy undoubtedly said, "Amen."[82]

In other primary contests, Governor Fitzgerald overwhelmed his opponent (Roscoe Conkling Fitch) by a vote of 455,876 to 53,249; Prentiss Brown narrowly defeated Louis Ward, Coughlin's Washington lobbyist, in the Democratic senatorial primary; former governor Wilber M. Brucker outpolled (328,560 to 199,204) Senator Couzens in the Republican senatorial primary; and Leo J. Nowicki, the Wayne County drain commissioner, won the Democratic nomination for lieutenant governor. Despite his own victory, Murphy had to view these results with a good deal of concern. The total Republican vote for governor in the primary exceeded the total Democratic vote for that office by about 100,000 even though Fitzgerald had run against token opposition and the Democratic choice had been hotly contested. Also, the Nowicki victory meant that the Democratic ticket in November would be headed by two Catholics, both of whom were from Detroit. The Polish-born Nowicki, moreover, was close to Van Wagoner, having helped to direct his campaign for the highway commissionership and having served with him on the PWA Advisory Board for Michigan. Murphy's private opinion was that Nowicki's presence on the ticket would cost him (Murphy) fifty thousand votes.[83]

Murphy's objectives as the Democrats prepared for their state convention in Battle Creek on September 25 were to harmonize the party's discordant elements and to select a state ticket that was "clean and invulnerable." He was not disappointed in the result. Describing the convention as "a humdinger," Picard reported to Hurja that the Murphy forces had been "in complete control" and had "straightened out a lot of people." Many party leaders wanted Murphy to place Welsh on the ticket as secretary of state, but Murphy preferred the Watervliet newspaper publisher, Leon D. Case, whom Nowicki had bested in the primary. The nomination went to Case, with a prominent Welsh supporter seconding the nomination. The remainder of the ticket consisted of Raymond W. Starr, a Grand Rapids attorney, for attorney general; Theodore I. Fry, the incumbent, for state treasurer; and the youthful George T. Gundry, former secretary of Michigan's Young Democrats, for auditor general. When it became evident that Starr was Murphy's choice for attorney general, University of Michigan regent Charles F. Hemans, who thought that he had been promised the post, berated Murphy so vigorously when the two men met in Battle Creek's Post Tavern that Murphy, childishly proud of his pugilistic ability, threatened to punch Hemans and to render him senseless. Fortunately, the two men were separated before any blows were struck. Although he had helped select his running mates, Murphy ungenerously characterized them to Josephine Gomon as "just so much dead wood" and as unlikely to help him in the election. This, however, was a "Murphyism" that was not to be taken seriously.[84]

"To a convention already burning with enthusiasm," a journalist reported, "the appearance and speech of Frank Murphy was like kerosene on a fire." In his address, Murphy rang the changes on themes he had developed in his primary campaign. "What we aim to achieve for the people of Michigan," he declared, "is restoration of a people's government, and deliverance from the neglect and misrule which they have endured for nearly two years under the gross mismanagement of Frank Fitzgerald and his senior partner, Frank McKay." Every citizen, Murphy declared, "within the means available to the government, and the limitations of practical administrative action,... should be protected from insecurity and unfair exploitation; should be provided with the opportunity for useful employment and a fair minimum return for his service; should be given an effective voice in the arrangements that govern his working conditions. This," Murphy explained, "is the new democracy," and it was "the meaning and the deeper essence of the New Deal." The platform adopted by the Democrats was a reflection of the "new democracy" and the Murphy influence in the party; it not only indicted the Fitzgerald administration for a series of alleged misdeeds and failures but also endorsed the reforms of the Roosevelt administration and adopted Murphy's campaign pledges as the party's goals.[85] The Murphy administration, it turned out, made a determined effort to implement the party's platform pledges.

Governor Fitzgerald, not surprisingly, dominated the Republican state convention, which convened in Grand Rapids on September 29. In his address to the convention the governor charged that the national administration had "used the tremendous power of its patronage, purchased with billions of dollars of the taxpayers' money, to thrust a handpicked candidate upon the people of Michigan." Quite in contrast to the party's record in office, the delegates adopted a platform that included many of the planks contained in the New Dealish platform of the Democrats.[86]

Murphy's campaign speeches, ghostwritten mainly by Ed Kemp and delivered before audiences that were consistently larger and more enthusiastic than those addressed by Fitzgerald, were largely a reprise of his speeches in the primary campaign, his address to the Democratic state convention, and the Democratic platform. There was the same praise of Roosevelt and the New Deal, the same attack on the shortcomings of the Fitzgerald administration and on McKayism, the same promise to provide a fiscally sound and socially progressive government, the same emphasis on social security, civil service reform, welfare reorganization, rural electrification, and compassion for the downtrodden.[87]

"We have a leader and an effective organization," Detroit's assistant corporation counsel wrote Farley during the campaign. "Everybody of consequence is pulling an oar and all are stroking at the same time." Much of the rancor of the Democratic primary had indeed been "dissipated," and the party was more united than it had been for years, but not "everyone of consequence" was "pulling an oar." Comstock and the men around him remained obdurate. One old-line Democrat wrote a friend that the Roosevelt administration had "dumped a truck load of Philippine fertilizer on the front porch of the Democratic Party of Michigan, which it will take them some time to clear away and to fumigate the place and get rid of the offensive odors.'' Comstock expressed his admiration for Fitzgerald and announced that he could not support Roosevelt and, presumably, Murphy. Welsh remained on the sidelines during the campaign, but Van Wagoner, possibly because $11 million in WPA funds had been made available to the Highway Department to ensure the commissioner's loyalty, responded to Murphy's appeal for support by endorsing the state Democratic ticket as ''the strongest . . . ever presented to the voters of Michigan'' and by contributing close to $2,000 to the campaign from the Highway Department campaign fund.[88]

As in the primary, Murphy enjoyed the support of blacks, Jews, and other ethnic groups. Moses Walker's Great Lakes Mutual Life Insurance Company had its agents distribute Murphy literature to the company's seventeen thousand policyholders, and the agents were instructed to preach ''the gospel'' of Murphy for governor. The Colored Voters League issued a broadside criticizing Fitzgerald as hostile to blacks and urging a straight Democratic vote, and the *Michigan Guide*, which declared that Murphy had assisted the blacks ''when they had no other friend,'' alleged that Fitzgerald had named his horse '' 'Nigger' '' because it was ''black, lazy and shiftless.'' Although Michigan's Republican national committeeman claimed that the Democrats appeared ''to have all kinds of funds to pass out to Negroes and by intimidation and otherwise seem to be holding them in line pretty well,'' it was the appeal of Murphy and the New Deal, not ''intimidation,'' that explained the ''trouble'' Republicans were having in winning black votes.[89]

The Michigan Council of Jewish Clubs worked closely with the Murphy organization. Three hundred and fifty club members canvassed Jewish neighborhoods, distributed Murphy literature, and served at the polls on election day, and sixteen speakers took to the hustings on Murphy's behalf. ''There has never been a man in public life in this city and state as beloved by the Jewish people . . . as Frank Murphy,'' a respected Jewish attorney asserted in Detroit's *Jewish Advocate* just before election day.[90]

Murphy undoubtedly gained a substantial number of votes among the seventy-five thousand families being supported by the WPA in Michigan as of October 1936. Fitzgerald claimed that WPA workers were being coerced by the Democrats and feared dismissal if a Republican governor were elected in November. The Republican charge, although predictable, was not without some basis: the WPA in Michigan was not entirely free of politics in 1936 despite ritualistic Democratic denials and despite a 6.6 percent reduction in WPA rolls in the state between September and November. In a report to Harry Hopkins shortly after the Michigan primary, Lorena Hickok, a WPA field observer, described "the WPA situation in Michigan" as "a little jittery." It appeared to her that "our own WPA crowd" and the Ed Shields and the "Murphy crowd" were "becoming irreconcilably . . . opposed to each other." Pierson and Haber, she noted, insisted that the WPA be administered in a nonpolitical manner, but "the other crowd," represented by Frederic S. Schouman, Pierson's administrative assistant, was "out-and-out, hand-in-glove with the political group. The Murphy people," in her opinion, "were getting bolder and bolder in their demands," seeking to win the state for Murphy and Roosevelt "according to traditional methods." She told Shields, who had complained to her that he had overheard Pierson say that he "didn't care a damn" about the party and was "only interested in the President," that Hopkins did not agree with the national committeeman's view that the WPA should be converted into "a Democratic machine."[91]

Although the WPA organization in Michigan did not become "a Democratic machine," it did not remain aloof from the 1936 campaign either. A Kalamazoo Democratic leader complained to Farley in the middle of October that the WPA was paying only "lip service" to the Democratic cause in some districts or was "secretly attempting to destroy the President," but he noted that the relief organization was cooperating 100 percent in other districts. When the campaign ended, Schouman supplied Murphy with a list of WPA officials whom the governor-elect should thank, notably district directors and members of the staff who, according to Schouman, had worked on their own time for Murphy and Roosevelt. Under the circumstances, it is not surprising that a Republican WPA worker wrote Fitzgerald during the campaign that he did not "dare" say anything about politics and would "hate to vote myself out of a job." How much Murphy knew about what was going on is problematical since it was his custom to keep himself ignorant about the grubbier aspects of politics, and Schouman, in any event, was assuring him that Republican charges of politics in the WPA were unfounded. It is worthy of note that when Pierson wished to resign just after the primary, Murphy urged him to stay on until after the election since this would guarantee that there would be "neither scandal nor political manipulation" in the WPA. Pierson resigned anyhow, but his successor was a Van Wagoner man, not a Murphy enthusiast.[92]

The Murphy campaign received a boost from the appearance in

Michigan of Franklin D. Roosevelt. When the Republican contender, Alfred M. Landon, visited Detroit on October 13, he was coolly received, with a maximum of twenty thousand persons in attendance to hear his principal address. Relatively small but more enthusiastic audiences greeted him the next day in Flint, Lansing, Battle Creek, and Jackson. Roosevelt, by contrast, was met by enormous crowds everywhere he went in Michigan in what the *Detroit Free Press* described as "the most extensive campaign tour ever made [in the state] by a White House incumbent." In Detroit on October 15 approximately one-half million people came out to see the president, and 150,000 persons massed in front of City Hall to hear him urge the election of "my old friend Frank Murphy." Murphy accompanied the president as he rode through the city, and Couzens left a hospital bed to be with Roosevelt. Schroeder thought that the president's visit "most certainly turned the tide for the Democrats."[93]

In her aforementioned report to Hopkins, Hickok reported that Shields had been informed by Farley and W. Forbes Morgan, the treasurer of the Democratic National Committee, that the committee would not provide the state party with "one red cent" to spend on the Michigan campaign. Shields, she noted, was "nearly crazy" because of the difficulty of raising money in Michigan. On the very day of the Hickok report, however, Farley, responding to a letter from Murphy that Harry Mead had delivered in person, advised Murphy that Morgan had dispatched $2,500 for the Murphy campaign. Murphy also received a contribution of $5,000 from Joseph E. Davies that almost certainly had been solicited for the Murphy campaign by the Democratic National Committee. Murphy turned over $1,500 of this sum to the Murphy campaign committee; he used $1,000 to meet the costs of his personal organization and his personal campaign expenses, necessary, he said, because the campaign had been "such a drain on my small purse"; and he returned $2,500 to Davies after the campaign. Davies considered this gesture "the most unique experience" of his "political life" and an example of Murphy's "high-mindedness," which, one may assume, was precisely the effect Murphy had hoped to produce.[94]

According to a post-election statement filed with the Wayne County clerk, the Murphy campaign committee raised $21,863 for Murphy's post-primary campaign, disbursed about the same sum, and had unpaid debts of $4,290 as of early December 1936. Although Michigan law required the candidate and the treasurer of a campaign committee to submit "a full, true and detailed account and statement . . . setting forth each and every sum of money received or disbursed for ... election expenses," the Murphy campaign statement did not include all the money raised for the Murphy campaign. Not all campaign funds, moreover, were channeled through the committee, as Murphy's allocation of the Davies gift indicates. The information compiled by Murphy's staff in preparing his 1936 income tax return reveals that $6,365 received for the Murphy campaign (including the $5,000 from Davies) had been deposited in Murphy's personal bank account, that $2,000 of this sum had been disbursed for campaign advertising, and that Murphy had "suggested" that the remainder, excluding the $2,500 returned to Davies, not be included "in making up ... [the 1936] returns" but rather be permitted to "ride" and "include[d] in the next campaign"![95]

Quite apart from the money handled by Murphy's personal organization, Edward F. Thomas, a Murphy supporter who had ties with the Republicans, reported to Murphy after the campaign that he had raised $11,000 among his friends for the Murphy campaign, probably including the primary, and had turned the money over to the Murphy campaign committee. Not all the contributions listed by Thomas, however, were included in the campaign committee's financial statement. Finally, Harry Mead asserted at a later time that he had collected some campaign money from gambling joints, some of which, he recalled, was given to him in return for the information that Murphy could be expected to close down gambling establishments. There is not the slightest reason to think that Murphy profited personally from contributions to his campaign, but he and his supporters handled campaign contributions in a haphazard manner, and his statement that less than $23,000 had been spent on his campaign was simply inaccurate.[96]

Unlike Frank Murphy, who offered the voters the vision of a better future under a Michigan New Deal, Frank Fitzgerald, a lackluster campaigner at best, failed to submit "a program of action" to the electorate. The lesson Fitzgerald claimed he had learned from the campaign was that a candidate had to offer the electorate "something more than the condemnation of the other fellow's ideas." The governor defended the record of his administration, as incumbents must, and he promised to support civil service reform, but what he emphasized in his addresses was the alleged follies of the New Deal, to which he linked the New Deal's candidate in Michigan.[97]

Fitzgerald injected a new issue into the campaign when he stated in an October 7 address that the question of whether to permit gambling and slot machines in Michigan should be decided on a local basis, which Michiganders understood to mean that gambling should be permitted to proceed without interference. On the attack, Murphy criticized the governor's "home rule for gamblers" pronouncement as an invitation to racketeers and as "the most shocking statement . . . made by a chief executive in the history of Michigan." After becoming governor, Murphy told a reporter that he had learned that the attorney general in the Fitzgerald administration had made "the gambling deal" for his party in the campaign.[98]

Fitzgerald himself made no reference to Murphy's religion, but Republican propaganda, especially in out-state Michigan, stressed the Catholic character of the Democratic ticket. Republicans also used "Keep Tammany Out of Michigan" billboard signs that left viewers free to decide whether it was Jim Farley or the pope or both who were to be kept out of the state. A flier entitled "God Save Michigan" listed all the Murphys running for office in Wayne County, characterized "the Murphy Clan" as "A Worthy Successor to the Ku Klux," and noted that "Intolerance" was "A Two-Edged Sword."[99]

The religious issue in the campaign may have been neutralized to some extent by the support that Father Coughlin openly gave to Fitzgerald. The Third party, as the Liberty party was listed on the ballot in Michigan, put together a ticket consisting of William Lemke for president, Thomas C. O'Brien for vice-president, Louis Ward for senator, and a few candidates for Congress, but it did not nominate a gubernatorial candidate. At a NUSJ rally at the State Fair Grounds Coliseum in Detroit—Fitzgerald had made the state facility available for the meeting because, he said, he wished to encourage a discussion of social justice!—Coughlin announced that he would vote for Fitzgerald in order to preserve home rule in Michigan as against "dictatorship" from Washington. The meeting ended abruptly when someone in the audience jumped onto the stage and showered Coughlin with feathers and the priest responded by pinning his assailant to the floor. Michigan's national committeewoman correctly judged that the meeting had been "a flop" and that Coughlin had "lost a great deal of ground" because of the affair.[100]

The Republican state chairman, Howard C. Lawrence, committed a blunder and probably antagonized Polish voters when he addressed letters on October 11 to both Murphy and Nowicki inquiring of the former whether he intended to resign his post if elected, as he had resigned his other positions, and asking the latter what his qualifications for the governorship were should he have to succeed Murphy. Murphy replied that he would not only serve out his term as governor if elected but would also rid the state government of men like

Lawrence who found it possible to serve simultaneously as state banking commissioner and chairman of the Republican State Central Committee. Shields and Fry responded to Lawrence by asking him whether Fitzgerald or McKay was "the actual governor of Michigan," and Prentiss Brown characterized the Lawrence letter as a "terrible slap at the people of Polish descent in Michigan" since it implied that Nowicki was unqualified to serve as governor.[101]

In the closing days of the campaign, employees of Michigan industrial firms, like employees across the nation, received notices in their pay envelopes informing them that, beginning on January 1, 1937, their employers were required by the Roosevelt administration to deduct 1 percent of their wages to finance the old-age pensions provided for in the Social Security Act. Employees were told that payroll deductions would eventually rise to 4 percent and that they would not receive pensions when they retired unless Congress appropriated the necessary funds. Murphy, who had stressed the importance of economic security throughout the campaign, struck hard at this "final desperate effort" of the enemies of the New Deal, noting that employers were prepared to spend large sums to maintain their machinery but were "outraged" about expenditures to maintain human beings. Attributing the scare campaign to the Industrial Division of the Republican National Committee and alleging that it operated in Michigan through a member of the state's Public Trust Commission, Murphy pointed out that it was a crime under Michigan law to attempt to influence the vote of an employee through his pay envelope. The Democrats in Michigan, viewing the matter with a good deal of concern since there was "an awful lot of objection" from workers about the impending deduction from their pay, sought to counter the pay-envelope notice and to set the record straight by passing out handbills at large plants and major streetcar stops and by using sound cars in various areas.[102]

The Republicans mounted a massive campaign in an effort to carry the state for Fitzgerald. The party's Speakers Bureau assigned speakers to 272 meetings, and county organizations were encouraged to arrange additional meetings. The party on three different occasions inserted twenty-inch advertisements in out-state publications with more than 1.6 million circulation; it also placed special display advertisements in the three Detroit daily newspapers. In addition, the Republicans paid special attention to the foreign-language press, and the state party's press service supplied newspapers with "items of interest" in behalf of the Republican cause. The party arranged for broadcast time early in the campaign so as to secure the most advantageous spots on the radio schedule, and it distributed a vast amount of campaign literature through the mail. Although billboard advertisers regarded 1,680 billboards as constituting "complete coverage" for the state, the Republicans used about 2,500 billboards to spread their message. The Michigan Republicans spent about $140,000 on the campaign, which vastly exceeded the sum expended in the Murphy campaign.[103]

Although Michigan Republicans, according to the party's state chairman, put together "the best precinct organization" in the history of the state party, a Wayne County democratic leader thought that the Republicans were actually "a lot more broken up" than the Democrats. There was tension in the party between Landon Republicans and the Republican Old Guard, between wets and drys, and between Couzens supporters and foes of Couzens. When Couzens on August 23 publicly proclaimed his support for Roosevelt, the Republican state chairman thought that this would "cost" his party "plenty of votes." Once it became evident that Landon could not win, Fitzgerald sought to dissociate himself from the Republican presidential nominee. "I have well-founded impressions," a Kalamazoo Democrat informed Farley, that Fitzgerald, "the best professional 'Hoss-trader' in politics that I have seen ... is attempting to trade Landon for Fitzgerald votes all over the State of Michigan." Shields also reported that the feeling among Republicans was that Fitzgerald had "sacrificed everybody else for himself," and the Democratic national committeeman wrote Farley late in October that "the whole Republican organization" had "broken down" and was "in desperation."[104]

Although the consensus among the state's politicians in the closing weeks of the election was that Roosevelt would carry the state, opinion was divided regarding the outcome of the gubernatorial race. Murphy's view was that "only a miracle" could save him from defeat but that Roosevelt would carry the state by 150,000–200,000 votes. In his celebrated November 2 prediction about the outcome of the 1936 campaign, Farley included Michigan among the forty-six states that Roosevelt would carry. What has not been noted heretofore, however, is that, in the same letter to the president, Farley was dubious about the prospects of a Murphy victory. "I have never been quite sold on the idea that Frank Murphy would win in Michigan, and that Brown would be elected to the Senate," Farley wrote. Because of "the religious situation," Farley thought that Murphy's chances were even slimmer than Brown's.[105]

Roosevelt had wanted Murphy to return to Michigan to help the president carry the state, but, as it turned out, it was Roosevelt who carried Murphy to victory. The president defeated Landon in Michigan by 317,000 votes, receiving 56.3 percent of the total vote for president to Landon's 36.8 percent, whereas Murphy bested Fitzgerald by only 48,919 votes, receiving 51 percent of the vote for governor compared to Fitzgerald's 48.2 percent. Out-state, Fitzgerald carried sixty counties, winning all the eighteen farm counties, all but one by more than 60 percent of the vote, eight of the nine farm-urban counties, and twenty-seven of the thirty Lower Peninsula forest counties. Murphy's strength out-state was concentrated in the economically depressed Upper Peninsula and in the urbanized counties: he carried four of the six mineral counties and five of the nine forest counties of the Upper Peninsula and five of the ten urban counties, winning 60 percent of the vote in Genesee County (Flint) and 58.5 percent of the vote in Muskegon County (Muskegon). Appealing far more to urban than to rural voters, he received 56.8 percent of the vote in the state's forty cities; and he won his victory in heavily urbanized Wayne County, where his margin over Fitzgerald was 119,427 votes, whereas he trailed his opponent by 70,508 votes in the remaining eighty-two counties.[106]

In Detroit, where the total vote in the gubernatorial election was 492,799 (80.7 percent of the registered voters), compared to about 300,000 votes in 1934 (56.2 percent of the registered voters), Murphy outpolled Fitzgerald by 100,000 votes, gaining 60 percent of the total vote as compared to 52.7 percent for Lacy in 1934 and 62.4 percent for Comstock in 1932, at the depth of the Depression in Detroit. The most spectacular change in voting habits in Detroit in 1936 occurred among black voters, who gave Murphy 63.5 percent of their vote, whereas Comstock had received only 36.7 percent of the Detroit black vote in 1932 and Lacy only 30 percent. Murphy also received 72.8 percent of the foreign-born vote in Detroit, including a phenomenal 84.9 percent of the Polish vote. Foreign-born voters supported Murphy in about the same proportion as they had supported Comstock in 1932 but to a greater extent than they had supported Lacy.[107]

Murphy received only 46.3 percent of the native-born white vote in Detroit, compared to 53.8 percent for Comstock and 44 percent for Lacy. He was strongly supported by lower-income, native-born whites (65.9 percent) but received less than half (44.2 percent) of the votes of middle-income, native-born whites and only 32.2 percent of the votes of upper-income, native-born whites, compared to Comstock's 45.8 percent. The pattern of the Murphy vote in Detroit resembled the pattern of the Comstock vote in 1932 except that Murphy fared far better among blacks than Comstock and fared far worse among upper-class, native-born whites. Murphy's principal electoral support in Detroit came from the same kinds of voters—blacks, the foreign-born, and lower-income, native-born whites—who had elected him Recorder's Court judge and mayor. These were the same voters who gave Roosevelt a 214,000 vote margin in Wayne County.[108]

The Democrats not only won the governorship but also all the other state offices. Although only Leon Case among the victorious candidates for state office won by a smaller plurality than Murphy, Murphy ran ahead of the other Democratic candidates in Wayne County. The Democrats won control of the Michigan Senate by a 17–15 margin and the Michigan House by a 60–40 margin. In the senatorial race, Prentiss Brown defeated his Republican opponent, Wilber Brucker.[109]

Michigan Republicans could and did take consolation in the fact that Michigan apparently still had "a great Republican rank and file" and that the Democratic victory in Michigan appeared to be "more national than state." "Straight tickets in Wayne County proved to be my undoing," Fitzgerald concluded. Lawrence correctly thought that Michigan remained a Republican state and that this would be demonstrated when there was no national ticket to confuse the issue. Frank McKay, who, according to a Republican newspaper, had been the "one vulnerable spot in Fitzgerald's armor," interpreted the election results as meaning that the country had gone "completely socialistic," and he did not wish to "mourn over a stupid people."[110]

Murphy's contribution to the 1936 Democratic victory in Michigan was well summed up by Joseph Hayden. "Frank," Hayden wrote Weldon Jones, "put on a terrific campaign. He did more than that, however, for he pulled a disorganized party together, forced it to nominate decent men on the state ticket, and gave it standing and leadership no one else could have furnished." Hayden was well aware that Roosevelt had carried the Democratic ticket to victory in Michigan, but the political scientist thought that Murphy was the only Michigan Democrat who could have run well enough to win the governorship. Murphy's mission, it will be recalled, had been "not primarily to be elected himself, but to pull the Democratic party in the state together and to help carry the state for Roosevelt," and he had played the role well. Although Murphy rode to victory on Roosevelt's coattails, blacks, Poles, and lower-income whites voted for him with enthusiasm in 1936, as they had before, and not simply because Roosevelt was on the ticket; and he had accustomed Detroit blacks to vote for a Democrat before they began to vote for Roosevelt in such large numbers. That Murphy did not win by a larger plurality can be explained by his religion (he became Michigan's first Catholic governor), his long absence from the state, Fitzgerald's demonstrated popularity with the voters (he had even survived the Democratic landslide in 1932), and the fact that Michigan, despite the 1936 result, was a Republican state. The election demonstrated that a solidly entrenched state party, as V. O. Key has pointed out, may be able to capitalize on traditional loyalties to muster enough support for its ticket to offset to some degree the surge of votes for the victorious presidential candidate of the rival party. This is especially so when the rival state party, in this instance Michigan's Democratic party, does not command the respect of the voters. Under the circumstances, Prentiss Brown was justified in asserting that Murphy won "a great victory against great odds." [111]

"... we, far away, think of you as one of the truly significant figures in the democratic leadership of America," the liberal New York rabbi, Stephen S. Wise, wrote to Murphy following his victory. The chairman of the association of state Democratic chairmen thought that the next step on the political ladder for Murphy was the presidency, and we may assume that this thought had crossed Murphy's mind as well. Murphy's admirers and his former colleagues in the Philippines were pleased for him but unhappy for the Philippines. "... we lose what others have gained," Evett D. Hester wrote the governor-elect. Just what "others" had "gained" remained to be seen, but in view of what was soon to occur in Michigan, there is a certain interest in Murphy's response to a congratulatory message from the president of the American Federation of Labor. "I am certain," Murphy wrote William Green, "that my administration in Lansing will mark a new day for labor in Michigan." [112]

7

"A 1937 Model" Governor

As Michigan's thirty-second governor Frank Murphy presided over a state whose 57,480 square miles of land surface and 40,000 square miles of Great Lakes water surface make it the second largest state east of the Mississippi. Physically, Michigan is distinguished by its two peninsulas, the mitten-shaped Lower Peninsula and the scenic, not entirely tamed, Upper Peninsula. The Straits of Mackinac, which separate the two peninsulas, was unbridged when Murphy took his oath of office.[1]

Agriculture was the predominant source of wealth in Michigan when it entered the union in 1837. Although lumbering had become important in the state before the Civil War, the industry reached its peak in the 1870–90 period, and Michigan became the nation's premier lumbering state. By 1890 the industry was on the decline, and production and employment plunged steadily downward in the twentieth century. Whereas the industry produced 5,478 billion board feet and employed 45,000 persons in 1889, it produced only 405 million board feet in 1936 and employed only about 9,000 workers. The decline of the industry and the abandonment of the sawmill towns in the lumbering counties of the Upper Peninsula and the northern part of the Lower Peninsula had a disastrous effect on farmers in the area who sold their produce to the logging communities and worked part-time in the logging towns. Many persons left the cut-over counties of the state in the 1920s, but some returned to the area in the next decade. The plight of those living in these counties in the 1930s "became hopeless and in some areas desperate."[2]

Although copper had been mined in Michigan before the first Europeans visited the region, commercial mining of the metal did not begin until the 1840s. One-half of the copper mined in the United States between 1847 and 1883 was mined in Michigan, principally in the western Upper Peninsula counties of Keweenaw, Ontonagon, and Houghton. At one time the Houghton mines alone employed as many as sixteen thousand workers, but the exhaustion of major deposits, the increasing depth of the functioning mines, the falling content of the copper portion of the rock mined, and, ultimately, the decline in the demand for copper substantially reduced the industry's output after World War I. Production fell from a range of 216–223 million pounds per annum in the years 1905–12 to 47 million pounds in 1933, and the state's copper companies employed less than two thousand persons in the latter year.[3]

Iron ore deposits were discovered near Negaunee and Ishpeming in the Upper Peninsula in 1844, but large-scale mining operations did not begin in the state until the opening of the Sault Canal in 1855. As of 1890, the yield from the mines of the Marquette, Menominee, and Gogebic districts made Michigan the leading producer of iron ore among the nation's states. Like the copper industry, Michigan's iron mining industry declined sharply in the twentieth century, especially after World War I. In 1923 Michigan's iron mines produced more than fourteen million tons of ore, and the industry employed about twelve thousand workers; ten years later, at the bottom of the Depression, only about 2.3 million tons of iron ore were mined in the state, and employment had fallen to 2,739. Production increased to a little more than 9 million tons in 1936, but employment in that year was less than five thousand; and the valuation of mining property, which constituted about 25 percent of the total property valuation in the Upper Peninsula, had decreased by almost 50 percent as compared to 1921.[4]

Although extractive industries dominated Michigan's economic life in the nineteenth century, the state became preeminent as a manufacturing state and the home of the automobile industry in the twentieth century. Michigan forged ahead of all other states in automobile manufacturing in 1904, and as of 1929 approximately 48 percent of the wage earners in the combined automobile manufacturing and automobile parts industries in the United States resided in Michigan, 73 percent of the state's total of these workers being concentrated in the Detroit industrial area. Whereas 28.9 percent of gainful workers in the United States were engaged in manufacturing and mechanical industries in 1930, 45.8 percent of Michigan's gainful workers were so employed. When Murphy became governor, Michigan ranked fifth among the states both in the value of its manufactured products and in the number of wage earners engaged in manufacturing.[5]

Although Michigan in the middle 1930s ranked only twenty-sixth among the states in the number of acres under cultivation, it was nevertheless an important producer of many field crops. General farming characterized the state's agriculture, but specialty crops were grown in several areas of the state. Truck farming, dairying, and poultry raising were concentrated near urban markets, beans and sugar beets were grown in the Thumb area and the Saginaw River Valley, a variety of fruits were grown in the western part of the state along the Lake Michigan shore, and dairy farming was the predominant agricultural activity in the Upper Peninsula. Michigan was not immune to the agricultural woes that plagued the nation in the 1920s: in that decade the number of farms in the state decreased 13.5 percent, to 169,000, and the number of acres under cultivation was reduced by about two million to a little over eleven million. As of 1930, 12.8 percent of the state's gainful workers were employed in agriculture (as compared to 21.4 percent nationally), the rural population constituted about 31.8 percent of the state's population, and about 20 percent of the state's inhabitants actually lived on farms.[6]

Of Michigan's population of 4,842,325 in 1930, which made it the nation's sixth most populous state, 17.5 percent (840,268) were foreign-born, and an additional 29.6 percent were native-born whites of foreign or mixed parentage. In twenty-four of the state's eighty-three counties the foreign stock comprised more than half the population. Among the foreign-born, English Canadians (20 percent), Poles (14.2 percent), British (13 percent), and Germans (9.7 percent) were the largest groups; among native-born whites of foreign and mixed parentage, persons of German origin (19.6 percent) were the most numerous, followed in order by those of English Canadian (16.4 percent), Polish (13.9 percent), and British (10.7 percent) extraction. Only 3.5 percent (169,453) of the state's inhabitants were blacks. The census also listed 13,336 Mexicans, most of whom had originally been brought to the state to work in the sugar beet fields, and 7,080 Indians, about one-third of whom lived on reservations. By 1940 the foreign-born among the population of 5,256,100 had decreased to 13 percent (686,165), and blacks had increased slightly to 4 percent (208,345). In a reversal of the historic pattern that is explained by the ravages of the Great Depression, Michigan's rural population increased from 31.8 to 34.3 percent in the 1930s.[7]

The Great Depression struck Michigan with terrible ferocity, largely because the state's major industry was peculiarly sensitive to the vicissitudes of the business cycle. In October 1932, at the height of the Depression, 722,400 persons, about 37 percent of the labor force as of 1930, were unemployed, compared to only 15,400 unemployed in May 1929. Statistics compiled by the Michigan Depart-

ment of Labor and Industry revealed that industrial employment in October 1932 was less than 41 percent of the average for 1923–26 and that the aggregate payroll of reporting companies had decreased 74 percent compared to "normal times." The number of unemployed in the state averaged 601,300 for the year 1932 but declined steadily thereafter to an average of 249,900 in 1936 (about 13 percent of the labor force as of 1930). In December 1936, however, there were still eight times as many workers unemployed in Michigan as in the month of highest unemployment in 1929.[8]

The high rate of unemployment in Michigan created a major relief problem for the state. Initially, the state relied on local government and private enterprise to carry the relief burden, but the federal and state governments increasingly became the source of Michigan relief funds. The Reconstruction Finance Corporation made $21.8 million available to the state in relief loans in 1932 and 1933, and in the spring of 1933 the state legislature diverted $12 million to relief purposes from the income yielded by the gasoline and weight taxes. In order to comply with the requirements of the Federal Emergency Relief Act of May 1933, Michigan established the State Emergency Welfare Relief Commission (SEWRC), which supervised the distribution of virtually all public relief funds in the state.[9]

Between July 1933 and December 1935 the SEWRC distributed more than $149 million in relief funds. About 72 percent of this sum was supplied by the federal government, about 17 percent by the state government, and about 11 percent by units of local government. From its establishment until the end of 1935 the state's Emergency Relief Administration provided relief assistance for a monthly average of more than 651,000 persons, about 13.2 percent of Michigan's population.[10]

The relief burden of the state government was eased after the establishment of the Works Progress Administration (WPA) on July 1, 1935. The WPA was supposed to provide work relief for the needy but employable unemployed, while the state government was to be responsible for unemployable cases. During 1936 the WPA provided for about 62 percent of the relief population in Michigan; the total cost of relief incurred by the state and local governments, which had been $66,377,000 in 1935, fell to $22,570,000, a 66 percent reduction. The average number of persons on relief cared for by the state dropped from 609,514 (170,000 cases and 12.6 percent of the population) in 1935 to 215,305 (72,000 cases and about 4.8 percent of the population) in 1936.[11]

The Great Depression, not surprisingly, had a differential impact on the diverse economic regions of Michigan. The Upper Peninsula was savaged by the economic downturn, which further depressed the already declining lumber and mineral industries. In the fiscal year 1934–35, 31.9 percent of the 318,000 persons in the area were on relief, compared to 14.5 percent for the state as a whole; in the four principal mining counties (Houghton, Gogebic, Keweenaw, and Iron), 40 to 75 percent of the population required relief. The cost of relief for the Upper Peninsula was 12.7 percent of the total cost for the state as a whole although only 6.6 percent of the state's population resided in the fifteen counties of the region. Michigan's Copper Country had the highest relief load in the United States in 1934.

In the thirty-two cutover counties of the northern part of the Lower Peninsula, where lumbering had declined and farming was rarely profitable because of the submarginal character of the soil, an average of 22.3 percent of the population, well above the state average, was on relief in the 1934–35 fiscal year. These counties contained 7 percent of the state's inhabitants but 10.7 percent of its relief population. In the twenty-one southern agricultural counties, where the soil was favorable for farming, an average of only 11.8 percent of the population received relief during the fiscal year; whereas these counties contained 14 percent of the state's population, their relief population was only 11.4 percent of the average number on relief, the best record for any economic region.

In terms both of the amount of money expended and the number of persons involved, the relief problem of Michigan centered in the fifteen industrial counties of the state and especially in the four counties (Wayne, Oakland, Genesee, Ingham) dependent on the automobile and related industries and in Kent County (Grand Rapids), which had depended on the furniture industry. In the early 1930s, 72.4 percent of the state's population was concentrated in these counties, 39 percent in Wayne County alone. During the fiscal year 1934–35 almost two-thirds (63.4 percent) of the average relief population of the state lived in these fifteen counties, and they received 71.6 percent of the funds the state expended for relief. Because of the economic recovery of the automobile industry, the average percentage of the population (12.7) on relief in these counties was below the statewide average for that fiscal year.[12]

II

The constitution of 1908, Michigan's third, set forth the outlines of Michigan's governmental structure.[13] The constitution provided for a two-house legislature, a House of Representatives of from sixty-four to one hundred members and a Senate of thirty-two members, all elected for two-year terms from single districts. The biennial legislative sessions began on the first Wednesday in January in odd-numbered years, and members received $3 per diem while the legislature was in session. Acts passed by the legislature and approved by the governor did not take effect until ninety days after the end of the session in which the measures were passed, except that the legislature could give a statute immediate effect by a two-thirds vote. The legislature's appropriation power was restricted by a constitutional provision limiting the state's indebtedness to $250,000, although the state could borrow up to $50 million to improve highways. Constitutional amendments approved in 1913 authorized the electorate to participate in the lawmaking process by resorting to the initiative and referendum.

The constitution specified that the governor, lieutenant governor, secretary of state, state treasurer, auditor general, and attorney general were to be elected for two-year terms at each general biennial election. The superintendent of public instruction and the highway commissioner were elected in a spring election in odd-numbered years. The "chief executive power" was vested in the governor who, in addition to possessing the usual powers of a chief executive in the American governmental system, could veto individual items in appropriation bills. The lieutenant governor was empowered to replace the governor under specified conditions; he also presided over the Senate but had no vote. The governor received a salary of $5,000, but the lieutenant governor was paid on the same per diem basis as legislators.

The Michigan constitution provided for a system of county and township governments. In addition to certain other officials, each township elected one supervisor annually as the principal township officer. The township supervisors in each county plus such representatives of the cities in the county as might be provided by law constituted the county board of supervisors, which was the governing board of the county. Cities and villages were granted home rule subject to limitations imposed on their taxing and borrowing powers.

In addition to eight elected state officers and three elected state boards, the state administration consisted of ninety-eight other officers and boards, mostly appointed by the governor with the advice and consent of the Senate. "There was," according to an analysis of the state administration, "almost total absence of machinery for making effective the nominal supervisory powers of the Governor. Duplication of function, contradictory effort, inefficiency, waste, and extravagance were the characteristic products of this system." In an effort to reduce the confusion, Governor Alex J. Groesbeck suggested a plan of reorganization that the legislature accepted in part in 1921. Forty-seven authorities were either abolished or merged with other agencies, and seventeen new agencies were created, including five new departments—welfare, labor and industry, agriculture, safety, and conservation. There was, however, a singular absence of uniformity in the reorganized state government and an insufficient degree of "central control" vested in the governor. Of the twelve departments, five were headed by single commissioners, three by boards, and four by a combination of individual officers and boards; boards administered most of the minor agencies. There was a similar lack of uniformity in the manner of appointment and removal of administrative officials and in their terms of office. The governor required the consent of the Senate for some appointments but not for others. Some department heads held office at the pleasure of the governor; others served for definite terms but were subject to removal for cause. In most minor agencies the terms of office of board members were longer than that of the governor, thus limiting his control over such personnel. Also, between 1921 and 1936 the legislature created about thirty new administrative agencies, many of them of little consequence, while abolishing two existing boards.

When Murphy became governor, the state's administrative organization was made up of 108 separate units consisting of elective offices and boards, ex-officio boards, major departments and commissions, examining and licensing boards, commissions of study and inquiry, and minor agencies. This was far too many agencies for any governor to administer effectively, even assuming that the heads of all the agencies were his own appointees, which they were not. As Joseph Hayden remarked, the Michigan "governmental machine" was "cumbersome, antiquated and perfectly designed to diffuse power and responsibility." Murphy complained that the state government was actually "a combination . . . of semi-independent governments . . . without an organization headquarters" that could "give the proper direction and control so as to get the right results . . . for the general public." The Michigan pattern of administrative organization was actually not unlike that in most other states, whose governors also had to contend with "an unplanned tangle of boards, commissions, departments and other agencies."[14]

In an effort to coordinate state administrative policy, Groesbeck persuaded the legislature to create the Administrative Board, consisting of the governor as chairman, the secretary of state, the state treasurer, the auditor general, the attorney general, the highway commissioner, and the superintendent of public instruction. The governor could veto any board action, but the legislature provided in 1927 that the veto could be overridden by the concurring vote of five members of the board. The board was given general supervisory power over the state's administrative agencies and state institutions, and it was given responsibility for the preparation of the state budget, state purchasing (except for the University of Michigan and Michigan State College), state accounting, state building and construction, and the investigation and settlement of certain kinds of claims against the state. In 1931 the legislature created the Augmented Administrative Board by providing that four legislators (the chairmen of the Ways and Means Committee of the House and the Finance and Appropriations Committee of the Senate and one additional member from each of these committees) were to sit with the board when it considered requests for emergency appropriations; in 1933 the legislature made the budget director responsible to the governor whereas, in theory, he had previously been responsible to the Administrative Board. To facilitate its activities, the Administrative Board organized itself into committees, generally consisting of three members; it appointed a secretary and director of accounting and purchasing; and it created accounting, purchasing, and traffic divisions and a building department.[15]

The Administrative Board, hardly an adequate solution for the inadequacies of the state's diffuse administrative structure, was not "well adapted to assist the chief executive in performing the vital functions of departmental coordination, policy-making, over-all supervision and management." Although the board consisted of elected officials independent of the governor and not necessarily even members of his political party, the governor required their consent in many matters. The board could not and did not function as a "Governor's cabinet or advisory council," many of the governor's advisors were not members of the board, and its committees met irregularly and functioned ineffectively.[16]

Not only did Michigan's governor have to share executive power with other elective officials, and not only did he lack full control over the state's Administrative Board and its multifarious administrative units, but he also lacked a staff of assistants to aid him in carrying out his duties. The executive office, Murphy discovered, consisted only of an executive secretary, a general secretary, a legal advisor, the director of the budget, and the commissioner of pardons and paroles. It is no wonder that Murphy concluded that Michigan had "an impossible government in its structural set-up." As he pointed out, although the governor "in the public mind and in political effect" was held responsible for the administration of the state's affairs, he lacked the authority and the staff to meet that responsibility.[17]

In 1935 Governor Frank Fitzgerald submitted a sweeping reorganization plan that, according to one authority, "would have given Michigan one of the best organized state governments in the United States." The legislature, however, largely rejected the governor's proposals. A variety of special-interest groups were perfectly content with the administrative status quo since, as Grant McConnell has pointed out, "disorganized and ill-coordinated administration" offers advantages to "narrow power-holding groups." Advantaged interests viewed the centralization of power in the hands of the governor as a "serious threat."[18]

Quite apart from the deficiencies of Michigan's administrative structure, the state's fiscal and tax system left a good deal to be desired when Murphy became governor. The state lacked a "centralized, simplified, modern system of machine accounting"; the state budget failed to provide "a simple clear picture" of what the state proposed to do and how it proposed to finance its activities; the budget director did not have sufficient authority to perform his duties satisfactorily; the State Tax Commission was riddled with politics; about a dozen agencies, none of them adequately staffed, were responsible for collecting the revenue, and some of the revenue due the state went uncollected; and payroll procedures were "exceedingly complicated, loose, and ineffective." Until 1932 the major source of revenue for the state government was the real property tax, but in November of that year the voters approved a constitutional amendment prohibiting the imposition of property taxes in excess of 15 mills (1.5 percent) per dollar of assessed valuation. This limit applied to the combined tax of the various units of government, but the Michigan Supreme Court ruled that the amendment did not apply to incorporated cities and villages unless they voted to amend their charters to this effect, as eleven such units decided to do. Since state revenue decreased during the Depression because of the 15-mill limitation, a 32 percent decline in assessed property valuations between 1930 and 1933, and mounting tax delinquency, the legislature in June 1933 enacted a 3 percent sales tax that became the state's major revenue producer. The state government abandoned the state real property tax in 1935, leaving this field entirely to local governments. The shift from the property to the sales tax as the principal source of state revenue meant the abandonment of a fairly stable source of revenue for a source that was "super-sensitive" to economic conditions, as became apparent in the recession of 1937-38. Unlike some other states, Michigan did not have a state income tax, the voters having decisively rejected constitutional amendments authorizing such a tax in 1922, 1924, 1934, and 1936.[19]

III

Following his election victory in November, a "weary and ill" Murphy took advantage of the hospitality of Joseph P. Kennedy to vacation in Palm Beach. When Norman Hill advised the governor-elect that his sojourn in Florida was creating a bad impression back home because of all the work that had to be done, Murphy testily replied that the campaign had set back his health, not that of his critics. "From now on," he wrote Hill, "I am going to give at least reasonable consideration to the care of my health." Murphy regularly made such vows after extreme tension, resulting from fear of a failure that might jeopardize his career, led to nervous exhaustion or an actual breakdown of his health.[20]

After about a month in Florida, Murphy devoted the remainder of his time before the inauguration to Philippine and state affairs. One state matter to which he had to attend was the biennial budget, which the governor was required to submit to the legislature within ten days after it convened in January. Budget hearings were supposed to be held in December, and, as the law required, Fitzgerald invited Murphy to sit with the budget director during these hearings or to designate a representative for that purpose. Murphy, who selected G. Donald Kennedy as his representative, learned that, although the general fund would be in balance as of the end of 1936, a deficiency appropriation of $8 million would be required to balance the budget for the fiscal year ending June 30, 1937. Fitzgerald attributed the impending deficit to relief and old-age assistance costs, but pay raises granted by the administration after the November election were also in part responsible.[21]

Before leaving for Florida, Murphy arranged for studies of social security, welfare administration, prison reform, the election laws, and workmen's compensation. The most pressing problem, one that could not await his inauguration, derived from the unemployment insurance section of the Social Security Act of 1935. The statute required employers in interstate commerce with eight or more employees to pay a payroll tax of 1 percent in 1936, 2 percent in 1937, and 3 percent in 1938 and thereafter, but they could be relieved of paying 90 percent of this tax if they contributed to a state unemployment insurance system that met certain federal standards.

Since employers did not have to begin paying the unemployment insurance tax until the end of 1936, the states had until that time to devise acceptable laws if they wished to retain most of what covered employers would have to pay in any event. Twenty states had taken appropriate action before the November elections, but Michigan, whose governor thought the Social Security Act unconstitutional, was not among them. The election results and the Supreme Court's validation of the New York unemployment insurance law persuaded many states that had not acted before November to call their legislatures into special session to pass the necessary statutes before the end of the year. Governor Fitzgerald, however, announced that there would not be a special session in Michigan. Because of Murphy's close relationship with Roosevelt, Congress, the governor declared, would not permit the Treasury to keep the unemployment tax money paid by Michigan employers. "I don't think we'll lose a dime," the lame-duck governor stated. Five days later Fitzgerald bowed to Murphy's wishes and summoned the legislature to meet in special session on December 21.[22]

Murphy, an advocate of unemployment insurance even before the New Deal, had sponsored an unemployment insurance bill that had been introduced in the Michigan legislature in 1931. He had stressed his commitment to social security during the gubernatorial campaign and had stated just after his victory that the enactment of legislation enabling Michigan to receive the full benefits of the Social Security Act would be "the immediate and supreme objective of the State's New Deal administration." Murphy assigned the task of drafting a Michigan unemployment insurance law to a study committee headed by University of Michigan economics professor William Haber. A Murphy advisor since the late 1920s, Haber was the state's relief administrator and was in the process of becoming one of the nation's social security experts.

Murphy instructed the Haber committee to draft "the most progressive and liberal" unemployment insurance law in the United States. The social security subcommittee of the Legislative Council, a bipartisan group of nine members drawn from the two houses of the legislature that functioned during the interim between legislative sessions, aided the Haber committee in drafting the bill. The principal draftsmen, however, were the students enrolled in Professor Haber's University of Michigan course, Social Insurance, whom Haber divided into committees to work on different sections of the bill. Eighteen of the students later found jobs with the Michigan Unemployment Compensation Commission.[23]

When the special session convened, Fitzgerald and the Republicans disclaimed any responsibility for the statute that might be enacted. Fitzgerald's advice to the legislature was to pass "purely a qualifying bill" that could be "thoroughly reviewed" and perhaps "remodelled" by the 1937 legislature. The measure adopted on December 23, signed by Fitzgerald the next day, and approved by the Social Security Board on December 29 was not, however, simply "a skeleton stop-gap bill." Although "hurriedly drawn," it was a detailed measure that satisfied Murphy's criterion of liberality. Thirty states had acted before the Michigan law was passed, and Michigan was one of twenty states to act after the November elections.[24]

Before passing the unemployment insurance bill, the legislature had to resolve two especially thorny issues: whether employees should also contribute to the unemployment insurance fund, a concept that had enjoyed a certain popularity before the election but had attracted virtually no support after that time, and which employers to exempt from the operation of the act. A House-Senate conference committee included an employee tax, but Detroit Democrats in the House balked at this, and the tax in the end was killed. Because the provision of the Michigan constitution requiring the legislature to provide "a uniform rule of taxation, except on property paying specific taxes" seemed to prohibit a state law relieving employers with fewer than eight employees from paying the required tax, as the federal law specified, the legislature accepted the Haber committee's recommendation that the first $6,000 in payrolls be exempted from the employer tax. The purpose of the exemption was to provide a legal Michigan equivalent of the exemption specified in the federal statute. The provision, which exempted about half of Michigan's employers from paying the tax, seemed likely to cost the state about $1 million in taxes in 1937 that employers would otherwise have had to pay and made an additional 300,000 employees ineligible for insurance. The act initially covered 18,859 employers and 1,338,635 workers.[25]

The administration of the Michigan unemployment insurance statute was entrusted to a four-man bipartisan commission. Employees qualifying under the law—they had to be unemployed for three consecutive weeks or for five weeks out of fifty-two—were to receive 50 percent of their average weekly wage but no more than $16 per week, the highest amount permitted by any state statute at that time. The length of the benefit period depended on the amount the employee had earned in covered employment during the preceding two years but was not to exceed sixteen weeks during the benefit year. Payments to employees were to begin on January 1, 1939.

The Michigan law provided for a pooled insurance fund and, like the laws in all but eleven states at that time, incorporated the principle of merit rating. Haber, however, later concluded that merit rating was "perhaps the weakest part" of the Michigan law. Although the "only purpose" of unemployment insurance, he contended in 1941, should be to provide protection for those employees who became unemployed through no fault of their own, merit rating shifted the emphasis from protection of the worker to encouraging employers to reduce unemployment so as to pay a smaller tax. The assumption was that this would lead to "more stable employment," but it should have been realized, Haber argued, that the individual employer had relatively little control over the amount of unemployment in his plant.[26]

IV

Murphy took his oath of office as governor at noon on January 1, 1937. "Guided by new visions of the social weal, with intelligent planning and progressive legislation," he declared in his inaugural address, "we may not only enhance the natural glories and aid the generous hand of nature; we may bring to men and women and children great security against misfortune and want, and to all our citizens wider enjoyment of the abundant blessings that modern life affords."

Hundreds of persons who held tickets for the inaugural banquet, which had been oversold, could not gain admission; Harry Mead, the chairman of the inaugural committee, Norman Hill, and many others had to dine at lunch counters in the basement of the Lansing hotel where the banquet was held. "The people," Murphy immodestly stated at the banquet, "have sensed that something big has happened; that we are going to try to do something big. In the whole flight of time in this state it is the first time anything of this kind has happened." About four thousand persons attended the inaugural ball, and Murphy, who was suffering from a cold, shook hands with the guests despite grumbling by his physician, who had ordered the governor to bed.[27]

In his state-of-the-state address to the fifty-ninth Michigan legislature on January 7, Murphy declared that, since the electorate had indicated its support for the New Deal on November 3, it was the "duty" of the governor and lawmakers "to translate into law and practice ... this new social and political philosophy, this broader conception of the responsibility of government for the economic health of the state and the social welfare of all its inhabitants." Presenting the lawmakers with a long agenda, Murphy called for improvements in the new unemployment insurance law, increased old-age benefits, an occupational disease law, fair labor standards legislation, recognition of the right of collective bargaining, industrial disputes legislation, "a thorough going system of civil service," consolidation of appropriations in a single appropriation bill, "a thorough-going program of administrative reorganization and integration," restructuring of the "chaotic" state and local welfare administration, a new securities law, a teacher-tenure law, and repeal of the teachers' oath law.[28] Legislators, the press, and others concluded from the address that Murphy was proposing "a little New Deal" for Michigan. Republicans thought the message "rather theoretical," wondered how Murphy's programs could be financed, and expressed concern that the governor had ignored agriculture in his address.[29]

Although Murphy's role as a strike mediator consumed the bulk of his official time at the outset of his administration, once the strike wave ebbed he devoted his time to the more conventional gubernatorial tasks of administration, political leadership, legislative leadership, and public relations. As could have been anticipated from his previous administrative service, Murphy did not consistently involve himself in the day-to-day affairs of the state government. His approach to administration was to select the best persons available to head the agencies subject to his appointment and to allow them, for the most part, to discharge their responsibilities without significant interference from above. The Murphy administrative style as governor did not mean that he lacked understanding of or interest in the affairs of state government. Newsmen, indeed, were impressed with how well informed he was at press conferences, and Carl Rudow, a *Detroit News* reporter who covered Lansing for many years, thought that Murphy could "see through issues and ... problems" as well as any government official whom Rudow had ever known. Even staunch Republicans conceded that the governor had "a remarkable comprehension of the problems and responsibilities of government." A friendly source, Dr. Haber, commented at the end of Murphy's term that "not in a generation, if ever" had Michigan had "a person in the Governor's office who grasped the problems of modern government as thoroughly" as Murphy had.[30]

He was "pleased" that Murphy was to become Michigan's governor, a Detroit official noted, because "if ever there was a place needed a clean-up," it was the "State Capitol, which became a veritable Augean stable" while Fitzgerald was governor. The Democratic party in Michigan was "weak and rotten" and the tone of state politics was "low," Republican Joseph Hayden wrote a friend, but Murphy was seeking to appoint "strong, honest, capable men" of both parties who would inspire public confidence. Murphy stated that he wanted his appointees to be in sympathy with "the Lansing New Deal" and to be able to "work in close co-operation" with the Roosevelt administration. He would appoint men and women to the key positions of government, he asserted, who were "high-minded, well-trained, and competent with a pro-public viewpoint." They would be "men and women unafraid of a new idea, and whose first objective ... [was] to do justice to the people." His goal, he declared, and he largely achieved it, was to give "character" to his administration and to provide the state with "the best possible, non-political administration."[31]

In seeking to provide the kind of administration he had promised, Murphy relied less on the recommendations of political leaders than on the advice of "experts" qualified to judge technical competence. Because of his profound respect for his alma mater, the University of Michigan, and his close relationship with Hayden, Murphy pressed the political scientist into service as an unofficial talent scout for the state administration, and Hayden exerted a considerable influence in this capacity. Academics from the University of Michigan and elsewhere played a conspicuous role in the Murphy administration and became Michigan's equivalent of the New Deal's brain trust.[32]

It was Hayden who first recommended Harold D. Smith for the important position of budget director, and Murphy eventually appointed Smith to the position. Characterized by an expert as "the one budget director whose previous work trained him for such a position," Smith was serving at the time as director of the University of Michigan's Bureau of Government, executive secretary of the Michigan Municipal League, and chairman of the Fitzgerald-appointed Welfare and Relief Study Commission. As Murphy knew, Smith was a registered Republican who had nevertheless voted for Eugene Debs in 1920 and Franklin D. Roosevelt in 1936. After distinguished service as Michigan's budget director, Smith was appointed by President Roosevelt in 1939 to head the federal government's Bureau of the Budget.[33]

As his commissioner of pardons and paroles, Murphy selected Hilmer Gellein, "a political unknown" who had once worked in the sociological department of the Cleveland Cliffs Iron Company and had served as Murphy's court stenographer when he was a Recorder's Court judge. "He has perfect integrity," Murphy said of Gellein, "and he doesn't know anything at all about politics." For state banking commissioner, Murphy selected Charles T. Fisher, Jr., a Republican of "New Deal tendencies" who had gained experience for the position as manager of the National Credit Corporation, vice-president of the First National Bank of Detroit, and head of the Michigan Division of the Reconstruction Finance Corporation. Detroit banker Joseph Dodge wrote the governor that he could not have made a better appointment insofar as the banks of Michigan were concerned. As head of the Michigan Corporation and Securities Commission, Murphy appointed Carl A. Olson, the regional chief of accounting for the Securities and Exchange Commission whom the commission's chairman characterized as "one of the ablest members" of the commission's staff. James G. Bryant, whom Murphy designated to serve as director of the state's Department of Welfare, had gained experience as regional representative of the Social Security Board, director of employment for the Kent County Relief Commission, and a CWA and WPA official; Ruth Bowen, who became the same department's deputy director, was recognized as a very able social worker.[34]

Before appointing Don W. Gudakunst, Detroit's deputy health commissioner, to become state health commissioner, Murphy had Hayden check out the appointment with University of Michigan physicians and also wrote to the surgeon general of the United States to assure himself that there was no one available outside of Michigan who might be better qualified. When Murphy had to appoint a new state hospital director, he contacted psychiatric sources both inside and outside Michigan and, on the basis of their advice, selected Dr. Joseph E. Barrett, the assistant commissioner of the Massachusetts Department of Mental Diseases. The board of directors of the National Committee of Mental Hygiene adopted a resolution lauding Murphy for the manner in which he had made the appointment.[35]

Murphy illustrated his disdain for conventional politics in making several key appointments. Although politicians understandably cast covetous eyes on the Liquor Control Commission, Murphy, ignoring the "importunities of various groups," selected Professor Edward W. McFarland, the head of Wayne University's social science department and a man with a long-standing interest in consumer and labor problems, to chair the commission. Professor Haber had long been anathema to politicians and was regarded by many legislators as too glib and self-assured, but, since he was an unemployment insurance expert, Murphy appointed him to the Michigan Unemployment Compensation Commission. Murphy recognized "the political inviolability" of the Conservation Commission by reappointing

Harry H. Whiteley, the manager of the *Dowagiac Daily News*, a Republican and a Murphy opponent, even though, as Whiteley observed, this was "at no small inconvenience to himself [Murphy] and in direct opposition to his party leaders." A reporter for the Republican-oriented Booth syndicate of Michigan newspapers doubted that Murphy had "ever been so disgusted" as when he received a letter from a Democratic justice of the Michigan Supreme Court urging the appointment of a new superintendent of the Girls' Training School in Adrian who had been recommended by the Lenawee County Democratic committee. " 'Imagine,' " Murphy sarcastically remarked, " 'placing the well-being and future of these girls . . . under the care and guidance of a liberal and progressive administrator selected by a democratic county committee.' "36

As his appointment of Democratic party leaders Frank Picard, Joseph M. Donnelly, and Charles S. Porritt indicates, Murphy did not always ignore party considerations in making major appointments. His most obvious political appointment was that of Edward J. Fry, the state party chairman, to be state racing commissioner. Senator Prentiss Brown objected to the appointment, noting that the Republicans had been hurt politically in 1936 because Howard Lawrence was both state banking commissioner and Republican state chairman just as the Democrats had earlier been subjected to criticism because Horatio Abbott and Alfred Debo had received major appointments while holding major party posts. In a letter to Brown that Murphy "heartily" approved, Democratic national committeeman Edmund C. Shields responded that Fry, who allegedly had an intimate knowledge of racing, would use his position to make the sport more popular, not to solicit contributions for the party. Reminding the senator that the position of the Democratic party in Michigan was "none too glamorous," Shields asserted that it would create "serious difficulty" for the party if Fry were forced to give up one of his two positions. Haber recalls that the governor told him the appointment was the price he had to pay to get his civil service bill through the legislature, but the record does not appear to substantiate this interpretation of the appointment.37

If the test of the civic mindedness of an executive is the quality of his major appointments, Murphy deserves high marks. The *Detroit Times* thought that the governor's appointments read "like a Michigan Who's Who of scholarship and civic endeavor," the *Detroit News* was impressed with the "exceptional qualifications" of the appointees, and Hayden reported that the reaction in the university community in Ann Arbor was "universally good." As became evident, however, Democratic politicians, noting the number of Republicans and independent Democrats selected, viewed the appointments in quite another light. It could hardly have escaped their notice, moreover, that the "goo-goo" types who lauded the appointments and some of the appointees themselves were not very likely to vote for Murphy and the Democrats as a result. "Most of our Governor's appointments," Harry Mead remarked, "are probably O.K. for the newspaper public and other fakers . . . [but] they are not much good when it comes to a definite commitment of themselves behind our leader!" A keen practitioner and student of politics in Michigan observed at a later time that gubernatorial appointments had to satisfy two major criteria, "competence" and acceptability by the community and the party organization. Murphy's major appointments certainly satisfied the criterion of competence, and they were well regarded by the "community," but they were not, on the whole, acceptable to the party organization.[38]

As mayor of Detroit, Murphy had demonstrated a remarkable ability not only to convince subordinates of varying backgrounds and beliefs of his high-mindedness but also to inspire them to give their best to the public service. The same was true of Murphy as governor, and a *Detroit Times* reporter was altogether correct when he said at the beginning of 1938 that persons close to the state government recognized "a different spirit throughout the intricate machinery of government." "Although I could not completely subscribe to your policies," Alvin Macauley, Jr., a conservative Detroit banker who had succeeded Fisher as banking commissioner, wrote Murphy at the close of his governorship, "I felt that every action was taken honestly and with a view to the public's best interest without regard to the political consequences, which to my mind is quite extraordinary." In similar fashion, Frank Isbey, a Detroit businessman whom Murphy had appointed to manage the Michigan State Fair, wrote the governor at the close of his term, "My life has been made richer in the realization of the high ideals and exemplary methods which you put into effect in administering the affairs of this State. . . . A new sense of dignity and worth of service to my fellowman has been derived by me as a consequence of having sat with you in the administration of governmental affairs." A well-to-do Detroit woman appointed by Murphy to head the state's new Consumers Bureau nicely reflected the views of the political amateurs whom Murphy attracted to state government when she observed of her experience in the Murphy administration, "Oh me! non partisan good government is such fun."[39]

The proper management of the state's affairs meant for Murphy not only the selection of able individuals to guide state agencies but the development of proper personnel policies for state employees, efficient and scandal-free conduct of the state's business, and reorganization and modernization of the state's administrative structure. Murphy, as we shall see, did not always attain his administrative objectives, but his efforts were consistently pointed in the proper direction, and it was his defeat in 1938 that prevented him from coming closer to the achievement of his goals.

As leader of his party in Michigan, Murphy was weakened by the fact that the multiplicity of statewide elective offices left ambitious politicians like Murray D. Van Wagoner and Leo J. Nowicki unbeholden to the governor and free, if they wished, to pursue their own political interests. Since many Democrats elected in 1936 had benefited from the $25,000 the Highway Department had distributed among Democratic candidates in the campaign and since the department disposed of more than 20 percent of the state's jobs, Van Wagoner was in an especially strong position to pursue an independent political course.

Murphy and Van Wagoner, G. Donald Kennedy observed, "were just two different peas in a pod." The difference between the two men was the difference between the politics of ideology and the politics of patronage; Murphy, the "idealist," and Van Wagoner, the "politician," simply did not speak the same language. They kept up appearances during Murphy's governorship, but there was no love lost between them. Van Wagoner thought that the governor did not give the Highway Department proper support, and he was miffed that the governor appointed only one key Van Wagoner man to an important position. As Van Wagoner saw it, Murphy neglected politics and thought that he was "bigger than the party." Murphy, on the other hand, received a confidential report shortly after his election that the Highway Department was "openly and viciously" against him and that Van Wagoner was not only providing legislators with patronage but also making promises to them regarding jobs that Murphy would award, thus setting a trap for the governor-elect.[40]

Nowicki, "a sensitive and sour fellow" with a "touchy disposition," had been a Welsh supporter. Although he later endorsed Murphy, he was not one of the governor's admirers. The lieutenant governor embarrassed Murphy and demonstrated his independence when he sought in December 1937 to take advantage of a 1840 statute that had never before been invoked by claiming the governor's salary for the seventy days in the year that Murphy had been out of the state. Murphy announced that he would surrender his salary for the absent days if the attorney general ruled in Nowicki's favor; he promptly sent the state treasurer part of the money in question, while Nowicki refunded to the state his $3 per diem for seventy days. The attorney general, however, ruled that the governor was entitled to his full salary and that the lieutenant governor could claim the salary only when he actually assumed the governor's duties, not simply when the governor was absent from the state. The state treasurer returned the money that Murphy and Nowicki had sent, and there the matter ended.[41]

Murphy was handicapped as a party leader not only by the independence of some of his associates but by the fact that he presided over a party that had so long been in the minority it had difficulty adjusting to its majority status. It was a party, also, that continued to be riven by factional discord. Picard was dismayed at how jealous of Murphy many Democrats were. Some Democrats, he told Emil Hurja, "would like to see Frank slip and break a leg."[42]

The Comstock wing of the party, composed of Democrats of the Grover Cleveland variety, loathed the New Deal and Michigan's ultra-New Dealish governor. Professor Mortimer E. Cooley, a Comstock Democrat, wrote his friend Van Wagoner that, if any Democrats survived the era, the record of the Murphy regime would cause them to "hang their heads in shame." ". . . the Democrat Party," he wrote, "is going—has gone to Hell. . . . [It] has failed the hopes of those whose opinions we have looked up to in the past. It is like a Mississippi steamboat with a nigger sitting on the safety valve. Or, maybe, there no longer is a Democratic party. The old time Democrat is more like a Republican than a New Dealer." Comstock, who did not regard Murphy as "our kind of Democrat," vented his political frustration in similar language. "We who have been called Old Line Democrats," he lamented, "have seen our party stolen from us." The Democratic party, which had become "the New Deal party," advocated principles that were closer to the historical doctrines of the Republican party than to the party of Jefferson, and it was the Republican party, Comstock thought, that now looked "suspiciously Jeffersonian."[43]

Murphy's understanding of what made for success in American politics necessarily influenced his style of political leadership. He explained his position candidly in an address to a meeting of Young Democrats in the fall of 1937 that was "not the kind of speech party leaders liked to hear." "I say," he declaimed, "that the problem of building political fences has been with us a definitely minor consideration." Some politicians, he asserted, thought that a party lost in "organization strength and solidarity" when it espoused causes like civil service or nonpartisan welfare administration. "Obsessed by the notion that patronage and other forms of political domination are the keys to party strength, they fail to see that in the long run there is never anything lost in advancing the interest of the general public. As a matter of fact, the party will flourish that puts the public interest first. . . . A party's true strength lies in its high principles and its lofty idealism. Let those principles remain high and noble, let an administration serve well and honestly, and a grateful public will do more for the party than organization or political fence-building ever can or will." As Murphy saw it, the most effective way to assure Democratic control in Michigan was to provide the state with the best government it had ever received. "He thinks that in the long run this will get the votes," Hayden explained.[44]

After his patronage policy and his unswerving support for civil service and the merit system had produced a serious rift in his party, Murphy sought to explain to party officials that he appreciated the importance of their service, but he did not alter his view as to what was more important and what less important in the world of politics. He had been too long associated with government affairs, he wrote the state party chairman, not to understand that the political party was "a valuable and necessary instrument of public service" and that party organization was important. However, the governor continued, the function of the party was "not to advance the private interests of party adherents but to provide a government responsive to the public needs, attuned to the public will, devoted to the public interest. . . . In the actual administration of government, the status of public officials as representatives of the party and its members is subordinate to their responsibility as servants of the general public."

Defending his patronage policy to protesting Democrats, Murphy explained that, although politics had to be "largely if not entirely disregarded" in filling certain positions, he believed that policy-making positions must go to party members sympathetic to its principles. He insisted, moreover, that insofar as routine jobs requiring no special qualifications were concerned, he had left matters to the State Central Committee and the county committees. "I never interfered, nor did I wish to have anything to do with it," he stated.[45]

Although Murphy paid little attention to Democratic regulars in making most of his major appointments, it is difficult to know what part he played in the turnover of routine jobs that occurred at the beginning of his administration when the victors sought to claim the spoils that they thought were rightfully theirs. When Fry stated after the election that he would be the patronage chief of the new administration, Murphy, who had criticized the Fitzgerald administration for channeling patronage through a patronage czar, responded, "There will be no patronage czar [in my administration]." Whereas the inefficient and "unworthy" would be discharged, he stated that "old and faithful employees" in departments subject to his control would be retained regardless of their politics, as would those with "technical training" who were performing creditably; and he instructed that employees of the State Emergency Relief Administration and the State Police, which had their own merit systems, "should be untouched."

Despite the governor's cautionary remarks, there was a substantial amount of turnover in state employment during the first six months of his administration. Of the approximately fifteen thousand state jobs as of June 1937, thirty-two hundred, primarily in the Highway Department, were held by Democrats appointed during previous administrations, another two hundred or so were under the merit system, but about four thousand jobs, roughly 27 percent of the total, had been awarded to "deserving" Democrats since January 1. The percentage of new employees in 1937 corresponded closely with the figures for the first year of both the Comstock and the Fitzgerald administrations and the average for the period 1926–35.[46]

What disturbed party men was less the manner in which routine jobs were filled than Murphy's major appointments, the extent to which he selected either Republicans or independents or failed to dismiss Republican incumbents, and his failure to consult the leadership about appointments or to heed their advice. Shields advised Murphy at the outset of his administration to alter the composition of the governing boards of the state hospitals since the Republicans had built up in several of these hospitals "some marvelous organizations" that controlled the vote in the counties in which the institutions were located. Murphy, however, told a reporter, " 'I do not intend to follow county committee recommendations in selecting state hospital superintendents,' " and the governor generally applied the same principle in dealing with hospital governing boards. At the close of Murphy's term the chairman of the Kent County Democratic committee was still complaining that Murphy, to the detriment of the Democratic party, had failed to change the composition of the boards of state institutions.

The president of a Democratic club in the Upper Peninsula resigned in the fall of 1937 because, he explained to the state party chairman, Murphy had appointed Republicans to "some of the best

Campaigning in Detroit, October 13, 1936. Franklin and Eleanor Roosevelt, Murphy, and G. Donald Kennedy.

Murphy and Father Coughlin

Murphy delivering his initial message to the Michigan legislature, January 7, 1937. Photo by the *Detroit News*.

Murphy announces the end of the GM strike, February 11, 1937. Seated left to right: Wyndham Mortimer, William S. Knudsen, James F. Dewey

Settlement of the Chrysler strike, April 6, 1937. Seated, left to right: John L. Lewis, Murphy, Walter Chrysler, Dewey. Standing, left to right: Homer Martin, Richard Frankensteen, Lee Pressman, K. T. Keller, Herman Weckler.

Murphy and Lewis

Murphy's law-and-order conference, March 17, 1937. Standing: E. Blythe Stason (sixth from left), H. Lynn Pierson (second from right), Father Frederick Seidenburg (extreme right). Seated: Frank Couzens (to Murphy's right), Frank Martel, Raymond W. Starr, William Haber (the first three persons to Murphy's left), Caroline Parker (at end of table to Murphy's left).

Murphy signs the civil service bill into law, August 5, 1937. James K. Pollock is the fourth person from the right.

Left to right: Edmund C. Shields, Theodore I. Fry, Murphy, Starr, Leo Nowicki.

Murray D. Van Wagoner (second from left) and G. Donald Kennedy (third from right). Photo by the *Detroit Free Press*.

At table, left to right: Prentiss Brown, James A. Farley, Murphy, Nowicki.

Murphy dedicates a Michigan State Employment Service office in Hamtramck, June 1938. Abner Larned is the third from the left, Frederic Schouman, the second from the right.

Murphy and John M. Carmody at the dedication of the Ubly REA project, June 18, 1938.

jobs'' and "you big shots sit on the sidelines and let him get away with that stuff.'' A prominent Michigan Democrat informed Roosevelt that seventy-five of the eighty-three county chairmen "secretly" opposed Murphy because he had failed to give them any recognition in the distribution of federal and state patronage. Another state Democrat wrote James A. Farley just after Murphy left office that the same number of county chairmen were "very much disgruntled because of the preferences shown strangers [by Murphy] within and without our own party.''[47]

Democratic regulars complained that the governor was often inaccessible to them and, when they did get to see him to discuss patronage matters, assumed a " 'cold, faraway look' " that embarrassed and humiliated them. They thought that Murphy did not understand that parties had to be organized "from the ground up" and that he had "thwarted every attempt, by his indifference, to develop an organization.'' He did not pay heed, they contended, to the men and women of the organization or to its regularly constituted committees ("his eye for fairness to his loyal workers and party management was shut all the time,'' one of them said). They claimed, with some reason, that he was more interested in his own career than in the success of the party.[48]

Democratic regulars also took issue with what Picard characterized as Murphy's "almost childish faith in the eventual triumph of truth and justice.'' It was simply wrong to assume that "doing a good job in public office in itself wins reelection,'' Joseph Donnelly told the governor. "I have never seen it happen myself without considerable political work on the side.'' The average political worker, Donnelly noted, needed the prestige that came from receiving an appointment or having had something to do with an appointment if he were to continue his party labors. "You can't work against that sentiment with anything except patronage when patronage is available.... you can't buck against jobs without jobs.'' Murphy's "interest in such matters,'' Donnelly accurately concluded, was "too fitful and not sufficiently sustained'' to enable his supporters to accomplish anything in his behalf. In similar vein, Picard asked ex-governor Murphy, "What good is altruism if because of failure to play *honest, fair, decent, practical politics* you lose the opportunity to render a service to your state or country [?]'' One state Democratic leader thought that the successful political leader had to have "the faculty of finding the road where *good government* and *good politics*'' met, and, like most party bigwigs, he thought that Murphy lacked this "faculty.''[49]

What party workers of the old school who thought that Murphy was politically "blind" failed to perceive was that he simply had a different conception of politics and how to win elections than they did. He was less concerned about rewarding the party's faithful, which was their preoccupation, than in using patronage to attract new groups to himself and the party. Of greater importance, he believed in an issue-oriented style of politics, a politics of ideology, that would win large numbers of voters to his side. The voters, in Murphy's view, would reward a government that was not only efficient and scandal-free but social-minded as well. He was, Russell B. Porter observed in the *New York Times* "a 1937 model" politician "with all the latest social and economic gadgets attached to the political body." Porter might have noted that Murphy was that kind of politician even before the New Deal.[50]

Murphy had gained his political experience in the nonpartisan ambience of Detroit. As a practitioner of the politics of nonpartisanship, which minimizes the influence of traditional party organization, he had learned the importance of attracting a large personal following and winning the favor of large voting blocs. Because of his personal magnetism and his record as judge and mayor, he had endeared himself to blacks, white ethnic groups, and organized labor, and they had rewarded him with their votes. Since the Democratic party in Michigan had such a narrow base and had been victorious less because of its own strength than because of Roosevelt's popularity, it was natural for Governor Murphy, anxious for reelection in 1938, to reach out to groups that had supported him in the past. These were groups that, on the whole, had played little part in the one-party factional politics of Michigan since, as V. O. Key pointed out with regard to the southern states, "the factional system simply provides no institutionalized mechanism for the expression of lower-bracket viewpoints." It was Murphy who began the process of affording these groups a political voice in the state Democratic party.[51]

Despite all that was said about Murphy's abhorrence of patronage, he understood its value in winning the support of voting blocs such as blacks and organized labor. He thus engaged a black secretary, only the second black to hold such a post in the governor's office; appointed a black deputy commissioner of the Department of Labor and Industry and a black assistant attorney general; and placed a black on the Michigan Corrections Commission, the first member of his race to serve as a commissioner of a state agency. Almost one thousand blacks were on the state payroll by the close of the Murphy administration, compared to less than one hundred under Fitzgerald, and state agencies that had once been lily-white, like the auditor general's office and the Department of Agriculture, now included black clerks, stenographers, and statisticians. "Never before in the history of America," a black newspaper in the state declared, "has a State administration so clearly demonstrated by actual appointments that they believe in equal opportunity and fair recognition for all, regardless of race, creed or color." Murphy seems to have made a less conscious effort to find places on the state payroll for members of white ethnic groups, but his position with Michigan Poles, Hungarians, Italians, and Jews was secure, as electoral results demonstrated.[52]

Murphy recognized that organized labor was "a growing force" in Michigan politics. This, he believed, would result in "fundamentally important changes in the location of political control" and in government policies, and he saw himself as "directing and controlling" this new force. He provided organized labor with greater representation than in any previous state administration, appointing unionists to more than thirty positions of importance. He was careful to recognize the claims of both the Michigan Federation of Labor and its affiliated organizations and the United Automobile Workers (UAW), the state's major CIO union. The Federation of Labor appointees were recommended to the governor by a committee representing the state federation and a number of the state's craft unions. This, according to Frank Martel, was the first time a Michigan governor had assigned the AFL "any major part" in his administration.[53]

The most noticed of Murphy's labor appointments was that of UAW vice-president Richard Frankensteen as a SEWRC member. When the chairman of one of the county relief commissions resigned in protest at the appointment of an "organizer for the racketeering UAW," Murphy, calling the official's charges "a disheartening piece of bigotry" and noting that government "belongs to all the people," retorted that it would be helpful if other local relief administrators who disliked the appointment also resigned.[54]

Although described by the female vice-chairman of the Democratic State Central Committee as "certainly no feminist," Murphy made an appeal for the feminine vote by appointing women to several important state posts, including the directorship of the Consumers Bureau, the deputy directorship of the Welfare Department, and membership on the Civil Service Commission, the Unemployment Compensation Commission, and the State Hospital Commission. He also pressed for the so-called 50–50 bill, which gave women equal representation with men throughout the state political party structure. Murphy also forged close links with the Young Democrats in the state, agreeing with a political ally that they were "the future hope of the Progressive wing of our Party" and seeing them as far more supportive of his own political ambitions than the regulars who controlled the State Central Committee.[55]

Murphy sought to rally support not only by patronage and the development of relations of amity with various voting groups but also by the articulation of programs and the support of legislation that appealed to blacks, labor, lower-income groups, and liberals. Blacks were especially pleased when Murphy signed a civil rights bill in June 1937 that greatly strengthened the requirement that blacks be treated equally with whites in "places of public accommodation, amusement, and recreation," helped to block an effort to segregate black school children in one Michigan county, and halted the extradition of black fugitives to southern states; and the black community and the unemployed knew that Governor Murphy like Mayor Murphy was committed to public relief for the jobless. Organized labor was enormously pleased with Murphy's role as a strike mediator and his vigorous support of legislation in which it had an interest. Liberals applauded his enthusiastic endorsement of the welfare state and his fashioning of a Michigan New Deal.[56]

Murphy attracted a large and devoted personal following as the result of his policies and his charismatic personality, but he devoted scant effort to the actual building of the Democratic party. Michigan largely follows the pattern of one-party Republican states in which the balance of party power was realigned as the result of a two-stage process that began in the New Deal era. In the first stage, there was a very substantial swing to the Democratic party at all electoral levels but especially at the presidential level. This initial wave soon receded for one reason or another, but later, in the second stage of the process, new issue-oriented leaders, "zealous to build the party and win elections," came to the fore, captured and restructured the party, and completed the process of party realignment. In Michigan, after Murphy's defeat in 1938 Van Wagoner gained control of the Democratic party, and he was elected governor in 1940; but the politics of patronage, of which he was reputedly a master practitioner, failed to win him reelection in 1942.

After 1942 the Democratic party in Michigan "descended from confusion into chaos." The second stage of the party realignment process was initiated in 1947. The lead was taken by the formidable team of G. Mennen Williams and Neil Staebler, who combined a liberal philosophy and an issue orientation, in the Murphy manner, with a "keen awareness of the importance of organization," which Murphy lacked. It was Murphy, however, who had brought Williams into state government as an assistant attorney general, and Williams's association with Murphy and the fact that he was viewed as a Murphy protégé evoked "a very warm response" to him among "power groups" in the state that remained devoted to Murphy. Labor and blacks, two groups to whom Murphy had special appeal, were especially important to the issue-oriented Democratic party that elected Williams to six successive terms as governor, beginning in 1948, and effectively realigned the Michigan political system. Thus, as Williams has observed, "there was a very definite continuation of the [Murphy] tradition, but it was not in the formal party sense; it was in the sense rather of groups of people dedicated to him [Murphy] personally and dedicated to him because of what he stood for."[57]

As legislative leader, Murphy confronted an inexperienced legislature in which no member of the Senate had served more than two previous terms and only six members had served that long, and only ten members of the House had served three terms or more. It was also a malapportioned body: almost 70 percent of the state's population in 1930 lived in urban places, but just under 60 percent of the senators and 56 percent of the House members represented districts with an urban majority. More important, although 39 percent of the state's population resided in Wayne County, only 24 percent of the members of the Senate and 21 percent of the members of the House represented that county.[58]

Not only was the legislature inexperienced and malapportioned, but its membership did not remotely correspond to the occupational distribution in the state. Of the thirty-two senators, nine (seven Republicans, two Democrats) were professional persons; fourteen (four Republicans, ten Democrats) were in the business-managerial category; five (three Republicans, two Democrats) were farmers; only one, a Democrat, was a salesman or clerk; and one, also a Democrat, was a manual worker. Of the one hundred representatives, fifteen (twelve Democrats, three Republicans) were professional persons; thirty-nine (twenty-two Democrats, seventeen Republicans) were in the business-managerial category; twenty-eight (eleven Democrats, seventeen Republicans) were farmers; three, all Democrats, were clerks or salesmen; one, a Democrat, may have been a manual worker; and only one, a Democrat, was a union official. The preponderant number of legislators lived in small towns, only eleven senators and thirty-one House members residing in cities of more than forty thousand population. The legislature was thus oriented toward small-town and rural Michigan, whereas Murphy was oriented toward Detroit and Wayne County. The result, as the *Detroit News* pointed out, was that the governor and the legislature did not speak the same language. The typical legislator, the *News* observed, was "skeptical of idealism," Murphy's stock-in-trade, and "antagonistic toward specialists and experts," conspicuous by their presence in the Lansing New Deal. "They are willing to use a little vision," the Detroit newspaper remarked, "but not too much."⁵⁹

When Murphy proclaimed his support for a unicameral legislature, he almost certainly added to the mistrust of rural-minded legislators since the proposal was commonly viewed as designed to reapportion legislative power in favor of urban interests. Committed to the idea largely because of his admiration for George Norris, Murphy failed to heed the warning of a University of Michigan political scientist that "questions of the apportionment of political power cut to the bone. They make people who are otherwise amenable antagonistic."⁶⁰

The nature of the leadership in the Michigan legislature also created problems for the governor in securing the passage of legislation that he favored. It would have been helpful had Lieutenant Governor Nowicki and Speaker Schroeder been on good terms, but relations between the two were "not altogether cordial," and Nowicki, as we have seen, was not a Murphy enthusiast. In the Senate, the Democratic floor leader not only lacked "the pugnacity and aggressiveness . . . essential to success with the Governor's program," but, since he was more conservative than Murphy, he sometimes refused to support administration bills. In the House, the Murphy floor leader was "pushed aside" by more powerful legislators. Murphy's problems in the Senate were compounded by the fact that when the legislature convened in January 1937, Democrat Anthony J. Wilkowski of Detroit was serving a four-to-five-year prison term for voting fraud. This left the Democrats one vote short of the seventeen votes needed to pass legislation in the Senate. Since the attorney general ruled that Wilkowski's seat was not legally vacant, Murphy could not call a special election in Wilkowski's district. When efforts by the Senate to oust the jailed Democrat failed, Democratic senators pressured Murphy to pardon or parole Wilkowski or to commute his sentence. Murphy refused to do so even though he commuted the sentences of others convicted of the same offense.⁶¹

Some have argued that Murphy was an ineffective legislative leader because he did not involve himself to any great extent in party affairs, did not take legislators into his confidence, and ignored the legislature in making appointments. These generalizations concerning the Murphy political style are largely accurate, but the conclusion derived from them is not. Because of his great powers of persuasion, his ability to arouse public opinion in his favor by the "idealistic ring" of his oratory and its "inspirational quality," and his effective use of the special session as a means of focusing attention on particular issues, Murphy was able to realize a substantial number of his legislative objectives, even though his role as a strike mediator severely limited the attention he could devote to legislative matters in the early weeks of his administration. Given the composition of the legislature and the institutional handicaps under which he labored, what is remarkable is not that Murphy sometimes lost in the legislature but how often he won. The governor was probably correct in stating that the first regular session of the 1937 legislature "enacted more progressive social legislation than any Legislature in Michigan's history" up to that time. "The ice of a conservative past has been broken," Murphy declared, "and Michigan stands today, in both legislative and administrative achievements, in the front rank of the progressive states of the Union."[62]

In his 1956 study of the office of governor, Coleman B. Ransone, Jr., concluded that public relations is "the most time-consuming" of the modern governor's functions. It is difficult to determine whether this was true of Governor Murphy, but there is no doubt that he attached considerable importance to the publicity aspect of public relations. He did not need a press agent, a Lansing newsman later observed, because "he says and does things that make news, and best of all he knows what is news, and has a very thorough understanding of mob psychology." Murphy cultivated the press, and although some newsmen found him to be "a little aloof even when he was most friendly"—a veteran Lansing reporter noted that, in his long experience in the state capital, Murphy was the only governor whom newsmen never addressed by his first name—most reporters respected and admired the governor. ". . . no man who has ever held political office in Michigan," a *Detroit News* reporter noted at the close of Murphy's governorship, "so fully held and justified the support and faith of the working newspaperman." Another reporter recalled that the conservative Lansing correspondent Guy H. Jenkins, who had initially been anti-Murphy, "almost cried" when Murphy left office.[63]

Whereas American governors "entered the thirties with a solemn indifference to national issues," Murphy was one of the new-style governors of the post-1933 era who appreciated "the clear necessity of being involved in national politics." The term "co-operative federalism" was coined in the 1930s to describe the "partnership between Washington and the states as they jointly sought solutions to their common problems."[64] A New Dealer among New Dealers, Murphy was acutely conscious of the change that was taking place in federal-state relations, and he eagerly sought Washington's aid in attempting to deal with Michigan's problems. Few governors, as we shall see, accepted cooperative federalism with quite the same enthusiasm as Michigan's Murphy.

Murphy was initially assisted in the performance of his duties by a miniscule staff consisting of Ed Kemp as legal advisor, Norman Hill as executive secretary, Eleanor Bumgardner as general secretary, Hilmer Gellein as commissioner of pardons and paroles, and George R. Thompson—a Fitzgerald holdover—and then Harold D. Smith as budget director. Seeking an aide to help with correspondence, speeches, and press releases, Murphy appointed Charles Hedetniemi, a Michigander of Finnish extraction who had majored in journalism at the University of Michigan. A Detroit source reported that one person whom Murphy had asked to recommend a stylist concluded that the only individuals who met the literary standards the governor had established for the post were George Bernard Shaw and G. K. Chesterton![65]

Murphy kept irregular hours as governor just as he had as mayor and governor-general. He liked the public to think that he came to the office after an early breakfast and worked until midnight, taking time out only for meals and an afternoon horseback ride; but this hardly describes the typical Murphy day as governor, if there was a typical Murphy day. A poor sleeper who kept state documents at his bedside for late night reading and telephoned persons on state business at hours when they were probably in bed, Murphy often did not come to the office until the latter part of the morning. He was no more able to budget his time effectively or maintain a sensible office routine as governor than he had been as mayor or governor-general.[66] The test of the Murphy administration, however, was what it was able to accomplish, not the orderliness with which the governor conducted the state's business.

V

Since Michigan did not provide its governor with an official residence, Murphy had to make his own living arrangements in Lansing. Claiming that the rental property shown him was either unsuitable or too expensive, he moved into the Hotel Olds and lived there for about seventeen months. It was hardly a satisfactory place for the governor to live. "They call up at all hours, drunk and sober," Murphy complained. "They even rap on the door at 3 o'clock in the morning." In May 1938 Murphy moved into a college-owned home on the Michigan State campus in East Lansing. Since he occupied the house rent-free, Murphy established an emergency fund to provide aid to needy Michigan State students. On weekends the governor often journeyed to Detroit, where he shared an apartment with his brother George and his sister Marguerite and her husband.[67]

Fatigued from his labors, weakened by a succession of colds, and having lost eighteen pounds since becoming governor, Murphy suffered a "physical breakdown" while visiting in California in August 1937 and had to spend three weeks in the University of Michigan Hospital in Ann Arbor. "Far from . . . well" when he left the hospital, he soon left for White Sulphur Springs to get some rest and to regain lost weight. After suffering from "a persistent sore throat" in the late fall and early winter, Murphy returned to the University of Michigan Hospital in late January 1938, this time with "a very severe attack of shingles." Shortly thereafter he went to Florida to recuperate. He seems to have developed "a case of nerves" as the result of his illnesses and feared that he might soon die. When a *Lansing State Journal* reporter, however, commented that the governor seemed to be falling apart physically and dubbed him " 'Fragile Frank,' " Murphy was furious. Once again giving vent to the bellicose streak in his nature, he childishly challenged the reporter to put on the gloves. The governor calmed down when the reporter suggested that, if the two men were to duel, he would select " 'adjectives' " as his weapon.[68]

Murphy made every effort to exercise daily while governor, in conformity with his view that physical fitness was an essential ingredient of political success. Horseback riding had been his favorite form of exercise for some time, and his enthusiasm for the sport did not diminish while he was governor. The governor on horseback was a familiar sight in East Lansing.[69]

"By the way," Joseph Kennedy wrote Murphy in May 1937, "I've yet to meet a girl in New York or Washington who doesn't know Frank Murphy. Where in hell do you find time to meet all these good looking women?" Murphy remained a bachelor as governor, but he continued to delight in the company of the opposite sex. Forty-six years of age when he became governor, he had lost none of his sex appeal, and women found Governor Murphy just as attractive and exciting as they had found federal attorney Murphy, Judge Murphy, Mayor Murphy, and Governor-General Murphy. The stunning Ann Harding, who had first met Murphy in 1922, decided that he was a lost cause, but at least one other Hollywood star demonstrated an extraordinary interest in Michigan's governor. Tongues began to wag when Murphy was seen taking his daily horseback ride in the company of a seventeen-year-old high school senior.[70]

Murphy's favorite girl friend while he was governor was the lovely

Ann Parker. A 1932 graduate of Smith College, where she had been selected the most beautiful girl, she had gone to the Philippines with her father, General Frank Parker, and had worked at Malacañan as an assistant to Norman Hill. After leaving the Philippines, she completed an M.A. at Northwestern University and then took a job in the governor's office in Lansing. She was overwhelmed when the governor revealed that he loved her, and in the early 1940s it seemed that she would become Mrs. Frank Murphy.[71]

Thanks to the investments that he had made during his Philippine service, Murphy's financial condition was "the best ever" for him while he was governor. In his first month as governor he made a handsome profit of more than $71,000 from the sale of common stock valued at $214,537. He continued to buy and sell securities during the remainder of his governorship, suffering losses during the 1937–38 recession but making a profit thereafter. He was by no means the poor man he pretended to be when his term came to an end.[72]

Just as it was characteristic of Murphy to seek to conceal the extent of his financial assets, so it was typical of him to make a show of his sincerely held religious beliefs. "He wore his religion on his sleeve," a Lansing reporter recalled. When he paraded into the Catholic church near the state capitol, it seemed to newsmen that the governor was looking for "a camera angle." Arriving late, he would walk down the center aisle accompanied by his state trooper bodyguard, and he would remain on his knees longer than other worshipers.

If Murphy wore his religion on his sleeve, he at least wore it correctly. The pundit Arthur Krock recalls in his memoirs an occasion when Cardinal Spellman said a requiem mass in Joseph Kennedy's Palm Beach house while Murphy, Krock, and the cardinal were Kennedy's guests. As the cardinal intoned the mass, Krock, a non-Catholic, sought to follow Kennedy in the performance of the ritual; but when it became evident that this was the wrong choice, the newsman followed Murphy, who knew exactly what was to be done. When Krock joshed Kennedy about this afterwards, he retorted, " 'That character . . . ought to have been a priest.' "[73]

Murphy took pleasure in the ritual of his church, but religion was more than a matter of ritual for him: it was a guide to life and to public policy. A member of the Third Order of St. Francis, into which he was received just before leaving for the Philippines and whose office he said every day, Murphy stated while he was governor, "I believe the principles of St. Francis not only can be practiced by governments but that they must be practiced if government is to fulfill its purpose." The failure to apply Christianity in the economic sphere, he declared in one of his addresses as governor, was "the Great Hypocrisy of American history."

"Throughout my public career," Murphy stated when he left the governorship, "I have tried ... to apply not only the ideals of democracy, but the precepts of [papal] encyclicals." He told a Catholic friend that, in dealing with the labor upheaval of his governorship, he had based his actions on the "great encyclicals" of Leo XIII and Pius XI because they "represent everything that is fair and just to both sides." Leo, the governor wrote an aide, spoke about labor with "matchless reason" because "a just order of things is necessary for the salvation of men's souls."

As Murphy saw it, Michigan was "a salient of the whole progressive movement—a social laboratory"—and offered a greater opportunity than any other place to apply "practical Christianity" and to "demonstrate Christianity's freshening influence in human relationships." For him, the application of "practical Christianity" meant the improvement of the condition of the workingman, government assistance to the afflicted and the needy, and the "carrying over into our social and economic order what in religion is called brotherhood."[74] It meant, in short, precisely the kind of policies Murphy pursued as mayor, governor-general, and governor. Whether he simply cited a Catholic source for actions that he would have taken in any event is impossible to say, but we may assume, at the very least, that his understanding of the teachings of his church intensified his belief in the correctness of his policies and strengthened his determination to press forward in the face of opposition.

The center of a good deal of national attention while he was governor, Murphy was viewed by reporters and others as something of an "enigma," an "odd" but "likeable chap" according to one paper, "hard to follow" according to another. "He talks quietly and with great self-restraint," Harold Ickes noted of Murphy, "but his expression is that of a zealot." There was much comment in the press about the austerity of Murphy's private life, his simple living arrangements in a less than fashionable hotel, his passion for exercise and physical conditioning, the cold morning showers that he took, his annoyance at press reports that he wore brightly colored pajamas, his allegedly "exaggerated idea of the virtue of chastity," his eschewal of alcohol and tobacco, and his spartan eating habits. Murphy's "approach to fleshly indulgence," *Fortune* noted, was "an occasional glut-fest of chocolate ice cream"; and after having had lunch in Murphy's office on one occasion, Harry Mead wrote the governor that "the delectable array of viands was about enough to take care of a canary or possibly a chipmunk at the most." He had "never learned how to live," Murphy told reporters, but the more discerning among them realized that despite his well-publicized austerity in some matters, Murphy, a bundle of contradictions, enjoyed many of "the good things in life" as well, the vacations at Palm Beach and White Sulphur Springs, the hospitality of the very rich, the company of attractive women, and the theater and music.[75]

"He is an actor," an unfriendly newspaper source said of Murphy, "he is always acting. Behind a priestly mien there is much pretense." Murphy even convinced some persons that he was humble and preferred not to talk about himself, but one had to be insensitive not to be aware that Murphy was an egocentric individual who had enormous confidence in himself and a profound belief in his own destiny. Although Murphy was entirely sincere in his desire to aid his fellowman, *Fortune* shrewdly observed that this "desire" was "bound up with a psychological need for personal aggrandizement." Murphy, the journal noted, "respects himself intensely," but he wanted to see that respect in the eyes of others also. "Always before him," *Fortune* remarked, "there dances an eidolon, the image of the perfect Frank Murphy—an image created in adolescence at the instance of an idealistic mother and kept alive far beyond the age at which most men get a little cynical about their early dreams." Harold Lasswell has described the political type as characterized by "an intense and ungratified craving for deference" that is "displaced upon public objects" and is "rationalized in terms of public interest."[76] Murphy seems to fit the model, but to see his career as designed simply to satisfy a deep-seated psychological need would be to ignore the extent to which he was influenced by conscience, idealism, religion, and a genuine compassion for the less fortunate among God's creatures. Like other men, Murphy was motivated by a variety of forces both from within and without, and he himself could not have fully explained why he acted as he did in any particular instance.

The interest in Governor Frank Murphy on the part of the press and public is explained by the fact that he was "different from the ruck of politicians who rise and fall without public excitement"[77] but even more by the great events with which he had to deal. None of these events was more dramatic or more significant in terms of its impact on the nation and on Murphy himself than the great General Motors sit-down strike that began a few days before Murphy took his oath as governor of Michigan.

8

The General Motors Sit-Down Strike

The principal contestants in the great General Motors sit-down strike of 1936–37[1] were the largest manufacturing corporation in the world and a small, weak union of automobile workers. The vital center of the conflict was Flint, Michigan. The tactic employed by the workers was the sit-down strike. The individual who most affected the outcome of the strike was the governor of Michigan, Frank Murphy.

General Motors (GM) at the end of 1936 was a concern of enormous economic strength. It was not simply "big"; as *Fortune* remarked, it was "colossal." It had sixty-nine automotive plants in thirty-five cities and fourteen states, and its total assets exceeded $1.5 billion. GM produced passenger cars for "every price and purpose," commercial vehicles, trucks, trailers, a great variety of automobile parts and accessories, and a considerable number of nonautomotive items. It accounted for 43.12 percent of all new passenger car registrations and 37.8 percent of new truck registrations in 1936, and the more than two million cars and trucks that it sold all over the world constituted 37 percent of world sales. GM had 171,711 hourly employees and 342,384 shareholders at the time of the sit-down strike. Wall Street rated it "the best managed big corporation in America."[2]

Although there had been relatively little need for GM to concern itself with unionism and collective bargaining before 1933, Section 7(a) of the National Industrial Recovery Act (NIRA) and the automobile manufacturing code adopted in pursuance of the statute led the corporation to formulate a set of principles regarding industrial relations to which it remained committed as 1936 drew to a close. GM would meet with the representatives of any group of employees who had specifically authorized these representatives to bargain for them, but it would not countenance the principle of majority rule in the selection of employee representatives, and it would not concede to any union representatives the exclusive right to bargain for employees. GM, furthermore, would not recognize a labor organization as such and would not enter into a written contract with a union on behalf of company employees. Finally, although expressing a willingness to engage in corporation-level talks with employee representatives regarding labor matters that affected the corporation as a whole, GM stipulated that employees or their representatives would have to take up such issues as wages, hours, seniority, and other conditions of employment with local plant managers.

GM not only construed the representation and bargaining rights of union officials in as narrow terms as possible, but it also discriminated against union workers, established company unions in GM plants and favored them over outside unions, and spied on its workers. The best corporate customer of the labor spy agencies, GM employed at least fourteen detective agencies between 1933 and 1936 and spent approximately $1 million for labor espionage between January 1, 1934, and July 31, 1936.[3]

The National Labor Relations Act (NLRA) of 1935 proscribed some of GM's labor practices and endorsed the principle of majority rule in the designation of employee representatives for bargaining purposes. GM, however, decided to ignore the statute, believing it unconstitutional. When a National Labor Relations Board (NLRB) examiner began a hearing on June 30, 1936, regarding complaints that the corporation had discharged numerous union employees, employed labor spies, and dominated the employee organizations at its St. Louis Chevrolet-Fisher Body plant, GM secured an injunction that restrained the NLRB from proceeding with the case. The injunction was still in effect at the beginning of the GM sit-down strike.[4]

The United Automobile Workers of America (UAW), the union that challenged GM in the sit-down strike, developed from the federal labor unions that had been established in most automobile and automobile parts plants following the enactment of the NIRA. When the constitutional convention of the union was held in August 1935, the paid-up membership of the organization was less that twenty-six thousand, and it had only a semi-industrial jurisdiction. Toward the end of 1935 the fledgling Committee for Industrial Organization (CIO) dispatched its first field representative, Adolph Germer, to the automotive centers of Michigan and Ohio to test the desire of the auto workers for organization. Germer discovered that there was "a quite general organization sentiment" but that it was "wholly" for the industrial form of organization. On the basis of information supplied by Germer, Sidney Hillman, at the December meeting of the CIO, recommended that the new committee should "centralize its efforts on the automobile industry." In August 1936 the UAW aligned itself with the CIO.[5]

The UAW had launched an organizing drive in June 1936, but the effort was lagging when Franklin D. Roosevelt's smashing victory over Alfred M. Landon in the presidential election provided an enormous stimulus to organization. Since Alfred P. Sloan, Jr., the president of GM and a major contributor to the Republican party, had made a thinly veiled appeal to GM workers to vote Republican, the UAW viewed the election results not only as a defeat for Landon but for GM and the other automobile manufacturers as well. "You voted New Deal at the polls, and defeated the Auto Barons—Now get a New Deal in the shop," the UAW told the auto workers.[6]

When leaders of the CIO met in Pittsburgh on November 7–8, 1936, they decided to step up the organizing campaign in the automobile industry to capitalize on "the favorable climate for the union" resulting from the Roosevelt and Murphy victories. The UAW enrolled approximately 15,500 new members in December, more than ten thousand of them in Michigan, where organization had been conspicuously weak. The union's paid-up membership in that month was close to sixty-three thousand, about 13.7 percent of the average employment in the industry for the year, compared to an average paid-up membership of about twenty-seven thousand between April 1 and the end of the year.[7]

The UAW's leadership recognized that if the automobile workers were to be organized, the union would have to penetrate GM's Flint stronghold, where the UAW had only 150 members as of June 1936. The home of Fisher Body No. 1, the largest automobile body plant in the world, Fisher Body No. 2, Chevrolet, Buick, and AC Spark Plug, Flint was to the nation's leading automobile manufacturer what Pittsburgh was to steel and Akron to rubber. GM's 47,247 Flint employees as of December 1936 constituted more than two-thirds of the gainfully employed workers in the city and more than one-fourth of the city's population of about 160,000. An estimated 80 percent of Flint's families were dependent on the GM payroll.[8]

The only difference between Flint and the usual company town, a clergyman observed during the GM strike, was that Flint workers did not have to buy at a company store. The company " 'owns the town,' " a character declares in Catherine Brody's Flint-based Depression novel, *Nobody Starves*. When the UAW pushed its organizing drive in Flint in the summer and fall of 1936, it was unable to secure a permit to pass out handbills, to purchase radio time, or to secure publicity in the *Flint Journal*, the city's only daily newspaper. Three of the city's nine commissioners worked for GM; the mayor of the city, Harold Bradshaw, was a Buick employee; the city manager, John M. Barringer, had come to Flint to establish a foundry that provided Buick with castings; the police chief, James V. Wills, had once been a Buick detective; one of the Genesee County Circuit Court judges held a sizeable bloc of GM stock; and the county prosecutor was a minor GM stockholder.[9]

When UAW vice-president Wyndham Mortimer arrived in Flint in June 1936 to take charge of organizational activity, he was immediately advised by an anonymous telephone caller, " 'You had better get the hell back where you came from if you don't want to be carried out in a wooden box!' " Although Mortimer spent about four months in Flint, his efforts did not result in any noteworthy increase in union membership despite the contrary impression created in some accounts. He was replaced at the beginning of October by Robert C. Travis, who had been born in Flint and had been president of the militant Toledo Chevrolet local. Travis, who was close to Mortimer—he later described Mortimer as "the main influence in my life"—was assisted in his organizational efforts by Roy Reuther, who had once been a teacher in the Federal Emergency Relief Administration's workers' education program in Flint. The UAW received material assistance from staff members of the United States Senate's La Follette Civil Liberties Committee, some of whom saw themselves more as allies of the UAW in the struggle with GM than as impartial investigators seeking to develop information for the committee's use. Capitalizing on a successful sit-down in the Fisher Body No. 1 plant on November 13, the UAW by the end of 1936 had enrolled about forty-five hundred workers in Flint, approximately 10 percent of the city's GM workers. Organization had proceeded most rapidly in the two Fisher Body plants.[10]

Mortimer and Travis had assumed from the start that only a strike would compel GM to grant the UAW the kind of recognition it desired. When they began their assignments in Flint, they were undoubtedly thinking in terms of a conventional strike as the culmination of their organizational efforts. By the end of 1936, however, the sit-down strike had captured the fancy of many automobile workers, and when the issue between the UAW and GM was finally and fully joined at the end of 1936, it was the sit-down tactic to which the union resorted.

It is hardly surprising that the sit-down became, for a season, the favored strike tactic of automobile unionists. Because of the closely interrelated processes of automobile production, a small group of automobile workers could tie up a large factory by closing down a few key departments, and they could paralyze even a major producer by stopping production in a few strategic plants that fabricated parts upon which its other plants depended. All this could be accomplished by a minority of workers in a given plant or a given company, which meant that the sit-down was a marvelously effective tactic for a union like the UAW that had succeeded in enrolling only a small percentage of the automobile workers. In Flint, in particular, a sit-down strike would deprive GM of the advantages it would enjoy in an outside strike because of its friendly association with public authorities and the forces of law and order. Whereas the Flint police could disperse or arrest pickets and protect the entry of strikebreakers into struck plants in a conventional strike, GM might hesitate to employ force to dislodge strikers inside its plants since this might damage expensive machinery and because sit-down strikers would be capable of putting up a more formidable defense than strikers on an exposed picket line could.[11]

Although Frank Murphy traced the origins of the sit-down strike to a group of masons in ancient Egypt and although there appears to have been a stay-in strike in the United States as early as 1884, it was not until 1936 that the sit-down or stay-in strike, meaning a strike in which workers remained in a plant at least overnight, became a conspicuous employee tactic. The first American work stoppage to focus public attention on the sit-down, even though the sit-down phase of the strike was very brief, was the Goodyear Rubber Company strike of February–March 1936. Two months after the settlement of the Goodyear strike, the first mass sit-down strike in history took place in France. The French strikes did not go unnoticed by elements of the UAW leadership, who probably concluded that what workers in the automobile and other mass production industries could accomplish in France could also be achieved in the United States.

The first significant sit-down strike in the American automobile industry occurred on November 17, 1936, in the South Bend plant of the Bendix Products Corporation, 24 percent of whose stock was owned by GM. Two days after this successful strike was settled, the UAW brought the sit-down tactic to the Detroit heart of the automobile industry by a strike at the plant of the Midland Steel Products Company, which made steel body frames for Chrysler and Ford. In addition to Midland Steel workers, employees of the Gordon Baking Company, the fabricating and extrusion plant of the Aluminum Company of America, Bohn Aluminum and Brass Corporation, National Automotive Fibres, and Kelsey-Hayes Wheel Company all sat down at their Detroit jobs for varying periods of time in December 1936.[12]

Observers of the auto scene were aware as 1936 drew to a close that the UAW would follow up its victories at Bendix, Midland Steel, and Kelsey-Hayes, all automobile parts producers, by a strike against the behemoth of the automobile industry, GM. "The successful sit-down strikes in the 'feeder' ... [plants]," observed the *Daily Worker*, which had excellent contacts within the UAW, "have been a prelude to the march forward upon the General Motors Corporation." When these words were written on December 21, GM's Atlanta and Kansas City Fisher Body plants were already on strike. The UAW's General Executive Board (GEB), however, had voted on December 4 against an immediate GM strike. If there were to be a GM strike, Germer, Mortimer, and others thought that it should not come until after January 1. They believed that the Christmas season was psychologically a poor time to strike and that it would be unwise to strike before GM workers received the $10 million in bonus money that the company was scheduled to pay them beginning on December 18 and before pro-labor Frank Murphy replaced Frank Fitzgerald as governor of Michigan on January 1, 1937. Homer Martin, the president of the UAW, contemplated calling out as many GM locals as could be persuaded to strike, but Germer advised union officials to strike only key GM plants. The most important of these were the Cleveland Fisher Body plant, which made all the stampings for two-door Chevrolet models and some parts for all Chevrolet bodies, Fisher Body No. 1, which made all the bodies for Buick and vital parts for Pontiac and Oldsmobile bodies as well, and Chevrolet No. 4 in Flint, the sole producer of engines for Chevrolets.[13]

On December 18 CIO and UAW representatives, including John L. Lewis, the head of the CIO, John Brophy, the CIO director of organization, Homer Martin, and Mortimer met to plot the auto union's GM strategy. They agreed that the UAW should immediately seek a general conference with GM to discuss outstanding grievances and should "move towards a climax in January" if the company refused to negotiate "on a broad scale."[14] When Martin on December 21 requested an "immediate general conference" between GM and the UAW, William Knudsen, the executive vice-president of the corporation, predictably advised the UAW president to take up the union's grievances with plant managers in the localities where the grievances had originated. Martin renewed his request for a general conference on December 24, but before Knudsen could reply, the GM strike had spread to the vital center of the GM domain. On December 28 a small number of workers, probably at Martin's instigation but without the required GEB approval, sat down at the Cleveland Fisher Body plant. When the mayor of Cleveland proposed that the union resume work while negotiations proceeded, the president of the local telephoned Mortimer, the former head of the Cleveland Auto Council, who happened to be in Flint. Mortimer advised the local president to keep the Cleveland strike going and also told Travis to strike the key Fisher Body No. 1 plant at the earliest possible moment.

On the morning of December 30 a maximum of fifty workers in the Fisher Body No. 2 plant, which employed about one thousand workers, sat down in the factory in what appears to have been an entirely spontaneous action. Later that same day a sit-in strike closed the more important No. 1 plant, which employed about seventy-three hundred workers. The initiative for the strike had been taken by Bob Travis in accord with Mortimer's instructions. In the days and weeks that followed, although Flint remained the center of the dispute, the strike spread to numerous GM plants across the nation, and other GM plants were forced to close because of a shortage of parts. Before the strike was over, it had idled 136,000 GM workers and brought the corporation's automotive production to an almost complete halt.[15]

Although the major phase of the GM strike was initiated at an earlier date than John L. Lewis had anticipated, he knew that the CIO had no choice but to support the strike. GM locals had sought to provoke a corporation-wide strike on three different occasions in 1934 and 1935 but had been thwarted by the cautious American Federation of Labor (AFL) leadership of the auto union. Aware that the AFL had impaired its standing among the auto workers because of its lack of militancy, the CIO had been promising the UAW support ever since the committee had been formed; and Lewis knew that if the CIO backed off now, "our movement," to use his words, "would have been gone." Recognizing the importance of the battle to the entire CIO campaign in the mass production industries, Lewis consequently stated at the strike's outset that his committee was "squarely behind" the UAW.[16]

On January 4 the UAW submitted strike demands to GM that had been agreed upon in a strategy conference in Flint the preceding day. The UAW stated that it wished to meet corporation executives to work out a national agreement providing for a national collective bargaining conference; the abolition of piecework systems in the corporation; the thirty-hour week, the six-hour day, and time-and-a-half compensation for overtime; a minimum rate of pay "commensurate with an American standard of living"; reinstatement of employees who had been "unjustly" dismissed; seniority based on length of service; mutual determination by management and union committees of the speed of production in GM plants; and recognition of the UAW as the "sole bargaining agency" for GM workers.[17]

From the point of view of the strikers, the speed of production was the most important of the working conditions that the UAW was seeking to adjust and was the major cause of the GM strike. "The essence of Flint is speed," a *New York Times* reporter who covered the sit-down asserted. "Speed, speed, speed—that is Flint morning, noon and night." The leader of the sit-down strikers in the No. 2 plant summed up the number one complaint of the strikers: "I ain't got no kick on wages, but I just don't like to be drove."

The UAW leadership, on the other hand, attached greatest significance among the strike demands to the recognition of the union as the exclusive bargaining agency for GM employees. Its "long and sad experience" with alternative methods of representation had convinced the UAW that collective bargaining pluralism was productive of "confusion, disruption and industrial strife." Exclusive representation, the UAW contended, was the indispensable prelude to the orderly determination of conditions of employment, and those who opposed it were really opposed to collective bargaining itself. The proper legal procedure for the UAW to have pursued in seeking to validate its claim to speak for GM workers was to have requested an NLRB election among the company's employees, but it realized that it probably could not win such an election. It was certain, moreover, that GM would contest an NLRB election order in the courts, and the UAW, like GM and most everyone else, assumed that the NLRA would be declared unconstitutional.[18]

GM contended that since the sit-downers were illegally trespassing on company property, it would refuse to bargain with them or their representatives until its plants had been evacuated. "We cannot have bona fide collective bargaining with sit-down strikers in illegal possession of plants," Knudsen declared. In an open letter to GM employees following the receipt of the January 4 demands, Sloan asserted that the UAW was seeking the closed shop and a labor dictatorship and stated categorically that GM would not accept any union as the sole bargaining agent for its employees. The corporation was supported in this position by the craft unions of the AFL: the Metal Trades and Building Trades Departments of the Federation and six international unions affiliated with them wired GM requesting the corporation to make no agreement that would give some other organization authority to represent workers over whom the craft unions claimed jurisdiction.[19]

GM sought to secure the evacuation of its two Flint plants by petitioning the Genesee County Circuit Court on January 2 for a "temporary restraining injunction" to prevent the union from "continuing to remain in said plants in idleness in a so-called 'sit-down' strike" and from otherwise interfering with entry into and exit from the plants. The injunction was promptly granted by the eighty-three-year-old Judge Edward D. Black. Sheriff Thomas Wolcott gave the sit-downers thirty minutes to leave the two factories, but they ignored the sheriff's order. Three days later, on January 5, the UAW discredited the injunction when it "exploded" the news that Black held 3,665 shares of GM stock worth $219,900 at the market price. Unaware of Black's large stockholdings and embarrassed by the whole affair, GM transferred further proceedings in the case to the court of Judge Paul V. Gadola. For the time being, however, the corporation made no effort to press for legal action against the strikers.[20]

Lewis wanted the settlement of the GM strike "put in the lap of one man, the President." He told Secretary of Labor Frances Perkins at the outset of the strike that only the president, who could " 'do anything he pleases,' " would be able to resolve the matter. Although Perkins, rather than Roosevelt, directed such efforts as the federal government made to resolve the dispute, the president played a larger role behind the scenes than was apparent at the time. Roosevelt's reluctance to intervene openly stemmed from his unwillingness to commit his prestige to the resolution of the strike when the intransigence of the parties made the chances for success problematical at best and also from his disinclination to become entangled in the fratricidal conflict between the AFL and the CIO.

When Vice-President John Nance Garner denounced the sit-down as " 'terrible' " at a cabinet meeting early in 1937 and advised that Perkins should instruct Murphy to eject the strikers, the president, according to Perkins, stated, " 'Well, we haven't yet gotten to the point where the President of the United States tells the Governors of sovereign states what they're to do inside their . . . states.' " Although both Perkins and Roosevelt regarded the sit-down tactic as "reprehensible," neither favored the forcible ejection of the sit-downers. Perkins apparently thought that Murphy might have dealt with the matter under the law of trespass, but neither the president nor she favored the use of "marching troops" against workers who had violated only a trespass law.[21]

The sit-down strike was to be settled not in Washington but in Michigan, and it was Frank Murphy who played the crucial mediatory role. Michigan's governor was well suited for the part. He enjoyed the confidence of both organized labor and many automobile magnates, and he had the patience, persistence, and ability to restrain his temper required of the skilled mediator. The austere habits of a lifetime had prepared him for the marathon bargaining that the settlement of the strike required, and he kept the strike talks going day and night until the weary negotiators resolved their differences. "He has the most excellent capacity for work of any negotiator I have ever known," Knudsen stated with regard to Murphy when the strike was concluded.[22]

As a mediator, Murphy impressed upon the union and the management that there was a "third party" in the dispute, the people of Michigan, to whom consideration must be given and that, as governor, he spoke for this party. "These difficulties in the days of mass production," he declared during the strike, "are no longer private affairs. The government must play a helpful part." His concern was less the right or wrong of the sit-down than the settlement of the dispute by the "method of reason," without the use of force. His strategy was to keep the talks going in the hope that somehow a solution would be found. "It must and will be settled peaceably, around the conference table," he declared as the negotiations got under way.[23]

Although Murphy regarded the sit-in as an illegal trespass and so advised union representatives privately and said as much publicly, the legal status of the tactic in Michigan was clouded, at least insofar as the criminal law was concerned. Forcible entry and detainer was not a statutory offense for which Michigan law expressly provided a penalty, but it was to be argued later that since it was an indictable offense under the common law, sit-downers were guilty of a felony according to the terms of a Michigan statute that made it felonious to commit an offense under the common law for which no statute had specified a punishment. The Wayne County prosecutor, on the other hand, had stated in December 1936 that although employers might seek redress in the civil courts, the police could not interfere with a peacefully conducted sit-down. The sit-downers, the prosecutor declared, were inside the plants they occupied by invitation of their employers, "so there can be no trespass."[24]

In contrast to the Wayne County prosecutor, Ed Kemp, who had more conventional views of law and order than the governor, regarded the sit-down as a criminal trespass. Both he and Attorney General Raymond W. Starr, however, agreed that the initiative in dealing with the sit-down must come from local authorities, to whom GM could turn for aid. As they interpreted the law, local officials, on the "proper showing of fact and complaint," could not only provide relief by injunction but could also arrest persons guilty of criminal trespass, "the State standing by to enforce peace and order."[25] Murphy received a request to maintain order in Flint at an early stage of the strike, and he complied with that request; but although some criticized him for failure to enforce the law during the strike, he did not receive an official request to authorize the use of force to eject the strikers until the final few days of the strike.

Even though Murphy regarded the sit-down as illegal, he was disinclined, as Roosevelt and Perkins were, to apply a remedy that would result in bloodshed or the loss of life. " 'My God,' " Murphy said to Perkins, " 'it seems an awful thing to shoot people for . . . trespass.' " The assertion that a liberal places human rights above property rights has become an almost meaningless cliché, but it is nonetheless an accurate characterization of Murphy's position regarding the enforcement of the law in the sit-down strike: he was not prepared to take the kind of action to protect property rights that might result in the death of strikers. "I would have relinquished my post as governor to prevent a fatality during the strike," Murphy declared when the dispute came to an end.[26]

Murphy was reinforced in his reluctance to use troops against trespassers who were "peacefully occupying their place of employment" by the knowledge that GM officials agreed with him, fearing that the loss of life in the strike might adversely affect the well-being of the corporation and the sale of its cars for years to come. Perkins recalled that Sloan wanted " 'this crazy government we've got here' " to send in troops to eject the strikers; then, he thought, " 'it'll be all right.' " Knudsen, however, stated publicly that GM wanted the strike settled by negotiation rather than by violence, and GM officials told Murphy privately that they did not want the strikers "evicted by force." As Murphy's executive secretary remembered the governor's account of the conversation, Fisher Body's Lawrence Fisher remarked to his good friend Frank Murphy at one point during the strike, " 'Frank, for God's sake if the Fisher . . . brothers never make another nickel, don't have bloodshed in that plant. We don't want to have blood on our hands. . . . Just keep things going . . . it'll work out.' "[27]

Murphy believed that, if the strikers had sinned, they had also been sinned against and that, in refusing to abide by the NLRA, GM was itself violating the law and had, to a degree, provoked the employee reaction about which it was complaining. Like some others at the time, Murphy seems to have believed that, although the sit-down was illegal under existing law, it might at some later date receive legal sanction. He thus remarked to union negotiators, "it is realized that what today may be a mere claim of equity, tomorrow may obtain recognition of law." The concept that a worker had a right to his job—the legal defense offered by strike sympathizers for the sit-down tactic—undoubtedly had a certain appeal for Murphy, and he was probably interested to learn that the sit-down, according to the *Catholic Worker*, had eminent defenders in the Catholic church.[28]

In serving as mediator during the GM strike, Murphy was influenced not only by his view of the law and his abhorrence of violence but by his long-standing sympathy for organized labor and his political ambition. "If I can only feel, when my day is done," he had written in a paper for a sociology course while an undergraduate at the University of Michigan, "that I have accomplished something towards uplifting the poor, uneducated, unfortunate, ten hour a day, laborer from the political chaos he now exists in, I will be satisfied that I have been worth while." He had never gone contrary to the wishes of organized labor in matters that concerned it, he asserted during his gubernatorial campaign, and he told one campaign audience that although it was the "duty" of a public official to avoid strikes, it was not his "duty or prerogative . . . to permit the use of the police power except to protect the public," and he should not deny welfare to strikers. "Outside of the integrity of government," Murphy told Germer after the strike, "the interest of the wage earner has been my main concern during the fifteen years I have been in public life and everything else has been subordinate to it." One can easily understand why a UAW attorney later observed, "Employers controlled everything in the State [Michigan]—except Murphy."[29]

As a political leader ambitious for the presidency, Murphy did not wish to take any action that might cost him labor support in the future. Lewis shrewdly capitalized on this fact during the negotiations leading to the end of the strike. He reminded Murphy, Lewis told Heber Blankenhorn just after the strike, that he had narrowly carried Michigan only because labor had supported him. " 'Labor put you here,' " Lewis said, and when Murphy conceded the point, the CIO head continued, " 'If you break this strike that washes us up and washes you up. General Motors fought you in the election and when we are gone you are gone. If you stand firm you will aggrandize your political position enormously and there will be talk of Governor Murphy in 1940.' " Murphy appreciated that the manner in which he played his role as mediator in the strike could "make or break him politically."[30]

In assessing the factors that influenced Murphy as a strike mediator, one can safely dismiss the fact that, unbeknownst to both GM and the UAW, when the strike began the governor owned 1,650 shares of GM stock then worth somewhat more than $100,000. Murphy sold the stock on January 18, 1937, at a profit of at least $52,800. How the UAW would have reacted to the knowledge that Governor Murphy, like Judge Black, owned a sizeable bloc of GM stock is an interesting speculation.[31]

Between January 1 and January 11 both Murphy and Perkins sought to compose the strike but without being able to bring the disputants together. Aided by the skilled federal conciliator James F. Dewey, Murphy, in separate meetings with GM officials and the UAW board of strategy, sought to devise a formula that would lead to negotiations. The two sides, however, chose to disagree, and the talks collapsed on January 9.[32]

The next day Murphy made a decision critical to the strike's outcome when he advised the state's relief administrator, William Haber, that relief should be provided to nonstrikers and strikers alike strictly on the basis of need. "I won't permit the women, children, [the] sick and the old folk to go hungry because of this situation," the governor declared. He sent Haber to Flint to survey the problem, and the State Emergency Welfare Relief Commission specifically ruled a few days later that relief should be "granted to workers striking in industry on the basis of individual need."

Whereas the relief case load in Genesee County under all public programs stood at 2,360 (8,448 persons) in December 1936, it rose to 7,161 (28,025 persons) in January and 11,168 in February (42,459 persons), about one-quarter of Flint's population. Of the 8,376 persons who applied for relief between January 1 and February 8, 1937, 6,032 were GM workers. Haber estimated that the strike increased relief costs in Flint by about $400,000, most of which was provided by the state government. Had the strike been conducted in an era when public relief assistance was less readily available or in a state whose governor was less committed to the principle of feeding the hungry regardless of the cause of their distress, the UAW might have been hard put to secure the funds needed to sustain its strike.[33]

The strike took a dramatic turn on January 11 when Flint police made a futile effort to dislodge the sit-downers from the lightly held Fisher Body No. 2 plant in what became known in trade union history as the Battle of the Running Bulls. The trouble began when GM turned off the heat in the plant—the temperature in Flint fell to 16° that day—and plant guards, for the first time, sought to prevent the entry of food into the factory. When the sit-downers successfully resited the effort to deny them food, the captain of the plant guards, claiming that his men and he had been "captured," phoned the police for assistance. The police, who were already present in the area, used tear gas in a vain effort to dislodge the strikers from the plant, but they were driven off by the sit-downers and by pickets outside the plant, who used fire hoses, automobile door hinges, bottles, stones, pieces of pavement, and assorted missiles as weapons. As the police retreated, they fired pistols and riot guns into the ranks of their pursuers. Fourteen strikers and strike sympathizers were wounded in the affray, thirteen of them by gunshot. Nine policemen, Sheriff Wolcott, and a deputy sheriff were also injured, all but one of them by flying missiles. "It was like a war or revolution," a union photographer who witnessed the scene recalled, "with broken glass and lumps of coal and hinges from Chevrolets, and a neon sign . . . on an overpass that said in flashes—Safety—Today—Tomorrow—Always."[34]

At about midnight on January 11 Governor Murphy left for Flint to appraise the situation. Flint officials informed him that they wanted the National Guard and State Police sent to the city. When the governor asked that this be put in writing, Mayor Bradshaw and Wolcott provided him with a handwritten note stating that "a serious situation" had developed in Flint endangering life and property, that local law enforcement agencies could not cope with the problem, and that the Guard and State Police were required to enforce law and order. Responding to the request, Murphy ordered four Guard units to Flint and instructed the State Police to be prepared to support local authorities. He also requested GM not to deny heat, water, or food to the strikers in the interest of the public health and because "such moves would only befuddle the already complicated situation."[35]

In statements on January 12 and 13 Murphy explained that neither party to the dispute would be permitted "by recourse to force and violence . . . to add public terror to the existing economic demonstration." The state, he indicated, had not wished to "*countenance the unlawful seizure of private property*" but had previously refrained from taking "strong measures" because it hoped that there would be an amicable settlement. Emphasizing that "the public peace and safety" were "paramount" and that "the public authority must prevail at all costs," Murphy stated that the troops would be used "only to protect the public interest and preserve peace and order" and that "[u]nder no circumstances" would they "take sides." He privately informed both Travis and Lewis that the troops would protect the strikers inside and outside the plants and would prevent the ejection of the sit-downers by local authorities.[36]

In addition to sending in the National Guard, Murphy on January 12 also sought to deal with a potentially dangerous problem created when Flint municipal court judges, with the approval of Genesee County's prosecuting attorney, Joseph R. Joseph, issued three hundred John Doe warrants authorizing the arrest of Fisher Body No. 2 strikers on the charge of kidnapping GM plant guards, malicious destruction of property, felonious assault, and criminal syndicalism. Since the warrants authorized the police, in Germer's words, to "pick up and arrest anybody and everybody," strike leaders were understandably concerned. Murphy, knowing from his experience as a criminal court judge that John Doe warrants were subject to abuse and concerned lest their use "provoke the sort of condition we are attempting to prevent," asked Joseph to hold the warrants in abeyance. He indicated, furthermore, that neither the National Guard nor the State Police would be permitted to serve the warrants without the governor's consent. Joseph, who would have needed the aid of the state to make large-scale arrests in Flint, reluctantly complied with Murphy's request.[37]

The intervention of state militia in labor disputes had in the past all too often weighted the scales of victory against strikers, but matters were to be different this time. Murphy kept a tight leash on the Guard and State Police throughout the period of their duty in Flint, and both Colonel Joseph H. Lewis, in command of the Guard, and Oscar G. Olander, the commissioner of the State Police, impressed upon their men that they must remain neutral. Since the troops were not used to eject the strikers but to preserve the status quo in Flint, it appeared to Kemp that public authority was being employed to protect "the private force . . . being unlawfully employed" in Flint and to "virtually force public picketing and unionization on employers" rather than to protect GM in the use of its property and to protect those employees who wished to work. Knudsen, however, stated that he did not want the Guard to evict the strikers, and GM for the time being had abandoned its efforts to secure a court injunction ordering the strikers to evacuate the company's property.[38]

On the same day that he dispatched the Guard to Flint, Murphy formally invited GM and the UAW to confer with him on January 14, "without condition or prejudice, in an effort to find a basis of agreement, tentative or otherwise, that . . . [would] avoid the possibility of further disorders and permit early resumption of work." Both sides accepted the invitation, GM drawing a distinction between its willingness to meet with the union to discuss the evacuation of its plants and its continued unwillingness to discuss the union's January 4 demands while its plants remained occupied by strikers. When

Knudsen, Donaldson Brown, and John T. Smith of GM met with union negotiators in Murphy's office in Lansing, it was the first time that the management and union high commands had met face to face since the initiation of the sit-down in the Cleveland Fisher Body plant. In the discussions that ensued, GM and UAW representatives conferred directly with one another for part of the time; for the remainder of the time they met in separate offices, with Murphy "taking the proposals and concessions of one to the other and then returning with compromises or suggestions."[39]

Shortly after 3:00 A.M. on January 15 Murphy, his face showing the strain of the prolonged discussions that had begun thirteen hours earlier, his voice hoarse, announced that the negotiators had "arrived at a peace." The terms of the agreement took the form of a letter from the GM negotiators to Murphy stating that since the UAW had agreed to evacuate the Fisher Body plants in Flint, the Cadillac and Fleetwood plants in Detroit, and the Guide Lamp plant in Anderson, Indiana, before January 18, GM would meet with the union on that date to bargain on its January 4 demands. Negotiations were to continue until an agreement had been reached, but the talks could be broken off by either side after fifteen days if no settlement had been effected. GM stated that it would continue its policy of nondiscrimination against unionists and that, during the period of the negotiations, it would not resume operations in the evacuated plants and would not remove "any dies, tools, machinery, material (except for export trade) or equipment." GM, by the terms of the agreement, did not yield on the issue of representation, but it had retreated on the matter of a general conference with the UAW. On the other hand, the UAW, despite CIO advice not to evacuate the plants it held until negotiations on the January 4 demands had been completed, surrendered its strongest weapon, the occupation of company plants, in return for a conference with GM and a GM guarantee not to operate the evacuated plants for a specified period.[40]

Observers accorded the chief credit for the truce to Governor Murphy. The pro-GM *Flint Journal*, which editorialized that Murphy had "done the state a great service," reported that he had received "the greatest flow of congratulatory messages" ever received by a Michigan governor in a comparable period of time. Chrysler's B. E. Hutchinson thought that Murphy had done "an extraordinarily good job in a most difficult situation," and the *Detroit News* congratulated the governor for his "dogged insistence on the priority of the public interest." "However the play ends," the Republican *Battle Creek Enquirer and Evening News* asserted, "Governor Murphy has displayed qualities of leadership and statesmanship during the first act.''[41]

In accordance with the Lansing agreement, the sit-down strikers evacuated the Cadillac, Fleetwood, and Guide Lamp plants on January 16. Shortly before the strikers were to evacuate the Flint Fisher Body plants on January 17, however, the UAW learned of a Knudsen telegram expressing his willingness to meet with the Flint Alliance for the Security of Our Jobs, Our Homes, and Our Country, an organization composed primarily of ''loyal'' GM employees that had been launched on January 7 and that the UAW viewed as a GM-inspired company union. [42] When Brophy was apprised of the wire, he realized that the UAW had been presented with a golden opportunity ''to get rid of the absurd preliminary agreement,'' the grounds being that GM, by agreeing to meet with the Flint Alliance, had, in effect, eliminated as a subject for negotiation the union's demand that it be the sole bargaining agency for GM employees. Brophy persuaded Martin to call off the scheduled evacuation of the Flint plants, a decision that brought the Lansing truce to an end despite Murphy's effort to induce Knudsen to cancel his arrangements with the Flint Alliance.[43]

Following the collapse of the Lansing truce, Frances Perkins took the lead in seeking to terminate the GM strike. She attempted to bring Sloan and Lewis together on the assumption that they were ''the real principals'' in the dispute, but she was unable at any time to persuade the GM president to meet with the CIO chairman. Perhaps, said Lewis, taunting his adversary, ''he feels his intellectual inferiority to me.'' The principal idea that Perkins explored with Sloan, according to her recollection, was an arrangement whereby GM would agree to negotiate with the UAW on behalf of its members rather than as the sole bargaining agency for GM workers. Walter Chrysler, to whom Myron Taylor of United States Steel had suggested the peace formula, brought this idea to the secretary of labor's attention, and she then presented it to Sloan. When he learned that United States Steel believed that it could '' 'endure' '' such an arrangement, he seemed willing to accept it for GM, but, according to Perkins, he then changed his mind.

If Perkins's recollection is correct, both Sloan and she were confused as to the nature of the representation issue at stake in the strike. GM was perfectly willing to meet with the UAW as the representative of UAW members only and, as the Lansing agreement indicated, was by that time even willing to do so at the summit—it is hard to believe that Sloan was unaware of this—but the procedure was unacceptable to the UAW. It is likely that what was actually being discussed in Washington was not what Perkins recalled but an arrangement whereby GM, although not granting the UAW exclusive bargaining rights, would provide certain guarantees that the corporation would not attempt to undermine the union in its plants. It may be that this is what Sloan first agreed to and then rejected.[44]

Murphy, who assisted Perkins in her mediation efforts, made several proposals to end the strike. Speaking to Lewis on January 19, the governor offered to surround the Fisher Body plants with the National Guard if the strikers would leave the two factories, which was a variant of the January 15 agreement. Lewis, however, refused to surrender his strongest bargaining weapon without a major concession from the company. Murphy and Perkins also proposed some kind of election plan as a means of ending the strike, but Sloan and Lewis, for different reasons, rejected a solution along these lines. They also rejected a Murphy proposal that the dispute be arbitrated, perhaps by three Michigan "religious leaders." "The realists in the background of this struggle and who are the controlling factors in it," the governor wrote an acquaintance, "drive their bargains hard, and are not enthused about the help of spiritual counsellors in the name of brotherhood and religion. But that doesn't mean they are right."[45]

Both Lewis and Sloan were publicly rebuked by the Roosevelt administration during the Washington talks of late January. In a press conference of January 21 Lewis indicated that he expected the administration to side with its supporters in the strike, not with its enemies. "We have advised the administration," he declared in his inimitable prose style, "that for six months the economic royalists represented by General Motors contributed their money and used their energy to drive this administration out of power. The administration asked labor for help to repel this attack and labor gave its help. The workers of this country expect the administration to help the workers in every legal way, and to support the auto workers in General Motors plants." When questioned about these remarks the next day, the president replied, "I think that, in the interests of peace, there come moments when statements, conversations and headlines are not in order."[46]

After Sloan refused an official invitation from Perkins to meet with Lewis and UAW representatives, the president called this "a very unfortunate decision," and an angry Perkins accused Sloan of shirking his moral responsibility and ignoring the public interest. Sloan made a secret visit to Washington on January 29 and, as Perkins understood, agreed to meet with Lewis and Sidney Hillman in a conference that Murphy would arrange. Sloan, however, phoned her that night to say that he had changed his mind. Furious, Perkins told Sloan that he was " 'a scoundrel and a skunk . . . a rotter . . . a quitter,' " that he had betrayed his government and deceived her, and that he would go to hell when he died. Sloan replied that he was worth $70 million and that she could not, therefore, speak to him in that way. Sloan, Perkins concluded, was "a frustrated and frightened personality" who was unable to cope with the problem presented by the sit-down strike. "It seems," Perkins ruefully but correctly told a reporter who reached her in the early hours of January 30, "that all of my work has gone to waste."[47]

Sloan's intransigence may have reflected a belief that the UAW would soon have to abandon its strike. About forty thousand Chevrolet workers, eleven thousand of them in Flint, returned to their jobs without incident on January 27, and there were indications that other nonunion auto workers idled by the strike were increasingly anxious to resume their employment. GM supplemented its back-to-work movement by going into Judge Paul V. Gadola's court in Flint on January 28 in quest of a new injunction. The judge ordered the UAW to appear in his courtroom on February 1 to show cause why the injunction should not be issued.[48]

As January drew to a close, the union leadership in Flint sensed that the morale of the strikers was beginning to sag and that the strike seemed to be "bogging down." "If we stand still," they thought, "we're through."[49] To regain the offensive, the strike leadership in Flint devised a daring plan to capture the strategic Chevrolet No. 4 plant, and they executed their plan to perfection on February 1. The operation began when unionists in the relatively unimportant Chevrolet No. 9 plant initiated what appeared to be a sit-down strike. Since the union had arranged for the Chevrolet management to receive advance information that a sit-down would occur in the plant, the company had concentrated two hundred plant police in the personnel building just east of the No. 9 plant. When the fracas began in No. 9, they rushed into the plant, but while they were subduing the apparent strikers inside the plant, unionists in Chevrolet No. 4, reinforced by comrades coming from nearby Chevrolet No. 6 and by unionists from outside, seized Chevrolet No. 4.[50] The union had regained the initiative, and the turning point of the strike had been reached. "We have the key plant of the G.M. and the eyes of the world are looking at us," a proud Chevrolet No. 4 striker wrote his wife. "We shure done a thing that G.M. said never could be done. . . ."[51]

The UAW's capture of Chevrolet No. 4 compelled Murphy to consider once again how the Michigan Guard should be deployed to preserve public order in Flint. While the battle was underway, the governor received conflicting information from the scene, and not until the strikers had gained control of Chevrolet No. 4 did both Mayor Bradshaw and Sheriff Wolcott agree that local authorities could no longer cope with the situation. When they so advised Murphy, he directed the state's adjutant general "to take immediate and effective steps to bring the situation under the control of the public authorities, suppress and prevent any breach of the peace, and ensure that the laws of the state are faithfully executed." The principal action taken by the Guard, on the instructions of the governor, was to establish a cordon guard (blockade) around Chevrolet and Fisher Body No. 2, whose location made it a part of the Chevrolet complex, to prevent anyone from entering the area, and to deny supplies of any kind, including food, to the occupants of the No. 4 plant. Additional Guardsmen were sent to Flint to reinforce the troops already there, the total number reaching 3,454 by February 7, about two-thirds of the Guard's entire complement.[52]

Murphy had decided to shut off the food supply to Chevrolet No. 4 because the Guard had advised him that outsiders had assisted materially in the capture of the plant and that a sizeable number of them remained in the factory. Murphy regarded the infiltration of plants by outsiders as "morally repulsive," a " 'wicked thing' " that could not be justified even by the UAW's right-to-one's-job thesis, and he did not wish to condone the practice by allowing food to pass through the Guard lines. Some time during the morning of February 2 Brophy called the governor and "berated" him for his action. " 'What do you want to do,' " Brophy asked, " 'starve to death poor workers who are only seeking their lawful rights?' " Murphy agreed to lift the food blockade once all nonemployees had left the factory. When the governor was officially informed later in the day that the outsiders had departed and that "practically all" the men inside the plant were "regular employees," he honored his pledge. The Guard continued to maintain its blockade of the area, but it made no attempt to eject the strikers or to deny them access to food.[53]

When Brophy telephoned Murphy after the food blockade had been lifted, the governor assured the CIO director, "The military will never be used against you. I'd leave my office first."[54] Brophy must have been aware that almost any governor but Murphy would have reacted to the union offensive of February 1 by ordering the ejection of the strikers from the No. 4 plant. In ordering the blockade of the

Chevrolet-Fisher No. 2 zone, Murphy had taken the least harmful action from the union's point of view that could have been expected in view of the riotous events of that day.

February 1, 1937, was a day of great tension in Flint both because of the expansion of the strike and because it was the day that Judge Gadola held a hearing to determine if he should grant the GM petition for an injunction against the strikers. The judge issued his opinion the next day, granting the preliminary mandatory injunction the corporation had requested. He ordered the UAW officers, the sit-downers, their attorneys, and their "agents" to evacuate the Fisher Body plants (he said that he would add Chevrolet No. 4 if the company requested this), not to picket or loiter near the plants, and not to prevent nonstrikers from working by "threats, personal violence, intimidation or any other unlawful means." He specified that the plants were to be evacuated by 3:00 P.M. on February 3 and that a penalty of $15 million would be levied upon the "lands, goods and chattels" of the defendants if they failed to comply with the injunction ("If the judge can get fifteen million bucks from us, he's welcome to it," a Fisher No. 1 sit-downer reportedly remarked).[55]

Sheriff Wolcott read the injunction to the sit-downers in the two Fisher Body plants in the early evening of February 2. The strike leadership decided to hold firm and to look to Murphy to forestall enforcement of the injunction. "Governor," the No. 2 strikers declared in one of two telegrams reaching Murphy from the Fisher Body plants, "we have decided to stay in the plant. We have no illusions about the sacrifices which this decision will entail. We fully expect that if a violent effort is made to oust us many of us will be killed and we take this means of making it known to our wives, to our children, to the people of the state of Michigan and of the country that if this result follows from the attempt to eject us you are the one who must be held responsible for our deaths." Ostensibly drafted by "those who are about to die," to quote Brophy's diary entry for February 2, the wires were more likely composed by UAW attorneys and the editor of the *Flint Auto Worker*, who were aware of Murphy's abhorrence of bloodshed and who thought that the bravado of the wires was precisely what was required to dissuade the governor from using force to implement the injunction.[56]

Wednesday, February 3, 1937, the day the injunction went into effect, was, in the opinion of a Detroit reporter, "the wildest day in Flint's history." It was the day when the Flint strike came closest to erupting into civil war. Early in the morning the roads leading to Flint were filled with vehicles carrying UAW members and sympathizers from Detroit, Toledo, and elsewhere to the scene of the strike. As the 3:00 P.M. zero hour approached, an enormous crowd of three thousand pickets and seven thousand spectators gathered outside Fisher Body No. 1. In "one of the most amazing labor demonstrations ever seen in America," singing pickets carrying "clubs, pieces of pipe, claw hammers, iron bars, sod cutters, spades," clothes trees, and auto body parts circled the plant, while the sit-downers leaned out of the factory windows to join in the singing and cheering and union sound cars "bombarded all ears." Strikers and strike sympathizers spilled over onto Saginaw Street, the city's principal artery on which the plant fronted, and the strikers directed such traffic as could get through. Chief of Police Wills drove up to the plant at one point but was chased away, "running for his life." When word came at about 3:00 P.M. that neither the sheriff nor the Guard would seek to eject the sit-downers—Wolcott and Gadola explained that no action could be taken until GM sought a writ of attachment against the sit-downers—about one thousand demonstrators broke away from the crowd in front of No. 1 and staged an auto parade through downtown Flint, honking their horns, shouting as they drove, and ignoring traffic regulations. There were reports of drinking by the demonstrators and of the beating and terrorization of Flint citizens.[57]

To worried middle-class citizens of Flint, the wild confusion of February 3 signaled the complete breakdown of law and order in the city and the arrival of mob rule. City Manager Barringer asked the Guard to break up the demonstration in front of Fisher No. 1 but was turned down by Colonel Lewis. The Guard commander was probably acting on instructions from Murphy, who thought that to comply with the request would "stir up things" and would interfere with the negotiations that had begun that day. Wolcott and Bradshaw wanted the State Police to disperse the crowd or at least to direct traffic in front of the plant, but their calls for help were also turned aside. Barringer decided under these circumstances to organize a five-hundred-man " 'army of our own' " in the form of a special police reserve. His intention was to use the reserve to eject the sit-downers from Fisher No. 1. ". . . we are going down there shooting," he declared. "The strikers have taken over this town and we are going to take it back."[58]

There was "near panic" in Flint when word spread that the city government was mobilizing a civilian police reserve that might attempt to eject the strikers. Knudsen, Murphy, and Colonel Lewis, however, interceded to quiet the situation, and Lewis helped to negotiate a peace treaty between the city government and the UAW.

The city agreed to "demobilize" the reserve police force, while the UAW agreed to keep its members from congregating in numbers that would create a traffic hazard or be "detrimental" to the enforcement of law and order and also to refrain from carrying "sundry pieces of wood and missiles."[59]

Events in Flint beginning with the seizure of Chevrolet No. 4 formed the backdrop for negotiations to settle the strike that were resumed in Detroit on February 3. In a call to Murphy on February 2, Perkins requested him to arrange a conference between Knudsen and John L. Lewis, already on his way to Detroit. Murphy learned that GM would agree to such a conference only if requested to do so by the president, and Roosevelt, still not wishing to become directly involved in the negotiations, authorized the governor to put the request to GM in these terms. "The President wants you to do it," Perkins told Murphy. "He doesn't want a conference in Washington and isn't going to have one."[60]

Negotiations between the UAW, represented by Martin, Lewis, and Lee Pressman, the CIO's general counsel, and the GM team of Knudsen, Brown, and Smith were conducted in cramped quarters in the Recorder's Court building in Detroit. On some occasions the two sides met together, but most of the time Murphy, assisted by James F. Dewey, carried proposals back and forth between the negotiators. "The governor," Martin declared, "is jumping around like a jack rabbit." Lewis replaced Martin with Mortimer after a few days because the strain of the negotiations had begun to tell on the unstable UAW president.[61]

In the initial days of the Detroit talks the UAW retreated from its demand that it be recognized as the exclusive bargaining agency for all GM workers and asked instead that it be accorded this privilege only in the twenty, later seventeen, plants that it claimed were on strike. GM, as expected, stated that it would recognize the union in the struck plants as the bargaining agency for its members, not as the sole bargaining agency, but it was now willing to assure the UAW in various ways that it would not seek to undermine the union's position in these plants.[62]

Murphy concluded that hope for a settlement lay in a formula that would accord the union the degree of recognition and the status in the struck plants that GM had indicated it was willing to concede but that deferred a decision on the thorny question of exclusive representation for six months, at which time it would be resolved by collective bargaining, the examination of union membership cards, or a board appointed by the president. Since Roosevelt had advised

Murphy that he was willing to speak to Knudsen and Lewis, the governor asked Perkins, with whom he was in daily communication, to request the president to express to the two men his approval of the Murphy peace formula. Roosevelt could tell Lewis, Murphy advised, that, since the plan would effectively give the UAW exclusive representation, he would yield nothing in accepting it. Murphy was probably assuming that the UAW would be able to win a majority in the struck plants during the six-month period and that GM would then have to accord it exclusive bargaining rights. On the basis of her conversation with Murphy, Perkins prepared a memorandum for the president to use in speaking to Lewis and Knudsen. It provided, however, for a truce period of only four months and did not specify how the issue of representation was to be resolved at the end of the truce period. Roosevelt spoke to Knudsen and Lewis by phone on February 6, but Lewis seems to have insisted on an immediate grant of exclusive representation.[63]

On that same day, February 6—we do not know whether it was before or after the president spoke to Knudsen—GM handed Murphy a confidential letter in which it agreed that, for a period of ninety days after a basic agreement with the UAW went into effect, it would not bargain with any other organization in the struck plants regarding matters of general corporation policy without first gaining Murphy's sanction for the procedure. This was a variant of a plan that Roosevelt had earlier suggested to Murphy, but Lewis responded that he would accept a ninety-day agreement only if it specifically granted the UAW exclusive representation. Although Murphy supported Lewis in this demand, GM would not agree to it. The next day, February 7, Murphy suggested to Perkins that the president ask Lewis to accept the GM proposal, and it is possible that the president did so. On the evening of the same day Murphy had a ''grand talk'' with Lewis and persuaded him to agree to the GM proposal if the truce were extended to six months. Murphy undoubtedly pointed out to Lewis that the union had already gained a good deal in the dispute because of the ''sympathetic government'' in both Washington and Lansing and that, since GM would not grant exclusive representation in so many words, he should content himself with the concession of the substance of the UAW's principal strike demand.[64]

Regarding the six-month peace formula as ''the best way out yet,'' Murphy told Assistant Secretary of Labor Edward F. McGrady that ''we ought to crowd it through.'' The governor explained that the proposal took the ''heat'' off Washington and placed the responsibility on him as the court of last resort. He therefore felt justified, no doubt, in asking for administration support in persuading GM to accept the plan. Since GM negotiators in Detroit were apparently unwilling to make the concession on their own, Murphy requested Perkins to speak to Sloan or, better still, to have the president do so. Murphy may have said that, if the president did not wish to do so, his secretary, Marvin McIntyre, should "insist on it at the request of the president" since Knudsen had said, "if the president told them they would do it." McIntyre telephoned Knudsen shortly thereafter, but he was either unwilling or unable to agree to the longer truce period. When McIntyre reported this to Murphy, he said, "The Boss has to get in touch with Sloane [sic] or the Duponts—tell them this is okay. This strike has got to go through tonight or we are done." The "Boss" did not himself follow the course that Murphy had recommended, but the administration did come to the governor's assistance within the next thirty-six hours. On February 9 Secretary of Commerce Daniel Roper had "a very long conversation" with Donaldson Brown, and the same day or the next morning, at Roper's request and in response to Perkins's desire that the aid of an "outstanding" business leader who knew Brown should also be enlisted, S. Clay Williams, the chairman of the board of the R. J. Reynolds Tobacco Company, talked with both Sloan and Brown.[65]

Although the strike talks appeared to be near collapse during prolonged, heated negotiations on February 8, discussions resumed the next day. When the two sides, however, agreed to disagree once again, a discouraged and weary Murphy decided to take a step that he had been contemplating for several days: he would have to clarify to Lewis the obligations of the state's chief executive with regard to law enforcement. Murphy had at no time been indifferent to the issue of legality and law enforcement in the strike, but it was only when the sit-down strikers decided to defy the Gadola injunction that the responsibility to act was clearly thrust on the governor. Hoping that GM would be satisfied with the "moral effect" of the injunction, he had sought to persuade company negotiators to delay seeking a writ of attachment. GM lawyers, however, went into Gadola's court on the morning of February 5 and, on the basis of an affidavit by the plant manager of Fisher Body Nos. 1 and 2 that the injunction had been violated, secured a writ commanding the sheriff "to attach the bodies" of all the sit-downers in the No. 1 and 2 plants, their "confederates" who were picketing, and UAW local and international officers.[66]

Shortly after Gadola issued the writ, Murphy received a wire from Wolcott asking whether the governor would authorize the use of the

National Guard to execute the writ or whether it would be necessary for the sheriff to swear in deputies to enforce the order. Murphy's initial reaction has been preserved in his handwritten scrawl on the face of the Wolcott wire. "Kemp," the governor wrote, "The conference is in session. Its deliberations should not be embarrassed or interferred [*sic*] with. Yet I should not say no [to] the sheriff. Perhaps it is best for him to proceed with the deputies first. What is the opinion of [Adjutant General] Col. Bersey and yourself?"

Perturbed that GM had sought the writ while the conference was in session, thus risking its breakup, Murphy told Perkins that GM had made a "serious mistake" and seemed to be trying to "embarrass" him and put him "in a bad position." Since he wished to be "obedient to the court" and at the same time to keep the strike talks going, Murphy decided that same day to prepare a law-and-order letter to Lewis and Martin but to accept neither of the alternatives posed to him by Wolcott as the means of enforcing the writ. He was not prepared to use the Guard for this purpose, and he had second thoughts about permitting the sheriff to move on the plants with a motley array of deputies. Instead, Murphy authorized the Guard, if it deemed the action necessary, to place a cordon guard around Fisher No. 1, as it already had around Fisher No. 2 and Chevrolet, to prevent the sheriff from attacking the plant. This proved to be unnecessary, however, since Wolcott, a loyal Democrat who had no desire to oppose the governor and who wished to avoid bloodshed and the imposition of martial law in Flint, agreed to Murphy's request to take no action on the writ unless advised to do so by the governor.[67]

Murphy counseled delay in part because he believed that enforcement of the writ would impede the chances for a settlement that he believed imminent. He was also influenced by his overwhelming desire to avoid the shedding of blood, which he feared would result from an effort to implement the court order. The writ of attachment, strictly speaking, did not order the ejection of the strikers but rather their arrest and transportation to Gadola's court to answer the contempt charge. Since Murphy, however, assumed that the strikers would resist arrest, which seems correct,[68] he was convinced that enforcement of the order would lead to violence and bloodshed. "I am not going to do it," he said to an Ann Arbor friend. "I'm not going down in history as 'Bloody Murphy.' If I sent those soldiers right in on the men there'd be no telling how many would be killed. It would be inconsistent with everything I have ever stood for in my whole life."[69]

Murphy may also have had some reservations about the National Guard's ability to subdue the sit-downers in the face of the expected resistance. The plants were large and well defended, and the militia was made up of youngsters without previous experience in riot duty and with little stomach for an assignment that might involve the shooting of fellow citizens. " '. . . what happens if we try to use the National Guard and they don't win?' " Murphy asked a Detroit reporter. After seeing the militia with his own eyes, the same reporter concluded that "the National Guard needed somebody to protect them." Even a GM official who was extremely bitter about Murphy's refusal to use the Guard to evacuate the occupied Flint plants thought the Guardsmen "too young and untrained" for the job.[70]

Unbeknownst to those who later criticized Murphy for delaying the enforcement of a court order, the military staff in Flint, impressed with the difficulty of apprehending and taking to court the several thousand persons inside and outside the plants against whom the court order was directed, was "quite unanimous" in advising the governor to delay using the Guard to enforce the writ. Disinclined to undertake a direct assault on the plants, the Guard devised an alternative strategy to secure the evacuation of the sit-downers should that prove necessary, namely, to place a cordon guard around Fisher Body No. 1 similar to the guard placed around Fisher No. 2 and Chevrolet and then, if so ordered, to secure the ouster of the strikers by denying them the necessities of life. Had the Guard carried out this plan, the strikers would have been forced to leave the occupied plants in short order. There were no significant reserves of food in Chevrolet No. 4 and Fisher No. 2, and the food stored in the No. 1 plant could have sustained the strikers there for only a week or so. Evacuation of the plants would not in itself have ended the strike, but the advantage in the dispute would certainly have passed to GM.[71]

Murphy had been assuming until he received the Guard plan that the enforcement of the court order meant the ejection of the sit-down strikers by force. He had, to be sure, denied food briefly to the occupants of Chevrolet No. 4, but he had done so only because out-siders had seized the plant. It may be that Murphy had privately and publicly equated enforcement of the writ with bloodshed because he could then justify to himself and others his reluctance to comply with the court order without delay. It undoubtedly would have been more difficult for him to explain a refusal to adopt the strategy of a food blockade, but even doctrinaire supporters of law and order were not advocating this course, and there is nothing in the record to suggest that Murphy had considered this possibility until the Guard on

February 8 recommended this course of action should he decide to enforce the court order.

As many Americans saw it, public officials had the responsibility of enforcing the law immediately and regardless of cost; otherwise the government would be one of men rather than of law. This, however, was not Murphy's view. The " 'faithful execution' " of the law that was required of him, he later told a United States Senate subcommittee in explaining, perhaps rationalizing, his conduct in the strike, included "wise administration of the law," not simply its "literal instantaneous application at any cost." He was faced, as he saw it, with "a difficult, practical question," not simply a problem of law enforcement. He was therefore justified, he contended, in exercising some discretion with regard to the manner in which he responded to the court order.[72] For six days the writ of attachment remained in abeyance, and Murphy, in effect, ranged the state on the side of the strikers, but the strike was settled in the meantime without the loss of a single life.

Murphy's delay in enforcing the writ of attachment was not without precedent, and even Gadola conceded that the sheriff possessed "the authority to wait indefinitely before serving it." Commenting in 1938 on the delay, Wolcott agreed that there was "no hurry about it especially when such great issues were at stake." Sheriffs in Michigan and elsewhere, after all, regularly delayed the execution of writs of attachment issued after property had been foreclosed or judgments made against merchants. "If the Governor is to be accused of obstructing justice," a member of the Michigan Parole Board wrote George Murphy, "then every sheriff and public officer might be accused of the same thing."[73]

Although Murphy delayed presenting his law-and-order letter to Lewis until February 9, he several times requested the CIO head to pull the men out of the plants since the sit-down was illegal. Lewis, however, had replied that it would take "bayonets" to get the men out of the plants. When Murphy said he had no intention of using bayonets, Lewis, if we are to believe what he told Heber Blankenhorn just after the strike, responded, " 'Then why bellyache to me about my getting those boys out to save you?' "[74]

When Murphy told Dewey on February 7 that he could not delay much longer explaining to Lewis that, as governor, he must enforce the law, the conciliator counselled him to discuss the matter with Roosevelt. Murphy phoned Roosevelt that night saying that he hoped to keep the conference going but that he must make clear his responsibility to "uphold the existing laws of the state." " 'You are absolutely right,' " Roosevelt said, " 'you are justified in doing that—go right ahead with it.' " When Congressman Andrew Transue, whose district included Flint, told Murphy the next evening that there was no support in Congress for "this sit-down business," Murphy responded, "alright [sic], Andy, I'll do something on it tonight." The letter to Lewis and Martin was completed that evening, but when Lewis accepted the GM proposal of February 6 provided it was extended to six months, Murphy decided to withhold the letter.

Since the Lewis concession did not break the strike stalemate, Murphy took Lewis aside on the night of February 9 and read him the law-and-order letter. The governor informed Lewis that he wished to make clear in writing, as he had "done verbally on several occasions," his position as chief executive of Michigan. It was still his hope that the strike would be settled by negotiation, but since the parties had thus far been unable to reach an agreement, "the time . . . [had] come for all concerned to comply fully with the decision and order of the court and take necessary steps to restore possession of the occupied plants to their rightful owners." It was his duty "to demand and require" obedience to the law and court orders, and he would be faithful to this obligation.[75]

The nature and significance of the Murphy letter to Lewis have been misrepresented by both the Murphy and Lewis camps. Murphy later referred to "that order" as "the turning point" in the strike. He had told Lewis, Murphy said, that if a settlement were not immediately reached, he would read the letter to the conferees the next morning and also make it public. The result, he claimed, was that terms were agreed upon a little more than twenty-four hours later. A Detroit newspaperman close to Murphy claimed that the governor "grabbed Lewis by the coat collar, and in no uncertain terms told him that the men would get out of the plants 'or else.' " George Murphy stated in an interview that Lewis had said to Frank after the letter had been read, "Governor—you win." Lewis took to his bed the next day, ill with the grippe, but some of those who attached great significance to the letter claimed that Lewis, a former coal miner prone to respiratory ailments, "was not sick. He was knocked out by Murphy's ultimatum."[76] The fact of the matter, though, is that Lewis did not alter his position in the slightest as the result of the February 9 letter. He had insisted on a six-month truce before the letter was read to him, and he continued to insist on a six-month truce after the letter had been read. It was GM, not Lewis, that yielded the next day.

The Lewis version of what occurred in the eyebrow-to-eyebrow confrontation with Murphy on February 9 is more dramatic than the Murphy version. As Lewis told the story in increasingly dramatic accounts to Heber Blankenhorn just after the strike, the UAW convention in 1940, and Saul Alinsky, probably also in 1940, the CIO leader said to the governor (Blankenhorn version), " 'You talk of the law. It is not law, it is General Motors law.... That is General Motors' strikebreaking law.' " Lewis claimed that he had expressed surprise that Murphy should advise obedience to the law when he had supported the Irish rebellion against England, his father had been imprisoned for Fenian activity, and his grandfather had been hanged—he had not—as a revolutionary. As for the warning in the letter, Lewis told the UAW delegates that he had said to Murphy, " 'I do not doubt your ability to call out your soldiers and shoot the members of our union out of those plants, but let me say that when you issue that order I shall leave this conference and I shall enter one of those plants with my own people. (Applause.) ... And the militia will have the pleasure of shooting me out of the plants with you [them?].' The order was not executed." As Alinsky tells the story, Lewis made an even more impassioned reply to Murphy than is presented in the UAW convention version ("as my body falls from the window to the ground, you listen to the voice of your grandfather as he whispers in your ear, 'Frank, are you sure you are doing the right thing?' "), and then Murphy, "white and shaking, seized the order from Lewis and tore out of the room." In the Blankenhorn version, the one closest to the event, Lewis says nothing about going into the plants himself but offers Murphy a choice of bayonets to use against the strikers—" 'the broad double blade or the four-sided French style? I believe the square style makes a bigger hole and you can turn it around inside a man.' "[77]

Just what Lewis said to Murphy we do not know, but although the various accounts we have may be nothing but retrospective fiction, they are correct insofar as they indicate that Lewis did not yield to an alleged Murphy ultimatum. However, the various Lewis versions of the affair, like most other treatments of the episode, are based on the presumption that Murphy was delivering a veiled threat to use troops to eject the strikers from the Flint plants by force. Actually, Murphy carefully avoided saying anything of this sort, and it is almost certain that he had no intention of following this course. The likelihood is that, following the advice of the military, he intended to place a guard around Fisher No. 1, as he already had around the other two occupied Flint plants, and then, if the negotiations broke down, to deny the occupants the necessities of life and thus compel their evacuation of the plants. The only other means of securing the evacuation of the plants that Murphy had considered was to capitalize on his immense prestige with the strikers by making a personal visit to the plants—he requested the union to invite him to do so—to ask the men to leave the plants because the law required this.[78] There is, at all events, no basis in fact for the assumption that Lewis's rhetoric and threats caused Murphy to abandon plans to shoot or bayonet the strikers out of the plants.

Allegedly because he did not want to "jeopardize" the consummation of a settlement by "disturbing" either party represented at the strike conference, Murphy did not make his letter known to the GM negotiators the next day. The contents of the document, as it turned out, were not revealed until January 13, 1939, when Murphy submitted a copy of the famous letter to a United States Senate subcommittee considering his nomination to be attorney general of the United States. Murphy claimed that he had remained silent about the matter while still governor because he had not wished to impair his "usefulness" as a mediator of the numerous labor disputes that he had helped resolve. Walter Lippmann believed that Murphy was right not to have used force when a settlement was near but wrong to have concealed the letter for so long since he should have left no doubt where he stood on the matter of law enforcement. Murphy, Lippmann thought, had chosen not to reveal the letter because he regarded it as "politically expedient" to appear to be an "unyielding partisan of labor."[79]

There is undoubtedly some truth in what Murphy and Lippmann both said about the February 9 letter. Murphy, however, may have remained silent about the letter for so long because it had not been a major factor in the outcome of the strike but rather was primarily a document for the record, a document that Murphy could cite at a later time as evidence of his belief in the sanctity of the law. Had Murphy used the letter just after the strike to support a claim that he had caused Lewis to capitulate, he knew that he would have been running the risk of instant and unanswerable repudiation.

The negotiations that finally brought the strike to an end began on the morning of February 10 and continued until 2:35 A.M. on February 11.[80] The position of GM had probably been weakened by that time as the result of testimony before the La Follette Committee on February 8 and 9 that linked the corporation to Pinkerton's National Detective Agency and labor espionage. A Pinkerton operative testified that he had visited Alexandria, Virginia, where Lewis lived, to gather information about the CIO and that GM had been billed for the trip; and other Pinkerton operatives revealed that when Assistant Secretary of Labor McGrady had been in Toledo in April 1935 seeking to mediate the Toledo Chevrolet strike, they had taken a hotel room next to his in an effort to listen in on his conversations. In his theatrical manner, Lewis taunted the GM negotiators with this information.[81]

The most important issues to be resolved in the final strike talks were the length of the period during which the UAW would enjoy a privileged position in the struck plants and the nature of that position. GM, as Brown had explained to Roper, was by then less interested in the length of the "experiment" than in "the phraseology relating to a definition of the words 'exclusive bargaining agents' in such an experiment," and since Lewis was willing to oblige GM on "phraseology," the corporation decided to accept a six-month rather than a three-month truce period.[82]

It was probably more than the inclusion of satisfactory "phraseology" in the agreement that caused GM to yield on the question of the length of the truce period. The corporation's automotive production was approaching zero—GM produced only 151 cars in the United States during the first ten days of February—and it must have appeared to the GM negotiators, unaware of Murphy's letter to Lewis, that the sit-downers were simply not going to be dislodged from the corporation's plants in the near future and that GM's automotive production would not be resumed until the corporation reached an agreement with the UAW. GM, undoubtedly, was also responding to pressure being exerted from the White House through McIntyre, Roper, Williams, and, in a sense, Murphy. When Knudsen later asserted that "the Government . . . practically ordered" the settlement of the strike, it may well have been the president to whom he was referring.[83]

After the conferees had agreed to the precise language of the agreement, a weary Murphy announced to reporters that the strike had been settled. The signing ceremony was held in the Recorder's Court on February 11, after which the agreement was taken to Lewis's hotel room, where the ill CIO chairman signed the document with a pen that Manuel Quezon had given Murphy.[84] By the terms of the agreement, GM recognized the UAW as the bargaining agency for employees of the corporation who were members of the union. It recognized and promised not to interfere with the right of its employees to be union members and agreed that it would not discriminate against them because of their union membership or their strike activity. The company agreed to begin bargaining with the UAW on February 16 regarding the union's January 4 demands. For its part, the union promised to terminate the strike and to evacuate the plants occupied by strikers. It agreed not to strike or interfere with production pending the negotiation of an agreement and to exhaust all efforts to settle a grievance or enforce a demand before striking or interfering with production during the life of that agreement. The UAW also promised not to coerce employees to join the union or to solicit members on company premises. After the plants had been evacuated and the strike ended, GM agreed to consent to the dismissal of injunction proceedings against the union (the company had also sought an injunction in Cleveland) and, subject to court approval, to discontinue contempt proceedings that it had instituted.[85]

Even more important to the UAW than the terms of the agreement was a supplementary letter from Knudsen to Murphy in which GM, on condition that the UAW refrained from "coercion and intimidation" inside or outside GM plants to increase its membership, promised not to "inspire" activities by other worker groups that might weaken the UAW. For six months after the resumption of work, GM would not "bargain with or enter into agreements with *any other union or representative of employes on strike*" regarding matters of "general corporate policy" specified in the UAW's January 4 letter unless Murphy sanctioned such action as "justified by law, equity or justice."[86] This meant that whereas GM in the general agreement recognized the UAW as the bargaining agency for its members only, the corporation, in effect, recognized the union as the sole bargaining agency for six months in the seventeen plants designated as having been on strike, unless Murphy permitted it to bargain with other groups. The governor, it was presumed, would not sanction such bargaining if he believed that GM had stimulated the organization of the rival group or was using it to undermine the position of the UAW. The union, obviously, felt secure in leaving this decision to Murphy.

Although permitting GM to save face on the principle of exclusive representation, the February 11 strike agreement must be regarded as a victory for the UAW. "Now," an auto worker told Lewis, "we got the sons of bitches." GM had been compelled to sign its first agreement with a union, and it had agreed for the first time to recognize the international union as a party to the collective bargaining process. It had accepted the UAW contention that all its January 4 demands should be discussed at a general conference and that even strikers guilty of acts of violence should be returned to their jobs without discrimination. Although the company had insisted that the sit-down was an illegal tactic, it had agreed to the dismissal of the injunctions against the strikers. The strike, above all, had been for organizational purposes, and it had been successful in this sense also. In seventeen plants, the UAW, in effect, was given six months to become the majority union free from any concern that GM might foster a rival organization; and the concession that GM made in these plants, the official recognition of the UAW as the bargaining agent for its members in all GM plants, the corporation's promise not to discriminate against union members, and the prestige the UAW gained from its apparent defeat of "the most powerful industrial aggregation" in the United States placed the union in a favorable position to spread its organization throughout the GM domain. The results obtained in a short space of time were remarkable: the union's dues-paying membership soared from about 88,000 in February to 254,000 in April and close to 400,000 in October. The effect of the strike, Mortimer recalled, was "like a huge reservoir bursting." It "seemed to open the flood gates of organization."[87]

The strike was a victory not only for the UAW but also for the CIO and unionism in the mass production industries. "The workers," an organizer in the steel industry reported during the strike, "regard the General Motors sit-down as a test of the C.I.O. . . . They hesitate to stick out their necks. 'Wait till you win the auto strike. Then we'll join,' " they said. "Future of C.I.O. Hangs on Auto Strike Result" was the *New York Times* headline for a January 24 story on the GM strike by its able labor reporter, Louis Stark.

The CIO's *Union News Service* observed on March 1 that the effects of the GM strike continued "to spread over the labor waters like waves and ripples in the wake of a boat that is forging ahead." As if to demonstrate the accuracy of this figure of speech, the next day United States Steel, long a stronghold of the open shop, came to terms with the Steel Workers Organizing Committee without a strike. Although other factors were also involved, the management of the company, observing what had occurred in the GM strike, undoubtedly concluded that a prolonged and costly strike would be pointless if United States Steel in the end would have to make concessions analogous to those GM felt compelled to make. Myron Taylor had told Frances Perkins during the GM strike that its outcome would be important for the mass production industries in general; when the steel settlement had been consummated, Lewis privately observed that the GM strike had broken "the united financial front" that had opposed the CIO and had had "a sweeping effect on steel."

"Labor was on the march," Edward Levinson reported, "as it had never been before in the history of the Republic."[88]

For its victory in the GM strike, the UAW could give credit not only to its own leadership and tactics and to the assistance of the CIO but also to the favorable political climate in Washington and Lansing. Despite Murphy's martyr-like complaints to some reporters after the strike that neither Roosevelt nor anyone else in Washington had "raise[d] his voice to help in the critical situation,"[89] the president, the secretary of labor, and the La Follette Committee had all been helpful to the union. It was, however, Governor Murphy, more than any other individual, who affected the outcome of the strike. It was Murphy who insisted that relief be provided to strikers; it was Murphy who sent the National Guard into Flint not to break the strike but to preserve public peace and, in effect, to protect the strikers against possible attack; it was Murphy who delayed the enforcement of a court order that could have broken the strike; it was Murphy who insisted that the strike be settled around the conference table and who kept the strike talks going day and night; and it was Murphy who threw his own support to, and gained Washington backing for, the six-month truce plan that was the key to the consummation of the February 11 agreement. Had Michigan's governor been Frank Fitzgerald or someone like Indiana's M. Clifford Townsend, whose reaction to the strike in GM's Guide Lamp plant in Anderson contrasted sharply with Murphy's behavior,[90] the strike would almost certainly have had a different outcome, and the coming to power of the UAW and the CIO would, at the very least, have been delayed. Murphy's contribution to the outcome of the dispute is a striking example of the truism that history is not the product of inexorable forces alone and that if man is not entirely the master of his fate he nevertheless helps to shape his own destiny.

Much of the comment following the strike centered on Murphy's role during the crisis. Union and management negotiators lauded his efforts as a mediator. Even Sloan, who came to dislike Murphy intensely, asserted that GM, its employees, and the general public were indebted to the governor for his "untiring and conscientious efforts, as well as the fairness with which he . . . handled a most difficult situation." The political community from President Roosevelt on down was full of compliments for Murphy. Arthur Krock reported that Washington opinion was perfectly summed up in a wire that he had received stating, "No praise [is] too great for Frank Murphy."

Murphy was particularly acclaimed for having so discharged his responsibilities that not a single life had been lost in the strike. "It is Governor Murphy's peculiar glory," the columnist Jay Franklin wrote, "that he sent in the troops and handled them so well that no man lost his life after their arrival, and that one of the bitterest industrial strikes on record passed off without the usual dreary lists of killed and wounded in the conventional struggle between scabs, strikers and their respective imported plug-uglies." [91]

There was, on the other hand, some criticism of Murphy for having failed to enforce the law and drive the sit-downers from the occupied plants. Organized labor, not the state of Michigan, had been "supreme" in the strike, the *Detroit Saturday Night* remarked, and "lawless strikers everywhere" now knew that they had "nothing to fear" from Murphy. The governor's correspondents who disapproved of his behavior told him that he had "made a joke of the laws of our state," had allowed the "seeds of Communism" to be "nurtured, fertilized and cultivated," was "a Yellow-Bellied Cur Dog" and "the rottenest Catholic in all Michigan," and was "not worth $5000 a year. Not a dam [sic] cent." It was generally recognized, however, that although a price had probably been paid in terms of law and order, the results achieved justified the expenditure. Lippmann thought that Murphy and GM were both "wiser" than those who had insisted on the vindication of property rights. "The essential fact," he wrote, "has been that certain rights of property were impaired and could not be repaired until the human rights to be represented had been established." [92]

After the strike Arthur Krock cited the views of an "eminent" conservative Democrat who said that he would have defended the rights of property had he been in Murphy's place but that conditions then would have been "permanently worse and the country would not have come out as well as it . . . [had] through the Governor's tactics." Murphy's "compromise" with law and order, the conservative Democrat concluded, was "in the spirit of wise statesmanship." The author of these remarks, Krock informed Murphy, was John Nance Garner, commonly thought of as an archenemy of the sit-down. [93]

Ed Kemp was correct in his later observation that, "in terms of public esteem and prestige," the GM sit-down was "the high point in Frank Murphy's entire career." Spencer Fullerton wrote in the *Cleveland Plain Dealer* a few days after the close of the strike that "few persons in American political life . . . [faced] quite as rosy a future" as Murphy, and *Time* thought that "the first vehicle to roll off General Motors' revived assembly lines" would be "a bandwagon labeled 'Frank Murphy for President in 1940.' ''[94] Contrary to the popular impression of a later day, Murphy gained enormously in stature as the result of his performance in the GM strike. Had not the dispute been followed by a rash of sit-downs across the land and especially in Michigan, it is unlikely that he would have been subjected to the severe criticism that was soon to be directed at him and that plagued him for the rest of his days.

9

"The Greatest Cause of Our Age"

I

"Oh, Michigan!" [1] the *New York Times* editorialized on March 13, 1937. "Isn't that uneasy place between the lakes the place where all the trouble that affects the nation starts?" As the *Times* saw it, the governor of the state appeared to be "a man of peace" with "a strong prejudice against enforcing the law." The newspaper wondered if Murphy, somehow, could be "induced to withdraw and let JOHN LEWIS take over Michigan as a kind of mandated territory.... Then the State could isolate itself as a social laboratory devoted exclusively to Mr. Lewis's experiments." [2]

It was the rash of sit-down strikes in Detroit following in the wake of the GM strike that provoked the *Times* editorial and that kept the nation's attention riveted on Michigan and its governor. There were thirty-four sit-down strikes in Detroit between February 12, the day after the GM strike was settled, and the end of the month, and seventy-eight such strikes in March. Detroit alone accounted for almost half the sit-down strikes in the nation in February and March, making it the undisputed sit-down strike capital of the United States. "Sitting down," a *Detroit News* reporter observed in March, "has replaced baseball as the national pastime, and sitter-downers clutter up the landscape in every direction." [3]

The strikes in Detroit were "happening with such suddenness," according to the National Labor Relations Board (NLRB) field agent in Detroit, that he found it "impossible to forecast just what ... [was] brewing." Many, probably most, of the strikes were staged by unorganized workers who did not even know how to present grievances but who used the sit-down tactic because it had become "a fad, the thing to do." They would call the offices of a Detroit newspaper, say that they wanted to organize, and inquire, "How can we get in touch with a union?" Sometimes they turned to the United Automobile Workers (UAW) for help, sometimes to AFL unions. Responding to requests for assistance, the UAW's General Executive Board (GEB) approved the granting of temporary charters to non-automotive workers pending their assignment to other CIO unions.[4]

Initially, the Detroit sit-downs occurred primarily in businesses with which the general public had little direct contact. On February 27, however, one hundred women sat down in the downtown store of F. W. Woolworth and Company, the first sit-down in Detroit in a mercantile establishment and the beginning of a rash of strikes among the city's nonunionized service employees. On March 8 employees of the eight Chrysler Corporation plants in the Detroit area began "the largest and most effectively organized sit-down strike on record," and this action precipitated a new "tidal wave" of sit-downs and outside strikes. Four hundred workers staged a sit-down in the Crowley-Milner Company department store on March 10, and Detroit's four largest downtown hotels were closed by strikes on March 16. At the Book-Cadillac Hotel, employees locked themselves in the dining room while organizers carrying meat cleavers rushed the rear entrance of the building and seized the establishment.[5]

It was not simply the number of strikes in Detroit and the fact that so many of them were of the sit-down variety that attracted attention but also the unusual places where strikes occurred and the unusual events sometimes associated with them. When employees sat down in the Fry Products Company, Walter L. Fry and two other company executives staged a sit-in of their own. One sit-down occurred in the office of Detroit's welfare superintendent, and there were also sit-downs in WPA offices. At noon on March 2 Fred Grubb, president of the Detroit local of the Waiters and Waitresses Union, walked into Stouffer's downtown restaurant with two organizers and called a strike. The waitresses thereupon stopped serving their customers. One patron rushed Grubb, shouting " 'Is this a free country or isn't it?' " An organizer grabbed the customer while other customers joined the fray. A waitress then jumped on a table and alleged that she and her associates were underpaid. The customers rushed toward her, and an organizer went to her defense. The management saved the situation by persuading the customers to leave the restaurant.

The Crowley-Milner sit-downers made merry until 2:00 A.M. on the first day of their strike while two orchestras entertained them and Woolworth strikers put on a floor show for their amusement. The hotel strike stranded opera star Lily Pons on the twelfth floor of the Statler Hotel and Michigan's Democratic national committeeman on the nineteenth floor of the Fort Shelby Hotel. In the Book-Cadillac Hotel, screen star Tyrone Power gallantly walked down fifteen flights of stairs to fetch a meal for the skater Sonja Henie, another celebrity inconvenienced by the hotel strike. Shock waves reverberated through the community when about 150 workers sitting down in the Newton Packing Company plant decided to ignore an injunction directing them to permit the removal of $170,000 in food products and then, of greater importance, when the Chrysler strikers also ignored an injunction to evacuate the plants that they occupied.[6]

The wave of strikes in Detroit, the places where they occurred, and the challenge to property rights posed by the sit-down tactic gave Detroit "the jitters" in the early months of 1937. Some housewives became reluctant to travel downtown to shop; others, preparing for the worst, began to hoard food; and stores, clubs, and other establishments took measures to protect themselves against "invasion." The J. L. Hudson Company, the city's largest department store, closed off some entrances to its downtown store and arranged for uniformed police and plainclothesmen to scan persons entering the building. "The entire country," the *Detroit Free Press* editorialized on March 12, "is pointing to Michigan as a place where mob rule can be instituted with impunity and can be used as an instrument to bring government to its knees." "Perhaps this IS the revolution," some of the fearful thought as the strike wave spread, and *Time* magazine was quite certain as March drew to a close that Detroiters had been "getting an idea of what a revolution feels like."[7]

The objective of the strikers, however, was not revolution but improved working conditions and collective bargaining. What was taking place was an uprising of the unorganized in an open shop city, and the astute *Detroit News* columnist W. K. Kelsey correctly observed that the strikers had "no more idea of 'revolution' than pussy-cats." They used the sit-down tactic to secure their ends because it had been effective in Flint and had become something of "a fad," not because they wished to challenge the nation's institutional structure. ". . . they all subscribed wholeheartedly to the profit system of free enterprise, and only infringed on it to the extent that they had to get a decent living," a UAW photographer of the period later remarked. "And it was for two cents an hour and seniority and a grievance system that they had to practically make a revolution. Having gotten it, they subsided."[8]

Much of the criticism about what was taking place in Michigan was directed at Governor Murphy, and his efforts to demonstrate that he too favored law and order did little to abate the unfavorable comment. Murphy's opponents were now increasingly inclined to view his conduct during the GM strike as "the beginning from which the rest arose." The "tacit blessing" given the GM sit-down by the "vacillating state administration," *Automotive Industries* declared, had opened the door "to any and all groups." The Flint experience taught "lawless strikers everywhere" that they could "safely defy the law" without fear of counteraction by Governor Murphy. By neglecting to enforce the law in Flint, a Michigan citizen complained, Murphy had started "a labor revolution" in America. "They should have turned the machine guns on them in Flint," was the way one Detroiter explained the city's strike wave. The use of force was also the way Murphy's critics thought the Detroit crisis should be resolved. "Words Won't Win This War, Mr. Murphy—Where Are Your Troops?" the *Detroit Saturday Night* asked the governor in a headline of March 20.

Murphy was criticized not only for failing to enforce the law but also for the "coddling of a minority class" at the expense of the public welfare and for having "practically turned over the management" of Detroit to "a rabble mob." Was he the governor of all the people of Michigan, one of his correspondents inquired, or was he only "a labor advocate"? The Detroit sit-downs deprived Murphy of much of the luster of his Flint achievement, and to an overwrought *Time* magazine it appeared that he was on his way to becoming "the Kerensky of the New Deal."[9]

Although Detroit was "the seething centre" of the sit-down, concern about the tactic and about law and order was by no means confined to Michigan. When the Chrysler sit-downers defied an injunction, "millions," according to *News-Week*, "sensed a threat against every man's right to keep what he owns, and against the courts' power to protect that right." An executive of the First Machinery Corporation of New York City wrote Murphy, "The insurrection against constituted authority is no longer a local concern within the confines of your State. It threatens the safety and security of private property everywhere in our land."[10]

Occurring at the same time that President Roosevelt was pressing his plan to reorganize the United States Supreme Court, the sit-downs in Detroit and across the nation aroused fears outside as well as inside Michigan that the very foundations of the Republic were being undermined. "Armed insurrection—defiance of law, order, and duly elected authority—is spreading like wildfire," a group of Boston civic leaders wired the United States Senate late in March. "If minority groups can seize premises illegally, hold indefinitely, refuse admittance to owners or managers, resist by violence and threaten bloodshed all attempts to dislodge them, and intimidate properly constituted authority to the point of impotence, then freedom and liberty are at an end, government becomes a mockery, superseded by anarchy, mob rule and ruthless dictatorship." A Gallup poll released on March 21 revealed that 67 percent of the respondents believed the states should make the sit-down strike illegal.[11]

Criticism of Murphy in Congress, which began during the GM strike, mounted once the sit-downs hit Detroit with full force. The chief critic was Clare Hoffman, a Republican congressman from Allegan, Michigan, who reflected "the provincialism and bigotry of undiluted Anglo-Saxon stock; the rugged individualism of the small-independent farmer." Accusing Murphy on March 19 of having "sowed the seeds of armed rebellion and anarchy" in Flint, Hoffman declared that "some of these questions cannot be settled until blood has been shed"; he thought the only question was whose blood it would be. Hoffman's colleague, Dewey Short of Missouri, declared a few days later that Michigan had once been a "State of law and order" but had become a "State of anarchy," and he contended that this would not have occurred had Michigan's governor possessed "a bone instead of a rubber band for a spine."

In the Senate, one of the leading critics of the sit-down was Michigan's Arthur H. Vandenberg. "America," Vandenberg declared on March 19, "could disintegrate in another swift and reckless 60 days" if the "illegal contagion" was not stemmed. On April 1, a day on which there was "a great explosion . . . on the floor of the Senate over sit-down strikes," Vandenberg rose to attack "this formula of violence." He read a letter from Mayor Frank Couzens of Detroit about the "epidemic of sit-down strikes" in Detroit in which Couzens noted that court orders had been "ignored and defied" and that thousands had been deprived of their livelihood by strikes often called against the wishes of the employees concerned. Vandenberg also quoted a Detroit strike leader as having told the hotel strikers, "You have nothing to fear from the police or from the courts. The President and the Governor of Michigan are back of you." The Senate on April 7 passed a concurrent resolution declaring the sit-down "illegal and contrary to sound public policy," but at the insistence of administration forces the resolution also condemned the unfair labor practices that the National Labor Relations Act (NLRA) declared illegal.[12]

Murphy's initial reaction to the Detroit sit-ins was to dispatch his commissioner of labor and industry, George A. Krogstad, to the city to mediate those strikes in which the disputants were willing to accept his assistance, this being the extent to which the state government could legally involve itself in the settlement of labor disputes. Arriving in Detroit on February 26, Krogstad worked "night and day" at his task. He achieved some success, but he advised Lansing after about a week that he could not do the job alone. Additional action was also sought by the Detroit Board of Commerce, which urged Murphy on March 12 to convene a conference of law-enforcement officials for the purpose of devising a "militant program" to deal with the "intolerable situation" that was allegedly endangering Detroit's "international civic reputation."[13]

Of greater importance than the plea of the Detroit Board of Commerce in influencing Murphy to intervene personally in the crisis was a memorandum prepared by Attorney General Raymond W. Starr. It was "opportune—if not necessary," Starr contended, for Murphy to make it evident that "the integrity of judicial orders and the law must be upheld" since organized labor, having "misconstrued" his role in Flint, had concluded that he would "not—under any circumstances—interfere or permit interference by lawful force with . . . Union activities in taking possession of factories, stores, etc." and would tolerate labor's "disregard" of the law and of court orders. Starr thought that "a proper first step" would be for the governor to meet with labor leaders to clarify his position, but Murphy decided instead to confer in Lansing on March 15 with the prosecuting attorneys of five southern Michigan counties and then to meet in Detroit on March 17 with representatives of labor, management, and the general public.[14]

Murphy told the prosecuting attorneys that both labor and management were obliged to obey the law and to respect the authority of the courts. He urged employers and employees to cooperate with local law-enforcement officials so that it would not be necessary for them to take "extreme measures" to preserve "public authority" and to protect the "rights of private property."[15]

Murphy's hopes of bringing together a representative group of persons for the Detroit law-and-order conference were frustrated when the UAW's General Executive Board (GEB), which contended that the real issue was not one of law and order but whether workers had a right to better their conditions of employment, voted unanimously to forbid any of its members to attend. Since public opinion had turned against labor unions and strikers, the UAW decision was a foolish one, and many persons undoubtedly agreed with the Michigan Manufacturers' Association that the action demonstrated that unions believed they were "a law unto themselves." Unlike the UAW, the Detroit and Wayne County Federation of Labor (DWCFL) and the Michigan Federation of Labor (MFL) sent representatives to the conference.[16]

Speaking, according to the *Detroit News*, with "a vigor few had seen the Governor display," Murphy told the twenty-three persons who gathered for the Detroit law-and-order conference that he had always counseled negotiation and the peaceful settlement of disputes but that there was a "limit" to this policy. It should not be assumed, he stated, that the state government would "forsake its responsibility to maintain order and protect citizens in the full enjoyment of their legal rights." He noted that public officials and the general public had become "gravely disturbed" by the numerous labor disputes and "a disposition in some quarters to ignore the law and violate the security and freedom of individuals and corporations in the exercise of their personal and property rights." Behavior of this sort, he declared, discredited labor organizations, impaired public confidence in liberal, democratic government, and impeded social progress. Although it was important to protect human rights, personal liberty, Murphy declared, would be of little value if the integrity of courts were not preserved and property rights went unprotected.

He was aware, the governor stated, that there was "fault on both sides" and that labor was responding to unjust conditions and the refusal of "backward employers" to recognize the right of collective bargaining. It was necessary, nevertheless, to find some way "to prevent these disorderly and unlawful methods of pursuing lawful and worthy objectives." Although he recommended the establishment of dispute-adjustment machinery within individual industries and in local communities to meet the immediate situation, he asserted that appropriate state legislation was required to make "wholly unnecessary" the kind of labor difficulties Michigan was experiencing. The conferees endorsed the governor's suggestions for dealing with the strike problem, but the only immediate action taken by Murphy was to appoint an Emergency Mediation Committee, consisting of three liberal clergymen, to assist in the settlement of the minor Detroit strikes.[17]

The different perspectives from which the law-and-order issue was viewed in Michigan in March 1937 are indicated by the contrasting reactions to Murphy's law-and-order remarks by Maurice Sugar, the UAW's counsel, and Ed Kemp. The employers, not the workers, were "the real criminals" and lawbreakers, Sugar protested to Murphy. The employers, he complained, had been "sitting down on the law" ever since the NLRA had been passed, whereas the workers were "liberty loving Americans rebelling against submission to the dictates of the criminal elements of the community." Why, Sugar asked, had Murphy called for law and order only after the sit-down strikes had occurred and not at an earlier time to protest employer defiance of the law? The cautious Kemp, by contrast, was afraid that Murphy, in his zeal "to assist labor groups or avoid losing the good will and confidence of their leaders and organizers," had placed too much emphasis in his Lansing and Detroit remarks on the peaceful settlement of disputes and labor's freedom to organize and its right to strike. These, he thought, were "secondary" or "collateral" matters compared to the state's primary obligation to enforce the law and to provide employers with some "practical alternative" to negotiating with groups or individuals, some of them "Communistic," who had "taken forcible possession of their business establishments and been allowed to keep them in defiance of the law." Despite Kemp's reservations, however, the arch-conservative *Detroit Free Press* applauded the governor's March 17 statement as "firm and clear" and something for which Michigan had "long been waiting."[18]

The turning point in the Detroit strike crisis occurred while the law-and-order conference was in session. Word was brought to the conferees that several "professional 'sit-downers' " had raided the Frank and Seder department store, instigated a sit-down strike, ejected customers and company executives, and prevented the 550 employees, most of whom apparently opposed the strike, from leaving the establishment. Mayor Couzens, who was attending the conference, ordered the police "to clear out all persons" who did not belong in the store. Murphy himself went to the store and found only one "professional" still there, a man he had once sent to jail for forgery. The governor was urging the employees to leave the building when the police arrived.[19]

Although the Frank and Seder dispute was quickly resolved, the advocates of law and order could now claim that "outsiders" were responsible for the Detroit strikes. Detroit, the executive secretary of the Detroit Board of Commerce proclaimed, was "swarming" with "imported organizers, agitators and labor racketeers." Even Murphy declared that, although a "legitimate strike" required a "neutral attitude" on government's part, "a raid is not a strike but a modified form of banditry and must be treated as such. Such matters are not going to be handled by red tape and technicalities and will be straightened out once and for all."[20]

For the next several days the Detroit newspapers contained pictures and accounts of persons with long police records, including even a former member of Detroit's infamous Purple Gang, who were allegedly responsible for some of the sit-down strikes in the city, especially those in retail stores. The *Detroit News* stated flatly that the sit-downs could now be placed in "the gangster racket class." Couzens ordered the police not to interfere with "peaceful" sit-downs if the strikers were employees but to take "proper action" where "total strangers" had "lawlessly" invaded stores and plants. The mayor's directive led to a series of police raids against establishments closed by sit-down strikes, including some in which no outsiders were present. On March 19 the police ejected strikers occupying six downtown shoes stores and a food products company. Two days later police and sheriff's deputies evicted and arrested sixty-four Newton Packing Company strikers for violating the injunction that had been served on them. On the same day about three hundred police, without benefit of a court order and without substantial evidence of the presence of outsiders, evicted 150 to 200 kicking, screaming, biting, hair-pulling, and mold-wielding women from the Bernard Schwarz Company cigar plant, while near the plant forty mounted police battled five hundred strike sympathizers who threw missile-laden snowballs at Detroit's finest. There were two more police raids the next day, in one of which the police evicted sit-downers from a city welfare station. To the shock of civil libertarians and his labor supporters, Murphy defended the police raids as "part of the campaign to make authority unquestioned and supreme in this community. That," he said, "is the Governor's duty." [21]

Protesting the "brutal eviction" of sit-downers and "ruthless clubbing" by the police and fearing that the raids were "a build-up" for a police attack on the Chrysler sit-downers, the UAW called a mass meeting for March 23 to register its disapproval of the antistrike tactics of the Detroit city government. When the Common Council rejected the union's application for a permit to hold the demonstration in Cadillac Square in downtown Detroit on the grounds that it would paralyze traffic, UAW vice-president Ed Hall retorted, "We don't give a good whoop in hell about the permit; we'll be there anyhow." Cooler heads prevailed, and the city and the UAW worked out an agreement for the union to hold the rally at 5:45 P.M., with the understanding that the meeting would be "peaceful and orderly" and that police would be present to direct traffic and to prevent "any unlawful or outside interference." At the request of the police, downtown stores and offices sent their employees home at 4:00 P.M. on the day of the rally.

A crowd of approximately fifty thousand attended the March 23 demonstration and resolved to support the Chrysler strikers and to stage two sit-down strikes for every police eviction. Headlining its story of the event, "UAWA Threatens Detroit Overturn," the *New York Times* reported DWCFL president Frank Martel as having proclaimed at the rally, "From this time on the constitutional rights of this community are going to be respected in the City Hall, the police station and the courts, or we'll turn them wrong-side up." Martel, however, was indulging in rabble-rousing and symbolic rhetoric, and neither he nor his audience had a coup d'etat in mind. Although the "tone of the city" was reported to have been "very uneasy" following the rally, the peaceful character of the demonstration punctured "the balloon of panic" that had been inflating in anticipation of the event. The police raids largely came to an end after the rally, perhaps to forestall a threatened UAW general strike in the city; and four days after the demonstration Murphy's Emergency Mediation Committee reported to the governor that it had successfully adjusted most of the strikes in Detroit and requested that its services be terminated.[22]

Murphy, in the meantime, was devoting his attention to the settlement of the Detroit area's most important dispute, the Chrysler sit-down strike, which idled more than sixty-eight thousand Chrysler employees. Although the major demand of the UAW, as in the GM strike, was exclusive bargaining rights, which the Chrysler Corporation, like GM, would not concede, the Chrysler strike differed in its origins from the GM strike. Negotiations between the union and the company had been initiated before the strike; the UAW had several times praised the company's labor-relations policy even though, as Irving Bernstein has observed, Chrysler's reputation in this regard was "almost certainly . . . exaggerated"; it is likely that the UAW from the start enjoyed the support of a majority of Chrysler employees; and the union initially requested the company to consent to an election "or any other fair medium" of determining the wishes of the employees. "It was a little easier" for Chrysler employees to conduct their strike, a Chrysler striker recalled, because "we had the experience of the General Motors boys and we knew, already, how Governor Murphy acted over there."[23]

The Chrysler Corporation petitioned the Wayne County Circuit Court on March 11 for an injunction to secure the evacuation of its plants. When the hearing on the petition was held, five thousand unionists demonstrated inside and outside the County Building while the twelve-piece UAW-Chrysler Flying Squadron Band played martial airs on the front steps. Judge Allan Campbell granted the corporation the writ it sought on March 15, ordering the evacuation of the Chrysler plants as of 9:30 A.M. on March 17. Murphy, who had already informed Germer that "he deplored the sit-down strikes—taking possession of other people's property," stated regarding the injunction that "the law should be obeyed and there should be no disobedience of court orders." [24]

Undoubtedly because of the pressure Murphy was exerting both publicly and privately, the UAW and CIO leadership was prepared to evacuate the Chrysler plants in return for a company promise not to operate its factories while negotiations proceeded. Since the union and the management were unable to work out such an arrangement despite the intercession of Murphy, John L. Lewis, and Frances Perkins, the UAW decided to defy Judge Campbell's injunction. The judge responded on March 19 by ordering the arrest of the approximately six thousand workers actually sitting in the eight Chrysler plants. Responsibility for executing the order fell on Sheriff Thomas C. Wilcox, but since he did not have the manpower to enforce the writ, his chief deputy stated, "it will be up to the Governor." While expressing his preference for "peace without bloodshed," Murphy asserted that the state would proceed "with vigor" if the sheriff requested the governor's assistance, and he instructed Kemp to have the matter of martial law "carefully reviewed." Although there is no documentary evidence indicating that Wilcox formally requested the governor for armed assistance, the sheriff must have known that Murphy preferred to negotiate the men out of the plants rather than to "shoot them out." [25]

Following the advice of James Dewey, Murphy decided to demand that the union comply with Judge Campbell's order but to request at the same time that Lewis and Walter Chrysler, with whom Murphy had long been on friendly terms, confer with the governor regarding means of implementing the evacuation. This decision, in Kemp's view, involved "a serious compromise on the fundamental issue of law and order." For Murphy, however, to have insisted on evacuation of the plants without a conference would have antagonized organized labor, which he was reluctant to do.

Murphy wired Lewis and Chrysler on March 23 that if the sheriff, as expected, requested the governor's assistance, the state would "employ all necessary and available means . . . to uphold public authority . . . and protect property rights. . . . In view of the large interests at stake, however, and [the] desirability of ascertaining whether adjustment . . . [was] possible before taking extreme and costly measures with possible unfortunate consequences," the governor requested the two men to confer with him the next day in an effort to find a "prompt satisfactory solution . . . in [the] enforcement of [the] court's order." Both Lewis and Chrysler accepted Murphy's invitation, although Lewis protested that he was being asked to confer "under duress" and Chrysler replied that the court order was "not a proper subject for negotiation" and the corporation would "not enter into any trade to get the men out of the plants."[26]

After eight hours of negotiation on March 24, Lewis and Chrysler agreed to terms. The UAW agreed to evacuate the Chrysler plants that it occupied, while the company committed itself not to operate these plants or to remove any dies or machinery pending negotiations with the union on its demand for exclusive bargaining rights. The State Police were to guard the gates of the factories to guarantee observance of the agreement. These terms were identical with a Murphy proposal that Lewis had rejected during the GM strike, but Lewis was aware that the mood of the country had changed since that time. Also, the presence in Murphy's office of the state's adjutant general, the commissioner of the Michigan State Police, and Colonel Joseph Lewis no doubt helped to persuade the CIO chief that Murphy was determined that the Chrysler plants be evacuated "at once."[27]

When Murphy read the truce terms to the press, he placed Lewis on his right and Chrysler on his left. Chrysler was "piqued" by this arrangement and, according to one observer, "clearly looked sick." The location of the dramatis personae led to a good deal of comment, prompting Murphy to remark, "the position at the right hand of Government is one that has [too?] long been enjoyed by great power, wealth and influence." No public official was doing more at that moment than the governor of Michigan to alter this state of affairs.[28]

Many Chrysler sit-downers, no doubt harking back to the collapse of the January 15 agreement in the GM strike, were dissatisfied with the March 24 truce terms, one angry striker declaring, "We might just as well not have sat down at all. We've been sold out." The union leadership and the union's CIO advisors, however, stressed to the "militants" that Murphy, one of the UAW's few friends in government, had given his word that the terms would be observed. Murphy kept his word, and the UAW, according to one strike leader, learned once again the importance of "getting the right people in positions where they could help us."[29]

The sit-downers marched out of the occupied Chrysler plants on March 25, eight days after the injunction deadline had expired. Murphy had accomplished his objective, but *News-Week* was correct in stating that the governor had "still put peace first, law second." The anti-Murphy *Detroit Free Press* nevertheless called the truce terms "a triumph for good sense and good order," and the columnist

Floyd Healey commented, "Two of the greatest threats American industry ever faced ... had been controlled within a period of two months—with one man holding the center of the arena, cracking the whip. This country has never seen anything like that before."[30]

Union and Chrysler negotiators in Detroit had made no progress whatsoever before the plants were evacuated. As Germer wrote John Brophy on March 18, "We have discussed the American Revolution, the French Revolution, the Paris Commune, the Civil War, the World War. We've been in Europe, Africa, South America and all over the United States and so far as the strike is concerned we are as near together as when you left [at the outset of the strike]." Following the Lansing truce arrangement, however, Murphy took personal charge of the negotiations and kept the talks going until the disputants agreed to terms. On March 29, during the course of the talks, Murphy sold twelve hundred shares of Chrysler stock that he had bought on February 9, sustaining a loss of about $6,000 on the transaction.[31]

Although Murphy's stockholdings had no bearing on the outcome of the Lansing strike talks, the April 5 election in Michigan, the composition of the negotiating teams, and the state of the union's treasury all had some effect on the negotiations. At a UAW mass meeting on April 1 Richard Frankensteen, the UAW's organizational director and one of the strike negotiators, pledged his union's support for the Michigan Democrats in the spring election "in appreciation for Governor Murphy's position" regarding the sit-downs. Lewis announced that Labor's Non-Partisan League, the political arm of the CIO, was also supporting the Democratic slate. Organized labor had every reason to support Democratic candidates on April 5, but Frankensteen and Lewis were no doubt also seeking to remind Murphy who his political friends were. On the other hand, the Chrysler negotiators, one of whom, B. E. Hutchinson, was the chief money-raiser for the Republican party in Michigan, were reluctant to come to terms with the UAW before the election lest this redound to the benefit of the Democrats. It is not entirely a coincidence that the peace terms were agreed to on April 6, the day following the election.[32]

At the outset of the Lansing talks Chrysler, described by *Fortune* as "a man of homely force, native shrewdness, and earthy intuition," refused to shake hands with "that bastard" Lewis. By the time the negotiations had been completed, however, the automobile executive was characterizing Lewis as the smartest man he had ever met. When members of the Chrysler negotiating team—" 'Chrysler's House of Lords,' " Lewis called them—talked "big," Chrysler would send them to speak with Lewis, and they would return with their "feathers all ruffled," much to Chrysler's amusement. Chrysler's associates, especially Hutchinson, a Chrysler vice-president and chairman of its finance committee, "took a harder line" than Chrysler himself. As Lee Pressman recalled, Hutchinson, whom Pressman regarded as the " 'secret brains of the outfit,' " said " 'No' " to everything. Similarly, members of the union strike committee, who were present in Lansing, were more militant than the principal negotiators for the union, Lewis, Pressman, Martin, and Frankensteen. Lewis had to convince them that the circumstances did not permit the negotiators to hold out for the union's maximum demands. The hard-liners must also have been aware that the union was running out of funds and many strikers were facing eviction and the loss of their cars. "Actually," R. J. Thomas, then president of one of the Chrysler locals, observed, "we were just building a union and we were in no position to hold out for too long a period for an item like sole collective bargaining."[33]

On April 4, near the end of the Lansing talks, fifteen hundred Chrysler strikers and sympathizers drove from Detroit to Lansing accompanied by a color guard and a seventy-piece band. In good spirits, the demonstrators cheered lustily when Murphy, Chrysler, Lewis, and some of the others went out on the balcony of the capitol building to greet them. Nicholas Kelley, the Chrysler counsel, thought the demonstration "a very moving thing," and Chrysler remarked to Thomas, " 'these people don't look like communists to me.' "[34]

The single issue that had to be resolved in the Lansing negotiations was the nature of the representation the corporation would accord the UAW. Although the union publicly insisted on exclusive bargaining rights, the principal union negotiators were prepared from the outset to accept a preferential status in Chrysler plants similar to that already enjoyed by the UAW in GM plants. The corporation, however, preferred an arrangement less favorable to the union; and since it did not wish a third party to "have any say after we got through," it was disinclined to provide Murphy with the kind of letter Knudsen had given him as part of the GM settlement. Murphy thought that he could have brought about an agreement much more readily had he been dealing with only Chrysler and Lewis. "Advice from others," the governor complained, slowed the negotiating process. Among the "others," Murphy did not seem to care for Kelley, who recalled that when he said that something the governor had proposed would simply not do, Murphy self-importantly replied, " 'Do you realize you're talking to the governor of Michigan?' "[35]

The negotiators considered draft after draft of language defining the UAW's status in Chrysler plants[36] until Murphy was able to announce on April 6 that an agreement finally had been reached. The corporation agreed to bargain with the union on behalf of its employees, and it recognized and promised not to interfere with the right of its employees to become union members and not to discriminate against union members. In the key provision of the agreement, the corporation stated that it would "not aid, promote or finance any labor group or organization which purports to engage in collective bargaining or make any agreement with any such group or organization for the purpose of undermining the Union." The corporation also promised to reemploy strikers as soon as possible and in accord with seniority and to consent to the dismissal of the Campbell injunction. For its part, the union promised not to coerce corporation employees to join the union and not to solicit members on company property or on company time, to end the strike, and not to engage in a sit-down strike or other work stoppage during the life of the agreement. The agreement was to run until March 31, 1938, and the parties were to begin negotiations for a supplementary agreement on April 8. The corporation did not accord the union exclusive bargaining rights in so many words, and it did not supplement the agreement with a Knudsen-type letter, but it nevertheless gave the union the substance of what it had been seeking. Chrysler may also have assured Lewis privately that the corporation would act on the presumption that the UAW represented all Chrysler plant workers. Those who then and later characterized the settlement as a UAW defeat were unaware of the union's realistic goals in the dispute and underestimated the significance of the settlement.[37]

Chrysler publicly praised Murphy's efforts to settle the strike and privately assured the governor that he had "meant every word." Speaking to a UAW audience of twenty-five thousand in Detroit just after the strike, Lewis expressed the wish that "we had more Frank Murphys as governors of our several states." Frankensteen also lauded Murphy, whereupon the audience rose and gave the governor an ovation that lasted several minutes. Although some complained that Murphy once again had failed to enforce the law, the general manager of the Michigan Manufacturers' Association praised the governor as "wise" and "right," and *News-Week* commented that he had "forced two titans to gulp his medicine."[38] The same "medicine" was gulped by Hudson Motor Car Company and Reo negotiators to resolve sit-down strikes in plants of these two companies.[39] This brought to a close the strike wave in the automobile industry that had occupied most of Murphy's time since he had assumed Michigan's governorship.

Three days after the Chrysler settlement James Dewey met with the UAW's GEB and reported Martin as saying that " 'the sit-down strategy was no longer necessary; that it had served its purpose; had been effective; that it was now necessary to abandon this practice which had attracted so much public attention; that public opinion was against it; and that it was unsafe to use it further.' " On April 12 the United States Supreme Court, in *NLRB* v. *Jones and Laughlin*, upheld the constitutionality of the NLRA, which made it far easier for unions to gain recognition without resorting to the sit-down tactic. There were only fifteen sit-downs in Detroit in April (compared to seventy-eight in March) and fifty-two in the nation (compared to 170 in March), and the total number of such strikes in the nation dwindled to four by December. "Place collective bargaining on a sane, civilized basis," Louis Stark had correctly observed, "and the sit-down strike will vanish." By a curious coincidence, Murphy was himself the victim of one of the few Detroit sit-downs in April. He was having lunch in the Book-Cadillac Hotel with his sister, a Detroit attorney, and a newspaper man and was explaining that the sit-down strike era had come to an end when someone walked into the dining room, blew a whistle, and announced a strike. Murphy, who laughed at first but then became angry, left the hotel, his meal unfinished. The police told the strikers to leave the hotel, and they complied.[40]

"My desk is cleared," Murphy stated at the close of the Chrysler strike. "I am ready to resume my other duties in the line of state business."[41] The governor, indeed, was now able to devote more time to his "other duties," but Michigan's "strike troubles" had not come to an end; and for the remainder of his term Murphy found it necessary to involve himself in one way or another in the labor disputes that continued to plague Michigan.

Following the Chrysler strike Murphy sought to resolve two Detroit strikes that had defied settlement for several weeks. The governor's office made a last-minute attempt to secure the evacuation of the Yale and Towne Manufacturing Company plant, which sit-down strikers had held since March 9 and which they had been enjoined to leave, by applying the same formula that had led to the evacuation of the Chrysler plants. When this effort failed, seemingly because management representatives were "in a belligerent mood," Sheriff Wilcox sought the governor's advice about enforcing an arrest order issued by the Wayne County Circuit Court on April 13, and Murphy told the sheriff to do his duty. Two hundred deputy sheriffs and police, firing tear gas and using riot sticks, forced the plant open on April 15 and arrested 120 sit-downers, two-thirds of them women, as well as sixteen unionists outside the plant, including Walter and Victor Reuther. The sit-downers were all sentenced for contempt, with twenty-two-year-old UAW organizer George Edwards, later to become Detroit's police commissioner and a federal judge, and twenty-year-old Peter P. Sedler, an assistant organizer, receiving the maximum sentence of thirty days and a $250 fine. The UAW requested Murphy to investigate what they alleged, with some cause, was the ''brutal'' police behavior in the ejection of the strikers and to pardon Edwards and Seidler. Murphy complied with neither request. He thought that complaints about the police behavior should be addressed to the county prosecutor, and he received legal advice that the governor's pardon power did not extend to convictions for contempt of court. When Yale and Towne decided shortly after the ejection of the strikers to close its Detroit plant, the union turned to Murphy for assistance, and he promised to attempt to persuade the company to reverse its decision. If he made the effort, he was unsuccessful.[42]

One week after the ejection of the Yale and Towne strikers Murphy interceded to settle a strike that had continued since mid-February in several Detroit cigar factories that employed about two thousand women under ''sweat shop conditions.'' The head of one of the companies involved in the strike explained in a letter to James Roosevelt why Murphy, who devoted about twenty continuous hours to arranging a settlement, was such an effective mediator. Murphy, the executive wrote, ''could give Trader Horn some points. Not only has he a most charming manner, but he has infinite patience and a real constructive approach to a problem.'' The industry was a small one, the businessman noted, but Murphy's ''patience and concentration was [sic] just as intense as if it were of vital interest to the State of Michigan. I was fascinated by his personality and ability, and he has a rare balance of humor, which, in a tense situation, comes to the foreground and gives everyone a breathing space.''[43]

Three labor events occurring in rapid succession—the Lansing Labor Holiday of June 7, 1937, a Consumers Power strike on June 9, and a clash on the picket line outside the Newton Steel plant in Monroe on June 10—led to renewed criticism of Murphy's labor policies and once again aroused concern about law and order in Michigan. When UAW Local 182 defied a June 3 injunction against picketing the Capitol City Wrecking Company of Lansing, the sheriff of Ingham County responded at 2:00 A.M. on June 7 by making home arrests of eight pickets, including the wife of the local's president, Lester Washburn. With Homer Martin's permission, Washburn thereupon proclaimed "a general labor holiday throughout the city to celebrate the brave act" of the sheriff and the prosecuting attorney and called on the city's numerous auto workers to absent themselves from their jobs that day. Several thousand UAW members and sympathizers, responding to Washburn's proclamation, took possession of Lansing's downtown that morning. They blocked traffic—"You could not have gotten a wheelbarrow through there," a Lansing reporter recalled—forced the closing of offices and stores, including the offices of the *Lansing State Journal*, jammed into the city-county building, where the pickets were being held, and listened to speeches by UAW leaders delivered from the steps of the state capitol.

Murphy was not in Lansing on the morning of June 7. When he returned to his office in the afternoon, he summoned Washburn and told him to clear the streets in ten minutes, something that was not revealed at the time. When Washburn said that the UAW had to educate the public, Murphy, whose "Irish was up," retorted, " 'the public will educate you.' " Knowing that there were not enough State Police troopers available to handle so large a crowd "without the use of extreme measures," Murphy went out on the capitol steps and, in what some thought was "too much of 'a welcoming address,' " cautioned the demonstrators against "extreme or unnecessary acts" but told them that the capitol could not be put to "better use" than the exercise by citizens of their freedom of speech and freedom of assembly. He also asserted that public officials had to "face and recognize new conditions" and that the demonstrators would suffer "no injustice" while he was governor.

Either Murphy's warning to Washburn or the release of the pickets, which the governor helped to arrange, brought the holiday to an end in the downtown area. Some "overeager" unionists, however, decided to close down East Lansing, the home of Michigan State College, but they were repulsed by hundreds of students who, after first being dissuaded by Murphy from riding down the unionists—" 'Boys, that's too Cossack-like,' " he reportedly said—threw eight demonstrators into the Red Cedar River. This led one legislator to suggest that the state give Michigan State College " 'two extra buildings,' " and about half the House members, including all the Republicans, sent a letter to the president of the college praising the students for "the very prompt and efficient way" that they had dealt with the labor invaders. The legislature went into session on the evening of the holiday and then, as one state senator recorded in his diary, "immediately adjourned to avoid any possible demonstration by strikers." Headlines such as "CIO Seizes Michigan Capital" gave the Lansing

Labor Holiday a rather frightening character. Senator Vandenberg later commented that the episode had "excited" his "critical attention" even more than the GM sit-down had.[44]

Two days after the Lansing Labor Holiday, while Murphy was in Pittsburgh to deliver a commencement address at Duquesne University, UAW members staged a wildcat strike against the Consumers Power Company that cut off electricity to one-half million people in the Saginaw Valley. An angry Murphy, who had successfully mediated a brief UAW strike against the same company in May and had then warned that the state government would not "tolerate any more strikes of this kind," called Martin and Robert Travis and told them to "Get those lights back on!" John L. Lewis, whom Murphy had also called, sent similar instructions to the UAW. After about fifteen hours the unauthorized strike, which Martin charged was being run by "a bunch of nuts," came to an end.[45]

As the lights went on in the Saginaw Valley, trouble erupted thirty-five miles southwest of Detroit, in Monroe, Michigan, the home of the Newton Steel Company, a Republic Steel subsidiary that the corporation had selected as the testing ground for a carefully orchestrated back-to-work movement designed to break the Little Steel strike then underway. The power structure of Monroe, an open-shop city of about eighteen thousand inhabitants that had lured Newton Steel to Monroe in 1929, feared that a prolonged strike might cause Republic to close the plant, which employed about 1,350 workers.

The recently organized and weak Monroe local of the Steel Workers Organizing Committee (SWOC) struck Newton on May 28 and established a picket line on the single road leading to the lake-shore plant. Until June 10 the line was maintained without any "serious disorder or untoward incident" since the company made no effort to operate the plant and the pickets did not interfere with company personnel wishing to enter the factory. The Steel Workers Association (SWA), an "independent" local union formed just before the strike, nevertheless requested state and local authorities to remove the pickets so that those who wished to return to work could do so safely. When a large SWA delegation visited Murphy on June 1, he advised that the wishes of the employees be determined by an NLRB election. Instead of an NLRB election, however, the anti-union and anti-strike mayor of Monroe, Daniel A. Knaggs, whose great grandfather had allegedly killed Tecumseh, conducted a referendum among the employees on June 7 to ascertain whether they wished to return to work. When the results of the referendum, which was boycotted by SWOC but in which about 60 percent of the workers participated, indicated that an overwhelming majority of those who had voted wished to return to work, the company announced that the plant would be reopened. Knaggs took the referendum results to Murphy and requested National Guard or State Police protection for the reopening of the plant. The governor, refusing to " 'take sides,' " advised that the state government could not comply with such a request unless it was officially informed in writing by local authorities that they could not control the situation. Claiming later that he had acted on a suggestion by Murphy, which is difficult to believe, Knaggs thereupon swore in 383 deputies as special police to augment the small force of twenty city police and a few sheriff's deputies available to him. The arms for the special police, some of whom were Newton employees, were paid for by the company.

The return to work in Monroe was scheduled for June 10. On the morning of that day a black SWOC organizer was dragged from his car by vigilantes, beaten, and run out of town while police looked on. Word of this transformed the men on the picket line into "an angry, unruly crowd." Although they had promised the sheriff not to interfere with the return to work, they now armed themselves with clubs and steel bars and blocked the road to the plant. Murphy, who had been urged by the American Civil Liberties Union to forestall the threatened violence "in line with your established policy heartening to us all," had sent Krogstad to Monroe to mediate the dispute. He also tried to delay the reopening of the plant for a few days pending a scheduled conference between the governor of Ohio and Republic Steel officials that Murphy hoped might end the strike. The head of the SWA, however, had told an audience of nine hundred workers on June 9 that they would reenter the plant the next day " 'regardless of what Governor Murphy says or does.' "

From Lansing, where he had been meeting with the interested parties, Murphy sought for several hours on June 10 to prevent a clash on the picket line. He told the pickets in no uncertain terms that, although they had a right to picket peacefully, they must not blockade the road, and he urged the police at the same time not to " 'go through that line.' " The pickets were willing to permit the plant to reopen but only if the city government disarmed and demobilized all vigilantes who were not Newton employees. City officials rejected these terms, and repeated calls from the governor failed to break the deadlock. While veterans deputized by Knaggs policed the downtown area with baseball bats, the special police moved against the pickets behind a barrage of nauseating gas fired by two gas squads that had reputedly been brought to Monroe by salesmen for the American Munitions Company, broke the picket line, and drove the "outnumbered, leaderless and bewildered" pickets from the road. A cavalcade of autos then carried the "loyal" workers into the plant. Murphy protested that there was "no excuse" for what had occurred, but the district manager of Republic Steel congratulated Knaggs for his efforts "in behalf of law and order."

On instructions from their locals, hundreds of auto workers from nearby Pontiac proceeded toward Monroe the day after the reopening of the plant in an effort to reactivate the picket line. Martin, however, called off the invasion before very many auto workers had reached the city, where bat-wielding American Legionnaires awaited them. Knaggs now wanted Murphy to declare martial law and send the National Guard to Monroe, but this proved to be unnecessary since the UAW, at the governor's behest, decided against a show of strength in Monroe and agreed instead to hold a protest rally on June 13 in a state park three miles north of the city. Murphy, who declined an invitation to speak at the affair, dispatched National Guardsmen and State Police to ensure that there would be no trouble and no interference with free speech. The rally, attended by about twenty thousand persons, proceeded without incident. Two days later the picketing of the Newton plant was resumed under severely restricted conditions.[46]

"The Battle of Monroe" received a tremendous amount of press coverage, as much as the "Memorial Day massacre" outside the Republic Steel plant in south Chicago, and it led to renewed criticism of the labor policies of Michigan's governor. Alleging concern because of Murphy's "yellow streak and previous protection to law violators," Congressman Hoffman offered to bring "a group of peaceably inclined but armed and well-equipped reliable citizens" to Monroe to aid in its "defense."[47]

The events of June 7–10 substantially heightened the concern about the state of law and order in Michigan and stimulated the formation of law-and-order leagues in several Michigan cities to support local law-enforcement agencies. "When the state's capitol is taken over, power lines are shut off and streets are barricaded," the *Michigan Manufacturer and Financial Record* declared, "there is an approach to anarchy which honest citizens cannot stomach." Judging from his mail that "a virtual state of terror " had "taken possession" of the people of Michigan, Senator Vandenberg concluded that the labor problem was ceasing to be "primarily a question of industrial relations" and was "rapidly approaching the naked question of sovereignty—who runs America? Is there a Government?'' He thought that the question was especially pertinent with regard to Michigan, ''where our amiable Governor has so far compromised with law and order that he has lost all chance to be effective except at a terrific price.''[48]

Responding to his critics and denouncing both ''Communist cliques'' that he alleged had sought to create disorder and ''hard boiled reactionaries who,'' he said, ''wanted to shoot it out in a revolutionary sort of way,'' Murphy stated that he would ''continue to steer the course I have taken down the reasonable middle road.'' He would be ''solicitous of every right of labor,'' but he would not tolerate irresponsible labor actions such as the denial of ''vital services'' to the public and the blockading of highways. To a correspondent accusing him of mouthing ''political swill and garbage'' and corrupting ''American ideals,'' Murphy replied that he was more determined than ever ''to do the kindly and right thing for the big and little alike. Sowing the seeds of kindness in the vineyard of 1937,'' he ruefully concluded, ''is not altogether an easy errand.''[49]

Strike activity in Michigan decreased after the Battle of Monroe,[50] but labor and management continued to turn to Murphy when they became locked in combat. One of the most bitter disputes into which the state government was drawn was a strike of six thousand lumberjacks in the Upper Peninsula that had begun on May 18. The union involved was the CIO's militant Lumber and Sawmill Workers Union, and it seems to have coerced many lumberjacks into joining the walkout. When the mayor of Munising, in Alger County, asked for State Police protection at the end of May, Murphy responded by instructing the commissioner of the State Police to '' 'keep an eye' '' on conditions and dispatching Krogstad to mediate the spreading dispute. On June 4 strikers from Munising sought to extend the strike to the village of Newberry, in Luce County, but they were repulsed by one thousand ''loyal'' employees armed with staves and clubs, and two persons were killed. The next day vigilantes drove the strikers from Munising. Most strikers then began returning to work, an action that was encouraged by the secretary of the Department of Labor and Industry, Joseph Ashmore, the former president of the Jackson Federation of Labor, who asserted that the Lumber and Sawmill Workers Union had ''adopted methods that even Soviet Russia wouldn't tolerate.''

In the latter part of June the union began to complain that the State Police were engaging in strikebreaking activities, but the federal conciliator who had been sent into the area refuted this allegation.

What seems to have occurred was that the strikers had threatened truck drivers hauling logs and had sometimes dumped their trucks, and so the State Police and sheriff's deputies began to provide escorts for the trucks. On June 30, by which time the strike was confined to the extreme western end of the Upper Peninsula, three hundred strikers attacked five logging trucks being escorted by state troopers, and fifty-three arrests resulted. Following this action, vigilantes raided union headquarters in Ironwood, in Gogebic County, beat up the union president, another union officer, and the union's attorney, Henry Paull, and took Paull across the state line to Wisconsin. Murphy now appointed a fact-finding committee to investigate the dispute, instructed the State Police to act in "an impartial manner to preserve order," and insisted that needy strikers receive relief and surplus commodities wherever these forms of assistance were being denied them. The union and the ACLU demanded that Murphy investigate Paull's "kidnapping," and Murphy requested Starr to do so. Because of lack of evidence, however, nothing came of this nor of an ACLU effort to persuade the federal government to prosecute the kidnappers under the Lindbergh Act. The Department of Labor and Industry in the meantime helped to negotiate agreements that finally brought the dispute to an end.[51]

Murphy also became involved in a series of actual or potential labor disputes that attracted relatively little public attention. He used small State Police detachments to keep highways open and to protect shipments on public highways in two strikes in July. He sent State Police and civilian observers to the gates of Ford's giant Rouge plant in the same month to discourage the company from interfering with the distribution of literature by the UAW, thus forestalling a possible repetition of the famous "battle of the overpass" of May 26, 1937. He also settled a Detroit cleaners and dyers strike in July that had tied up sixty-five plants for fifteen days, winning the praise of Sidney Hillman for his "great contribution toward the establishment of sound industrial relations." In August he persuaded the UAW to abandon a sit-down in the American Broach Company plant in Ann Arbor on the condition that he would meet with union and management representatives, and he was then instrumental in settling the dispute. He avoided a strike against the Detroit City Gas Company at the beginning of September, characterizing this kind of work stoppage as "unnecessary and unthinkable"; and the next month he settled another Consumers Power Company strike, helped to settle a jurisdictional dispute between the AFL and CIO involving a Saginaw laundry, and successfully mediated a strike at the Mueller Brass Company in Port Huron.[52]

Murphy's primary concerns as governor in 1938 were the recession that plagued Michigan and his own reelection, but Consumers Power and the CIO's Utility Workers Organizing Committee turned to him to resolve still another power strike that began when the unionists seized nineteen company plants at the beginning of April. The strike did not halt electric service to consumers since the strikers continued to operate the plants that they held. It appeared that the dispute, which Secretary of Labor Perkins characterized as "the most serious thing we have had happen in the labor field in the last five years," would be especially difficult to settle because it was a three-sided affair, involving not only the company and the CIO union but also a rival AFL union and an independent union. "You cannot justify the taking over of plants," Murphy said in rebuking the strikers. "It is illegal and plainly it must be opposed." Aided by Dewey, the governor brought representatives of the company and the strikers together and in eight hours of continuous negotiations on April 4 arranged a settlement providing for the renewal of the existing contract for four months (wage rates were not in dispute) and an NLRB election, previously opposed by the CIO union, to resolve the rival representation claims. "I pointed out everything I knew to be wrong about it [the strike]," Murphy wrote of his role as peacemaker, "because I believe the influence of government must be used against arbitrary, irresponsible acts on either side." Murphy's efforts elicited the praise of both Consumers Power and the CIO. "I wish we had more governors who could approach these complex economic problems in the intelligent and humane manner that you have done," Germer wrote the governor.[53]

As the public official most directly at the center of the great labor upheaval that began in the United States with the GM sit-down strike, Murphy devoted a good deal of attention in public and private to an analysis of the nation's labor problem and to a defense of his own labor record. He began with the assumption that the working-man was "the actor in the center of the stage" in 1937 and that the labor movement was "the greatest cause of our age." As he explained it, the "stability" of the nation and the preservation of democracy depended on the well-being of the workingman.[54]

Murphy complained about what he thought was the press's "traditional attitude of indifference toward the needs of labor and arrogance toward its efforts at self-improvement." The press, he asserted, had reacted with indignation to labor's excesses but not to employer misbehavior. It was thus critical of sit-down strikes but much less concerned about employer activities to combat organization. ". . . like many sedentary editors who have been dwelling for years on the same old theme," he wrote the publisher of a small-town Michigan newspaper who had criticized the Murphy labor policies, "you are out of touch with the realities of today. You quickly lose patience with actions of labor that are disturbing to your peace and quietude, but injustice to workers, their insecurity, the failure of the economic system to yield many of them a living wage seldom evoke from you anything more than pious platitudes." As for himself, Murphy said, he wanted "a square deal for both labor and management. That, and that alone, is what I have sought to achieve," he asserted.⁵⁵

Murphy rejected the view that the strike wave in Michigan was the result of what had occurred in Flint. He insisted rather that the labor turbulence was "a normal reaction" to the economic insecurity workingmen had experienced in the years of depression, the "humiliation of unemployment and the dole," and the refusal of employers to engage in collective bargaining. Had employers observed the terms of the NLRA and not interfered with the right of workers to organize and bargain—Detroit, he noted, was "the most avowed open shop city" in the nation—it would have "taken the edge off a great deal of the trouble in Michigan" and would have obviated the need for the sit-downs. Conceding that labor had been guilty of excesses, he attributed this to its "coming so suddenly into a new sense of power" and the inclination of the masses "to push beyond the legal structure of a country where the law provided no redress or help for them." Labor, however, was obliged to "discipline its forces." It was "axiomatic," he contended, that the "responsible leaders of responsible labor organizations should be accountable for the acts of such organizations."

Although regularly accused of lack of concern for law enforcement, Murphy just as regularly asserted the contrary. "We stand for law enforcement," he declared of his administration. "We believe in the protection of property rights. We believe in intelligent obedience to constituted authority." Murphy, however, contended that since the law often lagged behind the times and human needs, government, in the public interest, must sometimes refrain from "a blind and rigorous enforcement" of the law. He noted, furthermore, that "an apparent concern for the minute details of legality" had all too frequently served "to disguise or justify a denial of the basic rights of working people."

In the sit-down strikes, Murphy conceded, he had put a peaceful solution ahead of a "blind adherence to a legalistic formula." These strikes, he argued, were so "complicated" by the feeling of the workers that they were "the victims of injustice" that the issue could not be resolved by "the exact kind of justice that looks neither to the right nor the left and takes no heed of realities." "We must love justice, rather than its form," Murphy summarized, providing a significant clue as to the kind of justice he would later be on the United States Supreme Court.

Murphy's reluctance to resort to force to execute the law stemmed, as we have seen, from his unwillingness "to test authority at the risk of taking life" and his profound reluctance to be cast in the role of strikebreaker, "at the beck and call of industrialists." He also contended that the use of force by government in a strike only made matters worse. The use of force in the GM and other strikes, he insisted, would not have taught the workingman to respect government but would rather have made government for him "a horrible, oppressive thing," an instrument of capitalist brutality, and would have created animosities that it would have taken many years to remove. In his remarks about the law and the use of force, Murphy, of course, was rationalizing his own behavior in the GM and other strikes, but that does not mean that what he said was necessarily inaccurate.

"When a couple of mastodons collide," Murphy wrote Joseph Hayden just after the Chrysler strike, "it is difficult for them to become unentangled without the modest help and influence of the Government which, of course, should always speak for all the people." It was not sufficient, in Murphy's view, for the state government simply to play a role in bringing ongoing labor disputes to an end; it must also attempt to remove the causes of industrial warfare and to forestall threatened strikes and lockouts. This meant the enactment of "progressive and enlightened laws" designed to prevent "unhealthy conditions and unfair practices" that engendered labor unrest as well as the passage of comprehensive labor-relations legislation.[56]

Murphy could occasionally laugh about his strike role—he told an out-of-town friend whom he was about to visit that perhaps they could "stand around" a bit since "I refuse to 'sit-down' about anything"—but he more commonly struck the martyr pose that came to him so easily. "Sometimes," he wrote a former associate about what were surely "the most dramatic months" of Murphy's life, "I feel that I am standing alone against those who, however sincere, seem to be totally unable to appreciate the situation as it actually is." He wrote an admirer who had been active in the labor movement, "I paid with my body for the peaceful settlement of the great strikes.

That is as it should be—to do otherwise would have meant that the poor workers would have had to pay with . . . [their bodies] and that is the sort of thing you and I want to end forever."[57]

Murphy enjoyed remarkable success as a labor mediator, and despite the reiterated complaints that he had failed to enforce the law, the parties to the particular disputes in which he became involved were consistently appreciative of his efforts, even if some employers later had second thoughts. It is a truism today that labor became part of the "system" during the New Deal era, and the credit is generally given to the national administration and to such legislation as the NLRA, but the manner in which Murphy conducted himself during "the most serious" labor crisis in the nation's history[58] was of equal importance. No governor in American history played so large a role in the labor arena, and his refusal to shoot strikers out of the plants they occupied, even though it was at the expense of prompt enforcement of the law, helped to attract workers to their government rather than to alienate them from it.

II

Murphy appreciated that the strike is "only an index of the status of industrial relations" and that the problem of labor-management relations is "essentially . . . a problem of the daily adjustment of a person to his occupational environment." To improve the quality of that "environment" and to provide "a larger measure of social justice" in accordance with the spirit of the New Deal and his own campaign pledges, Murphy urged the state legislature to enact a variety of labor and social security laws. His efforts to secure labor legislation were encouraged and supported by the Division of Labor Standards and the Women's Bureau of the United States Department of Labor, and it was federal legislation that stimulated Michigan's action with regard to social security. The cooperative relationship between federal and state government in the era of the New Deal was nowhere more evident than in the labor-social security field.[59]

According to the secretary of the MFL, Michigan as of 1937 was "one of the most backward states in the Union" as far as labor legislation was concerned. The Federation had less reason to complain on this score at the end of the Murphy administration, although it was not entirely satisfied with what had been accomplished. During Murphy's governorship the Michigan legislature enacted more legislation favored by organized labor than any previous legislature in the state's history, but when Murphy left office Michigan still lacked a minimum-wage law and a law limiting the hours of male workers, and women were permitted to work longer hours in Michigan than in many other states. Insofar as labor legislation was concerned, the Michigan performance during Murphy's governorship was less impressive than that of Pennsylvania while George H. Earle was the state's governor and New York during the several gubernatorial terms of Herbert H. Lehman.[60]

As the MFL had anticipated, Murphy's election made it possible for Michigan, for the first time, to develop "a real Department of Labor." At Murphy's request, the Division of Labor Standards made a survey of the state's Department of Labor and Industry and suggested how it could be brought "in line with the best practices among other industrial states." The legislature in 1937 increased the number of commissioners of the department from three to six and also created a new Division of the Deaf and Deafened to collect statistics pertaining to the deaf and to find employment for them. The division succeeded in placing the deaf on WPA projects, Michigan thus becoming one of the few states in which the deaf were "generally employed" on such projects. The department's inspection powers, which the United States Department of Labor regarded as "entirely inadequate," were substantially increased so as to permit it, at long last, to conduct investigations at any time, inspect buildings in the course of construction, repair, or demolition, something long sought by organized labor, and regulate and inspect elevators, a measure favored by the Elevator Constructors' Union.

The Murphy administration also secured the passage of several measures that, although attracting little public attention, were of special interest to individual craft unions: a law requiring that all state printing be done in union shops or in shops that met labor standards equal to those in union shops; a statute sponsored by the United Master Barbers of Michigan providing for uniform prices and hours in barber shops; a Highway Reciprocity Act supported by the Drivers' Union that created a state board empowered to negotiate interstate compacts governing the operation of vehicles engaged in interstate commerce; a statute important to the Teamsters and Chauffeurs Union that limited the hours of drivers of commercial trucks and trailers; another hours law requiring that fire fighters on duty for twenty-four hours be off duty for the next twenty-four hours; and a measure extending the requirement that wages be paid on a semi-monthly basis to workers in dry-cleaning establishments, the petroleum industry, and gas-drilling operations.[61]

In an effort to set standards for the hiring of apprentices, to drive the "racket trade schools" out of existence, and to ease the shortage of skilled labor in the state despite the heavy unemployment at the time, Murphy created a State Apprenticeship Council in February 1938. The council, which was headed by Krogstad and included both labor and management representatives, drew up a model apprenticeship statute in cooperation with the Federal Committee on Apprenticeship of the Department of Labor, but it had not yet submitted the measure to the legislature as of the end of the year. It did, however, aid in the creation of state and local joint apprenticeship committees that voluntarily adopted the standards it had set. Its efforts were welcomed both by organized labor and the state's industrialists.[62]

In seeking legislation to ameliorate working conditions, Murphy devoted particular effort to securing the passage of an occupational disease law and a fair labor standards act. As of 1937, sixteen states had enacted occupational disease legislation, nine covering all such diseases and seven providing benefits for only certain listed diseases. Governor Fitzgerald had created a Commission of Inquiry Relative to Occupational Diseases in 1935, and in January 1937 a majority of its members recommended a schedule-type law. Krogstad, a member of the commission, filed a minority report favoring the "all-inclusive" type law, and organized labor also preferred a statute of this type. During the interregnum between his election and his inauguration Murphy appointed his own committee to study workmen's compensation in Michigan, and the Division of Labor Standards also supplied the governor with relevant information. After conferring with both the secretary of the MFL and the general manager of the Michigan Manufacturers' Association, Murphy announced his support for a "schedule" bill, claiming that New York had been compelled to abandon its all-inclusive law because of the difficulty of implementing it.

After one House member alleged that he had been offered a bribe to vote for a weak schedule bill favored by the Michigan Manufacturers' Association, the legislature on May 28, 1937, passed a measure covering thirty-nine specified diseases. Murphy signed the bill after being advised by the director of the Bureau of Industrial Hygiene of Detroit's Department of Health that its good features outweighed its shortcomings. The Michigan statute, one of five occupational disease laws enacted by the states in 1937, proved to be quite unsatisfactory. During the first year that it was in effect, there were only 337 occupational disease cases, and the awards totaled only $35,000. The obvious shortcomings of the statute led the legislature to enact an all-inclusive statute in 1943.[63]

At the beginning of 1937 Michigan limited the hours of working women to ten per day and fifty-four per week and prohibited the labor of children under eighteen years of age in "unapproved" occupations. Believing that it was "the duty of government to set minimum standards for workers," Murphy was "especially anxious" to secure a minimum-wage law for working women. In devising such legislation he sought assistance from the Women's Bureau of the Department of Labor, from Benjamin V. Cohen, the celebrated legislative draftsman of the Roosevelt administration, and from William Haber. A liberal bill providing a minimum wage for women and limiting their working hours to forty per week was introduced in the House. Opposed by retailers, canneries, the hotel and resort industry, and several women's organizations antagonistic to a measure that applied to women alone, the bill was amended to include working children of both sexes, to exempt canneries, and to raise maximum working hours to forty-eight; it passed the House in this form. The Senate, however, killed the wages portion of the bill and then approved a heavily amended forty-eight-hour bill by a vote of 14–13, short of the seventeen votes required for enactment. The two houses were unable to resolve their differences before adjournment.

When the governor convened the legislature for an adjourned session on July 29, 1937, and a special session the next day, he called upon it to enact a minimum-wage bill for women and children and a hours bill like that previously approved by the House. The legislature, however, refused to comply. Michigan thus was not among the fourteen states that in 1937 adopted minimum-wage laws for women and children or revived or strengthened existing minimum-wage laws (twenty-two states had such laws at the end of 1937, three of the laws applying to male workers also), or among the nine states that further restricted the permissible working hours of women, or the five states that limited the working hours of men as well as women. Murphy intended to submit a wages-and-hours bill applicable to both men and women to the 1939 session of the legislature, but he was no longer Michigan's governor by that time.[64]

Although Murphy failed to persuade the legislature to adopt fair labor standards legislation, he did secure the liberalization of the state's unemployment compensation and old-age assistance statutes. The most troublesome problem faced by Michigan's new Unemployment Compensation Commission (MUCC) derived from a provision of the December 1936 law requiring the commission to establish "a civil service merit system" for commission employees. Frank Picard, the MUCC chairman and a Democratic regular, characterized this provision as " 'Haber's doublecross,' " claiming that Haber, who was an MUCC member, had inserted the requirement in the bill while Picard was "out of the room." Once the commission was established, Haber and others offered a "course" in Detroit for those wishing to work for the commission, and the applicants then had to pass an examination prepared in accordance with the recommendations of an advisory committee on civil service. Picard was none too happy with this arrangement, fearing that it was a means by which welfare workers would infiltrate and then dominate the commission. He was running a " 'business' " agency, he fumed, "not a home for all the 'career' welfare workers in this state," who, he erroneously charged, were unsympathetic to the agency. He told the MUCC's personnel director to remember that the Democrats had won the election and ordered that applicants with endorsements from the Democratic State Central Committee were to receive job preference. According to Picard's estimate, about half of the commission's employees as of the end of July 1937 were graduates of Haber's "special classes" or had been appointed from civil service eligibility lists; the remainder, presumably, had the proper political endorsement.[65]

Picard and Haber came into open conflict over Picard's efforts to appoint Frederic S. Schouman to the key post of MUCC director. When Haber would not agree to the appointment since Schouman, a former newspaperman, a staunch Democrat, and a Murphy loyalist, lacked the necessary qualifications, and probably because Haber thought that Schouman had played politics when he had served as administrative assistant to the state's WPA administrator, Picard, believing that the University of Michigan professor was trying to make the agency "a 'Haber commission,' " decided to "rid" himself of his opponent. Since many legislators did not much care for "carpet bag professors and their like" and Professor Haber in particular, Picard's efforts met with success.[66]

Desirous of liberalizing the Michigan Unemployment Compensation Act, Murphy requested the legislature to strike the provision of the statute exempting employers with payrolls of less than $6,000 since this deprived about 300,000 workers of benefits under the act. He also urged the lawmakers to advance the initial payment date from January 1, 1939, to July 1, 1938, since increasing employment in the state indicated that the unemployment insurance fund would be adequate to satisfy claims on the earlier date, and to provide for monthly or quarterly rather than annual payments of the employer tax to facilitate compliance with Social Security Board regulations and to accommodate small businesses. The legislature, which approved a new unemployment compensation bill on July 29, 1937, obliged the governor with regard to the initial date for the payment of claims and the more frequent collection of the employment tax but not on the issue of coverage. Although it eliminated the $6,000 exemption, it limited the act's coverage to employers of eight or more persons, no longer viewing this as unconstitutional, rather than to employers of one or more persons, which Murphy and the MUCC favored. The bill also eliminated the civil service provision of the 1936 act, but its most unusual feature was the provision that no member of the MUCC could be an employee of any other state agency. This provision was specifically designed to force the removal from the commission of William Haber, an employee of the University of Michigan and the principal author of the 1936 unemployment compensation statute.[67]

Since he understandably regarded the provision barring university professors from serving on the MUCC as "bad in principle" and also opposed both the earlier payment date and exemption features of the bill, Haber wanted Murphy to veto the measure. Murphy, who was "in violent disagreement" with the anti-Haber amendment and was also unhappy about the bill's coverage and its elimination of civil service, was initially inclined to comply with Haber's request. He was dissuaded from doing so by a lengthy defense of the bill that Schouman submitted to him. Denying that he had "stabbed Dr. Haber in the back" and that Picard had been "a party to the assassination," Schouman pointed out that not a single Democrat in the legislature had risen to Haber's defense. Quite apart from the substantive merits of the bill, Schouman noted the "unquestionable [political] advantage" the Democrats could derive both from an earlier payment of benefits and from the opposition of the governor and most Democratic legislators to the Republican-sponsored "eight-or-more" amendment. As for the elimination of the civil service provision, Schouman observed that since the civil service statute that the legislature had just approved would go into effect on January 1, 1938, implementation by the MUCC of a separate civil service program until the general civil service statute went into effect would be "a useless duplication of effort and expense." Convinced that the benefits to be derived from the amended bill outweighed its shortcomings and probably concluding that a veto would be overridden—the final version of the bill had been unanimously approved by both houses of the legislature—Murphy signed the measure into law on August 5.[68]

Despite the elimination of the civil service requirement, the MUCC continued to fill at least some positions with persons on its civil service lists. At the same time, however, Picard wrote a member of the MUCC's civil service advisory committee, "it won't profit us very much if the only result of our efforts is to throw Frank Murphy out of office and let the state government get into the hands of somebody not entire[ly] sympathetic [to unemployment insurance]." Although he complained at the end of 1937 that he had "never [before] spent such a miserable year from the patronage angle," Picard was pleased that 90 percent of the commission's employees at that time were Democrats. Picard, however, was unable to secure the appointment of Schouman as the MUCC's director. Heeding Haber's advice, Murphy recommended that the commission appoint the highly re-garded businessman, Abner Larned, to the position. Since Larned was acceptable to Picard and Harry Mead, the MUCC obliged the governor.[69]

The Michigan Unemployment Compensation Act required that unemployment benefits be paid through free public employment offices maintained or operated by the state. To effectuate this pur-pose and to provide a free employment service for all workers and employers in the state, the statute authorized the creation of a state employment service as a division of the MUCC and provided that it was to affiliate with the United States Employment Service (USES). When Congress created the USES in 1933, it provided matching funds for state public employment agencies, but Michigan had failed to take advantage of the available federal money. In June 1937, however, the legislature appropriated funds for a state employment service, and in August the MUCC established the Michigan State Employment Service (MSES) and affiliated it with the USES. By the end of the year the MSES, which Schouman headed, had established employment offices in seventeen cities and was in the process of expanding its service across the state. In 1938 its fifty-five offices and eighty-eight itinerant service points found jobs for 64,651 Michigan workers.[70]

Interest in old-age assistance in Michigan goes back to 1919 when Governor Albert E. Sleeper appointed a commission to study indus-trial conditions in the state and advised it to consider the feasibility of legislation to provide old-age pensions. An old-age pension bill was introduced in the legislature that same year, but it did not pass, and the same fate befell a 1923 measure supported by the Fraternal Order of Eagles. When the Michigan Old Age Pension League was formed in 1930, Frank Murphy was elected to its board of directors, and he was one of the two principal authors of a liberal pension bill that the Michigan legislature failed to enact in 1931. In July 1933, while William Comstock was governor, the legislature finally approved an old-age pension measure that provided pensions up to $30 a month to persons aged seventy or more who had been citizens for fifteen years and had resided in the state for the ten preceding years or twenty years intermittently. The pensions were to be financed by a $2 head tax on all persons over twenty-one years of age, and the state was to place a lien against the estate of the recipient equal to the amount of pension money he received. The pensions actually paid under the act turned out to be "woefully small" since the state was able to collect only 7 percent of the head tax due it.

To conform to requirements of the federal Social Security Act and thereby to secure the matching grants provided by the statute, the Michigan legislature passed a new old-age assistance measure in 1935. It reduced the residence requirement to five of the nine preceding years, made any citizen eligible for a pension if otherwise qualified, lowered the age limit to sixty-five as of January 1, 1940, abolished the head tax, and provided that the cost of the program was to be met from general funds. The Michigan old-age assistance program was approved by the Social Security Board in December 1935, the first state program to receive such approval.[71]

The Bureau of Old Age Assistance, which administered the Michigan old-age statute, ran the program in a tight-fisted manner as long as Fitzgerald was governor. Although the law permitted monthly payments up to $30, half of which would be paid by the federal government, the bureau arbitrarily ruled that no grant could exceed $20. The average monthly payment in 1933 was only $14.33. About five thousand needy old persons were denied assistance because they refused to deed their homes to the state even though the law left this matter to the discretion of the director of the Welfare Department rather than making it a requirement for receiving aid. Politics dominated the agency, and it was allegedly in a state of "chaos and confusion" when the Fitzgerald administration came to an end.[72]

The administration of the old-age assistance program was liberalized once Murphy became governor, James G. Bryant became director of the State Welfare Department, and Herman M. Pekarsky assumed the post of supervisor of the Bureau of Old Age Assistance. Most of the 127 incumbent old-age pension investigators were replaced by social workers, the "property trusteeship" requirement for assistance was abandoned, and pensions were no longer limited to $20 per month. The average pension had risen to $17.54 per month by July 1937, and whereas a monthly average of 15,398 persons had received assistance in the fiscal year 1935–36 and 32,705 persons in December 1936, the number rose to 35,883 by June 1937.[73]

Accepting Murphy's recommendations, the legislature in June 1937 liberalized the old-age assistance eligibility requirements. The eligibility age was reduced to sixty-five years immediately; the citizenship requirement was abandoned; possible support by legally responsible relatives was no longer to be considered in determining eligibility; applicants were prohibited from assigning real or personal property to the state, and property and insurance already deeded or assigned were to be returned to the original owners; and the state was prohibited from seeking recoveries from the estates of deceased pensioners. Also, whereas the 1935 legislature had appropriated only $2 million for old-age assistance for 1936–37, a sum that the 1937 legislature supplemented by an additional $2 million, the legislature appropriated $10 million for 1937–38. Of the monthly average of 61,928 persons receiving old-age assistance in the fiscal year 1937–38, 26,500 persons, about 43 percent of the total, qualified under the liberalized eligibility requirements, 22,000 because they were under seventy years of age and 4,500 because they were aliens over seventy. The average monthly grant for 1937–38 was $18.60. As of March 1938, 249 of every thousand Michigan residents over sixty-five were receiving aid, as compared to a national average of 212 per thousand. On the other hand, the average grant of $18.82 in Michigan in that recession month compared with a national average of $19.30, placing Michigan twenty-third among the states in this respect.[74]

III

It is hardly surprising in view of the state of industrial relations in Michigan in 1937 that Murphy was even more concerned about the enactment of a state labor-relations law than he was about the improvement of the state's old-age assistance and unemployment insurance statutes and the passage of protective and ameliorative labor laws. "Something must be written on Labor," Murphy noted to Kemp with regard to the governor's initial message to the legislature. "We want a new co-operation between labor and industry in Michigan.... The State of Michigan must play a significant part in minimizing disturbances costly to the interest of the public." In his message to the legislature on January 7 Murphy talked about securing wage earners an "effective voice in the arrangements that govern their working conditions by upholding the principle and right of orderly collective bargaining," but he placed greater emphasis on the need for a solution to the problem of labor disputes and the part that government could play in that regard.[75]

Since Michigan lacked an appropriate agency to conciliate or mediate labor disputes, Murphy favored the establishment of some kind of state mediation board. The labor climate in Michigan at the time, however, convinced him that it also would be necessary for the state to place some "reasonable restraint" on the ability of labor to strike and of management to lock out. Murphy believed that workers must be protected against unfair labor practices by their employers, but the state's strike experience persuaded him that the time had come to hold labor, as well as management, to account. "Without suggesting undue restrictions on [the] freedom of labor to organize and act in its own best interests," he stated, "we may properly ask *whether such organizations should be subject to some degree of regulation.*"[76]

In advocating restraints on the right to strike and the behavior of labor organizations, Murphy was responding to what seemed to be overwhelming public support for such action. This was the message conveyed in the governor's mail and in Michigan press editorial opinion, and public opinion polls confirmed it. Polls released in March, April, and May 1937 revealed that among those with opinions 65 percent thought that state and local governments should use force to remove sit-down strikers, an astonishing 89 percent that employers and employees should be compelled by law to settle their differences before striking, 69 percent that unions should be regulated by government, and 86 percent that unions should be required to incorporate.[77]

Ambitious for the presidency, Murphy wanted to attract favorable national attention and to repair whatever damage his reputation may have suffered as the result of Michigan's well-publicized labor troubles by sponsoring "the first well-balanced" labor-relations statute in the nation. Other states were following the pattern of the NLRA—five states adopted "baby" Wagner Acts in 1937—and so it could be assumed that a different sort of statute, one responsive to the recent exercise of labor power, would not go unnoticed. In view of what had occurred in Flint and Detroit, this assumption was particularly pertinent with regard to a labor-relations measure emanating from Michigan, which Murphy now hoped to make "the proving ground of new Labor relations legislation in the United States."[78]

The kind of labor-relations bill that Murphy presented to the state legislature was influenced not only by the state of affairs in Michigan and the governor's political needs but also by the views of the two principal authors of the bill, Ed Kemp and E. Blythe Stason, a University of Michigan law professor and an accomplished legislative draftsman. Both men were "cautious conservatives" who viewed with dismay the developments in the labor field during the early months of Murphy's governorship. Kemp, in particular, was overwrought by what had occurred, fearing that Michigan, under its "new New Deal," was "apparently" heading in the direction of "workers' soviets" and the possibility of "a breakdown or dictatorship." Both Stason and he believed that a proper labor-relations statute must impose significant restraints on employees and employee organizations as well as on employers, and both favored a large role for the state in the conciliation, mediation, and arbitration of labor disputes.

In preparing their draft of a labor-relations bill, Stason and Kemp were particularly influenced by the Canadian Industrial Disputes Investigation Act and the railway labor legislation of the United States. The Canadian statute, which had been copied by Colorado, provided for a thirty-day strike notice and fact-finding and conciliation in the interim. It had a "very enthusiastic" supporter in Professor Haber, who briefly assisted Kemp and Stason and who believed that "the public can't stay out of a strike situation." Intent on finding a mechanism to forestall strikes, Kemp and Stason looked approvingly on the machinery for compulsory mediation, fact-finding, and possible arbitration provided by the Railway Labor Act of 1926 and by the 1934 amendments to the statute.[79]

The bill that Kemp and Stason prepared provided for the fairly detailed regulation of the internal affairs of labor unions. It prohibited the closed shop and sit-down, jurisdictional, sympathy, and political strikes, provided for minority representation and individual bargaining, and required the selection of employee representatives for bargaining purposes by secret ballot.[80] Murphy, however, excluded all of these restraints on unions from the bill he submitted to the legislature on April 29, 1937.

Whereas the purpose of the NLRA and the baby Wagner Acts was to enhance the bargaining power of organized labor, the major purpose of the Murphy administration's bill, so patently a product of the law-and-order crisis in Michigan, was "to remove some of the causes" of labor disputes and to "provide facilities for their prompt settlement." The bill, designated as House Bill 571, provided for a three-man board of industrial relations appointed by the governor. It asserted the right of employees to organize and to bargain through representatives of their own choosing and stated that it was "unfair" and "unlawful" for employers to (a) interfere with this right by "acts of repression and intimidation" such as espionage or the circulation of blacklists; (b) interfere with the formation or administration of a labor organization, although employers were permitted to provide facilities for shop councils or similar bodies; (c) discriminate against employees because of their membership or nonmembership in a labor organization or for signing complaints or providing information in accordance with the terms of the statute; (d) refuse to bargain; (e) violate the terms of a labor contract "knowingly and intentionally"; and (f) alter the terms of a contract when there was a dispute or declare a lockout without first submitting the matter to the board or, during a period not exceeding thirty days, while the matter was pending before the board or a special board of mediation.

House Bill 571 also contained a list of "unfair" employee practices. It made it "unlawful" for employees to (a) "interfere with, injure, restrain, or attempt to intimidate or to coerce" any employee with respect to his joining or not joining a labor organization, selecting representatives, or engaging in lawful employment; (b) strike without exhausting "every method of voluntary agreement and negotiation" specified in the measure and without giving notice to the employer and the board or during a period not exceeding thirty days while the issue was pending before the board or a special board of mediation; (c) refuse to bargain; (d) "prevent, obstruct, or interfere with" an employer, employee, or labor organization that was complying with the act; and (e) violate the terms of a contract. The union's books and records were made subject to examination by the board.

If there was a controversy regarding employee representation, the board, "on request of any party in interest" or on its own motion, was to investigate, and it could resolve the matter by an election or "any other suitable method." It was also the responsibility of the board to determine the appropriate unit for bargaining purposes. The board was empowered to mediate labor disputes, create special boards of mediation, encourage the parties to submit disputes to arbitration, adjudge complaints concerning labor contracts, issue "cease and desist" orders against employers, employees, or labor organizations found to be violating the act, and conduct investigations to protect employers or employees against "racketeering, extortion, and other unfair labor practices."

House Bill 571 vested extraordinary powers in the governor. If he decided that a strike or lockout would cause "grave injury, hardship, or inconvenience to the public" because it involved "a major industry or essential public service or for other substantial reason," it became illegal for any person or organization to order or encourage such a strike or lockout until the governor had had "reasonable opportunity" to consult with the disputants and the Administrative Board. If either party to the dispute violated this provision, the governor could take such action as he deemed necessary for "the due protection of the public peace, welfare, and safety." Also, if a strike or lockout occurred and the local police were unable to maintain order or protect the owners of the property in the peaceful exercise of their rights, the governor could place the establishment in the charge of the commissioner of the State Police pending further mediation efforts. The property in these circumstances was to remain closed or be permitted to operate under regulations approved by the governor.

House Bill 571 sought to restrain the use of the injunction in labor disputes and to authorize peaceful picketing, which had been declared illegal by the state's courts. It specified that no court was to issue injunctions in a labor dispute to prohibit persons "interested in such dispute" from striking, joining a union, paying strike benefits, giving publicity to the dispute by picketing or any other method not involving "fraud or violence, coercion or intimidation," and assembling peacefully. The measure, however, proscribed the picketing of a business affected by a labor dispute or the residence of any employee "in such manner as to be calculated to intimidate any such person, or to obstruct approach thereto or egress therefrom, or to lead to a breach of the peace."[81]

House Bill 571 was a far cry from the NLRA and the five state laws modeled on the federal statute even though the Michigan measure incorporated many of the provisions of these pro-labor statutes. It added contract violations and premature lockouts to the list of unfair employer practices, but it weakened the ban on company unions contained in the Wagner-type acts by specifically authorizing shop councils. By requiring the board, in effect, to hold an election for employee representatives at the employer's request, it authorized a procedure that the NLRB did not at that time permit lest it enable an employer to force a premature test of a union's strength or to challenge its majority status at the end of each contract term. The bill also left open the question of whether the board should apply the majority-rule criterion in the selection of employee representatives even though the Jones and Laughlin decision seemed to foreclose the issue, at least for interstate employers.

By including a list of unfair employee practices to "balance" the proscribed unfair employer practices, House Bill 571 departed from the model of the "protective" labor-relations statutes like the NLRA and anticipated the "restrictive" state labor laws of 1939 and later, and the Taft-Hartley Act of 1947. Advocates of the protective statutes insisted that it was necessary to place restraints on employer behavior because organized labor, the weaker of the two parties at that time, needed protection against the "abusive use of economic power" and unfair practices of employers if the unions were to acquire bargaining power equal to that of management. They contended, on the other hand, that it was unnecessary and unwise to specify unfair employee practices since most practices of this sort were already prohibited by law and since there was a "very real danger" that the courts would extend the impact of such provisions beyond the intent of the enacting legislatures. Kemp and Stason, however, thought that labor had the upper hand in Michigan and believed that events had demonstrated that employers, nonunion workers, and the general public required protection against abuses of union power, a point of view that influenced the restrictive labor laws that were to come. Similarly, the concept of an undefined public interest distinguishable from the interests of employers and employees, a concept present in the restrictive but not the protective laws, was very evident in House Bill 571's elaborate provisions regarding the settlement of strikes and threatened strikes.[82]

The press and Michigan employers found more to praise than to criticize in House Bill 571, viewing it as "vastly more rational and balanced" than the NLRA. They expressed concern, however, about the seizure power that the measure vested in the governor. The "aroma" of this provision, the *Detroit Free Press* thought, was "communistic rather than democratic." The strongest opposition to the bill came from organized labor, particularly the UAW. The DWCFL did not take a public stand on the measure since it did not wish to embarrass Murphy, but Martel wired the governor that his organization thought the bill "so hostile to the interests of labor both organized and unorganized and so dangerous to the peace of the community" that it would not even seek to have the measure amended. UAW spokesmen warned that passage of the bill, which Martin denounced as "one of the most dangerous pieces of legislation ever proposed in any state," would destroy Murphy's reputation as a liberal governor.

The UAW complained about the bill's failure to endorse majority rule. It feared that the authority granted the board to examine union records was the "opening wedge" leading to incorporation of unions in the state, a traditional union bugaboo. The UAW thought that the bill's language regarding shop councils might be construed as legalizing company unions, and it did not think that contract violations should be made a crime. It favored an anti-injunction section in the bill that conformed more closely to the terms of the Norris-LaGuardia Act. Above all, the UAW protested the provisions of House Bill 571 that dealt with unfair employee practices and that imposed restraints on the right to strike. "... in this period of growing organizations where labor is yet weak," Maurice Sugar said of the bill's proscription of certain employee practices, "the application of any of these provisions would furnish the employers with very effective weapons to destroy the labor movement and to hinder its growth." Martin alleged that even the "slightest restraint" on labor's right to strike marked "a long stride in the direction of destruction of labor unions and the introduction of fascism in this country." What the UAW favored was a statute similar to the NLRA that also included some mediation provisions and the terms of the Norris-LaGuardia Act. The ACLU, similarly, wired Murphy that it was "distressed" that "a great state under a liberal governor" was preparing to enact legislation that would infringe so important a civil liberty as the right to strike. All that was required, the ACLU advised, was for Michigan to enact a state version of the Norris-LaGuardia Act.[83]

Murphy had naively assumed that since organized labor knew that it had a friend in the governor's chair, it would not oppose a bill he deemed in the public interest. He now discovered that he had been mistaken, just as he discovered that it would be difficult to devise legislation to curb certain types of union behavior without antagonizing civil libertarians. Reacting to the criticism of House Bill 571, he arranged a series of conferences with members of the legislature, industrialists, and representatives of the UAW, the DWCFL, and the MFL. As the record makes clear, he was especially eager to conciliate his friends and supporters in the labor movement and in the ACLU, less willing to accommodate suggestions from manufacturers. Although he was "convinced" that a separate anti-injunction bill of the Norris-LaGuardia type, which the ACLU had proposed, could not be passed, he was willing to attach a section to House Bill 571 that would serve the same purpose. Roger Baldwin, the ACLU director, consequently had attorneys Isadore Polier and Nathan Greene prepare the draft of "a concentrated baby Norris-LaGuardia Act," and Murphy added it to the bill over Kemp's strenuous objections.[84]

Following Murphy's lead, the Michigan House, by a vote of 63 to 31, approved a substitute for House Bill 571 that the chairman of the Committee on Labor described as "Gov. Murphy's bill." The provisions of the original bill regarding shop councils and subjecting union records to examination were dropped, the measure now specifically provided that representatives of the majority in a bargaining unit were to be "the exclusive representatives," and the industrial relations board was no longer required to hold elections at the request of "any party in interest." Although the substitute bill still contained a list of unfair employee practices, contract violations were no longer included among them. Of particular importance to organized labor, the required strike notice was dropped from the bill, and the governor was no longer authorized to place struck establishments in the care of the State Police and to determine whether they remained closed or open. In addition to authorizing "all-union" (closed shop) agreements and prohibiting yellow-dog contracts, the substitute bill also included the anti-injunction section drafted by the ACLU. A hearing in open court that involved the taking of testimony and opportunity for cross-examination was now required before an injunction could be granted, injunctions were to be denied plaintiffs with "unclean hands," and jury trials were authorized in contempt cases.[85]

"Take a look at the Labor Relations Bill as I directed it out of committee," Murphy wrote Baldwin the day after the substitute bill passed the House. Baldwin replied that, "on quick reading," the measure appeared "to be beyond criticism as an example of progressive fair dealing in the most difficult field of lawmaking," and he urged the Michigan Conference for the Protection of Civil Rights to support the bill. Baldwin's favorable opinion of the bill was not shared by the UAW, which, although conceding that the measure was an improvement over its predecessor, attacked it as "a most reactionary piece of labor legislation." The major UAW objections were to the continued inclusion in the bill of unfair employee practices, the power still retained by the governor to declare strikes illegal under certain conditions, and a new provision banning strikes by public employees engaged in work "necessary for the public welfare and safety," which Sugar hyperbolically alleged would encourage "a psychology of submission and slavery" among such workers.

After learning that Baldwin had written approvingly of the substitute bill, Sugar, who was a sometimes attorney for the ACLU and who had sent a critical analysis of the bill to ACLU headquarters, wrote the ACLU director, "What in hell has happened to you!" A contrite Baldwin replied that the "only answer" he could give was that he had not read the substitute with sufficient care. Accepting Sugar's evaluation of the measure, the ACLU now informed Murphy that the substitute bill, in its view, interfered with the right to strike and nullified the guarantees of the NLRA. A few days later the ACLU forwarded to Murphy an analysis of the substitute bill that Nathan Greene had prepared at the organization's request. Professing to be "as much disturbed by the Michigan bill as I have ever been disturbed by anything,'' the labor lawyer charged that the measure made ''all organizational activity'' by labor an unfair practice, which was a considerable exaggeration. From here on, for all practical purposes, the ACLU and the UAW coordinated their strategy regarding a Michigan labor-relations bill, with Sugar, who had a foot in both camps, playing the key role. The cooperation of the two groups is a little-known example of the functioning of the libertarian-labor alliance in the New Deal era and of the way in which the ACLU identified itself with the goals of organized labor during that period.[86]

The UAW-ACLU criticisms of the House substitute bill were endorsed by Labor's Non-Partisan League and by John L. Lewis, who complained to Murphy that the measure would lead to ''a ghastly hamstringing of the organized labor movement'' and would ''put Michigan back a century in labor legislation.'' Because of the central position that Michigan occupied on the labor scene in 1937, organized labor feared that what happened in the Wolverine state would become a precedent for other states and perhaps for the national government as well. The Supreme Court had just validated the NLRA, and organized labor was unwilling to accept a state act that weakened the guarantees that unions had received in the federal statute.[87]

If organized labor thought that the House substitute bill imposed far too many restraints on unions, industrialists and businessmen in Michigan complained about the extent to which Murphy's original bill had been amended to accommodate labor criticism. The Detroit Board of Commerce urged the city's six hundred ''largest employers'' to seek the enactment of the original bill since the substitute, in the board's grossly overstated opinion, would make it ''almost impossible for you to maintain a payroll in Michigan.''[88] The impossibility of devising a labor-relations statute that would satisfy both the UAW and Michigan employers was becoming increasingly evident.

There was little likelihood that the Michigan Senate would approve the labor-relations bill the House had passed and even less likelihood that it would revise the measure in a manner that would please organized labor. Although the Democrats controlled the Senate, New Deal ideas had not yet penetrated that body, and, as Murphy observed, ''the Republicans and one or two Democrats'' were ''almost entirely sympathetic with the employer's viewpoint.''[89] Also, by the time the Senate turned its attention to labor-relations legislation, the tide of opinion was running heavily against organized labor and its friend in the governor's chair because of the Lansing Labor Holiday, the Consumers Power strike, and the Battle of Monroe.

The labor bill that the Senate approved on June 23 was characterized by its author as promoting "law and order instead of disorder." On the other hand, Murphy's personal secretary, echoing her boss, described the measure as "very regulatory and suppressive," blaming this on "present public opinion." The bill restored the provisions of House Bill 571 regarding representation, the examination of union books, and picketing. It also banned stranger picketing (picketing by persons other than employees of the affected plant) and picketing that interfered with "the free and unimpeded use of public highways," a provision recommended by Murphy because of what had occurred in the Battle of Monroe. The bill required a fifteen-day notice before a union could strike; and, if the dispute was not resolved in that time, the board of industrial relations was to publish a report identifying the party "mainly responsible or blameworthy." Labor organizations were required to include provisions in their constitutions, articles of association, or by-laws forbidding violation of a labor contract, sit-down strikes, and strikes that violated the terms of the bill, and requiring the expulsion of members who engaged in such strikes.[90]

The House overwhelmingly rejected the Senate bill, and a conference committee of the two chambers, ignoring the customary functions of such committees, then wrote a new bill. The conference bill omitted the provisions of the House substitute bill specifying unfair employer and employee practices and permitting the governor to delay strikes in major industries and essential public services; failed to include the restraints on the injunction contained in the House substitute; and, in addition to the House bill's restrictions on picketing, prohibited picketing that impeded the use of public highways and picketing by anyone other than an employee of the struck plant, a party to the dispute, or an official of a labor organization that was a party to the dispute. The conference bill was approved on June 25, the final working day of the session, by a vote of 72–3 in the House and 29–0 in the Senate. The measure was actually passed at 3:00 A.M. on June 26 (the clock was set back to make it appear that the bill had passed before midnight on June 25), and for the next twenty-four hours the UAW counsel was unable to contact any member of the legislature since, he reported, "they were drunk or in bed, or both." The legislators were reacting, each in his own fashion, to a typically insane conclusion of the regular session during which they had set off cannon crackers, thrown paper wads at their colleagues, and deluged one another with water guns. One House member had addressed the assemblage in his bathrobe. A reporter who had witnessed the scene was convinced that the legislators could "bat 1,000 in anybody's daffiness league."[91]

Business Week thought that businessmen in Michigan were "pretty well satisfied" with the industrial-relations bill, but the organ of the Michigan Manufacturers' Association concluded that the measure was "not much of an improvement over conditions which prevailed previously." Insofar as there was business opposition to the conference bill, however, it was far more muted than the opposition of the UAW, the AFL, the ACLU, and labor sympathizers, all of whom thought the measure flawed beyond redemption. They were dissatisfied with the bill's failure to prohibit unfair labor practices by employers, the deficiencies in its anti-injunction provisions, and language that they feared would make it possible for a hostile board and unfriendly courts to circumscribe labor's rights. Above all, the labor and libertarian critics of the bill focused on its picketing provisions and especially the ban on stranger picketing, which, they contended, reflected "a recognized community of interest among all workers" and was "the only realistic approach to unionism in modern industry." Public opinion, on the other hand, appeared to be opposed to all picketing, to say nothing of stranger picketing. According to polling data released by the American Institute of Public Opinion at the beginning of August, 54 percent of the respondents favored state laws prohibiting all picketing during strikes, and 63 percent believed that legal picketing should be limited to one or two pickets.[92]

Initially, Murphy seemed disposed to sign the conference bill, describing it as a "progressive step" and as "a truly pioneering measure" that was "broader than any other [industrial-relations] law." Accenting the positive, he noted that the statute guaranteed collective bargaining, legalized picketing, restricted the use of injunctions, and authorized the investigation of racketeering and extortion. The restraints on stranger picketing, he contended, were required to cope with "abuses" of a sort that had caused "a great deal of trouble." Above all, Murphy pointed to the measure's emphasis on conciliation, mediation, and arbitration as offering the means by which the state government could "impartially" assist in the resolution of labor disputes and the elimination of violence in the labor-relations field. Still bemused by the concept of the public interest, the governor seemed to view the opposition to the bill by both labor and management as proof of its reasonable character. Wanting an industrial-relations bill that would be "heralded nationally," he doubtlessly realized that the measure before him was the best that could be obtained from "the reactionary State Senate."[93]

Pressures exerted by the labor-libertarian alliance, however, began to have their effect on Murphy, and he "listened sympathetically" to its criticisms, particularly with respect to stranger picketing, an issue that took on exaggerated significance in the debate about possible industrial-relations legislation in Michigan. When the legislature reassembled for its brief adjournment session on July 29, the final day on which he could legally veto the June 25 measure, Murphy addressed a joint session of the two houses and noted that the conference bill, a measure he previously had praised, contained provisions that would make it difficult to gain the "cooperation and support" of labor and management that he now claimed were required if an industrial-relations measure were to be effectively implemented. It was, of course, the opposition of organized labor that was troubling Murphy, and he therefore requested that the bill be revised to permit picketing by members of a labor organization at a plant when any one of them was engaged in a dispute.

When the Senate proved unwilling to follow the governor's advice, Sugar feared that Murphy would feel obliged to sign the unamended bill. The UAW counsel, consequently, called for the "widest and most vigorous protest" by the foes of the measure before the day was out. The UAW, Lewis, Labor's Non-Partisan League, and the Conference for the Protection of Civil Rights all communicated with Murphy that day to urge a veto, and the governor obliged them by vetoing the bill that night, because, he said, it did not enjoy the support of the interests primarily affected by the legislation.[94]

Speaking informally after submitting his veto message, Murphy declared that he had not vetoed the bill because of the pressure of any group but because of "conscience." It is evident, though, that he had abandoned the amorphous concept of the "public interest" that had informed his defense of both House Bill 571 and the June 25 measure and was now assigning a veto power over industrial-relations legislation to organized labor and, presumably, to employers as well. In the final analysis, Murphy was simply not willing to defy a group with whose interests he had identified his career long before that group was as powerful as it had become in 1937. As he told the DWCFL after the veto, "I have never yet done anything to hurt Labor. . . . and I never will." The *Detroit News* thought that Murphy's "mental processes" in all this were "a puzzle," and even the *Nation*, which was friendly to Murphy, correctly remarked that the governor had gotten himself "tangled in as hopeless a web as ever troubled a well-meaning labor governor." The *Detroit Labor News*, however, thought that "a great governor" had been "doing a great job," and the ACLU informed Murphy "confidentially" that there were "very few governors—or any public officials for that matter—whose acts we so frequently endorse."[95]

Murphy had called a special session of the legislature to meet on July 30, just two hours after the adjournment of the regular session, and one of the three matters that he submitted to the legislators for their consideration was labor-relations legislation. Regarding the anti-picketing section of the bill as its "most important feature," a majority of the Senators repassed the June 25 measure. The House promptly substituted and then passed a version of the bill acceptable to Murphy that permitted picketing by persons employed in or residents of the municipality or township in which the dispute occurred or in an adjoining community. According to the diary entry of a state senator, half the House members who passed the bill were "so drunk they did not know whether they were in the House of Representatives or in a bar room." Refusing to yield, the Senate buried the House bill in committee and then illegally voted to adjourn. Senator James Burns, a Detroit Democrat who insisted that the Senate remain in session and pass the bill, thereupon strode to the desk of the anti-Murphy Democratic floor leader, William Palmer, jerked off his glasses, struck him twice in the face, and rushed from the chamber. The special session actually continued until August 12, but the two houses were unable to reconcile their differences on labor-relations legislation.[96]

When the special session came to a close, Murphy expressed "confidence" that Michigan could "work out a satisfactory [industrial-relations] law." He sought the advice of organized labor, the ACLU, employers, and the Department of Labor about the content of such a measure. The governor considered the possibility of convening another special session to deal with the problem, but legislators were cool to the idea; and, as the director of the Department of Labor's Division of Labor Standards pointed out, the time was hardly propitious for the enactment of the kind of measure that would have satisfied the labor-libertarian alliance.[97] It was not until 1939, after Murphy had left the governorship, that Michigan finally enacted a labor-relations statute. It was a measure of the restrictive type and presumably would have been vetoed by Murphy had he still been governor.[98]

The Michigan labor-relations experience of 1937 demonstrates how quickly a reaction set in against the kind of pro-labor sentiment that had led to the enactment of the NLRA. The sit-down strikes and the labor turbulence of the early months of 1937 adversely affected the public standing of organized labor, as polling data revealed,[99] and led to a spreading demand for law and order that influenced a governor known throughout the nation for his support of organized labor but anxious, at the same time, to further his own political career. Just as the sit-down strikes had focused national attention on Michigan at the beginning of 1937, so the attempt of the Murphy administration to devise legislation that would curb unions and restrain the use of the strike weapon became a matter of more than local interest; and it was deemed "a significant straw in the wind" that the reaction against the exercise of labor power had come in Murphy's Michigan.[100] Because of Murphy's inept and wavering legislative leadership, his veto of the only bill on which the two houses of the Michigan legislature could agree, and his unwillingness, in the end, to oppose organized labor on so important a matter, Michigan failed to enact a labor-relations law in 1937. The trend toward the passage of state and federal labor laws of the restrictive type, however, was foreshadowed by what took place in Lansing during the first year of Murphy's governorship.

10

The Battle against
"Privilege, Politics and Pull"

I

Although he was unsuccessful in securing the enactment of a labor-relations measure that he could sign, Murphy demonstrated considerable skill as a legislative leader in persuading a reluctant legislature to pass a strong civil service reform bill. The governor's performance won the plaudits of good-government advocates, but his conscientious enforcement of the reform measure impaired his standing with the leaders of his party.

The initial impetus for the civil service bill that Murphy pushed through the legislature was provided by his predecessor, Frank D. Fitzgerald. "Exasperated . . . with the job seekers' cigar ashes in his coffee," the Republican governor told an audience at the St. Joseph County Fair in September 1935, "I have endured almost nine months of an existence made burdensome by favor-hunters snapping at my heels, awakening me from my sleep, and taking up time in my office that should rightly be devoted to constructive work." He was consequently determined, he said, "to uproot the patronage evil from the government of the state of Michigan." On October 14, 1935, Fitzgerald appointed a Civil Service Study Commission, consisting of Professor James K. Pollock of the University of Michigan as chairman; Mrs. Siegel W. Judd of the League of Women Voters; Lent D. Upson, the director of the Detroit Bureau of Governmental Research; Haskell W. Nichols, a Republican member of the Michigan House of Representatives; and Edmund C. Shields, a prominent Democrat. The commission was aided in its work by the Public Administration Service and the Civil Service Assembly.[1]

The report of the Civil Service Study Commission, which was published on July 20, 1936, revealed how the spoils system had affected personnel practices in Michigan's state government. Information obtained from about twelve thousand of the state's 13,500 employees revealed that 40.8 percent had been appointed since January 1, 1935, mainly through a central patronage office, and new employees each year comprised about 25 percent of the total number of state jobholders. Twenty-five percent of the employees had only a grade school education, and only 27 percent had graduated from high school. Political considerations were "preeminent" in the recruitment of employees, nepotism was "rampant," employees were dismissed in an arbitrary and unfair manner, they were required to contribute 1–2 percent of their salaries as well as their time to their party, and morale was "of the lowest order." The titles of positions in the state service, the study commission reported, had little relationship to the work actually performed, and employees doing the same kind of work did not necessarily receive the same salaries. There was no promotion system, no system of in-service training, no formal system of individual service ratings, and hardly any use of personnel records. The commission's report, the *New York Herald Tribune* summarized, demonstrated that the government of Michigan was, "for the most part, in the hands of inexperienced men and women, who hold their jobs not because they know something but because they know somebody."[2]

The bill recommended by the study commission called for appointment by the governor of a four-member civil service commission, not more than two of whom could be from any one party. To avoid "any possible political angle," the commission was to appoint the state personnel director from among three persons recommended by an examining committee. The personnel director was to perform the executive and administrative functions of the civil service department, prepare classification and compensation plans encompassing all positions in the state service, investigate the need for every position in the classified service, and devise plans for employee training programs.

Positions in the state government with the exception of policy-making posts and positions exempted for constitutional or practical reasons were to be filled from eligible registers prepared on the basis of the performance of job applicants on competitive examinations, the appointing officer to make the selection from the three persons standing highest on the register. Appointees were to serve a probationary six-month period before receiving regular appointments. Insofar as possible, vacancies in the classified service were to be filled by promotion from within the state service. Incumbents in the classified service, rather than being "blanketed in" without an examination, were to retain their positions temporarily until the civil service commission, by open competitive examinations, could prepare eligible lists for all classes of positions. Provision was made for service ratings and the maintenance of adequate personnel records. To meet the objection that existing civil service systems made it difficult to get rid of inefficient employees, the study commission in its bill vested complete responsibility for the dismissal of employees in the appointing authority—the so-called "open back door system." Believing that civil service and "political service . . . simply cannot mix," the study commission specified in its bill that employees in the classified service were not to engage in political activity or to solicit or receive money for political purposes.

The most intriguing feature of the study commission bill was the provision permitting incumbents to retain their jobs only on the basis of their performance on competitive examinations. Since most state employees as of 1936 were Republicans, Frank Picard, who reflected Democratic opinion on the point, had warned a reform advocate that if the bill submitted to the legislature were "nothing more or less than an attempt to guarantee jobs to the republicans you're going to run up against a snag among democrats like myself who are really in favor of civil service." After the Democratic victory in November the Republicans thought it "quite evident," as one Republican senator put it, that "our Democratic brethren over in Lansing intend to ease out all of the Republicans and then throw over their successors the protective blanket of civil service." The Civil Service Study Commission sought to respond to the fears of men like Picard and the Republican senator by its unique recommendation regarding the status of incumbents.³

The widely circulated *Report of the Civil Service Study Commission* and its proposed bill created "nation-wide interest." Among the nine states that had merit systems as of the end of 1936, only Maryland had enacted its law after World War I. Arkansas and Tennessee adopted civil service statutes in 1937, both of them heavily influenced by the Civil Service Study Commission bill, and other states now looked to the Michigan bill as a model. ". . . our careful survey in Michigan," Pollock boasted, "has laid the ground work for the whole [civil service] movement throughout the country in the state field."⁴

The Michigan Merit System Association was formed in April 1936 to arouse citizen support for civil service reform in Michigan and to seek the enactment of the study commission bill. In the 1936 election campaign in Michigan, both parties and both gubernatorial candidates, responding to the commission's report and the efforts of the Merit System Association, pledged support for civil service reform. Twenty of the thirty-two senators and sixty-six of the one hundred House members elected were on record as favoring the commission's bill. On the other hand, thirty-one House candidates and eight senatorial candidates who had refused to respond to a Merit System Association questionnaire were defeated in the election, twenty of the former and three of the latter by civil service advocates.[5]

Consistent with his campaign pledge and believing that other state reforms could not be fully achieved unless the state government improved its personnel practices, Murphy wrote Pollock after the November election, "I am prepared to go straight ahead with the Civil Service program." Meeting with the political science professor a few days later, Murphy made the same commitment "after fluttering his feathers a little bit," as Pollock recalled, "and indicating that he felt pretty proud that unlike most politicians he saw what was his public duty." When Murphy conferred with Democratic party leaders late in December, he told them that merit must come first and politics second in the Lansing New Deal. "Special Emphasis Should be Placed Upon the Need for Civil Service," Murphy advised Kemp regarding what the governor wished to stress in his first message to the legislature. In his address, Murphy urged that "a thorough going system of civil service . . . be adopted at once," and he specifically endorsed the study commission bill.[6]

Because he was obliged to spend so much time on the strike front, Murphy could devote relatively little attention to legislative matters during the early weeks of his administration. As Kemp lamented on February 10, "while strike negotiations proceed, the legislative program languishes." One week after the end of the GM strike, however, Murphy listed civil service reform along with welfare reorganization, corrections legislation, and an occupational disease law as measures requiring "immediate and preferential consideration."[7]

Senate Bill No. 1, which largely replicated the provisions of the Civil Service Study Commission's bill, was reported out by the State Affairs Committee on February 23 with only minor changes. The most significant amendment was the requirement that the appointing officer select the top person on the eligible roster for any position rather than one of the top three. The author of this amendment, Senator Charles C. Diggs, a black Detroit undertaker, saw the rule-of-one as an anti-discrimination measure. Opposition to the bill on the Senate floor was led by a small band of Republicans, the most important of whom was the Republican floor leader, Miles Callaghan, a farmer, fruit grower, and former hardware-store owner of Reed City who was characterized by the executive secretary of the Michigan Merit System Association, William P. Lovett, as "unscrupulous and resourceful." Disabling amendments were defeated in the Senate, however, partly because Murphy, in between strikes, interceded with the Democratic leadership. The measure passed the Senate on March 4 by a vote of 23-7, the opposition consisting of two Democrats and five Republicans.[8]

The Michigan Merit System Association recognized that "the real battle" over the civil service bill would come in the House, where, an Association aide predicted, forty-one "hostile members" would attempt "to imitate Callaghan's tactics in the Senate." In the view of the Association staff, what was required to forestall defeat in the House was vigorous action by public officials, especially the governor, and "relentless pursuit of the citizen pressure campaign" of the Merit System Association.[9]

Returning to Lansing from Florida because of the Chrysler strike, Murphy summoned House leaders to inform them that civil service reform was "No. 1 on our legislative program." The reform bill, nevertheless, languished in the House State Affairs Committee, and the Democratic majority appeared to be hoping that the measure would die there. Pollock and the Michigan Merit System Association were convinced that the Democrats were delaying action at least until after the April 5 election, in which Van Wagoner was a candidate for reelection as highway commissioner, to make it possible for the "Highway Department controlled House . . . to amend the bill to suit Van Wagoner." It was one thing to say this privately, but Lovett, the Association's chief Lansing representative, "lost his head and blew off the lid" by declaring publicly on April 1 that if Van Wagoner were reelected, "we might as well say the bill is dead for this Legislature." Calling attention to the number of Democrats in the House to whose election campaign the Highway Department had contributed, Lovett stated that he was "convinced the House opposition to the bill" expressed "ideas of which Van Wagoner . . . [was] the responsible spokesman." A partisan Republican who had already written several persons that if Van Wagoner were reelected, "a virtual Tammany" would "be established in the State," Lovett had little hard evidence to support his allegations about Van Wagoner, who insisted that he favored the merit system. Moreover, it was "sheer suicide," as one Merit System Association lobbyist put it, to antagonize the Democratic majority in the House. Lovett was denounced on the floor of the House for making a " 'cowardly partisan attack,' " and a resolution was introduced in the chamber condemning the " 'vicious lobby' " that he headed.[10]

As an unidenitified Merit System Association source correctly noted, the organization's tactics in seeking the passage of the civil service bill—its petitions, the resolutions that it secured from civic organizations, and its organizational efforts in strategic counties—ceased to be of much value after the Lovett attack on Van Wagoner. Legislators, according to this source, resented the effort of civic organizations, newspapers, and the like to influence their vote and saw the civil service bill as a "measure which someone outside" was "trying to force down their throats." That "someone" represented "respectability" and "training," both of which were "foreign to the average legislator," especially the average Democratic legislator. If the legislature were to pass the bill, it was now apparent that pressure would have to be exerted from inside the political system, especially by the governor.

Understanding the governor's importance to their cause even if some Republicans were "skeptical" of his influence with the legislature, the good-government people sought to impress upon Murphy the leadership role that he would have to play if the bill were to pass. Merit System Association leaders met with the governor, and the director of the Civil Service Assembly of the United States and Canada, undoubtedly at the behest of Michigan friends, wrote Murphy that although Arkansas and Tennessee had overcome Michigan's "early lead" in the civil service field, "the eyes of the country" were "still on Michigan, and its reputation as well as that of its Governor would certainly be greatly enhanced by the final enactment of a personnel law." Murphy's task was not an easy one, however, since Democratic legislators saw little reason to deny their party the fruits of a rare electoral victory by enacting a strong civil service bill. "If the Democrats swallow this pill," the *Detroit News* observed, "the Governor will probably have to force it down their throats."[11]

The opposition to civil service in the legislature was in part based on the same antagonism toward intellectuals and "the university crowd" that inspired the anti-Haber amendment to the unemployment compensation bill. "In Michigan," declared Democrat Harry Glass, Jr., a House member from Grand Rapids and a junior college graduate, "we no longer have political parties—we have a coalition government headed by Doctors Pollock and Haber. If this trend keeps up, one will have to be a university professor, haughtily disdainful of any political faith, to be a janitor in the State Capitol." In similar vein, Representative Philip J. Rahoi, a Democrat from Iron Mountain who had left school at age fifteen, stated that he opposed civil service because it was "a scheme on the part of certain college heads to open up a market for college graduates, who can not acquire any other employment." Legislators expressed fear that civil service examinations would overstress "intelligence" and undervalue "personal appearance and personality." Although some jobs required college training, Rahoi asserted, all jobs required "honesty, courtesy and an industrious application" to the task at hand, and everyone knew, he continued, that "the average college does not teach any of these attributes." Since he believed that the University of Michigan was promoting the civil service measure, Chester B. Fitzgerald, the chairman of the House State Affairs Committee, introduced a bill requiring the university to apply civil service principles in selecting its president, faculty members, and athletic coaches. Professor Pollock's role in urging civil service reform created so much "ill feeling" among Democrats that a university regent advised President Alexander G. Ruthven to "curb" the political scientist.[12]

House Democrats were opposed to any civil service bill that failed to blanket in incumbents. This view, Picard noted, might appear "rather selfish to a lot of Republicans," but the Republicans, he maintained, had decided to oppose blanketing in only when it became evident that Michigan politics would not be "so entirely one-sided" any longer. "The democrats," Picard informed the Merit System Association, "rightly feel that if there is going to be any advantage in having 'one foot inside the door,' the democrats now ought to be the owners of that foot." Off the record, some Democrats conceded that they opposed the bill because they wanted to use jobs to strengthen their party. Whereas the Republicans, they alleged, could secure campaign funds from the wealthy, Democrats had to rely on state jobholders, which meant that Democrats were being asked to vote for a bill that would return the state to the Republicans. The American system of politics, Democrats also contended, depends on parties, and parties depend on jobs. " 'I don't believe in civil service. I believe in party government,' " Representative Charles T. Sundstrom candidly declared. " 'If a Democratic governor is elected he should clear out all Republicans. If a Republican is elected he should clear out all Democrats.' "[13]

As reported out of the House State Affairs Committee on June 10, an action taken at Murphy's insistence, the civil service bill provided that incumbents in the classified service were to remain in office until dismissed by the appointing officer; put the University of Michigan and Michigan State College as well as employees of courts of record under the merit system; provided for a three- rather than a four-member commission; reduced the personnel director to a figurehead, specified that he was to be appointed by the governor, not the commission, and fixed his salary at $5,000 rather than $10,000, as in the Senate bill; gave the governor and the Administrative Board the right to approve all civil service regulations and eliminated the penalties imposed by the Senate bill for violations of such regulations; returned to the rule-of-three; and prohibited political activity by state employees only during working hours. Surprisingly, Edward H. Litchfield, the executive secretary of the Merit System Association's legislative committee, advised Murphy that, although the House had " 'weakened' " the Senate bill, the House bill was nevertheless " 'stronger' " than most existing state civil service statutes. "This seemed to please" Murphy, but the governor sensed that further trouble lay ahead, telling Litchfield, " 'the wolves are fiercer today than in the past.' "

The governor was correct in his judgment, for the House on June 21 rejected the amended bill by a vote of 46–49, twenty-eight of the negative votes being cast by Democrats. The House then reconsidered its action and decided by a vote of 46–39 to table the measure, the necessary votes having been "herded in under the gubernatorial whip." The bill was removed from the table on June 24 and passed by a vote of 64 (44 Democrats, 20 Republicans)–29 (13 Democrats, 16 Republicans) after Murphy had persuaded some Democrats to switch their votes and Litchfield had similarly influenced a few Republicans. Other legislators voted in the affirmative once it became evident that the bill would pass. As passed, the measure provided that job applicants should receive no more than 50 percent credit for their performance on written tests and 50 percent credit for "actual practical experience in similar work."[14]

The Senate refused to concur in the House amendments, and two conference committees failed to break the deadlock because the two houses, despite the efforts of Murphy and Litchfield, could not reconcile their differences regarding the status of incumbents. The first conference committee, whose composition Murphy had substantially influenced, met four times in the governor's office, and the second committee also held one such meeting, but the Senate adjourned on June 25 without voting on the committee's report, which included a blanketing in provision. ". . . throughout the entire process," Litchfield reported to Merit System Association members, "Governor Murphy has been as sincere, as courageous, and as thorough in his efforts in our behalf as any man could possibly be expected to be. There were times when the Governor without hesitation took steps which might very possibly have jeopardized his own political future." "The civil service bill," Murphy declared when the Senate adjourned, "was lost in politics."[15]

Murphy decided to make a "last effort" to secure the passage of a civil service bill at the adjourned session of the legislature on July 29 and 30. If the legislature remained adamant, it was his intention to call a special session at a time "likely to embarrass candidates for reelection." Murphy turned to Pollock for advice regarding the kind of bill the Civil Service Study Commission would now be willing to accept. The political scientist, appreciating that compromise was necessary, responded that he could support the House bill if its "more vitiating amendments" were dropped. He was willing to accept the blanketing in of incumbents who had served at least four years if qualifying examinations were required for the remainder; he was opposed to the 50 percent credit for experience; he would accept the appointment of the personnel director by the governor if the selection was based on the recommendation of a committee of experts; and the salary of the director would have to be $10,000.[16]

Before the adjourned session convened, Murphy conferred with the second conference committee, legislative leaders, and Highway Department officials to gain their support for a compromise bill along the lines Pollock had suggested. Following these conferences, Murphy announced that he had won Highway Department support for his bill. In his message to the legislature, Murphy urged the lawmakers to pass a bill that provided qualifying examinations for incumbents, authorized the governor to appoint the first personnel director, and provided a salary for that official commensurate with his responsibilities.[17]

On July 30, the last day of the adjourned session and to the surprise of many, the House by a vote of 68 (53 Democrats, 15 Republicans)–20 (3 Democrats, 17 Republicans) and the Senate by a vote of 17 (16 Democrats, 1 Republican)–13 (all Republicans) approved a civil service bill along the lines the governor had recommended. The bill could not have passed the Senate had not Miles Callaghan unexpectedly deserted an otherwise solid bloc of Republicans to vote with the Democrats. When the Senate Republicans became aware that Callaghan would vote for the bill, they arranged for a one-hour recess to caucus. It became apparent to Lieutenant Governor Nowicki, the Senate's presiding officer, that the Republicans intended to hold Callaghan "a hostage in the Republican caucus room" and not to return to the Senate floor before the scheduled noon expiration time of the session. Not knowing how to deal with this situation, the inexperienced Nowicki consulted with the secretary of the Senate, who advised him to telephone the caucus room and to inform the caucus chairman that he, Nowicki, would request a call of the Senate, which required only a majority vote for adoption, and would then instruct the State Police to enter the locked caucus room and escort the Republicans to the floor unless they returned voluntarily. The Republicans promptly returned to the floor, and Callaghan provided the aye vote required for the bill's passage.[18]

The bill approved by the legislature provided for a three-member Civil Service Commission, not more than two of whom could be from the same party; a personnel director, appointed by the governor, whose salary was not to exceed $7,500 (the commission was to appoint subsequent directors); competitive examinations and appointment on the basis of the rule-of-three for applicants; qualifying examinations for incumbents, prepared "in collaboration with" department heads; and the open back door for dismissals. The measure also banned the solicitation of political assessments by state employees during working hours, stipulated that employees were under no obligation to contribute to political funds or to render political service, and specified that no state employee could use his official position to "influence or coerce" the political action of others. The measure was to go into effect on January 1, 1938.[19]

All the Republican senators save Callaghan signed a statement attacking the bill as creating "a completely political set-up." They criticized the provision authorizing the governor to appoint the first director, noted that the governor could appoint two members of his party to the three-member commission, alleged that the measure, "for all practical purposes," provided for the blanketing in of all state employees as of January 1, 1938, and claimed that state employees would be obliged to make political contributions. Pollock, on the other hand, asserted that the measure was "as good an act on the subject" as there was in the nation and was "perhaps the most constructive change ... made in Michigan State Government in a quarter of a century." After "several of the most competent personnel technicians" in the United States had examined the bill, the Michigan Merit System Association advised Murphy to sign the measure, Litchfield appraising the bill in terms of superlatives. When Murphy signed the bill into law on August 5, Michigan became one of the five states to enact civil service laws in 1937, "the first advance at the state level [in this field] since 1920."[20]

The defenders of the Michigan statute were much closer to the mark than the measure's critics. The Republicans complained about the three-man commission, but Harold Smith, a recognized public administration expert, noted that there was simply "no basis in theory or practice for the belief that a four-member, bi-partisan civil service commission" would "immunize personnel administration against the ... disease of partisan politics." Although the Civil Service Study Commission had attached a good deal of importance to the appointment of the personnel director by the commission on the basis of an examination by experts, the method of selection specified in the Michigan law, that is, appointment by the governor, had been applied successfully in Wisconsin and elsewhere. The Michigan law, moreover, required that the person the governor selected be "thoroughly familiar with the principles and experienced in the methods and techniques of personnel administration on the merit basis." It was unrealistic to have expected the legislature to approve a civil service bill that required competitive examinations for incumbents, and Smith, in any event, thought that such a bill would have been "unsound" administratively. Pollock had been assured by an expert in the field, the person, indeed, who was to become Michigan's personnel director, that anyone skilled in devising examinations could construct meaningful qualifying tests for incumbents, and Pollock was proved correct in his prediction that the qualifying examinations would be "a real test of merit and not a whitewash." Michigan, moreover, was the first state to adopt a civil service system that required incumbents to pass any kind of examination in order to keep their jobs. Although the ban on political activity in the Michigan law was "not as tight" as the comparable provision in Senate Bill No. 1, it was, assuming proper administration, "a sufficient guarantee against politicizing the state service." Much, of course, depended on the character of the personnel whom the governor would select to administer the new act, but the friends of civil service were confident that Murphy would not fail them in this regard.[21]

The Highway Department, how we do not know, was almost certainly responsible for switching Callaghan's vote and, in this way, contributed significantly to the Senate's approval of the civil service bill. The prevailing view among those closest to the scene, however, was that Murphy deserved the major credit for persuading a reluctant legislature to adopt a bill that most of its members openly or covertly opposed. ". . . if he hadn't come into this with both feet," Pollock said of the governor, "we would never have gotten that statute through." "What it means for a State to have a Governor with fine leadership qualities," the *St. Louis Post-Dispatch* editorialized, "has been demonstrated by the enactment of a model civil service law in Michigan."

The enactment of the civil service bill was probably "the most important single legislative achievement" of the Murphy administration. Legislators who bucked the governor on labor-relations legislation, sensing that public opinion was on their side and voting their own interests, apparently found it much more difficult to challenge him on the issue of civil service reform, perhaps because the press and vocal opinion supported the governor and the reformers and because it would have been difficult to justify a negative vote to their constituents. Republican opponents of the bill thus found it necessary to contend that they had opposed the governor only because they favored a stronger bill than the Democrats were willing to enact, not because they opposed the merit system.[22]

As members of the Civil Service Commission, Murphy on August 14 appointed Stuart H. Perry, the former president of the Michigan Merit System Association and the conservative Republican publisher of the *Adrian Telegram*, Mrs. Paul Jones, former president of the Michigan League of Women Voters and the state's "most active woman supporter" of the merit system other than Mrs. Judd, and George J. Burke, an attorney and a respected Democrat, as chairman. Pollock, who had declined Murphy's offer of the commission chairmanship, lauded the appointees, and the *Michigan Manufacturer and Financial Record* was pleased that the governor had selected a commission that appeared to be "far removed from partisan politics."[23]

Acting on Pollock's recommendation and after having gained the consent of the Civil Service Commission and the Civil Service Assembly, Murphy appointed William Brownrigg as the state's personnel director. A native of Manistee, Michigan, and a graduate of the University of Michigan, Brownrigg had been serving as the executive officer of the California State Personnel Board. He was regarded by civil service experts as "one of [the] best trained and most experienced men" in the field. Different groups in the state, Murphy told his brother George, hoped to be able to control the civil service system; in turning to Brownrigg, the governor asserted, he was "going to get someone that *no* one can control." After the appointment was announced, Pollock wrote Murphy that he had "never known anybody in the history of the State civil service to do so much—and no one could have done better."[24]

Brownrigg, who aptly compared his first months of service to the experience of someone who had to live in a house while simultaneously constructing it, had three principal tasks to perform as personnel director: classification of the state's employees, preparation of a compensation plan, and preparation and administration of qualifying and competitive examinations. The Civil Service Commission instructed

him to begin work at once on a classification system since the only practical way to administer the qualifying examinations, which were to be
initiated on January 1, 1938, was by classes and since a classification
system was the necessary foundation for "every personnel transaction." Brownrigg engaged Griffenhagen and Associates to aid in the
task, which was completed on May 18, 1938. The plan placed the
approximately seventeen thousand employees as of that time in twelve
hundred classes on the basis of their duties and responsibilities. The
plan proved to be "workable," although one of its authors conceded
that it was "definitely second rate."[25]

Since salaries accounted for 65 percent of the state budget, the
devising of a compensation plan was one of the most important
responsibilities of the Civil Service Department. To assist him in
performing the assignment, Brownrigg engaged a score of field men
and also enlisted the aid of the WPA in seeking to determine the
salaries and wages paid in private business for tasks comparable to
those performed in the public service. As presented to the Civil
Service Commission by Brownrigg on August 5, 1938, the compensation plan created fourteen salary grades and set minimum and maximum rates for each grade ranging from $75–90 per month at the
bottom to $650–750 per month at the top, with five salary steps,
generally speaking, in each grade. At public hearings on the compensation plan later that month, there were complaints that the minimum
pay was too low, a view that Murphy shared since he believed that
government should "lead the way a little" in setting pay scales. The
compensation plan put into effect by the Civil Service Commission
on September 1 largely followed the Brownrigg scheme, but the
number of grades was reduced to eleven, and the compensation for
the lowest grade was raised to $80–100, compared to a $70–75 range
in neighboring Ohio, Illinois, and Wisconsin. The plan implemented
the principle of equal pay for equal work for the first time in the
history of Michigan's state government. It raised the pay of six
thousand employees, mostly in the upper salary brackets, reduced the
pay of three thousand employees, mostly in the lower salary brackets,
and added $900,000 to the annual state payroll. Although the plan
was accepted with "a minimum of disapproval," unit heads, as
might have been expected, grumbled that the pay set for particular
positions was inadequate. Picard, for example, complained to Brownrigg, "we know what we need—you fellows can't and don't."[26]

The "most difficult, trying and thankless undertaking" of the
state's personnel director was the preparation of qualifying examinations for the approximately sixteen thousand employees in the classi-

fied service of the state government (about one thousand employees were exempted from the application of the civil service law). Between January 22 and July 30, by which time the law specified that the examinations were to have been completed, the Civil Service Department administered seven hundred different qualifying examinations, "the most extensive examination program of its kind ever to be undertaken by any civil service organization" up to that time. Brownrigg and the Civil Service Commission announced that the qualifying tests would be as difficult as the competitive examinations, and Murphy stated that he would oppose any effort to reduce the tests to a formality. Employees in the classified service became "temporary employees" on January 1, 1938, pending their successful completion of the qualifying examinations. They could have been laid off while in that status, but the governor warned against political dismissals.

The examination of each incumbent consisted of a written test, generally of the short-answer type, an evaluation of the employee's experience computed according to a formula, and a service or efficiency rating of the employee prepared by his superiors and approved by the department head. A definite weight was assigned to each of these elements depending on the type of work the employee performed. If he received a rating of 70 percent or better, he retained his position. Of the sixteen thousand persons examined, 1,225 (8.3 percent) failed, and an additional 518 (3.5 percent) were demoted as the result of their performance. Eighty-two employees sixty-five years of age or over failed to qualify, as did 152 employees with eight or more years of service.[27]

Murphy thought that it would be desirable to establish an appeals board to deal with "unfortunate cases" resulting from the qualifying examinations, and he advised the Civil Service Commission to consider the possibility of providing retirement pensions for ousted veteran employees. The commission rejected the idea of an appeals board, preferring to investigate hardship cases itself, but it endorsed the idea of pensions for elderly employees who failed the qualifying examinations. Murphy thereupon appointed a Retirement and Pension Study Commission, headed by a University of Michigan professor, to prepare a retirement plan for submission to the legislature. "Old age security for public employees," the governor declared, "is one of the most necessary steps to follow the installation of the merit system."[28]

Those who failed the qualifying examinations and their supporters complained that the tests had no relationship to the duty of the employees. The Civil Service Commission, however, asserted that the tests were "consistently of a practical nature" and noted that, as the law required, the departments involved had collaborated in the preparation of the examinations. Many false stories circulated concerning the questions on particular examinations. It was thus alleged that a janitor failed to retain his job because he could not answer algebra and calculus questions and such questions as "Does an undertaker deal with habeas corpus?"; a cook supposedly lost his job because he confused the size of the national debt with the distance from the earth to Jupiter and did not know if peacocks laid eggs. One alleged true-false question was: "People whose eyes are close together are usually narrow-minded."[29]

The first open, competitive examinations, like the first qualifying examinations, were administered beginning on January 22, 1938. More than forty-eight thousand examinations for 251 classes of work were administered by the Civil Service Department during the year, and eligible rosters containing the names of twenty-three thousand persons were prepared as a result. About twenty-eight hundred of these persons (17.8 percent of the total number in the classified service) had been placed on the state payroll by the end of the year. The principal complaint about the competitive examinations was that the Civil Service Department, as the law seemed to permit, limited the opportunity of taking some of the examinations to persons with a specified amount of schooling. According to one disgruntled Democratic leader, most Roosevelt supporters in the Upper Peninsula were debarred from taking the examinations for this reason. ". . . the Irish people in the Upper Peninsula," he declared, "would almost like to hang Brownrigg."[30]

The Civil Service Department played a negligible role in dismissals because of the open back door nature of the Michigan merit system. The open back door made it possible for department heads to dismiss inefficient employees, but it also enabled agency heads to discharge workers for political reasons, and the authority granted the Civil Service Commission to transfer such employees or to restore them to the eligible roster was insufficient protection for them. Murphy consequently proposed that the civil service law be amended to accord employees the right of a hearing before the commission and to grant the commission the "absolute right to reinstate."[31]

The necessity of devising a complete personnel program between October 1, 1937, and January 1, 1938, placed an enormous burden on Brownrigg and his staff. Pollock later asserted that Brownrigg was perhaps "the only man" in the country who could have discharged the responsibilities placed upon him by the "very restrictive time limits" of the Michigan law. By January 1, 1938, Brownrigg not only had begun work on a classification system and a compensation plan and the construction of competitive and qualifying examinations for thousands of persons but also had devised "a complete set of rules for the administration of the civil service system" and had established a working relationship with the personnel officers appointed by the various departments at his request. The Civil Service Commission estimated that the state saved $450,000 as the result of the decline in employee turnover during the first year. In addition, the Civil Service Department saved the state about $25,000 in payroll auditing costs, and it cooperated with the budget director in denying departmental requests for additional employees.[32]

Since neither Brownrigg nor Burke was "given to compromise" in the performance of his tasks, the civil service law and the civil service rules were "rigidly" enforced, and "administration not infrequently took on an arbitrary complexion in the eyes of many sincere persons." Picard, for one, complained to Brownrigg that 99 percent of the difficulties he encountered in discharging his responsibilities as chairman of the Unemployment Compensation Commission were "due to the failure of your [Brownrigg's] office to look upon our troubles from a common sense angle."[33]

Brownrigg, who characteristically declared that his "emphasis" was on "principles rather than individuals," was "long on the technical approach," to use Harold Smith's apt characterization, and lacked political judgment. He thus foolishly predicted in a public address that perhaps 2,500–3,000 incumbents would lose their jobs as the result of the qualifying examinations, which considerably overestimated the number of failures, and he indicated that some of the better-paying positions in the civil service would have to be filled by nonresidents since Michigan residents, presumably, lacked the necessary qualifications.[34]

Murphy gave the Civil Service Commission and the state personnel director his unstinting support. "You may belabor him on some things," Kemp wrote of Murphy to one of the governor's Republican newspaper critics, "but not on civil service. He saved it from legislative defeat and is doing everything possible to make it secure." The president of the Michigan Merit System Association, Arno R. Schorer, and the reporter closest to the Michigan civil service scene, Carl Rudow of the *Detroit News*, agreed with Kemp. "In my opinion," Schorer wrote Pollock, "it is only because the Governor has let it be known, in no uncertain terms, that he is for the Commission, for Brownrigg and for the law that the other state officials have not thrown monkey wrenches into the gears." Murphy, Rudow observed at the end of 1938, was "one of the few who kept full and complete faith with the spirit of this [civil service] law." Litchfield thought that the governor had "probably" been "as loyal to the ideas of sound civil service as any public official in America."[35]

Whereas Murphy consistently won the plaudits of civil service reformers for his devotion to the merit principle, Republicans charged that the civil service law and the manner in which it was being enforced were "only blinds to get Murphy Democrats on the payroll and keep them there." Democrats, by contrast, complained that the governor's nonpartisan administration of civil service was harming their party. "The enemies of civil service," Murphy noted, "are starting out to cut my throat. Well, let them cut away."[36]

Miffed because he incorrectly believed that his brother-in-law had been dismissed from a state hospital position at the instigation of Murphy and Brownrigg, former governor Fitzgerald grumbled to Mrs. Judd that, in selecting Brownrigg, Murphy " 'got somebody no one ever heard of who would be under his direct control.' " Mrs. Judd set Fitzgerald straight on this point, which probably explains why the ex-governor and his political associates did not make the same charge publicly. One accusation the Republicans did make was that the competitive examinations were rigged to favor Democrats, Fitzgerald protesting that "a Republican has no more chance of getting a job under this civil service system than a rabbit has with a pack of foxes." There was absolutely no substance to this allegation since the Civil Service Department was forbidden by law to elicit information regarding the political affiliation of examinees and test papers were graded "blindly."

More serious was the Republican charge that the Democrats had prepared for the qualifying examinations by "turning out Republicans by the hundreds" and replacing them with Democrats so that they would have the status of incumbents as of January 1, 1938. Although some agencies, apparently, did attempt to replace Repubicans with Democrats in advance of the qualifying examinations, Murphy put a stop to this when the matter was brought to his attention. In any event, an analysis of the state payroll at the end of the Murphy administration revealed the insubstantiality of the Republican charge. Of 16,143 state employees in the classified service on the last day of 1938, 54.9 percent had entered the service before Murphy took office (80 percent of them had been appointed in Republican administrations, the remainder during Comstock's governorship), and only 24.8 percent had received their jobs during the first year of the Murphy administration, nearly all of them, apparently, before the Civil Service Act went into effect. The remainder had been hired during the second year of Murphy's governorship as the result of their performance on competitive examinations (17.8 percent) or were temporary employees (2.4 percent). "The argument of hungry spoilsmen," concluded Mrs. Judd, who made the payroll analysis, "is therefore proved to be what it was from the beginning, a transparent and malicious untruth."[37] Mrs. Judd's figures were pleasing to civil service reformers, but they supported the contention of the "hungry spoilsmen" that the Murphy administration had failed to meet its obligations to deserving Democrats.

Democratic state and county leaders had been displeased from the outset of the Murphy administration about the governor's seeming lack of concern for the politics of patronage, and the rigorous enforcement by his administration of the civil service law greatly intensified that concern. If the governor permitted Brownrigg to have his way, a Saginaw Democrat remonstrated to the state party chairman, "his excellency and the rest of his official family might just as well apply now to the President for a ... WPA assignment." Gerald J. Cleary, a key Upper Peninsula Democrat, wrote the governor that the Civil Service Commission was "doing more harm" to the Murphy administration than the governor seemed to realize, and Cleary claimed that people came to his office daily to "assail" Brownrigg's actions. G. Donald Kennedy did not exaggerate when he said that Brownrigg was "a great irritant to the Democratic legislators and other party people."[38]

The differences between the governor and the state party leadership regarding civil service came into the open in June 1938 when Edward J. Fry, the chairman of the Democratic State Central Committee, launched a public attack on the administration of the state civil service system. The *Detroit News* correctly characterized what was taking place as "the official expression of a growing revolt against the merit system within Democratic ranks." In addition to criticizing the character of some of the questions asked on civil service examinations and deploring some of Brownrigg's public statements, Fry specifically challenged the personnel director's authority to deny any one the right to take an examination for a state job. To dramatize his point, Fry, who claimed he was simply trying to save civil service from "the fawning indulgence of its parents," stated that the State Central Committee was prepared to finance a court case against the commission by the next person who was denied the opportunity to take a civil service examination, an action that never materialized. As the *Detroit*

Times remarked, Murphy was now "in a familiar spot—backed against a wall before a firing squad of machine politicians."

Responding to Fry, Murphy praised Brownrigg for doing "an excellent pro-public job" and for following the law. Attacks on civil service, Murphy asserted, only caused him to support the system more strongly. The governor, who likened Fry's criticisms of civil service to those of Fitzgerald, said it was characteristic of opponents of civil service to allege their support of the merit principle but to criticize the manner in which it was being implemented. This, he tactlessly asserted, was a Tammany trait. In a letter to Murphy following these remarks, Fry criticized the governor for linking the state party chairman to ex-governor Fitzgerald and for characterizing the state Democratic organization as a "Tammany outfit. If they are a Tammany outfit," Fry asserted, "and loyalty to a leader compels them to accept that inference, . . . I thank God that I was chosen their spokesman and leader." Jabbing at the governor's oft-repeated statements that the voters would reward supporters of good government at the polls, Fry concluded, "This organization and no other will either elect or defeat, by their do-nothingness, you and every other State Officer on our ticket this fall."

Two days later, in what he said was his "last statement" on the subject, Fry told a Democratic audience that the party was not opposed to civil service, that Brownrigg was a good administrator, and that the state party chairman was "for Governor Murphy hook, line, and sinker." Despite Fry's protestations of loyalty, however, Murphy's unswerving support for the nonpartisan administration of civil service was a major factor in persuading some party leaders that "do-nothingness" was the proper response for them to the governor's effort to win reelection in 1938.[39]

II

Civil service reform was for Murphy only one aspect, although the most important aspect, of a general effort to eliminate "privilege, politics and pull" in Michigan's state government and to make it more efficient and businesslike in its operations. The good-government stress of the Murphy administration also manifested itself in the state's purchasing procedures, the policies of the Liquor Control Commission, the enforcement of the anti-gambling laws, the regulation of the securities business, state banks, and public utilities, the management of the state fair, and the activities of the State Tax Commission.[40]

Murphy appointed Charles S. Weber, an English instructor in the

Grand Rapids Junior College who had gained business experience in the textile trade, to serve as secretary and administrative officer of the Administrative Board, which was the purchasing agent for the state government. Politics and favoritism had characterized state purchasing during the Fitzgerald governorship, largely, it was alleged, because of the pervasive influence of Frank McKay. The state had awarded contracts to favored firms without meaningful competitive bidding, and political brokers representing advantaged firms had handled state accounts running to substantial sums. The state also had purchased certain items in quantities vastly exceeding existing needs—the state garage when Murphy became governor was, for example, overflowing with obsolete tires the state had recently bought. Murphy instructed Weber to institute "daylight procedures" for state purchasing, and the secretary duly implemented the governor's orders. The state began to require sealed bids for all purchases above $500, as compared to $3,000 in the previous administration; it took five bids, but not necessarily sealed bids, even for orders below that sum; and it invited far more firms to bid for state business than had been true previously. As a result, four times as many business concerns shared in the state's business under Murphy than under Fitzgerald. The Administrative Board also eliminated "curbstone brokers" by accepting bids only from established business houses and by requiring that bids name both the company that was to supply the material and its duly designated representative. Weber, in addition, warned merchants that they would be removed from the bidding lists if they provided gratuities to state employees with whom the merchants' firms were doing or wished to do business. The state realized substantial savings as the result of its altered purchasing procedures. The state garage, for example, netted a profit of $7,500 during Murphy's governorship as compared to an average monthly loss of $1,500 during Fitzgerald's tenure.[41]

When Murphy appointed Professor Edward McFarland to be chairman of the Liquor Control Commission, he told the professor that the public interest was to be his "only consideration" in running the commission. McFarland quickly discovered that he had taken over a "McKay guided" agency that was "hog-tied with political preferences." He inherited a purchasing system that had "all the ear-marks of large pay-offs" and that had loaded up the state liquor stores with "nondescript" and unsalable merchandise, a licensing system that was "honeycombed with petty chiselers," and a "political spoils ring" that monopolized the warehousing and the affixing of stamps on imported beer. Although the Liquor Control Commission was by no means problem-free during the Murphy governorship, it conducted its affairs in a businesslike manner; it netted the state a higher profit than the Fitzgerald commission had realized; and, as Murphy had instructed, it did not permit "insiders" to profit from its operations. It is hardly surprsing in view of the nature of the liquor business that political pressure caused the commission to modify one or another of its rules. Murphy, however, could rightfully point to the commission's behavior as another example of his successful effort to eliminate favoritism from the operation of the state government.[42]

The Liquor Control Commission directed the third largest liquor trade among the seventeen states that exercised a monopoly over the liquor business within their borders. Created in December 1933, the commission consisted of five commissioners, including the governor and the secretary of state, ex officio. It was the state's exclusive purchaser of liquor, it licensed private vendors and was empowered to inspect their premises and to designate the hours during which they could sell spirits, and it administered the law regulating the sale of beer and wine. As of January 31, 1937, the commission operated ninety-three stores and had issued licenses to 17,770 hotels, taverns, beer gardens, clubs, and Specially Designated Merchants (merchants licensed to sell beer and wine for consumption off the premises) as well as to 1,505 Specially Designated Distributors (SDD's). The latter were established businesses, mainly drugstores, selected by the Liquor Control Commission to sell packaged alcoholic beverages, other than beer, for consumption off the premises. The SDD privilege was a "sop" to private enterprise, the price the advocates of a system of state stores had had to pay to get the liquor control bill through the state legislature. There had been only 640 SDD's when Fitzgerald became governor on January 1, 1935, but the Liquor Control Commission had substantially increased their number during the next two years, awarding the licenses, allegedly, to "political pets" of the administration. ". . . you will appreciate," the chairman of the Wayne County Republican Committee wrote Fitzgerald in 1935, "that I cannot tell the newspapers that we are using [liquor?] licenses for political purposes."

The SDD's received a 10 percent discount (other licensees received a 15 percent discount) on the liquor they received from the state for sale, which netted them about $1.25 million in 1936. In that year, they accounted for about 50 percent of the liquor sold in the state (as compared to 29 percent sold by licensees and 21 percent by the state stores). Since they were theoretically designed to supplement rather than to compete with the state stores, the SDD's were permitted to sell liquor from 7:00 A.M. to 2:00 A.M. if they were located more than two miles from a state store but only from 7:00 A.M. to 9:00 A.M. and 6:00 P.M. to 2:00 A.M. if within that distance.[43]

Consistent with the purchasing procedures adopted by the Administrative Board, the Liquor Control Commission eliminated the "curbstone broker" from the state liquor business and made its purchasing decisions at public meetings of the full commission. Whereas vendors' bills had previously been discounted at selected banks by "preferred discount brokers," the commission now arranged to pay its bills within fifteen days, which enabled it to realize a saving on its purchases of 1.5 and later 2 percent—the commission saved $500,000 between April 15, 1937, and September 27, 1938, in this manner. In an effort to spotlight its purchasing and sales practices and to avoid even the appearance of favoritism, the commission toward the end of 1937 began to provide distillers with monthly figures indicating the sales of individual brands and stock on hand rather than simply reporting total monthly sales and purchases, as in the past.[44]

Since the Fitzgerald administration had " 'loaded up' " the state's liquor stock during and after the 1936 campaign, the Murphy Liquor Control Commission inherited a liquor inventory of more than $7 million, the largest in the history of the state-operated system to that time. More than $1 million of the inventory was made up of slow-moving, little-known brands. The commission cut its inventory to a record low of $4.2 million by the end of October, ridding itself in the process of some of its "frozen assets," but it then resumed heavy purchases and built up its stock to about $6.9 million in December. This angered the governor since it occurred at a time when the state was running a deficit. He accordingly instructed the commission to reduce its inventory to no more than $3.5 million by June, which would mean the release to the state of badly needed cash. Since the state stock by this time was made up of well-known and fast-selling brands and because of a purchasing policy based rigidly on sales that had been adopted toward the end of 1937, the commission was able to slash its inventory to $2.3 million by July 1, 1938.

The total net revenue of the commission for the fiscal years 1936-37 and 1937-38 was about $25 million, as compared to about $16 million for the combined fiscal years 1934-35 and 1935-36. It also added approximately $4.2 million more to the state treasury from liquor sales in the fiscal year 1937-38 than the commission had turned over to the state in any previous year. Because of its careful merchandising methods, a unit control system, the lower rents that it negotiated for its stores, and the reduction in the number of its employees, the commission was able to slash store expenses to 3.7 percent of sales, one of the lowest figures in the nation. It gained a reputation for operating one of the most efficient and economical liquor control systems in the United States.[45]

Anxious to increase the state government's share of liquor sales, the Liquor Control Commission opened ten new stores in the first half of 1937 and increased the hours during which its stores remained open (from 9:00 A.M. to 6:00 P.M. to 10:00 A.M. to 9:00 P.M. on weekdays and 10:00 A.M. to 10:00 P.M. on Saturday). It also announced a new set of rules at the beginning of July that prohibited the licensing of SDD's in towns of fifteen thousand population or less in which there was a state store, or within one mile of a state store rather than two miles, as before. Since the one-mile rule would have led to the termination of the licences of about 60 percent of the SDD's, it aroused the bitter opposition of the Michigan Associated Package Dealers. Pressure from the governor and legislators soon caused the commission to rescind the rule. A similar fate befell the efforts of the commission to reduce the hours during which the SDD's could sell liquor. The Associated Package Dealers supported Murphy for reelection in 1938, undoubtedly because he had backed the organization's efforts to prevent the state from reducing the number of SDD's and limiting their sales.[46]

The Liquor Control Commission created what the press called a " 'Snooper Squad' " to ensure that hotels, restaurants, and other licensees were observing the liquor regulations. Reacting to allegations that the squad was enticing licensees into violations, Speaker of the House George A. Schroeder complained in a letter to Murphy in November 1937 that the commission was responsible for a "despicable spy system" that compelled commission employees to act as "stool pigeons." He also protested that a commission rule prohibiting a licensed owner from mingling with his customers was "childish" and might cost the administration the support of licensees. The Liquor Control Commission, Schroeder concluded, should "reconsider its ill-considered rules and inject a bit of political sense into its views." Murphy interceded with the commission after receiving the Speaker's letter, and the commission promptly announced that it was halting the practice of enticing licensees to violate regulations, and it ended its "snooping" activities.[47]

Since gambling was illegal in Michigan, the commission in July 1937 banned slot machines and other gaming devices from establishments that sold liquor. The commission vigorously enforced its anti-gambling rule, revoking the licenses of offending establishments. As a result, gambling devices disappeared from Michigan drinking establishments for the first time since repeal of the prohibition amendment. The resort areas and the interests behind "organized gambling" in the state vociferously opposed the anti-gambling policy, creating what McFarland described as one of the commission's "toughest problems." Charging that the commission had "set itself up as a sort of Morals Commission," Schroeder protested that the commission was depriving the average workingman of any place where he could go "to play a friendly game of cards" and that the anti-gambling rule was "high-minded but not practical politically." If the rule were not revoked, he warned the governor, "we simply cannot carry Michigan again as we have alienated the very vote that put the Democratic party across—the liberal vote." Believing that the law had to be observed, Murphy refused to yield in this instance, and the anti-gambling rule remained in effect.[48]

Although the Liquor Control Commission was compelled by political realities to abandon or modify some of its rules, it did not, in the fashion of its predecessor, permit political considerations to influence the award of licenses and the purchase and distribution of the state's liquor supply. Whereas individual commissioners and even the commission's secretary had awarded licenses while Fitzgerald was governor, the McFarland group made decisions regarding licenses by majority vote of the entire commission at a weekly public meeting and only after the license applicant had received approval of the appropriate governing body in his jurisdiction.

Harry Mead, who, as the *Detroit News* observed, believed that "the victor is entitled to a few ladles of gravy," represented various licensees and distillers before the commission. The commission, however, seems largely to have observed Murphy's explicit instructions regarding his campaign manager, "Don't do a thing for him." When the commission cancelled a license because the licensee had introduced a striptease in his establishment, Mead, who wrote Murphy that the commission was "making a mountain out of a mole hill—or anyway out of a G string," succeeded in persuading the agency to reduce the penalty to a fifty-day license suspension. It would be difficult to demonstrate, however, that favoritism accounted for the commission's reversal. More important was Mead's failure as the representative of Indiana brewers to prevent the commission from enforcing an amendment to the liquor control statute banning the sale in Michigan of beer coming from states that discriminated against Michigan beer. After the commission successfully defended its action in the courts, it reached an agreement with Indiana authorities removing the economic barriers that had precipitated the controversy. As McFarland indicated, "a lot of Democrats" attempted to influence the commission's purchasing and licensing policies, but the commission was generally able to resist such advances because, the chairman noted, in its "fight against these men," Governor Murphy was "behind" the commission. "That," McFarland remarked, "is something that can be said of few past governors . . . in either political party."[49]

During the Christmas season in 1937 distillers' agents, as was their custom, sent gifts of whiskey to various state officials. When Murphy learned of this, he ordered the officials to pay for their gifts or to send the whiskey to liquor commission warehouses. At the governor's insistence, the commission then approved a rule prohibiting distillers' agents from making gifts of liquor or extending other favors to state employees. Commission employees who accepted such favors were made subject to dismissal, distillers that ignored the rule were warned that they might lose the right to do business in Michigan, and licensees guilty of the same offense were threatened with revocation of their licenses.[50]

When his term of office as chairman of the Liquor Control Commission came to an end, McFarland wrote Murphy, "The things of a worthwhile nature that have been accomplished by the L.C.C., I sincerely feel are credited to your idealism, noble incentives and unstinting support of those lines of endeavor in harmony with good government." When the commissioners had to make decisions, Mc-Farland told the governor, they were "ever conscious of your philosophy of what the public expects from its officials."[51]

Whereas the Fitzgerald administration had pursued a policy of "home rule" regarding the enforcement of the state's anti-gambling legislation, with the result that gamblers had been able to operate without significant molestation, Governor Murphy announced that there would no longer be "any such thing as a protected gambling place in Michigan." The State Police, he insisted, would "do their duty" in this regard if local enforcement agencies failed to do so. "I am not especially a moralist in government," Murphy declared, "but I am dead set against huge illegal profits amassed through the debauchery of our people and the collusion of public officials." "Commercial gambling," he contended, brought "racketeers, gunmen and crooks" into the state. Three weeks after Murphy became governor, William Lovett, the secretary of the Detroit Citizens League, reported that "the 'big shot' gamblers of Michigan" had "folded their tents and faded away." The same, however, could not be said of small gambling houses, bookie joints, and gambling in drinking establishments, although the Liquor Control Commission soon put a stop to the latter. Attorney General Starr concluded from his experience in enforcing the anti-gambling legislation that the state should experiment with the licensing of gambling establishments and slot machines. He nevertheless reacted swiftly and effectively when organized gambling and slot machines reappeared in the state in the summer of 1937. He also attempted to put an end to the more or less open gambling that had gone on for years in the Grand Hotel on Mackinac Island and other resort areas, but the evidence is conflicting as to whether he succeeded. What can safely be asserted, however, is that the record of the Murphy administration in enforcing the anti-gambling laws, as the goo-goos appreciated, compared very favorably with that of its predecessors and of other midwestern states and earned Murphy the bitter enmity of the organized gambling interests, as the 1938 Michigan election demonstrated.[52]

Despite its blue-sky act, before 1937 Michigan had the reputation of being a "sucker state" insofar as the sale of securities was concerned. Securities salesmen who had been driven from other states and who were little more than racketeers found Michigan a safe haven for their activities; the state's Corporation and Securities Commission permitted the registration of questionable securities; and it licensed securities dealers without adequate investigation of their credentials. Murphy's instructions to Commissioner Carl A. Olson were to "clean up conditions and keep them clean," and that is precisely what Olson did. The Securities Division of the commission revoked or suspended the licenses of numerous unscrupulous securities dealers, rejected the license applications of questionable stock salesmen, and carefully checked securities before permitting them to be registered. It adopted rigid rules that barred market speculation by commission employees and forbade them to purchase the securities of companies whose registration certificates were pending before the commission. The commission's Corporation Division, for the first time, systematically collected the filing and annual privilege fees required of domestic corporations and compelled foreign corporations to register with the state, as the law required, and to pay all fees due the state. Like the Securities Division, the Real Estate Division of the commission rid the state of "undesirable operators" while extending its service to rural areas and Detroit's black ghetto. "It is pleasant to observe a state office," the Republican *Grand Rapids Press* declared with regard to the Corporation and Securities Commission, "in which strict and honest administration appears to be of first concern."[53]

The state's Banking Department, ably directed first by Charles T. Fisher, Jr., and then by Alvin Macauley, Jr., enforced the state's banking legislation in the same rigorous, scandal-free manner as Commissioner Olson enforced the securities legislation. It established a Liquidation Division to deal with the large problem of liquidating closed banks, "rigorously" exercised its prerogative to specify the minimum quality of bonds in banking portfolios, scrutinized the practices of small-loan companies to ensure their compliance with the state's small-loan legislation, and aided credit unions in correcting errors resulting from their unfamiliarity with the law. Like the Corporation and Securities Commission, the Banking Department enjoyed the complete support of the governor in its efforts to enforce the law, and it was similarly "free from political influence."[54]

Murphy appointed Paul H. Todd, mayor of Kalamazoo and son of the first president of the National Municipal Ownership League, to serve as chairman of the state's Public Utilities Commission. Concerned because the commission maintained a rather low profile during 1937, Murphy made it plain that he wanted the agency to become "energized in behalf of the people." Todd promised that the commission would be "more aggressive in the future." And "more aggressive" it became.

After seeking to ascertain why Michigan Bell charged proportionately more for intrastate than interstate calls, the commission ordered the company in June 1938 to reduce state rates to the interstate level and also to eliminate the extra charge that it was imposing for the use of handset or French-type phones. Michigan Bell agreed to the latter, which saved 163,000 telephone users approximately $325,000 per annum; but it instituted a court challenge of the rate order, and the matter had not yet been resolved when Murphy's gubernatorial term came to an end. In August 1938 the commission ordered Consumers Power to reduce electricity rates by $700,000 annually, and the company did not contest the order. The new rates were the lowest for any state east of the Rockies not served by the Tennessee Valley Authority. The commission also issued regulations that aided the owners of gas wells by revising the "very one-sided contract" that the Fitzgerald commission had required well-owners to sign with Consumers Power and the Grand Rapids Gas Company, the two companies the commission had designated as the exclusive purchasers of the gas. The Todd commission failed, however, to sustain the charge that Consumers Power was conspiring to block the development of Michigan's natural gas field.

In an unprecedented action, in 1938 the Public Utilities Commission assumed jurisdiction over the Detroit City Gas Company by responding to a petition of the Wayne County prosecutor alleging that the company's rates were excessive. Although Starr authorized the action, the company blocked further proceedings by going to court. Finally, the commission established "a class rate tariff" for motor common carriers that brought stability to the previously "chaotic" motor carrier rate structure and satisfied both shippers and common carriers. Enjoying some successes and suffering some defeats, the commission in its second year had acted in the pro-public manner that the governor desired. "There are not many such commissions in the United States which are wholly uncontrolled by utility interests," the head of the federal government's Rural Electrification Administration asserted with regard to the Todd commission.[55]

When Murphy asked Frank N. Isbey, the president of the Detroit Fruit Auction Company, to become the manager of the Michigan State Fair, he told Isbey that he wanted the fair conducted "after the manner of a business, serving alike the interest of the farmer, the laborer, and the merchant." In two years Isbey converted "a corrupt and run-down organization" into a profitable and highly successful activity. The attendance at the fair, a measure of its success since the fair's purpose was to exhibit the products of agriculture and industry, rose from a little more than 200,000 in 1936 to 420,000 in 1937 and 728,000 in 1938, and the deficit of 1936 was converted into a profit in both 1937 and 1938.[56]

Everything that the State Tax Commission attempted, its chairman reported at the end of the Murphy governorship, was "highly controversial and opposed to the long entrenched policies of favoritism, political machination and slipshod supervision" of its Republican-appointed predecessor. When Murphy became governor, the Tax Commission, which appraised railroads, railroad car companies, and telephone, telegraph, and express companies, equalized the assessments of counties and other tax units, and supervised local assessors, had "degenerated into an organization . . . loaded with dry rot." Since commissioners served six-year terms, Murphy was not able to make an appointment to the three-member commission until November 1937, when he selected John N. Fegan, a former title attorney, judge, and assistant attorney general of Michigan, to be the commission's chairman in place of Melville B. McPherson, a highly influential Republican who had served on the commission since 1927. Claiming that the commission's system of assessment was "anything but scientific" and that McPherson had been guilty of "czarism," Fegan, whom Murphy had instructed to " 'modernize and im-

prove' '' the commission's administration, announced the dismissal
of most of the commission's twenty-two examiners, Republicans and
Democrats alike. McPherson fought unsuccessfully in the courts to
prevent the dismissals and also to retain his chairmanship. After
weeks of "political jockeying" the Murphy administration gained
control of the commission by the appointment of a second commissioner, and Fegan was then able to proceed with his reorganization
plans.[57]

In February 1938 Fegan initiated the first statewide, coordinated
effort to "ferret out" intangible wealth—stocks, bonds, bank deposits, accounts receivable, etc.—that had been evading taxes. In
Michigan, as in six other states, intangibles were taxed at the same
rate as real property, a practice deplored by almost all tax experts and
by Governor Murphy as well. The result was that only "a few ignorant, honest and unfortunate persons and corporations" paid the
tax while individuals and corporations holding substantial intangible
assets entirely evaded their tax obligation. Since Fegan initiated his
inquiry in the midst of a serious economic recession, Murphy, stating
that the time was "entirely inopportune to add to the difficulties of
taxpayers and of business," provided assurances that there would be
"no wholesale . . . effort to enforce intangible assessments." The
governor, however, belatedly gained permission for the tax commission to examine the federal income tax returns of some wealthy
Michigan citizens so that the commission could check on evasion of
the intangibles tax.

Predictably, the tax commission learned that "an astounding
amount of tax evasion" was being "openly countenanced" in the
state. Complaining of "vicious and unprecedented distortion [of the
commission's objectives] by partisan newspapers," Fegan asserted
that he was not "unsympathetic" to the claim that to tax intangibles
at the general property tax rate was tantamount to "confiscation."
He contended, however, that what he was doing would serve to
"focus public attention" upon tax evasion and compel "owners of
large fortunes" to pay "a reasonable share of the taxes" and might
also induce the legislature to address itself to the issue. Partly because
of Fegan's action, the legislature passed an intangibles tax measure in
1939, but the tax yielded only $2.5 million in 1941, the first year that
it was in effect.[58]

The Tax Commission's efforts to eliminate favoritism in assessments and to devise "a scientific and legally proper assessment
system" were designed to ensure that property subject to its jurisdiction was fairly assessed and also to aid local assessors in correctly

assessing property subject to the local general property tax. Conducting its assessments on the basis of data compiled by taxation and accounting experts, the commission discovered that several of the state's most profitable railroads were underassessed. It found that quite different standards were being used by local assessors in assessing utilities and that many industrial properties were either not being taxed or were being assessed at "ridiculously low figures." The commission concluded that assessed valuations of mining property in the Upper Peninsula indicated "constant shading," exaggeration of cost factors, and concealment of reserve tonnages, which led Fegan to charge that the mining interests had exercised "complete domination" over the Tax Commission and Conservation Department engineers.

The commission gave considerable assistance to local assessors in the state's 1,783 assessing jurisdictions. It prepared the first assessors' manual since 1914 to aid local assessors in making their 1938 assessments, met with them to explain principles of assessing, and helped sponsor a statewide assessors institute in Ann Arbor. It developed standard cost tables so that local officials could assess utilities in a uniform manner, and it created a Division of Industrial Appraisals to assist local assessors in appraising industrial property. Since the work of local assessors was often handicapped by a lack of proper records, the commission secured WPA aid to correct this defect. The newly created Research Division of the commission also obtained WPA approval for a statewide project to study assessment ratios, a project held up by the Republicans after Murphy's 1938 defeat. The efforts of the commission explain at least in part why assessed property valuations in the state increased from $5.72 billion in the fiscal year 1936–37 to $5.91 billion in 1937–38 even though the latter was a year of recession, and why the appraisal of public utilities subject to the state's jurisdiction increased by $12.5 million during the same period. Some Republicans saw politics in the commission's assessment efforts, one state senator charging at the outset of the commission's campaign that the "New Deal Michigan group" was planning an "assault" on large mining, lumber, and industrial properties identified with the Republican party so as to demonstrate that the McPherson-dominated commission had favored such property.[59]

Before 1937 Michigan had "an unenviable ranking as one of the most backward states in tax administration." While Murphy was governor, the State Tax Commission sought to improve and modernize the Michigan system of tax administration and to ensure that property was equitably assessed. "The advances that we made,"

Fegan noted at the close of the Murphy administration, "were all accomplished under the stress of bitter resistance by those who, unfortunately, will once again return to positions of power."[60]

Murphy had appointed a small "informal" taxation committee at the outset of his administration but had then ignored its work because of his preoccupation with strikes and other matters. Since he believed that Michigan's "muddled" and "archaic" tax system not only had been poorly and inequitably administered but that it also failed to provide the state with a certain and stable income or "a sufficiently equitable distribution of the cost of government according to ability to pay and benefits received," Murphy late in 1937 appointed an eleven-member bipartisan, multiinterest commission to examine the state's tax structure and to make recommendations for its improvement. Asserting that he regarded the income tax, which thirty-four states, not including Michigan, were then imposing, as "the soundest, most just tax" for the state, Murphy nevertheless assured taxpayers that he did not favor any new taxes for recession-plagued Michigan and only wished to see "a more equitable spread of existing taxes." The tax study commission did not report until January 30, 1939, by which time the governorship was in Republican hands. The commission did not recommend the imposition of any major new taxes but rather urged the more effective collection of existing taxes (the chairman of the commission regarded this as "the best new source of revenue"), the levying of a specific tax on intangibles at their market value, and the badly needed modernization of the state's revenue system.[61]

The policies of the Murphy administration regarding civil service reform; state purchasing; liquor control; gambling; the regulation of the securities business, the state's banks, and its public utilities; the State Fair; and the administration of the tax system were all designed to modernize the government, to make it more efficient, and to enable it to serve the people of the state more effectively and without political favoritism. Murphy had proclaimed his opposition to "privilege, politics and pull" in the state government, and even his critics, the *New York Times*'s Arthur Krock observed at the close of Murphy's governorship, would have to concede that "no cleaner State government existed than Michigan's during his tenure."[62]

11

"The Biggest Public Business
in Michigan"

Next to civil service, Professor James K. Pollock advised Murphy shortly after the 1936 election, administrative reorganization presented "the most important opportunity for improving the state government of Michigan." "It's an intriguing field," Murphy replied, "and I'd like to do a real job on this phase of government in our State." Pollock thereupon sent Murphy a memorandum on the subject as well as suggestions regarding reorganization that had been prepared by the Public Administration Service. Pollock thought it unwise to deal with structural reorganization in a piecemeal fashion, although he believed that certain changes, such as the creation of departments of finance and revenue and an integrated welfare department, might be initiated as first steps. The Public Administration Service recommended similar structural changes, according highest priority to the establishment of an integrated department of finance.[1]

Largely following this advice, Murphy, in his initial message to the legislature, called for a careful survey leading to "a thorough-going program of administrative organization and integration." He recommended immediate creation of a department of finance, the consolidation of state departments dealing with welfare, health, and corrections into three new departments, and establishment of county welfare departments subject to "reasonable state supervisory control." As it turned out, Murphy deferred a broad-scale survey of Michigan's governmental structure until late in his governorship but by that time his administration had introduced several piecemeal structural changes.[2]

Although Murphy appeared committed to the establishment of a unified department of finance from the outset of his administration, he became distracted by the state's labor troubles and did not pursue the matter. In June 1937 Harold D. Smith, the director of the budget, reminded the governor of the "great need" to improve the state's financial administration, and Murphy accepted Smith's recommendation for the state to commission a study of the matter by the Public Administration Service, which had developed an excellent system of accounting and financial control for Kentucky and was in the process of installing new accounting and budgetary procedures in Wayne County. In a report submitted in March 1938, the Public Administration Service once again urged the creation of a unified department of finance that would consolidate the functions of budgeting and accounting then being performed by two independent units, but it was mainly concerned with revised procedures for accounting control and for collecting and reporting budgetary data that, unlike the creation of a department of finance, could be implemented by administrative action.

After receiving the report, Murphy announced that he would put into effect the recommendations that did not require legislation. Michigan's new budgeting and accounting system, which replaced procedures established in 1921, were installed on July 1, 1938, the administration proclaiming that this would put an end to " 'political interpretations' " of the state's finances. The new procedures made it possible for the budget office to exercise accounting control over revenues and expenditures and made information on state finances available in an intelligible form.[3]

Murphy persuaded the state legislature to reorganize the state's relief and welfare structure, but opponents of reorganization were able to defeat it at the polls. Despite this setback, relief and public welfare services in Michigan "experienced greater change and development than . . . any other governmental function" in the 1930s, a decade in which the nation became "public welfare minded" for the first time in its history.[4]

Before the New Deal, outdoor relief in Michigan was administered by township supervisors (one of whom was elected annually in each township) and city relief agencies in twenty-three counties, including the most populous, and by county superintendents of the poor (three of whom were appointed in each county by the board of supervisors) in the remaining sixty counties. The supervisors, in some instances, also served as superintendents of the poor. In addition to local responsibility and "extreme decentralization," the Michigan Poor Law, which was codified in 1925 and was patterned on the Elizabethan system, made legal residence a prerequisite for receiving relief, placed primary responsibility for aiding the needy on their relatives, and discouraged outdoor relief, limiting assistance primarily to the permanently indigent. The latter were cared for in county infirmaries, which increasingly became repositories for "persons deficient in physical and mental competency."

In addition to general relief, local governments also provided categorical relief in the form of mothers' pensions and soldiers' and sailors' relief. County probate judges, under Michigan's mothers' pension legislation, could award mothers who were the sole support of their children from $2 to $10 per week for the first child and $2 for each additional child. The program was optional with the individual counties, and as of June 1936 only thirty-one counties were actually granting mothers' pensions, the sums ranging from sixty cents to $2 per child per week. The soldiers' and sailors' relief commissions, each consisting of three members appointed for three-year terms by county probate judges, provided assistance to indigent veterans and their dependents. A 1936 study of the welfare program in Michigan concluded that the soldiers' and sailors' relief commissions, which were providing relief in at least fifty-two counties, operated ineffectively and served "no real purpose."[5]

Michigan centralized the distribution of relief for the first time in the state's history when the legislature created the State Emergency Welfare Relief Commission (SEWRC) to qualify for federal relief funds made available by the Federal Emergency Relief Act of May 1933. Composed of three members appointed by the governor, the SEWRC, which was superimposed on the state's existing relief and welfare structure, supervised the distribution of all public relief funds in the state, appointed county relief commissions to administer relief locally, and supervised their operation. The principal responsibility for executing the SEWRC's policies and orders was vested in the state relief administrator, who was appointed by the commission and was responsible to it. The State Emergency Relief Administration (SERA) performed "an absolutely essential service at a criticial time" and functioned at a level "appreciably higher" than most other public welfare agencies in the state.[6]

Although the state did not centralize relief as much as it might have considering the modest amount contributed for relief by local governments (only 10.6 percent of the total expended for all forms of emergency relief in the state between July 1933 and June 1935), the "establishment" in many counties bitterly resented the diminished authority of local units in the distribution of relief, the intrusion of the state government in local affairs, and the presence in their midst of welfare workers, some of whom regarded what they were doing as "not merely social work but a crusade." A sensitive relief administrator in Manistee County reported early in 1935 that relief had replaced the younger generation as the "favorite" subject of discussion in the county. "Anything new here," she noted, "is regarded with suspicion." Local charitable organizations thought that they should have been placed in charge of relief administration, politicians were "disgruntled" because they could not control relief money, merchants complained about government distribution of surplus commodities ("this government food nonsense," one of them called the program), and the "moral" citizens were displeased that relief was not denied to the "immoral." Above all, the State Association of Supervisors, which represented Michigan's 1,267 township supervisors and was "one of the strongest political bodies" in the state, was anxious to regain the politically significant power to distribute relief funds that the supervisors had enjoyed before 1933. Made up of persons who were "predominantly republican and unbelievably reactionary," the association waged "a ceaseless battle" against Michigan's Emergency Relief Administration. The same was true, to a lesser extent, of the county superintendents of the poor.[7]

Opposed to the New Deal and all its works, the Fitzgerald administration wished to abolish the state and county emergency relief commissions and to return to the pre-1933 pattern for the distribution of relief. The Republican "machine" hoped in this way to gain control of federal relief funds—70.6 percent of the total expended for relief in Michigan between July 1933 and June 1935—and to supplant "the people who were running the [relief] show." As Howard O. Hunter, the Federal Emergency Relief Administration's (FERA) field man for Michigan, discovered, one of those "egging [Fitzgerald] on" was Melville B. McPherson, the president of the State Association of Supervisors and a major influence in the Fitzgerald administration. Since Hunter regarded the old system of relief as "atrocious," he informed Fitzgerald that the FERA would not permit federal relief funds to be funneled through the township supervisors and county superintendents of the poor. In March 1935 the Michigan Senate passed the kind of measure that Hunter had opposed, but it died in the House.[8]

Following the establishment of the Works Progress Administration (WPA) on July 1, 1935, the federal government no longer provided funds for direct relief, the burden shifting entirely to state and local government. Since local governments contributed 19.3 percent of the relief funds in 1935–36 (as compared to 13.1 percent in 1934–35 and 6.1 percent in 1933–34), township and county supervisors (the township supervisors in each county, it will be recalled, constituted the county board of supervisors) demanded that Michigan return to the traditional system of distributing relief or, at the very least, that there be some change in the manner of appointment of the county relief commissions. The return to the pre-1933 relief pattern was effectively precluded since the federal government was unwilling to accept the township supervisors and the county superintendents of the poor as certifying agents for the various federal relief programs. State and local officials, however, agreed in June 1936 that the SEWRC, although not surrendering any of its authority, would henceforth appoint the chairman of the county board of supervisors or someone designated by him to serve as a member of the county relief commission (supervisors had previously been debarred from service on the relief commissions), a second member of the commission would be a nominee of the county board of supervisors, but the SEWRC would continue to select the commission chairman.

Although the SERA continued to supervise the local administration of relief funds, the June 1936 agreement made the SEWRC "more of a financing agency and less of an administrative or supervisory body" than previously. In return for the concession that it made to the supervisors, the SEWRC stipulated that the relief staffs of the county governments, like that of the state government, would thereafter have to be selected on the basis of merit. McPherson protested that the SEWRC did not have authority to impose civil service requirements on local relief agencies, but his complaints were unavailing. Although McPherson was not entirely satisfied with the 1936 modification of the relief structure, the localities now effectively controlled the county relief commissions, and one county relief administrator reported that "virtually an edict had gone forth that everything . . . now [had to] be done to satisfy the Supervisors." Trying to persuade the supervisors to grant relief, she commented, was "a good deal like trying to sell a tribe of cannibals on the idea of becoming vegetarians." Michigan, to be sure, was by no means unique in restoring authority to local relief agencies in 1936: the cessation of direct relief by the federal government enabled local units in other states also to regain at least some of the control over public relief that they had exercised before 1933.[9]

Just as the requirements for obtaining federal relief funds led to a significant change in the method of distributing relief in Michigan, so the requirements imposed on the states to obtain the matching funds provided by the Social Security Act of 1935 induced Michigan to alter its procedures for granting assistance to the aged (as we have already seen) and to dependent children and to inaugurate a program for aiding the blind. Whereas mothers' pensions were financed entirely by the counties and no county was obliged to provide this form of assistance, the state could qualify for federal aid for dependent children ($1 for every $2 paid by the state) only if payments were made mandatory, the state appropriated money for the program, and the state administered or supervised the program. At the time the Social Security Act was approved, the needy blind in Michigan were being cared for as part of the relief population. To qualify for the $1-for-$1 matching grants available for the blind from the federal government, however, the state had to meet requirements analogous to those specified for the distribution of federal money for aid to dependent children (ADC). The SEWRC devised regulations in 1936 for aid to both dependent children and the blind that the Social Security Board approved, and the commission then transferred those eligible for these two types of categorical assistance from general relief to the new programs.[10] Just as the Federal Emergency Relief Act led to the centralization of relief policy in the states, so the effect of the Social Security Act was to transfer authority over at least some welfare programs from local governments to the state governments. Much has been written about the changed relationship between the federal government and the state governments as the result of New Deal legislation; much less attention has been paid to the transfer of power from local government to state government that the Roosevelt reforms also induced.

As an expert on the subject advised governor-elect Murphy at the end of 1936, the organization of welfare services in Michigan and in its eighty-three counties was "uncoordinated, loose, inefficient, and incapable of keeping step with modern needs." There was "a jumble of activities rather than an ordered state welfare program." The State Welfare Department, which dated from 1921, consisted of a director, a deputy director, and five independent and uncoordinated commissions, none of which was doing "a thoroughly satisfactory job" and some of which were doing "nothing at all." The Welfare Commission administered the Michigan Children's Institute (a state-supported placing-out system for dependent children), supervised boarding homes for dependents, housed a loosely controlled Old Age Bureau, and supervised private welfare agencies, hospitals, and jails. The Institute Commission supervised the School for the Deaf in Flint, the School for the Blind in Lansing, and the Employment Institute for the Blind in Saginaw. The Corrections Commission supervised the Vocational School for Delinquent Boys in Lansing and the Training School for Delinquent Girls in Adrian. The Prison Commission supervised the state prisons at Jackson, Marquette, and Ionia. The Hospital Commission supervised the hospitals for the mentally ill in Ypsilanti, Pontiac, Kalamazoo, Ionia, Traverse City, and Newberry, the institutes for the feebleminded in Lapeer, Mt. Pleasant, and Coldwater, and a hospital for epileptics in Wahjameja. In addition to the Welfare Department, the state welfare structure included the SEWRC; the Crippled Children's Commission, which supervised medical and hospital aid for crippled children and subsidized their education; the Soldiers' Home Commission, which administered the Soldiers' Home in Grand Rapids; the Crime Commission, which studied crime conditions in the state; and the commissioner of pardons and paroles, who recommended pardons and paroles to the governor and supervised parolees.

The organization of welfare services at the local level, the result of "unplanned growth and development," was just as "chaotic" as the organization at the state level. In addition to township supervisors and superintendents of the poor, who continued to dispense small amounts of relief, welfare functions at the county level were performed by county emergency relief commissions; probate courts; soldiers' and sailors' relief commissions; county agents (officials appointed by the state Welfare Commission who performed investigative chores for probate judges and the Welfare Department and served as probation officers for juvenile court judges); old-age assistance boards, which heard appeals from applicants for old-age assistance; and county infirmaries. Not only did a multitude of agencies perform the same or similar functions in the counties, but politics played an inordinately large role in the administration of programs and the selection of personnel, welfare personnel were all too often poorly educated, lacked an appreciation of their responsibilities, and did not possess "constructive social attitudes," and local officials assigned a higher priority to the cost of welfare services than to their quality or adequacy.[11]

Because he had concluded that Michigan's welfare and relief agencies were administered in "a hap-hazard, expensive and cumbersome manner," Governor Fitzgerald appointed a Welfare and Relief Study Commission on April 3, 1936, to examine the "organization and operation" of state and local welfare and relief services and to make appropriate recommendations for their reorganization in the interests of "efficiency, economy, [and] sound public policy." Harold Smith was designated chairman of the commission, Arthur Dunham, a faculty member of the Curriculum of Social Work at the University of Michigan, was its secretary, and Fred E. Levi, who had been the assistant executive secretary of the Governor's Commission on Unemployment Relief in New York, was the executive director. After his election Murphy let the commission know that he wished it to continue its work despite the impending change in the state administration. William J. Norton, a member of both the study commission and the SEWRC, informed his colleagues on the Smith commission that Murphy was "committed to the thing [welfare reorganization] very strongly."[12]

At one of the commission hearings, William Haber, who was a member, characterized welfare as "the biggest public business in Michigan today." The public relief aspects of the welfare problem received the greatest attention at the commission's hearings, the fundamental issue being the familiar one of state control versus local control. Smith and Haber sought to impress on local officials that as long as the state government provided the bulk of the funds for relief, it would set standards for the expenditure of the money just as it did with funds for health, highways, and old-age assistance. The state government, Smith summarized, wanted the local units to distribute relief but "with some strings on it."[13]

"The fundamental principle of American government is local government," a Kent County superintendent who was a member of the commission stated at one of the hearings. As local officials saw it, they were the persons best qualified to dispense relief. The members of the Calhoun County Board of Supervisors, one of them declared, were "not a bunch of hayseeds." The board, he asserted, was "made up of respectable people" who were well-regarded in their community and found it "obnoxious" to be told by the SEWRC that they were not qualified to decide how relief money should be expended. They were, indeed, better qualified than the SERA to dispense relief, another supervisor declared, because they had their "thumbs upon the situation" and would consequently be able to purge chiselers from the relief rolls.[14]

The majority report of the Welfare and Relief Study Commission, submitted on December 26, 1936, was informed by the axioms that (1) the Depression, changes in the nation's social and economic structure, and new conceptions of public responsibility had had a "revolutionary effect" on public welfare services; (2) the organization and administration of public welfare in Michigan had not adjusted to these developments; (3) the state government for some time to come would have to make substantial expenditures for relief; and (4) public welfare should provide not only "palliative relief" but should be developed along "the constructive paths of prevention and rehabilitation." "The modern emphasis," a draft of the report stated regarding the latter point, "must be upon prevention—the railway around the top of the precipice, rather than the ambulance at the bottom."[15]

Except for the School for the Deaf, the School for the Blind, and the Employment Institute for the Blind, which it entrusted to the State Board of Education, the commission recommended that the state welfare agencies be placed in three new departments: public welfare, mental hygiene, and corrections. Each department was to be headed by an unpaid commission, appointed by the governor, that would select the executive head of the department under its control. The department of public welfare was to assume the functions and duties of the director and deputy director of the Welfare Department, the Welfare Commission, the Old Age Assistance Bureau, the Corrections Commission, the SEWRC, and, after January 1, 1940, the Michigan Crippled Children's Commission. It would allocate state and federal funds for relief and public assistance to the county departments of public welfare, supervise these departments, promote programs for the prevention of dependency, neglect, delinquency, and other conditions that adversely affected the welfare of women and children, and seek to restore dependent individuals to "self-support and normal conditions of life." The department of mental hygiene was to assume the functions of the State Hospital Commission, and the department of corrections was to assume the functions of the State Prison Commission and the commissioner of pardons and paroles. Since it regarded qualified personnel as the "keystone" to successful administration, the commission recommended the adoption of the merit system for the entire state welfare system.

At the local level, the study commission recommended the creation of a county department of public welfare in each county, except that a city with a population of over 300,000 (only Detroit qualified) could establish its own welfare department and adjoining counties could establish a district department. The state department of public welfare was to select the chairman of the county department, and the county board of supervisors was to select the other two members, who did not "need to be" members of the board of supervisors, but all three members were to be residents of the county. If the county included a city whose population exceeded one-half of the county population (seventeen counties were in this category), the legislative body of the city was to select one of the two locally appointed members of the department; in a district department, each county was to appoint one member. The county public welfare board was to engage an executive officer to be known as the county welfare director, and all department employees were to be selected in accordance with the merit system. The study commission recommended the abolition of the county relief commissions, the superintendents of the poor, the soldiers' and sailors' relief commissions, the county agents, and the county old-age assistance boards. The county department of public welfare was to assume the functions of the agencies it replaced as well as the welfare functions of the township supervisors and the administration of mothers' pensions. Like the state department of public welfare, the county departments were to emphasize the prevention of dependency and the rehabilitation of the needy rather than "palliative relief."

The study commission recommended that the state government assume the entire cost (except for federal aid) of old-age assistance, ADC, aid to the blind, and the hospitalization of crippled and afflicted children and that the counties assume the cost of county infirmaries, the hospitalization of afflicted adults, the care of children not covered by the Social Security Act, and such miscellaneous costs as transportation of the indigent. The commission recommended that the state legislature appropriate $12 million per year for the next biennium for general relief and that the balance, estimated at $8 million for each year of the biennium, be raised by the counties.[16]

Dunham characterized the recommendations of the Welfare and Relief Study Commission as "the most statesmanlike social welfare proposal" in Michigan's history. He personally favored the creation of a single, integrated state department of social welfare, but he knew that state welfare personnel opposed the idea. The consolidation of the state's welfare agencies into three departments, on the other hand, enjoyed the support of "social work leaders," the more "progressive" state welfare employees, and some local officials. Dunham consequently recognized that this arrangement was the "best" that could be obtained at that time.[17]

The recommendations of the Welfare and Relief Study Commission were quite similar "in principle and in general direction" to proposals for welfare reorganization advanced in six other states (New York, Louisiana, Indiana, Missouri, Connecticut, and Minnesota) that, like Michigan, had responded to the termination of federal funding for direct relief and the "bait" of grants-in-aid provided under the Social Security Act by establishing commissions to study their welfare and relief systems. The various state study commissions generally sought to remove partisanship in the administration of welfare by providing that lay boards rather than the governor appoint the director of the welfare department and by urging the merit system for welfare employees. They were "startlingly unanimous" in recommending the retention of a local interest in welfare administration, but they insisted on local adherence to state standards as the condition for receiving state aid. All of them, also, rejected "the deterrent spirit of the old poor laws" and recognized that "welfare" meant something more than "public action to keep body and soul together."[18]

The difficulty that Murphy would face in gaining acceptance for the recommendations of the Welfare and Relief Study Commission were foreshadowed when four members of the nineteen-member commission submitted a minority report on December 28, 1936. Their principal complaint was that the majority report deprived local governments of control over purely local affairs, entrusting the responsibility instead to "so-called efficiency experts." "The State stuff isn't so bad," one dissenter stated, "but the local recommendations are terrible." The minority urged that the state Emergency Relief Act be repealed and "the tremendous and wasteful organization" maintained by the SERA be abolished, that the legislature appropriate $10 million for relief, the money to be distributed by the Administrative Board to meet "relief emergencies," and that the administration of relief be returned entirely to the counties. They recommended the creation of county relief commissions composed of three to five members appointed by the county boards of supervisors (except that the governing board of the largest city or township in the county could appoint at least one member). The superintendents of the poor and other county, city, or township officials were to be eligible to serve on the commissions. The commissioners were to distribute all federal and state funds for general relief, old-age assistance, ADC, aid to the blind, and hospitalization. They were to employ such persons as required to carry out the duties of the commission, subject to the approval of the county board of supervisors but not to the requirements of the merit system. The minority report was almost a carbon copy of a proposal agreed upon in November 1936 by the State Association of Supervisors.[19]

Although governor-elect Murphy had indicated that he wished the Welfare and Relief Study Commission to continue its work, he also requested William J. Norton, the executive vice-president of the Children's Fund of Michigan, who had advised and assisted Murphy on welfare matters when he had been mayor, to make an investigation of the same subject. Norton's recommendations, submitted to the governor-elect on December 9, were "more or less similar" to what the Welfare and Relief Study Commission proposed later in the month. ". . . the proposals," Norton wrote Murphy, "are not for a perfect system that will be impossible of attainment but for a much better system than the one now prevailing which with your backing probably can be secured." In his initial message to the legislature, the governor used the Norton report as the basis for remarks concerning the needed reorganization of state and local welfare services. Following his address, the Welfare and Relief Study Commission drafted eight bills embodying its recommendations, all of which were introduced in the Senate on February 17, 1937. The measures received the "full support" of the Murphy administration, Kemp stating that welfare reorganization was "one of the really big things in our program." Three additional bills prepared by the commission relating to prisons, parole, and probation were withheld in favor of proposals prepared by a separate committee that the governor-elect had appointed to study the reorganization of Michigan's correctional system.[20]

Opposition to the majority report of the Welfare and Relief Study Commission and to its bills centered on the proposed reorganization of welfare services at the local level and the degree of state supervision that would be exercised over the county boards of public welfare. Centralization of local relief functions in the county boards of public welfare and other study commission proposals regarding local welfare meant that 246 county superintendents of the poor, ninety county agents, and two hundred members of the soldiers' and sailors' relief commissions would lose their jobs and that 1,276 township and hence county supervisors would neither dispense relief themselves nor determine how it should be dispensed. Under these circumstances, it is hardly surprising that these officials and their legislative spokesmen found fault with the county reorganization bill. "We don't care about the rest of the plan," McPherson candidly declared, "but we think the supervisors should retain some control of welfare and relief activities."[21]

Opposition to the study commission bills derived to a considerable extent from resentment that had built up against New Dealish relief ideas and the state's emergency relief program among those who espoused traditional views of relief and welfare. Far more concerned with the cost of relief than "the humanitarian treatment of unfortunates," opponents of welfare reorganization alleged that relief was being administered by "immature and inexperienced students of sociology and psychology" and by "young folks fresh from school" who lacked the experience and "mental reserve" to resist the appeals of the undeserving poor. Township supervisors and county superintendents of the poor, by contrast, were said to be persons of practical experience who would dispense relief far more economically than the proposed county welfare boards. The purpose of the proposed legislation, one supervisor stated, was "to keep the parasitical social workers in jobs and build up a huge bureaucracy." Another supervisor alleged that if the county welfare bill were approved, " 'a bunch of kike social workers . . . will be coming up her[e] . . . and telling us how to run our own affairs.' "

The "kike" who most troubled the opponents of the county bill was William Haber, the state's capable relief administrator. " 'John L. Lewis and his C.I.O. communist agitators haven't got a thing on Dr. Haber and his social workers,' " one supervisor asserted. In what the *Detroit News* judged was "a new low for bad taste" in that session of the legislature, "if not for all time," members of the House on May 4 alleged that Haber had "educated his welfare clients not to work," that his associates and he favored "a big standing army of welfare clients" in order to keep their jobs, that the state needed a relief organization that was not dominated by "carpet-bag professors and their like," and that Haber had been on six different state payrolls, most of them concurrently, which was inaccurate. The *Detroit News* thought that the attack on Haber stemmed from "the stored-up rebellion of local public officials against a centralized relief administration," but it also reflected the same anti-intellectualism and anti-Semitism that manifested itself in the debate over the unemployment insurance and civil service bills in that session of the legislature. "I presume," Haber wrote the governor in response to what was being said in the legislature, "that it is one of the penalties that I have to pay for having left the secluded study of a Professor and going into public service."[22]

Proponents of welfare reorganization responded to the criticism of the commission bills by asserting that the opposition came from "a few selfish individuals who hope[d] to further their political well-being by gaining control of State relief funds." Defending the study commission recommendations regarding public relief, Norton pointed out that the pre-Depression relief pattern in the state had been designed for "the horse and buggy age," the existing arrangements were suitable only for an emergency, and the welfare reorganization plan was intended to "solve" the problem for the long run. Smith responded to the complaints about insufficient local control by arguing that the bills provided "the maximum local control compatible with sound administration, with the financial interests of the State and Federal governments in the enterprise and with the maintenance of suitable and uniform standards."[23]

Proponents of the study commission's bills formed a "citizens committee for public welfare organization'' to assist in securing their enactment. The study commission also lobbied in behalf of its bills, and Levi coached a Senate sponsor of the measures on ''matters'' that were ''strange to him.'' Senate Republicans attacked the ''welfare workers lobby,'' and a resolution was introduced in the House calling for an investigation of ''the lobbying activities of the Haber relief employes and their agencies''; but there was a counterattack in the Senate on the ''more vicious lobby'' of the State Association of Supervisors.[24]

The bills all passed the Senate in the middle of April. The county welfare bill, the most controversial of the measures, initially fell one vote short of the seventeen required for passage. After Murphy, however, interceded with the one Democrat who had voted against the bill, the measure was reconsidered and passed with two votes to spare. The bills received final legislative approval on June 25, and Murphy signed them into law on July 22, 1937. The legislature appropriated $12,075,000 for ''general public relief'' for each year of the biennium and specified that the state contribution for relief should constitute at least 50 percent of the total amount expended for relief by the counties.[25]

The legislature amended the original commission bills in several important respects.[26] Whereas the original county bill had specified that the locally appointed members of county public welfare boards ''need not be'' supervisors, the bill as approved prohibited supervisors from serving on the boards, which increased their antagonism toward the measure. On the other hand, the power of the state department of public assistance (as the legislature chose to name the welfare department) over the county boards was materially circumscribed by the legislature in the legislation's final form. In the bills as submitted, the state department, on its own initiative, could review any decision of a county board regarding old-age assistance, ADC, aid to the blind, or ''any other form of public aid or relief'' and could then determine the type and amount of assistance to be granted. As amended, the legislation provided that, except for programs involving federal funds, which required state administration or supervision, decisions of the county boards in granting relief were to be ''final in the absence of abuse of discretion or bad faith.'' If there was a disagreement between a relief client and a county board relative to the granting or denial of relief or the form or amount of relief granted, the jurisdiction of the state department of public assistance was ''limited to the fixing of reasonable minimum standards.'' Deferring still further to the local units, the legislature provided that the chairmen of the county welfare boards were to be selected by the boards themselves rather than by the state department of public assistance, as in the original county bill. Finally, the civil service requirements in the original bill were eliminated by the legislature for both the state and county welfare departments. This was of no importance insofar as the state was concerned since a civil service bill applicable to state employees was soon to be enacted by the legislature, but it had a good deal of meaning at the county level.[27]

The welfare reorganization acts of 1937 authorized the first significant reorganization of Michigan's welfare system in the state's history. "From being one of the lowest in the scale of modern and efficient welfare organization," Professor Ernest B. Harper of Michigan State College declared, "Michigan in one jump sets up a program that will compare favorably with that of any other state." Michigan was one of eighteen states providing for an integrated state welfare department in 1937; five additional states reorganized existing departments in the same year. Although the reorganization plans differed from state to state, they generally provided for the integration of welfare services at the state and local levels and for greater local responsibility for welfare services than had been characteristic of the emergency relief phase of the New Deal. Like the Michigan statute, they stressed not only assistance to the needy but "prevention and rehabilitation."[28]

Eight days after Murphy signed the welfare reorganization bills into law, the State Association of Supervisors and the State Association of Superintendents of the Poor agreed to hold a joint meeting to decide on a course of action regarding the measures. If they believed in "local control of local government," it was essential that they attend the meeting, the president of the superintendents advised the members of his organization. Shortly after the meeting was held, the supervisors announced that they would attempt to gather enough signatures to refer the act establishing the state department of public assistance to the decision of the voters in the November 1938 election. It was the county act to which the supervisors objected, but this act was not subject to a referendum since it was also an appropriation measure, and the state constitution forbade referenda on appropriation acts. This was only a technicality, however, since the county welfare act was not to take effect until sixty days after the state welfare act went into operation, and thus to kill the latter in a referendum was to kill the former as well. The attorney general, as a matter of fact, ruled that the welfare statutes were "allied acts" that "should be construed together" and must be suspended pending the referendum except for the few provisions that the legislature had given immediate effect. By the end of October the opponents of welfare reorganization had gathered a sufficient number of signatures to place the issue on the ballot. For Arthur Dunham, the question to be decided in the referendum was "how far Michigan . . . [had] progressed in state-wide social organization and in the understanding of her citizens in regard to the basic issues of public welfare."[29] The answer, Dunham discovered, was that Michigan had not "progressed" very far.

The principal advocates of a no vote on the referendum (a yes vote meant approving welfare reorganization) were the township supervisors. At their annual meeting in January 1938 the supervisors voted 300-8 to oppose the referendum and organized the Home Rule Committee to direct the campaign against welfare reorganization. The opposition had a decidedly Republican character. The State Association of Supervisors was theoretically a nonpartisan organization, but its composition was overwhelmingly Republican, and its 1938 meeting, at which McPherson-for-governor cards were distributed, was a pro-Republican, anti-Murphy affair. In the 1938 campaign, Republican candidate Fitzgerald joined the supervisors in urging a negative vote on the referendum.[30]

Opponents of reorganization sought to portray the issue as "just a part of the age-old battle between home rule and centralization." To affirm the reorganization acts, the more rabid among them declared, was to take a step in the direction of "dictatorship" and "totalitarian administration." The extravagant rhetoric about the threatened loss of local liberties is difficult to reconcile with the facts. Under the state emergency relief legislation of 1933 that was to be superseded by the welfare reorganization acts, an agency of the state government had the power to appoint all the members of the county relief commissions—the SEWRC could have revoked the June 1936 agreement at any time—whereas the welfare reorganization legislation permitted the state department of public assistance to appoint only one member of the county welfare board, and that person had to be a resident of the county. Also, whereas state government agencies exercised full control over state money appropriated for welfare and relief under existing law, the reorganization legislation gave county boards virtually complete control over the distribution of such funds except insofar as assistance programs were supported by federal grants.[31]

Why then did the sponsors of the referendum contend that the welfare reorganization acts limited the powers of local government when the reverse appears to have been true? " . . . the nub of the difference," the chairman of the Washtenaw County Board of Auditors thought, was "a matter of one man on the county welfare commission being appointed by the state welfare commission." The fear, as Fred Levi construed it, was that the state-appointed member would be "endowed with some magic mantle" and that the other two members would consequently be "impotent." Levi thought that the "kindest thing" he could say about this was that it was "foolish." More to the point, probably, was the fact that even though the boards of supervisors had the power to approve relief budgets under the reorganization legislation, the supervisors themselves could not serve on the county welfare boards and could not select the boards' employees, and they resented these restraints on their power.[32]

In part, one suspects, the opposition to welfare reorganization was simply a blind reaction among Michigan's conservative citizens against Mr. Roosevelt's New Deal and the New Dealish state government in Lansing. A Detroit doctor thus thought that welfare reorganization would lead to "regimentation" because of "our present state set-up cooperating with the set-up in Washington." The welfare reorganization scheme was "decidedly 'Pinkish,' " a handbill of the referendum opponents warned, and would "further centralize . . . states' rights in Washington."[33]

The anti-reorganization rhetoric did not mean that those who railed against centralization were willing to do without the federal and state funds that led to the modest restraints on local control imposed by the welfare reorganization legislation. The initiators of the referendum did not suggest that the state decline the offer of federal matching funds provided by the Social Security Act even though they recognized that this meant local government compliance with standards established in Washington and enforced by the state government. The supervisors, similarly, welcomed state funds for relief, favoring legislation that directed the state to distribute $15 million annually among the counties on the basis of population. The issue, as a senator who had sponsored the reorganization bills noted, was not one of "local control" versus "state control" but was rather between "two different kinds of local control." The senator was presumably distinguishing between township control and county control, but if the point of reference is the period of emergency relief in the state, the welfare reorganization legislation can be viewed as terminating a system of "absolute state control" and restoring considerable power over relief to local governments.[34]

The welfare reorganization statutes were endorsed by the Michigan League of Women Voters, the Michigan Municipal League, municipal government officials in Detroit and elsewhere, the Detroit Bureau of Governmental Research, the Detroit Citizens League, the Michigan Federation of Labor, and social workers. Believing that the opponents of welfare reorganization were guilty of a "campaign of misinformation," some friends of reorganization contended that it was "necessary for somebody to initiate and conduct a campaign of information" lest the referendum "go by default." They consequently created the Citizens Welfare Education Committee, with John A. McLellan, the executive secretary of the Michigan Conference of Social Work, as executive secretary.[35]

The strong municipal support for welfare reorganization is understandable since the cities stood to benefit materially from the new legislation. The welfare statutes provided that, except for Detroit, which was to continue to operate its own department, the cost of relief administered by the county departments could not be charged back to the cities or townships in the county. Direct relief was to be financed by the state and county, and old-age assistance, ADC, and aid to the blind entirely by the federal and state governments. The cities, moreover, no longer had to pay any part of the cost incurred in the hospitalization, medical care, and burial of indigents.[36]

Proponents of welfare reorganization charged that "greedy rural politicians" were the principal opponents of the referendum. Believing that welfare reorganization was, "next to Civil Service, . . . the most desirable of the new reforms" of his administration, Murphy lambasted the initiation of the referendum as "a shabby example of spoils politics, done only to advance the personal political ambitions of a single individual [McPherson] and to further a reactionary clique." Proponents of reorganization riddled the argument that the new welfare legislation increased the power of the state government at the expense of local governments. "Instead of local control by political officeholders who want to keep welfare administration because it increases their power," Murphy declared, "the reorganization laws provide local control by men who are chosen for their ability to administer the welfare laws." Mrs. Siegel Judd pointed out to Fitzgerald that health and highway functions had already been transferred from the townships to the county governments and that it was essential to do the same with welfare. The only way to preserve local government, she contended, was to strengthen county government. If local governments failed to deal with the welfare problem in a satisfactory manner, she warned, the state government would assume the task itself. As for the argument that the most economical way to dispense relief was to place the supervisors in charge, McLellan reported that a reliable survey of the problem had indicated that the integrated welfare system would save the state $200,000 a year in administrative costs alone.[37]

The Welfare Education Committee distributed factual information about welfare reorganization through various statewide organizations, arranged for speakers across the state, and set up subsidiary organizations, particularly in the larger counties. On the basis of an information test that they administered in several counties in the summer of 1938, two Michigan State College professors concluded that although the information disseminated by the committee was "intelligent, logical, lucid, and attractive in appearance," it was "too intellectual," was over the heads of the general public, and was not directed at "underlying emotional beliefs, group ideas and accepted values of the rural population."[38]

The issue presented to the voters by the welfare referendum was a complex one, and it was difficult for all but a minority to comprehend what was at stake. "To the average layman," the *Detroit News* observed, "the [welfare reorganization] act is just as clear as mud on a foggy morning." Wherever she went, the publicity director of the Democratic State Central Committee reported, she heard "the most conflicting reports and ideas" concerning welfare reorganization. "... even the best informed," she discovered, were "not able to talk on it coherently or answer the confusing questions asked." When the secretary of the Citizens Welfare Education Committee interviewed one hundred persons outside Detroit, he found that, even though the committee had sought to wage a nonpartisan campaign and had been reluctant to involve the governor too overtly in its efforts, forty-four thought that the issue was entirely political whereas only eleven persons saw it as a bona fide welfare question. Less than 20 percent of those interviewed had anything more than "a very hazy idea" of what they were supposed to decide.[39]

The welfare reorganization proposal was defeated at the polls in November 1938 by a vote of 572,756 to 497,569. Only 64 percent of those who went to the polls voted on this issue, whereas referenda proposals normally attracted the vote of 75 percent of those who cast ballots for the major office being decided in an election. Only eleven counties favored welfare reorganization, seven of them in the Upper Peninsula, where the percentage of persons on relief was very high compared to the rest of the state; the other four were the heavily industrialized counties of Wayne, Oakland, Muskegon, and Kent. In the eleven urban counties of the state, 52.5 percent of the voters favored welfare reorganization; but in the remainder of the state, where the supervisors enjoyed a good deal of political influence, only 35.4 percent approved. A majority of big-city voters, professional persons, and the unskilled apparently voted for welfare reorganization, whereas voters in small towns, farmers, and businessmen opposed it. Although the referendum was adopted as a progressive reform in the pre-World War I era, it is an electoral device that has all too often played into the hands of special-interest groups and has required voters to decide issues they only dimly comprehend, if they comprehend them at all.[40] The defeat of welfare reorganization in Michigan in 1938 is certainly a case in point.

II

The day before Murphy was elected governor, Arthur Evans Wood, a professor of sociology at the University of Michigan and a criminologist, expressed the hope that a victorious Murphy would "take hold of the penal situation" in Michigan since it lagged behind other states in the administration of its penal system and its treatment of offenders. The Michigan correctional system was "dominated by partisan politics." It also suffered from lack of "expert direction" and lack of coordination, state services in this area being distributed among the state welfare director, the commissioner of pardons and paroles, the Prison Commission, and the Corrections Commission.[41]

When Murphy became governor, there was no classification system in Michigan's three major prisons, the enormous Jackson Prison, which housed two-thirds of the state's prison population, the Marquette Branch Prison, and the Ionia Reformatory, to which juvenile offenders were sent. Each prison operated under its own rules, of which prisoners generally were not advised; the state employed only one prison psychiatrist; inadequate provision was made for the inspection of prisons; and prison industrial activity was sharply circumscribed by the Munshaw-Frey Act, which limited the distribution of prison-made goods to the state government and charitable institutions. Twenty-one counties were without adult probation officers as of January 1, 1937, and less than six of the 121 persons performing probation tasks were full-time salaried officers. The state government was supposed to supervise probation officers, but this was only an incidental duty of the officials charged with that task. The granting of paroles was "largely a hit and miss proposition" and was dominated by politics. As the Crime Commission advised the legislature at the beginning of 1937, the manner in which prisoners were selected for parole left a good deal to be desired, prisoners were not properly prepared for their paroles, and parolees were not adequately supervised.[42]

After his election Murphy, who had long been intensely interested in penal reform, asked Wood to prepare recommendations for reform of the correctional system. Although the Michigan professor gathered "a sort of informal committee" of academics and nonacademics to examine the problem, Murphy soon assigned the task to a new committee that included Wood. The chairman of the committee was Caroline Parker, whom Mayor Murphy had appointed to Detroit's House of Correction Commission, and its secretary was Hilmer Gellein, who had served as Judge Murphy's court stenographer. The Parker committee studied the federal prison system and the correctional systems in the states with the best-run penal institutions and the most effective parole procedures, and it examined the reports of the Osborne Association, a prison-reform organization. The committee entrusted legislative drafting responsibilities to Ephraim Gomberg, a Detroit attorney who had studied correctional reform for the Michigan Conference of Social Work, and Professor Burke Shartel of the University of Michigan Law School.

The Parker committee recommended the creation of a "unified" department of corrections, separate from the Welfare Department, because of its numerous responsibilities and Michigan's "vast problem in penology." The department was to be administered by a corrections commission appointed by the governor, and the commission was to select the department's director. There were to be three bureaus within the department, a bureau of prisons, a bureau of paroles, and a bureau of probation, each headed by an assistant director appointed by the director. The prison wardens were to be appointed by the director, and a classification committee was to be appointed for each prison. A parole board consisting of the head of the bureau of paroles, a psychiatrist, and a qualified third person was to replace the commissioner of pardons and paroles. The bureau of probation was to supervise probation officers in the state, and state grants-in-aid were to be made available to local governments so that they could hire additional probation officers. The committee recommended the application of the merit system throughout the proposed new department. Wood, as a matter of fact, had advised Murphy that it was "useless" to proceed with penal reform unless civil service was rigidly applied since "the major aspect of the problem," in his view, was the quality of the persons who would administer the department.[43]

The bills drafted by the Parker committee were introduced in the Senate on February 24, 1937, approved by the legislature on June 25 with little change, and signed into law by the governor on July 22. The Osborne Association hailed the legislation as providing "one of the best administrative structures for the control and management of prisons and prison industries, pardons and paroles, and probation ever established by any American governmental unit." Gellein, whom Murphy had already appointed to serve as commissioner of pardons and paroles, became the director of the new Department of Corrections; Joel R. Moore, the warden of Jackson Prison, was named acting assistant director in charge of the Bureau of Prisons; Ralph Hall Ferris, who had headed the Domestic Relations Division of the Detroit Recorder's Court's celebrated Probation Department, was placed in charge of the Bureau of Probation; and M. Hubert O'Brien, a well-known humanitarian, was made assistant director in charge of the Bureau of Pardons and Paroles.[44]

Whereas sentencing judges had previously determined the prison to which offenders should be sent, the head of the Bureau of Prisons now made the decision on the recommendation of classification committees at the Jackson Prison, the receiving prison for the Lower Peninsula, and the Marquette Prison, the receiving prison for the Upper Peninsula. To facilitate the work of the committees, each consisting of a psychiatrist as chairman, a doctor, a welfare worker, a chaplain, and the prison's vocational and educational directors, the Department of Corrections secured a WPA grant that enabled it to provide a more complete and uniform record both for the existing jail population, which numbered 6,600 in August 1937, and also for incoming inmates. Long-term prisoners requiring close supervision were sent to Marquette and youthful offenders to Ionia, and sex perverts and the mentally deficient were completely segregated. New and uniform rules adopted for the prisons spelled out the penalties for infractions and incorporated the regulations followed by the Parole Board.[45]

Seeking to increase employment opportunities for prisoners, the legislature amended the Munshaw-Frey Act in June 1937 to permit the sale of prison-made goods to local governments, not just to the state government and charitable institutions. The next month the lawmakers repealed the amendment. When Gellein asked Senator Earl W. Munshaw how the prisoners were to occupy their time, he replied, " 'Let them play ball.' " The Bureau of Prisons established a new tobacco factory at Marquette and a soap plant at Ionia and was able to persuade state institutions to use more prison-made goods. As a result, the number of employed inmates rose from 549 on January 1, 1937, to 1,470 on July 1, 1938. In a further effort to combat idleness, especially in the Marquette and Ionia institutions, the bureau persuaded some manufacturing firms to donate machinery for use in the vocational schools that had recently been established in both prisons. The number of inmates in the prison schools in the two institutions rose from 115 on September 1, 1937, to 355 by the end of 1938. An additional 1,800 persons were receiving full or part-time instruction at the Jackson Prison.

Acting under the authority of the new corrections legislation, the Bureau of Prisons inspected fifty-two county jails in 1938, finding many of them in "deplorable condition." The inspection of jails by county committees had apparently been perfunctory, and it was now necessary for the Department of Corrections to persuade local governments to improve the physical and sanitary condition of their correctional institutions. After advising Murphy that there was need for "much missionary work" in this field, Gellein in April 1938 announced the beginning of a joint state-county effort to improve county jails.[46]

The 1937 corrections legislation transferred the power to appoint and remove probation officers from the governor to the Department of Corrections. To carry out its duties, the Bureau of Probation, for the first time in Michigan's history, set minimum standards for the selection of local probation officers and provided for their supervision. The bureau offered grants-in-aid to impecunious counties so that they could employ probation officers, and it appointed twelve field probation officers to serve the counties that requested their services. As the result of the bureau's efforts, the courts began to make extensive use of probation officers in conducting pre-sentence investigations, and the supervision of probationers, whose number increased by 9 percent during the fiscal year 1937–38, was very much improved.[47]

Procedures for granting paroles and supervising parolees were greatly improved as the result of the reorganization of Michigan's correctional system. Murphy stated that he hoped to eliminate the "political aspects" of parole and to place parole on a "scientific basis," and that is essentially what occurred during his governorship. To his credit and in contrast to his predecessors, Murphy never once recommended that a prisoner be paroled despite the pressure sometimes brought on the governor's office.

Although the improvement in parole practices began while Gellein served as commissioner of pardons and paroles, the major reforms were initiated after the new corrections laws took effect. The parole staff had formerly consisted largely of part-time political appointees paid on a fee basis; now a trained, full-time, salaried staff of parole officers was recruited, and the ratio of parole officers to parolees was substantially reduced.

The new parole procedures required that each inmate receive a hearing on his parole application at least thirty days before the completion of his minimum term. A progress report covering every phase of his institutional record and containing the recommendation of the warden and the classification committee was then submitted to the Parole Board, which decided by majority vote whether to grant the parole. Before the board recommended to the governor that a prisoner be pardoned or his sentence commuted, there had to be a public hearing, which the sentencing judge and the prosecuting attorney could attend.

Prisoners granted parole and awaiting release were required to attend classes for three weeks to prepare themselves for life outside prison walls. Prisoners with a record of mental disturbance or sexual deviation were required as a condition of parole to visit a parole clinic during the period of their parole. The bureau engaged an employment director to help parolees find jobs, and, partly because the WPA provided some places for parolees with families, the number of employed parolees rose from 599 on January 1, 1937, to 1,470 on July 1, 1938. Thanks to the improved procedures, only 8 percent of the parolees violated parole in 1938 compared to 13 percent in 1937.[48]

When in the 1938 gubernatorial campaign Frank Fitzgerald found fault with the administration of the state's penal system during Murphy's governorship, the Republican *Grand Rapids Press* criticized the candidate for his remarks. The Murphy administration, the newspaper editorialized, had run Michigan's correctional system in a "scientific" manner and had kept it out of politics to a far greater extent than any of its recent predecessors. Gellein was correct in his assertion that the Murphy administration gave Michigan one of the best "penological systems" in the nation.[49]

Although there were more than seven thousand state prisoners in Michigan jails at the end of Murphy's governorship, it was the fate of a single federal prisoner, John Chebatoris, that caused Murphy the greatest anguish while he was governor. Chebatoris and an accomplice held up Midland's Chemical State Savings Bank, a national bank, on September 29, 1937, and killed a bystander in the process. The accomplice was killed while trying to escape, but Chebatoris was seized and was subsequently sentenced to be hanged at the federal prison in Milan on July 8, 1938—he was the first person to be tried and sentenced under the National Bank Robbery Act. Michigan had abolished capital punishment in 1846, and there had not been an execution in the state in 108 years. There was, moreover, no more dedicated and outspoken foe of capital punishment in Michigan than the state's governor, Frank Murphy. "The act of putting a noose around a man's neck and hanging him until he is dead is uncivilized," the governor stated. "That he too is uncivilized does not excuse it."

Murphy wrote President Roosevelt on June 22 requesting that Chebatoris's sentence be commuted or that the execution take place somewhere other than in Michigan since it would be "displeasing if not offensive to a majority of the people" of the state. A presidential aide correctly advised Roosevelt that this was "not a mere perfunctory request," that Murphy felt very deeply about the matter. Although Roosevelt saw no reason to commute the sentence, he asked the attorney general to ascertain if it were possible to carry out the sentence in a state other than Michigan. Joseph M. Keenan, assistant to the attorney general, directed John C. Lehr, the federal attorney for the Eastern District of Michigan, to advise the sentencing judge, Arthur Tuttle, that the Department of Justice did not object to his granting Murphy's request if this was permitted by state and federal law. Tuttle decided that there was no legal basis for the transfer of the execution and, also, that "it would not be in good taste to select the territory of a neighbor for the performance of an unpleasant duty." Chebatoris, who had slashed his throat and wrists after learning of his sentence, was accordingly hanged on July 8, although it would be more accurate to say that he was strangled to death since he apparently lived for twenty-one minutes after the trap was sprung.

The residents of Midland "seethed with indignation" at Murphy's efforts to have Chebatoris's sentence commuted or to have the execution take place outside Michigan. The press was critical of the governor's behavior, and Democrats feared that the party would suffer at the polls in November as a result. On the day of the execution Murphy, tormented by what had occurred, stated publicly that everyone in Michigan had been "debased and brutalized" by the hanging. "It is the duty of society to deter crime and rehabilitate a criminal," he declared. "You can't reform a man by hanging him."[50]

Just before his term came to an end, Murphy, who, it will be recalled, regarded the opportunity to perform "acts of personal kindness and mercy" as "the most satisfying experience in high public life," advised Gellein that he wanted to extend mercy to a deserving prisoner as his final official act. The individual selected was serving a life sentence for murder in the first degree, but ballistics experts had offered evidence that the conviction had been in error. Murphy commuted the sentence, delighted that his final act as governor could be "one of mercy."[51]

III

"One of the acute problems of Michigan," Fred R. Johnson, the secretary of Michigan's Children's Aid Fund, advised governor-elect Murphy, "is better organization in the field of mental hygiene." After World War I Michigan fell behind the nation's more progressive states in the care it provided for the mentally ill. As of May 1937 there were only 257.8 beds per 100,000 population in Michigan's mental hospitals, which placed it twenty-sixth among the states. The legislature had appropriated $19,517,300 in 1929 for a four-year hospital building program, but the program was discontinued in the depression year of 1932 after only $5 million had been spent. By a decisive 6–1 margin, Michigan voters in 1934 rejected a bond issue that would have permitted the resumption of the building program.[52]

Although the state's public mental and epileptic hospitals had a capacity for 12,645 persons at the beginning of 1937, they were actually caring for 15,601 patients at that time. About three to four thousand additional persons requiring care were on hospital waiting lists, were confined to jails or infirmaries, or were at large. ". . . we see inmates crowded into basements and halls," the Senate's State Hospital Committee reported in the spring of 1937, "tubercular patients housed in temporary sheds, the bed patients packed into fire traps, nearly every county jail detaining patients under conditions disgraceful to civilized society and fatal to the individuals. In short, the herds of cattle and swine of our various institutions are better housed and cared for than the human wards of the state."

The state was not only short of beds for the mentally ill but also of staff to look after them. Although known since 1911 as hospitals rather than "asylums," the state hospitals had increasingly become "places of *restraint* instead of *treatment*," and their superintendents, largely able men, took on the character of "wardens instead of healers." The state did not provide adequate follow-up care for those paroled from state hospitals, the out-patient service was inadequate, and the state did not have a mental hygiene program. The State Hospital Commission was a worthless body. Its members, Norton recalled, "just sat around at the hospitals once in a while and had a good meal and a good sleep and a good drink and that was it."[53]

In an effort to deal with the acute problem of the mentally ill, the Welfare and Relief Study Commission recommended the creation of a department of mental hygiene, independent of the Welfare Department, to administer the ten state institutions for the mentally ill, the mentally defective, and epileptics. It recommended that the department coordinate state services pertaining to mental hygiene, develop and supervise a state mental hygiene program that emphasized "educational and preventive measures," and license and supervise private institutions for the mentally ill. The legislature largely embodied these recommendations in a bill that it passed on June 25, 1937, and Murphy signed the measure into law on July 22. The next day the governor also approved a bill creating the Michigan Child Guidance Institute and authorizing it to inquire into the causes of child delinquency and to improve the methods of treating neglected, defective, and delinquent children.[54]

Acting under the authority of the hospital legislation, Murphy appointed men and women to the new seven-member bipartisan State Hospital Commission who took their responsibilities "seriously." He reached outside the state, as we have seen, to select the able, albeit tactless, Dr. Joseph E. Barrett as state hospital director. Taking a deep personal interest in the problem of mental health, Murphy was concerned that the state make "adequate institutional provision" and provide proper treatment for the mentally ill. To meet its legal obligation to the mentally afflicted and as "a matter of decency, humanity, and good government," the governor called on the legislature in May 1937 to appropriate $3–4 million for each year of the next biennium to provide accommodations for six thousand mental patients—construction was already underway to provide about one thousand beds. The legislature responded by appropriating $6,432,435 for the biennium to provide beds for additional patients and to renovate and fireproof existing facilities. Murphy instructed his budget director to see to it that the building program proceeded with dispatch.[55]

When he visited several state mental institutions in the fall of 1937, Murphy, who listened patiently to inmate complaints, was shocked by what he saw. He concluded that he had underestimated the cost of what was required to provide adequate medical care for the state's mentally afflicted. Turning to the Public Works Administration (PWA) for assistance, he asserted that there was "hardly a problem in Michigan more serious than the outmoded and overcrowded State hospitals." Late in June 1938 the PWA granted Michigan approximately $5 million for hospital construction, which expanded the hospital building program by about 45 percent. Barrett estimated that the program would provide approximately 4,300 new beds. By the end of October the building program had made it possible for the state to reduce to 1,721 the number of patients awaiting admission to the state hospitals.[56]

Because of the lack of funds, the expansion of hospital facilities was not matched by the badly needed expansion in hospital staffs. Whereas the American Psychiatric Association recommended the employment of one doctor per 150 mental patients as the minimum standard, the ratios in Michigan were one doctor per 349 patients in mental hospitals, one for every seven hundred patients in the hospitals for the feebleminded, and one for every 333 epileptic patients. "That," Murphy declared, is "shocking and inexcusable, and we must put an end to it." The state hospitals also suffered from a shortage of nurses and social service personnel. Per capita daily patient costs rose from 77.3 cents in the fiscal year 1935–36 to 81.6 cents in 1936–37, and 89.1 cents in 1937–38. States that provided better care than Michigan averaged at least $1.00 per day, and Barrett believed that Michigan should try to meet that standard.[57]

Murphy, who had great compassion for the unfortunate whether they were impoverished or ill, was concerned not only about providing additional beds for the mentally ill but also wished to alter public attitudes regarding mental illness. He thought that it was essential for the public to abandon the "archaic" belief that mental illness was entirely unlike physical illness, that it was a "disgrace" to be mentally ill, and that the mentally defective were simply victims of their own folly. "I want to get away from the ridicule directed at the 'medieval mad-house' and its patients," he asserted. Mental institutions, he urged, must be changed from asylums into hospitals, and the emphasis in dealing with mental illness must be on "curative hospitalization." Murphy thought that one of "the most tragic features" of the mental health problem was the failure of society to develop a "comprehensive, integrated program of prevention of mental illness" and the acceptance instead of the "thoroughly hopeless and defeatist theory" that this type of illness could not be prevented. He called for "a complete program of prevention" consisting of child guidance clinics, further development of out-patient clinics in the state hospitals, "sound, constructive paroling of patients," building up of research departments in the state hospitals, and a statewide program of mental hygiene education. The kind of approach to mental illness that he was urging, the governor stated, represented "a new departure in government service in Michigan" and was "the concrete embodiment of a new social spirit in the state."[58]

Murphy did not serve as governor for a sufficient length of time to implement fully his enlightened views about mental illness, but at least a beginning was made during his administration. The construction at the new and renovated state hospitals was planned "to put an entirely new face on the institutions," to make them look like "real hospitals" rather than asylums. The building program provided new facilities for research in the cure and prevention of mental disorders and included school and industrial units for epileptic and mentally retarded children designed to enable them to return to their communities "in due time." The quality of the out-patient service at the state hospitals was considerably improved, and Murphy forbade the jailing of mental patients. Also, the Crippled Children Commission began committing children with curable mental illnesses to the Neuro-Psychiatric Institute that the legislature had created in 1937 as a part of the University of Michigan Hospital.

In April 1938 the state government released $25,000 to the State Hospital Commission to launch a mental hygiene program in the state. Aided by the Children's Fund of Michigan, which was already financing a private clinic in Detroit, the state government opened its first child guidance clinic in September 1938, in Lansing, to deal with the problems of children under sixteen in an effort to correct maladjustments that might lead to mental illness or criminal behavior. Barrett hailed the event as "the start of our statewide program to prevent mental disorders." When the American Public Health Association surveyed public health facilities in Michigan in 1938, it specifically praised the achievements of the State Hospital Commission in the areas of mental hygiene and child guidance. "The state's mental hygiene program today is moving along the lines I have envisioned," Murphy proudly observed as his term of office drew to a close.[59]

Unlike the state hospitals, the Department of Health was not included in the reorganization plan proposed by the Welfare and Relief Study Commission. The freshening spirit of the Lansing New Deal, however, affected public health activities in Michigan just as it did the state's mental health program. By the time of his electoral defeat in 1938 Murphy was beginning to press beyond the conventional boundaries of state public health concerns into new and largely unexplored areas.

Like so many other state programs, public health activities in Michigan benefited enormously from the infusion of federal funds in the 1930s, in this instance funds for public health and maternal and child health services made available in accordance with the terms of the Social Security Act of 1935. These funds, which were the equivalent of 80 percent of the state appropriation for public health in 1936–37 and 53 percent of the appropriation in 1937–38, made it possible for the Health Department to sponsor the organization of twelve full-time county health departments in 1936, thus increasing the number of counties with such departments to fifty-two, to provide additional health services to other local departments, and to pay the tuition of public health personnel at major universities. The state also launched a program to improve child and maternal health care that included prenatal nursing services, child-care classes in the schools, women's health classes, infant welfare programs, and the assignment of public health nurses to counties that had lacked this service. Federal funds also made it possible for the Health Department to establish a Bureau of Industrial Hygiene in 1936 to promote the health of industrial workers and for Detroit to create a similar bureau. Finally, the PWA provided the state with $175,000 to construct a badly needed new building to house the department's biological and diagnostic laboratories, recognized as among the "finest" in the nation. "... the Michigan public health program," the head of the department declared in June 1937, was "a decade in advance of its normal progress" because of the impetus provided by federal funds.[60]

Despite the progress registered in 1936, Murphy learned that there was a good deal of room for improvement in the work of the Department of Health. The elderly commissioner of health, the governor was advised, was "a poor administrator" who did not "look after the work" and was not respected by the medical profession. The activities of the department were poorly coordinated, it provided insufficient health service to some sections of the state, and its new Bureau of Industrial Hygiene was largely inactive. It was his intention, Murphy indicated, "to energize the public health service and to broaden its work in accordance with modern principles." Replacing the incumbent health commissioner with the highly regarded Dr. Don W. Gudakunst, Murphy announced that he was making the change "to place the health service foremost of all government services." What he had in mind, the governor stated, was "a comprehensive campaign for the abatement and prevention of all contagious and infectious diseases in Michigan."[61]

Continuing to benefit from federal funds, the Department of Health aided in establishing departments of health in six additional counties in 1937 and 1938, bringing the total number of county departments to fifty-eight and providing health protection for about 75 percent of the state's population. For the first time, also, the State Department of Health specified the qualifications that had to be met by full-time county health officials if the counties wished to receive federal assistance. The Bureau of Industrial Hygiene finally became active, surveying various industries to determine possible health hazards to workers, establishing a laboratory where materials could be tested to ascertain if they posed a threat to health, and aiding management in preventing occupational diseases.[62]

As Murphy had wished, the Department of Health expanded its efforts to prevent and control disease, and it did not ignore the medically indigent in the process. Aided by a grant of $77,206 from the United States Public Health Service and a legislative appropriation of $50,000, the department initiated a broad-scale program to bring syphilis under control. It provided free diagnostic services, blood tests, and drugs to treat the disease, and it conducted a program of education among doctors, medical students, and the general public. The department "tremendously increased" its efforts to control tuberculosis, doubled the state subsidy for county sanatoria, and made care available to tuberculosis patients without regard to ability to pay. In an effort to combat pneumonia, the department established a new division of pneumonia control and set up typing stations throughout the state. A grant from the Commonwealth Fund enabled the department to manufacture and distribute pneumonia serum for two types of pneumonia to patients who could not afford to purchase the serum. The department also turned its attention to the previously ignored problem of dysentery, so prevalent in resort areas that it had come to be known as "Michigan Disease." The department, however, was insufficiently concerned about the content of food and milk, which may account for the typhoid epidemic in the state in 1938.[63]

Following the precedent set by Connecticut and Illinois, the Michigan legislature in 1937 enacted the Antenuptial Physical Examination Act, which required applicants for marriage licenses to submit to a medical examination, including a blood test for syphilis. During the first year the law was in effect, slightly more than 1 percent of the serological tests administered to marriage license applicants resulted in positive indications of syphilis. The director of the Bureau of Records and Statistics of the Health Department hailed the statute as "one of the best laws from the standpoint of eugenics that has ever been enacted."[64]

Murphy believed that government must help to provide medical care to those unable to pay for medical attention just as it provided relief for those unable to find work. It was essential, he stated, to protect the citizenry against illness as well as the debilities of old age, and he thought that government and the medical profession must join forces to "bridge the gap between [the] supply and demand" for medical care. In April 1938 the state government established a Committee on the Medical Needs of Governmental Assistance Clients to cooperate with the Michigan Medical Society, which, like the medical societies of forty-two other states, was studying the problem of medical care for the indigent.[65] The committee had hardly begun to function, however, before the scope of the governor's health concerns broadened, partly as the result of developments at the national level, partly because of conviction, and partly because of electoral concerns.

President Roosevelt convened the National Health Conference in Washington in July 1938 to consider a national health plan prepared by the Technical Committee on Medical Care of the Interdepartmental Committee to Coordinate Health and Welfare Activities. Among other things, the committee recommended a program of grants to the states to enable them to provide medical care for the indigent and the medically indigent, a " 'comprehensive program' " financed by taxation or insurance or both to improve and expand medical services, and the possible provision of a system of disability insurance. The conferees, who included representatives from farmer, labor, and consumer groups as well as the medical profession, evinced a good deal of enthusiasm for the Technical Committee's program. The American Medical Association (AMA) was perturbed about the general support for the program, especially the support evidenced for health insurance. Beginning in August, consequently, most state medical societies launched "a massive publicity campaign" against the health program presented at the conference.[66]

Soon after the close of the National Health Conference the "progressive" Michigan doctors Frederick C. Lendrum, director of the Medical Research Institute of the United Automobile Workers, Morris Raskin, and N. J. Bicknell met with Murphy and recommended that he convene a state health conference. The purpose of such a conclave, as they saw it, would be "to give articulate expression to the desires of the consumers of medical care in Michigan, so that the medical program for the fall election campaign" could "be based directly upon a wide popular demand." They also looked to the proposed conference to "mobilize mass backing for a progressive health policy in the state and nation" like that presented at the National Health Conference. Accepting the proposal of the three doctors, Murphy instructed Gudakunst to make the arrangements for a state health conference to be held on September 10.[67]

In announcing the conference, Murphy revealed that he had been in frequent contact with Washington regarding developments in the medical field. The purpose of the conference, he declared, would be to muster support behind the new federal health program, which

Washington, he stated, was likely to initiate in Michigan. Knowing that there was a liberal element within the Michigan Medical Society, Murphy indicated that he did not expect the same kind of opposition to health reform at the Michigan conference as the AMA had manifested at the National Health Conference.[68]

More than one thousand public health officials and other "producers and consumers" of medical care gathered in East Lansing on September 10 for the State Health Conference, the first meeting of its kind in any state. They heard speeches by Murphy, the assistant surgeon general, and others, listened to the preliminary report of the Committee on the Medical Needs of Governmental Assistance Clients, and discussed the expansion of health services, medical care for the indigent, and group hospital and health insurance. In his address, entitled "Catching Up with Human Needs," Murphy asserted that the 20 percent of the state's population then receiving relief in one form or another could not afford medical care, that another portion of the population, although not recipients of relief, could afford only "the most trivial medical attention," and that there was a disparity in the hospital and laboratory service available in different parts of the state. He declared that he was proceeding upon the assumption that every individual, regardless of his station, was entitled to the "best quality of medical service" and that government must play the leadership role in attaining this objective. Since this was a new role for government, he recognized that there would be criticism; but it was the duty of government, he contended, to promote the happiness and security of the people, and nothing was more bound up with their happiness and security than their health. Seeking to reassure the medical profession, traumatized by the specter of "socialized medicine," Murphy stated that the new medical care program must not come under "political influence or manipulation," its technical phase must be directed by the medical profession in conformity with its policies, and there must be no interference in the physician-patient relationship.

The conferees unanimously agreed on the need to establish additional laboratories in the state, and there was general support for health insurance and group hospital insurance supervised by the medical profession. Planning committees were approved to study the expansion of public health activities in the state, the medical needs of indigent groups, group hospital insurance, voluntary and compulsory health insurance, extension of the Social Security Act to cover loss of wages due to physical disability, and improvements in the state's workmen's compensation system.[69]

Doctors Raskin and Bicknell, who found the September 10 conference "a gratifying experience," thought that it reflected "a community of interest" among the medical profession, government, and the people. They reported to Murphy that there was great interest in the subject of health among workers in Detroit and that many "mass organizations" were establishing health committees. Lendrum told the governor that the UAW believed that the projected health program would play an "important part" in the 1938 campaign. At the annual convention of the Michigan Medical Society shortly after the conference, the society's Speaker of the House alleged that the federal government was intent upon promoting socialized medicine but that the Michigan health conference had pointed in the proper direction. The House of Delegates approved proposals calling for medical care for the indigent provided by local government, paid for out of taxes, and with the patient selecting his own doctor; state aid for medical care in the less affluent sections of Michigan, with the federal government providing the funds when the state was unable to meet emergencies; and an insurance plan to cover the costs of prolonged illness or medical emergencies. The delegates endorsed the principle of hospital insurance but opposed compulsory health insurance.[70]

Late in October 1938 Murphy appointed a seven-member Advisory Committee for the Expansion of Public Health Activities, headed by Dr. Henry A. Luce, the president of the Michigan Medical Society, to advise the governor regarding the implementation of the proposals advanced at the September 10 conference. A few days later Murphy announced that, if reelected, he would request the legislature to enact the principal proposals of the conference. The governor declared in a major campaign address that he planned "to mobilize a health organization covering every community in the state, under local control, [and] state supervision" to attack the causes of disease and death. The state government would provide assistance for the training of doctors to prepare them for their part in the campaign, and the federal government would aid in the construction of hospitals and treatment facilities. Michigan was on the verge of becoming the leading state in the nation in the matter of health care and of anticipating much that was to occur in the public health field in succeeding years, but Murphy's defeat in 1938 doomed the governor's plans. Although the legislature in 1939 enacted a measure permitting the establishment of group medical and hospital insurance plans, about all that could really be said concerning the ambitious health program of the Murphy administration was, to quote Gudakunst, that "at least the first sound steps . . . [had] been charted."[71]

It is unlikely that the defeat of Murphy's health plans disturbed many Michigan doctors and dentists despite the seeming support for those plans by the Michigan Medical Society. Four past presidents of the Michigan State Dental Society appealed to the dental profession to vote for Frank Fitzgerald in the 1938 gubernatorial election since Murphy had "done a good job to bring" them "closer to state medicine." After Murphy's defeat, the *Journal of the Michigan Medical Society*, in an editorial entitled "The Lesson," commented that the impression had been abroad that Michigan would be in the "vanguard" of the effort to "socialize" medicine in the United States. Doctors, however, could now feel confident, the editorial stated, that the victorious Republicans would not enact health legislation unacceptable to the medical and allied professions.[72]

IV

Although he had not taken steps during the first two-thirds of his administration to achieve the "thorough-going program of administrative reorganization and integration" to which he had referred in his initial message to the legislature, Murphy told Joe Hayden in June 1938 that, next to civil service reform and welfare reorganization, his "highest hopes" were for "the general reorganization of the central government" and that not a day went by without his seeing "the crying need for it." Hayden by this time had learned that, if reelected, Murphy intended "to reorganize and invigorate the government of the State in a way that ... [would] attract national attention and approbation."

Following the advice of Kemp and Arthur W. Bromage, a University of Michigan political scientist whom the governor had asked to examine the subject of reorganization, Murphy on August 17 appointed a Commission on Reform and Modernization of Government that ultimately consisted of eighty-six members selected so as to provide "a cross section of public sentiment." The commission was to survey the existing governmental structure and to make a preliminary report, following which the legislature in 1939 would create a new commission to draft the actual reorganization plan. Murphy selected Hayden to head the commission without having bothered to ask him if he wanted the assignment. "The whole framework of Michigan's archaic governmental system must be discarded," the governor stated in announcing the commission. He was thinking of such major reforms as a unicameral legislature, the elimination of partisanship in the selection of judges, a four-year term for the governor and other state officials, centralization of the state government into a few "efficient and economical units," and elimination of "the almost staggering duplication and waste in local government."[73] Murphy's remarks undoubtedly frightened a substantial number of state and local government officeholders as well as a variety of interest groups committed to the structural status quo.

When the commission held its first meeting on October 13, it accepted Murphy's recommendation that it create a small "working committee" and that it appoint Bromage the commission's secretary. What most concerned him, the governor declared, was "the lack of a modern efficient administrative mechanism" that would make it possible for the governor to "do the work expected of him, do it with intelligence and thoroughness, efficiency and dispatch." The governor, he justifiably complained, had far too small a staff, no one to analyze important economic problems, no one to advise him on the problems of local government, and no one to work out "a balanced legislative program" and to follow it through the legislature.[74]

The commission issued its preliminary report on December 20, 1938. Since a "minority" had become the "majority" in the legislature because of malapportionment, the commission recommended that consideration be given to a unicameral legislature and proportional representation as a basis for the selection of legislative members. It recommended that agencies dealing with overall problems of management such as planning, budget making, personnel administration, and administrative supervision be "tied directly" to the office of the governor and that he be given a staff of assistants to enable him to cope with the additional responsibilities that he had assumed in the preceding thirty years, including his enlarged role in the area of federal-state relations. It suggested that the sixty or so state agencies be consolidated into fifteen departments, that departments of taxation and finance be created, and that a post-audit be conducted at the conclusion of each fiscal year to determine the legality of expenditures, Michigan being one of only four states that did not already provide for this. The commission did not recommend the creation of a "true cabinet" such as existed in New York, California, and elsewhere, although it noted that the Administrative Board was an altogether unsatisfactory substitute for such a body.[75]

Tentative and sketchy as its preliminary report was, the Commission on Reform and Modernization of Government pointed to some of the major defects in Michigan's governmental structure and suggested reforms that would have enabled the governor, at least, to discharge his responsibilities in a more effective manner than the existing pattern of organization permitted. Eleven states adopted reorganization plans in the 1930s,[76] and, had he won his election, Murphy would have attempted to add Michigan to that number, difficult as that would have been.

The state administrative mechanism that Murphy inherited as governor functioned ineffectively because of "traditions of spoils, politics, and administrative disintegration." Murphy brought civil service to the state, ran the state government with far less regard for conventional politics than his immediate predecessors had, and was responsible for some piecemeal structural reforms, but his belated effort to deal with "administrative disintegration" in a comprehensive manner died aborning. "We don't need any 'streamlined' government in Michigan," Fitzgerald declared as he was about to succeed Murphy as Michigan's governor.[77]

12

"A Definite Farm Policy"

Scheduled to deliver an address at Michigan State College on February 4, 1937, as part of the state's celebration of Farmers' Week, Frank Murphy canceled the engagement because of his participation in the General Motors strike negotiations. Throughout Murphy's governorship the predominant opinion among Michigan's farmers, not too well disposed toward Democrats in any event, was that the governor assigned a higher priority to the problems of blue-collar workers than to the needs of the state's agriculturists and that his policies conspicuously favored organized labor to the detriment of other interest groups. "Propaganda," an official of the Farmers' Union in the state informed the governor, "has built in the minds of farmers an actual hatred of you because of your policies during the great labor disputes."[1]

Michigan Democrats believed that Murphy would have to "cultivate" the state's 195,000 farm operatives if he expected to be reelected in 1938. Murphy agreed that the state government should assist the farmers, but he asserted that this must be done because it was for the good of all the state's inhabitants. He also claimed that the farmers had a stake in his labor policies since they benefited from an increase in industrial payrolls and their children left the farm to work in the state's factories. Although even an admirer of the governor contended at the beginning of 1938 that one of the Murphy administration's "weak spots" was its lack of "a definite farm policy," the farmer was hardly a forgotten man in the Lansing New Deal.[2] He was the principal beneficiary of two extensions of the state's real-estate moratorium that Murphy secured from the legislature[3] and of the well-managed State Fair for which the governor could take credit. The Murphy administration spurred the electrification of Michigan's farms, it sought to aid the state's hard-pressed dairy farmers, and it enlarged the market for Michigan farm products by establishing grade standards for a variety of crops. Seeking to promote the general well-being, it evidenced concern not just for farm owners but also for migratory farm laborers and the consumers of farm products. In pursuing its farm policy, the Murphy administration linked its efforts with those of the federal government, another example of cooperative federalism in action in the Lansing New Deal.

In the 1936 gubernatorial campaign Murphy charged the Fitzgerald administration with blocking the efforts of the Rural Electrification Administration (REA) to electrify Michigan's farms. When President Roosevelt created the REA in May 1935, the assumption was that it would serve as a banker to private electric utility companies. Since these companies, however, generally refused to take advantage of the low-cost government loans made available to them, the REA began to establish rural electric cooperatives to apply for federal funds and to build the lines that would bring electric power to the farm. Increasingly, the REA not only allotted funds to cooperatives but offered them guidance and sought to promote their efforts.[4]

Solicitous of the interests of the privately owned electric companies, the Michigan Public Utilities Commission, which claimed jurisdiction over rural electric cooperatives, sought during the Fitzgerald administration to "crowd" the REA from the picture and to limit rural electrification to private companies. The REA as of the beginning of 1937 had not built a single mile of electrical line in the state, and not a single dollar of federal money had been allocated to Michigan in the form of REA loans. Creation of the REA, however, had stimulated the utility companies in Michigan, as elsewhere, to intensify their efforts to bring electricity to rural areas. Before the REA had been established, private utility companies in Michigan had been willing to supply electricity to areas where there were fewer than an average of ten consuming units per mile of line only if they would assume the full cost of construction or, at a later time, pay $1,000 per mile of line. After the REA was established, the state's two major electric utility companies, Consumers Power and Detroit Edison, decided to spread lines into the countryside at no cost to the consumers if they averaged at least five per mile of line—the REA standard was three per mile—and, in the case of Consumers Power, if they guaranteed the company that they each would consume about $12.50 worth of electricity per month. If the consumers averaged fewer than five per mile, the companies required them to pay $100 for each customer below the number necessary to bring the average per mile to five. Approximately nineteen thousand Michigan farms were electrified in 1935 and 1936 as the result of the liberalized policies of the private companies, raising the percentage of Michigan farms served by electricity from 22 at the beginning of 1935 to 33.3 at the end of 1936, compared to 15.3 percent of farms for the nation as a whole.[5]

"Rural Electrification," Ed Kemp advised Murphy, "furnished the only opportunity for this administration to benefit the farmers directly." Although this considerably overstated the matter, the Murphy administration placed a good deal of emphasis on rural electrification, which did so much to transform and improve the quality of rural life, and sought to make political capital of this fact. The administration supported a House bill in 1937 that provided for the formation of nonprofit "electric membership cooperatives" under the state's general corporation act and a Senate bill that sought, in effect, to prevent the privately owned utilities from invading areas being served by electric cooperatives. When the Senate Public Utilities Committee, one of whose members had received payments from Consumers Power for "professional services," blocked the latter measure in the regular session of the legislature, Murphy called for its enactment in the special session that he convened on July 30, 1937. Conservatives and power-company sympathizers, however, combined to prevent the bill's passage. The failure to enact the House bill turned out to be of little consequence since Attorney General Raymond W. Starr ruled that rural electric cooperatives could be formed under Michigan's corporation law without the need for additional legislation.[6]

Whereas the Fitzgerald Public Utilities Commission had been dominated by the power companies, the "new men" whom Murphy appointed to the commission were free of such taint. The governor requested John M. Carmody, the industrial engineer who had just succeeded Morris L. Cooke as the REA's head, to loan the state "a competent engineer" to aid the commission in promoting the electrification of Michigan's farms; Carmody obliged by assigning the very able Clarence A. Winder to the task. Arriving in Michigan in March 1937, Winder, whom the director of the National Popular Government League described as "a fighter in the public interest who . . . knows all the tricks in the power trust bag and is covered with scars from his many battles with them," was made chief engineer of the commission a few months later. Eight rural electric cooperatives were established in Michigan in 1937, and the Public Utilities Commission "aggressively" aided them both in getting underway and in securing federal aid. Winder, for his part, helped the cooperatives to devise soundly engineered electrification projects and saw to it that they engaged qualified contractors to build the lines. By July 1, 1938, the REA had allotted a total of $4,655,000 to ten Michigan projects designed to serve 13,446 farm homes, and 3,918 miles of line had been built or were under construction. Despite Michigan's late start, only seven states had received larger allotments.

The $2 million Ubly project, which served Michigan's Thumb area, was designed to provide electricity eventually to eight thousand farms. At the time of its dedication on June 18, 1938, it was the largest REA project in the nation. Both Carmody and Murphy were on hand for the dedication, the governor hailing the rural electric cooperative as "one of the most progressive and helpful achievements in behalf of the farming people of Michigan within a generation." Joseph M. Donnelly, the Public Utilities Commission member most directly concerned with rural electrification, thought it would be "very helpful" if the governor sent a letter to farm homes that had just been electrified as the result of an REA project. Murphy and Norman Hill, however, decided that a letter from the Public Utilities Commission would serve the same purpose and would be "more official and less political."[7]

The activity of the rural electric cooperatives during the Murphy governorship stimulated the private electric companies to speed up their efforts to bring electricity to rural areas of the state, particularly in the Lower Peninsula. The private companies expanded their service to more than twenty thousand farm customers in 1937, Consumers Power winning the Edison Electric Institute award for its contribution to rural electrification in that year. In July 1938, by which time it had built twelve thousand miles of rural lines and was serving fifty thousand of the ninety-four thousand rural homes receiving electricity, Consumers Power advised the Public Utilities Commission that it was prepared to construct rural lines without cost to the customers if they would jointly guarantee a monthly revenue to the company of $12.50 per mile. By the end of 1938 between 60 and 65 percent of Michigan's farms, compared to 20.6 percent of the nation's farms, were receiving electricity either from private companies or rural electric cooperatives.[8]

In its annual report for 1938 the REA noted that the private utility companies in Michigan and especially Consumers Power had tried to obstruct the rural electric cooperatives by resorting to "some of the most flagrant tactics in the history of rural electrification." In an effort to check "spite line construction"—construction by private companies in an area where a cooperative had received an REA allotment—the Public Utilities Commission, in May 1937, prohibited the private companies from building new lines or adding to existing lines without commission approval. There was some spite-line construction, however, despite the order. Consumers Power sought to block the Tri-County Electric Cooperative, which was dedicated in September 1938, by building lines wherever the cooperative was about to construct its lines, but the company effort was unsuccessful.

In one notable instance the REA put a crew to work on Saturday night to stop a power company from building a line to head off a government electrification project. By threatening law suits, Consumers Power also sought to prevent townships from granting permits to cooperatives to use township highways, a tactic that delayed but in the end did not prevent construction. The Public Utilities Commission, on the other hand, apparently impeded construction by Detroit Edison in the Thumb area before arranging a peace treaty between the Ubly project and the company. Like its counterparts in several states, the commission ordered the utilities to supply electricity to cooperatives at wholesale rates. Although two companies had proved amenable by June 1938, the others were either unwilling or unable to comply. The result was that four of the eighteen rural electric cooperatives in the nation to which the REA had allocated funds for generating plants as well as transmission lines as of July 1, 1938, were located in Michigan.[9]

The Murphy administration sought to raise the income of farmers by establishing uniform grades for their products and by stabilizing the state's important dairy industry. Although Michigan's agricultural marketing legislation dated from 1915, the lack of an effective inspection service had prevented the development of an adequate system of standardized grading of crops. In August 1937, however, the state Department of Agriculture, whose power to set grade standards had been increased by legislation enacted in 1937, concluded an agreement with the federal Department of Agriculture that made federal-state inspection and grading available for the first time to growers of fruits and vegetables in Michigan. Standard grades had been established for twenty-two fruits and vegetables by July 1, 1938. In the summer of 1937 Michigan also initiated a federal-state poultry products grading service to classify and standardize eggs. As the result of federal-state cooperation in inspection and grading, Michigan farmers were able to enlarge the market for several of their crops and to increase their sales to the Federal Surplus Commodities Corporation (FSCC). The state Department of Agriculture estimated that Michigan potato farmers received an additional $750,000 in 1938 because of uniform grading, and the FSCC purchased about $800,000 worth of apples, grapes, onions, and eggs in that year that it otherwise would have bought in other states. Few if any states in the nation had made as much progress in establishing uniform grades for their agricultural products as Michigan had by the end of Murphy's governorship.[10]

Michigan farmers derived about 30 percent of their agricultural income from dairy products, and milk was the principal source of income for sixty thousand farm operators. Although the industry had been stabilized and prices received by producers had risen substantially as the result of marketing agreements licensed by the federal government in accordance with the Agricultural Adjustment Act of 1933 and, later, the Marketing Agreement Acts of 1935 and 1937, conflicts between producers and distributors persuaded the secretary of agriculture in October 1937 to cancel the licenses in some of the marketing areas of the state, including the Detroit area. The result was that the price paid to producers of Class I milk, which had been $2.48 per cwt since February 1935, fell to $1.90 per cwt by June 1938. Despite the decline in prices received by producers to the lowest level since 1933, Murphy thought that the retail price of milk in Detroit was too high and wondered if this might be the result of a milk trust among dealers. There was, on the other hand, complaint about "cut-throat competition" among dealers notwithstanding the existence of a few large firms that allegedly exercised "great influence" over the marketing of milk. The Michigan Milk Producers Association, a cooperative group of about seventeen thousand farmers that supplied 85 percent of the milk consumed in the Detroit area, favored some sort of state regulation that would ensure producers a fair price for their product. The dealers also appeared to believe that state regulation of the industry was desirable.[11]

The federal government interested itself in Michigan's milk problem because of the possibility that the federal antitrust laws were being violated in the Detroit marketing area and also because the Department of Justice wished to test the feasibility of joint federal-state action in the antitrust field to minimize the possibility of jurisdictional conflict. "I am interested in taking some particular case and using it as a test tube to work out a general plan which may be offered to all the states," Thurman Arnold, head of the Antitrust Division of the Department of Justice, wrote the governor early in June 1938. "I would prefer to do it with you than with any other governor," Arnold, who had become acquainted with Murphy in the Philippines, asserted, "because of our personal relationships." Anxious to cooperate, Murphy dispatched Assistant Attorney General G. Mennen Williams to discuss the subject with Arnold, following which the antitrust head sent Robert E. Sher, one of the division's "best men," to investigate the milk industry in Detroit and surrounding areas. Arnold thought that a milk antitrust suit would aid Murphy with the farmers, but Williams contended that a successful suit would impair the governor's standing with dairy farmers because it would result in still lower milk prices to producers. Not dissuaded by this judgment, Murphy informed Arnold that he favored "a concerted effort" by the federal and state governments "to do an effective job on the Detroit and Michigan milk matter."[12]

Although Donald Gay, chairman of the Price and Investigation Committee of the Michigan Milk Producers Association, advised the Justice Department that some milk dealers and some officers of the association were engaged in a "conspiracy" to "demoralize" the milk market and thereby "to discredit the [Murphy] Administration," Sher found no evidence of any antitrust violation in the Detroit milk market, which, in any event, was almost entirely an intrastate market. Arnold came to Michigan in October, after Sher had completed his work, to join Starr in presenting Murphy with the results of "the first combined State-Federal investigation in the field of monopoly regulation." The report singled out the condition of producers as requiring "immediate attention," noting that the prices they received for milk were often below their cost of production. It called attention to the fact that distributors paid producers different prices for their milk even though "a strong body of opinion" favored uniform prices. The report concluded that although competition among dealers had benefited Detroit consumers, who, contrary to what Murphy had believed, were then paying the lowest price for milk since 1933, it was "contributing substantially" to the low prices received by producers.[13]

The Murphy administration had been awaiting the results of the federal antitrust investigation before deciding what the state government itself should do to stabilize the milk industry. Twenty-one states, beginning with New York in 1933, had adopted milk control legislation, most of them fixing prices at both the producer and retail levels. Since milk is sold in many forms and by many methods, it had proved vastly more difficult to set and enforce the prices distributors charged their customers than the prices distributors paid producers. Williams, to whom Murphy assigned the responsibility of drafting milk legislation, concluded that milk laws fixing retail prices had not only been difficult to enforce but had resulted in higher consumer prices without materially assisting producers—New York had found it necessary to replace its 1933 law in 1937 with a measure that sought to encourage collective bargaining between producers and distributors and then in 1938 had returned to price fixing, but only at the producer level. Williams feared that if prices were set at the consumer level in Detroit, it would freeze "an uneconomic situation" resulting from the overextension of distributor facilities and would also cause the workers to "howl 'Wall Street.' " Kemp, however, remonstrated that to fix prices only at the producer level was to treat producers as a favored group, and he thought that the administration was deluding itself if it believed that it could increase prices at the producer level without also increasing them at the consumer level or "pinching" distributors.[14]

Advised that his recognition of the plight of the producer and small dealer could mean "many votes," Murphy initially took the politically safe position that he favored legislation that was fair to both the producer and the consumer and yielded the distributor a "reasonable profit." After receiving the Starr-Arnold report, the governor indicated that drastic action might be necessary to deal not only with the problem of low producer prices but also with underconsumption, a subject that particularly concerned him. He appointed a Milk Marketing Study Commission on October 14 and indicated that he might recommend legislation permitting the regulation of producer prices so as to yield the farmer "a fair return for the labor and investment involved" and establishing a state milk board to stabilize the milk market. Although competition was desirable at the dealer level, the governor asserted, it might be necessary to authorize the milk board to set retail prices in certain circumstances. He believed that the milk board should have the power to eliminate wasteful, expensive, and unfair sales practices and to prescribe trade practices that would encourage consumption as well as the reserve power to engage in the distribution of milk. Alternatively, he thought, the board might temporarily subsidize certain low-cost forms of distribution by private operators, and it might also devise a method of furnishing milk to needy families and school children as a relief measure. Michigan, Murphy asserted, had "an unparalleled opportunity to take the lead in solving a national problem in conjunction with our national government." The governor's remarks were hardly of a sort to induce workers to "howl 'Wall Street,' " but his suggestions concerning what might be required to provide "high quality milk for the poor" undoubtedly alarmed the state's more conservative citizens, already concerned about the labor policies of their New Deal governor.[15]

Murphy's milk commission consisted of twelve producer representatives, ten distributor representatives, fifteen consumer representatives, two labor reepresentatives, and five state government officials. The task of drafting a suitable milk bill was delegated by the commission to Mennen Williams. Aided by the United States Department of Agriculture and Professor O. L. Ulrey of Michigan State College,

Williams prepared a bill that provided for price fixing only at the producer level. The bill, however, was revised by the commission's steering committee to permit the fixing of retail prices also. Since the Michigan Milk Producers Association, consumer representatives, and some large distributors were not entirely satisfied with the measure, the study commission decided late in December to delay formal action on the bill pending the inauguration of the state's new governor.[16]

The 1939 Michigan legislature enacted a milk bill that created a Milk Marketing Board to regulate the state's milk industry. The board could set the minimum price paid to producers, and, if an emergency developed in any milk marketing area, it could fix both the wholesale and retail price in that area. It was also empowered to appoint milk marketing committees for the various marketing areas; these committees could seek board consent to impose rules prohibiting unfair trade practices and unfair methods of competition in their areas. Differing chiefly in its administrative aspects from the draft bill finally approved by the steering committee of the Milk Marketing Study Commission, the 1939 milk law was declared unconstitutional by the Michigan Supreme Court.[17]

Although a milk control bill was not enacted in Michigan until after Murphy had left the governorship, he did succeed in persuading the legislature to pass another measure of considerable importance to the state's farmers: a crop insurance bill. The Agricultural Adjustment Act of 1938 did not permit the Commodity Credit Corporation to extend commodity loans on crops unless they were insured to the full amount of the loan. Since Michigan's insurance law did not provide for insurance of this type, the governor requested the legislature when it met in special session in August 1938 to amend the law accordingly. The lawmakers complied with the governor's request, thus making it possible for Michigan farmers to take advantage of federal crop loans.[18]

Consistent with its concern for the poor and afflicted, the Murphy administration sought to draft a code of rules to protect the ten thousand or so Mexican laborers who were annually imported into Michigan primarily to work in its sugar-beet fields. In December 1937 the Department of Labor and Industry worked out a voluntary agreement with the processors and growers using Mexican labor specifying that the workers were to be paid a living wage and provided with adequate housing, that their school-age children were to be sent to school, and that proper arrangements were to be made, without cost to the state, to return them to their homes when their work was completed. The secretary of the department noted in June 1938, however, that growers were violating the agreement, that five thousand laborers had been brought into the state jammed into trucks like cattle, and that they were living in "squalor" in violation of the housing and sanitation standards specified in the agreement. Although he threatened to turn to the legislature if the agreement were not observed in full, nothing further was done to improve the lot of imported farm laborers during the remaining months of the Murphy administration.[19]

Interested in the consumer as well as the producer, the Murphy administration took a pioneering step by establishing a Consumers' Bureau in the Department of Agriculture, the first state agency of its type in the nation. There had been consumer representatives in both the National Recovery Administration and Agricultural Adjustment Administration (AAA), but the results had been negligible. Beginning in 1934 the federal government also made an effort to establish county consumer councils under the direction of the Consumers Division of the National Emergency Council. It was Mrs. Stuart A. Fraser and the two other members of the Wayne County Consumer's Council who recommended to Murphy in the early weeks of his administration that he "do something about consumer protection."[20]

Murphy did not act on the Wayne County Consumer's Council suggestion until December 1937, when he decided to establish a Consumers' Bureau in the Department of Agriculture and to make Mrs. Fraser its director. Officially launched on January 3, 1938, the bureau was to make available to consumers product information supplied by the federal and state departments of agriculture, the National Bureau of Standards, and other agencies; encourage factual advertising, quality standards, and grade labeling; promote the use of informative labels; foster more "equitable" trade practices; and represent the consumer interest in the consideration of proposed legislation. The bureau included a Consumers' Advisory Board made up of specialists in consumer affairs. The expectation was that bureau activities would be supplemented by a statewide group of county consumer counsels.[21]

The principal activity of the bureau in 1938 was its effort to educate consumers to buy carefully by familiarizing themselves with grades and standards enforced by the state Department of Agriculture, studying product advertising in the press, and learning about practices that firms employed in merchandising their products. The bureau became best known to consumers through its "Tips to Housewives," which appeared weekly in seventeen Michigan newspapers. The bureau used this marketing service to advise consumers regarding supplies and prices of fruits, vegetables, and other products and the best buys for the week. The information was prepared in the wholesale marketing centers of the state by local committees consisting of the municipal market master, a food inspector, wholesale produce and meat representatives, and a woman consumer. Mrs. Fraser explained to the governor that the marketing tips were designed "to prevent merchants from buying in a plentiful supply market and selling on a scarcity supply basis." Donald E. Montgomery, the AAA Consumers' Counsel and a member of Michigan's Consumers' Advisory Board, thought that the market reports were "not professional and probably . . . not impartial" since most local committees included an Armour or Swift representative. He doubted, moveover, that a government agency should advise consumers regarding which products were cheap and which dear, an opinion that the Consumers' Bureau and the governor obviously did not share.

In addition to its weekly marketing tips, the bureau distributed to 460 newspapers a "Use, Don't Spend Money" column that advised consumers how to take advantage of local and seasonal merchandising factors. It also cooperated with the Bureau of Home Economics of Michigan State College in preparing consumer bulletins on such subjects as how to buy meat and textiles. The bureau, additionally, sought to persuade trade associations to modify trade practices that adversely affected consumers. Erroneously believing that Mrs. Fraser either had "no understanding of the consumer place in the merchandising picture" or had "a greater interest in the welfare of merchants than in the welfare of their customers," Montgomery informed Kemp that the bureau director was "extremely vague" about what could be accomplished through trade practice conferences. Mrs. Fraser, on the other hand, reported that the bureau had helped to improve business procedures and that trade groups had solicited its aid for that purpose.[22]

As the first state consumers' bureau, the Michigan agency was "under scrutiny" throughout the nation, and various state governments and numerous private organizations made inquiries concerning its activities. "It is hoped and expected," the Department of Agriculture asserted in the biennial report that it submitted in December 1938, "that the Bureau as it progresses and develops will be of untold benefit to the consumer."[23] The department's hopes and expectations for the bureau, however, did not survive Murphy's loss of the governorship. In consumer affairs as in so many other areas of state government, Murphy's defeat in 1938 signified a good deal more than the mere changing of the guard in Lansing.

13

"The Difference between
This Depression and the Last One"

I

Although the year, Murphy wrote a former aide in December 1937, was closing "peacefully" in Michigan, it was closing "somewhat uncertainly" because of the recession then plaguing the nation. As mayor of Detroit from 1930 to 1933, Murphy had found it necessary to cope with the effects of the Great Depression in the American city most ravaged by that depression; as governor of Michigan during the recession of 1937-38, he was again in the eye of the economic hurricane, presiding over the state that suffered the most severe downturn in the nation. As Detroit's depression mayor, Murphy had pioneered in seeking federal assistance for the nation's beleaguered cities; as Michigan's recession governor, he turned once again to the federal government for aid, and he found the Washington of the New Deal far more responsive to his pleas than the Washington of Herbert Hoover.

The economic decline from September 1937 to June 1938 has been characterized as "without parallel in American economic history." During those ten months industrial production decreased 33 percent; durable goods production, more than 50 percent; manufacturing employment, 23 percent; payrolls, 35 percent; profits, 78 percent; and the national income, 13 percent. Michigan did not begin to feel the effects of the recession until the last two months of 1937, and recovery in the state also lagged behind the rest of the nation. Unemployment in Michigan, which decreased in October 1937 as compared to September, increased every month thereafter until September 1938, rising from just under 190,000 in October to 680,000 in August 1938—about 35 percent of the state labor force as of 1930. The index of factory employment for the nation as a whole stood at 86 in August 1938 and the index of factory payrolls at 77 (1923-26 = 100), but the comparable figures in Michigan were 58.5 and 55 respectively. In addition to unemployment, there was a tremendous amount of underemployment in Michigan, especially in manufacturing industries.

453

The automobile and automobile parts industries, peculiarly sensitive to the ups and downs of the business cycle, contributed substantially to Michigan's high unemployment rate. About 65 percent of the hourly employees of General Motors, Ford, and Chrysler were unemployed as of late May 1938, and in March 1938 persons usually employed in the automobile and automobile parts industries accounted for 40.2 percent of all the emergency relief cases in the state.

Agriculture ranked second among the usual occupations of the heads of relief families in March 1938, accounting for 7.1 percent of the cases. Although Michigan farmers had been in a "relatively better [economic] position" at the beginning of the Murphy administration than at any time since the onset of the Great Depression, the very low farm prices resulting from the recession and the return to the countryside of workers who had lost their jobs in automobile and other plants adversely affected farm income and increased the relief load in agricultural counties. The income of Michigan farmers declined by 16 percent in 1938 as compared to 1937, falling from $249,734,000 to $207,530,000, while the combined emergency relief and WPA case load almost tripled in the southern agricultural counties between October 1937 and March 1938. The discontent of Michigan farmers intensified in the spring of 1938 when Secretary of Agriculture Henry A. Wallace ordered a 22 percent cut in the state's corn acreage.[1]

Murphy was not a systematic thinker—few political figures are—and his knowledge of economics was superficial. As governor of a state so afflicted with economic misfortune, however, he sought to explain what ailed the economy and to prescribe the remedies required for its recovery. He attributed the recession to a decline in government spending, which appears to have been a correct analysis, and to "fundamental economic maladjustments" that served to depress consumer buying power, such as the maldistribution of income and the "neglect of the masses' needs." The conservative and ever-cautious Ed Kemp thought the govenor's remarks about "economic maladjustments" betrayed "impatience with inequality, class sympathy, and pious social attitudes."[2]

In response to the recession and to avoid future economic crises, industry, Murphy thought, had to develop a "program of orderly and regulated production" and pay its workers a yearly wage, an idea that came quite naturally to the governor of a state whose major industry was notorious for the irregularity of its employment. The annual wage was "inevitable," the governor contended, if the existing economic system was to survive; if industry could not solve the problem, government, Murphy believed, would have to intercede to secure the objective. The press was saying that the principal responsibility of government in the recession was to encourage business confidence, but Murphy, who had said something similar at the beginning of the recession, attacked this approach in April 1938 as reminiscent of the Hoover policy that had brought the country to "its knees in chaos" during the Great Depression. Instead, the governor defended the New Deal's approach to the recession, namely, increased government spending to stimulate mass purchasing power. Before he left office, Murphy had concluded that data regarding the distribution of wealth in the United States "indicate[d] powerfully that Mr. Keynes['s] theory has considerable basis in truth."[3]

The job of "reconstruction" in the recession, Murphy believed, had to "begin with caring for the needs of the people . . . out on the streets unemployed, sick, too often weary with the strife." This meant action by the government in Lansing and the government in Washington, and, as the governor told a throng of Flint unionists in April 1938, "the difference between this depression and the last one is that you have a Governor who will fight your battles and do what he can to help you. And you have a President . . . who will do the same thing."[4]

II

Thanks to an improving economy and the availability of WPA jobs, the Michigan relief load was on the decline when Murphy became the state's governor. Whereas the state averaged 112,273 general relief cases (387,000 persons) during the fiscal year 1935–36, the number of such cases averaged only 55,252 (178,211 persons) in the last quarter of 1936 (an additional 31,821 persons received assistance under the ADC and aid-to-the-blind programs). The monthly average rose to just over 73,000 cases (246,860 persons) in the first quarter of 1937 largely because of the General Motors strike but then fell to 53,004 (166,255 persons) in the next quarter. Since the 1935 legislature had appropriated an insufficient amount to cover relief costs for the fiscal year 1936–37, the 1937 legislature, responding to the request of the Murphy administration, appropriated $6.9 million to meet the deficiency. The total state government cost for emergency relief for 1936–37 was almost $13.8 million.[5]

The state's cost for relief in 1936–37 would have been considerably less had the WPA actually provided work for all needy employable persons, but the work relief agency never did so in Michigan or anywhere else. In the last six months of 1936 from 12 to 19 percent of the needy employables were cared for by the State Emergency Relief

Administration (SERA), not the WPA, and the figure rose to a high of 32.1 percent in February 1937. In addition, since there was about a three-to-five-week delay between the time a needy person was certified for WPA employment and the time he actually went to work and an additional two-week delay before he received his first paycheck, the relief burden shouldered by the state was not immediately eased when it certified a reliefer for WPA employment. The WPA, moreover, provided employment for no more than one member of a family regardless of its size. Also, since the pay of WPA employees was determined by the number of hours they worked, not by the number of their dependents, the SERA sometimes had to supplement the wages of WPA workers.[6]

The WPA was always described as a federal program, and the role of the federal government in the WPA was substantially greater than it had been in the Federal Emergency Relief Administration, but state and local governments nevertheless had "very large responsibilities" in the operation of the WPA. State and local relief organizations certified the persons eligible for WPA employment, following federal standards in this regard, state and local governments sponsored nearly all the WPA projects and had to share their cost, and the state WPA office had to approve locally sponsored projects before they were forwarded to Washington for final approval. The principal contribution of local government was for the nonlabor costs of projects, the legal limitation on what the federal government could contribute for this purpose constituting the key factor affecting the share of the cost of a project that had to be borne by the local governmental unit—at the beginning of 1937 the average sponsor contribution for Michigan projects was about 18 percent of the cost of projects.[7]

The WPA employed a monthly average of 81,996 persons in Michigan in 1936, but because of improving economic conditions, the number fell to 46,677 by the beginning of August 1937. When Governor Herbert H. Lehman of New York called a conference of governors from some of the principal industrial states early in 1937 to protest the decline in WPA employment, Murphy expressed sympathy with the purpose of the conference. Preoccupied with other matters, however, and not yet overly concerned about the state of the economy, he did not attend the meeting, nor did he join the governors when they later conferred with the president to press their grievance.[8]

Projecting the state's needs against an uncertain future, the legislature in 1937 appropriated $8 million for general relief for each year of the next biennium in addition to $10 million for old-age assistance, $4 million for ADC, and $75,000 for aid to the blind. The appropriation for general relief proved woefully insufficient once Michigan began to feel the full effects of the recession, and a budget already out of balance was put under additional strain. Characterized as the " 'pennies from heaven legislature,' " the lawmakers appropriated about $125.5 million for the first fiscal year of the biennium and about $123 million for the second year even though the budget director estimated revenue for the first year at about $107.5 million and the state debt to meet deficits could not exceed $250,000. Responding to pressure groups, efforts of local governments to shift more of their expenses to the state government, the need to finance new social programs, and optimistic predictions that the revenues would exceed the budget director's projections, the legislature ignored the list of "excess appropriations" that the governor submitted to the finance committees of both houses, just as it paid no heed to his advice that it present him with a single appropriation bill lest separate bills lead to excessive expenditures. Had Murphy not found it necessary to devote so much of his time to the mediation of strikes at the beginning of his administration, it is possible that there would have been a different result. As it was, the appropriation process was already "completely out of control" by the time Murphy turned his attention to fiscal affairs and Harold D. Smith took up his duties on May 20, 1937, as budget director.[9]

The governor had the power to veto individual items in appropriation bills but not to reduce them. In 1935 the legislature authorized Governor Fitzgerald to make a 5 percent across-the-board cut in the legislative appropriation. Since Murphy, however, was opposed to this horizontal approach to budget reduction, the legislature granted him the unprecedented authority to keep expenditures in balance with income by making such reductions in spending as he thought necessary. Although Murphy had sought this power, its exercise meant that interest groups adversely affected by budget cuts would direct their criticism at the governor rather than at the legislature.[10]

Since the legislature appropriated funds for a biennium, it had to empower some agency to deal with emergencies arising between legislative sessions. In 1931 the legislature had vested that authority in the Augmented Administrative Board, consisting of four legislators in addition to the seven officials of the executive branch who served on the board. Dissatisfied with their minority position in this body, the legislators replaced it in 1937 with the Emergency Appropriation Commission, consisting of the governor, the Speaker of the House, the president of the Senate, and the members of the House Ways and Means Committee and the Senate Finance and Appropriations Committee. The governor was made chairman of the commission, which was to meet at his call, and he retained a suspensive veto over its actions. The commission received an appropriation of $1.5 million for each year of the biennium 1937–39.[11]

Promising to "whittle to the bone," Murphy vetoed appropriations totaling $3.406 million in the 1937–38 budget and $2.37 million in the 1938–39 budget, leaving a gap of $14–15 million between anticipated expenditures and anticipated income for each year of the biennium. A New Dealer who was a fiscal conservative, Murphy made a determined effort to close that gap. Early in October, on the eve of the recession in the state, he announced that he would withhold $12.3 million in appropriations, $7 million from various departments, $2.8 million in school aid, $2 million in old-age assistance, and $500,000 in welfare and relief funds. "More than anything else," Murphy declared in announcing his budget cuts, "the State needs a responsible government—a balanced budget." Even the anti-Murphy *Detroit Free Press* conceded that what the governor had done "required some grit."[12]

The most vociferous opponents of the Murphy budget reductions were the Highway Department and the Michigan Education Association (MEA). In addition to income earmarked for highways from the automobile weight tax (about $18 million), all of which was returned to the counties, and the gasoline tax, $6.55 million of which had to be surrendered to local units, the Highway Department persuaded the legislature in 1937 to appropriate $5 million for the department. The money, which was placed in a contingent fund, was to be reduced to the extent the gas tax yielded more than $27 million in the fiscal year. When Murphy reduced the $5 million contingency appropriation by $1.5 million, the Highway Department protested that it had made its budget plans on the assumption that it would receive $32 million from the state ($27 million from the gas tax plus the $5 million contingency appropriation). Because of the sum withheld, it contended, it would not have sufficient funds available after deducting the money already earmarked for state highways and required for working capital to take full advantage of the $13.5 million in matching funds for highways that the federal government was willing to provide. Murray D. Van Wagoner and G. Donald Kennedy were briefly mollified when at the end of February 1938 the administration advanced the Highway Department $1 million from the contingency fund, but the department was soon to make a determined effort to secure the full amount that the legislature had appropriated.[13]

Murphy pleased the state's teachers when he kept his promise to support a teacher-tenure law. Although the state superintendent of public instruction thought that it would be difficult to enact such a measure, Murphy recommended it in his initial message to the legislature, and it passed in the special session of July 1937 after failing of enactment in the regular session. The bill secured enough votes for passage, however, only after it had been amended to make it effective in a school district only if the voters in the district approved. During the next two years only two school districts exercised the local-option privilege to grant tenure to teachers who had served a probationary two or three years. Since aggrieved teachers could appeal to a state-appointed tenure board, a unique feature of the Michigan law, many school districts viewed the statute as still another encroachment by the Lansing New Deal on the prerogatives of local government.[14]

Whatever favor Murphy may have won with the teachers by his support of the tenure principle and his denunciation of the state's teachers' oath law as an "improper and unnecessary infringement on freedom of thought and liberty of opinion" he lost because of the money he withheld from the $43 million the legislature had appropriated for common schools in 1937–38, the largest single item in the state budget. Of the $43 million, an estimated $15 million was derived from the primary-school interest fund, composed of the income from several earmarked taxes. Although the 1937–38 appropriation was $5.6 million above the preceding year's appropriation, the MEA was dissatisfied with the legislative action, claiming that additional state aid was required because of the restriction imposed on the taxing power of local school districts by the fifteen-mill tax limitation. When Murphy pared $2.8 million from the appropriation, the MEA protested that this was actually a 10 percent cut in state aid over and above the yield of the primary interest fund and thus exceeded the 5–6 percent cut the governor had imposed on other state units. The advance of $1 million to the Highway Department only added to the grievance of public-school teachers.[15]

The $160,000 that Murphy eliminated from the general relief portion of the welfare and relief appropriation attracted scant attention at the time since the relief case load was declining in the fall of 1937. The SERA spent only $3 million of its $8 million appropriation during the first five months of the fiscal year, and George R. Granger, who became acting relief administrator after William Haber's resignation took effect on August 1, 1937, stated in the middle of November that there were "no indications" that the case load in the next few months would increase any more than it normally did in the winter months. Granger proved to be a rather poor prophet, for the general relief case load, which was 37,604 in October, rose every month thereafter until March 1938, when it stood at 161,213, and it did not fall below 100,000 until September. Between October 1937 and March 1938 the number of ADC cases rose from 11,227 to 12,354, the number of congregate shelter cases (transient, homeless, and un-attached males who were provided food, shelter, and other care in nine congregate shelters operated by the SERA) from 6,255 to 9,047, the number receiving old-age assistance from 52,835 to 71,310, and the number on WPA jobs from 44,397 to 113,320.

The largest increase in the emergency relief case load during the recession months took place in the twelve southern industrial counties of the state and especially in Wayne County. Whereas the cases receiving emergency relief increased in the state as a whole by 229.1 percent from October to March, the increase in the twelve southern industrial counties was 272.1 percent; and whereas the Wayne County case load constituted 37.8 percent of the total state case load in October, it constituted 44.7 percent of the state load in March. As of March 1938, 23.7 percent of the entire population of Michigan was receiving emergency relief of one kind or another or old-age assistance or was dependent on WPA employment. In the Upper Peninsula, 33.2 percent of the population was receiving aid; in the northern cut-over area, 22.5 percent; in the southern agricultural area, 15.2 percent; and in the southern industrial area, 25.3 percent. Michigan was the hardest hit of all the states during the recession: whereas the general relief case load for the nation as a whole rose 60.5 percent from July 1937 to March 1938, the Michigan case load increased by a staggering 301 percent. Michigan, however, was below the national average in the amount of relief it provided per case. The average grant per case in April 1938 for the forty states reporting to the Social Security Board was $24.01, whereas the Michigan average was $21.83, a reflection of the pressure placed on the Michigan budget by the extraordinary number of persons requiring public assistance.[16]

Although the general relief case load in Michigan fell after March 1938, this did not mean that the combined state and federal relief case load was also declining. The combined load did not reach its peak until July, when 26 percent of the state population as of 1930, representing 392,471 cases and about 1,159,000 persons, were receiving assistance. The number of state and federal public assistance cases declined after July, falling to 300,135 in December, which represented 19.3 percent of the state's population as of 1930. The smaller case load was primarily the result of improved economic conditions in the industrial counties of the state, especially Wayne County, where the percentage of the population receiving assistance had declined to 17.3. The case load had actually increased in the cut-over counties, where 23.9 percent of the population was on relief, and in the Upper Peninsula, where an astonishing 39.1 percent of the inhabitants were receiving one or another form of public assistance.[17]

In determining the amount of relief granted to relief families, county relief administrations worked out a budget of the family's minimum needs and then deducted from this sum any resources that the family might possess. Because of lack of funds, the allowances in many counties sometimes fell below "minimum needs." At the end of November 1937, for example, Granger informed Murphy that 75 percent of the counties were unable to provide families with a "minimum restricted budget," defined as a budget on which a family supposedly could live for a time without suffering ill health. Conditions worsened after that time as the average monthly grant per relief case began a steady decline, falling from a high of $24.61 in October 1937 to a low of $18.90 in August 1938. At the beginning of 1938 twenty-seven of seventy-five counties reporting to the State Emergency Welfare Relief Commission (SEWRC) alleged that relief families were keeping their children out of school because of lack of clothing, and forty-two counties had reduced individual relief budgets 10–52 percent below the minimum restricted level. In June Granger informed the governor that reduced budgets were "working real hardships" on relief clients and might "permanently damage [their] health and morale." Welfare workers, he noted, were under "emotional stress" as the result of "trying to explain the lack of necessities to those who need necessities."

In Genesee County (Flint), after relief allowances had been slashed to about $16.00 per case at the beginning of August 1938, the county relief administrator urged the sterilization of relief clients whose families had received aid for two generations. The administrator had previously advised unemployed auto workers with less than two years' seniority to leave Flint. This action led the SERA to remind county relief administrators that "domiciled indigents" were not to be returned to their former residence unless this was in the interests of the client and acceptable to officials of the previous residence. Unemployed industrial workers, the SERA stated, were not to be "shunted about the country like empty box cars" just because they were without work.[18]

The counties in the northern cut-over region of the state and the Upper Peninsula had long been afflicted with unemployment and were the least able of the state's counties to generate local funds for relief. Allowances for direct relief in the Upper Peninsula were "a disgrace," Murphy stated in May. "Must we bring in the bodies of starved lumber jacks to impress upon the State that relief is urgent?" the president of a local of the Michigan Timber and Sawmill Workers Union inquired of the governor. A delegation from the western part of the Upper Peninsula that visited the governor's office at the beginning of March 1938 alleged that some lumberjacks had actually starved or frozen to death. The WPA could do little for the woods- men, most of whom were single, since it gave preference to heads of families and since many of them were aliens and hence ineligible for WPA jobs. Under these circumstances, the SERA had to look after needy lumberjacks, a responsibility that it sought to meet by estab- lishing camps in the Upper Peninsula to provide for their care.[19]

Relief rolls in Michigan increased at a far more rapid rate during the recession of 1937–38 than at the outset of the Great Depression. This was not only because far more relief money was available but also because those who lost their jobs or were laid off during the recession had fewer financial resources to draw on than the jobless in 1930— unemployment in the state had been greater in 1936 than in 1929 (an average of 249,000 in 1936 compared to an average of 89,000 in 1929), and employment had been discontinuous in the pre-recession months of 1937 because of the numerous strikes and reduced hours of work. The needy unemployed, also, were far less reluctant to seek relief than they had been at the beginning of the Great Depression. "It is no longer considered a disgrace to go on relief," Granger reported to the governor. After studying local relief attitudes in the state during the recession, an investigator concluded, "There is no question but what the relief clients have come to the view that relief is rightfully theirs and they no longer wait until absolutely broke before applying."[20]

That the unemployed and needy were "good people," not "bums," that they were entitled to public relief, and that for them to receive aid was no disgrace was what Murphy had told his con- stituents in Detroit during the darkest days of the Great Depression. He did not alter his views as governor during the recession. Believing that it was "the first duty of those dedicated to the ministry of public service" to "take care of God's poor," Murphy saw no "excuse for failing to meet the needs of the unemployed intelligently." It would be "inhuman, unworthy of the Government and an enlightened community like the State of Michigan" to neglect the destitute, he asserted, and he would "not permit it." Those who complained about the state's finances, he alleged, were really complaining about what was being done to aid the distressed. His "only . . . regret," he declared, was that the state was "not doing well enough."[21]

Endeavoring to capitalize on his strong ties with the national administration, Murphy sought additional WPA aid for the state, and Harry Hopkins and Howard Hunter listened sympathetically to his pleas. Murphy announced at the beginning of December 1937 that Washington had promised the state five thousand jobs beyond the forty-four thousand allotted to Michigan for that month and an additional seven thousand jobs in January. Early in January Hopkins agreed to assign Detroit an "open quota," meaning that local WPA officials were authorized to employ as many persons as met the eligibility requirements regardless of the number of jobs allotted to the city. After Murphy spent two hours with the president on January 11 discussing the recession, the WPA assured the governor that it would employ every jobless man in Michigan who could prove his need; and on February 12, 1938, Murphy was able to announce that the federal agency had given the state as a whole an open quota. The WPA, Murphy wrote the agency's deputy administrator, had "done everything" for the state that "it reasonably could." Between the middle of May and the middle of August the number employed by the WPA in Michigan more than doubled, increasing from 74,705 to 198,190, which partly explains the decline in general relief cases in the state after March 1938. The rate of increase in WPA employment in Michigan from October 1937 to the latter part of August 1938 exceeded that in any other state. Despite the large increase in WPA employment, however, a substantial proportion of the persons receiving general relief during that time of adversity, amounting to about 45 percent of the case load in some months, were employables who were theoretically the responsibility of the WPA.[22]

The WPA's failure to provide jobs for all of Michigan's needy employables and thus further to reduce the relief burden of the SERA was the result to some extent of the inability of local units of government to pay the sponsor's share of project costs. Since some of the cities hardest hit by the recession, notably Detroit, Flint, and Pontiac, were the least able to sponsor WPA projects, Murphy pleaded with WPA authorities in February 1938 to reduce the local sponsor's share by allocating up to $10 per worker per month for materials rather than the $5 that the federal government was then contributing for nonwage costs. The Emergency Relief Appropriation Act of June 1938 raised the $5 federal limit to $7 and also provided $25 million that the WPA could use to exceed this figure. Michigan was one of the beneficiaries of the somewhat more generous federal contribution for nonlabor items after July 1: whereas sponsors' contributions in the state had averaged 23.1 percent at the end of 1937, the figure for the second half of 1938 was 12.9 percent, which was well below the national average of 18.2 percent for that period.[23]

Because of the shortage of funds in some localities, the SERA, acting on Murphy's suggestion, decided in April 1938 to pay the sponsor share, not exceeding $10-15 per worker per month, for projects in four southern industrial counties. Since the average monthly grant per family case in these counties exceeded $25 at that time, the SERA reasoned that it could reduce its expenditures to the extent that it was able to transfer employables in these counties from its rolls to the WPA projects that its contributions made possible. Within two months the SERA contribution had helped to provide WPA jobs for 10,732 persons, and the program was then expanded to two additional industrial counties. In November several county relief commissions, with SERA approval, also began making contributions to help local governments within these counties meet the cost of sponsoring projects.[24]

There was little the SERA could do about the lack of a sufficient number of eligible projects in some parts of the state, especially in rural areas, that was also a factor in the failure of the WPA to provide employment for all of Michigan's needy employables. At a meeting with local relief administrators in February 1938 the SERA reported that the WPA was prepared to take on forty thousand additional workers within the next two weeks if suitable projects could be devised for them. "We must have projects," Michigan's WPA administrator, Louis Nims, told the local officials. ". . . you have a responsibility to hang up a stocking for Santa Claus," William Norton said to the same group. There was "a mad scramble for projects in almost every section in the State" in 1938, but even hard-pressed Detroit was unable to devise enough projects to take full advantage of the open quota it had been granted.[25]

In addition to the WPA, three programs established as the result of the Social Security Act helped Michigan to cope with the consequences of the recession: the old-age assistance program, ADC, and unemployment insurance. Michigan's hard-pressed citizens also received assistance from the Civilian Conservation Corps (CCC), the National Youth Administration (NYA), and the Federal Surplus Commodities Corporation (FSCC). The availability of these programs while Murphy was governor and their absence while he was mayor of Detroit are an important measure of the difference in approach to economic adversity of the New Deal and the Hoover administration.

The liberalized old-age assistance eligibility requirements approved by the Michigan legislature in June 1937 coupled with the great need occasioned by the recession led to an increase in old-age assistance cases from 42,209 in July 1937 to a high of 71,310 cases in March 1938. The number of cases during the remainder of the calendar year leveled off at about 70,000, which constituted about 25 percent of the 285,000 persons over sixty-five years of age in the state. The average monthly grant received by these persons in the fiscal year 1937–38, which took into account the private resources of clients, was $18.60, ranging from $14.22 to $21.45 in the various counties. This sum, half of which was provided by the federal government, was slightly below the national average.[26]

When the Murphy administration at the beginning of October 1937 reduced the 1937–38 appropriation for old-age assistance from $10 million to $8 million, it was on the assumption that the legislature had overestimated the sum needed for old-age pensions. In late June 1938 the administration advised the Old Age Assistance Bureau that its $8 million allocation for 1938–39 would be further reduced to $7.2 million as part of the economy drive. This action induced the bureau, which had met the initial $2 million cut by reinvestigating its cases and limiting the number of persons it assisted, to cut the average monthly grant as of July 1 by about $1 since "merely closing the gates to newcomers" was no longer "enough."

Since the Old Age Assistance Bureau had about twenty-five thousand applications for assistance pending at the end of July and since about half of those who applied were usually deemed eligible for assistance, the director of the Welfare Department, James G. Bryant, pleaded with Murphy to restore at least $500,000 of the sum taken from the bureau. This, Bryant pointed out, would bring in an additional $500,000 in federal funds, permit the bureau to take on an additional nine thousand clients, and relieve much of the "concerted community and group pressure" being exerted on the administration. The July 1 cut appeared to necessitate still another reexamination of the old-age assistance case load, and Bryant wished the governor to know that "the constant checking" created "a feeling of insecurity" in the minds of the bureau's clients and did "not give them anything definite to look forward to." Persuaded by Bryant's arguments and probably thinking about the November election as well, Murphy restored $500,000 to the old-age assistance budget at the end of August and announced that the $1 cut in allowances would be rescinded as of September 1. The additional funds enabled the Old Age Assistance Bureau to take on an additional twenty-five hundred clients by the end of the calendar year, but the average grant for old-age assistance remained about the same.[27]

William C. Richards, the executive assistant for Michigan of the National Emergency Council, concluded at the end of 1938 that the old-age assistance program in Michigan was "ably run" but was "bogging down" because of lack of funds. In many instances, he observed, what the pensions made possible was "a slightly softened hunger and merely life itself." Norton, Richards noted, thought that Michigan provided " 'plenty' " for old-age assistance and had "skimped" other relief agencies for this purpose, but Murphy told the federal official that the average grant in Michigan was "entirely inadequate" and that the needy aged required $60 a month. "And then Murphy," Richards wrote, "after allowing his heart-beats to go up, says that this, of course, must be conditioned on sound finance."[28]

Because of mounting industrial unemployment, the United Automobile Workers, Frank Martel, and others urged Murphy to seek a change in the state's unemployment compensation law so that covered workers could begin filing for payments on January 1, 1938, as in twenty-four other states, rather than on July 1. Haber advised Murphy that the accumulated reserves in Michigan were insufficient for this and that to take this action would not only "confuse insurance with relief" but might discredit the system of unemployment insurance. When Murphy took the matter to Washington, he discovered that the Social Security Board agreed with Haber.[29]

On June 30, the day before Michigan workers began filing their claims for unemployment compensation, Murphy hailed unemployment insurance as "democracy's answer to a world at war. . . . It means that in this democracy we do not just talk social security—we build it." The first check was received as part of a "pretentious cerremony" on August 1 by a Detroit auto worker, the father of four, who had been unemployed since May 12. "This makes a new man out of me," he said. "It takes a great load off my mind for I've never accepted charity from any one." By the end of the year approximately 337,000 Michigan workers had received 2,958,000 benefit checks totaling almost $40 million. The typical beneficiary received nine checks netting him about $118, and about half of the beneficiaries received the $16 weekly maximum. Michigan's average weekly benefit of $13.49, which compared with a national average of $10.49, was the highest in the nation—the average was below $12 in every other state. Michigan also led the nation in the number of checks paid out, the total amount of unemployment compensation, and the rapidity with which it processed claims. "Had nothing else than unemployment insurance been accomplished during the past two years," Murphy wrote at the close of his governorship, "I would still be happy . . . that we had done something constructive to promote the economic security of those who work for a wage."[30]

The SERA was able to close more than 34,000 general relief cases in the last four months of 1938 because reliefers had received unemployment compensation, and an additional 10,536 persons had left the WPA rolls in Michigan by September 15 for the same reason. That unemployment compensation, however, was not a complete solution for the economic problems of the unemployed was documented in a study made by Paul L. Stanchfield of 55,260 workers, 20 percent of the Michigan total, who received unemployment compensation during the first three months that benefits were available and whose benefit year ended on June 30, 1939. Although 62 percent of these workers qualified for benefits for the full sixteen weeks and less than 10 percent of them received payments for less than twelve weeks, just about half had exhausted their benefits before they were reemployed. A study of fifteen thousand unemployment compensation beneficiaries in Wayne County during the fiscal year 1938–39 also revealed that unemployment compensation "fell far short of providing protection against all the unemployment experienced by workers who had sufficiently good job attachments to qualify for benefits." Of the approximately five thousand workers in the sample who had exhausted their benefits by the end of 1938, only about 28 percent were reemployed in the same quarter that their benefits expired, and about 30 percent of the Detroiters who had exhausted their benefits had to obtain relief after they stopped receiving unemployment compensation.[31]

Michigan averaged 10,910 ADC cases per month in 1937 and 12,187 cases in 1938. The average monthly grant per case in 1938, of which the federal government paid one-third, was $37.77, well below the figure in some other states. When Murphy, as part of his effort to reduce the 1938–39 deficit, cut the $4 million ADC appropriation by 10 percent, complaints came in from all over the state that the reduced grants made it impossible for the relief agencies to provide clothing for dependent children so that they would be able to attend school in the fall. Since the federal and state governments were supposed to bear the entire cost of ADC, local units became "more and more restive and critical" when the SERA asked them to contribute to the program so that minimum standards could be maintained. Granger consequently requested the governor to restore the 10 percent cut, and he did so in October.[32]

During the school year 1937–38 a total of 12,339 high school, college, and graduate students were employed on NYA projects, receiving an average monthly wage ranging from $4.78 to $15.57 depending on the level of their schooling. A modest supplement to family income, NYA wages enabled thousands of needy Michigan students to enter school and to remain there. Michigan also benefited from the CCC, whose forty-three Michigan camps housed a monthly average of 7,771 young men between the ages of seventeen and twenty-four in 1938. The enrollees earned just over $2 million in 1938, paid entirely by the federal government. At least $22 of the enrollees' monthly wage of $30 was assigned to their families, and since the SERA selected the young men from among relief families, this helped to reduce state and county relief costs. During 1938, also, the FSCC distributed about $4 million in surplus food, clothing, and household goods in Michigan. The cost of distribution was just under $600,000, of which the WPA paid 45 percent and state and county relief administrations paid the remainder. These supplies supplemented the often inadequate rations of relief families, adding $5–6 to the grants they received in some months.[33]

Although it was not, strictly speaking, a relief agency, the Public Works Administration (PWA) also aided Michigan during the recession by providing employment for workers who might otherwise have required public assistance. By April 20, 1938, the PWA had spent over $25 million on Michigan projects exclusive of low-cost housing, and the agency had also agreed to help Michigan with its hospital building program. The governor appointed a Public Works Study Commission on June 21 to examine the feasibility of particular work projects, advise applicants, and coordinate projects in the state. "We ought to do a real job on this," the governor urged. By the end of November the PWA had granted Michigan just over $31 million for 308 projects approved since the study commission had been formed. The projects included school buildings, libraries, sewage treatment plants and systems, waterworks, lighting and heating plants, hospitals, and roads. Frank Isbey, the head of the study commission, estimated that seventy-five thousand Michiganders would be employed on PWA projects by the end of 1938.[34]

The one federal relief agency that apparently failed Michigan during the recession was the Farm Security Administration (FSA). After talking with Washington officials in April 1938, Murphy announced that the FSA, which by then had spent $10 million in the state, would increase its relief efforts in rural areas of Michigan. About eleven thousand farmers or part-time farmers were receiving direct relief, and Murphy thought that it would be an "enormous help" to the state if FSA assistance made it possible to remove them from the relief rolls. Although the FSA was willing to help, lack of funds made it impossible for the agency to do so.[35]

The decline in Michigan's general relief case load after March 1938 was less the result of improving economic conditions than of the transfer of reliefers to some other program of assistance. Of the 138,735 cases closed during the last five months of 1938, only 13.5 percent resulted from the clients' having found private employment, whereas the WPA accounted for 26.1 percent of the closings, unemployment compensation for 25.3 percent, and old-age assistance, ADC, and aid to the blind for 1.6 percent.[36]

Despite the assistance the federal government provided Michigan, the SERA found it increasingly difficult to meet its share of the relief burden from money the legislature had appropriated. In late December 1937 Murphy restored the small amount of money that he had cut from the relief budget, and in January the Administrative Board made an additional $607,000 available. The entire 1937–38 relief appropriation, however, was soon exhausted, and the SERA had to begin meeting its obligations from its 1938–39 budget. At the end of April, by which time the state had already spent half of the 1938–39 relief appropriation, Murphy summoned the Emergency Appropriation Commission for its first meeting and persuaded it to appropriate $1 million for relief. Two months later the commission appropriated an additional $1.1 million for relief, which meant that $2.1 million of the $3 million the legislature had set aside for emergencies in the biennium had been expended for relief. By the end of the fiscal year on June 30, 1938, the state had spent $21,304,586 for emergency relief, leaving only $2.7 of the original combined 1937–38 and 1938–39 appropriation still available. About two-thirds of the remaining sum was expended in July.[37]

The governor and the SERA responded to the rapid drain on state relief funds by seeking to persuade the federal government to return to the policy of direct relief that it had abandoned in 1935, reducing the monthly allocation to counties below their estimates of need, and pressuring them to meet a larger proportion of their relief costs. The Michigan campaign to secure direct federal relief once again was initiated when in February 1938 Homer Martin and Richard Frankensteen presented President Roosevelt with a petition calling for the immediate expenditure in Michigan of $100 million in WPA funds and $30 million in direct relief. Three days later a huge throng variously estimated at 80,000 to 250,000 filled Cadillac Square in

Detroit to protest layoffs and " 'inadequate' " relief. In a speech to the crowd, Martin urged that the federal government provide Michigan $1 million a week in direct relief for unemployed auto workers. Although preferring work relief to direct relief, Murphy began to advocate the latter early in April since it had become apparent that the WPA would not be able to provide jobs for all the employables on the relief rolls. The governor's request for direct relief disturbed the WPA's Howard Hunter, who wired Murphy that the WPA was "in [a] position to take care of all [the] needy unemployed" in the state who were "willing to perform useful work." Although this was not entirely correct, it is likely that the agitation for direct relief prompted the WPA to intensify its efforts to provide work for Michigan's jobless citizens. Murphy looked to Congress to include a substantial sum for direct relief in the 1938 emergency relief appropriation, but his hopes were dashed when the legislators included only $25 million in discretionary relief funds in the bill.[38]

Month after month during the recession the SERA found itself unable to provide the counties with the sums that they requested to meet their relief needs, and the result was a steady decline in the average grant for emergency relief cases. Although the amount of money that the counties could appropriate was limited by restraints on their taxing power and rising tax delinquency as the result of the recession, the governor and the SERA agreed that it was essential "to put all possible pressure on counties to make local funds available." Those counties that contributed proportionately less for relief than the statewide average for counties were reminded of their dereliction, and the SERA sent tax experts to these counties to assist them in raising additional funds. The counties were advised to transfer mothers' pension cases to ADC and to use the funds released thereby for direct relief. They were also counseled to go into debt if necessary to provide adequate funds for relief. Granger informed the governor that some counties that were niggardly in meeting relief needs actually had "fat surpluses," and Murphy lamented that these and other counties "apparently" did not "care whether their people starve[d]."

When four counties cut relief allowances by 25 percent in July 1938, Murphy, who had been told that a relief commission member in one of these counties had stated that the commission was "putting the Governor on the spot," complained that the reductions were being made for "political reasons." A state investigator who visited eight counties that claimed they were "broke or nearly so" discovered that this was true of only four of these counties. He concluded that the Republican character of these counties might have been the cause for their refusal to provide additional funds for relief. " 'Well,' " one Republican relief official had stated in what the investigator thought was a typical remark, " 'Governor Murphy asked for it, now let him pay the shot. He told these people [relief clients] that there were ample funds to take care of them, now let him dig around for the money to pay for it all.' " In the end, despite pressure from Lansing, the proportion of the total funds expended for emergency relief contributed by the counties in 1937–38 (33.9 percent) was only slightly above the proportion they had contributed in 1936–37 (32.9 percent), although their contribution in absolute terms rose by about 58 percent (from $7,344,639 to $11,729,967).[39]

The SERA was faced with a unique situation in Midland County, where the board of supervisors informed the state in April 1938 that the county had sufficient local funds to meet its relief needs without any state subvention. The SERA thereupon withdrew from the county except for the role that it played in dispensing ADC funds and aid to the blind. A few months later a UAW local in Midland complained to the SERA that the county was distributing relief in accordance with the criteria of the old poor law and that the supervisors were subservient to the Dow Chemical Company, the most important business in Midland. The SERA, however, did not believe that it could set up "an opposition relief distribution agency" in the county.[40]

The SERA had a particularly disputatious relationship during the recession with Wayne County and Detroit. At the end of December 1937 the Detroit Common Council, claiming that city funds would soon be exhausted, requested the state to advance Detroit $1.5 million to cover its relief costs for January and February. This initiated a controversy between the city and county and the state about the sharing of relief costs that continued unabated until September, when economic conditions in Detroit took a decided turn for the better. Detroit and Wayne regularly alleged that their relief funds were about to run out and that they would be forced to discontinue relief—Wayne County did stop relief payments briefly in August 1938—and they would note that they were entitled to special consideration since they had met 63 percent of their relief costs in the last half of 1937, well above the average for the state. The state would respond that its funds were also nearing exhaustion, that it was running a deficit, that Detroit had not made a sufficient effort to solve its own problems, and that it should borrow to meet its needs. This led Detroit to complain that Governor Murphy was forgetting

Mayor Murphy's efforts to secure state aid for relief and his criticisms of Lansing's refusal to aid Detroit. The state would relent and release additional funds for Detroit and Wayne County but not as much as they had requested. In April Detroit agreed to borrow $1 million for direct relief, but in October, when the city had unpaid relief bills of $1.5 million, the governor and the SERA helped it to wipe out about half of its deficit. For the calendar year 1938 the state provided Wayne and Detroit with $11.3 million, which was about 45 percent of all relief funds distributed by the state during the year and about 54 percent of the total amount expended by the city and county for relief. Since the monthly average of Wayne County emergency relief cases was about 42 percent of the monthly average for the state as a whole in 1938, the SERA was not exactly niggardly in helping the county and its largest city to meet their relief needs.[41]

The differences between Detroit and the state involved not only the funding of relief but also the efforts of Mayor Richard W. Reading to tighten the conditions under which relief was granted and to purge the rolls of the allegedly undeserving. Concerned that many reliefers were "chiselers and drones," Reading, "a rigid conservative" who took office on January 1, 1938, ordered an investigation of all welfare clients by the Detroit Police Department and compelled the city's welfare superintendent to make confidential documents available to the police. A larger than usual number of clients were dropped from the rolls in the next several months, but the cost of the effort appears to have exceeded the savings to the city.[42]

At its meeting of February 15, 1938, the Detroit Public Welfare Commission accepted Reading's suggestion that all applicants for relief be required to sign a notarized affidavit attesting to their financial status and need. Such a document, Reading noted, could then be used to prosecute welfare clients who had defrauded the city. The SERA position was that an applicant for relief had to sign a state form provided for that purpose but that to require any additional certification was "costly and unnecessary." SEWRC member Richard Frankensteen promptly attacked the Detroit action as "probably the most backward step taken since the Elizabethan poor laws" and accused Reading of "impeding welfare progress" while "bleating about fraud and chiselers." Appearing at a Detroit Welfare Commission meeting, William Norton, also a SEWRC member, protested that he could not "conceive of an enlightened community like . . . Detroit punishing these poor devils who are thrown out of work by all the implications which go with standing up, raising your right hand, and swearing to God that you are a pauper." Murphy criticized welfare fraud "purges" in a public address and noted in a letter to Norton that the pauper's oath was "unjust, dilatory, and one of the things that substantially contributes to strikes in all eras following recovery. Those who have been humiliated in depressions organize as a reassertion of personality to the end that they won't be subjected to humiliation again." Faced with opposition from the state government, Detroit abandoned its efforts to have relief applicants sign a pauper's oath. In an ironic aftermath, Reading, after being defeated for reelection in 1939, was indicted, convicted, and sentenced to five years in prison for income tax evasion and "complicity in a Police Department graft ring."[43]

As the Michigan budget went ever more deeply into deficit as the result of increased relief expenditures and the slump in revenue, Murphy assigned a higher priority to relief than to balancing the budget. "Do you want me to balance the budget or meet the problem?" he asked. "For an intelligent and humane government," he continued, "there is only one answer." In the face of the relief crisis, he exclaimed in a Jefferson Day address, "the little politicians and exponents of reaction continue to orate about deficits and a balanced budget," but a democracy could "better afford a deficit in the public finances than a deficit in the morale of its people." Those who said otherwise, he asserted, wanted "to break down the morale of the multitudes" and to "starve them into submission."[44]

When Murphy stated early in April 1938 that expenditures for relief would have to take precedence over expenditures for roads in the absence of sufficient funds to provide for both, the rejoinder of the Highway Department was that the release of the $4 million still remaining in the highway contingency fund would do more to mitigate the effects of the recession than the expenditure of the same amount of money for direct relief. The Highway Department, Van Wagoner contended, could employ 12,945 persons (6,904 directly and 6,041 indirectly) in the next fiscal year with the $4 million, which would be more than matched by the federal government, whereas the state could assist only 6,410 persons with that sum. If his proposal were not approved, he asserted, the department would have to lay off its entire six-hundred-man construction force, and the state's three hundred highway contractors would also be adversely affected. In a speech to a Michigan Good Roads Federation banquet, Van Wagoner stated that, although he knew he was asking for money from an empty treasury, he did not believe that Murphy would "let the motorists down." Murphy, who was present at the affair, rose "with a stunned look" after hearing what the highway commissioner had to say. The *Detroit News* characterized Van Wagoner's proposal as "the 'hottest' political potato of the campaign year," and the *Detroit Free Press* wondered if the governor could afford to antagonize the "best organized and most far-flung vote-getting unit" of the Democratic party.[45]

There were several flaws in Van Wagoner's logic, as Murphy's aides pointed out to the governor. The Highway Department estimated the cost for assistance to a needy family at $52 a month, whereas the average cost at that time was about $26 and only about two-thirds of this sum was paid by the state. Van Wagoner overstated the amount of federal funds available for highway construction and assumed that the workers his department would employ with the $4 million would all be drawn from the relief rolls, which was obviously not so. Also, much of the "indirect labor" benefit to which Van Wagoner pointed would not have been realized by Michigan inhabitants. Murphy consequently rejected the highway commissioner's proposal, noting that to allocate the $4 million to the department would deprive the state of funds needed for welfare and other services.[46]

Replying to the governor, Van Wagoner stressed the consequences in terms of employment if the Highway Department were not granted additional funds. In a separate and quite brazen document, the department noted that the six hundred men that it would have to lay off had served the state and the Democratic party; the only certain way to ensure their continued loyalty as well as that of the thousands of workers who would benefit from the construction program, Van Wagoner contended, was for the governor to accept the department's proposal. Although Murphy still thought that relief must "come first," he decided at the end of May to compromise with Van Wagoner. He granted the Highway Department $750,000 from the contingency fund in addition to the $1 million that had already been advanced and a like sum of $1.75 million for 1938–39.[47] To protect itself against possible future raids on funds earmarked for roads, the Highway Department sponsored a constitutional amendment prohibiting the use of income from the gas and weight taxes for any purpose other than highways. The voters approved the amendment in the November 1938 election.[48]

According to the budget director, the state deficit for the fiscal year 1937–38 was $8.75 million. Since the state government spent $9 million more for emergency relief in the fiscal year than the legislature had appropriated, the budget would almost certainly have been in balance if not for the recession, despite the initial overappropriation by the legislature. Smith attributed the state's difficulties not only to relief expenditures but also to the decline in revenue yielded by the sales tax—the income from the tax for every month during the period February–November 1938 was at least 15 percent below the sum yielded in the same month in 1937. "Our fundamental difficulty," Smith declared, "is that the revenue system of the State is built on sand. It is of such a character that it will not withstand the onslaught of a depression."[49]

Anticipating a further deficit in 1938–39, the Murphy administration announced a $10 million economy program on July 1, 1938. The bulk of the saving was to be achieved by a reduction in positions, but about $2 million was to be realized by the imposition of salary cuts ranging from 6 percent on workers in the lowest brackets to 15 percent in the top brackets. The salary reductions, however, were in effect only until September 1, when the Civil Service Commission implemented the state's new compensation plan.[50]

Michigan's budget woes brought Murphy into conflict once again with the state's public-school teachers. The governor had pared the 1937–38 appropriation for education from $43 million to $40.2 million, but since the primary-school interest fund yielded $900,000 more than had been anticipated, the schools actually received $41.1 million. Although the teachers told Murphy that the schools required $44 million in 1938–39, the governor set the school budget at $39.5 million, which was a smaller reduction in percentage terms than was suffered by other departments and was above the 1936–37 figure by about $2.5 million. Since the primary-school interest fund, however, had increased from about $15 million in 1937–38 to more than $20 million because of the sum added to it from the estate of James Couzens, the MEA contended that the school-budget cut was greater than that imposed on any other state agency if the yield from the fund was also taken into account. Had the governor permitted the original legislative appropriation to stand, the schools would have received $48–49 million in 1938–39. One can therefore understand why the MEA protested the governor's decision and sought to muster the support of the " 'friends of education' " in opposition to the scheduled reduction in school aid. Murphy responded by restoring $1 million to the education budget, but the MEA was far from satisfied. The issue passed into the 1938 campaign, with Murphy defending his action in light of the state's needs and the cuts in other areas and Fitzgerald pledging the schools $44 million in 1939–40 and $46 million in 1940–41 and promising also that these sums would be earmarked so that they could not be "juggled" or "impaired." Both candidates stated their position in the October issue of the *Michigan*

Education Journal, which circulated to fifty thousand teachers. Their statements were followed by advice to the teachers from the MEA's executive secretary to vote for the candidate for governor "favorable toward adequate and guaranteed State-Aid for schools."[51]

Because of the drain on the state's budget, Murphy had all but decided as early as the end of January 1938 to call the legislature into special session at an early date to provide additional funds for emergency relief. His advisors dissuaded him from taking this step because it was wise, as they saw it, "to give the public an impression of careful and prudent management" before asking for larger appropriations; a special session might lead to "irresponsible talk or action" directed at the governor that "might revive . . . the issue of prodigality and free spending"; it was not yet certain how much money would be required; the legislature might refuse to vote the funds or might attach "strings" to the appropriation; and it would be politically damaging since it would "provide a sounding board for every . . . politically-minded Republican member of the legislature to jump on . . . the Administration for everything that could be talked about." The conventional wisdom in Lansing, indeed, was that a special session was generally "fatal" to an incumbent administration, one prominent Democrat telling the governor, "Frankly, I don't think we could survive a special session."[52]

Since it was apparent by the beginning of August that the state was about to spend the last dollar appropriated for relief for the biennium, Murphy had no choice but to call the legislature into special session that month. On August 10, consequently, the governor summoned the lawmakers to meet on August 29 to deal with relief, public housing, and the extension of the real-estate moratorium then in effect in the state. "Never before in Michigan's history," the *Detroit Times* commented, "has a governor dared to call the legislature back to Lansing practically on election eve. A greater political gamble hardly could be conceived." Some Democrats, however, credited Murphy with a "political coup" in setting the date of the session about two weeks before the primary since they believed that this would provide Democrats with an opportunity to show their concern for the "people" and Republicans would have to go along with the governor or incur the enmity of numerous voters.[53]

When Murphy delivered his message to the special session of the legislature, the galleries, according to a Republican senator, were "packed with [a] CIO crowd to furnish applause so as to make it appear [to the radio audience that the] Legislature was applauding his harangue." Murphy told the lawmakers that, despite his determined efforts to balance the budget, "an additional and immediate appropriation" of $10 million was required to enable the state to meets its relief needs until the legislature convened in regular session in January 1939. "This is elementary humanity," the governor declared, "and should not be confused with questions of economic policy or political strategy." Behaving precisely as some Democrats thought they would, Republican lawmakers attempted to embarrass the governor by seeking to appropriate additional money for education and old-age assistance, reminding teachers and the needy aged in this way that Murphy had recently made budget cuts in these areas. Republicans indicated their disapproval of the manner in which welfare funds had been expended by urging that a bipartisan legislative commission be made responsible for the monthly release of welfare money. Contending that they did not believe "the people of Michigan want[ed] Frankensteen handling welfare funds," Republicans suggested that the Senate be required to approve SEWRC members before the money the legislature was being asked to appropriate could be spent. They dwelt on the administration's "record-breaking" expenditures, forgetting that they had had "a lot of fun" offering amendments to increase those expenditures still further. They also attacked the governor as a "moral coward" for not recommending new taxes to provide the revenue for the additional relief money he was seeking. Murphy dismissed the Republican rhetoric as "just political hokum and plain bunk," and the Republicans in the end joined with the Democrats in appropriating the $10 million the governor had requested. The sum was sufficient to meet the state's relief costs for the remainder of the calendar year.[54]

In his call for the special session Murphy requested the legislature to amend the state's housing legislation to make it possible for any Michigan city with a population of more than ten thousand to apply for the federal grants and loans made available by the Housing Act of September 1937. When the measure became law, only Detroit among Michigan's cities had launched a public housing program, and only Detroit was eligible under Michigan law to take advantage of the federal subsidies that the statute authorized.

Suffering from an acute housing shortage and soaring rents, Detroit had secured PWA approval in November 1933 to clear an eleven-block area on the city's East Side that had both the highest percentage of substandard housing and the highest crime rate in the city and to build public housing units on the site. Known as Brewster Homes, the project was reserved for blacks. The Detroit Housing Commission, created by the mayor to run the project, later gained approval for a second project (Parkside), this one reserved for whites, to be constructed on vacant land near fashionable Grosse Pointe. For a variety of reasons, construction of the Brewster and Parkside homes had not yet begun when Murphy became Michigan's governor. New construction bids were approved in 1937; and both projects, Brewster consisting of 701 units (2,360 rooms) and Parkside consisting of 785 units (2,827 rooms), were completed in September 1938. The projects enjoyed the full support of the governor.[55]

When some of Murphy's advisors met at the beginning of 1938 to consider what the state might do to counteract the recession, they concluded that stimulation of the construction industry was of primary importance. Two months later Roosevelt urged Murphy to bring Michigan into line with the thirty other states that had passed enabling legislation to permit their cities to share in the $500 million in housing funds made available by the Housing Act. Responding to the president's prompting and his offer of United States Housing Authority (USHA) assistance in drafting the necessary legislation, Murphy conferred with the United States housing administrator, Nathan Straus, and gained his consent to reserve housing funds for out-state Michigan cities—$25 million had already been earmarked for Detroit—while the governor sought to persuade the legislature to enact the enabling legislation. The USHA dispatched Robert Frank to Lansing, and G. Mennen Williams, Kemp, and he drafted the housing bill that Murphy submitted to the special session on August 29. The legislature approved the measure on September 1 after amending it to provide that 3 percent of the registered voters in a city could force a referendum on an ordinance providing for the creation of a local housing authority.[56]

Anticipating favorable action by the legislature, Murphy on August 19 created the Michigan Housing Commission, headed by Robert W. Kelso, director of the University of Michigan's Institute of Public Administration. The commission was to study housing conditions in the state and to formulate "a comprehensive, sound and effective housing program" for Michigan, "one of the most backward of states" insofar as public housing was concerned. After the legislature passed the requisite housing legislation, the governor wired the mayors of thirty-eight cities that the Housing Commission was prepared to assist in drawing up ordinances that would enable them to secure federal housing aid. By the time Murphy left office, the federal government had earmarked more than $10 million in housing funds for five Michigan cities other than Detroit, and local surveys were underway in seven additional cities.[57]

In his message to the special session, Murphy informed the law-makers that the "abrupt and unconditional termination" of the state's real-estate moratorium law would result in the forced liquidation of a considerable amount of property. First enacted in 1933 and then extended in 1935 and again in 1937, the moratorium legislation empowered the courts on the application of one of the interested parties to forestall the foreclosure of mortgages and land contracts and to determine fair rental terms for the interim. When the legislature extended the moratorium statute in 1937, it specified that the measure was to expire on November 1, 1938, when the lawmakers would not be in session and in a position to take further action on the moratorium. Murphy now requested the legislature to extend the moratorium deadline until July 1, 1939, so that farmers and urban homeowners could take advantage of improving economic conditions to retain their property. The legislature approved Murphy's request, thus conceding to the governor on the three principal issues that had led him to call the special session. "I've won everything in the Special Session," Murphy exultantly told Harry Hopkins. "It's simply marvelous."[58]

Before he called the special session, Murphy had seemed less concerned about the extension of the real-estate moratorium than about the effect of the recession on installment credit. Troubled by the repossession of articles on which purchasers could not meet installment payments, deficiency judgments for the unpaid balance on repossessed items, and the garnishment of wages, Murphy thought that the state government could "stabilize and improve conditions" and aid in meeting a national problem by imposing "restrictions on the legal remedies available to vendors and purchasers of commercial paper." In January 1938 the governor consequently created a Credit Study Commission consisting of businessmen, local government officials, and college professors to investigate installment sales practices. Since the commission had not completed its work when he called the legislature into special session in August, Murphy did not make any recommendations regarding this subject.[59]

III

Unlike political leaders in states like Washington, Pennsylvania, Ohio, and New Mexico, Murphy did not take advantage of the state's relief program or the WPA to enhance his own political fortunes or those of his party. SERA employees had been selected on the basis of the merit system since July 1936, and of the ninety-nine on the payroll in June 1938, eighty-seven had been appointed before Murphy became governor. The SERA ordered both the state and county relief commissions " 'to refrain from any political activity on penalty of dismissal,' " and no member of a relief commission was permitted to use his office " 'for the purpose of politically advancing himself, or any other candidate for office.' " SERA employees appear to have observed these orders quite faithfully, but not all members of the county relief commissions paid heed to the specified limitations on their political activity. Insofar as they transgressed, however, Murphy was not necessarily the beneficiary.[60]

Murphy made no effort to staff the WPA organization in Michigan with deserving Democrats or Murphy supporters—there were Democratic complaints to the very end of his administration about Republican influence in the work relief agency. Louis Nims, who headed the state WPA throughout Murphy's governorship, was a Van Wagoner ally, and Hunter virtually had "to force" him to support Murphy in the 1938 election. A few WPA employees in the state, to be sure, violated the agency's regulations concerning political activity, but when they were caught, they were demoted or dismissed. It can be presumed that those receiving work relief as well as direct relief were not unmindful of the efforts of the Murphy administration in their behalf. On the other hand, WPA rolls in the state decreased in the weeks just before the 1938 election even though they were increasing in most neighboring states, and there was much grumbling among WPA workers about the adequacy of their wages and among relief clients about the amount of their grants.[61] It remained to be seen whether the voters would "punish" Murphy because the recession had occurred while he was governor or "reward" him because of his sympathy for the plight of the unfortunate and his efforts to alleviate their distress.

14

"Tragic Interruption"

I

However impressive Murphy's record as governor, his aspirations for still higher political office rested on his ability to win reelection in 1938. Before he faced that test, however, his party sought to win voter approval in the spring election of 1937, and the governor had to decide whether to involve himself in the heated Detroit mayoralty election in the fall of that year. The outcome of the two elections provided conflicting clues regarding Murphy's chances in 1938.

At stake in the April 5, 1937, Michigan election were the positions of highway commissioner and superintendent of public instruction, two seats on the Michigan Supreme Court, two seats each on the Board of Regents of the University of Michigan and the State Board of Agriculture of Michigan State College, and one seat on the State Board of Education. Claiming that the state was experiencing "evolution, not revolution," because of Murphy's efforts, Democrats urged the voters to show their support for the governor by voting for his party's candidates. The United Automobile Workers (UAW) and Labor's Non-Partisan League pledged support to the Democrats "in appreciation" of Murphy's conduct during the sit-down strikes; the Republicans, although concentrating their effort in rural Michigan, hoped that "disgusted" nonunionist voters in cities like Detroit and Flint would vote Republican. In the end, the Democrats captured six of the nine offices contested in the spring election, losing the race for superintendent of public instruction and for the seat on the Board of Education as well as one Supreme Court judgeship. This was a very satisfactory showing for the party in a spring election in Republican Michigan, but the switch of Genesee County (Flint), the scene of the General Motors strike, from the Democratic column in 1936 to the Republican column five months later was understandably of concern to Democrats thinking ahead to 1938.[1]

In the Detroit election in the fall of 1937 the UAW supported the mayoralty candidacy of Patrick H. O'Brien, who had been attorney general in the Comstock administration, and a labor slate of five UAW officials (Richard Frankensteen, Maurice Sugar, Walter Reuther, R. J. Thomas, and Tracy Doll) for councilmanic posts. The Detroit and Wayne County Federation of Labor (DWCFL), however, refused to support the UAW candidates. Murphy remained aloof from the Detroit primary, but after the UAW slate survived the contest and O'Brien and Richard W. Reading emerged as the two mayoralty candidates, the assumption was that the governor would "get into the race" in support of the liberal candidates.

Murphy was recuperating in White Sulphur Springs from a long bout with illness as the campaign reached its climax. When he returned to Michigan two days before the election, he remarked to newsmen that, although the election was "a local matter" and he did not wish to endorse any candidate, he believed that Frankensteen was an able man who deserved to be rewarded for helping to settle the auto strikes earlier in the year and that Sugar, a long-time Murphy acquaintance, was "good councilmanic material." Associates of the governor declared that he thought the UAW entitled to representation on the Detroit Common Council but not to "majority control" of the body. The UAW failed, however, to gain even a single seat on the council in the November 2 election, and its mayoralty candidate was also defeated.

The UAW, which had hoped for the "positive" support of the governor, was displeased with his "halfhearted" endorsement of Frankensteen and Sugar and his failure in his pre-election statement even to mention O'Brien. Criticizing the governor's behavior as "a betrayal" of the automobile workers and Detroit unionists, Homer Martin reminded Murphy that labor had supported him as a candidate for governor and asked, "What can labor expect if in its hour of need the governor of the state remains silent?" The only explanation that Murphy offered for his essentially neutral stance in the election was the nonpartisan character of Detroit's city government. Although this concern may have influenced the governor, other factors appear to have weighed more heavily. Murphy had scant regard for O'Brien, who had supported George Welsh in the 1936 Democratic primary and was linked in the campaign to the allegedly graft-ridden organization of Duncan McRea, the Wayne County prosecutor. Murphy had close ties with the DWCFL and its president, Frank Martel, and the governor had no desire to take sides in the fratricidal conflict between the AFL and the CIO. Murphy was also undoubtedly influenced by the warning of veteran Detroit newsman Carl Muller, a long-time Murphy enthusiast, that O'Brien was going to lose and that if the governor involved himself in the UAW's behalf in the divisive conflict, he himself would be defeated in 1938.[2]

Murphy's well-publicized role as peacemaker in the General Motors strike and his reputation as "the new type of leader" concerned about the poor and committed to social reform focused national attention on him early in his governorship as a possible Democratic presidential candidate in 1940. Not only did "hard-boiled" Lansing correspondents begin to think along these lines, but the national press also speculated about the possibility. "He has had more effective experience in American politics than any man now on the horizon who might be a candidate for the Democratic nomination in 1940," the *Emporia Gazette* declared of Murphy as the GM strike came to a close. In a Gallup poll of April 1937 in which the respondents expressed their opinion as to the best Democratic candidate in 1940 should Roosevelt decide not to run again, Murphy, who had not even been mentioned in a similar poll in December 1936, trailed only James A. Farley and Governor George H. Earle of Pennsylvania and led all potential candidates in the east northcentral region of the country.[3]

Although Murphy's chances for a presidential nomination were dimmed by the alleged collapse of law and order in Michigan following the GM strike, the governor was viewed as a possible Democratic presidential nominee right up to the state election in 1938. In a conversation with Harry Hopkins in the spring of 1938 President Roosevelt stated his opposition to Murphy as a presidential candidate, but in a memorandum some months later Farley asserted that the president favored Hopkins, Robert H. Jackson, and Murphy, in that order. If Roosevelt did not run in 1940, G. Gould Lincoln commented in the *Washington Star* in October 1938, Murphy appeared "to fill the bill more perfectly than any other." The previous month, however, the press quoted "one of the top members" of Roosevelt's staff as having said, "It's too bad Murphy's a Catholic. If he didn't have that political handicap to carry into the South, that bird would be just about what the boss is seeking for 1940 [—] a real New Dealer in viewpoint with both political experience and political 'it.' "[4]

"You know there's nothing to that," Murphy ritualistically responded in June 1937 when asked about the likelihood of his being the Democratic nominee in 1940. "I don't have any delusions of that sort." Murphy, of course, had long had "delusions of that sort" although he feared that his religion might be an insuperable obstacle to his chances. He tried to advance his possible candidacy by wooing the Young Democrats and by speaking from one end of the country to another. At Murphy's suggestion, Frederic Schouman attended the national convention of the Young Democrats in Indianapolis in August 1937. There, he sounded out "Murphy sentiment for 1940," secured a promise from the organization's new president to guarantee Murphy "a fair amount of time" to speak at the convention of the Young Democrats in 1939, and gained a position for Michigan on the organization's National Executive Board. Schouman was convinced that Murphy would be "the popular favorite of the young and progressive group in the party" in 1940.[5]

As one of the more glamorous figures in American politics and an orator of renown, Murphy was in demand as a speaker. He thus had ample opportunity to articulate his views on politics, industrial relations, and the welfare state before audiences outside his home state. Not only did he speak to such groups as the Knights of Columbus in Boston, the Consumers League in New York, the National Conference of Social Work in Indianapolis, the Democratic Women's Study Clubs of California in Long Beach, and the Women's Industrial League for Peace and Freedom in Washington, D.C., but he also made nationwide radio broadcasts on at least four occasions in 1937 and 1938. Murphy, of course, understood that Roosevelt could not be denied the nomination if he desired it, and he was one of six governors who in September 1937 expressed support for a possible third term.[6]

"... if he wins by a great Majority," Harold Murphy wrote of his brother and the 1938 gubernatorial election, "he will be the next President of the United States." Although Frank would not have stated the matter so categorically, Harold was no doubt echoing something he had heard his brother say regarding the election. The Michigan election was important, however, not only because of what it portended for Murphy's political ambitions; since Murphy was seen as "the one Democratic candidate for governor of a big state who personifie[d] the New Deal point of view" and since it was widely believed that his defeat would be "the deadliest blow" that the New Deal could suffer in that election year, the Michigan contest took on national significance as a "barometer" of popular feeling regarding the New Deal and President Roosevelt. Although Murphy told a newspaperman at the end of 1937 that he had "few fears" regarding the electoral outcome since "Republican statesmanship" had never caused him "any mental exercise," his victory in Republican Michigan was far from a certainty.[7]

Murphy's Republican opponent in the 1938 gubernatorial contest was ex-governor Frank D. Fitzgerald, who defeated Harry S. Toy, former Wayne County prosecutor, Michigan attorney general, and Michigan Supreme Court justice, by a two-to-one margin in the Republican primary. It seemed for a time that Melville B. McPherson would also be a candidate, but after Fitzgerald proclaimed his opposition to the welfare reorganization bills that Murphy had endorsed, McPherson threw his support to the former governor. It was widely believed in Michigan that Fitzgerald's disavowal of the welfare reorganization plan proposed by the commission that he himself had appointed was the result of a "political trade" that removed a potentially strong adversary from the primary race.[8]

There was never any doubt that Murphy would seek reelection, the governor declaring at one point that he would not announce his candidacy officially since "everybody" knew that he was "in the race." Murphy began to plan for the election as early as May 1937, and a campaign committee was by that time already gathering "a modest amount" of money for the contest. Preferring another candidate, some influential Democrats sought to persuade Senator Prentiss Brown to seek the governorship. They agreed, however, at a conference late in 1937 attended by Brown, Michigan's Democratic congressmen, and possibly Murray Van Wagoner and G. Donald Kennedy to back Murphy for reelection. Shortly after this conference, state party chairman Edward J. Fry sent out word that no Democrat in the state government was to use his position for a "personal build up. If Frank Murphy is built up," Fry stated, "that will take care of everything as far as our . . . party is concerned."[9] In the weeks that followed, however, it became evident that the party leadership and party workers were far from united in their support of the governor, largely because of his patronage policy and his commitment to civil service reform.

When Murphy toured the Upper Peninsula in late February in what the *Detroit News* thought might be "the real beginning" of his reelection campaign, spoils-minded party workers were perturbed by the governor's uncompromising support of the merit system. Joseph M. Donnelly, who had arranged the trip and then found it to be "a pain in the neck," informed the governor that rank-and-file Democrats were very "dissatisfied" with him and that some had even refused to sign his petitions. In May 1938 Fry also encountered a good deal of discontent with the Murphy administration when he conferred with the Democratic State Central Committee, county committees, legislators, and other prominent Democrats to test party sentiment in preparation for the fall campaign. At a meeting in Flint attended by representatives from seventeen county committees, party officials reported that Murphy's role in the sit-down strikes had hurt the party and that the welfare referendum was "going to cause trouble [for the Democrats] throughout the State." County committeemen were especially critical of Murphy's support of civil service and his alleged lack of concern for party workers and the party organization. "I say . . . that party organization is what makes the wheels go around," a member of the Genesee County committee declared.[10]

Opposition to Murphy was manifested before the primary not simply in the form of rhetoric but in an abortive Nowicki-for-governor boomlet and a last-minute effort by Van Wagoner supporters to have the highway commissioner enter the race. Detroit Poles who were disaffected with the Murphy administration for one reason or another initiated the circulation of Nowicki-for-Governor petitions in May 1938. Since Nowicki was regarded as a Van Wagoner ally, some suspected that the highway commissioner had instigated the lieutenant governor's candidacy. Van Wagoner, however, announced at the end of May that he was backing Nowicki for the lieutenant governorship, not the governorship. A few weeks later Nowicki, who later claimed that the petitions had been circulated without his approval, declared that, "in the interest of party harmony," he would not challenge Murphy in the primary.[11]

Although Murphy was in the end the sole Democratic candidate in the gubernatorial primary, it appeared on the eve of the July 26 filing deadline that the governor would face the formidable opposition of Murray Van Wagoner. Supporters of the highway commissioner, preferring his brand of organizational politics to the Murphy politics of ideology, met in several cities on July 24 to circulate Van Wagoner petitions, and the chief clerks of the Highway Department gathered in Lansing to await instructions. The Van Wagoner candidacy died aborning, however, when the highway commissioner announced, "There is a movement afoot to enter me in the Democratic primary for governor but we thought it over and I am not going to run." According to the *Detroit Free Press*, Van Wagoner had been dissuaded from running because the politically powerful Fry brothers had informed him that they would support Murphy, Edward Fry declaring that he would oppose any movement to "tear-up our party." The *Detroit News* speculated that Van Wagoner had remained out of the race because he feared that he would be defeated and that this would impair his chances of gaining control of the state Democratic party.[12]

The Detroit press analysis of the Van Wagoner decision, though plausible, ignores the behind-the-scenes role that Washington appears to have played. G. Hall Roosevelt, the president's brother-in-law and a Detroit official when Murphy had been the city's mayor, had become antagonistic to the governor and friendly with Van Wagoner and Kennedy. "Secretly trying to put the skids under Murphy," Hall had attempted to persuade the White House that Van Wagoner could win the governorship but Murphy could not. Hall apparently suggested to the president that Murphy should be offered a federal job, possibly a Supreme Court justiceship, thus paving the way for a Van Wagoner gubernatorial candidacy. The White House appears to have taken some tentative steps to implement this strategy or at least to explore its practicability, but Murphy refused to accept the bait. When Hall wired the president to "advise if the coast" were "clear," the president's secretary replied, "Our Michigan friend would not accept it." It is likely also that Harry Hopkins and Howard Hunter, both Murphy supporters, had advised Van Wagoner that the WPA, which provided funds for Michigan highways, would not look kindly on a Van Wagoner candidacy. In any event, Hunter wrote Hopkins on August 1, almost certainly with regard to a Van Wagoner candidacy, that the individual about whom Hopkins had expressed concern had attempted to interfere but that the Michigan matter had been settled and there would be "no competition."[13]

Hall Roosevelt continued to inject himself into Michigan politics once the primary campaign was underway. He apparently planted a story in the *Detroit Free Press* of September 1 that the president, after conferring with Hall, had decided not to visit Michigan during the campaign to dedicate the Blue Water Bridge because he had decided that Murphy could not win. Having seen administration-backed senatorial candidates go down to defeat in California and South Carolina the previous day, Roosevelt, according to this account, could not afford to suffer a further blow to his prestige by overtly supporting another losing candidate. Murphy sent copies of the *Free Press* article to James Roosevelt, Thomas Corcoran, and Hopkins, telling Hopkins, "You can gather from it what is in store for me in this campaign. The same sort of thing is going out all over the state."

Murphy telephoned Hopkins on the day the *Free Press* article appeared, asking the WPA head to talk the matter over with the president. Murphy attributed Hall's behavior to the fact that he was on the payroll of finance companies "controlled" by the auto manufacturers, who were opposed to both the president and the governor. Hall, Murphy said, "sits in with Comstock and his gang and tells them: 'Well boys it was tough but I finally got FDR talked off Murphy.' Then they hand the story down the line to the rest of the boys." In his press conference the next day the president denounced the "unjustified, absolutely unjustified, assumption" that he had decided not to visit Michigan because of the election campaign. "It is a deliberate distortion of . . . fact," Roosevelt asserted. Would he aid Murphy? the reporters asked. He would do the same for Murphy as for "other liberals," the president replied. "I am in favor of liberals. I am not taking part in party politics in the election," an assertion that hardly squared with the facts. The press story was not true, the president wrote Murphy that night, but, he asked, "what can one do about it?"[14]

Unopposed in the primary, Murphy did almost no formal campaigning before the balloting. He polled but 336,350 votes in the September 11 contest, well below the 627,731 votes garnered by the two major Republican candidates. Striking hard at his Republican opposition, Murphy declared in his address to the Democratic state convention, which met in Grand Rapids on September 30 and October 1, 1938, that the election would decide if the electorate could be "persuaded by expensive propaganda to embrace a sinister political machine that is totally devoid of ideals and has not the slightest interest in making democracy work. . . . It will decide whether that type of government shall return to power or whether a decent government that has placed the people's needs above partisanship, that has devoted itself every day of its existence to the strengthening . . . of democracy, will continue to serve." The delegates renominated all the elected state officers by acclamation and adopted a platform that praised the governor's conduct of the state's business and endorsed his principal reform proposals.[15]

Murphy faced the opposition in the campaign not only of the Republicans but also of the Constitutional Democratic party. Launched on August 17, 1938, the new party was the creation of the Comstock wing of the Democratic party. Its purpose was to "purge" the Democratic party of "rampant New Dealers" like Murphy and to restore control of the party to the "old line Democrats." "We don't like Gov. Murphy, he isn't our kind of Democrat," Comstock declared in an address at the party's organizational meeting. When the party met in convention on September 24, Comstock refused to accept its gubernatorial nomination; the delegates thereupon selected B. F. Stephenson of Detroit, who had been the Michigan supervisor of the National Union for Social Justice and had managed the Lemke campaign in the state and who, it was hoped, might draw Catholic votes from Murphy. Comstock promised to campaign for Stephenson and to raise funds for him, but when the former governor went hunting instead, Stephenson, on October 18, withdrew from the race, and the Constitutional Democrats virtually "folded" as a party. Toward the end of the contest, Comstock did some quiet campaigning in northern Michigan and advised his followers that he preferred Fitzgerald to Murphy. Making his final campaign appearance before a " 'mass' " meeting of the Constitutional Democrats on November 3—a grand total of seventy-eight persons, including eighteen candidates and four members of the band, were present—Comstock claimed that Murphy was a socialist. "I was off the New Deal and Mr. Roosevelt and all that he stands for in 1933," Comstock told his audience, "but I kept my mouth shut until I got out of office." If Murphy were defeated, Comstock asserted, it would be an easy matter for the old-line Democrats to "get the party back" by 1940; if he won, it would be "a tough battle" for them.[16]

There is reason to believe that Comstock concerted strategy with the Fitzgerald camp, the liaison man being the gambler Maurice Brown, "a political confidant and lobbyist" in the first Fitzgerald administration whose Detroit hotel suite served for a time as headquarters for the Constitutional Democrats. Initially, the Fitzgerald forces seem to have favored an independent Constitutional Democratic ticket, but after Stephenson had been nominated, Fitzgerald concluded that the new party's candidate might attract votes that would otherwise go to the Republicans. This probably explains why Comstock abandoned Stephenson and urged his followers to vote for Fitzgerald.[17]

Murphy, we can be certain, was much less concerned about the defection of the Comstock Democrats than he was about the degree to which Van Wagoner and the Highway Department would bestir themselves in behalf of the Murphy candidacy. That the highway commissioner had little enthusiasm for his party's nominee is hardly to be doubted—when Mortimer E. Cooley wrote Van Wagoner after voting in the primary, "I find myself up a tree. I am beginning to wonder whether our Democratic birthright has not become another Jacob-Esau affair," the highway commissioner replied that he found himself "in the same predicament." According to the press, Van Wagoner had demanded as a condition for his support that Murphy endorse in writing the proposed constitutional amendment prohibiting the diversion of gas and weight taxes for nonhighway purposes. The governor, however, announced on October 10 after a conference with Van Wagoner and Kennedy that the Highway Department had assured him of its "full support" and that the amendment had not even been discussed. Although he had initially favored diverting some highway money for relief, Murphy nevertheless endorsed the amendment at the end of the campaign because, he lamely stated, Michigan was "a motor state" and "the popular will" was "behind the proposal."[18]

Despite his assurances of "full support," Van Wagoner remained on the sidelines during most of the campaign. The highway commissioner was "an unknown quantity" to the Murphy campaign leadership, Josephine Gomon recorded in her diary on October 26. "They have no idea what he is doing or has done." Michigan's Democratic national committeeman advised Farley two days later that the Democrats in the state had been "working tooth and nail with the exception of the Highway Department." In the last week of the campaign, however, the key department personnel "promised to pitch in." Van Wagoner campaigned briefly in the Upper Peninsula toward the end of the electoral contest and called together 250 men in his organization and told them "to go down the line" for Murphy and the state ticket. Van Wagoner must have realized that it would not enhance his political prospects and his hopes of becoming "the Democratic spokesman for Michigan" if it appeared that he was openly sabotaging the Democratic ticket. The extent of his support for Murphy, however, was limited at best.[19]

If Murphy failed to gain anything more than the token support of the Van Wagoner wing of the party, he enjoyed the enthusiastic backing of the Young Democrats. The Young Democrats began to organize "Governor Frank Murphy Progressive Young Democratic Clubs" even before the primary, and they joined organized labor in a campaign to register voters in industrial centers. "The great hope and strength of our party," Murphy told the Young Democratic leadership in the state, "is the fact that it appeals to intelligent young people."[20]

As in his previous campaigns, Murphy was the favored candidate of organized labor, blacks, and many white ethnic groups in 1938. Both AFL and CIO unions, however much they disagreed on other matters, were generally agreed on the importance of supporting Murphy. "Defeat for Governor Murphy is a defeat for Labor," the DWCFL's Frank Martel asserted, and the *United Automobile Worker* stressed that it was labor's responsibility to secure Murphy's reelection. When the Michigan CIO held its first state convention in April 1938, Adolph Germer called on all CIO unions to stand behind the governor. The employers "want Murphy out," Germer stated, "so we want Murphy in." Murphy, Germer later declared, was "the greatest Governor that any state ever had." On October 5 the UAW's International Executive Board approved a resolution presented by Walter

Reuther to establish a political action committee that would seek a $25,000 loan from other CIO international unions and would attempt to raise an additional $25,000 in contributions from unions in Michigan to secure the reelection of Murphy and other progressive candidates. Although the UAW did not raise the full $50,000 contemplated in the resolution, the auto union and other CIO unions contributed at least $10,000 to the Democratic campaign.[21]

One CIO affiliate, the Detroit Newspaper Guild, deviated from a policy of nonparticipation in politics observed since its formation in January 1934 by endorsing Murphy as "a great governor—and a great man." The Guild reported that a straw poll among reporters of the three Detroit dailies revealed that 80 percent favored the governor. The reporters, Murphy had earlier stated, knew "the facts" even though the publishers did not.[22]

Inter- and intra-union differences probably prevented labor from mobilizing its full strength in Murphy's behalf. The effort to establish a single statewide campaign committee foundered because of AFL-CIO rivalry, and although Labor's Non-Partisan League officially endorsed Murphy, it was pushed into the background because the AFL saw it as a CIO front and because of allegations that it was Communist-dominated. The UAW had every reason to make a massive effort in Murphy's behalf, but the internecine warfare that was tearing the union apart distracted the leadership and absorbed energies that might otherwise have been devoted to the Murphy campaign. Also, although AFL leaders like Frank Martel gave Murphy unstinting support, some of "the AF of L boys" out-state were "not so cordial to his candidacy." A labor movement friend of the governor complained that some local leaders were "just piddling around and looking out for their own interests," and a Jackson AFL paper criticized both the sit-downs and politicians who had permitted them to continue.[23]

The CIO endorsement of Murphy may have hurt the governor more than it helped him. According to a Gallup poll released on September 7, 1938, 55 percent of the respondents asserted that they would vote against a congressional candidate if the CIO endorsed him, and only 12 percent said that they would favor him for that reason, the remaining respondents being indifferent to an endorsement. Twenty-five percent indicated that they would be disposed to vote against an AFL-endorsed congressional candidate, 22 percent that they would favor such a candidate, and 53 percent that the endorsement would not influence them. The poll, to be sure, was concerned with voter reaction to congressional, not gubernatorial, candidates; still, the Democratic state chairman seems to have preferred that the CIO not endorse Murphy lest this adversely influence "the great middle class and farm vote" that would "decide" the election. Late in the campaign Picard wrote Farley that Murphy and he agreed that "labor was being played up too much" in the contest. "The CIO," Picard observed, "is still offensive to certain people and those are the people we want to get." Picard tried to persuade the "CIO boys . . . to work for him [Murphy] secretly" so that it did not appear that only the CIO favored the governor. "As a matter of fact," Picard reported, "he [Murphy] has organized labor in this state as no man ever had it."[24]

The enthusiastic support for Murphy among rank-and-file auto workers posed a difficult problem for the Socialist party in Michigan, which a prominent Michigan Socialist characterized in August as "the toughest spot in the nation . . . politically" insofar as the party was concerned. The Socialist party had to decide whether to run a gubernatorial candidate of its own and then, when the state Executive Committee decided to do so, whether to permit the Socialist presidents of two important UAW locals, Walter Reuther and Emil Mazey, to support a capitalist candidate. Norman Thomas thought it a mistake for the Socialists to run a candidate for governor. ". . . the result of a gubernatorial race," he wrote, "may be to arouse working class irritation and to create an almost impossible situation in some locals for Socialists who are also very prominent in union affairs." The party should "merely say," he advised, "that since it cannot elect a candidate it will not vigorously oppose a man who is so clearly labor's choice even though it believes that judgment by labor badly mistaken." A majority of the state Executive Committee, however, apparently agreed that to withdraw the Socialist candidate would be "only the beginning of the oppositionist toboggan slide."

Ben Fischer, head of the Socialist caucus in the UAW, recognized that Reuther and Mazey would have to support Murphy "to maintain their positions and their influence." He thought, therefore, that they should be released from party discipline insofar as the gubernatorial election was concerned. Even though the Socialists had their own candidate, Fischer did not believe that the party was "obliged when running a candidate to insist on suicide for key people in the labor movement." Other Socialists, however, "shouted betrayal" and threatened to resign from the party if Reuther and Mazey were permitted to support Murphy. "If we make it kosher for Party members who happen to be big shots to fight the Party, then we have no party," one member asserted. In the end, the party permitted

Socialists who because of their union ties believed it necessary to endorse Murphy to resign from the party. Those who did not resign, however, escaped censure. Walter Reuther was among those who submitted a resignation, but the party leadership persuaded him to withdraw it. Socialists who remained loyal to the party evinced scant enthusiasm for its gubernatorial candidate, and he received the smallest share of the vote of any Socialist party candidate for governor in Michigan up to that time.[25]

Historians who contend that it was an anti-socialist trade union leadership in the United States that persuaded a passive and malleable rank and file to regard socialism as antithetical to trade union principles[26] would do well to examine the 1938 gubernatorial election in Michigan and the manner in which a pro–New Deal, pro-Murphy rank and file induced Socialist union leaders to support a nonsocialist candidate in preference to their party's candidate. What Fischer said of Reuther's West Side Local was true of socialism in Michigan as a whole. "The Murphy question," Fischer observed, "put a damper on whatever desire there was to build the [Socialist] party."[27] The dilemma faced by Michigan Socialists in the 1938 Michigan election is another example of the manner in which the New Deal virtually destroyed the Socialist party.

"It is the duty of every Negro to vote and work for his [Murphy's] re-election," a Michigan black newspaper asserted. The Murphy administration, black leaders claimed, had provided blacks with "more jobs and benefits" than any administration in the state's history. Blacks were admonished that they would be "traitors" to their race if they failed to support the governor. Like the blacks, numerous white ethnic groups, many of them identifying with the governor as a fellow Catholic, displayed their usual enthusiasm for Murphy. The long-time chairman of the Democratic party's Speakers' Bureau in Wayne County concluded that no Democratic candidate had ever been in so much demand to speak to ethnic groups as Murphy was in the 1938 campaign. This, Lewis Millman informed Murphy, was not because of "curiosity"; it was rather "an expression of the loyalty and love and affection of the people whose ancestors were oppressed in other countries and who look upon you as the Champion of Human Liberty."[28]

Jewish businessmen, professional persons, and workingmen organized "the Jewish Committee of One Thousand for the re-election of Governor Frank Murphy." Jews supported Murphy, a prominent Detroit Jewish attorney declared, not out of concern for Jewish matters but because Murphy's life was "one continuous battle for decency and honesty in dealing with ALL men.'' Rabbi Stephen Wise invited Murphy, who had expressed sympathy for the Jewish position regarding Palestine, to speak at an American Jewish Congress rally that was to be held in New York on October 30 or 31, at the height of the Michigan campaign, to protest a threatened British restriction of Jewish immigration to Palestine. ''I shall see to it,'' Wise wrote the governor, ''that the Lord make up for your absence from Michigan by giving you an extra twenty to forty thousand majority. You can safely leave it to us.'' Murphy, of course, was unable to accept the invitation, and the Lord in the end did not provide him with the extra votes that he needed for victory.[29]

Murphy thought that he would have ''a good chance to win'' if President Roosevelt visited Michigan during the campaign. If the president entered Michigan, Picard wrote Roosevelt, the press would say that he was interfering with the '' 'sovereign power' '' of a state, and if he remained away, the press would contend that he was ''at odds'' with Murphy. ''But we in Michigan have thought it all over,'' Picard concluded, ''and really would prefer that you interfere with our 'sovereign power.' '' Roosevelt replied that although it was ''entirely proper'' for him to express a preference as between candidates in a Democratic primary, which is precisely what he had said he could not do during the 1936 Michigan gubernatorial primary, he did not believe that, ''as President,'' he ''should take part in the November elections.'' It would be ''a mistake,'' he said, for him to appeal for the election of Democrats as Wilson had done in 1918—there were some Democrats, he noted, whom he could ''not honorably ... support''—but he did think that, without mentioning names, he could ask Michigan voters ''to choose between Liberals and Conservatives.'' Since the state's voters had ''ordinary human intelligence,'' they would know what that meant.[30]

Just why Roosevelt decided against visiting Michigan to aid Murphy, whose election he desired, is unclear. He may have been reacting to his failure to ''purge'' anti–New Deal Democrats in the 1938 Democratic primaries. Perhaps, as columnist Doris Fleeson thought, Democratic factionalism in Michigan was a factor. Possibly, the president thought that if he visited Michigan he would have to visit Pennsylvania, where there were charges of corruption in the Democratic party, and Wisconsin, where he did not wish to support the Democratic senatorial candidate opposing Robert La Follette, Jr. Roosevelt did seek to aid Murphy by sending him a letter on the occasion of the dedication of the Blue Water Bridge on October 5 that expressed the president's ''very real appreciation of the public service'' the governor had "rendered in a time when so many grave problems demand[ed] in their solution the best there is of leadership and statesmanship.'' In a nationwide broadcast just before the balloting, the president, going somewhat beyond his promise to Picard, called on voters to support candidates "known for their experience and their liberalism,'' mentioning only Murphy by name among candidates outside the state of New York.[31]

Some Michigan Democrats thought that, if the president did not visit Michigan, he could nevertheless dramatically aid Murphy's cause by approving PWA funding for a bridge across the Straits of Mackinac that would link the state's two peninsulas. If "the big fellow" were to make the Straits bridge "a Michigan Boulder Dam,'' Detroit's assistant corporation counsel, John W. Atkinson, wrote Murphy, the Democratic ticket would win out-state Michigan "hands-down.'' "This is the great chance and means a clean-up,'' Atkinson advised the president. Roosevelt indicated that he was "deeply interested" in the project and thought it "wholly feasible,'' and Farley "went across the board'' for the idea. The PWA, however, advised the president on October 14 that Michigan's application for funds had been disapproved for financial and other reasons.[32] The Straits bridge was eventually constructed but much too late to have any effect on Michigan's 1938 gubernatorial election.

Although the president did not visit Michigan, two members of his cabinet came to the state to lend support to the governor. Harold Ickes, in a speech to the Democratic state convention that was "just about fifty per cent Tom Corcoran and fifty per cent Harold Ickes,'' praised Murphy as "an aggressive and able cooperator with the Federal Government in the upbuilding of his State.'' Ickes pointedly remarked that, as a member of the cabinet, he wished to give "public challenge'' to the allegation that Roosevelt favored anyone but Murphy for the governorship. "There is no man running anywhere in the Nation at this time,'' Ickes wrote Murphy as the campaign neared its end, "in whose success I have greater interest than yours.''[33]

Advising Roosevelt that Murphy could win the election if he could get "an even break from the farmers,'' Picard urged that Secretary of Agriculture Henry Wallace or Senator George W. Norris visit Michigan in the governor's behalf. The administration responded by dispatching Wallace to Michigan, where he reminded the state's farmers how much the New Deal had done to improve their lot and praised Murphy as "a level-headed liberal and a progressive with common sense.'' Wallace, however, failed to alter prevailing attitudes among Michigan farmers concerning the New Deal's agricultural program.

He concluded after his visit that Michigan farmers were among the Department of Agriculture's most determined foes and that there was "perhaps a more complete misunderstanding of the [1938] farm act [in Lenawee County] . . . than anywhere in the Middle West."[34]

It is next to impossible to ascertain how much money the Democrats raised in the 1938 gubernatorial campaign. The Democratic State Central Committee reported receipts of $18,336, the Murphy-for-Governor Committee, $30,000 (including $200 from Charles Chaplin), the Wayne County Democratic Committee, $21,458, and the Wayne Political League, $22,000. These figures, however, understate the amount of money the Democrats received for the campaign. Both Harry Mead and Lee Pressman, for example, recalled that John L. Lewis made a very substantial contribution to the Murphy campaign, but no such contribution is listed in the filed statements of campaign receipts. Also, the Murphy Papers reveal that contributions of at least $4,145 went unreported, most likely because of sloppy bookkeeping.[35]

Democrats complained of lack of funds from the beginning of the campaign to its end. Murphy told a reporter that he could have received $250,000 for the campaign if he had made "just one statement of five words," namely, " 'Gambling is a local problem.' " However, the governor stated, "there isn't anybody who can give this government one penny, with my knowledge, and expect privileges or favors." Noting that his campaign receipts would be "very limited" because he refused to accept contributions from those doing business with the state or from illicit businesses, Murphy solicited the Democratic National Committee for "some modest help." According to the statement filed by the State Central Committee, the National Committee contributed $1,143, and Joseph E. Davies offered to help meet any deficit incurred in the campaign.[36]

The thorniest issue involving Democratic campaign finances is the extent to which state employees may have been coerced into contributing. When Picard informed Murphy early in September that state employees had formed a "Murphy for Governor Club" and would collect funds for the campaign, Murphy protested that it was a "mistake" to have established such a club and that he opposed the idea. Picard, however, disagreed, pointing out to the governor that, since state employees feared the consequences for civil service if Murphy were defeated, a Murphy club was in their best interests. They should, he thought, have the right "to show their belief actively." Murphy's opposition seems to have brought an end to the club, but it did not still Republican allegations that civil service employees were being "gouged" into contributing to the campaign in violation of the civil service law.[37]

Murphy's position regarding campaign contributions by state employees was unequivocal. "The practice just isn't right," he stated, "and I want it ended." It was an open secret, however, that certain state executives wanted their employees to contribute 1-5 percent of their salaries during the campaign. The state Republican chairman forwarded to the attorney general a letter signed by the chairman of the Ingham County Democratic Committee that solicited contributions from state employees on the basis of their salaries, telling them, "You may be assured that those vitally interested in Democratic success will know of the aid you have rendered." At least one state employee, also, acknowledged that he had urged fellow workers to contribute. None of this, however, necessarily violated the Civil Service Act. Nothing in the statute barred solicitation by party officials as distinguished from state employees, state officials could solicit funds as long as they did not do so during working hours, and state employees were free to contribute to political funds as long as they did so voluntarily.

Just before the election there were fanciful press reports that the Democrats had amassed a fund of $250,000 from state employees. Murphy, by contrast, claimed after the election that the total was no more than $6,000 and that the money had been contributed voluntarily. Responding to Republican requests, the Civil Service Commission initiated an investigation at the end of November to ascertain if state employees had been "forced" to contribute to the Democratic campaign, but the commission received only one specific allegation of a coerced contribution, and that came in the form of an anonymous letter. In February 1939 the majority members of a joint committee that the Republican legislature had established the previous month to investigate the operation of the civil service law reported that the Democrats had been guilty of wholesale violations of the statute in the campaign. The majority alleged that employees had been "coerced, bludgeoned and cajoled" into contributing to "flower funds," money had been collected for the campaign during working hours, campaign literature had been prepared at the taxpayers' expense, state employees had been assigned to Democratic campaign headquarters while on the state payroll, and state-owned automobiles had been used to distribute campaign literature.

It is difficult to place much credence in the majority report because of its rushed, biased, and obviously partisan character. The committee only heard witnesses hostile to the Civil Service Act and the

Murphy administration and refused to accept testimony from the Civil Service Department and the Michigan Merit System Association. Despite the one-sided character of the report, however, and despite the difficulty of proving whether a particular contribution was coerced or voluntary, we can be certain that some state employees contributed because they feared not to do so and that the sum they contributed was more than the $6,000 Murphy had claimed but far less than $250,000. There is, on the other hand, no substantial evidence to support Republican allegations that the administration pressured WPA workers to contribute to the campaign, although the Democrats did send a letter urging them to vote.[38]

In his addresses, nearly always delivered to large and enthusiastic audiences, Murphy consistently presented the issues in the campaign as "decency in government" versus "corruption and graft" and liberalism versus reaction. McKay and his cohorts, he charged, were "already booted and spurred, to ride into Lansing and raid the state." He contended that it was "nonsense" to say that because he was friendly to the worker he was unfriendly to business. "I have consistently held to the view," he stated, "that a square deal for the worker is the surest and most certain way to safeguard the interest of all." Defending the state budget deficit, Murphy asserted that his administration had "deliberately put off balancing the budget so that the poor and the jobless and the old folks could eat, have clothes on their backs, and a roof over their heads." It was time to recognize, he declared, that "governmental responsibility for the needy" was "here to stay" and would not be "sabotaged by politicians obsessed with the 'let em starve' attitude." His administration, he insisted, had sought "the right balance between dollars and humanity."[39]

The Republican old guard tightly controlled the state Republican convention, which was held in Grand Rapids on October 3, and the Young Republicans were "battered down" when they attempted to gain recognition. Fitzgerald handpicked the state Republican ticket, of whom only the candidate for auditor general was popular with the delegates. A Grand Rapids delegate who was making a seconding speech committed the oratorical blunder of the convention when he declared, "let's all go down the line and do as we are told to do." The Republican platform, which the delegates approved unread, alleged that the Murphy administration had dissipated a budget surplus left it by the Fitzgerald administration—this conveniently ignored the deficiency appropriation the 1937 legislature had been required to approve—and boosted payrolls by $9 million to "support the greatest spoils system in Michigan history." Murphy was also condemned for his strike policy, which, it was said, had led to "riot and lawlessness," for appointing "persons of known communistic tendencies and leanings" to state office, and for weakening the state's educational system.[40]

The Republican campaign did not lack for funds, although it is as difficult to know how much money the Republicans raised as it is to ascertain the size of the Democratic campaign chest. Quite apart from what the Republican State Central Committee may have raised, three separate committees filed reports in Wayne County revealing receipts totaling $67,396, but this was almost certainly just the tip of the iceberg. As early as June 1938 the press reported rumors that organized gamblers, who had been closed down by the Murphy administration, were gathering a huge "slush fund" to defeat Murphy and Attorney General Starr. A newsman who was close to the scene at the time later reported that he had no doubt that, as the Democrats suspected during the campaign, gambling money played a part in defeating Murphy, the funds coming from both "the big time gambling operators" and those seeking the legalization of slot machines. When Maurice Brown, the gambler through whom the slot machine money seems to have been funneled, told the *Detroit News* after the election about his close connection with the Fitzgerald camp, the *News* prepared a story to that effect but decided to secure Fitzgerald's comments about the matter before publishing the story. Before the governor could see the piece, however, he became ill and died. The *News* then decided not to publish the story.[41]

The Republicans did not have to depend on gamblers to secure money for their campaign. Potential contributors were no doubt impressed with Republican arguments that the continuation of "the New Deal administration in Lansing" meant higher valuations for railroad and mining property and higher taxes for all. Employers were probably motivated to contribute by the fear, as one Ohio businessman put it, that if Murphy were reelected, the state would be turned over "lock, stock and barrel" to "dictator" John L. Lewis and the Communist party, industry would be driven from Michigan, and the state would lie "prostrate under the heel of the C.I.O."[42]

Republicans enjoyed the almost unanimous support of the press during the campaign. A study by Edward Magdol and Robert Perlman of five daily and 376 weekly newspapers outside Detroit revealed that the Republicanism of the press was not only a matter of editorial policy: the news columns of the 381 papers, the two authors found, contained "a prevalence of propaganda devices aimed at influencing the reading voter to vote Republican.'' The *Detroit Free Press* was an especially important asset to the Republicans. It was "practically a bible to a good many of the people in the smaller communities and on the farms in the lower peninsula," one of Farley's Michigan correspondents reported, and the *Free Press*, the correspondent noted, "would stop at nothing to beat Murphy." The Michigan press would have been overwhelmingly Republican in any event, but its reaction to the labor upheaval of 1937 in Michigan and its animosity toward "anything that could be labeled as a part of the New Deal" substantially heightened its partisan ardor.[43]

As the party platform forecast, the essence of the Republican campaign strategy was to stress the alleged misdeeds of the Murphy administration and the Lansing New Deal. Since the Republican leadership sensed that there was no "crusading enthusiasm" for the Republican ticket,[44] this was undoubtedly the wisest strategy for the Fitzgerald forces to employ. Murphy's role in the sit-down strikes and his alleged ties to Communists came to dominate the Republican attack, but government spending and administration actions that were believed to have antagonized one interest group or another received their share of attention. Fitzgerald also sought to exploit differences within the Democratic party.

"The whole objective of our present type of government," Fitzgerald declared with reference to the Lansing and Washington New Deals, "is to spend, and spend, and spend, in an effort to prove that all blessings must flow from governmental coffers and that therefore that government should be kept in power." To reelect Murphy, the Republicans alleged, would be to approve "profligate extravagance and waste in state government such as this state has never witnessed before." If elected, Fitzgerald promised, he would slash state payrolls by $8.5 million in sixty days. His allegations about excessive spending by the Murphy administration did not prevent Fitzgerald from promising more state aid to schools than they had received during the Murphy governorship, criticizing Murphy for temporarily reducing assistance to the aged, and promising more generous relief than the Democrats had provided.[45]

Making a special appeal to old folks, Fitzgerald promised if elected to ensure that money intended for the aged would be spent for the aged and not to build up a political machine, as the Murphy administration allegedly had done. A district supervisor of the Old Age Assistance Bureau who had lost his position because he failed a qualifying examination sent a letter to persons receiving old-age assistance warning that, if Murphy remained in office, he would use funds set aside for them for other purposes, thus forcing them onto the welfare rolls. Since Fitzgerald, who had stated, "I like the Townsend plan," promised, if elected, to recommend that the legislature memorialize Congress in the plan's behalf, the Townsend organization in Michigan endorsed him as "a friend of our movement."[46]

Just as he sought to appeal to public-school teachers, the aged, and reliefers by promising them more than they had received from the Murphy administration, so Fitzgerald let the opponents of welfare reorganization know that he was on their side, and he exploited the fears of doctors concerning Murphy's health plans. Attacking the links Murphy had forged with the national government, Fitzgerald contended that Michigan was "no longer a sovereign state." Since the Republicans believed the New Deal was unpopular in Michigan, they claimed that what was at stake in the election had "originate[d] almost entirely with New Deal heads in Washington." Whereas Democratic regulars charged that Murphy's rigorous enforcement of the Civil Service Act was harming their party, Fitzgerald portrayed Murphy as simply "a tender-toned figurehead in the foreground" while "a machine more dangerous than Tammany at its worst operated in the background."[47]

Fitzgerald, not unexpectedly, sought to capitalize on divisions within Democratic ranks by avoiding criticism of Van Wagoner and by noting that the election was not a contest between the two parties since "many Democrats of Jeffersonian constitutional ancestry" had "mingled their strength" with Republican strength. At a meeting of the Eastern Michigan Tourist Association on October 13 Fitzgerald predicted a Nowicki victory in the contest for lieutenant governor. This apparent effort to woo dissident Polish and other Democratic voters who preferred Nowicki to Murphy infuriated the Republican candidate for lieutenant governor, the venerable Luren D. Dickinson, an important figure in the Republican party who had served as lieutenant governor from 1915 to 1920 and again from 1927 to 1932 and who as a prominent dry and Methodist enjoyed a good deal of support in rural areas. Before Dickinson could issue a statement that he had prepared attacking Fitzgerald, the Republican leadership effected a reconciliation between the two candidates, and Fitzgerald both over the radio and in a letter to Dickinson stated that he had only been joking. According to a leader of the Young Democrats, however, Fitzgerald, although angling for the Polish vote and attempting to "escape the odium of being allied to the dry vote," had made the Nowicki remark because he was "so drunk" at the time that "he was unable to read the prepared script of his speech and had to go into an extemporaneous talk."[48]

Despite his criticisms of the Lansing and Washington New Deals,

Fitzgerald actually embraced a good deal of the Murphy program before the campaign came to an end. He asserted that he favored rural electrification, the hospital building program, a generous relief program, medical care for the needy, and rigorous enforcement of the Civil Service Act. He claimed credit, with questionable accuracy, for the state's unemployment insurance and occupational disease statutes. In an effort to win the election, Murphy charged, Fitzgerald had embraced a program "as far removed from his reactionary philosophy as the sun is from the moon."[49]

The "principal battleground of the gubernatorial campaign," as one newspaper commented, was Murphy's role during the sit-down strikes.[50] In view of what had occurred in Michigan in 1937, the strikes would have been an issue of major importance under any circumstances. They acquired a special salience because they came to be associated with the specter of communism and because of hearings conducted at the height of the campaign by the Special House Committee on Un-American Activities, the so-called Dies Committee.

Speaking over a Detroit radio station on September 29, Clarence Hathaway, the editor of the *Daily Worker*, declared that "all progressive people must rally behind Governor Murphy." Although Murphy was "a defender of capitalism," it was essential, Hathaway stated, to defeat Ford, General Motors, and "their candidate, Fitzgerald," and by so doing to "block the road to facism and war." Two days later the Michigan State Committee of the Communist party announced support for Murphy, noting his "progressive, pro-labor record." Although Germer wondered whether the Communists were backing Murphy to ensure his defeat, the endorsement was entirely consistent with the Popular Front strategy the party was then pursuing. Just as the party accommodated itself to the New Deal at the national level, so it contended that it was essential to keep Michigan "a liberal, New Deal state."[51]

The Republicans, not surprisingly, promptly seized on the Communist endorsement of Murphy. "The red radicals are out in the open" supporting Murphy, Fitzgerald declared. "I glory in the fact that communists oppose me just as actively as they favor him." The link between Murphy and communism became a staple of the Republican campaign, the effectiveness of the tactic almost certainly being enhanced by Murphy's tardiness in repudiating Communist support. The most vicious propaganda piece used against Murphy as part of the campaign to tar him with the Communist brush was a pamphlet entitled *Communists Back Murphy in Fight to Turn Michigan Over to Reds*. By his "consenting silence," the pamphlet charged, Murphy demonstrated "a willingness to 'go forward' with Communist Hathaway and his Communist comrades." The Communists, the document alleged, had selected Murphy "to help the Soviet government . . . gain a foothold on American soil, because his philosophy of government . . . [offered] the result which Communism seeks." According to the pamphlet, "the first battle" to secure Soviet "domination" of America was being fought in Michigan "by Soviet agents, under immediate orders from Moscow."[52]

The issue of communism in the campaign became inextricably linked with the sit-down strikes when Chester Howe, an investigator for the Dies Committee, which was about to hold hearings on the strikes, stated in Detroit on October 11 that they had been instigated by Communist "agitators." The hearings were initiated in Washington a week later after Martin Dies had rejected the request of two committee members to delay the probe until after the elections. A parade of witnesses, not a single one friendly to Murphy, testified that the Communists had "engineered" the sit-downs in Michigan, linked UAW officials prominent in the strike to Communists in one way or another, and "effectively smeared" Murphy. Judge Paul Gadola claimed that Murphy had prevented Sheriff Thomas Wolcott from enforcing the injunction that Gadola had issued during the strike and that "civil authority had completely broken down" in Flint. Former Flint city manager, John Barringer, denounced Murphy's "treasonable action" in not coming to Flint's assistance when it needed help to preserve law and order. Fred Frahm, superintendent of the Detroit police, gave the committee an inaccurate account of the Frank and Seder strike that placed Murphy in a bad light and testified that the state government "never gave us [the Detroit Police Department] any assistance at all" in dealing with the Detroit sit-downs. Several witnesses testified about the Lansing Labor Holiday, leaving the impression that Murphy had failed to act to preserve law and order and quoting the governor as saying that the demonstration had been "conceived and engineered by the Communists." One witness later claimed that committee members had attempted to put words in his mouth to the effect that Murphy was a Communist.[53]

Having proclaimed at their state convention that the Communists had planned the sit-down strikes and that Murphy was their "benign godfather," the Republicans could now point to the Dies hearings as providing hard evidence for these allegations. They reminded voters that the Communists had endorsed Murphy and contended that Murphy's reelection meant approving the "illegal sit-down strikes" and his "sympathetic attitude toward known communistic labor racketeers." Murphy could have ended the sit-downs with "a nod of his head," Fitzgerald claimed. He promised to "use all the means" available "under the law" to halt such strikes should he be elected governor.[54]

Murphy responded more promptly to Republican criticism of his role during the sit-down strikes and to the inaccurate and misleading testimony before the Dies Committee than to the Communist support of his candidacy. It was "regrettable," he asserted, that the strikes had "become the subject of political manipulation by people whose scruples did not prevent them from dealing lightly with the truth for the sake of votes." He noted that he had "inherited" the sit-downs from his predecessors and rejected the "superficial" view that the strikes were "the work of a few radicals" rather than "a spontaneous expression of feeling by a large body of workers." He defended his conduct in the strikes in much the same manner as he had during and just after the great labor uprising in the state in 1937, taking credit for the fact that Michigan had "passed through the most terrifying industrial crisis in history without a life being lost and with its liberties intact."

Murphy contradicted the testimony before the Dies Committee that had been critical of him and denounced the committee's spread of "untruths" as "un-American and vicious." "It is, of course, just a coincidence that they go into these matters when we are in the midst of a political campaign," the governor stated. "There is no purpose and design in this—not much." Dies, the governor lashed out, was "running errands for the same vested interests" that were "determined to block every progressive measure advanced by the New Deal." One of those "errands," he insisted, was to secure the election of Fitzgerald, the friend of the utilities and the "willing servant of the advocates of force and violence in industrial relations."[55]

On October 23 Murphy prepared a letter to Dies asking to be heard by the committee immediately because of "inaccurate and misleading testimony" by Gadola and others. When the governor, however, informed the White House of his proposed action, he was told that the president himself would respond to Dies. In a statement released on October 25 that some constitutional historians regarded as an unprecedented presidential attack on a congressional committee, Roosevelt asserted that he was "disturbed, not because of the absurdly false charges made by a coterie of disgruntled Republican officeholders [Gadola and Barringer] against a profoundly religious, able and law-abiding Governor, but because a Congressional committee charged with the responsibility of investigating un-American activities should have permitted itself to be used in a flagrantly unfair and un-American attempt to influence an election." The president praised Murphy's handling of the sit-down strikes as "a great achievement of a great American." In the view of the *Detroit News*, Roosevelt's statement, allegedly "the strongest boost" he had accorded "a local candidate" since becoming president, made the Michigan gubernatorial election "the most important in the country as a symbol of New Deal success or failure."[56]

Responding to Roosevelt's thrust, Representative Dies contended that the president had been "wholly misinformed" and that testimony before the Un-American Activities Committee had demonstrated that "well-known Communists instigated and engineered the sit-down strike and the so-called Lansing holiday." Dies said regarding the latter that although felonies and misdemeanors had been committed "on that disgraceful day" under Murphy's very eyes, the governor had done nothing in response. It was his duty, Dies asserted, "to conduct a fearless investigation, regardless of political expediency," and it would be wrong for him to shield Murphy simply because he was a Democrat and the president's friend. Fitzgerald protested that the president was "attempting to select a Governor of Michigan," and eighty residents of Flint and Genesee County, after meeting in Gadola's courtroom, wired Roosevelt to condemn "any interference whatsoever, for political purposes, with the enforcement of law and order in our city, county and state." There was, on the other hand, a good deal of criticism of the behavior of the Dies Committee, including a magazine article by Paul Y. Anderson entitled "The Loaded Dies Committee" that assailed the "dirty political job" perpetrated on Murphy as both "crude" and "cowardly."[57]

Democratic leaders in Michigan were convinced that the one-sided testimony before the Dies Committee, which reopened an "old sore," was a severe blow to the Murphy campaign. "The impression" was "slowly" developing, Picard wrote Farley, that Murphy's re-election meant more sit-downs and that this would threaten the prosperity that was returning to the state. The Murphy for Governor Committee supplied the Civil Rights Federation of Michigan with $2,500 to defray the expenses of distributing sixty-five thousand copies of a leaflet alleging that the Dies Committee was using spies and strikebreakers to prove that the sit-down strikes were the product of a Red plot and announcing a mass meeting to protest committee behavior.[58]

Why Murphy hesitated so long to repudiate the Communist endorsement of his candidacy when those around him were convinced that it was inflicting grave wounds on his chances for victory remains a mystery. Earl Browder later claimed that Murphy "gladly" accepted Communist party support and held "many intimate conferences with Communists about how to conduct his campaign," but there is no independent corroboration of this assertion. Its timing, just after the Murphy-led Department of Justice had secured Browder's indictment for passport fraud, suggests that revenge may have been the motive for the Communist leader's assertion. What Murphy apparently told his associates was that, since he believed in "every man's inalienable right to express himself," he did not wish to offend "those few sincere, if misguided individuals, who . . . joined the Communist party solely in the hope of bettering their condition."⁵⁹ Although it is easy enough to imagine Murphy saying these things, it is difficult to believe that arguments of this sort fully explain his behavior.

Murphy's initial response to Republican use of the Communist support for his candidacy was to denounce the tactic as "the lowest possible level in shabby politics" and to deny that he was a Communist—"I am just a hundred per cent American and nothing else." He deplored Red-baiting as "a short-sighted and futile technic that only fans the flames of intolerance and prejudice," asserting that the allegation of radicalism was always directed at those "who want to fight the people's fight for social and economic justice." Those who accused public figures like himself and Roosevelt of being Communists, he charged, actually helped to prepare the ground for communism because they convinced uninformed persons that those who were interested in their welfare were Reds. Murphy recalled that in the 1936 campaign the Republicans had used "Keep Tammany out of Michigan" signs in an effort to make an issue of his religion whereas now he was being charged with being a Communist despite his Catholic faith. "They will stop at nothing," he declared.⁶⁰

Murphy was especially concerned about the reaction of the Catholic church and Catholic voters to the charge that he was a Communist sympathizer. He discussed the matter with Detroit's Archbishop Edward Mooney and, although unable to persuade the prelate to repudiate the allegation, arranged to have a Murphy address before the National Conference of Catholic Charities reprinted in the *Michigan Catholic*. Murphy also asked his friend, the lawyer and prominent Catholic layman Arthur D. Maguire, to consult with George Murphy and Tom Chawke about "means to offset the obscure and vicious Red propaganda." Maguire had already counseled Murphy against "too much delay" in responding to the Hathaway speech since to be blessed by a Communist, Maguire thought, was "nothing better than a political curse as far as Catholics are concerned." He reported back that everyone to whom he had spoken believed that the governor must make "a strong statement" about the Communist endorsement. ". . . your whole future is at stake" in the election, Maguire reminded Murphy. Maguire also wrote to Roosevelt to stress the importance of "a vigorous repudiation" by Murphy. When the president's secretary informed Murphy about the Maguire letter, the governor replied that he would take "appropriate action on the unfavorable endorsement."[61]

Speaking at a Communist rally in Detroit on November 1, William Z. Foster, the party chairman, and Earl Reno, the executive secretary, denied that the party had endorsed Murphy since it endorsed only Communist candidates but nevertheless left no doubt that their party favored Murphy's election. "Why don't they keep out of here, at least during the campaign," Germer wrote in his diary. "It's the same old meddling C.P." The chairman of the Republican State Central Committee publicly challenged Murphy to repudiate the Communist "endorsement," and the next night, in a statewide radio address, the governor reluctantly accepted the challenge. It was his policy, he stated, "to be tolerant of all political groups" and to permit them to "voice their views and grievances." If a Communist group had endorsed him, it had been done without his "knowledge, solicitation, or approval." The principles of the Communist party regarding religion, property rights, and political rights were "wholly at variance" with his principles, he said, and so anyone voting for him on the assumption that he had anything in common with the party was mistaken. He could not, of course, help it if some radicals endorsed him; after all, some Republicans also favored him. As for the sit-down strikes, the problem he faced was "not to find out who started the fire but to put it out with as little delay and as little damage as possible." If the Communists were responsible, he asserted, this was not known to him. The *Michigan Catholic* accorded due notice to Murphy's November 2 speech.[62]

Breaking political precedent in Michigan, Fitzgerald and Murphy campaigned up to election eve. "This is a test state," Fitzgerald declared in his last campaign statement. "Here the theories and ideas of our current administration have been given full play. No other state in the Union has been so severely affected [as a result] as Michigan." In a final radio appeal, Murphy stated that wherever he had traveled in the campaign, he had found "an amazing new interest in government" because the people knew it was "*their* government." "Running an honest government and making an earnest effort to give justice to the man who works for a wage is much more [important] than being elected," Murphy wrote Maurice Sugar on election day. "Perhaps now we will see if that sort of thing can be done with the support of a majority of the people."[63]

The verdict rendered on November 8 was that "that sort of thing" did not command the support of the majority of the electorate in Michigan in the year 1938, Fitzgerald defeating Murphy by a vote of 847,245 (52.8 percent of the total vote) to 753,752 (47 percent of the total vote). Whereas Murphy had captured twenty-two of the state's eighty-three counties in 1936, he carried only fourteen counties in 1938, defeating his opponent in five of the six depressed mineral counties and five of the nine depressed forest counties of the Upper Peninsula, three of the eight urban counties, and one of the thirty Lower Peninsula forest counties and losing all of the eighteen farm counties and all of the nine farm-urban counties. Murphy's percentage of the vote fell in seventy-six of the eighty-three counties compared to 1936, the most severe decline occurring in the farm counties, where his percentage of the vote ranged from only 18.4 to 37.3 in 1938 compared to a range of 22.6 to 46.6 in 1936, and in the farm-urban counties, where his percentage of the vote ranged from 28.7 to 48 in 1938 compared to 36.6 to 52.1 in 1936.[64]

In the forty cities of the state with populations of more than ten thousand, Murphy captured 54 percent of the vote in 1938 compared to 56.8 percent in 1936. In 1936 Murphy's margin of victory in the cities had been sufficient to overcome the rural vote for Fitzgerald; in 1938 reduced Democratic majorities in the cities coupled with an even greater decline in the Democratic vote in the countryside spelled defeat for Murphy and his party. In this sense, the pattern of the vote in Michigan was very similar to the pattern in Pennsylvania, where the Democrats also lost the governorship in 1938.[65]

Murphy's vote fell sharply in three cities that had experienced major labor disturbances during his administration: Flint, Lansing, and Monroe. The governor's percentage of the two-party vote declined from 62 to 51 in Flint, 54 to 48 in Lansing, and 51 to 43 in Monroe. Murphy's small majority in Flint in 1938 was wiped out in the small towns and rural areas of Genesee County, and his percentage of the vote in the remainder of Ingham and Monroe counties declined as compared to 1936 even more than it had in the cities of Lansing and Monroe.[66]

Murphy made his most impressive showing in Detroit, where his percentage of the vote only declined from 60 percent in 1936 to 59.1 percent (Murphy's Wayne County vote declined from 59.9 percent to

58.1 percent). Murphy won his Detroit majority among the blacks, the foreign born, and lower-income voters who made up the bulk of the New Deal coalition in the north. His percentage of the black vote increased from 63.5 in 1936 to 67.9, his percentage of the foreign-born vote from 72.8 to 73.9, and his percentage of the lower-income vote only declined from 66.6 to 66.2. On the other hand, his share of the native-born white vote fell from 46.3 in 1936 to 43.5, his share of the middle-income vote from 52.9 to 50.1, and his share of the upper-income vote from 44.6 to 37.9. The polarization of voters by income, ethnic origin, and race that was one of the political consequences of the New Deal was starkly revealed in the contest in Detroit.[67]

The Republicans not only captured the governorship in the election but also won all the statewide offices being contested (Van Wagoner was the only surviving Democrat on the Administrative Board), gained control of the legislature by a margin of 74–26 in the House and 24–8 in the Senate, and took three congressional seats from the Democrats. Among the Democrats contesting state offices, only Case ran ahead of Murphy, and narrowly so.[68]

The fact that 1938 was an off year in the American electoral cycle is a major explanation for Murphy's defeat. As compared to the "high-stimulus" presidential elections, off-year elections tend to be "low-stimulus" contests that are likely to follow party lines; they disadvantage the party that benefited in its vote in the preceding high-stimulus election and favor members of the party that lost the preceding election as compared to incumbents of the president's party. This is because there is a decline in the off-year in the number of "peripheral voters" who cast their ballots for the winning party in the presidential election and a return to normal voting patterns among "core voters" who supported the "advantaged party" in the presidential year. The decline in turnout in off-year as compared to presidential elections occurs, moreover, proportionately more among voters of low income and low social status, who in the New Deal years favored the Democratic party, than among wealthy voters and voters of high social status. The decision regarding a state party during the off year may also be the result of voter reaction to national political developments.[69]

All the above generalizations apply to some degree to the 1938 Michigan gubernatorial election. The total 1938 vote for governor was about 8.2 percent below that of 1936, when Roosevelt's presence on the ticket had swept Murphy into office; and the decline in turnout was greater in the cities, where Murphy and the Democrats were strong, than in the nonurban areas, where the governor and his party were weak. Whereas Fitzgerald received about the same total vote that he had received in 1936, Murphy's vote declined by 149,000 as compared to 1936. Since Michigan was "still pretty much Republican at the roots" and had deviated from its normal voting behavior only because of the extraordinary circumstances prevailing in 1932 and 1936, it is not surprising that "habit and tradition" reasserted themselves in 1938. Murphy, to some extent, was also the victim of a "national swing" against the New Deal that cost the Democrats eight United States Senate seats, eighty-one House seats, and a net of thirteen governorships. "Apparently it was not in the cards this year because the tide was running against us," Jim Farley wrote Murphy concerning his defeat. For those voters antagonistic to the New Deal—Michigan ruralists, for example, were "up in arms" against the national government and had "a terrific feeling against the President"—few if any local candidates more nearly symbolized what they disliked about national affairs than Frank Murphy.[70]

Among the national factors affecting the vote in Michigan, none was more important than the recession of 1937–38, which had hit Michigan harder than any other state. As Murphy himself put it, "a normal swing of the political pendulum was accentuated by low farm prices and continued unemployment." Although Murphy offered various reasons for his defeat, he eventually concluded that "the depression was the most important factor. It put the party on the defensive, nationally and locally, and good times did not return soon enough to become effective." Murphy undoubtedly found this a comforting explanation since it absolved him of personal responsibility for his defeat, but the argument is consistent with the hypotheses that the party division of the vote is generally altered because of a negative reaction of the voters to the party in power and that the party in power is more likely to be punished for bad times than rewarded for good. Thus the decline in the price of wheat from $1.38 in July 1937 to $0.61 in July 1938 and substantial declines in the price of corn and beans may in part explain why Murphy secured a smaller percentage of the vote in rural Michigan in 1938 than in 1936.[71]

The consensus regarding the principal reason for Murphy's defeat was that the voters had reacted negatively to his behavior during the sit-down strikes; this was the factor most often stressed by state and local Democratic leaders when Farley asked them to assess the causes for the electoral outcome. According to the *Michigan Manufacturer and Financial Record*, when the voters went to the polls, they carried "pictures of 1937" in the back of their heads. "Few will deny," the journal editorialized, "that it was the lax and ineffective manner in which Governor Murphy dealt with labor problems that was the chief cause for the downfall of his administration." The sit-downs, one Democratic leader thought, got Murphy "off to a bad start and plagued him throughout his administration," and the chairman of the Democratic State Central Committee remarked that "any grade-school pupil" could see that this was why the governor had been defeated. Even Murphy, in seeking an explanation for his defeat, spoke of "the labor rampage" in Michigan and "the prolonged and somewhat irresponsible labor conflicts."[72]

In contrast to most others, Frank Picard thought that votes Murphy might have lost because of his sit-down policy were offset or, perhaps, more than offset, by the solid labor support for his candidacy that had resulted from his strike policy and by votes that he gained because of his reputation as a " 'great peacemaker.' " Murphy also had second thoughts about the negative effect of his labor policy. "Take the labor vote out of the Democratic total," he asked rhetorically in the middle of December, "and what have you left?"[73]

It is, as a matter of fact, impossible to ascertain the extent to which the sit-down strike issue, in and of itself, affected the outcome of Michigan's 1938 gubernatorial election. There is little evidence that single issues decisively affect voters, their decision resulting rather from "a comparison of the total image of one of the candidate-party alternatives with the image of the other." Many voters, no doubt, had a negative "image" of Murphy and identified his candidacy with "lawlessness," the coercion of nonunion workers, and an "unholy alliance with the CIO and the Communists," but it is probable that a preponderant number of these voters would have voted Republican in any event.[74] Some voters who might otherwise have supported Murphy almost certainly voted against him because of his labor policy or what they understood to be his labor policy. It is difficult to determine, however, whether their number exceeded the voters attracted to his candidacy because of his "image" as a friend of the workingman.

Some Democrats thought that the Communist issue had contributed to Murphy's defeat, but a later study of the question by two students of public opinion reached inconclusive results. Although one Democratic county chairman thought that voters in general would not accept anyone "who has even the slightest suspicion of Communism hanging over him," the exploitation of the Communist issue was thought to have harmed Murphy particularly among his co-religionists. Complaining that "priests are awfully dumb," a prominent Catholic layman thus reported that he had learned that 50 percent of Detroit's priests had been "provoked" because of Murphy's tardy repudiation of Communist support and that he had lost forty thousand votes in Wayne County on this issue alone. Murphy bitterly complained at a later time that not more than six priests had voted for him even though he said " 'more prayers every day than any of them.' " Fitzgerald made a determined effort to attract Catholic voters—some Catholics complained about Fitzgerald advertising in Catholic publications—and it is possible that he reduced Murphy's majority among Catholic voters.[75]

One consequence of the Red scare in the campaign was that it compelled Murphy to stress his Catholicism in rebutting the accusations of communism. This, in turn, made the governor's religion a more important factor in the campaign than it otherwise would have been, and Democrats were convinced that this cut "very heavily" against Murphy. The Dickinson County Democratic chairman thus reported that a minister in his county had stationed himself at the polls, telling voters he knew not to cast their ballots for a Catholic. Although Democratic leaders thought that Murphy's religion had been a negative factor primarily in rural Michigan, Picard reported that he knew of one ward in Saginaw and several in Detroit where the governor's Catholicism also "hurt to beat the devil."[76]

Many Michigan Democrats attributed Murphy's defeat not only to the lack of a strong Democratic organization, particularly in out-state Michigan and in rural areas, but also to the fact that party workers gave the governor halfhearted support at best because of his slighting of party stalwarts and his "non-partisan nonsense." "It is my humble opinion," the Montcalm County Democratic chairman wrote Farley, "that there are very few individuals who can successfully turn their backs upon their political organizations and get away with it." According to the Mecosta County Democratic chairman, the election proved that Murphy's conception of government was simply wrong. It was "a mistaken idea," the chairman cynically wrote Farley, to think "that the average voter is interested in so-called 'good government.' The garden variety of voter does not given one damn about government. Give him a job and something to eat and the party in power can steal the dome off the capitol and the voter smiles and votes straight."[77]

Unlike those organization Democrats who sat on their hands during the election, Van Wagoner, some Michigan Democrats suspected, had "actually knifed" Murphy "in several areas." After the election Carl Muller sent Van Wagoner a wire reading: " 'Congratulations on the success of YOUR ticket.' " Murphy himself later told Josephine Gomon that Van Wagoner had "double crossed" him by "working with Fitzgerald." Frank Picard, who was in a position to know, thought that Van Wagoner "personally did everything he could" for Murphy but that his organization had failed to "take an active part." This, however, misstated the matter according to Joe Donnelly, who noted "the high glee and boastfulness among some rather highly placed people in the Highway Department" at Murphy's defeat and "their part in achieving that defeat." Van Wagoner's own recollection was that after some effort in Murphy's behalf he had quit the campaign because of the governor's opposition to the highway diversion amendment—Murphy eventually endorsed the amendment—and did not lift a finger for the governor thereafter. Van Wagoner's memory of what took place, whether or not correct in every detail, confirms at the very least how little he did in Murphy's behalf.[78]

Democratic officials also pointed to Murphy's policies regarding welfare, education, and health as causes for his defeat. Murphy's support of welfare reorganization almost certainly hurt him in rural areas, which voted heavily against the welfare referendum. Township and county supervisors, one Democrat reported, "made a house to house canvass in the rural sections all over the State" in an effort to defeat the referendum, and one may assume that this campaigning helped to diminish the Murphy vote. A Ludington Democrat wrote Farley that Murphy had lost fifty thousand votes by temporarily cutting old-age assistance. "The Administration," the Democrat noted, "must have forgotten it was an election year." There were a reputed 200,000 Townsendites in Michigan, and both Blair Moody and Frank Picard thought that Fitzgerald's seeming support of the Townsend plan had gained him thousands of votes. The medical profession had concluded that Murphy's health plans were socialistic, and not only did many of them oppose his candidacy, but if Carl Muller's doctor was typical, some also advised their patients how to vote. The executive secretary of the Michigan Education Association had recommended that public-school teachers vote for Fitzgerald; some Democrats thought that teachers in their parts of the state had followed this advice.[79]

Although one might assume that a substantial majority of WPA workers had voted for Murphy, Democrats from Harry Mead on down were convinced that the WPA was one of the causes for the governor's defeat. They believed that WPA workers had voted Republican or not voted at all because they regarded their average wage of $44 per month as totally inadequate, whereas the Republicans were promising them $60 per month if Fitzgerald were elected. Farmers resented the WPA, Democrats alleged, because they thought it deprived them of the road work on which some depended for supplementary income and made it difficult for them to obtain farm labor. The voters, it was also alleged, regarded WPA projects as "foolish," involving the "useless" expenditure of funds. Several county chairmen implied that the WPA would have been an asset in the campaign had key WPA positions been in Democratic rather than Republican hands. "We get the blame for using WPA and other Federal Agencies for political purposes," one county chairman lamented, "then why not see that good Democrats are place[d] in charge of the administration of these . . . agencies."[80]

Murphy's opposition to commercial gambling may also have contributed to his defeat. As Picard noted, the Murphy administration had put at least twenty-five thousand slot machines and gambling devices out of business, an action that offended the resort areas of the state and reduced the income of cigar stores, liquor stores, and pool rooms. Murphy's anti-gambling policy was popular with the "so-called 'good citizens' " and "very zealous church members," but these pietistic Protestants probably voted against Murphy because of their "deep rooted" Republicanism or because of religious bias.[81]

Prentiss Brown thought that Michigan's "practically 100 per cent Republican press" was the principal reason for Murphy's defeat, and others agreed that newspaper opposition had been a significant factor. "The poisoned press," Germer observed, "harped on a combination of things, magnified them a thousand fold and over a period of nearly two years built a feeling of hate and bitterness against anything that could be labeled as a part of the 'New Deal.' "[82]

Few Democrats thought that budget deficits, an issue much stressed by Republicans in the campaign, hurt Murphy at the polls, although some county chairmen believed that farmers and small businessmen were influenced to some degree by the allegations of "reckless spending." It may be that had Murphy thrown fiscal caution to the winds and sought larger expenditures for education, old-age assistance, and relief, he would have fared better at the polls.[83]

Sixty hours before the Michigan primary the Republican editor of the *Charlotte Republican Tribune*, Murl H. DeFoe, noted in his diary that Murphy would win the primary but lose the election. "No public man in Michigan," DeFoe recorded, "has ever accumulated the same amount of downright hatred in the same number of calendar days. The day after the result is known ... the state will be divided into Murphy haters and his defenders. The haters are in a majority. The conservative vote is solidly against him; small business actually despises him, the school men and doctors are two more groups hating him because they fear him, or rather his policies. And so it goes on ad infinitum. It isn't so much whom the Republicans nominate—that really doesn't matter.... The people are just fed up on Murphy and fourteen bridge dedications by F.D.R. wouldn't save him. He is just done, that's all."[84] One need not agree with everything DeFoe said, although it is true that Murphy excited strong emotions among both his opponents and supporters, but there is no doubt that the governor was "done" before the election campaign even began.

Politicians and pundits, who devoted so much effort to explaining why Murphy lost, failed to appreciate that he had actually made a respectable showing for a Democrat in Republican Michigan in an off-year election and in a state that had suffered a severe recession and a sharp labor upheaval during his incumbency. The 47 percent of the vote that he received compared favorably with the percentage of the gubernatorial vote that Democratic candidates had received in the off-year elections of 1930 (42 percent) and 1934 (45.8 percent); his popular vote was twice as great as the Comstock vote in 1930 and exceeded the Lacy vote by more than 175,000.[85] Murphy had run five percentage points behind Roosevelt in the 1936 election, and he might very well have been reelected had 1938 been a presidential year.

Conservative Michigan Republicans who saw Murphy as the archtypical New Dealer breathed a sigh of relief at his defeat. The former chairman of the Republican State Central Committee "shudder[ed]" when he thought "what would have happened had Murphy been re-elected. We would have been subjected to every crackpot idea that is conceivable and would have been the incubator for all of the New Deal ideas that come along," Howard C. Lawrence wrote Fitzgerald. For New Dealers across the land, however, Murphy's defeat, as Felix Frankfurter put it, was "a national misfortune." Ickes thought the Michigan result "the most serious defeat" for the Democrats in the 1938 elections, and columnist Paul Anderson deemed it the "worst blow" of the elections from the standpoint of Roosevelt, the New Deal, labor, "and everyone who values civilized, progressive, humanitarian government." The feelings of Murphy's distraught Michigan followers were best summed up by Carl Muller. "I could not believe," he wrote, "that Michigan wanted to turn out the best government it has ever had and turn it over to the McPhersons, McKays and McKeighhans [a McKay ally]. . . . I could not believe there were so many 'nice' people—smug, self-satisfied, self-sufficient, all-sufficient, in-sufficient people—who, whether they realized it or not, were rejecting the notion that man is his brother's keeper and that those of us in comfortable circumstances have an obligation to help our more unfortunate fellow-men.'' Incensed, Muller took a swing at a "Murphy hater"; the Murphy foe retaliated and broke Muller's dentures.[86]

Murphy said all the things that a defeated candidate is supposed to say in a democracy. "I fully accept the verdict of democracy," he declared. It had been "a great privilege to serve the people of Michigan," and his faith in the people was "unshaken." To suffer defeat and "to be humbled," he asserted, was "good for the man . . . and good for the public." A public servant who was not prepared to accept defeat did not belong in public life. He thought it "tragic" that his work had to be "interrupted," but, he commented to a friend, one had to "keep faith that in the long run the methods and policies that are best for the public will prevail."[87]

Privately, Murphy was embittered by his defeat, his first real rejection by the electorate.[88] Murphy, although capable of romantic flights of fancy, was enough of a political realist to understand that his hopes of becoming president had been dealt a shattering blow. When he visited the president after the election, Roosevelt, who also led others to believe that they were his preferred successor, told the lame-duck governor, according to his brother Harold, that "everything . . . [had been] set for him in *1940.*" Harold was very sorry for Frank since it had been his "dream since Boy-hood" to be president, and "he about had it in his hand, only to be Defeated."[89]

After the defeat in the 1938 elections of such liberals and progressives as Murphy, Elmer Benson of Minnesota, and Philip La Follette of Wisconsin, there was talk among progressives about the possible formation of a third party. At a meeting on November 12 with Fiorello LaGuardia and lame-duck Senator Robert J. Buckley of Ohio, Murphy repeated the counsel he had given when Philip La Follette had launched the National Progressives of America as a third party in the spring of 1938. The progressives, he contended, must seek to control the Democratic party, under Roosevelt's leadership, rather than form a third party. Murphy privately advised the president at the same time to move leftward. The "weakness" of the Democratic position, the governor wrote Roosevelt, was the administration's failure to solve the unemployment problem. If the Democrats were to prevent the existing electoral trend from becoming "a reactionary sweep with possible disastrous results to our democratic institutions," the federal government would have to provide jobs at a living wage for those able to work, the social security program would have to be expanded to provide more adequate unemployment insurance and assistance for unemployables and the sick, the treatment of the mentally ill would have to be improved, and the housing program would have to be carried forward in an energetic manner.[90] The lesson Murphy drew from New Deal and liberal setbacks in 1938, including his own, was that the need of the hour was an expanded New Deal, not a retreat from reform.

During the final six weeks of his governorship Murphy gave special attention to the completion of the work of the various study commissions he had appointed.[91] He also made every effort to ensure that there would be a smooth transition to the new administration. "We think the people of the State will not fail to be impressed by Gov. Murphy's bearing in these difficult days of his imminent retirement from office," the *Detroit News* editorialized on Murphy's last day in office.[92]

In his ex-augural address, submitted to the legislature on January 5, 1939, Murphy recommended the creation by the legislature of a special commission to study the "entire governmental procedure" as a follow-up to the work of his own study commission; supplementation of the civil service system with "a sound pension plan"; establishment of a special bureau and field staff in the Health Department to supervise and assist local health departments, more generous subsidization of such departments, and development of a plan to supply medical care and hospitalization to indigent persons; extending secondary schools to the thirteenth and fourteenth grades and a statewide teacher-tenure act if this could be implemented without preventing the dismissal of incompetent teachers; coordination of welfare functions on both the state and county levels; enactment of legislation to conserve Michigan's gas and oil resources and to control water pollution; enactment of a milk control law; legislation to facilitate the public operation of public utilities; and a labor relations law that met with "the substantial approval" of both labor and management and established appropriate agencies for the mediation and conciliation of industrial disputes.[93]

Murphy's ex-augural message is a good indication of the issues that would have concerned a second Murphy administration. In the message, the governor admonished the legislators not to conclude from the election that the people of the state wished to call a halt to what had been accomplished in the preceding two years. That the legislators did not agree with this judgment, however, was probably revealed by the reception they accorded the message: two minutes after the clerk had begun reading the document, a Republican legislator moved that it be "considered, read, and printed" in the journals of the House and Senate, and the motion was carried. The legislature had not dismissed an ex-augural message in so rude a fashion since 1931.[94]

The Fitzgerald-Dickinson administration returned Michigan to the old-style politics of favoritism and patronage, reversing the good-government approach that was a hallmark of the Murphy administration. The Republicans dismantled much of the Lansing New Deal, they evinced little interest in social legislation, and they enacted welfare and labor relations measures that Murphy would almost certainly have opposed.

Late in December 1938 a truck overturned on a Michigan highway and spilled slot machines onto the road, a graphic indication that commercial gambling was about to return to Michigan. Once the new governor reiterated his view that the enforcement of the gambling laws was "a local problem," gambling houses reopened, and operators of some of the major gambling establishments declared that they had an " 'understanding' " with Lansing. The public outcry that resulted and the demand of a Battle Creek minister that the governor " 'clean up the whole rotten gambling mess' " or face the possibility of a recall led Fitzgerald to abandon his home-rule position in March. The State Police then raided some of the worst offenders, but the gamblers were soon back in business, and slot machines were to be found everywhere in the state.[95]

Fitzgerald's victory meant the return of Frank McKay and the resumption of purchasing methods that the Murphy administration had abandoned as smacking of favoritism. Murphy's defeat also meant that the State Tax Commission would again be under the domination of Melville McPherson, who, the governor-elect announced, would be appointed commission chairman. On November 22, 1938, the commission voted to discontinue the survey of mining property valuations that John Fegan had instituted and to which the mining companies had objected.[96]

The new Republican legislature began its deliberations by appointing a committee composed principally of "enemies" of civil service to investigate the state's civil service system. After making "a clumsy and biased investigation," the committee submitted "a report replete with absurdities, partisan cliches, and manifest misstatements." Fitzgerald replaced two Murphy appointees on the Civil Service Commission with two "active Republican party workers," and Dickinson completed the dismantling of the original commission by replacing its sole surviving member with another partisan appointee. The legislature then passed a "ripper bill" that substantially reduced the number of state employees covered by the merit system, cut the salary of the personnel director, and reduced the appropriation for the operation of the Civil Service Department by more than 60 percent. When Murphy left office, 90.7 percent of the state employees were in the classified service; by March 1940 only 51 percent were included in this category.

The "partial destruction" of the civil service system by the Fitzgerald-Dickinson administration persuaded the Michigan Merit System Association to sponsor an amendment to the state constitution that placed over 90 percent of the state's employees in the classified service, provided for "a partially closed 'back door' " (because of the unsatisfactory experience with a "completely open 'back door' "), and required the legislature to appropriate not less than 1 percent of the aggregate payroll of the state service for the preceding fiscal year for the operation of the Civil Service Department. The amendment, which Murphy supported, was approved by the state's voters in November 1940 and went into effect the next year.[97]

The Murphy reforms in the areas of corrections, mental health, and welfare administration were diluted if not altogether vitiated during the Fitzgerald-Dickinson administration. The civil service ripper statute declassified 177 of 983 positions in the Department of Corrections, including wardens and deputy wardens, and partisan politics returned to the state's correctional system. A member of the State Hospital Commission wrote Murphy at the end of January 1939 that she was "heartsick" because of what was occurring at the state hospitals. "All your fine work for curative and preventative measures," Elsie Mershon informed Murphy, "[has been] shattered by [the] present administration." The legislature abolished the position of director of state hospitals, which led to the resignation of Dr. Joseph E. Barrett and the end of centralized control of the state hospitals. The new hospitals that were built remained unused because the legislature refused to appropriate funds for beds. The legislature in the end appropriated $39 million for school aid for the fiscal year 1939–40, not the $45 million Fitzgerald had promised; and rather than increasing old-age assistance payments to the promised monthly average of $30 per year, the Fitzgerald administration re-

duced the monthly average per person from \$17.11 at the close of the
Murphy administration to \$16.49 in May 1939.[98]

The legislature enacted a new welfare reorganization law in June
1939 that Arthur Dunham concluded contained "so many ambi-
guities, so many defects, and so many provisions for unsound forms
of organization and administration" that it was "a discredit rather
than a credit to the state." The statute created a new Department of
Social Welfare with "two coordinate executives" appointed by the
social welfare commission that administered the department: a
director of the department who supervised relief, child welfare, and
the employment institution for the blind, and a supervisor of the
Bureau of Social Security who supervised old-age assistance, ADC,
aid to the blind, and other forms of relief financed in whole or in part
by the federal government. To add to the administrative confusion
and further limiting the degree of welfare integration, the department also included an autonomous Juvenile Institute Commission
that supervised the state's juvenile training schools and the Michigan
Children's Institute. Although the state was to provide the counties
with at least 50 percent of the funds they expended for direct relief,
the state department was given no meaningful power to supervise the
manner in which relief funds were expended, nor did it have any
authority over the selection of personnel by the county departments.

The welfare statute provided for county departments of social
welfare consisting of a social welfare board of three members (two
appointed by the county board of supervisors and the other by the
state social welfare commission) and a supervisor of the bureau of
social aid, appointed by the supervisor of the state Bureau of Social
Security. The statute authorized the counties to distinguish between
county and township poor, which permitted township supervisors to
administer relief even though experience had discredited this practice. The county welfare relief commissions, the county old-age assistance boards, and the office of county superintendent of the poor
were abolished, but the measure did not abolish the mothers'
pension program, leaving the state in the "absurd position" of
having two forms of aid for dependent children. The soldiers' and
sailors' relief commissions were left intact as "a totally unintegrated
local public relief agency," and the position of county agent also
survived although that official lost his relief functions. Deferring
excessively to locally administered relief and welfare, the new welfare
statute was a far cry from the welfare reorganization legislation proposed by the Murphy administration, and it was partially responsible
for Michigan's recurring welfare crises in 1939 and 1940.[99]

In an action that clearly distinguished his administration from that of his predecessor, Fitzgerald appointed Daniel A. Knaggs, Murphy's antagonist in the Monroe strike, commissioner of the Department of Labor and Industry. The legislature approved a restrictive labor relations law that, although less stringent than the measure Fitzgerald had recommended, did not satisfy the criterion of acceptability by labor and management that Murphy had specified. The statute required a notice of at least five days before most strikes and lockouts, during which time the labor mediation board created by the act could seek to adjust the dispute. There was to be a thirty-day delay in the case of strikes or lockouts in public utilities, hospitals, and other industries "affected with a public interest" while a three-man commission appointed by the governor sought to mediate the difficulty. Although the act specified several unfair employer practices, this section of the law was little more than "an appendage" to the measure. The statute made it unlawful for anyone "by force, coercion, intimidation or threats" to compel any person to join a labor organization or to cease working; and, unlike House Bill 571, it made participation in sit-down strikes a misdemeanor. The labor-disputes machinery in the statute proved ineffective in the prolonged Chrysler strike in 1939, and the unfair labor practices section became a dead letter.[100]

Perturbed that his administration had been succeeded by an administration of "ambitious bossism grafted onto a basic pattern of small-town Republicanism," Murphy also suffered the humiliation of losing control of Michigan's Democratic party. The issue was resolved at a party convention on February 18, 1939, when the candidate of the Highway Department, Charles Porritt, was selected over the candidate of the Murphy wing of the party, William J. Delaney, to succeed Edward Fry as chairman of the Democratic State Central Committee. Murphy's initial choice for the chairmanship was George J. Burke, whom Murphy had appointed to head the Civil Service Commission. Van Wagoner would probably have accepted Burke as state chairman, but he resisted the pressure to become a candidate because of his wife's illness. After the Murphy men in the party failed to persuade the Van Wagoner camp to accept a compromise candidate, only Delaney, chairman of the Kent County Democratic Committee, was willing to challenge the Highway Department. He thus became the Murphy faction's candidate even though leaders of the faction would have preferred "a better and stronger candidate." Murphy's failure as governor to build a strong organization loyal to him and his principles handicapped his friends in the contest with the well-organized Highway forces, whose candidate won the chairmanship by a large majority. As Shields wrote Prentiss Brown, the Murphy people did not have "any definite votes whatever that they could point to; they had absolutely no organization." The Murphy-Roosevelt "New Deal crowd" was now "out," and the state party was "under the sway" of the Highway Department, which, according to Raymond Starr, stood for "everything but good government."[101]

II

The Murphy administration, the *Detroit News* noted as the governor's term came to an end, was "the most eventful and comment-provoking [Michigan] administration in decades."[102] It was also the most reform-minded and was responsible for one of the few successful little New Deals at the state level. The Murphy administration provided the state with a strengthened Department of Labor and Industry, an occupational disease law, and legislation to benefit a variety of craft unions in the state, and it made an effort to protect Mexican agricultural laborers imported into the state. It could claim credit for one of the most liberal unemployment insurance laws in the nation, and it greatly liberalized Michigan's old-age assistance statute. It not only energized the state's Health Department, which considerably expanded its disease control activities, but it also helped to focus attention on the needs of the medically indigent and on ways of improving the delivery of health care in the state. It launched a major hospital building program, stressed the prevention of mental illness, and provided Michigan with its first public child-guidance clinic. The Murphy administration provided the state with a public utilities commission that brought savings to the consumers of utility services. It was responsible for legislation that made it possible for Michigan's cities to take advantage of available federal housing funds. It spurred the electrification of the state's farms, provided uniform and standardized grading of fruits, vegetables, and poultry that benefited Michigan's farmers, and laid the groundwork for Michigan's 1939 Milk Act. As a Murphy supporter noted, the two years of the Murphy administration were a time when "Lansing thought and acted with social justice as the goal."[103]

Remembered primarily for its little New Deal and its friendship for organized labor, the Murphy administration was equally noteworthy for its administrative reforms and its commitment to good government. Murphy appointed able men to administrative posts and permitted them to discharge their responsibilities free from political interference. He played the decisive role in the enactment of Michigan's civil service law in 1937, and he insisted on its vigorous and nonpartisan enforcement even though this antagonized the leadership of his party. His administration reformed the state's purchasing system, introducing "daylight" procedures that eliminated favoritism. It administered the state's liquor control system in a businesslike manner, made an honest effort to enforce the anti-gambling laws, and converted the State Fair from a corrupt activity into an efficient, profit-making one. The Murphy administration provided Michigan with one of the best correctional systems in the nation, centralized the administration of state institutions for the mentally ill, and persuaded the state legislature to rationalize the state's disorganized welfare and relief structure. It introduced a new and effective budget and accounting system, cleaned up the securities business, and administered the state's banking legislation in an efficient and scandal-free manner. Although the *Detroit News* had opposed Murphy's reelection, it conceded at the close of his term that there had been "a coherence of effort toward 'good government' [in the Murphy administration] that was rare in Capitol experience." The veteran Lansing correspondent Carl Rudow stated many years later that Murphy had displayed "the highest governmental ethics" of the many governors whose administrations Rudow had covered.[104]

The Murphy administration failed to persuade the legislature to enact a labor relations measure that the governor could sign or to pass the labor standards legislation that he favored. Its welfare reorganization plan was rejected by the voters, and Murphy left office before he could accomplish the thoroughgoing program of administrative reform to which he was committed. Murphy himself was partly responsible for these failures—his leadership in the struggle to secure a labor relations law for Michigan was wavering at best, and he chose not to press the issue of overall as distinguished from piecemeal administrative reorganization until too late in his governorship to have any effect. Nevertheless, considering the ramifying effects first of the sit-down strikes and then the recession, the weakness of the state Democratic party, the character of the legislature, the power of business groups in the state, and the persistence of pre–New Deal attitudes concerning the proper role of government, what is remarkable is how much the Murphy administration accomplished in two years, not that it failed to reach all of its goals.

The Murphy administration is noteworthy not only for its reform legislation and administrative accomplishments but also for its impact on the labor movement and on Michigan's political structure. Because of the manner in which he reacted to the sit-down strikes and the great labor upheaval that occurred in Michigan during his administration, Murphy played a crucial role in the rise to power of the UAW and the CIO and the absorption of organized labor into the American "system." He also rallied organized labor, blacks, various white ethnic groups, and low-income voters to his support, and it was the "power groups" devoted to Murphy that helped to make Michigan become a two-party state after World War II.

To critics of the Murphy administration like the small-town editor and publisher, Floyd Josiah Miller, Murphy was "an impractical idealist," was "rather blind to the problem of how to pay for things," had "lessened respect for law and order," had justified "many dangerous steps" in trying to remove "wrongs" that admittedly existed, and had "little comprehension of the problems of running business and industry." To his admirers, he was the best governor Michigan had ever had, one who had "done more" for the state in two years than his predecessors in the preceding twenty. The Murphy administration was for them a time of excitement and high purpose, a welcome change from the lackluster administrations that had generally characterized state government in Michigan. "It's a shame that you are gone," state Supreme Court Justice Thomas F. McAllister wrote Murphy in 1939. "You came into the drab and murky light—and brought the flash of color and drama—and raised hearts to high things. And with your going it is as though night had fallen on the capitol and public affairs."[105]

In his study *The New Deal and the States*, James T. Patterson, who designates Murphy along with Governor Herbert H. Lehman of New York, Governor George H. Earle of Pennsylvania, and Governor Eurith D. Rivers of Georgia as "the most heralded little New Dealers," characterizes the achievements of the Murphy administration as "remarkable" when compared with the record of other states at the time.[106] Although the legislative accomplishments of the Lehman and Earle administrations were even more impressive than those of the Murphy administration, Lehman and Earle enjoyed advantages over Murphy as reform governors. Lehman, who was governor for ten years, presided over a state with a notable progressive heritage, a tradition of strong executives, and in which the urban influence was pronounced. Earle served for four years as compared to Murphy's two, and the ground had been prepared for the Pennsylvania New Deal during the second term of Earle's Republican predecessor, Gifford Pinchot. Such factors as the degree of urbanization, ethnic diversity, the extent of voter participation, the closeness of party conflict, and per capita wealth have been suggested as critical factors in determining whether or not a state will move in a reform direction. Since states with the same characteristics, however, have not necessarily behaved in the same manner and since the same states have behaved quite differently under the leadership of different governors—Michigan is a notable example—Patterson has correctly concluded that "the indispensable ingredient" in setting a state's course has probably been the character of the governor. Most state governors of the 1930s, we have been told, were "nobodies," but even Murphy's most rabid critics knew that he was a "somebody."[107]

The editors of a recent book concerned with the New Deal at the state and local levels concluded that, "for the most part, conflict rather than cooperation" characterized the federal-state relationship in the 1930s, and the author of a monograph on New York's little New Deal similarly has maintained that Albany and Washington largely "went their separate ways in the 1930s." Nevertheless, the term "cooperative federalism" that was coined in the New Deal years accurately describes the "partnership" relationship of Michigan and Washington while Murphy was Michigan's governor.[108] The Murphy administration conformed without complaint to federal standards required for the state to receive federal funds under the Social Security Act, and the WPA, in turn, sought to accommodate itself to Michigan's needs to the extent that federal funds and federal legislation permitted. Although the PWA did not approve all of Michigan's applications for aid, the relationship of the state and federal governments in the administration of the public works program was one of cooperation rather than conflict. The Department of Labor's Division of Labor Standards made a survey of Michigan's Department of Labor and Industry at Murphy's behest, the division responded to the state's request for assistance in devising a labor relations law, the Women's Bureau of the department stimulated and assisted Murphy's efforts to obtain minimum wage legislation, and the department's Federal Committee on Apprenticeship aided a Murphy-appointed committee in drawing up a model state apprenticeship statute. The Michigan and federal departments of agriculture cooperated in establishing federal-state inspection and grading of Michigan fruits, vegetables, and poultry. Responding to Murphy's request, the Rural Electrification Administration provided Michigan with an engineer to assist the state's Public Utilities Commission and to aid state efforts in electrifying Michigan's farms. The United States Housing Authority assisted the governor's aides in devising appropriate housing legislation and allocated funds to support public housing in the state. The Antitrust Division of the Department of Justice and the state of Michigan joined forces in a pioneering venture to test the feasibility of federal-state cooperation in enforcing the antitrust laws.

The enormous expansion of the functions of the federal government in the New Deal years led to expressions of concern at the time about "the passing of the states." The Michigan experience, however, confirms the judgment of the political scientist V. O. Key that state government was a growth industry in the 1930s and that the states in that decade began to play a more important part in the federal system than they had before.[109] Because of the impact of the Depression, the availability of federal funds as the result of the New Deal, and the example of the New Deal, Michigan state government substantially increased the scale of its operations in the 1930s. It assumed new responsibilities for general relief, old-age assistance, ADC, aid to the blind, public housing, rural electrification, and the public health, and it provided additional services to laborers, farmers, and consumers. Whereas local governments had been responsible for the needy aged, the needy blind, and dependent children before 1933, the nonfederal cost of these programs was shouldered by the state government after 1935, and it was responsible for the enforcement of the federal standards applicable to these programs. Whereas general public relief had been entirely the responsibility of local government before the Depression, the state met more than 60 percent of local relief costs while Murphy was governor, and relief was dispensed in accordance with standards established by the State Emergency Relief Administration. The cost of state government in Michigan (exclusive of state aid to local units) rose from $66.9 million in the fiscal year 1935–36 to $99.9 million in the fiscal year 1937–38, a 50 percent increase in two years.[110]

The growing importance of Michigan state government in the New Deal era was evidenced by the increase in the cost of state government as compared to local government and the extent to which the costs of the latter were met by state aid. Whereas state government costs consituted about 20 percent of the total cost of state and local government in Michigan in the fiscal year 1932–33, the figure rose to about 29 percent in the fiscal year 1937–38; the share of local government costs met by state government increased from 11.5 percent to 37 percent during the same years. In Michigan, as elsewhere in the 1930s, the share of the total taxes raised by local units decreased while the share of the state and federal governments increased, and state governments were increasingly raising funds that they funneled to the localities.[111]

As "the New Deal's most distinguished lame duck," Murphy, it was widely assumed, would be offered an important post by the president, one which would "change . . . [his] address from Lansing to Washington." Murphy told a reporter that he intended to return to the practice of law but "to keep very much in the public eye," preparatory, perhaps, to seeking the governorship again in 1940. Although he wrote Carlos Romulo that he had been "quite seriously intending to drop out of public life for a year or two," it is doubtful that he wished to do so. He alleged that he needed the money, but had that been a consideration, which it was not, he could have accepted the offer of a sizable "retainer" to look after Joseph P. Kennedy's legal affairs.[112]

There was a good deal of speculation late in 1938 that Murphy would be offered a Supreme Court post to fill the vacancy created by the death of Benjamin Cardozo. A defender of the president's plan to "pack" the Supreme Court, Murphy, as a matter of fact, had been a rumored nominee for each of the Supreme Court positions that became available while he was governor. It may be that Roosevelt offered to appoint Murphy to the court following Willis Van Devanter's resignation in May 1937, but even had Murphy wanted the position, and he did not, he could hardly have accepted it so soon after becoming governor. When Roosevelt nominated Hugo Black to fill the vacant seat, Murphy praised the selection, but he told a newsman two months later that he regarded Black as "judicially unqualified" for the job, primarily because of the revelation of his former membership in the Ku Klux Klan. Murphy was reportedly the Senate's choice to succeed Justice George Sutherland after he announced his retirement in January 1938; the columnist Raymond Clapper was told that the governor was one of four persons the president was considering. Roosevelt reportedly was anxious to "recoup from [the] loss" he had suffered as the result of the Black appointment by doing "something sensational that would click," such as appointing a second Catholic or a woman to the court. Stating that he was opposed to "the slightest effort, directly or indirectly," to secure the appointment, Murphy wrote a friend, "It is best for the Supreme Court and for myself that I am not appointed to that august [body]."[113]

Although Murphy had stated in August 1938 that he could not accept a nomination to succeed Cardozo and that Felix Frankfurter, who later became Murphy's great antagonist on the Supreme Court, was "the man best qualified in scholarship, training and judicial temperament" for the position, the governor's defeat renewed conjecture that he would become the nation's next Supreme Court justice. According to the *New York Times*, however, when the president's agents checked with the Senate, they learned that it might be difficult to get Murphy confirmed, presumably because he had temporized in enforcing the law during the General Motors strike. Murphy had not changed his mind about going on the bench, telling the *Detroit News*'s state editor that he believed the Supreme Court was " 'beyond his grasp,' " that he was not " 'qualified for it.' "[114]

In addition to a Supreme Court position, Murphy was rumored to be under consideration for five different cabinet posts as well as the high commissionership of the Philippines once again. Precisely what positions the president discussed with Murphy when the two men met on November 13 is uncertain, although we do know that the various proposals mentioned by Roosevelt did "not greatly appeal" to the lame-duck governor. Possibly, the president sought to ascertain Murphy's willingness to become secretary of commerce since, according to Farley, he had been under consideration for that position even before the November election; possibly, Roosevelt was thinking of Murphy as secretary of labor. In the end, it was the position of attorney general that Murphy accepted, with the understanding that he would soon be made secretary of war, the position he really wanted.[115]

In reporting on December 30 that Roosevelt would name Murphy attorney general, the *New York Times*'s Arthur Krock, who regarded Murphy as "one of the most earnest, interesting and able men in public life," speculated about the defeated governor's future. Describing Murphy as "an ascetic, an idealist, an able lawyer and administrator, a searcher after the Grail if ever there was one," Krock guessed that Murphy's "mistakes and defeat" might be "the stepping-stones to a remarkable comeback." As he was about to board the train for Washington in January to begin that "comeback," Murphy, according to his sister-in-law, "seemed a little sad to be leaving Detroit because . . . he felt that it closed that whole [Michigan] chapter of his life."[116] Murphy's New Deal years had come to an end; his Washington years were about to begin.

Abbreviations

ALHUA	Archives of Labor History and Urban Affairs, Wayne State University, Detroit, Michigan
DFP	*Detroit Free Press*
DLN	*Detroit Labor News*
DN	*Detroit News*
DT	*Detroit Times*
EG	Eugene Gressman
EG Papers	Eugene Gressman Papers, Michigan Historical Collections, Ann Arbor, Michigan
EGK	Edward G. Kemp
EGK Papers	Edward G. Kemp Papers, Michigan Historical Collections
EGK-BHC	Edward G. Kemp Papers, Burton Historical Collection, Detroit, Michigan
EMB	Eleanor M. Bumgardner
EMB Papers	Eleanor M. Bumgardner Papers, Michigan Historical Collections
FDR	Franklin D. Roosevelt
FDRL	Franklin D. Roosevelt Library, Hyde Park, New York
FM	Frank Murphy
FM Papers	Frank Murphy Papers, Michigan Historical Collections
GM	George Murphy
GM Papers	George Murphy Papers, Michigan Historical Collections
HM	Harold Murphy
HM Papers	Harold Murphy Papers, Michigan Historical Collections
HSB	Norman H. Hill Scrapbooks, Michigan Historical Collections
IM	Irene Murphy
IM Papers	Irene Murphy Papers, Michigan Historical Collections
JAF	James A. Farley
JRH	Joseph Ralston Hayden

JRH Papers	Joseph Ralston Hayden Papers, Michigan Historical Collections
LC	Library of Congress, Washington, D.C.
MDB	*Manila Daily Bulletin*
MHC	Michigan Historical Collections, Ann Arbor, Michigan
MM	Marguerite Murphy
MM Papers	Marguerite Murphy Papers, Michigan Historical Collections
MSB	Frank Murphy Scrapbooks, Michigan Historical Collections
MT	*Manila Tribune*
NARS	National Archives and Records Service, Washington, D.C.
NYT	*New York Times*
OF	Official File
PH	*Philippines Herald*
PPF	President's Personal File
PSF	President's Secretary's File
RG	Record Group

Notes

CHAPTER 1

1. Theodora McManus to FM [May 1933], FM Papers.

2. The summary of Murphy's career up to 1933 is based on Sidney Fine, *Frank Murphy: The Detroit Years* (Ann Arbor: University of Michigan Press, 1975).

3. *NYT*, June 15, 1933; *DN*, Apr. 9, 1933; *DT*, Apr, 9, 1933, MSB; Morris L. Ernst to FM, Apr. 7, 1933, Newell B. Wallace to FM, Apr. 8, 1933, M. B. Travis to FM, Apr. 10, 1933, FM to Pampangan Circle, May 10, 1933, FM Papers.

4. JAF to FM, Apr. 21, 1933, FM Papers; JRH to James R. Fugate, Apr. 8, 12, 1933, JRH to John A. Hackett, May 17, 1933, JRH Papers. Hayden's views were shared by W. Cameron Forbes, a former governor-general of the Philippines. Forbes to FDR, Apr. 10, 1933, OF 400, FDRL. See James Couzens to FM, Jan. 11, 1934, James Couzens Papers, Box 103, LC, for evidence of reservations about the appointment in the United States Senate.

5. Harry B. Hawes to FM, Apr. 11, 20, 1933, FM to Hawes, Apr. 19, 1933, George H. Dern to FM, Apr. 14, 1933, Manuel Roxas to FM, Apr. 15, 1933, FM to Roxas, Apr. 24, 1933, FM to Millard Tydings, Apr. 21, 1933, FM to Dwight F. Davis, May 5, 1933, F. LeJ. Parker to FM, Apr. 29, May 10, 1933, Norman H. Hill to Parker, May 10, 1933, Parker to John H. Holliday, Apr. 29, 1933, Edward Bruce to FM, May 2, 1933, JRH to Hill, May 5, 1933, FM Papers; JRH to Fugate, May 12, 1933, JRH Papers; Detroit Public Library, "Selected List of References on the Philippines," Apr. 1933, MM Papers; *DN*, Apr. 8, 24, 26, 1933; *DT*, Apr. 11, 1933, MSB; George A. Malcolm, *American Colonial Careerist* (Boston: Christopher Publishing House, 1957), p. 52.

6. See Fine, *Murphy*, passim.

7. *DN*, Apr. 10, 1933; *DT,* May 13, 1933, MSB; *San Francisco Examiner*, May 20, 1933, MSB; *Los Angeles Examiner*, May 17, 1933, MSB; *San Francisco Chronicle*, May 20, 1933, MSB; Memorandum for Records, May 17, 1933, Murphy file, Records of the Bureau of Insular Affairs, RG 350, NARS; MM to GM [May 1933], FM to GM, May 19, 1933, Joseph Mulcahy to GM, May 20, 1933, GM Papers; FM to GM, May 23, 1933, FM to Hearst, May 19, 1933, FM Papers.

8. *DT*, Apr. 11, 1933, MSB; *Japan Advertiser* [June 6, 1933], MSB; Malcolm to Charles A. Sink, Charles A. Sink Papers, MHC; Malcolm to FM, May 6, 1933, Parker to FM, May 10, 1933, FM to GM, May 23, 1933, FM Papers; Parker to FM, May 18, 1933, FM file, RG 350; MM to GM, May 24 [1933], [May 25, 1933], [May or June 1933], FM to GM, June 3, 1933, Cox to GM, Sept. 2, 1933, GM Papers; FM to HM, June 4, 1933, HM Papers; Malcolm, *Careerist*, p. 52.

9. MM to GM [May 26, June 8, 1933], GM Papers; Edwin S. Cunningham to Secretary of State, June 20, 1933, Quezon file, RG 350; Malcolm, *Careerist*, pp. 52-53; FM to Acting Secretary of Finance, May 26, 1933, FM to Vicente Singson Encarnacion, May [28], 1933, Holliday to FM, May 30 [1933], FM Papers; *Shanghai Evening Post and Mercury*, June 9, 1933, MSB; *China Press*, June 10, 1933, MSB; *Hongkong Daily Press*, June 13, 1933, MSB; *Japan Advertiser* [June 6, 1933], MSB; *PH*, June 14, 1933, MSB.

10. Joseph Ralston Hayden, *The Philippines* (New York: Macmillan Co., 1942), pp. 5-6; United States Tariff Commission (USTC), *United States-Philippine Trade...*, Report No. 118, Second Series (Washington: U.S. Government Printing Office, 1937), p. 1.

11. Garel A. Grunder and William Livezey, *The Philippines and the United States* (Norman: University of Oklahoma Press, 1951), p. 25.

12. Peter W. Stanley, *A Nation in the Making: The Philippines and the United States* (Cambridge, Mass.: Harvard University Press, 1974), p. 61; Ronald K. Edgerton, "Joseph Ralston Hayden and America's Colonial Experiment in the Philippines" (1969), p. 2, in my possession; Salvador P. Lopez, "The Colonial Relationship," in Frank H. Golay, ed., *The United States and the Philippines* (Englewood Cliffs, N.J.: Prentice-Hall, 1966), pp. 14-15.

13. For the development of civil government in the Philippines between 1901 and 1933, see Stanley, *Nation*, p. 60 ff.; John H. Romani, "The Philippine Presidency: An Evaluation in Terms of American Practices" (Ph.D. diss., University of Michigan, 1955), pp. 1, 25-34; Julius W. Pratt, *America's Colonial Experiment* (Englewood Cliffs, N.J.: Prentice-Hall, 1950), pp. 197-210; Grunder and Livezey, *Philippines*, pp. 67-81, 93-97; Hayden, *Philippines*, pp. 315-50; Michael Paul Onorato, *A Brief Review of American Interest in Philippine Development and Other Essays* (Berkeley: McCutchan Publishing Corp., 1968), pp. 35, 70-71, 73-74, 87-112, 134; Elting E. Morison, *Turmoil and Tradition: A Study of the Life and Times of Henry L. Stimson* (Boston: Houghton Mifflin Co., 1960), pp. 270-98; Dapen Liang, *The Development of Philippine Political Parties* (Hongkong: *South China Morning Post*, 1939), pp. 157-62, 192-96, et passim; Michael John Smith, "Henry L. Stimson and the Philippines" (Ph.D. diss., University of Indiana, 1970), pp. 65-76, 92-95, 102-6; and extract from letter of Arthur Fischer to Clinton R. Riggs, in Journals of W. Cameron Forbes, Second Series, 4:369-70, W. Cameron Forbes Papers, LC.

14. William H. Anderson, *The Philippine Problem* (New York: G. P. Putnam's Sons, 1939), pp. 150-51; E. D. Hester to JRH, July 1, 1933, Gouverneur Frank Mosher to JRH, July 20, 1933, JRH Papers.

15. Grunder and Livezey, *Philippines*, pp. 107-16, 211-12, 281; "Annual Report of the Governor-General of the Philippine Islands, 1933," Philippine Manuscript Reports, 1767:10-12, RG 350; Shirley Jenkins, *American Economic Policy toward the Philippines* (Stanford: Stanford University Press, 1954), pp. 32-33, 41; Theodore Friend, *Between Two Empires: The Ordeal of the Philippines, 1929-1946* (New Haven: Yale University Press, 1965), p. 6; Lopez, "Colonial Relationship," p. 23; USTC, *Philippine Trade*, pp. 11-12, 35-38.

16. Friend, "The Philippine Sugar Industry and the Politics of Independence, 1929-1935," *Journal of Asian Studies* 22 (Feb. 1963): 179-80, 181-84; Joint

Preparatory Committee on Philippine Affairs, *Report of May 20, 1938*, 4 vols. (Washington: U.S. Government Printing Office, 1938), 1:26, 38, 40–42; 2:382, 387–88; 3:152–53, 158–59, 577–78; USTC, *Philippine Trade*, pp. 45–46, 50–51; Stanley, *Nation*, p. 238; FM to Secretary of War, Sept. 8, 1933, File 4122, RG 350; Rafael Alunan to John Dalton, Mar. 29, 1935, Manuel L. Quezon Papers, microfilm copy in MHC.

17. Joint Preparatory Committee, *Report*, 1:49–56; USTC, *Philippine Trade*, pp. 64–71; FM to Cox, Oct. 20, 1933, FM Papers.

18. Joint Preparatory Committee, *Report*, 1:67–95 passim.

19. "Rice," Dec. 1935, File 4168, RG 350; Cornelio Balmaceda to Chief, Bureau of Insular Affairs, Nov. 7, 1934, ibid.; Lopez, "Colonial Relationship," p. 23; Robert Aura Smith, *Philippine Freedom, 1946–1958* (New York: Columbia University Press, 1958), pp. 65–66; USTC, *Philippine Trade*, p. 8.

20. Stanley, *Nation*, pp. 268–75; Lopez, "Colonial Relationship," pp. 21–24; Onorato, "The United States and the Philippine Independence Movement," *Solidarity* 5 (Sept. 1970), 15; Norman G. Owen, "Philippine Economic Development and American Policy: A Reappraisal," in Owen, ed., *Compadre Colonialism: Studies on the Philippines under American Rule* (Ann Arbor: University of Michigan, 1971), pp. 107, 113; Karl J. Pelzer, *Pioneer Settlement in the Asiatic Tropics* (New York: American Geographical Society, 1954), pp. 86, 92–95, 101; Hayden, *Philippines*, pp. 25–26, 378–79; Friend, *Two Empires*, pp. 19–20; Roy Manning Stubbs, "Philippine Radicalism: The Central Luzon Uprisings, 1925–1935" (Ph.D. diss., University of California, Berkeley, 1951), pp. 11–15; Romeo Cruz, *America's Colonial Desk and the Philippines, 1898–1934* (Quezon City: University of the Philippines, 1974), p. 16; Harlan R. Crippen, "Philippine Agrarian Unrest: Historical Backgrounds," *Science and Society* 10 (Fall 1946): 339–40; David R. Sturtevant, *Popular Uprisings in the Philippines, 1840–1940* (Ithaca: Cornell University Press, 1976), p. 174; Benedict J. Kerkvliet, *The Huk Rebellion* (Berkeley: University of California Press, 1977), pp. 1–25; Division of Labor Statistics, Department of Labor, "Fact-Finding Survey Report, 1936" (1936).

21. David Wurfel, "The Philippines," in George McTurnan Kahin, ed., *Government and Politics of Southeast Asia*, 2d ed. (Ithaca: Cornell University Press, 1964), pp. 691–93, 715; Hayden, *Philippines*, pp. 22–23, 26; Grunder and Livezey, *Philippines*, pp. 122–36; Friend, *Two Empires*, p. 18; Whitney T. Perkins, *Denial of Empire: The United States and Its Dependencies* (Leyden: A. W. Sythoff, 1962), pp. 209, 216; George E. Taylor, *The Philippines and the United States* (New York: Frederick A. Praeger, 1962), pp. 37–38, 82–85; Stubbs, "Philippine Radicalism," pp. 11, 126; Stanley, *Nation*, pp. 82, 156–60; Smith, "Stimson," pp. 17–20, 108–23.

22. Perkins, *Denial*, p. 209; Hayden, "News in and From the Philippines," undated, JRH Papers; press release, July 18, 1933, FM Papers.

23. Friend, *Two Empires*, pp. 31–32; Stanley, *Nation*, pp. 28–29; "Political Parties in the Philippine Islands," June 4, 1934, File 3427, RG 350; Hayden, *Philippines*, pp. 174, 316–50, 376–77; Liang, *Political Parties*, pp. 139–57, 164–67.

24. Stanley, *Nation*, pp. 182–83, 216; Malcolm, *Careerist*, pp. 88–94; James G. Wingo, "President of the Philippines," *Commonweal* 24 (July 3, 1936): 259–60;

Friend, *Two Empires*, pp. 26-27, 48-53; idem, "Manuel Quezon: Charismatic Conservative," *Philippine Historical Review* 1 (1965): 153-69; David Bernstein, *The Philippine Story* (New York: Farrar, Straus and Co., 1947), pp. 133-36; Smith, *Philippine Freedom*, p. 73; "Political Parties," June 4, 1934, File 3427, RG 350; Hayden, *Philippines*, pp. 321-50; JRH to Arthur E. Boak, Apr. 23, 1935, JRH Papers; J. Weldon Jones Memorandum for FM, Dec. 9, 1936, FM Papers; R. Custodio Salazar to FM, May 21, 1933, and enclosed memorandum, Norman H. Hill Papers, Burton Historical Collection, Detroit, Michigan.

25. Hayden, *Philippines*, pp. 173, 198; Robert Aura Smith, "Analysis of Proposed Constitution," Nov. 28, 1934, War Plans Division (WPD), File 3389-10, Records of the War Department General and Special Staffs, RG 165, NARS; *NYT*, Dec. 24, 1933; Friend, *Two Empires*, p. 157n.

26. Hayden, *Philippines*, pp. 87-103; Taylor, *Philippines*, pp. 76-77; Onofre D. Corpuz, *The Bureaucracy in the Philippines* ([Manila]: University of the Philippines, 1957), p. 183; "Thirty-Fourth Annual Report of the Bureau of Civil Service, Dec. 31, 1933," Philippine Manuscript Reports, 1769: Table 2, RG 350. As of July 31, 1933, 47 Americans and 3,361 Filipinos had been appointed to unclassified and exempted positions. Ibid.

27. Smith, "Analysis," WPD File 3389-10, RG 165; *MDB*, June 15, 1933, MSB; Taylor, *Philippines*, pp. 33-34; Corpuz, *Bureaucracy*, pp. 237-38.

28. Friend, *Two Empires*, pp. 22-23; Jean Grossholz, *Politics in the Philippines* (Boston: Little, Brown and Co., 1964), p. 87; Taylor, *Philippines*, p. 79; M. Ladd Thomas, "Centralism in the Philippines: Past and Present Causes," *Social Research* 30 (Summer 1963): 205, 206-7; Maximo M. Kalaw, "The New Constitution of the Philippine Commonwealth," *Foreign Affairs* 13 (July 1935): 693-94; Carl Lande, "Party Politics in the Philippines," in George M. Guthrie, ed., *Six Perspectives on the Philippines* (Manila: The Bookmark, 1968), p. 124.

29. Hayden, *Philippines*, pp. 11-12, 692-712; Friend, *Two Empires*, pp. 17-18.

30. Hayden, *Philippines*, pp. 12-14, 570-72; Grunder and Livezey, *Philippines*, pp. 137-39.

31. Stanley, *Nation*, pp. 127-29, 271-76; Hayden, *Philippines*, p. 397; A. V. Hartendorp, "The Philippines—When the East Is West," undated typescript in JRH Papers.

32. Hayden, *Philippines*, pp. 351-52, 912n; Friend, *Two Empires*, p. 6; Grayson L. Kirk, "Whither the Philippines?" *Current History* 43 (Nov. 1935): 133.

33. Bureau of Foreign and Domestic Commerce, Far East Series, No. 134, May 1, 1933, File 1239, RG 350; Harriet Moore, "The American Stake in the Philippines," *Foreign Affairs* 11 (Apr. 1933): 519-20; Friend, "American Interests and Philippine Independence, 1929-1933," *Philippine Studies* 11 (Oct. 1963): 507-10; Joint Preparatory Committee, *Report*, 1:96-97, 99, 101, 102; USTC, *Philippine Trade*, pp. 183-92; William R. Babcock to R. S. Swinton, Oct. 6, 1933, JRH Papers.

34. Friend, *Two Empires*, pp. 107-8; Grunder and Livezey, *Philippines*, pp. 196-99, 219-20.

35. Friend, "American Interests," pp. 510-12; idem, "Philippine Sugar Industry," pp. 180-81; idem, *Two Empires*, pp. 69, 82-83; Kirk, "Philippines," p. 314; Kirk, *Philippine Independence* (New York: Farrar & Rinehart, 1936), pp. 76, 90-93; Roy Veatch, "Sugar Production for the American Market...," Feb. 6, 1934,

811.6135/119, Records of the Department of State, RG 59, NARS; Rafael Alunun, "Sugar under the New Program," *American Chamber of Commerce Journal* 15 (Nov. 1935): 46; Joint Preparatory Committee, *Report*, 3:615; Camillus Gott, "William Cameron Forbes and the Philippines" (Ph.D. diss., University of Indiana, 1974), p. 199.

36. Friend, "American Interests," pp. 512–13; Kirk, "Philippines," p. 134; Kirk, *Philippine Independence*, pp. 79, 81, 84–87; Friend, *Two Empires*, p. 82; Grunder and Livezey, *Philippines*, pp. 212–15; USTC, *Philippine Trade*, p. 71.

37. Friend, *Two Empires*, pp. 69, 83; idem, "American Interests," pp. 513–16. According to the United States census, there were 5,603 Filipinos in the United States in 1920 and 45,028 in 1930. Bureau of the Census, *Fifteenth Census of the United States, Population*, vol. 2 (Washington: U.S. Government Printing Office, 1933): 32.

38. Friend, "American Interests," pp. 516, 518; Gerald E. Wheeler, "Republican Philippine Policy, 1921–1933," *Pacific Historical Review* 28 (Nov. 1959): 384–85; Louis Morton, "War Plan Orange: Evolution of a Strategy," *World Politics* 11 (1959): 231–37; Frederic S. Marquardt, *Before Bataan and After* (New York: Bobbs-Merrill Co., 1943), p. 144; Cox Memorandum for Secretary of War, Feb. 2, 1934, PSF, War Department, 1934–1936, FDRL.

39. Key Pitman to FM, Apr. 14, 1933, FM Papers; Grunder and Livezey, *Philippines*, pp. 203–6.

40. Friend, "Philippine Interests and the Mission for Independence, 1929–1932," *Philippine Studies* 12 (Jan. 1964): 70–72; idem, *Two Empires*, p. 87; Pittman to FM, Apr. 14, 1933, FM Papers; JRH to Charles W. Franks, Mar. 31, 1933, JRH Papers.

41. Friend, "Veto and Repassage of the Hare-Hawes-Cutting Act: A Catalogue of Motives," *Philippine Studies* 12 (Oct. 1964): 672–73; Grunder and Livezey, *Philippines*, pp. 206–8; Cox Memorandum for Secretary of War, Feb. 2, 1934, PSF, War Department, 1934–1936.

42. Friend, *Two Empires*, pp. 58–62, 98–104; idem, "Philippine Independence and the Last Lame-Duck Congress," *Philippine Studies* 12 (Apr. 1964): 260–75; Hayden, *Philippines*, p. 351.

43. Quezon to Roy Howard, Mar. 23, Apr. 1, 1933, Quezon to Jose Clarin and Quintin Paredes, Apr. 25, 1933, Quezon Papers; Pittman to FM, Apr. 14, 1933, Parker to Holliday, Apr. 28, 1933, FM Papers; Hill draft of article, undated, Hill Papers; Vicente Albano Pacis, *President Sergio Osmeña*, 2 vols. (Quezon City: Osmeña Memorial Foundation, 1971), 2:35, 44–45, 411n; Friend, *Two Empires*, pp. 110–13. Friend provides a slightly different account of the meeting in Pittman's office. See also Pittman to Camilo Osias, Feb. 5, 1934, Key Pittman Papers, Philippine File, LC.

44. MM to GM [June 16, 1933], MM to ——— [June 1933], MM Papers; Antonio de las Alas to FM, May 26, 1933, FM Papers; Russell B. Porter, "Governor Murphy's Star in the Ascendant," *NYT*, Feb. 21, 1937; *News-Week* 9 (Feb. 20, 1937): 14; *MDB*, June 15, 1933, MSB; *PH*, June 15, 16, 1933, MSB; *Manila Sunday Tribune*, June 18, 1933, MSB; *Inaugural Address of Governor-General Frank Murphy, June 15, 1933* (Manila: n.p., 1933).

45. "Governor General of the Philippine Islands," Mar. 17, 1933, File 3038, RG

350; Parker Memorandum for FM, Apr. 18, 1933, FM file, ibid.; Grunder and Livezey, *Philippines*, pp. 155–56.

46. JRH to Fugate, May 3, 1933, JRH to H. Otley Beyer, May 14, 1933, JRH Papers; Friend, *Two Empires*, p. 20; Louis J. Van Schaick Memorandum for FM, July 3, 1933, FM Papers; Henry L. Stimson and McGeorge Bundy, *On Active Service in Peace and War* (New York: Harper and Brothers, 1948), pp. 130–31; Edgerton, "Hayden," pp. 25–27; Smith, *Philippine Freedom*, pp. 75–76; Forbes to T. Roosevelt, Jr., Forbes Journals, Second Series, 4:237–38, Forbes Papers.

47. Forbes to FDR, Apr. 10, 1933, OF 400; Interview with Mrs. Fielding H. Yost, Oct. 28, 1963, pp. 1–2, MHC; FM to Mr. and Mrs. Yost, Nov. 20, 1933, Fielding H. Yost Papers, MHC; Edgerton, "Hayden," pp. 7–9, 21–23, 29–30; FM to Parker, May 18, 1933, Pittman to FM, Apr. 14, 1933, Malcolm to FM, Sept. 12, 1933, FM Papers; FM to Secretary of War, July 5, 1933, Parker to JRH, July 8, 1933, JRH to Parker, July 10, 1933, Parker Memorandum for Secretary of War, July 13, 1933, Dern to FDR, Aug. 18, Nov. 2, 1933, Cox to JRH, Sept. 9, 1933, Hayden file, RG 350; Parker to JRH, Aug. 19, 1933, JRH to Cox, Sept. 6, 1933, Basil D. Edwards to JRH, Sept. 23, 29, Oct. 9, 1933, JRH to Edwards, Sept. 27, 1933, JRH Papers; IM to D. M. Roots [Dec. 11, 1933], IM Papers; Malcolm to Sink, Nov. 21, 1932, Mar. 15 [1933], Sink to Malcolm, Mar. 27, 1933, Sink Papers; Malcolm to Mrs. C. M. Malcolm, Sept. 21, 1933, George A. Malcolm Papers, MHC; [*PH*, Nov. 3, 1933], HSB; Francis Burton Harrison, *Origins of the Philippine Republic: Extracts from the Diaries of Francis Burton Harrison*, ed. and annotated by Michael P. Onorato (Ithaca: Cornell University, 1974), p. 6.

48. JRH to Jesse Reeves, Feb. 9, 1934, JRH to George Lewis, Dec. 16, 1934, JRH Papers; Jones to Richard D. Lunt, Jan. 25, 1963, Richard D. Lunt Papers, MHC; Hester to T. Roosevelt, Jr., Sept. 8, 1936, Theodore Roosevelt, Jr., Papers, Box 21, LC.

40. Press Release, Sept. 6, 1933, Jones file, RG 350; Jones to Lunt, Jan. 25, 1963, Lunt Papers; Jones to Fine, Jan. 29, 1966.

50. FM to Parker, May 3, 1933, FM to Cox, Apr. 7, 1934, EGK to FM, Apr. 9, 1934, FM to W. S. Gilmore, Apr. 17, 1934, FM Papers; IM to Roots, Mar. 31 [1934], IM Papers; [*PH*, Apr. 7, 1934], MSB; *PH*, Jan. 13, 1934, HSB.

51. *PH*, Jan. 13, 1934, HSB; *PH*, July 9, 1935, MSB; *MDB*, Apr. 30, 1934, MSB; *DT*, May 13, 1933, MSB; Roosevelt, Jr., to Parker, Feb. 18, 1933, FM to Parker, May 10, 1933, Hill to Parker, May 10, 1933, FM to Cox, Apr. 7, 1934, FM Papers; typed sheet [May 2, 1934], ibid.; Hester to Roosevelt, Jr., Sept. 8, 1936, Roosevelt Papers, Box 21; Jones to Lunt, Jan. 25, 1963, Lunt Papers; Parker Memorandum for FM, Apr. 18, 1933, Murphy file, RG 350.

52. Juan F. Hilario to FM, Mar. 21, 1934, FM Papers; *DN*, June 10, 1934.

53. IM to Roots [Dec. 11, 1933], IM Papers; Stimson and Bundy, *Active Service*, p. 129; *Japan Advertiser* [June 6, 1933], HSB; *MT*, Apr. 13, 1934, MSB; *MT*, May 13, 1936, HSB; *NYT*, June 16, 1933; FM to Ann Joachim, June 3, 1933, FM to Louis Howe, July 18, 1933, FM to Jones, May 25, 1936, FM Papers; FM notes, Feb. 1935, ibid.; FM to Blair Moody, May 11, 1935, Blair Moody Papers, MHC; FM to Couzens, Nov. 17, 1935, Couzens Papers, Box 16; FM to Raymond Moley, July 18, 1933, Raymond Moley Papers, Hoover Institution, Stanford University, Stanford, California

(I saw the relevant Murphy items in the Moley Papers before they were transferred to the Hoover Institution).

54. Unsigned document [July 24, 1933], FM Papers; *San Francisco Chronicle*, Mar. 28, 1935, clipping in ibid.; Hester to JRH, Nov. 8, 1933, JRH to Reeves, Feb. 9, 1934, JRH to James Clement Wheat, Feb. 26, 1934, JRH to Eugene A. Gilmore, July 11, 1934, JRH Papers; *PH*, Dec. 5, 1933, HSB; [*MT*, Dec. 6, 1933], HSB; *MDB*, Dec. 7, 1933, HSB; *DN*, June 10, 1934; JRH, "The Changing Orient," *Michigan Alumnus Quarterly Review* 42 (Spring 1936): 116; JRH, "The Philippine Policy of the United States" (New York: Institute of Pacific Relations, 1939), p. 25; EGK, Re—Frank Murphy, Oct. 1961, EGK Papers; EGK draft of "Frank Murphy as Government Administrator," ibid.; Melchor P. Aquino, "Frank Murphy," *Bulletin of the American Historical Collection* 1 (July 1973): 16.

55. Marquardt, *Bataan*, p. 186; Anderson, *Philippine Problem*, p. 152; JRH to Boak, Apr. 20, 1935, JRH to Nicholas Roosevelt, Mar. 20, 1937, JRH Papers; FM to Tydings, Sept. 14, 1934, Quezon to FM, Aug. 23, 1934, Apr. 26, May 16, 1936, JRH to FM, Mar. 12, 1936, FM Papers; FM notes on conversation with Quezon, Aug. 23, 1934, ibid.; FM notes, Feb. 1935, ibid.; MM diary, May, Aug. 14, 1935, MM Papers; Quezon to FM, June 15, 1934, Quezon Papers; Cox Memorandum: Conversation with Mr. Q . . . , Oct. 13, 1934, Quezon Mission, 1934, Records of the Office of the U.S. High Commissioner to the Philippine Islands, RG 126, NARS; Dern, "Confidential Report to the President," Part 2, Dec. 20, 1935, PSF, War Department (Dern), FDRL; Hilario, "American-Philippine Relations," *National Review*, Apr. 23, 1937, p. 17, FM Papers; [DLN, Nov. 30, 1934], MSB; Interview with Norman H. Hill, Aug. 21, 1963, p. 16, MHC; Interview with IM, July 30, 1964, pp. 49, 51, MHC; Interview with Mrs. Joseph R. Hayden, Feb. 15, 1965, p. 4, MHC; Jones to Fine, Jan. 29, 1966; Harrison, *Origins*, pp. 19, 22, 40, 43, 73, 78, 120.

56. A. Quezon to FM, June 8, 1936, FM Papers; IM interview, p. 54.

57. Hill to Frank Picard, Oct. 23, 1933, Hill Papers; Hester to JRH, Nov. 8, 1933, JRH Papers; Hester to Roosevelt, Jr., Jan. 11, 1934, Roosevelt Papers, Box 19; *PH*, July 3, 1934, *MDB*, June 25, 1934, *Philippines Free Press*, Aug. 4, 1934, clippings in FM Papers; Hayden, *Philippines*, pp. 183, 886–87; Anderson, *Philippine Problem*, p. 152.

58. Minutes of Cabinet Meetings, July 19, 26, 1934, FM Papers; unsigned document [July 24, 1933], ibid.; *PH*, July 3, 1934, clipping in ibid.; *Advertiser*, Aug. 6, 1933, MSB. Despite Murphy's advice, the cabinet continued to discuss trivial patronage matters. Murphy eventually devised a procedure whereby the cabinet first disposed of minor matters and then discussed general policy questions. See Cabinet Minutes, Sept. 12, 1934, FM Papers.

59. Staff Meetings [Mar. 20, 1934], FM Papers; *PH*, Mar. 31, Apr. 3, 1934, MSB; *MDB*, Apr. 5, 1934, MSB; *NYT*, Apr. 5, 1934; Hayden, *Philippines*, pp. 148–49.

60. "Civil Service Report, 1933," 1769: 18–20, RG 350; FM to Speaker, Dec. 3, 1934, File 2223, ibid.; Executive Order No. 446, Sept. 29, 1933, FM Papers; [Hester] Confidential Memorandum for the Governor General . . . [Sept. 16, 1933], ibid.; Cabinet Meeting notes, Dec. 2, 1934, ibid.; Hill to W. Steele Gilmore, Aug. 29, 1934, *DN*—Murphy file, in my possession; Hester to Roosevelt, Jr., Jan. 11, 1934, Roosevelt Papers, Box 19; *MDB*, Apr. 24, 1934, Nov. 5, 1935, MSB; *PH*, Jan. 8,

1934, MSB; *MT*, Apr. 13, 1934, HSB; *MT*, Jan. 22, 1935, clipping in FM Papers.

61. *MDB*, Aug. 31, 1933, clipping in FM Papers; Hester to Roosevelt, Jr., Jan. 11, 1934, Roosevelt Papers, Box 19; FM to Alex Rivers, Dec. 13, 1934, FM to Ann Walker, May 7, 1934, July 31, 1935, FM Papers; Hill to Picard, Oct. 23, 1933, Hill Papers; JRH to Cox, Dec. 27, 1933, Hayden file, RG 350; JRH to Reeves, Feb. 9, 1934, JRH Papers; MM to GM, Aug. 25 [1934], Dec. 12, 1934, Aug. 7, 1935, GM Papers; MM to Mrs. Walker [Oct. or Nov. 1935], MM Papers; Jones to Fine, Jan. 29, 1966; *Manila Sunday Tribune*, Oct. 23, 1933, HSB; [*MDB*, Feb. 1, 1934], MSB; JRH, "Changing Orient," p. 116.

62. FM to GM, July 25, 1933, GM Papers; Garfinkel to EMB, undated, FM Papers; Press Release, July 18, 1933, ibid.; Executive Order No. 428, June 29, 1933, ibid.; Cabinet Minutes, June 28, 1933, ibid.; Staff Meetings, Oct. 3, 1933, ibid.; Notes of Staff Meeting, 1934, ibid.; Notes of a meeting of . . . Hayden with his Staff, Jan. 25, 1935, ibid.; Hester to Roosevelt, Jr., Jan. 11, 1934, Roosevelt Papers, Box 19; "Civil Service Report, 1933," 1769: 20-21, RG 350; *PH*, June 22, 1933, MSB; *PH*, June 30, 1933, HSB; *MDB*, June 15, 1933, MSB; *MDB*, Sept. 15, 1933, clipping in FM Papers; *MT*, Apr. 13, 1934, MSB.

63. Cabinet Minutes, June 28, 1933, FM Papers; MM to GM [Oct. 1933], GM Papers; Roosevelt, Jr., to Hester, Feb. 14, 1934, F. Theo Rogers to Roosevelt, Jr., Sept. 15, 1934, Roosevelt Papers, Box 19; Richard D. Lunt, *The High Ministry of Government: The Political Career of Frank Murphy* (Detroit: Wayne State University Press, 1965), pp. 87-88; *MDB*, Nov. 5, 1935, MSB; *MDB*, May 13, 1936, clipping in FM Papers.

64. *PH*, Feb. 24, 26, 28, 1934, HSB; *PH*, Jan. 22, 1934, clipping in FM Papers; *PH*, Mar. 14, June 22, 1934, MSB; *MDB*, Jan. 22, Mar. 2, June 27, 1934, clippings in FM Papers; *MDB*, Feb. 26, 1934, HSB; *MDB*, Feb. 27, 28, Mar. 8, 14, [June 21], June 23, 1934, MSB; *MT*, Feb. 28, Mar. 1, 10, 11, 1934, MSB; *DN*, June 10, 1934; Hill to Moody, June 24, 1934, Moody Papers; Jones to Fine, Jan. 29, 1966; Stanley, *Nation*, p. 109; Harrison, *Origins*, p. 15.

65. JRH to Reeves, Feb. 9, 1934, JRH Papers; Hilario to FM, Aug. 7, 1933, Encarnacion to FM, July 25, 1934, JRH to FM, Nov. 27, 1935, FM Papers; Jones to Fine, Jan. 29, 1966; [*PH*, Nov. 2, 1935], MSB.

66. *DN*, Apr. 23, 1933; MM to GM, July 22 [1933], FM to GM, July 25, 1933, Mar. 28, 1934, IM to GM [Jan. 11, 1934], GM Papers; FM to Walker, June 30, July 7, Sept. 5, 1934, FM to Mulcahy, Sept. 17, 1934, Arthur Garfield Hays to FM, Sept. 20, 1935, Garfinkel to EMB, undated, FM Papers; *PH*, July 18, 1933, MSB; Anderson, *Philippine Problem*, p. 152; "Lay Bishop," *Time* 34 (Aug. 28, 1939): 16; Hill interview, p. 16; IM interview, pp. 48-49, 53.

67. *DN*, Apr. 9, 1933; FM to Alex Blain, July 9, 1933, FM to John E. Murphy, Sept. 19, 1933, FM to GM, Sept. 17, 1934, FM to Homer Cummings, Apr. 2, 1934, FM Papers; FM to GM, Mar. 28, 1934, GM Papers; FM to JRH, Mar. 16, 1936, JRH Papers.

68. IM to Roots [Dec. 11, 1933], IM Papers; FM to GM, July 25, 1933, IM to GM [Jan. 11, 1934], GM Papers; MM to —————— [1935 or 1936], MM Papers; Jones to Fine, Jan. 29, 1966; Forbes to Roosevelt, Jr., Feb. 18, 1932, Forbes Journals, 4:237-38, Forbes Papers; [(Ann Arbor) *Voice of Democracy*, Oct. 30, 1936], MSB; Marquardt,

Bataan, p. 169; Grossholz, *Politics*, p. 95; Friend, *Two Empires*, pp. 24–25, 30; Smith, *Philippine Freedom*, pp. 35, 37, 39; Guthrie, "The Philippine Temperament," in Guthrie, ed., *Six Perspectives*, p. 58; Mrs. Hayden interview, p. 5; IM interview, p. 52.

69. IM to Roots [Dec. 11, 1933], IM Papers; FM notes, Feb. 1935, FM Papers; John J. Burke to FM, May 6, 1933, ibid.; HM to GM, Dec. 10, 1933, GM Papers; draft of Hill article, Hill Papers; Marquardt to Roosevelt, Jr., Dec. 25, 1933, Roosevelt Papers, Box 29; *MDB*, Nov. 23, 1933, clipping in FM Papers; *MDB*, June 16, 1933, MSB; *MT*, June 16, 1933, MSB; *PH*, Apr. 28, 1933, MSB; *Shanghai Evening Post and Mercury*, June 9, 1933, MSB; *DN*, June 10, 1934; *Philippines Free Press*, Dec. 14, 1935, MSB; Moody, "High Commissioner to Manila," *Survey Graphic* 24 (Dec. 1935): 610; Manuel Luis Quezon, *The Good Fight* (New York: D. Appleton-Century Co., 1946), p. 150; Marquardt, *Bataan*, pp. 169, 175; J. Woodford Howard, *Mr. Justice Murphy* (Princeton: Princeton University Press, 1968), pp. 67–69; Hill interview, pp. 15–16; IM interview, p. 51.

70. Burke to FM, May 6, 1933, FM to Burke, May 22, 1933, Angel A. Ansaldo to FM, Sept. 13, 1933, Pastor Santiago Memorandum for FM, Dec. 7, 1933, FM Papers; *Christian Century*, Aug. 23, 1933, clipping in ibid.; *La Defensa*, July 22, 1933, HSB; [*Baltimore Catholic Review*, Apr. 5, 1935], MSB; *America* 52 (Oct. 20, 1934): 28; Marquardt, *Bataan*, pp. 169–70; EG notes on interview with MM, undated, EG Papers; Jones to Lunt, Jan. 25, 1963, Lunt Papers.

71. A. Quezon to FM, Jan. 26, 1938, Mosher to FM, Nov. 3, 1933, William Piani to FM, Dec. 18, 1933, E. Cardinal Pacelli to FM, Jan. 14, 1934, Edward F. Casey to FM, Dec. 31, 1934 [1933], Leo Butler to FM, Nov. 10, 1936, FM Papers; Mosher to JRH, Nov. 4, 1933, JRH Papers; *Christian Century*, Aug. 23, 1933, clipping in FM Papers.

72. *Graphic*, June 29, 1933, clipping in FM Papers; *La Defensa*, July 22, 1933, HSB; Pedro de la Llana, "The Unknown Murphy," *Philippines Free Press* [Nov. 30, 1935], MSB; [*Atlanta Constitution*, Jan. 1936], MSB; *PH*, Aug. 3, 1934, MSB; *MDB*, Aug. 4, 1934, MSB; Piani to FM, Dec. 18, 1933, Michael J. O'Doherty to FM, July 8, Aug. 29, Nov. 21, 1934, Josefa J. Martinez to FM, Nov. 22, 1934, FM Papers; FM notes on conversation with Quezon, Aug. 23, 1934, ibid.; Cabinet Minutes, Aug. 7, 1935, ibid.; Hester to Roosevelt, Jr., Jan. 11, 1934, Roosevelt Papers, Box 19; IM to GM, Jan. 11, 1934, GM Papers; Jones to Lunt, Jan. 25, 1963, Lunt Papers; Smith, *Philippine Freedom*, pp. 25–26; Marquardt, *Bataan*, p. 170; Mrs. Hayden interview, pp. 2–3; The Reminiscences of Roger N. Baldwin (1954), 1:217, Oral History Research Office, Columbia University, New York, New York. Like his predecessors, Murphy declined to intervene when an auditor's report revealed that the banks of the church were insolvent. Jones to Lunt, Jan. 25, 1963, Lunt Papers.

73. Jones to Fine, Jan. 29, 1966; Friend, *Two Empires*, p. 37; Florence Horn, *Orphans of the Pacific: The Philippines* (New York: Reynal and Hitchcock, 1941), p. 90; Hester to Roosevelt, Jr., Jan. 11, 1934, C. M. Cotterman to Roosevelt, Jr., May 22, 1934, Roosevelt Papers, Box 19; J. A. Wolfson to John K. Watkins, Sept. 11, 1933, Kenneth B. Day to FM, Jan. 23, 1935, John Hausserman to FM, Mar. 20, 1936, FM Papers; Helen Yearsley to Andrew C. Baird, Aug. 24, 1933, enclosed with Baird to GM, Sept. 30, 1933, GM Papers; M. W. H. and D. to MM, Sept. 18,

1933, MM Papers; Hausserman to FDR, June 30, 1936, OF 400; Dern, "Confidential Report," Part 2, Dec. 20, 1935, PSF, War Department (Dern); F. G. Roth to JRH, Mar. 5, 1938, JRH Papers; *American Chamber of Commerce Journal*, Dec. 1935, MSB; IM interview, p. 51; Interview with Martin S. Hayden, Oct. 6, 1964, p. 37, MHC; Howard, *Murphy*, p. 68; Harrison, *Origins*, pp. 9, 61.

74. FM to Bain, June 29, 1933, FM to Byron Foy, Aug. 12, 1933, May 7, 1936, FM to Sam Ledner, Aug. 10, 1933, FM to Walker, June 30, 1934, June 6, 1936, FM to Hernando J. Abaya, Jan. 24, 1938, FM Papers; FM to GM, Mar. 28, 1934, GM Papers; FM to JRH, Mar. 16, 1936, JRH Papers; IM interview, p. 48.

75. FM to John and Venus Perkins, Aug. 21, 1933, FM to Walker, Sept. 25, 1934, Garfinkel to EMB, undated, FM Papers; IM to Roots [Nov. 28, Dec. 11, 1933], Mar. 31 [1934], IM Papers; MM to GM, July 5 [1933], Oct. 4, 1933, GM Papers; Marquardt, *Bataan*, p. 175.

76. Fine, *Murphy*, p. 194; MM to GM, Sept. 14, 1933, GM Papers; Murphy file, RG 350; Jones to Lunt, Jan. 25, 1963, Lunt Papers; Jones to Fine, Jan. 29, 1966; Howard, *Murphy*, pp. 67–68.

77. FM to GM, July 7, Dec. 18, 1934, IM to GM, Nov. 29 [1933], MM to GM [Nov. 12, 1934], [Aug. 1935], GM Papers; FM to Walker, Sept. 14, 1935, FM Papers; FM notes, Feb. 1935, ibid.; Jones to Lunt, Jan. 25, 1963, Lunt Papers.

78. FM to GM, July 25, 1933, MM to GM, Aug. 26, 1933, GM Papers; FM to Walker, May 7, Sept. 23, 1934, July 31, 1935, FM to General and Mrs. Parker, Apr. 24, 1934, FM to John Hammond, Feb. 21, 1936, FM Papers; EMB to Ethel [Holt], May 1, 1934, EMB Papers; Rogers to Roosevelt, Jr., Sept. 15, 1934, Roosevelt Papers, Box 19; *MT*, Feb. 18, 1934, MSB; [*MDB*, Dec. 9, 1935], *MDB*, Mar. 24, 1936, MSB; de la Llana, "Unknown Murphy," MSB; *La Defensa*, July 22, 1933, MSB; *News-Week* 5 (Mar. 16, 1935): 17.

79. Fine, *Murphy*, p. 256; FM to Foy, Aug. 12, 1933, FM to Walker, June 6, 1936, F. W. Manley to FM, July 26, 1936, Hayden, Stone and Co. to FM, Oct. 3, 1936, A. L. Yacto to Ely, Jan. 10, 1936, FM Papers; copy of FM's 1936 income tax return, ibid.; MM to GM, Sept. 14, 1933, HM to GM, Dec. 10, 1933, GM Papers; IM to Roots [Dec. 11, 1933], IM Papers; Giles Kavanagh notes [1951], Josephine Gomon Papers, MHC.

80. FM to Charles L. Palms, Mar. 28, 1935, FM Papers; Robert Dollar Co. receipt, May 23, 1934, ibid.; FM to GM, Oct. 11, 1934, GM Papers; FM file, RG 350.

81. Fine, *Murphy*, pp. 195–96, 256, 456; MM to GM [May or June 1933], GM Papers; IM to Roots [Dec. 11, 1933], IM Papers; ——— to FM [Oct. 8, 1933], ——— to FM, Nov. 22, 1934, ——— to FM, Nov. 4 [1935], FM Papers.

82. [*PH*, Nov. 3, 1933], HSB; [*PH*, Apr. 21, 1934], clipping in FM Papers; MM Diary, Apr. 18, 1934, MM Papers; IM to Aunt Irene [Mar. 11, 1935], IM Papers; Walker to FM, Sept. 19, 1930, [Apr. 1934], [Apr. 25, 1934], [1935], June 9 [1935], FM to Walker, May 7, June 2, 30, July 7, 17, 30, Aug. 20, Sept. 5, 23, Oct. 8, Nov. 7, 28, Dec. 2, 1934, May 14, 15, [16], 17, 21, Aug. 7, Sept. 4, Oct. 9, 1935.

83. Rogers to Roosevelt, Jr., Sept. 15, 1934, Roosevelt Papers, Box 19; *News-Week* 5 (Mar. 16, 1935): 17; *PH*, May 13, 1936, MSB; [*Atlanta Constitution*, Jan. 1936], MSB; IM to FM [May 1946], FM Papers; Aquino, "Murphy," p. 17.

84. *PH*, Dec. 15, 1933, HSB; FM to Walker, May 7, 1934, Nov. 20 [1934], FM to

Robert Aura Smith, Apr. 16, 1934, FM to John A. Ruskowski, Jr., Sept. 2, 1935, FM Papers.

85. FM to Howe, July 18, 1933, FM to Marvin H. McIntyre, June 17, 1933, OF 400; Cox to Secretary of War, June 16, 1933, FM to Mulcahy, June 20, 1933, Van Schaick Memoranda for the Governor-General, July 17, 18, 1933, Roxas to FM, July 19, 1933, Dern to FM, Aug. 19, 1933, Hilario to FM, Aug. 21, 1933, Wolfson to Watkins, Sept. 11, 1933, FM Papers; FM to GM, July 25, 1933, GM Papers; Walter Robb to JRH, July 5, 1933, Mosher to JRH, July 20, Nov. 4, 1933, Hill to JRH, July 22, 1933, JRH to Fugate, Aug. 19, 1933, JRH Papers; Hill to Picard, Oct. 3, 1933, Hill Papers; Hester to Roosevelt, Jr., Jan. 11, 1934, Roosevelt Papers, Box 19; *MDB*, July 18, Aug. 21, 1933, MSB; *MT*, June 16, July 18, 1933, MSB; *PH*, June 22, July 18, 1933, MSB; *NYT*, June 16, July 18, 1933; July 18, 1933 release, FM Papers.

CHAPTER 2

1. EG notes on interview with GM, 1949, EG Papers. George Murphy used slightly different phraseology to describe the episode in an interview with Sidney Fine and Robert M. Warner, Mar. 28, 1957, p. 12, MHC.

2. Hawes to FDR, Jan. 23, 1933, PPF 3947, FDRL.

3. FM to Hester Everard, Apr. 12, 1922, Hester Everard Papers, Burton Historical Collection, Detroit, Michigan; *DN*, Apr. 9, 1933; *PH*, Apr. 28, 1933, clipping in FM Papers; Interview with IM, July 30, 1964, p. 49, MHC; Sidney Fine, *Frank Murphy: The Detroit Years* (Ann Arbor: University of Michigan Press, 1975), pp. 47, 197.

4. Frederic S. Marquardt column in unidentified newspaper [May 13, 1933], MSB; Marcial P. Lichauco, *Roxas* (Manila: Kiko Printing Press, 1952), pp. 102–3.

5. *Inaugural Address of Governor-General Frank Murphy, June 15, 1933* (Manila: Bureau of Printing, 1933), p. 6; *Message of Governor-General Frank Murphy to the Ninth Philippine Legislature, July 17, 1933* (Manila: Bureau of Printing, 1933), p. 4; FM to Heraclio Abistado, July 5, 1933, FM to Frank L. Riordon, Aug. 14, 1933, FM to Secretary of War, Nov. 25, 1933, FM Papers; FM to GM, July 25, 1933, GM Papers; FM to JRH, Nov. 4, 1933, JRH Papers; IM to D. T. Roots [Dec. 11, 1933], IM Papers; Norman H. Hill to Frank Picard, Oct. 23, 1933, Norman H. Hill Papers, Burton Historical Collection; [*PH*, Oct. 17, 1933], HSB; JRH, "The Philippine Policy of the United States" (New York: Institute of Pacific Relations, 1939), p. 25; Manuel Luis Quezon, *The Good Fight* (New York: D. Appleton-Century Co., 1946), pp. 149–50.

6. Hawes to FM, May 5, 1933, FM Papers; F. LeJ. Parker, Memorandum for the Secretary of War, May 11, 1933, File 364, Records of the Bureau of Insular Affairs, RG 350, NARS.

7. FM to Secretary of War, Nov. 25, 1933, FM Papers; Theodore Friend, *Between Two Empires: The Ordeal of the Philippines, 1929–1946* (New Haven: Yale University Press, 1965), pp. 114–15; idem, "The Philippine Sugar Industry and the Politics of Independence, 1929–1935," *Journal of Asian Studies* 22 (Feb. 1963): 185–87; E. D. Hester to EGK, Nov. 24, 1933, EGK Papers; Hester to Theodore Roosevelt, Jr., Theodore Roosevelt, Jr. Papers, Box 19, LC.

8. Parker to John M. Holliday, Apr. 28, 1933, Quezon to FM, Nov. 7, 19, 1933, FM Papers; Quezon to Roy Howard, Apr. 1, 1933, Manuel L. Quezon Papers, microfilm copy in MHC; Creed F. Cox Memorandum, Dec. 18, 1933, OF 400, FDRL; Quezon to Roosevelt, Jan. 15, 1934, File 364, RG 350; Friend, "Sugar," p. 186; Quezon, *Good Fight*, p. 149.

9. Quezon to Jose Clarin, Apr. 27, 1933, Quezon to Roy Howard, July 11, 1933, Quezon to Key Pittman, Aug. 11, 1933, Quezon Papers; *PH*, June 29, 1933, HSB; Friend, *Two Empires*, p. 113; FM to Secretary of War, Nov. 25, 1933, FM Papers.

10. Friend, *Two Empires*, pp. 126-34; FM to Secretary of War, July 10, 19, Nov. 25, 1933, Cox to FM, Sept. 12, 1933, FM Papers; George H. Dern to Wallace, Aug. 10, 1933, FM to Cox, Aug. 29, 1933, FM to Secretary of War, Sept. 8, 14, Oct. 6, 19, 1933, Wallace to Secretary of War, Oct. 6, 1933, File 4122, RG 350; Statement of Parker..., Aug. 10, 1933, ibid.; *MT*, June 25, 1933, HSB; *MT*, July 11, Aug. 13, Sept. 15, 1933, MSB; *MT*, Aug. 31, Oct. 4, 1933, clippings in FM Papers; *PH*, July 15, 1933, MSB; [*PH*, Aug. 29, 1933], MSB; *MDB*, Sept. 28, 1933, [Oct. 2, 1933], MSB.

11. Dern to FM, Oct. 31, 1933, FM to Secretary of War, Nov. 21, 25, 28, Dec. 1, 1933, FM Papers; Dern to FDR, Dec. 20, 1933, OF 400.

12. Pittman to FM, Sept. 8, 1933, FM Papers; Pittman to Camilo Osias, Feb. 5, 1934, Key Pittman Papers, Philippine File, LC; Hester to EGK, Nov. 24, 1933, EGK Papers; Cox Memorandum for Secretary of War, Nov. 24, 1933, File 364, RG 350. The bureau recommendation was based on the advice of Joseph R. Hayden. Office Memorandum, Nov. 8, 1933, JRH Papers; "... notes ... dictated by ... Hayden...," Nov. 9, 1933, ibid.

13. Quezon Memorandum for FM, Nov. 3, 1933, Quezon Papers; Quezon note, Nov. 4, 1933, FM Papers; Quezon to FM, Nov. 7, 1933 (two letters), FM Papers; M. J. Smith, "Henry L. Stimson and the Philippines...," *Michigan Academician* 5 (Winter 1973): 345.

14. Hester to Roosevelt, Jr., Jan. 11, 1934, Roosevelt Papers, Box 19; FM Radio Message, Nov. 15, 1933, Quezon file, RG 350; Quezon to FDR, Jan. 15, 1934, File 364, ibid.; Joaquin Elizalde to Quezon, Nov. 20, 1933, Quezon to Guillermo Cabrera, Dec. 28, 1933, Quezon Papers; Henry L. Stimson Diary, Dec. 11, 1933, Jan. 24, 1934, Henry L. Stimson Papers, Sterling Library, Yale University, New Haven, Connecticut; Cox Memoranda, Dec. 18, 20, 1933, OF 400; *MDB*, Nov. 16, 1933, HSB; *MT*, Nov. 16, 1933, HSB; Roosevelt, Jr., *Colonial Policies of the United States* (Garden City: Doubleday, Doran, and Co., 1937), p. 181.

15. Quezon to Cabrera, Dec. 28, 1933, Quezon to J. G. Harbord, Feb. 6, 1934, Quezon Papers; Rafael Alunan to Elizalde [Dec. 29, 1933], Quezon to Elizalde, Jan. 3, 1934, FM Papers; Quezon to Dern, Jan. 23, 1934, Dern to FDR, Jan. 30, 1934, OF 400; Cox Memorandum for Secretary of War, Feb. 12, 1934, Cox to Tydings, Mar. 1, 1934, File 364, RG 350; Cox, Conference with ... Tydings, Feb. 28, 1934, Confidential Diary Notes on Miscellaneous Subjects, 1933-1935, File 9-7-2, Records of the Office of Territories, RG 126, NARS.

16. Quezon note, Nov. 4, 1933, FM Papers; Hawes to FM, May 5, 1933, ibid.; Cox Memorandum, Dec. 18, 1933, OF 400; Tydings to FDR, Feb. 26, 1934, ibid.; Quezon to FDR, Jan. 15, 1934, File 364, RG 350; Quezon to Quintin Paredes, Feb.

22, 1934, Quezon Papers; Cox Memorandum for Secretary of War, Feb. 2, 1934, PSF, War Department, 1934–1936, FDRL; Cox, Conference with Tydings, Feb. 28, 1934, Confidential Diary Notes, RG 126.

17. Quezon to Howard, Nov. 30, 1933, Quezon to Cabrera, Dec. 28, 29, 1933, Quezon Papers; Vicente Madrigal et al. to Quezon, Jan. 2, 1934, FM Papers; Dern to FDR, Jan. 30, 1934, OF 400; Cox Memorandum for Secretary of War, Feb. 12, 1934, File 364, RG 350; Vicente Albano Pacis, "Murphy—P. I. Benefactor," *Philippines Herald Year Book* 3 (1935–36): 20, MSB; FDR to Roosevelt, Jr., Feb. 17, 1934, Roosevelt Papers, Box 30; Stimson Diary, May 17, 1934, Stimson Papers.

18. Quezon to FM, Feb. 17, 1934, FM Papers; FDR to Roosevelt, Jr., Feb. 17, 1934, Roosevelt Papers, Box 30; Tydings to FDR, Feb. 26, 1934, OF 400; Friend, *Two Empires*, pp. 140–41; *NYT*, Mar. 3, 1934.

19. Tydings to FDR, Feb. 26, 1934, OF 400; Quezon to FM, Mar. 23, 1934, FM Papers; FM account of conversation with Quezon, Aug. 23, 1934, ibid.; *La Vanguardia*, Nov. 15, 1933, clipping in ibid.; draft of Hill article, Hill Papers; Pacis, "Murphy," p. 20. For the terms of the Tydings-McDuffie Act, see *The Statutes at Large of the United States of America* 48, pt. 1 (Washington: U.S. Government Printing Office, 1934): 456–65.

20. *PH*, Mar. 26, 1934, HSB; FM to W. S. Gilmore, Apr. 17, 1934, FM Papers; FM comments on "Hester Notes on the Hare-Hawes-Cutting Bill" [1934], ibid.; HM to GM, Dec. 10, 1933, GM Papers; IM to Mrs. E. V. Hawkins, Mar. 27 [1934], IM Papers; Stimson Diary, Dec. 11, 1933, Stimson Papers.

21. *Monday Mail*, Mar. 26, 1934, HSB; *MT*, Apr. 13, 1934, MSB; Cox to FM, Apr. 4, 1934, FM to Secretary of War, Apr. 9, 1934, FM Papers.

22. *MDB*, May 1, 2, 1934, *MT*, May 1, 1934, clippings in FM Papers; FM speech, Apr. 30, 1934, ibid.; FM to Secretary of War, May 2, 1934, ibid.; [*PH*, Dec. 31, 1934], HSB; "Annual Report of the Governor-General of the Philippine Islands, 1934," Philippine Manuscript Reports 1789: 1–2, RG 350; Friend, *Two Empires*, pp. 146–47.

23. FM to Cox, Aug. 1, 1934, FM to Tydings, Sept. 4, 1934, FM Papers; Joseph Ralston Hayden, *The Philippines* (Macmillan Co., 1942), p. 40; JRH to Jesse Reeves, Oct. 6, 1934, JRH Papers; George A. Malcolm, *American Colonial Careerist* (Boston: Christopher Publishing House, 1957), pp. 115–20; Gerald E. Wheeler, "Manuel L. Quezon and the Philippine Constitution," *University of the East . . . Journal* 1 (1964): 167, 171.

24. Pedro Guevara to Sumners, June 2, 1934, OF 400; Quezon to Guevara, June 29, 1934, Cox to FM (from Sumners), July 6, 8, 1934, FM to Cox, July 10, 1934, FM Papers; FM to Secretary of War, Sept. 4, 5, 1934, File 364, RG 350; Draft Memorandum by Cox, Dec. 27, 1934, File 41, ibid.; Cox Memorandum, May 23, 1934, Confidential Diary Notes, RG 126. For evidence that drafters of the constitution sought to follow the advice of the United States government on at least one matter, see FM to Secretary of War, Oct. 5, 1934, Cox Memorandum, Oct. 6, 1934, Confidential Diary Notes, RG 126; and FM to Secretary of War, Oct. 15, 1934, Quezon file, RG 350.

25. [*MDB*, July 31, 1934], MSB; Louis J. Van Schaick Memorandum for the Governor-General, July 31, 1934, FM Papers; Notes of Staff Meeting, July 27, 1934,

ibid.; FM to Ann Walker, Sept. 5, 1934, FM to JRH et al., Dec. 12, 1934, Claro M. Recto to FM, Jan. 7, 1934 [1935], ibid.; Hayden, *Philippines*, pp. 39-40; Malcolm, *Careerist*, p. 121; Robert Aura Smith, *Philippine Freedom, 1946-1958* (New York: Columbia University Press, 1958), pp. 80-81. Although the president of the convention asked Murphy to refer the sections of the constitution to Washington with his comments and recommendations, Murphy forwarded the sections without comment. FM to Secretary of War, Jan. 15, 1935, FM Papers.

26. *Message . . . July 17, 1933*, pp. 16-17; Pura Villanueva Kalaw, *How the Filipina Got the Vote* (Manila: n.p., 1952), pp. 7, 12, 17-21, 28-30; *NYT*, Nov. 12, 1933; *PH*, Dec. 7, 1933, HSB; Robert Aura Smith, "Analysis of the Proposed Constitution of the Philippine Commonwealth," War Plans Division (WPD) File 3389-10, Records of the War Department General and Special Staffs, RG 165, NARS.

27. Smith, "Analysis," WPD File 3389-10, RG 165; FM account of conversation with Quezon, Aug. 23, 1934, FM Papers; FM account of conversation with Osmeña, Aug. 25, 1934, ibid.; *Constitution of the Philippines* (Mar. 1935), Article V; Kalaw, *Filipina*, pp. 37-45.

28. Fine, *Murphy*, pp. 427, 441; Cox to FM (Quezon for Recto), Nov. 2, 1934, FM to Norris, Jan. 5, 1935, FM Papers; Smith, "Analysis," WPD File 3389-10, RG 165; Wheeler, "Quezon," p. 170; Hayden, *Philippines*, p. 44; *Constitution*, Article II, Section 5, Article VI, Article XIII, Section 6. The Filipinos returned to a bicameral legislature in 1939.

29. *Constitution*, Article II, Section 2, Article III, Article VI, Sections 9, 11, 16, Article XII, Sections 1, 6, Article XVII; John H. Romani, "The Philippine Presidency: An Evaluation in Terms of American Practices and Procedures" (Ph.D. diss., University of Michigan, 1955), pp. 1, 39; Wheeler, "Quezon," pp. 168-69; Hayden Memorandum for the Governor-General, Dec. 31, 1934, JRH Papers; Maximo M. Kalaw, "The New Constitution of the Philippine Commonwealth," *Foreign Affairs* 13 (July 1935): 689; Conrado Benitez, "The New Philippine Constitution," *Pacific Affairs* 8 (Dec. 1935): 430-31; Friend, *Two Empires*, p. 151; George E. Taylor, *The Philippines and the United States* (New York: Frederick A. Praeger, 1964), pp. 69-70; Hayden, *Philippines*, pp. 42-59; Smith, *Philippine Freedom*, pp. 82, 86-87, 89, 92-93; Smith, "Analysis," WPD File 3389-10, RG 165; J. Weldon Jones Weekly Report . . . , May 24, 1936, FM Papers; Jose Yulo to FM, Feb. 9, 1935, ibid.; [*PH*, Feb. 28, 1935], MSB.

30. Cox Memoranda, Mar. 16, 18, 22, 1935, Murphy Visit, 1935, Records of the Office of U.S. High Commissioner to the Philippine Islands, RG 126; FM to Cox, Mar. 18, 1935, Harry Woodring to FDR, Mar. 22, 1935, FM Papers; FM, "Statement," undated, ibid.; "Certification of Philippine Constitution," Mar. 23 [1935], ibid.; *PH*, Mar. 19, 1935, MSB; [*MT*, Mar. 24, 1935], MSB; [*MDB*, Mar. 25, 1935], MSB.

31. Elizalde and Yulo to FM, Mar. 22, 1935, Juan F. Hilario to FM, Mar. 23, 1935, JRH to Secretary of War, Mar. 27, 1935, FM Papers; *Honolulu Star-Bulletin*, Feb. 8, 1935, *MT*, Mar. 24, 1935, *PH*, June 3, 1935, clippings in ibid.; [*PH*, Feb. 14, Mar. 29, 1935], MSB; *PH*, Mar. 25, 1935, MSB; [*MDB*, Mar. 25, Apr. 9, 1935], HSB; Pacis, "Murphy," p. 20; draft of Hill article, Hill Papers.

32. JRH to Secretary of War, Mar. 27 (two messages), May 1, 1935, Cox to FM, May 1, 8, 1935, FM to EGK, May 2, 1935, FM to Cox, May 6, 1935, FM Papers; Minutes of the Cabinet Meeting, Apr. 24, 1935, ibid.; *MT*, Mar. 24, 1935, clipping in ibid.

33. Hayden, *Philippines*, p. 400; Roy Manning Stubbs, "Philippine Radicalism: The Central Luzon Uprisings, 1925–1935" (Ph.D. diss., University of California, Berkeley, 1951), pp. 1, 12–15, 24–128; JRH to Secretary of War, May 8, 1935, File 4865, RG 350; Carlos Romulo to Quezon, May 20, 1935, Quezon Papers; Benigno Ramos to FDR, May 14, 1935, Benigno Ramos file, RG 350; extract of letter from Jose P. Fausto to Ramon Torres, May 26, 1935, JRH Papers; "Report of the Committee . . . to Investigate the Uprisings of May 2 and 3," especially Appendix I, FM Papers; Teofilo Sison to FM, June 5, 1935, FM to Secretary of War, Aug. 3, 1935, ibid.; *PH*, May 4, 5, 1935, MSB; *MDB*, May 8, 1935, MSB; "The Sakdal Protest," *Philippine Magazine* 32 (May 1935): 273. Sakdalism is placed in the context of earlier "popular" uprisings in the Philippines in David R. Sturtevant, *Popular Uprisings in the Philippines, 1840–1940* (Ithaca: Cornell University Press, 1976).

34. Grant K. Goodman, "Japan and Philippine Radicalism: The Case of Benigno Ramos," in Goodman, *Four Aspects of Philippine-Japanese Relations, 1930–1940* ([New Haven]: n.p., 1967), pp. 135–40; Stubbs, "Philippine Radicalism," pp. 130–60; Sturtevant, "Philippine Social Structure and Its Relation to Agrarian Unrest" (Ph.D. diss., Stanford University, 1958), pp. 105, 150–52, 159.

35. Goodman, "Ramos," pp. 137–38, 140; Stubbs, "Philippine Radicalism," pp. 160–65; Sturtevant, "Agrarian Unrest," pp. 166–70; idem, "Sakdalism and Philippine Radicalism," *Journal of Asian Studies* 21 (Feb. 1962): 202–4; Hayden, *Philippines*, pp. 384–87; H. H. Slaughter, Memorandum by Far Eastern Section, G-2, May 4, 1935, File 28875, RG 350.

36. Goodman, "Ramos," pp. 144, 147–50; Sturtevant, "Agrarian Unrest," pp. 173, 175–81; idem, "Sakdalism," pp. 205–6n; Stubbs, "Philippine Radicalism," pp. 16–69, 172–73, 182–84; Ramos to FDR, Nov. 19, 1934, Grew to Cordell Hull, May 13, 1935, Ramos file, RG 350; Grew to JRH, May 13, 1935, JRH Papers; *NYT*, May 5, 1935.

37. Eulogio Rodriguez to JRH, Apr. 2, 1935, JRH to H. A. Gosnell, Apr. 24, 1935, JRH Papers; JRH to Secretary of War, May 8, 1935, File 4185, RG 350; Robert G. Woods to F. W. Manley, May 22, 1935, enclosing Miguel Nicdao to Adjutant General, Philippine Constabulary, May 16, 1935, FM Papers; Manley Memorandum for FM, June 13, 1935, and enclosed pamphlet, ibid.; "Report of Uprisings Committee," ibid.; Sturtevant, "Agrarian Unrest," pp. 173–74, 195–96; Hayden, *Philippines*, pp. 387–89; [*PH*, Apr. 27, 1935], MSB.

38. *Free Filipinos*, Apr. 1, 1935, JRH Papers; Sturtevant, "Agrarian Unrest," pp. 176, 177–80; idem, "Sakdalism," pp. 205–7.

39. Cabinet Minutes, Mar. 6, 20, Apr. 3, 17, 1935, FM Papers; Rodriguez to JRH, Mar. 16, 1935, JRH Papers; Department of Agriculture and Commerce, General Circular No. 11, Apr. 12, 1935, ibid.; Jorge Vargas to Quezon, Apr. 21, 24, 27, 1935, Quezon to Vargas, Apr. 24, May 1, 1935, Quezon Papers; Sturtevant, "Agrarian Unrest," pp. 174–75; Stubbs, "Philippine Radicalism," pp. 186–89.

40. Sturtevant, "Agrarian Unrest," pp. 194–96; idem, "Sakdalism," pp. 207–8;

Stubbs, "Philippine Radicalism," pp. 197-98; Hayden, *Philippines*, p. 391; Nicdao to Adjutant General, May 16, 1935, Sison to FM, June 5, 1935, FM Papers; Grew to JRH, May 13, 1935, and enclosed [*Japan Advertiser*, May 7, 1935], JRH Papers; *MDB*, May 7, 1935, [*MDB*, Aug. 11, 1939], clippings in ibid.

41. JRH to Secretary of War, May 1, 1935, Confidential Memorandum for Superintendent, May 2, 1935, JRH Papers; JRH to Secretary of War, May 8, 1935, File 4865, RG 350; "Report of Uprisings Committee," FM Papers; Nicdao to Adjutant General, May 16, 1935, Sison to FM, June 5, 1935, ibid.; *MT*, May 3, 1935, MSB; [*MDB*, May 6, 1935], MSB; Sturtevant, "Agrarian Unrest," pp. 181-84; idem, "Sakdalism," p. 207.

42. The account of the Sakdalista revolt is based on the following: JRH to Secretary of War, May 8, 1935, File 4865, RG 350; Ely to Secretary of War, May 3, 1935, Telesforo Martinez Memorandum for District Adjutant, May 10, 1935, Nicdao Memorandum for Siguiyon Reyna, May 11, 1935, Nicdao to Adjutant General, May 16, 1935, Sison to FM, June 5, 1935, FM Papers; "Report of Uprisings Committee," ibid.; Ely Memorandum for the Governor-General, May 4, 1935, Van Schaick Memorandum for the Governor-General, May 4, 1935, JRH Papers; *PH*, May 4, 1935, MSB; *MDB*, May 4, 1935, MSB; Sturtevant, "Agrarian Unrest," pp. 184-93; idem, "Sakdalism," pp. 199-200; Stubbs, "Philippine Radicalism," pp. 191-94; Hayden, *Philippines*, pp. 389-90.

43. Van Schaick Memorandum, May 4, 1935, JRH Papers; Nicdao to Adjutant General, May 16, 1935, Sison to FM, June 5, 1935, FM Papers; "Report of Uprisings Committee," ibid.; "Sakdal Protest," p. 233.

44. Yulo to FM, May 7, 27, 1935, Sison to FM, June 5, 1935, FM to Secretary of War, Aug. 3, 1935, FM Papers; Stubbs, "Philippine Radicalism," p. 198.

45. *PH*, May 7, 1935, MSB; [*Japan Advertiser*, May 7, 1935], clipping in JRH Papers; FM to Secretary of War, Apr. 6, 1936, Quezon to FM, Apr. 9, 1936, FM Papers; Arthur Garells to Secretary of State, May 11, 1936, enclosing Stenographic Transcript..., Apr. 24, 1936, Ramos file, RG 350; Goodman, "Ramos," pp. 148-50, 158-59, 172, 179-82; Taylor, *Philippines*, p. 106; Friend, *Two Empires*, p. 244.

46. *NYT*, May 3, 5, 1935; Rodriguez Memorandum for JRH, May 8, 1935, JRH to Stephen Duggan, June 4, 1935, JRH Papers; Cox Memorandum for Secretary of War, May 7, 1935, File 4865, RG 350; Romulo to Quezon, May 20, 1935, Quezon Papers; Yulo to FM, May 27, 1935, FM Papers; MDB, May 4, 6, 1935, MSB.

47. Cox Memoranda for Secretary of War, May 4, 7, 1935, JRH to Secretary of War, May 9, 1935, File 4865, RG 350; FM to United Press Associations, May 3, 1935, FM to Cox, May 3, 6, 1935, F. Theo Rogers to FM, May 4, 1935, FM to JRH, May 11, 1935, FM to Blair Moody, May 11, 1935, JRH to FM, May 25, 27, 1935, FM Papers; Cabinet Minutes, May 15, 1935, ibid.; FM, "The Legislative Program," June 7, 1935, ibid.; Jose Robles to Quezon [May 11, 1935], Vargas to Quezon, May 16, 1935, Quezon to Vargas, May 20, 1935, Quezon Papers; JRH Notes for ... Rotary Talk, Feb. 25, 1936, JRH Papers; *MDB*, May 7, 24, 1935, MSB; *MT*, June 9, 1935, MSB; *NYT*, July 14, 1935.

48. "Report of Uprisings Committee," FM Papers; FM to Tydings, July 16, 1935, FM to ... Philippine Constabulary, July 20, 1935, ibid.; Cabinet Minutes, Aug. 21, 1935, ibid.; *MT*, June 9, 1935, MSB; Hayden, *Philippines*, pp. 392-97.

49. Jose P. Guido Memorandum for Superintendent, May 9, 1935, JRH Papers; JRH to Secretary of War, May 13, 1935, File 4865, RG 350; Cox to FM, May 13, 1935, Alberto Ramos Memorandum for Manley, July 10, 1935, Manley Memorandum for FM, Aug. 23, 1935, and enclosed reports, FM Papers; Your Comrades of Bulacan, "An Open Letter...," May 23, 1935, ibid.; MM to GM, June 1935, GM Papers; Sturtevant, "Agrarian Unrest," pp. 215–18; idem, *Popular Uprisings*, pp. 54–55n, 248; Stubbs, "Philippine Radicalism," pp. 198–99; Hayden, *Philippines*, pp. 428–29; *Fifth Annual Report of the United States High Commissioner..., Fiscal Year 1941* (Washington: U.S. Government Printing Office, 1943), pp. 34–35; Leo C. Stine, "The Economic Policies of the Commonwealth Government of the Philippine Islands," *University of Manila Journal of East Asiatic Studies* 10 (Mar. 1966): 37–51.

50. "Report of the Governor-General ... covering the period January 1, to November 14, 1935," Philippine Manuscript Reports 1865:28, RG 350; Hayden, *Philippines*, pp. 366–73; *MDB*, June 17, 1935, MSB. The agreement to coalesce did not extend to candidates for the National Assembly.

51. Hayden, *Philippines*, pp. 401–27; *PH*, Dec. 24, 1934, HSB; [*MDB*, July 29, 1935], HSB.

52. [*MT*, Feb. 21, 1935], MSB; *PH*, June 8, 1935, [Sept. 6, 1935], MSB; [*MDB*, Sept. 7, 1935], MSB; Rufo M. San Juan to FM, Aug. 14, 22, 29, 1935, C. W. Franks to Governor-General, Aug. 17, 1935, Franks to San Juan, Aug. 31, 1935, FM to San Juan, Aug. 31, 1935, FM Papers; Cabinet Minutes, July 24, Aug. 14, 1935, ibid.; A Resolution ... [Sept. 5, 1935], ibid.; MM to GM, Sept. 8, 1935, GM Papers.

53. Hayden, *Philippines*, pp. 426–27. The vote was limited to males by a special act of the legislature. [*MDB*, June 24, 1935], MSB.

54. MM Diary, Sept. [18], 1935, [Oct. 1935], MM Papers; 110 to Joe, Oct. 21, 1935, FM.

55. 110 to Joe, Oct. 21, 1935, 110 to Basilio J. Valdes, Oct. 23, 1935, [110 to Joe], Nov. 1, 1935, Guido Memorandum for Superintendent, Sept. 27, 1935, Ramon de Gaviola Memorandum for Adjutant General [Sept. 28, 1935], Severo C. Cruz Memorandum for Adjutant General, Oct. 1, 1935, FM Papers.

56. *MT*, Sept. 22, 1935, clipping in FM Papers; Memorandum for Superintendent, Intelligence Division, Sept. 21, 25, 1935, Guido Memoranda for Superintendent, Sept. 27, Oct. 5, 19, 1935, de Gaviola Memorandum [Sept. 28, 1935], E. Kolimlim Memorandum for Superintendent, Intelligence Division, Oct. 3, 1935, Guido Memorandum for Superintendent, enclosed with Valdes to Manley, Oct. 5, 1935, Memoranda for Superintendent, Intelligence Division, Oct. 7, 15, 30, 1935, Cruz Memoranda for Adjutant General, Oct. 1, 9, 12, 14, 15, 17, 23, 26, Nov. 1, 1935, Cruz Memorandum for District Adjutant, Oct. 7, 1935, A. G. Gabriel Memorandum for Superintendent, Oct. 9, 1935, Leon Angeles Memorandum for District Adjutant, Oct. 17, 1935, 110 to Joe, Oct. 21, 1935, 110 to Valdes, Oct. 23, 1935, FM Papers; Aguinaldo Statement, Oct. 28, 1935, ibid.; JRH to Jesse Reeves, Oct. 21, 1935, JRH Papers; *MDB*, Oct. 19, 1935, HSB; *NYT*, Oct. 30, 1935.

57. Cruz Memoranda for Adjutant General, Oct. 9, 11, 1935, Gabriel Memorandum, Oct. 9, 1935, Guido Memorandum, Oct. 9, 1935, Aguinaldo to FM, Oct. 11, 1935, Memorandum for Adjutant General, Oct. 15, 1935, Van Schaick Memoran-

dum for FM, Oct. 21, 1935, FM Papers; JRH to Reeves, Oct. 12, 1935, JRH Papers; MM Diary [Oct. 1935], MM Papers.

58. JRH to Reeves, Sept. 29, Oct. 7, 12, 1935, JRH to James R. Fugate, Oct. 12, 1935, JRH to Paul F. Russell, Oct. 17, 1935, JRH Papers; MM Diary [Oct. 1935], MM Papers.

59. Aguinaldo to FM, Oct. 11, 17, 1935, FM to Aguinaldo, Oct. 16, 19, 1935, EGK to FM, Oct. 16, 1935, FM to Secretary of Justice, Oct. 16, 1935, Yulo to Aguinaldo, Oct. 17, 1935, Aguinaldo to Secretary of Justice, Oct. 18, 1935, Sison and Prospero Sanidad to Aguinaldo, Oct. 19, 1935, FM to Secretary of War, Oct. 21, 1935, Aguinaldo to Chairmen. . ., Oct. 21, 1935, FM to FDR, Oct. 23, 1935, FDR to FM, Dec. 7, 1935, FM Papers; Joint Resolution of the Elections Committee and enclosed Report, Oct. 22, 1935, ibid.; JRH to Reeves, Nov. 7, 1934 [1935], JRH Papers; Dern, "Confidential Report to the President," Part 2, Dec. 20, 1935, PSF, War Department (Dern); [*MDB*, Oct. 19, 1935], MSB; Hayden, *Philippines*, pp. 430, 433, 435.

60. JRH to Reeves, Oct. 21, 1935, JRH Papers.

61. "Quezon—Methods. . .," Oct. 2, 1935, ibid.; JRH to Reeves, Nov. 7, 1934 [1935], ibid.; FM Notes on Conference, Jan. 19 [1935], FM Papers; Van Schaick Memorandum for Governor-General, Oct. 1, 1935, [110] to Joe, Nov. 1, 1935, 110 to Joe, Nov. 3, 1935, FM Papers. Aguinaldo had lost some of the friar land that he had purchased because he was in arrears in tax payments. In the end, his land was repossessed by the government—1,200 hectares were involved. Jones Weekly Report. . ., July 12, 1936, Jones to Acting Secretary of War, Sept. 10, 1936, FM Papers; Aguinaldo and Vicente Albano Pacis, *A Second Look at America* (New York: Robert Spiller and Sons, 1957), pp. 179–80.

62. [110 to Joe], Nov. 1, 1935, 110 to Joe, Nov. 3, 1935, FM Papers.

63. [110 to Joe], Nov. 1, 1935, Memorandum for Superintendent of Intelligence Division, Nov. 4, 1935, Memorandum for Adjutant General, Nov. 4, 1935, ibid.; JRH to Reeves, Oct. 12, 1935, Nov. 7, 1934 [1935], JRH Papers; *DT*, Nov. 16, 1935, MSB; [*DT*, Dec. 15, 1935], HSB; Hayden, *Philippines*, pp. 433–34. According to some accounts of the Murphy-Aguinaldo confrontation, Murphy took the general to the window, pointed to the American ships in the harbor, told him how many troops were available, and even threatened to hang him. This is probably a melodramatic version of what actually happened. See *Ann Arbor News*, July 19, 1949, clipping in FM Papers; and Interview with Martin S. Hayden, Oct. 6, 1964, pp. 13–14, MHC. For still another version, see [*DN*, Jan. 16, 1936], HSB.

64. Cruz Memorandum, Oct. 26, 1935, Valdes to Manley, Oct. 29, 1935, Manley Memorandum for Governor-General, Oct. 29, 1935, FM Papers; Aguinaldo to Dern, Nov. 3, 9, 1935, Quezon Papers; Dern, "Confidential Report," Part 2, Dec. 20, 1935, PSF, War Department (Dern); *MT*, Nov. 12, 1935, MSB.

65. R. Alejandre Memoranda for District Adjutant, Oct. 18, Nov. 17, 1935, Guido Memoranda for Superintendent, Oct. 21, Nov. 1, 2, 1935, Cruz Memorandum for Adjutant General, Oct. 23, 1935, FWM [Manley] Memorandum for Governor-General, Oct. 23, 1935, enclosing Ramos for Marcos, Oct. 10, 1935, Valdes to Manley, Oct. 25, 1935, and enclosed "Notes," FM to Vicente Villamin, Oct. 17, 1939, FM Papers; *San Francisco Examiner*, Feb. 6, 1943, clipping in ibid.;

High Commissioner's notes, Nov. 21, 1935, EG Papers; [*MDB*, Oct. 23, 24, 1935], HSB; *NYT*, Oct. 24, Nov. 15, 1935; [*MDB*, Aug. 11, 1939], clipping in JRH Papers; Frederic S. Marquardt, *Before Bataan and After* (New York: Bobbs Merrill Co., 1943), p. 198.

66. Dern to FDR (from FM), Nov. 16, 1935, FM Papers.

CHAPTER 3

1. *Inaugural Address of Governor-General Frank Murphy, June 15, 1933* (Manila: Bureau of Printing, 1933), pp. 7–8.

2. Ibid., p. 6; FM to Acting Secretary of Finance, May 26, 1933, FM to Vicente Singson Encarnacion, May 28 [1933], FM Papers; *Message of Governor-General Frank Murphy to the Ninth Philippine Legislature, July 17, 1933* (Manila: Bureau of Printing, 1933), pp. 5–6; Norman H. Hill to Blair Moody, July 24, 1934, Blair Moody Papers, MHC.

3. FM to Tydings, May 10, 1934, Sen 73A, F25, Tray 26, Records of the United States Senate, RG 46, NARS; FM to Caroline Parker, Jan. 9, 1934, FM to Joseph Sanders, May 8, 1934, FM to Cresencio T. Balasbas, Oct. 25, 1935, FM to Ann Walker, June 6, 1936, FM Papers; *Los Angeles Times*, Mar. 3, 1935, MSB.

4. "Annual Report of the Governor-General of the Philippine Islands, 1933," Philippine Manuscript Reports 1767:1, 3, Records of the Bureau of Insular Affairs, RG 350; "Annual Report of the Governor-General of the Philippine Islands, 1934," ibid. 1789:2, 3, ibid.; "Report of the Governor-General of the Philippine Islands covering the period January 1, to November 14, 1935," ibid. 1865:42, ibid.; Joint Preparatory Committee on Philippine Affairs, *Report of May 20, 1938*, 4 vols. (Washington, 1938), 1:108; *DN*, June 10, 1934; John H. Holliday to Theodore Roosevelt, Jr., Nov. 16, 1933, Theodore Roosevelt, Jr., Papers, Box 18, LC; Frederic S. Marquardt, *Before Bataan and After* (New York: Bobbs-Merrill Co., 1943), pp. 163–64.

5. "Governor-General Report, 1933," 1767:2–3, RG 350; *MDB*, July 5, 27, 1933, Sept. 8, 1934, Aug. 23, 24, 1935, MSB; *MDB*, Dec. 13, 21, 1933, [*MDB*, May 24, July 26, Aug. 4, 1934], HSB; [*MDB*, Dec. 7, 10, 1934], MSB; *MDB*, July 28, 1933, Jan. 11, 1935, clippings in FM Papers; *MT*, July 15, 28, Aug. 4, 28, 1933, May 26, 1934, Nov. 15, 1935, MSB; *MT*, Aug. 19, 1933, [*MT*, Sept. 29, 1933], HSB; *PH*, July 27, 1933, May 11, Dec. 6, 1934, [Aug. 24, 1935], [*PH*, Dec. 7, 1934, June 24, 1935], MSB; [*PH*, Sept. 27, Oct. 18, 1933, July 21, 1934], HSB; *PH*, Jan. 8, 1935, clipping in FM Papers; *Philippines Free Press*, Dec. 15, 1934, MSB; unsigned document [July 24, 1933], FM Papers; Minutes of Meetings of the Cabinet, Aug. 9, Dec. 20, 1933, Oct. 10, 1934, Jan. 9, 1935, ibid.; Office of the Governor-General, Financial Statement, undated, ibid.; Minutes of Council of State Meeting, July 21, 1934, ibid.; FM to L. G. Lenhardt, Oct. 2, 1933, Hill to John L. Lovett, Dec. 13, 1934, ibid.; Executive Order No. 437, Aug. 18, 1933, JRH Papers; Cabinet Minutes, Oct. 31, 1934, ibid.; Hester to Roosevelt, Jr., Jan. 11, 1934, Roosevelt Papers, Box 19; FM to Secretary of War, May 7, 1934, Jan. 22, Aug. 16, 1935, OF 400, FDRL. For Governor-General Stimson's efforts to curb the pork-barrel evil, see Michael John Smith, "Henry L. Stimson and the Philippines" (Ph.D. diss., University of Indiana,

1970), pp. 124–25. For Quezon's views on the subject, see Francis Burton Harrison, *Origins of the Philippine Republic: Extracts from the Records and Diaries of Francis Burton Harrison*, ed. and annotated by Michael P. Onorato (Ithaca: Cornell University, 1974), p. 19.

6. Joseph Ralston Hayden, *The Philippines* (New York: Macmillan Co., 1942), pp. 294–95; "Governor-General Report, 1933," 1767:3–5; [*MT*, Aug. 5, 1933], MSB; [*PH*, Aug. 26, 1933], HSB; [*MDB*, July 10, 1934], MSB; *PH*, Aug. 13, 1933, clipping in FM Papers; Louis J. Van Schaick Memorandum for FM, Aug. 1, 1933, ibid.; Cabinet Minutes, Aug. 2, 1933, ibid.; FM speech to Provincial Governors [Oct. 30, 1934], ibid.; FM to Secretary of War, May 7, 1934, OF 400; Hester to Roosevelt, Jr., Jan. 11, 1934, Roosevelt Papers, Box 19; J. Weldon Jones to Richard D. Lunt, Jan. 25, 1963, Richard D. Lunt Papers, MHC; Hill to Moody, June 24, 1934, Moody Papers.

7. *MDB*, June 17, 29, 1933, Sept. 11, 1934, MSB; *MDB*, Nov. 17, 1933, HSB; *MDB*, July 10, 1934, clipping in FM Papers; *PH*, June 28, 1933, Dec. 7, 1934, MSB; *PH*, Jan. 17, 1934, HSB; "Staff Meetings," Oct. 11, 1933 (with Staff Meeting [Mar. 20, 1934]), FM Papers; FM speech [Oct. 30, 1934], ibid.; Jones to Lunt, Jan. 25, 1963, Lunt Papers; Cabinet Minutes, Dec. 14, 1934, JRH Papers; George A. Malcolm, *The Commonwealth of the Philippines* (New York: D. Appleton-Century Co., 1939), pp. 227–28.

8. FM to Secretary of War, May 7, 1934, Aug. 16, 1935, OF 400; "Governor-General Report, 1933," 1767:5, RG 350; "Governor-General Report, 1934," 1789:4, ibid.; *MDB*, Sept. 11, 1935, clipping in FM Papers; *MDB*, Nov. 15, 1935, MSB; Hayden, *Philippines*, pp. 295–96.

9. Peter W. Stanley, *A Nation in the Making: The Philippines and the United States, 1899–1921* (Cambridge, Mass.: Harvard University Press, 1974), pp. 226, 232–39; Hester to Roosevelt, Jr., Jan. 11, 1934, Roosevelt Papers, Box 19; FM to Secretary of War, May 7, 1934, Jan. 22, Aug. 16, 1935, OF 400; *PH*, July 8, 1933, July 5, 1935, HSB; *PH*, Oct. 8, 1933, Dec. 5, 6, 1934, MSB; *MT*, July 15, Dec. 23, 1933, MSB; *MDB*, Jan. 5, 1934, HSB; *MDB*, Nov. 15, 1935, MSB; "Governor-General Report, 1933," 1767:4, RG 350; "Governor-General Report, 1934," 1789:4, ibid.; Report of Committee . . . , undated, JRH Papers.

10. *MDB* [Dec. 6, 1934], HSB; *MT*, Nov. 15, 1935, MSB; "Governor-General Report, 1935," 1865:42, RG 350. For some minor unfinished fiscal business at the inauguration of the Commonwealth, see FM Memorandum for Quezon, Oct. 24, 1935, J. Weldon Jones Papers, Harry S. Truman Library, Independence, Missouri.

11. "Governor-General Report, 1933," 1767:1, RG 350; "Governor-General Report, 1934," 1789:5, ibid.; FM to C. W. Franks, Dec. 30, 1935, FM Papers; *News-Week* 5 (Mar. 16, 1935): 17.

12. Hayden, *Philippines*, pp. 637–38, 650, 654; "Governor-General Report, 1934," 1789:5, RG 350; George C. Dunham Memoranda for FM [Dec. 14, 1933], Oct. 26, 1935, FM Papers; FM speeches, Oct. 28, 1933, Feb. 5, 1934, ibid.; Dunham, "Progress of Public Health and Social Work in the Philippine Islands . . . ," Jan. 18, 1935, ibid.; undated document, ibid.; Juan F. Hilario to FM, July 18, 1934, FM to Walker, July 30, 1934, ibid.; *Message of Governor-General Frank Murphy to the Tenth Philippine Legislature, July 16, 1934* (Manila: Bureau of Printing, 1934), pp. 12–13; *MT*, Feb. 28, Mar. 1, 2, 1934, MSB; *PH*, Feb. 28, 1934, HSB; *PH*, June

22, 1934, [*PH*, Jan. 25, 1935], MSB; *MDB*, Mar. 12, 1934, MSB; *DN*, June 10, 1934; Jones to Lunt, Jan. 25, 1963, Lunt Papers; O. D. Corpuz, "Cultural Foundations," in Jose Veloso Abueva and Raul P. De Guzman, eds., *Foundations and Dynamics of Filipino Government and Politics* (Manila: The Bookmark, Inc., 1969), p. 13; George M. Guthrie, "The Philippine Temperament," in Guthrie, ed., *Six Perspectives on the Philippines* (Manila: The Bookmark, Inc., 1968), p. 55; Robert Aura Smith, *Philippine Freedom, 1946-1958* (New York: Columbia University Press, 1958), p. 69.

13. FM to Walker, July 30, 1934, FM Papers; Dunham Memoranda for FM, Mar. 8, 16, 1934, Oct. 26, 1935, ibid.; Dunham Memorandum for FM, June 23, 1933, JRH Papers; Hayden, *Philippines*, pp. 638-47, 681-83; Mariano D. Gana, *Social Legislation in the Philippine Islands* (n.p.: Institute of Pacific Relations, 1931), pp. 3-34.

14. *Inaugural Address*, pp. 7-10.

15. *NYT*, Dec. 3, 1933; FM speeches, Aug. 4, Oct. 28, Dec. 12, 1933, Feb. 5, 1934, Sept. 1, 1935, FM Papers; FM to President of Senate, July 6, 1935, ibid.; Dunham Memorandum for FM, Oct. 26, 1935, ibid.; undated document, ibid.; "Governor-General Report, 1934," 1789:5, RG 350; *Message, 1934*, pp. 12-15; Hayden, *Philippines*, pp. 651, 666; *PH*, July 27, 1933, [June 24, 1935], MSB; [*MDB*, July 26, 1934], HSB; *MDB*, Sept. 3, 1934, clipping in FM Papers; *MDB*, July 9, 1935, MSB.

16. Hayden, *Philippines*, p. 649; Hill to Moody, Aug. 27, 1935, Moody Papers; JRH to William C. Harllee, July 17, 1935, JRH to Commanding General, Philippine Department, Nov. 18, 1935, JRH Papers; FM to Commanding General, Philippine Department, Nov. 18, 1935, FM Papers; *PH*, July 9, 1935, clipping in ibid.

17. Dunham Memorandum for Vice-Governor, Apr. 14, 1934, Dunham Memoranda for FM [Dec. 14, 1933], Sept. 18, 1934, Oct. 26, 1935, FM Papers; Notes for Conference with Governor-General, Sept. 30, 1933, ibid.; FM speech, Sept. 5, 1933, ibid.; *NYT*, Aug. 19, 1934.

18. "A Brief Statement of Social Welfare Activities in the Philippines To-Day" [Mar. 3, 1932], FM Papers; "Brief Annual Report of the Bureau of Health for 1933," Philippine Manuscript Reports 1768:27, 29, RG 350; "Brief Annual Report of the Bureau of Health for 1934," pp. 22-24, JRH Papers; Dunham Memoranda for FM, June 23, 1933, Mar. 8, 1934, ibid.; Dunham Memorandum for FM, Oct. 26, 1935, FM Papers; Hayden, *Philippines*, p. 651.

19. "Governor-General Report, 1933," 1767:8, RG 350; Dunham, "Progress," Jan. 18, 1935, FM Papers; "Health Report for 1934," pp. 22-24, JRH Papers; JRH to Jose Fabella, Jan. 3, 1935, ibid.; Hayden, *Philippines*, p. 651.

20. Unidentified clipping, with JRH to Shirley Smith, Aug. 12, 1934, Shirley Smith Papers, MHC; Notes for Conference with Governor-General, Sept. 30, 1933, FM Papers; Dunham Memoranda for FM [Dec. 14, 1933], Mar. 16, 1934, Oct. 26, 1935, ibid.; "Governor-General Report, 1933," 1767:7-8, RG 350; "Governor-General Report, 1934," 1789:5, ibid.; "Brief Annual Report of the Bureau of Health for 1935," Philippine Manuscript Reports 1865:34-44, ibid.; Hayden, *Philippines*, pp. 652-53; *MT*, Dec. 30, 1933, MSB; [*MDB*, Sept. 12, 1934], HSB.

21. Dunham Memoranda for FM, Mar. 10, 1934, June 8, Oct. 26, 1935, Dunham Memorandum for JRH, June 11, 1935, FM Papers; *MT*, July 9, 1935, MSB.

22. JRH to Harry R. Hayden, Oct. 30, 1934, Fabella to JRH, Dec. 24, 1935, JRH

Papers; JRH note for the press, Jan. 22, 1935, ibid.; F. Calderon to JRH, Dec. 1, 1935, FM Papers; Hayden, *Philippines*, p. 659; [*MDB*, Nov. 13, 1934], HSB.

23. Dunham Memorandum for FM, June 23, 1933, JRH Papers; Dunham Memoranda for FM [Dec. 14, 1933], Oct. 26, 1935, FM Papers; "Governor-General Report, 1934," 1789:8–9, RG 350.

24. Hayden, *Philippines*, p. 657; Dunham Memorandum for FM, Oct. 26, 1935, FM Papers.

25. FM to Walker, July 30, 1934, FM Papers.

26. *PH*, Nov. 3, 1933, MSB.

27. *MDB*, July 20, 1934, MSB; [*PH*, June 21, 1935], MSB; Hayden, *Philippines*, pp. 657–58; Dunham Memorandum for FM, Apr. 18, 1934, JRH to FM, June 29, 1935, JRH Papers; Dunham Memoranda for FM, July 24, Aug. 16, 1934, Oct. 26, 1935, FM Papers; Minutes of Staff Meeting, July 27, 1934, ibid.; unidentified clipping, with JRH to Smith, Aug. 12, 1934, Smith papers; *Iloilo Times*, July 22, 1934, HSB.

28. [*MT*, July 27, 1934], *MT*, Aug. 22, 1934, HSB; *PH*, Jan. 22, [July 5, 1935], July 30, 1935, MSB; Dunham Memoranda for FM, Aug. 5, Oct. 26, 1935, FM Papers; Hill to Moody, Aug. 27, 1935, Moody Papers; Hayden, *Philippines*, p. 658.

29. FM speech, Sept. 2, 1934, FM Papers; Fabella Memorandum for FM, June 19, 1935, FM to President of Senate, July 6, 1935, Dunham Memorandum for FM, Oct. 26, 1935, ibid.; Hayden, *Philippines*, p. 659.

30. "Partial Report of the Leprosy Commission," Sept. 18, 1935, FM Papers; Dunham Memorandum for FM, Oct. 26, 1935, ibid.; FM Statement, Sept. 27, 1935, ibid.; Dunham to Juan Nolasco, July 3, 1935, JRH Papers; *MT*, Mar. 10, 1934, MSB; *MDB*, July 24, 1935, MSB; Hayden, *Philippines*, pp. 661–64. The 1936 legislature appropriated funds for three new leper colonies. Ibid., p. 664.

31. *Graphic*, Aug. 31, 1933, *PH*, Nov. 17, 1933, clippings in FM Papers; [*MDB*, Sept. 12, 1934], HSB; *PH*, Dec. 10, 1934, MSB; *MT*, Jan. 6, 1934, HSB; *MT*, Feb. 21, 1934, HSB; Dunham Memoranda for FM, Mar. 16, 1934, Jan. 10, 30, Oct. 26, 1935, FM to Dunham, Feb. 16, Apr. 14, 1934, Paulino Santos to FM, Aug. 17, 1935, FM Papers; Minutes of Conference with . . . Hayden, Feb. 2, 1935, ibid.; Dunham Memorandum for FM, Nov. 30, 1934, Charles H. Forster to FM, July 29, 1935, and enclosed Report of Committee . . . , C. M. Hoskins to JRH, Aug. 8, 1935, JRH Papers; Hayden, *Philippines*, pp. 653–54; "Governor-General Report, 1934," 1789:6, RG 350.

32. "Governor-General Report, 1933," 1767:9, RG 350; Hayden, *Philippines*, p. 661; *Graphic*, Aug. 31, 1933, clipping in FM Papers; *MT*, Aug. 15, 1933, MSB.

33. "Twenty-Fifth Annual Report of the Bureau of Labor, Dec. 31, 1933," Philippine Manuscript Reports 1769:41–42, RG 350; "Annual Report for 1933 of Bureau of Public Welfare," ibid. 1768:7, 11–12, 19–20, ibid.; "Governor-General Report, 1933," 1767:9–10, ibid.; "Governor-General Report, 1934," 1789:7, ibid.; Hayden, *Philippines*, pp. 654–55; FM to Dunham, Aug. 30, 1933, Aug. 30, 1934, FM to John E. Murphy, Sept. 19, 1933, Dunham Memoranda for FM, July 19, Aug. 30, Nov. 10, 1933, Oct. 26, 1935, FM to Tomas Earnshaw, Aug. 22, 1934, FM Papers; "Report of the Sub-Committee No. 4 . . ." [1933], ibid.; Minutes of the Unemployment Committee, June 2, 1934, ibid.; *MDB*, July 19, 1933, MSB; *PH*,

July 20, Nov. 30, 1933, HSB; [*MT*, July 21, Aug. 26, Nov. 9, 1933], MSB; [*MT*, Aug. 21, 1933], clipping in FM Papers. Cf. the inflated unemployment figures in Philippine Economic Association, *Economic Problems of the Philippines* (Manila: Bureau of Printing, 1934), p. 68.

34. Cabinet Minutes, Sept. 26, 1934, FM Papers; Dunham Memorandum for FM, Oct. 26, 1935, ibid.; Press Release [May 23, 1935], ibid.; Fabella Memorandum for FM, June 6, 1935, JRH Papers; Bureau of Public Welfare, "Annual Report, Jan. 1–Nov. 15, 1935," Philippine Manuscript Reports 1865:30, RG 350; Hayden, *Philippines*, p. 655; *MT* [Oct. 11, 1934], MSB.

35. "Governor-General Report, 1934," 1789:8, RG 350; Dunham Memorandum for FM, Apr. 17, 1934, JRH to H. R. Hayden, Oct. 30, 1934, Fabella to JRH, Nov. 5, 1934, JRH Memorandum for Governor-General, Nov. 28, 1934, Dunham to Fabella, Apr. 17, 1935, JRH Papers; Fabella Press Statement, Mar. 8, 1935, ibid.; Memorandum of Meetings, Nov. 15, 1934, and attached draft of press statement, ibid.; Fabella Memorandum for FM, Nov. 5, 1934, Fabella to JRH, Nov. 5, 1934, Fabella to FM, Mar. 29, 1935, Dunham Memorandum for FM, Oct. 26, 1935, FM Papers; Press release, Oct. 17, 1934, ibid.; Meeting in Office of . . . Fabella, Oct. 17, 1934, ibid.; Cabinet Minutes, Oct. 17, 20, 1934, ibid.; Jones to Lunt, Jan. 25, 1963, Lunt Papers; [*MDB*, Oct. 17, 1934], HSB; *MDB*, Oct. 20, 1934, HSB; *MT*, Dec. 1, 1934, MSB; Hayden, *Philippines*, pp. 656–57.

36. [*PH*, Aug. 15, 1935]; *PH*, Sept. 21, 27, 28, 1935, MSB; *MDB*, Sept. 21, 1935, MSB; Cabinet Minutes, Sept. 4, 11, 20, 1935, FM Papers; Council of State Minutes, Sept. 26, 1935, ibid.; FM Proclamation [Sept. 23, 1935], ibid.; Executive Order No. 872, Sept. 27, 1935, ibid.; Elpidio Quirino et al. to FM, Sept. 21, 1935, Forster Memorandum to FM, Oct. 15, 1935, Eulogio Rodriguez Memorandum for FM, Oct. 23, 1935, Hester Memorandum for FM, Oct. 25, 1935, R. J. Alejandre for Adjutant General, Philippine Constabulary, Oct. 16, 1935, Dunham Memorandum for FM, Oct. 26, 1935, FM Papers; JRH to Reeves, Oct. 12, 1935, JRH Papers; Charles O. Houston, Jr., "Rice in the Philippine Economy," *Journal of Asiatic Studies* 3 (Oct. 1953): 25–28, 39, 41, 80.

37. Executive Order No. 436, Aug. 18, 1933, FM Papers; Stanton Youngberg Memorandum for FM, Aug. 30, 1933, Youngberg to FM, Feb. 17, 1934, Dunham Memorandum for FM, Oct. 26, 1935, ibid.; "Governor-General Report, 1933," 1767:9, RG 350; "Governor-General Report, 1934," 1789:7, ibid.; "Narrative Report of the Director of Plant Industry . . . ," Nov. 14, 1935, Philippine Manuscript Reports 1866:27, RG 350; "Annual Report of the Director of Plant Industry . . . Dec. 31, 1936," ibid. 1869:188, RG 350; [*MDB*, Aug. 6, 1934], MSB; Hayden, *Philippines*, pp. 660–61.

38. Cabinet Minutes, Aug. 23, 1933, FM Papers; Meeting of the Rural Improvement Committee, Aug. 26, 1933, ibid.; Notes of Staff Meeting, July 27, 1934, ibid.; Hilario to FM, Aug. 21, 1933, [FM] to Board of Directors [June 18, 1935], ibid.; "Twenty-Fifth Annual Report of the Bureau of Labor for . . . 1933," Philippine Manuscript Reports 1769:47, RG 350; FM to V. Carmona, Dec. 22, 1933, Joseph Mills Papers, Burton Historical Collection, Detroit, Michigan; [Rafael Corpuz] to Board of Directors, Jan. 25, 1935, Executive Committee to Board of Directors, Jan. 25, 1935, JRH Papers; Cabinet Minutes, Apr. 24, 1935, ibid.; [*PH*, June 8, 1935],

PH, July 8, 11, 19, HSB; *PH*, Apr. 3, 1934, MSB; *MT*, Dec. 23, 1933, MSB; Philippine Economic Association, *Economic Report*, p. 220.

39. Dunham Memorandum for FM, Oct. 26, 1935, FM Papers; *MDB*, Nov. 15, 1935, MSB; Hernando Abaya, "Frank Murphy, Champion of Social Justice," *Anti-Usury Bulletin* 1 (Nov. 1935): 2 + .

40. FM to Tydings, July 16, 1935, FM Papers; JRH to Reeves, June 14, 1934, JRH to Wilfred B. Shaw, June 30, 1934, JRH to Eugene A. Gilmore, July 11, 1934, JRH to Harllee, July 17, 1935, JRH Papers.

41. Hayden, *Philippines*, pp. 669, 673–74; Jones Weekly Report … Oct. 25, 1936, FM Papers; Abaya to FM, Dec. 26, 1937, ibid.; David R. Sturtevant, *Popular Uprisings in the Philippines, 1840–1940* (Ithaca: Cornell University Press, 1976), pp. 248–49. Cf. Theodore Friend, *Between Two Empires: The Ordeal of the Philippines, 1929–1946* (New Haven: Yale University Press, 1965), pp. 269–70; idem, "Manuel Quezon: Charismatic Conservative," *Philippine Historical Review* 1 (1965): 157; and J. Woodford Howard, *Mr. Justice Murphy* (Princeton: Princeton University Press, 1968), pp. 79–80. The Commonwealth government established a court of industrial relations, legitimized labor organizations, provided for mine safety, established a minimum wage for laborers employed by government contractors and on public works, enacted a general eight-hour law and required premium pay for over-time, raised the pay of government laborers, purchased large estates for resale to tenants, provided storage facilities for small farmers, sought to prevent the concentration of public domain lands in the hands of the few, set up a National Housing Commission to provide low-rent housing and to engage in slum clearance, and established an Agricultural and Industrial Bank. "Report of the United States High Commissioner to the Philippine Islands covering the Period from Nov. 15, 1935 to Dec. 31, 1936," Philippine Manuscript Reports 1867:23–31, RG 350; *Third Annual Report of the United States High Commissioner … 1938 and First Six Months, 1939* (Washington: U.S. Government Printing Office, 1943), pp. 39, 48–49, 52, 61–64; *Fourth Annual Report … July 1, 1939–June 30, 1940* ((Washington: U.S. Government Printing Office, 1943), pp. 52–53; *Fifth Annual Report … 1941* (Washington: U.S. Government Printing Office, 1943), pp. 37–38.

42. Jose G. Hilario to FM, July 28, 1933, FM Papers.

43. Ibid.; Epipano A. Taok et al. to FM, May 25, 1933, Holliday Memorandum for the Governor-General, Aug. 1, 1933, FM to Frank Martel, Nov. 9, 1933, ibid.; Cabinet Minutes, June 28, Aug. 2, 1933, ibid.; unidentified clipping [Nov. 9, or 10, 1933], ibid.; Marquardt to Roosevelt, Jr., Dec. 25, 1933, Roosevelt Papers, Box 29; *MDB*, Nov. 8, 1933, HSB; *PH*, Jan. 22, 1934, MSB.

44. "Bureau of Labor Report, 1933," 1769:43–44, 46, RG 350; "Annual Report of the Department of Labor for the Calendar Year Ending Nov. 14, 1935," pp. 17–18, FM Papers; Ramon Torres to FM, Dec. 9, 1933, Mar. 7, 1936, and enclosed report, Ruperto S. Cristobal to FM, July 18, 1934, ibid.; unsigned document [July 24, 1933], ibid.; Cabinet Minutes, Apr. 27, July 26, 1934, Jan. 9, 1935, ibid.; *Herald Mid-Week Magazine*, May 2, 1934, clipping in ibid.; Quezon to Roosevelt, Jr., Roosevelt Papers, Box 30; *PH*, Dec. 11, 1933, [*PH*, May 1, 1934], MSB; *MT*, Dec. 9, 1933, MSB. For somewhat different figures on job placement and colonization, see Torres to FM, May 7, 1936, FM Papers.

45. [*MT*, July 13, 1933], MSB.

46. Cabinet Minutes, Aug. 29, 1934, FM Papers; Memorandum for the Superintendent, Aug. 29, 1934, C. E. Piatt to Secretary of Interior, Sept. 20, 1934, Teofilo Sison to FM, Sept. 20, 1934, Miguel Unson et al. to FM, Jan. 19, 1935, ibid.; *MT*, Sept. 29, 1934, clipping in ibid.; *MT*, Sept. 11, 1934, MSB; [*MT*, Sept. 19, 1934], HSB; George H. Dern, "Confidential Report to the President," Part 2, Dec. 20, 1935, PSF, War Department (Dern), FDRL.

47. *PH*, Sept. 18, 1934, *MDB*, Sept. 11, 21, 1934, clippings in FM Papers; [*MDB*, Sept. 18, 1934], MSB; Piatt to Secretary of Interior, Sept. 20, 1934, Sison to Secretary of Interior, Sept. 20, 1934, ACLU to FM, Sept. 30, 1934, FM to Baldwin, Oct. 2, 1934, Baldwin to FM, Nov. 6, 1934, FM Papers. For the GM strike, see Sidney Fine, *Sit-Down* (Ann Arbor: University of Michigan Press, 1969).

48. See Fine, *Frank Murphy: The Detroit Years* (Ann Arbor: University of Michigan Press, 1975), p. 417.

49. MM Reminiscences, Sept. 10 [1934], MM Papers; FM Memorandum Order, Sept. 14, 1934, FM Papers; Unson et al. to FM, Jan. 19, 1935, ibid.; Cabinet Minutes, Mar. 6, 13, 1934, JRH Papers; *MDB*, Sept. 11, 13, 26, 27, 1934, *MT*, Sept. 11, 14, 1934, *PH*, Sept. 11, 21, 1934, clippings in FM Papers. The Fact Finding Board thought that the Torres settlement permitted too large a differential between Manila and the provinces.

50. Torres to FM, May 2, 1935, JRH Papers; Torres to FM, Sept. 6, 1935, FM Papers. On labor union membership, see Kenneth K. Kurihara, *Labor in the Philippine Economy* (Stanford: Stanford University Press, 1945), p. 70. On working conditions, see Leo C. Stine, "The Economic Policies of the Commonwealth Government of the Philippine Islands," *University of Manila Journal of East Asiatic Studies* 10 (Mar. 1966): 87–90.

51. *Message, July 17, 1933*, p. 13; Fine, *Murphy*, pp. 109, 135–36, et passim.

52. Hayden, *Philippines*, pp. 42–43; EGK to FM, Jan. 25, 26, 27, 1934, FM Papers; Executive Order No. 501, Aug. 24, 1934, ibid.; Hill to W. Steele Gilmore, Aug. 29, 1934, *DN*—Murphy file, in my possession; Memorandum for Secretary of War from F. LeJ. Parker, Apr. 14, 1933, File 6128, RG 350; *PH*, Aug. 10, 1934, MSB; *PH*, Aug. 10, 1935, clipping in FM Papers.

53. Fine, *Murphy*, pp. 109, 126; [*MT*, Nov. 24, 1934], MSB; *DN*, Nov. 19, 1935, MSB; "Department of Labor Report, 1935," pp. 30–35, FM Papers; Hayden, *Philippines*, p. 259.

54. FM to F. W. Manley, Jan. 13, 1934, FM to Caroline Parker, July 12, 1934, FM Papers; Cabinet Minutes, May 4, 1934, ibid,; Memorandum [1934], ibid,; Hilmer Gellein, "United States Supreme Court Justice Frank Murphy . . . ," undated, p. 32, Hilmer Gellein Papers, MHC; *MDB*, July 4, 23, 1933, [*MDB*, Oct. 24, 1933], MSB; *MDB*, Mar. 2, 1934, clipping in FM Papers; *PH*, Jan. 13, 1934, MSB; [*PH*, Apr. 19, 1934], HSB; *NYT*, Dec. 3, 1933.

55. *MDB*, July 23, 25, 1933, [*MDB*, Nov. 7, 1933, Jan. 8, 1934], MSB; *MT*, Jan. 7, 1934, MSB; *PH*, July 25, 1933, [*PH*, Nov. 9, 10, 1933], MSB; FM to Joel R. Moore, Dec. 4, 1933, FM Papers; "Message of Governor-General Frank Murphy to the Philippine Legislature in Its Final Session, Nov. 14, 1935," p. 21, ibid.; Jones to Lunt, Jan. 25, 1963, Lunt Papers.

56. MM Diary, Aug. 9, 1935, MM Papers; FM to Raymond Moley, Aug. 30, 1934, FM to Charles Edward Russell, Aug. 5, 1935, FM to Arsenio C. Roldan, Feb. 24, 1936, Roldan to FM, Feb. 27, 1936, FM Papers; Cabinet Minutes, Aug. 8, Nov. 7, 1934, ibid.; [*PH*, Aug. 9, 1934], *PH*, Aug. 6, 1935, MSB; *MT*, July 4, 1935, MSB; *MDB*, Aug. 9, 1934, clipping in FM Papers; unidentified clipping [Aug. 8, 1935], in ibid.; *Herald Mid-Week Magazine*, May 13, 1936, MSB; *Philippines Free Press*, Sept. 11, 1937, MSB.

57. Fine, *Murphy*, pp. 186-88; Cabinet Minutes, July 31, 1935, FM Papers; Quezon to FM, Aug. 3, 1935, FM to Russell, Aug. 5, 1935, ibid.; Jones to Lunt, Jan. 25, 1963, Lunt Papers; Marquardt, *Bataan*, p. 178; *PH*, Aug. 10, 1934, clipping in FM Papers; *PH*, July 31, Aug. 3, 1935, [*PH*, Aug. 2, 1935], MSB.

58. Hayden, *Philippines*, pp. 240-41; *Message, July 17, 1933*, p. 13; *PH*, May 22, 1935, HSB.

59. Executive Order, Feb. 23, 1934, FM Papers; *MT*, Feb. 24, 1934, HSB; *MT*, Mar. 1, 1934, MSB.

60. Cabinet Minutes, July 10, Sept. 11, 1935, FM Papers; FM to Baldwin, Sept. 6, 1935, American Civil Liberties Union Archives (ACLU), vol. 862, Princeton University, Princeton, New Jersey.

61. *PH*, Sept. 21, Dec. 16, 1933, May 22, 1935, HSB; *MDB*, Aug. 21, 1933, clipping in FM Papers; [*MDB*, Dec. 26, 1934], HSB; Abaya, "Murphy," p. 93; Casim L. Garcia to FM, Apr. 27, 1934, FM Papers.

62. Alvin Scaff, *The Philippine Answer to Communism* (Stanford: Stanford University Press, 1955), pp. 7-13; "History of Communism in the Philippines" [Apr. 1936], FM Papers; Lucille B. Milner to Jacinto G. Manahan, May 25, 1933, Baldwin to FM, Nov. 22, 1933, Jan. 27, May 10, 1934, ibid.; "Annual Report of the Department of Interior and Labor for ... 1933," Philippine Manuscript Reports 1767:16-17, RG 350; Ben J. Kerkvliet, "Peasant Rebellion in the Philippines: The Origin and Growth of the HMB" (Ph.D. diss., University of Wisconsin, 1972), pp. 181-82.

63. FM to Baldwin, Oct. 14, 1933, Kemp Memorandum to Elbridge G. Chapman, Aug. 2, 1934, Chapman Memorandum for EGK, Aug. 3, 1934, EGK to FM, Oct. 8 [1934], FM Papers; Cabinet Minutes, Aug. 7, 1935, ibid.; Baldwin to Ignacio Nabong, Jan. 8, 1934, ACLU Archives, vol. 758.

64. Baldwin to Nabong, Jan. 8, 1934, ACLU Archives, vol. 758; FM to Baldwin, Sept. 6, 1935, ibid., vol. 862; FM to Baldwin, Dec. 24, 1935, Baldwin to FM, Feb. 4, 1936, ibid., vol. 952; Chapman Memorandum for FM, Oct. 11, 1934, Dana H. Allen Memorandum for Acting High Commissioner, Oct. 22, 1936, FM Papers; [*PH*, Apr. 11, 12, 1934], *PH*, Nov. 16, 1935, MSB; *PH*, Aug. 17, 1935, HSB; Harrison, *Origins*, p. 78.

65. Baldwin to Nabong, Jan. 8, 1934, Hayden to Milner, Feb. 20, 1934, ACLU Archives, vol. 758; Baldwin to FM, Nov. 22, 1933, Jan. 27, 1934, FM Papers.

66. JRH, "The Government of the Sulu Archipelago," Dec. 16, 1936, JRH Papers; JRH, "What Next for the Moro?" *Foreign Affairs* 6, (July 1938): 637-43; G. de los Santos to FM, Sept. 21, 1933, Teopisto Guingona to FM, Feb. 23, 1934, FM Papers; Ralph Benjamin Thomas, "Muslim but Filipino: The Integration of Philippine Muslims, 1917-1946" (Ph.D. diss., University of Pennsylvania, 1971), pp. 6-47.

67. JRH, "What Next," pp. 633, 637; JRH, "Sulu," JRH Papers; Malcolm, *Commonwealth*, p. 43; Guingona to FM, Feb. 23, 1934, FM Papers; Robert Aura Smith, "The Gloomy Philippine Future," *Asia* 35 (May 1935): 294.

68. JRH, "What Next," p. 636; Hayden, "Sulu," JRH Papers; Guingona to FM, Feb. 23, 1934, FM Papers; Thomas, "Muslim but Filipino," pp. 48–49, 95.

69. JRH, "Sulu," JRH Papers; "Notes on the Sulu Situation," Dec. 1933, ibid.; J. C. Early Memorandum for the Governor-General, Dec. 18, 1930, H. Gulamu Rasul to Abad Santos, Aug. 5, 1931, James R. Fugate to JRH, Dec. 28, 1933, Jan. 31, 1935, C. P. Vidamo to JRH, Sept. 18, 1934, ibid.; Roth Memorandum on Policy for . . . Sulu, Sept. 8, 1934, ibid.; [Lt. Tando], "Agama Court Problem" [Mar. 26, 1934], ibid.; Extract from the Narrative Report of the Provincial Governor for June 1936, ibid.; Guingona to Provisional Governor of Sulu, Aug. 5, 1920, FM Papers; Thomas, "Muslim but Filipino," pp. 66–69, 157–61, 214.

70. JRH, Memorandum Concerning the Province of Sulu, Mar. 25, 1933, Hayden file, RG 350; JRH, "Sulu," JRH Papers; Ludovico Hidrosollo to Secretary of Interior, Aug. 26, 1929, Fugate to JRH [Fall 1933], Dec. 28, 1933, Hester to JRH, July 1, 1933, ibid.; *Philippines Free Press*, Jan. 2, 1937, clipping in ibid.; Thomas, "Muslim but Filipino," pp. 168–74, 186–88, 191–92.

71. JRH Memorandum, Mar. 25, 1933, Hayden file, RG 350; JRH, "Sulu," JRH Papers; Arolas Tulawie to Fugate, Mar. 31, 1933, Fugate to JRH, Apr. 26, 1933, Caroline S. Spencer to FM, Nov. 17 [1933], JRH to Frank W. Carpenter, Feb. 26, 1934, ibid.; JRH to FM, Dec. 2, 1936, FM Papers. Cf. Spiller to FM, Nov. 24, 1933, ibid.

72. JRH to Fugate, Mar. 7, Apr. 8, May 2, 3, 12, 1933, JRH to Spencer, Oct. 31, 1933, [JRH to ——— 1933], JRH Papers; Parker to FM, May 9, 1933, FM Papers.

73. Van Schaick to FM, Aug. 5, 1933, FM to Guy D. Fort, Aug. 5, 1933, FM Papers; unidentified clippings, Sept. 11, 14, 1933, in ibid.; *Mindanao Herald*, Sept. 30, 1933, clipping in ibid.; *NYT*, Oct. 29, 1933; [*MT*, Nov. 22, 1933], HSB.

74. Guingona to Secretary of Interior and Labor, Sept. 27, 1933, Sison to FM, Oct. 2, 1933, JRH to N. M. Saleeby, Dec. 29, 1933, JRH to Reeves, Feb. 9, 1934, JRH to Carpenter, Feb. 26, 1934, JRH Papers. My italics.

75. See excerpt from [Clarence H. Bowers to Secretary of Interior, Jan. 31, 1934], ibid.; Spiller to Guingona, Dec. 8, 1934, ibid.; "Notes on Sulu," Dec. 1933, ibid.; Van Schaick Memoranda for FM, Aug. 5, Sept. 8, 1933, Spencer to FM, Sept. 13, 17, Oct. 2, 1933, and de los Santos to FM, Sept. 21, 1933, FM Papers.

76. JRH to Roth, Jan 18, 1934, JRH Memorandum for FM, Jan. 22, 1934, JRH to Reeves, Feb. 9, 1934, JRH to Carpenter, Feb. 26, 1934, JRH Papers; FM to JRH, Nov. 11, 1933, FM to Secretary of Interior, Feb. 19, 1934, FM to Spencer, Oct. 13, 1945, FM Papers; *PH*, Feb. 21, 1934, clipping in ibid.; [*MT*, Nov. 22, 1933], HSB.

77. FM to Spiller, Feb. 14, 1934, FM Papers; Cabinet Minutes, Feb. 21, 1934, ibid.; Fugate to JRH [Fall 1933], Chapman to JRH, Mar. 2, 1934, JRH Papers; Jones to Lunt, Jan. 25, 1963, Lunt Papers; [*MT*, Feb. 22, 1934], MSB; [*MT*, Mar. 1, 1934], HSB; *PH*, Mar. 2, 1934, HSB; *MDB*, Feb. 21, 1934, HSB; *MDB*, Mar. 5, 1934, MSB; [*MT*, Mar. 23, 1934], *MDB*, Mar. 2, 12, 1934, clippings in FM Papers.

78. Bureau of Non-Christian Tribes, Circular No. 13, July 11, 1924, JRH Papers; excerpt from "Annual Report of the Provincial Governor of Lanao for the Year 1933," ibid.; "Annual Report of the Provincial Governor of Lanao for . . . 1935,"

ibid.; "Annual Report of the Director of the Bureau for . . . 1934," ibid.; "Annual Report of the Provincial Governor of Sulu for 1935," ibid.; FM to Fugate, Apr. 10, 1934, JRH to Fugate, Apr. 11, 1934, Roth to JRH, May 24, 1934, Roth to FM, May 30, July 25, 1934, Roth Memorandum, July 23, 1934, JRH to Edward M. Kuder, Sept. 10, 1934, Akuk Sangkula to JRH, Jan. 14, 1937, ibid.; FM to JRH, Mar. 12, 1934, Camins to FM, Apr. 12, 1934, FM to Camins, Apr. 19, 1934, FM to Fugate, Aug. 21, 1934, FM Papers; Jones to Lunt, Jan. 25, 1963, Lunt Papers; Thomas, "Muslim but Filipino," pp. 202, 206–9, 212.

79. FM to Secretary of Interior and Labor, Feb. 19, 1934, Chapman to FM, July 29, 1934, FM to Fugate, Aug. 21, 1934, Dunham Memorandum for FM, Oct. 26, 1935, FM Papers; JRH to Fugate, May 31, 1934, Jan. 12, 1935, JRH to Kuder, Sept. 10, 1934, Aug. 27, 1935, JRH Papers; *MDB*, Sept. 28, 1935, HSB; "Annual Report of Director, 1934," ibid.; "Sulu Report, 1935," ibid.; "Lanao Report, 1935," ibid.; Hayden, *Philippines*, p. 657.

80. FM to Secretary of Interior and Labor, Feb. 19, 1934, FM to Fugate, Aug. 21, 1934, Nov. 12, 1935, FM Papers; Cabinet Minutes, Jan. 23, 1935, ibid.; Fugate to JRH, Dec. 28, 1933, July 16, 1934, Rasul to JRH, Apr. 27, 1934, JRH to Albert W. Herre, June 12, 1934, JRH to H. R. Hayden, Oct. 30, 1934, Roth Memorandum, Feb. 26, 1935, Roth to JRH, May 19, 1935, JRH to D. Gutierrez, Sept. 26, 1935, JRH Papers; Roth, Memorandum on Policy for the Province of Sulu, Sept. 8, 1934, ibid.; "Sulu Report, 1935," ibid.; *Philippines Free Press*, Jan. 2, 1937, clipping in ibid.

81. Fugate to Deputy Governor. . . , Sulu, Apr. 17, 1934, JRH to Fugate, May 12, 1934, Fugate to JRH, July 8, 1934, JRH Papers; Roth Memorandum, Sept. 8, 1934, ibid.

82. Kiram to FM, Sept. 21, 1934, FM to Kiram, Oct. 17, 1934, FM to Fugate, Oct. 17, 1934, FM Papers; FM to GM, Oct. 2, 1934, GM Papers; JRH to Fugate, Oct. 5, 1934, Jan. 12, 1935, Aug. 21, 1936, Roth to JRH, Jan. 5, 1935, JRH Papers; Thomas, "Muslim but Filipino," p. 223.

83. Rasul to Sison, Dec. 9, 1934, Fugate to JRH, Jan. 1, 1934 [1935], Roth to JRH, Jan. 5, 1935, and enclosures, JRH to Fugate, Jan. 12, July 13, 1935, Aug. 21, 1936, JRH Papers; "Sulu Report, 1935," ibid.; Thomas, "Muslim but Filipino," pp. 227–29.

84. Hayden, "Sulu," JRH Papers.

85. "Lanao Report, 1935," JRH Papers; M. Guiambañgan et al. to FM, May 15, 1934, Sultan Aragon Samporna to FDR, May 26, 1934, Fugate to JRH, Apr. 20, 1935, JRH Papers; Hadji Bogabong et al. to FDR, Mar. 18, 1935, OF 400; Dern, "Confidential Report," Part 2, Dec. 20, 1935, PSF, War Department (Dern).

86. Hayden, "Sulu," JRH Papers; FM to JRH, Dec. 5, 1936, [Ombra Amilbungsa] to JRH, Mar. 4, 1938, Roth to Billy and Joe, Mar. 5, 1938, Fugate to JRH, Aug. 25, 1938, ibid.; "Annual Report of the Provincial Governor of Sulu," Jan. 16, 1937, ibid.; JRH to FM, Dec. 2, 1936, Quezon to FM, Mar. 15, 1938, FM Papers; Harrison, *Origins*, p. 69.

87. There were a total of 421,484 pagans living in eight provinces, six of them in Mindanao. Guingona to FM, Feb. 23, 1934, FM Papers.

88. JRH to Roth, June 7, 1934, JRH to Herre, June 12, 1934, William E. Dosser et

al. to FM, June 16, 1934, JRH Memorandum for FM, Nov. 13, 1934, JRH to Dosser, May 16, 1935, Dosser to JRH, May 20, 1935, Dosser to Director, Bureau of Non-Christian Tribes, Nov. 15, 1935, Rodolfo Baltasar to Secretary of Interior, Jan. 9, 1937, JRH Papers; Press Statement, May 1, 1935, ibid.; Dunham Memorandum for FM, Oct. 26, 1935, FM Papers; *Monday Mail*, Jan 1, 1934, MSB.

CHAPTER 4

1. FM, "Jan. 19 [1935] Conference...," FM Papers. See also Carlos Quirino, *Quezon* (Manila: Filipiniana Book Guild, 1971), pp. 270, 271–72.

2. Joseph Ralston Hayden, *The Philippines* (New York: Macmillan Co., 1942), pp. 712–13, 715–16; JRH, "Japanese Interests in the Philippine Islands" [1935], JRH Papers; Hilario A. Roxas, Memorandum to Director, Bureau of Science, Jan. 19, 1935, ibid.; Charles Burnett, Memorandum: Japanese Penetration of the Philippine Islands [1937], PSF, Japan, FDRL.

3. For the Japanese in Davao, see JRH, "Japanese Interests" [1935], JRH Papers; Alfredo Fajardo et al. to Secretary of Agriculture and Commerce, Feb. 11, 1935, ibid.; Grant K. Goodman, *Davao: A Case Study in Japanese-Philippine Relations* ([Lawrence, Kan.]: University of Kansas, 1967), Introduction, pp. 1–32; idem, "Davaokuo: Japan in Philippine Politics, 1931–1941," in Robert K. Sakai, ed., *Studies in Asia, 1963* (Lincoln: University of Nebraska Press, 1963), pp. 185–88; Teopisto Guingona to Secretary of Interior, Dec. 8, 1932, Aug. 23, 1934, Eulogio Rodriguez to FM, Feb. 19, 1934, FM Papers; [Toyoji Kaneko], "The Japanese in Davao," undated, File 6144, Records of the Bureau of Insular Affairs, RG 350, NARS; "Far East," Feb. 23, 1935, ibid.; Serafin Quiason, "The Japanese Colony in Davao, 1904–1941," *Philippine Social Science Review* 23 (July–Dec. 1958): 215–30; James G. Wingo, "The Philippines and the New Regime," *Contemporary Review* 151 (Jan. 1937): 73; *NYT*, May 24, 1936; Hayden, *Philippines*, pp. 717–19; United States Tariff Commission (USTC), *United States-Philippine Trade*, Report No. 118, Second Series (Washington: U.S. Government Printing Office, 1937), p. 128; and Theodore Friend, *Between Two Empires: The Ordeal of the Philippines* (New Haven: Yale University Press, 1965), p. 179.

4. Hayden, *Philippines*, pp. 722–23; Chargé d'Affaires ad interim to Secretary of State, Sept. 29, 1934, 811 B.01/230, Records of the Department of State, RG 59, NARS; RV [Roy Veatch] Conversation with Vicente Villamin, Jan. 9, 1935, 611 B.003/143, ibid.; unsigned document, Feb. 19, 1935, File 6144, RG 350; "Far East," Feb. 23, 1935, ibid.; Edwin L. Neville to Cordell Hull, Sept. 3, 1935, ibid.; Sidney H. Brown to Hull, Sept. 4, 1934, Quezon file, ibid.; Henry L. Stimson Diary, Feb. 2, 1935, Henry L. Stimson Papers, Sterling Library, Yale University, New Haven, Conn.; Guingona to Secretary of Interior, Aug. 23, 1934, JRH to Secretary of War, Feb. 23, 1935, FM Papers; FM notes on conference, Jan. 21, 1935, ibid.; [*PH*, Sept. 24, 1934], HSB; Friend, *Two Empires*, p. 176; Thomas Harrington, "The Philippines on the Eve of Change," *International Affairs* 15 (Mar.–Apr. 1936): 282–83.

5. FM notes, Jan. 28, Feb. 1, 1935, FM Papers; [Notes when Governor-General

talked with President Roosevelt, Apr.–May 1935], ibid.; Stimson Diary, Mar. 5, 1935, Stimson Papers; Conversation. Murphy, [Stanley K.] Hornbeck, [Maxwell M.] Hamilton, Mar. 27, 1935, 811 B.01/246, RG 59; George H. Dern to FDR, Mar. 9, 1935, OF 400, FDRL.

6. FM notes, Feb. 1, 1935, FM Papers.

7. FM to Secretary of War, Sept. 15, Oct. 5, 12, 18, Dec. 18, 1934, Koki Hirota to Grew, Dec. 17, 1934, Grew to Hull, Mar. 8, 1935, Edward S. Maney to Grew, Apr. 17, 1935, File 6144, RG 350; Minutes of Cabinet Meetings, Sept. 19, Oct. 10, 1934, Jan. 30, 1935, FM Papers; Creed F. Cox to FM, Oct. 11, 1934, FM to Grew, Oct. 18, 1934, Grew to FM, Oct. 19, 28, Nov. 22, 1934, JRH Memorandum for FM, Dec. 5, 1934, ibid.; EGK Memorandum, Oct. 17 [1934], ibid.; Press release, Oct. 17, 1934, ibid.; [*PH*, Sept. 17, 1934, Jan. 14, 24, 1935], MSB; [*PH*, Oct. 4, 19, 1934], HSB; *MDB*, Oct. 25, 1934, MSB; [*MT*, Jan. 30, 1935], MSB; Hayden, *Philippines*, pp. 716–17.

8. Hayden, *Philippines*, p. 717.

9. Friend, *Two Empires*, p. 179; Hayden, *Philippines*, pp. 719–20; Guingona to Secretary of Interior, Aug. 23, 1934, FM Papers; Rodriguez Memorandum for FM, Dec. 12, 1934, JRH Papers; Notes of a Meeting of . . . JRH with his staff, Feb. 15, 1935, ibid.; [*MT*, Dec. 6, 1934], HSB; [*MDB*, Apr. 19, 1935], MSB.

10. Notes of a Meeting of JRH with His Staff, Feb. 1, 1935, FM Papers; JRH staff meeting, Feb. 15, 1935, JRH Papers; Cabinet Minutes, Jan. 30, 1935, ibid.; [*MT*, Jan. 26, 1935], MSB; Goodman, *Davao*, pp. 39–40.

11. JRH staff meeting, Feb. 15, 1935, JRH Papers.

12. Kimura to Kaneko, Jan. 18, 1935, Kaneko to Hirota, Mar. 20, 1935, Japanese Ministry of Foreign Affairs Archives, Reel S460, Asia Library, University of Michigan, Ann Arbor, Mich.; Rodriguez to Governor-General, Feb. 19, 1935, JRH to Secretary of War, Feb. 23, 1935, FM Papers; Rodriguez to JRH, Mar. 20, 1935, JRH Papers.

13. JRH Memorandum for FM, Feb. 19, 1935, E. G. Chapman Memorandum for Governor-General, Feb. 16, 1935, Louis J. Van Schaick Memorandum for Governor-General, Feb. 19, 1935, JRH Papers; Cabinet Minutes, Feb. 20, 1935, FM Papers; JRH to Secretary of War (for FM), Feb. 23, 1935, [Mar. 9, 1935], ibid.; FM to JRH, Mar. 14, 1935, File 212, RG 350; Cox Memorandum, Mar. 14, 1935, FM file, ibid.

14. Memorandum Order [Proposed], Feb. 20, 1935, JRH Papers; JRH to Rodriguez, Mar. 12, 29, 1935, Rodriguez to JRH, Mar. 15, 26, 1935, Rodriguez Memorandum for JRH, Mar. 21, 1935, Chapman Memorandum for the Governor-General, Apr. 2, 1935, JRH Papers; Memorandum for the Press, Apr. 8, 1935, ibid.; Cox Memorandum, Mar. 16, 1935, FM Visit, 1935, Records of the Office of the United States High Commissioner to the Philippine Islands, RG 126, NARS; Office Memorandum, Apr. 15, 1935, ibid.; Cabinet Minutes, June 19, 1935, FM Papers; *MDB*, Apr. 9, 1935, MSB.

15. Rodriguez to FM, June 20, 1935, FM Papers; *Graphic*, June 27, 1935, clipping in ibid.; Goodman, *Davao*, p. 153; *PH*, June 27, 1935, HSB.

16. Goodman, "Davaokuo," p. 190; idem, *Davao*, pp. 53–59; [*PH*, Sept. 14, 1935], MSB; *MDB*, Oct. 11, 1935, HSB; Notes Verbal, Sept. 18, 1935, and enclosed Memorandum, undated, FM Papers; Fajardo Memorandum for Secretary of Agriculture and Commerce, Sept. 21, 1935, ibid.; Cabinet Minutes, Sept. 25, Oct. 2, 1935,

ibid.; Uchiyama to Kaneko, Sept. 7, 1935, Kaneko to Hirota, Sept. 9, 1935, Uchiyama to Hirota, Sept. 20, 1935, Japanese Archives, Reel S460; [Cox], "The Inauguration of the Philippine Commonwealth" [1935], Confidential Diary Notes on Miscellaneous Subjects, 1933–1935, File 9-7-2, Records of the Office of Territories, RG 126, NARS; Friend, *Two Empires*, p. 180.

17. Uchiyama to Hirota, Nov. 7, 1935, Japanese Archives, Reel S460; Goodman, *Davao*, pp. 56–58, 63–65, 114n; Francis Burton Harrison, *Origins of the Philippine Republic: Extracts from the Diaries and Records of Francis Burton Harrison*, ed. and annotated by Michael Paul Onorato (Ithaca: Cornell University, 1974), p. 103.

18. FM notes, Dec. 26 [1935], EG Papers; FM to Richard R. Ely, Dec. 30, 1935, FM Papers.

19. Goodman, *Davao*, pp. 65–76; idem, "Davaokuo," pp. 189–90; Quezon to FM [May 5, 1936], FM Papers.

20. Memorandum for the Interdepartmental Committee..., Mar. 11, 1936, File C-1247, RG 350.

21. Uchiyama to Arita, May 9, 1936, Japanese Archives, Reel S461; Goodman, *Davao*, pp. 72–106; idem, "Davaokuo," p. 193; EGK to FM, May 23, 1936, FM Papers; "Situation in Davao," Feb. 1, 1936, 811 B.5294/2, RG 59; FM to Secretary of War, File 2074-A, RG 350; Friend, *Two Empires*, pp. 180–81.

22. Embick to Commanding General, Philippine Department, Apr. 19, 1935, FM Papers; Ronald Schaffer, "General Stanley D. Embick: Military Dissenter," *Military Affairs* 37 (Oct. 1973): 87–91; Louis Morton, "War Plan Orange: Evolution of a Strategy," *World Politics* 11 (Jan. 1959): 237–38.

23. D. Clayton James, *The Years of MacArthur*, vol. 1 (*1880–1941*) (Boston: Houghton Mifflin Co., 1970), pp. 473–76; Morton, "Orange," pp. 238–44; idem, *The Fall of the Philippines* (Washington: Department of the Army, 1953), pp. 8–9; [James F.] McKinley to Parker, July 26, 1934, Bureau of Insular Affairs (BIA) File 364, in AG 313.3 (6-26-39), Office of the Adjutant General, Central Files, 1926–1939, RG 407, NARS; Parker to Adjutant General, Aug. 17, 20, 1934, War Plans Division (WPD) File 3251-22, Records of the War Department General and Special Staffs, RG 165, NARS. Parker first sent a brief radio message and then followed it up with a more detailed letter. See also Parker to Chief of Staff, Feb. 28, 1935, WPD File 3251-27, ibid.

24. Parker to Adjutant General, Aug. 20, 1934, WPD File 3251-22, RG 165; F. W. Manley Memorandum for the Governor-General [1934], FM Papers; Morton, *Philippines*, p. 9.

25. FM to Secretary of Interior and Labor, Mar. 12, 1934, FM to Officers and Men of Philippine Constabulary, Apr. 4, 1934, Admiring Philippine Constabulary Officers to FM [June 25, 1934], FM Papers; Manley Memorandum [1934], ibid.; *Philippines Free Press*, Mar. 31, 1934, clipping in ibid.

26. [*MDB*, Nov. 12, 1934], HSB; "Message of ... Frank Murphy to the Philippine Legislature...," Nov. 14, 1935, p. 12, FM Papers.

27. FM to Secretary of War, Dec. 24, 1934, File 3326, RG 350.

28. JRH 3rd Indorsement [*sic*], Nov. 23, 1934, JRH Papers; Norman H. Hill Memorandum for JRH, Dec. 4, 1934, FM to Speaker of House, Dec. 7, 1934, ibid.; Robert L. Collins to Commanding General, Philippine Department, Dec. 10, 1934,

BIA File 364, RG 407; Cox to FM, Dec. 29, 1934, File 3326, RG 350; Parker to Adjutant General, Aug. 20, 1934, WPD File 3251-22, RG 165.

29. F. LeJ. Parker Memorandum for Assistant Chief of Staff, WPD, May 10, 1933, Dern to Chief, BIA, May 16, 1933, Parker to FM, May 17, 1933, File 21499, RG 350.

30. R. L. Maughan to FM, June 24, 1933, FM to F. LeJ. Parker, June 27, 1933, Maughan Memorandum to the Governor-General, June 29, 1933, FM to Cox, Sept. 28, 1933, FM to Secretary of War, Nov. 22, 1933, ibid.; Leighton V. Rogers, Informal Memorandum for Hornbeck, enclosing Rogers Memorandum for Evans Young, May 3, 1933, 811 B.7961/3, RG 59; *MDB*, Aug. 4, 1933, MSB; Philippine Economic Association, *Economic Problems of the Philippines* (Manila: Bureau of Printing, 1934), p. 167.

31. Maughan to FM, June 24, 1933, File 21499, RG 350; C. F. C. [Cox] Memorandum, Nov. 15, 1933, ibid.; *Message of Governor-General Frank Murphy to the Ninth Philippine Legislature, July 17, 1933* (Manila: Bureau of Printing, 1933), p. 10; *MT*, Aug. 20, 1933, MSB.

32. FM to Secretary of War, Nov. 15, 22, 24, 1933, Dern to Chief, BIA, Dec. 1, 1933, File 21499, RG 350; *MDB*, Nov. 25, 1933, MSB; *MT*, Nov. 26, 1933, MSB.

33. Dern to Chief, BIA, Dec. 1, 1933, FM to Secretary of War, Jan. 21, 1935, J. Carroll Cone to Marvin H. McIntyre, Jan. 24, 1935, D. C. McDonald Memorandum for Chief, BIA, Apr. 23, 1935, File 21499, RG 350; "Text of Veto by ... Murphy" [Dec. 11, 1933], ibid.; Daniel Roper to Secretary of State, Apr. 18, 1934, Hull to Roper, May 8, 1934, 811 B.7961/5, RG 59. Despite Murphy's veto, the two airlines were permitted to continue flying the routes they were already servicing. *PH*, Dec. 11, 14, 1933, MSB.

34. Extract from BIA Radio No. 398, Aug. 28, 1934, File 21499, RG 350; FM to Secretary of War, Sept. 8, 1934, Secretary of War to Secretary of State, Sept. 21, 1934 (draft), Cox Memorandum for Chief of Staff, Sept. 22, 1934, ibid.

35. Trippe to Secretary of State, Oct. 2, 1934, C. E. Kilbourne Memorandum to Chief of Staff, Oct. 15, 1934, Cox Memoranda to Chief of Staff, Oct. 10, 20, 1934, Dern to Secretary of State, Dec. 17, 1934, Jan. 22, Apr. 16, 1935, Hull to Dern, Jan. 9, Mar. 13, May 13, 1935, William F. Pearson to Chief, BIA, Jan. 31, 1935, McDonald Memorandum for Chief of Bureau, Apr. 25, 1935, ibid.; Cox Memorandum, Apr. 27, 1935, ibid.; Cox Memorandum, Mar. 14, 1935, FM file, RG 350; Roper to Hull, Feb. 19, 1935, 811 B.79656D/10, RG 59; RS [Richard Southgate], Memorandum of Conversation between the Governor-General..., ... [R. Walton] Moore, and ... Southgate, Mar. 4, 1935, 811 B.79656D/11, ibid.

36. McDonald Memorandum for Chief of Bureau, Apr. 25, 1935, FM to Cox, Apr. 16, May 19, 1935, Cox to FM, May 14, 1935, FM to Secretary of War, July 17, 1935, BIA File 21499, RG 350; Cox Memoranda, May 3, 8, 1935, ibid.; C. F. C. [Cox] Memorandum, May 3, 1935, Confidential Diary Notes, RG 126; FM to President of Senate, July 5, 1935, Trippe to FM, Dec. 26, 1935, FM to Hill, Feb. 28, 1936, FM Papers; *PH*, Sept. 27, 1935, clipping in ibid.; Quezon to Roy Howard, July 17, 1935, Manuel L. Quezon Papers, microfilm copy in MHC; *MDB*, Apr. 27, Oct. 17, 18, 1935, MSB; *MT*, Dec. 11, 1935, HSB.

37. K. F. Baldwin Memorandum for the Records, Sept. 21, 1934, File 21499, RG 350; FM to Cox, Apr. 16, 1935, McDonald Memoranda for Chief, BIA, Apr. 23,

May 1, 1935, Stanley Reed to Hull, Oct. 23, 1936, ibid.; Minutes of Meeting of Interdepartmental Committee on Civil International Aviation, June 4, 1936, ibid.; EGK, Memorandum—Philippine Aviation, Mar. 18, 1935, FM Papers; Moore to Dern, June 13, 1936, 811 B.79656D/25, RG59; Hull to Homer Cummings, June 10, 1936, 811 B.79656D/26, ibid.

38. *MDB*, Oct. 25, 1935; [Jacob A. Metzger] Memorandum, Nov. 4, 1935, File 21499, RG 350; Dern to Secretary of State, Jan. 28, 1936, W. Kruger Memorandum for Chief of Staff, May 29, 1936, Malin Craig to Secretary of War, June 6, 1936, Secretary of War to FM [June 1936], Moore to Harry H. Woodring, Nov. 5, 1936, FM to Cox, Nov. 20, 1936, ibid.; Interdepartmental Committee on Aviation Minutes, June 4, 1936, ibid.; SL [Stephen Latchford] to Moore, Nov. 5, 1935, 811 B.79656D/17, Metzger for Moore and Latchford, May 4, 1935, 811 B.7961/9, RG 59; SL Memorandum, May 6, 1935, ibid.; J. Weldon Jones Memoranda for High Commissioner, Sept. 23, Oct. 13, 22, 1936, Jones to Secretary of War, Oct. 4, 1936, McDonald to High Commissioner, Oct. 30, 1936, Cox to FM, Nov. 23, 1936, FM Papers.

39. Antonio de las Alas to Jose Clarin, Apr. 17, 1934, Maughan to FM, July 5, 1934, Maughan Memoranda for Governor-General, Aug. 6, 19, Nov. 17, 1934, FM Papers; Cabinet Minutes, Oct. 24, Nov. 7, 1934, ibid.; *MDB*, Sept. 27, 1935, clipping in ibid.

40. "Murphy Message," Nov. 14, 1935, p. 11, ibid.; Parker to Adjutant General, Sept. 13, 1934, Parker to FM, Oct. 29, 1935, FM to Parker, Nov. 2, 1935, ibid.; Cabinet Minutes, Sept. 19, 1934, Aug. 21, 1935, ibid.; *MT*, Sept. 29, 1935, clipping in ibid.; *MDB*, Sept. 11, 1934, MSB.

41. *PH*, Aug. 2, 1933, MSB; *MDB*, Aug. 4, 1933, MSB; *MDB*, Sept. 27, 1935, clipping in FM Papers; *MDB*, Oct. 30, 1935, HSB; *MT*, Sept. 29, 1935, clipping in FM Papers; Maughan Memorandum for Governor-General, Feb. 5, 1935, JRH Papers; FM to Secretary of War, File 21499, RG 350; Cabinet Minutes, May 22, 1935, FM Papers.

42. *Inaugural Address of Governor-General Frank Murphy, June 15, 1933* (Manila: Bureau of Printing, 1933), p. 10; *Message, July 17, 1933*, pp. 7–8. See also *MDB*, Aug. 18, 1934, clipping in FM Papers.

43. Catherine Porter, *Crisis in the Philippines* (New York: Alfred A. Knopf, 1942), p. 73; Philippine Economic Association, *Economic Problems*, p. 121; Bureau of Foreign and Domestic Commerce, "Far Eastern Series, No. 134," May 1, 1933, File 1239, RG 350; FM to Secretary of War, Aug. 8, 1933, File 28813, ibid.; Robert Aura Smith, "Analysis of the Proposed Constitution of the Philippine Commonwealth" [Nov. 28, 1934], WPD File 3389-10, RG 165; Cabinet Minutes, July 3, 1934, FM Papers; Rodriguez to FM, Sept. 7, 1934, ibid.; *PH*, Aug. 18, 1933, clipping in ibid.; [*MT*, Aug. 17, 18, 1933], *MT*, Oct. 11, 1934, MSB.

44. Elizalde to FM, Oct. 18, 1934, Nov. 12, 1935, FM to Elizalde, Oct. 23, 1934, FM Papers; *MDB*, May 10, 1934, HSB; [*MDB*, Oct. 2, 1934], MSB; *PH*, Oct. 15, 1934, MSB; [*MT*, Oct. 19, 1934], MSB; USTC, *Philippine Trade*, p. 167; Charles O. Houston, Jr., "Other Philippine Crops and Industries: 1934-1950," *University of Manila Journal of Asiatic Studies* 4 (Jan. 1955): 18-19; Porter, *Crisis*, pp. 73-74; *Second Annual Report of the United States High Commissioner to the Philip-*

pines . . . 1937 (Washington: U.S. Government Printing Office, 1939), pp. 99–103; *Third Annual Report of the . . . High Commissioner, 1938 and the First Six Months of 1939* (Washington: U.S. Government Printing Office, 1943), pp. 114–24; *Fourth Annual Report of the . . . High Commissioner, July 1, 1939–June 30, 1940* (Washington: U.S. Government Printing Office, 1943), pp. 92, 153–72; Leo C. Stine, "The Economic Policies of the Commonwealth Government of the Philippine Islands," *University of Manila Journal of East Asiatic Studies* 10 (Mar. 1966): 65–87, 132.

45. *MT*, June 30, 1933, MSB; *PH*, Apr. 24, 1934, [*PH*, June 21, 25, 1935], HSB; [*MDB*, June 30, 1934, June 21, 1935], *MDB*, July 17, 1935, Mar. 26, 1936, HSB; FM to Cox, June 25, 1935, Quezon to FM, Mar. 9, 1936, FM Papers; *Philippines Free Press*, Mar. 23, 1935, clipping in ibid.; Dern to FDR, Mar. 9, May 4, 1934, FDR to Congress, Mar. 1934 (not sent), Douglas Memoranda for the President, Mar. 26, Apr. 2, 1934, FDR to Robert L. Doughton, May 7, 1934, OF 400, FDRL; Cox Memorandum: Telephone Conversation with FM, Mar. 18, 1935, FM Visit, 1935, RG 126; Cox Memoranda, Apr. 25, 1934, June 28, 1935, Confidential Diary Notes, ibid.; Jones to EGK, Feb. 21, 1941, EGK Papers.

46. *MDB*, Jan. 16, Feb. 1, 1936, HSB; *MT*, May 20, 1936, HSB; Cox Memorandum, Jan. 29, 1936, Confidential Diary Notes, RG 126; Quezon to FM, Mar. 9, 1936, FM Memorandum for EGK, May 21, 1936, FM to Jones, May 25, 1936, Jones to Dern, June 9, 1936, Jones to EGK, June 21, 1936, FM Papers; FM to FDR, May 29, 1936, FDR Memorandum for Mac [McIntyre], June 4, 1936, OF 400. As a sop to the Philippines, Roosevelt allowed the Commonwealth government to earn a profit of P1.2 million on United States government coins that it had acquired before December 28, 1933, and that were being held by the United States Treasury. Memorandum for the High Commissioner, July 6, 1936, Jones to Quezon, June 10, 1936, FM Papers.

47. Jones to EGK, Feb. 21, 1941, EGK Papers; Philippine Economic Association, *Economic Problems*, pp. 79, 81; Dern, "Confidential Report to the President," Part 2, Dec. 20, 1935, PSF, War Department (Dern), FDRL; "Report of the United States High Commissioner to the Philippine Islands Covering the Period from November 15, 1935 to December 31, 1936," Philippine Manuscript Reports 1867:45, RG 350; USTC, *Philippine Trade*, pp. 122–25; *Second Report of High Commissioner*, p. 117.

48. Philippine Economic Association, *Economic Problems*, pp. 35, 46; "Annual Report of the Governor-General of the Philippine Islands, 1933," Philippine Manuscript Reports 1767:17; Houston, Jr., "Philippine Crops and Industries," pp. 18–32; Stine, "Economic Policies," pp. 30–31. See Chapter 3.

49. F. LeJ. Parker to FM, Aug. 14, 1933, FM to Cox, Aug. 28, 1933, FM to Secretary of War, Dec. 16, 1933 (two messages), Feb. 3, 1934, Cox to FM, Dec. 19, 1933, Dern to Wallace, Dec. 20, 1933, File 4122, RG 350; Mills to FM, Dec. 5, 1933, Joseph Mills Papers, Burton Historical Collection, Detroit, Michigan; *MDB*, Dec. 11, 1933, clipping in FM Papers; *MDB*, Dec. 12, 1933, MSB; *Sugar News*, Jan. 1934, HSB; Joint Preparatory Committee on Philippine Affairs, *Report of May 20, 1938*, 4 vols. (Washington: U.S. Government Printing Office, 1938), 3:162.

50. M [Mills] Memorandum, Jan. 13, 1934, FM Papers; Sugar Committee to FM,

Mar. 19, 1934, FM to Philippine Sugar Planters, Mar. 24, 1934 (draft), FM to Hester, Apr. 5, 1934, Hester to FM, Apr. 14, 1934, FM to Renton Hind, May 3, 1934, ibid.; [*MT*, Feb. 1, 1934], *MT*, Feb. 2, 7, 13, 17, 28, Mar. 20, 1934, MSB; [*PH*, Feb. 5, 1934], MSB; *MDB*, Feb. 2, 8, 10, 14, Mar. 19, 29, 1934, MSB; *MDB*, Mar. 3, 1934, HSB.

51. M [Mills] Memorandum, Jan. 13, 1934, FM Papers; Rodriguez to Secretary of War, Mar. 13, 1934, FM to Secretary of War, Mar. 13, 1934, OF 400; Harry Hawes to FM, Apr. 18, 1934, FM to Secretary of War, Apr. 23, 1934, Cox Memorandum for Secretary of War, Apr. 24, 1934, Dern to Wallace, Apr. 24, 1934, Quezon to Chief, BIA, Apr. 28, 1934, Rexford Guy Tugwell to Secretary of War, May 18, 1934, File 4122, RG 350; Veatch, "*Sugar Production* for the American Market, with Special Reference to the Philippine Islands," Feb. 6, 1934, 811.6135/19, RG 59; Theodore Friend, Jr., "The Philippine Sugar Industry and the Politics of Independence, 1929–1935," *Journal of Asian Studies* 22 (Feb. 1963): 189; Thomas Janney Heston, "Sweet Subsidy: The Economic and Diplomatic Effects of the U.S. Sugar Acts—1934–1974" (Ph.D. diss., Case Western Reserve University, 1975), pp. 272–73.

52. Cox to FM, May 17, 1934, FM Papers; *MT*, May 20, 1934, MSB; *MT*, May 26, 1934, HSB; *MT*, June 9, 1934, clipping in FM Papers; *MDB*, May 21, 25, 26, 1934, HSB; *MDB*, June 21, 1934, MSB; *PH*, May 26, 1934, clipping in FM Papers. The twenty-three largest centrals would have received 77.99 percent of the quota under the averaging method and 73.49 percent under the best-year method. *MDB*, May 26, 1934.

53. *MT*, June 27, 1934, [*MT*, June 30, 1934], MSB; [*MDB*, June 28, 1934], *MDB*, Aug. 9, 1934, MSB; *MDB*, July 6, 1934, HSB; FM to Secretary of War, June 28, 1934, File 4122, RG 350. The small 1934 quota of 69,665 short tons of refined sugar was to be allocated on the basis of shipments of refined sugar to the United States in 1933. *MT*, June 27, 1934, MSB.

54. Hester Memorandum for FM, Aug. 2, 1934, FM Papers; *MT*, Aug. 3, 1934, MSB; [*PH*, Dec. 5, 1934], MSB; "Report of the Governor-General of the Philippine Islands covering the period January 1, to November 14, 1935," Philippine Manuscript Reports 1865:53–54, RG 350. The emergency reserve quota was to be not less than 100,000 tons or 10 percent of the combined export and domestic quotas, whichever was larger.

55. [*PH*, July 2, Oct. 8, 1934], HSB; [*MT*, Dec. 8, 1934], HSB; "Report of Governor-General, 1935," 1865:55, 57, 59–66, RG 350; FM to Secretary of War, Sept. 25, 1934, FM Papers; [Statement by Sugar Administration, Dec. 1934], ibid.; "Sugar Report" [1936], ibid,; Rafael Alunan to John E. Dalton, Mar. 28, 1935, Quezon Papers.

56. "Report of Governor-General, 1935," 1865:58–59, RG 350; Murray R. Benedict, *Farm Policies of the United States, 1790–1950* (New York: Twentieth Century Fund, 1953), pp. 349–50; FM to Wallace, Mar. 14, 1935, Cox to FM, Jan. 8, 1936, FM Papers; FM to Cox, Aug. 3, 1934, enclosing FM to Amando Avanceña, Aug. 2, 1934, File 4122, RG 350; Joint Preparatory Committee, *Report*, 1:42, 44; *PH*, Aug. 1, 1934, MSB; [*MDB*, Mar. 29, 1935], MSB; *MDB*, Aug. 19, 1935, HSB. Actual shipments of Philippine sugar in 1935 came to 529,180 short tons, 23,500 short tons below the quota.

57. Joint Preparatory Committee, *Report*, 1:42, 44; Cox to FM, Jan. 8, 1936, FM to Secretary of War, May 7, 1936, Jones to Secretary of War, June 9, Aug. 7, 1936, FM Papers; "Report of High Commissioner, 1936," 1867:61–63, RG 350; [*MDB*, Dec. 30, 1935], *MDB*, Apr. 13, June 26, 1936, HSB; *MDB*, Jan. 16, 22, 1936, MSB.

58. Cox to FM, June 19, 1934, File 4122, RG 350; McDonald Memorandum for the Records, Dec. 13, 1934, File 1239, ibid.; Hester to Theodore Roosevelt, Jr., Sept. 8, 1936, Theodore Roosevelt, Jr., Papers, Box 21, LC; [*MDB*, July 27, 1934, Aug. 23, 1935], HSB.

59. "Report of Governor-General, 1935," 1865:67–69, RG 350; "Report of High Commissioner, 1936," 1867:64, ibid.; Heston, "Sweet Subsidy," pp. 274–75; [*MT*, Dec. 8, 1934], MSB; *Philippines Free Press*, Nov. 23, 1935, MSB; "Sugar Report" [1936], FM Papers; Jones to Secretary of War, Aug. 7, 1936, FM Papers; FM to BIA, Oct. 16, 1935, BIA to Governor-General, Oct. 16, 1935, File 4168, RG 350. A congressional resolution of June 19, 1936, continued the quota provision of the Jones-Costigan Act but halted its other features. Benedict, *Farm Policies*, pp. 355–56. Because of compliance failures, 564 benefit payment contracts had to be rescinded. Jones to Secretary of War, Aug. 7, 1936, FM Papers.

60. *MT*, Sept. 29, 1934, MSB; [*MT*, Mar. 17, 1934], HSB; [*MDB*, July 2, 1934], *MDB*, Apr. 27, 1935, MSB; [*MDB*, July 19, 1934], HSB; Wallace to FM, June 21, 1934, [Arnold and Rosenquist] Memorandum for Governor-General [Sept. 1934], Hester Memorandum for Governor-General, Nov. 20, 1934, FM to Wallace, Mar. 14, 1935, FM Papers; "N. Hill," Apr. 12, 1935, ibid.; JRH to Secretary of War, May 3, 1935, JRH Papers; McDonald Memorandum: Sugar, July 30, 1935, File 4122, RG 350; FM to FDR, Apr. 26, 1935, D. W. Bell to Louis Howe, Sept. 21, 1935, FDR to Secretary of War [Sept. 23, 1935], OF 400. Two days before the attack on Pearl Harbor Congress authorized the Philippines to use the sugar processing tax money for defense purposes. Friend, *Two Empires*, p. 204; Garel A. Grunder and William E. Livezey, *The Philippines and the United States* (Norman: University of Oklahoma Press, 1951), p. 208.

61. Hester to FM, Feb. 20, 1935, FM to Secretary of War, May 7, 1936, FM Papers; FM to Cox, Aug. 3, 1934, File 4122, RG 350; Alunan to Dalton, Mar. 29, 1935, Quezon Papers; Hester to Roosevelt, Jr., Sept. 8, 1936, Roosevelt Papers, Box 21; "Report of Governor-General, 1935," 1865:69–70, RG 350; John E. Dalton, *Sugar: A Case Study of Government Control* (New York: Macmillan Co., 1937), pp. 234–35. Cf. Thurman Arnold, *Fair Fights and Foul* (New York: Harcourt, Brace & World, 1965), p. 134.

62. "Sugar Report" [1936], FM Papers; Joint Preparatory Committee, *Report*, 1:42; Dalton, *Sugar*, p. 236; Friend, "Sugar Industry," p. 181.

63. [*PH*, Oct. 2, 1933], MSB; [*MT*, Oct. 4, 1933], clipping in FM Papers; *MDB*, Oct. 21, 1933, MSB; Cox to FM, Oct. 13, 1933 (two messages), FM to Cox, Oct. 20, 1933, FM Papers.

64. Pedro E. Abelarde, *American Tariff Policy toward the Philippines* (New York: Kings Crown Press, 1947), p. 130; L. J. Taber et al. to FDR, Apr. 17, 1934, OF 400; *PH*, Jan. 30, Feb. 3, 6, 1934, MSB; *MT*, Feb. 25, 1934, HSB; [*MDB*, Jan. 30, 1934], *MDB*, Feb. 3, 10, 1934, MSB. Murphy estimated the total supply of coconut oil used in the United States at 327,000 metric tons and assumed that 25 percent of the total

was used for edible purposes. The average extraction rate from copra was 60 percent. *MDB*, Jan. 30, 1934.

65. [*MDB*, Jan. 31, 1934], *MDB*, Feb. 3, 10, Apr. 11, 1934, MSB; *MDB*, Feb. 28, 1934, HSB; *PH*, Mar. 3, 17, 1934, MSB; *MT*, Feb. 9, 1934, MSB; *NYT*, May 2, 4, 1934; Cox to FM, Apr. 26, 1934, FM Papers; Dern to FDR, Feb. 24, 1934 (two messages), FDR to Mac [McIntyre], Feb. 25, 1934, FM to Secretary of War, Mar. 13, 1934, FDR to Byron Harrison, Mar. 24, 1934, Stephen Early Memorandum for the President, Apr. 19, 1934, OF 400; Grayson V. Kirk, *Philippine Independence* (New York: Farrar and Rinehart, 1936), pp. 134–35.

66. FM to Secretary of War, May 1, 1934, Quezon and Quintin Paredes to Pedro Guevara, May 1, 1934, Howard Kellogg to FDR, May 2, 1934, John B. Gordon to FDR, May 4, 1934, OF 400; Press Release, Jan. 27 [1935], ibid.; Salvador Araneta to FM, Apr. 19, 1934, FM Papers; Memorandum: Meeting of . . . Murphy with Interdepartmental Committee, Mar. 13, 1935, File C–1247, RG 350; Joint Preparatory Committee, *Report*, 1:63.

67. Joint Preparatory Committee, *Report*, 1:53, 54, 108, 3:449, 451, 791–92, 1375; Quezon to FM, Jan. 8, 1935, Quezon Papers; Dern, "Confidential Report," Dec. 20, 1935, PSF, War Department (Dern); Hester Memorandum for EGK, Apr. 3, 1936, Jones to Secretary of War, July 14, Sept. 10, 1936, FM Papers; FM to Dern, Mar. 2, 1936, File 2074–A, RG 350; Jones to EGK, Feb. 21, 1941, EGK Papers; USTC, *Philippine Trade*, pp. 101–3; *Second Report of High Commissioner*, pp. 2, 65–69; *Third Report of High Commissioner*, p. 2; *Fourth Report of High Commissioner*, pp. 16–23; *Fifth Annual Report of the United States High Commissioner to the Philippine Islands* (Washington: U.S. Government Printing Office, 1943), pp. 75–79; Friend, *Two Empires*, pp. 159–60. The value of copra and coconut oil shipped to the United States in 1936 was $1,798,545 more than in 1935. Joint Preparatory Committee, *Report*, 1:53–54. In 1936 Congress imposed the excise on several previously exempt competing oils. Jones to Secretary of War, July 4, 1936, FM Papers. The Commonwealth government netted $51 million in receipts and transfers in 1936. Joint Preparatory Committee, *Report*, 1:108. Congress specified in 1939 that the proceeds from the excise were to be used to help readjust the Philippine economy to independence. *Fourth Report of High Commissioner*, pp. 117–18.

68. Joint Preparatory Committee, *Report*, 1:71; USTC, *Philippine Trade*, pp. 130, 133.

69. Raul P. DeGuzman, "The Formulation and Implementation of the Philippine Independence Policy of the United States, 1929–1946" (Ph.D. diss., Florida State University, 1957), pp. 110–11; Abelarde, *Tariff Policy*, pp. 165–66; *MT*, Mar. 31, 1935, [*MT*, Apr. 10, 1935], MSB; *MDB*, Mar. 23, 1935, HSB; *MDB*, June 5, 1935, MSB; Cox Memorandum, Mar. 26, 1935, Quezon Mission, 1935, Records of the Office of U.S. High Commissioner to the Philippine Islands, RG 126, NARS; JRH to Secretary of War (Rodriguez to Quezon), Mar. 24, 1935, JRH Papers; FM to J. S. McDaniel, Apr. 25, 1935, FM Papers; "N. Hill," Apr. 12, 1935, ibid.; Cox Memorandum for Records, Nov. 15, 1934, Confidential Diary Notes, RG 126.

70. Tydings to FM, May 6, 1935, Sen 74A–F23, Tray 142, Records of the United States Senate, RG 46, NARS; General Cordage Committee—Aide Memoire, undated, FM Papers; FM to Secretary of War, July 22, Aug. 12, 1935, ibid.; Executive

Order No. 846, Aug. 28, 1935, ibid.; Joint Preparatory Committee, *Report*, 1:71, 72, 73. Elizalde and Co., which received 63 percent of the quota under the formula adopted, would have received 34 percent had the allocation been based on spindle capacity and 59 percent had it been based on shipments in the twelve preceding months. FM to Secretary of War, July 22, 1935, FM Papers. Shipments totaled 3,918,622 pounds in 1936 and 4,660,333 pounds in 1937. Joint Preparatory Committee, *Report*, 1:71.

71. J. W. Martyn to Early, Oct. 12, 1934, enclosing Cox, "The Philippine Islands," Oct. 11, 1934, OF 400.

72. Veatch, "Future Trade Relations between the United States and the Philippine Islands," Sept. 7, 1934, OF 400. See also Walter Robb to Hal O'Flaherty, Jan. 17, 1935, FM Papers.

73. Cox Memoranda of Conversations with Quezon, Oct. 13, Nov. 19, 1934, Quezon Mission, 1934, RG 126. Cf. "Quezon's Visit to the U.S.," Oct. 12, 1934, ibid. See Roy Watson Curry, *Woodrow Wilson and Far Eastern Policy* (New York: Bookman Associates, 1957), pp. 79-81, 93.

74. FM notes, Aug. 25, 1934, FM Papers.

75. See ibid.

76. Veatch, "Trade Relations," Sept. 7, 1934, OF 400.

77. Richard R. Ely, Memorandum for the Governor-General [Jan. 1934], Carl H. Boehringer to FM, Aug. 1, 1934, FM Papers; Joint Preparatory Committee, *Report*, 1:26.

78. Philippine Economic Association, *Economic Problems*, p. 193; Joint Preparatory Committee, *Report*, 1:96-97; "Report of Governor-General, 1935," 1865:72, RG 350; "Report of the Cotton and Cotton Goods Committee on the Philippine Market for American Textiles," May 7, 1935, OF 23-Q, FDRL; Francis B. Sayre to Howe, Apr. 6, 1934, 611 B.003/39, RG 59; Philippine Committee of Textile Export Association of the United States to United States Congressional Mission, Dec. 20, 1934, FM Papers; A. G. Kempf to FM, Jan. 14, 1935, ibid.; Suggested Terms of a Voluntary Agreement..., May 7, 1935, ibid.; Frank A. Waring to Interdepartmental Committee, Mar. 23, 1935, and enclosed Memorandum on the Application of Quota Restrictions ... [Mar. 23, 1935], File C-1247, RG 350.

79. "The question of Philippine tariff rates" [Mar. 9, 1935], File C-1247, RG 350; USTC, Summary of Memorandum on Philippine-United States Trade Relations [Jan. 1935], ibid.; Memorandum Concerning Possible Adjustments in Philippine-United States Trade Relations [Apr. 3, 1935], ibid.; Sayre to Howe, Apr. 6, 1934, 611 B.003/39, RG 59; USTC, *Philippine Trade*, pp. 30, 172-73, 179-80.

80. Veatch Memorandum to Livesey, Aug. 15, 1934, 611 B.003/54, RG 59; Veatch Memorandum, Nov. 2, 1934, 611 B.003/134, ibid.; Veatch, "Trade Relations," Sept. 7, 1934, OF 400.

81. *Message of Governor-General Frank Murphy to the Tenth Philippine Legislature, July 16, 1934* (Manila: Bureau of Printing, 1934), pp. 11-12; Boehringer to FM, Aug. 1, 1934, FM to Secretary of War, Aug. 9, 1934, FM Papers; FM to Sayre, July 26, 1935, File C-1247, RG 350; Minutes of the Interdepartmental Committee on Philippine Affairs, Mar. 20, 1935, ibid.; [PH, Aug. 10, 1934], HSB.

82. *PH*, Sept. 1, 1934, MSB; [*MT*, Aug. 18, 1934], HSB; *MDB*, Sept. 1, 3, 4, 1934, MSB; Hester, "Notes Re Philippine-United States Reciprocal Trade Policy,"

Sept. 10, 1934, FM Papers; Veatch, "Trade Relations," Sept. 7, 1934, OF 400; Interdepartmental Committee Minutes, Mar. 20, 1935, FIle C-1247, RG 350.

83. The American share in 1933 and 1934 was 65 percent. Joint Preparatory Committee, *Report*, 1:26.

84. FM to Secretary of War, Sept. 11, 1934, Cox to FM, Sept. 15, 1934, FM Papers; Memorandum: Interdepartmental Committee on Philippine-United States Trade Relations, Mar. 28, 1935, File C-1247, RG 350; "Philippine tariff rates" [Mar. 19, 1935], ibid.; Veatch Memorandum, Nov. 2, 1934, 611 B.003/134, RG 59; Veatch Memorandum, May 10, 1935, OF 355, FDRL.

85. Cox to FM, Aug. 29, Sept. 5, 15, 19, 1934, Hull to FM, Sept. 18, 1934, Robert L. O'Brien to Secretary of War, Sept. 20, 1934, FM Papers; O'Brien to Secretary of War, File C-21, RG 350; "Philippine tariff rates" [Mar. 19, 1935], File C-1247, ibid.; USTC, Summary of Memorandum [Jan. 1935], ibid.; Memorandum on Quota Restrictions [Mar. 23, 1935], ibid.; Hull to Dern, Sept. 18, 1934, 611 B.003/43, Herbert Feis to Secretary of War, Oct. 29, 1934, 611 B.003/84, RG 59.

86. Veatch Memorandum, May 10, 1935, OF 355; Hull to FM, Sept. 18, 1934, Dern to FM, Sept. 22, 1934, FM Papers; Cox to FM, Sept. 19, 1934, Hull to Dern, Sept. 19, 1934, File C-21, RG 350.

87. FM to Secretary of War, Sept. 26, Oct. 9, 1934, [Cox] to FM, Oct. 1, 1934, FM Papers; Veatch Memorandum, Oct. 12, 1934, 611 B.003/62, RG 59; Veatch Memorandum of Conversation . . . with . . . Fish. . ., Jan. 17, 1935, 611 B.003/146, ibid.; Frederic S. Marquardt to Roosevelt, Jr., Oct. 4, 1934, Roosevelt Papers, Box 29; [*MT*, Oct. 9, 1934], MSB.

88. Veatch Memorandum, May 10, 1935, OF 355; Hull to Dern, Oct. 8, 1934, Cox to Hull and Dern, Oct. 15, 1934, File C-21, RG 350; Cox to FM, Oct. 9, 13, 23, [24], Oct. 9, 1934, FM Papers; Cox Memorandum: Conversation with Quezon. . ., Oct. 13, 1934, Quezon Mission, 1934, RG 126.

89. Veatch Memorandum, Nov. 2, 1934, 611 B.003/134, RG 59; Veatch Memorandum, May 10, 1935, OF 355; FM to Secretary of War, Oct. 19, 1934, FM Papers. The Philippine tariff committee did submit a "much revised" bill on October 26 that raised rates on a few items that competed with local industries, but this apparently was for the record only. *MDB*, Oct. 26, 1934.

90. Press Release, Oct. 26, 1934, FM Papers; Veatch Memorandum, May 10, 1935, OF 355; *MDB*, Oct. 26, 1934, HSB; M. J. McDermott Memorandum to Early, May 14, 1935, OF 355.

91. Howard E. Coffin to McIntyre, Oct. 26, 1934, American Chamber of Commerce to War Department, Oct. 27, 1934, OF 400; William Philipps to Sayre, Oct. 27, 1934, 611 B.003/82, Veatch to Feis, Oct. 27, 1934, 611 B.003/100, RG 59; Veatch Memorandum, May 10, 1935, OF 355.

92. Philipps to Sayre, Oct. 27, 1934, 611 B.003/82, Veatch Memorandum to Feis, Oct. 27, 1934, 611 B.003/100, Feis to Secretary of State, Oct. 29, 1934, 611 B.003/84, Philipps to Dern, Nov. 1, 1934, 611 B.003/79A, RG 59; Stimson Diary, Oct. 31, 1934, Stimson Papers; Cox to FM, Nov. 1, 1934, FM to Secretary of War, Nov. 8, 1934, FM Papers; Veatch Memorandum, May 10, 1935, OF 355; Cox Memorandum for Records, Oct. 31, 1934, Confidential Diary Notes, RG 126; Cox Memorandum of Conversation re P.I. Tariff Revision, Nov. 7, 1934, ibid.

93. Philippine Committee of Textile Export Association to Congressional Mission,

Dec. 20, 1934, Kempf to FM, Jan. 14, 1935, Kempf to EGK, Jan. 21, 1935, FM Papers; [Hull] Memorandum [Nov. 20, 1934], 611 B.003/106, RG 59; Hull to Martin, Jan. 19, 1935, OF 355; *MDB*, Mar. 11, 1935, MSB; Richard V. Leopold, *The Growth of American Foreign Policy* (New York: Alfred A. Knopf, 1962), p. 525.

94. Memorandum: Interdepartmental Committee, Mar. 28, 1935, File C-1247, RG 350; Interdepartmental Committee Minutes, Apr. 14, 1935, ibid.; FDR Memorandum for Secretary of State, Nov. 19, 1934, OF 20, FDRL.

95. Memorandum on Quota Restrictions [Mar. 23, 1935], File C-1247, RG 350; Memorandum: Interdepartmental Committee, Mar. 28, 1935, ibid.; Interdepartmental Committee, Memorandum Concerning Possible Adjustments in Philippine-United States Trade Relations [Apr. 3, 1935], ibid.; Interdepartmental Committee Minutes, Mar. 20, 28, Apr. 4, 1935, ibid.; Cox Memorandum, Mar. 14, 1935, FM file, RG 350; Cox Memorandum, Mar. 16, 1935, FM Visit, 1935, RG 126; Hull to FDR, Mar. 18, 1935, OF 400; [Cox] Office Memorandum, Apr. 15, 1935, FM Visit, 1935, RG 126.

96. Interdepartmental Committee, Memorandum Concerning Adjustments in Trade Relations [Apr. 3, 1935], File C-1247, RG 350; Interdepartmental Committee Minutes, Mar. 25, Apr. 4, 1935, ibid.; MMH [Hamilton] Conversation, Apr. 4, 1935, 611 B.003/148, RG 59; Hull to FDR, Apr. 6, 1935, FDR Memorandum for Early, Apr. 8, 1935, OF 400; Veatch Memorandum, May 10, 1935, OF 355; FM to Early, Apr. 9, 1935, FM Papers.

97. *Foreign Relations of the United States, 1935*, vol. 3 (Washington: U.S. Government Printing Office, 1953), pp. 952, 954-55, 964, 973, 976; Allen J. Treadway et al. to Quezon, June 14, 1935, Cox Memoranda for Secretary of War, June 28, July 8, 1935, Secretary of War to Tydings, July 8, 1935, and Cox note of July 5 on letter, Cox to FM, July 13, 1935, FM to Secretary of War, July 15, 1935, File C-1094, RG 350; Cox Memorandum, July 11, 1935, ibid.; FM to Sayre, July 26, 1935, Sayre to FM, Sept. 26, 1935, File C-1247, ibid.; Cox to FM, Apr. 27, 1935, Fish to Quezon, June 17, 1935, FM to Speaker of House, July 9, 1935, FM Papers; FM to Secretary of War, July 9, 1935, OF 400; Cox Memorandum, July 8, 1935, Confidential Diary Notes, RG 126; Confidential Summary of Intelligence for the Phil. Dept., July 15, 1935, ibid.; *MDB*, July 19, 1935, HSB.

98. Proposition Suggested by U.S.A. Government, Apr. 18, 1935, FM Papers; Cox to FM, May 8, 1935, enclosing Sayre to Cox, May 8, 1935, Cox to FM, May 16, 1935, FM to Cox, May 9, 1935, FM to JRH, May 10, 1935, Sayre to FM, Oct. 29, 1935, FM Papers; Interdepartmental Committee Minutes, July 19, Sept. 28, 1935, File C-1247, RG 350; FM to Secretary of War, Sept. 30, Oct. 3, 1935, ibid.; Conversation, Oct. 11, 1935 (two documents), ibid.; Department of State Press Release, Oct. 12, 1935, ibid.; Subcommittee to Sayre, Mar. 23, 1936, ibid.; *Foreign Relations of United States, 1935*, 3:998, 1000-2, 1006-8.

99. FM to Secretary of War, Oct. 29, 1935, McDonald to FM, Oct. 30, 1935, FM to Sayre, Dec. 4, 1935, Hester Memorandum for High Commissioner, Dec. 11, 1935, Cox to FM, Dec. 24, Mar. 30, Apr. 6, 18, 1936, [E. A.] Stockton to FM, Dec. 12, 1935, FM Papers; Stockton to FM, Dec. 5, 1935, Subcommittee to Sayre, Mar. 23, 1936, FM to Secretary of War, Apr. 4, 1936, File C-1247, RG 350; Interdepartmental Committee Minutes, Dec. 13, 1935, Feb. 5, 27, Mar. 17, 24, Apr. 17,

July 23, 1936, ibid.; Memorandum for Interdepartmental Committee, Mar. 13, 1936, ibid.; *Foreign Relations of United States, 1935*, 3:1025–30; ibid., *1936*, vol. 4 (Washington: U.S. Government Printing Office, 1954), pp. 807, 819–20; Sayre to Claudius T. Murchison, Sept. 19, 1936, 611 B.9417/220A, RG 59; "Report of High Commissioner, 1936," 1867:67–69, RG 350; *MDB*, Mar. 3, Apr. 17, 1936, clippings in FM Papers; *MDB*, Sept. 23, 1936, HSB.

100. *Foreign Relations of United States, 1935*, 3:1022–25; ibid., *1936*, 4:808, 930–31, 934; Interdepartmental Committee Minutes, Mar. 17, 24, July 23, 1936, File C-1247, RG 350; Subcommittee to Sayre, Mar. 23, 1936, ibid.; Cox to FM (from Sayre), May 9, 1936, FM to Jones, May 25, 1936, FM Papers; "Report of Governor-General, 1935," 1865:73, RG 350; "Report of High Commissioner, 1936," 1867:67, ibid.; *MDB*, Sept. 23, 1936, HSB; *Second Report of High Commissioner*, pp. 110, 163–64; *Third Report of High Commissioner*, pp. 137–38; *Fourth Report of High Commissioner*, pp. 85–86; *Fifth Report of High Commissioner*, p. 56; *Sixth Annual Report of the United States High Commissioner to the Philippine Islands, . . . July 1, 1941–June 30, 1942* (Washington: U.S. Government Printing Office, 1943), p. 100.

101. FM to Secretary of War, May 8, 9, 1934, Cox Memoranda for Secretary of War, May 18, June 14, 1934, Cox to FM, June 18, 1934, BIA to FM, June 20, 1934, Tydings to FM, Oct. 6, 1934, File 22639, RG 350; Cox Memorandum, June 14, 1934, ibid.; Cox Memorandum, May 23, 1934, Confidential Diary Notes, RG 126; FM to Secretary of War, May 10, 1934, Dern to FDR, May 24, 1934, FDR to FM, May 24, 1934, MHM [McIntyre] Memorandum for President, June 15, 1934, FDR to Speaker [June 16, 1934], FDR to Vice-President [June 16, 1934], OF 400.

102. Cox to FM, June 23, 1934, File 22639, RG 350; C. Hayden to Tydings, Aug. 6, 1934, FM Papers; Sayre Conversation in Office of . . . Tydings, Oct. 1, 1934, 611 B.003/63, RG 59; Hull to C. Hayden, Sept. 6, 1934, 611 B.003/45, ibid.; [*MDB*, July 23, 1934], MSB.

103. Cox to FM, Oct. 6, 1934, FM Papers; K. F. Baldwin Memorandum, Dec. 5, 1934, File 1239, RG 350; Memorial of Chamber of Commerce of Philippine Islands . . . , Dec. 9, 1934, File 22639, ibid.; [*MT*, Dec. 27, 1934], HSB; [*PH*, Dec. 24, 27, 1934], HSB; Veatch Conversation with Villamin, Jan. 9, 1935, 611 B.003/143, RG 59; Veatch Memorandum to Feis and Sayre, Feb. 9, 1935, 811 B.001/241, ibid.; Sayre Memorandum of Conversation between Tydings, Ryder, and Sayre . . . , Feb. 26, 1935, 811 B.001/241, ibid.; Asociacion de los Veteranos de la Revolucion Memorial . . . , Dec. 23, 1935, Emilio Aguinaldo file, RG 350; F. A. Delgado to FDR, Feb. 4, 1935, OF 400. For the Tydings address, see *Senate Miscellaneous Documents*, 74 Cong., 1 sess., Sen. Doc. No. 119 (Washington: U.S. Government Printing Office, 1935).

104. *Senate Miscellaneous Documents*, 74 Cong., 1 sess., Sen. Doc. No. 57, 2 parts (Washington: U.S. Government Printing Office, 1935); [*PH*, Feb. 8, 1935], MSB; [*MT*, May 5, 1935], MSB; Sayre Memorandum of Conversation, Feb. 26, 1935, 811 B.01/241, RG 59; FM to Secretary of War, Dec. 31, 1934, File C-1247, RG 350; Cox Memorandum, Feb. 12, 1935, Confidential Diary Notes, RG 126.

105. Hull to Dern, Jan. 10, 1935, File C-1247, RG 350; Interdepartmental Committee Minutes, Jan. 11, Mar. 7, 1935, ibid.; Hull to FDR, Jan. 15, 1935, 611 B.003/125B, RG 59. The January 11 action was anticipated in an informal meeting

of the interested departments on December 11, 1934. See Interdepartmental Meeting on the Philippines, Dec. 12, 1934, File 1239, RG 350; McDonald Memorandum for Records, Dec. 13, 1934, File 1239, ibid.; and Sayre to Cox, Dec. 14, 1934, 611 B.003/111A, RG 59.

106. FM Notes on Conference, Jan. 19 [1935], FM Papers; FM notes, Feb. 1, 1935, ibid.; "Conference," Jan. 21, 1935, ibid. See also Robert Aura Smith, "The Gloomy Philippine Future," *Asia* 35 (May 1935): 290-97.

107. FM to Joseph Sanders, May 8, 1934, FM Papers; FM notes, Feb. 1935, ibid.; [*MDB*, Jan. 23, 1935], MSB.

108. FM notes, Feb. 1935, FM Papers; [*MDB*, Jan. 24, 1935], MSB.

109. [*PH*, Jan. 12, 1935], MSB; [*MDB*, Jan. 26, 1935], *MDB*, May 20, 1935, MSB; *NYT*, Feb. 9, 1935; *Honolulu Star Bulletin*, Feb. 8, 1935, clipping in FM Papers; FM speech, Feb. 13, 1935, ibid.; Kenneth R. McDonald Interview with FM, Feb. 24 [1935], ibid.; FM Notes, May 7-9, 1935, ibid.; Cox Memorandum, Mar. 5, 1935, FM file, RG 350; Interdepartmental Committee Minutes, Mar. 7, 1935, File C-1247, ibid.; Dern to FDR, Mar. 9, 1935, OF 400; MMH [Hamilton] Conversation, Apr. 4, 1935, 611 B.003/148, RG 59; Stimson Diary, Mar. 5, 1935, Stimson Papers.

110. Interdepartmental Committee Minutes, Mar. 7, 9, 13, 1935, File C-1247, RG 350; Memorandum: Meeting of . . . Murphy with Interdepartmental Committee, Mar. 13, 1935, ibid.; "Outline for a Philippine Trade Act . . ." [Mar. 7, 1935], ibid.; FM notes [Mar. 1935?], FM Papers.

111. Hull to FDR, Mar. 18, 1935, and enclosed Confidential Memorandum. . . , Hull to FDR, Apr. 6, 1935, OF 400.

112. FDR Memorandum for Secretary of State, Mar. 19, 1935, File C-1247, RG 350; FDR to FM, Apr. 10, 1935, OF 400; *NYT*, Apr. 11, 1935; [*MT*, Apr. 12, 1935], MSB; *Philippines Free Press*, June 8, 1935, clipping in FM Papers; *PH*, Apr. 13, 1935, MSB; [*PH*, Apr. 29, 1935], HSB; Vicente Albano Pacis, "Murphy—P.I. Benefactor," *Philippine Yearbook* 3 (1935-36): 20.

113. Cox to Sayre, May 17, 1935, Cox to FM, May 27, June 8, 1935, FM to Secretary of War, July 10, 1935, FM to Sayre, July 26, 1935, Philipps to Cox, Aug. 1, 1935, File C-1247, RG 350; Interdepartmental Committee Minutes, July 13, 17, 1935, ibid.; *MT*, July 18, 1935, HSB; *MT*, Sept. 11, 1935, clipping in FM Papers; [*PH*, July 12, 1935], HSB; *PH*, Sept. 9, 12, 1935, clippings in FM Papers; Cox to FM, May 27, 1935, and enclosed Suggested Studies. . . , ibid.; Memorandum for Governor-General, Sept. 11, 1935, ibid.

114. *MDB*, Jan. 1, 11, 1936, HSB; Memorandum for the High Commissioner, Jan. 11, 1936, FM Papers; "Preliminary Report to the Interdepartmental Committee . . . by the Survey Committee . . . ," Mar. 31, 1936, File C-1247, RG 350.

115. Benito Razon, "The Trade Conference," *Commonwealth Advocate*, Jan. 3, 1936, FM Papers; *MDB*, May 1, 1936, clipping in ibid.; Roxas, *Philippine Independence May Succeed without Free Trade* (Manila: n.p., 1936), ibid.; Hester to FM, Apr. 16, 1936, and enclosed Confidential Memorandum, Apr. 16, 1936, Quezon to FM [May 5, 1936], May 14, 1936, Jones to Acting Secretary of War, Oct. 8, 1936, ibid.

116. FM to Sayre, Dec. 4, 1935, FM to Secretary of War, Jan. 20, Feb. 10, 1936, FM to Hester, Apr. 24, May 14, 1936, FM Memorandum to EGK, May 21, 1936, FM

to Jones, May 25, 1936, FM to James G. Wingo, June 6, 1936, FM Papers; Cabinet Minutes, July 10, 1935, ibid.; FM to Dern, May 2, 1936, File 2074-A, RG 350; FM to Secretary of War, Jan. 24, 1936, File C-1247, ibid.; FM to Secretary of State, May 13, 1936, OF 400; *MDB*, Sept. 4, Oct. 8, 1935, clippings in FM Papers; [*PH*, Apr. 12, 1935], *PH*, May 11, 1936, HSB; *NYT*, Apr. 11, 1935.

117. Dern, "Confidential Report," Dec. 20, 1935, PSF, War Department (Dern); FM to Secretary of War, Jan. 24, 1936, FM to Hull, May 13, 1936, File C-1247, RG 350; Interdepartmental Committee Minutes, Jan. 6, July 23, 1936, ibid.; [Dorfman], Memorandum for Interdepartmental Committee..., Mar. 11, 1936, ibid.; State Department Release, Dec. 29, 1936, ibid.; Cox to FM, Jan. 10, May 9, 1936, [Jorge] Vargas to Hill, Jan. 22, 1936, FM to EGK, Sept. 3, 1936, FM to Sayre, Dec. 2, 1936, FM to Salvador and Victoria Araneta, Dec. 2, 1936, Sayre to FM, Dec. 21, 1936, Cox to High Commissioner, Dec. 22, 1936, FM to Quezon, Dec. 28, 1936, FM Papers; Interdepartmental Committee Minutes, Dec. 18, 1936, ibid.; JRH Notes, Mar. 3, 1936, JRH Papers; Joint Preparatory Committee, *Report*, 1:11; *PH*, June 22, July 9, 1936, HSB; *MDB*, Nov. 7, 1936, HSB.

118. Sayre to FDR, Feb. 19, 1937, and enclosed *Memorandum*, 711 B.00111/8A, RG 59; Sayre to FM, Feb. 25, 1937, FM Papers; Joint Preparatory Committee, *Report*, 1:3.

119. Joint Preparatory Committee, *Report*, 1:5, 10–13, 161–73; Sayre to FM, Nov. 29, 1938, FM Papers; David Vawter DuFault, "Francis B. Sayre and the Commonwealth of the Philippines, 1936–1942" (Ph.D. diss., University of Oregon, 1972), pp. 146–65.

120. Ethel B. Dietrich, "United States Commercial Relations with the Far East" (Institute of Pacific Relations, 1939), p. 41, JRH Papers; Friend, *Two Empires*, pp. 158–59. Cf. DuFault, "Sayre," pp. 193–94. For the terms of the Economic Adjustment Act of 1939, see *Fourth Report of High Commissioner*, pp. 195–201.

CHAPTER 5

1. Joseph Ralston Hayden, *The Philippines* (New York: Macmillan Co., 1942), pp. 762–63, 777; idem, "The Philippines in Transition: From Commonwealth to Independence," *Foreign Affairs* 14 (July 1936): 639–42.

2. *The Statutes at Large of the United States of America* 48, pt. 1 (Washington: U.S. Government Printing Office, 1934): 454–65.

3. *Philippines Free Press*, Oct. 5, 1935, MSB; [*PH*, June 8, 1935], MSB; [*MT*, Nov. 3, 1934], MSB; Hayden, "Transition," p. 643; [Frank McIntyre], "US Participation in the Philippine Government under the Independence Act," June 27, 1934, File 3038-B, Records of the Bureau of Insular Affairs, RG 350, NARS; Creed F. Cox Memorandum for Secretary of War, Nov. 19, 1936, ibid.; Quezon to FDR, Jan. 15, 1934, Cox to FM, June 23, 1934, File 364, ibid.; [Cox], "Notes on the Administration of the Philippine Independence Act...," July 2, 1934, ibid.

4. *MDB*, Mar. 28, 1934, *PH*, Apr. 2, 1935, clippings in FM Papers; Press Release, May 3 [1934], ibid.; FM to Ann Walker, July 7, Nov. 7, 1934, ibid.; FM notes, May 7–9, 1935, ibid.; IM to Mrs. E. V. Hawkins, Mar. 27, 1934, IM Papers; FM to GM,

Mar. 28, [July 1934], GM Papers; Cox Memoranda of Conversations with Quezon, Oct. 13, Nov. 19, 1934, Quezon Mission, 1934, Records of the Office of the U.S. High Commissioner to the Philippine Islands, RG 126, NARS; [Cox] Memorandum, Mar. 18, 1935, FM Visit, 1935, ibid.; Cox Memorandum, Feb. 12, 1935, Confidential Diary Notes on Miscellaneous Subjects, 1933–1935, Records of the Office of Territories, ibid.; Harry B. Hawes to Rafael R. Alunan, Nov. 8, 1934, Manuel L. Quezon Papers, MHC; Henry L. Stimson Diary, Mar. 20, 1935, Henry L. Stimson Papers, Sterling Library, Yale University, New Haven, Conn. Cf. [*MDB*, Mar. 15, 1935], MSB.

5. Marvin H. McIntyre to Secretary of War, June 25, 1935, FM file, RG 350; FM to GM, June 19, 1935, Cox to FM, June 25, 1935, FM to Walker, July 10, 1935, FM Papers; *PH*, June 27, 1935, MSB; *MT*, July 3, 1935, MSB. See also FM to GM, Aug. 24, 1935, GM Papers.

6. D. Clayton James, *The Years of MacArthur*, vol. 1 (*1880–1941*) (Boston: Houghton Mifflin Co., 1970), pp. 486–89; Quezon to MacArthur, May 21, 1935, RG 18, MacArthur Memorial Library, Norfolk, Virginia (hereafter MML); MacArthur to FDR, Sept. 9, 1935, FDR to MacArthur, Sept. 19, 1935, PSF, War Department, 1934–1936, FDRL; FDR Memorandum for Secretary of War, Feb. 10, 1936, ibid.

7. *MDB*, June 27, 1935, *PH*, June 26, 1935, clippings in FM Papers; *MT*, June 27, 1935, MSB; Claro M. Recto to FM, June 27, 1935, Jorge B. Vargas to FM, June 27, 1935, FM Papers; Joint Resolution . . . , July 3, 1935, copy in ibid.; Quezon speech, July 3, 1935, ibid.

8. FM to Secretary of War, May 21, 1934, Harry H. Woodring to FDR, June 5, 1934, OF 400, FDRL; FM to FDR, Nov. 28, 1934, FM Papers; Cox Memorandum for Judge Advocate General, May 26, 1934, Cox to FM, June 23, 1934, File 364, RG 350; Cox, "Philippine Independence," June 14, 1934, Confidential Diary Notes, RG 126; C. E. Kilbourne to Governor-General, July 9, 1934 (draft), Kilbourne Memorandum for Chief, Bureau of Insular Affairs (BIA), July 9, 1934, Edward A. Stockton Memorandum for Assistant Chief of Staff, War Plans Division (WPD). Aug. 17, 1934, BIA File 364, in File 313 (6-26-39), Records of the Adjutant General's Office, 1917–, RG 407, NARS; C. Hayden to Tydings, Sept. 27, 1934, Sen 73-A, F 25, Tray 126, Records of the United States Senate, RG 46, ibid.

9. Cox to FM, Feb. 23, 1935, FM Papers; [Cox] Notes . . . J., Mar. 7, 1935, ibid.; Cox Memoranda for Secretary of War, Feb. 26, 1935, Nov. 19, 1936, File 3038-B, RG 350; Cox Memorandum for Judge Advocate General, Mar. 13, 1935, OF 400; Cox Memorandum, Mar. 14, 1935, FM file, RG 350; FM to Cox, Apr. 16, 1935, File 141, ibid.; Memorandum, Mar. 22, 1935, FM Visit, RG 126.

10. [Cox] Memorandum, Apr. 9, 1935, File 3038-B, RG 350; Cox Memoranda for Secretary of War, Aug. 15, 1935, Nov. 19, 1936, Cox to FM, Sept. 10, 1935, ibid.; Office Memorandum, Apr. 15, 1935, FM Visit, 1935, RG 126; FM to Blair Moody, May 11, 1935, Blair Moody Papers, MHC; Dern to FM, Aug. 16, 1935, FM Papers (FDR's agreement is indicated on the letter); Dern to FDR, Aug. 16, 1935, OF 400; Dern, "Confidential Report to the President," Part 2, Dec. 20, 1935, PSF, War Department (Dern), FDRL; JRH to Jesse Reeves, Sept. 29, 1935, JRH Papers.

11. Cox to FM, Aug. 16, 1935, and enclosed "Notes Re Inaugural Ceremony . . . ," FM to Secretary of War, Aug. 23, Sept. 3, 1935, FM Papers; FM to Secretary of War,

Aug. 17, 1935, File 3038-B, RG 350; JRH to Reeves, Sept. 29, 1935, Reeves Papers.

12. MacArthur Memorandum for Secretary of War, Aug. 20, 1935, General Correspondence of the Secretary of War, 1932–1942, Philippine Islands, Records of the Office of the Secretary of War, RG 107, NARS (Dern's agreement is indicated on the memorandum); Cox to FM, Sept. 6, 1935, FM Papers; McDonald to FM, Sept. 27, 1935, File 3038-B, RG 350; JRH to Reeves, Sept. 29, 1935, JRH Papers; James, *MacArthur*, 1:497–98.

13. FM to Secretary of War, Sept. 11, 1935, File 3038-B, RG 350.

14. FM to Secretary of War, Sept. 12, 13, 1935, ibid.; JRH to Reeves, Sept. 29, 1935, JRH Papers.

15. FM to FDR, Sept. 22, 1935, FM Papers.

16. FM to Secretary of War, Sept. 23, 1935, File 3038-B, RG 350.

17. Cox Memorandum for Secretary of War, Nov. 19, 1936, ibid.; JRH to Reeves, Sept. 29, Nov. 7, 1934 [1935], FM to JRH, Dec. 5, 1935, JRH Papers; E. T. Conley to Commanding General, Philippine Department, Sept. 18, 1935, WPD File 3389-31, Records of the War Department General and Special Staffs, RG 165, NARS; Keith D. McFarland, *Harry H. Woodring* (Lawrence: University of Kansas Press, 1975), p. 82.

18. Memorandum for Records, Sept. 17, 1935, File 3038-B, RG 350; McDonald to Cox [Sept. 23, 1935], ibid.; [McDonald] notations on Secretary of War to President [Sept. 24, 1935] (draft), ibid.; McDonald Memorandum for the Records, Sept. 26, 1935, ibid.; J. C. Holmes to Secretary [of State], Sept. 24, 1935, 811 B.0151/6, Records of the Department of State, RG 59, NARS; Hornbeck Memorandum, Sept. 25, 1936, ibid.

19. McDonald Memorandum for the Records, Sept. 26, 1935, File 3038-B, RG 350.

20. MacArthur to FDR, Sept. 26, 1935, ibid.

21. McDonald Memorandum for the Records, Sept. 26, 1935, ibid.; McDonald to War Department, Sept. 27, 1935, ibid.; William Philipps Memorandum, Sept. 26, 1935, 811 B.0151/6, RG 59; Stanley Reed to FDR, Sept. 26, 1935, FDR to FM, Sept. 27, 1935, OF 400; JRH to Reeves, Oct. 7, 1935, JRH Papers; James, *MacArthur*, 1:489–93.

22. *PH*, Oct. 4, 1935, clipping in FM Papers; [Cox], ''The Inauguration of the Philippine Commonwealth'' [1935], Confidential Diary Notes, RG 126; William F. Pearson Memorandum for File, Sept. 6, 1935, File 093.5, RG 407; JRH to Reeves, Oct. 7, 1935, JRH Papers; McDonald to FM, Sept. 28, Oct. 7, 8, 11, 1935, FM to McDonald, Oct. 7, 1935, FM to Dern. Oct. 7, 9, 1935, FM Papers.

23. Quezon to FM, Oct. 29, 1935, Quezon to Hawes, Oct. 30, 1935, Quezon Papers; JRH to Reeves, Sept. 29, Nov. 7, 1934 [1935], JRH Papers; Quezon to FDR, Jan. 15, 1934, OF 400; Quezon Memorandum for Governor-General, Nov. 2, 1935, File 3038-B, RG 350; Francis Burton Harrison, *Origins of the Philippine Republic: Extracts from the Diaries and Records of Francis Burton Harrison*, ed. and annotated by Michael P. Onorato (Ithaca: Cornell University, 1974), p. 6.

24. FM to EGK, Nov. 21, 1935, EGK-BHC, Box 12; undated document, signed by FM, analyzing Quezon's Nov. 2 Memorandum, File 3038-B, RG 350; FM to Dern, Dec. 4, 1935, FM Papers.

25. [Cox], "Inauguration" [1935], RG 126; JRH to Reeves, Nov. 7, 1934 [1935], JRH Papers.

26. JRH to Reeves, Nov. 7, 1934 [1935], JRH Papers; Cox Memorandum for Secretary of War, Nov. 4, 1935, File 3038-B, RG 350; FM to Dern, Nov. 7, 1935, FM Papers; [Cox], "Inauguration" [1935], RG 126; Dern, "Confidential Report," Dec. 20, 1935, PSF, War Department (Dern).

27. [Cox], "Inauguration" [1935], RG 126; JRH to Reeves, Nov. 7, 1934 [1935], JRH Papers; Dern, "Confidential Report," Dec. 20, 1935, PSF, War Department (Dern).

28. [Cox], "Inauguration" [1935], RG 126; FM to Dern, Nov. 7, 9, 1935, Dern to FDR, Nov. 8, 1935 (draft), FM Papers; JRH to Reeves, Nov. 7, 1934 [1935], JRH Papers; EGK, "Re—FM," Oct. 1961, EGK Papers, MHC.

29. Dern to FDR, Nov. 9, 1935, FDR to Dern, Nov. 9, 1935, OF 400.

30. Dern to Quezon, Nov. 10, 1935, FM Papers; Dern to Secretary of War (for FDR), Nov. 12, 1935, OF 400; Dern, "Confidential Report," Dec. 20, 1935, PSF, War Department (Dern); Quezon to Osmeña, Sept. 15, 1936, enclosed with Jones Memorandum for High Commissioner, Sept. 30, 1936, FM Papers; *MDB*, Nov. 12, 1935, *PH*, June 5, 1936, clippings in ibid.; George A. Malcolm to EGK, Oct. 10, Nov. 5, 1936, EMB Papers; "Nov. 10, 1947," George A. Malcolm Papers, MHC; Memorandum of Conversation, Mar. 3, 1937, 811B.001/Quezon, Manuel L./84 (two documents), RG 59; JRH to Norman H. Hill, May 24, 1939, JRH Papers; Harrison, *Origins*, pp. 18–19; Jones to Richard D. Lunt, Jan. 25, 1963, Richard D. Lunt Papers, MHC; Jones to Fine, Jan. 29, 1966; Theodore Friend, *Between Two Empires: The Ordeal of the Philippines, 1929–1946* (New Haven: Yale University Press, 1965), p. 185; Carlos Quirino, *Quezon* (Manila: Filipiniana Book Guild, 1971), p. 284.

31. FDR to Dern, Nov. 13, 1935, Dern to FDR, Nov. 16, 1935, FM to Secretary of War, Nov. 16, 1935, FM Memorandum for Acting Secretary of War, Nov. 22, 1935, FM to FDR, Dec. 16, 1935, OF 400; Dern, "Confidential Report," Dec. 20, 1935, PSF, War Department (Dern); [Cox], "Inauguration" [1935], RG 126; Hornbeck Statement, Nov. 12, 1935, 811B.001/Quezon/19, RG 59; RS [Richard Southgate] to Philipps, Nov. 12, 1935, and J. E. Holmes note of Nov. 13 on same, ibid.; FM to Cox, Nov. 20, 1936, FM Papers; *MDB*, Nov. 12, 1935, clipping in ibid.

32. Hornbeck, " 'Protocol'—and Philippine Affairs," Mar. 2, 1937, 811B.001/ Quezon/83, RG 59; Memorandum of Conversation, Mar. 3, 1937, ibid.

33. Secretary of War to FM, Nov. 13, 1935, FM to Secretary of War [Nov. 14, 1935], FM Papers; Cox Memorandum for Secretary of War, Nov. 19, 1936, File 3038-B, RG 350; Dern, "Confidential Report," Dec. 20, 1935, PSF, War Department (Dern).

34. FM to Elinor Greene, Nov. 5, 1935, FM to Dern (for FDR), Nov. 18, 1935, Ettie Garner to FM, Nov. 24, 1935, J. Garner to FM, Dec. 24, 1936, FM Papers; George Malcolm, *First Malayan Republic* (Boston: Christopher Publishing House, 1951), p. 115.

35. "Report of the Governor-General covering the period January 1, to November 14, 1935," Philippine Manuscript Reports 1865:7–8, RG 350; "Message of . . . Frank Murphy to the Philippine Legislature . . . ," Nov. 14, 1935, FM Papers; *MT*, Nov. 15,

1935, MSB; J. P. McEvoy, "Little Brother, What Next?" *Saturday Evening Post* 208 (Jan. 25, 1936): 30.

36. *Official Program of the Inauguration* . . . [Manila: n.p., 1935], FM Papers; FDR, "A Proclamation" [Nov. 14, 1935], ibid.; Cox to Commanding General, Philippine Department, Nov. 12, 1935, ibid.; [Cox], "Inauguration" [1935], RG 126; *MDB*, Nov. 15, 16, 1935, MSB; *MT*, Nov. 16, 1935, clipping in FM Papers; *New York Herald Tribune*, Nov. 15, 1935, MSB; "Report of the United States High Commissioner to the Philippine Islands Covering the Period from Nov. 15, 1935 to Dec. 31, 1936," Philippine Manuscript Reports 1867:7, RG 350.

37. *PH*, Nov. 16, 1935, MSB; George A. Malcolm, *American Colonial Careerist* (Boston: Christopher Publishing House, 1957), pp. 47–48; Kemp, "Re—FM," Oct. 1961, EGK Papers; FM to EGK, Oct. 13, 1936, FM Papers; Jones to Lunt, Jan. 25, 1963, Lunt Papers; Jones to Fine, Jan. 29, 1966.

38. FM to Secretary of War, Nov. 16, 29, 1935, McDonald to FM, Nov. 25, Dec. 2, 1935, FM to JRH, Nov. 26, 1935, FM to Miguel Espinos y Bosch, Dec. 10, 1935, FM Papers; FM to JRH, Dec. 11, 1935, JRH Papers; Dern to FDR, Nov. 16, 1935, OF 400; Memorandum for Acting Secretary of War, Nov. 22, 1935, ibid.

39. Frank Parker to Adjutant General, Nov. 26, 1935, Conley to Parker, Nov. 26, 1935, File 093.5, RG 407; *NYT*, Dec. 1, 1935; *MDB*, Nov. 30, 1935, HSB; Jones to JRH, Nov. 28, 1935, Feb. 11, 1936, JRH Papers; FM to Hill, Feb. 28, 1936, Hill Memorandum to Acting High Commissioner, Sept. 16, 1936, Hill Memorandum for High Commissioner, Oct. 5, 1936, and enclosed Jones to Secretary of War, undated, EGK to FM, Nov. 20, 1936, FM Papers; Patricia R. Mamot, "Paul V. McNutt: His Role in the Birth of Philippine Independence" (Ph.D. diss., Ball State University, 1974), pp. 74–75; I. George Blake, *Paul V. McNutt* (Indianapolis: Central Publishing Co., 1966), pp. 190–91.

40. Jones Memorandum for High Commissioner, Sept. 30, 1936, FM Papers. Although there was no formal exchange of calls, Osmeña suggested that Jones call first on Quezon in Manila and Quezon call first on Jones in Baguio, and this was done. Jones to Lunt, Jan. 25, 1963, Lunt Papers.

41. RS [Southgate] to [Joseph E.] Jacobs, Jan. 9, 1937, 811B.001/Quezon/58, Cordell Hull to FDR, Feb. 12, 1937, ibid., RG 59; James, *MacArthur*, 1:511–12; Friend, *Two Empires*, pp. 185–86.

42. FM to Secretary of War [Nov. 14, 1935], Dec. 4, 1935, FM to JRH, Dec. 5, 1935, FM to Woodring, Dec. 10, 1936, FM Papers; Cox Memorandum for Secretary of War, Nov. 19, 1936, File 3038-B, RG 350; FM to EGK, Nov. 21, 1935, EGK-BHC, Box 12; FM to JRH, Dec. 11, 1935, JRH Papers.

43. FM to Dern, Dec. 10, 1935, File 3038-B, RG 350; FM to JRH, Dec. 11, 1935, JRH Papers.

44. Cox Memorandum for Judge Advocate General, Dec. 18, 1935, Hugh C. Smith Memorandum for Cox, Dec. 24, 1935, Cox Memorandum for Secretary of War, Dec. 30, 1935, Jan. 17, 1936, A. W. Brown Memorandum for Chief, BIA, Jan. 17, 1936, Dern to FDR, Jan. 21, 1936, Dern to FM, Jan. 21, 1936, File 3038-B, RG 350; EGK Memorandum to the High Commissioner, Feb. 20, 1936, FM Papers.

45. Jones Memorandum for High Commissioner, Aug. 13, 1936, Jones to EGK, Aug. 18, 1936, FM to EGK, Sept. 1, Oct. 13, 1936, EGK to FM, Oct. 8, 26, 1936,

FM to JRH, Nov. 20, 1936, FM to Secretary of War, Dec. 31, 1936, FM Papers; Cox Memorandum for Secretary of War, Nov. 17, Dec. 29, 1936, Cox to FM, Dec. 29, 1936, enclosing "Suggested Draft of Letter for New High Commissioner," File 3038-B, RG 350; Memorandum of Conversation, Dec. 28, 1936, Francis B. Sayre File, R. Walton Moore Papers, FDRL.

46. S. D. Embick to FM, Jan. 26, 1937, FM Papers; Sayre to FM, Feb. 3, 25, 1937, FM to Sayre, Feb. 10, 1937, Francis B. Sayre Papers, LC; FDR to McNutt, Mar. 1, 1937, File 3038-B, RG 350; David Vawter DuFault, "Francis B. Sayre and the Commonwealth of the Philippines, 1936–1942" (Ph.D. diss., University of Oregon, 1972), pp. 135–36.

47. FM to Secretary of War, Sept. 10, Nov. 9, 1934, F. W. Manley Memorandum to Governor-General, Dec. 6, 1934, File 3038-B, RG 350; W. Cameron Forbes to FM, Aug. 28, 1934, FM to Secretary of War, Sept. 5, 6, 1934, FM to Forbes, Oct. 6, 1934, FM Papers; C. Hayden to Tydings, Sept. 27, 1934, Sen 73-A, F 25, Tray 126, RG 46; MM to GM, Aug. 7, 1935, GM Papers.

48. Cox Memorandum of Conversation with Quezon, Oct. 13, 1934, Quezon Mission, 1934, RG 126; Office Memorandum, Apr. 8, 1935, FM Visit, 1935, ibid.; [Cox], "Inauguration" [1935], ibid.; Cox to FM, Oct. 16, 1934, Aug. 12, 1935, Dern to Daniel Bell, Mar. 6, 1935, FM to Cox, Apr. 17, 1935, File 3038-B, RG 350; Cox to FM, July 9, Aug. 16, Nov. 6, 1935, Dern to FM, Nov. 18, 1935, EGK to FM, Nov. 28, 1935, [Nov. 1935], FM to Dern, Nov. 30, 1935, FM to James Byrnes, Dec. 6, 13, 1935, FM Papers; Dern to FDR, Jan. 26, 1935, Cox Memorandum for FM, Apr. 9, 1935, OF 400; Quezon to Vargas, Feb. 18, 1937, Quezon Papers; "Report of High Commissioner, 1935," 1867:9–10; *Fourth Annual Report of the United States High Commissioner to the Philippine Islands . . . July 1, 1939–June 30, 1940* (Washington: U.S. Government Printing Office, 1943), pp. 10–11.

49. Hester, Memorandum and Budget for High Commissioner, May 16, 1934, FM Papers; FM to Cox, May 28, 1934, FM Papers; Woodring to FDR, June 5, 1934, FM to Secretary of War, May 21, 29, 1934, OF 400; Cox to FM, June 23, 1934, July 9, 12, Sept. 10, 1935, FM to Secretary of War, Sept. 6, 7, 10, 1934, Aug. 17, 1935, Secretary of War to Bell, Dec. 7, 1934, File 3038-B, RG 350; Cox Memorandum, Mar. 18, 1935, Quezon Mission, 1935, RG 126; *MT*, Mar. 17, 22, 1935, clippings in FM Papers; Richard S. Maxwell, "A Historical Study of the Office of the United States High Commissioner to the Philippine Islands, 1935–1946" (M.A. thesis, American University, 1966), p. 37.

50. William Teahan to GM, Feb. 7, 1936, GM Papers; FDR to FM, Apr. 15, 1936, Jones to Acting Secretary of War, Oct. 8, 1936, FM Papers; Harrison, *Origins*, p. 28; *NYT*, Jan. 26, 1936; McEvoy, "Little Brother," p. 30; "Report of High Commissioner, 1936," 1867:14–16.

51. FM to FDR, Dec. 16, 1935, FM to Claude Bowers, Jan. 24, 1936, EMB Papers; FM to JRH, Dec. 5, 11, 1935, Jones to JRH, Apr. 21, 1936, JRH Papers; FM to Secretary of War, Mar. 10, 1936, Hull to FDR, Mar. 23, 1936, OF 400; FM to Al Dale, Feb. 17, 1936, FM to Quezon, Mar. 16, 1936, Cox to FM, Apr. 6, 1936, EGK to FM, Apr. 9, 1936, FM to Cox, Apr. 14, 1936, Jones to FM, June 2, 1936, Jones Memorandum to High Commissioner, June 6, 1936, Jones to Secretary of War, July 14, 1936, FM Papers. The effort of the Commonwealth government to impose duties

on army and navy imports despite a 1929 comptroller general's ruling that such goods were not subject to duty was dealt with by Jones as acting high commissioner but with Murphy's concurrence. See Quezon to Lucius R. Holbrook, Sept. 15, 1936, Jones to FM, Sept. 18, 1936, Jones Memoranda for FM, Sept. 30, Dec. 1, 9, 1936, Jones to Secretary of War, Sept. 22, Nov. 28, Dec. 5, 7, 1936, Jones to Acting Secretary of War, Oct. 8, 1936, Cox to FM, Nov. 30, 1936, J. W. Rankin to E. J. Marquart, Nov. 27, 1936, Marquart to Jones, Dec. 1, 1936, Jones to Quezon, Dec. 3, 1936, and V. Aldanese to Marquart, Dec. 4, 1936, ibid.

52. FM to EGK, Nov. 21, 1935, EGK-BHC, Box 12; EGK to Edward T. Gushee, Jan. 10, 1936, ibid., Box 18; Jones to High Commissioner, Nov. 23, 1935, FM to Quezon, Dec. 5, 1935, FM to Hill, Dec. 30, 1935, FM to Jones, July 31, 1936, FM Papers; Jones to JRH, Dec. 27, 1935, JRH Papers.

53. Harrison, *Origins*, p. 120; V. Carmona to President of Philippines, Apr. 22, 1936, FM to Quezon, May 10, 1936 (draft), FM to Jones, May 19, 1936, Jones Memoranda to High Commissioner, June 6, July 6, Aug. 12, 13, 21, 1936, Jones to EGK, Aug. 18, 1936, FM Papers; Jones to EGK, Jan. 28, 1937, EGK Papers.

54. FM to Jones, Apr. 20, May 19, 25, July 31, Sept. 2, 1936, Quezon to FM, May 4, July 20, 1936, Jones Memoranda for High Commissioner, May 8, 12, July 6 (two memoranda), Aug. 12, 21, 1936, Kemp to FM, May 10, 1936, FM to Quezon, May 10, 1936 (draft), Quezon to National Assembly, June 23, 1936, FM Papers; Harrison, *Origins*, pp. 115, 120.

55. FM to Hester, Dec. 27, 1935, FM to Secretary of War, Feb. 28, 1936, JRH to FM, Mar. 12, 1936, Jones to FM, Nov. 10, 1936, FM Papers; FM notes, Dec. 26 [1935], Mar. 4, 1936, EG Papers; EGK to Osborn, Nov. 29, 1935, EGK-BHC, Box 15; FM to JRH, Dec. 5, 1935, Feb. 9, Mar. 16, 1936, Jones to JRH, Dec. 27, 1935, JRH Papers; FM to Secretary of War, Jan. 21, Feb. 1, 1936, File 2074-A, RG 350; FM to FDR, Dec. 16, 1935, OF 400; Jones to EGK, June 8, 1936, EGK Papers.

56. FM notes, Feb. 9, 11, 1936, EG Papers; FM to JRH, Mar. 16, 1936, JRH Papers; Quirino, *Quezon*, pp. 290–91; Marcial P. Lichauco, *Roxas* (Manila: Kiko Printing Press, 1952), pp. 112–13. For Quezon's version of the Roxas affair, see Harrison, *Origins*, p. 51.

57. Jones Memoranda for High Commissioner, Dec. 2, 1935, June 7, Aug. 11, 1936 (and enclosed exhibits), FM to Jones, Feb. 24, Apr. 20, 1936, Jones to FM, June 1, 1936, Quezon to FM, Aug. 5, 1936, FM to McDonald, Sept. 2, 1936, FM to Woodring, Dec. 31, 1936, FM Papers; FM notes, Feb. 12, 1936, EG Papers; Jones to EGK, June 21, 1936, EGK Papers; *MDB*, Aug. 3, 1936, [Aug. 4, 1936], Aug. 15, 1936 (copy), *MT*, Aug. 4, 1936, clippings in FM Papers; Harrison, *Origins*, p. 97.

58. *Iloilo Times*, Mar. 1, 1936, copy in FM Papers; William H. Anderson, *The Philippine Problem* (New York: G. P. Putnam's Sons, 1939), pp. 156–58, 162, 165; Frederic S. Marquardt, *Before Bataan and After* (New York: Bobbs-Merrill Co., 1943), p. 179; Grunder and Livezey, *The Philippines and the United States* (Norman: University of Oklahoma Press, 1951), p. 228; Hayden, "Transition," pp. 643–44; idem, "The United States and the Philippine Commonwealth" (New York: Institute of Pacific Relations, 1937) p. 10, JRH Papers; Charles Orville Houston, Jr., "The Philippine Commonwealth, 1934–1936 . . . " *University of Manila Journal of East Asiatic Studies* 2 (July 1953): 35–36; F. B. Acasiano, "Frank Murphy . . . ," with

Pedro de la Llana to FM, Feb. 17, 1936, FM Papers; FM to Clark Howell, Feb. 18, 1936, Jones to Dern, June 9, 1936, ibid.; FM to JRH, Dec. 5, 1935, Mar. 16, 1936, Jones to JRH, Mar. 2, 1936, JRH Papers; Secretary of War to FDR (for Quezon) [July 6, 1936], OF 400; R. Veatch Memorandum, June 19, 1936, 124.11B/5, RG 59; EGK, "Frank Murphy as Government Administrator" (Mar. 6, 1951), pp. 4–5, EGK Papers; *NYT,* July 10, 1936; *MDB,* Feb. 1, 1936, MSB; *MT,* May 13, 1936, MSB; *Philippines Free Press,* May 16, 1936, MSB; *PH,* June 5, 1936, *MDB,* Nov. 14, 1936, clippings in FM Papers.

59. FM to Moody, May 11, 1935, Moody Papers; FM to Arthur D. Maguire, Dec. 5, 1935, FM to George J. Jenks, Dec. 9, 1935, William D. Murphy to FM, Dec. 13, 1935, FM to Hale V. Sattley, Jan. 24, 1936, FM to Joan Swift, Feb. 11, 1936, FM Papers; Jones to Fine, Jan. 29, 1966; *Herald Mid-Week Magazine,* May 6, 1936, MSB.

60. See Chapter 3, n. 41.

61. FM to Secretary of War, Jan. 21, 1936, FM to Howell, Feb. 18, 1936, Smith to FM, Nov. 18, 1936, Jones Memorandum for High Commissioner, Dec. 19, 1936, and enclosed Malcolm Memorandum to Jones, Dec. 17, 1936, FM Papers; *MDB,* Nov. 14, 1936, clipping in ibid.; FM to JRH, Mar. 16, 1936, JRH Papers; Memorandum of Conversation, Dec. 28, 1936, Sayre File, Moore Papers.

62. Quezon to Dern, Nov. 19, 1934, Quezon to John McDuffie, Nov. 19, 1934, Quezon Papers; Cox Memorandum of Conversation with Quezon, Nov. 19, 1934, Quezon Mission, 1934, RG 126; Dern to Tydings and McDuffie, Dec. 5, 1934, File 28864, RG 350; [*MT,* Jan. 11, 1935], HSB; *MDB,* May 8, 1935, MSB; James, *MacArthur,* 1:479–80, 483–84.

63. Quezon, *The Good Fight* (New York: D. Appleton-Century Co., 1946), pp. 152–54; James, *MacArthur,* 1:481. MacArthur stated in his *Reminiscences* that he told Quezon that the Philippines were defensible only if the Commonwealth had ten years to prepare its defenses and the United States provided a good deal of aid. *Reminiscences* (New York: McGraw-Hill Co, 1964), p. 102.

64. *DN,* Sept. 18, 1935; *MDB,* Sept. 19, 1935, clipping in FM Papers; James, *MacArthur,* 1:480–83.

65. MacArthur to Quezon, June 1, 1935, Quezon Papers; James, *MacArthur,* 1:486–87.

66. The two memoranda are in RG 1, MML. See also Quezon to MacArthur, Dec. 31, 1935, ibid.

67. James, *MacArthur,* 1:484–85; Conley to MacArthur, Sept. 18, 1935, Conley to Commanding General, Philippine Department, Sept. 18, 1935, WPD File 3389–31, RG 165.

68. Memorandum of Conversation, Dec. 28, 1936, Sayre File, Moore Papers; JRH to Reeves, Nov. 7, 1934 [1935], JRH Papers; Parker to Dern, Nov. 14, 1935, WPD File 3389–31, RG 165; Dern, "Confidential Report," Dec. 20, 1935, PSF, War Department (Dern).

69. FM to EGK, Dec. 20, 1935, Feb. 1, Apr. 21, 1936, EGK to FM, undated, EGK Memorandum for High Commissioner, Feb. 7, 1936, FM to Secretary of War, May 8, 1936, FM Papers; FM notes, May 7–9, 1935, ibid.; "When Discussing Defense Matter...," July 1936, ibid.; JRH to Reeves, Sept. 29, Nov. 7, 1934

[1935], JRH Papers; Hornbeck to Secretary, Dec. 9, 1935, 811B.01/274, RG 59; Courtney Whitney, *MacArthur* (New York: Alfred A. Knopf, 1956), p. 5; Friend, *Two Empires*, p. 166.

70. Kemp to High Commissioner, July 30, 1936, Embick to FM, Aug. 5, 1936, FM to Woodring, Nov. 30, 1936, FM Papers; [Embick] Memorandum for Chief of Staff, Aug. 5, 1936, Secretary of War Memorandum for President, Nov. 16, 1936, and enclosed draft of letter to MacArthur, WPD File 3389-31, RG 165; James, *MacArthur*, 1:514-15.

71. Eisenhower, Diary of the American Military Mission in the Philippine Islands, Dec. 27, 1935, Dwight D. Eisenhower Library, Abilene, Kansas; MacArthur to FM, Nov. 28, 1935, Manley Memorandum for High Commissioner, Dec. 10, 1935, [EGK] Memorandum for High Commissioner, Feb. 7, 1936, FM to Secretary of War, May 8, 1936, Malin Craig to FM, Aug. 13, 1936, FM Papers; Louis Morton, "The Philippine Army, 1935-1939: Eisenhower's Memorandum to Quezon," *Military Affairs* 12 (Summer 1948): 164; idem, *The Fall of the Philippines* (Washington: Department of the Army, 1953), pp. 9-10.

72. Dwight D. Eisenhower, *At Ease* (Garden City, N.Y.: Doubleday and Co., 1967), p. 221; James, *MacArthur*, 1:482; MacArthur to Quezon, June 1, 1935, Quezon Papers; Kiyoshi Uchiyama to Koki Hirota, Nov. 7, 1935, Archives of the Japanese Ministry of Foreign Affairs, 1865-1945, Reel S460, Asia Library, University of Michigan, Ann Arbor, Michigan.

73. MacArthur to Quezon [Nov. 1935], Quezon to MacArthur, Dec. 31, 1935, June 13, 1936, Vargas to MacArthur, July 1, 30, 1936, RG 1, MML; MacArthur, *Report on National Defense in the Philippines* (Manila: Bureau of Printing, 1936), pp. 23-24, ibid.; *PH*, Nov. 16, 1935, [*MT*, May 3, 1936], clippings in FM Papers; MacArthur to Adjutant General, Dec. 26, 1935, ibid.; FM to Secretary of War, Jan. 21, 1936, File 2074-A, RG 350; James, *MacArthur*, 1:503-4. There are copies of Quezon's message to the National Assembly and of Commonwealth Bill No. 1 in RG 1, MML. Osmeña did not regard the defense plan as viable and was "a silent critic of the Quezon-MacArthur alliance." James K. Eyre, Jr., *The Roosevelt-MacArthur Conflict* (Chambersburg, Pa.: Craft Press, 1950), p. 29.

74. MacArthur to FM, Nov. 28, 1935, Jones Memoranda for High Commissioner, Dec. 2, 4, 12, 1935, FM to Jones, Dec. 3, 1935, Manley Memorandum for High Commissioner, Dec. 10, 1935, EGK Memorandum for High Commissioner, Jan. 23, 1936, and enclosed memorandum, FM Papers; High Commissioner notes, Nov. 30, Dec. 1, 1935, EG Papers; Jones to JRH, Feb. 11, 1936, JRH Papers.

75. FM to Jones, Dec. 3, 1935, Feb. 13, 24, 1936, Jones Memoranda for High Commissioner, Dec. 4, 12, 1935, Manley Memorandum for High Commissioner, Dec. 10, 1935, EGK Memorandum for High Commissioner, Jan. 23, 1936, and enclosed memorandum, FM to Secretary of War, Jan. 29, May 8, 1936, FM to EGK, Apr. 21, 1936, FM Papers; EGK, "Financial Section," Mar. 30, 1936, ibid.; Jones to JRH, Feb. 11, 1936, JRH Papers; Hayden, *Philippines*, pp. 751-52; *MDB*, Feb. 1, 1936, clipping in FM Papers.

76. MacArthur, *National Defense*, pp. 29-30, RG 1, MML.

77. Parker to Adjutant General, Aug. 20, 1934, WPD File 3251-22, RG 165; Manley Memorandum for FM, Aug. 20, 1934, Embick to FM, Jan. 2, 1935, FM to Embick,

Jan. 4, 1935, FM to Forbes, Oct. 16, 1935, FM Papers; Embick, "Confidential Data on Corregidor Island," Nov. 27, 1934, ibid.; Maxwell M. Hamilton, Conversation, Apr. 4, 1935, 611B.003/148, RG 59; [*San Francisco Chronicle*, Aug. 4, 1935], HSB.

78. Hamilton, Conversation, Apr. 4, 1935, 611B.003/148, RG 59; FM notes, May 7-9, 1935, FM Papers; "Notes on the Far Eastern Situation," Nov. 17, 1936, ibid.; [Embick], "Military Aspects of the Situation...," Dec. 20, 1934, BIA File 364, in File 313.3 (6-26-39), RG 407; Cox Memorandum for Secretary of War, Dec. 20, 1935, ibid.; Edgar B. Nixon, ed., *Franklin D. Roosevelt and Foreign Affairs*, 3 vols. (Cambridge, Mass.: Harvard University Press, 1969), 2:495-96; Stephen E. Pelz, *Race to Pearl Harbor* (Cambridge, Mass.: Harvard University Press, 1974), p. 158; Louis Morton, "War Plan Orange: Evolution of a Strategy," *World Politics* 11 (1959): 241-44; Ronald Schaffer, "General Stanley D. Embick: Military Dissenter," *Military Affairs* 37 (Oct. 1973): 91; Dorothy Borg, *The United States and the Far Eastern Crisis, 1933-1938* (Cambridge, Mass.: Harvard University Press, 1964), pp. 111-12, 248-52.

79. Embick, "Military Aspects," Appendix B, Dec. 20, 1935, BIA File 364, in File 313 (6-26-39), RG 407; idem, "Notes on Military Establishment of Philippine Commonwealth Government," Aug. 8, 1936, WPD File 3389-31, RG 165; Manley Memorandum for FM, Dec. 10, 1935, FM to EGK, Feb. 1, Apr. 15, 1936, FM to Secretary of War, May 8, 1936, FM Papers; Schaffer, "Embick," p. 91; James, *MacArthur*, 1:502.

80. FM to Grew, Dec. 5, 1935, Manley Memorandum for High Commissioner, Dec. 10, 1935, FM to Secretary of War, Jan. 29, May 8, 1936, [EGK] Memorandum to High Commissioner, Feb. 7, 1936, FM Papers; F. W. M. [Manley], "National Defense Act" [Jan. 1936], ibid.

81. Jones to JRH, Feb. 11, 1936, JRH Papers; MacArthur to Adjutant General, Dec. 26, 1935, Cox to FM, Jan. 16, 1936, Conley to MacArthur, Jan. 16, 1936, [EGK] Memorandum for High Commissioner, Feb. 7, 1936, FM to EGK, Mar. 23, 1936, FM Papers; SKH [Hornbeck] Memorandum, Jan. 6, 1936, 811B.24/1, RG 59; Embick, Memorandum for Chief of Staff, Jan. 7, 1936, WPD File 3389-18, RG 165.

82. Memorandum for High Commissioner, Jan. 17, 1936, FM Papers; FM notes, Jan. 18, 1936, EG Papers; Eisenhower Diary, Jan. 20, 1936.

83. FM to Secretary of War, Jan. 21, 1936, Cox to FM, Jan. 29, 1936, FM Papers; Dern Memorandum for Chief, BIA, Jan. 28, 1936, BIA File 1184-A, in File 313.3 (6-26-39), RG 407; Eisenhower Diary, Jan. 20, Feb. 6, 1936; Quezon to MacArthur, Jan. 30, 1936, RG 1, MML.

84. FM to Secretary of War, May 8, 1936, FM Papers.

85. MacArthur to Craig, July 9, Sept. 10, 1936, Craig to MacArthur, Aug. 5, 1936, H. R. Bull Memorandum for Adjutant General, Sept. 29, 1936, File 093.5, RG 407; Cox Memorandum for Secretary of War, July 14, 1936, F. J. Monaghan to Cox, Oct. 27, 1936, enclosing excerpts from letters of Frank S. Jonas, BIA File 1184-A, in File 313.3 (6-26-39), ibid.; Embick to FM, Aug. 5, 1936, FM to Craig, Aug. 10, 1936, FM Papers; "National Defense Matter," July 1936, ibid.; [Embick?] Memorandum to the Chief of Staff, Aug. 5, 1936, and enclosed Memorandum for President, Craig Memorandum for McIntyre, Sept. 11, 1936, Robert L. Collins to Commanding General, Philippine Department, Oct. 6, 1936, Craig Memorandum

for Secretary of War, Dec. 17, 1936, WPD File 3389-31, RG 165; James, *MacArthur*, 1:543–45; MacArthur, *National Defense*, p. 31, RG 1, MML. Cf. John Callan O'Laughlin to MacArthur, Aug. 7, 1936, ibid.

86. Craig to FM, Aug. 13, 1936, FM to EGK, Sept. 1, 1936, FM Papers; Acting Secretary of War Memorandum for McIntyre, Sept. 11, 1936, FDR Memorandum for McIntyre, Sept. 12, 1936, FDR Memorandum for Acting Secretary of War, Sept. 17, 1936, OF 178, FDRL.

87. SKH [Hornbeck] to Sayre, Sept. 5, 1936, 811B.20/11, Hull to Woodring, Sept. 18, 1936, 811B.20/7A, Woodring to Hull, Sept. 19, 1936, 811B.20/8, RG 59; Woodring to FM, Sept. 19, 1936, FM Papers.

88. Sayre Memorandum, Nov. 16, 1936, 711B.00111/6, RG 59; Borg, *Far Eastern Crisis*, pp. 244–46.

89. Memorandum of Conversation, Dec. 28, 1936, Sayre File, Moore Papers.

90. Frazier Hunt, *The Untold Story of Douglas MacArthur* (New York: Devin-Adair Co., 1954), pp. 186–88; James, *MacArthur*, 1:521–22.

91. James, *MacArthur*, 1:522–23.

92. Memorandum of Conversation, Dec. 28, 1936, Sayre File, Moore Papers; Sayre to Roosevelt, Feb. 19, 1937, and enclosed Memorandum, 711B.00111/8A, RG 59; Joint Preparatory Committee on Far Eastern Affairs, *Report of May 20, 1938*, 4 vols. (Washington: U.S. Government Printing Office, 1938), 1:107–23, 168–91; Borg, *Far Eastern Crisis*, p. 253.

93. Morton, *Philippines*, p. 12; Monaghan to Cox, May 23, 1936, and enclosed excerpts from Jonas letters, File 1184-A, with File 313.3 (6-26-39), RG 407; Eisenhower Diary, Jan. 1, May 29, 1936.

94. Morton, "Philippine Army," p. 105; idem, *Philippines*, pp. 12–13; Hayden, *Philippines*, p. 741; James, *MacArthur*, 1:527–33, 594; Friend, *Two Empires*, p. 167; Catherine Porter, *Crisis in the Philippines* (New York: Alfred A. Knopf, 1942), pp. 115–16; Jones to FM, Aug. 6, 1936, FM Papers.

95. Friend, *Two Empires*, p. 193; James, *MacArthur*, 1:535–36, 581, 590; Du-Fault, "Sayre," p. 350.

96. *PH*, Apr. 4, 1936, HSB; *PH*, May 14, 1936, MSB; *MT*, May 5, 1936, MSB; *MDB*, May 5, 1936, MSB; FDR to FM, Apr. 30, 1936, OF 400; Jones to Dern, June 9, 1936, FM to EMB [July 1936], and enclosed "Pending Philippine Matters," FM Papers; EGK to Osborn, May 9, 1936, Chase S. Osborn Papers, MHC.

97. FM notes, May 13, 21, 23, and undated, 1936, EG Papers; *PH*, May 13, 15, 1936, HSB; *MDB*, May 19, 23, 1936, HSB; *Tokyo Nichi Nichi*, May 22, 1936, MSB; FM to Walker, June 6, 1936, FM Papers.

98. FM to Byron Foy, May 17, 1936, Frank Martel to FM, June 10, 1936, FM to Louis Mayer, June 15, 1936, FM to Chaplin, June 15, 1936, FM to Hearst, June 15, 1936, Jones to Secretary of War, July 14, 1936, FM to Salvador and Victoria [Araneta], Dec. 2, 1936 (possibly not sent), FM Papers; EMB to Cox [Nov. 27, 1936], FM file, RG 350; *MT*, June 16, 1936, clipping in FM Papers; *MT*, June 28, July 1, 2, 9, 25, 1936, HSB; *DT*, June 20, 21, 1936, MSB; *PH*, May 11, June 30, July 2, 8–10, Nov. 2, 6, 1936, HSB; *MDB*, June 22, 23, July 10, Nov. 7, 1936, HSB.

99. JRH to William H. Hobbs, Jan. 29, 1935, JRH to Parker, May 29, 1936, JRH Papers; Juan F. Hilario to Dern, Nov. 4, 1935, Joseph W. Byrns to FM, Jan. 2, 1936,

FM Papers; Gregorio F. Zaide, *Philippine Political and Cultural History*, 2 vols. (Manila: Philippine Education Co., 1949), 2:262; Julius C. Edelstein, "A Friend in Court...," *Philippines* 1 (1941): 3, 19; *PH*, May 13, 1936, MSB; *American Chamber of Commerce Journal* (Dec. 1935), MSB; Dern, "Confidential Report," Dec. 20, 1935, PSF, War Department (Dern).

100. Hilario to FM, Dec. 24, 1934, Ricardo S. Santos to FM, Feb. 22, 1935, Hilario to Dern, Nov. 4, 1935, Eulogio Rodriguez to FM, Apr. 13, 1936, Carlos Quirino to FM, Sept. 30, 1936, Jones to FM, Jan. 23, 1937, F. Theo Rogers to FM, July 1, 1937, Hernando J. Abaya to FM, Dec. 30, 1937, Antonio de las Alas to FM, Dec. 9, 1938, FM Papers; JRH to Reeves, Feb. 9, 1934, JRH Papers; Rogers to Theodore Roosevelt, Jr., Sept. 15, 1934, Theodore Roosevelt, Jr., Papers, Box 19, LC; Rogers to Roosevelt, Jr., July 6, 1935, ibid., Box 21; Jones to Fine, Jan. 29, 1966; Reeves to EGK, Dec. 24, 1934, EGK-BHC, Box 15; John W. Hausserman to FDR, June 30, 1936, OF 400; *DN*, June 10, 1934; *NYT*, Aug. 4, 1935; [(Ann Arbor) *Voice of Democracy*, Oct. 30, 1936], MSB; J. Woodford Howard, *Mr. Justice Murphy* (Princeton: Princeton University Press, 1968), pp. 79-80, 114-15; [*Atlanta Constitution*, Jan. 1936], MSB; *MT*, Apr. 13, June 15, 1934, MSB; *MT*, May 13, 1936, HSB; *MT*, Jan. 22, 1935, *MDB*, July 16, 1934, *PH*, May 8, 1934, *PH*, July 3, 1935, clippings in FM Papers; *PH*, Nov. 2, 1935, HSB; *PH*, Nov. 14, 1935, MSB.

CHAPTER 6

1. FM to GM, June 3, 1933, MM to GM [Oct. 1933], [Nov. 21, 1934], Raymond Moley to GM, Dec. 19, 1934, GM Papers; Norman H. Hill to Blair Moody, June 24, 1934, FM to Moody, July 3, 1936, Blair Moody Papers, MHC; Arthur F. Lederle to FM, Sept. 7, 1933, FM to Louis Howe, Apr. 2, 1934, Carl Hayden to Hill, Mar. 2, 1936, FM to Moody, Apr. 2, 1936, and enclosures, [EMB] to Hill, May 14, 1936, FM Papers; *Washington Herald* [Jan. 28, 1934], *Washington Star*, Mar. 9, 1935, clippings in ibid.; Jerome Barry, "Headed up the Ladder," *Today* (July 6, 1935), copy in ibid.; Moody, "High Commissioner to Manila," *Survey Graphic* 24 (Dec. 1935): 610-11 + .

2. Sidney Fine, *Frank Murphy: The Detroit Years* (Ann Arbor: University of Michigan Press, 1975), pp. 254-55; FM to Coughlin, Sept. 16, 1933, Feb. 9, 1934, FM to B. C. Fassio, Nov. 20, 1933, William M. Walker to FM, Nov. 19, 1933, Jan. 19, 1934, JAF to FM, Feb. 2, 1934, Coughlin to FM, July 26, 1934, FM Papers.

3. FM to GM, July 7, Oct. 11, 1934, GM Papers; FM to Louis Howe, Apr. 2, 1934, FM to Ann Walker, Sept. 23, 1934, FM Papers.

4. FM to Harry Bitner, May 15, 1935, FM to GM, June 19, 1935, FM Papers; [*DN*, Mar. 25, 1935], MSB; [*PH*, Mar. 5, Apr. 3, 17, 1935], MSB; [*Washington Herald*, Apr. 3, 1935], MSB; James A. Gross, *The Making of the National Labor Relations Board*, vol. 1 (*1933-1937*) (Albany: State University of New York Press, 1974), pp. 149-50n.

5. For the history of the Democratic party in Michigan to 1932, see Stephen B. Sarasohn and Vera H. Sarasohn, *Political Party Patterns in Michigan* (Detroit: Wayne State University Press, 1957), pp. 5-9, 24; Stephen B. Sarasohn, "The Regulation of

Parties and Nominations in Michigan: The Politics of Election Reform'' (Ph.D. diss., Columbia University, 1953), pp. 218-21; John F. Fenton, *Midwest Politics* (New York: Holt, Rinehart and Winston, 1966), pp. 5-6; and Richard Theodore Ortquist, Jr., "Depression Politics in Michigan, 1929-1933" (Ph.D. diss., University of Michigan, 1968), pp. 12-13, 19-22, 80-89, 205-18.

6. Christine J. McDonald to JAF, Democratic National Campaign Committee, 1936, Correspondence of James A. Farley, 1936, Michigan folder, Democratic Party, National Committee Papers, FDRL (hereafter cited as DNC-JAF); *DN*, Jan. 22, 29, 1933, May 16, 17, 1938; Ortquist, Jr., "Depression Politics," pp. 226-27; John P. White, "The Governor of Michigan as Party Leader: The Case of William A. Comstock," *Papers of the Michigan Academy of Science, Arts, and Letters* 42 (1957): 181-84.

7. *DN*, Jan. 9, 1933, June 11, July 25, 1934, Nov. 22, 1936; Cathy Abernathy, "The 1934 Election . . ." (1973), pp. 7-12, in my possession; Ortquist, Jr., "Depression Politics," pp. 225-38; Don W. Canfield to JAF, July 7, 1936, DNC-JAF; Arthur J. Lacy to Congressmen, Feb. 5, 1933, Arthur J. Lacy Papers, MHC; unidentified analysis of 1934 election, ibid.; Loren N. O'Brien to FM, May 2, 1933, Newell B. Wallace to FM, June 21, 1933, Wright W. Gedge to FM, June 30, 1933, FM Papers; White, "Comstock," p. 184.

8. For the conflict within the Democratic party, see White, "Comstock," pp. 184-92; Gloria Warden Newquist, "James A. Farley and the Politics of Victory, 1928-1936" (Ph.D. diss., University of Southern California, 1966), pp. 415-16; Ortquist, Jr., "Depression Politics," pp. 220-25; Abernathy, "1934 Election," pp. 17-18; Sarasohn and Sarasohn, *Party Politics*, pp. 45-46; Carl M. Weideman to John F. Hamilton, Mar. 17, 1933, Weideman to T. Emmett McKenzie, Mar. 22, 1933, Weideman et al. to JAF [Nov. 1933], June 12, 1934, J. C. Lehr to JAF, June 12, 1934, Carl M. Weideman Papers, MHC; Giles Kavanagh to JAF, June 6, 1934, Emil Hurja Papers, FDRL; Canfield to JAF, July 17, 1936, DNC-JAF; Lesinski to JAF, Oct. 20, 1933, Will R. McDonald to Marvin McIntyre, Dec. 11, 1933, Patrick H. O'Brien to FDR, Jan. 26, 1935, OF 300 (Michigan), FDRL; W. H. Bannan to JAF, Dec. 10, 1938, OF 300 (Election . . . Results, 1938), ibid.; Clyde V. Fenner to FM, Sept. 20, 1933, Edmund C. Shields to FM, June 21, 1934, FM Papers; James Couzens to Thomas W. Payne, Mar. 19, 1934, Payne to Couzens, Mar. 26, 1934, James Couzens Papers, Box 102, LC; *DN*, June 27, 1933, Jan. 19, May 18, 22, 1934; and Interview with James A. Farley, Nov. 11, 1964, p. 4, MHC.

9. Fine, *Murphy*, pp. 368-70, 440-42; FM to J. Pomfret, Jan. 23, 1933, Mayor's Office Records, Burton Historical Collection, Detroit, Michigan; FM to JAF, May 23, 1933, FM to Gedge, Aug. 3, 1933, FM to Edward Fremsdorf, June 25, Sept. 4, 1934, FM to GM, Sept. 17, 1934, FM Papers; FM to GM, July 10, [11], 1934, GM Papers, GM to MM, Nov. 10, 1933, MM Papers; FM to Couzens, June 25, 1934, Couzens Papers, Box 104. Cf. Frank Picard to Hill, Norman H. Hill Papers, Burton Historical Collection.

10. FM to JAF, May 23, 1933, FM to Lacy, May 23, 1933, FM to Bushnell, May 23, 1933, FM to GM, May 23, 1933, Bushnell to FM, June 3, 30, 1933, JAF to FM, June 6, 1933, FM Papers; GM to Lacy, June 3, 1933, Lacy to FM [Spring 1935], Lacy Papers; Bushnell notes, Oct. 28, 1951, Josephine Gomon Papers, MHC.

11. George Sadowski et al. to FM, May 12, 1933, FM to JAF, May 16, July 10, 1933, FM to Sadowski, May 16, 1933, FM to Dingell, Sept. 17, 1934, FM to GM, Sept. 17, 1934, FM Papers.

12. John Braeman et al., eds., *The New Deal*, vol. 2, *The State and Local Levels* (Columbus: Ohio State University Press, 1975), pp. xiii–xiv; Lacy to Congressmen, Feb. 5, 1933 (not sent), Lacy to FM [Spring 1935], Lacy Papers; 1934 election analysis, ibid.; Lacy to FDR, May 8, 1934, H. M. K. [Kanee] Memorandum for McIntyre, May 17, 1934, Fenner to Lacy, May 22, 1934, and enclosed "Michigan Ballots," May 21, 1934, with Lacy to McIntyre, May 31, 1934, Norman M. Snider to FDR, Aug. 10, 1934, McIntyre to Snider, Aug. 16, Sept. 1, 1934, Snider to McIntyre, Aug. 21, 1934, Abbott to G. Hall Roosevelt, Aug. 31, 1934, G. H. Roosevelt to Howe, Sept. 5, 1934, OF 300 (Michigan); *DN*, May 12, 1934; Richard T. Ortquist, Jr., and Marvin Petroelje Interview with Arthur J. Lacy, undated, pp. 63, 71–72, copy in my possession.

13. Lacy to FM [Spring 1935], Lacy Papers; GM to Comstock, May 22, 1934, GM Papers; Coughlin to FM, July 26, 1934, FM to GM, Sept. 17, 1934, FM Papers; G. H. Roosevelt to Howe, Sept. 5, 1934, FDR Memorandum for McIntyre, Sept. 13, 1934, OF 300 (Michigan); HMK Memorandum, Sept. 13, 1934, ibid.; Lacy interview, p. 64; *MT*, Sept. 7, 1934, HSB. The *Detroit Times* claimed that George had said that Frank favored Comstock's reelection, but this seems incorrect. *DT*, Sept. 5, 1934.

14. FM to Fremsdorf, June 25, 1934, FM to GM, Sept. 29, 1934, GM to FM, Oct. 26, 1934, FM Papers; FM to GM, Aug. 27, Oct. 11, 1934, GM Papers; Lacy to FM [Spring 1935], Lacy Papers; Lacy interview, pp. 67–68; *DN*, Sept. 5, 1934.

15. Picard speech [Sept. 8, 1934], Frank Picard Papers, MHC; Lacy to FM, Sept. 9, 1934, FM to Lacy, Sept. 9, 1934, FM Papers; Lacy to FM [Spring 1935], Lacy Papers.

16. *DN*, Sept. 29, Oct. 1, 1934; 1934 election analysis, Lacy Papers; GM to FM, Oct. 10, 1934, FM to GM, Oct. 15, 1934, FM Papers.

17. John P. White, *Michigan Votes: Election Statistics, 1928–1956* (Ann Arbor: University of Michigan, 1958), pp. 26–27, 29–35; FDR to FM, Oct. 22, 1934, John K. Stack to FM, Jan. 10, 1935, FM Papers; JAF to FDR, Nov. 3, 1934, PSF, Post Office, FDRL; Norbert Blank to Abbott, Nov. 8, 1934, Picard to JAF, Nov. 9, 1934, Picard to FDR, Nov. 10, 1934, G. Foulkes to JAF, Nov. 10, 1934, McDonald to McIntyre, Nov. 12, 1934, OF 300 (Michigan); 1934 election analysis, Lacy Papers; Lacy to FM [Spring 1935], ibid.; Lehr to Prentiss M. Brown, Feb. 2, 1935, Prentiss M. Brown Papers, Box 1, MHC; McDonald to JAF, Aug. 5, 1936, DNC-JAF; Lacy interview, pp. 64–65; Richard J. Drew, "The Survival of a Senator: The Vandenberg-Picard Senatorial Race, 1934" (1967), p. 58, in my possession. Lacy, who was far from being an ardent New Dealer, remained a Democrat until 1936, but, as he put it, he "woke up" shortly thereafter and voted Republican for the rest of his life. Lacy to F. A. Perine, Feb. 22, 1949, Lacy Papers.

18. Picard to FM, Nov. 11, 1932, L. O'Brien to FM, May 2, 1933, Frank Sparks to FM, Nov. 2, 1933, Walker to FM, Nov. 9, 1933, Jan. 19, 1934, Frank Martel to FM, Jan. 26, Apr. 9, 1934, Fenner to FM, Jan. 26, 1934, Giles Kavanagh to FM, Feb. 12, 1934, Henry Montgomery to FM, Feb. 22, 1934, John E. Kinnane to FM, Mar. 9,

1934, FM Papers; HM to MM, Sept. 26, 1933, Frank Bright to MM, Dec. 13, 1933, MM Papers, MHC; *DN* [Oct. 23, 1933], HSB; Drew, "Survival," pp. 35, 37.

19. *Grand Rapids Chronicle*, Dec. 22, 1933, clipping in FM Papers; [*MDB*, Nov. 25, 1933], HSB; *MDB*, Jan. 30, 1934, MSB; *MT*, Nov. 25, 1933, HSB; *PH*, Dec. 19, 1933, HSB; FM to Kinnane, Nov. 6, 1933, FM to Edgar DeWitt Jones, Jan. 9, 1934, FM to George W. Welsh, Jan. 25, 1934, Dingell to FM, Jan. 26, 1934, FM to Lee M. Beard, Mar. 22, 1934, FM to Howe, Apr. 2, 1934, FM Papers; FM to GM, Mar. 4, 28, 1934, GM Papers; IM to Mrs. E. V. Hawkins, Mar. 27, 1934, IM Papers, MHC.

20. GM to L. O'Brien, Mar. 26, 1934, McAllister to GM, Mar. 28, Apr. 5, 1934, McAllister to FM, Mar. 28, 1934, GM to McAllister, Apr. 4, 1934, GM to FM, Apr. 4, 1934, GM Papers; Martel to E. W. Crockett, Apr. 4, 1935, Wayne County AFL-CIO Papers, Box 11, ALHUA; Joseph Sanders to FM, Apr. 11, 1934, FM Papers.

21. FM to JRH, Mar. 16, 1936, JRH Papers; *La Vanguardia*, May 12, 1934, MSB; EG notes on interview with GM [1949], EG Papers, MHC; Interview with GM, Mar. 28, 1957, pp. 18–19, MHC; Frederic S. Marquardt to Theodore Roosevelt, Jr., Mar. 30, 1934, Theodore Roosevelt, Jr., Papers, Box 29, LC; Dingell to FM, May 12 (letter and radiogram), July 30, 1934, Dingell to JAF, May 12, 1934, FM to Dingell, May 18, 1934, JAF to FM, May 21, 1934, FDR to FM, June 30, 1934, FM Papers; PLS [Shannon] Memorandum for Stephen Early, June 27, 1934, PPF 1662, FDRL; *DN*, June 28, 1934; *NYT*, Jan. 7, 1934; Drew, "Survival," pp. 35, 37.

22. FM to Lyle C. Wilson, Apr. 17, 1934, FM to Shields, May 22, 1934, FM to Couzens, June 25, 1934, FM to Dingell, June 26, 1934, FM to GM, Apr. 30, 1947, FM Papers; Kinnane to FM, July 10, 1934, FM to GM, July [11], 1934, GM Papers; Hill to Martel, Aug. 21, 1934, Wayne County AFL-CIO Papers, Box 11.

23. FM to GM [July 11, 1934], P. H. O'Brien to GM, July 20, 1934, Dingell to GM, Mar. 18, 1936, GM Papers; Dingell to FM, July 30, Oct. 29, 1934, GM to FM, Aug. 25, 1934, Vandenberg to FM, Aug. 21, 1934, FM Papers. Cf. Richard Drew, Interview with Wilber Brucker, undated, pp. 7–9, MHC.

24. Sarasohn and Sarasohn, *Party Patterns*, pp. 26–33; Queena M. Fitzgerald, "Frank D. Fitzgerald: A Tribute," *Michigan History Magazine* 24 (May 1940): 13–14; Brown to FM, Oct. 2, 1935, Brown Papers, Box 1; Howard O. Hunter to Hopkins, Dec. 11, 1934, WPA-FERA Narrative Field Reports, 1933–1936, Harry L. Hopkins Papers, FDRL; Fitzgerald to Joseph H. Brewer, Nov. 15, 1935, Frank D. Fitzgerald Papers, MHC; Peter Fagan to FM, June 11, 1935, EGK to FM, Oct. 23, 1936, Hill to FM, Dec. 11, 1936, FM Papers; Picard to Sidney T. Miller, May 31, 1935, Picard Papers; George J. Burke to JAF, Aug. 3, 1936, DNC-JAF; *DN*, Dec. 27, 1936, Nov. 17, 1963; Cash Asher, *Ten Thousand Promises* (Grass Lake, Mich.: The Author, 1936), passim.

25. Picard to JAF, Mar. 5, 1935, Picard Papers; Picard to GM, Apr. 3, 1935, GM to FM, July 18, 1935, GM Papers; Picard to FM, May 1, 1935, George Maines to FM, Oct. 10, 1935, FM Papers; *DN*, May 23, June 7, July 6, 17, 20, Aug. 30, 31, Sept. 1, 1935, Feb. 9, July 28, 1936; *Port Huron Times-Herald*, July 20, 1935, HSB.

26. Kenneth B. Withrow to McIntyre, Sept. 6, 1935, Malcolm Hatfield to Howe, Jan. 9, 1936, OF 300 (Michigan); Abbott to Mary W. Dewson, Nov. 26, 1935,

Democratic Party, National Committee, Women's Division Papers, 1933–1944 (Michigan), FDRL (hereafter cited as DNC-WD); Lacy to FM [Spring 1935], Lacy Papers; Picard to FM, Mar. 4, 1935, Adelaide Williams to FM, Sept. 5, 1935, FM Papers; Fagan, "Report on Matters Affecting the Democratic Party in Michigan" [1934], ibid.; Howard R. Marsh to EGK, Mar. 10, 1936, EGK-BHC, Box 18.

27. "Governor Murray D. Van Wagoner," *Michigan History Magazine* 25 (Winter 1941): 5–13; Interview with G. Donald Kennedy, May 11, 1965, pp. 1–7, MHC; Burke to JAF, Aug. 3, 1936, McDonald to JAF, Aug. 5, 1936, DNC-JAF; Elizabeth Belen to FM, Sept. 11, 1935, FM Papers; Sarasohn and Sarasohn, *Party Patterns*, pp. 46–47; *DN*, Sept. 27, 1936, May 19, 1937.

28. Picard to JAF, Nov. 9, 1934, Picard to FDR, Nov. 10, 1934, Hurja Papers; Howe to [William Stanley], Feb. 12, 1935, Howe to JAF, Mar. 4, 1935, FM Papers; Elmer B. O'Hara speech, Apr. 18, 1935, Picard Papers; *DN*, Nov. 9, 1934, Mar. 19, 1935; Newquist, "Farley," p. 417.

29. *DN*, Mar. 6, 15, 19, July 6, 1935; *DT*, Feb. 27, 28, Mar. 3, 9, 1935, MSB; [*DT*, Mar. 12, Apr. 3, 1935], MSB; unidentified newspaper clippings, Mar. 14, 21, 1935, and undated, MSB; Lacy to FM [Spring 1935], Lacy Papers; FM to A. J. Sawyer, Feb. 27, 1935, Howe Memorandum for JAF, Mar. 4, 1935, FM to Picard, Mar. 8, 1935, Feb. 15, 1936, FM to Edward H. Williams, Mar. 18, 1935, FM to Martin W. Baginski, Mar. 25, 1935, FM to Nina K. Easton, Apr. 8, 1935, W. W. Howes to FM, Apr. 12, 1935, FM to James H. Lynch, Apr. 15, 1935, FM to JAF, Apr. 15, May 13, 1935, FM to Howe, Apr. 18, 1935, FM to Jesse Jones, Apr. 27, 1935, FM to Hurja, May 13, 1935, FM to Chawke, May 17, June 15, 1935, JAF to FM, June 14, 1935, FM to Ernest F. Rossi, July 1, 1935, FM to Sadowski, Aug. 8, 1935, FM to James K. Watkins, Oct. 8, 1935, FM Papers; FM to GM, May 15, 21, 1935, Hurja to GM, June 4, 1935, GM to FM, July 11, 1935, GM Papers; Brown to Lehr, Mar. 29, 1935, Lehr to Brown, Apr. 3, Aug. 22, 1935, Brown Papers, Box 1; L. G. Lenhardt to Moody, Mar. 27, 1935, Moody Papers; O'Hara speech, Apr. 18, 1935, Picard Papers; Interview with Thomas F. Chawke, Mar. 1965, p. 164, MHC; Fine, *Murphy*, p. 164.

30. *DT*, Apr. 10, 1935, MSB; *DT*, May 18, June 30, 1935, clippings in FM Papers; *DN*, Apr. 11, May 4, 1935; FM to Lynch, Apr. 15, 1935, Evelyn S. Mershon to FM, May 1, 1935, FM to Lehr, May 11, 1935, FM to Lesinski, May 11, 1935, Picard to FM, May 13, 1935, FM to Charles Roehm, May 13, 1935, FM to G. H. Roosevelt, May 14, 1935, FM to Hopkins, May 14, 1935, FM to Martel, May 15, 1935, Pierson to FM, May 18, 1935, Dingell to FM, May 28, 1935, Hurja to FM, June 4, 1935, Rossi to FM, June 6, 1935, JAF to FM, June 14, 1935, FM to Dingell, June 22, 1935, FM to Rossi, July 1, 1935, FM Papers; O'Hara speech, Apr. 18, 1935, Picard Papers; Frank Hook to FDR, May 14, 1935, OF 300 (Michigan); FM to GM, May 15, 21, 1935, GM Papers; Martin Edward Sullivan, " 'On the Dole': The Relief Issue in Detroit, 1929–1939" (Ph.D. diss., University of Notre Dame, 1974), p. 172.

31. FM to Martel, May 15, 1935, Pierson to FM, July 10, 1935, Martel to FM, July 15, Sept. 16, 1935, Belen to JAF, Aug. 17, 1935, Dingell to FM, Aug. 29, 1935, FM Papers; Charles E. Varcoe to Abbott, Aug. 2, 1935, with Abbott to FDR, Aug. 15, 1935, Sadowski to Hopkins, Aug. 9, 1935, with Sadowski to McIntyre, Aug. 22, 1935, Roland S. Philipps to McIntyre [Sept. 1935], OF 300 (Michigan); Varcoe, "Appeal . . ." [Aug. 25, 1935], ibid.; Harry Glass, Jr., to Marguerite LeHand, July

7, 1935, Canfield to McIntyre, Feb. 25, 1936, Hook to McIntyre, Apr. 18, 1936, OF 444-Misc., FDRL; Schroeder to JAF, Feb. 27, 1936, Confidential Political File, 1933–1938, Hopkins Papers; Sadowski to GM, July 3, 1935, H. F. Donahue to GM, Aug. 13, 1935, Dingell to GM, Sept. 6, 1935, GM Papers.

32. Hopkins telephone conversation with . . . Pierson, July 9, 1935, Transcripts of Telephone Conversations, 1934–1938, FERA-WPA, Hopkins Papers; Pierson and Hopkins Conversation, Jan. 2, 1936, ibid.; Lorena Hickok to Hopkins, Dec. 21, 1935, FERA-WPA Reports, ibid.; GM to Sadowski, July 5, 1935, FM to GM, Aug. 12, 1935, Dingell to GM, Sept. 6, 1935, GM Papers; GM to FM, Aug. 2, 1935, FM to Pierson, Aug. 12, 1935, Dingell to FM, Aug. 29, 1935, FM Papers.

33. MM to GM [Nov. 21, 1934], FM to GM, Dec. 18, 1934, GM Papers; Theodora F. McManus to FM, Nov. 27, 1934, Fenner to FM, Nov. 30, 1934, Dora Woodruff to FM, Dec. 10, 1934, FM to Andrew J. Sawyer, Jan. 4, 1935, FM to James F. Healey, Jan. 17, 1935, FM Papers; Brown to FM, Jan. 7, 1935, Brown Papers, Box 1.

34. Donald McCoy, *Angry Voices: Left of Center Politics in the New Deal Era* (Lawrence: University of Kansas Press, 1958), p. 119; Charles J. Tull, *Father Coughlin and the New Deal* (Syracuse: Syracuse University Press, 1965), pp. 61, 80, 82, 91; Picard to FM, Dec. 14, 1934, FM Papers; Daniel Tobin to JAF, Apr. 23, 1935, OF 306, FDRL. See also James P. Shenton, "The Coughlin Movement and the New Deal," *Political Science Quarterly* 73 (Sept. 1958): 354n.

35. FM to GM, Feb. 6, 13, 1935, FM to E. Williams, Feb. 8, 1935, Arthur D. Maguire to FM, Mar. 2, 1935, FM to Maguire, Mar. 5, 1935, FM Papers; FM speeches, Feb. 22, 25, 1935, ibid.; FM to GM, Feb. 14, 1935, GM Papers; IM to Mrs. D. T. Roots [Mar. 11, 1935], IM Papers; *DN*, Feb. 20–23, May 4, 1935; [*DT*, Feb. 20–24, 26, 1935], MSB.

36. Vincent J. Toole to FM, Mar. 19, 1935, FM to Kennedy, May 9, 10, 1935, Kennedy to FM, May 9, 12, 1935, FM to LeHand, May 12, 1935, FM to Early, May 13, 1935, FM to Moley, May 14, 1935 (not sent), FM to JAF, May 17, 1935, JAF to FM, June 14, 1935, FM Papers; FM speech, May 11, 1935, ibid.; Hill to Moody, May 10, 1935, Moody Papers; FM to Early, May 18, 1935, OF 400, FDRL; *DT*, May 7, 15, 1935, MSB; James A. Farley, *Jim Farley's Story* (New York: McGraw-Hill, 1938), p. 52. My impression of what Murphy probably said to Coughlin is based on FM to Louis Ward, July 11, 1935, FM Papers.

37. T. Harry Williams, *Huey Long* (New York: Alfred A. Knopf, 1970), pp. 641–42, 800–802, 845–47; Long, *My First Days in the White House* (Harrisburg, Pa.: The Telegraph Press, 1935), pp. 50–58; Tull, *Coughlin*, p. 101. The newsman William Hutchinson claimed that he had convinced Long to name Murphy his attorney general in the book, the manuscript of which, Hutchinson stated, Long had given him "to brighten or freshen or authenticate." George H. Maines, a Long publicist, claimed that he had introduced Murphy to Long and that they had spent several hours together during which time Long promised to appoint Murphy attorney general if he (Long) were elected president. After Long's death Murphy described himself as "a friend and admirer" of Long. Hutchinson to FM, July 10, 1935, FM to Hutchinson, Sept. 13, 1935, Feb. 4, 1936, FM Papers; Maines to EMB, undated, EMB Papers.

38. Kennedy to FM, Sept. 4, 1935, EMB Papers; JAF to FM, June 14, 1935, Coughlin to FM, Sept. 5, Nov. 13, 1935, Ward to FM, Sept. 18, 1935, FM to William F. Murphy, Oct. 16, 1935, FM to Coughlin, Oct. 22, 1935, FM Papers; *NYT*, Sept. 12, 1935; McCoy, *Angry Voices*, pp. 131–34; Tull, *Coughlin*, pp. 102–3. For the gradualness of Coughlin's break with Roosevelt, see Richard Akin Davis, "Radio Priest: The Public Career of Father Charles Edward Coughlin" (Ph.D. diss., University of North Carolina, 1974), pp. 155–58.

39. JAF to FDR, Sept. 26, 1935, and enclosed Hurja, Special Memorandum, PSF, Democratic National Committee, FDRL; Hatfield to Richard F. Roper, Apr. 9, 1935, OF 300 (Michigan); Hickok to Hopkins, May 27, 1935, enclosing Hickok, "Confidential Report on Michigan," Hickok to Hopkins, Dec. 21, 1935, FERA-WPA Reports, Hopkins Papers; Hunter to Hopkins, Oct. 21, 1935, General Correspondence, 1933–1940, ibid.; Frank McHale to GM, July 29, 1935, GM Papers; G. H. Roosevelt to FM, Nov. 1, 1935, FM Papers; JRH to Louis Van Schaick, Nov. 3, 1936, JRH Papers. Cf. Davis, "Radio Priest," pp. 163–64, 184.

40. Harry Barnard, *Independent Man: The Life of Senator James Couzens* (New York: Charles Scribner's Sons, 1958), pp. 306–10, 357n; FM to Couzens, May 11, 1935, Couzens Papers, Box 119; Couzens to Clarence E. Wilcox, Jan. 27, 1936, ibid., Box 113; Wilcox to Couzens, Feb. 5, 15, 1936, Couzens to Wilcox, Feb. 19, 1936, Couzens to George Averill, Feb. 20, 1936, Couzens to Payne, Apr. 14, May 21, 1936, Payne to Couzens, May 25, 1936, ibid., Box 110; Couzens to Fitzgerald, Feb. 4, 1936, Fitzgerald Papers; Brown to FDR, May 29, 1936, OF 300 (Michigan); *DN*, June 16, 1936.

41. McAllister to FM, May 13, 1935, FM to Montgomery, May 17, 1935, Gedge to FM, June 15, 1935, FM to GM, June 19, 1935, MM to GM, July 15, 1935, FM Papers; GM to Nicholas V. Olds, Apr. 9, 1935, FM to GM, June 17, 1935, GM Papers; Brown to Roger Andrews, Apr. 13, 1935, Brown Papers, Box 1. See also McHale to GM, July 29, 1935, GM Papers; *Philippines Free Press*, June 8, 1935, clipping in FM Papers; and *Sault Ste. Marie Evening News*, June 7, 1935, HSB.

42. Fagan to FM, June 11, 1935, FM to Dingell, June 22, 1935, James L. Smith to FM, June 23, 1935, William Stearn and Joseph E. Sears to FM, June 24, 1935, FM to Coughlin, July 5, 1935, FM to Fagan, July 8, 1935, FM to Smith, July 22, 1935, Jacob P. Sumeracki to FM, Aug. 5, 1935, Schroeder to FM, Aug. 7, 1935, McAllister to FM, Aug. 12, 1935, A. Williams to FM, Sept. 5, 1935, Coughlin to FM, Sept. 5, 1935, W. D. Murphy to FM, Sept. 11, Dec. 13, 1935, Charles Rydzewski to FM, Sept. 9, 1935, FM to McAllister, Sept. 12, 1935, Burr Lincoln to FM, Sept. 29, 1935, Frederic S. Schouman to FM, Sept. 30, 1935, Abner Larned to FM, Oct. 7, 1935, FM to A. Williams, Oct. 10, 1935, Dingell to FM, Dec. 5, 1935, HM to FM, Dec. 17, 1935, FM Papers; FM to GM, July 10, 1935, MM to GM, July 15, 1935, Fagan to GM, Sept. 1, 7, 1935, GM Papers; Brown to FM, Oct. 2, 1935, Brown Papers, Box 1; George Malcolm to EGK [1935], EGK Papers; Abbott to Dewson, Nov. 26, 1935, DNC-WD; *Port Huron Times-Herald*, July 20, 1935, HSB; *MDB*, July 22, 1935, MSB; [*DN*, Oct. 3, 1935], clipping in FM Papers; *DN*, Mar. 1, 1936.

43. GM to FM, July 27, 1935, Feb. 5, 1936, Jack Manning to FM, Nov. 19, 1935, FM Papers; FM to GM, Aug. 22, 24, 1935, GM Papers; Guy Hugh Jenkins to George C. Booth, Guy Hugh Jenkins Papers, MHC; *DN*, July 20, Aug. 31, 1935.

44. G. D. Kennedy to GM, Sept. 29, 1935, A. Williams to FM, Oct. 21, 1935, FM to G. D. Kennedy [Oct. 28, 1935], Nov. 22, 1935, FM to Casper Cutler, Nov. 18, 1935, Montgomery to FM, Nov. 20, 1935, FM to Andrews, Dec. 9, 1935, FM to A. Williams, Dec. 30, 1935, FM to Hill, Jan. 4, 1936, FM to Shields, Jan. 30, 1936, GM to FM, Feb. 5, 1936, FM Papers; FM instructions for GM [Dec. 1935], ibid.; GM to MM, Dec. 13, 1935, MM Papers; GM to Kinnane, Jan. 28, 1936, GM Papers; FM to Montgomery, Jan. 7, 1936, EMB Papers; Kennedy interview, pp. 7-8.

45. FDR to FM, Jan. 7, 1936, PSF, FM, FDRL; FDR Memorandum for JAF, Jan. 7, 1936, PPF 1662, FDRL. Roosevelt told Hayden on March 3 "something to the effect that the state should be saved if possible." JRH, "The President—Notes on conversation with," Mar. 3, 1936, JRH Papers.

46. FM to William Donnelly, Feb. 4, 1936, Donnelly to FM, Feb. 7, 1936, FM file, Records of the Bureau of Insular Affairs, RG 350, NARS; FM to Hurja et al., Feb. 4, 1936, Joseph M. Donnelly to FM, Feb. 6, 1936, Chawke to FM, Feb. 6, 1936, Howard Starrett to War Department Message Center, Feb. 8, 1936, FM to JRH, Feb. 9, 1936, FM to Homer Cummings, Feb. 16, 1936, FM Papers; FM to GM, Feb. 4, 5, 1936, and draft of GM reply on latter, GM Papers; Martel to FM, Feb. 6, 1936, Wayne County AFL-CIO Papers, Box 11; FM to FDR, Feb. 12, 1936, PSF, FM.

47. E. H. Williams speech, Jan. 24, 1936, FM Papers; Coughlin to FM, Feb. 5, 1936, GM to FM, Feb. 5, 1936, Dingell to FM, Feb. 13, 1936, FM to Picard, Feb. 15, 1936, FM to W. D. Murphy, Feb. 17, 1936, FM to Mary E. Moore, Feb. 18, 1936, FM to Coughlin, Feb. 27, 1936, FM to Rossi, Feb. 27, 1936, FM to J. Donnelly, Mar. 4, 1936, FM Papers; FM to GM, Feb. 18, 1936, Dingell to GM, Mar. 18, 1936, GM Papers; *MT*, Jan. 25, 1936, MSB; *MDB*, Feb. 24, 1936, MSB; *DN*, Feb. 5, 1936.

48. FM to Joseph Mulcahy, Feb. 7, 1936, Edward F. Thomas to FM, Feb. 20, 1936, FM to Martel, Feb. 29, 1936, FM to Hurja, Mar. 3, 1936, FM to FDR, Mar. 3, Apr. 25, 1936, FM Papers; FM to JRH, Mar. 16, 1936, JRH Papers; GM to George E. Manting, Mar. 19, 1936, GM Papers.

49. J. Weldon Jones to JRH, May 25, July 10, 1936, JRH Papers; FM to Al Dale, Feb. 17, 1936, E. Williams to FM, Feb. 21, 1936, Fenner to FM, Mar. 3, 1936, Shields to FM, Mar. 7, 1936, Coughlin to FM, Mar. 13, 1936, John Berghage to FM, Mar. 23, 1936, A. Williams to FM, Mar. 25, 29, Apr. 10, 1936, Kinnane to FM, Mar. 25, 1936, FM to George A. Osborn, Mar. 31, 1936, J. Donnelly et al. to FM, Apr. 27, 1936, FM to J. Donnelly, May 7, 1936, GM to FM, May 16, 1936, FM Papers; FM to Moses L. Walker, Mar. 3, 1936, GM to Dingell, Apr. 15, 1936, GM to Manuel L. Quezon, July 30, 1936, GM Papers; Hill to Murl H. Defoe, Apr. 11, 1936, Hill Papers; Hill to Richard D. Lunt, Feb. 19, 1964, Richard D. Lunt Papers, MHC; EGK to Chase S. Osborn, May 9, 1936, EGK Papers; Interview with Martin S. Hayden, Oct. 6, 1964, p. 37, MHC; *Herald Mid-Week Magazine*, May 6, 1936, MSB; *MT*, May 5, 1936, MSB; *DN*, May 20, 1936. Cf. *DT*, Dec. 1, 1936, MSB.

50. *DN*, Apr. 14, May 3, 9, June 22, 26, Sept. 16, 1936; Kennedy to Hurja, May 15, 1936, Hurja Papers; Schroeder to Edward J. Flynn, Nov. 25, 1940, FM Papers; Picard to Moody, Nov. 12, 1936, Moody Papers.

51. *DN*, May 20-22, June 16, 1936; *PH*, May 21, 22, 1936, HSB; *MDB*, May 22, 1936, HSB; Picard to Hurja, May 25, 1936, Hurja Papers; JRH to Jones, May 25, 1936, JRH Papers.

52. *DN*, June 4, 20, 24, 1936; *DT*, June 21, 1936, MSB; [*DT*, June 24, 1936], MSB; *San Francisco Bulletin*, June 4, 1936, HSB; *NYT*, June 21, 1936; *PH*, June 30, 1936, HSB; Statement to Press by E. Williams, June 4, 1936, FM Papers; FM to MM, June 21, 1936, MM Papers; Tull, *Coughlin*, pp. 116–19; McCoy, *Angry Voices*, p. 134; George Q. Flynn, *American Catholics and the Roosevelt Presidency* (Lexington: University of Kentucky Press, 1968), pp. 318–23, 335; Davis, "Radio Priest," p. 639.

53. Jones to Secretary of War, July 14, 1936, FM Papers; *DN*, June 4, 22, 23, 27, 28, 1936; *MT*, June 28, 1936, HSB.

54. Hurja to FM, May 25, 29, 1936, G. D. Kennedy to FM, June 1, 1936, enclosing "Report on a Poll of the Voters of the State of Michigan Taken in the Spring of 1936," FM Papers; FM notes, June 29, 1936, EG Papers; JRH to A. V. Hartendorp, July 20, 1936, JRH Papers; *NYT*, June 30, July 15, 1936. See also FM to Mrs. Robert Aura Smith, July 10, 1936, FM Papers.

55. *DN*, July 3, 1936; [*DT*, July 3, 1936], MSB.

56. Shields to FM, July 6, 7, 8, 1936, FM Papers; FM notes, July 9, 1936, EG Papers; *DN*, July 5–9, 1936; [*DT*, July 9, 1936], MSB.

57. FDR to FM, July 8, 1936, OF 400, FDRL; Press Release, July 9, 1936, FM Papers; FM notes, July 9, 1936, EG Papers; *DN*, July 10, 1936; *NYT*, July 10, 1936; *Time* 28 (July 20, 1936): 19; [*DN*, July 11, 1936], MSB; FM to Jones, July 10, 1936, FM file, RG 350.

58. *DN*, July 10, 1936.

59. *DN*, July 10, 11, 1936; *MDB*, July 10, 11, 18, HSB; *PH*, July 14, 1936, HSB; [*Bay City Times*, July 10, 1936], MSB; [*Lansing State Journal*, July 11, 1936], MSB; *DFP*, July 11, 1936.

60. JRH to Jones, May 25, July 21–22, 1936, JRH Papers; Samuel T. Metzger to FDR, July 9, 1936, OF 300 (Michigan); FM to JAF, July 20, 1936, FM Papers; Canfield to JAF, July 17, 1936, Shields to JAF, July 21, 1936, McDonald to JAF, Aug. 5, 1936, DNC-JAF; *DN*, July 31, Aug. 19, Sept. 10, 1936.

61. FM to JAF, July 20, 1936, Thomas to FM, Nov. 24, 1936, FM Papers; J. H. Eliasohn to GM, Aug. 21, 1936, GM Papers; McDonald to JAF, Aug. 5, 1936, James F. Murphy to JAF, Sept. 8, 1936, John J. McGinty to JAF, Sept. 14, 1936, Clara Van Auken to JAF, Oct. 7, 1936, DNC-JAF; Hook to JAF, Aug. 12, 1936, OF 300 (Farley Correspondence on Political Trends, 1936) (hereafter cited as JAF, 1936); Picard to Hurja, Aug. 8, 1936, Hurja Papers; [*DT*, July 9, 16, 1936], MSB; *DN*, July 28, 1936.

62. *DN*, July 28, 30, 1936; [*DT*, July 29–31, 1936], MSB; [*DFP*, July 31, 1936], MSB; *Saginaw News*, July 29, 1936, MSB; McDonald to JAF, Aug. 5, 1936, J. F. Murphy to JAF, Sept. 8, 1936, DNC-JAF; E. J. Fry to FDR, July 30, 1936, OF 300 (Michigan); FM to Thomas E. Roberts, July 31, 1936, enclosed with Roberts to GM, Aug. 1, 1936, GM to Roberts, Aug. 6, 1936, GM Papers.

63. Hurja to JAF, July 21, 1936, Hurja Papers; JAF to FM, July 27, 1936, FM Papers; JAF to GM, Aug. 29, 1936, GM Papers; McDonald to JAF, Aug. 5, 1936, J. F. Murphy to JAF, Sept. 8, 1936, DNC-JAF; *DN*, Aug. 7, 1936; *DFP*, Aug. 5, 1936; [*DFP*, Aug. 6, 1936], MSB.

64. *DN*, June 29, July 10, 11, 1936; Burke to JAF, Aug. 3, 1936, Lesinski to JAF, Aug. 20, 1936, DNC-JAF.

65. Canfield to JAF, July 17, 1936, Burke to JAF, Aug. 3, 1936, McDonald to JAF, Aug. 5, 1936, Michael J. Hart to JAF, Aug. 11, 1936, Lesinski to JAF, Aug. 21, 1936, J. F. Murphy to JAF, Sept. 8, 1936, McGinty to JAF, Sept. 14, 1936, DNC-JAF; Louis Rabaut to JAF, Aug. 24, 1936, OF 300 (JAF, 1936); JRH to FM, July 30, 1936, Toole to FM, Aug. 17, 1936, FM to Lee Kreiselman, Sept. 17, 1936, FM to James Baker, Sept. 19, 1936, FM Papers; *DN*, Aug. 23, Sept. 1, 7, 1936; *NYT*, Aug. 10, 1936; [*DT*, Sept. 2, 1936], MSB.

66. Report of Evelyn Mershon [July 29, 1936], DNC-WD; J. Newton Colver to Stanley High, July 31, 1936, Hurja Papers; Kent Torrey to FM, Sept. 14, 1936, FM to Torrey, Sept. 16, 1936, FM Papers; WHP [Phelps] to Ernest S. Lyons, Aug. 13, 1936, EGK Papers; Lesinski to JAF, Aug. 20, 1936, DNC-JAF; Ben F. Searight to JAF, Sept. 9, 1936, OF 300 (JAF, 1936). As of 1936, whereas 21 percent of the population in metropolitan areas of the state was Catholic, only 13 percent of the nonmetropolitan population was of this faith. On the other hand, of Michigan's 1,196,406 church members over 13 years of age, 510,352 were Catholic. V. O. Key, *American State Politics* (New York: Alfred A. Knopf, 1965), p. 239; Bureau of the Census, *Religious Bodies*, 2 vols. (Washington: U.S. Government Printing Office, 1941), 1:226, 230.

67. Colver to High, July 31, 1936, Hurja Papers; JHR to Jones, July 21–22, 1936, JRH Papers; FM to JAF, July 20, 1936, FM to Hearst, Aug. 4, 1936, FM to Richard E. Berlin, May 14, 1947, FM Papers; Hilmer Gellein to Elmer J. Hanna, Sept. 21, 1936, Hill Papers; G. Mennen Williams to EMB, July 8, 1957, EMB Papers; McDonald to JAF, Aug. 5, 1936, Dingell to JAF, Aug. 10, 1936, DNC-JAF; Interview with Jack Manning, Dec. 4, 1964, pp. 6–7, MHC; [*DT*, Aug. 7, 1936], MSB; [*Redford Record*, July 16, 1936], MSB.

68. Shields to JAF, July 21, 1936, Burke to JAF, Aug. 3, 1936, McDonald to JAF, Aug. 5, 1936, JAF to Aubrey Williams, Aug. 21, 1936, J. F. Murphy to JAF, Sept. 8, 1936, McGinty to JAF, Sept. 14, 1936, DNC-JAF; FM to JAF, July 20, 1936, FM Papers; JRH to Jones, July 21–22, 1936, JRH Papers; Kennedy interview, p. 11; *DFP*, Aug. 5, 1936.

69. Fine, *Murphy*, pp. 215–16, 433; Gomon Diary, July 13, 1936, Gomon Papers; FM to Harold Ickes, July 20, 1936, FM Papers; *DN*, Aug. 2, 1936.

70. FM to Mead, July 14, 26, Aug. 12, Sept. 3, 1936, FM to Mead and Howell Van Auken, undated, Zygmunt Kowalski and Constantine Dobrowoloski to FM, Aug. 6, 1936, Marie Hendry to Mead, Sept. 10, 1936, FM Papers; *DN*, July 14, Aug. 3, 6, 7, 12, 17, Sept. 11, 1936; [*DT*, Sept. 2, 1936], MSB; Rabaut to JAF, Aug. 24, 1936, OF 300 (JAF, 1936); Ida Z. Kleinman speech, Sept. 13, 1936, FM Papers.

71. FM to Mead, Aug. 12, Sept. 7, 1936, Walker to FM, Feb. 6, July 3, Aug. 31, Sept. 10, 1936, Walker to My Dear Rev., Sept. 4, 1936, FM Papers; [*Detroit People's News*, Aug. 15, Sept. 12, 1936], MSB.

72. *DLN*, July 7, Aug. 7, 14, 21, 28, 1936; *DN*, July 31, 1936; Fred Pettinga to Martel, Aug. 8, 1936, Martel to Pettinga, Aug. 11, 1936, H. Van Auken to DWCFL, Sept. 4, 1936, Wayne County AFL-CIO Papers, Box 7.

73. FM to Mead and H. Van Auken, undated, FM to JAF, July 20, 1936, Schroeder to FM, Aug. 18, 1936, FM to Trendle, Aug. 19, 1936, FM to Mead, Sept. 7, 1936, Trendle to FM, Sept. 9, 1936, R. L. Maughan to FM, Feb. 4, 1937, FM

Papers; FM to GM [Aug. 22, 1936], GM Papers; Colver to High, July 31, 1936, Picard to JAF, Sept. 17, 1936, Hurja Papers; Van Wagoner to JAF, Sept. 10, 1936, DNC-JAF. Murphy sought to assist WMBC, which was also friendly to him, in securing a channel reallocation. FM to Gedge, Aug. 19, 1936, FM Papers.

74. EGK to FM, Aug. 11, 1936, J. B. Bannick to Bob, Sept. 8, 1936, FM Papers; Bannick to FM, Sept. 8, 1936, EMB Papers; FM speech, Sept. 3, 1936, FM Papers; *DN*, Sept. 4, 1936; *DFP*, Sept. 4, 1936; [*Muskegon Chronicle*, Sept. 4, 1936], MSB.

75. Paul Todd to FM, July 11, 18, 1936, FM to JAF, July 20, 1936, FM to Early, July 25, 1936, Welsh to FM, Sept. 1, 1936, FM to Welsh, Sept. 3, 1936, Picard to FM, Sept. 3, 1936, FM to Mead and H. Van Auken, undated, FM Papers; FM release, Sept. 2, 1936, ibid.; FM to GM [Aug. 22, 1936], GM Papers; "Mr. Early: Hyde Park" folder, July 31, 1936, OF 200-EE, FDRL; [*DT*, Aug. 26, 1936], MSB; *DN*, Sept. 2, 3, 10, 1936.

76. *DN*, Sept. 10, 1936; FM to Kreiselman, Sept. 17, 1936, H. Van Auken to FM, Dec. 7, 1936, and enclosed Committee Treasurer's Detailed Statement of Nomination and Election Expenses, FM Papers. The Van Auken statement erroneously lists the Democratic National Committee's loan as having been made on September 24, after the primary. See W. Forbes Morgan to FM, Oct. 16, 1936, FM Papers.

77. *DN*, July 13, 22, 25, 27-29, Aug. 7, 8, 10, 18, 20, 23, Sept. 1, 7, 9, 11, 13, 1936; *DFP*, July 18, 1936; FM to EGK, July 14, 1936, FM to H. Van Auken, July 14, 1936, FM to Hearst, Aug. 4, 1936, FM to JRH, Sept. 1, 1936, FM Papers; FM speech, July 17, 1936, ibid.; Dingell to JAF, Aug. 10, 1936, DNC-JAF; *Michigan Democratic Forum* 1 (Sept. 1936): 3, MSB.

78. FM speeches, July 17, 18, Aug. 14, Sept. 5, 13, 1936, FM Papers; *DN*, July 12, 22, 27, 28, Aug. 11, 12, 16, 19, 21, 25, 29, Sept. 2-4, 13, 1936.

79. FM speeches, July 17, 18, Aug. 6, Sept. 13, 1936, FM Papers; *DN*, July 22, 25, 30, Aug. 7, 19, 23, 28, 31, 1936; *DLN*, Sept. 11, 1936; Lynd A. Walkling, July 24, Aug. 11, 28, 1936, Schroeder to FM, Aug. 4, 1936, FM to Birt Darling, Aug. 10, 1936, FM Papers.

80. Shields to JAF, July 21, 1936, McGinty to JAF, Sept. 14, 1936, DNC-JAF; Welsh to FM, Sept. 1, 1936, Burke to FM, Sept. 4, 1936, FM Papers; H. O. Weitschat to Howard Lawrence, Aug. 18, 1936, Fitzgerald Papers; *DN*, July 17-19, 28, Aug. 1, 7, 9, 13, 17, 26, 27, Sept. 2, 5, 10, 12, 13, 1936; *DFP*, Aug. 9, Sept. 8, 11, 1936; [*DT*, July 13, 1936], MSB; FM speech, Sept. 13, 1936, FM Papers.

81. G. D. Kennedy to FM, Sept. 10, 1936, and enclosed polls, FM Papers; *Michigan Official Directory and Legislative Manual, 1937-38* (n.p., n.d.), pp. 210-11; *DN*, Sept. 16, 1936; [*DN*, Oct. 4, 1936], MSB; Bledsoe to JAF, Sept. 25, 1936, OF 300 (Michigan).

82. *DFP*, Sept. 17, 18, 1936; [*Detroit Saturday Night*, Sept. 16, 1936], MSB; [*Richmond Times Dispatch*, Sept. 17, 1936], MSB; Marvin A. Bacon, *Income as an Index of the Fiscal Capacity of Michigan Counties* (Ann Arbor: University of Michigan Press, 1941), pp. 24-25.

83. *Michigan Manual, 1937-38*, pp. 205, 209; *DN*, June 5, Sept. 20, 1936; Picard to JAF, Sept. 13, 1936, Hurja Papers; Kennedy interview, p. 5; Gomon Diary, Oct. 13, 1936, Gomon Papers; Nick Arthur Masters, "Father Coughlin and Social Justice: A Case Study of a Social Movement" (Ph.D. diss., University of Wisconsin, 1955),

p. 197; Leo J. Nowicki, "Profile of an American by Choice" (1975), pp. 50–52, MHC.

84. P. H. O'Brien to JAF, Sept. 28, 1936, OF 300 (JAF, 1936); A. C. Baird to JAF, Oct. 9, 1936, DNC-JAF; Picard to Hurja, Sept. 28, 1936, Hurja Papers; FM to JRH, Oct. 2, 1936, FM Papers; JRH to Jones, Nov. 6, 1936, JRH Papers; Gomon Diary, Oct. 13, 1936, Gomon Papers; *DN*, Sept. 25–28, 1936; [*DT*, Sept. 27, 1936], MSB.

85. [*Kalamazoo Gazette*, Sept. 27, 1936], MSB; FM speech, Sept. 26, 1936, FM Papers; "Democratic Platform, 1936," ibid.; *DN*, Sept. 27, 1936.

86. *DN*, Sept. 29, 30, 1936.

87. *DN*, Oct. 7–11, 17, 18, 20, 21, 23, 25, 26, 28, 29, Nov. 2, 1936; FM speeches, Oct. 6, 13, 18, 27, 29, Nov. 1, 2, 1936, FM Papers.

88. Lehr to JAF, Sept. 17, 1936, Baird to JAF, Oct. 9, 1936, DNC-JAF; John Atkinson to JAF, Oct. 28, 1936, OF 300 (JAF, 1936); C. Van Auken to JAF, Oct. 26, 1936, OF 300 (Election Forecasts, 1936); Henry M. Wallace to Roscoe Fertich, Oct. 6, 1936, Mortimer E. Cooley Papers, MHC; Comstock to Fitzgerald, Nov. 5, 1936, Fitzgerald Papers; FM to Van Wagoner, Oct. 16, 1936, Van Wagoner to FM, Oct. 20, 1936, Murray D. Van Wagoner Papers, MHC; Thomas to FM, Nov. 24, 1936, and enclosed Report, H. Van Auken to FM, Dec. 7, 1936, and enclosed Committee Treasurer's Statement, FM Papers; *DN*, Oct. 6, 27, 1936; [*DT*, Oct. 24, 1936], MSB.

89. Walker to Mead, Oct. 16, 1936, FM Papers; James E. Davidson to Charles D. Hilles, Oct. 20, 1936, Charles D. Hilles Papers, LC (this letter was called to my attention by Dr. Donn Neal); Colored Voters League, "Questions Colored Voters Want Governor Fitzgerald to Answer," with Fitzgerald to David B. Stenton, Nov. 13, 1936, Fitzgerald Papers; *Michigan Guide*, Oct. 26, 1936, copy in ibid. Cf. *Detroit Herald*, Oct. 17, 1936.

90. Frank Schwarz to FM, Oct. 19, 1936, FM; [*Jewish Advocate*, Oct. 31, 1936], MSB.

91. Schouman to FM, Oct. 12, 1936, FM Papers; Hickok to Hopkins, Sept. 19, 1936, FERA-WPA Reports, Hopkins Papers. For WPA employment in Michigan, see Michigan Emergency Relief Administration, *Monthly Bulletin on Public Relief Statistics* 3 (Sept. 1934): 5; ibid. (Oct. 1936): 4; ibid. (Nov. 1936): 4.

92. John P. Kirk to JAF, Sept. 14, 1936, Claude S. Carney to JAF, Oct. 13, 1936, OF 300 (JAF, 1936); Schouman to FM, Oct. 12, Nov. 4, 1936, FM Papers; F. Brownson to Fitzgerald, Sept. 27, 1936, Fitzgerald Papers; FM to Pierson, Sept. 20, 1936, and enclosed FM to Hopkins, Sept. 20, 1936, Harry Lynn Pierson Papers, MHC; *DN*, Sept. 29, Oct. 22, 1936.

93. *DN*, Oct. 13–16, 20, 1936; *DFP*, Oct. 16, 1936; FM to McIntyre, Oct. 7, 1936, EGK to Fred W. Manley, Oct. 21, 1936, FM to Harry Barnard, Feb. 9, 1946, FM Papers; FDR speech, Oct. 15, 1936, ibid.; Schroeder to JAF, Oct. 22, 1936, OF 300 (Election Forecasts, 1936); Barnard, *Independent Man*, pp. 320–23.

94. Hickok to Hopkins, Sept. 19, 1936, FERA-WPA Reports, Hopkins Papers; FM to JAF, Sept. 16, 1936, JAF to FM, Sept. 19, 1936, FM to H. Van Auken, Sept. 22, 1936, Morgan to FM, Oct. 16, 1936, Todd to FM, Oct. 20, 1936, FM to Davies, Dec. 17, 1936, FM Papers; Davies to FM, Dec. 28, 1936, EMB Papers; T. I. Fry to JAF, Oct. 19, 1936, DNC-JAF.

95. *Public Acts of the Legislature of . . . Michigan . . . 1925* (Lansing: Robert Smith Co., 1925), pp. 636–37; H. Van Auken to FM, Dec. 7, 1936, and enclosed Committee Treasurer's Statement, FM Papers; "Donations Received for Governor's Campaign and Deposited in His Personal Bank Account," with EMB to Kavanagh, Mar. 13, 1937, EMB Papers.

96. Thomas to FM, Nov. 24, 1936, and enclosed Report and Exhibit A, FM to Davies, Dec. 17, 1936, FM Papers; Interview with Harry Mead, Aug. 16, 1963, pp. 17–20, MHC. Calvin Look, a district sales manager for Frankfort Distilleries and a friend of Picard, testified during the Frank McKay trial in 1941 that he had paid some Murphy campaign bills in 1936. The treasurer's statement, noted above, lists Look as having made a $300 contribution. G. M. Williams to FM, May 25, 1941, and enclosed Extract of Testimony, FM Papers; *DN*, May 23, 1941; Alice Smuts notes on interview with Van Wagoner, May 1, 1969, in my possession.

97. Fitzgerald to John C. Beukema, Nov. 16, 20, 1936, Fitzgerald Papers; *DN*, Oct. 5, 6, 9–11, 13, 19, 22, 23, 27, Nov. 1, 2, 1936.

98. *DN*, Oct. 8, 13, 1936; Fitzgerald to Frank J. Russell, Oct. 21, 1936, H. E. Duttweiler to Fitzgerald, Oct. 21, 1936, Fitzgerald Papers; Jenkins to Booth, Dec. 1, 1937, Jenkins Papers; FM speech, Oct. 18, 1936, FM Papers; William Lovett to Joseph A. Vance, Sept. 24, 1937, Detroit Citizens League Papers, Box 33, Burton Historical Collection.

99. Weideman to JAF, Oct. 3, 1936, Atkinson to JAF, Oct. 28, 1936, OF 300 (JAF, 1936); J. C. Cahalan, Jr., to JAF, Oct. 28, 1936, OF 300 (Election Forecasts, 1936); "God Save Michigan," FM Papers; *DN*, Oct. 8, 1936.

100. *DN*, Oct. 7, 18, 26, Nov. 8, 1936; Coughlin to Fitzgerald, Sept. 22, 1936, Fitzgerald to Coughlin, Sept. 24, 1936, Fitzgerald Papers; Edward J. Hickey to McIntyre, Oct. 14, 1936, OF 200-HH, FDRL; MM to Ann ——— [1936], MM Papers; C. Van Auken to JAF, Oct. 26, 1936, OF 300 (Election Forecasts, 1936); Tull, *Coughlin*, p. 160.

101. Lawrence to Nowicki, Oct. 10, 1936, Howard C. Lawrence Papers, MHC; *DFP*, Oct. 11–13, 1936; *DN*, Oct. 12, Nov. 8, 1936; FM speech, Oct. 11, 1936, FM Papers.

102. Kleinman to FM, Oct. 10, 1936, and enclosed "Notice to Employees," FM Papers; FM speeches, Oct. 25, 27, [28], Nov. 2, 1936, ibid.; Canfield to JAF, Oct. 21, 1936, C. Van Auken to JAF, Oct. 26, 1936, OF 300 (Election Forecasts, 1936); Lenhardt to Moody, Oct. 29, 1936, Moody Papers; Dewson to Murphy for Governor Headquarters, Oct. 28, 1936, DNC-WD; *DN*, Oct. 21, 22, 24, Nov. 2, 1936. For the social security scare campaign in the nation, see Arthur M. Schlesinger, Jr., *The Age of Roosevelt: The Politics of Upheaval* (Boston: Houghton Mifflin Co., 1960), pp. 635–37.

103. Lawrence to Augustine Lonergan, Dec. 9, 1936, Lawrence Papers; Lawrence to Fitzgerald, Oct. 16, Nov. 24, 1936, Fitzgerald Papers.

104. Baird to JAF, Oct. 9, 1936, DNC-JAF; Carney to JAF, Oct. 16, 1936, Shields to JAF, Oct. 22, 1936, OF 300 (Election Forecasts, 1936); Barnard, *Independent Man*, p. 314; Lawrence to Robert J. Laubengayer, Sept. 8, 1936, Lawrence Papers; Picard to Francis B. Drolet, Oct. 8, 1936, Fitzgerald Papers; H. Van Auken to FM, Sept. 14, 1940, FM Papers; *DN*, Oct. 9, 16, 20, 25, 28, 1936.

105. G. H. Roosevelt Memorandum [Oct. 1936], PPF 285 (Special Folder Drawer 2-36), FDRL; Canfield to JAF, Oct. 21, 1936, Shields to JAF, Oct. 22, 1936, C. Van Auken to JAF, Oct. 26, 1936, Atkinson to JAF, Oct. 28, 1936, Van Wagoner to JAF, Oct. 29, 1936, OF 300 (Election Forecasts, 1936); MHM [McIntyre] Memorandum for the President, Oct. 22, 1936, OF 300 (Michigan); FM to Hill, Oct. 26, 1936 (note on back of speech), FM Papers; JAF to FDR, Nov. 2, 1936, PSF, Post Office.

106. White, *Michigan Votes*, p. 40; Gerald Cleary to FM, Nov. 27, 1936, enclosing "General Election Results...," FM Papers; James K. Pollock and Samuel J. Eldersveld, *Michigan Politics in Transition* (Ann Arbor: University of Michigan Press, 1942), p. 45. In the classification of counties, I have relied on Bacon, *Income*, pp. 8–13, 24–25.

107. Edward H. Litchfield, *Voting Behavior in a Metropolitan Area* (Ann Arbor: University of Michigan Press, 1941), pp. 7, 12, 28; Thomas R. Solomon, "Participation of Negroes in Detroit Elections" (Ph.D. diss., University of Michigan, 1939), p. 139; *DN*, Nov. 5, 1936. Detroit's 120,066 blacks constituted 7.6 percent of Detroit's population in 1930; the city's 149,109 blacks made up 9.7 percent of its population in 1940. Bureau of the Census, *Fifteenth Census of the United States: 1940, Population*, vol. 2, pt. 3 (Washington: U.S. Government Printing Office, 1943), p. 889. Foreign-born registered voters in Detroit, including 20,597 Poles, made up 21.5 percent of the total number of registered voters in 1938. Donald S. Hecock and Harry A. Trevelyan, *Detroit Voters in Recent Elections* (Detroit: Bureau of Governmental Research, 1938), p. 66. See also E. Williams to FM, Nov. 5, 1936, and Sadowski to FM, Dec. 30, 1936, and enclosed "Complete Results ... Nov. 3, 1936," FM Papers.

108. Litchfield, *Voting Behavior*, pp. 28, 39. As defined in Litchfield's study, from which my Detroit voting data were derived, members of the upper-income group (25 percent of the city's population) had annual incomes of at least $2,501; members of the middle-income group (52 percent of the population), $1,000–$2,500; and members of the lower-income group (23 percent of the population), less than $1,000. For the methods used by Litchfield, see ibid., pp. 71–82.

109. *Michigan Manual, 1937–38*, pp. 272, 293–315.

110. Vandenberg to Fitzgerald, Nov. 5, 1936, McKay to Fitzgerald, Nov. 5, 1936, Fitzgerald to Vandenberg, Nov. 9, 1936, Fitzgerald to McKay, Nov. 12, 1936, Vernon J. Brown to Fitzgerald, Nov. 17, 1936, Lawrence to Fitzgerald, Nov. 24, 1936, Fitzgerald to Lawrence H. Fish, Dec. 8, 1936, Fitzgerald Papers; Lawrence to Brinton F. Hall, Nov. 16, 1936, McKay to Lawrence, Nov. 16, 1936, Lawrence Papers.

111. JRH to Van Schaick, Nov. 3, 1936, JRH to Jones, Nov. 6, 1936, JRH Papers; Brown to FM, Nov. 4, 1936, Herbert Bayard Swope to FM, Nov. 5, 1936, FM Papers; Key, *State Politics*, pp. 36–37; James L. Sundquist, *Dynamics of the Party System* (Washington: Brookings Institution, 1973), p. 239.

112. Wise to FM, Nov. 4, 1936, Walker to FM, Nov. 4, 1936, Hester to FM, Nov. 5, 1936, Charles E. Misner to FM, Nov. 7, 1936, FM to Green, Nov. 7, 1936, FM Papers.

CHAPTER 7

1. *Michigan: A Guide to the Wolverine State* (New York: Oxford University Press, 1941), pp. 16–18.

2. Ibid., pp. 60–62; F. Clever Bald, *Michigan in Four Centuries* (New York: Harper and Brothers, 1954), pp. 206, 230, 281; George F. Granger and Lawrence R. Klein, *Emergency Relief in Michigan, 1933–1939* (Lansing: n.p., 1939), pp. 96–97.

3. *Michigan*, p. 63; William Haber and Paul L. Stanchfield, *Unemployment, Relief and Economic Security* (Lansing: n.p., 1936), pp. 139–40; William B. Gates, Jr., *Michigan Copper and Boston Dollars* (Cambridge, Mass.: Harvard University Press, 1951), pp. 143–46; Granger and Klein, *Emergency Relief*, pp. 100–101.

4. *Michigan*, pp. 63–64; Granger and Klein, *Emergency Relief*, pp. 98–99.

5. Bald, *Michigan*, pp. 360, 378; *Michigan*, p. 69; Sidney Fine, *The Automobile under the Blue Eagle* (Ann Arbor: University of Michigan Press, 1963), p. 4; *Unemployment and Relief in Michigan* (Lansing: Franklin DeKleine Co., 1935), p. 32; Bureau of the Census, *Fifteenth Census of the United States: 1930, Population*, vol. 3, pt. 1 (Washington: U.S. Government Printing Office, 1932), p. 1123; Bureau of the Census, *Biennial Census of Manufactures, 1937*, pt. 1 (Washington: U.S. Government Printing Office, 1939), pp. 20–21.

6. Bald, *Michigan*, pp. 392–93; *Michigan*, p. 60; "Agriculture" [Dec. 12, 1938], FM Papers; *Unemployment and Relief*, p. 32.

7. Bureau of the Census, *Fifteenth Census, Population*, vol. 3, pt. 1, pp. 1115, 1122; idem, *Sixteenth Census of the United States: 1940, Population*, vol. 2, pt. 3 (Washington: U.S. Government Printing Office, 1943), pp. 760, 776; *Michigan*, pp. 32, 55, 103–11.

8. *Unemployment and Relief*, p. 2; Granger and Klein, *Emergency Relief*, p. 85.

9. *Unemployment and Relief*, pp. 3–4, 36–37.

10. Haber and Stanchfield, *Economic Security*, pp. 1, 6.

11. Granger and Klein, *Emergency Relief*, pp. 5–6, 31.

12. Haber and Stanchfield, *Economic Security*, pp. 85–86; Gates, Jr., *Michigan Copper*, p. 167; *Unemployment and Relief*, pp. 9–12.

13. There is a copy of the constitution in *Michigan Official Directory and Legislative Manual, 1937-38* (n.p., n.d.), pp. 28–54.

14. Harold M. Dorr, *Administrative Organization of State Government in Michigan, 1921-1936* (Ann Arbor: University of Michigan, 1936), pp. 1–3, 7–26; JRH to Bishop Mosher, Dec. 26, 1936, JRH Papers; "Statement of JRH," Oct. 13, 1938, in Arthur W. Bromage, comp., "Documents and Proceedings of the Commission on Reform and Modernization of Government," Bulletin No. 1 (1938), pp. 14–15; Hearing of Meeting of Commission . . . , Oct. 13, 1938, Commission on the Reform and Modernization of Government Papers, MHC; Coleman B. Ransone, Jr., *The Office of Governor in the United States* (University, Ala.: Alabama University Press, 1956), pp. 235–36.

15. Dorr, *Administrative Organization*, pp. 2, 9–10; John A. Perkins, *The Role of the Governor in the Enactment of Appropriations* (Ann Arbor: University of Michigan Press, 1943), pp. 97, 118; George C. S. Benson and Edward H. Litchfield, *The Administrative Board in Michigan* (Ann Arbor: University of Michigan Press, 1938),

pp. 35–38; Frank R. Woodford, *Alex J. Groesbeck* (Detroit: Wayne State University Press, 1962), pp. 129–32, 135–39.

16. EGK to FM, Jan. 11, 1937, EGK–BHC, Box 8; James K. Pollock to FM, Dec. 8, 1936, and enclosed Public Administration Service, "Suggestions for the Administrative Improvement of the Michigan State Government," FM Papers; William Brownrigg, "Confidential Report to the State Civil Service Commission," Jan. 15, 1938, ibid.; Michigan Commission on Reform and Modernization of Government, "Report of a Preliminary Survey," Dec. 20, 1938, p. 11, ibid.

17. Dorr, *Administrative Organization*, pp. 8–9; [*Lansing State Journal*, Mar. 16, 1938], MSB; Commission on Reform and Modernization of Government, "Report," pp. 11–12, FM Papers; "Address of . . . Murphy," Oct. 13, 1938, in Bromage, comp., "Documents," pp. 2–3.

18. Dorr, *Administrative Organization*, pp. 2–4; Pollock to FM, Dec. 8, 1936, and enclosed Memorandum, FM Papers; Grant McConnell, *Private Power and American Democracy* (New York: Random House, Vintage Books, 1970), pp. 182–84.

19. Public Administration Service, "Suggestions," FM Papers; Brownrigg, "Confidential Report," Jan. 15, 1938, FM Papers; Harold D. Smith Memorandum to FM, Aug. 9, 1938, ibid.; [FM Executive Order], Dec. 22, 1937, ibid.; Bald, *Michigan*, p. 412; Robert S. Ford, *Financing Michigan's Government: 1930–1938* (Ann Arbor: University of Michigan Press, 1939), pp. 2–5; idem, "Recent Fiscal Policy in Michigan," *Papers of the Michigan Academy of Science, Arts and Letters* 30 (1936): 223–31; *Michigan Manual, 1937–38*, pp. 57–59; *Report of the Tax Study Commission, January 30, 1939* (Detroit: The Commission, n.d.), p. 9.

20. FM to William M. Walker, Nov. 11, 1936, FM to Kennedy, Nov. 17, Dec. 17, 1936, Hill to FM, Dec. 4, 1936, FM to Hill, Dec. 7, 1936, FM Papers; *DN*, Nov. 24, 1936; Sidney Fine, *Frank Murphy: The Detroit Years* (Ann Arbor: University of Michigan Press, 1975), pp. 117, 175.

21. *DN*, Nov. 24, Dec. 11, 17, 18, 20, 1936; Perkins, *Role of Governor*, pp. 83–84, 98–99; Fitzgerald to FM, Nov. 16, Dec. 10, 1936, FM to Fitzgerald, Dec. 6, 1936, FM to Kennedy, Dec. 17, 1936, FM to Emil Hurja, Dec. 23, 1936, FM to Smith, Mar. 2, 1938, and enclosed copy of *DT* article, Dec. 3, 1936, FM Papers; FM, *Message . . . Jan. 7, 1937* (n.p., n.d.), p. 6, ibid.

22. *DN*, Nov. 29, Dec. 6, 10, 11, 15, 16, 1936; Raymond Louis Koch, "The Development of Public Relief Programs in Minnesota, 1929–1941" (Ph.D. diss., University of Minnesota, 1967), p. 331; William P. Smith to Fitzgerald, Dec. 7, 1936, Fitzgerald to Smith, Dec. 9, 1936, Frank D. Fitzgerald Papers, MHC; Haber to FM, Aug. 27, 1936, Fitzgerald to FM, Dec. 15, 1936, FM to Fitzgerald, Dec. 15, 1936 (two letters), FM Papers; Harry Malisoff, "The Emergence of Unemployment Compensation I," *Political Science Quarterly* 44 (June 1939): 252, 255–56.

23. Fine, *Murphy*, pp. 189–90; Michigan Unemployment Compensation Commission (MUCC), *Annual Report for the Year Ending December 31, 1937* (Lansing: n.p., 1938), pp. 4–5; *DN*, Nov. 6, 22, 29, Dec. 14, 16, 18, 20, 1936; *Michigan Manual, 1937–38*, p. 591; Reminiscences of William Haber, Aug. 11, 1965, p. 27, Oral History Research Office, Columbia University, New York, New York; Interview with Haber, Sept. 24, 1976.

24. *DN*, Dec. 21–23, 25, 29, 1936; MUCC, *Annual Report, 1937*, p. 6; Haber to FM, Dec. 24, 1936, FM Papers; Malisoff, "Unemployment Compensation," p. 252.

25. *DN*, Dec. 18, 19, 21–23, 26, 1936, Jan. 2, 1937; Malisoff, "The Emergence of Unemployment Compensation II," *Political Science Quarterly* 44 (Sept. 1939): 413; *Michigan Manual, 1937–38*, p. 45; *Michigan Manufacturer and Financial Record* 59 (Jan. 9, 1937): 5; FM, *Message, Jan. 7, 1937*, pp. 8–9, FM Papers; MUCC, *Annual Report, 1937*, p. 26.

26. MUCC, *Annual Report, 1937*, p. 7; *DN*, Feb. 4, 1937, May 26, 1939; Malisoff, "Unemployment Compensation II," p. 415; Haber to Guy Hugh Jenkins, Mar. 22, May 7, 1941, Guy Hugh Jenkins Papers, MHC; Haber interview.

27. *DN*, Jan. 1, 2, 1937; *Governor Frank Murphy's Inaugural Address, Jan. 1, 1937* (n.p., n.d.), FM Papers; *Program for the Inauguration of Frank Murphy* . . . (Lansing: n.p., 1937), MSB.

28. FM, *Message, Jan. 7, 1937*, FM Papers.

29. *DN*, Jan. 7–9, 1937; *DFP*, Jan. 8, 1937; [*DT*, Jan. 8, 1937], MSB; [*Grand Rapids Herald*, Jan. 9, 1937], MSB; [*Port Huron Times-Herald*, Jan. 8, 1937], MSB; [*Muskegon Chronicle*, Jan. 9, 1937], MSB; [*Michigan Catholic*, Jan. 14, 1937], MSB; *Michigan Manufacturer and Finanacial Record* 59 (Jan. 9, 1937): 8.

30. *DN*, Sept. 2, Nov. 13, 1938; Fine, *Murphy*, pp. 227–29; Interview with Norman H. Hill, Aug. 21, 1963, p. 8, MHC; Interview with Carl Rudow, Oct. 6, 1964, p. 2, MHC; Blair Moody to FM, May 22, 1937, EMB Papers; Haber to FM, Nov. 16, 1938, FM Papers.

31. L. G. Lenhardt to Moody, Nov. 10, 1936, Blair Moody Papers, MHC; JRH to Bishop Mosher, Dec. 26, 1936, JRH to George C. Dunham, Dec. 23, 1937, JRH Papers; FM to Hill, Dec. 7, 1936, FM to Hurja, Dec. 22, 1936, FM Papers; FM to EGK, Oct. 24, 1937, EGK-BHC, Box 8; *DN*, Dec. 17, 21, 1936, Jan. 1–3, 1937.

32. JRH to FM, Nov. 14, 20, 1936, Feb. 2, Sept. 30, Dec. 4, 8, 1937, Mar. 7, 1938, FM Papers; JRH to FM, Dec. 10, 17, 1937, Feb. 1, 1938, JRH Papers.

33. JRH to FM, Nov. 14, 1936, Feb. 2, 1937, FM Papers; *DN*, Apr. 23, 1937; Perkins, *Role of Governor*, p. 102.

34. *DN*, Jan. 1, 11, 1937; Dodge to FM, Jan. 2, 1937, James M. Landis to FM, Jan. 8, 1937, FM Papers.

35. JRH to FM, Sept. 28, 30, 1937, FM to Thomas Parran, Nov. 10, 1937, Parran to FM, Nov. 17, 1937, FM Papers; "Resolution . . . ," Dec. 28, 1937, ibid.; *DN*, Nov. 11, Dec. 21, 1937.

36. *DN*, Jan. 5, 10, Feb. 19, 20, 1937; Whiteley to FM, Jan. 5, 1939, and enclosed editorial, FM Papers; Jenkins to George G. Booth, Oct. 22, 1937, Jenkins Papers.

37. FM to Hill, Dec. 7, 1936, Brown to FM et al., May 13, 1937, Shields to FM, May 17, 1937, and enclosed Shields to Brown, May 17, 1937, EMB to Florence M. Strudley, May 20, 1937, FM Papers; *DN*, Apr. 27, May 20, 1937; Haber interview.

38. Interview with James K. Pollock, July 12, 1966, p. 15, MHC; Ransone, Jr., *Governor*, p. 388; *DT*, Feb. 27, 1937, cited in Penelope Helen Sawkins, "Executive Leadership of Frank Murphy as Governor of Michigan" (M.A. thesis, Wayne State University, 1950), p. 31; *DN*, Jan. 2, 31, Apr. 25, 1937; [*DT*, Mar. 2, 1937], MSB; JRH to Dunham, Dec. 23, 1937, JRH Papers; Mead to Martel, Jan. 16, 1939, Wayne

County AFL-CIO Papers, Box 8, ALHUA; Robert Lee Sawyer, Jr., *The Democratic State Central Committee in Michigan, 1949–1959* (Ann Arbor: University of Michigan, 1960), p. 185.

39. Fine, *Murphy*, pp. 231–32; [*DT*, Jan. 2, 1938], MSB; *DN*, Jan. 5, 1938; Macauley, Jr., to FM, Jan. 4, 1938, FM Papers; "Report of the 1938 Michigan State Fair," ibid.; Mrs. Stuart Fraser to FM [Mar. 10, 1938], EGK–BHC, Box 18.

40. V. O. Key, *American State Politics* (New York: Alfred A. Knopf, 1956), p. 216; Ransone, Jr., *Governor*, pp. 151, 223; Interview with G. Donald Kennedy, May 11, 1965, p. 19, MHC; Alice Smuts notes on interview with Murray D. Van Wagoner, May 1, 1969, in my possession; *DN*, Oct. 17, 1937; [*DT*, Aug. 12, 1938], MSB; Kennedy to FM, Nov. 21, 1936, Edward F. Thomas to FM, Nov. 24, 1936, and enclosed "Report," FM Papers. The one appointment was that of Charles Porritt, whom Murphy appointed to the Public Utilities Commission.

41. FM to Hill, Dec. 7, 1936, Hill to FM, Dec. 12, 1936, John Atkinson to FM, Dec. 27, 1937, Hill Memo for EGK, Dec. 30, 1937, FM Papers; FM to EGK, Dec. 21, 1937, EGK–BHC, Box 8; Rudow interview, p. 47; *DN*, Apr. 1, Dec. 21, 22, 24, 26, 1937, Jan. 6, 7, 1938.

42. Picard to Hurja, Jan. 6, 1937, Emil Hurja Papers, FDRL; *DN*, Aug. 14, 1938.

43. Cooley to Van Wagoner, Mar. 23, 1937, Murray D. Van Wagoner Papers, MHC; *DN*, Feb. 17, May 8, Aug. 11, 17, 18, 1938.

44. FM speech, Oct. 16, 1937, FM Papers; FM to Perry J. Breece, Jan. 14, 1938, FM Papers; *DN*, Oct. 17, 1937, Dec. 31, 1938; JRH to Dunham, Dec. 23, 1937, JRH Papers.

45. FM to Sherman McDonald, June 28, 1938, FM to Fry, June 30, 1938, FM Papers.

46. *DN*, Nov. 13, 29, Dec. 11, 27, 30, 1936, Jan. 3, 4, 30, Mar. 19, May 5, June 3, Aug. 5, 1937; FM to Hill, Dec. 7, 1936, Hill to E. J. Hanna, Dec. 16, 1936, FM Papers; *Report of the Civil Service Study Commission* (Lansing: n.p., 1936), pp. 42–44.

47. Shields to FM, Jan. 16, 1937, G. Hall Roosevelt to FM, June 28, 1937, Joseph Donnelly to FM, July 20, 1938, FM Papers; Minutes of Meeting Held in Flint, May 19, 1938, ibid.; Jenkins to Booth, Oct. 27, 1937, Jenkins Papers; *DN*, Oct. 10, Nov. 14, 1937; [*Saginaw News*, Mar. 26, 1938], MSB; [*Iron Mountain News*, June 7, 1938], MSB; Malcolm Hatfield to FDR, June 4, 1937, Hatfield to Lawrence Wood Robert, Jr., Nov. 26, 1938, OF 300 (Michigan), FDRL; Charles Cronenworth to JAF, Dec. 14, 1938, William J. Delaney to JAF, Dec. 15, 1938, Lonnie Henderson to JAF, Dec. 16, 1938, Charles E. Misner to JAF, Jan. 6, 1939, OF 300 (Election Forecasts and Analysis of Election Results, 1938; hereafter cited as 1938).

48. McDonald to Fry, June 9, 1938, Donnelly to FM, Jan. 23, 1939, Hatfield to FM, Apr. 7, 1939, FM Papers; Loren N. O'Brien to Editor [Nov. 1938], clipping in ibid.; E. W. Murphy to Hurja, Feb. 21, 1939, Hurja Papers; *DN*, June 9, 1938; Molle Franklin Gibney to JAF, Nov. 9, 1938, Giles Kavanagh to JAF, Dec. 12, 1938, Cronenworth to JAF, Dec. 14, 1938, Glen Greene to JAF, Dec. 23, 1938, Claude B. Root to JAF, Dec. 28, 1938, OF 300 (1938); Kennedy interview, p. 17.

49. Picard to Prentiss Brown, Feb. 3, 1939, Frank Picard Papers, MHC; Donnelly to FM, July 22, 1938, July 26, 1939, Picard to FM, Mar. 25, 1939, FM Papers;

Hatfield to Robert, Jr., Nov. 26, 1938, OF 300 (Michigan); Greene to JAF, Dec. 23, 1938, Martin R. Bradley to JAF, Dec. 23, 1938, OF 300 (1938); *DN*, July 3, 1938.

50. Gibney to JAF, Nov. 9, 1938, OF 300 (1938); Porter, "Governor Murphy's Star in the Ascendant," *NYT*, Feb. 21, 1937.

51. Fine, *Murphy*, pp. 95-97, 167, 178-83, 233-39 et passim; Moody to FM, Mar. 22, 1937, EMB Papers; Key, *Southern Politics in State and Nation* (New York: Random House, Vintage Books, 1949), pp. 307-10.

52. [*Detroit Tribune*, Jan. 16, 1937], MSB; [*Pittsburgh Courier*, Jan. 16, 1937], MSB; [*Guardian*, May 29, 1937], MSB; unidentified clipping in MSB; *Michigan Guide*, Nov. 5, 1938; *DN*, Apr. 30, May 22, 1937, Mar. 10, 1938; *United Automobile Worker*, Oct. 29, 1938; Mead to FM [Oct. 1937], FM Papers; F. J. Kolodziejski to GM, Feb. 12, 1938, GM Papers.

53. FM to Howell Van Auken, Feb. 10, 1937, Martel to FM, May 17, June 9, 1937, JRH to FM, Feb. 7, 1938, FM Papers; *DLN*, Dec. 31, 1937, Oct. 21, Nov. 4, 1938; Martel to Joseph Cummings, Sept. 29, 1938, Wayne County AFL-CIO Papers, Box 11.

54. *DN*, Dec. 15, 23, 1937, Lewis to FM, Jan. 19, 1938, FM to John J. O'Brien, Jan. 21, 1938, FM Papers.

55. Mrs. James H. McDonald to Dorothy McAllister, Aug. 24, 1937, Democratic Party, National Committee, Women's Division Papers (Michigan), FDRL; "Women Appointments Made by Governor Murphy," FM Papers; F. E. Levi to FM, Jan. 25, 1938, Lydia Levin to ———[1938], and enclosed "A Brief Outline...," John C. Cahalan to FM, May 26, 1938, FM to Cahalan, June 13, 1938, ibid.; John J. McGinty to JAF, Sept. 14, 1936, OF 300 (Farley Correspondence on Political Trends, 1936); *DN*, Sept. 29, 1936.

56. For examples of Murphy's welfare state ideas, see FM, *Message, Jan. 7, 1937*, FM Papers; FM speeches, Mar. 8, May 13, 1938, ibid.; FM, Guest Column for Federated Press, Jan. 5, 1938, ibid.; and *DN*, Nov. 14, 1937. For Murphy and black issues, see *DN*, May 5, 1937; *Public and Local Acts of the Legislature of ... Michigan ...1937* (Lansing: Franklin DeKleine Co., 1937), pp. 185-86; [*Detroit Tribune*, July 3, 1937], MSB; and *United Automobile Worker*, Oct. 29, 1938.

57. James L. Sundquist, *Dynamics of the Party System* (Washington: Brookings Institution, 1973), pp. 218-19, 239-43; John H. Fenton, *Midwest Politics* (New York: Holt, Rinehart and Winston, 1966), pp. 11-12; Sawyer, Jr., *State Central Committee*, pp. 5-9; Interview with Carl Muller, William Muller, and Martin S. Hayden, Dec. 9, 1964, pp. 47-48, MHC; Interview with G. Mennen Williams, Dec. 1964, pp. 1-2, 3-5, MHC.

58. Josiah L. Sayre, "Some Aspects of the Legislative Process in Michigan, 1925 to 1937" (Ph.D. diss., University of Michigan, 1938), p. 22; David O. Walter, "Reapportionment and Urban Representation," *Annals of the American Academy of Political and Social Science* 195 (Jan. 1938): 14; *Michigan Manual, 1937-38*, pp. 33-34, 166, 668-99; FM, *Message, Jan. 7, 1937*, p. 13, FM Papers. The state legislature had failed to meet its constitutional obligation to redraw electoral district lines to reflect the results of the 1930 census.

59. *Michigan Manual, 1937-38*, pp. 115-28, 668-99; *DN*, Dec. 20, 1936, Apr. 25, May 5, June 20, 1937, July 31, 1938. For Michigan as a whole in 1940, 11.7

percent of the labor force was engaged in agriculture, 38.4 percent in manufacturing, 16 percent in wholesale and retail trade, 6.9 percent in professional and related services, 5.5 percent in transportation, communication, and other public utilities, 6.9 percent in personal service, and 3 percent in government. Bureau of the Census, *Fifteenth Census: 1940, Population*, vol. 2, pt. 3, pp. 780–82. See Gordon E. Baker, *Rural versus Urban Power* (Garden City, N.Y.: Doubleday & Co., 1951), for the policy consequences of unbalanced representation in state legislatures.

60. *NYT*, Apr. 11, 1937; FM to Norris, Sept. 9, 1937, FM Memorandum to EGK, Dec. 17, 1937, FM Papers; Bromage to JRH, Feb. 10, 1938, EGK–BHC, Box 16; Fine, *Murphy*, pp. 427, 441, 448.

61. Sayre, "Legislative Process," pp. 25, 101; Hill to FM, Dec. 12, 1936, FM Papers; EGK to FM, Jan. 26, Mar. 31, 1937, EGK–BHC, Box 8; William P. Lovett to Pollock, Feb. 19, 1937, Civil Service Study Commission Papers, MHC; *DN*, Dec. 8, 10, 20, 1936, Jan. 8, 9, Feb. 3, July 8, Nov. 7, 1937.

62. Perkins, *Role of Governor*, p. 155; *DN*, June 26, 27, 1937, July 20, 1949; FM, "First Quarterly Accounting," July 10, 1937, MSB; William L. Stidger to FM, July 28, 1937, FM Papers; Ransone, Jr., *Governor*, pp. 211–12.

63. Ransone, Jr., *Governor*, p. 116; FM to George W. Trendle, Sept. 3, 1937, FM Memorandum to Hill, Dec. 15, 1937, S. L. A. Marshall to R. E. Thomason, Jan. 5, 1939, FM Papers; Jenkins to Joseph A. Mulcahy, Sept. 5, 1939, Jenkins Papers; Interview with Jack Manning, Dec. 4, 1964, p. 16, MHC; W. Muller interview, p. 9; Interview with Charles J. Hedetniemi, Oct. 20, 1964, p. 16, MHC; Marvin J. Petroelje and Richard T. Ortquist, Jr., interview with Joseph H. Creighton, undated, pp. 18, 30–31, MHC.

64. Glenn E. Brooks, *When Governors Convene: The Governors' Conference and National Politics* (Baltimore: Johns Hopkins Press, 1961), pp. 27–36.

65. JRH to FM, Nov. 20, 1936, Hedetniemi to FM, Nov. 24, 1936, FM Papers; Hedetniemi interview, pp. 1–6; *DN*, Jan. 31, 1937.

66. *St. Louis Post-Dispatch*, Jan. 23, 1938, clipping in FM Papers; *DN*, Feb. 28, 1937; Hedetniemi interview, p. 4; Hill interview, p. 8; Hayden interview, p. 2; Interview with Hilmer Gellein, Aug. 21, 1963, p. 18, MHC; Pollock, "Notes on FM...," p. 3, James K. Pollock Papers, MHC; Fine, *Murphy*, p. 241.

67. *DN*, Dec. 27, 1936, Jan. 29, Feb. 28, 1937; *St. Louis Post-Dispatch*, Jan. 23, 1938, clipping in FM Papers; FM to Bruce Anderson, May 23, 1938, FM to Robert S. Shaw, May 19, June 29, Dec. 28, 1938, Shaw to FM, June 3, 1938, FM Papers; FM to Shaw, Nov. 10, 1938, FM to John A. Hannah, Oct. 18, 1939, EMB Papers.

68. [*Los Angeles Herald Express*, Aug. 16, 1937], MSB; [*DT*, Aug. 31, 1937], MSB; [*DFP*, Sept. 1, 1937], MSB; *DN*, Aug. 31, Sept. 1, 2, 21, 1937; FM to Mrs. Murad Saleeby, Aug. 31, 1937, FM to Manuel L. Quezon, Sept. 5, 1937, FM to Charles Chaplin, Sept. 5, 1937, FM to Dunham, Sept. 28, 1937, FM to Kennedy, Oct. 25, 1937, FM to Julian A. Wolfson, Jan. 19, 1938, FM Papers; University of Michigan Hospital Receipt, Jan. 9, 1939, ibid.; GM to O'Brien, Sept. 9, 1937, GM Papers; Jenkins to Booth, Oct. 22, 1937, Jenkins Papers; JRH to Dunham, Dec. 23, 1937, JHR to James R. Fugate, Mar. 31, 1938, JRH Papers; Creighton interview, pp. 20–21; Jenkins to Michael A. Gorman, Mar. 12, 1938, Michael Gorman Papers, MHC.

69. FM to Clarence Lehr, May 27, 1937, FM to Wolfson, Jan. 19, 1938, FM Papers; *St. Louis Post-Dispatch*, Jan. 23, 1938, clipping in ibid.

70. Harding to FM, July 17, Nov. 3, 1936, Kennedy to FM, May 18, 1937, FM Papers; interview with Harry Mead, Aug. 15, 1963, pp. 30-32, MHC; Interview with Sharon Keyes, July 30, 1964, pp. 22-23, MHC; [*DT*, May 25, 1937], MSB; Interview with Albert K. Steigerwalt, Jr., Aug. 4, 1976.

71. HSB No. 2, p. 175; FM to F. Parker, Dec. 12, 1936, A. Parker to FM [Oct. 1937], [Dec. 1937], FM Papers; *DN*, July 24, 1938. See the typed statement announcing the marriage of Ann Parker and FM [Jan. 1943?], in FM Papers.

72. FM to Ann Walker, July 28, 1936, FM to LeRoy Pelletier, Jan. 3, 1937 [1938], FM Papers; Kavanagh notes [1951], Josephine Gomon Papers, MHC; *DN*, Dec. 27, 1936; *St. Francis Chronicle*, Mar. 18, 1937, MSB; *St. Louis Post-Dispatch*, Jan. 23, 1938, clipping in FM Papers; copy of FM's income tax return for 1937, EMB Papers. The FM and the MM Papers for 1937 and 1938 document Murphy's stock transactions.

73. Creighton interview, pp. 21-22; Hayden interview, pp. 24-25; Krock, *Memoirs* (New York: Funk and Wagnalls, 1968), pp. 353-54.

74. Stanley High, *Roosevelt—And Then?* (New York: Harper and Brothers, 1937), p. 320; FM to Edward Mooney, June 2, 1937, FM to Hedetniemi, Jan. 26, 1938, FM to Francis B. Sayre, Apr. 27, 1938, Arthur D. Maguire to Editor of *America*, Jan. 17, 1939, Maguire to Mooney, Jan. 17, 1939, FM to Theophane Maguire, Feb. 21, 1939, FM Papers; [Francis M. Donahue], "Interview" with FM, undated, ibid.; FM speech, Oct. 9, 1938, ibid.; Donahue, "Michigan's Murphy," *St. Anthony's Messenger*, Apr. 1938, p. 661, MSB; *Selected Addresses of Frank Murphy . . . , January 1, 1937, to September 30, 1938* (Lansing: n.p., 1938), pp. 42, 73-74; FM, "Politics," *Christian Front* 4 (Mar. 1939): 38-39; Leona Garrity to Sidney Fine, Apr. 1, 1977.

75. Creighton, "Frank Murphy—Off the Record," Part Two (Aug. 1938), p. 29, FM Papers; *Boston Sunday Globe*, Feb. 7, 1937, MSB; *Detroit Saturday Night*, Aug. 7, 1937; "Murphy of Michigan," *Literary Digest* 124 (Aug. 14, 1937): 7; *DN*, Nov. 4, 1936; [*Grand Rapids Times*, Jan. 22, 1937], MSB; Porter, "Murphy's Star"; *The Secret Diary of Harold L. Ickes*, 3 vols. (New York: Simon and Schuster, 1953-1954), 2:181, 372; "The Labor Governors," *Fortune* 15 (June 1937): 81; Mead to FM, Apr. 30, 1937, FM Papers; *St. Louis Post-Dispatch*, Jan. 27, 1938, clipping in ibid.; [*Milwaukee Journal*, Oct. 26, 1938], MSB; [*DT*, Jan. 12, 1939], MSB.

76. *Detroit Saturday Night*, Aug. 7, 1937; High, *Roosevelt*, p. 320; Interview with Arthur Krock, May 22, 1969; *News-Week* 9 (Feb. 20, 1937): 13; Williams interview, p. 15; Pollock interview, p. 17; C. Muller interview, p. 5; Hayden interview, p. 7; "Labor Governors," pp. 79-80, 81; Lasswell, *Power and Personality* (New York: W. W. Norton and Co., 1948), pp. 137-38.

77. *DN*, Dec. 25, 1938.

CHAPTER 8

1. This chapter is largely adapted from Sidney Fine, *Sit-Down: The General Motors Strike of 1936-1937* (Ann Arbor: University of Michigan Press, 1969). Although a few manuscript and published sources containing information on the

strike have become available since 1969, they do not, in my judgment, alter in any fundamental way the account of the strike presented in *Sit-Down*. The Reminiscences of Frances Perkins, 1955, Book 6, Oral History Research Office, Columbia University, New York, New York, include an interesting section on the strike that describes the secretary of labor's efforts to mediate the dispute. The account of the strike in George Martin, *Madam Secretary* (Boston: Houghton Mifflin Co., 1976), is largely based on the Perkins oral history. The principal item pertaining to the strike in the Heber Blankenhorn Papers, ALHUA, is a fascinating document prepared by Blankenhorn on the basis of a conversation with John L. Lewis on February 25, 1937, in which Lewis analyzes the negotiations that led to the settlement of the strike. I have reproduced the document in "John L. Lewis Discusses the General Motors Sit-Down Strike: A Document," *Labor History* 15 (Fall 1974): 563–70.

The Maurice Sugar Papers, ALHUA, are disappointing insofar as the GM strike is concerned, but there are a few important items in the Edward G. Kemp Papers, Burton Historical Collection, Detroit, Michigan. Roger Roy Keeran somewhat exaggerates the admittedly important role of communists in the strike in "Communists and Auto Workers: The Struggle for a Union, 1919–1941" (Ph.D. diss., University of Wisconsin, 1974). There are some observations on the strike by Len DeCaux in *Labor Radical* (Boston: Beacon Press, 1970), but Wyndham Mortimer, *Organize!*, ed. Leo Fenster (Boston: Beacon Press, 1971), adds nothing of substance to the Mortimer oral history transcripts in the MHC. Melvyn Dubofsky and Warren Van Tine, *John L. Lewis* (New York: Quadrangle/New York Times Book Co., 1977), does not differ from *Sit-Down* in its account of the strike.

2. Fine, *Sit-Down*, pp. 16, 19, 21–22.

3. Ibid., pp. 30–50.

4. Ibid., pp. 50–51.

5. Sidney Fine, *The Automobile under the Blue Eagle* (Ann Arbor: University of Michigan Press, 1963), pp. 416–17.

6. Fine, *Sit-Down*, pp. 94–96.

7. Ibid., pp. 96–98.

8. Ibid., pp. 100, 105, 107.

9. Ibid., pp. 107–8.

10. Ibid., pp. 91–93, 95, 108–19; Mortimer, *Organize!*, p. 104.

11. Fine, *Sit-Down*, pp. 120–22.

12. Ibid., pp. 122–23; Murphy speech, Oct. 21, 1938, FM Papers.

13. *Daily Worker*, Dec. 21, 1936; UAW General Executive Board (GEB) Minutes, Nov. 30, Dec. 1–2, 4–5, Henry Kraus Papers, Box 7, ALHUA; Adolph Germer Diary, Nov. 22, 28, Dec. 1, 4, 1936, Adolph Germer Papers, State Historical Society of Wisconsin, Madison, Wisconsin; Germer to John L. Lewis, Nov. 30, 1936, Germer to Philip Murray, Nov. 30, 1936, ibid.; Germer to Brophy, Dec. 5, 1936, CIO File (notes on this file were made available to me by Irving Bernstein); Oral History Interview of Wyndham Mortimer, June 20, 1960, pp. 27, 34–35, MHC; Henry Kraus, *The Many and the Few* (Los Angeles: Plantin Press, 1947), p. 73; Fine, *Sit-Down*, pp. 27, 73, 133–39, 266.

14. Brophy to Germer, Dec. 19, 1936, Germer Papers; *Proceedings of the Fifth Annual Convention of the ... United Automobile Workers ... 1940* (n.p., n.d.), p. 104.

15. Martin to Knudsen, Dec. 21, 1936 (telegram and letter), Martin to Alfred P. Sloan, Jr., and Knudsen, Dec. 24, 1936, Knudsen to Martin, Dec. 31, 1936, GM, Labor Relations Diary, Appendix Documents to Accompany Section 1, Docs. 62-64, GM Building, Detroit, Michigan; *DN*, Dec. 23, 24, 1936; *NYT*, Dec. 23-25, 1936; Fine, *Sit-Down*, pp. 141-46, 305-6.

16. Fine, *Blue Eagle*, pp. 263-67, 381-403; H. B. [Heber Blankenhorn] Personal Note, Feb. 25, 1937, "Settlement of General Motors Strike, February, 10 [11]," Heber Blankenhorn Papers, Box 1, ALHUA; *NYT*, Jan. 2, 1937; *DN*, Jan. 4, 1937; *Flint Journal*, Jan. 19, 1937; Frank N. Trager, "Autos...," Jan. 11, 1937, Norman Thomas Papers, New York Public Library, New York, New York; Lorin Lee Cary, "Adolph Germer: From Labor Agitator to Labor Professional" (Ph.D. diss., University of Wisconsin, 1968), pp. 109-10, 227-28n.

17. Martin to Sloan, Jr., and Knudsen, Jan. 4, 1937, Kraus Papers, Box 9; *Flint Auto Worker*, Jan. 5, 1937; *DN*, Jan. 4, 1937.

18. Hartley W. Barclay to Harry W. Anderson, Jan. 20, 1937, and enclosed Memorandum, FM Papers; Harry Weiss, "What Caused the G.M. Strike?" *New Masses* 22 (Feb. 23, 1937): 11; Porter, "Speed, Speed...," *NYT*, Jan. 31, 1937; *News-Week* 9(Feb. 20, 1937): 14-15; Department of Research and Education, Federal Council of the Churches of Christ, *Information Service*, Feb. 6, 1937; *Flint Auto Worker*, Nov. 1936; "Why Did the Auto Workers Strike?" *Social Action* 3 (Feb. 15, 1937): 11; Oral History Interview of Jack Palmer, July 23, 1960, p. 9, MHC; Interview with Joe Devitt, July 14, 1966, pp. 3-4, MHC; Interview with Roy Reuther, July 12, 1966, pp. 20-21, MHC; *NYT*, Jan. 24, Feb. 1, 1937; Porter, "Assembly Lines Hum," *NYT*, Feb. 28, 1937; UAW Releases, Jan. 7, 16, 1937, Edward Levinson Papers, Box 4, ALHUA; *DN*, Jan. 13, 23, 1937; *Flint Journal*, Jan. 6, 1937.

19. *NYT*, Jan. 1, 1937; Sloan, Jr., to All Employes..., Jan. 5, 1937, Kraus Papers, Box 9; Minutes of the Meeting of the Executive Council, AFL, Feb. 10, 1937, pp. 43, 45-47, 49-51, 55-56; copy of John Frey telegram [Jan. 9, 1937], GM, Labor Relations Diary, Appendix Doc. 73.

20. *Flint Journal*, Jan. 3-5, 1937; *DN*, Jan. 3, 5, 7, 1937; *NYT*, Jan. 3, 6, 1937; Germer Diary, Jan. 3, 5, 1937, Germer Papers; Roy E. Brownell to H. W. Arant, Feb. 3, 1937, Edward D. Black Papers, MHC.

21. Blankenhorn to J. Warren Madden, Jan. 6, 1937, Blankenhorn Papers, Box 1; Perkins Reminiscences, Book 6, pp. 135-41, 144-45; *DN*, Jan. 31, Feb. 9, 1937; "Mr. Lewis and the Auto Strike," *New Republic* 89 (Feb. 3, 1937): 398; FDR to Samuel I. Rosenman, Nov. 13, 1940, PPF 64, FDRL.

22. *New York Post*, Jan. 16, 1937, MSB; Porter, "Governor Murphy's Star in the Ascendant," *NYT*, Feb. 21, 1937; *NYT*, Feb. 12, 1937; Interview with Wyndham Mortimer, Dec. 9, 1964, p. 35, MHC; Interview with IM, July 30, 1964, p. 35, MHC.

23. [*MT*, July 13, 1933], MSB; *Flint Journal*, Jan. 19, 1937; *DN*, Jan. 4, Feb. 11, 1937; *NYT*, Feb. 12, 1937; Porter, "Murphy's Star"; *Liberty*, Feb. 25, 1937, p. 7; Interview with Norman H. Hill, Aug. 21, 1963, p. 22, MHC; FM to JRH, Apr. 8, 1937, FM to Stuart H. Perry, June 1, 1938, FM Papers.

24. *DN*, Dec. 20, 1936; Merlin Wiley, "Was the Sit-Down Strike a Crime in

Michigan?'' *Michigan State Bar Journal* 19 (Feb. 1940): 66, 68–69, 85; William L. Brunner to Duncan McRea [Mar. 1937], Samuel D. Pepper Papers (privately held).

25. Kemp Memorandum to FM, Jan. 27, 1937, FM Papers.

26. Perkins Reminiscences, p. 128; FM to Warren E. Kelley, Apr. 2, 1937, FM to George O. Hackett, June 18, 1937, FM Papers; FM, ''First Quarterly Accounting,'' July 10, 1937, MSB; *NYT*, Jan. 29, Feb. 12, 1937; [*Catholic Worker,* Oct. 1937], MSB; *Cleveland Plain Dealer* [Feb. 12, 1937], MSB.

27. Perkins Reminiscences, p. 121; Norman Beasley, *Knudsen* (New York: Whittlesey House, 1947), pp. 166–69; FM to Mark Sullivan, Jan. 4, 1939, FM Papers; [*Charlotte Republican-Tribune*, Apr. 16, 1937], clipping in ibid.; John L. Lovett speech [Apr. 1937], p. 6, ibid.; Joseph H. Creighton Memorandum to FM, May 11, 1938, ibid.; FM speech, Oct. 21, 1938, ibid.; Hill interview, pp. 22–23; *NYT*, Jan. 30, Feb. 9, 1937.

28. *NYT*, Jan. 14, Feb. 1, 1937; FM to James Bryant, Sept. 28, 1937, FM to P.H. Callahan, May 25, 1937, FM Papers; FM, ''First Quarterly Accounting,'' July 10, 1937, MSB; Oral History Interview of Stanley Brahms, Nov. 23, 1959, p. 25, MHC; Local 156 Release, Feb. 8, 1937, Joe Brown Collection, ALHUA; Pontiac notes [Jan. 1937], Kraus Papers, Box 10; Joel Seidman, ''*Sit-Down*'' (New York: League for Industrial Democracy, 1937), p. 30; *Auto Worker,* Jan. 12, 1937; Leon Green, ''The Case for the Sit-Down Strike,'' *New Republic* 90 (Mar. 24, 1937): 199–201.

29. FM, ''Politics and the Laborer'' ([1911]), pp. 1–2, FM Papers; *DLN*, Sept. 11, Dec. 25, 1936; *DN*, Oct. 21, 1936; FM to Germer, Mar. 24, 1938, Germer Papers; Sugar notes [1940s], Sugar Papers, Box 3.

30. H. B. Personal Note, Feb. 25, 1937, Blankenhorn Papers, Box 1; JRH to Frank Parker, Jan. 21, 1937, JRH Papers; JRH to FM, Feb. 26, 1937, FM Papers.

31. Hayden, Stone and Co. to FM, Oct. 3, 5, 1936, EMB to EGK [Dec. 31, 1936], FM Papers; copy of FM's 1936 income tax return, ibid.; J. E. Swan to Margaret [Marguerite] Teahan, Dec. 29, 1937, Feb. 16, 1939, MM Papers; *NYT*, Jan. 1, 1937; Fine, *Sit-Down*, p. 372n.

32. *NYT*, Jan. 3–10, 1937; *DN*, Jan. 4–10, 1937; Germer Diary, Jan. 4, 6–9, 1937, Germer Papers; ''Following information from James F. Dewey to Hugh L. Kerwin,'' Jan. 7, 1937, File 182-2067-A, Records of the Federal Mediation and Conciliation Service, Record Group 280, NARS; draft of agreement, Jan. 7, 1937, FM Papers; Knudsen to FM, Jan. 8, 1937, ibid.; FM notes, Jan. 8, 1937, ibid.; GM Release, Jan. 9, 1937, Levinson Papers, Box 4.

33. *DN*, Jan. 11, 16, Feb. 12, Mar. 12, 1937; [*DT*, Jan. 11, 1937], MSB; *Flint Journal*, Jan. 17, Feb. 9, 11, 1937; Kraus, *Many and Few*, pp. 171–72; George F. Granger and Lawrence R. Klein, *Emergency Relief in Michigan, 1933–1939* (Lansing: n.p., 1939), pp. 134, 138, 172. The UAW welfare committee ungenerously accused SEWRC, despite the aid it provided, of being ''the 'tool of General Motors.' '' Ella Lee Cogwill to Haber, Feb. 11, 1937, EGK-BHC, Box 20.

34. For an account of the Battle of the Running Bulls, see Fine, *Sit-Down*, pp. 1–8, 11–12. The quotation is from Barbara Willson to Josephine Gomon [1951], Josephine Gomon Papers, MHC.

35. Typed notes, Jan. 11, 12, 1937, FM Papers; John S. Bersey to FM, Jan. 12, 1937, Hill to FM, Jan. 12, 1937, Bradshaw and Wolcott to FM, Jan. 12, 1937, FM

Papers; "E. Kemp narrative" [Jan. 13, 1939], ibid.; Germer Diary, Jan. 12, 1937, Germer Papers; *DN*, Jan. 12, 13, 1937; House Special Committee on Un-American Activities, *Investigation of Un-American Propaganda Activities in the United States, Hearings...*, 75 Cong., 3 sess., 4 vols. (Washington: U.S. Government Printing Office, 1938), 2:1686–87 (hereafter cited as *Dies Hearings*).

36. *DN*, Jan. 12–14, 1937; *NYT*, Jan. 13, 1937; Kraus, *Many and Few*, p. 141; Marie Hempel to Roger N. Baldwin, Jan. 20, 1937, American Civil Liberties Union (ACLU) Archives, vol. 1046, Princeton University, Princeton, New Jersey. My italics.

37. Hill to FM, Jan. 12, 1937, FM Papers; *DN*, Jan. 13, 17, 21, 1937; *NYT*, Jan. 14, 1937.

38. Hempel to Baldwin, Jan. 20, 1937, ACLU Archives, vol. 1046; Bersey to Commanding Officer, Jan. 12, 1937, Records of the Michigan Military Establishment Relating to the Flint Sit-Down Strike, 1937, microfilm copy in MHC (hereafter cited as National Guard Records); "Michigan National Guard Bulletin No. 1," Jan. 19, 1937, ibid.; Kemp to FM, Jan. 27, 1937, EGK-BHC, Box 8; Western Union Press Message, Jan. 13, 1937, Levinson Papers, Box 4; *DN*, Feb. 3, 1937; Fine, *Sit-Down*, pp. 243–44.

39. FM to Knudsen and Martin, Jan. 12, 1937, Martin to FM, Jan. 13, 1937, Knudsen to FM, Jan. 13, 1937, FM Papers; FM notes, Jan. 12–15, 1937, ibid.; FM speech, Jan. 14, 1937, ibid.; Germer Diary, Jan. 14, 1937, Germer Papers; *NYT*, Jan. 15, 1937.

40. *DN*, Jan. 15, 1937; *NYT*, Jan. 16, 1937; Knudsen, Brown, and Smith to FM, Jan. 15, 1937, FM Papers; John Brophy, "The Struggle for an Auto Union," undated, pp. 10–11, John Brophy Papers, Catholic University, Washington, D.C.; idem, *A Miner's Life*, ed. and supplemented by John O. P. Hall (Madison: University of Wisconsin Press, 1964), pp. 269–70.

41. *Flint Journal*, Jan. 16, 17, 1937; Hutchinson to FM, Jan. 16, 1937, FM Papers; *DN*, Jan. 16, 1937; *Battle Creek Enquirer and Evening News*, Jan. 17, 1937, MSB.

42. For the origins of the Flint Alliance, see Fine, *Sit-Down*, pp. 187–90.

43. *NYT*, Jan. 16–19, 24, 1937; *DN*, Jan. 17, 18, 1937; *Flint Journal*, Jan. 17, 18, 1937; GM Releases, Jan. 17, 18, 1937, Levinson Papers, Box 4; UAW Release, Jan. 17, 1937, ibid.; Brophy, *Miner's Life*, p. 270; *Daily Worker*, Jan. 19, 1937; Kraus, *Many and Few*, pp. 161–65; Mortimer interview, Dec. 9, 1964, pp. 6–7; William H. Lawrence to Sidney Fine, May 1, 1967; Brophy, "Struggle for Auto Union," pp. 12–13, Brophy Papers; AFL Executive Council Minutes, Feb. 10, 1937, p. 57.

44. Perkins Reminiscences, pp. 173–94; Perkins Memorandum to the President, Jan. 19, 1937, PSF, Department of Labor, FDRL; "General Motors Situation," undated, File 182-2067-A, RG 280; *DN*, Jan. 22, 23, 1937; *Flint Journal*, Jan. 21, 1937.

45. Perkins Memorandum, Jan. 19, 1937, PSF, Department of Labor; *NYT*, Jan. 20, 24, 1937; *DN*, Jan. 23, 24, 1937; FM to William Lovett, Jan. 25, 1937, Detroit Citizens League Papers, Candidate Files, Box 23, Burton Historical Collection.

46. *DN*, Jan. 22, 1937; Press Conference No. 338, pp. 99–100, FDRL.

47. Perkins Reminiscences, pp. 201–6, 211–13; *DN*, Jan. 24, 27, 30, 31, 1937; *NYT*, Jan. 26, 27, 30, 31, 1937; *Flint Journal*, Jan. 27, 1937; Press Conference No.

339, pp. 106–7, FDRL; Brophy, "Struggle for Auto Union," p. 15, Brophy Papers; GM Releases, Jan. 25, [30], 1937, Levinson Papers, Box 4.

48. Fine, *Sit-Down*, pp. 260–64.

49. Germer Diary, Jan. 31, 1937, Germer Papers; Brophy, "Struggle for Auto Union," p. 16, Brophy Papers; Mortimer interview, Dec. 9, 1964, p. 10; William Weinstone, "The Great Auto Strike," *Communist* 16 (Mar. 1937): 217–18; Kraus, *Many and Few*, pp. 189–90; *NYT*, Feb. 2, 1937; *United Automobile Worker*, Feb. 25, 1937; *Socialist Call*, Feb. 13, 1937; Paul Gallico, "Sit-Down Strike," *Cosmopolitan* 104 (Apr. 1938): [176].

50. See Fine, *Sit-Down*, pp. 266–71, for an account of the seizure of Chevrolet No. 4.

51. Edwin Chapman to Dear Liz and all, Feb. 3, 1937, Kraus Papers, Box 9.

52. Strike Chronology, Feb. 1, 1937, FM Papers; Wolcott to FM, Feb. 1, 1937 (letter and telegram), FM Executive Order to Bersey, Feb. 1, 1937, ibid.; John H. Steck to Joseph H. Lewis, Feb. 20, 1937, National Guard Records; G-3 Report for Feb. 1, 1937, ibid.; 63rd Brigade S-3 Report, Feb. 2, 1937, ibid.; 63rd Brigade Field Order No. 1, Feb. 2, 1937, ibid.; G-1 Reports, Feb. 1–7, 1937, ibid.; *NYT*, Feb. 2, 3, 1937; *DN*, Feb. 2, 1937; *Flint Journal*, Feb. 3, 1937.

53. Frances Perkins, *The Roosevelt I Knew* (New York: Viking Press, 1946), pp. 322–23; Perkins Reminiscences, p. 149; Brophy, "Struggle for Auto Union," pp. 18–19, Brophy Papers; Brophy Diary, Feb. 2, 1937, ibid.; Strike Chronology, Feb. 2, 1937, FM Papers; Kraus, *Many and Few*, pp. 222–26; Local 156 Release, Feb. 2, 1937, Kraus Papers, Box 9; UAW Release, Feb. 2, 1937, ibid.; Official Strike Bulletin No. 10, Brown Collection; G-3 Report for Feb. 2, 1937, National Guard Records.

54. Strike Chronology, Feb. 2, 1937, FM Papers.

55. Strike Chronology, Feb. 1, 1937, ibid.; Gadola opinion, Feb. 2, 1937, Kraus Papers, Box 9; *Flint Journal*, Feb. 1–3, 1937; *DN*, Feb. 2, 1937; *NYT*, Feb. 3, 1937; *Daily Worker*, Feb. 8, 1937.

56. G-3 Report for Feb. 2, 1937, National Guard Records; *DN*, Feb. 3, 1937; *Flint Journal*, Feb. 3, 1937; *NYT*, Feb. 3, 1937; Mortimer interview, Dec. 9, 1964, p. 29, MHC; Interview with Larry S. Davidow, May 12, 1967, p. 2 (first draft), MHC; Kraus, *Many and Few*, pp. 232–33; Fisher No. 1 Sit-In Employes to FM, Feb. 3, 1937, Stay In Strikers of the Fisher Body Plant No. 2 to FM, Feb. 3, 1937, FM Papers; Brophy Diary, Feb. 2, 1937, Brophy Papers.

57. Brophy, "Struggle for Auto Union," pp. 20–21, Brophy Papers; O. H. Walburn to Robert Wohlforth, Feb. 3, 1937, Sen 78, F 9, La Follette Committee Papers, Box 124, Records of the United States Senate, RG 46, NARS; H. A. Hudgins to Editors, *Michigan Christian Advocate*, Feb. 24, 1937, William H. Phelps Papers, MHC; W. S. Needham and Purlett Hinckley to Lawrence Lyon, Feb. 3, 1937, State Police File 5977, Michigan State Police Records, Lansing, Michigan; State Police Daily Log, Feb. 3, 1937, ibid.; G-2 Journal, Feb. 3, 1937, National Guard Records; *DT*, Feb. 4, 1937, Brown Scrapbooks, Brown Collection; *DN*, Feb. 4, 1937; *NYT*, Feb. 4, 1937; *Flint Journal*, Feb. 4, 1937; *Flint Auto Worker*, Feb. 3, 1937; Germer Diary, Feb. 3, 1937, Germer Papers.

58. *NYT*, Feb. 4, 1937; *DT*, Feb. 4, 1937, Brown Scrapbooks; State Police Daily Log, Feb. 3, 1937, File 5977, State Police Records; Harold Mulbar to Olander, undated, ibid.; *Dies Hearings*, 2:1687–88; Barringer to FDR, Oct. 27, 1938, OF 320, FDRL; *DN*, Feb. 4, 1937; *Flint Journal*, Feb. 4, 1937; *Flint City Proceedings* 5 (Feb. 6, 1937): 2109; Interview with Colin J. MacDonald, May 15, 1967.

59. *Flint Journal*, Feb. 4, 1937; *DN*, Feb. 4, 1937; *NYT*, Feb. 4, 1937; *DT*, Feb. 4, 1937, Brown Scrapbooks; *Dies Hearings*, 2:1689; Vern C. Snell to Lyon, Feb. 4, 1937, File 5977, State Police Records; Mulbar to Olander, undated, ibid.; [*Detroit Legal Record*], Apr. 8, 1937, MSB; MacDonald interview; "Phone Call from . . . [Wolcott]," Oct. 23, 1938, FM Papers; undated text of agreement, National Guard Records.

60. Strike Chronology, Feb. 2, 1937, FM Papers; FM to Knudsen, Feb. 2, 1937, Knudsen to FM, Feb. 2, 1937, ibid.; Donaldson Brown, *Some Reminiscences of an Industrialist* (Privately printed [1957]), pp. 95–98; Alfred P. Sloan, Jr., *My Years with General Motors*, ed. John McDonald with Catherine Stevens (Garden City, N.Y.: Doubleday & Co., 1964), p. 393; *NYT*, Feb. 3, 1937.

61. *Flint Journal*, Feb. 9, 1937; *DN*, Feb. 6, 11, 1937; Saul Alinsky, *John L. Lewis* (New York: G. P. Putnam's Sons, 1949), pp. 136–37; Kraus, *Many and Few*, pp. 264–65; *Iron Age* 139 (Feb. 25, 1937): 57; UAW Release, Feb. 9, 1937, Kraus Papers, Box 9; Mortimer interview, Dec. 9, 1964, pp. 12–13.

62. Proposals of UAW, Feb. 4, 1937, FM Papers; typed sheet, Feb. 4, 1937, ibid.; GM to FM, Feb. 5, 1937, ibid.; Proposal for General Motors-Lewis Agreement [Feb. 5, 1937], PSF, Department of Labor; *NYT*, Feb. 10, 1937.

63. Strike Chronology, Feb. 5, 1937, FM Papers; Perkins Reminiscences, pp. 111, 142; Memorandum for the President, Feb. 5, 1937, PSF, Department of Labor; Memorandum for the President's Conversation with . . . Lewis and with Knudsen and Brown, Feb. 5, 1937, ibid. The latter document contains Perkins's handwritten note, "get exclusive agreement for 2 months."

64. Strike Chronology, Feb. 5, 8, 1937, FM Papers; GM to FM, Feb. 6, 1937, ibid.; FM statement, Feb. 6, 1937, ibid.; Perkins Memorandum for the President, Feb. 8, 1937, OF 407-B, FDRL; *NYT*, Feb. 7, 1937; *DN*, Feb. 9, 1937; Alinsky, *Lewis*, pp. 133–34; The Reminiscences of Lee Pressman, 1958, p. 73, Oral History Research Office; Mortimer interview, June 20, 1960, pp. 41–42.

65. Strike Chronology, Feb. 8, 1937, and enclosed pencil notes, FM Papers; Beasley, *Knudsen*, p. 169; Roper Memorandum for McIntyre, Feb. 10, 1937, OF 407-B.

66. *DN*, Feb. 5, 8, 1937; *NYT*, Feb. 3, 9, 10, 1937; GM Statement, Feb. 8, 1937, Brown Collection; Lewis Press Conference, Feb. 8, 1937, Kraus Papers, Box 9; Alinsky, *Lewis*, p. 138; Strike Chronology, Feb. 2, 1937, FM Papers; GM to FM, Feb. 9, 1937, FM Papers; Subcommittee of the Senate Committee on the Judiciary, *Nomination of Frank Murphy*, 76 Cong., 1 sess. (Washington: U.S. Government Printing Office, 1939), pp. 9–10; E. J. Parker Affidavit, Feb. 4, 1937, National Guard Records; Gadola Court Order, Feb. 5, 1937, ibid.

67. Wolcott to FM, Feb. 5, 1937, and FM note on same, EGK-BHC, Box 10; Strike Chronology, Feb. 5, 1937, FM Papers; Minutes of a Meeting Held in Flint, May 19, 1938, ibid.; Wolcott to FM, Aug. 17, 1938, FM to Hill, Jan. 23, 1939, ibid.;

Statement by Wolcott, Oct. 21, 1938, ibid.; *Nomination of Murphy*, p. 10; *DN*, Feb. 6, 7, 1937; *NYT*, Feb. 7, 1937.

68. On this point, see Fine, *Sit-Down*, pp. 295-96, 405-6n; and H. B. Personal Note, Feb. 25, 1937, Blankenhorn Papers, Box 1.

69. Strike Chronology, Feb. 5, 8, 1937, FM Papers; typed sheet, Oct. 22, 1938, ibid.; FM to Florence H. Mann, July 17, 1937, FM to Garner, Dec. 28, 1938, FM to Josiah W. Bailey, Jan. 19, 1939, ibid.; *Nomination of Murphy*, pp. 3-4, 10; *NYT*, Feb. 6, 1937; Interview with Mrs. Fielding H. Yost, Oct. 28, 1963, p. 6, MHC.

70. Interview with Martin S. Hayden, Oct. 6, 1964, p. 45, MHC; Wolburn to Wohlforth, Feb. 3, 1937, La Follette Committee Papers, Box 124, RG 46; [L. G. Lenhardt], "It Can Happen Here," Mar. 9, 1937, Blair Moody Papers, MHC; EGK to FM, Aug. 9, 1937, EGK-BHC, Box 8.

71. Copy of clipping from Port Huron newspaper, Mar. 18, 1937, FM Papers; Pepper to Starr, Mar. 22, 1937, Pepper to FM, Dec. 23, 1938, Pepper to EGK, Jan. 12, 1939, ibid.; John H. Steck to Joseph Lewis, Feb. 5, 1937, Pepper to Lewis, Feb. 20, 1937, Steck Memorandum to Lewis, undated, National Guard Records; Steck to Pepper, Mar. 11, 1937, Pepper Papers; Minutes of Fisher Body No. 1 Strike Committee, Jan. 25, 1937, and Kraus notes on same, Harry Van Nocker Notebook, Kraus Papers, Box 9; Devitt interview, p. 27. Cf. Interview with Robert C. Travis, Dec. 10, 1964, pp. 40-41, MHC.

72. *NYT*, Feb. 12, 1937; FM to Perry, June 1, 1938, Bailey to FM, Jan. 30, 1939, FM Papers; *Nomination of Murphy*, pp. 3-4.

73. *DN*, Feb. 8, 1937; Statement by Wolcott, Oct. 21, 1938, FM Papers; John H. Eliasohn to GM, Oct. 24, 1938, ibid.

74. H. B. Personal Note, Feb. 25, 1937, Blankenhorn Papers, Box 1; DeCaux, *Labor Radical*, p. 267.

75. Strike Chronology, Feb. 7, 8, 1937, FM Papers; FM to Lewis and Martin, Feb. 8, 1937, ibid. The original of the letter in the Murphy Papers bears the date February 9. When the letter was typed, probably on February 8, the space for the day of the month was left blank, and the "9" was later added, presumably to make the date conform to the date of its presentation to Lewis. When a copy of the letter was first publicly revealed on January 13, 1939, it bore the date February 8 and a notation that it had been read and delivered at 9:15 P.M. on February 9.

76. Pencil notes by FM, Aug. 1938 folder, ibid.; *Nomination of Murphy*, p. 10; Carl Muller, "Frank Murphy, Ornament of the Bar," *Detroit Lawyer* 17 (Sept. 1949): 183; Interview with GM, Mar. 28, 1957, p. 4, MHC; [Lenhardt], "It Can Happen Here," Mar. 9, 1937, Moody Papers; *DN*, Jan. 15, 16, 1939.

77. H. B. Personal Note, Feb. 25, 1937, Blankenhorn Papers, Box 1; UAW, *Proceedings, 1940*, p. 105; Alinsky, *Lewis*, pp. 144-46.

78. Sugar notes [1940s], Sugar Papers, Box 3; *NYT*, Feb. 9, Mar. 16, 1937; Kraus, *Many and Few*, p. 275.

79. FM to Guy H. Jenkins, Jan. 28, 1939, FM Papers; *NYT*, Jan. 6, 1939; EGK, "Frank Murphy as Government Administrator" (1951), EGK Papers; *DN*, Jan. 15, 1939; [*Washington Post*, Jan. 17, 1939], MSB.

80. *DN*, Feb. 10, 11, 1937.

81. Subcommittee of Senate Committee on Education and Labor, *Violations*

of Free Speech and Rights of Labor, Hearings..., 75 Cong., 1 sess. (Washington: U.S. Government Printing Office, 1937), pt. 5:1460, 1465, 1467-68, 1511-14, 1518-23; H. B. Personal Note, Feb. 25, 1937, Blankenhorn Papers, Box 1.

82. Roper Memorandum for McIntyre, Feb. 10, 1937, OF 407-B.

83. Maurice Wyss to Sidney Fine, Aug. 30, 1967; *DN*, Oct. 29, 1937; Stephen M. DuBrul, "The Problem of Union Agreements," Dec. 31, 1936, GM, Labor Relations Diary, Appendix Doc. 74-A. Lewis reported that the banks were pressing GM for the payment of outstanding promissory notes. H. B. Personal Note, Feb. 25, 1937, Blankenhorn Papers, Box 1.

84. *DN*, Feb. 11, 1937; *NYT*, Feb. 12, 1937; Alinsky, *Lewis*, p. 146; Kraus, *Many and Few*, p. 285.

85. The original agreement is in the FM Papers.

86. Knudsen to FM, Feb. 11, 1937, ibid. My italics.

87. H. B. Personal Note, Feb. 25, 1937, Blankenhorn Papers, Box 1; GM, Labor Relations Diary, Section 1, pp. 80-81; *Socialist Call*, Feb. 20, 1937; *United Automobile Worker*, Feb. 13, 1937; Brophy, "Struggle for Auto Union," p. 23, Brophy Papers; "Report of John Brophy to CIO Meeting," Oct. 11, 1937, ibid.; "Report of George F. Addes to the GEB...," Sept. 13, 1937, Kraus Papers, Box 11; "After the Motors Strike," *Christian Century* 54 (Feb. 24, 1937): 240; Mortimer interview, June 20, 1960, pp. 43-44.

88. Robert R. R. Brooks, *As Steel Goes* (New Haven: Yale University Press, 1940), p. 120; Trager, "Autos," Jan. 11, 1937, Thomas Papers; *NYT*, Jan. 10, 24, 31, 1937; Edward Levinson, "Detroit Digs In," *Nation* 144 (Jan. 16, 1937): 64; *DN*, Feb. 8, 1937; *New Republic* 90 (Feb. 24, 1937): 60-61; *Daily Worker*, Feb. 12, 1937; *Union News Service*, Mar. 1, 1937; *NYT*, Feb. 14, 1937; Perkins Reminiscences, p. 171; Minutes of CIO Meeting, Mar. 9, 1937, Katherine Pollak Ellickson CIO File, FDRL; Edward Levinson, *Labor on the March* (New York: University Books, 1956), pp. 173-74.

89. Jenkins to George G. Booth, Dec. 1, 1937, Guy Hugh Jenkins Papers, MHC; Creighton Memorandum to FM, May 11, 1938, FM Papers. See also H. B. Personal Note, Feb. 25, 1937, Blankenhorn Papers, Box 1.

90. See Fine, *Sit-Down*, pp. 215, 216, 218, 311, 314-15.

91. FDR to FM, Feb. 11, 1937, Perkins to FM, Feb. 11, 1937, Felix Frankfurter to FM, Feb. 12, 1937, Josephus Daniels to FM, Feb. 12, 1937, Newton D. Baker to FM, Feb. 12, 1937, John M. Carmody to FM, Feb. 15, 1937, Sloan, Jr., to Margery Abrahams, Feb. 7, 1939, FM Papers; *NYT*, Feb. 12, 1937; *DN*, Feb. 12, 1937; *Flint Journal*, Feb. 12, 1937; Franklin column in unidentified newspaper, MSB; miscellaneous clippings in MSB.

92. *Detroit Saturday Night*, Feb. 13, 1937; White E. Gibson to FM, Feb. 12, 1937, Mitchell E. Foster to FM, Feb. 23, 1937, Frank Gaines to FM, Feb. 25, 1937, xxx to FM, undated, FM Papers; *Flint Journal*, Feb. 17, 1937; *Commercial and Financial Chronicle* 144 (Feb. 20, 1937): 1164; George E. Sokolsky, "The Law and Labor," *Atlantic Monthly* 159 (Apr. 1937): 433-34.

93. *NYT*, Feb. 12, 1937; Krock to FM, Feb. 12, 1937, FM.

94. EGK, "Murphy," FM Papers; [*Cleveland Plain Dealer*], Feb. 16, 1937, MSB; *Time* 29 (Feb. 22, 1937): 14. See also Porter, "Murphy's Star."

CHAPTER 9

1. Portions of this chapter have been adapted from Sidney Fine, "Frank Murphy, Law and Order, and Labor Relations in Michigan, 1937," in David B. Lipsky, ed., *Union Power and Public Policy* (Ithaca: Cornell University Press, 1975), pp. 1–23.

2. *NYT*, Mar. 13, 1937.

3. There is a list of sit-down and conventional strikes in Detroit in House Special Committee on Un-American Activities, *Investigation of Un-American Propaganda Activities in the United States, Hearings* . . . , 75 Cong., 3 sess., 4 vols. (Washington: U.S. Government Printing Office, 1938), 2:1609–21 (hereafter cited as *Dies Hearings*). The totals for the nation are given in "Number of Sit-Down Strikes in 1937," *Monthly Labor Review* 47 (Aug. 1938): 361. The figure of 217 sit-down strikes in February and March given in the latter does not include sit-downs lasting less than one day. The quotation is from *DN*, Mar. 14, 1937.

4. Frank H. Bowen to NLRB, Feb. 27, 1937, La Follette Committee Papers, Sen 78A–F9, Box 85, Records of the United States Senate, RG 46, NARS; *DN*, Mar. 17, 19, 1937.

5. *DN*, Feb. 16–Mar. 19, 1937; *NYT*, Mar. 7, 10, 17, 1937; Burnham Finney, "Worse than the Plague," *American Machinist* 81 (Apr. 7, 1937): 286–87; *Business Week*, Mar. 27, 1937, pp. 13–14; *Time* 29 (Mar. 29, 1937): 11–13; Carlos A. Schwantes, ". . . The 1937 Non-Automotive Sit Down Strikes in Detroit," *Michigan History* 56 (Fall 1972): 179–99; Carol A. Westenhoefer, "Non-Automotive Sit-Down Strikes in Detroit" (1964), in my possession.

6. *DN*, Feb. 20, 21, 23, 25, Mar. 2, 7, 8, 11, 16, 1937; *DFP*, Mar. 3, 1937; *NYT*, Mar. 17, 1937; Shields to Prentiss Brown, Mar. 16, 1937, Prentiss Brown Papers, Box 1, MHC.

7. *NYT*, Mar. 17, 1937; *Business Week*, Mar. 27, 1937, pp. 13–14; *DFP*, Mar. 12, 1937; Mary Heaton Vorse, "Detroit Has the Jitters," *New Republic* 90 (Apr. 7, 1937): 256; *Time* 29 (Mar. 12, 1937): 12; *DN*, Mar. 19, 21, Apr. 5, 1937.

8. *DN*, Mar. 24, 1937; Barbara Willson to Josephine Gomon [1951], Josephine Gomon Papers, MHC.

9. *DN*, Mar. 13–15, 1937; *NYT*, Mar. 16, 21, 1937; *Automotive Industries* 76 (Mar. 20, 1937): 452; Vorse, "Detroit," p. 256; [*New York Herald Tribune*, Mar. 23, 1937], clipping in EGK-BHC, Box 10; Dwight S. Bobb to FM, Mar. 18, 1937, Cecile Bass to FM, Mar. 18, 1937, P. D. Jones to FM, Mar. 18, 1937, Lois Landon to FM, Mar. 19, 1937, G. H. Hoffman to FM, Mar. 20, 1937, FM Papers; *Michigan Manufacturer and Financial Record* (hereafter *MMFR*) 49 (Mar. 13, 1937): 12; L. C. Persons to Arthur H. Vandenberg, Mar. 17, 1937, Arthur H. Vandenberg Papers, MHC; *Detroit Saturday Night*, Feb. 27, Mar. 20, 1937; *Time* 29 (Mar. 29, 1937): 12.

10. *Time* 29 (Mar. 29, 1937): 12; *News-Week* 9 (Mar. 27, 1937): 9; F. Howard Mason to FM, Mar. 24, 1937, FM Papers.

11. *NYT*, Mar. 27, 1937; *DN*, Mar. 21, 1937.

12. Stephen K. Bailey, *Congress Makes a Law* (New York: Columbia University Press, 1950), pp. 199–200; *Congressional Record*, 75 Cong., 1 sess., pt. 1:246–47, 325–26, 825–26, 1068, pt. 3:2485, 2520–22, 3022–24, 3042–43, 3018–19, 3121, 3136, 3232–33, 3248; Vandenberg to Frank Knox, Apr. 2, 1937, Vandenberg Papers; Apr. 2, 1937 entry, Vandenberg Scrapbook No. 9, ibid.

13. *DN*, Feb. 26, 1937; *Public Acts of the Legislature of . . . Michigan . . . 1915* (Lansing: Wynkoop Hallenbeck Crawford Co., 1915), pp. 387–92; *DLN*, Mar. 5, 1937; Norman H. Hill to FM, Mar. 12, 1937, Harvey Campbell to FM, Mar. 12, 1937, FM Papers.

14. Starr to EGK, Mar. 12, 1937, EGK-BHC, Box 10; FM to EGK, Mar. 12, 1937, and EGK note on same, FM Papers; *DN*, Mar. 14, 1937.

15. *DN*, Mar. 16, 1937; Samuel D. Pepper to John S. Bersey, Mar. 17, 1937, Samuel D. Pepper Papers, privately held.

16. UAW GEB Minutes, Mar. 15, 1937, Henry Kraus Papers, Box 7, ALHUA; UAW Release, Mar. 20, 1937, Joe Brown Collection, ibid.; FM statement [Mar. 13, 1937], FM Papers; FM to Hill, Mar. 16, 1937, UAW GEB and General Executive Officers to FM, Mar. 17 [1937], ibid.

17. "Statement by Governor Murphy," Mar. 17, 1937, FM Papers; Minutes of Mar. 17, 1937 meeting, ibid.; *DN*, Mar. 17–19, 1937.

18. Sugar to FM, Mar. 22, 1937, EGK-BHC, Box 10; EGK to FM [Mar. 20, 1937], FM Papers; *DFP*, Mar. 19, 1937.

19. *DN*, Mar. 18, 19, 1937, Oct. 21, 22, 1938; *Dies Hearings*, 2:1630–31; *Time* 29 (Mar. 29, 1937): 12–13; Vincent W. Sincere to FM, Jan. 14, 1939, FM Papers.

20. *DN*, Mar. 18, 19, 1937; *NYT*, Mar. 21, 1937.

21. Couzens to M. Udale, Mar. 25, 1937, Couzens to Martin W. Rolnick, Mar. 27, 1937, Mayor's Office Records, 1937, Box 15, Burton Historical Collection, Detroit, Michigan; *DN*, Mar. 19–22, 1937; *DFP*, Mar. 21, 1937; *NYT*, Mar. 21, 24, 1937; Roger N. Baldwin to FM, Mar. 18, 1937, American Civil Liberties Union (ACLU) Archives, vol. 1047, Princeton University, Princeton, New Jersey; J. H. Bollens to FM, Mar. 20, 1937, EGK-BHC, Box 10; "Dodge Main News," Mar. 23, 1937, Brown Collection.

22. *United Automobile Worker*, Mar. 23, 1937; *DN*, Mar. 21–24, 1937; *DFP*, Mar. 25, 1937; copy of agreement, Mayor's Office Records, 1937, Box 5; Adolph Germer Diary, Mar. 22, 1937, Adolph Germer Papers, State Historical Society of Wisconsin, Madison, Wisconsin; *NYT*, Mar. 23, 24, 1937; Vorse, "Detroit," pp. 257–58; Interview with Wyndham Mortimer, Dec. 9, 1964, p. 22, MHC; Frederic Seidenburg et al. to FM, Mar. 27, 1937, FM Papers. The *DLN* of Mar. 26, 1937, reported Martel as having said that the people would "wipe out" (not "overturn") public officials who disregarded labor's rights.

23. *DN*, Jan. 31, Feb. 22, 24, 28, Mar. 1, 2, 4, 6, 8, 10–13, 1937, June 7, 1940; *NYT*, Mar. 4, 5, 18, 1937; Dodge Main Plant Employee Representatives' Meeting, Feb. 9, 1937, John A. Zaremba Papers, Box 1, ALHUA; K. T. Keller, "Chrysler Corporation . . . to the Employees," Mar. 20, 1937, ibid., Box 9, ALHUA; "Dodge Main News," Mar. 9, 21, 1937, ibid.; UAW Release, Mar. 13, 1937, CIO-UAW Papers, Catholic University, Washington, D.C.; John Brophy Diary, Mar. 8, 1937, John Brophy Papers, ibid.; UAW Release, Mar. 20, 1937, Brown Collection; *Time* 29 (Mar. 22, 1937): 17; Bernstein, *The Turbulent Years* (Boston: Houghton Mifflin Co., 1970), pp. 552–53; Doris McLaughlin, ". . . The Chrysler Strike of 1937" (undated), pp. 20–26, in my possession; Oral History Interview of Nick Digaetano, Apr. 29, May 7, 1959, p. 57, MHC; Oral History Interview of Richard Harris, Nov. 16, 1959, pp. 22, 24, 27, MHC; Oral History Interview of Harry Ross, July 10, 1961,

p. 20, MHC; Oral History Interview of Frank B. Tuttle, Apr. 27, 1959, pp. 14–15, 21, MHC.

24. *NYT*, Mar. 11, 14, 16, 1937; *DN*, Mar. 9–11, 13–15, 1937; Germer Diary, Mar. 12, 1937, Germer Papers.

25. Germer Diary, Mar. 12, 13, 15, 18, 1937, Germer Papers; Germer to Brophy, Mar. 18, 1937, CIO File (notes on this file in possession of Irving Bernstein); EGK to FM, Mar. 17, 1937, FM to EGK, Mar. 22, 1937, FM Papers; Martin to FM, Mar. 22, 1937, EGK-BHC, Box 10; George S. Wilson to Frank Reid, Mar. 20, 1937, Zaremba Papers, Box 9; "Dodge Main News," Mar. 11, 19, 1937, ibid.; "Dodge Main News," Mar. 15, 20, 21, 1937, Brown Collection; *DN*, Mar. 16–20, 1937; *NYT*, Mar. 17–23, Apr. 1, 1937; *DFP*, Mar. 22, 1937; *DT*, Mar. 21, 1937, MSB; J. Woodford Howard, "Frank Murphy and the Sit-Down Strikes of 1937," *Labor History* 1 (Spring 1960): 120; The Reminiscences of Nicholas Kelley, 1957, p. 376, Oral History Research Office, Columbia University, New York, New York; Oral History Interview of R. J. Thomas, Mar. 26, 1963, p. 12, MHC.

26. EGK Memorandum, Mar. 22, 1937, FM Papers; FM to Lewis and Chrysler, Mar. 23, 1937, Lewis to FM, Mar. 23, 1937, Chrysler to FM, Mar. 23, 1937, ibid.; *NYT*, Mar. 24, 1937.

27. FM to UAW, Mar. 24, 1937, FM Papers; Germer Diary, Mar. 24, 1937, Germer Papers; *DN*, Mar. 24, 25, 1937; *NYT*, Mar. 25, 1937.

28. Notes on Doris McLaughlin interview with William Haber, Mar. 25, 1963, in my possession; *DN*, Mar. 25, May 2, 1937.

29. *DN*, Mar. 25, 1937; *NYT*, Mar. 26, 1937; *Time* 29 (Apr. 5, 1937): 14; "UAW Strike Against Chrysler Corp. (3–8–1937)," Brown Collection; The Reminiscences of R. J. Thomas, 1956, Book 3, pp. 12–13, Oral History Research Office; Ross interview, pp. 23–24; Digaetano interview, pp. 69–70.

30. *DN*, Mar. 26, 1937; *News-Week* 9 (Apr. 3, 1937): 7; *DFP*, Mar. 26, 1937; *San Francisco Chronicle*, Mar. 28, 1937, MSB.

31. *DN*, Mar. 12, 24, Apr. 11, 1937; *NYT*, Mar. 14, 19, Apr. 6, 1937; *DT*, Apr. 7, 1937, MSB; *New York American*, Apr. 1, 1937, MSB; Germer Diary, Mar. 10, 12, 26, 1937, Germer Papers; Germer to Brophy, Mar. 18, 22, 1937, CIO File; Martin to FM, Mar. 22, 1937, EGK-BHC, Box 10; Guy H. Jenkins to Carl Sanders, Apr. 12, 1937, Guy Hugh Jenkins Papers, MHC; John L. Lovett speech [Apr. 1937], FM Papers; FM to JRH, Apr. 8, 1937, Joseph H. Creighton Memorandum to FM, May 11, 1938, ibid.; Margaret [Marguerite] Teahan, In Account with Hayden, Stone and Co. [1937], ibid. Frank Murphy's account with Hayden, Stone and Co. was transferred to Marguerite's name on February 11, 1937. It was only a nominal transfer. J. E. Swan to MM, Feb. 16, 1939, MM Papers. Murphy's income tax return for 1937, EMB Papers, shows him sustaining a loss of $6,196 on the sale of his Chrysler stock.

32. *DN*, Apr. 2, 5, 1937; McLaughlin, "Chrysler Strike," p. 53; *NYT*, Apr. 4, 1937.

33. "Chrysler," *Fortune* 12 (Aug. 5, 1937): 37; Interview with Norman H. Hill, Aug. 21, 1963, MHC; Kelley Reminiscences, pp. 376, 377, 384; Harris interview, pp. 28–29; Oral History Reminiscences of Lee Pressman, 1958, pp. 82–83, Oral History Research Office; Thomas Reminiscences, Book 3, pp. 9–10, 17; Frankensteen, "Introduction," *Agreement . . . Apr. 1937*, Joseph A. Labadie Collection,

University of Michigan, Ann Arbor, Michigan; *DN*, Apr. 6, 20, 1937; McLaughlin, "Chrysler Strike," p. 56.

34. *DN*, Apr. 5, 1937; *NYT*, Apr. 5, 1937; UAW Release, Apr. 6, 1937, Kraus Papers, Box 11; Kelley Reminiscences, pp. 379–80; Thomas Reminiscences, Book 3, p. 14.

35. Germer to Brophy, Mar. 22, 1937, CIO File; Germer Diary, Mar. 26, 1937, Germer Papers; Kelley Reminiscences, pp. 378, 386; Thomas Reminiscences, Book 3, pp. 16–17; Martin to FM, Mar. 22, 1937, EGK–BHC, Box 10; FM to JRH, Apr. 10, 1937, FM Papers; Advance on FM speech, Oct. 25, 1938, ibid.; *DN*, Mar. 11, 30, Apr. 11, 1937; *NYT*, Mar. 28, 1937; [*New York American*, Apr. 1, 1937], MSB.

36. See the drafts in the FM Papers dated Mar. 24, 25, 26, 27, 28, 30, Apr. 4, 5, 1937; and Germer Diary, Mar. 26, 1937, Germer Papers.

37. *DN*, Apr. 7, 1937; *NYT*, Apr. 8, 1937; *DT*, Apr. 7, 1937, MSB; *Business Week*, Apr. 10, 1937, p. 16; *Automotive Industries* 76 (Apr. 10, 1937): 543–44; *DFP*, Apr. 13, 1937; Interview with Lee Pressman, Nov. 12, 1964, p. 39, MHC; McLaughlin, "Chrysler Strike," p. 55; Walter Galenson, *The CIO Challenge to the AFL* (Cambridge, Mass.: Harvard University Press, 1960), p. 149; J. Woodford Howard, *Mr. Justice Murphy* (Princeton: Princeton University Press, 1968), p. 154. There is a copy of the agreement in the FM Papers.

38. Chrysler to FM, Apr. 7, 1937, Keller to FM, Apr. 14, 1937, FM Papers; Lovett speech [Apr. 1937], ibid.; Lewis speech, Apr. 7, 1937, Kraus Papers, Box 11; *DN*, Apr. 7, 8, 1937; *NYT*, Apr. 8, 1937; *United Automobile Worker*, Apr. 7, 1937; *News-Week* 9 (Apr. 17, 1937): 10; *Review of Reviews* 95 (May 1937): 9–10.

39. On the Hudson and Reo strikes, see *DN*, Mar. 8, 9, 11, Apr. 5–10, 1937; "Following Information from Dewey," Apr. 9, 1937, File 182–2259, Records of the Federal Mediation and Conciliation Service, RG 280, NARS; Georges Schreiber, "Roosevelt's Successor," *Common Sense* 6 (June 1937): 9; Oral History Interview of Tracy Doll, Apr. 21, 1961, pp. 22–25, MHC; and Oral History Interview of Joseph Pagano, May 23, 1937, pp. 9–11, MHC.

40. "Information from Dewey," Apr. 9, 1937, File 182–2259, RG 280; *Dies Hearings*, 2:1614, 1620; "Number of Sit-Down Strikes in 1937," p. 361; Stark, "Sit-Down," *Survey Graphic* 26 (June 1937): 320; Sidney Fine, *Sit-Down: The General Motors Strike of 1936–1937* (Ann Arbor: University of Michigan Press, 1969), p. 331; *DN*, Apr. 2, 1937; Interview with John Manning, Dec. 4, 1964, pp. 10–11, MHC.

41. *DT*, Apr. 9, 1937, MSB; *DN*, Apr. 9, 1937.

42. *DN*, Apr. 4, 8, 12–16, 28, May 14, 22, 26, 1937; UAW Releases, Apr. 4, 15, May 21, Kraus Papers, Box 11; NHH [Hill] Memorandum to FM, Apr. 13, 1937, Martin to FM, Apr. 15, May 4, 1937, Lawrence A. Lyon to FM, Apr. 16, 1937, EGK to FM, May 5, 14, 1937, FM Memorandum to Hill, May 5, 1937, Hilmer Gellein to FM, May 21, 1937, Edwards to FM, Aug. 2, 1937, FM Papers; Charles A. Weeks, Jr., "The Yale and Towne Sit-Down Strike of 1937" (1964), in my possession.

43. *DN*, Feb. 18–20, 27, Mar. 8, 16, 19, 30, Apr. 9, 16, 17, 23, 28, May 14, 22, 26, 1937; [*DT*, Apr. 22, 1937], clipping in FM Papers; "Report of the Citizens' Fact Finding Committee...," undated, ibid.; "Resume for the Meeting with ... Murphy...," Apr. 22, 1937, ibid.; Frank Ingram to FM, Mar. 6, 1937, Krogstad to Hill,

Apr. 20, 1937, James Cullman to J. Roosevelt, Apr. 26, 1937, ibid. See also T. P. Jackman to FM, Apr. 23, 1937, and Mary Cebula to FM, Apr. 27, 1937, ibid.

44. For the Lansing Labor Holiday, see Albert A. Blum and Ira Spar, "The Lansing Labor Holiday," *Michigan History* 49 (Mar. 1965): 1-11; *DN,* June 7, 8, 13, 1937, Oct. 25, 29, 1938; *DFP,* June 8, 1937; *Lansing State Journal,* June 8, 1937; [*DT,* June 8, 1937], clipping in FM Papers; *Lansing Industrial News,* June 4, 11, 1937; *United Automobile Worker,* June 12, 1937; *NYT,* June 8, 13, 1937; *MMFR* 49 (June 12, 1937): 4; Birt Darling, *City in the Forest: The Story of Lansing* (New York: Stratford House, 1950), pp. 238-42; EGK, "Frank Murphy as Government Administrator" (1951), p. 11, EGK Papers; *Dies Hearings,* 2:1695-1710, 3:2063-72; Interview with Charles Hedetniemi, Oct. 20, 1964, p. 8, MHC; Creighton Memorandum to FM, May 11, 1938, Vandenberg to FM, Jan. 16, 1939, Hill to FM, Jan. 11, 1939 [1940], FM Papers; draft of statement, undated, ibid.; and Diary of George P. McCallum, June 7, 1937, George P. McCallum Papers, MHC.

45. *DN,* May 19-21, June 5, 9, 10, 1937, June 7, 1938; *DT,* May 20, 1937, MSB; *Pittsburgh Press,* June 9, 1937, *Pittsburgh Post-Gazette,* June 10, 1937, clippings in FM Papers; Mortimer interview, pp. 22-26.

46. For the Newton strike and the Battle of Monroe, see Donald G. Sofchalk, "The Little Steel Strike of 1937" (Ph.D. diss., Ohio State University, 1961), pp. 208-22; idem, "The Chicago Memorial Day Incident...," *Labor History* 6 (Winter 1965): 34; Tom M. Girdler, *Boot Straps: The Autobiography of Tom M. Girdler* (New York: Charles Scribner's Sons, 1943), pp. 312-13, 318-22, 326; *DN,* June 1-4, 8-16, 20, 1937; *Lansing State Journal,* June 1, 2, 1937, MSB; Hill to FM, June 10, 1937, FM to F. J. Thieme, June 14, 1937, Robert Wohlforth to FM, Aug. 6, 1938, and FM comments on enclosed transcript, Heber Blankenhorn Memorandum for Robert La Follette, Apr. 29, 1939, FM Papers; Baldwin to FM, June 9, 1937, ACLU Archives, vol. 1047; Senate Committee on Education and Labor, *Violations of Free Speech and Rights of Labor,* 76 Cong., 1 sess., Rept. no. 6, pt. 3 (*Industrial Munitions*) (Washington: U.S. Government Printing Office, 1939), pp. 148-55; Subcommittee of the Senate Committee on Education and Labor, *Violations of Free Speech and Rights of Labor, Hearings...,* 75 Cong., 3 sess. (Washington: U.S. Government Printing Office, 1939), pt. 27:11364-65, pt. 28:11515-29, 11547-48, 11586-88, 11599-603, 11750-56, 11779-80, 11784-800, 12057-59, pt. 42:16302-9, 16313-14, 16323-26; and William H. Hackett, "The Influence of the Back to Work Movement in the Monroe Michigan Steel Strike of 1937" (undated), in my possession.

47. Sofchalk, "Incident," p. 34; *DN,* June 15, 1937.

48. *MMFR* 59 (June 12, 1937): 3; ibid. 60 (July 17, 1937): 12; Vandenberg to Couzens, June 11, 1937, Couzens to Vandenberg, June 14, 1937, Vandenberg Papers; Vandenberg to Howard C. Lawrence, June 16, 1937, Howard C. Lawrence Papers, MHC; *DN,* June 13, July 4, 1937; *NYT,* June 13, 1937; *Ann Arbor News,* June 16, 1937.

49. *DFP,* June 12, 1937; *DN,* July 2, 1937; *Lansing State Journal,* July 2, 1937, clipping in FM Papers; Thieme to Alexander Ruthven, June 9, 1937, FM to Thieme, June 14, 1937, ibid.

50. There were 76 strikes involving 57,609 workers in the final six months of 1937

compared to 205 strikes involving 264,565 workers in the first six months. There were only 76 strikes involving 75,639 workers in all of 1938. These strike figures were derived from vols. 44-48 of the *Monthly Labor Review*. The annual strike figures for 1937 and 1938 on p. 1193 of vol. 46 and p. 1117 of vol. 48, respectively, do not coincide with the totals derived from the monthly strike figures.

51. *DN*, June 4-7, July 1, 1937; Joe Liss et al. to FDR, June 2, 1937, John W. Maki to FDR, June 22, 1937, Charles O. Houston to John Steelman, June 28, 1937, J. S. Landon to Steelman, July 3, Aug. 2, 1937, Steelman to Brown, July 19, 1937, File 199-203, RG 280; Houston, "Preliminary Report...," June 20, 1937, ibid.; John W. Hannah to FM, May 28, 1937, FM to Hannah, June 2, 1937, Hill Memorandum for FM, June 2, 1937, Luke Raik to FM, June 4, 10, 23, July 2, 1937, FM to Raik, June 10, 23, 1937, FM to Maki, June 14, 1937, R. W. Nebel to Hill, June 16, 1937, Oscar Olander to FM, June 24, 1937, EMB to Raik, June 30, 1937, Krogstad to FM, July 1, 1937, FM to Arthur Erickson, July 2, 6, 1937, Henry Paull to Nathaniel Clark, July 4, 1937, Hill to Erickson, July 16, 1937, Hill to James G. Bryant, July 30, 1937, Bryant Memorandum to Hill, Aug. 6, 1937, Hedetniemi to FM, Dec. 27, 1937, FM Papers; Statement to Press by Governor's Committee, undated, ibid.; unidentified clipping, June 11, 1937, ibid.; Baldwin to FM [July 7, 1937], FM to Baldwin, July 7, 14, 1937, ACLU to Homer Cummings, July 7, 1937, Starr to Baldwin, July 8, 1937, Starr to A. L. Wirin, July 24, 1937, FM to Wirin, Aug. 4, 1937, [Brien] McMahon to Arthur Garfield Hays, Mar. 18, 1938, ACLU Archives, vol. 1048; Application for Federal Investigation and Prosecution..., undated, ibid.; Lucille B. Milner to ———, Dec. 8, 1938, ibid., vol. 2037.

52. Kenneth O. Doyle to FM, July 4, 1937, FM to Olander, July 4, 1937, U.S. Truck Co. to FM, July 15, 1937, Hill to U.S. Truck Co., July 15, 1937, William Stidger to FM, July 18 [1937], Hillman to FM, July 23, 1937, Hill Memorandum to FM, Aug. 5, 1937, Walter C. Sadler to FM, Aug. 5, 7, 1937, Victor Reuther to FM, Aug. 5, 1937, and FM note on same, Reuther et al. to Sadler, Aug. 6, 1937, George W. Eastley to FM, Oct. 5, 14, 1937,——— to Eastley, Oct. 6, 1937, Howard G. Welch to FM, Oct. 6, 14, 1937, FM to William Green, Oct. 11, 1937, F. L. Riggin to FM, Nov. 10, 1937, FM Papers; Germer Diary, Sept. 1, 2, 1937, Germer Papers; Sugar to FM, June 28, July 23, Aug. 6, 1937, Maurice Sugar Papers, Box 13, ALHUA; *DN*, July 4, 7, 17, Aug. 11, 31, Sept. 2, 13, Oct. 2, 13, 1937; [*DT*, July 23, 1937], MSB; *Michigan Daily*, Aug. 5, 7, 1937, clippings in FM Papers; *DFP*, July 23, 1937.

53. Steelman to Perkins, Apr. 5, 7, 1938, and enclosed "Public Utility Strike...," File 199-1516, RG 280; Sugar to FM, Apr. 5, 1938, Germer to FM, Apr. 6, 1938, Perkins to FM, Apr. 7, 1938, FM to Archibald McNeil, Apr. 12, 1938, FM Papers; *DN*, Apr. 2-5, June 7, 1938.

54. *Selected Addresses of Frank Murphy ... January 1, 1937, to September 30, 1938* (Lansing: n.p., 1938), p. 47; *DN*, Feb. 22, 1938; FM to Martel, Nov. 10, 1938, Wayne County AFL-CIO Papers, Box 11.

55. *Adrian Daily Telegram*, Apr. 20, 1938, clipping in FM Papers; Stuart H. Perry to FM, May 18, 1938, FM to Perry, June 1, 1938, FM to John M. Connolly, Dec. 15, 1938, ibid.

56. The description of Murphy's views on the labor problem is based on *Selected*

Addresses, pp. 7–9, 12–17, 20–23, 25, 27, 30–31, 35–38, 45, 47, 56; FM statement, Mar. 17, 1937, FM Papers; FM speech, Mar. 29, 1937, ibid.; FM to Vandenberg, Mar. 15, 1937, FM to JRH, Apr. 8, 1937, FM to P. H. Callahan, May 25, 1937, FM to Hutchinson, June 24, 1937, FM to Perry, June 1, 1938, ibid.; FM to EGK, Mar. 23, 1937, EGK–BHC, Box 10; FM to Martel, Nov. 10, 1938, Wayne County AFL-CIO Papers, Box 11; FM, "First Quarterly Accounting," July 10, 1937, MSB; FM, "New Era," *American Hungarian* 1 (July 1, 1937), MSB; *New York American*, Apr. 1, 1937, MSB; *Lansing State Journal*, Apr. 29, 1937, MSB; unidentified New York newspaper [June 30, 1937], MSB; [*DT*, Oct. 22, 1936], *DT*, Mar. 24, 1937, MSB; *DLN*, Nov. 6, Dec. 25, 1936, Mar. 11, 1938; *DN*, Mar. 20, 25, 26, 30, Apr. 11, 30, 1937, Feb. 22, 1938; *NYT*, Mar. 20, 26, Apr. 1, 1937; *DFP*, Mar. 25, 1937; FM, "The Shaping of a Labor Policy," *Survey Graphic* 26 (Aug. 1937): 411–13, 450; FM, "Industrial Peace," *Christian Front* 2 (Nov. 1937): 157–58; and Schreiber, "Roosevelt's Successor," p. 9.

57. FM to Frank D. Adams, Apr. 2, 1937, FM to Arthur B. Moehlman, Apr. 15, 1937, FM to Sarraine Andrews, Sept. 17, 1937, FM to Hill, Jan. 9, 1945, FM Papers.

58. Unidentified New York newspaper, June 30 [1937], MSB.

59. FM, "Labor Policy," p. 450; James T. Patterson, *The New Deal and the States* (Princeton: Princeton University Press, 1969), pp. 121–23.

60. *DLN*, May 28, 1937; Richard C. Keller, "Pennsylvania's Little New Deal," *Pennsylvania History* 29 (Oct. 1962): 405; Robert P. Ingalls, *Herbert H. Lehman and New York's Little New Deal* (New York: New York University Press, 1975), pp. 108, 114–15, 131–42.

61. John Reid to Martel, Dec. 9, 1936, Wayne County AFL-CIO Papers, Box 8; FM to Hill, Jan. 25, 1937, Krogstad to Department of Labor, Feb. 24, 1937, V. A. Zimmer to Krogstad, Feb. 25, 1937, FM to EGK, Apr. 30, Oct. 8, 1937, Division of Labor Standards to FM, July 16, 1937, EGK–BHC, Box 10; *Michigan Official Directory and Legislative Manual, 1937–38* (n.p., n.d.), p. 370; "State Labor Legislation, 1937," *Monthly Labor Review* 46 (Jan. 1938): 143; Penelope Helen Sawkins, "Executive Leadership of Frank Murphy as Governor of Michigan" (M.A. thesis, Wayne University, 1950), pp. 141–42, 143; [*DT*, Apr. 18, 1937], MSB; *DLN*, June 18, July 9, 30, Aug. 6, Dec. 31, 1937, Apr. 1, 1938; *DN*, Apr. 13, Dec. 9, 16, 1937, Jan. 7, 1938; Krogstad, "Department of Labor and Industry" [Dec. 1938], FM Papers.

62. [*Lansing State Journal*, Feb. 9, 1938], MSB; unidentified clipping [Feb. 9, 1938], MSB; *DLN*, Feb. 18, Apr. 15, 1938; *DN*, Feb. 26, 1938; FM to Martel, Feb. 14, 1938, Krogstad to FM, Dec. 16, 1938, and enclosed Krogstad to FM, undated, and Krogstad to All the Members, undated, FM Papers.

63. Krogstad, "From the Department of Labor and Industry . . . ," undated, FM Papers; Krogstad, "Department" [Dec. 1938], ibid.; FM to Hill, Dec. 7, 1936, Henry F. Vaughan to FM, June 17, 1937, and enclosed [Carey] McCord, ". . . Michigan's Occupational Disease Law," June 15, 1937, ibid.; "Minority Report of Commission of Inquiry . . . ," Jan. 28, 1937, Wayne County AFL-CIO Papers, Box 12; Reid to Martel, Mar. 11, 1937, ibid., Box 8; "State Labor Legislation, 1937," p. 149; *DN*, Nov. 29, 1936, Jan. 23, Mar. 12, 23, Apr. 1, May 13, 26, 28, Oct. 24, 1937; Zimmer to FM, Jan. 18, 1937, EGK–BHC, Box 10; [*DT*, Apr. 18, 1937],

MSB; *Ann Arbor News*, May 26, 1937; *DFP*, Oct. 28, 1938; *Message of Frank Murphy...*, *January 7, 1937* (n.p., n.d.), p. 5, FM Papers; *DLN*, May 28, Dec. 31, 1937; Betty W. Allie, "History of Workmen's Compensation in Michigan," *Michigan History Magazine* 30 (Apr.-June 1946): 324-25.

64. Krogstad, "From the Department," FM Papers; FM Memorandum to EGK, Feb. 27, 1937, F. E. Levi Memorandum to Hill, Dec. 13, 1937, EGK Memorandum for Hill, Dec. 14, 1937, Perkins to FM, Jan. 26, 1938, FM to Mrs. Thomas F. McAllister, Mar. 16, 1938, EGK to FM, Oct. 18, Nov. 19, 1937, ibid.; FM, "Message to Legislature," June 29, 1937, ibid.; "Proclamation of Governor for Extraordinary Session of the Legislature," July 30, 1937, ibid.; Mary Anderson to Lionel Heap, Mar. 14, 1937, Marguerite Kloepell to FM, Mar. 29, 1937, Mrs. George T. Hendrie to EGK, Mar. 31, 1937, Cohen to EGK, Apr. 7, 1937, Haber to EGK, Apr. 8, Aug. 5, 1937, Charlotte Stott to EGK, Apr. 18, 1937, Jennie McKibben to EGK, Apr. 24, 1937, Corrinne Hutto and Ann Steele to FM, Apr. 27, 1937, Heap to EGK, Apr. 28, 1937, Louise Stitt to FM, May 17, 1937, EGK to FM, Jan. 3, 1938, FM to Hedetniemi, July 21, 1938, Anderson to FM, July 7, 1938, FM to Anderson, July 22, 1938, FM to EMB, Aug. 16, 1938, EGK-BHC, Box 11; FM to EGK, Mar. 31, 1937, EGK to FM, Nov. 17, 1937, ibid., Box 8; Clare M. Beyer to FM, Oct. 19, 1937, FM to EGK, Oct. 22, 1937, ibid., Box 16; FM to EGK, Nov. 3, 1937, ibid., Box 7; *DN*, Mar. 30, Apr. 21-23, 30, June 10, 18, Aug. 4, 6, 1937; *DLN*, May 28, June 4, 18, 1937; FM, "Labor Policy," pp. 450-51; "State Labor Legislation, 1937," p. 139; Patterson, *New Deal*, pp. 123-24.

65. *Public Act of the Legislature of Michigan ... Extra Session of 1936* (Lansing: Franklin DeKleine Co., n.d.), p. 5; Michigan Unemployment Compensation Commission (MUCC), *Annual Report for the Year Ending December 31, 1937* (n.p., n.d.), pp. 8-9; Edward H. Litchfield to James K. Pollock, Feb. 9, 1937, Civil Service Study Commission Papers, MHC; Picard to Pollock, Aug. 21, 1937, James K. Pollock Papers, Box 6, MHC; Picard to William F. Pyper, Sept. 4, 1937, Jenkins Papers; The Reminiscences of William Haber, 1965, p. 28, Oral History Research Office; Interview with Haber, Sept. 24, 1976; *DN*, Feb. 10, 1937.

66. Haber interview; Haber Reminiscences, pp. 28-29; Picard to Brown, Dec. 16, 1937, Brown Papers, Box 2; *DN*, Feb. 3, 1937.

67. *FM Message, Jan. 7, 1937*, p. 4, FM Papers; FM, "Message," July 29, 1937, ibid.; *Journal of the House of Representatives of ... Michigan, 1937 Regular Session*, 2 vols. (Lansing: Franklin DeKleine Co., n.d.), 2:2265; Harry E. Slavin to Robert E. Hilton, July 19, 1937, Starr to EGK, July 22, 1937, EGK-BHC, Box 15; Haber to EGK, June 24, 1937, ibid., Box 20; Olga to FM, June 24 [1937], ibid., Box 8; Schouman to FM, Aug. 2, 1937, FM Papers; *DN*, Apr. 16, June 4, 9, July 30, Aug. 1, 1937; MUCC, *Report, 1937*, pp. 11-12.

68. Schouman to FM, Aug. 2, 1937, Haber to FM, Aug. 4, 1937, FM to Haber, Aug. 5, 1937, FM Papers; Haber interview.

69. Picard to Pollock, Aug. 21, Sept. 22, 1937, Pollock Papers, Box 6; Picard to Brown, Dec. 16, 1937, Brown Papers, Box 2; FM to Haber, Sept. 9, 1937, Haber to FM, Oct. 20, 1937, FM to Picard, Oct. 20, 1937, Picard to FM, Oct. 21, 22, 1937, Larned to FM, Oct. 21, 1937, Mead to FM [Oct. 1937], FM Papers; *DN*, Aug. 26, 1937.

70. MUCC, *Report, 1937*, pp. 8, 10-11, 27-29; Schouman to FM, Oct. 15, 1937, Feb. 19, 1938, FM Papers; *DN*, July 13, Oct. 15, Nov. 2, 1937; MUCC, *Unemployment Compensation in Michigan—1938* (Detroit: n.p., 1939), p. 51.

71. State Welfare Department, Bureau of Old Age Assistance, *Old Age Assistance in Michigan, 1933-1937* (Lansing: n.p., 1938), pp. 2-7; ibid., *1937-1938* (Lansing: State Welfare Department, 1938), p. 1; Bryant speech, July 25, 1937, FM Papers; Fine, *Murphy*, pp. 188-89; *Public and Local Acts of the Legislature of . . . Michigan . . . 1935* (Lansing: Franklin DeKleine Co., 1935), pp. 243-50.

72. Haber to FM, Aug. 27, 1936, Herman M. Pekarsky to Hedetniemi, Oct. 13, 1938, and enclosed statement, FM Papers; *DN*, Jan. 7, 1937; Claude R. Tharp, *Social Security and Related Services in Michigan* (Ann Arbor: University of Michigan Press, 1946), p. 8.

73. Pekarsky to Hedetniemi, Oct. 13, 1938, and enclosed statement, FM Papers; Bureau of Old Age Assistance, *Old Age Assistance, 1937-1938*, p. 8; *DN*, Feb. 17, Apr. 28, 1937.

74. *FM Message, Jan. 7, 1937*, p. 4, FM Papers; Levi Memorandum to FM, July 14, 1938, and enclosed Memorandum, July 14, 1938, ibid.; *DN*, Mar. 16, June 26, 1937; Bureau of Old Age Assistance, *Old Age Assistance, 1937-1938*, pp. 2-4, 6, 8, 15.

75. FM to EGK, Nov. 24, 1936, EGK-BHC, Box 10; FM, *Message, Jan. 7, 1937*, pp. 3, 5, FM Papers.

76. FM statement, Mar. 17, 1937, FM Papers; FM to Robert J. Caldwell, July 6, 1937, ibid.; *DN*, Dec. 21, 1936, Mar. 26, 30, Apr. 11, 30, 1937; FM, "Labor Policy," p. 412; FM, "New Era," p. 1; *Selected Addresses*, pp. 24-25, 38.

77. *DN*, Mar. 21, Apr. 29, 1937; *MMFR* 59 (Apr. 10, 1937): 8; George Gallup, *The Gallup Poll: Public Opinion, 1935-1971*, 3 vols. (New York: Random House, 1972), 1:55, 58; Hadley Cantril, ed., *Public Opinion, 1935-1946* (Princeton: Princeton University Press, 1951), pp. 14, 872.

78. EGK to FM, Jan. 27, 1937, E. Blythe Stason to EGK, Mar. 18, Apr. 13, 1937, FM Papers; *Lansing State Journal*, Apr. 14, 1937, clipping in ibid.; *DLN*, Apr. 2, 23, 1937; *DN*, Apr. 18, 1937.

79. EGK to FM, Jan. 27, Mar. 20, 23, 1937, Stason to FM, Mar. 18, 24, 1937, and enclosed "Outline. . . ," Stason to EGK, Apr. 13, 1937, FM Papers; EGK drafts and notes, undated, ibid.; Haber to FM, Jan. 31, 1937, EGK to FM [Mar. 19, 1937], EGK-BHC, Box 10; EGK drafts and notes, undated, ibid.; document dated May 3, 1937, ibid.; *DN*, Mar. 30, Apr. 9, 1937; *Ann Arbor News*, May 21, 1937; Howard S. Kaltenborn, *Governmental Adjustment of Labor Disputes* (Chicago: The Foundation Press, 1943), pp. 37-60, 193n, 195-96; Charles C. Killingsworth, *State Labor Relations Acts* (Chicago: University of Chicago Press, 1948), pp. 219-20.

80. Stason to EGK, Mar. 31, 1937, and enclosed "Bill," Stason to EGK, Apr. 9, 1937, and enclosed draft, FM Papers; EGK draft of bill, Apr. 22, 1937, EGK Papers.

81. "House Bill No. 571," in State of Michigan, Legislature of 1937-1938, Regular Session, House Bills, University of Michigan Law Library, Ann Arbor, Michigan.

82. Harry A. Millis and Emily Clark Brown, *From the Wagner Act to Taft-Hartley* (Chicago: University of Chicago Press, 1950), pp. 161-62; Stason to EGK, Apr. 13,

1937, FM Papers; Killingsworth, *State Labor Acts*, pp. 1–2, 42–107, 215, 221–22, 230; Sanford Cohen, *State Labor Legislation, 1937–1939* (Columbus: Ohio State University Press, 1948), pp. 36, 43; Nathan Greene to Wirin, June 12, 1937, and enclosed "Analysis of proposed Michigan labor law. . . ," ACLU Archives, vol. 1048; Isadore Polier, "An Analysis of the Michigan Industrial Relations Bill" [July 2, 1937], ibid.; Zimmer to FM, Dec. 9, 1937, EGK–BHC, Box 11; document dated May 3, 1937, Box 10, ibid.; *DN*, June 17, 1937.

83. *MMFR* 59 (May 8, 1937): 8; *DN*, May 1–4, 6, 13, 1937; *DFP*, May 1, 1937; *Ann Arbor News*, May 1, 11, 12, 1937; *Flint Journal*, May 9, 1937, MSB; *United Automobile Worker*, May 8, 1937; Martel to FM, May 4, 1937, Travis to FM, May 1, 1937, EGK–BHC, Box 10; document dictated by Sugar, May 11, 1937, ibid.; Sugar draft of bill, undated, ibid.; ACLU Bulletin, May 4, 1937, ACLU Archives, vol. 1048; A. G. Mezerik to ——, undated, ACLU to FM, May 6, 1937, ibid., vol. 1049.

84. *DN*, Dec. 21, 1936, May 6, 11–13, 23, 26, 1937; *Ann Arbor News*, May 8, 11, 12, 1937; FM statement, Mar. 17, 1937, FM Papers; document dated May 3, 1937, EGK–BHC, Box 10; FM to Travis, May 3, 1937, EGK to Alkouri, undated, and enclosed copy of bill, ibid.; Baldwin to FM, May 15, 1937, ACLU Archives, vol. 1048; Minutes of ACLU Board of Directors' Meeting, May 17, 1937, ibid.; Polier to FM, May 16, 1937, Wirin to Greene, May 17, 1937, Wirin to Polier, May 20, 1937, Baldwin to FM, May [21], 1937, ibid., vol. 1049.

85. *DN*, May 26, 29, June 3, 4, 1937; *Ann Arbor News*, June 6, 1937; Polier to FM, May 16, 1937, ACLU Archives, vol. 1049; *House Journal, 1937*, 2:1285–95, 1379–80, 1397–99.

86. FM to Baldwin, June 3, 1937, Baldwin to FM, June 4, 1937, Sugar to Baldwin, June 9, 1937, Baldwin to Sugar, June 10, 1937, ACLU to FM, June 15, 1937, Wirin to Sugar, June 15, 1937, ACLU Archives, vol. 1049; Baldwin to Mezerik, June 4, 1937, Wirin to Greene, June 7, 1937, Greene to Wirin, June 12, 1937, and enclosed "Analysis," Wirin to Mezerik, June 15, 1937, ibid., vol. 1048; Sugar Memo on Substitute for House Bill 571, June 7, 1937, ibid.; Baldwin and Hays to FM, June 9, 1937, EGK–BHC, Box 9; *United Automobile Worker*, June 12, 1937; Jerold S. Auerbach, *Labor and Liberty: The La Follette Committee and the New Deal* (Indianapolis: Bobbs-Merrill Co., 1966), pp. 213–15 et passim.

87. Lewis to FM, June 11, 1937, E. L. Oliver to All Michigan Members, June 14, 1937, EGK–BHC, Box 9; *DN*, June 15–17, 1937; *United Automobile Worker*, July 31, 1937.

88. *MMFR* 59 (Jan. 5, 1937): 7; Carl F. Clarke to FM, June 14, 1937, Campbell to Hill, undated, and enclosed "Help Influence Enactment. . . ," June 7, 1937, EGK–BHC, Box 10; *DN*, June 15, 1937.

89. *DN*, June 20, 24, 1937; Josiah L. Sayre, "Some Aspects of the Legislative Process in Michigan, 1925–1937" (Ph.D. diss., University of Michigan, 1938), p. 10; FM to Polier, Aug. 11, 1937, EGK–BHC, Box 9.

90. *Journal of the Senate of the State of Michigan, 1937 Regular Session*, 2 vols. (Lansing: Franklin DeKleine Co., 1937), 2:1534–35, 1657–64; FM draft of picketing clause, EGK–BHC, Box 10; EMB to Baldwin, June 23, 1937, ACLU Archives, vol. 1049; *NYT*, June 16, 1937; *DN*, June 24, 1937.

91. *House Journal, 1937*, 2:2054, 2060, 2092, 2123, 2165, 2171–79; *Senate*

Journal, 1937, 2:1884; Sayre, "Legislative Process," pp. 121–22; Sugar to Baldwin, July 6, 1937, ACLU Archives, vol. 1048; *DN*, June 27, 1937.

92. *Business Week*, July 3, 1937, p. 14; *MMFR* 60 (July 3, 1937): 3, 8; *DN*, June 27, July 1, 29, 1937; *NYT*, July 1, 1937; *United Automobile Worker*, July 10, 1937; Sugar to Baldwin, June 29, 1937, Polier to FM, July 2, 1937, and enclosed "Analysis," Baldwin to FM, July 3, 1937, ACLU Archives, vol. 1049; Sugar to Baldwin, July 6, 1937, and enclosed Memo, Baldwin to Sugar, July 7, 1937, ibid., vol. 1048; ACLU Release, July 12, 1937, ibid.; Arthur J. Hartley to FM, June 30, 1937, W. Green to FM, July 20, 1937, EGK–BHC, Box 9; Harold A. Cowell to FM, July 25, 1937, Sugar to FM, July 29, 1937, ibid., Box 10; *DLN*, July 23, 1937; Cantril, ed., *Public Opinion*, p. 817.

93. *NYT*, June 29, 1937; FM to C. C. Chase, July 7, 1937, FM Papers; *Lansing State Journal*, July 2, 1937, clipping in ibid.; FM, "Labor Policy," pp. 411–13; *DN*, July 2, 3, 1937; Polier to FM, July 2, 1937, ACLU Archives, vol. 1049; Sugar to Baldwin, July 6, 12, 1937, ibid., vol. 1048.

94. Sugar to Baldwin, July 6, 12, 1937, Sugar to ACLU, July 29, 1937, ACLU Archives, vol. 1048; UAW Release, July 29, 1937, ibid., vol. 1049; Sugar to FM, July 29, 1937, EGK–BHC, Box 10; Lewis to FM, July 29, 1937, ibid., Box 9; Conference for Protection of Civil Rights to FM, July 29, 1937, FM Papers; *NYT*, July 28, 1937; *DN*, July 30, 1937; *House Journal, 1937*, 2:2265–66, 2279–80.

95. *DN*, July 30, Aug. 8, 1937; *NYT*, July 30, 1937; FM to Lee Jaffe, Aug. 13, 1937, FM Papers; FM to Lewis, Aug. 12, Sept. 3, 1937, EGK–BHC, Box 9; *DLN*, Aug 6, 1937; *Nation* 145 (Aug. 7, 1937): 142; Wirin to FM, Aug. 9, 1937, ACLU Archives, vol. 1049.

96. *Journal of the Senate of the State of Michigan, Extra Session of 1937* (Lansing: Franklin DeKleine Co., 1937), pp. 2, 4, 13–20, 29, 30, 33–40, 50; *Journal of the House of Representatives of the State of Michigan, Extra Session of 1937* (Lansing; Franklin DeKleine Co. [1937]), pp. 9, 17, 24, 43, 44, 48; *DN*, July 16, 31, Aug. 1, 4–6, 8, Nov. 7, 1937; *DFP*, July 30, 31, 1937; *Ann Arbor News*, July 31, Aug. 2, 1937; *MMFR* 60 (Aug. 4, 1937): 18; *DLN*, Dec. 17, 1937; Polier to FM, Oct. 1, 1937, ACLU Archives, vol. 1048; "Conference of . . . the MFL . . . ," Dec. 12, 1937, Wayne County AFL-CIO Papers, Box 8; McCallum Diary, July 30, 1937, McCallum Papers.

97. FM to Baldwin, Aug. 11, 1937, FM to Polier, Aug. 11, 1937, FM to Pierson, Aug. 11, 1937, FM to Kelley, Aug. 11, 1937, FM to Lawrence Fisher, Aug. 11, 1937, FM to Perkins, Aug. 11, 1937, FM to Green, Aug. 12, 1937, FM to Lewis, Aug. 12, 1937, FM to Hartley, Aug. 12, 1937, EGK–BHC, Box 9; Zimmer to FM, Dec. 9, 1937, and enclosed memorandum, EGK to Zimmer, Jan. 4, 1938, Zimmer to EGK, Jan. 20, 1938, ibid., Box 11; Wirin to Sugar, Sept. 14, 1937, ACLU Archives, vol. 1049; Polier to Baldwin, Oct. 1, 1937, [Oct. 8, 1937], Baldwin to Sugar, Oct. 11, 1937, ibid., vol. 1048; ACLU Minutes, Oct. 11, 1937, ibid.; *DN*, Sept. 26, 1937.

98. See Chapter 14.

99. A Gallup poll released on July 4, 1937, revealed that among the 50 percent of those responding who indicated that their attitude toward labor unions had changed during the preceding six months, 71 percent were less well disposed toward unions. Gallup, *Gallup Poll*, 1:63.

100. See, for example, *DN*, May 2, July 1, 1937; *NYT*, June 29, 30, July 30, 1937;

Washington Post, June 30, 1937, clipping in FM Papers; FM, "Labor Policy," pp. 411–13 +; and "For and Against—Governor Murphy's Labor Policy," *Survey Graphic* 26 (Sept. 1937): 464–69.

CHAPTER 10

1. Testimony concerning the Civil Service System..., Oct. 25, 1936, in Mrs. Siegel W. Judd, "Origins of the Michigan Merit System, 1935–1941" (undated), Dorothy Judd Papers, Box 2, MHC; unidentified newspaper clipping, Sept. 19 [1935], in ibid.; Frank D. Fitzgerald, "Why I Favor the Merit System," *Michigan Municipal Review* 9 (May 1936): 67; idem, "Public Personnel," *State Government* 9 (July 1936): 153–54; *Report of the Civil Service Study Commission* (Lansing: n.p., 1936), pp. 11–12; *DN*, Oct. 14, 1935; Interview with James K. Pollock, July 12, 1966, pp. 1–2, MHC.

2. *Civil Service Report*, pp. 15–55; *New York Herald Tribune*, Feb. 28, 1937.

3. *Civil Service Report*, pp. 59–80; "Summary of the Bill Proposed by the Civil Service Study Commission," Civil Service Study Commission (hereafter CSSC) Papers, MHC; Picard to David V. Addy, June 4, 1936, Pollock to George Meader, Jan. 18, 1937, Pollock to Christian Matthews, Mar. 1, 1937, ibid.; G. P. McCallum to Meader, Jan. 11, 1937, James K. Pollock Papers, Box 5, MHC; Shields to FM, May 15, 1937, and enclosed Memorandum in Regard to the Civil Service Bill, EGK-BHC, Box 18.

4. *DN*, Feb. 10, 1937; Pollock to Leland Stowe, Feb. 19, 1937, CSSC Papers; *New York Herald Tribune*, Feb. 28, 1937.

5. Edward H. Litchfield, "Michigan's Experience with Civil Service," *Personnel Administration* 2 (Dec. 1939): 3; *DN*, Nov. 8, 1936.

6. FM to Pollock, Nov. 20, 1936, Pollock Papers, Box 5; Pollock to Upson, Dec. 4, 1936, ibid., Box 7; Pollock to Judd, Jan. 7, 1937, ibid., Box 4; Pollock interview, pp. 3–4; "Notes on Frank Murphy...," Pollock Papers; FM to EGK, undated, with FM to EGK, Nov. 24, 1936, FM Papers; *Message of Frank Murphy..., Jan. 7, 1937* (n.d., n.p.), pp. 5–6, ibid.; FM article for *Democratic Digest*, Jan. 6, 1938, ibid.; *DN*, Dec. 20, 1936.

7. EGK to FM, Feb. 10, 1937, EGK-BHC, Box 8; Pollock to Judd, Feb. 2, 1937, Pollock Papers, Box 4; Upson to Pollock, Feb. 10, 1937, ibid., Box 7; Pollock to Eliot Kaplan, Mar. 23, 1937, ibid., Box 5; William P. Lovett to Pollock, Feb. 8, 1937, CSSC Papers; *DN*, Feb. 18, 1937.

8. *DN*, Feb. 10, 21, 23, 24, 26, Mar. 3, 5, 1937; Lovett to Pollock, Feb. 19, 27, 1937, Pollock to W. S. Gilmore, Feb. 19, Mar. 26, 1937, Litchfield to Pollock, Feb. 24, 1937, Pollock to Diggs, Mar. 1, 1937, Pollock to Matthews, Mar. 1, 1937, Pollock to William Palmer, Mar. 2, 1937, Pollock to Lovett, Mar. 8, 1937, CSSC Papers; *Journal of the Senate of the State of Michigan, 1937 Regular Session*, 2 vols. (Lansing: Franklin DeKleine Co., 1937), 1:261; *Michigan Official Directory and Legislative Manual, 1937–38* (n.p., n.d.), p. 670.

9. Lovett to Pollock, Mar. 5, 13, 20, 1937, CSSC Papers; *DN*, Mar. 5, 1937. Cf. Pollock to Judd, Mar. 12, 1937, Pollock Papers, Box 4.

10. *DN*, Mar. 11, 21, Apr. 1, 2, 1937; Pollock to Gilmore, Mar. 26, 1937, CSSC

Papers; Litchfield to Judd, Apr. 1, 1937, Michigan Merit System Association Papers, MHC; Pollock to Upson, Apr. 3, 1937, Pollock Papers, Box 7; Lovett to George A. Schroeder, Apr. 3, 1937, EGK-BHC, Box 18; Litchfield, "Michigan's Experience," p. 3. For Lovett's partisanship, see Lovett to Miller Dunckel, Detroit Citizens League Papers, Box 32, Burton Historical Collection, Detroit, Michigan.

11. Undated typed sheet, in Michigan Merit System Association Papers, MHC; Litchfield to Pollock, Apr. 15, 19, 23, 1937, Pollock Papers, Box 5; Shields to Pollock, Oct. 19, 1937, ibid., Box 6; G. Lyle Belsley to FM, Apr. 7, 1937, EGK-BHC, Box 18; *DN*, May 5, 30, 1937.

12. Picard to Litchfield, July 2, 1937, Pollock Papers, Box 5; *DN*, Mar. 5, 10, 12, 23, Apr. 22, June 22, 1937; *Journal of the House of Representatives of the State of Michigan, 1937 Regular Session*, 2 vols. (Lansing: Franklin DeKleine Co., n.d.), 2:1867, 2010; *Michigan Manual, 1937–38*, pp. 683, 692; Charles F. Hemans to Alexander G. Ruthven, Apr. 1, 1937, Alexander G. Ruthven Papers, Box 21, MHC.

13. *DN*, Mar. 21, 23, May 4, 23, June 22, 1937; Picard to Litchfield, July 2, 1937, Pollock Papers, Box 5.

14. *DN*, June 10, 22, 25, 27, 1937; *House Journal, 1937*, 2:1577–80, 1853–67, 2007–11; Litchfield to Pollock, June 16, 24, 1937, Pollock Papers, Box 5.

15. Litchfield to Pollock, June 24, 1937, Litchfield to Members, June 30, 1937, Litchfield to Picard, July 9, 1937, Pollock Papers, Box 5; *DN*, June 26, 27, 1937; Josiah L. Sayre, "Some Aspects of the Legislative Process in Michigan, 1925 to 1937" (Ph.D. diss., University of Michigan, 1938), pp. 118, 237.

16. Litchfield to Pollock, May 4, 12, 1937, Pollock Papers, Box 5; Pollock to Upson, June 29, 1937, ibid., Box 7; Pollock to Gilmore, July 2, 1937, Lovett to Pollock, July 2, 1937, CSSC Papers; Lovett to George A. Osborn, June 28, 1937, Lovett to Dunckel, July 13, 1937, Detroit Citizens League Papers, Box 32; *DN*, June 22, 26, July 2, 3, 8, 1937; Pollock to FM, July 2, 1937, and enclosed Memorandum on Civil Service, EGK-BHC, Box 18.

17. FM to Henry F. Shea, July 15, 1937, Callaghan to FM, July 19, 1937, Pollock to EGK, July 19, 1937, EGK-BHC, Box 18; FM to Representatives and Senators, July 25, 1937, ibid., Box 14; *House Journal, 1937*, 2:2264–65; *DN*, July 28, 29, 1937; *Lansing State Journal*, July 28, 1937, MSB. See also Pollock to Upson, Apr. 3, 1937, Box 7; and Interview with G. Donald Kennedy, May 11, 1965, p. 16, MHC.

18. *Senate Journal, 1937*, 2:1975; *House Journal, 1937*, 2:2290–95; Leo J. Nowicki, "Profile of an American by Choice" (1975), pp. 63–65, 80.

19. *Public and Local Acts of the Legislature of . . . Michigan . . . 1937* (Lansing: Franklin DeKleine Co., 1937), pp. 830–43.

20. *DN*, July 31, Aug. 1, 2, 5, 13, 1937; Pollock to Kaplan, July 31, 1937, Litchfield to FM, Aug. 3, 1937, Pollock Papers, Box 5; Michigan Merit System Association News Letter, Aug. 11, 1937, ibid.; Pollock to William Brownrigg, July 31, 1937, ibid., Box 3; Pollock to Upson, Aug. 3, 1937, ibid., Box 7; Statement of Pollock, Aug. 3, 1937, CSSC Papers; Belsley, "The Advance of the Merit System," *State Government* 12 (Jan. 1939): 7.

21. [Smith], "Comments on Senate Bill #1" [1937], EGK-BHC, Box 18; *Civil Service Report*, p. 61; Brownrigg to Pollock, May 10, July 31, 1937, CSSC Papers; Pollock statement, Aug. 3, 1937, ibid.; Michigan Merit System Association News

Letter, Aug. 1, 1937, Pollock Papers, Box 5; Pollock to Kaplan, July 31, 1937, ibid.

22. FM to Kennedy, July 31, 1937, G. Donald Kennedy Papers, MHC; *Lansing State Journal*, July 28, 1937, MSB; *DN*, Aug. 1, 6, 22, 1937; Nowicki, "Profile," p. 65; Sayre, "Legislative Process," pp. 192–93, 197–98, 235, 238; Kennedy interview, p. 16; Pollock to Kaplan, July 31, 1937, Litchfield to FM, Aug. 3, 1937, Pollock Papers, Box 5; Pollock to Brownrigg, July 31, 1937, ibid., Box 3; Shields to Pollock, Oct. 19, 1937, ibid., Box 6; Lovett to Mrs. Harry R. Applegate, Aug. 5, 1937, Lovett to James T. Milliken, Sept. 22, 1937, Detroit Citizens League Papers, Box 32; Pollock to FM, Sept. 8, 1937, FM Papers; JRH to George C. Dunham, Dec. 23, 1937, JRH Papers; Litchfield, "Michigan's Experience," p. 3; [*St. Louis Post-Dispatch*, Aug. 21, 1937], clipping in FM Papers; Pollock interview, pp. 3, 5; Penelope Helen Sawkins, "Executive Leadership of Frank Murphy as Governor of Michigan" (M.A. thesis, Wayne University, 1950), pp. 61–62.

23. *DN*, Aug. 14, 1937; Pollock to Brownrigg, Aug. 16, 1937, Pollock Papers, Box 3; *Michigan Manufacturer and Financial Record* 60 (Aug. 21, 1937): 8.

24. *DN*, Aug. 14, Sept. 8, 9, 1937; press release, Sept. 7, 1937, FM Papers; Belsley to FM [Sept. 1937], Pollock to FM, Sept. 8, 1937, ibid.; Pollock to Lovett, Sept. 8, 1937, CSSC Papers; Pollock to Thomas Barclay, Sept. 8, 1937, Pollock Papers, Box 3; Pollock interview, p. 7; Interview with GM, Mar. 28, 1957, p. 11, MHC. Brownrigg initially accepted the job only for one year, taking a leave of absence from his California position because he feared that, if he resigned, the opponents of the merit system would influence the choice of his successor. At the end of twelve months Brownrigg decided to remain in Michigan. Brownrigg to FM, Aug. 24, Sept. 9, 1937, FM to Brownrigg, Sept. 4, 8, 1937, FM Papers; *DN*, Sept. 24, 1938.

25. Litchfield, "Michigan's Experience," p. 4; Brownrigg, "Confidential Report to the State Civil Service Commission," Jan. 25, 1938, CSSC Papers; Warren M. Huff to Pollock, Nov. 25, 1938, ibid.; "Radio Dialog," Apr. 10, 1938, FM Papers; EGK to FM, July 28, 1938, ibid.; Michigan State Civil Service Department, "First Annual Report" (1938), pp. 6, 7–8; Pollock, "Michigan's First Year of Civil Service," *National Municipal Review* 28 (Jan. 1939): 5; EGK to FM, July 1, 1938, EGK-BHC, Box 12; *DN*, Sept. 30, Oct. 19, 1937, May 18, 1938.

26. *DN*, May 11, Aug. 6, 23, 30, Sept. 12, 1938; Civil Service Department, "First Report," pp. 9–11, 36–42; Huff to Pollock, Nov. 25, 1938, CSSC Papers; Litchfield, "Michigan's Experience," p. 4; Picard to Brownrigg, Sept. 13, 1938, FM Papers.

27. *DN*, Aug. 22, Nov. 18, Dec. 16, 1937; Brownrigg, "Confidential Report," CSSC Papers; "Report of the Civil Service Commission to the Governor on the Qualifying Examination Program," Sept. 25, 1938, ibid.; Huff to Pollock, Nov. 25, 1938, ibid.; "Radio Dialog," Apr. 10, 1938, FM Papers; Civil Service Department, "First Report," pp. 9, 13–14; Pollock, "First Year," p. 4; Litchfield, "Michigan's Experience," p. 5.

28. *DN*, Sept. 15, 16, 20, 24, 25, Oct. 5, 1938; Burke to Brownrigg, Sept. 16, 1938, FM Papers; "Report on Qualifying Examination Programs," CSSC Papers. The commission was also to consider the advisability of a pension plan for local government employees and was to investigate the actuarial soundness of the Teachers' Retirement Fund.

29. Gerald J. Cleary to FM, June 24, 1938, FM Papers; "Report on Qualifying Examination Program," CSSC Papers; *DN*, July 3, Sept. 13, 1938.

30. Civil Service Department, "First Report," pp. 9, 16; *DN*, June 4, 5, Sept. 22, 1938; Judd analysis of payroll [1939], CSSC Papers; Cleary to FM, June 9, 1938, FM Papers; *Public Acts of Michigan, 1937*, p. 837.

31. Litchfield, "Another Chapter in Michigan Civil Service Reform," *American Political Science Review* 35 (Feb. 1941): 80; Advance on FM speech, Oct. 20, 1938, FM Papers; *DN*, Oct. 21, 1938.

32. Brownrigg, "Confidential Report," CSSC Papers; Pollock, "First Year," p. 1; Pollock to Brownrigg, Feb. 15, 1939, William Brownrigg Papers, MHC; Civil Service Department, "First Report," pp. 7, 21–22.

33. Pollock, "First Year," p. 3; Litchfield, "Michigan's Experience," p. 6; Brownrigg, "Confidential Report," CSSC Papers; Picard to Brownrigg, Sept. 3, 1938, FM Papers.

34. *DN*, Oct. 14, 1937, May 15, 19, June 4, 1938; Daily Memorandum, May 18, 1939, Harold D. Smith Papers, FDRL; Pollock interview, p. 8; Kennedy interview, p. 16.

35. EGK to M. H. DeFoe, Mar. 8, 1938, EGK-BHC, Box 17; Schorer to Pollock, June 28, 1938, Pollock Papers, Box 6; *DN*, Dec. 25, 1938; Litchfield, "Michigan's Experience," p. 6.

36. Judd analysis [1939], CSSC Papers; *DN*, May 19, 1938.

37. Judd to Fitzgerald, June 6, 1938, in "Origins of Merit System," Judd Papers, Box 2; Judd to Pollock, Apr. 18, 1938, R. L. Dixon to Judd, June 1, 1938, Fitzgerald to Judd, June 7, 1938, ibid.; Floyd Josiah Miller Diary, Dec. 30, 1937, Floyd Josiah Miller Papers, MHC; *DN*, Dec. 3, 26, 28, 1937, Jan. 16, May 22, 1938; Lovett to Applegate, Aug. 16, 1937, Detroit Citizens League Papers, Box 32; EGK to DeFoe, Mar. 8, 1938, EGK-BHC, Box 17; Judd analysis [1939], CSSC Papers; *Public Acts of Michigan, 1937*, p. 842. See above, p. 276.

38. Minutes of Meeting Held in Flint, May 19, 1938, FM Papers; Cleary to FM, June 24, 1938, ibid.; Kennedy interview, p. 16; *DFP*, June 1, 1938.

39. *DN*, June 4–6, 1938; *DT*, June 5, 1938, clipping in FM Papers; Fry to FM, June 7, 1938, Sherman McDonald to Fry, June 9, 1938, ibid.; "Remarks of Edward J. Fry," June 9, 1938, ibid. See Chapter 14 and Litchfield, "Michigan's Experience," pp. 6–7.

40. See *DN*, Sept. 12, 1937, and FM article for *Democratic Digest*, Jan. 6, 1938, FM Papers.

41. *DN*, Jan. 12, Sept. 21, 26, Nov. 10, 1937, Jan. 18, Feb. 11, 26, 1938; Weber speech, Oct. 27, 1938, FM Papers; Weber Memorandum to Norman H. Hill, Dec. 19, 1938, ibid. For a possible exception to Weber's generally competent administration of state purchasing, see *Michigan Times*, Aug. 11, 1939, FM Papers.

42. McFarland speech, Nov. 3, 1938, FM Papers; "Suggestions for Governor Murphy . . ." [1938], ibid.; *DN*, Feb. 27, 1937; *DFP*, July 20, 1937; EGK to FM, Jan. 27, 1937, EGK-BHC, Box 18.

43. *Public Acts of the Legislature of . . . Michigan . . . Extra Sessions of 1933–1934* (Lansing: Franklin DeKleine, Co., 1934), pp. 16–34; Harold M. Dorr, *Administrative Organization of State Government in Michigan, 1921–1936* (Ann Arbor:

University of Michigan, 1936), p. 16; *DN*, Jan. 12, Feb. 21, Apr. 28, May 1, July 1, 14, 15, 1937; "Suggestions" [1938], FM Papers; Picard to FM, Sept. 24, 1938, ibid.; George C. Ackers, *Michigan Liquor Control Commission Activities, 1933–1945* (n.p., n.d.), p. 11; *Activities of the Michigan Liquor Control Commission for the Fiscal Year Ending June 30, 1938* (n.p., n.d.), pp. 31, 43; Paul W. Tara to Fitzgerald, Jan. 10, 1935, Picard to Francis B. Drolet, Oct. 8, 1936, Frank D. Fitzgerald Papers, MHC; Leo D. Woodworth and Lent D. Upson, eds., "Staff Studies of the Tax Study Commission," 3 pts. (Detroit: Office of the Commission [1938–1939]), pt. 2, pp. 453–58. The closing hours were changed to 1:00 A.M. (1:30 in Wayne County) in 1935, but the original hours were restored on May 1, 1937. *DN*, May 1, 1937. Six Michigan counties as of the beginning of 1937 had exercised their option to limit the sale of alcoholic beverages to beer and wine; only 291 cities, villages, and townships in the state permitted the sale of liquor by the glass. Woodworth and Upson, eds., "Staff Studies," pt. 2, p. 455.

44. *DN*, Feb. 27, Mar. 10, June 7, Nov. 17, 25, Dec. 10, 1937; [*DT*, Nov. 23, 1937], MSB; McFarland speech, Nov. 3, 1938, FM Papers; "Suggestions" [1938], ibid.

45. *Activities of Liquor Commission, 1938*, pp. 9–10, 21–25, 27–29, 47, 63; Ackers, *Activities*, p. 18; Michigan Liquor Control Commission Release [May 4, 1938], FM Papers; L. D. Rahilly to Jerome G. Thomas, May 4, 1938, Irwin Huston to FM, June 30, 1938, and enclosed sheet of same date, Huston to FM, Oct. 4, 1938, FM Papers; McFarland speech, Nov. 3, 1938, ibid.; "Suggestions" [1938], ibid.; *DN*, Apr. 15, 28, June 7, Sept. 5, 1937, Mar. 21, 25, May 5, 13, July 7, 1938. The price of liquor was increased by 7 percent in September 1937. *DN*, Sept. 5, 1937. The average markup in 1937–38 was 45.7 percent, compared to 42.5 percent in 1935–36 and 43.7 percent in 1936–37. Woodworth and Upson, eds., "Staff Studies," pt. 2, p. 457.

46. *DN*, Apr. 28, June 26, July 1, 2, 14, 15, 22, 28, 29, Aug. 5, 25, 26, Nov. 4, 28, 1937; *DFP*, July 2, Nov. 24, 1937; Schroeder to FM, Nov. 19, 1937, and enclosed notes, Cleary to FM, Aug. 18, 1938, McFarland to FM, Jan. 20, 1938, Picard to FM, Sept. 28, 1938, Drolet to SDD's, Nov. 2, 1938, FM Papers; *Activities of Liquor Commission, 1938*, p. 31. An amendment to the Liquor Control Act that went into effect on July 22, 1937, authorized the establishment of state stores in cities or villages of 3,000 population or more. *DN*, July 22, 1937. Although SDD sales declined to 48 percent of total liquor sales in 1937, they increased to 51 percent in 1938. Acker, *Activities*, p. 11.

47. Schroeder to FM, Nov. 19, 1937, and enclosed notes, Cleary to FM, Aug. 18, 1938, FM Papers; [*DT*, Nov. 23, Dec. 3, 1937], MSB; *DFP*, Nov. 25, 1937; *DN*, Nov. 25, 1937.

48. *DN*, July 16, Aug. 29, Sept. 3, Oct. 5, 9, Nov. 4, 1937; Schroeder to FM, Nov. 19, 1937, and enclosed notes, FM Papers.

49. William F. Pyper article [July 10, 1937], Guy Hugh Jenkins Papers, MHC; Picard to Pyper, July 13, 1937, Pyper to Picard, July 14, 1937, ibid.; *Activities of the Liquor Commission, 1938*, pp. 20–21, 40, 43; McFarland speech, Nov. 3, 1938, FM Papers; "Suggestions" [1938], ibid.; Mead to FM, June 24, 1937, ibid.; Mead

statement, May 4, 1938, ibid.; Liquor Commission Release [May 4, 1938], ibid.; *DN*, May 1, June 7, July 22, Oct. 7, 14, Dec. 15, 1937, Mar. 13, May 5, 1938.

50. *DN*, Dec. 28, 31, 1937.

51. McFarland to FM, Dec. 30, 1938, FM Papers.

52. *DN*, Jan. 7, July 14, 15, 29, 30, Aug. 8, 22, 26, 29, 31, Sept. 20, Nov. 22, 23, Dec. 5, 9, 1937, Feb. 9, Apr. 3, July 8, 13, 19, 29, Aug. 6, 1938; *Michigan Christian Advocate*, Jan. 21, 1937; *DFP* [Aug. 11, 1939], MSB; Starr speech, Dec. 8, 1937, FM Papers; Starr to Hill, Dec. 20, 1938, ibid.; Starr to Lovett, Dec. 14, 1937, Detroit Citizens League Papers, Box 33.

53. *DN*, Feb. 10, 11, 19, Dec. 5, 1937; *Achievement* (Sept. 1938): 36; "A Brief Resume of the Accomplishments of the Michigan Corporation and Securities Commission . . ." [Oct. 18, 1938], FM Papers; Olson speeches, Oct. 25, 28, 1938, ibid.; Olson to FM, Dec. 27, 1937, Dec. 21, 1938, ibid.; *Grand Rapids Press*, Oct. 29, 1938, clipping in ibid.

54. State Banking Department, "Summary Report of Activities during 1937 . . .," FM Papers; FM to Fisher, Jr., Jan. 4, 1938, EMB to Mary Hayden, Sept. 13, 1938, Macauley, Jr., to FM [Nov. 1938], Harold G. Hudson to Hill, Dec. 14, 1938, FM Papers; document dated Oct. 28, 1938, ibid.; "Prepared for EGK by Macauley, Jr." [Dec. 19, 1938], ibid.; *DN*, June 23, 1937.

55. *DN*, Jan. 1, 1937, Mar. 14, 16, Nov. 30, 1937, Jan. 30, 31, Feb. 18, Mar. 14, 16, Apr. 6, 21, 26, 27, May 20, June 29, July 30, 1938; Glenwood C. Fuller, "The Public Interest," Aug. 4, 1937, FM Papers; Lucille Belen to EMB [July 25, 1938], Todd to FM, July 28, 1938, Howell Van Auken to FM, July 29, 1938, ibid.; Todd speech, Oct. 26 [1938], ibid.; *Achievement* (Sept. 1938): 34; John M. Carmody to H. O. Clines, Aug. 19, 1937, John M. Carmody Papers, Box 87, FDRL.

56. *DN*, Aug. 15, 1937; "Report of the 1937 Michigan State Fair," MSB; "Report of the 1938 Michigan State Fair," FM Papers; FM to James W. Clapp, Dec. 19, 1938, FM to Hill, Jan. 9, 1945, ibid.

57. EGK to FM, Jan. 11, 1937, EGK-BHC, Box 18; WAB to EMB, Sept. 8, 1938, Fegan to FM, Dec. 13, 1938, [Fegan] Memorandum to FM, Dec. 23, 1938, FM Papers; Robert S. Ford and Albert Waxman, *Financing Government in Michigan* (Ann Arbor: University of Michigan Press, 1942), p. 40; *DN*, Dec. 9, 15, 16, 22, 24, 1937, Jan. 4, 5, 1938; *DFP*, Nov. 24, Dec. 23, 24, 1937; [*Lansing State Journal*, Dec. 14, 1937, Feb. 2, 1938], MSB; *Report of the Tax Study Commission, Jan. 30, 1939* (Detroit: The Commission [1939]), p. 10. As a compromise, Fegan agreed to permit the examiners to remain on the job until their status could be determined by their performance on the qualifying examinations. *DFP*, Dec. 23, 24, 1937.

58. *DN*, Feb. 15, 19, Mar. 12, May 1, 1938, June 22, 1939; *DFP*, Apr. 6, 7, 1938; [*Lansing State Journal*, Apr. 6, 7, 1938], MSB; Arthur Lyon Cross to FM, Mar. 10, 1938, Hill to Cross, Mar. 17, 1938, WAB to EMB, Sept. 8, 1938, [Fegan] Memorandum to FM, Dec. 23, 1938, FM Papers; Jenkins to Michael A. Gorman, Mar. 16, 1938, Jenkins Papers; *Report of Tax Study Commission*, pp. 36–37; Arthur W. Stace et al., *Taxation in Michigan* (Ann Arbor: Booth Newspapers, Inc., 1938); Ford and Waxman, *Financing Government*, p. 66.

59. WAB to EMB, Sept. 8, 1938, Fegan to FM, Dec. 13, 1938, [Fegan] Memoran-

dum to FM, Dec. 23, 1938, FM Papers; [Fegan], "The State Tax Commission" [1938], FM Papers; *DN*, Apr. 19, 1938; Woodworth and Upson, eds., "Staff Studies," pt. 3, p. 538; *Ex-Augural Message of Frank Murphy. . ., Jan. 5, 1939* (n.p., n.d.), p. 8; George P. McCallum to Gentlemen, Feb. 21, 1938, Howard C. Lawrence Papers, MHC.

60. WAB to EMB, Sept. 8, 1938, [Fegan] Memorandum to FM, Dec. 23, 1938, FM Papers.

61. Upson to FM, Nov. 27, 1936, Detroit Bureau of Governmental Research Papers, Box 41, Burton Historical Collection; Upson to P. A. Herbert, Mar. 9, 1937, ibid., Box 42; Upson to Brownrigg, Sept. 9, 1938, ibid., Box 43; Arthur Elder to FM, Dec. 22, 1937, EGK-BHC, Box 15; [Executive Order] Dec. 22, 1937, FM Papers; FM to Claude G. Bowers, Jan. 3, 1938, FM to Charles B. Van Dusen, Jan. 25, 1938, F. E. Levi to EGK, Jan. 31, 1938, Upson to EGK, Mar. 24, 1938, ibid.; *DT*, Mar. 1, 1938, clipping in ibid.; *Report of Tax Study Commission*; [*Lansing State Journal*, Jan. 8, 13, 1938], MSB; [*Saginaw News*, Jan. 18, 1938], MSB; unidentified clipping, Jan. 27, 1938, MSB. See Box 43 of the Detroit Bureau of Governmental Research Papers for the work of the Tax Study Commission.

62. *NYT*, Feb. 3, 1939.

CHAPTER 11

1. Pollock to FM, Nov. 9, 1936, and enclosed Memorandum and Public Administration Service, "Suggestions for Administrative Improvement of the Michigan State Government," undated, FM Papers.

2. *Message of Frank Murphy . . . January 7, 1937* (n.p., n.d.), p. 8, ibid.; Interview with G. Donald Kennedy, May 11, 1965, MHC.

3. FM to Norman H. Hill, Feb. 9, 1937, EGK-BHC, Box 18; Smith to FM, June 1, 1937, Harold W. H. Burrows to Hill, Dec. 20, 1938, Smith to John H. Brennan, Aug. 2, 1940, FM Papers; Smith press release [Mar. 9, 1938], ibid.; Smith, "Need for Installation of Revised Financial System," Apr. 6, 1938, ibid.; Public Administration Service, "Report on Financial Administration in the Michigan State Government" ([Chicago], 1938); *DN*, Mar. 10, July 18, 1938; *DFP*, Apr. 29, 1938.

4. Frank M. Landers, *Administration and Financing of Public Relief* ([Ann Arbor]: University of Michigan, 1942), p. 1; Charles F. Ernst, "New Trends in Public Welfare Legislation," *State Government* 11 (May 1938): 85.

5. Landers, *Public Relief*, pp. 2–4; Ernest B. Harper and Duane L. Gibson, *Reorganization of Public Welfare in Michigan* (East Lansing: Michigan State College, 1942), pp. 7–8; Isabel Campbell Bruce and Edith Eickhoff, *The Michigan Poor Law* (Chicago: University of Chicago Press, 1936), pp. 11, 14, 23–24, 31, 62–63, 148–49; Margaret F. Gordon, "The Organization and Functions of the Local . . . Public Welfare Agencies in Michigan" (M.A. thesis, University of Michigan, 1945), pp. 30, 34; George F. Granger and Lawrence R. Klein, *Emergency Relief in Michigan, 1933–1939* (Lansing: n.p., 1939), pp. 1, 9; "Public Welfare in Michigan, A Report Prepared under the Auspices of the State of Michigan Welfare and Relief Study Commission [WRSC] by the Staff" (1937), pp. 259–60, 270–75, 280, 332, 388;

Constance L. Pontello, "Welfare Reorganization in Michigan, 1936 to 1939" (1964), p. 9, in my possession.

6. Landers, *Public Relief*, pp. 6–9, 24–25; Fred R. Johnson, "The Crisis in State Welfare," *Compass Needle* 2 (Jan.–Feb. 1936): 8; William Haber and Paul L. Stanchfield, *Unemployment, Relief and Economic Security* (Lansing: n.p., 1936), p. 7; Granger and Klein, *Emergency Relief*, pp. 2–4; "Staff Report on Welfare," pp. 228–29.

7. *Unemployment and Relief in Michigan* (Lansing: n.p., 1935), pp. 45–48; Haber and Stanchfield, *Unemployment*, p. 31; Interview with William J. Norton, undated, p. 13, MHC; "Staff Report on Welfare," pp. 227, 391; Louise V. Armstrong, *We Too Are the People* (Boston: Little, Brown and Co, 1938), pp. 79, 106, 269, 466–67; [Armstrong] to Haber, Feb. 7, 1935, Louise V. Armstrong Papers, MHC; Norton to FM, Dec. 9, 1936, and enclosed Memorandum, FM Papers; WRSC, Hearing..., Sept. 18, 1936, Records of the WRSC, RG 35, Box 2, State Archives, Michigan History Division, Lansing, Michigan; Howard O. Hunter to Harry L. Hopkins, Dec. 11, 1934, WPA-FERA Narrative Field Reports, Harry L. Hopkins Papers, FDRL.

8. Hunter to Hopkins, Dec. 11, 1934, Jan. 20, Mar. 25, 1935, Hunter to Fitzgerald, Dec. 27, 30, 1934, Fitzgerald to Hunter, Dec. 28, 1934, FERA-WPA Reports, Hopkins Papers; *DN*, Nov. 22, 1936; Haber and Stanchfield, *Unemployment*, p. 31.

9. Granger and Klein, *Emergency Relief*, pp. 5, 11–12; Haber and Stanchfield, *Unemployment*, p. 52; Landers, *Public Relief*, p. 11; Charles H. Bender to Members of Board of Supervisors, Oct. 1, 1935, SEWRC Papers, MHC; SERA Letter #589, June 4, 1936, ibid.; SERA Letter #594, June 17, 1936, ibid.; Haber to Fitzgerald, May 1, 1936, Haber to Norton, May 1, June 22, 1936, Children's Fund of Michigan Papers, Box 13, MHC; "President's Address," 38th Annual Meeting, State Association of Supervisors, Jan. 26–28, 1937, Minutes of the WRSC, RG 52-4, Box 2, State Archives, Michigan History Division; Armstrong, *People*, pp. 466–67; Granger to FM, Apr. 12, 1938, FM Papers; Raymond Louis Koch, "The Development of Public Relief Programs in Minnesota, 1929–1941" (Ph.D. diss., University of Minnesota, 1967), pp. 297, 300–2; Dwayne Charles Cole, "The Relief Crisis in Illinois during the Depression, 1930 to 1940" (Ph.D. diss., St. Louis University, 1973), pp. 339–41.

10. Haber and Stanchfield, *Unemployment*, pp. 12–14; Granger and Klein, *Emergency Relief*, pp. 8–11, 68–69; *Report of the Welfare and Relief Study Commission* (Lansing: n.p., 1936), p. 41.

11. Norton to FM, Dec. 9, 1936, and enclosed Memorandum, FM Papers; *Report of the State Welfare Department of the State of Michigan, December, 1938* (n.p., n.d.), p. 14; Public Administration Service, "Suggestions," FM Papers; "Staff Report on Welfare," pp. 268–70, 289–98, 322, 334, 387–91; *WRSC Report*, pp. 18–19, 29–31; Johnson, "Crisis," pp. 8–9.

12. First Meeting of WRSC, Apr. 20, 1936, pp. 2–6, RG 35, Box 1; WRSC, Verbatim Minutes, Nov. 10, 1936, pp. 6–10, 16, ibid.; *WRSC Report*, pp. 9–11; Arthur Dunham, "Public Welfare and the Referendum in Michigan," *Social Service Review* 12 (Sept. 1938): 419–20.

13. WRSC, Hearing . . . , Sept. 18, 1936, pp. 1-4, RG 35, Box 2; Hearing Held by WRSC for Supervisors, Nov. 10, 1936, pp. 52-55, ibid., Box 1.

14. WRSC, Hearing, Sept. 18, 1936, pp. 4-5, ibid., Box 2; WRSC, Hearing, Nov. 10, 1936, pp. 6-7, 28-29, 35-38, 46, ibid.; Minutes of a Meeting and Hearing . . . of the . . . WRSC . . . , Oct. 22, 1936, pp. 8-11, 15, ibid., Box 1; Minutes of WRSC, Nov. 20, 1936, ibid., Box 2.

15. "First Draft of a Report Submitted to the WRSC . . . ," Nov. 30, 1936, p. 16, ibid., Box 3; *WRSC Report*, p. 11.

16. *WRSC Report*, pp. 11-42.

17. "Weaknesses in Recommendations of Michigan WRSC, Comments by Arthur Dunham," Jan. 11, 1937, RG 52-4, Box 2; Dunham, "A Public Welfare Program in Michigan," "Citizen's News" (Feb. 12, 1937): 3; Norton to FM, Dec. 9, 1936, and enclosed Memorandum, FM Papers.

18. Martha Chickering, "States Look at Public Welfare," *Survey* 73 (May 1937): 135-37; Robert P. Ingalls, *Herbert H. Lehman and New York's Little New Deal* (New York: New York University Press, 1975), pp. 55-58.

19. "Minority Report of the Governor's WRSC," Dec. 28, 1936, Children's Fund Papers, Box 13; "President's Address," Jan. 26-28, 1937, RG 52-4, Box 2; *DN*, Dec. 29, 1936, Jan. 27, 1937.

20. Norton to FM, Dec. 9, 1936, and enclosed Memorandum, FM Papers; *FM Message, Jan. 7, 1937*, pp. 9-11, ibid.; EGK to FM, Jan. 9, 27, Feb. 10, Mar. 31, 1937, EGK-BHC, Box 8; *DN*, Nov. 6, 1936; Dunham, "Referendum," p. 430.

21. [H.] Donald Reed to EGK, Jan. 29, 1937, EGK-BHC, Box 20; *DN*, Jan. 27, Mar. 11, 26, Apr. 16, 1937; [*DT*, June 26, 1937], MSB; "House Bill No. 227," in State of Michigan, Legislature of 1937-1938, Regular Session, House Bills, University of Michigan Law Library, Ann Arbor, Michigan.

22. Reed to EGK, Jan. 29, 1937, Reed to Ernest Brooks, Apr. 3, 1937, EGK-BHC, Box 20; EGK to FM, Mar. 31, 1937, ibid., Box 8; Levi to Smith, Feb. 15, 1937, RG 35, Box 9; Landers, "Meeting of Supervisors . . . , July 2, 1937," ibid.; *DN*, Feb. 27, Apr. 16, May 5, 1937; Haber to FM, Apr. 19, 1937, FM to Haber, Apr. 21, 1937, FM Papers; Haber, "Social Work and Politics," *Survey* 74 (May 1938): 138-39. Haber was only on the University of Michigan payroll at the time. When he served as WPA deputy director, he did not draw a salary as the state's relief administrator or as its National Youth Administration director. Haber to Clarence S. Yoakum, May 1, 1937, Haber to FM, May 7, 1937, FM Papers.

23. *DN*, Feb. 7, 9, 27, Mar. 18, 1937; Dunham, "Referendum," p. 438; Norton speech, Feb. 7, 1937, FM Papers.

24. *DN*, Feb. 7, Mar. 7, 12, Apr. 16, 1937; Levi to Smith, Feb. 15, Mar. 5, 1937, RG 35, Box 9; Smith to FM, May 6, 1937, EGK-BHC, Box 16.

25. *Journal of the Senate of the State of Michigan, 1937 Regular Session*, 2 vols. (Lansing: Franklin DeKleine Co., 1937), 1:554-55, 574-76, 2:1802, 1893-94; *Journal of the House of Representatives of the State of Michigan, 1937 Regular Session*, 2 vols. (Lansing: Franklin DeKleine Co., n.d.), 2:1610, 2024-25, 2121-23, 2189-93; EGK to FM, Mar. 3, 1937, EGK-BHC, Box 16; EGK to FM, Apr. 14, 1937, ibid., Box 8; *Public and Local Acts of the Legislature of . . . Michigan . . . 1937* (Lansing:

Franklin DeKleine Co., 1937), pp. 442–79; Dunham, "Referendum," pp. 430–31; *DN*, Apr. 15, 18, June 15, 20, 1937.

26. Among the minor amendments were those providing that the state public assistance commission and the county welfare boards were to be bipartisan rather than nonpartisan, specifying that the heads of the bureaus of the state department and of the institutions under its control were to be appointed by the state public assistance commission rather than by the director with the commission's approval, deleting the provision for field services by the state department, and placing the Employment Institute for the Blind under the state department of public assistance rather than the Board of Education.

27. "Senate Bills Nos. 111, 112," in Michigan Legislature, 1937, Senate Bills, Michigan Law Library; *Senate Journal, 1937*, 1:386–87, 509–12, 531–37, 2:1791–93, 1838–42; *House Journal, 1937*, 2:1510–11, 1608–10, 1754–56, 2121–23, 2189–93; *Public Acts of Michigan, 1937*, pp. 445, 451, 453; Dunham, "Referendum," pp. 445, 453; *DN*, Apr. 14, 1937.

28. *DN*, July 4, Oct. 1, 1937; Levi to Fred Hoehler, July 6, 1937, RG 35, Box 9; FM to M. J. O'Doherty, Aug. 10, 1937, FM Papers; Ernst, "Welfare Legislation," pp. 85–88. For the reorganization plan in Minnesota, see Koch, "Minnesota," pp. 324–25, 336–38; for Washington, see Bruce Dudley Blumell, "Development of Public Assistance in the State of Washington during the Great Depression" (Ph.D. diss., University of Washington, 1973), pp. 284, 373–79; and for Ohio, see David Joseph Maurer, "Public Relief Programs and Policies in Ohio, 1929–1939" (Ph.D. diss., Ohio State University, 1962), p. 138.

29. M.A. Van Gisen to All Superintendents of the Poor . . . , July 30, 1937, RG 35, Box 2; *DN*, Aug. 26, 29, Oct. 12, 28, 29, 1937; Dunham, "Referendum," pp. 434–35, 439.

30. *DN*, Aug. 29, Oct. 8, 1937, Jan. 26, 27, 30, May 22, June 7, July 29, Oct. 30, 1938; *DFP*, Oct. 23, 1938; Dunham, "Referendum," p. 438.

31. *DN*, Apr. 16, Oct. 8, 1937, June 1, 26, Oct. 25, 26, Nov. 7, 1938; D. Hale Brake, "Local Welfare Reorganization," *Proceedings of the Michigan Municipal League, 1937* (Ann Arbor, 1937), pp. 62–65, 70; "Suggestions for Speech on Welfare Referendum . . . ," undated, SEWRC Papers.

32. WRSC, Hearing, Dec. 2, 1936, pp. 35, 38–39, RG 35, Box 1; Reed to EGK, Jan. 17, 1938, Levi to EGK, Jan. 26, 1938, EGK-BHC, Box 20; *Proceedings of Michigan Municipal League, 1937*, p. 78; "Citizen's News" (Oct. 1938): 6–7; "Suggestions for Speech," undated, SEWRC Papers; *DN*, Oct. 26, 30, 1938.

33. Clark D. Brooks to William Lovett, Oct. 27, 1938, Detroit Citizens League Papers, Box 33, Burton Historical Collection, Detroit Michigan; *DN*, Oct. 25, 30, 1938; handbill in FM Papers.

34. "House Bill No. 227," in 1937 House Bills; *DN*, Jan. 27, June 1, 1938; Brake, "Welfare Reorganization," p. 60; "Citizen's News" (Oct. 10, 1938): 10; Citizens Welfare Education Committee, "How Michigan Can Obtain Economy . . . ," undated, EGK-BHC, Box 16.

35. *DN*, Oct. 1, Dec. 2, 1937, June 1, July 11, Sept. 27, Oct. 9, 25, 26, 30, Nov. 2, 1938; Lovett to Francis B. Creamer, Oct. 11, 1938, Detroit Citizens League

Papers, Box 33; Minutes of . . . the Welfare Education Committee, Dec. 1, 1937, RG 35, Box 2; Grand Rapids League of Women Voters to FM, Oct. 17, 1938, FM Papers; "Citizen's News" (Oct. 1938): 12.

36. Committee on Welfare, Michigan Municipal League, *How Municipalities Will Benefit from Welfare Reorganization* (Ann Arbor: n.p., 1938), SEWRC Papers; *Public Acts of Michigan, 1937*, p. 458; *DN*, July 1, Sept. 27, Oct. 9, 16, 1938.

37. *DT*, Nov. 9, 1937, clipping in FM Papers; *DN*, July 4, Oct. 8, Dec. 9, 1937, June 1, 2, 26, Oct. 26, Nov. 4, 1938; Haber, "Social Work," p. 139; *Proceedings of Michigan Municipal League, 1937*, p. 79; Brake, "Welfare Reorganization," pp. 66–68; "Suggestions for Speech," SEWRC Papers; Judd to Fitzgerald, June 6, 1938, Dorothy Judd Papers, Box 2, MHC; FM article for *Democratic Digest*, June 11, 1938, FM Papers; FM speech, Oct. 11, 1938, ibid.; "Citizen's News" (Oct. 1938): 6, 10–11.

38. [Welfare Education Committee] Memorandum, July 21, 1938, RG 35, Box 2; Laura N. LaShelle, "Frank Murphy's Welfare and Relief Programs While Governor of Michigan, 1937–1938" (1963), p. 28, in my possession; Harper and Gibson, *Public Welfare*, p. 48.

39. *DN*, Dec. 15, 17, 1937, Jan. 26, July 17, Oct. 24, 1938; [Welfare Education Committee] Memorandum, July 21, 1938, RG 35, Box 2; "Survey to Determine Public Attitudes toward the Welfare Referendum in Michigan," undated, ibid.; Harper and Gibson, *Public Welfare*, pp. 48–49; Thelma Bailey to Hill, June 4, 1938, FM Papers.

40. *DN*, Dec. 9, 1938; Harper and Gibson, *Public Welfare*, pp. 40–41, 46, 49–50; Samuel T. McSeveney, "The Michigan Gubernatorial Campaign of 1938," *Michigan History* 45 (June 1961): 104; Norton interview, p. 16; Lloyd Sponholz, "The Initiative and Referendum: Direct Democracy in Perspective," *American Studies* 14 (Fall 1973): 43, 53, 58.

41. Wood to FM, Nov. 2, 1936, FM Papers; Osborne Association, *1940 Survey of Michigan Penal Institutions* (n.p., n.d.), pp. 8, 43–44.

42. [Richard E. Derick], "The Michigan Correctional System and the Reforms of 1937" [1964], pp. 4, 8, in my possession; *DN*, Jan. 6, 11, 18, 1937; State Department of Corrections, *Michigan's Correctional System: First Biennial Report, 1937–38* (Lansing: State Department of Corrections, n.d.), pp. 7, 9, 16, 20, 23–24; Gellein, "Department of Corrections," Dec. 10, 1937, FM Papers; Public Administration Service, "Suggestions," ibid.; Minutes of the Committee . . . , Nov. 30, 1936, Hilmer Gellein Papers, MHC; Wood to FM, Nov. 21, 1936, Parker to Members [Jan. 1937], ibid.; Ralph Hall Ferris, "The Michigan Department of Corrections," in Michigan Probation Association, *Probation in Theory and Practice* (n.p., n.d.), pp. 10, 11; Department of Corrections, *History of Probation, Prisons, Pardons and Paroles in Michigan* (n.p., 1938), p. 14.

43. Wood to FM, Nov. 21, 1936, Gellein Papers; Minutes of Committee . . . , Nov. 30, Dec. 2, 7, 12, 1936, ibid.; FM to Gellein, Nov. 21, 1936, Gellein to FM, Nov. 27, 1936, FM Papers; Sidney Fine, *Frank Murphy: The Detroit Years* (Ann Arbor: University of Michigan Press, 1975), pp. 122, 230; *DN*, Nov. 29, Dec. 17, 1936; Parker to FM, Dec. 15, 1936, enclosing [Study Committee to FM], Dec. 14, 1936, Detroit Citizens League Papers, Candidate Files, Box 23; Parker to FM,

Jan. 14, 1937, EGK-BHC, Box 16; Osborne Association, *Survey*, p. 44.

44. *WRSC Report*, pp. 15-17; EGK to Parker, Feb. 10, 1937, Levi to EGK, Feb. 19, 1937, EGK-BHC, Box 16; Levi to Gellein, Feb. 19, 1937, RG 35, Box 10; *DN*, Feb. 23, June 26, Aug. 11, 1937; Osborne Association, *Survey*, pp. 8, 45; Ferris, "Department of Corrections," pp. 10-11; [Derick], "Michigan Correctional System," p. 19; *Public Acts of Michigan, 1937*, pp. 424-42.

45. Department of Corrections, *History*, pp. 7-8; Department of Corrections, *Michigan Correctional System*, pp. 9, 11-12, 14-15; Gellein, "Department of Corrections," Dec. 10, 1937, FM Papers; *DN*, Aug. 6, 15, 1937. The department purchased land near Marquette Prison in 1938 to build a barracks for young offenders serving sentences of one year or less, to save the expense of sending them to Ionia. Gellein, "A New Penal System," *Achievement* (Sept. 1938): 39.

46. [Derick], "Michigan Correctional System," p. 22; Department of Corrections, *Michigan Correctional System*, pp. 9-10, 15-18; Gellein, "Department of Corrections," Dec. 10, 1937, FM Papers; Gellein to FM, Mar. 10, 1938, ibid.; "Progress Highlights in Corrections in Michigan from January 1, 1937 to July 1, 1938," ibid.; copy of article by FM for *Official Detective Stories Magazine*, May 23, 1938, ibid.; *DN*, Nov. 29, 1937.

47. Department of Corrections, *History*, p. 43; Department of Corrections, *Michigan's Correctional System*, pp. 20, 24-27; Gellein, "Department of Corrections," Dec. 10, 1937, FM Papers; *DN*, Oct. 28, 1937, Dec. 29, 1938.

48. *DN*, Jan. 6, 18, Feb. 2, 20, Aug. 11, 15, Dec. 7, 1937, Jan. 11, Nov. 8, Dec. 29, 1938; Gellein, "Department of Corrections," Dec. 10, 1937, FM Papers; Gellein to FM, Dec. 12, 1938, ibid.; "Progress Highlights," ibid.; Department of Corrections, *History*, pp. 38-41; Department of Corrections, *Michigan's Correctional System*, pp. 18-20; Gellein, "What About Parole?" *Michigan Police Journal* 7 (Sept. 1938): 13-14; Gellein, "United States Supreme Court Justice Frank Murphy...," undated, pp. 49-50, Gellein Papers; Interview with Gellein, Aug. 21, 1963, pp. 25-26, MHC; Ferris, "Department of Corrections," pp. 11-12. There were 1,904 parolees in 1937 and 2,264 in 1938, compared to an average of 2,934 in the period 1931-36. *DN*, Jan. 11, 1938; Department of Corrections, *Michigan's Correctional System*, p. 72.

49. [*Grand Rapids Press*, Oct. 12, 1938], MSB; Gellein to Charles Hedetniemi, Mar. 27, 1939, FM Papers. See also *DN*, Dec. 19, 1937, Dec. 2, 1938.

50. For the Chebatoris affair, see FM to FDR, June 22, 1938, FDR to FM, July 6, 1938, EGK to FM, July 8, 1938, Mrs. Donald H. Bacon to FM, July 18, 1938, FM Papers; Memorandum for the President, June 23, 1938, Keenan to Lehr, July 6, 1938, OF 3100, FDRL; *DN*, July 1, 3, 5-8, 1938; [*Rochester Clarion*, July 8, 1938], MSB; [*Marshall Evening Chronicle*, July 29, 1938], MSB; and *Ann Arbor News*, Apr. 9, 1977. For Murphy's views on capital punishment, see Fine, *Murphy*, pp. 63-66, 137-38.

51. FM to Ann Walker, June 30, 1934, FM Papers; Gellein, "Murphy," pp. 58-59, Gellein Papers.

52. Johnson to FM, Dec. 10, 1936, EGK-BHC, Box 16; FM to Members of Legislature, May 4, 1937, FM Papers; *Senate Journal, 1937*, 1:681-82.

53. Susan Miller, "Michigan's Health" (1964), p. 2, in my possession; *Senate*

Journal, 1937, 1:676, 680–81, 682–86; FM to Members of Legislature, May 4, 1937, FM Papers; *DN*, Feb. 26, Apr. 25, Oct. 19, 1937; *DFP*, Apr. 28, 1937; [*Lansing State Journal*, Oct. 12, 1937], MSB; Howard Titus to EGK, Dec. 19, 1936, EGK-BHC, Box 20; Norton interview, p. 17.

54. *WRSC Report*, p. 15; *DN*, June 26, 27, 1937; *Public Acts of Michigan, 1937*, pp. 147–66, 530–32.

55. *DN*, May 9, Nov. 9, 11, 17, 25, 1937; *DFP*, Apr. 28, Nov. 11, 1937; [*DT*, Apr. 28, 1937], MSB; FM to Members of Legislature, May 4, 1937, FM to Smith, Oct. 18, 1937, FM Papers; *Public Acts of Michigan, 1937*, pp. 406–8.

56. *DN*, Oct. 14, 15, 19, Nov. 6, 1937, Jan. 23, Apr. 17, May 19, 20, June 9, 22, 1938; [*Lansing State Journal*, Oct. 12, 15, Nov. 2, 1937], MSB; FM to Harold L. Ickes, May 19, 1938, Barrett to Hill, Dec. 12, 1938, FM Papers; *Ex-Augural Message of Frank Murphy . . . Jan. 5, 1939* (n.p., n.d.), p. 11.

57. Barrett Memorandum to FM, Jan. 31, 1938, Smith Memorandum to FM, July 20, 1938, Barrett to Hill, Sept. 8, Dec. 12, 1938, FM Papers; FM speech, Apr. 29, 1938, ibid.; *DN*, July 28, 1937, June 28, July 23, Oct. 18, 1938.

58. FM to Members of Legislature, May 4, 1937, FM Papers; FM speeches, Apr. 29, Sept. 9, 1938, ibid.; FM article for *Democratic Digest*, Apr. 30, 1938, ibid.; [*DT*, Apr. 28, 1937], MSB; *DN*, Oct 14, 19, Nov. 4, 6, 11, 1937, Oct. 18, 1938.

59. Barrett Memorandum to FM, Jan. 31, 1938, Barrett to Hill, Sept. 8, 1938, W. S. Ramsey to FM, Dec. 15, 1938, FM to Barrett, Dec. 29, 1938, FM Papers; *DN*, Mar. 3, Apr. 29, June 28, July 21, Sept. 13, 1938; *Michigan Public Health* 26 (Feb. 1938): 37–38; American Public Health Association, "Michigan's Health, 1938," p. 101, RG 52-4, Box 1.

60. *WRSC Report*, p. 42; "The Health of the State—A Review of 1936," *Michigan Public Health* 24 (Dec. 1936): 223–25; C. C. Slemons, "Public Health Progress in Michigan under the Social Security Act," ibid. 24 (June 1937): 111–16; *Sixty-Fifth Annual Report of the Commissioner of the Michigan Department of Health for the Fiscal Year Ending June 30, 1937* (Lansing: Franklin DeKleine Co., 1938), pp. 341, 346; *Sixty-Sixth Annual Report . . . June 30, 1938* (Lansing: Franklin DeKleine Co., 1940), pp. 9–10; Don W. Gudakunst to FM, July 25, 1938, FM Papers; American Public Health Association, "Michigan's Health," p. 25, RG 52-4, Box 1.

61. Message from GM to FM, Sept. 18, 1937, FM to JRH, Nov. 26, 1937, FM to Jabin Hsu, Dec. 17, 1937, Carey P. McCord to FM, Jan. 25, 1938, FM Papers; FM release, Dec. 21, 1937, ibid.; FM article for *Democratic Digest*, Feb. 10, 1938, ibid.; *DN*, Sept. 21, Dec. 21, 1937.

62. W. J. Myers, "The Health of Michigan in 1937," *Michigan Public Health* 25 (Dec. 1937): 241–42, 244–45; "The Health of the State in 1938," ibid. 26 (Dec. 1938): 228; *DN*, Mar. 3, 1938; Gudakunst, "The Health of the State" [Dec. 1938], FM Papers; American Public Health Association, "Michigan's Health," pp. 2, 25, RG 52-4, Box 1.

63. Myers, "Health of Michigan," p. 242; "Health of State in 1938," pp. 228–29; Gudakunst to FM, July 25, Aug. 16, 1938, FM Papers; Gudakunst, "Health of State," ibid.; [Gudakunst], "Public Health in Michigan" [Dec. 1938], ibid.; American Public Health Association, "Michigan's Health," p. 25, RG 52-4, Box 1.

64. "Antenuptial Physical Examination Law," *Michigan Public Health* 25 (Aug. 1937): 151–52; W. J. V. Deacon, "The First Year of the Prenuptial Examination Law," ibid. 26 (Nov. 1938): 220–22.

65. *DN*, Feb. 1, Apr. 8, 1938; FM article for *Democratic Digest*, Feb. 10, 1938, FM Papers; FM to Gudakunst, Feb. 26, 1938, Gudakunst to FM, Mar. 11, 1938, FM to Hill, Mar. 11, 1938, FM to Henry Cook, Mar. 16, 1938, Hill to Gudakunst, Mar. 17, 1938, and enclosed "Some of the Purposes," Gudakunst to Hill, May 13, 1938, and enclosed "Report...," ibid.; FM speech, Mar. 8, 1938, pp. 10–11, ibid.; FM release [Apr. 7, 1938], ibid.

66. Daniel S. Hirshfield, *The Lost Reform* (Cambridge, Mass.: Harvard University Press, 1970), pp. 102–30; Roy Lubove, "The New Deal and National Health," *Current History* 45 (Aug. 1963): 84–85.

67. Lendrum, Bicknell, and Raskin to FM, Aug. 3, 1938, FM to Gudakunst, Aug. 5, 1938, FM Papers.

68. *DN*, Aug. 16, 1937; [*DT*, Aug. 27, 1938], MSB; Hirshfield, *Lost Reform*, pp. 77–78. See also *DLN*, Sept. 8, 1938.

69. Gudakunst, "Health Conference, Sept. 10, 1937," FM Papers; FM, "Catching Up with Human Needs," Sept. 10, 1938, ibid.; *DN*, Sept. 8, 10, 11, 1937; "The State Health Conference," *Michigan Public Health* 26 (Sept. 1938): 167–70.

70. Raskin and Bicknell to FM, Sept. 21, 1938, Lendrum to FM, Sept. 29, 1938, FM Papers; *DN*, Sept. 19, 20, 1938.

71. *DN*, Oct. 21, 25, 1938, May 28, 1939; FM speech, Oct. 26, 1938, FM Papers; Gudakunst, "Health of State," ibid.

72. W. H. Elliott et al. to the Dental Profession [1938], FM Papers; "The Lesson," *Journal of the Michigan Medical Society* 37 (Dec. 1938): 1113.

73. *FM Message, Jan. 7, 1937*, p. 8, FM Papers; Bromage to FM, Apr. 23, 1938, EGK Memorandum to FM, Aug. 5, 1938, FM to Lovett, Sept. 13, 1938, ibid.; FM to JRH, June 21, 1938, JRH to James R. Fugate, Mar. 31, Nov. 16, 1938, JRH Papers; EGK to JRH, July 15, 1938, EGK to FM, July 23, 1938 (two letters), EGK-BHC, Box 13; [*Lansing State Journal*, Mar. 16, 1938], MSB; *DT*, Aug. 21, 1938, MSB; *DN*, Apr. 1, 1937, Aug. 21, 22, 1938; Bromage, comp., "Documents and Proceedings of the Commission on Reform and Modernization of Government" (Lansing, 1938), Doc. Nos. 1, 2.

74. Bromage, comp., "Documents," Doc. No. 4; FM to Hedetniemi, undated, JRH to FM, Sept. 5, 1938, FM to JRH, Sept. 15, 1938, FM Papers; Commission on Reform and Modernization of Government, "Report of a Preliminary Survey" (1938), pp. iv–vii, ibid.; *DN*, Oct. 13, 1938.

75. Commission on Reform and Modernization of Government, "Report," pp. 3–16, FM Papers; Bromage, "Michigan Surveys Its State Government," *National Municipal Review* 28 (Mar. 1939): 234–37.

76. James T. Patterson, *The New Deal and the States* (Princeton: Princeton University Press, 1969), p. 195.

77. George C. S. Benson, *The New Centralization* (New York: Farrar and Rinehart, 1941), p. 112; *DN*, Dec. 5, 1938.

CHAPTER 12

1. *DN*, Feb. 5, 1937; Chester A. Graham to FM, Aug. 11, 1938, FM Papers.

2. Joseph M. Donnelly Memorandum to FM, Jan. 31, 1938, FM to Robert S. Shaw, Feb. 3, 1938, Esther Lincoln to FM, Mar. 8, 1938, John Cahalan, Jr., to FM, May 26, 1938, FM to Cahalan, Jr., June 13, 1938, John Dingell to FM, June 26, 1938, ibid.; James Lincoln manuscript [1938], ibid.

3. See Chapter 13.

4. Murray R. Benedict, *Farm Policies of the United States, 1790–1950* (New York: Twentieth Century Fund, 1953), p. 338; Frederick William Muller, *Public Rural Electrification* (Washington: American Council on Public Affairs, 1944), pp. 22–24; *Report of Rural Electrification Administration, 1937* (Washington: U.S. Government Printing Office, 1938), p. 31.

5. George A. Schroeder to FM, Aug. 1, 1936, FM Papers; FM speech, Oct. 17, 1936, ibid.; Memorandum for FM speech, May 8, 1938, ibid.; FM article for *Democratic Digest*, Aug. 23, 1938, ibid.; Donnelly, "Electrification of the Farm Areas of Michigan" [1938], ibid.; Donnelly speeches, Feb. 6, July 8, 1938, ibid.; R. M. Burr, "Rural Electrification in Michigan," "Citizen's News" (Apr. 7, 1937): 3; *DN*, July 27, 1938; *Report of Rural Electrification Administration, 1938* (Washington: U.S. Government Printing Office, 1939), p. 5; Twentieth Century Fund, *Electric Power and Government Policy* (New York: Twentieth Century Fund, 1948), p. 470.

6. EGK to FM, June 10, 1937, EGK-BHC, Box 8; "House Bill No. 51," State of Michigan, Legislature of 1937–1938, Regular Session, House Bills, University of Michigan Law Library, Ann Arbor, Michigan; "Senate Bill No. 224," Michigan Legislature, 1937, Senate Bills, ibid.; FM speech, July 30, 1937, FM Papers; memorandum for FM speech, May 8, 1938, ibid.; "Proclamation by the Governor...," July 30, 1937, ibid.; "A Brief Outline of the Accomplishments of the Democratic Party of Michigan, 1936–1938," p. 4, ibid.; Donnelly Report ... to Dec. 1, 1937, undated, ibid.; Paul H. Todd to FM, July 20, 28, 1938, ibid.; John M. Carmody to FM, May 10, 1937, John M. Carmody Papers, Box 86, FDRL; *DN*, June 8, 19, Aug. 1, 1937, July 15, 1938; Arthur M. Schlesinger, Jr., *The Politics of Upheaval* (Boston: Houghton Mifflin Co., 1960), pp. 379–80, 384.

7. The Reminiscences of John A. Carmody, 1957, p. 383, Oral History Research Office, Columbia University, New York, New York; Judson Knight to Frank Martel, Apr. 3, 1937, Wayne County AFL-CIO Papers, Box 7, ALHUA; Donnelly, "Electrification," FM Papers; Donnelly speeches, Nov. 24, 1937, May 4, 1938, ibid.; FM addresses, July 30, Sept. 3, 1938, ibid.; "Brief Outline," p. 4, ibid.; Carmody to FM, Mar. 31, 1938, Donnelly to FM, Apr. 23, 1938, Hill to Donnelly, May 25, 1938, ibid.; Press Release, June 18, 1938, ibid.; Carmody to C. L. Brody, Dec. 16, 1937, Carmody Papers, Box 87; *DN*, Dec. 23, 1937, June 19, July 25, 31, Sept. 4, 1938; *Saginaw News*, June 18, 1938, MSB; *Time* 22 (July 4, 1938): 12; Schlesinger, Jr., *Politics of Upheaval*, p. 384.

8. Donnelly speeches, Nov. 24, 1937, July 8, 1938, FM Papers; Donnelly, "Electrification," ibid.; Guy H. Jenkins article in unidentified newspaper [June 1938], MSB; *DN*, June 27, 1938; *REA Report, 1938*, p. 261; Muller, *Rural Electrification*, p. 17; Schlesinger, Jr., *Politics of Upheaval*, pp. 383–84.

9. *REA Report, 1937*, pp. 23, 36, 97–98; *REA Report, 1938*, pp. 79, 93, 96, 152–53; Carmody Reminiscences, pp. 383, 429; Donnelly speeches, May 4, July 8, 1938, FM Papers; "Brief Outline," p. 4, ibid.; Raymond C. Miller, *Kilowatts at Work: A History of the Detroit Edison Company* (Detroit: Wayne State University Press, 1957), pp. 238–40.

10. Michigan State Department of Agriculture, *Eighth Biennial Report ...* (Lansing: Franklin DeKleine Co., 1939), pp. 74–77; "Department of Agriculture" [1938], MSB; "Agriculture" [Dec. 12, 1938], FM Papers; Leo V. Card, Memo on the ... Agricultural Program ... [1938], ibid.; John B. Strange, Jr., to Charles Hedetniemi, Feb. 18, 1938, ibid.; FM speech, Feb. 22, 1938, ibid.; [*DT*, June 29, 1937], MSB; *Achievement* (Sept. 1938): 42.

11. Department of Agriculture, *Eighth Biennial Report*, p. 84; Department of Agriculture, *Ninth Biennial Report ...* (Lansing: Franklin DeKleine Co., 1940), p. 100; Murray R. Benedict and Oscar C. Stine, *The Agricultural Commodity Programs* (New York: Twentieth Century Fund, 1956), pp. 206–7; "A Report to FM by Raymond W. Starr and Thurman Arnold" [Oct. 1938], FM Papers; ——— to Burr Lincoln, Mar. 9, 1937, Strange, Jr., to FM, May 23, July 19, 1938, E. Lincoln Memorandum to FM, July 8, 1938, J. Lincoln to FM, July 8, 1938, J. Lincoln to GM, Aug. 4, 1938, and enclosed memorandum, ibid.; [*DT*, May 27, 1938], MSB; *DN*, June 3, 1938.

12. Arnold to FM, June 9, 1938, G. Mennen Williams Papers, Box A-1, MHC; Arnold to John C. Lehr, July 12, 1938, FM to Arnold, July 21, 1938, File 60-139-7, Records of the Department of Justice, RG 60, NARS; Department of Justice Release, Oct. 15, 1938, ibid.; EGK Memorandum for FM, July 11, 1938, Williams Memorandum for FM, July 12, 1938, FM to Williams, July 14, 1938, Williams to FM, July 20, 1938, FM Papers; *DN*, June 30, 1938.

13. Gay to Department of Justice, Aug. 20, 1938, Sher to Arnold, Aug. 20, 1938, File 60-139-7, RG 60; Department of Justice Release, Oct. 15, 1938, ibid.; Gay to FM, Aug. 12, 1938, FM Papers; "Starr and Arnold Report," ibid.; Memorandum for Press Conference, Oct. 13, 1938, EGK-BHC, Box 11.

14. EGK Memoranda to FM, July 11, 24, 1938, FM to E. Lincoln, July 19, 1938, Williams Memoranda to FM, Aug. 1, Sept. 22, 1938, FM Papers; Williams to FM, July 12, 1938, EGK-BHC, Box 11; American Municipal Association, *Milk Control* (Chicago: Public Administration Service, 1937), pp. 5, 7; Benedict and Stine, *Commodity Programs*, pp. 455–56; Leland Spencer, "Public Regulation of the Milk Industry," *State Government* 12 (Oct. 1939): 179–80; Robert P. Ingalls, *Herbert H. Lehman and New York's Little New Deal* (New York: New York University Press, 1975), pp. 148–72.

15. J. Lincoln manuscript [1938], FM Papers; FM to Williams, July 14, 1938, FM to J. Lincoln, July 15, 1938, MH [Marie Hendry] to FM, Sept. 14, 1938, ibid.; Press Releases, July 21 (not released), Oct. 12, 1938, ibid.; Advance on FM speech, Oct. 13, 1938, ibid.; Executive Order, Oct. 14, 1938, ibid.; *DN*, July 13, Oct. 13, 1938.

16. Executive Order, Oct. 14, 1938, FM Papers; MH to FM, Sept. 14, 1938, White to FM, Dec. 28, 1938, Williams to EGK, Dec. 28, 1938, FM Papers; "A Tentative Draft Marketing Bill...," Dec. 27, 1938, Williams Papers, Box A-1; William Ramsey, Jr., to Williams, Jan. 22, 1940, ibid., Box A-3; Interview with G. Mennen

Williams, Dec. 1964, p. 3, MHC; *DN*, Oct. 14, 29, Nov. 5, 16, Dec. 28, 1938.

17. *Public and Local Acts of the Legislature of . . . Michigan . . . 1939* (Lansing: Franklin DeKleine Co., 1939), pp. 274-90; Williams interview, p. 3. Cf. Martin Bigelow to Williams, Jan. 31, 1940, Williams Papers, Box A-3, and *DFP*, Nov. 8, 1948.

18. [*Lansing State Journal*, Aug. 29, 1938], MSB; *DN*, Aug. 30, Sept. 1, 1938; *Public Acts of the Legislature of . . . Michigan . . . Extra Session of 1938* (Lansing: Franklin DeKleine Co., 1938), pp. 4-7.

19. *DN*, Dec. 9, 16, 1937, June 7, 1938.

20. Benedict, *Farm Policies*, pp. 335-37; Persia Campbell, *Consumer Representation in the New Deal* (New York: Columbia University Press, 1940), pp. 70, 81-84; *DN*, Dec. 14, 1937; Hester Renwick Fraser et al., "Recommendations of the Wayne County Consumer's Council to FM," Feb. 1937, EGK-BHC, Box 18; FM to EGK, undated, ibid.

21. *DN*, Dec. 12, 1937; EGK to Frazer [*sic*], Dec. 6, 1937, Fraser to FM and Strange, Jr. [Dec. 1937], EGK-BHC, Box 18; EGK to Strange, Jr., Jan. 19, 1938, ibid., Box 17; Press Release, Jan. 3, 1938, FM Papers; [*Lansing State Journal*, Dec. 8, 1937], MSB; Department of Agriculture, *Eighth Biennial Report*, pp. 80-81.

22. Department of Agriculture, *Eighth Biennial Report*, p. 81; "Marketing Tips to Housewives," Feb. 9, 1938, EGK-BHC, Box 18; Fraser to FM, Feb. 11, 1938, Fraser to Robert Littell, Feb. 16, 1938, Montgomery to EGK, Oct. 4, 1938, ibid.; Fraser to Prentice [*sic*] Brown, Mar. 28, 1939, FM Papers.

23. Fraser to FM [Mar. 10, 1938], Montgomery to EGK, Oct. 4, 1938, EGK-BHC, Box 18; Department of Agriculture, *Eighth Biennial Report*, pp. 81-82.

CHAPTER 13

1. FM to Louis Van Schaick, Dec. 14, 1937, George F. Granger to FM, Aug. 12, 1938, FM Papers; Kenneth D. Roose, *The Economics of Recession and Revival: An Interpretation of 1937-38* (New Haven: Yale University Press, 1954), p. 237; George F. Granger and Lawrence R. Klein, *Emergency Relief in Michigan, 1933-1939* (Lansing: n.p., 1939), pp. 85-87, 110; United States Bureau of the Census, *Fifteenth Census of the United States: 1930, Population*, vol. 3, pt. 1 (Washington: U.S. Government Printing Office, 1932), p. 1123; Michigan State Emergency Relief Administration (SERA), *Public Relief Statistics* 4 (Dec. 1937): 4-5; ibid. 5 (Feb. 1938): 5; ibid. (Mar. 1938): 6, 10; ibid. (Dec. 1938): 17; Louis M. Nims to Leon Henderson, May 27, 1938, OF 444-C, FDRL; Michigan State Department of Agriculture, *Tenth Biennial Report . . .* (Lansing: Franklin DeKleine Co., 1943), p. 33; Murray R. Benedict and Oscar L. Stine, *The Agricultural Commodity Programs* (New York: Twentieth Century Fund, 1956), pp. 206-7.

2. [*DT*, Apr. 24, 1938], MSB; FM to EGK, July 20, 1938, FM Papers; [EGK] manuscript [Aug. 1, 1938], ibid.

3. *Selected Addresses of Frank Murphy . . . , January 1, 1937, to September 30, 1938* (Lansing: n.p., 1938), pp. 65-66; FM speeches, Mar. 4, May 4, 1938, FM Papers; "Notes for . . . speech," July 15, 1938, ibid.; FM to James Cromwell, Nov. 19, Dec. 21, 1938, ibid.; FM, "The Democratic Way of Life," *Democratic Digest* 15

(June 1938): 18–19; *DN*, Jan. 7, Feb. 8, Mar. 16, Apr. 24, May 5, 21, July 15, 1938.

4. FM to Al Dale, July 23, 1938, FM Papers; *DN*, Jan. 15, Apr. 10, 1938.

5. Granger and Klein, *Emergency Relief*, pp. 31, 51, 85; William J. Norton and William Haber to FM, Jan. 5, 1937, Haber to FM, Feb. 12, 17, Mar. 15, 1937, Fred E. Levi Memorandum for FM, Mar. 11, 1938, FM Papers.

6. SERA, *Public Relief Statistics* 3 (Dec. 1936): 6, 11; ibid. 4 (Dec. 1937): 25; Granger to FM, Jan. 25, 1938, FM Papers; *Final Report on the WPA Program, 1935–1943* (Washington: U.S. Government Printing Office [1946]), pp. 8–9, 17, 27–29; Donald S. Howard, *The WPA and Federal Relief Policy* (New York: Russell Sage Foundation, 1943), pp. 200–206. The WPA employed only 33 percent of the unemployed in the United States in 1936 and even less in 1937 and 1938. Arthur W. McMahon et al., *The Administration of Federal Work Relief* (Chicago: Public Administration Service, 1941), p. 182.

7. *Final Report on WPA*, pp. 8, 101; Howard, *WPA*, pp. 144–47; McMahon et al., *Federal Work Relief*, pp. 89, 303–14, 332–36; *DN*, Feb. 16, 1937; Raymond Louis Koch, "The Development of Public Relief Programs in Minnesota, 1929–1941" (Ph.D. diss., University of Minnesota, 1967), pp. 370–71, 375–76, 378. Sponsor contributions nationally averaged 14.7 percent in fiscal 1937, 21.4 percent in fiscal 1938, and 19.3 percent in fiscal 1939. Howard. *WPA*, p. 149.

8. *DN*, Jan. 26, June 21, Aug. 3, 1937; Howard, *WPA*, p. 538; Lehman to FM, Feb. 19, 1937, FM to Lehman, Feb. 28, 1937, Elmer Benson et al. to FDR, Feb. 28, 1937, Herbert H. Lehman Papers, Reel 98, Columbia University, New York, New York. The Lehman items were made available to me by Richard Storatz.

9. *Public and Local Acts of the Legislature of . . . Michigan . . . 1937* (Lansing: Franklin DeKleine Co., 1937), pp. 458–59, 473; John A. Perkins, *The Role of the Governor of Michigan in the Enactment of Appropriations* (Ann Arbor: University of Michigan Press, 1943), pp. 29–30, 70, 101; State of Michigan, Office of the Budget Director, *Finances of the State Government, July 1, 1937–June 30, 1938*, p. 6, FM Papers; *DN*, June 9–11, 26, 1937.

10. Perkins, *Role of Governor*, pp. 70–72; *DN*, June 24, 26, July 7, 1937.

11. Perkins, *Role of Governor*, pp. 117–19.

12. *DN*, July 22, 24, 30, Oct. 3, 8, 1937; *DFP*, Oct. 11, 1937; *Journal of the House of Representatives of the State of Michigan, 1937 Regular Session*, 2 vols. (Lansing: Franklin DeKleine Co., n.d.), 2:2367; [FM statement], Sept. 30, 1937, FM Papers; Smith Memorandum for FM, Sept. 30, 1937, ibid.

13. Robert S. Ford and Albert Waxman, *Financing Government in Michigan* (Ann Arbor: University of Michigan Press, 1942), pp. 82–86, 158; Smith to FM, May 6, 1937, EGK to Smith, Nov. 10, 1937, EGK-BHC, Box 17; EGK to FM, Feb. 18, 1938, FM to EGK, Feb. 19, 1938, EGK Memorandum for FM, Apr. 20, 1938, ibid., Box 19; Mortimer E. Cooley to FM, Jan. 17, 1938, FM Papers; *DN*, Oct. 12, Dec. 8, 1937, Mar. 1, Apr. 30, 1938.

14. Otto C. Marckwardt to FM, Nov. 24, 1936, Arthur B. Moehlman to FM, Dec. 17, 1936, FM Papers; *Message of Frank Murphy . . . Jan. 7, 1937* (n.p., n.d.), p. 13, ibid.; Eugene B. Elliott to FM, Jan. 27, 1938, EGK-BHC, Box 20; *Michigan Education Journal* 14 (Jan. 1937): 226; George A. Male, "The Michigan Education Association as an Interest Group, 1852–1950" (Ph.D. diss., University of Michigan,

1951), pp. 399–402; *DN*, Aug. 6, 1937; Arthur Elder, "Launching Teacher Tenure," "Citizen's News" (Aug. 20, 1938): 4.

15. Robert J. Mowitz, "Michigan," in Walter Gellhorn, ed., *The States and Subversion* (Ithaca: Cornell University Press, 1957), pp. 196–97; Ford and Waxman, *Financing Government*, pp. 79–80; Male, "MEA," pp. 468–72; *FM Message, Jan. 7, 1937*, p. 13, FM Papers; *Michigan Education Journal* 14 (Jan. 1937): 226; ibid. 15 (Oct. 15, 1937): 89; FM, "Michigan's Responsibility to Education," ibid. (May 1938): 449–51; *DN*, Jan. 25, Mar. 5, Sept. 10, 14, Dec. 12, 1937.

16. *DN*, Nov. 17, 1937; Haber to Members..., July 20, 1937, Haber to FM, July 20, 1937, FM to Haber, July 21, 1937, Granger to FM, Nov. 30, 1937, FM Papers; Granger and Klein, *Emergency Relief*, p. 92; SERA, *Public Relief Statistics* 4 (Oct. 1937): 2–3; ibid. 5 (Mar. 1938): 3–4, 9–11, 15; ibid. (Apr. 1938): 14, 15; ibid. (Dec. 1938 and Supplement): 16, 30–31.

17. SERA, *Public Relief Statistics* 5 (July 1938): 3, 4; ibid. (Dec. 1938 and Supplement): 3, 4.

18. Ibid. 4 (Dec. 1937): 25; ibid. 5 (May 1938): 15–16; ibid. (Aug. 1938): 8; Granger to FM, Nov. 30, 1937, Jan. 25, Feb. 9, Apr. 12, May 3, June 21, 1938, L. E. Howlett to Granger, Dec. 9, 1937, FM Papers; SERA News Letter, May 3, 1938, ibid.; SEWRC Minutes, Mar. 9, 1938, Minutes of the State Welfare Commission, RG 53–12, Box 2, State Archives, Michigan History Division, Lansing, Michigan; Harold Bradshaw to FM [Aug. 2, 1938], EGK-BHC, Box 16; Senate Special Committee to Investigate Unemployment and Relief, *Unemployment and Relief, Hearings...*, 75 Cong., 3 sess., 2 vols. (Washington: U.S. Government Printing Office, 1938), 1:668–69, 674; *DN*, Apr. 28, May 3, Aug. 5, 1938; Granger and Klein, *Emergency Relief*, p. 170.

19. Granger to FM, Jan. 25, Mar. 14, 1938, Norman H. Hill to FM, Mar. 4, 1938, FM to Harry H. Woodring, Mar. 15, 1938, FM Papers; Matt Savola to FM, Jan. 22, 1938, Richard Frankensteen Papers, Box 4, ALHUA; Philip J. Rahoi to FM [July 1938], EGK-BHC, Box 14; SEWRC Minutes, Mar. 9, 1938, RG 53–12, Box 2; *DN*, Feb. 24, 1938; [*Greenway Press Gazette*, May 11, 1938], MSB. SERA had operated two camps since early in 1936. "An Outline of S.E.R.A. Camps" (Feb. 1938), Children's Fund of Michigan Papers, Box 14, MHC. The WPA also established work camps for unattached and nonresident males. Howard, *WPA*, p. 338.

20. Granger and Klein, *Emergency Relief*, p. 85; Granger to Smith, Jan. 29, 1938, Frank Landers to Smith [1938], EGK-BHC, Box 16; Granger to FM, Apr. 12, 27, 1938, FM Papers; *DN*, Jan. 31, 1938.

21. Sidney Fine, *Frank Murphy: The Detroit Years* (Ann Arbor: University of Michigan Press, 1975), pp. 257–58; *DN*, Dec. 2, 1937, Jan. 25, Mar. 16, Aug. 10, 18, 1938; [*Daily Evening Gazette*, Oct. 18, 1938], MSB; FM to Claude Bowers, Jan. 3, 1938, FM Papers.

22. *DN*, Dec. 2, 8, 29, 1937, Jan. 8, 12, Feb. 10, 12, Mar. 2, Apr. 16, 17, May 10, June 10, Dec. 8, 28, 1938; *DFP*, Jan. 11, 1938; Howard, *WPA*, pp. 603–4; FM to Williams, Feb. 10, 1938, File 610, Records of the Work Projects Administration, RG 69, NARS; Granger to FM, Jan. 25, Apr. 7, 11, May 13, Dec. 28, 1938, Nims to Hill, Dec. 8, 1938, FM Papers; Granger and Klein, *Emergency Relief*, pp. 88–89;

Michigan Social Welfare Commission, *Fourth Biennial Report, July 1944-June 1946* (Lansing: n.p., 1946), p. 16.

23. *DN*, Feb. 10, Apr. 14, 1938; [*DFP*, June 21, 1938], MSB; SEWRC Minutes, Apr. 18, 1938, RG 53-12, Box 2; Richard W. Reading to FDR, Jan. 3, 1938, Hopkins to Reading, June 24, 1938, Williams to Prentiss Brown, June 30, 1938, File 610, RG 69; C. A. Sirrine, "Report of Division of Operations...," Oct. 17-18, 1938, File 132.4 (July 1938 folder), ibid.; George D. O'Brien to G. E. Textor, Jan. 22, 1938, File 650, ibid.; James G. Bryant to FM, Apr. 12, 1938, and enclosure, FM Papers; "The New WPA Regulations," *National Municipal Review* 12 (July 1938): 101-2; McMahon et al., *Federal Work Relief*, p. 314; [*Lansing State Journal*, Apr. 8, 1938], MSB.

24. Granger to Norton, Mar. 18, 1938, and enclosed "Factors to be Considered...," Frankensteen Papers, Box 4; SEWRC Minutes, June 23, 1938, ibid.; SEWRC Minutes, Apr. 8, 27, Nov. 23, 1938, RG 53-12, Box 2; Sirrine, "Report," File 132.4, RG 69; Richard L. Grills, "Murphy, Michigan, and the WPA in the 1938 Recession" (1963), p. 21, in my possession.

25. *DN*, Feb. 16, 17, Apr. 10, June 9, 19, 1938; [*Lansing State Journal*, Apr. 8, 1938], MSB; Granger to FM, Feb. 15, 1938, FM Papers.

26. SERA, *Public Relief Statistics* 4 (Dec. 1937): 20; ibid. 5 (Mar. 1938): 7; William C. Richards, "Old-Age Assistance in Michigan," Dec. 6, 1938, Records of the National Emergency Council, RG 44, Box 295, NARS; State Welfare Department, Bureau of Old Age Assistance, *Old Age Assistance in Michigan, 1937-1938* (Lansing: State Welfare Department, 1938), pp. 6, 8, 19; Levi Memorandum to FM, July 14, 1938, and enclosed Memorandum, July 14, 1938, FM Papers.

27. EGK Memorandum to FM, June 3, 1938, Bryant to FM, July 14, 29, Aug. 11, 17, Dec. 13, 1938, FM Papers; EGK to FM, Feb. 1, June 27, 1938, FM to Bryant, June 27, 1938, EGK-BHC, Box 16; Levi Memorandum, June 27, 1938, ibid.; *DN*, July 2, 3, 8, 14, Aug. 30, Sept. 23, Oct. 23, 1938.

28. Richards, "Old-Age Assistance," RG 44, Box 295.

29. Martel to FM, Dec. 16, 1937, Wayne County AFL-CIO Papers, Box 11, ALHUA; Haber to FM, Dec. 17, 1937, FM to Haber, Dec. 21, 1937, FM Papers; D. Hale Brake to FM, Jan. 3, 1938, FM to Brake, Jan. 13, 1938, EGK-BHC, Box 14; *DLN*, Dec. 17, 24, 1937; *DN*, Dec. 5, 1937, Jan. 11, 1938; Michigan Unemployment Compensation Commission, *Unemployment Compensation in Michigan— 1938* (Detroit: n.p., 1939), p. 9.

30. FM speeches, June 30, Aug. 1, Oct. 21, 1938, FM Papers; *Flint Journal*, June 30, 1938, MSB; [*DT*, Aug. 1, 1938], MSB; *DN*, July 1, 31, Aug. 2, 7, Sept. 15, 1938; Unemployment Compensation Commission, *Unemployment Compensation— 1938*, pp. 7-9, 64; Frank Picard to FM, Sept. 6, 1938, Abner Larned to FM, Dec. 22, 28 (and enclosed Report), 1938, FM to Larned, Dec. 30, 1938, FM Papers.

31. SERA, *Public Relief Statistics* 5 (Nov. 1938): 13; ibid. (Dec. 1938): 8; Granger to FM, Sept. 16, 1938, FM Papers; Stanchfield, "Adequacy of Benefit Duration in Michigan...," *Social Security Bulletin* 3 (Sept. 1940): 19-28; Daniel Creamer and Arthur C. Wellman, "Adequacy of Unemployment Benefits in the Detroit Area during the 1938 Recession," ibid. (Nov. 1940): 3-11.

32. SERA, *Public Relief Statistics* 4 (Dec. 1937): 25; ibid. 5 (Dec. 1938 and Supplement): 27–28; Granger to FM, Sept. 19, 30, 1938, FM Papers; SEWRC Minutes, Oct. 19, 1938, RG 53–12, Box 2; *DN*, Oct. 7, 1938.

33. SERA, *Public Relief Statistics* 5 (Aug. 1938): 15; ibid. (Dec. 1938 and Supplement): 30–31; Hill to FM, Aug. 3, 1938, EGK-BHC, Box 16; SEWRC Minutes, July 18, 1938, RG 53–12, Box 2; *DN*, June 25, Aug. 29, 1938; Granger and Klein, *Emergency Relief*, pp. 6, 71.

34. *DN*, Apr. 17, May 10, June 22, Oct. 9, 1938; Executive Order, June 21, 1938, FM Papers; FM to Smith, July 18, 20, 1938, ibid.; "Report of the Public Works Commission," Nov. 30, 1938, notebook in G. Donald Kennedy Papers, Box 1, MHC. See Chapter 11 for the hospital building program.

35. *DN*, Apr. 17, May 10, 1938; [*Lansing State Journal*, Apr. 21, 1938], MSB; Hunter to Hopkins, Apr. 19, 1938, Hunter to Williams, Apr. 28, 1938, File 610, RG 69.

36. SEWRC Minutes, Sept. 16, 1938, RG 53–12, Box 2; SERA, *Public Relief Statistics* 5 (Dec. 1938 and Supplement): 22.

37. SERA, *Public Relief Statistics* 5 (July 1938): 9; Granger to FM, Nov. 30, 1937, Jan. 25, Feb. 9, Apr. 12, 1938, FM Papers; Granger to FM, Apr. 7, 1938, Frankensteen Papers, Box 4; Granger to Emergency Appropriations Board, July 14, 1938, EGK-BHC, Box 16; SEWRC Minutes, Dec. 22, 1937, May 25, 1938, RG 53–12, Box 2; *DN*, Jan. 31, Mar. 14, Apr. 8, 28, 1938; *DFP*, Apr. 28, 1938; Granger and Klein, *Emergency Relief*, p. 5; Perkins, *Governor's Role*, pp. 129–32.

38. Martin E. Sullivan, " 'On the Dole': The Relief Issue in Detroit, 1920–1939" (Ph.D. diss., University of Notre Dame, 1974), p. 216; *DN*, Feb. 1, 5, Apr. 7, June 9, 10, 15, 1938; *DFP*, Feb. 2, 1938; *NYT*, Feb. 5, 10, 1938; SEWRC Minutes, Feb. 9, 1938, RG 53–12, Box 2; Hunter to FM, Apr. 11, 1938, FM to Hunter, Apr. 12, 1938, FERA-WPA Confidential Political File, 1933–1938, Harry L. Hopkins Papers, FDRL; Hunter to Hopkins, June 8, 1938, File 610, RG 69; Granger to FM, Apr. 12, 1938, Levi Memorandum to FM, Apr. 12, 1938, Brown to FM, Aug. 24, 1938, FM Papers; [*Lansing State Journal*, Apr. 8, 1938], MSB.

39. Granger to FM, Feb. 9, 15, Apr. 12, 21, May 4, June 21, 1938, FM to Lloyd Burger, Mar. 3, 1938, FM Memorandum to Granger, Mar. 16, 1938, FM Papers; Granger to Emergency Appropriations Board, July 14, 1938, Landers to Smith [1938], EGK-BHC, Box 16; SEWRC Minutes, Mar. 9, 1938, RG 53–12, Box 2; *DN*, Dec. 17, 1937, May 26, July 23, Aug. 4, 24, 1938; *Lansing State Journal*, Mar. 24, 1938, clipping in FM Papers.

40. Granger to Hill, Aug. 10, 1938, Granger to FM, Sept. 22, 1938, FM Papers.

41. *DN*, Dec. 30, 31, 1937, Jan. 2, 7, 13, 27, Mar. 10, 27, Apr. 17, 18, May 27, June 21, 26, July 27, Aug. 7, 22, 24, Sept. 23, 24, Oct. 7, 1938; Proceedings of the [Detroit] Public Welfare Commission, Dec. 14, 29, 1937, Apr. 12, 1938, Burton Historical Collection, Detroit, Michigan; Fred W. Castator to FM, Dec. 31, 1937, G. R. Harris to Granger, Dec. 31, 1937, Mayor's Office Records, 1937, Box 7, ibid.; Harris to Frankensteen, Apr. 15, 1938, Frankensteen Papers, Box 1; Smith to FM, Apr. 15, 1938, Granger to FM, May 27, June 15, Oct. 6, 1938, Levi Memorandum to FM, June 6, 1938, FM to Edward J. Jeffries, June 24, 1938, FM Papers; SEWRC Minutes, Feb. 9, 16, Apr. 18, 1938, RG 53–12, Box 2; Sullivan, " 'On the Dole,' " p. 214; SERA,

Public Relief Statistics 5 (Dec. 1938 and Supplement): 16, 18, 25; Granger and Klein, *Emergency Relief*, pp. 137, 141, 156. After 1933 the lines of authority between the Wayne County Relief Commission and the Detroit Public Welfare Commission were "often clouded and confusing." Department of Public Welfare, *The Department of Public Welfare, 1930 to 1940* (Detroit: n.p., n.d.), p. 3.

42. Sullivan, " 'On the Dole,' " pp. 205, 209–11; Proceedings of Public Welfare Commission, Feb. 15, 1938; *DN*, Mar. 10, 1938; *DFP*, Apr. 25, 1940.

43. Proceedings of Public Welfare Commission, Feb. 15, 1938; Public Welfare Commission Minutes, Feb. 23, 1938, Mayor's Office Records, 1938, Box 9; Frankensteen to Reading, Feb. 15, 1938, Frankensteen Papers, Box 1; Granger to FM, Feb. 17, 1938, enclosing Granger to Harris, Feb. 13, 1938, FM to Norton, Feb. 26, 1938, FM Papers; SEWRC Minutes, Feb. 16, 1938, RG 53-12, Box 2; *DN*, Feb. 17, 27, Mar. 9, 1938; Sullivan, " 'On the Dole,' " pp. 209–11; Granger and Klein, *Emergency Relief*, p. 169.

44. *DN*, Feb. 24, May 5, 1938; FM speeches, Apr. 20, May 4, 1938, FM Papers; FM to Carlos Young, Aug. 9, 1938, ibid.; Marvin J. Petroelje and Richard T. Ortquist, Jr., interview with J. H. Creighton, undated, pp. 15–16, MHC.

45. Van Wagoner to FM, Apr. 18, 1938, FM Papers; *DN*, Apr. 8, 29, 1938; [*DFP*, Apr. 29, 1938], MSB.

46. Smith Memorandum to FM, Apr. 21, 1938, FM Memorandum to EGK, Apr. 28, 1938, EGK Memorandum to FM, Apr. 28, 1938, FM to Van Wagoner, May 6, 1938, FM Papers.

47. Since the gas tax yield for the year appeared to be $28.5 million rather than the $27 million originally estimated, the Highway Department could claim only $3.5 of the $5 million contingency fund. Draft of statement [May 1938], FM Papers.

48. Van Wagoner to FM, May 18, 1938, FM to Van Wagoner, May 24, 1938 (not sent), Van Wagoner to Hill, Dec. 13, 1938, FM Papers; Highway Department Release [May 1938], ibid.; "Final Press Statement," May 27, 1938, ibid.; *DN*, June 1, 1938; Robert S. Ford and Marvin A. Bacon, *Michigan Highway Finance* (Ann Arbor: University of Michigan Press, 1943), pp. 30, 31.

49. Office of the Budget Director, *Finances of State Government, July 1, 1937–June 30, 1938*, pp. 4–5, 9, 11; Ford and Waxman, *Financing Government*, pp. 149, 163; Perkins, *Role of Governor*, p. 72; Granger and Klein, *Emergency Relief*, p. 51; Smith to State, County and Municipal Workers of America, July 15, 1939, Smith Memorandum to FM, Aug. 9, 1938, FM Papers; Release, July 1, 1938, ibid.; "The Financial Condition of the State" [1938], ibid.; *Ex-Augural Message of Frank Murphy . . . January 5, 1939* (n.p., n.d.), pp. 6–7; *DN*, Mar. 16, July 3, 25, Aug. 4, 19, 1938. According to the copy of the budget in the FM Papers, disbursements in 1937–38 exceeded those of 1936–37 by $24.45 million, social welfare measures accounting for $13 million of this sum, education for $6.7 million, and health and hospitals for $3.4 million.

50. *DN*, July 2, 5, 6, Sept. 2, 7, Oct. 30, 1938; Smith Memorandum to FM, Mar. 7, 1938, FM Papers.

51. Raymond W. Starr to EGK, Oct. 11, 1938, FM to Local School Authorities, Oct. 19, 1938, FM Papers; [*Lansing State Journal*, Aug. 26, 1938], MSB; *DFP*, Aug. 31, Sept. 1, 1938; *DN*, June 2, Aug. 28, 31, Sept. 1, 1938; "How Much for Schools?"

Michigan Education Journal 15 (Sept. 1938): 3–6; "Gubernatorial Candidates State Their Plans for Education," ibid. 16 (Oct. 1938): 76–78, 100; Male, "MEA," pp. 473–75.

52. FM to EGK, Jan. 28, 31, 1938, EGK to FM, Feb. 1, 18, 1936, EGK-BHC, Box 16; EGK manuscript, Apr. 5, 1938, ibid.; FM to EGK, Mar. 3, 1938, ibid., Box 8; Joseph Donnelly to FM, Apr. 13, 1938, ibid., Box 14; FM to Martin, Feb. 4, 1938, Smith Memorandum to FM, May 16, 1938, FM Papers; *DN*, Feb. 20, Aug. 7, 1938; *NYT*, Feb. 5, 1938.

53. *DN*, Aug. 5, 11, 12, 23, 26, 1938; [*DT*, Aug. 27, 1938], MSB; Joseph C. Murphy to FM, Aug. 15, 1938, EGK-BHC, Box 14; "Proclamation by Governor for Extraordinary Session of the Legislature," Aug. 10, 1938, FM Papers.

54. George P. McCallum Diary, Aug. 29, 1938, George P. McCallum Papers, MHC; *Journal of the House of Representatives of the State of Michigan, Extra Session of 1938* (Lansing: Franklin DeKleine Co., n.d.), pp. 9–12; *DN*, Aug. 15, 23–31, Sept. 1–4, 1938.

55. *DN*, Nov. 21, 1937, Aug. 11, 1938; Sullivan, " 'On the Dole,' " pp. 183–88; National Emergency Council, Digest of Monthly Reports Due Oct. 15, 1937, RG 44, Box 512; FM to Harold Ickes, May 17, 1937, FM Papers; Proceedings of Public Welfare Commission, July 20, 1937; Detroit Housing Commission, "Third Annual Report" [1937], pp. 1, 5–6, 20; idem, "Fourth Annual Report" [1938], pp. 2–3; idem, "Fifth Annual Report" (1939), pp. 11–12, 17–20, 55–56.

56. EGK to FM, Jan. 3, 1937 [1938], EGK–BHC, Box 7; FDR to FM, Mar. 3, 1938, FM to FDR, Mar. 14, 1938, Straus to FM, Mar. 25, May 4, June 9, 1938, FM to Straus, May 31, 1938, FM to Starr, Aug. 13, 1938, Leon Keyserling to FM, Aug. 18, 27, Sept. 3, 1938, ibid., Box 9; FM Press Release, Apr. 22, 1938, ibid.; Hill to Williams, Aug. 18, 1938, EGK Memorandum to Williams, Aug. 19, 1938, FM Papers; *House Journal, Extra Session of 1938*, p. 13; *DN*, June 9, 10, Sept. 1, 7, 1938; *Public Acts of the Legislature of ... Michigan ... Extra Session of 1938* (Lansing: Franklin DeKleine Co., 1938), pp. 8–10.

57. Executive Order, Aug. 19, 1938, FM Papers; EGK to Western Union, Sept. 14, 1938, Clarence Smazel to Hill [Dec. 20, 1938], ibid.; Press Release, Sept. 14, 1938, ibid.; *Housing in Michigan ... A Preliminary Report of the Michigan Housing Commission* (n.p., n.d.); FM, *Ex-Augural Message*, p. 18.

58. *House Journal, Extra Session of 1938*, pp. 12–13; *DN*, Jan. 28, Feb. 9, 18, 1937, Aug. 11, Sept. 2, 1938; A. M. Mellier to FM, Feb. 18, 1937, FM Papers; Summary of Conversation with Governor Murphy, Sept. 1, 1938, PSF, Frank Murphy, FDRL. See also Hill to Ickes, Sept. 22, 1938, FM Papers.

59. *DN*, Jan. 12, 1938; *DFP*, Jan. 21, 1938; Press Releases, Jan. 14, Feb. 4, 1938, FM Papers; FM to Chase S. Osborn, Feb. 2, 1938, FM to Martin, Feb. 4, 1938, ibid.; Executive Order, Jan. 20, 1938, ibid.; FM article for *Democratic Digest*, Mar. 10, 1938, ibid.

60. Bruce Dudley Blumell, "Development of Public Assistance in the State of Washington during the Great Depression" (Ph.D. diss., University of Washington, 1973), pp. 229–30, 255–66; Priscilla Ferguson Clement, "The Works Progress Administration in Pennsylvania, 1935 to 1940," *Pennsylvania Magazine of History and Biography* 90 (Apr. 1971): 246–47, 254–55, 259; John Braeman et al., eds.,

The New Deal, vol. 2, *The State and Local Level* (Columbus: Ohio State University Press, 1975), pp. 342–43, 388–90, 414; Searle F. Charles, *Minister of Relief: Harry Hopkins and the Depression* (Syracuse: Syracuse University Press, 1963), pp. 174–205; Senate Special Committee to Investigate Senatorial Campaign Expenditures and Use of Governmental Funds in 1938, *Investigation of Senatorial Campaign Expenditures and Use of Governmental Funds*, 76 Cong., 1 sess., Sen. Report No. 1, 2 pts. (Washington: U.S. Government Printing Office, 1939); Hill to Granger, May 6, 1938, Granger to FM, June 16, 1938, FM Papers; Granger to FM, Aug. 4, 11, 18, 1938, EGK–BHC, Box 16; *DN*, June 1, 9, Sept. 7, 9, 1938; *DT*, June 14, 1938, copy of clipping in FM Papers; Granger and Klein, *Emergency Relief*, p. 171.

61. William H. Carpenter to FM, July 9, 1938, FM Papers; L. E. Fisher to Williams, Aug. 30, 1938, Nims to Williams, Oct. 31, Nov. 8, 1938, File 610, RG 59; Paul H. Todd to EGK, Oct. 15, 1938, EGK–BHC, Box 16; Hunter to Hopkins, Dec. 6, 1938, Confidential Political File, 1938–1940, Hopkins Papers; SERA, *Public Relief Statistics* 5 (Apr. 1938): 3; ibid. (Sept. 1938): 3; ibid. (Oct. 1938): 3; Howard, *WPA*, p. 591.

CHAPTER 14

1. *DN*, Feb. 11, 12, 14, Apr. 2, 6, 7, 1937; handbill in FM Papers; FM speeches, Mar. 28, 29, 1937, ibid.; Emerson Boyles to Arthur H. Vandenberg, Feb. 24, 1937, Emerson Boyles Papers, Box 2, MHC; *Michigan Official Directory and Legislative Manual, 1937–38* (n.p., n.d.), pp. 642–54.

2. *DN*, Sept. 5, Nov. 1, 1937; William Markland to Ralph [Johnson] [Oct. 1937], *DN*—Murphy File, in my possession; Muller to FM, Oct. 11, 1937, Martin to FM, Nov. 1, 1937 (two telegrams), FM Papers; Guy Hugh Jenkins to George G. Booth, Oct. 22, 1937, Guy Hugh Jenkins Papers, MHC; William Lovett to FM, Nov. 3, 1937, EGK–BHC, Box 19; Josephine Gomon Diary, Nov. 3, 1937, Josephine Gomon Papers, MHC; Michael Craine, "Labor in the 1937 Detroit Municipal Election" (1971), pp. 15–26, 30–32, 39–44, 47–48, in my possession. Cf. Frank Cormier and William J. Eaton, *Reuther* (Englewood Cliffs, N.J.: Prentice-Hall [1970]), p. 123.

3. [*DT*, Jan. 20, 1937], MSB; *New York Post*, Jan. 16, 1937, MSB; [*Grand Rapids Times*, Jan. 22, 1937], MSB; *DN*, Jan. 17, 19, Apr. 11, 1937; [*Emporia Gazette*, Feb. 11, 1937], MSB; *Michigan Democratic Forum* (Mar. 1937): 9, MSB; Walter Karig, "Who Will Succeed Roosevelt?" [*Liberty* (Sept. 18, 1937)], MSB; James Wingo to FM, July 6, 1937, FM Papers.

4. Robert Sherwood, *Roosevelt and Hopkins*, 2 vols. (New York: Bantam Books, 1950), 1:114–16; [*New York World*, May 13, 1938], MSB; [*Washington Star*, Oct. 11, 1938], MSB; *DN*, Sept. 4, Nov. 7, 1938.

5. *Pittsburgh Sun-Telegraph*, June 10, 1937, MSB; Lee Kreiselman Jaffe to FM, May 17, 1937, Schouman to FM, Aug. 24, 1937, FM Papers.

6. *Selected Addresses of Frank Murphy . . . January 1, 1937, to September 30, 1938* (Lansing: n.p., 1938), passim; *DN*, Sept. 10, 1937; [*Chicago Herald Examiner*, Aug. 31, 1937], MSB.

7. HM to Ruth Treglown, Oct. 5, 1938, HM Papers; [*Gratiot County Herald*, June

2, 1938], MSB; *DN*, Nov. 7, 1938; Jenkins to Booth, Dec. 1, 1937, Jenkins Papers.

8. For the Republican primary, see *DN*, Dec. 8, 1937, Mar. 25, May 15, 22, June 7, 26, July 13, 29, Aug. 21, Sept. 10, 11, 14, 23, 1938; *DFP*, Mar. 18, 1938; Edward H. Litchfield, "Michigan's Experience with Civil Service," *Personnel Administration* 2 (Dec. 1939): 6; Floyd Josiah Miller Diary, Sept. 14, 1938, Floyd Josiah Miller Papers, MHC; Adolph Germer to FM, Mar. 18, 1938, FM Papers; Frank Picard speech, Sept. 22, 1938, ibid.; and *Michigan Official Directory and Legislative Manual, 1939-1940* (n.p., n.d.), p. 196. A third Republican candidate, Roscoe Conkling Fitch, received only 14,253 votes.

9. FM to Gar Wood, May 27, 1937, Fry to FM, Feb. 1, 1938, FM Papers; *DN*, Jan. 2, May 4, 1938. The report of the anti-Murphy meeting first appeared in the *Detroit Free Press* on December 15, 1937. That the meeting occurred appears to be confirmed by the following: *DN*, Jan. 22, 1938; FM to Brown, Jan. 22, 1938, FM Papers; and Brown to FDR, June 6, 1938, OF 300 (Michigan), FDRL.

10. *DN*, Feb. 27, June 9, 1938; Mead to FM, Mar. 2, 1938, Fry to FM, June 7, 1938, Donnelly to FM, July 22, 1938, FM Papers; Minutes of Meeting Held in Flint, May 19, 1938, ibid.

11. Germer to FM, May 10, 1938, Marie Hendrie to FM, May 10, 1938, Frank C. Rommeck to Dear Friend, May 10, 1938, FM Papers; *DN*, May 8, 15, 31, July 10, 1938; [*DT*, July 10, 1938], MSB; Leo J. Nowicki, "Profile of an American by Choice" (1935), p. 68, MHC.

12. *DN*, July 24, 25, 31, 1938; *DFP*, July 24, 25, 1938; [*Dallas Dispatch-Journal*, Sept. 5, 1938], MSB; Jenkins column in unidentified newspaper [June 1938], MSB.

13. Brigid McKenna to James Roosevelt, July 24, 1938, OF 300 (Michigan); G. H. Roosevelt to FDR, July 12, 1938, Marvin H. McIntyre to G. H. Roosevelt, July 13, 1938, PPF 285, FDRL; FM to J. Roosevelt, Aug. 30, 1938, and enclosed clipping from *New York Mirror*, Aug. 29, 1938, PSF, FM; Hunter to Hopkins, Aug. 1, 1938, Confidential Political File, 1933-1938, Harry L. Hopkins Papers, FDRL.

14. *DFP*, Sept. 1, 3, 1938; *DN*, Sept. 2, 4, 1938; [*New York Daily Mirror*, Sept. 9, 20, 1938], MSB; FM to J. Roosevelt, Aug. 30, Sept. 1, 1938, FM to Hopkins, and enclosed Summary of Conversation with . . . FM, Sept. 1, 1938, PSF, FM; FM to Corcoran, Sept. 1, 1938, FDR to FM, Sept. 2, 1938, FM Papers; Press Conference #482, Sept. 2, 1938, FDRL.

15. *DN*, May 14, Sept. 5, 6, Oct. 1, 2, 1938; *DFP*, Oct. 1, 2, 1938; FM speech, Oct. 1, 1938, FM Papers; *Michigan Manual, 1939-1940*, p. 194.

16. *DN*, May 8, Aug. 11, 17, 18, Sept. 24, 25, Oct. 2, 14, 18, 30, Nov. 4, 1938; [*Muskegon Observer*, Sept. 1938], clipping in FM Papers; unreleased *DN* article [Mar. 1939], in my possession; Samuel T. Metzger to Comstock, Nov. 1, 1940, William Comstock Papers, MHC; Edmund C. Shields to JAF, Oct. 28, 1938, OF 300 (Election Forecasts and Analysis of Election Results, 1938) (hereafter cited as 1938).

17. *DN*, Mar. 4, 1939; unreleased *DN* article [Mar. 1939]; Martin S. Hayden to Fine, Oct. 8, 1964. Brown discussed his role in the campaign in an interview with Martin S. Hayden of the *Detroit News* following the election. Unreleased *DN* article [Mar. 1939]. Hayden provided me with a copy of this article.

18. Cooley to Van Wagoner, Sept. 13, 1938, Van Wagoner to Cooley, Sept. 22, 1938, Murray D. Van Wagoner Papers, MHC; *DN*, Oct. 10, 11, Nov. 6, 1938.

19. Gomon Diary, Oct. 26, 1938, Gomon Papers; Shields to JAF, Oct. 28, 1938,

Clara Van Auken to JAF, Oct. 30, 1938, Picard to JAF, Oct. 31, 1938, OF 300 (1938); John McGinty to JAF, Oct. 29, 1938, John Barc to JAF, Oct. 31, 1938, OF 300 (Supplementary State Reports, 1938, Michigan) (hereafter cited as Supplementary); *DN*, Oct. 29, 1938.

20. John C. Sullivan to FM, July 9, 1938, FM to Sullivan, Aug. 9, 1938, Sullivan and Harry J. Davenport to FM, Aug. 12, 1938, FM to Sullivan and Davenport, Aug. 31, 1938, FM Papers; McGinty to JAF, Oct. 29, 1938, OF 300 (Supplementary).

21. [*Daily Record Progresssive Weekly*, Sept. 1938], MSB; *United Automobile Worker*, Apr. 23, July 9, Oct. 29, Nov. 5, 1938; UAW Release, Oct. 6, 1938, Joe Brown Collection, ALHUA; UAW International Executive Board Minutes, Oct. 5, 1938, p. 7, Henry Kraus Papers, Box 7, ALHUA; *DLN*, Dec. 17, 1937, Oct. 7, 14, 1938; *DFP*, Oct. 7, 1938; *NYT*, Oct. 21, 1938; *DN*, Dec. 13, 1937, Feb. 11, Mar. 21, Apr. 24, Oct. 8, 1938; Wayne Political League, Committee Treasurer's Detailed Statement of Nomination and Election Expenses, Nov. 8, 1938, FM Papers.

22. Text of Detroit Newspaper Guild broadcast [Oct. 27, 1938], MSB; Daniel J. Leab, *A Union of Individuals: The Formation of the American Newspaper Guild, 1933–1936* (New York: Columbia University Press, 1970), p. 78; *DN*, Sept. 24, 1938.

23. *DN*, Mar. 21, Aug. 12, 1938; *NYT*, Oct. 21, 1938; Labor's Non-Partisan League Release, Oct. 3, 1938, Brown Collection; Germer Diary, July 20, 1938, Adolph Germer Papers, State Historical Society of Wisconsin, Madison, Wisconsin; Brophy to Germer, July 23, 1938, ibid.; Germer to Brophy, Sept. 8, 1938, notes on CIO File, in possession of Irving Bernstein; Germer to FM, June 18, 1938, Sarraine Andrews to FM, Nov. 10, 1938, Vera Brown to FM, Nov. 11, 1938, FM Papers; Mead to JAF, Dec. 24, 1938, Charles E. Misner to JAF, Jan. 16, 1939, OF 300 (1938); Samuel T. McSeveney, "The Michigan Gubernatorial Campaign of 1938," *Michigan History* 45 (June 1961): 116.

24. *DN*, Sept. 7, 1938; Ben Fischer, "On Political Action in Michigan," Jan. 15, 1938, Daniel Bell Papers, Tamiment Library, New York, New York; Picard to JAF, Oct. 31, 1938, OF 300 (1938).

25. Fischer, "Confidential Report of the Socialist Party...," June 7, 1938, Kraus Papers, Box 16; [Fischer] to Herb Zam, Aug. 10, 1938, Thomas to Fischer and Tucker Smith, Aug. 19, 1938, Fischer to Paul Porter, Sept. 20, 1938, Willie Barrash to Gus Tyler, Sept. 21, 1938, Fischer to Comrades, Sept. 26, 1938, Thomas to Fischer, Sept. 26, 1938, Zam to Comrades, Sept. 29, 1938, Judah —— to Fischer, Oct. 1, 1938, Bell Papers; Daniel Bell, "The Development and Background of Marxian Socialism in the United States," in Donald Drew Egbert and Stow Persons, eds., *Socialism in American Life*, 2 vols. (Princeton: Princeton University Press, 1952), 1:390–91; Frank Warren, *An Alternative Vision: The Socialist Party in the 1930's* (Bloomington: University of Indiana Press, 1974), pp. 106–7; McSeveney, "1938," p. 117n. Fischer, Roy Reuther, and Hy Fish were originally censured by the national office for introducing resolutions in their unions calling for the election of Murphy and of Charles Sawyer in Ohio. Warren, *Alternative Vision*, p. 224n.

26. See William Dick, *Labor and Socialism in America: The Gompers Era* (Port Washington, N.Y.: Kennikat Press, 1972), pp. 78–80, for the presentation of this argument for the Gompers era.

27. Fischer to Tyler, Jan. 31, 1938, Bell Papers.

28. [*State Echo*, Nov. 6, 1938], MSB; *Michigan Guide*, Nov. 5, 1938; *United Automobile Worker*, Oct. 29, 1938; *DN*, June 22, 1938; [*Detroit Hungarian News*, Sept. 9, 1938], MSB; [*Italian-American Outlook*, Oct. 28, 1938], MSB; John C. Lehr to JAF, Oct. 31, 1938, OF 300 (1938); Millman to FM, Nov. 7, 1938, FM Papers.

29. *Detroit Jewish Voice*, Nov. 4, 1938, in FM Papers; FM to S. Margoshes, Oct. 13, 1938, Wise to FM, Oct. 18, 1938, FM to Wise, Oct. 21, 1938, ibid.

30. FM to Frank Walker, Aug. 7, 1938, Stephen Early to FM, Sept. 30, 1938, FM Papers; FM to Hopkins, Sept. 1, 1938, and enclosed Summary of Conversation, Sept. 1, 1938, PSF, FM; Hunter to Hopkins, Sept. 1, 1938, Correspondence 1933–1940, Hopkins Papers; Picard to FDR, Sept. 3, 1938, FDR to Picard, Sept. 11, 1938, PPF 5503, FDRL.

31. Fleeson column, Oct. 6, 1938, clipping in FM Papers; FDR to FM, Oct. 5, 1938, FM Papers; *DN*, Oct. 26, Nov. 5, 1938; *NYT*, Nov. 5, 1938.

32. Atkinson to FM, Sept. 11, 19, 1938, FM Papers; Atkinson to FDR, Oct. 11, 1938, Elbert K. Burlew Memorandum for the President, Oct. 14, 1938, FDR to Atkinson, Oct. 18, 1938, FDR to FM, Oct. 18, 1938, OF 725, FDRL; Atkinson to JAF, Oct. 28, 1938, OF 300 (1938).

33. *DN*, Sept. 28, 1938; Ickes speech, Sept. 30, 1938, FM Papers; Ickes to FM, Nov. 1, 1938, ibid.; *The Secret Diary of Harold L. Ickes*, 3 vols. (New York: Simon and Schuster, 1953–54), 2:482.

34. Picard to FDR, Oct. 12, 18, 1938, FDR to Picard, Oct. 21, 1938, PPF 5503; FM to JAF, Oct. 7, 1938, FM Papers; *DN*, Oct. 21, 1938; McSeveney, "1938," pp. 105–6.

35. Wayne County Democratic Committee, Committee Treasurer's Detailed Statement of Nomination and Election Expenses, Nov. 8, 1938, FM Papers; Wayne Political League, Detailed Statement . . ., Nov. 8, 1938, ibid.; Murphy for Governor Committee, Detailed Statement . . ., Nov. 8, 1938, ibid.; Howell Van Auken to FM, Aug. 7, 1939, ibid.; *DN*, Nov. 29, 30, 1938; Interview with Harry Mead, Aug. 15, 1963, p. 23, MHC; Interview with Lee Pressman, Nov. 12, 1964, p. 41, MHC.

36. *DN*, May 9, Oct. 2, 6, 1938; *DFP*, Dec. 1, 1938; Jenkins to Booth, Dec. 8, 1937, Jenkins Papers; FM to Walker, Aug. 7, Dec. 5, 1938, Walker to FM, Sept. 14, 1938, FM Papers; Shields to JAF, Oct. 28, 1938, OF 300 (1938); McGinty to JAF, Oct. 28, 1938, OF 300 (Supplementary).

37. Picard to FM, Sept. 8, 10, 1938, FM to Picard, Sept. 9, 1938; *DN*, Oct. 11, 19, Nov. 2, 1938.

38. *DN*, Sept. 23, Oct. 6, 7, 30, Nov. 11, 28, Dec. 7, 1938, Feb. 22, 1939; *DFP*, Oct. 25, 1938; unidentified clipping [Oct. 7, 1938], MSB; James F. Thomson to FM, Oct. 15, 1938, enclosing Thomson to Raymond W. Starr, Oct. 15, 1938, and undated letter signed by W. J. Barber, EGK–BHC, Box 20; *Journal of the Senate of the State of Michigan, 1939 Regular Session*, 2 vols. (Lansing: Franklin DeKleine Co., 1939), 1:273–78, 311–13.

39. *DN*, Oct. 12, 14, 17, 20, 23, Nov. 1, 2, 4, 6, 1938; advances on FM speeches, Oct. 12, 14, 16, 25, 28, 1938, FM Papers; FM speeches, Sept. 23, Oct. 22, Nov. 3, 1938, ibid.; Notes for FM speech, Oct. 31, 1938, ibid.; FM article for *Democratic Digest*, Oct. 11, 1938, ibid.; M. Hayden to Fine, Oct. 8, 1964.

40. *DN*, Oct. 4, 9, 1938; [*Lansing State Journal*, Oct. 4, 1938], MSB; Martin R. Bradley to JAF, Oct. 28, 1938, OF 300 (1938); McGinty to JAF, Oct. 29, 1938, OF 300 (Supplementary).

41. *DN*, June 26, Nov. 30, 1938, Mar. 4, 1939; unreleased *DN* article [Mar. 1939]; *DFP*, Nov. 30, 1938; George Sadowski to FM, Oct. 18, 1938, FM Papers; John Luecke to JAF, Oct. 23, 1938, John Dingell to JAF, Oct. 26, 1938, OF 300 (1938); Interview with Martin S. Hayden, Oct. 6, 1964, p. 41, MHC; Hayden to Fine, Oct. 8, 1964.

42. Mrs. George W. Rogers to Mrs. Theodore D. Buhl, Apr. 11, 1938, Jerome C. Nadolney to FM, Dec. 31, 1938, FM Papers; A. E. Holland to Fitzgerald for Governor Headquarters, Nov. 3, 1938, Leland S. Bisbee to Fitzgerald, Dec. 8, 1938, Frank D. Fitzgerald Papers, MHC; George P. McCallum to Gentlemen, Feb. 21, 1938, Howard C. Lawrence Papers, MHC.

43. FM to A. E. Dale, July 23, 1938, Germer to FM, Dec. 12, 1938, FM Papers; Magdol and Perlman, "The Press of Michigan in the 1938 Election . . ." (Jan. 15, 1939), in Mr. Magdol's possession; McGinty to JAF, Oct. 29, 1938, OF 300 (Supplementary); Blair Moody to Picard, Dec. 12, 1938, Blair Moody Papers, MHC.

44. *DN*, Oct. 29, 1938.

45. *DN*, Oct. 3, 8, 12, 13, 15, 21, 26, 29, Nov. 6, 1938; [*Gratiot County Herald*, Oct. 27, 1938], MSB; "Gubernatorial Candidates State Their Plans for Education," *Michigan Education Journal* 16 (Oct. 1938): 76; *Civic Echo*, undated, in FM Papers; Donnelly to FM, Sept. 15, 1938, ibid.

46. *Republican Digest*, Sept. 23, 1938, in FM Papers; John T. Howell to Dear Friend, Oct. 10, 1938, and enclosed pamphlet, Hill to FM, undated, ibid.; *DN*, Sept. 10, 11, Oct. 28, 30, Nov. 6, 1938. Murphy ignored the Townsend plan until the very end of the campaign, when he lamely stated that he favored the "principle" of the plan and that it had been "a helpful influence" in the nation. *DN*, Nov. 6, 1938.

47. *DN*, Oct. 11, 15, 26, 27, 29, 30, Nov. 2, 6, 1938; [*Gratiot County Herald*, Oct. 27, 1938], MSB.

48. *DN*, Oct. 14–18, 23–28, 1938; McGinty to JAF, Oct. 29, 1938, OF 300 (Supplementary). See also McSeveney, "1938," pp. 102–3.

49. *DN*, Oct. 28, 29, Nov. 2–4, 6, 1938.

50. *DN*, Nov. 6, 1938.

51. *DN*, Sept. 30, 1938; Legislative News Letter, Oct. 1, 1938, Brown Collection; Communist Party of Michigan, *The People of Michigan vs Re-Action in 1938*, pamphlet in Vertical File, MHC; Germer to Brophy, Sept. 30, 1938, notes on CIO File.

52. *DN*, Oct. 3, 4, 25, 26, 30, Nov. 4, 1938; *Civic Echo*, undated, in FM Papers; *Communists Back Murphy. . .*, pamphlet in ibid.; Atkinson to JAF, Oct. 28, 1938, Lehr to JAF, Oct. 31, 1938, OF 300 (1938).

53. *DN*, Oct. 18–22, 1938; *Congressional Record*, 76 Cong., 1 sess., Appendix, p. 486; Special House Committee on Un-American Activities, *Investigation of Un-American Propaganda Activities in the United States, Hearings. . .*, 75 Cong., 3 sess., 4 vols. (Washington: U.S. Government Printing Office, 1938), 2:1454, 1493–96, 1528, 1531–32, 1551, 1594, 1596, 1606, 1630–32, 1649, 1675–80, 1683–

91, 1695-1710, 3:2063-72 (hereafter cited as *Dies Hearings*); August Raymond Ogden, *The Dies Committee* (Washington: Catholic University Press, 1943), pp. 75-78; Marvin Petroelje and Richard T. Ortquist, Jr., Interview with Joseph Creighton, undated, pp. 29-30, MHC. For the extent of Communist participation in the GM strike, see Sidney Fine, *Sit-Down: The General Motors Strike of 1936-1937* (Ann Arbor: University of Michigan Press, 1969), pp. 220-23.

54. *DN*, Oct. 3, 22, 27, 31, Nov. 4, 6, 1938; *NYT*, Oct. 21, 1938; [*Gratiot County Herald*, Oct. 27, 1938], MSB.

55. Advance on FM speech, Oct. 12, 1938, FM Papers; FM speeches, Oct. 21, 24, Nov. 4, 1938, ibid.; *Kalamazoo Gazette*, Oct. 26, 1938, clipping in ibid.; Press Release, Oct. 27, 1938, ibid.; *DN*, Oct. 22, 26, 27, 29, 1938; *DFP*, Oct. 25, 1938.

56. FM to Dies, Oct. 23, 1938, FM Papers; *DN*, Oct. 27, 29, 30, 1938, Jan. 15, 1939; *NYT*, Oct. 26, 30, 1938.

57. *Dies Hearings*, 2:2019-20; *United Automobile Worker*, Oct. 22, 1938; Press Release, Oct. 27, 1938, FM Papers; John B. Waite to FM, Oct. 28, 1938, Dorothy Detzer to FM, Oct. 28, 1938, enclosing Hanna Clothier Hull et al. to FDR, Oct. 27, 1938, ibid.; *Flint Journal*, Oct. 27, 1938, clipping in ibid.; *DN*, Oct. 27, 1938; Citizens of Flint and Genesee County to FDR, Oct. 27, 1938, Barringer to FDR, Oct. 27, 1938, Edward J. Fry to FDR, Oct. 30, 1938, OF 320, FDRL; Frances Perkins to FM, Oct. 30, 1938, EMB Papers; Anderson, "The Loaded Dies Committee," *Nation* 147 (Oct. 29, 1938): 443.

58. Rudolf G. Tenerowicz to JAF, Oct. 25, 1938, Edwin A. Bolger to JAF, Oct. 27, 1938, Bradley to JAF, Oct. 28, 1938, Lehr to JAF, Oct. 31, 1938, Picard to JAF, Oct. 31, 1938, OF 300 (1938); J. H. Bollens to Murphy for Governor Committee, Nov. 2, 1938, Civil Rights Congress of Michigan Papers, Box 31, ALHUA.

59. *NYT*, Jan. 23, 1940; *Daily Worker*, Jan. 24, 1940; Arthur Maguire to FM, Oct. 21, 1938, Ida Z. Kleinman to FM, Oct. 25, 1938, Maguire to Edward Cardinal Mooney, Nov. 6, 1938, FM Papers.

60. FM speeches, Oct. 12, 29, 1938, FM Papers; Advance on FM speech, Oct. 12, 1938, ibid.; FM to Maguire, Oct. 13, 1938, ibid.; *DN*, Oct. 12, 24, 26, 28, 30, 1938. See also Atkinson to JAF, Oct. 28, 1938, OF 300 (1938).

61. Maguire to FM, Oct. 8, 1938, enclosing Maguire to Mooney, Oct. 8, 1938, Maguire to FM, Oct. 12, 21, Nov. 6, 1938, FM to Maguire, Oct. 13, 1938, Maguire to FDR, Oct. 26, 1938, McIntyre to FM, Oct. 28, 1938, FM to McIntyre, Nov. 2, 1938, Maguire to Mooney, Nov. 6, 1938, FM Papers; Mead interview, pp. 25-26.

62. *DN*, Nov. 2, 3, 1938; Germer Diary, Nov. 1, 1938, Germer Papers; FM speech, Nov. 2, 1938, FM Papers; *Michigan Catholic*, Nov. 3, 1938.

63. *DN*, Nov. 6, 7, 1938; FM speech, Nov. 7, 1938; FM to Sugar, Nov. 8, 1938, FM Papers.

64. John P. White, *Michigan Votes: Election Statistics, 1928-1956* (Ann Arbor: University of Michigan, 1958), pp. 40, 47. I have followed the classification of counties in Marvin A. Bacon, *Income as an Index of Fiscal Capacity in Michigan Counties* (Ann Arbor: University of Michigan Press, 1941), pp. 24-25.

65. James K. Pollock and Samuel J. Eldersveld, *Michigan Politics in Transition* (Ann Arbor: University of Michigan Press, 1942), pp. 43, 45; John Braeman et al., eds., *The New Deal*, vol. 2, *The State and Local Levels* (Columbus: Ohio State University Press, 1975), pp. 70-72; McSeveney, "1938," pp. 120-21.

66. *Michigan Manual, 1939-1940,* pp. 324-27, 334-35, 357.

67. Edward H. Litchfield, *Voting Behavior in a Metropolitan Area* (Ann Arbor: University of Michigan Press, 1941), pp. 12, 28; Pollock and Eldersveld, *Michigan Politics,* p. 45; Thomas R. Solomon, "Participation of Negroes in Detroit Elections" (Ph.D. diss., University of Michigan, 1939), p. 139; McSeveney, "1938," p. 123; White, *Michigan Votes,* pp. 40, 47. See Chapter 6, n. 108.

68. *DN,* Nov. 10, Dec. 9, 1938.

69. Angus Campbell et al., *Elections and the Political Order* (New York: John Wiley and Sons, 1966), pp. 43-44, 61; V. O. Key, *American State Politics* (New York: Alfred A. Knopf, 1956), pp. 15, 37; James L. Sundquist, *Dynamics of the Party System* (Washington: Brookings Institution, 1973), pp. 219, 239; James T. Patterson, *The New Deal and the States* (Princeton: Princeton University Press, 1969), p. 157; McSeveney, "1938," pp. 97-98; J. Stephen Turell, "The Vulnerability of American Governors, 1900-1969," in Thad Beyle and J. Oliver Williams, eds., *The American Governor in Behavioral Perspective* (New York: Harper and Row, 1972), pp. 27-28.

70. White, *Michigan Votes,* pp. 40, 47; McSeveney, "1938," pp. 122-23; *DN,* Nov. 13, 27, 29, 1938; *NYT,* Nov. 3, 1938; Esther Van Wagoner Tufty to FM, Nov. 10, 1938, Elinor Greene to FM, Nov. 11, 1938, Charles M. Novak to FM, Nov. 11, 1938, JAF to FM, Nov. 14, 1938, FM to Frank Markey, Nov. 22, 1938, William Allen White to FM, Nov. 23, 1938, and enclosed *Emporia Gazette* editorial [Nov. 17, 1938], FM Papers; Neil S. Purdy to JAF, Dec. 14, 1938, Mead to JAF, Dec. 24, 1938, OF 300 (1938).

71. FM to Ruth and Edward Treglown, Dec. 20, 1938, EMB Papers; Mrs. Thomas F. McAllister to Mrs. McDonald, Nov. 10, 1938, Democratic Party, National Committee, Women's Division Records, Michigan, FDRL; Picard to Moody, Nov. 28, 1938, Moody to Picard, Dec. 12, 1938, Moody Papers; Paul H. Todd to FM, Nov. 12, 1938, FM Papers; E. A. Wooten speech [1939], ibid.; FM to JAF, Dec. 7, 1938, W. H. Bannan to JAF, Dec. 10, 1938, William M. J. Baird to JAF, Dec. 12, 1938, Francis T. McDonald to JAF, Dec. 21, 1938, John Kladzyk to JAF, Dec. 22, 1938, OF 300 (1938); FM, "Tragic Interruption," *Nation* 147 (Dec. 3, 1938): 590; Angus Campbell et al., *The American Voter* (New York: John Wiley and Sons, 1964), pp. 554-57; [*Washington Star,* Oct. 11, 1938], MSB.

72. *Michigan Manufacturer and Financial Record* 62 (Nov. 12, 1938): 52; ibid. (Dec. 10, 1938): 8; *DN,* Nov. 10, 27, 29, Dec. 14, 25, 1938; *DFP,* Nov. 10, 1938; *Battle Creek Evening News,* Nov. 29, 1938, clipping in FM Papers; *DLN,* Nov. 11, 1938; *NYT,* Nov. 10, 1938; Luecke to JAF, Nov. 15, 1938, Paul F. Voelker to JAF, Nov. 18, 1938, FM to JAF, Dec. 7, 1938, Bannan to JAF, Dec. 10, 1938, Baird to JAF, Dec. 12, 1938, Charles Beaudin to JAF, Dec. 15, 1938, Charles H. Snyder to JAF, Dec. 19, 1938, G. A. Gale to JAF, Dec. 19, 1938, Bradley to JAF, Dec. 23, 1938, Mead to JAF, Dec. 24, 1938, Earl M. LaFreniere to JAF, Dec. 28, 1938, Claude B. Root to JAF, Dec. 28, 1938, A. E. Henwood to JAF, Jan. 9, 1939, Walter Denning to JAF, Jan. 17, 1939, OF 300 (1938); Donnelly to FM, Nov. 9, 1938, John J. O'Brien to FM, Nov. 10, 1938, Claude S. Hyman to FM, Nov. 14, 1938, Dingell to FM, Nov. 15, 1938, FM to G. A. Richards, Nov. 19, 1938, FM to David Dubinsky, Nov. 21, 1938, FM to JAF, Nov. 23, 1938, Shields to FM, Nov. 25, 1938, FM Papers; Moody to Picard, Dec. 12, 1938, Moody Papers.

73. Picard to Moody, Nov. 28, 1938, Moody Papers; *DN*, Dec. 14, 1938; FM to Brown [Dec. 1938], Prentiss Brown Papers, Box 2, MHC. See also William J. Delaney to JAF, Dec. 15, 1938, and McDonald to JAF, Dec. 21, 1938, OF 300 (1938).

74. Campbell et al., *American Voter*, pp. 168–87, 544–46; Voelker to JAF, Nov. 18, 1938, OF 300 (1938); John J. Krault to Editor, *DN* [Nov. 1938], *DN*—Murphy File.

75. Steuart Henderson Britt and Selden C. Menefee, "Did the Publicity of the Dies Committee in 1938 Influence Public Opinion?" *Public Opinion Quarterly* 3 (July 1939): 456n, 457; James A. Farley, *Jim Farley's Story* (New York: McGraw-Hill, 1938), p. 149; Voelker to JAF, Nov. 18, 1938, LaFreniere to JAF, Dec. 28, 1938, OF 300 (1938); [Atkinson] to Mooney, Oct. 5, 1938, and enclosed handbill, Edward J. Hickey to Atkinson, Oct. 10, 1938, Maguire to Mooney, Nov. 6, 1938, Atkinson to FM, Nov. 9, 1938, Feb. 18, 1939, Donnelly to FM, Nov. 9, 1938, Maguire to FM, Nov. 10, 1938, Nadolney to FM, Nov. 16, 1938, Mrs. Louise F. Ransome to Mooney, Nov. 16, 1938, FM Papers; *Secret Diary of Ickes*, 3:229. Cf. FM to Maguire, Nov. 15, 1938, ibid.

76. Picard to Moody, Nov. 28, 1938, Moody Papers; Robert Dahne to JAF, Dec. 8, 1938, Michael F. DeFant to JAF, Dec. 11, 1938, Beaudin to JAF, Dec. 15, 1938, LaFreniere to JAF, Dec. 28, 1938, James R. Burke and C. Henry Bennett to JAF, Jan. 17, 1939, OF 300 (1938); Gerald J. Cleary to FM, Nov. 19, 1938, FM Papers; *Secret Diary of Ickes*, 2:498–99.

77. Molle Franklin Gibney to JAF, Nov. 19, 1938, DeFant to JAF, Dec. 11, 1938, Giles Kavanagh to JAF, Dec. 12, 1938, Charles Cronenworth to JAF, Dec. 14, 1938, Beaudin to JAF, Dec. 15, 1938, Delaney to JAF, Dec. 15, 1938, Lonnie Henderson to JAF, Dec. 16, 1938, George Marble to JAF, Dec. 16, 1938, Glen Greene to JAF, Dec. 23, 1938, Oral Levan to JAF, Dec. 24, 1938, LaFreniere to JAF, Dec. 28, 1938, Root to JAF, Dec. 28, 1938, Misner to JAF, Jan. 6, 1939, Henwood to JAF, Jan. 9, 1939, Chet P. Emunson to JAF, Jan. 9, 1939, Burke and Bennett, Jan. 17, 1939, OF 300 (1938); F. D. Moses to FM, Nov. 9, 1938, Dingell to FM, Nov. 15, 1938, Nadolney to FM, Dec. 31, 1938, FM Papers; Wooten speech [1939], ibid.; L. O'Brien to Editor [Nov. 1938], clipping in ibid.; L. O'Brien to GM, Dec. 3, 1938, GM Papers; *United Automobile Worker*, Nov. 12, 1938.

78. Pollock to Paul Scott Mowrer, Nov. 28, 1938, James K. Pollock Papers, Box 5, MHC; *United Automobile Worker*, Nov. 12, 1938; Picard to Moody, Nov. 28, 1938, Moody to Picard, Dec. 12, 1938, Moody Papers; Gomon Diary, May 11, 1939, Gomon Papers; Muller to FM, Nov. 11, 1938, Donnelly to John W. Kushing, July 26, 1939, Starr to FM, Jan. 10, 1940, Hill to FM, Dec. 10, 1942, FM Papers; *Wayne County Democrat*, Apr. 10, 1943, FM Papers; Interview with G. Mennen Williams, Dec. 1964, p. 5, MHC; Alice Smuts notes on interview with Van Wagoner, May 1, 1969, in my possession. Cf. Interview with G. Donald Kennedy, May 11, 1965, p. 19, MHC.

79. Ernest B. Harper and Duane L. Gibson, *Reorganization of Public Welfare in Michigan* (East Lansing: Michigan State College, 1942), pp. 41, 50; Pamela Sawkins, "Executive Leadership of Frank Murphy as Governor of Michigan" (M.A. thesis, Wayne University, 1950), 60n; McSeveney, "1938," pp. 104–5; Pollock to Mowrer,

Nov. 28, 1938, Pollock Papers, Box 5; Picard to Moody, Nov. 28, 1938, Moody to Picard, Dec. 12, 1938, Moody Papers; Muller to FM, Nov. 11, 1938, Cleary to FM, Nov. 19, 1938, Nadolney to FM, Dec. 31, 1938, FM Papers; Gibney to JAF, Nov. 9, 1938, Leo M. Mitchell to JAF, Dec. 12, 1938, Clines to JAF, Dec. 12, 1938, H. Lester Farnum to JAF, Dec. 16, 1938, Misner to JAF, Jan. 6, 1939, Henwood to JAF, Jan. 9, 1939, OF 300 (1938).

80. Cleary to JAF, Nov. 19, 1938, James B. Sumner to JAF, Dec. 9, 1938, Bannan to JAF, Dec. 10, 1938, Harold E. Nilsen to JAF, Dec. 12, 1938, Beaudin to JAF, Dec. 15, 1938, Delaney to JAF, Dec. 15, 1938, McDonald to JAF, Dec. 21, 1938, Bradley to JAF, Dec. 23, 1938, Mead to JAF, Dec. 24, 1938, LaFreniere to JAF, Dec. 28, 1938, Henwood to JAF, Jan. 9, 1939, Emunson to JAF, Jan. 9, 1939, Luecke to JAF, Feb. 8, 1939, OF 300 (1938); Nadolney to FM, Nov. 16, 1938, Matt Savola to FM, Nov. 17, 1938, Cleary to FM, Nov. 19, 1938, FM Papers; Pollock to Mowrer, Nov. 28, 1938, Pollock Papers, Box 5; McSeveney, "1938," p. 106.

81. Picard to Moody, Nov. 28, 1938, Moody Papers; Basil G. Larke to JAF, Dec. 19, 1938, Henwood to JAF, Jan. 9, 1939, OF 300 (1938); Wooten speech [1939], FM Papers; Krault to Editor, *DN* [Nov. 1938], *DN*—Murphy File.

82. Brown to FM, Nov. 10, 1938, EMB Papers; Dale to FM, Nov. 9, 1938, J. J. O'Brien to FM, Nov. 10, 1938, Roy H. Hagerman to FM, Nov. 10, 1938, Germer to FM, Nov. 11, 1938, FM Papers; Picard to Moody, Nov. 28, 1938, Moody to FM, Dec. 12, 1938, Moody Papers; McGinty to JAF, Oct. 29, 1938, OF 300 (Supplementary); Greene to JAF, Dec. 23, 1938, Mead to JAF, Dec. 24, 1938, Misner to JAF, Jan. 6, 1939, OF 300 (1938).

83. Shields to FM, Nov. 25, 1938, FM Papers; DeFant to JAF, Dec. 11, 1938, Clines to JAF, Dec. 12, 1938, Denning to JAF, Jan. 17, 1939, OF 300 (1938).

84. DeFoe Diary, Sept. 11, 1938, Murl H. DeFoe Papers, MHC.

85. White, *Michigan Votes*, pp. 17, 31, 47. See *DN*, Dec. 1, 25, 1938, and FM to Corcoran, Nov. 10, 1938, FM Papers.

86. Lawrence to Arthur H. Vandenberg, Nov. 9, 1938, Lawrence to Fitzgerald, Nov. 9, 1938, Howard C. Lawrence Papers; Detzer to FM, Nov. 9, 1938, Donnelly to FM, Nov. 9, 1938, Frankfurter to FM, Nov. 10, 1938, Bessie M. Garner to FM, Nov. 10, 1938, Ethel Vorce to FM, Nov. 13, 1938, William Haber to FM, Nov. 16, 1938, FM Papers; *United Automobile Worker*, Nov. 12, 1938; *Secret Diary of Ickes*, 2:498; *New Republic* 97 (Nov. 23, 1938): 58; Anderson, "What the Election Means," *Nation* 147 (Nov. 19, 1938): 527.

87. *DN*, Nov. 9, 11, 1938; FM to Sy Bartlett, Nov. 22, 1938, FM to Julian Wolfson, Dec. 13, 1938, FM to Hernando J. Abaya, FM Papers; FM, "Tragic Interruption," p. 590.

88. See Interview with Irene Murphy, July 30, 1964, p. 68, MHC; FM to Pollock, Feb. 23, 1939, Pollock Papers, Box 5; and FM to Mark Wells, Oct. 30, 1939, FM Papers.

89. HM to Ruth [Treglown], Dec. 7, 1938, HM Papers.

90. *DN*, Sept. 10, 1937, Nov. 13, 14, Dec. 1, 1938; *NYT*, Nov. 13, 14, 1938; *DT*, May 8, 1938, *New York Mirror*, Nov. 13, 1938, clippings in FM Papers; FM to Clarence McConnell, May 4, 1938, ibid.; [*Greenway Press Gazette*, May 11, 1938], MSB; FM to FDR, Dec. 2, 1938, EMB Papers.

91. The following study commissions had not yet reported: Reform and Modernization; Tax; Public Works; Housing; Milk Marketing; Pensions; and Credit.

92. *DN*, Nov. 10, 12, 23, 27, Dec. 6, 29, 31, 1938; FM to Sam Ledner, Nov. 21, 1938, Hill to ———, Dec. 2, 1938, FM to Fitzgerald, Dec. 7, 1938, FM Papers.

93. *Ex-Augural Message of Frank Murphy . . . Jan. 5, 1939* (n.p., n.d.).

94. Ibid., p. 3; Richard Lunt, *The High Ministry of Government: The Political Career of Frank Murphy* (Detroit: Wayne State University Press, 1965), pp. 161–62.

95. Edward H. Litchfield, "Pipe-Line Government in Michigan," *New Republic* 103 (Aug. 26, 1940): 270; *Detroit Harper Van Dyke Press*, Jan. 15, 1939, MSB; *DN*, Jan. 4, 5, 10, Mar. 4, 1939; *DN*, Mar. 3, 1939, *Detroit News* Lansing Bureau Scrapbooks, MHC; unreleased *DN* article [Mar. 3, 1939]; FM to Marguerite LeHand, Apr. 12, 1939, and enclosed clippings, OF 117, FDRL.

96. Litchfield, "Pipe-Line Government," pp. 271, 272; *DN*, Nov. 23, 1938; Lee M. Mitchell to JAF, Dec. 12, 1938, OF 300 (1938).

97. Litchfield, "Michigan's Experience," pp. 7–9; idem, "Another Chapter in Michigan Civil Service," *American Political Science Review* 35 (Feb. 1941): 76–81; William H. Combs, "Michigan's Civil Service Amendment," *State Government* 14 (Feb. 1941): 34, 45; Meeting of Editors, Booth Newspapers, Oct. 9, 1939, Emil Hurja Papers, FDRL; Lovett to EGK, Apr. 1, 24, 1939, EGK Papers; FM to Pollock, June 9, 1939, Pollock Papers, Box 5.

98. Austin H. MacCormick, "The Michigan Corrections Law and Partisan Politics," *Osborne Association News Bulletin* 11 (Dec. 1940): 7; Mershon to FM, Jan. 30, 1939, FM Papers; "History of . . . the Mental Health Program in Michigan," undated, Children's Fund of Michigan Papers, Box 14, MHC; *DN*, Feb. 4, May 22, June 24, 30, 1939; Meeting of Editors, Oct. 9, 1939, Hurja Papers; Litchfield, "Pipe-Line Government," p. 272.

99. *Public and Local Acts of the Legislature of . . . Michigan . . . 1939* (Lansing: Franklin DeKleine Co., 1939), pp. 513–40; Dunham, *The Michigan Welfare Reorganization Act of 1939* (Lansing: Michigan Conference of Social Work, 1939), pp. 7–11, 43–44; Litchfield, "Pipe-Line Government," p. 272.

100. *DN*, Jan. 5, Feb. 7, 1939; *Public Acts of Michigan, 1939*, pp. 336–40; Charles C. Killingsworth, *State Labor Relations Acts* (Chicago: University of Chicago Press, 1948), pp. 132–33, 220–22; Litchfield, "Pipe-Line Government," p. 272.

101. Litchfield, "Pipe-Line Government," p. 272; FM to Burke, Jan. 17, Feb. 9, 1939, Donnelly to FM, Jan. 23, Feb. 27, 1939, Burke to FM, Feb. 4, 13, 1939, Picard to FM, Feb. 13, 20, 1939, Starr to FM, Mar. 3, 1939, FM Papers; *Muskegon Chronicle*, Feb. 24, 1939, clipping in ibid.; FDR to Burke, Feb. 11, 1939, PPF 5829, FDRL; Shields to Brown [Feb. 13], Feb. 20, 1939, Brown to Burke, Feb. 14, 1939, Brown Papers, Box 3; E. W. Murphy to Emil Hurja, Feb. 21, 1939, Hurja Papers; *NYT*, Feb. 19, 1939.

102. *DN*, Dec. 25, 1938.

103. Harold Titus to FM, Nov. 9, 1938, FM Papers.

104. *DN*, Dec. 25, 1938; Interview with Carl Rudow, Oct. 6, 1964, p. 2, MHC. See also Haber to FM, June 1, 1938, James Lincoln to FM, Nov. 13, 1938, FM Papers; Picard to Moody, Nov. 28, 1939, Moody Papers; and Litchfield, "Pipe-Line Government," p. 270.

105. Miller Diary, May 12, 1938, Miller Papers; Miller to Dear Gang, June 10, 1938, copy in ibid.; Haber to FM, June 1, 1938, Arthur Evans Wood to FM, Nov. 6, 1938, Donnelly to FM, Nov. 9, 1938, Burton K. Wheeler to FM, Nov. 25, 1938, McAllister to FM [Sept. 6, 1939], FM Papers.

106. Patterson, *New Deal and States*, pp. 142–52. Patterson concludes that the reform administrations of Floyd Olson in Minnesota and Philip La Follette in Wisconsin owed more to the farmer-labor and progressive traditions, respectively, than to the influence of the New Deal. Ibid., pp. 130, 132. For New York's little New Deal, see Robert P. Ingalls, *Herbert H. Lehman and New York's Little New Deal* (New York: New York University Press, 1975). For Pennsylvania, see Braeman et al., *New Deal*, 2:45–76. For New Deal legislation in Massachusetts, see ibid., p. 21.

107. Patterson, *New Deal and States*, pp. 153, 161–66; Richard E. Dawson, "Social Development, Party Competition, and Policy," in William Nisbet Chambers and Walter Dean Burnham, eds., *The American Party System* (New York: Oxford University Press, 1967), pp. 211–37; Ingalls, *Lehman*, pp. 252–53; Braeman et al., *New Deal*, 2:51.

108. Braeman et al., *New Deal*, 2:xiii; Ingalls, *Lehman*, p. 251; Glen E. Brooks, *When Governors Convene* (Baltimore: Johns Hopkins Press, 1961), p. 34. See also Jane Perry Clark, *The Rise of a New Federalism* (New York: Columbia University Press, 1938), pp. 24, 36–37, 66–70, et passim.

109. Key, *State Politics*, pp. 7–9. See also Arthur Howard Benedict, "Federal Centralization through Congressional Legislation, 1924 to 1939" (Ph.D. diss., Ohio State University, 1948), pp. 547–51, 560.

110. George F. Granger and Lawrence R. Klein, *Emergency Relief in Michigan, 1933–1939* (Lansing: n.p., 1939), p. 51; Robert S. Ford and Albert Waxman, *Financing Michigan's Government*, p. 72.

111. Ford and Waxman, *Financing Government*, pp. 72–73; George C. S. Benson, *The New Centralization: A Study of Intergovernmental Relationships in the United States* (New York: Farrar and Rinehart, 1941), pp. 104–5; Key, *State Politics*, p. 8.

112. *New Republic* 97 (Dec. 14, 1938): 171; *DN*, Nov. 11, 12, 1938; Charles and Esther Gitlin to FM, Nov. 11, 1938, FM to Richards, Nov. 11, 1938, FM to Romulo, Dec. 28, 1938, FM Papers; [Ralph] Reed to [Fred Gaertner] [Nov. 11, 1938], *DN*— Murphy File; Ickes Diary, Apr. 23, 1939, p. 3389, Harold L. Ickes Papers, Box 14, LC; Joseph P. Lash, *From the Diaries of Felix Frankfurter* (New York: W. W. Norton & Co., 1975), p. 311.

113. FM to Hyman, Mar. 9, 1937, William D. Murphy to FM, July 29, 1937, FM to Elinor Greene, Jan. 18, 1938, Osborn to FM, Jan. 24, 1938, FM Papers; Brown to FM, May 20, 1937, FM to Brown, May 20, 1937, Brown Papers, Box 1; Jenkins to Booth, Oct. 22, 1937, Jenkins Papers; Reed to [Gaertner] [Nov. 1938], *DN*— Murphy File; *DN*, June 11, July 15, 29, Aug. 1, 13, 1937, Jan. 9, 14, 1938; *NYT*, May 19, June 12, Aug. 3, 1937, Jan. 9, 1938; Stanley High, *Roosevelt—And Then?* (New York: Harper and Brothers, 1937), p. 320.

114. *DN*, Aug. 29, Nov. 14, 1938; *NYT*, Nov. 10, Dec. 3, 1938; Reed to [Gaertner] [Nov. 1938], *DN*—Murphy File.

115. *DN*, Nov. 13, 14, 17, Dec. 1, 1938; *NYT*, Nov. 14, Dec. 29, 30, 1938; FM to Richards, Nov. 19, 1938, Kleinman to FM, Nov. 26, 1938, FM Papers; Farley, *Farley's Story*, pp. 134-35. I shall discuss the complexities surrounding Murphy's appointment as attorney general in *Frank Murphy: The Washington Years*, forthcoming.

116. *NYT*, Dec. 30, 1938; IM to Mrs. D. T. Roots [Jan. 3, 1939], IM Papers.

Bibliography

MANUSCRIPT COLLECTIONS

Michigan Historical Collections, Ann Arbor, Michigan. The Frank Murphy Papers are the single most important manuscript collection for Murphy's New Deal years. The Murphy Papers are richer for Murphy's career after than before 1933. The George Murphy, Marguerite Murphy, Harold Murphy, and Irene Murphy Papers supplement the Frank Murphy Papers, the George Murphy Papers being especially valuable for Michigan politics in the 1930s and the Marguerite and Irene Murphy Papers for Frank's Philippine service. The Eleanor M. Bumgardner Papers and the Eugene Gressman Papers are really part of the corpus of Frank Murphy Papers. The Gressman Papers include notes and memoranda that Murphy made of some of his most important conversations.

The Edward G. Kemp Papers, a small collection, include some significant items. The Josephine Gomon Papers are valuable mainly for Murphy's mayoralty but include scattered material pertaining to his post-1933 career. The Blair Moody and Guy Hugh Jenkins Papers, the collections of Michigan newspapermen, include material on Murphy's New Deal years.

The Joseph Ralston Hayden Papers, one of the most important collections in the United States for the study of the Philippines and Philippine-American relations, are particularly valuable for the period of Murphy's governor-generalship. The Michigan Historical Collections has a microfilm copy of the Manuel L. Quezon Papers, which help to illuminate the quest for Philippine independence, the politics of sugar, and the Murphy-Quezon relationship. The George A. Malcolm Papers are unrevealing. There is a long letter from J. Weldon Jones dealing with Murphy's Philippine service in the Richard D. Lunt Papers.

The Prentiss M. Brown and Arthur J. Lacy Papers shed light on Michigan Democratic politics in the 1930s. There are scattered items on the same subject in the following collections: Elizabeth Lehman Belen, William A. Comstock, Mortimer E. Cooley, G. Donald Kennedy, Frank Picard, H. Lynn Pierson, Lawrence Rubin, Murray D. Van Wagoner, and Carl M. Weideman. Picard, unfortunately, destroyed most of his personal correspondence before his death in 1963, and the Comstock, Kennedy, and Van Wagoner Papers are obviously far from complete. The Frank D. Fitzgerald Papers, thin on Fitzgerald's gubernatorial service, are more revealing for his 1936 and 1938 gubernatorial campaigns. The Howard C. Lawrence Papers are most useful for the 1936 and 1938 Republican campaigns. Republican politics in the 1930s also receive some attention in the following collections: Emerson Richard

Boyles, Wilber Marion Brucker, Murl H. DeFoe, George P. McCallum (a few interesting diary entries), Floyd Josiah Miller, Chase S. Osborn, Charles A. Sink, and Arthur H. Vandenberg (also of interest for the sit-down strikes in Michigan).

The Records of the Michigan Military Establishment Relating to the Flint Sit-Down Strike, 1937, available on microfilm, are an indispensable source for the General Motors sit-down strike. The James Kerr Pollock Papers and the Civil Service Study Commission Papers are superb sources for the background, enactment, and implementation of the Civil Service Act of 1937. There is some additional material on the same subject in the Dorothy Judd Papers, the William Brownrigg Papers, and the Michigan Merit System Association Papers. The State Emergency Welfare Relief Commission Papers contain the releases and directives issued by the SEWRC. There is pertinent material on welfare and relief in Michigan in the 1930s in the Children's Fund of Michigan Papers. The Louise V. Armstrong Papers are mainly concerned with the fine Armstrong book, *We Too Are the People*. The Hilmer Gellein Papers are primarily useful for the study of Michigan's correctional system during the Murphy governorship. The Commission on Reform and Modernization of Government Papers contain some of the records of the commission to study government reorganization that Murphy appointed in 1938. The G. Mennen Williams Papers are useful for the Murphy administration's efforts to regulate Michigan's milk industry. The Raymond W. Starr Papers were of no value for this study.

Burton Historical Collection, Detroit, Michigan. The Edward G. Kemp Papers, second in importance only to the Murphy Papers as a source for Murphy's governorship, are unequaled for the information they provide on the legislative history of the Lansing New Deal. The Detroit Citizens League Papers include correspondence on civil service reform and some other aspects of Murphy's governorship. The Detroit Bureau of Governmental Research Papers contain some material on the work of the Tax Study Commission, of which the bureau's director was chairman. There is a good deal of information on Detroit's welfare problems in 1937 and 1938 and a few items on the labor strife in Detroit in 1937 in the Mayor's Office Records. The minutes of the Detroit Public Welfare Commission for 1937–38 are bound together in the Proceedings of the Public Welfare Commission. Both the Joseph E. Mills and Norman H. Hill Papers include some Philippine items.

Archives of Labor History and Urban Affairs, Wayne State University, Detroit, Michigan. There are numerous letters pertaining to Michigan politics and Michigan labor in the 1930s in the Wayne County AFL-CIO Papers. The Richard Frankensteen Papers are useful for the activities of the SEWRC while Frankensteen was one of its members. The Henry Kraus Papers are a major source for the GM sit-down strike and various UAW matters. The Edward Levinson Papers contain copies of the press releases issued by the UAW and GM during the GM strike. The John A. Zaremba Papers are an important source for the Chrysler sit-down strike. There is much miscellaneous information on labor affairs in Michigan in the 1930s in the Joe Brown Collection. The Civil Rights Congress of Michigan Papers, primarily useful for a later period, include a few items pertinent to Murphy's governorship. The Maurice Sugar Papers, Philip Rahoi Papers, R. J. Thomas Papers, and Edward McFarland Papers are of little value for Murphy's governorship.

State Archives, Michigan History Division, Lansing, Michigan. The Records of the

Welfare and Relief Study Commission (RG 35) and the Minutes of the Welfare and Relief Study Commission (RG 52-4) provide abundant information on welfare and relief problems in Michigan in the 1930s and on the work of the Welfare and Relief Study Commission. The Minutes of the State Welfare Commission (RG 53-12) include the minutes of the SEWRC. The Records of the Executive Office (RG 44), much of which was destroyed by fire, contain nothing for Murphy's governorship and little of value for Fitzgerald's governorship.

National Archives and Records Service, Washington, D.C. The Records of the Bureau of Insular Affairs (RG 350) are an indispensable source for the Philippines and Philippine-American relations. The record group is difficult to use because the availability of confidential and ''with'' files that are part of the numbered files is not always self-evident. The few files relevant to this study in the Records of the United States High Commissioner to the Philippine Islands (RG 126) and the Records of the Office of Territories (RG 126) tend to be of considerable value. The Records of the Department of State (RG 59) contain abundant information on the Philippine-American trade relationship, the troublesome issue of rank and precedence as between the American high commissioner and the president of the Philippine Commonwealth, Philippine defense, and Philippine-American-Japanese relations. There is material on the Philippines for the years of Murphy's service in the islands in the Records of the Senate Committee on Territories and Insular Affairs for the 73rd (Sen 73A-F25) and 74th (Sen 74A-F23) Congresses, included in the Records of the United States Senate (RG 46). The La Follette Committee Papers (Sen 78A-F9), in the same record group, contain some interesting information on the GM sit-down strike. Several War Plans Division files, in Records of the War Department General and Special Staffs (RG 165), deal with the problem of Philippine defense and, hence, with the Murphy-MacArthur relationship. The Records of the Adjutant General's Office, 1917- (RG 407), which include two important confidential files transferred from RG 350, are useful for the same subject. The Records of the Office of the Secretary of War (RG 107) are of minimum value for Philippine defense during the 1933-36 period.

The Records of the Department of Justice (RG 60) reveal Thurman Arnold's interest in using the Michigan milk problem as a test case of federal-state cooperation in the antitrust field. There are files on the GM and Chrysler sit-down strikes, the Consumers Power strike, and the strike of the Lumber and Sawmill Workers Union in the Records of the Federal Mediation and Conciliation Service (RG 280). The Records of the Work Projects Administration (RG 69) include files on the operation of the FERA and the WPA in Michigan. The Records of the National Emergency Council, part of the Records of the Office of Government Reports (RG 44), include miscellaneous information pertaining to the operation of federal programs in Michigan.

Library of Congress, Washington, D.C. The Theodore Roosevelt, Jr., Papers include letters from Philippine correspondents while Murphy served in the Philippines. The letters of Evett D. Hester are of special interest. There is a small Philippine file in the Key Pittman Papers, and there are some relevant items in the Journals of W. Cameron Forbes, Second Series. The Francis B. Sayre Papers contain little of significance for this volume. There is material on Michigan politics in the

1930s in the James Couzens Papers. The James A. Farley Papers became available at too late a time for me to examine the collection.

Franklin D. Roosevelt Library, Hyde Park, New York. The Official File, the President's Personal File, and the President's Secretary's File in the Roosevelt presidential papers all contain material relevant to Murphy's New Deal years. Official File 300 is indispensable for Michigan politics in the 1933–38 period; Official File 400 is the major file for Philippine matters. There is additional material on Michigan politics in the Emil Hurja Papers, the Democratic Party, National Committee Papers, and the Democratic Party, National Committee, Women's Division Papers. The Harry L. Hopkins Papers are important both for federal relief efforts in Michigan and Michigan politics. There is some interesting information on rural electrification in Michigan in the John M. Carmody Papers.

Miscellaneous Manuscript Collections. The American Civil Liberties Union Archives, in the Firestone Library, Princeton University, Princeton, New Jersey (there is a microfilm copy in the New York Public Library), are a major source for civil liberties issues in the Philippines and Michigan that involved Frank Murphy. The collection is of great value for Murphy's effort to secure the enactment of labor-relations legislation in Michigan in 1937. The Henry L. Stimson Diary, in the Henry L. Stimson Papers, Sterling Library, Yale University, New Haven, Connecticut, has some interesting entries relating to Philippine independence. There is essential documentation pertaining to the MacArthur defense plan for the Philippines in Record Group 1 in the MacArthur Memorial Library, Norfolk, Virginia, and a few relevant items in Record Group 18. I examined the pertinent documents on microfilm. I also examined a microfilm copy of the Philippine items for the years 1933–36 in the J. Weldon Jones Papers, in the Harry S. Truman Library, Independence, Missouri. Dwight D. Eisenhower's Diary of the American Military Mission in the Philippine Islands, in the Dwight D. Eisenhower Library, Abilene, Kansas, includes significant material on Douglas MacArthur's role as military advisor to the Commonwealth government. I examined a photocopy of the diary. Raymond Moley permitted me to examine his Murphy file, now part of the Moley Papers in the Hoover Institute, Stanford University, Stanford, California. The documents brought together from the Japanese Ministry of Foreign Affairs Archives on Reels S459, S460, and S461, a copy of which is in the Asia Library, University of Michigan, Ann Arbor, Michigan, shed light on Japanese-Philippine relations and especially on the Davao problem.

The dilemma faced by the Socialist party of Michigan in the 1938 Michigan gubernatorial election is strikingly revealed in the Daniel Bell Papers, Tamiment Institute Library, New York University, New York, New York. The Adolph Germer Papers, State Historical Society of Wisconsin, Madison, Wisconsin, are a major source for labor matters in Michigan between 1935 and 1938. There is some material on the GM strike in the John Brophy Papers, Catholic University, Washington, D.C. I could not locate the CIO files for the period of Murphy's governorship, but Professor Irving Bernstein permitted me to examine his notes on this material. There are a few pertinent items on the GM strike in the Samuel D. Pepper Papers, which are privately held. Martin S. Hayden gave me the *Detroit News*'s Murphy file, which contains several items of interest. Case File #5977, Michigan State Police Records,

Lansing, Michigan, which I examined on microfilm, documents the role of the State Police in the GM strike. There is an interesting analysis of the strike by Frank N. Trager in the Norman Thomas Papers, New York Public Library, New York, New York. There is a brief account of the strike in General Motors, Labor Relations Diary, Section 1, and some pertinent documents among the Appendix Documents to Accompany Section 1, located in the General Motors Building in Detroit. The Frances Perkins Papers, Butler Library, Columbia University, New York, New York, proved to be a disappointment insofar as this study is concerned.

INTERVIEWS AND CORRESPONDENCE

My interviews with the following persons proved to be helpful: Thomas F. Chawke, Larry S. Davidow, Joe Devitt, James A. Farley, Hilmer Gellein, William Haber, Mrs. Joseph R. Hayden, Martin S. Hayden, Charles J. Hedetniemi, Norman H. Hill G. Donald Kennedy, Sharon Keyes, Arthur Krock, Colin J. MacDonald, Jack Manning, Harry Mead, Wyndham Mortimer, Carl Muller, William Muller, George Murphy, Irene Murphy, William Norton, James K. Pollock, Lee Pressman, Roy Reuther, Robert Travis, G. Mennen Williams, and Mrs. Fielding H. Yost. There are transcripts in the Michigan Historical Collections of most of these interviews as well as of interviews conducted with Joseph H. Creighton by Marvin Petroelje and Richard T. Ortquist, Jr., and with Wilber M. Brucker by Richard J. Drew. The notes deriving from an interview that Alice Smuts conducted with Murray D. Van Wagoner are in my possession.

About two-thirds of the 127 oral history interviews resulting from the UAW Oral History Project of the Institute of Industrial Relations of the University of Michigan and Wayne State University contain information pertinent to the GM sit-down strike. There are transcripts of these interviews in both the Michigan Historical Collections and the Archives of Labor History and Urban Affairs. The interviews with Nick Digaetano, Richard Harris, Harry Ross, R. J. Thomas, and Frank B. Tuttle are of interest for the Chrysler sit-down strike. The Reminiscences of John Brophy, John M. Carmody, William Haber, Nicholas Kelley, Frances Perkins, Lee Pressman, and R. J. Thomas, all located in the Oral History Research Office, Columbia University, include information on Murphy's New Deal years. J. Weldon Jones responded to my numerous questions concerning Murphy in a fascinating forty-eight page letter. Letters from Martin S. Hayden and Leona Garrity also proved helpful.

NEWSPAPERS AND PERIODICALS

Although haphazardly arranged, the Frank Murphy Scrapbooks, in the Michigan Historical Collections, provide abundant coverage of Murphy's service in the Philippines and Michigan. They consist primarily of newspaper clippings but also include journal articles and numerous photographs. The Norman H. Hill Scrapbooks, also in the Michigan Historical Collections, are better arranged than the Murphy Scrapbooks and are more complete for the Philippine phase of Murphy's career. I consulted the *Detroit News* and *Detroit Free Press* for Murphy's governorship and Michigan politics. The other Detroit daily for the period, the *Detroit Times*, is well represented in the Murphy Scrapbooks. The Detroit News Lansing Bureau Scrapbooks, in the Michigan Historical Collections, provide a record of the activities of Michigan's state government. Frequent entries in the *New York Times* attest to the significance of the issues with which Murphy dealt in both the Philippines and Michigan. The *Ann Arbor News* and the *Flint Journal* proved helpful for selected topics.

The *Philippine Magazine* for the years 1933–36 and the four volumes of the *Philippine Yearbook* for 1933–37 were of limited significance for this volume. The *Detroit Labor News* and the *United Automobile Worker* are important sources for labor developments in Michigan during the Murphy governorship; the employer perspective on labor and other matters is reflected in the *Michigan Manufacturer and Financial Record*. There are many interesting pieces on Michigan state government in the "Citizen's News," the publication of the Ann Arbor Citizens' Council. Public health developments while Murphy was governor are covered in the volumes of *Michigan Public Health*, published by the state's Department of Health. Philippine and Michigan events and Murphy's part in them were the subject of comment from time to time in *Time, News-Week, Nation, New Republic, Survey, Survey Graphic*, and *State Government*.

PUBLISHED AND UNPUBLISHED GOVERNMENT DOCUMENTS

Philippines. I relied on the Philippine Manuscript Reports, in Record Group 350, National Archives and Records Service, for Murphy's annual reports as governor-general and high commissioner since they are more extensive than the published version. The Manuscript Reports also include the reports of the departments of the Philippine government. The six *Annual Reports of the United States High Commissioner to the Philippine Islands* are a convenient source for the history of the Philippine Commonwealth and its relations with the United States. United States Tariff Commission, *United States-Philippine Trade with Special Reference to the Philippine Independence Act and Other Recent Legislation*, Report No. 118, Second Series (Washington: U.S. Government Printing Office, 1937), and Joint Preparatory Committee on Philippine Affairs, *Report of May 20, 1938*, 4 vols. (Washington: U.S. Government Printing Office, 1938), provide invaluable substantive information and statistical data on the United States-Philippine trade relationship. *Foreign Relations of the United States, 1935*, vol. 3 (Washington: U.S. Government Printing Office, 1953), and *1936*, vol. 4 (Washington: U.S. Government Printing Office, 1954), reproduce the diplomatic correspondence pertaining to the negotiation and implementation of the textile quota agreement with Japan. The documents resulting from the Tydings Mission are collected in *Senate Miscellaneous Documents*, 74 Cong., 1 sess., Docs. Nos. 57, 119, 120 (Washington: U.S. Government Printing Office, 1935). Division of Labor Statistics, Department of Labor, "Fact-Finding Survey Report, 1936" (1936), provides graphic evidence of the depressed condition of Philippine tenants in eighteen provinces.

Michigan. The *Journal of the House of Representatives of the State of Michigan.* and the *Journal of the Senate of the State of Michigan* for the regular session of 1937 and the extra sessions of 1937 and 1938 make it possible to trace the course of legislation in the Michigan legislature. Michigan does not publish an official record of the debates in its legislature. The statutes enacted by the legislature are compiled in *Public and Local Acts of the Legislature of the State of Michigan*. There are copies of the bills introduced in the legislature in 1937–38 in the University of Michigan Law Library. *Michigan Official Directory and Legislative Manual, 1937-38* (n.p., n.d.), and the similar volume for 1939–40 contain brief biographies of the state's legislators, detailed election and census statistics, information on state agencies and institutions, and a miscellany of other information about the state.

There is a good deal of one-sided testimony concerning the GM and other strikes and the Lansing Labor Holiday in House Special Committee on Un-American Activities, *Investigation of Un-American Propaganda Activities in the United States, Hearings...*, 75 Cong., 1 sess., 4 vols. (Washington: U.S. Government Printing Office, 1938). GM's use of labor spies is revealed in Subcommittee of Senate Committee on Education and Labor, *Violations of Free Speech and Rights of Labor, Hearings...*, 75 Cong., 1 sess., pts. 5–7 (Washington: U.S. Government Printing Office, 1937), and Senate Committee on Education and Labor, *Violations of Free Speech and Rights of Labor*, 76 Cong., 1 sess., Rept. 6, pt. 6 (Washington: U.S. Government Printing Office, 1939). There is abundant information on the Monroe strike in the same series of hearings, 75 Cong., 3 sess., pts. 27–29, and 76 Cong., 1 Sess., pt. 42 (Washington: U.S. Government Printing Office, 1939).

The need for civil service reform in Michigan is made evident in *Report of the Civil Service Study Commission* (Lansing: n.p., 1936). The implementation of the Civil Service Act of 1937 is described in Michigan State Civil Service Department, "First Annual Report ..." (Lansing: Civil Service Commission, 1938). Michigan Liquor Control Commission, *Activities of the Michigan Liquor Control Commission for the Fiscal Year Ending June 30, 1938* (n.p., n.d.), and George Ackers, *Michigan Liquor Control Commission Activities, 1933-1945* (n.p., n.d.), present data on the policies and record of the Liquor Control Commission during Murphy's governorship. *Report of the Tax Study Commission, January 30, 1939* (Detroit: Office of the Commission [1939]), and Leo Day Woodworth and Lent D. Upson, eds., "Staff Studies of the Tax Study Commission," 3 pts. (Detroit: Office of the Commission [1938-1939]), are the products of the Tax Study Commission Murphy appointed in 1938.

Unemployment and Relief in Michigan (Lansing: Franklin DeKleine Co., 1935); William Haber and Paul L. Stanchfield, *Unemployment, Relief and Economic Security* (Lansing: n.p., 1936); and George F. Granger and Lawrence R. Klein, *Emergency Relief in Michigan, 1933-1939* (Lansing: n.p., 1939), are the first, second, and third reports, respectively, of the SEWRC and are superb sources for the history of public relief in Michigan in all of its ramifications. Michigan State Emergency Relief Administration, *Monthly Bulletin on Public Relief Statistics*, vols. 3–5, is indispensable for relief trends and relief statistics. The national context for the operation of the WPA in Michigan is provided in *Final Report on the WPA Program, 1935-43* (Washington: U.S. Government Printing Office [1946]). There is some Michigan testimony in Senate Special Committee to Investigate Unemployment Relief, *Unemployment and Relief, Hearings...*, 75 Cong., 3 sess. (Washington: U.S. Government Printing Office, 1938).

"Public Welfare in Michigan. A Report Prepared under the Auspices of the State of Michigan Welfare and Relief Study Commission by the Staff of the Commission'' (1937), reveals the jumbled nature of Michigan's state and local welfare structure. The *Report of the Welfare and Relief Study Commission* (Lansing: n.p., 1936), presents the recommendations that shaped the welfare reorganization legislation approved by the state legislature in 1937. The activities of the State Welfare Department are described in *Report of the State Welfare Department of the State of Michigan, December, 1938* (n.p., n.d.). State Welfare Department, Bureau of Old Age Assistance, *Old Age Assistance in Michigan, 1933-1937* (Lansing: n.p., 1938), and the same agency's *Old Age Assistance in Michigan, 1937-1938* (Lansing: State Welfare Department, 1938), are the official account of the implementation of Michigan's old-age assistance program. The history of unemployment insurance in Michigan and the enforcement of the state's old-age insurance law during Murphy's governorship are treated in two reports of the Michigan Unemployment Compensation Commission: *Annual Report for the Year Ending December 31, 1937* (n.p., 1938), and *Unemployment Compensation in Michigan—1938* (Detroit: n.p., 1939). The achievements of the Murphy administration in the area of penology and corrections are set forth in Department of Corrections, *History of Probation, Prisons, Pardons and Paroles* (n.p., 1938), and State Department of Corrections, *Michigan's Correctional System: First Biennial Report, 1937-38* (Lansing: n.p., n.d.).

The *Sixty-Fifth* and *Sixty-Sixth Annual Reports of the Commissioners of the Michigan Department of Health* detail state public health activities in 1937 and 1938. Some basic documents relating to the work of the Murphy-appointed Commission on Reform and Modernization of Government are contained in Arthur W. Bromage, comp., ''Documents and Proceedings of the Commission on Reform and Modernization of Government'' (Lansing, 1938); the commission's conclusions are set forth in ''Report of a Preliminary Survey'' (Lansing, 1938). The *Reports of the Rural Electrification Administration* for 1937 and 1938 include information on Michigan. Other aspects of agricultural policy during the Murphy governorship are described in Michigan State Department of Agriculture, *Eighth Biennial Report for the Fiscal Years Ending June 30, 1937, and June 30, 1938* (Lansing: Franklin DeKleine Co., 1939). The ''Annual Reports'' of the Detroit Housing Commission for 1936-38 recount the slow progress of public housing construction in Detroit.

MISCELLANEOUS UNPUBLISHED SOURCES

Philippines. Joseph Ralston Hayden, ''The Philippine Policy of the United States'' (New York: Institute of Pacific Relations, 1939), is an earlier version of Hayden's major book on the Philippines. Violet Elizabeth Wurfel, ''American Implementation of Philippine Independence'' (Ph.D. diss., University of Virginia, 1951), and Raul P. DeGuzman, ''The Formulation and Implementation of the Philippine Independence Policy of the United States, 1929-1946'' (Ph.D. diss., Florida State University, 1957), limit themselves to published sources. Karen Wells Borden, ''Persuasive Appeals of Imperialist and Anti-Imperialist Congressmen in the Debates on Philippine Independence, 1912-1934'' (Ph.D. diss., University of California, Los Angeles, 1972), is a content analysis of speeches for and against Philippine independence. Thomas Janney Heston, ''Sweet Subsidy: The Economic and Diplomatic

Effects of the U.S. Sugar Acts—1934-1974'' (Ph.D. diss., Case Western Reserve University, 1975), provides a context for the appraisal of American policy regarding sugar imports from the Philippines. The Philippine careers of two of Murphy's predecessors as governor-general are described and appraised in Camillus Gott, "William Cameron Forbes and the Philippines, 1904-1946'' (Ph.D. diss., University of Indiana, 1974), and Michael John Smith, "Henry L. Stimson and the Philippines'' (Ph.D. diss., University of Indiana, 1970). Murphy's successors as high commissioner to the Philippines are the subject of David Vawter Dufault, "Francis B. Sayre and the Commonwealth of the Philippines, 1936-1942'' (Ph.D. diss., University of Oregon, 1972), a useful and well-researched work, and Patricia R. Mamot, "Paul V. McNutt: His Role in the Birth of Philippine Independence'' (Ph.D. diss., Ball State University, 1974), which is very thin. Murphy's vice-governor is appraised in Ronald K. Edgerton, "Joseph Ralston Hayden and America's Colonial Experiment'' (1969), in my possession.

Roy Manning Stubbs, "Philippine Radicalism: The Central Luzon Uprisings, 1925-1935'' (Ph.D. diss., University of California, Berkeley, 1951), is concerned with the Sakdalista and predecessor revolts. David R. Sturtevant, "Philippine Social Structure and Its Relation to Agrarian Unrest'' (Ph.D. diss., Stanford University, 1958), which deals with the same subject in a more comprehensive context, is especially good on the Sakdalista uprising. Frances Lucille Starner, "The Agrarian Impact on Philippine Politics'' (Ph.D. diss., University of California, Berkeley, 1958), emphasizes the period since 1953. Ralph Benjamin Thomas, "Muslim but Filipino: The Integration of Philippine Muslims, 1917-1946'' (Ph.D. diss., University of Pennsylvania, 1971), is an excellent study of the Moro problem. Joseph R. Hayden, "The Government of the Sulu Archipelago'' (1936), in the Hayden Papers, is a superb brief account of the region in Moroland with which the Murphy regime was primarily concerned.

Richard S. Maxwell, "A Historical Study of the Office of the United States High Commissioner to the Philippine Islands, 1935-1946'' (M.A. thesis, American University, 1966), contains some of the essential information on the office whose first incumbent was Frank Murphy. Charles Orville Houston, Jr., "The Philippines: Commonwealth to Republic. An Experiment in Applied Politics. Part I. The Economic Bases'' (Ph.D. diss., Columbia University, 1952), is concerned with the principal Philippine crops. The evolution of the Philippine presidency is appraised in John H. Romani, "The Philippine Presidency: An Evolution in Terms of American Practices and Procedures'' (Ph.D. diss., University of Michigan, 1955).

Michigan. Stephen B. Sarasohn, "The Regulation of Parties and Nominations in Michigan: The Politics of Election Reform'' (Ph.D. diss., Columbia University, 1953), contains some general information on Michigan politics in the 1930s. Richard Theodore Ortquist, Jr., "Depression Politics in Michigan, 1929-1933'' (Ph.D. diss., University of Michigan, 1968), provides the necessary background for the appraisal of Michigan politics in the New Deal years. There are some references to Michigan politics in Gloria Winden Newquist, "James A. Farley and the Politics of Victory, 1928-1936'' (Ph.D. diss., University of Southern California, 1966). Penelope Helen Sawkins, "Executive Leadership of Frank Murphy as Governor of Michigan'' (M.A. thesis, Wayne University, 1950), is a mechanical account. Leo J. Nowicki, "Profile of an American by Choice" (1975), in the Michigan Historical Collections, is a revealing autobiography of Michigan's lieutenant governor in 1937–38. There are some interesting observations on the 1937 Michigan legislature in Josiah L. Sayre, "Some Aspects of the Legislative Process in Michigan, 1925 to 1937" (Ph.D. diss., University of Michigan, 1938). Richard Akin Davis, "Radio Priest: The Public Career of Father Charles Edward Coughlin" (Ph.D. diss., University of North Carolina, 1974), is the most comprehensive and best-researched account of Coughlin's public career. Nick Arthur Masters, "Father Coughlin and Social Justice: A Case Study of a Social Movement" (Ph.D. diss., University of Wisconsin, 1955), is of limited value. There is an analysis of the black vote in Detroit in Thomas R. Solomon, "Participation of Negroes in Detroit Elections" (Ph.D. diss., University of Michigan, 1939).

Roger Roy Keeran, "Communists and Auto Workers: The Struggle for a Union, 1919–1941" (Ph.D. diss., University of Wisconsin, 1974), is a well-researched work that is insufficiently critical of its sources. Doris McLaughlin, ". . . The Chrysler Strike of 1937" (undated), in my possession, is a discriminating account of the Chrysler sit-down strike. The "Battle of Monroe" is successfully placed in the context of the Little Steel strike of 1937 in Donald G. Sofchalk, "The Little Steel Strike of 1937" (Ph.D. diss., Ohio State University, 1961). Lorin Lee Cary, "Adolph Germer: From Labor Agitator to Labor Professional" (Ph.D. diss., University of Wisconsin, 1968), focuses on the CIO's man in Michigan while Murphy was governor.

Public Administration Service, "Report on Financial Administration in the Michigan State Government" ([Chicago], 1938), is a detailed study of the state's financial administration, with recommendations for its improvement. The status of local welfare organization in Michigan is presented in a rather mechanical manner in Margaret F. Gordon, "The Organization and Functions of the Local and Locally Operated Public Welfare Agencies of Michigan" (M.A. thesis, University of Michigan, 1945). Isadore Pastor, "Public Old Age Assistance in Michigan" (M.A. thesis, Wayne University, 1937), is a history of the movement for old-age assistance before Murphy became governor. There is much useful information on public welfare in Detroit in Martin E. Sullivan, " 'On the Dole:' The Relief Issue in Detroit, 1920–1939" (Ph.D. diss., University of Notre Dame, 1974). The following dissertations make it possible to examine relief and welfare problems in Michigan in a comparative perspective: David Joseph Maurer, "Public Relief Programs and Policies in Ohio, 1929–1939" (Ph.D. diss., Ohio State University, 1962); Raymond Louis Koch, "The Development of Public Relief Programs in Minnesota, 1929–1941" (Ph.D. diss., University of Minnesota, 1967); Bruce Dudley Blumell, "Development of Public Assistance in the State of Washington during the Great Depression" (Ph.D. diss., University of Washington, 1973); and Dwayne Charles Cole, "The Relief Crisis in Illinois during the Depression, 1930–1940" (Ph.D. diss., St. Louis University, 1973). George A. Male, "The Michigan Education Association as an Interest Group, 1852–1950" (Ph.D. diss., University of Michigan, 1951), is concerned, *inter alia*, with the school-aid problem during Murphy's governership. The Republican bias of the Michigan press in the state's 1938 gubernatorial election is documented in Edward Magdol and Robert Perlman, "The Press of Michigan in the 1938 Election (Exclusive of Detroit)" (1939), in Mr. Magdol's possession. Arthur Howard Benedict, "Federal Centralization through Congressional Legislation, 1924 to 1939" (Ph.D. diss., Ohio State University, 1948), is a surface treatment of an important subject.

PUBLISHED SOURCES

Murphy. There are chapters on Murphy's New Deal years in Richard D. Lunt, *The High Ministry of Government: The Political Career of Frank Murphy* (Detroit: Wayne State University Press, 1965), and J. Woodford Howard, *Mr. Justice Murphy: A Political Biography* (Princeton: Princeton University Press, 1968). Howard's book is decidedly the superior of the two, but there are substantial gaps in the research of both authors. Howard's "Frank Murphy and the Philippine Commonwealth," *Pacific Historical Review* 33 (Feb. 1964): 45-68, is an introduction to the subject. Blair Moody, "High Commissioner to Manila," *Survey Graphic* 24 (Dec. 1935): 610-11 +, is an appraisal by a newspaperman friendly to Murphy. Melchor P. Aquino, "Frank Murphy," *Bulletin of the American Historical Collection* 1 (July 1973): 11-17, is anecdotal. There is a discriminating portrait of Murphy in "The Labor Governors," *Fortune* 15 (June 1937): 78-81 +. Many of Murphy's speeches as governor have been collected in *Selected Addresses of Frank Murphy . . . January 1, 1937, to September 30, 1938* (Lansing: n.p., 1938).

Philippines. Peter W. Stanley, *A Nation in the Making: The Philippines and the United States, 1899-1921* (Cambridge: Harvard University Press, 1974), is the best study of American-Philippine relations to the close of the Wilson administration. Michael Onorato, *A Brief Review of American Interest in Philippine Development and Other Essays* (Berkeley: McCutchan Publishing Corp., 1968), is a well-researched collection of pieces that departs from the conventional treatment of Leonard Wood's governor-generalship. Theodore Friend, *Between Two Empires: The Ordeal of the Philippines, 1929-1946* (New Haven: Yale University Press, 1965), a splendid work in every respect, is indispensable for the period in Philippine-American history that it covers. Garel A. Grunder and William E. Livezey, *The Philippines and the United States* (Norman: University of Oklahoma Press, 1951), once the standard account of the Philippine-American relationship, has been largely supplanted by better-researched and more sophisticated studies. There are interesting insights on the relationship of the Philippines and the United States in George E. Taylor, *The Philippines and the United States* (New York: Frederick A. Praeger, 1964), and Frank H. Golay, ed., *The United States and the Philippines* (Englewood Cliffs, N.J.: Prentice-Hall, 1966). Romeo V. Cruz, *America's Colonial Desk and the Philippines, 1898-1934* (Quezon City: University of the Philippines, 1974), is a history of the Bureau of Insular Affairs.

The following general works on the Philippines rarely probe beneath the surface: Florence Horn, *Orphans of the Pacific: The Philippines* (New York: Reynal and Hitchcock, 1941); David Bernstein, *The Philippine Story* (New York: Farrar, Straus and Co., 1947); Usha Mahajani, *Philippine Nationalism: External Challenge and Filipino Response, 1565-1946* (St. Lucia, Queensland: University of Queensland Press, 1971); and Gregorio F. Zaide, *Philippine Political and Cultural History*, 2 vols. (Manila: Philippine Education Co., 1949). William H. Anderson, *The Philippine Problem* (New York: G. P. Putnam's Sons, 1939), is the work of an American businessman long resident in the Philippines who had a poor opinion of Murphy. Frederic S. Marquardt, who was associate editor of the *Philippines Free Press*, includes a chapter on Murphy in his "personalized history of our Philippine experiment," *Before Bataan and After* (New York: Bobbs-Merrill Co., 1943). Robert Aura

Smith, *Philippine Freedom, 1946-1958* (New York: Columbia University Press, 1958), the work of the *New York Times* correspondent in Manila while Murphy was governor-general, includes some material on the pre-World War II period. George A. Malcolm, *First Malayan Republic: The Story of the Philippines* (Boston: Christopher Publishing House, 1951), is mainly concerned with the period since 1936. Joseph Ralston Hayden, "The Changing Orient," *Michigan Alumnus Quarterly Review* 42 (Spring 1936): 111-17, is an encomium of Murphy.

Joseph Ralston Hayden, *The Philippines* (New York: Macmillan Co., 1942), remains unequaled as an institutional history of the Philippines for the period before World War II. It is of special value for Murphy's governor-generalship. George M. Guthrie, ed., *Six Perspectives on the Philippines* (Manila: Bookmark, 1968), and David Wurfel, "The Philippines," in George McTurnan Kahin, ed., *Governments and Politics of Southeast Asia*, 2d ed. (Ithaca: Cornell University Press, 1964), help one to understand Philippine society, politics, and personal relations. Philippine politics is examined historically in Dapen Liang, *The Development of Philippine Political Parties* (Hongkong: South China Morning Post, 1939), and structurally in Jean Grossholtz, *Politics in the Philippines* (Boston: Little, Brown and Co., 1964), and Carl H. Landé, *Leaders, Factions, and Parties: The Structure of Philippine Politics* ([New Haven]: Yale University, 1965). Pura Villanueva Kalaw, *How the Filipina Got the Vote* (Manila: n.p., 1952), is a history of female suffrage in the Philippines. The standard work on the Philippine bureaucracy is Onofre D. Corpuz, *The Bureaucracy in the Philippines* ([Manila]: University of the Philippines, 1957).

The substance of Theodore Friend's four excellent articles in vols. 11 and 12 of *Philippine Studies* on the background and enactment of the Hare-Hawes-Cutting Act is reproduced in *Between Two Empires*. Friend's work supersedes Grayson V. Kirk, *Philippine Independence* (New York: Farrar and Rinehart, 1936), but the latter book as well as the succinct summary of Kirk's thesis in "Whither the Philippines?" *Current History* 43 (Nov. 1935): 131-38, are still of interest. The Republican reaction to the possibility of Philippine independence is described in Gerald E. Wheeler, "Republican Philippine Policy, 1921-1933," *Pacific Historical Review* 28 (Nov. 1959): 377-90. Henry L. Stimson's performance as governor-general and his views regarding Philippine independence are delineated in Stimson and McGeorge Bundy, *On Active Service in Peace and War* (New York: Harper and Brothers, 1948); Elting E. Morison, *Turmoil and Tradition: A Study of the Life and Times of Henry L. Stimson* (Boston: Houghton Mifflin Co., 1960); and M. J. Smith, "Henry L. Stimson and the Philippines: American Withdrawal from Empire, 1931-1935," *Michigan Academician* 5 (Winter 1973): 335-48. Gerald E. Wheeler, "The Movement to Reverse Philippine Independence," *Pacific Historical Review* 33 (May 1964): 167-81, is primarily concerned with the period after 1936. There is a summary account of the independence movement in Michael Onorato, "The United States and the Philippine Independence Movement," *Solidarity* 5 (Sept. 1970): 2-15. The doubts at the time about the viability of Philippine independence are reflected in Robert Aura Smith, "The Gloomy Philippine Future," *Asia* 35 (May 1935): 290-97.

Pedro E. Abelarde, *American Tariff Policy towards the Philippines, 1898-1946* (New York: Kings Crown Press, 1947), is primarily concerned with the content of tariff legislation and is insufficiently analytical. Shirley Jenkins, *American Economic Policy toward the Philippines* (Stanford: Stanford University Press, 1954), emphasizes the period since World War II. Theodore Friend, "The Philippine Sugar Policy and the Politics of Independence, 1929-1935," *Journal of Asian Studies* 22 (Feb. 1963): 179-92, is the best brief treatment of the subject. The implementation of the Jones-Costigan Act in the Philippines is treated in John E. Dalton, *Sugar: A Case Study of Government Control* (New York: Macmillan Co., 1937). There are chapters on various aspects of the Philippine economy in Philippine Economic Association, *Economic Problems of the Philippines* (Manila: Bureau of Printing, 1934). A. V. Hartendorp, *History of Industry and Trade of the Philippines* (Manila: American Chamber of Commerce, 1958), contains a mass of unassimilated data. Charles O. Houston, Jr., has dealt with the principal Philippine crops in four articles in vols. 3 and 4 of the *University of Manila Journal of Asiatic Studies*. There is a brief summary of the social legislation enacted in the Philippines during the first three decades of American rule in Mariano D. Gana, *Social Legislation in the Philippine Islands* (n.p.: Institute of Pacific Relations, 1931).

There is no satisfactory biography of Manuel L. Quezon, but Carlos Quirino, *Quezon* (Manila: Filipiniana Book Guild, 1971), presents most of the essential facts. There is a finely developed portrait of Quezon in Theodore Friend, "Manuel Quezon: Charismatic Conservative," *Philippine Historical Review* 1 (1965): 153-69. Quezon's view of his place in Philippine history is set forth in his autobiography, *The Good Fight* (New York: D. Appleton-Century Co., 1946). The standard biographies of the leaders of the OsRox mission are Vicente Albano Pacis, *President Sergio Osmeña*, 2 vols. (Quezon City: Philippine Constitution Association, 1971), and Marcial Lichauco, *Roxas* (Manila: Kiko Printing Press, 1952). Emilio Aguinaldo presents his version of events in Aguinaldo and Vicente Albano Pacis, *A Second Look at America* (New York: Robert Spiller and Sons, 1957). George A. Malcolm includes some observations on Murphy's Philippine career in *American Colonial Careerist* (Boston: Christopher Publishing House, 1957). Ronald K. Edgerton's paper on Hayden is reproduced in somewhat different form in Norman G. Owen, ed., *Compadre Colonialism: Studies on the Philippines under American Rule* (Ann Arbor: University of Michigan, 1971). Owen, "Philippine Economic Development and American Policy: A Reappraisal," in the same work, is critical of American rule.

The nature of Philippine tenantry and the reasons for the Sakdalista and similar uprisings are set forth in Karl J. Pelzer, *Pioneer Settlement in the Asiatic Tropics* (New York: American Geographical Society, 1945), a very helpful study; Harlan R. Crippen, "Philippine Agrarian Unrest: Historical Backgrounds," *Science and Society* 10 (Fall 1946): 337-60, a Marxist view of the problem; Benedict J. Kerkvliet, *The Huk Rebellion* (Berkeley: University of California Press, 1977); and David R. Sturtevant, *Popular Uprisings in the Philippines, 1840-1940* (Ithaca: Cornell University Press, 1976), the fullest treatment of the subject. Sturtevant's "Sakdalism and Philippine Radicalism," *Journal of Asian Studies* 21 (Feb. 1962): 199-213, is a good, brief treatment of the Sakdalista uprising. Grant K. Goodman, "Japan and Philippine Radicalism: The Case of Benigno Ramos," in Goodman, *Four Aspects of Philippine-Japanese Relations, 1930-1940* ([New Haven]: n.p., 1967), pp. 133-94, is the best piece on the leader of the Sakdalistas and his ties with Japan. The response of Philippine officialdom to communism is the subject of Alvin H. Scaff, *The Philippine Answer to Communism* (Stanford: Stanford University Press, 1955). Kenneth K. Kurihara, *Labor in the Philippine Economy* (Stanford: Stanford University Press, 1945), is superficial and ignores the Murphy regime. Joseph Ralston Hayden, "What Next for the Moro?" *Foreign Affairs* (July 1928): 633–44, provides some of the setting for the Moro New Deal.

The best study of the Japanese colony in Davao and Japanese interest in the Philippines is Grant K. Goodman, *Davao: A Case Study in Japanese-American Relations* ([Lawrence, Kan.]: University of Kansas, 1967). Goodman treats the same subject in summary form in "Davaokuo: Japan in Philippine Politics, 1931–1941," in Robert K. Sakai, ed., *Studies on Asia, 1963* (Lincoln: University of Nebraska Press, 1963), pp. 185–96. There is additional material on the Davao problem in Serafin Quiason, "The Japanese Colony in Davao, 1904–1941," *Philippine Social Science and Humanities Review* 23 (July–Dec. 1958): 215–30; and Josefa M. Saniel, "The Japanese Minority in the Philippines before Pearl Harbor: Social Organization in Davao," *Asian Studies* 4 (Apr. 1966): 103–26. The context in which the United States viewed Japan's interest in the Philippines is provided in Dorothy Borg, *The United States and the Far Eastern Crisis of 1933–1938* (Cambridge, Mass.: Harvard University Press, 1964).

The United States plan to defend the Philippines in the event of war with Japan is the subject of Louis Morton, "War Plan Orange: Evolution of a Strategy," *World Politics* 11 (1959): 221–50. Ronald Schaffer, "General Stanley D. Embick: Military Dissenter," *Military Affairs* 37 (Oct. 1973), summarizes the career and strategic thought of the army's principal critic of War Plan Orange. D. Clayton James, *The Years of MacArthur*, vol. 1 (*1880–1941*) (Boston: Houghton Mifflin Co., 1970, is the most substantial study of the MacArthur defense plan for the Philippines and its implementation. The same subject is treated in the following: Dwight D. Eisenhower, *At Ease* (Garden City, N.Y.: Doubleday and Co., 1967); Louis Morton, contributor, "The Philippine Army, 1935–1939: Eisenhower's Memorandum to Quezon," *Military Affairs* 12 (Summer 1948): 103–7; Louis Morton, *The Fall of the Philippines* (Washington: Department of the Army, 1953); Douglas MacArthur, *Reminiscences* (New York: McGraw-Hill Co., 1964); Frazier Hunt, *The Untold Story of Douglas MacArthur* (New York: Devin-Adair Co., 1954); James K. Eyre, *The Roosevelt-MacArthur Conflict* (Chambersburg, Pa.: Craft Press, 1950); and Courtney Whitney, *MacArthur* (New York: Alfred A. Knopf, 1956).

The constitution of the Philippine Commonwealth is analyzed in the following: Maximo M. Kalaw, "The New Constitution of the Philippine Commonwealth," *Foreign Affairs* 13 (July 1935): 687–94; Conrado Benitez, "The New Philippine Constitution," *Pacific Affairs* 8 (Dec. 1935): 428–32; Jessie S. Reeves, "The Constitution of the Philippines," *American Journal of International Law* 29 (July 1935): 476–78; Ifor B. Powell, "The Commonwealth of the Philippines," *Pacific Affairs* 9 (Mar. 1936): 33–43; and Gerald E. Wheeler, "Manual L. Quezon and the Philippine Constitution," *University of the East . . . Journal* 1 (1964): 165–79. J. P. McEvoy, "Little Brother, What Next?" *Saturday Evening Post* 208 (Jan. 25, 1936): 29–30, is a cynical account of the launching of the Commonwealth.

Francis Burton Harrison, *Origins of the Philippine Republic: Extracts from the*

Diaries and Records of Francis Burton Harrison, ed. and annotated by Michael P. Onorato (Ithaca: Cornell University, 1974), is a major source for the period July 6, 1935–January 21, 1937, and is especially valuable for Harrison's account of his conversations with Quezon. Quezon, one must be aware, knew that the diary would eventually be published. The economic policies of the Commonwealth are delineated in Leo C. Stine, "The Economic Policies of the Commonwealth Government of the Philippine Islands," *University of Manila Journal of East Asiatic Studies* 10 (Mar. 1966): 1–136, which summarizes Stine's doctoral dissertation.

The Commonwealth of the Philippines is also the subject of the following: George A. Malcolm, *The Commonwealth of the Philippines* (New York: D. Appleton-Century Co., 1939); Joseph Ralston Hayden, "The Philippines in Transition: From Commonwealth to Independence," *Foreign Affairs* 14 (July 1936): 639–53; Catherine Porter, *Crisis in the Philippines* (New York: Alfred A. Knopf, 1942); Charles O. Houston, Jr., "The Philippine Commonwealth, 1936–1946: A Study," *University of Manila Journal of East Asiatic Studies* 2 (July 1953): 29–38; and Gerald E. Wheeler, "The American Minority in the Commonwealth Period," *Asian Studies* 4 (Aug. 1966): 362–73. The material on the Philippines in I. George Blake, *Paul V. McNutt* (Indianapolis: Central Publishing Co., 1966), is singularly unrevealing. Francis B. Sayre, *Glad Adventure* (New York: Macmillan Co., 1957), is the memoir of McNutt's successor as high commissioner.

Michigan. Although oriented toward the present, Coleman B. Ransone, Jr., *The Office of Governor in the United States* (University, Ala.: Alabama University Press, 1956), and Thad Beyle and J. Oliver Williams, eds., *The American Governor in Behavioral Perspective* (New York: Harper and Row, 1972), raise questions that are pertinent to Murphy's governorship. Michigan is not among the states considered in Leslie Lipson, *The American Governor from Figurehead to Leader* (Chicago: University of Chicago Press, 1939). The belated interest in national affairs on the part of the governors is noted in Glenn E. Brooks, *When Governors Convene: The Governors' Conference and National Politics* (Baltimore: Johns Hopkins Press, 1961).

There is, unfortunately, no really satisfactory history of Michigan. I found F. Clever Bald, *Michigan in Four Centuries* (New York: Harper and Brothers, 1954), more suitable for my purposes than the antiquated George N. Fuller, ed., *Michigan*, 5 vols. (Chicago: Lewis Publishing Co., 1939), or the more recent Willis Frederick Dunbar, *Michigan* (Grand Rapids: W. B. Eerdmans Publishing Co., 1965). There is an excellent profile of Michigan at about the time of Murphy's governorship in *Michigan: A Guide to the Wolverine State* (New York: Oxford University Press, 1941). Frank B. Woodford, *Alex J. Groesbeck* (Detroit: Wayne State University Press, 1962), is the biography of one of Murphy's more eminent predecessors as governor. There is a good analysis of William A. Comstock's shortcomings as governor and party leader in John P. White, "The Governor of Michigan as Party Leader: The Case of William A. Comstock," *Papers of the Michigan Academy of Science, Arts, and Letters* 42 (1957): 179–99. Cash Asher, *Ten Thousand Promises* (Grass Lake, Mich.: The Author, 1936), purports to be the "inside story of the Fitzgerald-McKay spoils machine." Queena M. Fitzgerald, "Frank D. Fitzgerald: A Tribute," *Michigan History Magazine* 24 (Winter 1940): 13–22, provides some biographical information about Murphy's predecessor and successor as governor, and "Governor Murray D.

Van Wagoner: A Biography,'' *Michigan History Magazine* 25 (Winter 1941): 5-13, does the same for Murphy's Democratic rival. The structure of Michigan's state government is set forth in Harold M. Dorr, *Administrative Organization of State Government in Michigan, 1921-1936* (University of Michigan, 1936). The Michigan state government's substitute for a cabinet is the subject of George C. S. Benson and Edward H. Litchfield, *The State Administrative Board in Michigan* (Ann Arbor: University of Michigan Press, 1938).

Sidney Fine, *Sit-Down: The General Motors Strike of 1936-1937* (Ann Arbor: University of Michigan Press, 1969), is a detailed account of what was probably the most important strike in American history. The bibliography on pp. 417-26 of *Sit-Down* appraises the principal manuscript and published sources for the strike and is brought up to date in Chapter 8, n. 1, of this volume. Melvyn Dubofsky and Warren Van Tine, *John L. Lewis* (New York: Quadrangle/New York Times Book Co., 1977), supersedes earlier biographies of Lewis. Carlos A. Schwantes, ''. . . The 1937 Non-Automotive Sit Down Strikes in Detroit,'' *Michigan History* 56 (Fall 1972): 179-200, is a graphic account of the Detroit labor upheaval that followed the GM strike. Albert A. Blum and Ira Spar, ''The Lansing Labor Holiday,'' *Michigan History* 49 (Mar. 1965): 1-11, is a more reliable account of the Lansing Labor Holiday than is provided in Birt Darling, *City in the Forest: The Story of Lansing* (New York: Stratford House, 1950). The importance of Monroe in the Little Steel strike is indicated in Donald G. Sofchalk, ''The Chicago Memorial Day Incident: An Episode of Mass Action,'' *Labor History* 6 (Winter 1965): 3-43.

Murphy's effort to secure the enactment of a state labor-relations law is placed in the context of the labor upheaval in the state in Sidney Fine, ''Frank Murphy, Law and Order, and Labor Relations in Michigan,'' in David B. Lipsky, ed., *Union Power and Public Policy* (Ithaca: New York State School of Industrial and Labor Relations, 1975), pp. 1-23. Murphy defended his approach to labor relations legislation in ''The Shaping of a Labor Policy,'' *Survey Graphic* 26 (Aug. 1937): 411-13 + ; the reaction to the article is given in ''For and Against—Governor Murphy's Labor Policy,'' *Survey Graphic* 26 (Sept. 1937): 464-69. A yardstick by which to measure the type of state labor-relations legislation supported by Murphy is provided in Charles C. Killingsworth, *State Labor Relations Acts* (Chicago: University of Chicago Press, 1948), and Sanford Cohen, *State Labor Legislation, 1937-1939* (Columbus: Ohio State University Press, 1948). The labor legislation enacted in Michigan in 1937-38 can be compared with what was accomplished in other states by examining ''State Labor Legislation, 1937,'' *Monthly Labor Review* 46 (Jan. 1938): 132-62, and ''State Labor Legislation, 1938,'' *Monthly Labor Review* 47 (Oct. 1938): 807-20.

Edward H. Litchfield, ''Michigan's Experience with Civil Service,'' *Personnel Administration* 2 (Dec. 1939): 1-7, is the best study of the enactment and implementation of the Civil Service Act of 1937. The implementation of the statute is also appraised in James K. Pollock, ''Michigan's First Year of Civil Service,'' *National Municipal Review* 28 (Jan. 1939): 1-8, and Litchfield, ''The 'Open Back Door'—A Case Study,'' *National Municipal Review* 30 (Feb. 1941): 1-6. The adoption of the civil service amendment to the Michigan constitution is examined in Litchfield, ''Another Chapter in Michigan Civil Service Reform,'' *American Political Science Review* 35 (Feb. 1941): 76-82, and William H. Combs, ''Michigan's Civil Service

Amendment," *State Government* 14 (Feb. 1941): 34–35 + . G. Lyle Belsley, "The Advance of the Merit System," *State Government* 12 (Jan. 1939): 7–8 + , measures the progress of civil service reform in the various states.

The pre-New Deal system of relief in Michigan is described in Isabel Campbell Bruce and Edith Eickhoff, *The Michigan Poor Law* (Chicago: University of Chicago Press, 1936). Louise V. Armstrong, *We Too Are the People* (Boston: Little, Brown and Co., 1938), is a sensitive account of the human side of the relief problem by the relief administrator in Manistee County in the early years of the New Deal. There is a succinct description of the relief structure in Michigan in the 1930s in Frank M. Landers, *Administration and Financing of Public Relief* ([Ann Arbor]: University of Michigan, 1942). The state studies in Michigan and elsewhere that followed the termination of federal relief are examined in Martha A. Chickering, "States Look at Public Welfare," *Survey* 73 (May 1937): 135–37. Arthur Dunham, "Public Welfare and the Referendum," *Social Service Review* 12 (Sept. 1938): 417–39, is the best account of the controversy engendered by the welfare reorganization legislation of 1937. James G. Bryant, Ernest C. Brooks, and D. Hale Brake defend welfare reorganization in *Proceedings of the Michigan Municipal League, 1937*, pp. 43–57, 71–86. Ernest B. Harper and Duane L. Gibson, *Reorganization of Public Welfare in Michigan* (East Lansing: Michigan State College, 1942), a revealing study of public attitudes regarding welfare reorganization, contains an analysis of the vote on the welfare referendum. In *The Michigan Welfare Reorganization Act of 1939* (Lansing: Michigan Conference of Social Work, 1939), Arthur Dunham points out the shortcomings of the 1939 welfare statute. The nature of the state welfare reorganization plans is summarized in Charles F. Ernst, "New Trends in Public Welfare Legislation," *State Government* 11 (May 1938): 85–88. The standard economic analysis of the recession of 1937–38 that added so greatly to Michigan's welfare problems is Kenneth D. Roose, *The Economics of Recession and Revival: An Interpretation of 1937–38* (New Haven: Yale University Press, 1954).

Arthur W. McMahon et al., *The Administration of Federal Work Relief* (Chicago: Public Administration Service, 1941), and Donald S. Howard, *The WPA and Federal Relief Policy* (New York: Russell Sage Foundation, 1943), satisfactorily explain how the WPA functioned. Federal-state relations in the administration of relief is one of the topics examined in Searle F. Charles, *Minister of Relief: Harry Hopkins and the Depression* (Syracuse: Syracuse University Press, 1963), which does not do justice to its subject.

Claude R. Tharp, *Social Security and Related Services in Michigan* (Ann Arbor: University of Michigan Press, 1946), provides an overview of the nature of social insurance, public assistance, and welfare programs in Michigan. The history of workmen's compensation in Michigan is summarized in Betty W. Allie, "History of Workmen's Compensation in Michigan," *Michigan History Magazine* 30 (Apr.–June 1946): 317–30. Harry Malisoff, "The Emergence of Unemployment Compensation," *Political Science Quarterly* 54 (June 1939): 237–58, (Sept. 1939): 391–420, (Dec. 1939): 577–99, describes how the states reacted to the unemployment insurance section of the Social Security Act. The extent to which unemployment insurance met the needs of the unemployed in Michigan during the 1937–38 recession is appraised in Paul Stanchfield, "Adequacy of Benefit Duration in Michigan: A Survey of Experience in a Minor Depression," *Social Security Bulletin* 3 (Sept. 1940): 19-28, and Daniel Creamer and Arthur C. Wellman, "Adequacy of Unemployment Benefits in the Detroit Area during the 1938 Recession," *Social Security Bulletin* 3 (Nov. 1940): 3-11. National public health developments in the 1930s that had an impact on Michigan are described in Roy Lubove, "The New Deal and National Health," *Current History* 45 (Aug. 1963): 77-86, and Daniel S. Hirschfield, *The Lost Reform: The Campaign for Compulsory Health Insurance in the United States from 1932 to 1943* (Cambridge, Mass.: Harvard University Press, 1970).

The changes in Michigan's correctional system introduced by the Murphy administration are set forth in the following: "The Michigan Department of Corrections," in Michigan Probation Association, *Probation in Theory and Practice* (n.p., n.d.), pp. 9-16; Hilmer Gellein, "New Department of Corrections," *Michigan Police Journal* 7 (June 1938): 9-10; Gellein, "What about Parole?" *Michigan Police Journal* 7 (Sept. 1938): 12-14; Austin H. MacCormick, "The Michigan Corrections Law and Partisan Politics," *Osborne Association News Bulletin* 11 (Dec. 1940): 1-3 + ; and Osborne Association, *1940 Survey of Michigan Penal Institutions* (n.p., n.d.).

The essential data regarding state government finance in Michigan in the 1930s are provided in Robert S. Ford and Albert Waxman, *Financing Government in Michigan* (Ann Arbor: University of Michigan Press, 1942), and Robert S. Ford, *Financing Government in Michigan: 1930-1938* ([Ann Arbor]: University of Michigan 1939). John A. Perkins, *The Role of the Governor of Michigan in the Enactment of Appropriations* (Ann Arbor: Univeristy of Michigan Press, 1943), focuses on the manner in which Murphy and other Michigan governors shaped Michigan's budget in the 1920s and 1930s. The extent to which Michigan benefited from the infusion of federal funds is indicated in Claude R. Tharp, *Federal Expenditures in Michigan* (Ann Arbor: University of Michigan, 1941).

The regulation of the milk industry by state governments in the 1930s is described in American Municipal Association, *Milk Control: Governmental Regulation of the Dairy Industry in the United States* (Chicago: Public Administration Service, 1937), and Leland Spencer, "Public Regulation of the Milk Industry," *State Government* 12 (Oct. 1939): 179-80 + . Frederick William Muller, *Public Rural Electrification* (Washington: American Council on Public Affairs, 1944), sets forth the accomplishments of the Rural Electrification Administration.

The following help one to understand political developments and voting behavior in Michigan in the 1930s: V. O. Key, *American State Politics* (New York: Alfred A. Knopf, 1956); Angus Campbell et al., *The American Voter* (New York: John Wiley and Sons, 1960); Angus Campbell et al., *Elections and the Political Order* (New York: John Wiley and Sons, 1966); John H. Fenton, *Midwest Politics* (New York: Holt, Rinehart and Winston, 1966); and James L. Sundquist, *Dynamics of the Party System* (Washington: Brookings Institution, 1973). Stephen B. and Vera H. Sarasohn, *Politcal Party Patterns in Michigan* (Detroit: Wayne State University Press, 1957), contains a brief account of Michigan's political history. Murphy is portrayed as a member of Huey Long's cabinet in the latter's *My First Days in the White House* (Harrisburg: Telegraph Press, 1935). The relationship between the Roosevelt administration and Father Charles E. Coughlin is described in Charles J. Tull, *Father Charles Coughlin and the New Deal* (Syracuse: Syracuse University Press, 1965); Donald R. McCoy, *Angry Voices: Left-of-Center Politics in the New Deal Era* (Lawrence: University of Kansas Press, 1958); James P. Shenton, "The Coughlin Movement and the New Deal," *Political Science Quarterly* 73 (Sept. 1958): 352-73; David H. Bennett, *Demagogues in the Depression: American Radicals and the Union Party, 1932-1936* (New Brunswick: Rutgers University Press, 1969); and Sheldon Marcus, *Father Coughlin* (Boston: Little, Brown and Co., 1973). The more general question of Catholicism and the New Deal is delineated in George Q. Flynn, *American Catholics and the Roosevelt Presidency* (Lexington: University of Kentucky Press, 1968). The chairman of the Democratic National Committee during Murphy's New Deal years provides his version of events in James A. Farley, *Jim Farley's Story: The Roosevelt Years* (New York: McGraw-Hill, 1938). There is material on James Couzens's role in the 1936 Michigan election in Harry Barnard, *Independent Man: The Life of Senator James Couzens* (New York: Charles Scribner's Sons, 1958).

The best study of the 1938 Michigan gubernatorial election is Samuel T. Mc-Seveney, "The Michigan Gubernatorial Campaign of 1938," *Michigan History* 45 (June 1961): 97-127. The hearings on the sit-down strikes conducted by the Dies Committee during the course of the 1938 election campaign are appraised in August Raymond Ogden, *The Dies Committee* (Washington: Catholic University Press, 1943). The dilemma that the election posed for Michigan socialists is evident in Daniel Bell, "The Background and Development of Marxian Socialism in the United States," in Donald Drew Egbert and Stow Persons, eds., *Socialism and American Life*, 2 vols. (Princeton: Princeton University Press, 1952), 1:213-405, and Frank Warren, *An Alternative Vision: The Socialist Party in the 1930's* (Bloomington: University of Indiana Press, 1974). Murphy reflects on the consequences of his 1938 defeat in "Tragic Interruption," *Nation* 147 (Dec. 3, 1938): 589-90.

John P. White, *Michigan Votes: Election Statistics, 1928-1956* (Ann Arbor: University of Michigan, 1958), contains the results, county by county, of elections in Michigan in the 1930s. The following enable one to analyze the results of the 1936 and 1938 gubernatorial elections in Michigan: James K. Pollock and Samuel J. Eldersveld, *Michigan Politics in Transition* (Ann Arbor: University of Michigan Press, 1942), useful for its examination of the urban vote; Edward H. Litchfield, *Voting Behavior in a Metropolitan Area* (Ann Arbor: University of Michigan Press, 1941), an invaluable analysis of the voting behavior of ethnic and income groups in Detroit from 1930 to 1938; and Donald S. Hecock and Harry A. Trevelyan, *Detroit Voters and Recent Elections* (Detroit: Bureau of Governmental Research, 1938), which lists the country of origin, precinct by precinct, of foreign-born registered voters in Detroit as of February 1, 1938. Michigan's counties are conveniently grouped according to their economic character in Marvin A. Bacon, *Income as an Index of the Fiscal Capacity of Michigan Counties* (Ann Arbor: University of Michigan Press, 1941). The principal sources for polling data relevant to Michigan during Murphy's New Deal years are Hadley Cantril, ed., *Public Opinion, 1935-1946* (Princeton: Princeton University Press, 1951); and George H. Gallup, *The Gallup Poll: Public Opinion, 1935-1971*, 3 vols. (New York: Random House, 1972).

Michigan politics and the Lansing New Deal can be compared with developments in other states by consulting James T. Patterson, *The New Deal and the States* (Princeton: Princeton University Press, 1969); Patterson, "The New Deal and the States," *American Historical Review* 73 (Oct. 1967): 70–84; John Braeman et al., eds., *The New Deal*, vol. 2, *The State and Local Levels* (Columbus: Ohio State University Press, 1975); and Robert P. Ingalls, *Herbert H. Lehman and New York's Little New Deal* (New York: New York University Press, 1975). Michael S. Holmes, *The New Deal in Georgia* (Westport: Greenwood Publishing Corp., 1975), an administrative history of New Deal agencies in Georgia, lacked relevance for this study. Jane Perry Clark, *The Rise of a New Federalism* (New York: Columbia University Press, 1938), and George C. S. Benson, *The New Centralization: A Study of Intergovernmental Relationships in the United States* (New York: Farrar and Rinehart, 1941), assess the impact of the New Deal on the federal system. There are accounts of post-1938 developments in Michigan in Edward H. Litchfield, "Pipe-Line Government in Michigan," *New Republic* 103 (Aug. 26, 1940): 270–72, and Robert Lee Sawyer, Jr., *The Democratic State Central Committee in Michigan, 1949–1959* (Ann Arbor: University of Michigan, 1960).

Index

Abaca and cordage, 10, 101–2, 117; and Hare-Hawes-Cutting bill, 18, 43, 131; and Quezon, 43; state of industry, 131; and Cordage Act (1935), 131–32, 151, 154, 567–68 n.70

Abbott, Horatio, 205, 207, 208, 215, 271

AC Spark Plug, 291

Adams, Alva, 121

Adrian Telegram, 385

Agama. *See* Moros

Aglipay, Gregorio, 14, 58, 59

Agricultural Adjustment Act (1933), 447

Agricultural Adjustment Act (1938), 450

Agricultural Adjustment Administration, 126–27, 129, 451, 452

Agricultural and Industrial Bank, 554 n.41

Agriculture, Department of, 147, 446, 449, 496, 525

Aguinaldo, Emilio, 5, 14; and Tydings-McDuffie Act, 45; and 1935 presidential election, 58, 59–64, 548 n.63; Paliparan estate of, 63, 548 n.61; and independence, 146

Air Commerce Act, 115

Alinsky, Saul, 318

Alka-Seltzer, 238

Allegan, Michigan, 330

Allen, Robert S., 204

Alpena, Michigan, 205

Aluminum Company of America, 293

American Broach Company, 348

American Chamber of Commerce (Manila), 15

American Civil Liberties Union: and Philippines, 84, 89, 90; and Monroe strike, 345; and lumberjack strike, 348; and Michigan labor-relations bills, 366, 367–78, 370, 372. *See also* Baldwin, Roger N.

American Cordage Institute, 16–17, 132

American Federation of Labor, 253, 279, 295,

326, 348, 349, 370, 482; and Philippine independence, 17; and GM sit-down strike, 296, 297; and 1938 election, 490, 491; value of endorsement by, 491

American Institute of Public Opinion, 370

American Jewish Congress, 494

American Legion, 346

American Medical Association, 436, 437

American Munitions Company, 346

American Public Health Association, 433

American Psychiatric Association, 432

American Red Cross (Philippine chapter), 73, 77, 78, 79

American Textile Export Association, 136

Anderson, Paul Y., 505, 515

Angeles, Leon, 92–93, 94, 95, 99

Ann Arbor, Michigan, 271, 348

Antenuptial Physical Examination Act, 435

Arkansas: and civil service reform, 376, 379

Armour and Company, 452

Army War College, 188

Arnold, Thurman, 127; and Michigan milk industry, 447–48, 449

Ashmore, Joseph, 347

Associated Charities (Philippines), 78, 79

Association of Japanese Exporters of Cotton Goods to the Philippine Islands, 143, 144

Atkinson, John W., 495

Atlanta Fisher Body plant, 294

Automotive Industries, 329

Baguio, 9, 21, 30, 34, 101, 114; and Mansion House, 179, 180

Baker, Newton D., 158

Balabac, Palawan, 104

Baldwin, Roger N., 193; and Philippines, 84, 89, 90; and Michigan Labor relations bills, 366, 367. *See also* American Civil Liberties Union

Barrett, Joseph E.: appointment of, 270; and

679